W9-BBS-890

The Best Books for Academic Libraries
10 Volumes (ISBN 0-7222-0014-5)

**Volume 1 — Science, Technology, and Agriculture
(ISBN 0-7222-0011-0)**
Q   Science
S   Agriculture
T   Technology, Engineering

**Volume 2 — Medicine
(ISBN 0-7222-0012-9)**
BF   Psychology
R   Medicine
RM-RS   Therapeutics
RT   Nursing

**Volume 3 — Language and Literature
(ISBN 0-7222-0013-7)**
P   Language and Literature
PA   Classical Language and Literature
PB-PH   Modern European Languages and Slavic
          Languages and Literature
PJ-PL   Oriental Language and Literature
PN   Literature: General and Comparative
PQ   Romance Literatures
PR   English Literature
PS   American Literature
PT   German, Dutch and Scandinavian Literature
PZ   Juvenile Literature

**Volume 4 — History of the Americas
(ISBN 0-7222-0014-5)**
E   America
E151-E970   United States
F1-975   US Local History
F1001-3799 Canada, Latin America

**Volume 5 — World History
(ISBN 0-7222-0015-3)**
C   Auxiliary Sciences of History
D   History

**Volume 6 — Social Sciences
(ISBN 0-7222-0016-1)**
G-GF   Geography, Oceanography, Human Ecology
GN   Anthropology, Ethnology, Archaeology
GR-GT   Folklore, Customs, Costumes
GV   Recreation, Physical Training, Sports
H-HA   Social Sciences. General Statistics
HB-HJ   Economics, Population
HM-HV   Sociology, Social History, Social Pathology
HX   Socialism, Communism, Anarchism

**Volume 7 — Political Science, Law, Education
(ISBN 0-7222-0017-X)**
J   Political Science
L   Education
K   Law

**Volume 8 — Religion and Philosophy
(ISBN 0-7222-0018-8)**
B-BJ   Philosophy
BL-BX   Religion

**Volume 9 — Music & Fine Arts
(ISBN 0-7222-0019-6)**
ML, MT Music
N-NX   Fine Arts

**Volume 10 — General Works, Military & Naval,
Library Science Author Index, Title Index,
Subject Guide
(ISBN 0-7222-0020-X)**
A   General Works
U   Military Science
V   Naval Science
Z   Bibliography, Library Science
          Author and Title Indexes
          Subject Guide

The Best Books for Academic Libraries

World History

Volume 5

First Edition

The Best Books, Inc.
P. O. Box 893520
Temecula, CA. 92589-3520

ISBN 0-7222-0010-2 (10 Volume Set)
ISBN 0-7222-0015-3 (Volume 5)

Library of Congress Cataloging-in-Publication Data

The best books for academic libraries.-- 1st ed.
      v. cm.
Includes indexes.
Contents: v. 1. Science, technology, and agriculture -- v. 2. Medicine
-- v. 3. Language and literature -- v. 4. History of the Americas -- v.
5. World history -- v. 6. Social sciences -- v. 7. Political science,
law, education - v. 8. Religion and philosophy -- v. 9. Music & fine
arts -- v. 10. General works, military & naval, library science.
    ISBN 0-7222-0020-21-0.(set : alk. paper) -- ISBN 0-7222-0011-0 (v. 1 :
alk. paper. ISBN 0-7222-0012-9 (v. 2 : alk. paper) -- ISBN 0-7222-
0013-7 (v.3 : alk. paper) -- ISBN 0-7222-0014-5 (v. 4 : alk.
paper) -- ISBN 0-7222-0015-3 (v. 5 : alk. paper) ISBN 0-7222-0016-1
(v. 6 : alk. paper) -- ISBN 0-7222-0017-X (v. 7 : alk. paper) -- ISBN
0-7222-0018-8 (v. 8 : alk. paper) -- ISBN 0-7222-0019-6 (v. 9 : alk.
paper) -- ISBN 0-7222-0020-X (v. 10 : alk. paper).
    1.   Academic libraries--United States--Book lists. I. Best Books,
Inc.

Z1035 .B545 2002
011'.67—dc21   2002013790

For further information, contact:

The Best Books, Inc.
P.O. Box 893520
Temecula, CA 92589-3520
(Voice) 888-265-3531
(Fax) 888-265-3540

For product information/customer service, e-mail: customerservice@thebbooks.net

Visit our Web site: www.bestbooksfor.com

Table of Contents

Introduction

ABOUT THE PROJECT:

The Best Books for Academic Libraries was created to fill a need that has been growing in collection development for undergraduate and college libraries since the late 1980's. Our editorial department organized *The Best Books Database* (designed as a resource for university libraries) by consulting the leading book review journals, bibliographies, and reference books with subject bibliographies. It was compiled based upon the bibliographic standard from the Library of Congress (LC) MARC records. Each section was arranged by Library of Congress Classification Numbers.

PROCESSES FOR SUBJECT SELECTION AND COMPILATION:

To create *The Best Books for Academic Libraries,* the Editor conducted a comprehensive search of prominent Subject Librarians and Subject Specialists, experts in their area(s), to participate as Subject Advisors. The editorial processes utilized by The Best Books editorial staff are as follows:

1. Subject Advisors were asked to select the best books recommended for undergraduate and college libraries. Those who volunteered selected approximately one-third from over 170,000 books in *The Best Books Database* that they felt were essential to undergraduate work in their area(s) of expertise. Each Subject Advisor made their selections from subject surveys that were arranged by LC Classification Number. They added their choices of titles that were omitted from the surveys, and updated titles to the latest editions.

2. The Best Books editorial staff tabulated the returned surveys, and added the omissions into the database, following the LC MARC record standard, to arrive at a consensus of approximately the best 80,000 books.

3. Senior Subject Advisors were selected to conduct a final review of the surveys. They added any other titles they felt were essential to undergraduate work in their area(s) of expertise.

4. The final results were tabulated to create the First Edition of the 10 Volume set – *The Best Books for Academic Libraries.*

The actual title selection was left to the Subject Advisors. Each Advisor used the bibliographic resources available to them in their subject areas to make the best possible recommendations for undergraduate and college libraries. In order to achieve results that were well rounded, two to three Subject Advisors reviewed each section.

When there were discrepancies in the LC sorting and/or the description of any titles, The Best Books editorial staff defaulted to the information available on the LC MARC records.

The intention of this project, and The Best Books editorial staff, was to include only books in this listing. However, other titles may have been included, based upon recommendations by Subject Advisors and Senior Subject Advisors. In some cases, the Advisors did select annual reviews and multi-volume sets for inclusion in this work.

The editorial department has made every attempt to list the most recent publications for each title in this work. In the interest of maintaining a current core-collection bibliographic list, our Advisors were asked to note the most recent publications available, especially with regards to series and publishers that regularly produce new editions. Books were listed as the original edition (or latest reprint) when no information of a recent publication was available.

ARRANGEMENT BY LC CLASSIFICATION SCHEDULE:

Each section of this work was arranged by Library of Congress Classification Numbers (LCCN), using the Library of Congress Classification Schedule for ready reference. For the purposes of this project, we have organized a system of varying font sizes and the incorporation of Em-dashes (—) to identify whether the subject headings herein are **primary** (Main Class), **secondary** (Sub-Class), or **tertiary** (Sub-Sub-Class) in the LC Classification Schedule outline. The primary heading is presented in 14 point Times New Roman, the secondary in 12 point, and the tertiary in 10 point. This distinction can be viewed in the examples that follow:

Primary Classification:
(14 Point Times New Roman)

P49 Addresses, essays, lectures

P49.J35 1985
Jakobson, Roman,
  Verbal art, verbal sign, verbal time / Roman Jakobson ; Krystyna Pomorska and Stephen Rudy, editors ; with the assistance of Brent Vine. Minneapolis : University of Minnesota Press, c1985. xiv, 208 p. :
84-007268 808/.00141 0816613583
  Philology. Semiotics. Space and time in language.

Secondary Classification:
(12 Point Times New Roman)

P51 Study and teaching. Research — General

P51.L39 1998
  Learning foreign and second languages : perspectives in research and scholarship / edited by Heidi Byrnes. New York : Modern Language Association of America, 1998. viii, 322 p.
98-039497 418/.007 087352800X
  Language and languages -- Study and teaching. Second language acquisition.

Tertiary Classification:
(10 Point Times New Roman)

P92 Communication. Mass media — By region or country — Individual regions or countries, A-Z

P92.C5.C52 2000
  Chinese perspectives in rhetoric and communication / edited by D. Ray Heisey. Stamford, Conn. : Ablex Pub. Corp., 2000. xx, 297 p. ;
99-053426 302.2/0951 1567504949
  Communication and culture -- China. Rhetoric -- Political aspects -- China.

ERRORS, LACUNAE, AND OMISSIONS:

The Subject Advisors and Senior Subject Advisors were the sole source for recommending titles to include in the completed work, and no titles were intentionally added or omitted other than those that the Subject Advisors and Senior Subject Advisors recommended. There is no expressed or implied warranty or guarantee on this product.

The Best Books editorial department requests that any suggestions or errors be sent, via e-mail or regular mail, to be corrected in future editions of this project.

BEST BOOKS EDITORIAL STAFF:

This work is the ongoing product and group effort of a number of enthusiastic individuals: The Best Books editorial staff includes: Assistant Editor, Annette Wiles; Database Administrator, Richelle Tague; and Editor, Ashley Ludwig.

CONTRIBUTING ADVISORS:

This volume would not be possible without the dedicated work of our Subject Advisors and Senior Subject Advisors who donated their time, resources and knowledge towards creating this Best Books list. To them, we are truly grateful. *(Denotes Senior Subject Advisors for *Volume 5 – World History*.)

SUBJECT ADVISORS:

Chris Africa, *Collection Management – Classics, University of Iowa Libraries*
Subject Advisor for: DE – History of the Greco Roman World, DF – History of Greece, DG – History of Italy

Brenda E. Bickett, *Middle Eastern & Islamic Studies Bibliographer, Georgetown University Library*
Subject Advisor for: DR – History of Turkey, Istanbul, DS – History of Islamic Countries, Iraq, Lebanon, History of Asia: Afghanistan, Pakistan, India, Sri Lanka, etc., DT – History of Northwest Africa

Hugo Chapa-Guzman, *Language Librarian, University of Texas, Austin*
Subject Advisor for: DP – History of Spain, Portugal

Su Chen,* *Head, East Asian Library, University of Minnesota Libraries - Twin Cities*
Subject Advisor for: DS – History of East Asia – China

Laurie Cohen,* *Collection Services Librarian for Jewish Studies, Hillman Library, University of Pittsburgh*
Subject Advisor for: C – Auxiliary Sciences of History: Biographies, DS – Jewish History, DP – History of Spain

Donald C. Johnson,* *South Asia Bibliographer, University of Minnesota Libraries - Twin Cities, Ames Library*
Subject Advisor for: DS – History of Asia: Afghanistan, Pakistan, India, Sri Lanka, etc.

Abbie Landry, *Head of Reference, Northwestern State University of Louisiana*
Subject Advisor for: DA – History of Great Britain: Irish History; Tudor-Stuart & 19th Century British History

AnnMarie Dorwart Mitchell, *Curator, Romance Collections (Europe), University of California – Berkeley*
Subject Advisor for: DK – Polish History

Michael P. Olson,* *Germanic Language & Literature Librarian, Widener Library, Harvard University*
Subject Advisor for: DAW – History of Central Europe, Austria, Liechtenstein, DD – History of Germany, DH – History of Low Countries, Benelux Countries, DJ – History of the Netherlands, DL – History of Northern Europe, Scandinavia

Joan G. Packer, *Head, Reference Department, Central Connecticut State University*
Subject Advisor for: D – History, General, DA – History of Great Britain, DD – History of Germany, DC – History of France

Karen Peacock, *Curator, Pacific Islands Collection, University of Hawaii, Hilo*
Subject Advisor for: DU – History of Oceania (South Seas)

Daniel M. Pennell,* *Slavic Bibliographer, University of Pittsburgh*
Subject Advisor for: DJK – History of Eastern Europe, DK – History of Poland, DL – History of Northern Europe, Scandinavia, DB – History of Hungary, Czechoslovakia, DAW – History of Central Europe, Austria, Liechtenstein, DR – History of the Balkan Peninsula

Brent Roberts, *Reference & Instruction Librarian, Montana State University – Billings*
Subject Advisor for: DS – History of Asia

SENIOR SUBJECT ADVISORS:

Su Chen, *Head, East Asian Library, University of Minnesota Libraries - Twin Cites.* Su Chen received her Masters of Library Science from McGill University, Montreal, Canada. She earned her Masters in Chinese Philosophy from The Huazhong University of Science and Technology in Wuhan, China. Currently, Chen serves as the Head of The East Asian Library at the University of Minnesota Libraries. Previously, she worked as the East Asian Studies Librarian at McGill University Library.

Senior Subject Advisor for: DS – Title in relation to East Asia – China

Laurie Cohen, *Collection Services Librarian for Jewish Studies, Hillman Library, University of Pittsburgh.* Laurie Cohen earned her Masters in Library and Information Science at Indiana University, Bloomington, where she had an Association of Jewish Libraries Scholarship. She received her Bachelor of Arts degree in Sociology and Jewish Studies from Kent State University. Laurie currently serves at the University of Pittsburgh Hillman Library as the Collections Services Librarian for Education, Hispanic Languages & Literatures, Jewish Studies, Religious Studies, and Women's Studies. She also serves as a Reference Consultant, providing editorial and verification services for authors. Previously, Ms. Cohen served as a Bibliographer and Reference Librarian at the Hillman Library. She has worked as Adjunct Instructor at Wright State University in Dayton, Ohio where she also served as a Humanities Reference Librarian. While serving at the Hillman Library, Cohen has worked on many committees to evaluate and recommend changes in operations, patron services, and facilities, including: the Acquisitions Budget Committee, the Oakland Library Consortium Task Force on Shared Databases, the Strategic Planning Steering Committee, and the Networked Resources Committee.

Senior Subject Advisor for: C-CT – Auxiliary Sciences of History, DS – History of Asia, including Arab countries, Middle East, Iraq, Israel (Palestine). The Jews, Jordan. Transjordan

Donald Clay Johnson, *Curator, Ames Library of South Asia, University of Minnesota Libraries -Twin Cities.* Dr. Johnson, Curator of the Ames Library of South Asia, University of Minnesota, earned his Masters from the University of Chicago and his Ph.D. from the University of Wisconsin-Madison Library School. Other positions he held include Head of the Reader Services Division at the College of William and Mary, Lecturer and Teaching Assistant at the Library School of the University of Wisconsin-Madison, Assistant Librarian for Reader Services at the National University of Malaysia (Universiti Kebangsaan Malaysia), and Curator of the Southeast Asia Collection, Yale University. Donald Clay Johnson has published many reference books on Southeast Asia. He has written articles, chapters, etc. for such publications as the Encyclopaedia Britannica, Libraries and Culture, Jain Journal, South Asia Library notes & queries, and the Journal of library history, philosophy, and comparative librarianship. He has given many presentations and lectures at such institutions as the University of Minnesota Libraries, Duke University, Carleton College, The University of Wisconsin-Madison, and The Siketu Shah Trust, Ahmedabad, India, among many others. Some of the many contributions Johnson has made for South Asia include: the Portal to Asian Internet Resources (PAIR) program for the Department of Education Technological Innovation and Cooperation for Foreign Information Access, he has served as a Reviewer for the Senior Scholars Program for the Council for International Exchange of Scholars, and has contributed to the Digital Asia Library Project. Most recently he published Agile Hands and Creative Minds: a bibliography of the textile traditions of Afghanistan, Bangladesh, Bhutan, India, Nepal, Pakistan, and Sri Lanka.

Senior Subject Advisor for: DS History of Asia, including Afghanistan, Pakistan, India (Bharat), Sri Lanka, etc.

Michael P. Olson, *Librarian for Germanic Collections, Harvard University – Widener Library.* Michael P. Olson received his Masters of Library Science and his Ph.D. in Germanic Languages from the University of California, Los Angeles. His undergraduate studies were conducted at the University of Washington. Olson currently is serving as the Librarian for Germanic Collections at the Widener Library of Harvard University. He previously was employed as the Germanic Studies Bibliographer at the University Research Library, UCLA. Michael Olson previously taught German at the Johann Wolfgang Goethe-Universität, Frankfurt, Germany.

Senior Subject Advisor for: C-CT – Auxiliary Sciences of History, DAW – History of Central Europe, Austria, DD – History of Germany, DH – History of Low Countries. Benelux Countries, DJ – History of Netherlands (Holland), DL – History of Northern Europe, Scandinavia

Daniel M. Pennell, *Bibliographer for Russian, East European, and Germanic Studies, University of Pittsburgh, Hillman Library.* Daniel M. Pennell received his Masters in Russian History and his Masters of Library Science from Indiana University where he is a Ph.D. Candidate in Eastern European History. Pennell currently works as Bibliographer at the University of Pittsburgh. Previously, he served as Assistant to the Slavic Bibliographer at Indiana University. He has given conference presentations for the AAASS National Convention, and the Babes-Bolyai University, Cluj-Napoca, Romania. His publications include articles for the Cluj University Press, Harvard University, and various other publications. He has written reviews for Balkanistica, Balkan Academic News, and Slavic and East European Information Resources. Daniel Pennell speaks and/or reads the languages of Czech, German, Hungarian, Romanian, Russian, Serbo-Croatian, and Slovak.

Senior Subject Advisor for: C-CT – Auxiliary Sciences of History, DB – History of Hungary, Czechoslovakia, DJK – History of Eastern Europe (General), DK – History of Russia. Soviet Union. Former Soviet Republics. Poland, DL – History of Northern Europe. Scandinavia, DR – History of Balkan Peninsula

David S. Sullivan, *Classics Librarian, University of California - Berkeley.* David S. Sullivan earned his Masters in Library and Information Science from the University of California, Berkeley. He achieved his Ph.D. in Classics at Stanford University. He currently serves as the Classics Librarian at the University of California, Berkeley. Sullivan has worked as a Rare Books and Technical Services Librarian and Bibliographer for Classics at the Stanford University Library. He has lectured on Classics at both Colby College and Stanford University.

Senior Subject Advisor for: C-CT – Auxiliary Sciences of History, DE – History of Greco Roman World, DF – History of Greece, DG – History of Italy, DR – History of Turkey

CB History of Civilization

CB5 Collected works (nonserial) — Several authors

CB5.R4 57
Shinoda, Minoru.
The founding of the Kamakura shogunate, 1180-1185. With selected translations from the Azuma kagami. New York, Columbia University Press, 1960. xii, 385 p.
59-010433   952.02
Japan -- History -- Kamakura period, 1185-1333.

CB9 Dictionaries. Encyclopedias

CB9.D53 1997
The dictionary of global culture/ edited by Kwame Anthony Appiah and Henry Louis Gates, Jr.; Michael Colin Vazquez, associate editor. New York: Knopf: 1997. xiv, 717 p.
93-043132   903   039458581X
Civilization -- Dictionaries.

CB15 Historiography — General works

CB15.S74 1993
Stearns, Peter N.
Meaning over memory: recasting the teaching of culture and history/ Peter N. Stearns. Chapel Hill: University of North Carolina Press, c1993. xiii, 254 p.
92-050815   907/.1/073   0807820903
Civilization -- Historiography -- History. Civilization -- Study and teaching -- United States. Humanities -- Study and teaching -- United States.

CB18 Historiography — Biography of historians — Individual, A-Z

CB18.E44.M46 1989
Mennell, Stephen.
Norbert Elias: civilization, and the human self-image/ Stephen Mennell. Oxford, UK; Blackwell, 1989. xi, 319 p.
88-028117   901   0631155333
Elias, Norbert.   Civilization -- Philosophy. Sociology -- Europe -- History -- 20th century.

CB18.T65.P47 1982
Perry, Marvin.
Arnold Toynbee and the crisis of the West/ Marvin Perry. Washington, D.C.: University Press of America, c1982. xiii, 138 p.
81-040162   907/.2024   0819120251
Toynbee, Arnold Joseph, -- 1889-1975. Civilization, Western. History -- Philosophy. Historians -- Great Britain -- Biography.

CB19 Philosophy. Theory

CB19.A35 1983
Adams, Robert Martin, 1915-
Decadent societies/ Robert M. Adams. San Francisco: North Point Press, 1983. 196 p.
82-073710   901   0865471037
Civilization -- Philosophy. Civilization -- History.

CB19.B69 1985
Brown, Norman Oliver, 1913-
Life against death: the psychoanalytical meaning of history/ by Norman O. Brown. Middletown, Conn.: Wesleyan University Press; 1985, c1959. xx, 366 p.
85-017928   150.19/52   0819551481
Civilization -- Philosophy. Civilization -- Psychological aspects. Psychohistory.

CB19.K686 1963
Kroeber, A. L. 1876-1960.
An anthropologist looks at history. With a foreword by Milton Singer. Edited by Theodora Kroeber. Berkeley, University of California Press, 1963. xix, 213 p.
63-016250   901.9
Civilization -- History -- Addresses, essays, lectures.

CB19.N59 1971
Northrop, F. S. C. 1893-
Ideological differences and world order; studies in the philosophy and science of the world's cultures. Edited by F. S. C. Northrop. Westport, Conn., Greenwood Press [1971, c1949] xi, 486 p.
74-136078   901.9/4   0837152283
Civilization -- Philosophy.

CB19.N6
Northrop, F. S. C. 1893-
The meeting of East and West, an inquiry concerning world understanding, by F. S. C. Northrop. New York, The Macmillan company, 1946. xxii p.
46-004813   901
Civilization -- Philosophy.

CB19.T6.P3
The Pattern of the past: can we determine it? Boston, Beacon Press, 1949. 126 p.
49-011504   901
Toynbee, Arnold Joseph, -- 1889-1975. Civilization -- Philosophy. History -- Philosophy.

CB19.V58 1956
Voegelin, Eric, 1901-
Order and history. [Baton Rouge] Louisiana State University Press [1956]-c1987. 5 v.
56-011670   901
Civilization -- Philosophy. Order (Philosophy)

CB19.W48 1969
White, Leslie A., 1900-1975.
The science of culture; a study of man and civilization, by Leslie A. White. New York, Farrar, Straus and Giroux [1969] xl, 444 p.
75-007130   301.2
Culture. Civilization.

CB19.W53 1956a
Wilson, Colin, 1931-
The outsider. Boston, Houghton Mifflin, 1956. 288 p.
56-011983   901
Civilization -- Philosophy.

CB53-59 General works — 1801- — American

CB53.L58
Lovejoy, Arthur O. 1873-1962.
A documentary history of primitivism and related ideas; general editiors: Arthur O. Lovejoy, Gilbert Chinard, George Boas [and] Ronald S. Crane. Baltimore, The Johns Hopkins press, 1935. 1v.
35-012598
Progress. Civilization.

CB53.L8 1953
Lucas, Henry Stephen,
A short history of civilization. 2d ed. New York, McGraw-Hill, 1953. 1002 p.
53-006045   901
Civilization--History.

CB53.M8 1973
Mumford, Lewis,
The condition of man. New York, Harcourt Brace Jovanovich [1973] xii, 467 p.
72-091160   901.9   0156215500
Civilization--History.

CB53.M82
Mumford, Lewis, 1895-
The transformations of man. New York, Harper, [1956] 249 p.
56-006030   901
Man. Civilizations -- History.

CB53.T5 1948
Thorndike, Lynn, 1882-1965.
A short history of civilization, by Lynn Thorndike... New York, Appleton-Century-Crofts [1948] xiii, 751 p.
48-007724   901
Civilization -- History.

CB53.W5
Whitehead, Alfred North, 1861-1947.
Adventures of ideas, by Alfred North Whitehead. New York, The Macmillan company, 1933. xii, 392 p.
33-005611   901
Civilization -- History. Sociology -- History. Cosmology -- History.

CB57.M9
Muller, Herbert Joseph, 1905-
The uses of the past; profiles of former societies. New York, Oxford University Press, 1952. xi, 394 p.
52-006168   901
Civilization -- History.

CB57.R32 1940
Randall, John Herman, 1899-
The making of the modern mind. Boston, Houghton Mifflin company [c1940] xiii, 696 p.
41-000357   901
Civilization -- History. Europe -- Civilization.

CB59.B6 1963
Bowle, John.
Man through the ages: from the origins to the eighteenth century/ Little, 1962. v.
62-017032   901.9
Civilization -- History.

CB59.K7 1962a
Kroeber, A. L. 1876-1960.
A roster of civilizations and culture. Chicago, Aldine Pub. Co. [1962] 96 p.
62-014933   901.902
Civilization -- History -- Outlines, syllabi, etc.

CB59.Q5
Quigley, Carroll.
The evolution of civilizations; an introduction to
historical analysis. New York, Macmillan, 1961.
281 p.
61-014345 901.9
History -- Methodology. Civilization -- History.

CB59.W4
Weyl, Nathaniel, 1910-
The geography of intellect, by Nathaniel Weyl and
Stefan T. Possony. Chicago, H. Regnery Co., 1963.
xiii, 299 p.
63-012889 901.9
Intellectual life -- History. Intelligence.
Ethnopsychology.

CB63-68 General works — 1801- — English

CB63.B8 1964
Buckle, Henry Thomas, 1821-1862.
History of civilization in England. Summarized and
abridged by Clement Wood. Introd. by Hans Kohn.
New York, Ungar [1964] xvi, 137 p.
64-015688 914
Civilization -- History.

CB63.T613
Toynbee, Arnold Joseph, 1889-1975.
A study of history. London, Oxford University
Press [1948]-61. 12 v.
49-000777 909
Civilization. History -- Philosophy. Historical
geography -- Maps.

CB63.T68.G3
Gargan, Edward T., 1922-
The intent of Toynbee's History; a cooperative
appraisal. Pref. by Arnold J. Toynbee. Chicago,
Loyola University Press, 1961. viii, 224 p.
61-010704 901.9
Toynbee, Arnold Joseph, -- 1889- -- A study of
history.

CB63.T68.S3
Samuel, Maurice, 1895-1972.
The professor and the fossil; some observations on
Arnold J. Toynbee's A study of history. New
York, Knopf, 1956. 268 p.
56-008929 901
Toynbee, Arnold Joseph, -- 1889-1975. -- Study of
history. Jews -- History.

CB63.T68M6
Montagu, Ashley, 1905-
Toynbee and history; critical essays and reviews.
Boston, Porter Sargent [1956] xiii, 385 p.
56-003047 901
Toynbee, Arnold Joseph, -- 1889- -- A study of
history. History -- Philosophy.

CB67.B8 1932
Bury, J. B. 1861-1927.
The idea of progress: an inquiry into its origin and
growth, by J. B. Bury...introduction by Charles A.
Beard. New York, The Macmillan company, 1932.
xl, 357 p.
32-011686 901
Progress. History -- Philosophy.

CB68.C55 1970
Clark, Kenneth, 1903-
Civilisation: a personal view [by] Kenneth Clark.
New York, Harper & Row [1970, c1969] xviii,
359 p.
75-097174 901.9
Civilization -- History. Art -- History.

CB68.F4
Ferguson, John, 1921-
Foundations of the modern world. Cambridge
[Eng.] University Press, 1963. 183 p.
63-005743 901.9
Civilization -- History.

CB69 General works — 1801- — American and English, 1974-

CB69.B66 1983
Boorstin, Daniel J. 1914-
The discoverers/ Daniel J. Boorstin. New York:
Random House, c1983. xvi, 745 p.
83-042766 909 0394402294
Civilization -- History. Discoveries in geography.
Science -- History.

CB69.C37 1993
Carruth, Gorton.
The encyclopedia of world facts and dates/ Gorton
Carruth. New York: HarperCollins, c1993. ix,
1310 p.
89-046521 902/.02 006270012X
Civilization -- History -- Chronology.
Chronology, Historical. Civilization -- History --
Encyclopedias.

CB69.M33
McNeill, William Hardy, 1917-
The human condition: an ecological and historical
view/ William H. McNeill. Princeton, N.J.:
Princeton University Press, c1980. viii, 81 p.
80-007547 304.2 0691053170
Civilization -- Addresses, essays, lectures.
Human ecology -- Addresses, essays, lectures.

CB83-88 General works — 1801- — German

CB83.E413 1994
Elias, Norbert.
The civilizing process/ Norbert Elias; translated by
Edmund Jephcott. Oxford [England]; Blackwell,
c1994. xvii, 558 p.
93-037350 909.220 0631192220
Civilization--History. Civilization--Philosophy.

CB83.S63 1991
Spengler, Oswald,
The decline of the West/ Oswald Spengler; an
abridged ed. by Helmut Werner; English abridged
ed. prepared by Charles Francis Atkinson;[with a
new introduction by H. Stuart Hughes]. New York:
Oxford University Press, 1991. xxxix, 414 p.
90-041662 909.220 0195066340
Civilization--History.

CB88.R84213
Rustow, Alexander, 1885-1963.
Freedom and domination: a historical critique of
civilization/ Alexander Rustow; abbreviated
translation from the German by Salvator Attanasio;
edited, and with introd., by Dankwart A. Rustow.
Princeton, N.J.: Princeton University Press, c1980.
xxix, 716 p.
80-010575 909 0691053045
Civilization -- History.

CB103 General works — 1801- — Spanish

CB103.O713 1993
Ortega y Gasset, José,
The revolt of the masses/ Jose Ortega y Gasset.
New York: W.W. Norton, 1993. 190 p.
93-029295 901.220 0393310957
Civilization. Proletariat.

CB113 General works — 1801- — Other languages, A-Z

CB113.D3.B513
Birket-Smith, Kaj, 1893-
The paths of culture; a general ethnology.
Translated from the Danish by Karin Fennow.
Madison, University of Wisconsin Press, 1965. xi,
535 p.
64-008488 301.2
Civilization -- History. Ethnology.

CB151 General special

CB151.F574 1989
Fiske, John.
Understanding popular culture/ John Fiske. Boston:
Unwin Hyman, 1989. xi, 206 p.
89-005720 306.4 0044454384
Popular culture. Capitalism.

CB151.J34 1970
Jacob, Heinrich Eduard, 1889-1967.
Six thousand years of bread; its holy and unholy
history. Translated by Richard and Clara Winston.
Westport, Conn., Greenwood Press [1970, c1944]
xiv, 399 p.
75-110043 901.9 0837144310
Bread. Civilization -- History.

CB151.L36 1972
Laski, Harold Joseph, 1893-1950.
Faith, reason, and civilization; an essay in
historical analysis. Freeport, N.Y., Books for
Libraries Press [1972, c1944] 187 p.
74-167375 901.9 0836926625
Civilization. Christianity. Socialism.

CB151.R25
Rabinowitch, Eugene, 1901-
The dawn of a new age; reflections on science and
human affairs. Chicago, University of Chicago
Press [1963] viii, 332 p.
63-020898 901.9
Science and civilization.

CB151.T56 1991
Tomlinson, John, 1949-
Cultural imperialism: a critical introduction/ John
Tomlinson. Baltimore, Md.: Johns Hopkins
University Press, c1991. ix, 187 p.
90-053700 306 0801842492
Politics and culture. United States -- Relations -
- Foreign countries.

CB155 Relations to special topics

CB155.E26
Edelstein, Ludwig, 1902-1965.
The idea of progress in classical antiquity. Baltimore, John Hopkins Press [1967] xxxiii, 211 p.
67-016483   901
Progress. Philosophy, Ancient.

CB155.L95
Lynch, Kevin, 1918-
What time is this place? Cambridge, MIT Press [1972] viii, 277 p.
72-007059   301.24   0262120615
Progress -- Addresses, essays, lectures. Cycles -- Addresses, essays, lectures. Time perception -- Addresses, essays, lectures.

CB155.M323
Ceram, C. W., 1915-1972.
Yestermorrow: notes on man's progress, with a glossary-index by Kurt W. Marek (C. W. Ceram) Translated from the German by Ralph Manheim. New York, Knopf, 1961. 151 p.
61-013218   901.9
Progress.

CB156 Terrestrial evidence of interplanetary voyages. Influence of extraterrestrial life on human civilization

CB156.C56 1990
Clube, Victor.
The cosmic winter/ Victor Clube and Bill Napier. Oxford, UK; B. Blackwell, 1990. vi, 307 p.
89-018011   001.9   0631169539
Civilization -- Extraterrestrial influences. Glacial epoch. Catastrophical, The.

CB158 Forecasts of future progress — Methodology

CB158.B45 1996
Bell, Wendell.
Foundations of futures studies: human science for a new era/ Wendell Bell. New Brunswick, NJ: Transaction Publishers, 1996-c1997. 2 v.
96-022496   303.49/09/04   1560002719
Forecasting.

CB158.C67
Cornish, Edward, 1927-
The study of the future: an introduction to the art and science of understanding and shaping tomorrow's world/ by Edward Cornish with members and staff of the World Future Society. Washington, D.C.: The Society, c1977. x, 307 p.
77-075308   001.4/33   0930242033
Forecasting.

CB158.H415 1983
Helmer, Olaf, 1910-
Looking forward: a guide to futures research/ Olaf Helmer. Beverly Hills, Calif.: Sage Publications, c1983. 376 p.
83-004520   003/.2   0803920172
Forecasting -- Methodology. Forecasting -- Research.

CB158.P6213 1973
Polak, Fred.
The image of the future. [By] Fred Polak. Translated from the Dutch and abridged by Elise Boulding. Amsterdam, Elsevier Scientific Pub. Co., 1973. x, 321 p.
72-083209   901.94
Forecasting -- History. Civilization -- History. Eschatology -- Comparative studies.

CB158.S23 1990
Saaty, Thomas L.
Embracing the future: meeting the challenge of our changing world/ Thomas L. Saaty and Larry W. Boone. New York: Praeger, 1990. ix, 176 p.
90-031963   303.49   0275935736
Forecasting. Human behavior. Social evolution.

CB160 Forecasts of future progress — Special forecasts. By author or title — Published through 1950

CB160.D3 1953a
Darwin, Charles Galton, 1887-1962.
The next million years. Garden City, N.Y., Doubleday, 1953. 210 p.
52-013372   901.9   0837168767
Forecasting. Civilization -- History.

CB160.K3 1967
Kahn, Herman, 1922-
The year 2000; a framework for speculation on the next thirty-three years, by Herman Kahn and Anthony J. Wiener, with contributions from other staff members of the Hudson Institute. Introd. by Daniel Bell. New York, Macmillan [1967] xxviii, 431 p
67-029488   301.2
Twentieth century -- Forecasts.

CB161 Forecasts of future progress — Special forecasts. By author or title — 1951-

CB161.B4
Beckwith, Burnham P. 1904-
The next 500 years; scientific predictions of major social trends. With a foreword by Daniel Bell. New York, Exposition Press [1967] xvi, 341 p.
67-026389   901.9
Twenty-fifth century -- Forecasts.

CB161.C36 1994
Carlson, Richard C.
Fast forward: where technology, demographics, and history will take America and the world in the next thirty years/ Richard Carlson and Bruce Goldman. New York, NY: HarperBusiness, c1994. viii, 246 p.
93-039546   330.973/001/12   0887305970
Twenty-first century -- Forecasts. Economic forecasting -- United States. Social prediction -- United States.

CB161.C52 1979
Clarke, I. F.
The pattern of expectation, 1644-2001/ I. F. Clarke. New York: Basic Books, 1979. xi, 344 p.
78-019669   909.08   0465054579
Forecasting -- History. Twentieth century -- Forecasts. Progress.

CB161.K44 1994
Kennedy, Paul M.,
Preparing for the twenty-first century/ Paul Kennedy.1st Vintage Books ed. New York: Vintage Books, 1994. xvi, 428 p.
93-006327   303.49/09/05.220   0679747052
Twenty-first century.

CB161.M3
McHale, John.
The future of the future. New York, G. Braziller [1969] ix, 322 p.
69-015827   301.3
Technology and civilization. Twenty-first century -- Forecasts.

CB161.P35 1981
Peccei, Aurelio.
One hundred pages for the future: reflections of the president of the Club of Rome/ Aurelio Peccei. New York: Pergamon Press, c1981. 191 p.
82-133898   303.4/9   0080281109
Twenty-first century -- Forecasts. Twentieth century -- Forecasts. Civilization, Modern -- 1950-

CB195 Civilization and race — General works

CB195.D72 1987
Drake, St. Clair.
Black folk here and there: an essay in history and anthropology/ St. Clair Drake. Los Angeles: Center for Afro-American Studies, University of c1987-c1990. 2 v.
86-016045   305.8/96   0934934282
Racism -- History. Blacks -- History. Blacks -- Nile River Valley -- History. Nile River Valley -- History.

CB197 Civilization and race — General special

CB197.P6
Platt, Washington.
National character in action; intelligence factors in foreign relations. New Brunswick, N.J., Rutgers University Press [1961] xix, 250 p.
61-010265   136.49
National characteristics. Intelligence service -- United States. Diplomatic and consular service, American.

CB201-206 Civilization and race — Special civilizations — Caucasian. Aryan

CB201.E53 1997
Encyclopedia of Indo-European culture/ editors, J.P. Mallory and D.Q. Adams. London; Fitzroy Dearborn, 1997. xlvi, 829 p.
98-101334   305.8/034   1884964982
Indo-Europeans -- Encyclopedias.

CB203.B87 1978
Burke, Peter.
Popular culture in early modern Europe/ Peter
Burke. London: T. Smith, 1978. 365 p.
78-314304 940.2 0851171508
Popular culture -- Europe.

CB203.E54
The Enlightenment in national context/ edited by
Roy Porter and Mikulas Teich. Cambridge;
Cambridge University Press, 1981. xii, 275 p.
80-041750 940.2/53 0521237572
*Enlightenment -- Europe. Europe -- Intellectual
life. Europe -- History -- 18th century.*

CB203.G47
Gerhard, Dietrich, 1896-
Old Europe: a study of continuity, 1000-1800/
Dietrich Gerhard. New York: Academic Press,
c1981. xii, 147 p.
81-014872 940 0122807200
*Social history -- Medieval, 500-1500. Europe --
Civilization. Europe -- Social conditions.*

CB203.L32
Lach, Donald F. 1917-
Asia in the making of Europe [by] Donald F. Lach.
Chicago, University of Chicago Press [1965]-
c1993 v. 1-3
64-019848
*East and West -- Asia -- History. Europe --
Civilization -- Oriental influences. Asia --
Discovery and exploration.*

CB203.L38
The Legacy of Greece: a new appraisal/ edited by
M. I. Finley. Oxford: Clarendon Press; 1981. 479,
[16] p.
80-040188 940 0198219156
*Civilization, Greek. Europe -- Civilization --
Greek influences.*

CB203.M35 1989
McKnight, Stephen A., 1944-
Sacralizing the secular: the Renaissance origins of
modernity/ Stephen A. McKnight. Baton Rouge:
Louisiana State University Press, c1989. xi, 131 p.
88-009048 940.2 0807114499
*Hermetism -- Italy -- Influence. Philosophy,
Renaissance. Philosophy, Modern. Europe --
Intellectual life.*

CB203.P3 1993
Pagden, Anthony.
European encounters with the New World: from
Renaissance to Romanticism/ Anthony Pagden.
New Haven: Yale University Press, 1993. vi,
216 p.
92-021947 303.48/2407 0300052855
*Europe -- Intellectual life. Europe -- Relations
-- America. America -- Relations -- Europe.*

CB203.S76
Stone, Lawrence.
The past and the present/ Lawrence Stone. Boston:
Routledge & K. Paul, 1981. xii, 274 p.
80-041657 940 0710006284
Historiography. Europe -- Civilization.

CB203.T73 1990
The Transmission of culture in early modern
Europe/ Anthony Grafton and Ann Blair, editors.
Philadelphia: University of Pennsylvania Press,
c1990. 326 p.
89-070326 940.2 0812281918
*Culture diffusion -- Europe -- History. Europe -
- Intellectual life. Europe -- Civilization.*

CB203.W63
Wohl, Robert.
The generation of 1914/ Robert Wohl. Cambridge,
Mass.: Harvard University Press, 1979. ix, 307 p.
78-021124 909.82/1 0674344650
*Youth -- Europe -- History. Conflict of
generations -- United States. World War, 1914-
1918 -- Influence. Europe -- Intellectual life -- 20th
century.*

CB204.B87 2000
Burrow, J. W. 1935-
The crisis of reason: European thought, 1848-1914/
J.W. Burrow. New Haven: Yale Univeristy Press,
c2000. xv, 271 p.
99-059165 940.2/8 0300083904
*Philosophy, Modern -- 19th century. Philosophy,
Modern -- 20th century Europe -- Intellectual life -
- 19th century. Europe -- Intellectual life -- 20th
century.*

CB205.E37 1987
Eisenstadt, S. N. 1923-
European civilization in a comparative perspective:
a study in the relations between culture and social
structure/ S.N. Eisenstadt. Oslo: Norwegian
University Press; c1987. 162 p.
87-139999 940.55 8200058190
*Europe -- Civilization -- 20th century. Europe -
- Social conditions -- 20th century*

CB205.L53 2000
Lichtheim, George,
Europe in the twentieth century/ George
Lichtheim; with an introduction by Mark
Mazower. London: Phoenix Press, 2000. xiv,
409 p.
2001-3698 940.5.221 0297643835

CB206.C44 1982
The Celtic consciousness/ edited by Robert
O'Driscoll. New York: Braziller, 1982, c1981.
xxxi, 642 p.
82-001269 909/.0974916 0807610410
Civilization, Celtic -- Congresses.

CB235 Civilization and race — Special civilizations — Black

CB235.G55 1993
Gilroy, Paul.
The black Atlantic: modernity and double
consciousness/ Paul Gilroy. Cambridge, Mass.:
Harvard University Press, 1993. ix, 261 p.
93-016042 305.896/073 0674076052
*Blacks -- Intellectual life. Afro-Americans --
Intellectual life. Afrocentrism.*

CB245 Civilization and race — Special civilizations — Occidental. Western

CB245.B64 1987
Bondanella, Peter E., 1943-
The Eternal City: Roman images in the modern
world/ by Peter Bondanella. Chapel Hill:
University of North Carolina Press, c1987. xiv,
286 p.
86-030847 909/.09821 0807817406
*Civilization, Western -- Roman influences.
Renaissance -- Italy. Italy -- Intellectual life.*

CB245.C362
Columbia College (Columbia University)
Chapters in Western civilization, edited by the
Contemporary civilization staff of Columbia
College, Columbia University. New York,
Columbia University Press, 1961- v.
61-013862 914
Civilization -- History. Civilization, Western.

CB245.D76 1992
Duignan, Peter.
The rebirth of the West: the Americanization of the
democratic world, 1945-1958/ Peter Duignan and
L.H. Gann. Cambridge, Mass., USA: Blackwell,
1992. xii, 733 p.
90-000417 909.82 1557860890
*Civilization, Western -- 20th century. Political
culture -- History -- 20th century. United States --
Civilization -- 1945- Canada -- Civilization --
1945- Europe, Western -- Civilization.*

CB245.G55 1993
Girling, J. L. S.
Myths and politics in western societies: evaluating
the crisis of modernity in the United States,
Germany, and Great Britain/ John Girling. New
Brunswick, N.J., U.S.A: Transaction Publishers,
c1993. xi, 191 p.
92-021504 909/.09713 1560000929
*Civilization, Western. Mythology -- Political
aspects.*

CB245.H35
Hayes, Carlton Joseph Huntley, 1882-1964.
Christianity and Western civilization. Stanford,
Stanford University Press [1954] 63 p.
54-011786 901
Civilization, Western. Civilization, Christian.

CB245.H429 1997
Herman, Arthur, 1956-
The idea of decline in Western history/ Arthur
Herman. New York: Free Press, c1997. 521 p.
96-036285 909/.09812 0684827913
*Civilization, Western -- Philosophy. Regression
(Civilization)*

CB245.K544 1988
King, David B.
The crisis of our time: reflections on the course of
Western civilization, past, present, and future/
David Burnett King. Selinsgrove [Pa.]:
Susquehanna University Press; c1988. 265 p.
86-063055 909/.09821 0941664783
Civilization, Western.

CB245.M8
Muller, Herbert Joseph, 1905-
Freedom in the Western World, from the Dark
Ages to the rise of democracy. New York, Harper
& Row [1963] 428 p.
63-008427 914
Civilization, Western. Liberty.

CB245.W28 1997
Waswo, Richard.
The founding legend of western civilization: from
Virgil to Vietnam/ Richard Waswo. Hanover, NH:
Wesleyan University Press: c1997. xvii, 373 p.
96-032079 909/.09812 0819552968
*Civilization, Western -- History. Legends --
History and criticism. European literature --
History and criticism. Europe -- Territorial
expansion.*

CB245.W4 1964
Webb, Walter Prescott, 1888-1963.
The Great Frontier. Introd. by Arnold J. Toynbee. Austin, University of Texas Press [1964] xviii, 434 p.
64-010321   914
Civilization, Western -- Philosophy. Social history. Frontier and pioneer life.

CB251 Civilization and race — Special civilizations — Eastern and Western

CB251.A213
Abegg, Lily.
Mind of East Asia. Thames, 1952. 344 p.
52-012912   901
Civilization, Oriental. National characteristics.

CB251.B3813
Baudet, E. H. P. 1919-
Paradise on earth; some thoughts on European images of non-European man. Translated by Elizabeth Wentholt. New Haven, Yale University Press, 1965. xii, 87 p.
65-011174   301.154
East and West

CB251.T69 1953a
Toynbee, Arnold Joseph, 1889-1975.
The world and the West. New York, Oxford University Press, 1953. 99 p.
53-005911   901
Civilization -- History. East and West.

CB251.T69 1960
Toynbee, Arnold Joseph, 1889-1975.
Civilization on trial and The world and the West/ by Arnold Toynbee. New York: Meridian Books, 1958, 1960 pr 348 p.
58-008525   901.9
History -- Philosophy. East and West. Civilization.

CB253 Civilization and race — Special civilizations — Oriental. Eastern

CB253.D4
Dean, Vera (Micheles) 1903-
The nature of the non-Western World. [New York] New American Library [1957] 284 p.
57-008030   901
Civilization, Oriental. Africa -- Civilization. Latin America -- Civilization.

CB253.S3813 1984
Schwab, Raymond.
Oriental renaissance: Europe's rediscovery of India and the East, 1680-1880/ Raymond Schwab; translated by Gene Patterson-Black and Victor Reinking; foreword by Edward W. Said. New York: Columbia University Press, 1984. xx, 542 p.
83-025279   909/.09811   0231041381
East and West. Europe -- Civilization -- Oriental influences. Europe -- Civilization -- Indic influences. Europe -- Intellectual life.

CB301 By period — Prehistory

CB301.C57
Clark, Grahame, 1907-
Aspects of prehistory [by] Grahame Clark. Berkeley, University of California Press, 1970. xiii, 161 p.
73-094989   913.03/1   0520015843
Prehistoric peoples. Evolution.

CB301.L48
The epic of man, by the editors of Life. New York, Time, inc., 1961. 307 p.
61-017388   901.91
Civilization, Ancient.

CB301.L513
Lissner, Ivar, 1909-1967.
Man, God, and magic; translated from the German by J. Maxwell Brownjohn. New York, Putnam [1961] 344 p.
61-005698   901.91
Civilization, Ancient. Primitive societies. Evenki (Asian people)

CB301.P5 1961
Piggott, Stuart,
The dawn of civilization; the first world survey of human cultures in early times. Texts by Grahame Clark [and others] New York, McGraw-Hill [1961] 403 p.
61-011703   901.91
Civilization, Ancient.

CB311 By period — Ancient — General works

CB311.B3
Bacon, Edward,
Vanished civilizations of the ancient world. Texts by Henri Lhote [and others] 802 illus. (211 in color, 539 photos. and drawings, 52 maps and charts) New York, McGraw-Hill [1963] 360 p.
63-014869   901.91
Civilization, Ancient.

CB311.B5 1973
Bibby, Geoffrey.
Four thousand years ago; a world panorama of life in the second millennium B.C. New york, Knopf, 1961. 398 p.
61-014367   901.91
Civilization, Ancient.

CB311.C85
Cottrell, Leonard.
The anvil of civilization. [New York] New American Library [1957] 256 p.
57-010111   901
Civilization, Ancient.

CB311.E535 2000
Encyclopedia of the ancient world/ editor, Thomas J. Sienkewicz. Pasadena, Calif.: Salem Press, 2001. p. cm.
2001-049896   930/.03   0893560383
Civilization, Ancient -- Encyclopedias.

CB311.G69
Green, Peter, 1924-
Essays in antiquity. Cleveland, World Pub. Co. [1960] 224 p.
60-013359   901.91
Civilization, Ancient.

CB311.H35 1993
Hawkes, Jacquetta Hopkins, 1910-
The atlas of early man/ Jacquetta Hawkes; assisted by David Trump. New York: St. Martin's Press, 1993. 255 p.
93-014330   930.220   0312097468
Civilization, Ancient. Prehistoric peoples.

CB311.H65
The Horizon book of lost worlds, by the editors of Horizon magazine. Editor in charge: Marshall B. Davidson. Narrative by Leonard Cottrell. New York, American Heritage Pub. Co.; book trade distribut [1962] 431 p.
62-019438   901.91
Civilization, Ancient.

CB311.M27 1999
Maisels, Charles Keith.
Early civilizations of the old world: the formative histories of Egypt, the Levant, Mesopotamia, India, and China/ Charles Keith Maisels. London; Routledge, 1999. xvi, 479 p.
99-220327   930   0415109752
Civilization, Ancient.

CB311.P44 1983
Peoples and places of the past: the National Geographic illustrated cultural atlas of the ancient world. [Washington, D.C.]: National Geographic Society, c1983. 424 p.
83-002208   909.07   087044462X
Civilization, Ancient. Civilization, Medieval.

CB311.T245 1988
Tainter, Joseph A.
The collapse of complex societies/ Joseph A. Tainter. Cambridge, Cambridgeshire; Cambridge University Press, 1988. xiv, 250 p.
86-033432   930   0521340926
Civilization, Ancient. Comparative civilization. Civilization -- Philosophy.

CB311.W55
White, Leslie A., 1900-1975.
The evolution of culture; the development of civilization to the fall of Rome. New York, McGraw-Hill, 1959. 378 p.
58-011197   901.91
Civilization, Ancient.

CB311.W66
Woody, Thomas, 1891-.
Life and education in early societies. New York, Macmillan Co., 1949. xx, 825 p.
49-008741   901
Civilization, Ancient. Education -- History. Physical education and training -- History.

CB351 By period — Medieval — General works

CB351.A56 1980
Artz, Frederick Binkerd,
The mind of the Middle Ages, A.D. 200-1500:an historical survey/ Frederick B. Artz.3d ed., rev. Chicago: University of Chicago Press, 1980. xiv, 586 p.
79-016259   909.07   0226028402
Civilization, Medieval.

CB351.B35 1992
Barber, Malcolm.
The two cities: medieval Europe, 1050-1320/ Malcolm Barber. London; Routledge, 1992. 581 p.
91-002464   940.1   0415087804
Civilization, Medieval. Europe -- History -- 476-1492.

CB351.C25
Cantor, Norman F.
The meaning of the Middle Ages; a sociological and cultural history [by] Norman F. Cantor. Boston, Allyn and Bacon [1973] viii, 321 p.
77-190550   901/.93
Civilization, Medieval.

CB351.C54 1997
Colish, Marcia L.
Medieval foundations of the western intellectual tradition, 400-1400/ Marcia L. Colish. New Haven: Yale Univesity Press, c1997. xii, 388 p.
97-024370   940   0300071426
Learning and scholarship -- History -- Medieval, 500-1500. Comparative civilization. Europe -- Intellectual life.

CB351.D24 1984
Dahmus, Joseph Henry, 1909-
Dictionary of medieval civilization/ Joseph Dahmus. New York: Macmillan, c1984. p. cm.
83-025583   909.07/03/21   0029078709

CB351.D27 1992
Dales, Richard C.
The intellectual life of Western Europe in the Middle Ages/ by Richard C. Dales.2nd rev. ed. Leiden; E.J. Brill, 1992. 322 p.
92-010587   940.1.220   9004096221
Civilization, Medieval.

CB351.E76
Erickson, Carolly, 1943-
The medieval vision: essays in history and perception/ Carolly Erickson. New York: Oxford University Press, 1976. vii, 247 p.
75-010179   940.1   0195019644
Civilization, Medieval. Religious thought -- Middle Ages.

CB351.E78
Essays on medieval civilization/ by Richard E. Sullivan ... [et al.]; introd. by Bryce Lyon; edited by Bede Karl Lackner & Kenneth Roy Philp. Austin: University of Texas Press, c1978. xxi, 178 p.
77-017068   940.1/4   0292720238
Civilization, Medieval -- Addresses, essays, lectures.

CB351.H3 1958
Haskins, Charles Homer, 1870-1937.
Studies in mediaeval culture. New York, F. Ungar Pub. Co. [1958] viii, 294 p.
58-007726   901
Civilization, Medieval. Latin literature, Medieval and modern -- History and criticism.

CB351.H4
Herlihy, David,
Medieval culture and society. New York, Harper & Row [1968] xv, 410 p.
68-013326   914.03/1
Civilization, Medieval.

CB351.H6 1966
Hoyt, Robert S.
Europe in the Middle Ages.   Harcourt, Brace, and World, 1966. 684 p.
66-016060   940.1
Civilization, Medieval.   Europe -- History -- 476-1492.

CB351.L26
Laistner, M. L. W. 1890-1959.
The intellectual heritage of the early Middle Ages; selected essays. Edited by Chester G. Starr. Ithaca, N.Y., Cornell University Press [1957] xvii, 285 p.
57-002704   901
Middle Ages -- Intellectual life.

CB351.L44 2001
Levine, David, 1946-
At the dawn of modernity: biology, culture, and material life in Europe after the year 1000/ David Levine. Berkeley: University of California Press, c2001. vii, 431 p.
00-034384   940.1   0520220587
Civilization, Medieval. Social history -- Medieval, 500-1500. Body, Human -- Social aspects -- History. Europe -- Church history -- 600-1500.

CB351.M565 1989
The Middle Ages: a concise encyclopaedia/ general editor, H.R. Loyn. New York, N.Y.: Thames and Hudson, 1989. 352 p.
88-050254   909.07   0500251037
Middle Ages -- Dictionaries. Civilization, Medieval -- Dictionaries.

CB351.M7813 1986
The Cambridge illustrated history of the Middle Ages/ edited by Robert Fossier; translated by Janet Sondheimer. Cambridge; Cambridge University Press, 1986-1997. 3 v.
85-021268   909.07   0521266440
Civilization, Medieval.

CB351.R3 1957
Rand, Edward Kennard, 1871-1945.
Founders of the Middle Ages. New York, Dover Publications [1957, c1928] 365 p.
57-059148   901
Civilization, Medieval. Literature, Medieval -- History and criticism. Middle Ages.

CB351.S6 1953a
Southern, R. W. 1912-
The making of the Middle Ages. New Haven, Yale University Press, 1953. 280 p.
53-005280   940.1
Civilization, Medieval. Middle Ages.

CB351.W613 1968
Wolff, Philippe, 1913-
The cultural awakening. Translated from the French by Anne Carter. New York, Pantheon Books, [c1968] 314 p.
68-013014   914/.03/1
Civilization, Medieval.

CB353 By period — Medieval — General special

CB353.B6 1997
Boas, George,
Primitivism and related ideas in the Middle Ages/ by George Boas.Johns Hopkins paperbacks ed. Baltimore: Johns Hopkins University Press, 1997. xii, 227 p.
96-029536   940.1.221   0801856108
Primitivism. Civilization, Medieval.

CB353.C837 1996
The cultural patronage of medieval women/ edited by June Hall McCash. Athens: University of Georgia Press, c1996. xix, 402 p.
94-013063   920.72/094   0820317020
Women benefactors -- Europe -- History. Women -- History -- Middle Ages, 500-1500.

CB353.D26
Daniel, Norman.
The Arabs and mediaeval Europe/ Norman Daniel. London: Longman, 1975. xiv, 378 p.
73-093276   301.29/4/0174927   0582780454
Europe -- Relations -- Islamic Empire. Islamic Empire -- Relations -- Europe.

CB353.G7
Grabois, Aryeh, 1930-
Illustrated encyclopedia of medieval civilization/ by Aryeh Grabois. New York: Mayflower Books, 1979 p. cm.
79-013630   909/.1/03   070640856X
Civilization, Medieval -- Dictionaries.

CB353.G8713 1988
Gurevich, Aron IAkovlevich.
Medieval popular culture: problems of belief and perception/ Aron Gurevich; translated by Janos M. Bak and Paul A. Hollingsworth. Cambridge [Cambridgeshire]; Cambridge University Press; 1988. xx, 275 p.
87-009318   940.1   0521303699
Civilization, Medieval. Popular culture -- Europe.

CB353.L38 2001
The late medieval age of crisis and renewal, 1300-1500: a biographical dictionary/ edited by Clayton J. Drees. Westport, Conn.: Greenwood Press, 2001. xiv, 546 p.
00-022335   940.1   0313305889
Civilization, Medieval -- Dictionaries. Europe -- History -- 476-1492 -- Biography -- Dictionaries. Europe -- History -- 1492-1517 -- Biography -- Dictionaries. Europe -- Social conditions -- To 1492 -- Dictionaries.

CB353.L48 1988
Lewis, Archibald Ross, 1914-
Nomads and Crusaders, A.D. 1000-1368/ Archibald R. Lewis. Bloomington: Indiana University Press, c1988. ix, 213 p.
87-045588   940.1   0253347874
Civilization, Medieval. Comparative civilization. Middle ages -- History. Europe -- Territorial expansion.

CB353.M83 1987
Mullett, Michael A.
Popular culture and popular protest in late medieval and early modern Europe/ Michael Mullett. London; Croom Helm, c1987. 176 p.
87-022146   940   0709935668
Civilization, Medieval. Popular culture -- Europe. Insurgency -- Europe -- History. Europe -- Social conditions -- To 1492. Europe -- Social conditions -- 16th century. Europe -- Social conditions -- 17th century.

CB353.P5413 2001
Pleij, Herman.
Dreaming of Cockaigne: medieval fantasies of the perfect life/ Herman Pleij; translated by Diane Webb. New York: Columbia University Press, c2001. ix, 533 p.
00-051916   398/.42/0940902   0231117027
Cockaigne. Civilization, Medieval. Social history -- Medieval, 500-1500.

CB354.6 By period — Medieval — 12th century

CB354.6.P32
Packard, Sidney Raymond, 1893-
12th century Europe; an interpretive essay, by Sidney R. Packard. Amherst, University of Massachusetts Press, 1973. ix, 362 p.
73-079507   914/.03/17
Civilization, Medieval -- 12th century. Twelfth century. Europe -- Civilization.

CB355 By period — Medieval — 13th century

CB355.D3
Davis, William Stearns, 1877-1930.
Life on a medieval barony; a picture of a typical feudal community in the thirteenth century, by William Stearns Davis. New York and London: Harper, [1936?] 414 p.
37-007526
Feudalism. Chivalry. Civilization, Medieval.

CB358 By period — Modern — General special

CB358.G76 1992
Gross, David, 1940-
The past in ruins: tradition and the critique of modernity/ David Gross. Amherst: University of Massachusetts Press, c1992. xi, 175 p.
92-010935   901   0870238213
Civilization, Modern -- Philosophy. Tradition (Philosophy)

CB358.P53 1962
Plaine, Henry L.
Darwin, Marx, and Wagner; a symposium. [Columbus] Ohio State University Press [1962] viii, 165 p.
61-012066   901
Marx, Karl, -- 1818-1883. Darwin, Charles, -- 1809-1882. Wagner, Richard, -- 1813-1883. Civilization, Modern.

CB358.T84 1989
Twitchell, James B., 1943-
Preposterous violence: fables of aggression in modern culture/ James B. Twitchell. New York: Oxford University Press, 1989. 338 p.
88-031227   302.2/34   0195058879
Popular culture -- History. Amusements -- History. Violence in mass media -- History.

CB359-369 By period — Modern — Renaissance

CB359.L8 1960
Lucas, Henry Stephen, 1889-1961.
The Renaissance and the Reformation. Harper & Row, c1960. 757 p.
60-007014   901.93
Renaissance. Reformation.

CB359.S65
Spitz, Lewis William, 1922-
The Reformation: material or spiritual? Boston, Heath [1962] 104 p.
62-013573
Reformation -- Addresses, essays, lectures.

CB361.B43 1987
Bergin, Thomas Goddard, 1904-
Encyclopedia of the Renaissance/ Thomas G. Bergin, Jennifer Speake. New York, N.Y.: Facts on File Publications, c1987. 454 p.
87-013433   940.2/1/0321   0816013152
Renaissance -- Dictionaries.

CB361.C5 1959
The Civilization of the Renaissance, by James Westfall Thompson [and others] New York, Ungar [1959] 136 p.
58-059873   901.93
Renaissance. Art, Renaissance.

CB361.D27
Dannenfeldt, Karl H.,
The Renaissance: medieval or modern? Boston, Heath [1959] 115 p.
59-008438   901.93
Renaissance -- Addresses, essays, lectures. Civilization, Medieval.

CB361.E52 1999
Encyclopedia of the Renaissance/ Paul F. Grendler, editor in chief. New York: Scribner's, 1999. 6 v.
99-048290   940.2/1/03   0684805146
Renaissance -- Encyclopedias.

CB361.F373
Ferguson, Wallace Klippert, 1902-
The Renaissance in historical thought; five centuries of interpretation. Boston, Houghton Mifflin Co. [1948] xiii, 429 p.
48-009685   940.21
Renaissance. Historiography.

CB361.G6213 1993
Goetz, Hans-Werner.
Life in the Middle Ages: from the seventh to the thirteenth century/ Hans-Werner Goetz; translated by Albert Wimmer; edited by Steven Rowan. Notre Dame, Ind.: University of Notre Dame Press, c1993. ix, 316 p.
92-056868   940.1   0268013004
Civilization, Medieval. Europe -- Social life and customs.

CB361.G69 1991
Grafton, Anthony.
Defenders of the text: the traditions of scholarship in an age of science, 1450-1800/ Anthony Grafton. Cambridge, Mass.: Harvard University Press, 1991. 330 p.
90-037895   001.1   0674195442
Renaissance. Learning and scholarship -- History. Europe -- Intellectual life.

CB361.J34 2000
Jardine, Lisa.
Global interests: Renaissance art between East and West/ Lisa Jardine and Jerry Brotton. Ithaca, N.Y.: Cornell University Press, 2000. 223 p.
00-025362   940.2/1   080143808X
Renaissance. Material culture -- Europe. Europe -- Civilization -- Turkish influences. Turkey -- Civilization -- European influences.

CB361.P27 1981
Patronage in the Renaissance/ edited by Guy Fitch Lytle and Stephen Orgel. Princeton, N.J.: Princeton University Press, c1981. xiv, 389 p.
81-047143   940.2/1   0691053383
Renaissance -- Congresses. Art patronage -- Europe -- History -- Congresses.

CB361.R39
Renaissance letters: revelations of a world reborn/ edited with introd., commentary, and translation by Robert J. Clements and Lorna Levant. [New York]: New York University Press, c1976. xxvi, 468 p.
75-021806   940.2/1   0814713629
Renaissance -- Sources.

CB361.S93 1959
The Renaissance: a reconsideration of the theories and interpretations of the age. Edited by Tinsley Helton. Contributors: Garrett Mattingly [and others] Madison, University of Wisconsin Press [c1961] 1964 xiii, 160 p.
61-005903   901.93
Renaissance -- Congresses.

CB361.T74 1983
Trinkaus, Charles Edward, 1911-
The scope of Renaissance humanism/ Charles Trinkaus. Ann Arbor: University of Michigan Press, c1983. xxvii, 479 p.
83-006650   001.3/09/024   0472100319
Renaissance. Humanism.

CB361.U43
Ullmann, Walter, 1910-
Medieval foundations of renaissance humanism/ Walter Ullmann. Ithaca, N.Y.: Cornell University Press, c1977. xii, 212 p.
77-000278   144/.094   0801411106
Humanism. Renaissance. Civilization, Medieval.

CB365.U8
Utley, Francis Lee, 1907-
The forward movement of the fourteenth century. Columbus, Ohio State University Press [1961] 166 p.
60-014642   901.903
Fourteenth century.

CB367.A5 1963
Allen, P. S. 1869-1933.
The age of Erasmus: lectures delivered in the universities of Oxford and London/ by P. S. Allen. New York: Russell & Russell, 1963, 1914. 303 p.
63-011026   922.2492
Erasmus, Desiderius, -- d. 1536. Renaissance.

CB367.C57 1991
Circa 1492: art in the age of exploration/ edited by Jay A. Levenson. Washington: National Gallery of Art; c1991. 671 p.
91-050590   909/.4074753   0300051670
Fifteenth century -- Exhibitions.

CB367.H35 1994
Hale, J. R. 1923-
The civilization of Europe in the Renaissance/ John Hale. New York: Atheneum; 1994. xx, 648 p.
93-046246   940.2/1   0689122004
Renaissance. Europe -- Civilization -- 16th century.

CB369.M36 1992
Manchester, William Raymond, 1922-
A world lit only by fire: the medieval mind and the Renaissance: portrait of an age/ William Manchester. Boston: Little, Brown, c1992. xvii, 318 p.
91-039928   940.2/1   0316545317
Renaissance. Learning and scholarship -- History -- Medieval, 500-1500.

CB401 By period — Modern — 16th-17th centuries

CB401.E43
Elliott, John Huxtable.
The old world and the new 1492-1650, by J. H. Elliott. Cambridge [Eng.] University Press, 1970. x, 118 p.
73-121362   914/.03   0521079373
Europe -- Civilization. America -- Discovery and exploration.

CB401.E94 2000
Bouwsma, William James, 1923-
The waning of the Renaissance, 1550-1640/ William J. Bouwsma. New Haven: Yale University Press, c2000. xi, 288 p.
00-049538   940.2/1   0300085370
Renaissance. Science and civilization. Astronomy, Renaissance. Europe -- Intellectual life -- 16th century. Europe -- Intellectual life -- 17th century.

CB401.F7
Friedrich, Carl J. 1901-
The age of power [by] Carl J. Friedrich and Charles Blitzer. Ithaca, N.Y., Cornell University Press [1957] 200 p.
57-004449   909/.06
Europe -- Civilization -- 17th century.

CB401.H3 1969b
Hatton, Ragnhild Marie.
Europe in the age of Louis XIV [by] Ragnhild Hatton. [New York] Harcourt, Brace & World [1969] 263 p.
70-078869   914/.03/25
Europe -- Civilization -- 17th century.

CB411 By period — Modern — 18th century

CB411.C6 1969
Cobban, Alfred.
The eighteenth century: Europe in the age of enlightenment. Texts by Alfred Cobban [and others] Edited by Alfred Cobban. New York, McGraw-Hill [1969] 360 p.
78-075160   914/.03/25
Europe -- Civilization -- 18th century.

CB411.H38 1968
Hampson, Norman.
A cultural history of the Enlightenment. New York, Pantheon Books [c1968] 304 p.
68-026043   914/.03/253
Enlightenment -- History.

CB411.K7 1961
Kraus, Michael, 1901-
The Atlantic civilization: eighteenth-century origins. New York, Russell & Russell, 1961 [c1949] 334 p.
61-012131   901.93
Civilization, Modern -- 18th century. United States -- Relations -- Europe. Europe -- Relations -- United States.

CB411.M3
Mazzeo, Joseph Anthony, 1923-
Reason and the imagination; studies in the history of ideas, 1600-1800. New York, Columbia University Press, 1962. viii, 321 p.
62-007773   901.93
Nicolson, Marjorie Hope, -- 1894- Eighteenth century. Seventeenth century.

CB417 By period — Modern — 19th century

CB417.M36
Masur, Gerhard, 1901-1975.
Prophets of yesterday; studies in European culture, 1890-1914. New York, Macmillan, 1961. 481 p.
61-009729   914
Civilization, Modern -- 19th century. Europe -- Intellectual life.

CB417.R4
Regin, Deric.
Culture and the crowd; a cultural history of the proletarian era. Philadelphia, Chilton Book Co. [1968] xii, 512 p.
68-019178   901.9/4
Civilization, Modern -- 19th century. Civilization, Modern -- 20th century.

CB425-427 By period — Modern — 1900-1970

CB425.A89
Ayres, Clarence Edwin, 1891-1972.
Toward a reasonable society: the values of industrial civilization/ by C.E. Ayres. Austin: University of Texas, c1961. 301 p.
61-012911   901.94
Civilization, Modern -- 20th century.

CB425.B458 1988
Berman, Marshall,
All that is solid melts into air: the experience of modernity/ Marshall Berman. New York, N.Y., U.S.A.: Viking Penguin, 1988. 383 p.
87-029174   909.82.219   0140109625
Civilization, Modern--20th century. Civilization, Modern--19th century.

CB425.B668
Boulding, Kenneth Ewart, 1910-
The meaning of the twentieth century; the great transition [by] Kenneth E. Boulding. New York, Harper & Row [1964] xvi, 199 p.
64-020540   301.24
Civilization, Modern -- 1950-

CB425.C28 1988
Cantor, Norman F.
Twentieth-century culture: modernism to deconstruction/ Norman F. Cantor. New York: P. Lang, 1988. xx, 452 p.
87-017024   909.82   082040358X
Civilization, Modern -- 20th century. Modernism (Art) Modernism (Literature)

CB425.H24
Harrington, Michael, 1928-
The accidental century. New York, Macmillan [1965] 322 p.
65-016935   901.94
Civilization, Modern -- 20th century.

CB425.H86 1962
Huxley, Julian, 1887-1975.
The humanist frame. New York, Harper [1962, c1961] 432 p.
62-007898   144
Civilization -- Philosophy. Humanism -- 20th century. Civilization, Modern.

CB425.K45
Kerr, Walter, 1913-
The decline of pleasure. New York, Simon and Schuster, 1962. 319 p.
62-009607   136.4973
Intellectual life.

CB425.K75
Krutch, Joseph Wood, 1893-1970.
Human nature and the human condition. New York, Random House c1959. 211 p.
59-010808   901.94
Civilization, Modern -- 1950-

CB425.M79
Mumford, Lewis, 1895-
In the name of sanity. New York, Harcourt, Brace [1954] 244 p.
54-011324   901
Civilization, Modern -- 20th century.

CB427.C48
Chase, Stuart, 1888-
The most probable world. New York, Harper & Row [c1968] xii, 239 p.
67-028803   901.9/4
Civilization, Modern -- 20th century -- Addresses, essays, lectures.

CB427.F25
Fabun, Don.
The dynamics of change, by Don Fabun, assisted by Niels Sundermeyer. Art director: Bob Conover. Englewood Cliffs, N.J., Prentice-Hall [1967] 1 v.
67-025569   901.94
Civilization, Modern -- 1950-

CB427.K6 1961
Koestler, Arthur, 1905-
The lotus and the robot. New York, Macmillan, 1961 [c1960] 296 p.
61-006583   915
Yoga. Zen Buddhism. Civilization.

CB427.M287 2001
Manifesto: a century of isms/ edited by Mary Ann Caws. Lincoln: University of Nebraska Press, c2001. xxxiv, 713 p.
00-033783   909.82   0803264070
Civilization, Modern -- 20th century -- Sources. Intellectual life -- History -- 20th century -- Sources. Arts, Modern -- 20th century -- Sources. Europe -- Civilization -- 20th century -- Sources. America -- Civilization -- 20th century -- Sources.

CB427.S2313 1968
Sakharov, Andrei, 1921-
Progress, coexistence, and intellectual freedom, by Andrei D. Sakharov. Translated by the New York Times. With introd., afterword, and notes, by Harrison E. Salisbury. New York, Norton [1968] 158 p.
68-057368   901.94/5   0393054284
Civilization, Modern -- 1950-

CB428-430 By period — Modern — 1971-

CB428.C58 1989
Clark, Mary E.
Ariadne's thread: the search for new modes of thinking/ Mary E. Clark. New York: St. Martin's Press, 1989. xxviii, 584 p
88-028185   909.82   0312015801
Civilization, Modern -- 1950-

CB428.H38 1989
Harvey, David, 1935-
The condition of postmodernity: an enquiry into the origins of cultural change/ David Harvey. Oxford [England]; Blackwell, 1989. ix, 378 p.
88-039135 909.82 0631162925
Civilization, Modern -- 1950- Capitalism. Space and time.

CB428.H44 1974
Heilbroner, Robert L.
An inquiry into the human prospect [by] Robert L. Heilbroner. New York, Norton [1974] 150 p.
73-021879 909.82 0393055140
Civilization, Modern -- 1950- Regression (Civilization)

CB428.M356 1989
Marcus, Greil.
Lipstick traces: a secret history of the twentieth century/ Greil Marcus. Cambridge, Mass.: Harvard University Press, 1989. 496 p.
88-024678 306/.4/0904 0674535804
Popular culture -- History -- 20th century. Avant-garde (Aesthetics) Art and society -- History -- 20th century.

CB428.M854
Muller, Herbert Joseph, 1905-
Uses of the future [by] Herbert J. Muller. Bloomington, Indiana University Press [1974] xviii, 264 p.
73-015240 901.94 0253362105
Civilization, Modern -- 1950- Twenty-first century -- Forecasts. United States -- Civilization -- 1970-

CB428.P4
Pawley, Martin.
The private future: causes and consequences of community collapse in the West. New York, Random House [1974] 217 p.
73-005044 901.94 0394480724
Civilization, Modern -- 1950- Regression (Civilization)

CB428.R67
Roszak, Theodore, 1933-
Where the wasteland ends; politics and transcendence in postindustrial society. Garden City, N.Y., Doubleday, 1972. xxxiv, 492 p.
78-170179 910/.03/0904 0385027281
Civilization, Modern -- 1950-

CB428.S8
Stavrianos, Leften Stavros.
The promise of the coming dark age/ L. S. Stavrianos. San Francisco: W. H. Freeman, c1976. x, 211 p.
76-008232 909.82 0716704978.
Civilization, Modern -- 1950- Civilization -- History. Regression (Civilization)

CB428.T69 1971
Toynbee, Arnold Joseph, 1889-1975.
Surviving the future [by] Arnold Toynbee. London, Oxford University Press, 1971. xii, 164 p.
77-167854 901.9 0192152521
Civilization, Modern -- 1950- Civilization -- Philosophy.

CB430.P637 1999
Postman, Neil.
Building a bridge to the 18th century: how the past can improve our future/ by Neil Postman. New York: Alfred A. Knopf: 1999. 213 p.
99-018923 909.82/5 0375401296
Civilization, Modern -- 1950- Enlightenment. Technology and civilization. United States -- Civilization -- 1970-

CB430.Y33 1997
Yack, Bernard, 1952-
The fetishism of modernities: epochal self-consciousness in contemporary social and political thought/ Bernard Yack. Notre Dame, Ind.: University of Notre Dame Press, c1997. ix, 182 p.
97-012144 301/.01 0268028508
Civilization, Modern -- 1950- -- Philosophy. Social sciences -- Philosophy. Postmodernism.

CB475 Relation to special topics — Symbolism and civilization

CB475.B3 1951
Bayley, Harold.
The lost language of symbolism; an inquiry into the origin of certain letters, words, names, fairy-tales, folklore, and mythologies. New York, Barnes & Noble [1951] 2 v.
51-013169 401
Symbolism. Printers' marks. Watermarks.

CB475.O37 1992
Olderr, Steven.
Reverse symbolism dictionary: symbols listed by subject/ compiled by Steven Olderr. Jefferson, N.C.: McFarland, c1992. ix, 181 p.
90-053517 302.2/22 0899505619
Signs and symbols -- Dictionaries. Symbolism -- Dictionaries. Emblems -- Dictionaries.

CB478 Relation to special topics — Technology and civilization. Science and civilization

CB478.A34 1996
Adams, Robert McCormick, 1926-
Paths of fire: an anthropologist's inquiry into Western technology/ Robert McC. Adams. Princeton, NJ: Princeton University Press, 1996. xvi, 332 p.
96-012733 303.48/3 0691026343
Technology and civilization. Civilization, Western -- History.

CB478.B73 1978
Bronowski, Jacob, 1908-1974.
Magic, science, and civilization/ J. Bronowski. New York: Columbia University Press, 1978. 88 p.
78-001660 909.08 0231044844
Science and civilization -- Addresses, essays, lectures. Science -- Europe -- History -- Addresses, essays, lectures. Philosophy -- Europe -- History -- Addresses, essays, lectures.

CB478.F6
Foster, George McClelland, 1913-
Traditional cultures, and the impact of technological change. New York, Harper [1962] 292 p.
62-010483 301.24
Technology and civilization.

CB478.M78
Mumford, Lewis, 1895-
The myth of the machine. New York, Harcourt, Brace & World [1967-1970] 2 v.
67-016088 901.9
Technology and civilization.

CB478.N4
Nef, John Ulric, 1899-
Cultural foundations of industrial civilization. Cambridge, Eng., University Press, 1958. xiv, 163 p.
59-000642
Technology and civilization. Civilization -- History.

CB478.P4
Peccei, Aurelio.
The chasm ahead. [New York] Macmillan [1969] xvi, 297 p.
69-011395 901.9
Technology and civilization.

CB478.T38 1970b
Taylor, Gordon Rattray.
The doomsday book; can the world survive? New York, World Pub. Co. [1970] 335 p.
75-124280 301.31
Technology and civilization. Human ecology.

CB481 Relation to special topics — War and civilization

CB481.S58 1998
Sowell, Thomas, 1930-
Conquests and cultures: an international history/ Thomas Sowell. New York: Basic Books, c1998. xvi, 493 p.
97-050290 325/.32 0465013996
War and civilization. Conquerors -- History. Imperialism -- History.

CC Archaeology

CC65 Collected works (nonserial) — Several authors

CC65.S2
New roads to yesterday; essays in archaeology. Articles from Science, edited by Joseph R. Caldwell. New York, Basic Books [1966] viii, 546 p.
65-025225 913.03108
Archaeology.

CC70 Dictionaries. Encyclopedias

CC70.C58 1993
Collins dictionary of archaeology/ edited by Paul Bahn. Santa Barbara, Calif.: ABC-CLIO, c1993. 654 p.
93-037784 930.1/03 0874367441
Archaeology -- Dictionaries.

CC70.C59 1999
Companion encyclopedia of archaeology/ edited by Graeme Barker and Annie Grant. London; Routledge, 1999. p. cm.
98-007621   930.1   0415064481
Archaeology -- Encyclopedias.

CC70.F32 1984
The Facts on File dictionary of archaeology/ editor, Ruth D. Whitehouse. New York, N.Y.: Facts on File, 1984. p. cm.
83-016396   930.1/03/21   0871960486
Archaeology -- Dictionaries.

CC70.K56 2000
Kipfer, Barbara Ann.
Encyclopedic dictionary of archaeology/ compiled by Barbara Ann Kipfer. New York: Kluwer Academic/Plenum, c2000. xi, 708 p.
99-053995   930.1/03   0306461587
Archaeology -- Dictionaries.

CC70.M45 1993
Mignon, Molly Raymond.
Dictionary of concepts in archaeology/ Molly Raymond Mignon. Westport, Conn.: Greenwood Press, 1993. xii, 364 p.
92-043151   930.1/03   0313246599
Archaeology -- Dictionaries.

CC70.O96 1996
The Oxford companion to archaeology/ editor in chief, Brian M. Fagan; editors, Charlotte Beck ... [et al.]. New York: Oxford University Press, 1996. xx, 844 p.
96-030792   930.1/03   0195076184
Archaeology -- Dictionaries.

CC72 Philosophy. Theory — General works

CC72.W37 1984
Watson, Patty Jo, 1932-
Archeological explanation: the scientific method in archeology/ Patty Jo Watson, Steven A. LeBlanc, Charles L. Redman. New York: Columbia University Press, 1984. xi, 309 p.
84-005014   930.1/01   0231060289
Archaeology -- Philosophy. Archaeology -- Methodology.

CC72.4 Philosophy. Theory — Social archaeology

CC72.4.C43 2000
Gender and material culture in archaeological perspective/ edited by Moira Donald and Linda Hurcombe. New York: St. Martin's Press, 2000. xxiv, 275 p.
99-039504   930.1   0312223986
Social archaeology. Feminist archaeology. Material culture -- History.

CC72.4.F54 1995
Fletcher, Roland.
The limits of settlement growth: a theoretical outline/ Roland Fletcher. Cambridge; Cambridge Unversity Press, 1995. xxiii, 276 p.
94-018290   930.1   0521430852
Social archaeology. Human settlements -- History. Cities and towns -- Growth.

CC72.4.G53 1984
Gibbon, Guy E., 1939-
Anthropological archaeology/ Guy Gibbon. New York: Columbia University Press, 1984. xii, 455 p.
84-004321   930.1   0231056621
Social archaeology. Ethnoarchaeology.

CC72.4.G55 1999
Gilchrist, Roberta.
Gender and archaeology: contesting the past/ Roberta Gilchrist. London; Routledge, 1999. xviii, 190 p.
99-028835   930.1/082   0415215994
Feminist archaeology. Sex role -- History -- Philosophy.

CC72.4.L56 2000
Lines that divide: historical archaeologies of race, class, and gender/ edited by James A. Delle, Stephen A. Mrozowski, and Robert Paynter. Knoxville: University of Tennessee Press, c2000. xxxi, 328 p.
99-050986   907/.2   1572330864
Social archaeology. Archaeology and history. Racism -- History.

CC72.4.M55 1987
Miller, Daniel, 1954-
Material culture and mass consumption/ Daniel Miller. Oxford, OX, UK; B. Blackwell, 1987. viii, 240 p.
87-014627   930.1   0631156054
Social archaeology -- Philosophy. Material culture. Consumption (Economics)

CC72.4.N45 1997
Nelson, Sarah M., 1931-
Gender in archaeology: analyzing power and prestige/ by Sarah Milledge Nelson. Walnut Creek, Calif.: AltaMira Press, c1997. 240 p.
97-004860   930.1   0761991158
Feminist archaeology.

CC72.4.R46 1984
Renfrew, Colin, 1937-
Approaches to social archaeology/ Colin Renfrew. Cambridge, Mass.: Harvard University Press, 1984. viii, 430 p.
83-022548   306/.093   0674041658
Social archaeology. Anthropology, Prehistoric. Prehistoric peoples.

CC72.7 Philosophy. Theory — Classification

CC72.7.A33 1991
Adams, William Yeudale, 1927-
Archaeological typology and practical reality: a dialectical approach to artifact classification and sorting/ William Y. Adams and Ernest W. Adams. Cambridge [England]; Cambridge University Press, 1991. xxiii, 427 p.
90-041556   0521393345
Archaeology -- Classification. Antiquities -- Classification. Typology (Linguistics)

CC75 Philosophy. Theory — Methodology — General works

CC75.A3 1974
Aitken, M. J.
Physics and archaeology/ by M. J. Aitken. Oxford: Clarendon Press, 1974. viii, 291 p.
75-310409   930/.1/028   0198519222
Archaeology -- Methodology.

CC75.A654 2000
Archaeological method and theory: an encyclopedia/ editor, Linda Ellis. New York: Garland Pub., 2000. 705 p.
99-039140   930.1.221   0815313051
Archaeology--Methodology--Encyclopedias. Archaeology--Philosophy--Encyclopedias.

CC75.B47
Biek, Leo.
Archaeology and the microscope; the scientific examination of archaeological evidence. New York, Praeger [1963] 287 p.
63-020391   571.018
Archaeology -- Methodology.

CC75.B73 1970
Brothwell, Don R.,
Science in archaeology; a survey of progress and research. Edited by Don Brothwell and Eric Higgs. With a foreword by Grahame Clark. New York, Praeger [1970] 720 p.
76-092580   913.03/1/018
Archaeology -- Methodology.

CC75.C45 1956a
Childe, V. Gordon 1892-1957.
Piecing together the past; the interpretation of archeological data [by] V. Gordon Childe. London, Routledge & Kegan Paul [1956] vii, 176 p.
56-002114
Archaeology -- Methodology.

CC75.C535 1978
Clarke, David L., d. 1976.
Analytical archaeology/ David L. Clarke. New York: Columbia University Press, 1978. xxi, 526 p.
78-016957   930/.1/028   0231046308
Archaeology -- Methodology.

CC75.D36
Dating techniques for the archaeologist. Coedited by Henry N. Michael and Elizabeth K. Ralph. Cambridge, MIT Press [1971] xi, 226 p.
79-153296   913.03/10285   0262130742
Archaeology -- Methodology.

CC75.D63
Doran, J. E.
Mathematics and computers in archaeology/ J. E. Doran and F. R. Hodson. Edinburgh: Edinburgh University Press, [1975] xi, 381 p.
75-313615   930/.1/0285   0852242506
Archaeology -- Methodology -- Data processing. Archaeology -- Classification -- Data processing.

CC75.G66 1990
Gould, Richard A.
Recovering the past/ Richard A. Gould. Albuquerque: University of New Mexico Press, c1990. x, 258 p.
90-012589   930.1   0826312292
Archaeology. Archaeology and history. Ethnoarchaeology.

CC75.H44
Heizer, Robert Fleming, 1915-
The application of quantitative methods in archaeology, edited by Robert F. Heizer and Sherburne F. Cook. Chicago, Quadrangle Books, 1960. x, 358 p.
61-000987   913.018
Archaeology -- Methodology.

CC75.H445 1975
Heizer, Robert Fleming,
The archaeologist at work: a source book in archaeological method and interpretation/ edited by Robert F. Heizer. Westport, Conn.: Greenwood Press, 1975, c1959. xiv, 522 p.
75-025516   930/.1/028   0837183464
Archaeology--Methodology.

CC75.L297 1997
Lambert, Joseph B.
Traces of the past: unraveling the secrets of archaeology through chemistry/ Joseph B. Lambert. Reading, Mass.: Addison-Wesley, c1997. 319 p.
97-011454   930.1/028   0201409283
Archaeology -- Methodology Archaeological chemistry.

CC75.O15
Oakley, Kenneth Page, 1911-
Frameworks for dating fossil man [by] Kenneth P. Oakley. Chicago, Aldine Pub. Co. [c1964] x, 355 p.
64-008452   571.018
Archaeology -- Methodology.

CC75.P5
Piggott, Stuart.
Approach to archaeology.   Cambridge, Harvard University Press, 1959. 134 p.
59-016950   571
Archaeology.

CC75.P9
Pyddoke, Edward
The scientist and archaeology.   New York, Roy Publishers [c1963] xiii, 208 p.
64-013618   571.018
Archaeology -- Methodology.

CC75.T68 1978
Trigger, Bruce G.
Time and traditions: essays in archaeological interpretation/ Bruce G. Trigger. New York: Columbia University Press, 1978. xii, 273 p.
77-028524   930.1   0231045484
Archaeology -- Methodology -- Addresses, essays, lectures. Archaeology -- History -- Addresses, essays, lectures.

CC75.7 Philosophy. Theory — Methodology — General special

CC75.7.S6
Social archeology: beyond subsistence and dating/ edited by Charles L. Redman ... [et al.]. New York: Academic Press, c1978. xiv, 471 p.
78-016390   930/.1/028   0125851502
Archaeology -- Methodology. Social archaeology. Prehistoric peoples.

CC75.7.S68
Spatial archaeology/ edited by David L. Clarke. London; Academic Press, 1977. xi, 386 p.
76-055909   930/.1/028   0121757501
Archaeology -- Methodology -- Addresses, essays, lectures.

CC76-76.3 Philosophy. Theory — Methodology — Field methods

CC76.A3.D4
Deuel, Leo.
Flights into yesterday; the story of aerial archaeology. Pref. by Glyn Daniel. New York, St. Martin's Press, 1969. xx, 332 p.
73-086386   913/.031/028
Aerial photography in archaeology.

CC76.J68
Joukowsky, Martha.
A complete manual of field archaeology: tools and techniques of field work for archaeologists/ Martha Joukowsky. Englewood Cliffs, N.J.: Prentice-Hall, c1980. x, 630 p.
79-025847   930.1   0131621645
Archaeology -- Field work -- Handbooks, manuals, etc.

CC76.3.A74 1990
The Archaeology of regions: a case for full-coverage survey/ edited by Suzanne K. Fish and Stephen A. Kowalewski. Washington, D.C.; Smithsonian Institution Press, c1990. xiv, 277 p.
89-006249   930.1/028   0874744040
Archaeological surveying -- Congresses.

CC77 Philosophy. Theory — Methodology — Special types of archaelogy and archaeological sites, A-Z

CC77.B3
Bass, George Fletcher.
Archaeology under water [by] George F. Bass. New York, Praeger [1966] 224 p.
66-012992   913.031028
Underwater archaeology.

CC77.B8.L37 1997
Larsen, Clark Spencer.
Bioarchaeology: interpereting behavior from the human skeleton/ Clark Spencer Larsen. New York: Cambridge University Press, 1997. xii, 461 p.
96-051571   599.97   0521496411
Human remains (Archaeology) Human skeleton - - Analysis.

CC77.B8.L375 2000
Larsen, Clark Spencer.
Skeletons in our closet: revealing our past through bioarchaeology/ Clark Spencer Larsen. Princeton, N.J.: Princeton University Press, c2000. xvii, 248 p.
99-053724   930.1   0691004900
Human remains (Archaeology) Human skeleton - - Analysis. Population -- History.

CC77.C48
Chang, Kwang-chih.
Rethinking archaeology [by] K. C. Chang. New York, Random House [1967] xiv, 172 p.
67-010916   913/.001/8
Archaeology -- Methodology.

CC77.H5.H58 1991
Historical archaeology in Global perspective/ edited by Lisa Falk. Washington, D.C.: Smithsonian Institution Press, c1991. xiv, 122 p.
90-038918   930.1   087474413X
Archaeology and history. Netherlands -- Colonies -- History. Netherlands -- Territorial expansion. America -- Discovery and exploration.

CC77.H5.H59 1993
History from things: essays on material culture/ edited by Steven Lubar and W. David Kingery. Washington: Smithsonian Institution Press, c1993. xvii, 300 p.
92-020535   930.1   1560982047
Archaeology and history. Material culture.

CC77.H5.O78 1996
Orser, Charles E.
A historical archaeology of the modern world/ Charles E. Orser, Jr. New York: Plenum Press, c1996. xvi, 247 p.
95-026380   930.1   0306451735
Archaeology and history.

CC77.U5.E53 1998
Encyclopedia of underwater and maritime archaeology/ edited by James P. Delgado. New Haven: Yale University Press, 1998, c1997. 493 p.
97-061539   930.1/028/04   0300074271
Underwater archaeology -- Encyclopedias. Shipwrecks -- Encyclopedias.

CC77.W48.C65 1989
Coles, Bryony.
People of the wetlands: bogs, bodies, and lake-dwellers/ Bryony and John Coles. New York, N.Y.: Thames & Hudson, 1989. 215 p.
89-050546   0500021120
Water-saturated sites (Archaeology) Bog bodies. Lake-dwellers and lake-dwellings.

CC77.5 Philosophy. Theory — Methodology — Special types of archaeology and archaeological sites, A-Z

CC77.5.A73 1985
Archaeological geology/ edited by George Rapp, Jr. and John A. Gifford. New Haven: Yale University Press, c1985. xvii, 435 p.
84-040201   930.1   0300031424
Archaeological geology.

CC78 Philosophy. Theory — Methodology — Dating methods. Chronology

CC78.A73 1990
Archaeomagnetic dating/ edited by Jeffrey L. Eighmy and Robert S. Sternberg. Tucson: University of Arizona Press, c1990. xvi, 446 p.
90-011110   930.1/028/5   0816511322
Archaeological dating. Archaeometry.

CC78.D85
Dunnell, Robert C., 1942-
Systematics in prehistory [by] Robert C. Dunnell. New York, Free Press [1971] x, 214 p.
76-142359   913.03/1
Archaeology -- Classification. Anthropology, Prehistoric.

CC78.F54 1977
Fleming, Stuart James.
Dating in archaeology: a guide to scientific techniques/ Stuart Fleming. New York: St. Martin's Press, 1977, c1976. 272 p.
76-020199   930/.1/0285
Archaeological dating.

CC78.I87 2000
It's about time: a history of archaeological dating in North America/ edited by Stephen E. Nash. Salt Lake City: University of Utah Press, c2000. viii, 296 p.
99-046316   930.1/028/5   0874806216
Archaeological dating -- United States -- History.

CC79 Philosophy. Theory — Methodology — Special methods borrowed from other disciplines, A-Z

CC79.E85.G68
Gould, Richard A.
Living archaeology/ R. A. Gould. Cambridge [Eng.]; Cambridge University Press, 1980. xv, 270 p.
79-020788   930/.1   0521230934
Ethnoarchaeology. Australian aborigines -- Australia -- Western Desert. Australia -- Antiquities.

CC79.5 Philosophy. Theory — Methodology — Remains of special materials, A-Z

CC79.5.A5.O36 2000
O'Connor, T. P. 1954-
The archaeology of animal bones/ Terry O'Connor. College Station, TX: Texas A&M University Press, 2000. ix, 206 p.
   930.10285   0890969590
Animal remains (Archaeology) -- ((AGSN:49937950)) SAF:150 Archaeology -- Methodology. -- ((AGSN:49926585)) SAF:150

CC79.5.P5 P43 2000
Pearsall, Deborah M.
Paleoethnobotany: a handbook of procedures/ Deborah M. Pearsall.2nd ed. San Diego: Academic Press, c2000. xxxii, 700 p.
99-068199   930.1.221   0125480423
Plant remains (Archaeology) Paleoethnobotany.

CC79.5.P6.C48 1991
Ceramic ethnoarchaeology/ edited by William A. Longacre. Tucson: University of Arizona Press, c1991. viii, 307 p.
90-020982   930.1   0816511985
Pottery -- Analysis -- Congresses. Ethnoarchaeology -- Congresses.

CC79.5.P6.R93
Rye, Owen S.
Pottery technology: principles and reconstruction/ Owen S. Rye. Washington, D.C.: Taraxacum, 1981. ix, 150 p.
80-053439   738.1   096028222X
Pottery -- Analysis. Archaeology -- Methodology.

CC80 Philosophy. Theory — Methodology — Analysis and interpretation of archaeological evidence

CC80.S33
Schiffer, Michael B.
Behavioral archaeology/ Michael B. Schiffer. New York: Academic Press, c1976. xviii, 222 p.
75-032035   930/.1/028   0126241503
Archaeology -- Methodology. Human behavior -- History. Ethnoarchaeology. Joint site, Ariz. Arizona -- Antiquities.

CC80.S335 1996
Schiffer, Michael B.
Formation processes of the archaeological record/ Michael B. Schiffer. Salt Lake City: University of Utah Press, 1996. xx, 428 p.
96-011651   930.1/028.220   0874805139
Archaeology--Methodology. Archaeology--Philosophy.

CC81 Philosophy. Theory — Methodology — Environmental archaeology

CC81.B87 1982
Butzer, Karl W.
Archaeology as human ecology: method and theory for a contextual approach/ Karl W. Butzer. Cambridge; Cambridge University Press, 1982. xiii, 364 p.
81-021576   930.1   0521246520
Environmental archaeology. Human ecology.

CC81.D56 2000
Dincauze, Dena Ferran.
Environmental archaeology: principles and practice/ Dena Ferran Dincauze. Cambridge, UK Cambridge University Press, 2000. xxx, 587 p.
99-039090   930.1   0521310776
Environmental archaeology.

CC81.E93 1978
Evans, John G.
An introduction to environmental archaeology/ John G. Evans. Ithaca, N.Y.: Cornell University Press, 1978. xii, 154 p.
77-090903   930/.1   0801411726.
Environmental archaeology.

CC95 Study and teaching. Research — By region or country — United States

CC95.A73 1989
Archaeological thought in America/ edited by C.C. Lamberg-Karlovsky. Cambridge [England]; Cambridge University Press, 1989. viii, 357 p.
88-007303   973.1   0521354528
Archaeology -- United States. Archaeology -- Case studies.

CC100 History of the science of archaeology — General works

CC100.B3 1961
Bacon, Edward.
Digging for history; archaeological discoveries throughout the world, 1945 to 1959. With an introd. by William Foxwell Albright. New York, J. Day Co. 1961 318 p.
61-005680   913
Excavations (Archaeology)

CC100.D27 1975
Daniel, Glyn Edmund.
A hundred and fifty years of archaeology/ Glyn Daniel. London: Duckworth, 1975. 410 p.
75-316779   930/.1   0715607758
Archaeology -- History.

CC100.M313 1994
Ceram, C. W.,
Gods, graves & scholars: the story of archaeology/ C.W. Ceram; translated from the German by E.B. Garside and Sophie Wilkins.2nd, rev. and substantially enl. ed. New York: Wings Books; xiv, 441 p.
94-015215   930.1.220   0517119811
Archaeology--History.

CC100.S3613 1997
Schnapp, Alain, 1946-
The discovery of the past/ Alain Schnapp; [translated from the French by Ian Kinnes and Gillian Varndell]. New York: Harry N. Abrams, 1997. 384 p.
96-029269   930.1   0810932334
Archaeology -- History. Antiquarians.

CC100.T73 1989
Tracing archaeology's past: the historiography of archaeology/ edited by Andrew L. Christenson. Carbondale: Southern Illinois University Press, c1989. xi, 252 p.
88-027278   930/.1/072   0809315238
Archaeology -- Historiography. Archaeology -- History.

CC101-105 History of the science of archaeology — By region or country, A-Z

CC101.A35.H57 1990
A History of African archaeology/ edited by Peter Robertshaw. London: J. Currey; 1990. vii, 378 p.
89-026733   960/.1   0435080415
Archaeology -- Africa -- History. Africa -- Antiquities.

CC101.I75.S57 1982
Silberman, Neil Asher, 1950-
Digging for God and country: exploration, archeology, and the secret struggle for the Holy Land, 1799-1917/ Neil Asher Silberman. New York: Knopf: 1982. xv, 228 p.
81-048104   956.94/03   0394511395
Archaeology -- Palestine -- History. Palestine -- History -- 1799-1917.

CC101.U6.R57 1997
The rise and fall of culture history/ [edited by] R.
Lee Lyman, Michael J. O'Brien, and Robert C.
Dunnell. New York: Plenum Press, 1997. p. cm.
97-014507   930.1   0306455374
*Archaeology -- United States -- History -- 20th
century. Archaeology -- North America -- History -
- 20th century. Indians of North America --
Antiquities.*

CC105.R9 M613 1970
Mongaæit, A. L.
Archaeology in the USSR [by] A. L. Mongait.
Translated and adapted by M. W. Thompson.
Gloucester, Mass., P. Smith, 1970 [c1961] 320 p.
78-018591   914.7/03/1
Archaeology--History.

CC107 Archaeology as a profession

CC107.A77 1999
Assembling the past: studies in the
professionalization of archaeology/ edited by Alice
B. Kehoe and Mary Beth Emmerichs.
Albuquerque: University of New Mexico Press,
c1999. vi, 241 p.
99-006846   930.1   0826319394
*Archaeology -- History. Archaeologists --
History. Professional socialization -- History.*

CC110 Biography — Collective

CC110.E54 1999
Encyclopedia of archaeology. edited by Tim
Murray. Santa Barbara, Calif.: ABC-CLIO, c1999
v. 2
99-052159   930.1/092/2   1576071995
Archaeologists -- Biography -- Encyclopedias.

CC110.G75 1999
Grit tempered: early women archaeologists in the
southeastern United States/ edited by Nancy Marie
White, Lynne P. Sullivan, and Rochelle A.
Marrinan; foreword by Jerald T. Milanich.
Gainesville: University Press of Florida, c1999.
xviii, 392 p.
98-050942   930.1/092/275   081301686X
*Women archaeologists -- Southern States --
Biography. Archaeology -- Southern States --
History -- 20th century. Indians of North America -
- Southern States -- Antiquities. Southern States --
Antiquities. Southern States -- Biography.*

CC110.W66 1994
Women in archaeology/ edited by Cheryl Claassen.
Philadelphia: University of Pennsylvania Press,
c1994. x, 252 p.
94-008818   930.1/082   0812232771
*Women archaeologists -- United States --
Biography. Women archaeologists -- United States.*

CC115 Biography — Individual, A-Z

CC115.C45.M38
McNairn, Barbara.
The method and theory of V. Gordon Childe:
economic, social, and cultural interpretations of
prehistory/ Barbara McNairn. Edinburgh:
Edinburgh University Press, c1980. vii, 184 p.
81-145332   930.1/092/4   0852243898
*Childe, V. Gordon -- (Vere Gordon), -- 1892-1957.
Anthropology, Prehistoric. History -- Philosophy.
Culture.*

CC115.C45.T74 1980
Trigger, Bruce G.
Gordon Childe, revolutions in archaeology/ Bruce
G. Trigger. New York: Columbia University Press,
c1980. 207 p.
79-026410   930/.1/0924   0231050380
*Childe, V. Gordon -- (Vere Gordon), -- 1892-1957.
Prehistoric peoples. Antiquities, Prehistoric.
Archaeologists -- Great Britain -- Biography.*

CC115.C74.A3 1988
Cressman, Luther Sheeleigh, 1897-
A golden journey: memoirs of an archaeologist/
Luther S. Cressman. Salt Lake City: University of
Utah Press, c1988. xvii, 506 p.
87-030286   930.1/092/4   0874802938
*Cressman, Luther Sheeleigh, -- 1897-
Archaeologists -- United States -- Biography.
Indianists -- United States -- Biography.*

CC115.W58.H38 1982
Hawkes, Jacquetta Hopkins, 1910-
Adventurer in archaeology: the biography of Sir
Mortimer Wheeler/ by Jacquetta Hawkes. New
York, N.Y.: St. Martin's Press, c1982. x, 387 p.
81-021493   930.1/092/4   0312006586
*Wheeler, Robert Eric Mortimer, -- Sir, -- 1890-
Archaeologists -- Great Britain -- Biography.*

CC125 Directories — By region or country — Other regions or countries, A-Z

CC125.N7.W55 1991
Williams, Stephen, 1926-
Fantastic archaeology: the wild side of North
American prehistory/ Stephen Williams.
Philadelphia: University of Pennsylvania Press,
c1991. xi, 407 p.
90-029189   973.1   0812282388
*Archaeology -- North America -- History. North
America -- Antiquities.*

CC135 Preservation, restoration, and conservation of antiquities. Antiquities and state — General works

CC135.C29 2000
Caple, Chris, 1958-
Conservation skills: judgement, method, and
decision/ Chris Caple. London; Routledge, 2000. p.
cm.
00-032183   363.6/9   0415188806
*Antiquities -- Collection and preservation.
Historic sites -- Conservation and restoration.
Cultural property -- Protection.*

CC135.E84 1999
The ethics of collecting cultural property: whose
culture? whose property?/ edited by Phyllis Mauch
Messenger; foreword by Brian Fagan.2nd ed.,
updated and enl. Albuquerque: University of New
Mexico Press, 1999. 301 p.
99-031907   363.6/9.221   0826321259
*Cultural property--Protection--Moral and ethical
aspects. Antiquities--Collection and preservation--
Moral and ethical aspects.*

CC135.G74 1996
Greenfield, Jeanette.
The return of cultural treasures/ Jeanette
Greenfield.2nd ed. Cambridge [England];
Cambridge University Press, xix, 351 p.
95-001256   363.6/9.220   0521477468
*Cultural property--Protection. Cultural property-
-Protection (International law) Restitution.*

CC135.H467 2001
Historic cities and sacred sites: cultural roots for
urban futures/ Ismail Serageldin, Ephim Shluger,
Joan Martin-Brown, editors. Washington, D.C.:
World Bank, 2001. xix, 420 p.
00-069698   363.6/9   082134904X
*Historic preservation. Historic preservation --
Planning. Historic sites -- Conservation and
restoration.*

CC165 General descriptive works — 1801-

CC165.A85 2000
The atlas of world archaeology/ edited by Paul
Bahn. New York: Checkmark Books, c2000. 208 p.
00-025225   930.1/09   0816040516
*Archaeology. Civilization, Ancient. Civilization,
Ancient -- Maps.*

CC165.B48 2002
Binford, Lewis Roberts,
In pursuit of the past: decoding the archaeological
record: with a new afterword/ Lewis R. Binford,
with the editorial collaboration of Joyn F. Cherry
and Robin Torrence.1st Calif. pbk. Berkeley:
University of California Press, [2002] 260 p.
2001-0539   930.1.221   0520233395
*Archaeology. Antiquities, Prehistoric.
Civilization, Ancient.*

CC165.C3 1980b
The Cambridge encyclopedia of archaeology/
editor, Andrew Sherratt; foreword by Grahame
Clark. New York: Crown Publishers, 1980. 495 p.
78-016232   930/.1/03   0517534975
*Archaeology. Prehistoric peoples. Civilization,
Ancient.*

CC165.C6613 1988
Courbin, Paul.
What is archaeology?: an essay on the nature of
archaeological research/ Paul Courbin; translated
by Paul Bahn. Chicago: University of Chicago
Press, 1988. xxv, 197 p.
88-001727   930.1/01   0226116565
Archaeology.

CC165.J35 1993
James, Peter
Centuries of darkness: a challenge to the
conventional chronology of Old World
archaeology/ Peter James, in collaboration with I.J.
Thorpe ... [et al.].; foreword by Colin Renfrew.
New Brunswick, N.J.: Rutgers University Press,
1993. xxii, 434 p.
92-037722   930.1   0813519500
History, Ancient -- Chronology. Archaeology.

CC165.T48 1998
Thomas, David Hurst.
Archaeology/ David Hurst Thomas.3rd ed. Fort Worth: Harcourt College Publishers, c1998. xxix, 735 p.
97-080982   930.1.221   0155013696
Archaeology.

CC173 Addresses, essays, lectures

CC173.B56 1989
Binford, Lewis Roberts, 1930-
Debating archaeology/ Lewis R. Binford. San Diego: Academic Press, c1989. xv, 534 p.
88-008098   930.1   0121000451
Archaeology.

CC175 General special

CC175.P65 1994
The politics of the past/ edited by Peter Gathercole, David Lowenthal. London; Routledge, 1994. xxvi, 319 p.
94-236326   930.1.220   0415095549
Archaeology--Political aspects--Congresses. Archaeology--Political aspects--Developing countries--Congresses. Archaeology and state--Congresses.

CC205 Miscellaneous subjects — Bells. Campanology — General works

CC205.C6 1971b
Coleman, Satis N. (Satis Narrona),
Bells, their history, legends, making, and uses. With a foreword by Otis W. Caldwell. Westport, Conn., Greenwood Press [1971] ix, 462 p.
70-109722   681/.81/9509   0837142121
Bells. Chimes.

CC350 Miscellaneous subjects — Crosses — By region or country

CC350.U6 I76 1982
Iron spirits/ editors, Nicholas Curchin Vrooman, project director, Patrice Avon Marvin; photographers, Jane Gudmundson, Wayne Gudmundson. 1st ed. Fargo, ND: North Dakota Council on the Arts, c1982. x, 116 p.
82-062157   739/.47784.219   0911205004
Crosses--North Dakota. Folk art--North Dakota. Blacksmiths--North Dakota.

CD Diplomatics. Archives. Seals

CD105 Diplomatics — Collections of documents, facsimiles, etc., for study — By region or country

CD105.H3
Harmer, Florence Elizabeth
Anglo-Saxon writs. [Manchester, Eng.] Manchester University Press [1952] xxii,604p.
52-010196
Writs -- Great Britain.

CD950 Archives — General works on the science of archives — American and English

CD950.D8
Duckett, Kenneth W.
Modern manuscripts: a practical manual for their management, care, and use/ Kenneth W. Duckett. Nashville: American Association for State and Local History [1975] xvi, 375 p.
75-005717   025.17/1   0910050163
Archives -- Handbooks, manuals, etc.

CD950.S29 1988
Schellenberg, T. R.
The management of archives/ T.R. Schellenberg; foreword by Jane F. Smith. Washington, DC: National Archives and Records Administration, xxxvi, 383 p.
88-600028   025.17/1.219   091133372X
Archives--Administration.

CD950.S3
Schellenberg, T. R. 1903-1970.
Modern archives: principles and techniques/ T.R. Schellenberg. [Chicago]: University of Chicago Press, [1975, c1956] xv, 247 p.
56-058525   025.171   0226736849
Archives.

CD986.5 Archives — Buildings — Access control to public records

CD986.5.M33 1992
MacNeil, Heather.
Without consent: the ethics of disclosing personal information in public archives/ Heather MacNeil. [Chicago, Ill.]: Society of American Archivists; 1992. 224 p.
92-016754   350.71/46   0810825813
Archives -- Access control. Privacy, Right of.

CD996 Archives — History and statistics — By period

CD996.P67
Posner, Ernst.
Archives in the ancient world. Cambridge, Mass., Harvard University Press, 1972. xvii, 283 p.
79-158426   930/.007/2   0674044630
Archives -- History -- To 500. Archives -- History -- 500-1400.

CD996.S53 1999
Sickinger, James P.
Public records and archives in classical Athens/ James P. Sickinger. Chapel Hill: University of North Carolina Press, c1999. x, 274 p.
98-030098   352.3/87/09385   0807824690
Archives -- Greece -- Athens -- History -- To 500. Paleography, Greek -- Greece -- Athens. Public records -- Greece -- Athens -- History -- To 500. Greece -- History -- To 146 B.C. -- Archival resources.

CD1001-3050 Archives — History and statistics — By region or country

CD1001.T4 1975
Thomas, Daniel H.,
The new guide to the diplomatic archives of Western Europe/ edited by Daniel H. Thomas and Lynn M. Case. [Philadelphia]: University of Pennsylvania Press, c1975. xi, 441 p.
75-010127   027.5/094   0812276973
Archives -- Europe.

CD1048.U5.C7
Crick, Bernard R.
A guide to manuscripts relating to America in Great Britain and Ireland. Edited by B. R. Crick and Miriam Alman under the general supervision of H. L. Beales. [London] Published for the British Association for Americ 1961 xxxvi, 667 p.
61-065029   016.973
Archives -- Great Britan -- Inventories, calendars, etc. Archives -- Catalogs -- Ireland. United States -- History -- Sources -- Bibliography.

CD1101.D57 1999
Directory of Irish archives/ edited by Seamus Helferty and Raymond Refaussé.3rd ed. Dublin: Four Courts Press, c1999. 192 p.
00-269350   027.0415/025.221   1851824693
Archives--Ireland--Directories. Archives--Northern Ireland--Directories.

CD1586. 1998
Vatican Archives: an inventory and guide to historical documents of the Holy See/ Francis X. Blouin, Jr., general editor; Leonard A. Coombs, archivist, Elizabeth Yakel, archivist; Claudia Carlen, historian, Katherine J. Gill, historian. New York: Oxford University Press, 1998. xl, 588 p.
97-029248   016.282   0195095529
Church history -- Sources -- Bibliography -- Catalogs.

CD1710.A76 2000
Archives of Russia: a directory and bibliographic guide to holdings in Moscow and St. Petersburg/ edited by Patricia Kennedy Grimsted; compiled by Patricia Kennedy Grimsted, Lada Vladimirovna Repulo, and Irina Vladimirovna Tunkina; with an introduction by Vladimir Petrovich Kozlov. Armonk, N.Y.: M.E. Sharpe, c2000. 2 v.
96-047237   027/.002547/31   076560034X
Archives -- Russia (Federation) -- Moscow -- Directories. Archives -- Russia (Federation) -- Saint Petersburg -- Directories. Russia -- Archival resources -- Directories. Russia (Federation) -- Archival resources -- Directories.

CD3020.D49 1988
Directory of archives and manuscript repositories in the United States/ National Historical Publications and Records Commission. Phoenix: Oryx Press, 1988. xv, 853 p.
87-030157   016.091/025/73   0897744756
Archives -- United States -- Directories.

CD3021.R47 1988
Researcher's guide to archives and regional history sources/ edited by John C. Larsen; foreword by John Y. Cole. Hamden, Conn.: Library Professional Publications, 1988. xiv, 167 p.
88-015081   973/.072   0208021442
Archives -- United States. Archival materials. United States -- History -- Research. United States -- History -- Archival resources.

CD3022.A45
United States.
A guide to archives and manuscripts in the United States. Philip M. Hamer, ed. New Haven, Yale University Press, 1961. xxiii, 775 p.
61-006878   025.171
Archives -- United States. Manuscripts -- United States.

CD3024.W37 1995
Warner, Robert Mark, 1927-
Diary of a dream: a history of the National Archives independence movement, 1980-1985/ by Robert M. Warner. Metuchen, N.J.: Scarecrow Press, 1995. viii, 211 p.
94-037951   353.0071/46   0810829568

CD3026. 1988
Szucs, Loretto Dennis.
The Archives: a guide to the National Archives field branches/ by Loretto Dennis Szucs & Sandra Hargreaves Luebking. Salt Lake City, UT: Ancestry Pub., 1988. xvii, 340 p.
87-070108   016.973   091648923X
Public records -- United States -- Bibliography -- Catalogs.   United States -- History -- Sources -- Bibliography -- Catalogs.   United States -- Genealogy -- Bibliography -- Catalogs.

CD3029.82.S35 1989
Schick, Frank Leopold, 1918-
Records of the presidency: presidential papers and libraries from Washington to Reagan/ by Frank L. Schick with Renee Schick and Mark Carroll; foreword by Gerald R. Ford. Phoenix, Ariz.: Oryx Press, 1989. xv, 309 p.
88-028222   353.0085/2   089774277X
Presidents -- United States -- Archives.

CD3045.W44 1989
Wehmann, Howard H.
A guide to pre-federal records in the National Archives/ compiled by Howard H. Wehmann; revised by Benjamin L. DeWhitt. Washington, DC: National Archives and Records Administration, 1989. xiii, 375 p.
88-600400   016.973   0911333754
United States -- History -- Colonial period, ca. 1600-1775 -- Sources -- Bibliography -- Catalogs. United States -- History -- Revolution, 1775-1783 -- Sources -- Bibliography -- Catalogs. United States -- History -- Confederation, 1783-1789 -- Sources -- Bibliography -- Catalogs.

CD3050.P67
Posner, Ernst.
American State archives. Chicago, University of Chicago Press [1964] xiv, 397 p.
64-023425   350
Archives -- United States -- States.

CE Technical Chronology. Calendar

CE6 History — General works

CE6.S74 2000
Steel, Duncan, 1955-
Marking time: the epic quest to invent the perfect calendar/ Duncan Steel. New York: J. Wiley, c2000. ix, 422 p.
99-051369   529/.3   0471298271
Calendar -- History.

CE11 General works — 1801-

CE11.B66 1982
The Book of calendars/ Frank Parise, editor. New York: Facts on File, c1982. 387 p.
80-019974   529/.3
Calendars.

CE11.R5 1999
Richards, E. G.
Mapping time: the calendar and its history/ E.G. Richards. New York: Oxford University Press, 1999. xxi, 438 p.
98-024957   529/.3   0198504136
Calendar -- History. Calendars -- History.

CE59 Medieval and modern — Medieval

CE59.F7 1977
Freeman-Grenville, G. S. P.
The Muslim and Christian calendars: being tables for the conversion of Muslim and Christian dates from the Hijra to the year A.D. 2000/ G. S. P. Freeman-Grenville. London: R. Collings, 1977. vii, 87 p.
78-309244   529/.32/7   0860360598
Calendar, Islamic. Church calendar.

CE73 Medieval and modern — Reform of the calendar

CE73.A7
Archer, Peter, 1873-
The Christian calendar and the Gregorian reform/ Peter Archer. New York: Fordham University Press, 1941. xi, 124 p.
41-015354   529.4
Calendar. Calendar, Gregorian.

CE76 Medieval and modern — Special systems — Gregorian

CE76.H65 1990
Holidays and anniversaries of the world: a comprehensive catalogue   containing detailed information on every month and day of the year .../ Jennifer Mossman, editor.2nd ed. Detroit: Gale Research, c1990. xxix, 1080 p.
90-127165   394.2/6.220   0810348705
Calendar, Gregorian. Holidays. Chronology, Historical.

CJ Numismatics

CJ59 History — General works

CJ59.C75 1990
Cribb, Joe.
The coin atlas: the world of coinage from its origins to the present day/ Joe Cribb, Barrie Cook, Ian Carradice; cartography by John Flower, with an introduction by the American Numismatic Association. New York: Facts on File, c1990. 337 p.
89-001353   737.494   0816020973
Coins -- History. Coinage -- History. Coins -- History -- Maps.

CJ67 Dictionaries. Encyclopedias — General works

CJ67.J86 1984
Junge, Ewald.
World coin encyclopedia/ Ewald Junge. New York: W. Morrow, c1984. 297 p.
84-060663   737.4/03   0688040829
Coins -- Encyclopedias. Numismatics -- Encyclopedias.

CJ335-401 Coins — Ancient — Greek

CJ335.H45 1967
Head, Barclay Vincent,
Historia numorum; a manual of Greek numismatics, by Barclay V. Head. Assisted by G. F. Hill, George MacDonald, and W. Wroth.New and enl. [1st American] ed. Chicago, Argonaut, 1967. 966 p.
67-025818   737.49/38
Numismatics, Greek.

CJ401.K72
Kraay, Colin M.
Archaic and classical Greek coins/ Colin M. Kraay. Berkeley: University of California Press, c1976. xxvi, 390 p.
76-014303   737.4/9/38   0520032543
Numismatics, Greek.

CJ843-1001 Coins — Ancient — Roman

CJ843.H35 1996
Harl, Kenneth W.
Coinage in the Roman economy, 300 B.C. to A.D. 700/ Kenneth W. Harl. Baltimore: Johns Hopkins University Press, 1996. x, 533 p.
95-050043   737.4937   0801852919
Coins, Roman. Coinage -- Rome -- History. Rome -- Economic conditions.

CJ969.H37 1987
Harl, Kenneth W.
Civic coins and civic politics in the Roman East, A.D. 180-275/ Kenneth W. Harl. Berkeley: University of California Press, c1987. viii, 253 p.
85-020854   737.4937   0520055527
Coins, Roman. Politics in numisatres -- Rome. Rome -- Politics and government -- 30 B.C.-476 A.D.

CJ1001.S76 1987
Sutherland, C. H. V. 1908-
Roman history and coinage, 44 BC-AD 69: fifty points of relation from Julius Caesar to Vespasian/ C.H.V. Sutherland. Oxford: Clarendon Press; 1987. xii, 131 p.
86-018165 737.4937 0198721242
Coins, Roman.   Rome -- History -- Civil War, 43-31 B.C. Rome -- History -- The five Julii, 30 B.C.-68 A.D.

CJ1755 Coins — Medieval and modern — By period

CJ1755.K72
Krause, Chester L.
Standard catalog of world coins.   [Iola, Wis., Krause Publications] "1901-present." v.
79-640940 737.4/021/6
Coins -- Catalogs.

CJ1826 Coins — Medieval and modern — By region or country

CJ1826.C635 1990
Coin world comprehensive catalog & encyclopedia of United States coins including pre-federal coinage, pioneer gold, and patterns/ edited by David T. Alexander. New York: World Almanac: c1990. 456 p.
89-077554 737.4973 088687484X
Coins, American -- Catalogs.

CJ4867 Tokens — By period — Ancient

CJ4867.S364 1996
Schmandt-Besserat, Denise.
How writing came about/ Denise Schmandt-Besserat.1st abridged ed. Austin: University of Texas Press, 1996. xii, 193 p.
95-041829 737/.3/0956.220 0292777043
Tokens--Middle East. Writing--History.

CN Inscriptions. Epigraphy

CN120 By period — Ancient inscriptions — General works

CN120.C55 1961
Cleator, P. E. 1908-
Lost languages. New York, John Day Co. [1961] 192 p.
61-008278
Inscriptions.

CN350-510 By period — Ancient inscriptions — Classical languages

CN350.W65 1992
Woodhead, A. G.
The study of Greek inscriptions/ by A. Geoffrey Woodhead.2nd ed. Norman: University of Oklahoma Press, c1992. 150 p.
92-054148 481/.1.220 0806124318
Inscriptions, Greek.

CN362.J44 1990
Jeffery, L. H.
The local scripts of archaic Greece: a study of the origin of the Greek alphabet and its development from the eighth to the fifth centuries B.C./ by L.H. Jeffery. Oxford [England]: New York: Oxford University Press, 1990. xx, 481, 80 p
88-020921 481/.7 0198140614
Inscriptions, Greek -- Greece. Greek language -- Alphabet. Greek language -- Dialects.

CN362.V4
Ventris, Michael.
Documents in Mycenaean Greek; three hundred selected tablets from Knossos, Pylos, and Mycenae with commentary and vocabulary by Michael Ventris and John Chadwick. With a foreword by Alan J.B. Wace. Cambridge [Eng.] University Press, 1956. xxx, 452 p.
57-000404 481.7
Inscriptions, Linear B. Inscriptions -- Mycenae.

CN405.W4
Welles, C. Bradford 1901-
Royal correspondence in the Hellenistic period; a study in Greek epigraphy, by C. Bradford Welles. New Haven, Yale University Kondakov Institute; 1974 c, 403 p.
35-004012 481.7
Seleucids. Inscriptions, Greek -- Turkey. Greek letters. Greek language, Hellenistic (300 B.C.-600 A.D.) Pergamum -- History -- Sources.

CN510.K46 1991
Keppie, L. J. F.
Understanding Roman inscriptions/ Lawrence Keppie. Baltimore: Johns Hopkins University Press, 1991. 158 p.
91-019853 980 0801843227
Inscriptions, Latin.

CR Heraldry

CR13 Dictionaries. Encyclopedias

CR13.F7 1970
Franklyn, Julian.
An encyclopaedic dictionary of heraldry, by Julian Franklyn and John Tanner. Illustrated by Violetta Keeble. Oxford, Pergamon Press [1970] xiii, 367 p.
79-015403 929.6/03 0080132979
Heraldry -- Encyclopedias.

CR23 General works — 1801-

CR23.G8 1976
Grant, Francis James,
The manual of heraldry: a concise description of the several terms used, and containing a dictionary of every designation in the science/ edited by Francis J. Grant.New and rev. ed. Detroit: Gale Research Co., 1976. viii, 142 p.
75-023365 929.6 0810342529
Heraldry.

CR31 Handbooks, manuals, etc.

CR31.C5
Child, Heather.
Heraldic design; a handbook for students. With a foreword by A. Colin Cole. London, G. Bell [1965] 180 p.
66-021223 745.66
Heraldry. Heraldry, Ornamental.

CR69 Crests, monograms, devices, badges, mottoes, etc. — Devices and badges — By region or country, A-Z

CR69.U6.O38 1991
Olson, Lester C.
Emblems of American community in the revolutionary era: a study in rhetorical iconology/ Lester C. Olson. Washington: Smithsonian Institution Press, c1991. xxi, 306 p.
90-024523 704.9/46/0973 1560980664
Emblems -- United States -- History -- 18th century. United States -- History -- Revolution, 1775-1783 -- Art and the revolution.

CR101 Flags, banners, and standards — General works

CR101.C3 1974
Campbell, Gordon, 1886-1953.
The book of flags/ [by] Gordon Campbell, and I. O. Evans. London: Oxford University Press, 1974. xii, 120 p.
74-196829 929.9 0192731327
Flags.

CR101.T3413 1982
Talocci, Mauro.
Guide to the flags of the world/ Mauro Talocci; illustrations by Guido Canestrari, Carlo Giordana, Paolo Riccioni; translated from the Italian by Ronald Strom. New York: Morrow, 1982. 271 p.
81-016890 929.9/2 0688011039
Flags. Heraldry.

CR109 Flags, banners, and standards — By period — Modern

CR109.F555 1998
Flags of the world.   Danbury, CT: Grolier Educational, 1998. 9 v.
97-024204 929.9/2.221 0717291685
Flags--Juvenile literature. Flags.

CR113 Flags, banners, and standards — By region or country — United States

CR113.E35 1964
Eggenberger, David.
Flags of the U. S. A. New York, Crowell [1964] 222 p.
64-012115 929.90973
Flags -- United States.

CR113.G57 1995
Goldstein, Robert Justin.
Saving Old Glory: the history of the American flag desecration controversy/ Robert Justin Goldstein. Boulder, CO: Westview Press, 1995. xv, 263 p.
94-029362   929.9/2/0973   0813323258
Flags -- Desecration -- United States.

CR113.G83 1990
Guenter, Scot M., 1956-
The American flag, 1777-1924: cultural shifts from creation to codification/ Scot M. Guenter. Rutherford, N.J.: Fairleigh Dickinson University Press; c1990. 254 p.
89-045578   929.9/2/0973   0838633846
Flags -- United States -- History.

CR191 Public and official heraldry — General works

CR191.P55 1970b
Pine, L. G. 1907-
International heraldry, by L. G. Pine. Rutland, Vt., C. E. Tuttle Co. [1970] 244 p.
72-109405   929.6   0804809003
Heraldry.

CR1605-1619 Family heraldry — By region or country — Europe

CR1605.L68 1991
Louda, Jiri.
Lines of succession: heraldry of the royal families of Europe/ tables by Jiri Louda; text by Michael Maclagan. New York: Macmillan; c1991. 308 p.
91-035681   929.7   0028972554
Heraldry -- Europe. Europe -- Kings and rulers.

CR1612.H7 1953
Hope, W. H. St. John (William Henry St. John), 1854-1919.
A grammar of English heraldry, by the late W. H. St. John Hope. Cambridge [Eng.] University Press, 1953. xii, 99 p.
53-007594   929.8
Heraldry -- Great Britain.

CR1619.B73 1969
Burke, Bernard, 1814-1892.
The general armory of England, Scotland, Ireland, and Wales; comprising a registry of armorial bearings from the earliest to the present time. With a supplement. Baltimore, Genealogical Pub. Co., 1969. cxxx, 1185 p.
73-011215   929.8
Heraldry -- Great Britain.

CR3515 Titles of honor, rank, precedence, etc. — General works — 1801-

CR3515.M4 1970
Measures, Howard, 1894-
Styles of address; a manual of usage in writing and in speech. New York, St. Martin's Press [1970, c1969] vii, 161 p.
72-085142   395
Forms of address.

CR4513 Chivalry and knighthood (Orders, decorations, etc.) — History — By period

CR4513.B33
Barber, Richard W.
The reign of chivalry/ Richard Barber. New York: St. Martin's Press, [c1980] 208 p.
79-003747   394/.7/0902   0312669941
Chivalry -- History. Knights and knighthood. Middle Ages -- History.

CR4513.K44 1984
Keen, Maurice Hugh.
Chivalry/ Maurice Keen. New Haven: Yale University Press, 1984. x, 303 p.
83-023282   394/.7   0300031505
Chivalry. Knights and knighthood -- Europe. Nobility -- Europe -- History.

CR4529 Chivalry and knighthood (Orders, decorations, etc.) — By region or country, A-Z

CR4529.G7.F4
Ferguson, Arthur B.
The Indian summer of English chivalry: studies in the decline and transformation of chivalric idealism/ Arthur B. Ferguson. Durham, N.C.: Duke University Press, 1960. xviii, 242 p.
60-008743   942.04
Chivalry. Great Britain -- Civilization.

CR4595 Chivalry and knighthood (Orders, decorations, etc.) — Duels and dueling — By region or country, A-Z

CR4595.G3.M35 1994
McAleer, Kevin, 1961-
Dueling: the cult of honor in fin-de-siecle Germany/ Kevin McAleer. Princeton, N.J.: Princeton University Press, c1994. xiii, 268 p.
94-004401   394/.8/0943   0691034621
Dueling -- Germany -- History.

CR4595.U5 S78 2000
Steward, Dick,
Duels and the roots of violence in Missouri/ Dick Steward. Columbia: University of Missouri Press, c2000. 286 p.
00-028669   394/.8/09778.221   0826212840
Dueling--Missouri. Violence--Missouri--History.

CR4723-4755 Chivalry and knighthood (Orders, decorations, etc.) — Orders, etc. — Military-religious orders

CR4723.S5 1994
Sire, H. J. A.
The Knights of Malta/ by H.J.A. Sire. New Haven: Yale University Press, c1994. xiii, 305 p.
92-047283   271/.7912   0300055021

CR4743.B27 1994
Barber, Malcolm.
The new knighthood: a history of the Order of the Temple/ Malcolm Barber. Cambridge [England]; Cambridge University Press, 1994. xxi, 441 p.
92-033821   271/.7913   0521420415

CR4743.R4 1999
Read, Piers Paul, 1941-
The Templars/ Piers Paul Read. New York: St. Martin's Press, 2000. xiii, 350 p.
00-056144   271/.7913   0312266588

CR4755.F7.S45 1999
Selwood, Dominic, 1970-
Knights of the cloister: Templars and Hospitallers in central-southern Occitania, c. 1100-c. 1300/ Dominic Selwood. Woodbridge, Suffolk; Boydell Press, 1999. xvii, 261 p.
99-012004   944/.8   0851157300
Templars -- France, Southern -- History. Hospitallers -- France, Southern -- History. France, Southern -- History.

CR4755.G7.P3 1963
Parker, Thomas William, 1921-
The Knights Templars in England.   Tucson, University of Arizona Press, 1963. 195 p.
63-011983   271
Templars -- England.

CR6020 Chivalry and knighthood (Orders, decorations, etc.) — Orders, etc. — By region or country

CR6020.A2.J33 1999
Jackson, Beverly.
Ladder to the clouds: intrigue and tradition in Chinese rank/ Beverly Jackson and David Hugus. Berkeley, CA: Ten Speed Press, 1999. p. cm.
99-042578   929.9/0951/0903   1580081274
Insignia -- China. China -- Costume -- History - - Ming-ching dynasty, 1368-1912. China -- Officials and employees.

CS Genealogy

CS5 Directories

CS5.W5 1990
Meyer, Mary Keysor.
Who's who in genealogy & heraldry/ Mary Keysor Meyer and P. William Filby, editors. Savage, Md. (8944 Madison St., Savage 29763): Who's Who in Genealogy & Heraldry, c1990. xvi, 331 p.
91-122269   929/.1/02573
Genealogists -- Directories. Heraldists -- Directories. Genealogists -- Biography.

CS9 General works — American and English

CS9.P76 2001
Professional genealogy: a manual for researchers, writers, editors, lecturers, and librarians/ editor, Elizabeth Shown Mills; editorial board, Donn Devine, James L. Hansen, Helen F.M. Leary. Baltimore: Genealogical Pub. Co., 2001. p. cm.
00-067225   929/.1   0806316489
Genealogy -- Methodology.

CS21 Popular works — General special

CS21.B55
Blockson, Charles L.
Black genealogy/ Charles L. Blockson with Ron Fry. Englewood Cliffs, N.J.: Prentice-Hall, c1977. 232 p.
77-003150   929/.1/028   0130776858
Afro-Americans -- Genealogy -- Handbooks, manuals, etc.

CS21.K46 1997
Kemp, Thomas Jay.
Virtual roots: a guide to genealogy and local history on the World Wide Web/ Thomas Jay Kemp. Wilmington, Del.: Scholarly Resources, 1997. xix, 279 p.
97-018954   929/.1/028   0842027181
Genealogy -- Computer network resources -- Directories.

CS27 Genealogical lists, etc., covering more than one country or continent — By class — Royalty, ruling families, chief magistrates, etc.

CS27.M67 1989
Morby, John E.
Dynasties of the world: a chronological and genealogical handbook/ John E. Morby. Oxford; Oxford University Press, 1989. xv, 254 p.
87-036438   909   0192158724
Kings and rulers -- Genealogy.

CS44 By region or country — United States — Directories

CS44.C46
Cemeteries of the U.S.: a guide to contact information for U.S. cemeteries and their records. Detroit: Gale Research, c1994- v.
94-640777   929/.5/02573
Cemeteries -- United States -- Directories. United States -- Genealogy -- Directories.

CS44.S33 1996
Schaefer, Christina K.
The center: a guide to genealogical research in the national capital area/ Christina K. Schaefer. Baltimore, MD: Genealogical Pub., c1996. vii, 148 p.
96-075861   929/.1/0720753   0806315156
Archival resources -- Washington (D.C.) -- Directories. Library resources -- Washington (D.C.) -- Directories. United States -- Genealogy -- Library resources -- Directories. United States -- Genealogy -- Archival resources -- Directories.

CS47 By region or country — United States — General works

CS47.G79 2000
Greenwood, Val D.
The researcher's guide to American genealogy/ Val D. Greenwood.3rd ed. Baltimore, MD: Genealogical Pub. Co., c2000. xiv, 662 p.
99-073349   929/.1/072073.221   0806316217
Archives--United States.

CS49 By region or country — United States — General special

CS49.A55 1989
Ancestry's red book: American state, county, and town sources/ edited by Alice Eichholz. Salt Lake City, UT: Ancestry Pub., 1989. p. cm.
89-039227   929/.1/072073   0916489477
United States -- Genealogy -- Handbooks, manuals, etc.

CS49.C63 1989
Colletta, John Philip, 1949-
They came in ships/ by John Philip Colletta. Salt Lake City, UT: Ancestry Pub., c1989. 65 p.
89-017742   929/.1/072073   0916489426
Ships -- United States -- Passenger lists -- Handbooks, manuals, etc.   United States -- Genealogy -- Handbooks, manuals, etc.

CS49.H57 2000
History comes home: family stories across the curriculum/ Steven Zemelman ... [et al.]. York, Me.: Stenhouse Publishers, c2000. ix, 164 p.
99-032842   929/.1/071273   1571103082
Genealogy -- Study and teaching (Elementary) -- United States.

CS49.K4 2001
Kemp, Thomas Jay.
The American census handbook/ Thomas Jay Kemp. Wilmington, Del.: Scholarly Resources, 2001. xiii, 517 p.
00-059500   016.929/1/072073   0842029249
United States -- Genealogy -- Handbooks, manuals, etc. United States -- Census -- Handbooks, manuals, etc.

CS49.S28 1997
Schaefer, Christina K.
Guide to naturalization records of the United States/ Christina K. Schaefer. Baltimore, MD: Genealogical Pub. Co., c1997. xii, 394 p.
96-080366   929/.373   0806315326
Naturalization records -- United States -- States -- Directories. Naturalization records -- United States -- Handbooks, manuals, etc. United States -- Genealogy -- Archival resources -- Directories. United States -- Emigration and immigration -- Archival resources -- Directories. United States -- Genealogy -- Handbooks, manuals, etc.

CS65 By region or country — United States — By period

CS65.P37
Parker, J. Carlyle.
City, county, town, and township index to the 1850 Federal census schedules/ J. Carlyle Parker. Detroit: Gale Research Co., c1979. xvii, 215 p.
79-011644   929/.373   0810313855
Cities and towns -- United States -- Indexes. United States -- Genealogy -- Indexes. United States -- Census, 7th, 1850 -- Indexes.

CS69-71 By region or country — United States — Family history

CS69.B82 1981
Burke's presidential families of the United States of America/ [edited by Hugh Montgomery-Massingberd].2nd ed. London: Burke's Peerage; 597 p.
81-132895   973/.09/92.219   0850110335
Presidents--United States--Genealogy.

CS71.A2. 1983
Nagel, Paul C.
Descent from glory: four generations of the John Adams family/ Paul C. Nagel. New York: Oxford University Press, 1983. xiv, 400 p.
82-006505   929/.2/0973   0195031725
Adams family.

CS71.A85. 1979
Cowles, Virginia.
The Astors/ Virginia Cowles. New York: Knopf, 1979. 256 p.
79-002219   929/.2/0941   0394414780
Astor family.   Great Britain -- Genealogy.

CS71.B4405 1970
Stowe, Lyman Beecher,
Saints, sinners and Beechers.   Freeport, N.Y., Books for Libraries Press [1970, c1962] 450 p.
71-117847   929.2/0973   0836917200
Beecher family.

CS71.D77. 1970
Bowen, Catherine Drinker, 1897-1973.
Family portrait.   Boston, Little, Brown [1970] xvi, 301 p.
75-105569   917.3/03/90922
Drinker family.

CS71.H4 1951
Loggins, Vernon, 1893-
The Hawthornes; the story of seven generations of an American family.   New York, Columbia University Press, 1951. 365 p.
51-012495
Hathorne family (William Hathorne, -- 1607?-1681)

CS71.L915. 1946
Greenslet, Ferris, 1875-1959.
The Lowells and their seven worlds ...   Boston, Houghton Mifflin Company, 1946. xi, 442 p.
46-025260
Lowell family. Lowell, Percival, -- 1571-1664 -- Family.   New England -- History.

CS71.P35 1949
Tharp, Louise Hall, 1898-
The Peabody sisters of Salem.   Boston, Little, Brown, 1950. x, 372 p.
49-049265
Peabody, Elizabeth Palmer, -- 1804-1894. Mann, Mary Tyler Peabody, -- 1806-1887. Peabody family.

CS71.W26. 1956
Tharp, Louise Hall, 1898-
Three saints and a sinner: Julia Ward Howe, Louisa, Annie, Sam Ward. Boston, Little, Brown [1956] 406 p.
56-010638
Howe, Julia Ward, -- 1819-1910. Terry, Louisa (Ward) -- 1823-1897. Mailliard, Anne Eliza (Ward) -- 1824-1895.

CS414 By region or country — Europe — Great Britain. England

CS414.H47 1997
Herber, Mark D.
Ancestral trails: the complete guide to British genealogy and family history/ Mark D. Herber; foreword by John Titford. Baltimore, Md.: Genealogical Pub. Co., Inc, 1998, c1997. xiv, 674 p.
97-071594   929/.1/072041   0806315415
Great Britain -- Genealogy -- Handbooks, manuals, etc.

CS483 By region or country — Europe — Ireland

CS483.G74 1999b
Grenham, John.
Tracing your Irish ancestors: the complete guide/ John Grenham.2nd ed. Baltimore, MD: Genealogical Pub. Co., 1999. xxii, 374 p.
00-267279   929/.1/0720415.221   0806316179
Irish   Americans--Genealogy--Handbooks, manuals, etc.

CS587 By region or country — Europe — France

CS587.B68 2001
Bouchard, Constance Brittain.
Those of my blood: constructing noble families in medieval Francia/ Constance Brittain Bouchard. Philadelphia: University of Pennsylvania Press, c2001. ix, 248 p.
00-048831   929.7/4   0812235908
Nobility -- France -- History -- To 1500. Nobility -- France -- Genealogy. Knights and knighthood -- France -- History -- To 1500.

CS2305 Personal and family names — General works

CS2305.I54 1996
Ingraham, Holly, 1953-
People's names: a cross-cultural reference guide to the proper use of over 40,000 personal and familial names in over 100 cultures/ Holly Ingraham. Jefferson, N.C.: McFarland & Co., 1996. xxiv, 613 p.
96-028638   929.4   0786401877
Names, Personal.

CS2309 Personal and family names — General special

CS2309.A7 1990
Arthur, William,
An etymological dictionary of family and christian names: with an essay on their derivation and import/ by William Arthur. Detroit: Omnigraphics, 1990, c1856. 300 p.
89-063009   929.4.220   155888839X
Names, Personal.

CS2367 Personal and family names — Forenames (Christian names) — General works

CS2367.D83 1984
Dunkling, Leslie, 1935-
The Facts on file dictionary of first names/ Leslie Dunkling and William Gosling. New York, N.Y.: Facts on File Publications, 1984, c1983. xiv, 305 p.
84-004175   929.4/4/0321   0871962748
Names, Personal -- English. English language -- Etymology -- Names.

CS2367.L54 2000
Lieberson, Stanley, 1933-
A matter of taste: how names, fashions, and culture change/ Stanley Lieberson. New Haven: Yale University Press, c2000. xvi, 334 p.
00-104460   0300083858
Names, Personal -- United States. Fashion. Fads.

CS2375 Personal and family names — Forenames (Christian names) — By region or country, A-Z

CS2375.G7 W5 1977
Withycombe, Elizabeth Gidley,
The Oxford dictionary of English Christian names/ by E. G. Withycombe.3d ed. Oxford [Eng.]; Clarendon, 1977. xlvii, 310 p.
77-373402   929.4   0198691246
Names, Personal--English.

CS2377 Personal and family names — Forenames (Christian names) — General special

CS2377.S48 1997
Sierra, Judy.
Celtic baby names: traditional names from Ireland, Scotland, Wales, Brittany, Cornwall & the Isle of Man/ Judy Sierra. Eugene, Or.: Folkprint, c1997. 121 p.
96-052432   929/.4/4/0899162   0963608959
Names, Personal -- Celtic -- Dictionaries.

CS2385 Personal and family names — Surnames — General works

CS2385.H27 1988
Hanks, Patrick.
A dictionary of surnames/ Patrick Hanks and Flavia Hodges; special consultant for Jewish names, David L. Gold. Oxford [England]; Oxford University Press, 1988. (1990) liv, 826 p.
88-021882   929.4/2/0321   0192115928
Names, Personal -- Dictionaries.

CS2389 Personal and family names — Surnames — General special

CS2389.K87 1990
Kupper, Susan J., 1949-
Surnames for women: a decision-making guide/ by Susan J. Kupper. Jefferson, N.C.: McFarland, c1990. ix, 147 p.
89-043654   929.4/2/0973   0899504965
Names, Personal -- United States. Married women -- United States -- Names.

CS2481-2505 Personal and family names — By country, nationality, etc. — Teutonic

CS2481.S55
Smith, Elsdon Coles, 1903-
Dictionary of American family names. New York, Harper [1956] xxxiv, 244 p.
56-008766   929.4
Names, Personal -- United States.

CS2485.R6 1995
Robb, H. Amanda.
Encyclopedia of American family names/ H. Amanda Robb and Andrew Chesler. New York: HarperCollins, c1995. x, 710 p.
94-028719   929.4/0973   0062700758
Names, Personal -- United States -- Dictionaries.

CS2487.H66 1982
Hook, J. N. 1913-
Family names: how our surnames came to America/ J.N. Hook. New York: Macmillan; c1982. 388 p.
81-018646   929.4/2/0973   0025521004
Names, Personal -- United States. Ethnology -- United States.

CS2505.C67
Cottle, Basil.
The Penguin dictionary of surnames. Harmondsworth, Penguin, 1967. 334 p.
67-112240   929.4/0941
Names, Personal -- Great Britain.

CS2505.D65 1972
Dolan, J. R.
English ancestral names; the evolution of the surname from medieval occupations [by] J. R. Dolan. New York, C. N. Potter; distributed by Crown Publishers [1972] xvi, 381 p.
73-139349   929.4
Names, Personal -- English. English language -- Etymology -- Names. Occupations -- England -- History -- To 1500.

CS2505.R39 1997
Reaney, Percy H.
A dictionary of English surnames/ by P.H. Reaney.Rev. 3rd ed. /with corrections and additions by R.M. Wilson. Oxford [England]: Oxford University Press, 1997. lxx, 520 p.
97-216995   929.4/2/03.221   0198600925
Names, Personal--Great Britain--Dictionaries. Names, English--Dictionaries.

CS2745 Personal and family names — By country, nationality, etc. — Romance

CS2745.P55 1996
Platt, Lyman De.
Hispanic surnames and family history/ Lyman D. Platt. Baltimore, MD: Genealogical Publishing Co., 1996. 349 p.
95-081292   929/.4/0946   080631480X
Names, Personal -- Spanish -- Genealogy. Hispanic Americans -- Genealogy -- Bibliography. Latin America -- Genealogy -- Bibliography.

CS3010 Personal and family names — By country, nationality, etc. — Oriental

CS3010.G84 1992
Guggenheimer, Heinrich W. 1924-
Jewish family names and their origins: an etymological dictionary/ by Heinrich W. Guggenheimer and Eva H. Guggenheimer. [Hoboken, N.J.]: Ktav Pub. House, 1992. xliii, 882 p.
91-046313   929.4/2/089924   0881252972
Names, Personal -- Jewish -- Dictionaries.

CT Biography

CT21 Biography as an art or literary form — General works

CT21.B28 1999
Backscheider, Paula R.
Reflections on biography/ Paula R. Backscheider. Oxford; Oxford University Press, 1999. xxii, 289 p.
99-034521   808/.06692   019818641X
Biography as a literary form.

CT21.B564
Bowen, Catherine Drinker, 1897-1973.
Biography: the craft and the calling.   Boston, Little, Brown [1969] xvi, 174 p.
69-011259   808.06/6/92
Biography as a literary form.

CT21.B65 1994
Brian, Denis.
Fair game: what biographers don't tell you/ Denis Brian. Amherst, N.Y.: Prometheus Books, 1994. 373 p.
94-005401   808/.06692   0879758996
Biography as a literary form. Biographers -- United States.

CT21.E414 2000
Ellis, David, 1939-
Literary lives: biography and the search for understanding/ David Ellis. New York: Routledge, 2000. ix, 195 p.
00-044631   809/.93592   0415928478
Biography as a literary form. Authors -- Biography -- History and criticism.

CT21.E83 1999
Evans, Mary, 1946-
Missing   persons: the   impossibility   of auto/biography/ Mary Evans. London; Routledge, 1999. vii, 164 p.
98-019232   808/.06692   0415099757
Biography as a literary form. Autobiography.

CT21.N68 1986
Novarr, David.
The lines of life: theories of biography, 1880-1970/ David Novarr. West Lafayette, Ind.: Purdue University Press, 1986. xvii, 202 p.
85-024562   808/.06692   0911198792
Biography as a literary form.

CT21.T44
Telling lives, the biographer's art/ by Leon Edel ... [et al.]; edited by Marc Pachter. Washington: New Republic Books, 1979. 151 p.
79-000698   808/.066/92   0915220547
Biography as a literary form.

CT25 Autobiography

CT25.A49 1998
Amelang, James S., 1952-
The flight of Icarus: artisan autobiography in early modern Europe/ James S. Amelang. Stanford, Calif.: Stanford University Press, 1998. 497 p.
98-023284   609/.2/24   0804733406
Parets, Miquel. -- Molts successos que han succeit dins Barcelona i molts altres llocs de Catalunya, dignes de memoria.   Artisans -- Europe -- Biography -- History and criticism. Autobiography. Europe -- Biography -- History and criticism.

CT25.E25 1999
Eakin, Paul John.
How our lives become stories: making selves/ Paul John Eakin. Ithaca, N.Y.: Cornell University Press, 1999. xii, 207 p.
99-028793   808/.06692   0801436591
Autobiography.   Self-perception.   Identity (Psychology)

CT25.I58 1987
Inventing the truth: the art and craft of memoir/ Russell Baker ... [et al.]; edited with a memoir and an introduction by William Zinsser. Boston: Houghton Mifflin, 1987. 172 p.
87-003875   973.91/092/2   0395445264
Autobiography. Authors, American -- Biography -- History and criticism.   United States -- Biography -- History and criticism.

CT25.R56 2000
Rios, Theodore.
Telling a good one: the process of a Native American collaborative biography/ by Theodore Rios and Kathleen Mullen Sands. Lincoln: University of Nebraska Press, c2000. xix, 365 p.
00-029920   808/.06692   0803242654
Rios, Theodore. Sands, Kathleen M. Authorship -- Collaboration.   Autobiography -- Authorship. Biography   as   a   literary   form.   Arizona -- Biography.

CT25.W28 1999
Watson, Martha, 1941-
Lives of their own: rhetorical dimensions in autobiographies of women activists/ Martha Watson. Columbia, S.C.: University of South Carolina Press, c1999. x, 149 p.
97-045361   809/.93592072   1570032009
Autobiography -- Women authors. Biography as a literary form. Women social reformers -- United States -- Biography.

CT34 History — By region or country, A-Z

CT34.G7.S67
Stauffer, Donald A. 1902-1952.
The art of biography in eighteenth century England, by Donald A. Stauffer. Princeton, Princeton university press; 1941. xiv, 572 p.
41-003950   920
Biography as a literary form. English literature -- History and criticism.   Great Britain -- Biography -- Bibliography.

CT34.U6.O5
O'Neill, Edward Hayes.
A history of American biography, 1800-1935, by Edward H. O'Neill. Philadelphia, University of Pennsylvania Press, 1935. xi, 428 p.
35-019710   920
Biography   as   a   literary   form.   American literature -- History and criticism.

CT95 General collective biography — Universal in scope. By language — Other early works

CT95.B33
Bayle, Pierre, 1647-1706.
Selections from Bayle's dictionary. Edited by E. A. Beller and M. du P. Lee, Jr. Princeton, Princeton University Press 1952. xxxiv, 312 p.
52-008760   920.02
Biography -- Dictionaries.

CT100-120 General collective biography — Universal in scope. By language — American and English

CT100.C8
Current biography yearbook.   New York, H.W. Wilson Co. v.
40-027432   920/.009/04
Biography -- 20th century -- Periodicals.

CT103.C25 1996
The Cambridge biographical dictionary/ edited by David Crystal. Cambridge; Cambridge University Press, 1996. x, 495 p.
95-040299   920/.003   0521567807
Biography -- Dictionaries.

CT103.E56 1998
Encyclopedia of world biography.   Detroit: Gale Research, c1998-c1999. 18 v.
97-042327   920/.003   0787622214
Biography -- Dictionaries -- Juvenile literature. Biography.

CT103.M47 1995
Merriam-Webster's   biographical   dictionary. Springfield, Mass.: Merriam-Webster, c1995. xiii, 1170 p.
94-043025   920.02   0877797439
Biography -- Dictionaries.

CT103.W66 1990
The World almanac biographical dictionary/ the editors of the World almanac. New York, N.Y.: World Almanac, 1990. x, 390 p.
90-045309   920.02   0886875641
Biography -- Dictionaries.

CT104.D54 1998
Dictionary of world biography/ Frank N. Magill, editor;   Christina J. Moose, managing editor; Alison   Aves,   researcher   and   bibliographer. Chicago: Fitzroy Dearborn Publishers; 1998- v. 1-2
97-051154   920.02   0893562734
Biography. World history.

CT104.S78
Strachey, Lytton, 1880-1932.
Biographical essays. New York, Harcourt, Brace [1949] 294 p.
49-011684   920.02
Biography.

CT105.S63 1998
Slomanson, Joan Kanel.
A short history: thumbnail sketches of 50 little giants/ Joan Kanel Slomanson; illustrated by T.R. Nimen. New York: Abbeville Press, c1998. 110 p.
97-009911   920.02   0789203332
Short people -- Biography. Celebrities -- Biography.

CT107.C44 1987
Christ, Henry I. 1915-
World biographies/ Henry I. Christ, Marie E. Christ, contributing author; [illustrations, Robert Shore]. New York: Globe Book Co., c1987. viii, 296 p.
87-131445   920/.02   0870650394
Biography -- Juvenile literature. Celebrities -- Biography -- Juvenile literature.

CT108.T83
Twentieth century American nicknames/ edited by Laurence Urdang; compiled by Walter C. Kidney and George C. Kohn; with a foreword by Leslie Alan Dunkling. New York: H. W. Wilson, 1979. xi, 398 p.
79-023390   929.4/0973   0824206428
Nicknames -- United States.

CT114.S56
Snodgrass, Mary Ellen.
Who's who in the Middle Ages/ Mary Ellen Snodgrass; illustrations research by Linda Campbell Franklin. Jefferson, N.C.: McFarland, 2001. 312 p.
00-056243   920/.009/02   0786407743
Biography -- Middle Ages, 500-1500 -- Dictionaries. Civilization, Medieval -- Dictionaries. Europe -- History -- 476-1492 -- Biography -- Dictionaries.

CT120.B53
Biography news. Detroit, Gale Research Co.
74-642922   920/.009/04
Biography -- 20th century -- Periodicals.

CT120.D53 1992
A Dictionary of twentieth-century world biography/ consultant editor, Asa Briggs. Oxford; Oxford University Press, 1992. vi, 615 p.
91-027696   920/.009/04   0192116797
Biography -- 20th century -- Dictionaries.

CT120.I5
The International who's who.   London, Europa Publications Ltd. [1935- v.
35-010257   920.01
Biography.

CT120.W5
Who's who in the world.   Wilmette, Ill. [etc.] Marquis Who's Who, Macmillan Directory Division, v.
79-139215   920.02
Biography -- 20th century -- Periodicals.

CT213-310 National biography — By region or country — North America

CT213.A68 1999
American national biography/ general editors, John A. Garraty, Mark C. Carnes. New York: Oxford University Press, 1999. 24 v.
98-020826   920.073   0195206355
United States -- Biography -- Dictionaries.

CT213.C36 1995
The Cambridge dictionary of American biography/ edited by John S. Bowman. Cambridge; Cambridge University Press, 1995. xxxviii, 903 p.
94-005057   920.073   0521402581
United States -- Biography -- Dictionaries.

CT213.N47
The New York times obituaries index.   New York: New York times, 1970-1980. 2 v.
72-113422   920/.02   0667005986
Obituaries -- Indexes.

CT214.R47 1988
Research guide to American historical biography/ Robert Muccigrosso, editor; Suzanne Niemeyer, editorial dirrector. Washington, D.C.: Beacham Pub., c1988-c1992 v. 1-5
88-019316   920/.073   0933833091
United States -- Biography -- Handbooks, manuals, etc. United States -- Bio-bibliography.

CT244.D53 1999
Dictionary of Missouri biography/ edited by Lawrence O. Christensen ... [et al.]. Columbia: University of Missouri Press, c1999. viii, 832 p.
99-015518   920.0778. 221   0826212220

CT253.R65 1987
Rolfsrud, Erling Nicolai,
Notable North Dakotans/ by Erling Nicolai Rolfsrud. Farwell, Minn.: Lantern Books, c1987. 110 p.
88-134658   920/.0784. 219   0914689118

CT253.W48
Who's who in North Dakota.   Mandan, N.D.: Dakota West Enterprise, 1984- v.
84-649116   920/.0784.219

CT269.W66 1991
Woods, L. Milton
Wyoming biographies/ Lawrence M. Woods. Worland, Wyo.: High Plains Pub. Co., 1991. 224 p.
91-070461   920.0787. 220   0962333379

CT274.A43.B63 1980
Boggs, Marion Alexander, 1877-
The Alexander letters, 1787-1900/ edited by Marion Alexander Boggs; foreword by Richard Barksdale Harwell. Athens: University of Georgia Press, [c1980] 387 p.
79-005187   929/.2/0973   0820304921
Alexander family.

CT274.F58.G66 1991
Goodwin, Doris Kearns.
The Fitzgeralds and the Kennedys/ Doris Kearns Goodwin. New York: St. Martin's Press, [1991] xvii, 932 p.
91-021711   929/.2/0973   0312063547
Fitzgerald family. Kennedy family.   United States -- Biography.

CT274.L48.L48 2000
The Leverett letters: correspondence of a South Carolina family, 1851-1868/ edited by Frances Wallace Taylor, Catherine Taylor Matthews, and J. Tracy Power. Columbia: University of South Carolina Press, c2000. 543 p.
99-050784   975.7/03/0922   1570032122
Leverett family -- Correspondence.   South Carolina -- Biography. South Carolina -- History -- Civil War, 1861-1865 -- Personal narratives. United States -- History -- Civil War, 1861-1865 -- Personal narratives.

CT274.R59.H37 1988
Harr, John Ensor, 1926-
The Rockefeller century/ John Ensor Harr and Peter J. Johnson. New York: Scribner, c1988. xviii, 621 p.
87-032437   973.9/092/2   0684189364
Rockefeller family.   United States -- Biography.

CT274.W375.B66 1995
Bonfield, Lynn A., 1939-
Roxana's children: the biography of a nineteenth-century Vermont family/ Lynn A. Bonfield and Mary C. Morrison. Amherst: University of Massachusetts Press, c1995. xviii, 267 p.
95-002417   929/.2/0973   0870239724
Watt family. Watts, Roxana Brown Walbridge, -- 1802-1862 -- Family. Family -- Vermont -- Peacham -- History -- 19th century. Peacham (Vt.) -- Biography. United States -- Social life and customs -- 19th century.

CT275.A186.A25 1996
Acosta, Oscar Zeta.
Oscar "Zeta" Acosta: the uncollected works/ edited by Ilan Stavans. Houston, Tex.: Arte Publico Press, 1996. xxi, 312 p.
95-033398   973/.046872/0092   1558850996
Acosta, Oscar Zeta.   Mexican Americans -- Biography. Mexican American authors -- Biography. American literature -- Mexican American authors.

CT275.A847.A3
Astor, Brooke.
Patchwork child New York, Harper & Row [1962] 224 p.
62-017083   920.7

CT275.B144
Barrows, Robert G. 1946-
Albion Fellows Bacon: Indiana's municipal housekeeper/ Robert G. Barrows. Bloomington, Ind.: Indiana University Press, 2000. xx, 229 p.
00-025134   303.48/4/092   0253337747
Bacon, Albion Fellows, -- 1865- Women social reformers -- Indiana -- Biography. Authors, American -- 20th century -- Biography. Indiana -- Social life and customs. Indiana -- Biography.

CT275.B316.A3
Baldrige, Letitia.
Of diamonds and diplomats.   Boston, Houghton Mifflin, 1968. 337 p.
68-026055   917.3/03/920924
Baldrige, Letitia. Baldrige, Letitia. Socialites -- United States -- Biography.

CT275.B546.A3
Beck, Daisy (Woodward) 1876-
All the years were grand; with drawings by Rosemary Emerson. Chicago, Erle Press [c1951] 257 p.
51-011565   920.7
Beck, Daisy (Woodward) -- 1876-

CT275.C3.A3
Carnegie, Andrew, 1835-1919.
Autobiography of Andrew Carnegie.   Boston, Houghton Mifflin company, 1920. xii p.
20-019520
Carnegie, Andrew, -- 1835-1919. Industrialists -- United States -- Biography. Philanthropists -- United States -- Biography.

CT275.C4564.A3
Chambers, Whittaker.
Cold Friday. Edited and with an introd. by Duncan Norton-Taylor. New York, Random House [1964] xviii, 327 p.
64-020025   818.54

CT275.C578.A3
Chrysler, Walter Percy, 1875-1940.
Life of an American workman/ by Walter P. Chrysler in collaboration with Boyden Sparkes. New York: Dodd, Mead, [1950] 219 p.
50-010162   923.373
Chrysler, Walter Percy, -- 1875-1940. Industrialists -- United States -- Biography. Automobile industry and trade -- United States -- History.

CT275.C684.A3
Coleman, Ann Raney Thomas, 1810-1897.
Victorian lady on the Texas frontier; the journal of Ann Raney Coleman. Edited by C. Richard King. Norman, University of Oklahoma Press [1971] xxi, 206 p.
69-016721   917.64/03   0806109068
Coleman, Ann Raney Thomas, -- 1810-1897 -- Diaries. Frontier and pioneer life -- Texas. Women pioneers -- Texas -- Diaries.

CT275.C757.A3
Conant, James Bryant, 1893-1978.
My several lives; memoirs of a social inventor, by James B. Conant. New York, Harper & Row [1970] xvi, 701 p.
72-083590   370/.924
Conant, James Bryant, -- 1893-1978.

CT275.D2374.A3 1957
Darrow, Clarence, 1857-1938.
The story of my life. New York, Grosset & Dunlap [1957, c1932] viii, 465 p.
57-003510   923.473
Lawyers -- United States -- Correspondence, reminiscences, etc.

CT275.D463.A34 1976
Dienstag, Eleanor Foa.
Whither thou goest: the story of an uprooted wife/ by Eleanor Dienstag. New York: Dutton, 1976. 187 p.
75-025751   973.92/092/4   0525233148
Dienstag, Eleanor Foa.

CT275.E357 1996
Edwards, Madaline Selima, 1816-1854.
Madaline: love and survival in antebellum New Orleans/ edited by Dell Upton. Athens: University of Georgia Press, c1996. xviii, 366 p.
95-014156   976.3/3505/092   0820317586
Edwards, Madaline Selima, -- 1816-1854. Women -- Louisiana -- New Orleans -- Biography. Women pioneers -- California -- San Francisco -- Biography. Pioneers -- California -- San Francisco -- Biography. San Francisco (Calif.) -- Biography. New Orleans (La.) -- Biography.

CT275.E97.A35
Exner, Judith Katherine Campbell, 1934-
My story/ Judith Exner as told to Ovid Demaris. New York: Grove Press, 1977. 299 p.
76-049722   973.922/092/4   0802101399
Exner, Judith, -- 1934- Kennedy, John F. -- (John Fitzgerald), -- 1917-1963 -- Relations with women. Presidents -- United States -- Biography. United States -- Biography.

CT275.F5586.B83 1984
Buel, Joy Day.
The way of duty: a woman and her family in revolutionary America/ Joy Day Buel and Richard Buel, Jr. New York: Norton, c1984. xviii, 309 p.
83-012176   973.3/092/4   0393017672
Silliman, Mary Fish Noyes, -- 1736-1818. Women -- United States -- History -- 18th century. Family -- United States -- History -- 18th century. United States -- History -- Revolution, 1775-1783 -- Women. United States -- Biography.

CT275.F68.B78
Burlingame, Roger, 1889-1967.
Henry Ford, a great life in brief. New York, Knopf, 1955 [i.e. 19 194, vii p.
54-005268   923.373
Ford, Henry, -- 1863-1947.

CT275.F68.S55 1937a
Sinclair, Upton, 1878-1968.
The flivver king, a story of Ford-America, Detroit, Mich., The United automobile workers of America: [1937] 2 p.
43-040418
Ford, Henry, -- 1863-1947.

CT275.G3917.A3 1954
Gilbert, A. C. 1884-
The man who lives in paradise; the autobiography of A. C. Gilbert, with Marshall McClintock. New York, Rinehart, [1954] 374 p.
54-009126   920

CT275.G47.A35
Glass, Willie Elmore.
Miss Willie: happenings of a happy family, 1816-1926/ by Willie Elmore Glass. Essington, Pa.: Huntingdon Press, c1976. 419 p.
77-356482   976.1/47/050924
Elmore family. Glass, Willie Elmore. United States -- Biography.

CT275.G6.O27
O'Connor, Richard, 1915-1975.
Gould's millions. Doubleday, 1962.
62-007669   0837168759
Gould, Jay, -- 1836-1892. Capitalists and financiers.

CT275.G855.G8 1971
Gunther, John, 1901-1970.
Death be not proud. Pref. by Cass Canfield. New York, Harper & Row [1971] 264 p.
75-138730   616.9/94/810924   006011634X
Gunther, John, -- 1929-1947.

CT275.H28743.A36
Halsey, Margaret, 1910-
No laughing matter: the autobiography of a WASP/ Margaret Halsey. Philadelphia: Lippincott, c1977. 250 p.
77-022949   974.7/04/0924   0397012403
Halsey, Margaret, -- 1910- Halsey, Margaret, -- 1910- WASPs (Persons) -- Biography. United States -- Biography. United States -- Biography.

CT275.H645515.A38
Holmes, Marjorie, 1910-
You and I and yesterday. New York, W. Morrow, 1973. 191 p.
73-007386   917.3/03/916   068800153X
Holmes, Marjorie, -- 1910- -- Childhood and youth. Storm Lake (Iowa) -- Biography. Storm Lake (Iowa) -- Social life and customs.

CT275.H6678.A3
Hughes, Howard, 1905-1976.
My life and opinions [by] Howard Hughes. Edited by Robert P. Eaton. [Chicago] Best Books Press [1972] 244 p.
70-188090   670/.92/4
Hughes, Howard, -- 1905-1976.

CT275.H6678.I78
Irving, Clifford.
Clifford Irving: what really happened; his untold story of the Hughes affair, by Clifford Irving with Richard Suskind. New York, Grove Press [1972] vi, 378 p.
72-088115   364.1/63
Hughes, Howard, -- 1905-1976.

CT275.J29.A3 1964
James, Alice, 1848-1892.
The diary of Alice James. Edited with an introd. by Leon Edel. New York, Dodd, Mead [1964] x, 241 p.
64-018879   920.7
James family. James, William, -- 1842-1910. James, Henry, -- 1843-1916.

CT275.J29.S77
Strouse, Jean.
Alice James, a biography/ Jean Strouse. Boston: Houghton Mifflin, c1980. xv, 367 p.
80-022103   929/.2/0973   0395277876
James, Alice, -- 1848-1892. James family. United States -- Biography.

CT275.J97.A3
Julian, Hubert Fauntleroy, 1897-
Black Eagle: Colonel Hubert Julian, as told to John Bulloch. [London]: Jarrolds Publishers, [1964] 200 p.
66-080307

CT275.K26.M3
Phillips-Matz, Mary Jane.
The many lives of Otto Kahn./ By Mary Jane Matz. New York, Macmillan Co. [1963] x, 299 p.
63-015288   923.373
Kahn, Otto Hermann, -- 1867-1934.

CT275.K49.A3
King, Alexander, 1900-1965.
Mine enemy grows older. New York, Simon and Schuster, 1958. 375 p.
58-013170
King, Alexander, -- 1900-1965.

CT275.K5764.A33 1976
Kingston, Maxine Hong.
The woman warrior: memoirs of a girlhood among ghosts/ Maxine Hong Kingston. New York: Knopf: distributed by Random House, 1976. 209 p.
76-013674   979.4/61/050924   0394400674
Kingston, Maxine Hong -- Childhood and youth. Chinese Americans -- California -- Social life and customs. United States -- Biography.

CT275.K897.A3
Kushin, Nathan, 1884-
Memoirs of a new American/ Nathan Kushin. New York: Bloch, 1949. xii, 157 p.
49-009874   920

CT275.L44.A3
Lilienthal, Meta, 1876-
Dear remembered world; childhood memories of an old New Yorker. New York, R. R. Smith, 1947. 248 p.
47-012436   920.7

CT275.L69244.A36
Loud, Pat, 1926-
Pat Loud: a woman's story, by Pat Loud with Nora Johnson. New York, Coward, McCann & Geoghegan [1974] 223 p.
73-088543 917.3/03/924 0698105788
Loud, Pat, -- 1926-

CT275.L838.A3 1999
Luhan, Mabel Dodge, 1879-1962.
Intimate memories: the autobiography of Mabel Dodge Luhan/ edited by Lois Palken Rudnick. Albuquerque: University of New Mexico Press, c1999. xxii, 265 p.
99-024085 973.9/092 0826318576
Luhan, Mabel Dodge, -- 1879-1962. Intellectuals -- United States -- Biography. Taos (N.M.) -- Biography.

CT275.L838.A4 1996
Luhan, Mabel Dodge, 1879-1962.
A history of having a great many times not continued to be friends: the correspondence between Mabel Dodge and Gertrude Stein, 1911-1934/ Patricia R. Everett. Albuquerque: University of New Mexico Press, c1996. xx, 303 p.
95-004345 818/.5209
Luhan, Mabel Dodge, -- 1879-1962 -- Correspondence. Stein, Gertrude, -- 1874-1946 -- Correspondence. Intellectuals -- United States -- Correspondence. Women authors, American -- 20th century -- Correspondence.

CT275.M23.A3 1975
McAllister, Ward, 1827-1895.
Society as I have found it/ Samuel Ward McAllister. New York: Arno Press, 1975, c1890. xv, 469 p.
75-001855 301.44/1 0405069219
McAllister, Ward, -- 1827-1895.

CT275.M43.A43
MacDonald, Betty Bard.
Who, me! The autobiography of Betty MacDonald. Philadelphia, Lippincott [c1959] 352 p.
59-013252 920.7

CT275.M46518.A34
Maynard, Joyce, 1953-
Looking back; a chronicle of growing up old in the sixties. Garden City, N.Y., Doubleday, 1973. 160 p.
72-076233 917.3/03/920924 0385029721
Maynard, Joyce, -- 1953-

CT275.M498.A3
Mesta, Perle (Skirvin)
Perle--my story, by Perle Mesta with Robert Cahn. New York, McGraw-Hill [1960] 251 p.
60-010478 923.273

CT275.M5124.A3
Meyer, Agnes Elizabeth Ernst, 1887-
Out of these roots, the autobiography of an American woman. Boston, Little, Brown [1953] 385 p.
53-010236 920.5

CT275.M59444.A3
Morris, Willie.
North toward home. Boston, Houghton Mifflin, 1967. 438 p.
67-025803 973.92/0924
Morris, Willie. Authors, American -- 20th century -- Biography. Journalists -- United States -- Biography. United States -- Intellectual life -- 20th century. Mississippi -- Biography.

CT275.M6.S32
Satterlee, Herbert Livingston, 1863-1947.
J. Pierpont Morgan; an intimate portrait, by Herbert L. Satterlee. New York, The Macmillan company, 1939. xvi p.
39-029473 923.373
Morgan, J. Pierpont -- (John Pierpont), -- 1837-1913.

CT275.M668.A3
Hughes, Lora Wood.
No time for tears. Decorations by Edwin Earle. Boston: Houghton Mifflin company, 1946. 305 p.
46-001227 920.7

CT275.M73.M8
Mumford, Lewis, 1895-
Green memories; the story of Geddes Mumford. New York, Harcourt, Brace [1947] vi, 342 p.
47-031499 920
Mumford, Geddes, -- 1925-1944.

CT275.M734.A35
Mumford, Lewis, 1895-
My works and days: a personal chronicle/ Lewis Mumford. New York: Harcourt Brace Jovanovich, c1979. 545 p.
78-053893 818/.5/209 0151640874
Mumford, Lewis, -- 1895- Social reformers -- United States -- Biography. City planners -- United States -- Biography. Architects -- United States -- Biography.

CT275.M755.A3 1970
Mungo, Raymond, 1946-
Famous long ago; my life and hard times with Liberation News Service. Boston, Beacon Press [1970] 202 p.
77-103937 070/.924 0807061824
Mungo, Raymond, -- 1946- Mungo, Raymond, -- 1946- Authors, American -- 20th century -- Biography. Baby boom generation -- United States. Intellectuals -- United States -- Biography.

CT275.O24 A3 2001
O'Brien, John,
At home in the heart of Appalachia/ John O'Brien. 1st ed. New York: Knopf, 2001. 306 p.
2001-0897 975.04.221 0394564510
O'Brien, John.   Mountain whites (Southern States)--Appalachian Region, Southern--Social

CT275.O552.A36
Onassis, Jacqueline Kennedy, 1929-
One special summer/ written and illustrated by Jacqueline and Lee Bouvier. New York: Delacorte Press, [1974] [63] p.
74-193210 914/.04/550924 0440060370
Onassis, Jacqueline Kennedy, -- 1929- Radziwill, Lee Bouvier, -- 1933- Europe -- Description and travel.

CT275.P3875.A3
Parsons, Schuyler Livingston, 1892-
Untold friendships. Boston: Houghton Mifflin, 1955. 252 p.
55-009001
Parsons, Schuyler Livingston, -- 1892-

CT275.P488.A3
Peabody, Marian Lawrence, 1875-
To be young was very heaven. Boston, Houghton Mifflin, 1967. 366 p.
67-011756 974.4/61/040924
Peabody, Marian Lawrence, -- 1875- Boston (Mass.) -- Social life and customs. Massachusetts -- Biography.

CT275.R6.A29
Riis, Jacob A. 1849-1914.
The making of an American, by Jacob A. Riis ... New York, The Macmillan Company; [etc., etc.] 1924. xi, 284 p.
25-009728

CT275.R62.A32
Rivers, Caryl.
Aphrodite at mid-century; growing up Catholic and female in post-war America. Garden City, N.Y., Doubleday, 1973. 283 p.
73-079706 917.52/84/0340924 038505632X
Rivers, Caryl.

CT275.R75.C47 1998
Chernow, Ron.
Titan: the life of John D. Rockefeller, Sr./ Ron Chernow. New York: Random House, c1998. xxii, 774 p.
97-033117 338.7/622382/092 0679438084
Rockefeller, John D. -- (John Davison), -- 1839-1937. Capitalists and financiers -- United States -- Biography. Industrialists -- United States -- Biography. Philanthropists -- United States -- Biography.

CT275.R75.L3
Latham, Earl,
John D. Rockefeller, robber baron or industrial statesman? Boston, Heath [1949] 115 p.
59-042022 923.373
Rockefeller, John D. -- (John Davison), -- 1839-1937.

CT275.R772.A33
Romanoff, Alexis Lawrence, 1892-
Diaries through war and peace: one life in two worlds/ by Alexis Lawrence Romanoff. Ithaca, N.Y.: Ithaca Heritage Books c1977. viii, 217 p.
77-074621 947.084/092/4
Romanoff, Alexis Lawrence, -- 1892- -- Diaries. Biologists -- United States -- Diaries.   Soviet Union -- Social life and customs.

CT275.S3442.A2
Schiff, Jacob H. 1847-1920.
Jacob H. Schiff; his life and letters, by Cyrus Adler. Garden City, N.Y., Doubleday, Doran, 1928. 2 v.
28-030273 332.6/0924
Schiff, Jacob H. -- (Jacob Henry), -- 1847-1920.

CT275.S5233.A3 1970
Sloan, Alfred P. 1875-1966.
Adventures of a white-collar man [by] Alfred P. Sloan, Jr., in collaboration with Boyden Sparkes. Freeport, N.Y., Books for Libraries Press [1970, c1941] xv, 208 p.
74-126258 338.7/62/920924 0836954858

CT275.S5233.A35
Sloan, Alfred P. 1875-1966.
My years with General Motors. Edited by John McDonald, with Catharine Stevens. Garden City, N.Y., Doubleday, 1964 [c1963] xxv, 472 p.
64-011306 338.7/6292/0973

CT275.S59.A3
Solomon, Hannah (Greenebaum) 1858-1943.
Fabric of my life, the autobiography of Hannah G. Solomon. New York, Bloch publishing company, 5707-1946, c1946. xiv, 263 p.
47-000734
Solomon, Hannah (Greenebaum) -- 1858-1943.

CT275.S6763.A3
Steinbeck, John, 1946-
In touch [by] John Steinbeck, IV. New York,
Knopf, 1969. xiv, 202 p.
69-010685 917.3/03/9230924
*Steinbeck, John, -- 1946- Vietnamese Conflict,
1961-1975 -- Personal narratives, American.
Marijuana.*

CT275.S898.A3 1993
Sturrock, John.
The language of autobiography: studies in the first
person singular/ John Sturrock. Cambridge;
Cambridge University Press, 1993. 296 p.
92-029784 808/.06692 0521412900
Autobiography.

CT275.S954.A4 1978
Sulzberger, Marina.
Marina: letters and diaries of Marina Sulzberger/
edited by C.L. Sulzberger. New York: Crown
Publishers, c1978. xii, 530 p.
78-007926 909.82 0517533758
*Sulzberger, Marina. Sulzberger, C. L. -- (Cyrus
Leo), -- 1912- United States -- Biography.*

CT275.T523.A33
Theroux, Phyllis.
California and other states of grace: a memoir/
Phyllis Theroux. New York: W. Morrow, 1980.
300 p.
79-027848 973/.0994 0688036414
Theroux, Phyllis. United States -- Biography.

CT275.T554.A34
Thomas, Lowell Jackson, 1892-1981.
Good evening everybody: from Cripple Creek to
Samarkand/ by Lowell Thomas. New York:
Morrow, 1976. 349 p.
76-010668 070/.92/4 0688030688
*Thomas, Lowell, -- 1892-1981. United States --
Biography.*

CT275.V23.L3
Lane, Wheaton Joshua, 1902-
Commodore Vanderbilt; an epic of the steam age,
by Wheaton J. Lane. New York, A. A. Knopf,
1942. xiv, 357 p.
42-036093 923.373
Vanderbilt, Cornelius, -- 1794-1877.

CT275.V233.A28
Vanderbilt, Gloria (Morgan) 1904-
Double exposure, a twin autobiography, by Gloria
Vanderbilt and Thelma Lady Furness. New York,
D. McKay Co. [1958] 369 p.
57-011077

CT275.W272A7
Appel, Joseph Herbert, 1873-
The business biography of John Wanamaker. New
York, The Macmillan company, 1930. 471 p.
30-004504
*Wanamaker, Thomas Brown, -- 1861-1908.
Wanamaker, John, -- 1838-1922. Wanamaker,
Rodman, -- 1863-1928.*

CT275.W5543.A3 1971
Whitney, Eleanor Searle.
Invitation to joy; a personal story. New York,
Harper & Row [1971] ix, 195 p.
70-148435 248/.0924
Whitney, Eleanor Searle.

CT275.W58458.A34
Winfrey, Carey.
Starts and finishes: coming of age in the fifties/
Carey Winfrey. New York: Saturday Review Press,
[1975] 183 p.
74-028086 917.3/03/920924 0841503710
Winfrey, Carey.

CT275.W58465.A3
Winkler, Max, 1888-
From A to X: reminiscences of Max Winkler. New
York: Crown Publishers, c1957. x, 178 p.
57-008701 926.555
Winkler, Max, -- 1888-

CT310.G728.A3
Gray, James Henry, 1906-
The boy from Winnipeg [by] James H. Gray.
Illustrated by Myra Lowenthal. Toronto,
Macmillan of Canada [c1970] 204 p.
79-587925 917.127/4
Gray, James Henry, -- 1906-

CT506-552 National biography — By region or country — Latin America

CT506.W48 1971
Who's who in Latin America; a biographical
dictionary of notable living men and women of
Latin America. Edited by Ronald Hilton. Detroit,
B. Ethridge, 1971 [c1945] 2 v.
76-165656 920.08 0879170212
Latin America -- Biography -- Dictionaries.

CT552.C36 1988
Camp, Roderic Ai.
Who's who in Mexico today/ Roderic Ai Camp.
Boulder: Westview Press, 1988. xix, 183 p.
87-029823 920/.072 0813373972
Mexico -- Biography -- Dictionaries.

CT759-1203 National biography — By region or country — Europe

CT759.R46 2001
Renaissance and Reformation, 1500-1620: a
biographical dictionary/ edited by Jo Eldridge
Carney. Westport, Conn.: Greenwood Press, c2001.
xvii, 417 p.
99-462063 920.04 0313305749
*Renaissance -- Biography -- Dictionaries.
Reformation -- Biography -- Dictionaries. Europe
-- Biography -- Dictionaries.*

CT775.S55 1957
Sitwell, Edith, 1887-1964.
English eccentrics. New York, Vanguard Press
[1957] 376 p.
57-014192 920.042
Eccentrics and eccentricities.

CT782.R6
Rosenbaum, Robert A., 1926-
Earnest Victorians; six great Victorians as
portrayed in their own words and those of their
contemporaries. New York, Hawthorn Books
[1961] 383 p.
61-005955 920.042
Great Britain -- Biography.

CT788.H5.A53 1962
Hickey, William, b. 1749.
The prodigal rake; memoirs of William Hickey.
Edited by Peter Quennell. New York, Dutton, 1962
[c1960] 452 p.
62-008217 920

CT788.T566.F6
Forster, E. M. 1879-1970.
Marianne Thornton, a domestic biography, 1797-
1887. New York, Harcourt, Brace [1956] 337 p.
56-006662 920.7
Thornton, Marianne, -- 1797-1887.

CT808.B9.A3
Byrne, John Francis, 1880-
Silent years; an autobiography with memoirs of
James Joyce and our Ireland. New York, Farrar,
Straus and Young [1953] 307 p.
53-009680 920.5
Joyce, James, -- 1882-1941.

CT862.B69 1998
Boylan, Henry.
A dictionary of Irish biography/ Henry Boylan.
Niwot, Colo.: Roberts Rinehart, c1998. xviii,
462 p.
98-065825 1570982368
Ireland -- Biography -- Dictionaries.

CT1017.D46.F67
Forster, Robert, 1926-
Merchants, landlords, magistrates: the Depont
family in eighteenth-century France/ Robert
Forster. Baltimore: Johns Hopkins University
Press, c1980. xii, 275 p.
80-014944 305.5/0944 0801824060
*Depont family. Social mobility -- France --
History -- 18th century. Family -- France --
History -- 18th century. France -- Social
conditions -- 18th century.*

CT1063.W48 1982
Wistrich, Robert S., 1945-
Who's who in Nazi Germany/ Robert Wistrich.
New York: Macmillan, 1982. 359 p.
82-004704 920/.043 002630600X
*Nazis -- Biography -- Dictionaries. Brain drain -
- Germany -- History -- 20th century --
Dictionaries. Germany -- History -- 1933-1945 --
Biography -- Dictionaries.*

CT1098.S45.A282 1949
Schweitzer, Albert, 1875-1965.
Out of my life and thought, an autobiography; tr.
by C. T. Campion. Postscript by Everett Skillings.
New York, H. Holt [1949] 274 p.
49-009927 922.443
*Schweitzer, Albert, -- 1875-1965. Schweitzer,
Albert, -- 1875-1965. Missionaries, Medical -
Gabon -- Biography. Theologians -- Europe --
Biography. Musicians -- Europe -- Biography.
France -- Biography.*

CT1098.S45.A33 1949
Schweitzer, Albert, 1875-1965.
Memoirs of childhood and youth. Translated by C.
T. Campion. New York, Macmillan Co. 1949. 78 p.
49-010619 922.443
*Schweitzer, Albert, -- 1875-1965. Physicians --
biography*

CT1203.W47 1993
Who's who in Russia and the new states/ edited by
Leonard Geron and Alex Pravda. London; I.B.
Tauris & Co., c1993. 77, ca. 525 p.
93-130316 920.047 1850434875
*Former Soviet republics -- Biography --
Dictionaries.*

CT1343-1474 National biography — By region or country — Europe

CT1343.D53 1996
Dictionary of Hispanic biography/ Joseph C. Tardiff & L. Mpho Mabunda, editors; foreword by Rudolfo Anaya. New York: Gale Research, c1996. xxv, 1011 p.
95-038261 920.046.220 0810383020
Hispanic Americans--Biography--Dictionaries.

CT1474.T8
Tugay, Emine Foat, 1897-
Three centuries; family chronicles of Turkey and Egypt. With a foreword by the Dowager Marchioness of Reading. London, Oxford University Press, 1963. x, 324 p.
63-006071 929.2
Muhammad Ali Basha, -- Governor of Egypt, -- 1769-1849. Egypt -- Biography. Turkey -- Biography.

CT1503-1828 National biography — By region or country — Asia

CT1503.R53 1998
Riddick, John F.
Who was who in British India/ John F. Riddick. Westport, Conn.: Greenwood Press, 1998. xv, 445 p.
98-023311 920/.0092 0313292329
British -- India -- Biography -- Dictionaries. India -- History -- British occupation, 1765-1947 -- Biography -- Dictionaries.

CT1512.B56 1997
Biographical encyclopedia of Pakistan. [Lahore]: Biographical Encyclopedia of Pakistan, [1997] 958 p.
97-930651
Pakistan -- Biography -- Dictionaries.

CT1828.C5.A3
Chao, Buwei Yang, 1889-
Autobiography of a Chinese woman/ Buwei Yang Chao; put into English by her husband Yuenren Chao. New York: The John Day Company, 1947. xvi, 327 p.
47-001800 920.7
Chao, Buwei Yang, -- 1889-   China -- Social life and customs.

CT1828.W785.A3 1993
Wu, Ningkun.
A single tear: a family's persecution, love, and endurance in Communist China/ Wu Ningkun, in collaboration with Li Yikai. New York: Atlantic Monthly Press, c1993. xiv, 367 p.
92-023054 951.05/092 0871134942
Wu, Ningkun.   China -- Biography. China -- Politics and government -- 1949-

CT2508 National biography — By region or country — Africa

CT2508.K94
Kyei, T. E.
Our days dwindle: memories of my childhood days in Asante/ T.E. Kyei; edited with an introduction by Jean Allman. Portsmouth, NH: Heinemann, c2001. xxiii, 239 p.
00-063248 966.7 0325070423
Kyei, T. E. -- (Thomas E.) -- Childhood and youth. Ashanti Region (Ghana) -- Biography. Ashanti Region (Ghana) -- Social life and customs.

CT2804 National biography — By region or country — Oceania. Pacific Islands

CT2804.A97 1998
Australian lives: an Oxford anthology/ edited by Joy Hooton. Melbourne: Oxford University Press, 1998. xiv, 298 p.
98-201344   0195537858
Autobiographies. Australia -- Biography.

CT3202 Biography. By subject — Biography of women (Collective) — General works

CT3202.L37 1996
Larousse dictionary of women/ editor, Melanie Parry. New York: Larousse, 1996. x, 741 p.
95-082384 920.72 0752300156
Women -- Biography -- Dictionaries.

CT3203 Biography. By subject — Biography of women (Collective) — General special

CT3203.G57 1992
Golemba, Beverly E., 1935-
Lesser-known women: a biographical dictionary/ Beverly E. Golemba. Boulder: Lynne Rienner Publishers, 1992. xi, 380 p.
91-041182 920.72 1555873014
Women -- Biography -- Dictionaries.

CT3220 Biography. By subject — Biography of women (Collective) — Medieval

CT3220.A56 1992
Echols, Anne.
An annotated index of medieval women/ by Anne Echols and Marty Williams. New York: M. Wiener Pub.; c1992. xxiv, 635 p.
90-039810 920.72/094 0910129274
Women -- Europe -- Biography -- Dictionaries. Women -- History -- Middle Ages, 500-1500 -- Dictionaries. Social history -- Medieval, 500-1500 -- Dictionaries.

CT3234 Biography. By subject — Biography of women (Collective) — Modern

CT3234.W65
The Women's book of world records and achievements/ edited by Lois Decker O'Neill. Garden City, N.Y.: Anchor Press/Doubleday, 1979. xiii, 798 p.
77-082961 920.72 0385127324
Women -- Biography. Biography -- 19th century. Biography -- 20th century.

CT3260-3290 Biography. By subject — Biography of women (Collective) — America

CT3260.M36 2002
McMillen, Margot Ford.
Called to courage: four women in Missouri history/ Margot Ford McMillen and Heather Roberson. Columbia: University of Missouri Press, c2002. xi, 136 p.
2002-0179 920.72/09778 221 0826213995
Ignon Ouaconisen, ca. 1700-ca. 1751. Boone, Olive Van Bibber, 1783-1858. Tolton, Martha Jane Chisley, b. 1833. Women pioneers--Missouri--Biography.

CT3260.N57
Notable American women, 1607-1950; a biographical dictionary. Edward T. James, editor. Janet Wilson James, associate editor. Paul S. Boyer, assistant editor. Cambridge, Mass., Belknap Press of Harvard University Press, 1971. 3 v.
76-152274 920.72/0973 0674627318
Women -- United States -- Biography -- Dictionaries.

CT3260.N573
Notable American women: the modern period: a biographical dictionary/ edited by Barbara Sicherman, Carol Hurd Green with Ilene Kantrov, Harriette Walker. Cambridge, Mass.: Belknap Press of Harvard University Press, 1980. xxii, 773 p.
80-018402 920.72/0973 0674627326
Women -- United States -- Biography.

CT3260.W56 1973
Willard, Frances Elizabeth, 1839-1898,
American women: fifteen hundred biographies with over 1,400 portraits; a comprehensive encyclopedia of the lives and achievements of American women during the nineteenth century. Edited by Frances E. Willard and Mary A. Livermore. Newly rev. with the addition of a classified index. New York, Mast, Crowell & Kirkpatrick. Detroit, Gale Research Co., 1973-[c1897] v.
73-007985 920.72/0973
Women -- United States -- Biography -- Encyclopedias.

CT3290.N68 2001
Notable twentieth-century Latin American women: a biographical dictionary/ edited by Cynthia Margarita Tompkins and David William Foster. Westport, Conn.: Greenwood Press, 2001. xxiii, 324 p.
00-027631 920.72/098 0313311129
Women -- Latin America -- Biography. Latin America -- Biography.

CT3320 Biography. By subject — Biography of women (Collective) — Europe

CT3320.S85 1993
Sweeney, Patricia E., 1950-
Biographies of British women: an annotated bibliography/ Patricia E. Sweeney. Santa Barbara, Calif.: ABC-CLIO, c1993. xi, 410 p.
93-013325 920.72/0941 0874366283
Women -- Great Britain -- Biography.

CT3990 Biography. By subject — Academicians. Scholars. Savants

CT3990.W36.C64 1974
Cohen, Paul A.
Between tradition and modernity: Wang T'ao and reform in late Ch'ing China/ Paul A. Cohen. Cambridge: Harvard University Press, 1974. x, 357 p.
74-075109   301.2/4/0951   0674068750
Wang, Tao, -- 1828-1897.   Scholars -- China -- Biography.   China -- History -- Reform movement, 1898.

D History (General)

D1 Societies. Serials

D1.J62
Journal of world history: official journal of the World History Association.   Honolulu, HI: University of Hawaii Press, c1990- v.
90-640778   905
World history -- Periodicals.

D5 Sources and documents

D5.H25 1993
Haskell, Francis, 1928-
History and its images: art and the interpretation of the past/ Francis Haskell. New Haven: Yale University Press, c1993. x, 558 p.
92-041145   909   0300055404
Art and history. History -- Sources.

D6 Collected works (Monographs, essays, etc.) — Several authors

D6.G35
Gay, Peter, 1923-
Historians at work. Edited by Peter Gay and Gerald J. Cavanaugh. New York, Harper & Row [1972-75] 4 v.
75-123930   908   0060114738
History -- Addresses, essays, lectures.

D7 Collected works (Monographs, essays, etc.) — Individual authors

D7.B7513
Braudel, Fernand.
On history/ Fernand Braudel; translated by Sarah Matthews. Chicago: University of Chicago Press, c1980. ix, 226 p.
80-011201   901   0226071502
History.

D7.H823
Huizinga, Johan, 1872-1945.
Men and ideas: history, the Middle Ages, the Renaissance; essays. Translated by James S. Holmes and Hans van Marle. New York, Meridian Books [1959] 378 p.
59-007177   940.1
History.

D7.K73
Kohn, Hans, 1891-1971.
Reflections on modern history; the historian and human responsibility.   Princeton, N.J., D. Van Nostrand [1963] xvi, 360 p.
63-006466   908
History, Modern

D7.M77
Mommsen, Theodor Ernst, 1905-1958.
Medieval and Renaissance studies. Edited by Eugene F. Rice, Jr. Ithaca, N.Y., Cornell University Press [1959] xiii, 353 p.
60-000125   908.1
Petrarca, Francesco, -- 1304-1374.   Christian literature, Early -- History and criticism.   Italy -- History -- 1265-1492. Italy -- History -- 1492-1559.

D7.T79 1957
Trevor-Roper, H. R. 1914-
Historical essays/ by H. R. Trevor-Roper. London: Macmillan; [1958, c1957] viii, 298 p.
58-006157
History.

D7.W43
Wedgwood, C. V. 1910-
Velvet studies, by C. V. Wedgwood. London, J. Cape [1946] 159 p.
47-000980   904
History

D8 Pamphlets, etc.

D8.W4
Wedgwood, C. V. 1910-
The sense of the past.   [London] Cambridge University Press, 1957. 26 p.
58-001771
James, Henry, -- 1843-1916. -- The sense of the past.   History.

D9 Dictionaries

D9.C37 1991
Carper, N. Gordon.
The meaning of history: a dictionary of quotations/ N. Gordon Carper and Joyce Carper. New York: Greenwood Press, 1991. xiii, 374 p.
90-013977   903   0313268355
History -- Quotations, maxims, etc. -- Dictionaries.   Historians -- Quotations -- Dictionaries.

D9.D53 2000
A dictionary of world history/ [editors, Alan Isaacs ... et al.]. Oxford; Oxford University Press, 2000. 697 p.
00-702307   0192801058
History -- Dictionaries.

D9.K63 1990
Kohn, George C.
Dictionary of historic documents/ George C. Kohn; introduction by Leonard Latkovski. New York: Facts on File, c1991. viii, 408 p.
90-042305   016.909   0816019789
History -- Sources -- Dictionaries.

D9.W47 1994
Wetterau, Bruce.
World history: a dictionary of important people, places, and events from ancient times to the present/ Bruce Wetterau. New York: H. Holt, 1994. xvi, 1173 p.
93-034819   903   080502350X
History -- Dictionaries.

D11 Chronological tables, etc.

D11.A76 1991
Asimov, Isaac, 1920-
Asimov's chronology of the world/ Isaac Asimov. New York, N.Y.: HarperCollins Publishers, c1991. 674 p.
91-055007   902/.02   0062700367
Chronology, Historical.

D11.M39 1999
Mellersh, H. E. L.
Chronology of world history/ H.E.L. Mellersh. Santa Barbara, Calif.: ABC-CLIO, c1999. 4 v.
99-019300   902/.02   1576071553
Chronology, Historical.

D11.S83 1986
Steinberg, S. H. 1899-1969.
Historical tables, 58 BC-AD 1985/ by S.H. Steinberg; foreword by G.P. Gooch. New York: Garland Pub., c1986. ix, 277 p.
86-018326   902/.02   0824089510
Chronology, Historical -- Tables.

D11.W65 1999
The Wilson calendar of world history/ edited by John Paxton and Edward W. Knappman; based on S.H. Steinberg's Historical tables; contributors, Rodney Carlisle ... [et al.]. New York: H.W. Wilson, 1999. xiv, 460 p.
98-050998   902/.02   0824209370
Chronology, Historical. Calendars.

D11.5 Chronological tables, etc. — Special

D11.5.L64 1992
Long, Kim.
The almanac of anniversaries/ Kim Long. Santa Barbara, Calif.: ABC-CLIO, c1992. xvi, 270 p.
92-028945   394.2   0874366755
Anniversaries -- Calendars.

D13 Historiography — General works

D13.B33
Barraclough, Geoffrey, 1908-
History in a changing world. Oxford, Blackwell, 1955. viii, 246 p.
56-002540   907
Historiography.

D13.B333
Barzun, Jacques, 1907-
Clio and the doctors: psycho-history, quanto-history, & history/ Jacques Barzun. Chicago: University of Chicago Press, c1974. xi, 173 p.
74-005723   155
Historiography. Psychohistory.

D13.B334 1970
Barzun, Jacques, 1907-
The modern researcher [by] Jacques Barzun & Henry F. Graff. New York, Harcourt, Brace & World [1970] xvii, 430 p.
72-115861   907.2   0151614822
Historiography. Academic writing.

D13.B38 1972
Becker, Carl Lotus, 1873-1945.
Detachment and the writing of history: essays and letters of Carl L. Becker. Edited by Phil L. Snyder. Westport, Conn., Greenwood Press [1972, c1958] xvi, 240 p.
70-152590   907/.2   0837160235
Historiography -- Addresses, essays, lectures.

D13.B427 1999
Bentley, Michael, 1948-
Modern historiography: an introduction/ Michael Bentley. London; Routledge, 1999. xii, 182 p.
98-039603   907/.2   0415202671
Historiography.

D13.B54 1997
Black, Jeremy.
Maps and history: constructing images of the past/ Jeremy Black. New Haven: Yale University Press, c1997. 267 p.
96-041293   907.2   0300069766
Historiography. History -- Methodology. Historical geography -- Maps.

D13.B686 1983
Breisach, Ernst.
Historiography: ancient, medieval, & modern/ Ernst Breisach. Chicago: University of Chicago Press, c1983. xii, 487 p.
82-020246   907/.2   0226072746
Historiography -- History.

D13.B79
Butterfield, Herbert, 1900-
Man on his past: the study of the history of historical scholarship. Cambridge [Eng.] University Press, 1955. xvi, 237 p.
55-013806   907/.2   521095670
Historiography.

D13.B8
Butterfield, Herbert, 1900-
The whig interpretation of history, by H. Butterfield ... London: G. Bell and Sons, 1959. vi p. 1 . 1
31-035009   907
Historiography.

D13.C6
Collingwood, R. G. 1889-1943.
The idea of history/ by R. G. Collingwood. Oxford: Clarendon Press, 1946. xxvi, 339 p.
47-000113   907
Historiography. History -- Philosophy.

D13.C626 1997
Companion to historiography/ edited by Michael Bentley. London; Routledge, 1997. xvii, 997 p.
97-202105   907.2   0415030846
Historiography.

D13.C674 1993
Costello, Paul.
World historians and their goals: twentieth-century answers to modernism/ Paul Costello. DeKalb [Ill.]: Northern Illinois University Press, 1993. x, 315 p.
92-015134   907.2   0875801730
Historiography -- History -- 20th century.

D13.C682 1970
Croce, Benedetto, 1866-1952.
History as the story of liberty. [Translated by Sylvia Sprigge] Chicago, Regnery [1970] 320 p.
71-105123   907/.2
Historiography. History -- Philosophy. Historicism.

D13.G47 1998
A global encyclopedia of historical writing/ editor, D.R. Woolf; managing editor, Kathryn M. Brammall; editorial assistant, Greg Bak; advisory editors, Peter Burke ... [et al.]. New York: Garland Pub., 1998. 2 v.
97-042982   907/.2   0815315147
Historiography. Historians.

D13.G7 1959
Gooch, G. P. 1873-1968.
History and historians in the nineteenth century. With a new introd. by the author. Boston, Beacon Press [1959] 547 p.
59-006390   907.2
Historiography -- History -- 19th century. Historians.

D13.H282 1996
Hamilton, Richard F.
The social misconstruction of reality: validity and verification in the scholarly community/ Richard F. Hamilton. New Haven: Yale University Press, c1996. xiii, 289 p.
95-030970   907.2   0300063458
Historiography -- Case studies. Knowledge, Sociology of -- Case studies.

D13.H75 2000
Hughes-Warrington, Marnie.
Fifty key thinkers on history/ Marnie Hughes-Warrington. London; Routledge, 2000. xix, 363 p.
00-710864   907.2   041516981X
Historiography.

D13.H87 1993
Hutton, Patrick H.
History as an art of memory/ Patrick H. Hutton. [Burlington, Vt.]: University of Vermont; c1993. xxv, 229 p.
93-017246   907/.2   0874516315
Historiography. Memory. History -- Philosophy.

D13.J314 1953a
Jaspers, Karl, 1883-1969.
The origin and goal of history. [Translated from the German by Michael Bullock] New Haven, Yale University Press, 1953. 294 p.
53-011595   907
Historiography.

D13.K315 1992
Kaye, Harvey J.
The education of desire: Marxists and the writing of history/ Harvey J. Kaye; foreword by Christopher Hill. New York: Routledge, 1992. xiv, 211 p.
92-011609   335.4/119   0415905877
Marxian historiography.

D13.K7 1989
Krieger, Leonard.
Time's reasons: philosophies of history old and new/ Leonard Krieger. Chicago: University of Chicago Press, 1989. xii, 202 p.
88-029407   907/.2   0226453006
Historiography. History -- Philosophy.

D13.L26 1985
LaCapra, Dominick, 1939-
History & criticism/ Dominick LaCapra. Ithaca, N.Y.: Cornell University Press, 1985. 145 p.
84-016990   907/.2   0801417880
Historiography.

D13.M363 1984
McCullagh, C. Behan.
Justifying historical descriptions/ C. Behan McCullagh. Cambridge; Cambridge University Press, 1984. x, 252 p.
84-007028   907.2   0521267226
Historiography.

D13.M86 2000
Munslow, Alun, 1947-
The Routledge companion to historical studies/ Alun Munslow. London; Routledge, 2000. xv, 271 p.
99-027243   907/.2   0415184940
Historiography -- History -- 20th century. History -- Philosophy.

D13.N367 1975
Nevins, Allan, 1890-1971.
Allan Nevins on history/ compiled and introduced by Ray Allen Billington. New York: Scribner, [1975] xxvii, 420 p.
75-004870   907/.2   0684143208
Historiography. Historians -- United States -- Biography.

D13.N45 1992
New perspectives on historical writing/ edited by Peter Burke. University Park, Pa.: Pennsylvania State University Press, 1992. 254 p.
91-029380   907/.2   027100827X
Historiography.

D13.R32
Ranke, Leopold von, 1795-1886.
The theory and practice of history. Edited with an introd. by Georg G. Iggers and Konrad von Moltke. New translations by Wilma A. Iggers and Konrad von Moltke. Indianapolis, Bobbs-Merrill [1973] lxx, 514 p.
79-167691   901   067251673X
Historiography.

D13.R44 2000
Richardson, R. C.
The study of history: a bibliographical guide/ compiled by R.C. Richardson. Manchester [England]; Manchester University Press; 2000. p. cm.
00-021461   016.907/2   0719058996
Historiography -- Bibliography. History -- Methodology -- Bibliography. History -- Philosophy -- Bibliography.

D13.R49 1986
Ritter, Harry.
Dictionary of concepts in history/ Harry Ritter. Westport, Conn.: Greenwood Press, 1986. xix, 490 p.
85-027305   907/.2/0321   0313227004
Historiography -- Dictionaries.

D13.S5 1939
Shotwell, James Thomson, 1874-1965.
The history of history, by James T. Shotwell... New York, Columbia University Press, 1939- v.
39-004448   907
Historiography.

D13.S567 1998
Smith, Bonnie G., 1940-
The gender of history: men, women, and historical practice/ Bonnie G. Smith. Cambridge, Mass.: Harvard University Press, 1998. viii, 306 p.
98-011926   907/.2   0674341813
Historiography. Historians. Women historians.

D13.W42
Wedgwood, C. V. 1910-
Literature and the historian.   [London, Oxford University Press] 1956. 15 p.
56-058675   907
Literature and history. Historiography.

D13.W624 1997
Windschuttle, Keith, 1942-
The killing of history: how literary critics and social theorists are murdering our past/ Keith Windschuttle. New York: Free Press, 1997. 298 p.
97-018957   907/.2   0684844451
Historiography. Historicism.

D13.W97 1998
Wyschogrod, Edith.
An ethics of remembering: history, heterology, and the nameless others/ Edith Wyschogrod. Chicago: University of Chicago Press, 1998. xxi, 280 p.
97-041458   901   0226920445
Historiography -- Moral and ethical aspects. Difference (Psychology) -- Moral and ethical aspects.

D13.2 Historiography — Criticism and reviews

D13.2.I3413 1997
Iggers, Georg G.
Historiography in the twentieth century: from scientific objectivity to the postmodern challenge/ Georg G. Iggers. Hanover, NH: Wesleyan University Press, published by Universi c1997. x, 182 p.
96-024058   907/.2   0819553026
Historiography -- History -- 20th century. History -- Philosophy. History -- Methodology.

D13.2.R54 1987
Rigby, S. H. 1955-
Marxism and history: a critical introduction/ S.H. Rigby. New York: St. Martin's Press, 1987. 314 p.
87-009723   907/.2   0312009216
Historiography.   Marxism.   Historical materialism.

D13.5 Historiography — By region or country, A-Z

D13.5.E85.F66 1995
Fontana i Lazaro, Josep.
The distorted past: a reinterpretation of Europe/ Josep Fontana; translated by Colin Smith. Oxford; Blackwell Publishers, 1995. p. cm.
94-039077   940/.072   0631176225
Europe -- Historiography.

D13.5.E85.H57 1980
The Historian at work/ edited by John Cannon. London; Allen & Unwin, 1980. xiv, 210 p.
81-217031   907/.204   0049010255
Historiography -- Europe. Historians -- Europe -- Biography.

D13.5.U6.V65 1999
Voices of women historians: the personal, the political, the professional/ edited by Eileen Boris and Nupur Chaudhuri. Bloomington: Indiana University Press, c1999. xx, 295 p.
98-051191   907/.202273   0253334942
Women -- United States -- History -- 20th century. Women historians -- United States -- Biography. Feminism -- United States -- History -- 20th century.

D14 Historiography — Biography of historians — Collective

D14.B58 1988
The Blackwell dictionary of historians/ edited by John Cannon ... [et al.]. New York: Blackwell Reference, 1988. xiv, 480 p.
88-019361   907/.202/2   063114708X
Historians -- Biography -- Dictionaries.

D14.G75 1991
Great historians of the modern age: an international dictionary/ Lucian Boia, editor-in-chief; Ellen Nore, Keith Hitchins, and Georg G. Iggers, associate editors. New York: Greenwood Press, 1991. xxiv, 841 p.
89-026009   907/.2022   0313273286
Historians -- Biography -- Dictionaries.

D14.H3
Halperin, Samuel William.
Some 20th-century historians; essays on eminent Europeans. Contributors: James L. Cate and others. Chicago, University of Chicago Press, 1961. xxiv, 298 p.
61-005608   928
Historians.

D15 Historiography — Biography of historians — Individual, A-Z

D15.A25.H487 2000
Hill, Roland, 1920-
Lord Acton/ Roland Hill; foreword by Owen Chadwick. New Haven: Yale University Press, c2000. xxiv, 548 p.
99-053065   907/.202   0300079567
Acton, John Emerich Edward Dalberg Acton, -- Baron, -- 1834-1902. Historians -- Great Britain -- Biography.

D15.A25.H5 1952a
Himmelfarb, Gertrude.
Lord Acton; a study in conscience and politics. London, Routledge & Paul [1952] 260 p.
53-000477   928.2
Acton, John Emerich Edward Dalberg Acton, -- baron, -- 1834-1902.

D15.B33.W5
Wilkins, Burleigh Taylor.
Carl Becker: a biographical study in American intellectual history/ by Burleigh Taylor Wilkins. Cambridge, Mass.: M.I.T. Press, 1967, c1961. ix, 246 p.
61-007870   928.1
Becker, Carl Lotus, -- 1873-1945.   Historians -- United States -- Biography.

D15.B596.F56 1989
Fink, Carole, 1940-
Marc Bloch: a life in history/ Carole Fink. Cambridge; Cambridge University Press, 1989. xix, 371 p.
88-032216   944/.0072024   052137300X
Bloch, Marc Leopold Benjamin, -- 1886-1944. Historians -- France -- Biography.

D15.B596.F75 1996
Friedman, Susan W.
Marc   Bloch,   sociology   and   geography: encountering changing disciplines/ Susan W. Friedman. Cambridge; Cambridge University Press, 1996. xii, 258 p.
95-037598   304.2/3   0521561574
Bloch, Marc Leopold Benjamin, -- 1886-1944. Social sciences and history. Historical geography.

D15.B8 A422 1955
Burckhardt, Jacob, 1818-1897.
Letters/ Selected, edited and translated by Alexander Dru. Pantheon Books, 1955. 242 p.
55-002791   928.3
Burckhardt, Jacob, -- 1818-1897.

D15.D87.A33
Durant, Will, 1885-
A dual autobiography/ by Will and Ariel Durant. New York: Simon and Schuster, c1977. 420 p.
77-024590   973/.07/2022   0671229257
Durant, Will, -- 1885- Durant, Ariel. Historians -- United States -- Biography.

D15.G64.A3
Gooch, G. P. 1873-1968.
Under six reigns.   London, Longmans, Green [1958] 344 p.
59-001259   928.2
Historians -- Correspondence, reminiscences, etc.

D15.H88.A3 1990
Hughes, H. Stuart 1916-
Gentleman rebel: the memoirs of H. Stuart Hughes. New York: Ticknor & Fields, 1990. x, 326 p.
90-040272   940/.07202   039556316X
Hughes, H. Stuart -- (Henry Stuart), -- 1916- Historians -- United States -- Biography. Europe -- Historiography.

D15.L3.C45 1993
Chickering, Roger, 1942-
Karl Lamprecht: a German academic life (1856-1915)/ Roger Chickering. New Jersey: Humanities Press, 1993. xviii, 491 p.
92-009140   907/.202   0391037668
Lamprecht, Karl, -- 1856-1915.   Historians -- Germany -- Biography.

D15.M34.A32
Marshall, S. L. A. 1900-1977.
Bringing up the rear: a memoir/ by S. L. A. Marshall; edited by Cate Marshall. San Rafael, Calif.: Presidio Press, c1979. xiii, 310 p.
79-014949   355/.0092/4   0891410848
Marshall, S. L. A. -- (Samuel Lyman Atwood), -- 1900-1977.   Historians -- United States -- Biography.

D15.N3.N35 1971
Namier, Julia,
Lewis Namier: a biography by Julia Namier. London, Oxford University Press, 1971. xvii, 347 p.
76-852488   907/.2/024   0192117068
Namier, Lewis Bernstein, -- Sir, -- 1888-1960.

D15.N4.M3
Manuel, Frank Edward.
Isaac Newton, historian.   Cambridge, Belknap Press of Harvard University Press, 1963. viii, 328 p.
63-010869   925.3
Newton, Isaac, -- Sir, -- 1642-1727.   Historians -- Great Britain -- Biography. Mathematicians -- Great Britain -- Biography.

D15.R3.K74
Krieger, Leonard.
Ranke: the meaning of history/ Leonard Krieger. Chicago: University of Chicago Press, 1977. xii, 402 p.
76-025633   907/.2/024   0226453499
Ranke, Leopold von, -- 1795-1886.   History -- Philosophy. Historicism. Historians -- Germany -- Biography.

D15.S85.A3 1996
Strausz-Hupe, Robert, 1903-
In my time/ Robert Strausz-Hupe; with a new introduction by the author. New Brunswick, NJ: Transaction Publishers, c1996. 284 p.
95-031867   943.605   1560008539
Strausz-Hupe, Robert, -- 1903- Historians -- Austria -- Biography. Diplomats -- Austria -- Biography. Historians -- United States -- Biography.

D15.V6.B7
Brumfitt, J. H.
Voltaire, historian/ J.H. Brumfitt. London: Oxford University Press, 1958. 178 p.
58-000923
Voltaire, -- 1694-1778.

D16 Methodology. Relation to other sciences — General works

D16.B15 1976
Barbu, Zevedei, 1919-
Problems of historical psychology/ by Zevedei Barbu. Westport, Conn.: Greenwood Press, 1976, c1960. x, 222 p.
75-028659   301.24/7   0837184762
Psychohistory. National characteristics, English. Civilization -- History.

D16.B464 1995
Berkhofer, Robert F.
Beyond the great story: history as text and discourse/ Robert F. Berkhofer, Jr. Cambridge, Mass.: Belknap Press of Harvard University Press, 1995. xii, 381 p.
95-002005   901   0674069072
History -- Methodology. History -- Philosophy.

D16.B94 1990
Burke, Peter.
The French historical revolution: the Annales school, 1929-89/ Peter Burke. Stanford, Calif.: Stanford University Press, 1990. vi, 152 p.
90-070699   907/.2044   0804718369
History -- Methodology. History -- Philosophy. Annales school.

D16.D48
The Dimensions of the past; materials, problems, and opportunities for quantitative work in history. Edited by Val R. Lorwin and Jacob M. Price. New Haven, Yale University Press, 1972. vi, 568 p.
78-151587   907/.2073
History -- Statistical methods -- Addresses, essays, lectures.

D16.E32 1997
Egmond, Florike.
The mammoth and the mouse: microhistory and morphology/ Florike Egmond and Peter Mason. Baltimore: Johns Hopkins University Press, c1997. xiii, 245 p.
96-047416   907.2   0801854776
History -- Methodology. Historiography.

D16.G78 1993
Green, William A., 1935-
History, historians, and the dynamics of change/ William A. Green. Westport, Conn.: Praeger, 1993. x, 260 p.
92-026023   902   0275939022
History -- Methodology. Social change.

D16.P8
The Psychoanalytic interpretation of history, edited by Benjamin B. Wolman. Foreword by William L. Langer. New York, Basic Books [1971] x, 240 p.
71-135561   907.2/2   0465065937
Stalin, Joseph, -- 1879-1953. Herzl, Theodor, -- 1860-1904. Hitler, Adolf, -- 1889-1945. Psychohistory -- Addresses, essays, lectures.

D16.W59
White, Morton Gabriel, 1917-
Foundations of historical knowledge, by Morton White. New York, Harper & Row [1965] 299 p.
64-025124   901
History -- Methodology. History -- Philosophy.

D16.12 Methodology. Relation to other sciences — Special topics — Data processing

D16.12.G74 1994
Greenstein, Daniel I.
A historian's guide to computing/ Daniel I. Greenstein. Oxford; Oxford University Press, 1994. xiii, 268 p.
93-046381   902/.85   0198242352
History -- Data processing.

D16.13 Methodology. Relation to other sciences — Special topics — Historiometry

D16.13.S58 1990
Simonton, Dean Keith.
Psychology, science, and history: an introduction to historiometry/ Dean Keith Simonton. New Haven [CT]: Yale University Press, c1990. xi, 291 p.
90-035617   901   0300047711
Historiometry.

D16.14 Methodology. Relation to other sciences — Special topics — Oral history

D16.14.B38
Baum, Willa K.
Transcribing and editing oral history/ by Willa K. Baum. Nashville: American Association for State and Local History c1977. 127 p.
77-003340   907/.2   0910050260
Oral history. English language -- Transcription. Editing.

D16.14.F65 1988
Foley, John Miles.
The theory of oral composition: history and methodology/ John Miles Foley. Bloomington: Indiana University Press, c1988. xv, 170 p.
87-045402   901   0253342600
Oral history.

D16.14.I55 1994
Interactive oral history interviewing/ edited by Eva M. McMahan, Kim Lacy Rogers. Hillsdale, N.J.: Erlbaum, 1994. ix, 172 p.
94-010437   907/.2   0805805761
Oral history. Interviewing.

D16.14.O74 1990
Oral history index: an international directory of oral history interviews. Westport: Meckler, c1990. 434 p.
90-043972   909.82/025   0887363490
Oral history -- Indexes.

D16.14.P67 1990
Portelli, Alessandro.
The death of Luigi Trastulli, and other stories: form and meaning in oral history/ Alessandro Portelli. Albany, N.Y.: State University of New York Press, c1991. xvi, 341 p.
89-026260   907   0791404293
Oral history. Working class -- Italy -- Terni -- History -- 20th century. Working class -- Kentucky -- Harlan County -- History -- 20th century. Terni (Italy) -- Social conditions. Harlan County (Ky.) -- Social conditions.

D16.16 Methodology. Relation to other sciences — Special topics — Psychohistory

D16.16.L64 1983
Loewenberg, Peter, 1933-
Decoding the past: the psychohistorical approach/ Peter Loewenberg. New York: Knopf: 1983, c1982. xiv, 300 p.
82-047796   901/.9   0394481526
Psychohistory.

D16.16.L65 1995
Loewenberg, Peter, 1933-
Fantasy and reality in history/ Peter Loewenberg. New York: Oxford University Press, 1995. viii, 235 p.
94-043804   901/.9   0195067630
Psychohistory. Irrationalism (Philosophy)

D16.16.P87 1988
Psychology and historical interpretation/ edited by William McKinley Runyan. New York: Oxford University Press, 1988. xiii, 306 p.
87-025708   901/.9   0195053273
Psychohistory. History -- Psychological aspects. Personality and history.

D16.163 Methodology. Relation to other sciences — Special topics — Public history

D16.163.L44 1989
Leffler, Phyllis K.
Public and academic history: a philosophy and paradigm / Phyllis K. Leffler and Joseph Brent. Malabar, Fla.: R.E. Krieger, 1990. viii, 97 p.
89-002628   907.2   0894642987
Public history. Historiography.

D16.166 Methodology. Relation to other sciences — Special topics — Social sciences and history

D16.166.P53 1997
Pickering, Michael.
History, experience, and cultural studies/ Michael Pickering. New York: St. Martin's Press, 1997. x, 274 p.
96-051470   306/.07   0312173458
Social sciences and history. Culture -- Study and teaching.

D16.17 Methodology. Relation to other sciences — Special topics — Statistical methods

D16.17.J37 1991
Jarausch, Konrad Hugo.
Quantitative methods for historians: a guide to research, data, and statistics/ Konrad H. Jarausch and Kenneth A. Hardy. Chapel Hill: University of North Carolina Press, c1991. xv, 247 p.
90-040746   907/.2   0807819476
History -- Statistical methods.

D16.25 Study and teaching — General special

D16.25.B5 2000
Beyond the area studies wars: toward a new international studies/ Neil L. Waters, editor. [Middlebury, Vt.]: Middlebury College Press; c2000. vi, 243 p.
00-009483   907/.2   1584650745
Area studies. World politics -- Study and teaching. International relations -- Study and teaching.

D16.25.R68 1998
Roth, Stacy Flora.
Past into present: effective techniques for first-person historical interpretation/ Stacy F. Roth. Chapel Hill: University of North Carolina Press, c1998. 254 p.
97-036874   907/.1   0807824070
History -- Study and teaching. Historic sites -- Interpretive programs. Historical reenactments.

D16.255 Study and teaching — Special topics, A-Z

D16.255.C65.H58 2000
The history highway 2000: a guide to Internet resources/ [edited by] Dennis A. Trinkle, Scott A. Merriman. Armonk, N.Y.: M.E. Sharpe, c2000. xiv, 600 p.
99-052019   025.06/9   0765604779
History -- Computer network resources. Internet.

D16.3 Study and teaching — By region or country — United States

D16.3.T35 1993
Teaching social studies: handbook of trends, issues, and implications for the future/ edited by Virginia S. Wilson, James A. Litle, and Gerald Lee Wilson. Westport, Conn.: Greenwood Press, 1993. xi, 296 p.
92-017837   907/.1273   0313278814
History -- Study and teaching -- United States. Social sciences -- Study and teaching -- United States.

D16.4 Study and teaching — By region or country — Other regions or countries, A-Z

D16.4.G3.A793
Antoni, Carlo.
From history to sociology; the transition in German historical thinking. With a foreword by Benedetto Croce. Translated from the Italian by Hayden V. White. Detroit, Wayne State University Press, 1959. 249 p.
58-062837   901.8
Historians -- Germany. Sociology -- Methodology. History -- Philosophy.

D16.7 Philosophy of history — General works — Through 1800

D16.7.I24
Ibn Khaldun, 1332-1406.
An Arab philosophy of history: selections from the Prolegomena of Ibn Khaldun of Tunis (1332-1406)/ translated and arranged by Charles Issawi. London: J. Murray, 1950. xiv, 190 p.
50-014293   901
History -- Philosophy -- Early works to 1800. Civilization -- Philosophy -- Early works to 1800.

D16.7.I2413 1969
Ibn Khaldun, 1332-1406.
The Muqaddimah, an introduction to history. Translated from the Arabic by Franz Rosenthal. Abridged and edited by N. J. Dawood. [Princeton, N.J.] Princeton University Press [1969] xiv, 465 p.
72-008164   901.9   0691017549
History -- Philosophy -- Early works to 1800. Civilization -- Early works to 1800.

D16.7.P45 2000
Philosophies of history: from enlightenment to post-modernity/ introduced and edited by Robert M. Burns and Hugh Rayment-Pickard. Oxford, UK; Blackwell Publishers, 2000. xv, 360 p.
99-056272   901   0631212361
History -- Philosophy.

D16.8 Philosophy of history — General works — 1801-

D16.8.A638 1994
Ankersmit, F. R.
History and tropology: the rise and fall of metaphor/ F.R. Ankersmit. Berkeley: University of California Press, c1994. vii, 244 p.
93-012081   901   0520082044
History -- Philosophy. Historiography.

D16.8.A65
Arendt, Hannah.
Between past and future: six exercises in political thought/ Hannah Arendt. Cleveland: World Pub. Co., 1968, c1961. 246 p.
61-007281   901
History -- Philosophy. Civilization, Modern -- 1950-

D16.8.A725
Aron, Raymond, 1905-
Politics and history: selected essays/ by Raymond Aron; collected, translated, and edited by Miriam Bernheim Conant. New York: Free Press, c1978. xxx, 274 p.
78-054122   901   0029010004
History -- Philosophy -- Addresses, essays, lectures. Political science -- Addresses, essays, lectures. Social sciences -- Addresses, essays, lectures.

D16.8.A75
Atkinson, R. F. 1928-
Knowledge and explanation in history: an introduction to the philosophy of history/ R. F. Atkinson. Ithaca, N.Y.: Cornell University Press, 1978. x, 229 p.
77-090896   901   0801411165.
History -- Philosophy.

D16.8.B318 1966
Becker, Carl Lotus, 1873-1945.
Everyman his own historian; essays on history and politics, by Carl L. Becker. Chicago, Quadrangle Books [1966] 325 p.
67-001041   901
History -- Philosophy.

D16.8.B812 1964
Burckhardt, Jacob, 1818-1897.
Force and freedom; reflections on history [by] Jacob Burckhardt. Edited by James Hastings Nichols. New York, Pantheon Books [1964, c1943] vi, 382 p.
64-005204   901
History -- Philosophy.

D16.8.C33 1962
Carr, Edward Hallett, 1892-
What is history? New York, Knopf, 1962 [c1961] 209 p.
61-017812   901
History -- Philosophy.

D16.8.D49 1962
Dilthey, Wilhelm, 1833-1911.
Pattern & meaning in history; thoughts on history & society. Edited & introduced by H. P. Rickman. New York, Harper [1962, c1961] 170 p.
62-005023   901
History -- Philosophy.

D16.8.D69
Dray, William H.
Perspectives on history/ William Dray. London; Routledge and K. Paul, 1980. ix, 142 p.
79-042651   901   0710005695
History -- Philosophy -- Addresses, essays, lectures.

D16.8.D7
Dray, William H.
Philosophy of history. Englewood Cliffs, N.J., Prentice-Hall [1964] ix, 116 p.
64-016442   901
History -- Philosophy.

D16.8.E847 1999
Evans, Richard J.
In defense of history/ Richard J. Evans. New York: W.W. Norton, c1999. 287 p.
98-024422   907   0393046877

D16.8.F45213 1990
Ferry, Luc.
Rights: the new quarrel between the Ancients and the Moderns/ Luc Ferry; translated by Franklin Philip. Chicago: University of Chicago Press, c1990. vii, 151 p.
89-020335   901   0226244717
History -- Philosophy. Historicism.

D16.8.G413 1989
Gellner, Ernest.
Plough, sword, and book: the structure of human history/ Ernest Gellner. Chicago: University of Chicago Press, 1989, c1988. 288 p.
88-032452   901   0226287017
History -- Philosophy.

D16.8.G532 1990
Gilbert, Felix, 1905-
History: politics or culture?: reflections on Ranke and Burckhardt/ Felix Gilbert. Princeton, N.J.: Princeton University Press, c1990. x, 109 p.
90-037417   901   0691031630
Ranke, Leopold von, -- 1795-1886 -- Contributions in the philosophy of history. Burckhardt, Jacob, -- 1818-1897. -- Contributions in the philosophy of history. History -- Philosophy.

D16.8.G6985 1997
Graham, John T. 1928-
Theory of history in Ortega y Gasset: "The dawn of historical reason"/ John T. Graham. Columbia, Mo.: University of Missouri Press, c1997. xix, 384 p.
96-031839   901   0826210848
Ortega y Gasset, Jose, -- 1883-1955 -- Contributions in philosophy of history. History -- Philosophy.

D16.8.H462
Hegel, Georg Wilhelm Friedrich, 1770-1831.
Reason in history, a general introduction to the philosophy of history; translated, with an introd., by Robert S. Hartman. New York, Liberal Arts Press [1953] xlii, 95 p.
53-004476   901
History -- Philosophy.

D16.8.H6241742 2000
Historians on history: an anthology / edited and introduced by John Tosh. Harlow, Essex, England: Pearson Education, 2000. p. cm.
00-020360   901   0582357950
History -- Philosophy. Historiography.

D16.8.H626 1997b
Hobsbawm, E. J. 1917-
On history/ Eric Hobsbawm. New York: New Press: c1997. xi, 305 p.
   901   1565843932
History -- Philosophy. Historiography.

D16.8.H913 1996
Hyppolite, Jean.
Introduction to Hegel's philosophy of history/ Jean Hyppolite; translated by Bond Harris and Jacqueline Bouchard Spurlock; with a foreword by Arkady Plotnitsky. Gainesville: University Press of Florida, c1996. xix, 88 p.
96-032322   901   0813014581
Hegel, Georg Wilhelm Friedrich, -- 1770-1831 -- Contributions in philosophy of history. History -- Philosophy.

D16.8.K37 1998
Kelley, Donald R., 1931-
Faces of history: historical inquiry from Herodotus to Herder/ Donald R. Kelley. New Haven, Conn.: Yale University Press, 1998. p. cm.
98-010979   901   0300073089
History -- Philosophy. Historicism.

D16.8.M286 1973
Maritain, Jacques, 1882-1973.
On the philosophy of history. Edited by Joseph W. Evans. Clifton [N.J.] A. M. Kelley, 1973 [c1957] xi, 180 p.
73-128059   901   0678027609
History -- Philosophy.

D16.8.M294.F4 1971
Federn, Karl, 1868-1942.
The materialist conception of history; a critical analysis. Westport, Conn., Greenwood Press [1971] xiv, 262 p.
75-114523   901   0837147891
Marx, Karl, -- 1818-1883. History -- Philosophy.

D16.8.M4613 1972b
Meinecke, Friedrich, 1862-1954.
Historism; the rise of a new historical outlook. [Translated by J. E. Anderson. New York] Herder and Herder [1972] lxi, 524 p.
73-186993   907/.2
History -- Philosophy. Historiography -- History.

D16.8.O72 1961
Ortega y Gasset, Jose, 1883-1955.
History as a system, and other essays toward a philosophy of history. With an afterword by John William Miller New York, Norton [1961] 269 p.
61-005613   901
History -- Philosophy.

D16.8.O94 1994
Owensby, Jacob, 1957-
Dilthey and the narrative of history/ Jacob Owensby. Ithaca: Cornell University Press, 1994. x, 193 p.
94-015982   901   0801430119
Dilthey, Wilhelm, -- 1833-1911 -- Contributions in philosophy of history. History -- Philosophy.

D16.8.P57 1964
Popper, Karl Raimund, 1902-
The poverty of historicism, by Karl R. Popper. New York, Harper & Row [1964, c1961]. x, 166 p.
64-003717   901
History -- Philosophy.

D16.8.P737 1999
Price, David W. 1957-
History made, history imagined: contemporary literature, poiesis, and the past/ David W. Price. Urbana: University of Illinois Press, c1999. x, 338 p.
98-058031   901   0252024680
History -- Philosophy. History -- Methodology.

D16.8.R29 1981
Ranke, Leopold von, 1795-1886.
The secret of world history: selected writings on the art and science of history/ Leopold von Ranke; edited, with translations, by Roger Wines. New York: Fordham University Press, 1981. x, 276 p.
80-065600   901   0823210502
History -- Philosophy. Historiography.

D16.8.R6813 1984
Rossi, Paolo, 1923-
The dark abyss of time: the history of the earth & the history of nations from Hooke to Vico/ Paolo Rossi; translated by Lydia G. Cochrane. Chicago: University of Chicago Press, c1984. xvi, 338 p.
84-008481 901 0226728358
Vico, Giambattista, -- 1668-1744.   History -- Philosophy -- History. Science -- Philosophy -- History.

D16.8.R842
Rotenstreich, Nathan, 1914-
Between past and present; an essay on history. With a foreword by Martin Buber. New Haven, Yale University Press, 1958. 329 p.
58-005462 901
History -- Philosophy.

D16.8.R95
Russell, Bertrand, 1872-1970.
History as an art. Aldington, Kent, Hand and Flower Press [1954] 23 p.
55-021195 901
History -- Philosophy.

D16.8.S28 1888
Schlegel, Friedrich von, 1772-1829.
The philosophy of history, in a course of lectures, delivered at Vienna by Frederick von Schlegel. Tr. from the German, with a memoir of the author, by James Burton Robertson. London, G. Bell & sons, 1888. 2 p.
15-025145
History -- Philosophy.

D16.8.S46 1961
Seligman, Edwin Robert Anderson, 1861-1939.
The economic interpretation of history. New York, Columbia University Press 1965. ix, 166 p.
61-065021 901
Economics. History -- Philosophy.

D16.8.S688 2000
Southgate, Beverley C.
Why bother with history?: ancient, modern and postmodern motivations/ Beverley Southgate. -- Harlow: Longman, 2000. xi, 184 p.
901 0582423902
Histoire -- Philosophie.

D16.8.T76
Trompf, G. W.
The idea of historical recurrence in Western thought: from antiquity to the Reformation/ G. W. Trompf. Berkeley: University of California Press, c1979. x, 381 p.
77-076188 901 0520034791
History -- Philosophy.

D16.8.V46 1991
Versions of history from antiquity to the Enlightenment/ edited by Donald R. Kelley. New Haven: Yale University Press, c1991. xii, 515 p.
90-026606 901 0300047754
History -- Philosophy.

D16.8.W38 1960a
Wedgwood, C. V. 1910-
Truth and opinion; historical essays. New York, Macmillan, 1960. 254 p.
60-008943 907.2
History -- Philosophy. Great Britain -- History -- Early Stuarts, 1603-1649.

D16.8.W597
Wilkins, Burleigh Taylor.
Has history any meaning?: A critique of Popper's philosophy of history/ Burleigh Taylor Wilkins. Ithaca, N.Y.: Cornell University Press, 1978. 251 p.
78-058054 901 0801411874
Popper, Karl Raimund, -- Sir, -- 1902- History -- Philosophy.

D16.9 Philosophy of history — Special topics

D16.9.B4
Berlin, Isaiah.
Historical inevitability.   London, Oxford University Press [1955] 79 p.
55-014152 901
History -- Philosophy.

D16.9.B493 2000
Blaut, James M.
Eight Eurocentric historians/ J.M. Blaut. New York: Guilford Press, c2000. xii, 228 p.
00-039339 940/.072 1572305908
Historians -- Europe. Eurocentrism. Historians -- United States.

D16.9.C56 1978b
Cohen, G. A. 1941-
Karl Marx's theory of history: a defence/ by G. A. Cohen. Oxford: Clarendon Press; 1978. xv, 369 p.
78-040242 335.4/11 0198721964
Marx, Karl, -- 1818-1883. Historical materialism.

D16.9.C7613 1966
Croce, Benedetto, 1866-1952.
Historical materialism and the economics of Karl Marx. Translated by C.M. Meredith and with an introd. by A.D. Lindsay. New York, Russell & Russell, 1966. xxiii, 188 p.
66-015950 335.4/119
Historical materialism. Marxian economics.

D16.9.E57 1979
Engels, Friedrich, 1820-1895.
On historical materialism/ by Frederick Engels. New York: AMS Press, 1979. 30 p.
76-042699 335.4/11 0404153704
Historical materialism.

D16.9.G47
Giddens, Anthony.
A contemporary critique of historical materialism/ Anthony Giddens. Berkeley: University of California Press, c1981-1985 v. 1-2
81-043382 335.4/119 0520045351
Historical materialism.

D16.9.H39 1991
Hawthorn, Geoffrey.
Plausible worlds: possibility and understanding in history and the social sciences/ Geoffrey Hawthorn. Cambridge; Cambridge University Press, 1991. p. cm.
90-021801 901 0521403596
History -- Philosophy. History -- Methodology. Social sciences -- Philosophy.

D16.9.M26
Mandelbaum, Maurice, 1908-
The anatomy of historical knowledge/ Maurice Mandelbaum. Baltimore: Johns Hopkins University Press, c1977. viii, 230 p.
76-046945 901 0801819296
History -- Philosophy. Causation.

D16.9.M276 1993
Margolis, Joseph, 1924-
The flux of history and the flux of science/ Joseph Margolis. Berkeley: University of California Press, c1993. x, 238 p.
93-004134 907/.2 0520083199
Historicism. Historiography.

D16.9.N5
Niebuhr, Reinhold, 1892-1971.
Faith and history; a comparison of Christian and modern views of history. New York, C. Scribner's Sons [1949] viii, 257 p.
49-008484 901
History -- Philosophy. Apologetics -- 20th century. Christianity -- Philosophy.

D16.9.P2654 1999
Parker, Noel, 1945-
Revolutions and history: an essay in interpretation/ Noel Parker. Cambridge, UK: Polity Press; 1999. p. cm.
99-010927 303.6/4/09 0745611354
Revolutions -- History. History -- Philosophy.

D16.9.P755 1987
Post-structuralism and the question of history/ edited by Derek Attridge, Geoff Bennington, and Robert Young.   Cambridge [Cambridgeshire]; Cambridge University Press, 1987. viii, 292 p.
86-012972 901 0521327598
History -- Philosophy. Poststructuralism.

D17 World histories — Chronicles and works written before 1525

D17.O85
Otto I, Bishop of Freising, d. 1158 d. 1158.
The two cities. By Otto, Bishop of Freising; translated in full with introduction and notes by Charles Christopher Mierow, edited by Austin P. Evans and Charles Knapp. New York, Columbia university press, 1928. 523 p.
28-025768
World history -- Early works to 1800.

D17.T513 1982
Theophanes, d. ca. 818.
The chronicle of Theophanes: an English translation of anni mundi 6095-6305 (A.D. 602-813)/ with introduction and notes by Harry Turtledove.   Philadelphia: University of Pennsylvania Press, 1982. xxiv, 201 p.
82-004861 909/.1 0812278429
World history -- Early works to 1800.

D20 World histories — General works, 1801-

D20.P37 1931
Pirenne, Henri, 1862-1935.
La fin du moyen age ... par Henri Pirenne ... Augustin Renaudet ... Edouard Perroy ... Marcel Handelsman ... Louis Halphen ... Paris, F. Alcan, 1931. 2 v.
31-021558 940.17
Middle Ages -- History.

D20.P37 t.3, 1967
Piganiol, Andre, 1883-1968.
La Conquete romaine. Paris, Presses universitaires
de France, 1967. 656 p.
67-093437   937
*Rome -- History -- Republic, 510-30 B.C. Italy
-- History -- Ancient to 476 A.D.*

D20.P37 vol. 5, 2d set
Halphen, Louis, 1880-1950.
Les barbares, des grandes invasions aux conquetes
turques du XIe siecle, par Louis Halphen ... Paris,
F. Alcan, 1930. 2 p.
35-001839   940.1
*Migrations of nations. Middle Ages -- History
Rome -- History -- Germanic Invasions, 3rd-6th
centuries. Islamic Empire.*

D20.P513
Pirenne, Jacques, 1891-
The tides of history. Translated from the French by
Lavett Edwards. New York, Dutton, 1962- v.
62-007800   909
World history.

D20.R42 1998
Rietbergen, P. J. A. N.
Europe: a cultural history/ Peter Rietbergen.
London; Routledge, 1998. xxvii, 516 p.
98-022241   940   0415172292
Europe -- History. Europe -- Civilization.

D20.R65 1993
Roberts, J. M.
History of the world/ J.M. Roberts. New York:
Oxford University Press, 1993. xiii, 952 p.
93-014431   909.220   0195210433
World history.

D20.W717 1997
Williams, Glyndwr.
The great South Sea: English voyages and
encounters, 1570-1750/ Glyndwr Williams. New
Haven: Yale University Press, c1997. xv, 300 p.
97-018028   995   0300072449
*Oceania -- Discovery and exploration --
British. Pacific Coast (South America) --
Discovery and exploration -- British.*

D21 World histories — Compends. Textbooks. Outlines. Syllabi. Questions

D21.B745513 1976
Bossuet, Jacques Benigne, 1627-1704.
Discourse on universal history/ Jacques-Benigne
Bossuet; translated by Elborg Forster; edited and
with an introd. by Orest Ranum. Chicago:
University of Chicago Press, 1976. xlvi, 376 p.
75-009062   909   0226067084
World history -- Early works to 1800.

D21.B973
Burckhardt, Jacob, 1818-1897.
Judgements on history and historians. Translated
by Harry Zohn, with an introd. by H. R. Trevor-
Roper. London, Allen & Unwin [1958] 258 p.
58-006250
World history.

D21.E577 2000
Encyclopedia of world history/ [introduction by
Patrick K. O'Brien]. New York: Facts On File,
c2000. 524 p.
00-034721   903   0816042497
*World history -- Encyclopedias. History --
Outlines, syllabi, etc.*

D21.L27 1972
Langer, William L. 1896-1977.
An encyclopedia of world history; ancient,
medieval, and modern, chronologically arranged.
Compiled and edited by William L. Langer.
Boston, Houghton Mifflin, 1972. xxxix, 1569 p.
72-186219   902/.02   0395135923
History -- Outlines, syllabi, etc.

D21.3 World histories — General special

D21.3.M29 1995
McNeill, William Hardy, 1917-
Keeping together in time: dance and drill in human
history/ William H. McNeill. Cambridge, Mass.:
Harvard University Press, 1995. viii, 198 p.
95-008794   306.4/84   0674502299
*World history. Military history. Unit cohesion
(Military science)*

D21.3.M3
McNeill, William Hardy, 1917-
The shape of European history [by] William H.
McNeill. New York, Oxford University Press,
1974. vi, 181 p.
73-090359   940/.07/2   0195018060
Europe -- History. Europe -- Historiography.

D21.3.M55 2000
Minahan, James.
One Europe, many nations: a historical dictionary
of European national groups/ by James B.
Minahan. Westport, Conn.: Greenwood Press,
2000. xvii, 781 p.
99-046040   940/.03   0313309841
*Ethnology -- Europe -- Dictionaries. Europe --
History -- Dictionaries.*

D21.3.P55 1997
Pipes, Daniel, 1949-
Conspiracy: how the paranoid style flourishes and
where it comes from/ Daniel Pipes. New York:
Free Press, c1997. xiii, 258 p.
97-020949   909.8   0684831317
World politics. Conspiracies.

D21.3.W27 1996
Walt, Stephen M., 1955-
Revolution and war/ Stephen M. Walt. Ithaca, NY:
Cornell University Press, 1996. x, 365 p.
95-045006   303.6/4   0801432057
World politics. Revolutions -- History. War.

D21.3.W48 1997
Who's who in democracy/ Seymour Martin Lipset,
editor in chief. Washington, D.C.: Congressional
Quarterly, c1997. xxii, 247 p.
96-048342   920.02   1568021216
*Statesmen -- Biography. Heads of state --
Biography. Revolutionaries -- Biography.*

D21.5 World histories — Historical geography

D21.5.G4713 1996
Geremek, Bronislaw.
The common roots of Europe/ Bronislaw Geremek;
translated by Jan Aleksandrowicz ... [et al.].
Cambridge, MA: Polity Press, 1996. p. cm.
96-026695   940   0745611214
*Europe -- Historical geography. Europe --
Civilization.*

D21.5.P634
Pounds, Norman John Greville.
An historical geography of Europe, 1500-1840/ N.
J. G. Pounds. Cambridge [Eng.]; Cambridge
University Press, 1979. xvi, 438 p.
79-011528   940.2   0521223792
Europe -- Historical geography.

D25.A2 Military history — Dictionaries. Chronological tables, etc.

D25.A2.D38 1996
Davis, Paul K., 1952-
Encyclopedia of invasions and conquests from
ancient times to the present/ Paul K. Davis. Santa
Barbara, Calif.: ABC-CLIO, c1996. x, 443 p.
96-049452   355/.003   0874367824
History, Military -- Encyclopedias.

D25.A2.H2 1981
Harbottle, Thomas Benfield, d. 1904
Harbottle's Dictionary of battles. New York: Van
Nostrand Reinhold, 1981, c1979. 303 p.
80-053498   904.7   0442223366
Battles -- Dictionaries.

D25.A2.H64 1995
Hogg, Ian V., 1926-
Battles: a concise dictionary/ edited by Ian V.
Hogg. New York: Harcourt Brace, c1995. x, 210 p.
95-045950   904/.7   0151002126
*Battles -- Dictionaries. Military biography --
Dictionaries.*

D25.A2.K63 1999
Kohn, George C.
Dictionary of wars/ George Childs Kohn. New
York: Facts On File, c1999. viii, 614 p.
98-049684   355/.009   0816039283
Military history -- Dictionaries.

D25.A2.M34 2001
Magill's guide to military history/ editor, John
Powell; managing editor, Christina J. Moose;
project editor, Rowena Wildin. Pasadena, Calif.:
Salem Press, c2001. 5 v.
00-066072   355/.009   0893560146
*Military history -- Dictionaries. Generals --
Biography -- Dictionaries.*

D25.A2.M66 2000
Montagu, John Drogo.
Battles of the Greek and Roman worlds: a
chronological compendium of 667 battles to 31
B.C., from the historians of the ancient world/ John
Drogo Montagu. London: Greenhill Books; c2000.
256 p.
00-023945   938/.002/02   1853673897
*Military history, Ancient -- Chronology. Battles -
- Greece -- Chronology. Battles -- Rome --
Chronology.*

D25.A2.O94 2001
The Oxford companion to military history/ edited
by Richard Holmes; consultant editor, Hew
Strachan; Associate editors, Christopher Bellamy
and Hugh Bicheno. Oxford; Oxford University
Press, 2001. xvii, 1048 p.
01-273896   0198662092
Military history.

D25.D86-25.K43 Military history — General works

D25.D86 1993
Dupuy, R. Ernest 1887-1975.
The Harper encyclopedia of military history: from 3500 BC to the present/ R. Ernest Dupuy and Trevor N. Dupuy. New York, NY: HarperCollins, c1993. xxi, 1654 p.
92-017853   355/.009   0062700561
Military history -- Dictionaries. Military art and science -- History -- Dictionaries.

D25.F935
Fuller, J. F. C. 1878-1966.
A military history of the Western World.   New York, Funk & Wagnalls, 1954-56. 3 v.
54-009733   909
Military history.

D25.K43 1976
Keegan, John, 1934-
The face of battle/ John Keegan. New York: Viking Press, 1976. 354 p.
76-010611   355.4/8   0670304328
Battles. Military history.

D25.5 Military history — General special

D25.5.B3 1991
Baumgartner, Frederic J.
From spear to flintlock: a history of war in Europe and the Middle East to the French Revolution/ Frederic J. Baumgartner. New York: Praeger, 1991. xii, 353 p.
91-010421   355/.0094   0275939553
Europe -- History, Military. Middle East -- History, Military.

D25.5.C34 1992
Carlton, Eric.
Occupation: the policies and practices of military conquerors/ Eric Carlton. Savage, Md.: Barnes & Noble Books, 1992. viii, 198 p.
91-030623   355.4/9   0389209813
Military government -- History. Military occupation -- History. Colonies -- Administration.

D25.5.O34 2000
Official military historical offices and sources/ edited by Robin Higham. Westport, Conn.: Greenwood Press, 2000. 2 v.
99-049148   355/.009   0313286841
Military history. Military history -- Archival resources.

D25.9 Military history — Pamphlets, etc.

D25.9.D38 1998
Davis, Paul K., 1952-
Encyclopedia of warrior peoples and fighting groups/ Paul K. Davis and Allen Lee Hamilton. Santa Barbara, Calif.: ABC-CLIO, c1998. ix, 294 p.
98-036079   355/.003   0874369614
Military history.

D27 Naval history

D27.S37 1981
Sea power: a naval history/ editor, E.B. Potter; assistant editors, Roger Fredland, Henry H. Adams; authors, Henry H. Adams ... [et al.]. Annapolis, Md.: Naval Institute Press, c1981. vii, 419 p.
81-081668   359/.009   0870216074
Naval history. Sea-power.

D31 Political and diplomatic history — General works

D31.R37 1994
Rasler, Karen A., 1952-
The great powers and global struggle 1490-1990/ Karen A. Rasler & William R. Thompson. Lexington, Ky.: University Press of Kentucky, c1994. xx, 275 p.
94-031406   320.1/2   0813118891
World politics. World politics -- 1945- Geopolitics.

D32 Political and diplomatic history — General special

D32.A54 1997
Alexseev, Mikhail A., 1963-
Without warning: threat assessment, intelligence, and global struggle/ Mikhail A. Alexseev. New York: St. Martin's Press, 1997. xv, 348 p.
97-028936   327   0312175388
World politics. International relations.

D32.B5713 1989
Bitterli, Urs.
Cultures in conflict: encounters between European and non-European cultures, 1492-1800/ Urs Bitterli; translated by Ritchie Robertson. Stanford, Calif.: Stanford University Press, 1989. 215 p.
88-064050   940   0804717370
Culture conflict. Europe -- Relations -- Foreign countries. Europe -- Civilization -- Foreign influences.

D34 Political and diplomatic history — Relations between Europe and individual countries, A-Z

D34.R9
Poe, Marshall.
A people born to slavery: Russia in early modern European ethnography, 1476-1748/ Marshall T. Poe. Ithaca [N.Y.]: Cornell University Press, 2000. xi, 293 p.
00-010045   947   0801437989
Public opinion -- Europe.   Russia -- Foreign public opinion, European. Russia -- Relations -- Europe. Europe -- Relations -- Russia.

D56 Ancient history — Historiography. Methodology — General works

D56.H57 1990
History as text: the writing of ancient history/ edited by Averil Cameron. Chapel Hill: University of North Carolina Press, 1990, c1989. 208 p.
89-014675   930/.072   0807818895
History, Ancient -- Historiography.

D56.M37 1997
Marincola, John.
Authority and tradition in ancient historiography/ John Marincola. Cambridge; Cambridge Univesity Press, 1997. xvi, 361 p.
96-018630   930/.072   0521480191
History, Ancient -- Historiography.

D56.52 Ancient history — Historiography. Methodology — Biography of historians

D56.52.H45.E93 1991
Evans, J. A. S. 1931-
Herodotus, explorer of the past: three essays/ J.A.S. Evans. Princeton, N.J.: Princeton University Press, c1991. x, 166 p.
90-008734   938/.007202   0691068712
Herodotus. Herodotus. -- History. History, Ancient -- Historiography. Historiography -- Greece. Biography -- To 500.

D56.52.H45.R66 1998
Romm, James S.
Herodotus/ James Romm; foreword by John Herington. New Haven: Yale University Press, c1998. xv, 211 p.
98-010983   938/.0072/02   0300072295
Herodotus. Herodotus. -- History. History, Ancient -- Historiography. Historians -- Greece -- Biography.

D57 Ancient history — General works — 1525-

D57.C252
The Cambridge ancient history.   Cambridge [England]; Cambridge University Press, 1970-1998 v. 1; v. 2, p
75-085719   930
History, Ancient.

D57.D28 1996
Davies, Norman.
Europe: a history/ Norman Davies. Oxford; Oxford University Press, 1996. xvii, 1365 p.
96-042032   940   0195209125
Europe -- History.

D57.I88 1991
Early antiquity/ I.M. Diakonoff, volume editor; Philip L. Kohl, project editor; translated by Alexander Kirjanov. Chicago: University of Chicago Press, 1991. xxiii, 461 p.
90-024148   930   0226144658
History, Ancient.

D57.R8 1971
Rostovtzeff, Michael Ivanovitch, 1870-1952.
A history of the ancient world, by M. Rostovtzeff. Westport, Conn., Greenwood Press [1971] 2 v.
73-109834   930   0837144167
History, Ancient.

D58 Ancient history — Works by classical historians

D58.H46 1949
Herodotus.
Herodotus. Translated by J. Enoch Powell. Oxford, Clarendon Press, 1949. 2 v.
  49-049720 888.1
  History, Ancient. Greece -- History.

D58.H7
Harrison, Thomas, 1969-
Divinity and history: the religion of Herodotus/ Thomas Harrison. Oxford; Clarendon Press, 2000. xii, 320 p.
  99-039300 938/.007202
Herodotus. -- History. Herodotus -- Religion.

D58.P7 1967
Polybius.
The histories. Newly translated by Mortimer Chambers. New York, Twayne Publishers [1967, c1966] xliv, 340 p.
  68-000113 930
  History, Ancient.

D58.T46 2000
Thomas, Rosalind, 1959-
Herodotus in context: ethnography, science, and the art of persuasion/ Rosalind Thomas. Cambridge, U.K.; Cambridge University Press, 2000. viii, 321 p.
  99-045516 938/.007/202 0521662591
Herodotus. -- History. History, Ancient -- Historiography.

D59 Ancient history — Compends. Textbooks. Outlines. Syllabi. Questions

D59.G6 1979
Glover, T. R. 1869-1943.
The ancient world: a beginning/ by T. R. Glover. Westport, Conn.: Greenwood Press, 1979. 350 p.
  79-011456 930 031321459X
  History, Ancient.

D59.G6878
Grant, Michael, 1914-
Ancient history. New York, Harper & Row [1965, c1952] 247 p.
  52-002842
  History, Ancient.

D59.L373
Larousse encyclopedia of ancient and medieval history/ general editor: Marcel Dunan; English advisory editor: John Bowle; foreword by Arnold Toynbee. New York: Harper & Row, 1963. 413 p.
  63-012711 909
  Middle Ages -- History. History, Ancient.

D59.S75 1974
Starr, Chester G., 1914-
A history of the ancient world/ Chester G. Starr. New York: Oxford University Press, 1974. xvii, 742 p.
  74-079633 930 0195018141
  History, Ancient.

D65 Ancient history — Earliest history. Dawn of history — General works

D65.C5 1958
Childe, V. Gordon 1892-1957.
The dawn of European civilization. New York, Knopf, 1958 [c1957] xii, 367 p.
  58-005914 901
  Archaeology. Man, Prehistoric. Europe -- Civilization.

D70 Ancient history — Earliest history. Dawn of history — Celts. Celtic antiquities

D70.A8313 1992
Audouze, Francoise.
Towns, villages, and countryside of Celtic Europe: from the beginning of the second millennium to the end of the first century BC/ Francoise Audouze and Olivier Buchsenschutz; translated by Henry Cleere. Bloomington: Indiana University Press, c1992. 256 p.
  91-037593 936 0253310822
  Celts -- Europe. Excavations (Archaeology) -- Europe. Europe -- Antiquities, Celtic.

D70.C38 1995
The Celtic world/ edited by Miranda J. Green. London; Routledge, 1995. xxiii, 839 p.
  94-019311 940/.04916 0415057647
  Celts.

D70.C47
Chadwick, Nora K. 1891-1972.
The Celts [by] Nora Chadwick. With an introductory chapter by J. X. W. P. Corcoran. [Harmondsworth, Eng.] Penguin Books [1970] 301 p.
  70-025718 909.04/916
  Celts.

D70.R36 1987
Rankin, H. D.
Celts and the classical world/ H.D. Rankin. London: Croom Helm; 1987. 319 p.
  87-019141 306/.089916038 0918400066
  Celts. Celts -- Public opinion. Public opinion -- Greece.

D102 Medieval and modern history, 476- — General works

D102.M4 1980, vol. 4
Waugh, W. T. 1884-1932.
A history of Europe from 1378 to 1494/ by W. T. Waugh. Westport, Conn.: Greenwood Press, 1980. xiii, 545 p.
  80-023759 940.1 0837180910
  Civilization, Medieval. Europe -- History -- 476-1492.

D104 Medieval and modern history, 476- — General special

D104.H27 1968
Hay, Denys.
Europe: the emergence of an idea. Edinburgh, Edinburgh U.P., 1968. xxiv, 151 p.
  68-019886 911.4 0852240112
  Europe -- Name. Europe -- Historical geography.

D106 Medieval and modern history, 476- — Biography and memoirs — Collective

D106.K36 2000
Kamen, Henry Arthur Francis.
Who's who in Europe, 1450-1750/ Henry Kamen. London; Routledge, 2000. x, 321 p.
  00-267243 920.04 0415147271
  Europe -- History. Europe -- Biography.

D107 Medieval and modern history, 476- — Biography and memoirs — — Rulers, kings, etc.

D107.T36 1983
Tapsell, R. F., 1936-
Monarchs, rulers, dynasties, and kingdoms of the world/ compiled by R.F. Tapsell. New York: Facts on File Publications, 1983. 511 p.
  82-015726 920/.02 0871961210
  Kings and rulers -- Biography. Kings and rulers -- Genealogy. Royal houses -- History.

D107.6 Medieval and modern history, 476- — Biography and memoirs — Claimants to royalty. Pretenders

D107.6.C44 2000
Cheesman, Clive.
Rebels, pretenders & imposters/ Clive Cheesman and Jonathan Williams. New York: St. Martin's Press, 2000. 192 p.
  00-040437 364.16/3 0312238665
  Pretenders to the throne -- History. Impostors and imposture -- History. Insurgency -- History.

D108 Medieval and modern history, 476- — Biography and memoirs — Public men

D108.C44 1991
Chambers dictionary of political biography/ editor, John Ransley. Edinburgh: Chambers, 1991. 436 p.
  94-148795 920.02 0550172513
  Statesmen -- Biography -- Dictionaries. Political scientists -- Biography -- Dictionaries. Statesmen -- Quotations.

D108.C65 1991
The Columbia dictionary of political biography/
the Economist Books. New York: Columbia
University Press, c1991. 335 p.
90-024439 920.02 0231075863
Heads of state -- Biography -- Dictionaries.
Statesmen -- Biography -- Dictionaries.

D113 Medieval history — Sources and documents. Collections. Chronicles

D113.F77 1968
Froissart, Jean, 1338?-1410?
Chronicles. Translated and edited by John Jolliffe.
New York: Modern Library, [1968, c1967] xxiii,
448 p.
66-021508 944/.025
Hundred Years' War, 1339-1453. France --
History -- House of Valois, 1328-1589. Great
Britain -- History -- 14th century. Flanders --
History.

D113.5 Medieval history — Sources and documents. Collections. Chronicles — Minor collections

D113.5.C7 1943
Crump, Charles G. 1862-1935.
The legacy of the middle ages, edited by C.G.
Crump & E.F. Jacob. Oxford, The Clarendon Press
[1943] xii, 549 p.
44-007247 901
Middle Ages, 600-1500. Civilization, Medieval.
Art, Medieval.

D113.5.D6
Downs, Norton.
Basic documents in medieval history. Princeton,
N.J., Van Nostrand [1959] 189 p.
59-009758 940.1082
Middle Ages -- History -- Sources.

D114 Medieval history — Dictionaries

D114.D5 1982
Dictionary of the Middle Ages/ Joseph R. Strayer,
editor in chief. New York: Scribner, c1982-c1989.
13 v.
82-005904 909.07 0684190737
Middle Ages -- Dictionaries.

D116 Medieval history — Historiography — General works

D116.C35 1991
Cantor, Norman F.
Inventing the Middle Ages: the lives, works, and
ideas of the great medievalists of the twentieth
century/ Norman F. Cantor. New York: W.
Morrow, c1991. 477 p.
91-022748 940.1/072 0688094066
Middle Ages -- Historiography -- History -- 20th
century.

D116.M4
Medieval studies: an introduction/ edited by James
M. M. Powell. Syracuse, N.Y.: Syracuse University
Press, 1976. x, 389 p.
76-008870 940.1/07/2 0815621752.
Middle Ages -- Historiography.

D116.7 Medieval history — Historiography — Biography of historians

D116.7.I3.M3 1964
Mahdi, Muhsin.
Ibn Khaldun's philosophy of history: a study in the
philosophic foundation of the science of culture.
[Chicago] University of Chicago Press [1964]
325 p.
64-023414 901
Ibn Khaldun, -- 1332-1406.　　History --
Philosophy.

D117 Medieval history — General works — Early

D117.B7 1969
Brooke, Z. N. 1883-1946.
A history of Europe from 911 to 1198 [by] Z. N.
Brooke. London, Methuen, 1969. xx, 553 p.
76-402132 940.1 0416296408
Civilization, Medieval. Middle Ages. Europe --
History -- 476-1492.

D117.C32
The Cambridge medieval history.　　Cambridge
[Eng.] University Press, 1966- v. in
66-004537 909.07
Middle Ages -- History.

D117.N48 1995
The New Cambridge medieval history.　Cambridge
[England]; Cambridge University Press, 1995-1998
v. 2, 7 in
93-039643 940.1 052136292X
Middle Ages -- History.　　Europe -- History --
476-1492.

D117.T53 1960
Thompson, James Westfall, 1869-1941.
Economic and social history of Europe in the later
Middle Ages (1300-1530)　New York, F. Ungar
Pub. Co. [1960] 545 p.
60-009106 940.17
Middle Ages -- History.　　Europe -- Social
conditions. Europe -- Economic conditions.

D117.T6 1983
Tierney, Brian.
Western Europe in the Middle Ages, 300-1475:
formerly entitled a History of the Middle Ages,
284-1500/ Brian Tierney, Sidney Painter. New
York: Knopf, c1983. xiv, 633 p.
82-010034 940.1 0394330609
Middle Ages -- History.

D118 Medieval history — General works — Modern

D118.C3
Cantor, Norman F.
Medieval history; the life and death of a
civilization. New York, Macmillan [1963] 622 p.
63-003927 909
Middle Ages -- History.

D118.T49 1998
Thomson, J. K. J.
Decline in history: the european experience/ J.K.J.
Thomson. Malden, MA: Polity Press, 1998. p. cm.
98-039778 909/.0982201 0745614248
Middle Ages -- History. Regression (Civilization)
Progress. Europe -- History -- 476-1492. Europe --
History -- 1492-

D121 Medieval history — By period — General works

D121.G64 1989
Goffart, Walter A.
Rome's fall and after/ Walter Goffart. London;
Hambledon Press, 1989. 371 p.
88-034556 936 1852850019
Europe -- History -- 392-814. Rome -- History -
- Empire, 284-476.

D121.P52 1968
Pirenne, Henri, 1862-1935.
Mohammed and Charlemagne; [translated from the
French by Bernard Miall]. London, Allen &
Unwin, 1968. 293 p.
72-363566 940.1/1
Europe -- History -- 392-814. Islamic empire --
History.

D121.W3 1967
Wallace-Hadrill, J. M.
The barbarian West, 400-1000 [by] J.M. Wallace-
Hadrill. London, Hutchinson, 1967. 176 p.
67-074988 940.1
Middle Ages -- History. Migrations of nations

D125 Medieval history — Antiquities

D125.F4413 1992
Fehring, Gunter P.
The archaeology of medieval Germany: an
introduction/ Gunter P. Fehring; translated by Ross
Samson. London; Routledge, 1991. xix, 266 p.
91-011241 936.3 0415040620
Archaeology　　(Medieval)　　Excavations
(Archaeology)　　--　　Europe.　　Excavations
(Archaeology) -- Germany. Germany -- Antiquities.

D127 Medieval history — Social life and customs

D127.C6 1930
Coulton, G. G. 1858-1947.
Life in the middle ages/ selected, translated &
annotated by G. G. Coulton. New York: The
Macmillan Company; 1930. 4 v. in 1
31-009494 940.1
Middle Ages -- History -- Sources. Literature,
Medieval.

D128 Medieval history — Military and naval history

D128.B34 2001
Bachrach, Bernard S., 1939-
Early Carolingian warfare: prelude to empire/
Bernard S. Bachrach. Philadelphia: University of
Pennsylvania Press, c2001. xii, 430 p.
99-087239 355/.0094/0902 0812235339
Military art and science -- History -- Medieval,
500-1500. Europe -- History, Military.

D128.F68 2001
Fowler, Kenneth Alan.
Medieval mercenaries/ Kenneth Fowler. Oxford; Blackwell, 2001- p. cm.
00-009323   355.3/54/09409023   0631158863
Mercenary troops -- Europe -- History -- To 1500. Military history, Medieval. Military art and science -- Europe -- History -- Medieval, 500-1500.

D131 Medieval history — Political history and institutions — General works

D131.B513 1961
Bloch, Marc Leopold Benjamin, 1886-1944.
Feudal society/ Marc Bloch; translated by L.A. Manyon. Chicago: University of Chicago Press, 1961. 2 v.
61-004322   940.14   0226059782
Feudalism. Europe -- History -- 476-1492.

D135 Medieval history — Migrations — General works

D135.B8 1963
Bury, J. B. 1861-1927.
The invasion of Europe by the barbarians. New York, Russell & Russell, 1963. 296 p.
63-008359   937.09
Migrations of nations. Rome -- History -- Germanic Invasions, 3rd-6th centuries.

D135.M8813
Musset, Lucien.
The Germanic invasions: the making of Europe, AD 400-600/ Lucien Musset; translated by Edward and Columba James. University Park: Pennsylvania State University Press, c1975. xiii, 287 p.
75-014261   940.1/1   027101198X
Migrations of nations. Germanic peoples. Europe -- History -- 392-814.

D135.P33 2001
Pagden, Anthony.
Peoples and empires: a short history of European migration, exploration, and conquest, from Greece to the present/ Anthony Pagden. New York: Modern Library, 2001. xxv, 206 p.
00-066204   909   0679640967
Migrations of nations. Emigration and immigration -- History. Germanic peoples. Mediterranean Region -- Civilization. Rome -- History -- Germanic Invasions, 3rd-6th centuries.

D137 Medieval history — Migrations —Goths (General). Visigoths

D137.H425 1996
Heather, P. J.
The Goths/ Peter Heather. Oxford, OX, UK; Blackwell Publishers, 1996. xv, 358 p.
96-006725   909/.0439   0631165363
Goths -- History.

D137.W6213 1988
Wolfram, Herwig.
History of the Goths/ Herwig Wolfram; translated by Thomas J. Dunlap. Berkeley: University of California Press, c1988. xii, 613 p.
85-029044   940.1   0520052595
Goths.

D141 Medieval history — Migrations — Huns. Attila

D141.M33
Manchen-Helfen, Otto.
The world of the Huns; studies in their history and culture, by J. Otto Maenchen-Helfen. Edited by Max Knight. Berkeley, University of California Press, 1973. xxix, 602 p.
79-094985   910/.039/42   0520015967
Attila, -- d. 453.   Huns.

D141.T5 1948
Thompson, E. A.
A history of Attila and the Huns.   Oxford, Claredon Press, 1948. xii, 228 p.
48-009260
Attila, -- d. 453.   Huns.

D147 Medieval history — Migrations — Slavs

D147.D84
Dvornik, Francis, 1893-
The Slavs in European history and civilization. New Brunswick, N.J., Rutgers University Press [1962] xxviii, 688 p.
61-010259   947
Slavs -- History.

D148 Medieval history — Migrations — Normans

D148.C48
Chibnall, Marjorie.
The Normans/ Marjorie Chibnall. Malden, MA: Blackwell Publishers, 2001. p. cm.
00-033665   909/.04395   0631186719
Normans -- History.   Europe -- History -- 476-1492. Normandy (France) -- History -- To 1515.

D151 Medieval history — Crusades — Sources and documents

D151.S5
Chronicles of the Crusades/ Joinville & Villehardouin. Translated with an introduction by M.R.B. Shaw. Baltimore: Penguin Books, 1963. 362 p.
63-005725   940.18
Crusades.

D157 Medieval history — Crusades — General works

D157.B88
Brundage, James A.
The Crusades, a documentary survey.   Milwaukee, Marquette University Press, 1962. 318 p.
62-012897   940.18
Crusades.

D157.E713
Erdmann, Carl, 1898-1945.
The origin of the idea of crusade/ Carl Erdmann; translated from the German by Marshall W. Baldwin and Walter Goffart; foreword and additional notes by Marshall W. Baldwin. Princeton, N.J.: Princeton University Press, 1977. xxxvi, 446 p.
77-071980   909.07   0691052514
Crusades.

D157.R53 1987
Riley-Smith, Jonathan Simon Christopher, 1938-
The Crusades: a short history/ Jonathan Riley-Smith. New Haven [Conn.]: Yale University Press, 1987. xxx, 302 p.
87-050214   909.07   0300039050
Crusades.

D158 Medieval history — Crusades — Compends. Textbooks. Outlines. Syllabi. Questions

D158.P413 1963
Pernoud, Regine, 1909-
The Crusades/ edited by Regine Pernoud; translated by Enid McLeod. New York: Putnam, 1963, c1962. 295 p.
63-007751
Crusades.

D160 Medieval history — Crusades — Other

D160.F73 1999
France, John.
Western warfare in the age of the Crusades, 1000-1300/ John France. Ithaca, N.Y.: Cornell University Press, 1999. xv, 327 p.
98-048997   940.1/8   0801486076
Crusades. Military history, Medieval. Military art and science -- History.

D161.2 Medieval history — Crusades — First crusade, 1096-1099

D161.2.R485 1997
Riley-Smith, Jonathan Simon Christopher, 1938-
The first crusaders, 1095-1131/ Jonathan Riley-Smith. Cambridge, U.K.; Cambridge University Press, 1997. x, 300 p.
96-036669   940.1/8   0521590051
Crusades -- First, 1096-1099.

D162.2 Medieval history — Crusades — Second crusade, 1147-1149

D162.2.S43 1992
The Second Crusade and the Cistercians/ edited by Michael Gervers. New York: St. Martin's Press, 1992. xxi, 266 p.
91-026968   909.07   0312056079
Bernard, -- of Clairvaux, Saint, -- 1090 or 91-1153. Crusades -- Second, 1147-1149.

D163 Medieval history — Crusades — Third crusade, 1189-1193

D163.A3.A52
Ambroise, fl. ca. 1196 fl. ca. 1196.
The crusade of Richard Lion-Heart/ by Ambroise, translated from the Old French by Merton Jerome Hubert; with notes and documentation by John L. La Monte. New York: Columbia University Press, 1941. xi, 478 p.
42-001708
Crusades -- Third, 1189-1192.   Great Britain -- History -- Richard I, 1189-1199.

D164 Medieval history — Crusades — Fourth crusade, 1196-1198; 1204-1219

D164.A3.C55 1996
Clari, Robert de, 12th/13th cen
The conquest of Constantinople/ Robert of Clari; translated with introduction and notes by Edgar Holmes McNeal. Toronto; University of Toronto Press in association with c1996. 150 p.
97-114367   949.61/8013   0802078230
Crusades -- Fourth, 1202-1204.   Istanbul (Turkey) -- History -- Siege, 1203-1204.

D164.B37 2000
Bartlett, W. B.
An ungodly war: the sack of Constantinople & the fourth crusade/ W.B. Bartlett. Stroud: Sutton, 2000. xviii, 229 p.
                 0750923784
Crusades -- Fourth, 1202-1204.

D164.N57 1996
Nirenberg, David, 1964-
Communities of violence: persecution of minorities in the Middle Ages/ David Nirenberg. Princeton, N.J.: Princeton University Press, c1996. viii, 301 p.
95-033589   305.8/0094   0691033757
Minorities -- Europe -- Crimes against -- History. Persecution -- Europe. Civilization, Medieval. Europe -- Race relations. Europe -- Ethnic relations.

D181 Medieval history — Latin Kingdom of Jerusalem. Latin Orient. 1099-1291 — Biography, memoirs, journals

D181.G56.E33 1997
Edbury, P. W.
John of Ibelin and the Kingdom of Jerusalem/ Peter W. Edbury. Woodbridge, Suffolk, UK; Boydell Press, 1997. x, 222 p.
97-009898   956.94/4203/092   0851157033
Giovanni, -- di Ibelin, -- 13th cent. Giovanni, -- di Ibelin, -- 13th cent. -- Livre des assises. Statesmen -- Jerusalem -- Biography. Jerusalem -- History -- Latin Kingdom, 1199-1244.

D183 Medieval history — Latin Kingdom of Jerusalem. Latin Orient. 1099-1291 — General special

D183.P45 1996
Phillips, Jonathan
Defenders of the Holy Land: relations between the Latin East and the West, 1119-1187/ Jonathan Phillips. Oxford [England]: Clarendon Press; 1996. xiii, 314 p.
95-043444   909.07   0198205406
Crusades. Christians -- Latin Orient. Europe -- Foreign relations -- Latin Orient. Latin Orient -- Foreign relations -- Europe.

D184.4 Medieval history — Latin Kingdom of Jerusalem. Latin Orient. 1099-1291 — Individual rulers

D184.4.H36 2000
Hamilton, Bernard, 1932-
The leper king and his heirs: Baldwin IV and the Crusader Kingdom of Jerusalem/ Bernard Hamilton. Cambridge, UK; Cambridge University Press, 2000. xxv, 288 p.
99-038628   956.94/03/092   052164187X
Baudouin -- IV, -- King of Jerusalem, -- 1160-1185 Jerusalem -- Kings and rulers -- Biography. Jerusalem -- History -- Latin Kingdom, 1099-1244.

D198.2-199.3 Medieval history — Arab (Islamic) Empire

D198.2.R67 1968
Rosenthal, Franz, 1914-
A history of Muslim historiography. Leiden, E. J. Brill, 1968. xvi, 656 p.
68-113306
Historians -- Islamic countries. Islam -- Historiography. Middle East -- Historiography.

D199.3.I8.2
Coulson, Noel J.
A history of Islamic law, by N. J. Coulson. Edinburgh, University Press [1964] viii, 264 p.
64-014916   348.9709
Mohammedan law -- History.

D199.3.I8 no. 4
Watt, W. Montgomery
A history of Islamic Spain [by] W. Montgomery Watt, with additional sections on literature by Pierre Cachia. Edinburgh, Edinburgh U. P. [1965] xi, 210 p.
66-002646   946.02
Islam -- Spain. Muslims -- Spain. Spain -- History -- 711-1516.

D199.3.V62 1961
Von Grunebaum, Gustave E. 1909-1972.
Islam: essays in the nature and growth of a cultural tradition. London, Routledge & Paul [1961] 266 p.
61-066666
Civilization, Mohammedan.

D200 Medieval history — Later medieval. 11th-15th centuries — General works

D200.B27 1993
Bartlett, Robert, 1950-
The making of Europe: conquest, colonization, and cultural change, 950-1350/ Robert Bartlett. Princeton, N.J.: Princeton University Press, c1993. 432 p.
92-043925   940.1   069103298X
Social history -- Medieval, 500-1500. Conquerors -- Europe. Social change. Europe -- Colonization. Europe -- History -- 476-1492.

D201 Medieval history — Later medieval. 11th-15th centuries — 11th-12th centuries

D201.M66 2000
Moore, R. I. 1941-
The first European revolution, c. 970-1215/ R.I. Moore. Oxford [England]; Blackwell, c2000. xiii, 237 p.
00-031022   943/.02   0631184791
Civilization, Medieval.   Holy Roman Empire -- History -- 843-1273.

D202-203 Medieval history — Later medieval. 11th-15th centuries — 13th-15th centuries

D202.C76 1997
Crosby, Alfred W.
The measure of reality: quantification and Western society, 1250-1600/ Alfred W. Crosby. Cambridge [England]; Cambridge University Press, 1997. xii, 245 p.
96-003092   940   0521554276
Historiometry.   History   --   Methodology. Civilization, Medieval. Europe -- History -- 476-1492. Europe -- History -- 1492-1648.

D202.F4
Ferguson, Wallace Klippert, 1902-
Europe in transition, 1300-1520.   Boston, Houghton Mifflin [c1962] 625 p.
63-002312   940.17
Civilization, Medieval. Renaissance. Europe -- Civilization. Europe -- History -- 476-1492.

D202.H68 1992
Housley, Norman.
The later crusades, 1274-1580: from Lyons to Alcazar/ Norman Housley. New York: Oxford University Press, 1992. viii, 14, 528
91-022260   940.1   0198221371
Crusades.   Europe -- History -- 476-1492. Europe -- History -- 1492-1648.

D202.8.J67 1996
Jordan, William C., 1948-
The great famine: northern Europe in the early fourteenth century/ William Chester Jordan. Princeton, N.J.: Princeton University Press, 1996. 317 p.
95-026684   940.1/92   0691011346
Famines -- Europe -- History.   Europe -- Economic conditions -- To 1492. Europe -- Social conditions -- To 1492. Europe -- History -- 476-1492.

D203.H36 1994
Handbook of European history, 1400-1600: late Middle Ages, Renaissance, and Reformation/ edited by Thomas A. Brady, Jr., Heiko A. Oberman, James D. Tracy. Leiden; E.J. Brill, 1994- v. (1)
94-001290   940.2   9004097627
Reformation -- Europe. Renaissance. Middle Ages. Europe -- History -- 1492-1648. Europe -- History -- 15th century.

D203.J64 2000
Johnson, Paul, 1928-
The Renaissance: a short history/ Paul Johnson. New York: Modern Library, 2000. viii, 196 p.
00-035491   940.2/1   067964086X
Renaissance. Civilization, Medieval. Europe -- History -- 15th century. Europe -- History -- 1492-1648. Europe -- Intellectual life -- 16th century.

D208 Modern history, 1453— General works

D208.N4
The New Cambridge modern history. Cambridge [Eng.] University Press, 1957-79. 14 v.
57-014935   940.2
History, Modern.

D209 Modern history, 1453— Compends. Textbooks. Outlines

D209.P26 1984
Palmer, R. R. 1909-
A history of the modern world/ R.R. Palmer, Joel Colton. New York: Knopf, c1984. xvi, 1106 p.
83-047988   909.08   0394335961
History, Modern.

D209.W59 1994b
Williams, Neville, 1924-
Chronology of the modern world, 1763 to 1992. New York: Simon & Schuster, 1994. p. cm.
94-030477   909.08/02/02   0133266958
History, Modern -- 18th century -- Chronology. History, Modern -- 19th century -- Chronology. History, Modern -- 20th century -- Chronology.

D210 Modern history, 1453— General special. Addresses, essays, lectures

D210.G58 1991
Goldstone, Jack A.
Revolution and rebellion in the early modern world/ Jack A. Goldstone. Berkeley: University of California Press, c1991. xxix, 608 p.
89-049052   904/.7   0520067584
Revolutions -- History. History, Modern. State, The -- History.

D210.K46 1987
Kennedy, Paul M., 1945-
The rise and fall of the great powers: economic change and military conflict from 1500 to 2000/ by Paul Kennedy. New York, NY: Random House, c1987. xxv, 677 p.
87-009690   909.82   0394546741
History, Modern. Economic history. Military history, Modern.

D210.N32
Namier, Lewis Bernstein, 1888-1960.
Personalities and powers. London, H. Hamilton [1955] 157 p.
55-003092
History, Modern.

D210.T3
Taylor, A. J. P. 1906-
Englishmen and others. London, H. Hamilton [1956] 192 p.
57-002855
Europe -- History -- 1789-1900. Europe -- History -- 20th century.

D210.T6813 1995
Touraine, Alain.
Critique of modernity/ Alain Touraine; translated by David Macey. Cambridge, Mass.: Blackwell, 1995. p. cm.
94-021504   901
History, Modern -- Philosophy. Civilization, Modern -- Philosophy.

D210.T89 1984
Tuchman, Barbara Wertheim.
The march of folly: from Troy to Vietnam/ Barbara W. Tuchman. New York: Knopf: 1984. xiv, 447 p.
83-022206   909.08   0394527771
History, Modern. History -- Errors, inventions, etc. Power (Social sciences)

D210.Z33 1982
Zagorin, Perez.
Rebels and rulers, 1500-1660/ Perez Zagorin. Cambridge; Cambridge University Press, 1982. 2 v.
81-017039   940.2   0521244722
Revolutions -- Europe -- History -- 16th century. Revolutions -- Europe -- History -- 17th century. Europe -- History -- 1492-1648. Europe -- History -- 17th century.

D214 Modern history, 1453— Military history

D214.B56 1994
Black, Jeremy.
European warfare, 1660-1815/ Jeremy Black. New Haven; Yale University Press, 1994. x, 276 p.
94-060602   940.2   0300061706
Military history, Modern. War and society -- History. Europe -- History -- 1648-1789. Europe -- History -- 1789-1815. Europe -- History, Military -- 1648-1789.

D214.B58 1998
Black, Jeremy.
War and the world: military power and the fate of continents, 1450-2000/ Jeremy Black. New Haven, Conn.: Yale University Press, c1998. 334 p.
97-028169   355/.009   0300072023
Military history, Modern. War and society -- History. History, Modern. Europe -- History.

D214.B585 1998
Black, Jeremy.
Why wars happen/ Jeremy Black. New York: New York University Press, 1998. 271 p.
98-005805   904/.7   0814713335
Military history, Modern. War.

D214.B83 1997
Bucholz, Arden.
Delbruck's modern military history/ Hans Delbruck; edited and translated by Arden Bucholz. Lincoln: University of Nebraska Press, 1997. 244 p.
96-050000   355/.009/04   080321698X
Delbruck, Hans, -- 1848-1929. Military history, Modern.

D214.C55 1991
Clodfelter, Micheal, 1946-
Warfare and armed conflicts: a statistical reference to casualty and other figures, 1618-1991/ by Micheal Clodfelter. Jefferson, N.C.: McFarland, c1992. 2 v.
91-052632   904/.7   0899505449
Military history, Modern -- Encyclopedias. Military history, Modern -- Statistics.

D214.T35 1992
Tallett, Frank.
War and society in Early-Modern Europe: 1495-1715/ Frank Tallett. London; Routledge, 1992. xiii, 319 p.
91-043901   940.2   0415024765
Europe -- History, Military -- 1492-1648. Europe -- History -- 1492-1648. Europe -- History -- 1648-1715. Europe -- History, Military -- 1648-1789.

D214.T54 1993
Tilly, Charles.
European revolutions, 1492-1992/ Charles Tilly. Oxford, UK; Blackwell, 1993. xv, 262 p.
92-039019   940.2   0631173986
Revolutions -- Europe -- History. Europe -- History -- 1492-

D217 Modern history, 1453— Political and diplomatic history. European concert. Balance of power

D217.C46 2000
Chamberlain, Muriel Evelyn.
The Longman companion to the formation of the European empires, 1488-1920/ Muriel E. Chamberlain. Harlow: Longman, 2000. vii, 267 p.
01-267994   0582369800
History, Modern. Imperialism -- History. Europe -- Colonies -- History.

D217.K32 1990
Kaiser, David E., 1947-
Politics and war: European conflict from Philip II to Hitler/ David Kaiser. Cambridge, Mass.: Harvard University Press, 1990. 435 p.
90-004166   322/.5/094   0674688155
Europe -- Politics and government. Europe -- History, Military.

D217.L82 1991
Luard, Evan, 1926-
The balance of power: the system of international relations, 1648-1815/ Evan Luard. New York: St. Martin's Press, 1992. xv, 399 p.
91-009249   327.1/12   0312062087
Balance of power. World politics. International relations

D220-221 Modern history, 1453——1453-1648— Sources and documents

D220.M33 1993
Mackenney, Richard.
Sixteenth century Europe: expansion and conflict/ Richard Mackenney. New York: St. Martin's Press, 1993. xxxi, 393 p.
90-023292   940.2/3   031206036X
Sixteenth century. Europe -- History -- 1517-1648.

D221.V4.D3 1970
Davis, James C.
Pursuit of power; Venetian ambassadors' reports on Spain, Turkey, and France in the age of Philip II, 1560-1600. Edited and translated by James C. Davis. New York, Harper & Row [1970] xi, 283 p.
70-134281   940.2/32
Europe -- History -- 1517-1648 -- Sources.

D228 Modern history, 1453-
— 1453-1648
— General works

D228.C52
Clark, G. N. 1890-
Early modern Europe from about 1450 to about 1720. London, Oxford University Press, 1957. 261 p.
57-059170   940.2
Europe -- History -- 1492-1648. Europe -- History -- 1648-1715.

D228.G74 1964
Green, Vivian Hubert Howard.
Renaissance and Reformation; a survey of European history between 1450 and 1660, by V.H.H. Green. New York, St. Martin's Press, 1964. 462 p.
64-020945   940.21
Renaissance. Reformation. Europe -- History -- 1492-1648.

D228.H4 1964
Helm, P. J. 1916-
History of Europe, 1450-1660/ [by] P.J. Helm. New York: F. Ungar Pub. Co., 1964, c1961. 371 p.
64-025555   940.23
Renaissance. Reformation. Europe -- History -- 1492-1648.

D228.K6 1971
Koenigsberger, H. G.
The Habsburgs and Europe, 1516-1660, by H.G. Koenigsberger. Ithaca [N.Y.] Cornell University Press [1971] xv, 304 p.
73-145868   940.2/3   0801406242
Habsburg, House of. Europe -- History -- 1517-1648.

D228.O26 1974
O'Connell, Marvin Richard.
The Counter Reformation, 1559-1610, by Marvin R. O'Connell. New York, Harper & Row [1974] xv, 390 p.
73-014278   940/.08 s   0060132337
Counter-Reformation. Europe -- History -- 1517-1648.

D228.W54
Wilson, Charles, 1914-
The transformation of Europe, 1558-1648/ Charles Wilson. Berkeley: University of California Press, c1976. xi, 301 p.
75-017283   940.2/3   0520030753
Europe -- History -- 1517-1648.

D231 Modern history, 1453-
— 1453-1648
— General special

D231.C86 2000
Cunningham, Andrew,
The Four Horsemen of the Apocalypse: religion, war, famine, and death in Reformation Europe/ Andrew Cunningham and Ole Peter Grell. Cambridge, UK; Cambridge University Press, c2000. xiii, 360 p.
00-025314   940.2/2   0521461359
Four Horsemen of the Apocalypse. Apocalyptic literature -- History and criticism. Reformation -- Europe. Europe -- History -- 1517-1648

D231.I55 1997
Israel, Jonathan Irvine.
Conflicts of empires: Spain, the low countries and the struggle for world supremacy, 1585-1713/ Jonathan I. Israel. London; Hambledon Press, c1997. xxv. 420 p.
97-016021   940   1852851619
Europe -- History -- 1517-1648. Europe -- History -- 1648-1715. Europe -- Relations -- Spain.

D231.T42 1998
Te Brake, Wayne Ph.
Shaping history: ordinary people in European politics, 1500-1700/ Wayne te Brake. Berkeley: University of California Press, c1998. xiii, 221 p.
97-036930   940.2   0520211707
Europe -- Politics and government -- 1492-1648. Europe -- Politics and government -- 1648-1715.

D246 Modern history, 1453-
1601-1715. 17th century
— General works

D246.F74 1952
Friedrich, Carl J. 1901-
The age of the baroque, 1610-1660. New York, Harper [1952] xv, 367 p.
52-005435   940.22
Europe -- History -- 17th century.

D246.O4 1971
Ogg, David, 1887-1965.
Europe in the seventeenth century. London, A. and C. Black, 1971. viii, 576 p.
72-190787   940.2/52   0713612584
Europe -- History -- 17th century.

D246.W55 2001
Wills, John E. 1936-
1688: a global history/ John E. Wills. New York: Norton, c2001. xii, 330 p.
00-060077   909.6   039304744X
History, Modern -- 17th century.

D247 Modern history, 1453-
— 1601-1715. 17th century
— General special

D247.M23 1979
Maland, David.
Europe at war 1600-1650/ David Maland. Totowa, N.J.: Rowman and Littlefield, 1980. viii, 219 p.
79-018053   940.2/4   0847662136
Thirty Years' War, 1618-1648. Europe -- History -- 17th century. Netherlands -- History -- Wars of Independence, 1556-1648.

D247.M6813 1970
Mousnier, Roland.
Peasant uprisings in seventeenth-century France, Russia, and China. Translated from the French by Brian Pearce. New York, Harper & Row [1970] xx, 358 p.
72-095975   322/.42
Peasant uprisings -- History -- 17th century.

D258-271 Modern history, 1453-
— 1601-1715. 17th century
— Thirty Years' War, 1618-1648

D258.A83 1997
Asch, Ronald G.
The Thirty Years War: the Holy Roman Empire and Europe, 1618-48/ Ronald G. Asch. New York: St. Martin's Press, 1997. xiv, 247 p.
96-041029   940.2/4   0312165846
Thirty Years' War, 1618-1648. Europe -- History -- 17th century. Holy Roman Empire -- History -- Ferdinand II, 1619-1637.

D258.W4
Wedgwood, C. V. 1910-
The thirty years war/ by C. V. Wedgwood ... London: Cape, 1944. -- 544 p.
39-015988   940.24
Habsburg, House of. Thirty Years' War, 1618-1648. Germany -- History -- 1618-1648. Europe -- History -- 1517-1648.

D263.L63 1996
Lockhart, Paul Douglas, 1963-
Denmark in the Thirty Years' War, 1618-1648: King Christian IV and the decline of the Oldenburg State/ Paul Douglas Lockhart. Selinsgrove: Susquehanna University Press; c1996. 347 p.
95-035090   940.2/4   0945636768
Christian -- IV, -- King of Denmark and Norway, -- 1577-1648. Thirty Years' War, 1618-1648. Denmark -- History -- Christian IV, 1588-1648.

D271.R8.P67 1995
Porshnev, B. F. 1905-1972.
Muscovy and Sweden in the Thirty Years' War, 1630-1635/ B.F. Porshnev; edited by Paul Dukes; translated by Brian Pearce. Cambridge; Cambridge University Press, 1995. xxi, 256 p.
95-010293   940.2/4   0521451396
Thirty Years' War, 1618-1648. Russia -- History -- 1613-1689.

D273-282 Modern history, 1453-
— 1601-1715. 17th century
— 1648-1715

D273.B4
Beloff, Max, 1913-
The age of absolutism, 1660-1815. London, Hutchinson's University Library [1954] 191 p.
54-012579   940.22
Despotism. Europe -- History -- 1648-1789.

D273.5.H32 1953a
Hazard, Paul, 1878-1944.
The European mind, the critical years, 1680-1715. New Haven, Yale University Press, 1953. xx, 454 p.
53-012258   914
Seventeenth century. Eighteenth century. Philosophy, Modern -- History. Europe -- Intellectual life.

D273.5.M36 1983
McKay, Derek.
The rise of the great powers, 1648-1815/ Derek McKay and H.M. Scott. London; Longman, 1983. xi, 378 p.
82-000159   940   0582485541
Great powers -- History -- 17th century. Great powers -- History -- 18th century. Great powers -- History -- 19th century. Europe -- History -- 1648-1789. Europe -- History -- 1789-1815.

D274.J3.A3
James II, King of England, 1633-1701 1633-1701.
The memoirs of James II: his campaigns as Duke of York, 1652-1660. Translated by A. Lytton Sells from the Bouillon manuscript. Edited and collated with the Clarke edition. With an introd. by Sir Arthur Bryant. Bloomington, Indiana University Press, 1962. 301 p.
62-008916 940.25
James -- II, -- King of England, -- 1633-1701. Europe -- History -- 1648-1715 -- Sources.

D274.M37.S88 1994
Stoye, John, 1917-
Marsigli's Europe, 1680-1730: the life and times of Luigi Ferdinando Marsigli, soldier and virtuoso/ John Stoye. New Haven: Yale University Press, 1994. xii, 356 p.
93-024053 940.2/52 0300055420
Marsili, Luigi Ferdinando, -- 1658-1730. Generals -- Europe -- Biography. Scientists -- Europe -- Biography. Europe -- History -- 1648-1789. Bologna (Italy) -- Intellectual life.

D277.5.S66 1988
Sonnino, Paul.
Louis XIV and the origins of the Dutch War/ Paul Sonnino. Cambridge [England]; Cambridge University Press, 1988. xii, 226 p.
88-001889 940.2/52 0521345901
Louis -- XIV, -- King of France, -- 1638-1715. Dutch War, 1672-1678 -- Causes.

D279.5.C48 1991
Childs, John Charles Roger.
The Nine Years' War and the British Army, 1688-1697: the operations in the Low Countries/ John Childs. Manchester, England; Manchester University Press; c1991. vii, 372 p.
91-016633 940.2/525 0719034612
Grand Alliance, War of the, 1689-1697 -- Campaigns -- Benelux countries. Benelux countries -- History, Military.

D281.5.K36 1969
Kamen, Henry Arthur Francis.
The War of Succession in Spain, 1700-15 [by] Henry Kamen. Bloomington, Indiana University Press [1969] xii, 436 p.
75-085088 940.25/26 0253190258
Spanish Succession, War of, 1701-1714. Spain -- History -- Philip V, 1700-1746.

D282.T74 1995
The treaties of the War of the Spanish Succession: an historical and critical dictionary/ edited by Linda Frey and Marsha Frey. Westport, Conn.: Greenwood Press, 1995. xxvi, 576 p.
95-003804 940.2/526 0313278849
Spanish Succession, War of, 1701-1714 -- Treaties -- Dictionaries.

D285.1-285.8 Modern history, 1453-
— 1715-1789. 18th century
— Biography and memoirs

D285.1.D6
Dobree, Bonamy, 1891-
Three eighteenth century figures: Sarah Churchill, John Wesley [and] Giacomo Casanova. London, Oxford University Press, 1962. 248 p.
62-001635 920.02
Marlborough, Sarah Jennings, -- Duchess of, -- 1660-1744. Wesley, John, -- 1703-1791. Casanova, Giacomo, -- 1725-1798.

D285.8.C32 1959
Casanova, Giacomo, 1725-1798.
The memoirs of Jacques Casanova de Seingalt; the first complete and unabridged English translation by Arthur Machen. Illustrated with old engravings. New York, Putnam [1959-61] 6 v.
59-016015 920
Casanova, Giacomo, 1725-1798. Europe -- History -- 18th century -- Biography. Adventure and adventurers -- Biography. Courts and courtiers -- Biography.

D285.8.C4.C448 1988
Childs, J. Rives 1893-1987.
Casanova, a new perspective/ J. Rives Childs. New York: Paragon House Publishers, c1988. xvii, 346 p.
87-008915 940.2/53/0924 0913729698
Casanova, Giacomo, -- 1725-1798. Europe -- Biography.

D286 Modern history, 1453-
— 1715-1789. 18th century
— General works

D286.A5
Anderson, M. S.
Europe in the eighteenth century, 1713-1783. New York, Holt, Rinehart and Winston [1961] 364 p.
61-012769 940.25
Europe -- History -- 18th century.

D286.M33
Manuel, Frank Edward.
The age of reason. Ithaca, Cornell University Press [1951] ix, 146 p.
51-003056 940.22
Eighteenth century. Enlightenment. Europe -- History -- 18th century.

D286.R63
Roberts, J. M. 1928-
Revolution and improvement: the Western World, 1775-1847/ John Roberts. Berkeley: University of California Press, c1976. xii, 290 p.
75-017288 909.7 0520030761
History, Modern -- 18th century. History, Modern -- 19th century. Revolutions -- History.

D289 Modern history, 1453-
— 1715-1789. 18th century—
1740-1789

D289.V4613 1991
Venturi, Franco.
The end of the Old Regime in Europe, 1776-1789/ Franco Venturi; translated by R. Burr Litchfield. Princeton, N.J.: Princeton University Press, c1991. 2 v.
90-008050 940.2/53 0691031568
Europe -- History -- 1648-1789.

D292 Modern history, 1453-
— 1715-1789. 18th century
— War of Austrian Succession,
1740-1748

D292.B76 1993
Browning, Reed.
The War of the Austrian Succession/ by Reed Browning. New York: St. Martin's Press, 1993. xv, 445 p.
93-012439 940.2/532 0312094833
Austrian Succession, War of, 1740-1748.

D295 Modern history, 1453-
— 1715-1789. 18th century —
1750-1789

D295.E55 1990
Enlightened absolutism: reform and reformers in later eighteenth-century Europe/ edited by H.M. Scott. Ann Arbor: University of Michigan Press, 1990. ix, 385 p.
89-020231 940.2/53 0472101730
Despotism -- Europe -- History -- 18th century. Enlightenment. Europe -- Politics and government -- 1648-1789.

D295.P3
Palmer, R. R. 1909-
The age of the democratic revolution: a political history of Europe and America, 1760-1800/ by R.R. Palmer. Princeton, N.J.: Princeton University Press, 1959-64. 2 v.
59-010068 940.25 0691005699
Constitutional history. Europe -- Politics and government -- 18th century.

D295.T73 1994
Schroeder, Paul W.
The transformation of European politics, 1763-1848/ by Paul W. Schroeder. Oxford: Clarendon Press: 1994 xxii, 894 p.
93-026439 940 0198221193
Europe -- Politics and government -- 1648-1789. Europe -- Politics and government -- 1789-1815. Europe -- Politics and government -- 1815-1848.

D299 Modern history, 1453-
— 1789-
— General works

D299.B484 1982
Best, Geoffrey Francis Andrew.
War and society in revolutionary Europe, 1770-1870/ Geoffrey Best. New York: St. Martin's Press, 1982. 336 p.
82-003261 940.2/8 0312855516
Social classes -- Europe -- History -- 18th century. Social classes -- Europe -- History -- 19th century. Europe -- History -- 1789-1900. Europe -- History, Military -- 18th century. France -- History -- 1789-1900.

D299.H6 1969
Hobsbawm, E. J. 1917-
The age of revolution: Europe 1789-1848 [by] E. J. Hobsbawm. New York, Praeger Publishers [1969, c1962] xvi, 356 p.
75-099597 914/.03/28
Industrial revolution. Europe -- History -- 1789-1900.

D299.T49 1984
Tholfsen, Trygve R.
Ideology and revolution in modern Europe: an essay on the role of ideas in history/ Trygve R. Tholfsen. New York: Columbia University Press, 1984. xv, 287 p.
84-003178 940/.01 0231058861
Revolutions -- Europe -- Philosophy. Ideology -- Political aspects -- Europe. Europe -- History -- 1789-1900 -- Philosophy. Europe -- History -- 20th century -- Philosophy. Europe -- Intellectual life.

D308 Modern history, 1453-
— 1789-
— 1789-1815.
Period of the French Revolution

D308.F65 1970
Ford, Franklin L. 1920-
Europe, 1780-1830 [by] Franklin L. Ford. New York, Holt, Rinehart and Winston [c1970] xvii, 423 p.
76-110097 914/.03/27 0030861470
Europe -- History -- 1789-1815. Europe -- History -- 1815-1848.

D308.W66 1991
Woolf, S. J.
Napoleon's integration of Europe/ Stuart Woolf. London; Routledge, 1991. ix, 319 p.
90-024135 940.2/7 041504961X
Napoleon -- I, -- Emperor of the French, -- 1769-1821 -- Influence. Europe -- History -- 1789-1815. Europe -- Relations -- France. France -- Relations -- Europe.

D351-397 Modern history, 1453-
— 1789-
— 19th century. 1801-1914/1920

D351.P86 1969
Postgate, Raymond William, 1896-
Revolution from 1789 to 1906; documents selected and edited with notes and introductions by Raymond Postgate. Gloucester, Mass., P. Smith, 1969. xvi, 398 p.
70-010678 940.2/7
Revolutions -- Europe -- History -- Sources. Europe -- History -- 1789-1900 -- Sources.

D358.G55 1987
Gildea, Robert.
Barricades and borders: Europe 1800-1914/ Robert Gildea. Oxford [Oxfordshire]; Oxford University Press, 1987. xvi, 498 p.
86-028577 940.2 0198730284
Europe -- History -- 1789-1900. Europe -- History -- 1871-1918.

D358.H56 1975b
Hobsbawm, E. J. 1917-
The age of capital, 1848-1875/ E. J. Hobsbawm. New York: Scribner, c1975. xv, 354 p.
75-029583 940.2/8 0684144506
History, Modern -- 19th century. Economic history -- 1750-1918.

D358.R8 1934a
Russell, Bertrand, 1872-1970.
Freedom and organization, 1814-1914, by Bertrand Russell. London, G. Allen & Unwin ltd. [1934] viii, 528 p.
34-041076 909.81
Europe -- Politics -- 1789-1900. Political science -- History. Liberty. United States -- Politics and government -- 19th century.

D359.C37 1980
Carr, Edward Hallett, 1892-
From Napoleon to Stalin, and other essays/ by E.H. Carr. New York: St. Martin's Press, c1980. ix, 277 p.
80-018439 940 0312307748
Intellectuals. Socialism. Europe -- History -- 1789-1900. Europe -- History -- 20th century. Soviet Union -- History -- 20th century.

D359.C73
Croce, Benedetto, 1866-1952.
History of Europe in the nineteenth century. Translated from the Italian by Henry Furst. London, Allen & Unwin [1953] 375 p.
63-022991 940.28
Europe -- History -- 1780-1900.

D359.R48 1977
Rich, Norman.
The age of nationalism and reform, 1850-1890/ Norman Rich; [cartography by Harold K. Faye, picture research by Liesel Bennett]. New York: Norton, c1977. xv, 270 p.
76-021080 940.2/8 0393056074.
Europe -- History -- 1848-1871. Europe -- History -- 1871-1918.

D359.T3
Taylor, A. J. P. 1906-
From Napoleon to Stalin, comments on European history. London, Hamilton [1950] 224 p.
51-000446 940.27
Europe -- History -- 20th century. Europe -- History -- 1789-1900.

D359.T33
Taylor, A. J. P. 1906-
The struggle for mastery in Europe, 1848-1918. Oxford, Clarendon Press, 1954. xxxvi, 638 p.
54-013436
Europe -- History -- 1848-1871. Europe -- History -- 1871-1918.

D359.7.G73 1996
Gran, Peter, 1941-
Beyond Eurocentrism: a new view of modern world history/ Peter Gran. Syracuse, N.Y.: Syracuse University Press, 1996. xiii, 440 p.
95-035939 909.08 0815626924
History, Modern -- 19th century. History, Modern -- 20th century.

D359.7.H63 1987
Hobsbawm, E. J. 1917-
The age of empire, 1875-1914/ E.J. Hobsbawm. New York: Pantheon Books, c1987. 404 p.
87-043055 909.81 0394563190
History, Modern -- 19th century.

D360.A5
Anderson, Eugene Newton.
Europe in the nineteenth century; a documentary analysis of change and conflict, by Eugene N. Anderson, Stanley J. Pincetl, Jr., [and] Donald J. Ziegler. Indianapolis, Bobbs-Merrill, 1961] 2 v.
61-013154 940.2082
Europe -- History -- 1815-1871. Europe -- History -- 1871-1918. Europe -- Social conditions.

D361.P64 2000
Porch, Douglas.
Wars of empire/ Douglas Porch. London: Cassell, 2000. 224 p.
01-326036 355.0209034 0304352713
Military history, Modern -- 19th century. Military art and science -- History -- 19th century.

D363.A58
Albrecht-Carrie, Rene, 1904-
A diplomatic history of Europe since the Congress of Vienna. New York, Harper [1958] 736 p.
58-006131 940.28
Europe -- History -- 1789-1900. Europe -- History -- 20th century.

D363.I46 2001
Ikenberry, G. John.
After victory: institutions, strategic restraint, and the rebuilding of order after major wars/ G. John Ikenberry. Princeton: Princeton University Press, c2001. xiii, 293 p.
00-034681 327.1 0691050910
World politics. Military history, Modern -- 19th century. Military history, Modern -- 20th century.

D363.M29 1988
Mandelbaum, Michael.
The fate of nations: the search for national security in the nineteenth and twentieth centuries/ Michael Mandelbaum. Cambridge; Cambridge University Press, 1988. xi, 416 p.
87-033838 327.1/1 0521355273
World politics -- 19th century. World politics -- 20th century. National security.

D363.M37 1974b
Marx, Karl, 1818-1883.
Political writings. Edited and with an introd. by David Fernbach. New York, Random House, 1974- v. 3
73-020559 320.9/4/028 0394489381
World politics -- 19th century. Socialism. Europe -- History -- 1848-1849.

D363.V273 1951
Valery, Paul, 1871-1945.
Reflections on the world today; translation by Francis Scarfe. London, Thames and Hudson [1951] 199 p.
52-001850
World politics.

D371.D35 1998
Dalby, Andrew, 1947-
Dictionary of languages: the definitive reference to more than 400 languages/ Andrew Dalby. New York: Columbia University Press, 1998. xvi, 734 p.
98-087178 403 0231115687
Language and languages -- Dictionaries.

D376.G7.S4 1972
Seton-Watson, R. W. 1879-1951.
Disraeli, Gladstone, and the Eastern question; a study in diplomacy and party politics, by R. W. Seton-Watson. New York, Norton [1972] xiii, 590 p.
72-200972 327.42 0393005941
Eastern question. Great Britain -- Foreign relations -- 1837-1901. Great Britain -- Politics and government -- 1837-1901. Europe -- Politics and government -- 1871-1918.

D376.U6.K4
Kertesz, Stephen Denis, 1904-
The fate of East Central Europe: hopes and failures of American foreign policy. [Notre Dame, Ind.]: University of Notre Dame Press, 1956. 463 p.
56-009731 943
Europe, Eastern -- Politics and government. United States -- Foreign relations -- Europe, Eastern.

D377.5.S65.P47 1985
Petrovich, Michael Boro.
The emergence of Russian Panslavism, 1856-1870/ by Michael Boro Petrovich. Westport, Conn.: Greenwood Press, 1985. xiv, 312 p.
84-025242 320.5/4 0313247420
Panslavism. Soviet Union -- Intellectual life -- 1801-1917.

D383.D7
Droz, Jacques, 1909-
Europe between revolutions, 1815-1848.
Translated by Robert Baldick. New York, Harper
& Row [1967] 286 p.
67-022496   914/.03/282
Europe -- History -- 1815-1848.

D383.K5 1957a
Kissinger, Henry, 1923-
A world restored; Metternich, Castlereagh and the
problems of peace, 1812-22. Boston, Houghton
Mifflin, 1957. 354 p.
57-010969   940.27
Metternich, Clemens Wenzel Lothar, -- Furst von, -
- 1773-1859. Castlereagh, Robert Stewart, --
Viscount, -- 1769-1822.   Europe -- Politics and
government -- 1815-1848.

D383.T4 1966a
Temperley, Harold William Vazeille.
The foreign policy of Canning, 1822-1827,
England, the Neo-Holy Alliance, and the New
World. Hamden, CT, Archon Books, 1966 636 p.
66-004116   327.42
   Great Britain -- Foreign relations -- 1820-
1830. Europe -- History -- 1815-1848.

D385.B58 1993
Blum, Jerome, 1913-
In the beginning: the advent of the modern age,
Europe in the 1840's/ Jerome Blum. New York: C.
Scribner's Sons; c1994. xx, 405 p.
93-001572   940.2/83   0684195674
Europe -- History -- 1815-1848.

D385.L36 1969
Langer, William L. 1896-1977.
Political and social upheaval, 1832-1852, by
William L. Langer. New York, Harper & Row
[1969] xviii, 674 p.
69-017284   940.2/83
   Europe -- Politics and government -- 1815-
1848. Europe -- Social conditions -- 1789-1900.
Europe -- Economic conditions -- 19th century.

D387.E8713 2001
Europe in 1848: revolution and reform/ edited by
Dieter Dowe ... [et al.]; translated by David
Higgins. New York: Berghahn Books, 2001. xiv,
994 p.
00-027750   940.2/85   1571811648
Revolutions -- Europe -- History -- 20th century.
Europe -- History -- 1848-1849.

D387.H413
Herzen, Aleksandr, 1812-1870.
From the other shore, and The Russian people and
socialism, an open letter to Jules Michelet. Introd.
by Isaiah Berlin. New York, G. Braziller, 1956.
208 p.
56-041455   940.28
Europe -- History -- 1848-1849.

D387.N3 1964
Namier, Lewis Bernstein, 1888-1960.
1848: the revolution of the intellectuals/ by Lewis
Namier. Garden City, N.Y.: Anchor Books, 1964.
153 p.
64-003105
Europe -- History -- 1848-1849.

D387.S7 1974
Stearns, Peter N.
1848: the revolutionary tide in Europe [by] Peter
N. Stearns. New York, Norton [1974] 278 p.
73-016474   940.2/84   0393055108
Europe -- History -- 1848-1849.

D387.T3 1970
Taylor, A. J. P. 1906-
The Italian problem in European diplomacy, 1847-
1849, by A. J. P. Taylor. [Manchester, Eng.]
Manchester University Press; [1970] viii, 252 p.
73-021516   327.4/045   0719003997
   Italian question, 1848-1870. Europe -- Politics
and government -- 1848-1871. Italy -- History --
Revolution of 1848. Italy -- Foreign relations --
1849-1870.

D388.A55
Albrecht-Carrie, Rene, 1904-
The Concert of Europe. New York, Walker [1968]
384 p.
68-013327   341.184
   Concert of Europe.

D395.F55 1990
Fin de siecle and its legacy/ edited by Mikulas
Teich and Roy Porter. Cambridge; Cambridge
University Press, 1990. xii, 345 p.
89-022347   909.8   0521341086
   History, Modern -- 19th century. History,
Modern -- 20th century.

D395.F67 1988
Ford, Ford Madox, 1873-1939.
A history of our own times/ Ford Madox Ford;
edited by Solon Beinfeld and Sondra J. Stang.
Bloomington: Indiana Unversity Press, c1988. xxv,
262 p.
87-045441   909.81   0253328187
   History, Modern -- 19th century.

D395.H24 1971
Hale, Oron J.
The great illusion, 1900-1914, by Oron J. Hale.
New York, Harper & Row [c1971] xv, 361 p.
76-123933   914/.03/288
   Europe -- History -- 1871-1918.

D395.S77 1984
Stone, Norman, 1941-
Europe transformed, 1878-1919/ Norman Stone.
Cambridge, Mass.: Harvard University Press, 1984,
c1983. 447 p.
83-022830   940.2/8   0674269225
   Europe -- History -- 1871-1918.

D396.B63 1983
Bond, Brian.
War and society in Europe, 1870-1970/ Brian
Bond. New York: St. Martin's Press, 1983. 256 p.
83-040281   940.2/8   0312855478
   Europe -- History, Military -- 19th century.
Europe -- History, Military -- 20th century. Europe
-- Social conditions -- 1789-1900.

D397.G58 1969
Gooch, G. P. 1873-1968.
Studies in diplomacy and statecraft.   New York,
Russell & Russell [1969] vii, 373 p.
77-075464   327.2
   Europe -- History -- 1871-1918.

D397.L282 1951
Langer, William L. 1896-1977.
The diplomacy of imperialism, 1890-1902.   New
York, Knopf, 1951 [c1950] xxii, 797 p.
51-000343
   Colonies. Imperialism. World politics.

D397.M28
Mansergh, Nicholas.
The coming of the First World War; a study in the
European balance, 1878-1914.   London,
Longmans, Green [1949] xiv, 257 p.
49-011284   940.28
   Balance of power.   Europe -- Politics and
government -- 1871-1918.

D412-497 Modern history, 1453-
— 1789-
— 20th century

D412.W67 2000
World leaders of the twentieth century/ edited by
the editors of Salem Press. Pasadena, Calif.: The
Press, c2000. 2 v.
99-017017   920/.009/04   0893563374
   Heads of state -- Biography. Statesmen --
Biography. Biography -- 20th century.

D412.6.A2 1961
Acheson, Dean, 1893-1971.
Sketches from life of men I have known/ Dean
Acheson. New York: Harper, c1961. xiv, 206 p.
61-009701   923.2
   Statesmen.

D412.7.L66 1973b
Longford, Frank Pakenham, 1905-
The history makers; leaders and statesmen of the
20th century. Edited by Lord Longford & Sir John
Wheeler-Bennet.   Chronologies and editorial
assistance by Christine Nicholls. New York, St.
Martin's Press [1973] 448 p.
73-079066   920/.02
   Heads of state -- Biography. Statesmen --
Biography.

D413.E36.A3
Einstein, Lewis, 1877-1967.
A diplomat looks back. Edited by Lawrence E.
Gelfand, with a foreword by George F. Kennan.
New Haven, Yale University Press, 1968. xxxiv,
269 p.
67-024497   327.73
   Diplomats -- United States -- Biography. United
States -- Foreign relations -- 20th century.

D413.M56.A3313 1978b
Monnet, Jean, 1888-
Memoirs/ Jean Monnet; introd. by George W. Ball;
translated from the French by Richard Mayne.
Garden City, N.Y.: Doubleday, 1978. 544 p.
76-056322   940.5/092/4   0385125054
   Monnet, Jean, -- 1888- Statesmen -- Europe --
Biography. Economists -- Europe -- Biography.

D413.M56.D73 1994
Duchene, Francois.
Jean Monnet: the first statesman of
interdependence/ Francois Duchene. New York:
Norton, 1994. 478 p.
93-034404   940.5/092   0393034976
   Monnet, Jean, -- 1888- Statesmen -- Europe --
Biography. European federation.   France --
Politics and government -- 20th century.

D413.5.B83 2000
Buck-Morss, Susan.
Dreamworld and catastrophe: the passing of mass
utopia in East and West/ Susan Buck-Morss.
Cambridge, Mass.: MIT Press, c2000. xvi, 368 p.
99-045165   909.82   0262024640
   History, Modern -- 20th century --
Historiography. History, Modern -- 20th century --
Philosophy. Popular culture -- History -- 20th
century.

D415.B4
Beloff, Max, 1913-
The great powers; London, Allen & Unwin [1959]
240 p.
62-053403
World politics.

D415.S75 1962
Strachey, John, 1901-1963.
The strangled cry, and other unparliamentary
papers. New York, W. Sloane Associates [1962]
256 p.
62-016885
History, Modern -- 20th century.

D419.C58 1997
Cook, Chris, 1945-
What happened where: a guide to places and events
in twentieth-century history/ Chris Cook and
Diccon Bewes. New York: St. Martin's Press,
1997. x, 310 p.
96-045597   909.82/03   0312172788
*History, Modern -- 20th century -- Dictionaries.
Historic sites -- Dictionaries.*

D419.L36 1974
Laqueur, Walter, 1921-
A dictionary of politics/ edited by Walter Laqueur,
with the assistance of Evelyn Anderson ... [et al.].
New York: Free Press, 1974, c1973. 565 p.
74-009232   320/.03
World politics -- 20th century -- Dictionaries.

D419.T44 1992
Teed, Peter.
A dictionary of twentieth century history: 1914-
1990/ Peter Teed. Oxford; Oxford University
Press, 1992. 520 p.
92-218815   909.82/03   0192116762
History, Modern -- 20th century -- Dictionaries.

D421.F33 1999
Facts about the world's nations/ edited by Michael
O'Mara. New York: H.W. Wilson, c1999. xi,
1065 p.
98-051148   909.82/03   0824209559
*History, Modern -- 20th century. State, The --
Directories.*

D421.G65 1984
Grenville, J. A. S. 1928-
A world history of the twentieth century/ J.A.S.
Grenville. Hanover, N.H.: Published for Brandeis
University Press by Unive 1984- c1980 v. 1
84-040300   909.82   0874513154
History, Modern -- 20th century.

D421.H582 1994
Hobsbawm, E. J. 1917-
The age of extremes: a history of the world, 1914-
1991/ Eric Hobsbawm. New York: Pantheon
Books, c1994. xii, 627 p.
94-028981   909.82   0394585755
History, Modern -- 20th century.

D421.J64 1983
Johnson, Paul, 1928-
Modern times: the world from the twenties to the
eighties/ Paul Johnson. New York: Harper & Row,
c1983. ix, 817 p.
82-048836   909.82   0060151595
History, Modern -- 20th century.

D421.L85 1993
Lukacs, John, 1924-
The end of the twentieth century and the end of the
modern age/ John Lukacs. New York: Ticknor &
Fields, 1993. 291 p.
92-034081   909.82   0395584728
*History, Modern -- 20th century. Nationalism --
History -- 20th century. World War, 1914-1918 --
Influence.*

D421.P66 1999
Ponting, Clive.
The twentieth century: a world history/ Clive
Ponting. New York: H. Holt, 1999. 584 p.
98-037613   909.82   080506088X
History, Modern -- 20th century.

D421.R413 1969
Renouvin, Pierre, 1893-1974.
World War II and its origins; international
relations, 1929-1945. Translated by Remy Inglis
Hall. New York, Harper & Row [1968, c1969] x,
402 p.
72-001076   940.53
History, Modern -- 20th century.

D421.R47 2000
Richards, Michael D.
Term paper resource guide to twentieth-century
world history/ Michael D. Richards and Philip F.
Riley. Westport, Conn.: Greenwood Press, 2000.
xiii, 335 p.
99-088458   909.82   0313305595
*History, Modern -- 20th century. History,
Modern -- 20th century -- Bibliography. History,
Modern -- 20th century -- Sources -- Bibliography.*

D421.T58 1965
Thomson, David, 1912-
World history from 1914 to 1961. New York,
Oxford University Press, 1964 [i.e. 19 iv, 154 p.
68-002207
History, Modern -- 20th century.

D421.W36 1999
War and remembrance in the twentieth century/
edited by Jay Winter and Emmanuel Sivan.
Cambridge, United Kingdom; Press Syndicate of
the University of Cambridge, 1999. p. cm.
98-024909   909.82   0521640350
*History, Modern -- 20th century. Memory. War
and society.*

D424.C65 1992
The Columbia dictionary of European political
history since 1914/ John Stevenson, general editor.
New York: Columbia University Press, c1992.
437 p.
91-029693   940.2/8   0231078803
*Europe -- History -- 20th century --
Dictionaries.*

D424.H83 1987
Hughes, H. Stuart 1916-
Contemporary Europe: a history.   Englewood
Cliffs, N.J.: Prentice-Hall, c1987. xiii, 615 p.
86-030434   940.5   0131699474
Europe -- History -- 20th century.

D424.M39 1999
Mazower, Mark.
Dark continent: Europe's twentieth century/ Mark
Mazower. New York: A.A. Knopf: 1999. xvi,
487 p.
98-015886   940.55   0679438092
Europe -- History -- 20th century.

D424.R66 1983
Ross, Graham, 1933-
The great powers and the decline of the European
states system, 1914-1945/ Graham Ross. London;
Longman, 1983. vii, 181 p.
83-000686   327.4   0582491886
*Europe -- Foreign relations -- 1871-1918.
Europe -- Foreign relations -- 1918-1945. Europe -
- Politics and government -- 1871-1918.*

D429.E5 1951
Ellis, Havelock, 1859-1939.
The genius of Europe. New York, Rinehart [1951]
viik, 288 p.
51-010504
Europe -- Civilization.

D431.A7
Aron, Raymond, 1905-
The century of total war.   Garden City, N.Y.,
Doubleday, 1954. 379 p.
54-005714   940.5
*Military history, Modern -- 20th century. World
politics -- 20th century.*

D431.H68 1991
Howard, Michael Eliot, 1922-
The lessons of history/ Michael Howard. New
Haven [Conn.]: Yale University Press, c1991.
217 p.
90-037654   909.82   0300047282
*History, Modern -- 20th century. Military
history, Modern -- 20th century. World history.*

D442.S82
Documents on international affairs.   London:
Oxford University Press, 1929-1973. v.
30-010914   341.08
*International relations -- Sources -- Periodicals.
World politics -- 1933-1945 -- Periodicals.*

D443.B58
Borsody, Stephen, 1911-
The triumph of tyranny; the Nazi and Soviet
conquest of Central Europe.   New York,
Macmillan, 1960. 285 p.
61-008601
Europe, Central -- Politics and government.

D443.B713 1988
Brecher, Michael.
Crises in the twentieth century/ by Michael
Brecher, Jonathan Wilkenfeld, Sheila Moser.
Oxford; Pergamon Press, 1988. 2 v.
87-010412   909.82   0080349811
World politics -- 20th century.

D443.B7135 2000
Brecher, Michael.
A study of crisis/ Michael Brecher and Jonathan
Wilkenfeld. Ann Arbor: University of Michigan
Press, 2000. xxii, 322 p.
00-712578   909.82   047208707X
World politics -- 20th century.

D443.C29 1947
Carr, Edward Hallett, 1892-
International relations between the two world wars,
1919-1939. London: Macmillan, 1947. viii,302 p.
48-008249   909.82
*World politics. World War, 1914-1918 --
Influence. Europe -- Politics and government --
1918-1945.*

D443.C34 1999
A century's journey: how the great powers shape the world/ edited by Robert A. Pastor. New York: Basic Books, c1999. x, 415 p.
99-040493   327.1/09/04   0465054757
World politics -- 20th century. Great powers.

D443.E77 2001
Ethnopolitical warfare: causes, consequences, and possible solutions/ edited by Daniel Chirot and Martin E.P. Seligman. Washington, DC: American Psychological Association, c2001. xvii, 379 p.
00-059351   305.8   1557987378
World politics -- 20th century. Ethnic relations. Minorities.

D443.L4964 1998
Liska, George.
Expanding realism: the historical dimension of world politics/ George Liska. Lanham, Md.: Rowman & Littlefield, c1998. x, 307 p.
97-022607   909.82/07/2   0847686795
World politics -- 20th century -- Historiography. Historicism.

D443.L4966 1999
Liska, George.
Resurrecting a discipline: enduring scholarship for evolving world politics/ George Liska. Lanham, Md.: Lexington Books, c1999. vi, 361 p.
99-021500   327.1/01   0739100661
World politics -- 20th century -- Historiography.

D443.M289 1998
Mangold, Peter.
From Tirpitz to Gorbachev: power politics in the twentieth century/ Peter Mangold. Basingstoke, Hampshire: Macmillan Press; 1998. viii, 210 p.
97-038347   909.82/9   0333673522
World politics -- 20th century.

D443.S588 1972
Snow, Edgar, 1905-
Journey to the beginning.   New York, Vintage Books [1972, c1958] 434 p.
72-004257   909.82   039471847X
Snow, Edgar, -- 1905-   World politics -- 20th century.

D443.S65
Spengler, Oswald, 1880-1936.
The hour of decision, part one: Germany and world-historical evolution. Translated from the German for the first time by Charles Francis Atkinson. New York, A. A. Knopf, 1934. xvi, 230 p.
34-002638   909.82
Civilization -- History. Economic history -- 1918-1945. World politics.

D443.Y63
Yost, Charles Woodruff.
The insecurity of nations; international relations in the twentieth century, by Charles Yost. New York, Published for the Council on Foreign Relations [[1968] x, 276 p.
68-011324   909.82
History, Modern -- 20th century.

D445.B765 1997b
Brooker, Paul.
Defiant dictatorships: communist and Middle-Eastern dictatorships in a democratic age/ Paul Brooker. Washington Square, N.Y.: New York University Press, 1997. v, 223 p.
97-015332   909.82   0814713114
History, Modern -- 1945- Dictatorship.

D445.C735 1997
Contested social orders and international politics/ edited by David Skidmore. Nashville: Vanderbilt University Press, 1997. xi, 273 p.
97-004573   327/.09/04   0826512844
World politics -- 20th century. International relations. International economic relations.

D445.G54 1995
Gleason, Abbott.
Totalitarianism: the inner history of the Cold War/ Abbott Gleason. New York: Oxford University Press, 1995. 307 p.
94-008750   320.9/04   0195050177
World politics -- 20th century. Totalitarianism. Cold War.

D445.G57 1990
Gormly, James L., 1946-
From Potsdam to the Cold War: Big Three diplomacy, 1945-1947/ James L. Gormly. Wilmington, Del.: SR Books, 1990. xviii, 242 p.
90-008662   940.53/14   0842023348
World politics -- 1945- Cold War.

D445.G7313 1978
Grimal, Henri, 1910-
Decolonization: the British, French, Dutch, and Belgian Empires, 1919-1963/ Henri Grimal; translated by Stephan De Vos. Boulder, Colo.: Westview Press, 1978. xi, 443 p.
77-000922   909.82   0891587322
History, Modern -- 20th century. Newly independent states. Decolonization -- History. Netherlands -- Colonies -- History. Belgium -- Colonies -- History. Great Britain -- Colonies -- History.

D445.H32 1990
Hamerow, Theodore S.
From the Finland station: the graying of revolution in the twentieth century/ Theodore S. Hamerow. New York: Basic Books, c1990. xvi, 386 p.
89-043092   909.82   0465069509
History, Modern -- 20th century. Revolutions -- History -- 20th century. Military history, Modern -- 20th century.

D445.N58 1990
Nixon, Richard M. 1913-
Leaders/ Richard Nixon; with a new introduction by President Nixon. New York: Simon & Schuster, 1990. xiii, 371 p.
90-032311   909.82/092/2   0671706187
Nixon, Richard M. -- (Richard Milhous), -- 1913- World politics -- 20th century. Statesmen -- Biography.

D445.R58 1989
Rock, Stephen R.
Why peace breaks out: great power rapprochement in historical perspective/ Stephen R. Rock. Chapel Hill: University of North Carolina Press, c1989. x, 220 p.
88-033824   909.82/1   0807818577
World politics -- 1900-1918. Great powers. Peace -- History -- 20th century.

D445.V73 1987
Von Laue, Theodore H.
The world revolution of Westernization: the twentieth century in global perspective/ Theodore H. Von Laue. New York: Oxford University Press, 1987. xx, 396 p.
86-033246   909.82   0195049063
History, Modern -- 20th century.

D447.M4
Meyer, Henry Cord, 1913-
Mitteleuropa in German thought and action, 1815-1945. The Hague, Nijhoff, 1955. xv, 378 p.
56-002311
Pangermanism.   Europe, Central -- Politics. Germany -- History -- Historiography.

D453.L43
Lee, Dwight Erwin, 1898-
Europe's crucial years: the diplomatic background of World War I, 1902-1914, by Dwight E. Lee. Hanover, N.H., Published for Clark University Press by the Univ 1974. xiv, 482 p.
73-091315   940.3/112   0874510945
World War, 1914-1918 -- Diplomatic history. Europe -- Politics and government -- 1871-1918.

D463.S7
Stavrianos, Leften Stavros.
Balkan federation. A history of the movement toward Balkan unity in modern times, by L. S. Stavrianos. Northampton, Mass., The Dept. of history of Smith college [1944] x, 338 p.
45-035016   949.6
Eastern question (Balkan)   Balkan Peninsula -- History.   Balkan Peninsula -- Politics and government.

D465.G753 1984
The Great powers and the end of the Ottoman Empire/ edited by Marian Kent. London; G. Allen & Unwin, 1984. x, 237 p.
83-015896   327.5604   0049560131
Eastern question (Balkan)   Great powers.   Europe -- Foreign relations -- Turkey.   Turkey -- Foreign relations -- Europe.   Europe -- Foreign relations -- 1871-1918.

D465.S33 1970
Schmitt, Bernadotte Everly, 1886-1969.
The annexation of Bosnia, 1908-1909. New York, H. Fertig, 1970. viii, 264 p.
71-080588   949.7/42
Eastern question (Balkan)   Bosnia and Hercegovina -- Annexation to Austria.   Europe -- Politics and government -- 1871-1918.

D469.G7.S75
Storrs, Ronald, 1881-1955.
The memoirs of Sir Ronald Storrs.   New York: Putnam, 1937. xvii, 563 p.
37-029409
Storrs, Ronald, -- Sir, -- 1881-1955.   Colonial administrators -- Great Britain -- Biography.   Colonial administrators -- Middle East -- Biography.   Middle East -- Politics and government -- 1914-1945.

D497.H4A37
Haydon, Benjamin Robert, 1786-1846.
Diary. Edited by Willard Bissell Pope. Cambridge, Harvard University Press, 1960-1963. 5 v.
60-005394   927.5

D505 World War I (1914-1918)
— Sources and documents

D505.G2713 1968
Geiss, Imanuel,
July 1914; the outbreak of the First World War; selected documents.   New York, Scribner [1968, c1967] 400 p.
68-011752   940.3/112/08
World War, 1914-1918 -- Diplomatic history.

D505.S7
Snyder, Louis Leo, 1907-
Historic documents of World War I. Princeton, N.J., Van Nostrand [1958] 192 p.
58-014438 940.3082
World War, 1914-1918 -- Sources.

D507 World War I (1914-1918) — Biography — Collective

D507.H47 1982
Herwig, Holger H.
Biographical dictionary of World War I/ Holger H. Herwig and Neil M. Heyman. Westport, Conn.: Greenwood Press, 1982. xiv, 424 p.
81-004242 940.3/092/2 0313213569
World War, 1914-1918 -- Biography -- Dictionaries.

D510 World War I (1914-1918) — Dictionaries

D510.E97 1996
The European powers in the First World War: an encyclopedia/ edited by Spencer C. Tucker; associate editors, Laura Matysek Wood, Justin D. Murphy. New York: Garland Pub., 1996. xxix, 783 p.
95-041418 940.3/4/03 0815303998
World War, 1914-1918 -- Encyclopedias. World War, 1914-1918 -- Europe -- Encyclopedias.

D510.U65 1995
The United States in the First World War: an encyclopedia/ editor, Anne Cipriano Venzon, consulting editor, Paul L. Miles. New York: Garland Pub., 1995. xx, 830 p.
95-001782 940.3/73/03 0824070550
World War, 1914-1918 -- Encyclopedias.

D511 World War I (1914-1918) — Causes. Origins. Aims — General works. Triple Entente, 1907

D511.A574
Albertini, Luigi, 1871-1941.
The origins of the War of 1914. Translated and edited by Isabella M. Massey. London; Oxford University Press, 1952-57. 3 v.
52-012126 940.311
World War, 1914-1918 -- Diplomatic history. World War, 1914-1918 -- Causes. Europe -- Politics and government -- 1871-1918.

D511.C623 1988
The Coming of the First World War/ edited by R.J.W Evans and Hartmut Pogge von Strandmann. Oxford [England]: Clarendon Press; 1988. viii, 189 p.
88-023880 940.3/11 0198228996
World War, 1914-1918 -- Causes.

D511.C626 2000
Copeland, Dale C., 1960-
The origins of major war/ Dale C. Copeland. Ithaca: Cornell University Press, 2000. xi, 322 p.
00-024040 940.3/11 0801437504
World War, 1914-1918 -- Causes. World War, 1939-1945 -- Causes. Balance of power.

D511.G592
Gooch, G. P. 1873-1968.
Recent revelations of European diplomacy, by G.P. Gooch. London, Longmans, Green [1940] viii, 475 p.
42-004455
World War, 1914-1918 -- Causes. Europe -- Politics -- 1871-

D511.K34 1984
Kennan, George Frost, 1904-
The fateful alliance: France, Russia, and the coming of the First World War/ George F. Kennan. New York: Pantheon Books, c1984. xx, 300 p. [
84-042709 940.3/11 0394534948
World War, 1914-1918 -- Causes. France -- Foreign relations -- Russia. France -- Foreign relations -- 1870-1940. Russia -- Foreign relations -- 1894-1917.

D511.M53 1985
Military strategy and the origins of the First World War: an International security reader/ edited by Steven E. Miller. Princeton, N.J.: Princeton University Press, [1985] 186 p.
84-061326 940.3/1 0691076790
World War, 1914-1918 -- Causes. Strategy.

D511.S28 1918
Schmitt, Bernadotte Everly, 1886-1969.
England and Germany, 1740-1914, by Bernadotte Everly Schmitt. Princeton, Princeton University Press, 1918. ix, 524 p.
18-020642
World War, 1914-1918 -- Causes. Germany -- Foreign relations -- Great Britain. Great Britain -- Foreign relations -- Germany.

D511.S815 1996
Stevenson, D. (David), 1954- 1954-
Armaments and the coming of war: Europe, 1904-1914/ David Stevenson. Oxford: Clarendon Press; 1996. xi, 463 p.
95-040415 940.3/112 0198202083
World War, 1914-1918 -- Causes. Military weapons. Europe -- Politics and government -- 1871-1918.

D511.S816 1988
Stevenson, D. (David), 1954- 1954-
The First World War and international politics/ David Stevenson. Oxford [Oxfordshire]; Oxford University Press, 1988. 392 p.
87-022912 940.32 0198730497
World War, 1914-1918 -- Influence. World War, 1914-1918 -- Diplomatic history. World politics -- 20th century. Europe -- Politics and government -- 20th century.

D515 World War I (1914-1918) — Causes. Origins. Aims — Germany

D515.B4665
Bethmann Hollweg, Theobald von, 1856-1921.
Reflections on the world war, by Th. von Bethmann-Hollweg; tr. by George Young. London, T. Butterworth [1920- v.
21-000831
World War, 1914-1918. Europe -- Politics -- 1871-1918.

D517 World War I (1914-1918) — Causes. Origins. Aims — Great Britain

D517.S816 1977
Steiner, Zara S.
Britain and the origins of the First World War/ Zara S. Steiner. New York: St. Martin's Press, 1977. 305 p.
76-055861 940.3/11 0312098189
World War, 1914-1918 -- Causes. World War, 1914-1918 -- Great Britain. Great Britain -- Foreign relations -- 1901-1910. Great Britain -- Foreign relations -- 1910-1936.

D521 World War I (1914-1918) — General works

D521.C513
Churchill, Winston, 1874-1965.
The world crisis. London, T. Butterworth [1923-31] 6 v.
65-059059
World War, 1914-1918. World War, 1914-1918 -- Great Britain. Reconstruction (1914-1939)

D521.C7 1936
Cruttwell, Charles Robert Mowbray Fraser, 1887-1941.
A history of the great war, 1914-1918, by C. R. M. F. Cruttwell. Oxford, The Clarendon Press, 1936. xii 655 p.
38-002895 940.3
World War, 1914-1918.

D521.D35 2000
De Groot, Gerard J., 1955-
The First World War/ Gerard J. De Groot. Houndmills, Basingstoke, Hampshire; Palgrave, 2001. x, 225 p.
00-030891 940.3 0333745345
World War, 1914-1918. World War, 1914-1918 -- Campaigns -- Western Front. World War, 1914-1918 -- Campaigns -- Eastern Front.

D521.K345 1999
Keegan, John, 1934-
The First World War/ John Keegan. New York: A. Knopf; 1999. xvi, 475 p.
98-031826 940.3 0375400524
World War, 1914-1918.

D521.L48 1963
Liddell Hart, Basil Henry, 1895-
The real war, 1914-1918. Boston, Little, Brown [1963, c1930] xii, 508 p.
63-024492 940.4
World War, 1914-1918.

D521.S367 1984
Schmitt, Bernadotte Everly, 1886-1969.
The world in the crucible, 1914-1919/ by Bernadotte E. Schmitt and Harold C. Vedeler. New York: Harper & Row, c1984. xvii, 553 p.
83-048384 940.3 0060152680
World War, 1914-1918. World War, 1914-1918 -- Influence. Revolutions -- Europe -- History -- 20th century. Europe -- History -- 1871-1918. Europe -- History -- 1918-1945.

D521.T83 1998
Tucker, Spencer, 1937-
The great war, 1914-18/ Spencer C. Tucker.
Bloomington: Indiana University Press, 1998. xx,
272 p.
97-031430 940.3 0253333725
World War, 1914-1918.

D522.23 World War I (1914-1918) — Motion pictures about the war

D522.23.D43 1997
DeBauche, Leslie Midkiff.
Reel patriotism: the movies and World War I/
Leslie Midkiff DeBauche. Madison, Wis.:
University of Wisconsin Press, c1997. xviii, 244 p.
96-045979 940.3 0299154009
*World War, 1914-1918 -- Motion pictures and
the war. Motion pictures -- United States --
History. War films -- United States -- History and
criticism.*

D522.23.F57 2000
The First World War and popular cinema: 1914 to
the present/ edited by Michael Paris. New
Brunswick, N.J.: Rutgers University Press, 2000. p.
cm.
99-055762 940.4/8 0813528240
*World War, 1914-1918 -- Motion pictures and
the war. World War, 1914-1918 -- Propaganda.*

D522.25 World War I (1914-1918) — Posters

D522.25.R38 1988
Rawls, Walton H.
Wake up, America!: World War I and the
American poster/ by Walton Rawls; foreword by
Maurice Rickards. New York: Abbeville Press,
c1988. 288 p.
88-014638 940.3/022/2 0896598888
*World War, 1914-1918 -- Posters. Political
posters, American.*

D522.42 World War I (1914-1918) — Historiography

D522.42.F56 1991
The First World War and British military history/
edited by Brian Bond. Oxford: Clarendon Press;
1991. xiv, 330 p.
91-010894 940.4/072 0198222998
*World War, 1914-1918 -- Historiography.
Historiography -- Great Britain -- History -- 20th
century.*

D522.5 World War I (1914-1918) — Outlines, syllabi, tables, etc.

D522.5.H43 1991
Herman, Gerald.
The pivotal conflict: a comprehensive chronology
of the First World War, 1914-1919/ Gerald
Herman. New York: Greenwood Press, 1992. xv,
800 p.
91-022245 940.3/02/02 0313227934
World War, 1914-1918 -- Chronology.

D523 World War I (1914-1918) — General special

D523.A546
Albrecht-Carrie, Rene, 1904-
The meaning of the First World War. Englewood
Cliffs, N.J., Prentice-Hall [1965] x, 181 p.
65-013180 940.3
World War, 1914-1918 -- Influence.

D523.A756 1980
Ashworth, Tony.
Trench warfare, 1914-1918: the live and let live
system/ Tony Ashworth. New York, N.Y.: Holmes
& Meier, 1980. xi, 266 p.
80-013696 940.4/14 0841906157
World War, 1914-1918 -- Trench Warfare.

D523.E85 1999
European culture in the Great War: the arts,
entertainment, and propaganda, 1914-1918/ edited
by Aviel Roshwald and Richard Stites. Cambridge,
UK: Cambridge University Press, 1999. xii, 430 p.
98-027978 940.3/1 0521570158
*World War, 1914-1918 -- Social aspects --
Europe. World War, 1914-1918 -- Influence.
Popular culture -- Europe. Europe -- Intellectual
life -- 20th century.*

D523.H96 1991
Hynes, Samuel Lynn.
A war imagined: the First World War and English
culture/ Samuel Hynes. New York: Atheneum:
1991. xiv, 514 p.
90-021873 940.3 0689121288
*World War, 1914-1918 -- Influence. Great
Britain -- Civilization -- 20th century.*

D523.L443
Leed, Eric J.
No man's land: combat & identity in World War I/
Eric J. Leed. Cambridge; Cambridge University
Press, 1979. xii, 257 p.
78-026396 940.3/14 0521224713
*World War, 1914-1918 -- Psychological aspects.
World War, 1914-1918 -- Influence. World War,
1914-1918 -- Moral and ethical aspects.*

D523.T47 2001
Total war and historical change: Europe, 1914-
1955/ edited by Arthur Marwick and Wendy
Simpson. Buckingham; Open University Press,
2001. p. cm.
00-055054 940.5 0335207944
*World War, 1914-1918 -- Influence. World War,
1939-1945 -- Influence. World War, 1914-1918 --
Social aspects -- Europe. Europe -- History -- 20th
century.*

D523.U7 1988
The Upheaval of war: family, work, and welfare in
Europe, 1914-1918/ edited by Richard Wall and
Jay Winter. Cambridge [England]; Cambridge
University Press, 1988. vii, 497 p.
88-010229 940.3/16 0521323452
*World War, 1914-1918 -- Europe. World War,
1914-1918 -- Women. Europe -- Social conditions
-- 20th century. Europe -- Economic conditions --
20th century.*

D523.W578 1996
Winter, J. M.
Capital cities at war: Paris, London, Berlin, 1914-
1919/ Jay Winter and Jean-Louis Robert.
Cambridge [England]; Cambridge University
Press, 1997. xvii, 622 p.
96-000796 940 0521571715
*World War, 1914-1918 -- France -- Paris. World
War, 1914-1918 -- England -- London. World War,
1914-1918 -- Germany -- Berlin. Paris (France) --
History. London (England) -- History. Berlin
(Germany) -- History.*

D523.W58 1995
Winter, J. M.
Sites of memory, sites of mourning: the Great War
in European cultural history/ Jay Winter.
Cambridge; Cambridge University Press, 1995. x,
310 p.
94-044586 940.4/2 0521496829
*World War, 1914-1918. Memory. Europe --
Intellectual life -- 20th century. Europe --
Civilization -- 20th century.*

D523.W745 2000
World War I and the cultures of modernity/ edited
by Douglas Mackaman and Michael Mays.
Jackson, MS: University Press of Mississippi,
2000. xxv, 197 p.
99-057734 909.82 1578062438
*World War, 1914-1918 -- Influence. Civilization,
Modern -- 20th century.*

D529.3 World War I (1914-1918) — Military operations — Special arms

D529.3.S26 1992
Samuels, Martin.
Doctrine and dogma: German and British infantry
tactics in the First World War/ Martin Samuels.
New York: Greenwood Press, 1992. 225 p.
91-000822 940.4/14 0313279594
World War, 1914-1918 -- Campaigns.

D530-549 World War I (1914-1918) — Military operations — Western

D530.A77 1991
Asprey, Robert B.
The German high command at war: Hindenburg
and Ludendorff conduct World War I/ Robert B.
Asprey. New York: W. Morrow, c1991. 558 p.
90-022733 940.4/144 0688082262
*Hindenburg, Paul von, -- 1847-1934. Ludendorff,
Erich, -- 1865-1937. World War, 1914-1918 --
Campaigns -- Western Front. World War, 1914-
1918 -- Germany.*

D530.B76 1998
Brown, Ian Malcolm, 1965-
British logistics on the Western Front, 1914-1919/
Ian Malcolm Brown. Westport, Conn.: Praeger,
1998. xvi, 261 p.
97-021444 940.4/144 0275958949
*World War, 1914-1918 -- Campaigns -- Western
Front. World War, 1914-1918 -- Logistics -- Great
Britain.*

D530.P75 1991
Prior, Robin.
Command on the western front: the military career of Sir Henry Rawlinson, 1914-18/ Robin Prior and Trevor Wilson. Oxford, UK; Basil Blackwell, 1992. viii, 421 p.
91-011089   940.4/144   0631166831
Rawlinson, Henry, -- Sir. World War, 1914-1918 -- Personal narratives, British. World War, 1914-1918 -- Campaigns -- Western Front. Soldiers -- Great Britain -- Biography.

D530.T73 1987
Travers, Timothy.
The killing ground: the British Army, the western front, and the emergence of modern warfare, 1900-1918/ Tim Travers. London; Allen & Unwin, 1987. xxiv, 309 p.
86-028684   940.4/144   0049422057
World War, 1914-1918 -- Campaigns -- Western Front.

D530.T8
Tuchman, Barbara Wertheim.
The guns of August. New York, Macmillan, 1962. 511 p.
62-007515   940.421
World War, 1914-1918 -- Campaigns -- Western Front.

D531.H464 1997
Herwig, Holger H.
The First World War: Germany and Austria-Hungary, 1914-1918/ Holger H. Herwig. London; Arnold: 1997. xix, 490 p.
96-028152   940.4/147   0340677538
World War, 1914-1918 -- Germany. World War, 1914-1918 -- Austria.

D531.L7713 1971
Ludendorff, Erich, 1865-1937.
Ludendorff's own story, August 1914-November 1918; the Great War from the siege of Liege to the signing of the armistice as viewed from the grand headquarters of the German Army. Freeport, N.Y., Books for Libraries Press [1971, c1920] 2 v.
72-165647   940.4/09/43   0836959566
Ludendorff, Erich, -- 1865-1937.   World War, 1914-1918 -- Germany.

D538.5.B47.D38 2000
Davis, Belinda.
Home fires burning: food, politics, and everyday life in World War I Berlin/ Belinda Davis. Chapel Hill: University of North Carolina Press, 2000. p. cm.
99-032578   943/.155084   0807825263
World War, 1914-1918 -- Germany -- Berlin. Women -- Germany -- History -- 20th century. World War, 1914-1918 -- Women -- Germany. Berlin (Germany) -- History -- 1918-1945.

D542.Y72.P75 1996
Prior, Robin.
Passchendaele: the untold story/ Robin Prior and Trevor Wilson. New Haven: Yale University Press, c1996. xv, 237 p.
96-000754   940.4/31   0300066929
Ypres, 3rd Battle of, Ieper, Belgium, 1917.

D544.H29.W56 1991
Winter, Denis.
Haig's command: a reassessment/ Denis Winter. London, England; Viking, 1991. xi, 362 p.
90-050956   0670802255
Haig, Douglas, -- Sir, -- 1861-1928.   Command of troops. History -- Errors, inventions, etc. Generals -- Great Britain -- Biography.

D544.P49 1996
Philpott, William James.
Anglo-French relations and strategy on the Western Front 1914-18/ William James Philpott. New York: St. Martin's Press, 1996. x, 227 p.
95-053241   940.4/012   0312129440
World War, 1914-1918 -- Campaigns -- Western Front. Strategy. France -- Military relations -- Great Britain. Great Britain -- Military relations -- France.

D544.T49 1999
Thompson, J. Lee, 1951-
Politicians, the press & propaganda: Lord Northcliffe & the Great War, 1914-1919/ J. Lee Thompson. Kent, Ohio: Kent State University Press, c1999. xii, 319 p.
99-024205   940.4/88941   087338637X
Northcliffe, Alfred Harmsworth, -- Viscount, -- 1865-1922.   World War, 1914-1918 -- Great Britain. Press and politics -- Great Britain -- History -- 20th century. Press and propaganda -- Great Britain -- History -- 20th century.

D545.V3.H6
Horne, Alistair.
The price of glory; Verdun 1916. New York, St. Martin's Press [1963, c1962] 371 p.
62-019735   940.427
Verdun, Battle of, 1916.

D546.G47 1999
Graham, Dominick.
Against odds: reflections on the experiences of the British army, 1914-45/ Dominick Graham. New York: St. Martin's Press, 1999. xiv, 240 p.
98-017691   940.54/0941   0312215916
World War, 1914-1918 -- Great Britain. World War, 1939-1945 -- Great Britain.

D546.H43
Hankey, Maurice Pascal Alers Hankey, Baron.
Supreme Command, 1914-1918. Allen, 1961.
61-003901   940.40942
World War, 1914-1918 -- Great Britain. Great Britain. Committee of Imperial Defense. Great Britain. War Cabinet.

D546.L5 1933
Lloyd George, David, 1863-1945.
War memoirs of David Lloyd George. London, I. Nicholson & Watson [1933-36] 6 v.
33-028755
World War, 1914-1918.

D546.S56 1988
Simkins, Peter, 1939-
Kitchener's army: the raising of the new armies, 1914-16/ Peter Simkins. Manchester; Manchester University Press; c1988. xvi, 359 p.
88-006857   355/.00941   0719026377
Kitchener, Horatio Herbert Kitchener, -- Earl -- 1850-1916.

D546.W28 1987
Waites, Bernard.
A class society at war, England, 1914-1918/ Bernard Waites. Leamington Spa, UK; Berg; 1987. 303 p.
87-006564   940.3/1   0907582656
World War, 1914-1918 -- Great Britain. Social classes -- Great Britain -- History -- 20th century. Social classes -- Europe -- History -- 20th century.

D546.W59 1998
Woodward, David R., 1939-
Field Marshal Sir William Robertson: chief of the Imperial General Staff in the Great War/ David R. Woodward. Westport, Conn.: Praeger, 1998. xiv, 230 p.
97-024549   940.3/092   0275954226
Robertson, William Robert, -- Sir, -- 1860-1933. World War, 1914-1918 -- Great Britain. Marshals -- Great Britain -- Biography.

D547.A8.A53 1993
Andrews, E. M. 1933-
The Anzac illusion: Anglo-Australian relations during World War I/ E.M. Andrews. Cambridge; Cambridge University Press, 1993. xiv, 274 p.
93-001484   940.3/2241   052141914X
World War, 1914-1918 -- Australia. World War, 1914-1918 -- Great Britain. Australia -- Military relations -- Great Britain. Great Britain -- Military relations -- Australia. Australia -- Foreign relations -- Great Britain.

D547.I6.D86 1997
Dungan, Myles.
They shall grow not old: Irish soldiers and the Great War/ Myles Dungan. Dublin; Four Courts Press, c1997. 218 p.
98-128773   940.54/12415   1851823476
World War, 1914-1918 -- Ireland. Soldiers -- Ireland -- History. Ireland -- History, Military.

D548.C28 1985
Cassar, George H.
The tragedy of Sir John French/ George H. Cassar. Newark: University of Delaware Press; c1985. 324 p.
82-049302   940.54/21   087413241X
French, John Denton Pinkstone, -- Earl of Ypres, -- 1852-1925. World War, 1914-1918 -- Campaigns -- France.   France -- History -- German occupation, 1914-1918.

D549.I53.I53 1999
Indian voices of the Great War: solders' letters, 1914-18/ selected and introduced by David Omissi. New York: St. Martin's Press, 1999. p. cm.
98-042208   940.4/8154   0312220618
World War, 1914-1918 -- Personal narratives, Indian. World War, 1914-1918 -- Campaigns -- France. Soldiers -- India -- Correspondence.

D550-569 World War I (1914-1918) — Military operations — Eastern

D550.C4
Churchill, Winston, 1874-1965.
The unknown war; the eastern front, by the Rt. Hon. Winston S. Churchill ... New York, C. Scribner's Sons, 1931. xv, p.
31-032920   940.4147
World War, 1914-1918. World War, 1914-1918 -- Campaigns -- Eastern Front.

D550.C62 1998
Cockfield, Jamie H.
With snow on their boots: the tragic odyssey of the Russian Expeditionary Force in France during World War I/ Jamie H. Cockfield. New York: St. Martin's Press, 1998. xi, 396 p.
97-021440   940.4/147   0312173563
World War, 1914-1918 -- Campaigns -- France. World War, 1914-1918 -- Regimental histories -- Russia.

D550.S76
Stone, Norman, 1941-
The eastern front, 1914-1917/ by Norman Stone. New York: Scribner, c1975. 348 p.
75-018914 940.4/147 0684144921
World War, 1914-1918 -- Campaigns -- Eastern Front. Soviet Union -- History -- Revolution, 1917-1921 -- Causes.

D551.L58 2000
Liulevicius, Vejas G.
War land on the Eastern Front: culture, national identity and German occupation in World War I/ Vejas Gabriel Liulevicius. Cambridge, UK; Cambridge University Press, 2000. viii, 309 p.
00-693294 940.4/143 0521661579
World War, 1914-1918 -- Eastern Front. World War, 1914-1918 -- Germany. World War, 1914-1918 -- Influence. Germany -- Relations -- Europe, Eastern. Europe, Eastern -- Relations -- Germany. Germany -- History -- 1918-1933.

D558.M6 1957
Morley, James William, 1921-
The Japanese thrust into Siberia, 1918. New York, Columbia University Press, 1957 [c1954] xiii, 395 p.
57-005805 940.4385
Japanese -- Siberia (R.S.F.S.R.) Japan -- Foreign relations. Soviet Union -- History -- Allied intervention, 1918-1920.

D558.W5
White, John Albert.
The Siberian intervention. Princeton, Princeton University Press, 1950. xi, 471 p.
50-005604 940.4385
Soviet Union -- History -- Allied intervention, 1918-1920.

D568.3.H5
Higgins, Trumbull.
Winston Churchill and the Dardanelles, a dialogue in ends and means. New York, Macmillan [1963] 308 p.
63-014536 940.425
Churchill, Winston, -- Sir, -- 1874-1965 -- Military leadership. World War, 1914-1918 -- Campaigns -- Turkey -- Gallipoli Peninsula.

D568.3.J3 1965a
James, Robert Rhodes, 1933-
Gallipoli. New York, Macmillan, 1965. xi, 384 p.
65-012661 940.425
World War, 1914-1918 -- Campaigns -- Turkey -- Gallipoli Peninsula.

D568.4.L32 1989
Lawrence, T. E. 1888-1935.
The selected letters/ T.E. Lawrence; edited by Malcolm [sic] Brown. New York: Norton, 1989. xxxi, 568 p.
89-003153 940.4/15/0924 0393026841
Lawrence, T. E. -- (Thomas Edward), -- 1888-1935 -- Correspondence. Soldiers -- Great Britain -- Correspondence. World War, 1914-1918 -- Campaigns -- Middle East.

D568.4.L4 1966
Lawrence, T. E. 1888-1935.
Seven pillars of wisdom; a triumph. Garden City, N.Y., Doubleday, 1966 [c1935] xiv, 622 p.
65-029663 940.415
World War, 1914-1918 -- Campaigns -- Arabian Peninsula. Arabs. Bedouins. Arabian Peninsula -- Social life and customs.

D568.4.L45.A43
Lawrence, T. E. 1888-1935.
T.E. Lawrence to his biographers, Robert Graves and Liddell Hart. Garden City, N.Y., Doubleday, 1963. viii, 187 p.
63-011220 940.4150924
Lawrence, T. E. (Thomas Edward), 1888-1935. World War, 1914-1918 -- Campaigns -- Middle East. British -- Middle East -- History -- 20th century. Soldiers -- Great Britain -- Biography. Biography as a literary form.

D568.4.L45.A633 1998
Crawford, Fred D.
Richard Aldington and Lawrence of Arabia: a cautionary tale/ Fred D. Crawford. Carbondale: Southern Illinois University Press, 1998. xvii, 263 p.
97-025418 940.4/15 0809321661
Aldington, Richard, -- 1892-1962. -- Lawrence of Arabia. Lawrence, T. E. -- (Thomas Edward), -- 1888-1935. Aldington, Richard, -- 1892-1962 -- Censorship. British -- Middle East -- History -- 20th century. Publishers and publishing -- Great Britain. Freedom of the press -- Great Britain.

D568.4.L45.L52 1936
Liddell Hart, Basil Henry, 1895-
'T. E. Lawrence' in Arabia and after, by Liddell Hart. London, J. Cape [1936] 2 p.
36-031721 940.4153
Lawrence, T. E. -- (Thomas Edward), -- 1888-1935. World War, 1914-1918 -- Arabian Peninsula. World War, 1914-1918 -- Campaigns -- Turkey and the Near East.

D568.4.L45.M28
Mack, John E., 1929-
A prince of our disorder: the life of T. E. Lawrence/ John E. Mack. Boston: Little, Brown, c1976. xxviii, 561 p.
75-022481 941.083/092/4 0316542326
Lawrence, T. E. -- (Thomas Edward), -- 1888-1935. Orientalists -- Great Britain -- Biography. Archaeologists -- Middle East -- Biography. Soldiers -- Great Britain -- Biography.

D568.4.L45.W55 1990
Wilson, Jeremy.
Lawrence of Arabia: the authorized biography of T.E. Lawrence/ Jeremy Wilson. New York: Atheneum, 1990, c1989. p. cm.
89-049008 940.4/15/092 0689119348
Lawrence, T. E. -- (Thomas Edward), -- 1888-1935. Soldiers -- Great Britain -- Biography. World War, 1914-1918 -- Campaigns -- Middle East. Middle East -- History -- 20th century.

D568.5.D38 1994
Davis, Paul K., 1952-
Ends and means: the British Mesopotamian campaign and commission/ Paul K. Davis. Rutherford, N.J.: Fairleigh Dickinson University Press; c1994. 279 p.
92-055121 940.4/15 083863530X
World War, 1914-1918 -- Campaigns -- Iraq.

D568.5.W6
Wilson, Arnold Talbot, 1884-1940.
Loyalties; Mesopotamia, 1914-1917; a personal and historical record. London, Oxford University Press, H. Milford, 1930. xxxvi, 340 p.
31-001104 940/.415
World War, 1914-1918 -- Campaigns -- Turkey and the Near East -- Iraq.

D569.I69
Schindler, John R.
Isonzo: the forgotten sacrifice of the Great War/ John R. Schindler. Westport, Conn.: Praeger, 2001. xiv, 409 p.
00-061108 940.4/145 0275972046
Isonzo, Battles of the, Italy, 1915-1917.

D570-570.9 World War I (1914-1918) — Military operations — United States

D570.A1.Z54 2000
Zieger, Robert H.
America's Great War: World War I and the American experience/ Robert H. Zieger. Lanham, Md.: Rowman & Littlefield Publishers, c2000. xxii, 275 p.
00-038742 940.4/0973 0847696448
World War, 1914-1918 -- United States. World War, 1914-1918 -- Social aspects -- United States. United States -- Politics and government -- 1913-1921.

D570.A46 1997
Harries, Meirion, 1951-
The last days of innocence: America at war, 1917-1918/ Meirion and Susie Harries. New York: Random House, c1997. xiii, 573 p.
96-021756 940.4/0973 0679418636
World War, 1914-1918 -- United States.

D570.C6
Coffman, Edward M.
The war to end all wars; the American military experience in World War I [by] Edward M. Coffman. New York, Oxford University Press, 1968. xvi, 412 p.
68-029715 940.4/12/73
World War, 1914-1918 -- United States.

D570.P32
Palmer, Frederick, 1873-1958.
Newton D. Baker: America at war: based on the personal papers of the Secretary of War in the World War, his correspondence with the President and important leaders at home and abroad, the confiden by Frederick Palmer. New York: Dodd, Mead, 1931. 2 v.
31-028311 940.373
Baker, Newton D. -- (Newton Diehl), -- 1871-1937. World War, 1914-1918 -- United States.

D570.P44 1931
Pershing, John J. 1860-1948.
My experiences in the World War/ by John J. Pershing ... with sixty-nine reproductions from photographs and numerous maps. New York: Frederick A. Stokes Company, 1931. 2 v.
31-010662 940.4173
Pershing, John J. -- (John Joseph), -- 1860-1948. World War, 1914-1918 -- United States.

D570.1.E27 1997
Early, Frances H.
A world without war: how U.S. feminists and pacifists resisted World War I/ Frances H. Early. Syracuse, N.Y.: Syracuse University Press, 1997. xxi, 265 p.
97-016767 940.3/16 0815627459
World War, 1914-1918 -- United States. World War, 1939-1945 -- Women -- United States -- History -- 20th century. Pacifism.

D570.1.H38
Herbert Hoover--the Great War and its aftermath, 1914-23/ edited with introd. by Lawrence E. Gelfand. Iowa City: University of Iowa Press, c1979. xii, 242 p.
79-010139   940.3/14   0877450951
Hoover, Herbert, -- 1874-1964 -- Congresses. World War, 1914-1918 -- United States -- Congresses. World War, 1914-1918 -- Diplomatic history -- Congresses. Reconstruction (1914-1939) -- Congresses. United States -- Foreign relations -- 1913-1921 -- Congresses.

D570.1.M45 1997
Meigs, Mark.
Optimism at Armageddon: voices of American participants in the First World War/ Mark Meigs. Washington Square, N.Y.: New York University Press, 1997. ix, 269 p.
96-023869   940.4/0973   0814755488
World War, 1914-1918 -- United States. World War, 1914-1918 -- Campaigns -- France. Soldiers -- United States -- History -- 20th century. United States -- Civilization -- French influences.

D570.348.C43 1999
Clark, George B.
Devil dogs: fighting marines of World War I/ George B. Clark. Novato, CA: Presidio Press, c1999. xxxii, 463 p.
98-021853   940.4/1273   0891416536
World War, 1914-1918 -- Regimental histories -- United States. World War, 1914-1918 -- Campaigns -- France.

D570.3 82nd.C66 1999
Cooke, James J.
The All-Americans at war: the 82nd Division in the Great War, 1917-1918/ James J. Cooke. Westport, Conn.: Praeger, 1999. x, 142 p.
98-021782   940.4/1273   0275957403
World War, 1914-1918 -- Campaigns -- Western Front. World War, 1914-1918 -- Regimental histories -- United States.

D570.65.L43 1998
Lebow, Eileen F.
A grandstand seat: the American Balloon Service in World War I/ Eileen F. Lebow. Westport, Conn.: Praeger, 1998. viii, 205 p.
98-005240   940.54/1273   0275962555
World War, 1914-1918 -- Aerial operations, American.

D570.8.C8.M63 1991
Chrislock, Carl Henry.
Watchdog of loyalty: the Minnesota Commission of Public Safety during World War I/ Carl H. Chrislock. St. Paul: Minnesota Historical Society Press, 1991. p. cm.
91-011228   977.6/051   0873512634
World War, 1914-1918 -- Minnesota. Civil rights -- Minnesota -- History -- 20th century. Internal security -- Minnesota -- History -- 20th century. Minnesota -- History -- 1858-

D570.8.I6.B75 1997
Britten, Thomas A. 1964-
American Indians in World War I: at home and at war/ Thomas A. Britten. Albuquerque: University of New Mexico Press, c1997. x, 253 p.
97-004685   940.4/03   0826318045
World War, 1914-1918 -- Participation, Indian. Indians of North America -- History -- 20th century. Indian veterans -- United States. United States -- Armed Forces -- Indians.

D570.9.C82 1970
Cummings, E. E. 1894-1962.
The enormous room. [Introd. by Robert Graves] New York, Liveright [1970, c1922] xix, 271 p.
77-114387   940.4/81/73
Cummings, E. E. -- (Edward Estlin), -- 1894-1962. World War, 1914-1918 -- Personal narratives, American. World War, 1914-1918 -- Prisoners and prisons, French. Soldiers -- United States -- Biography.

D570.9.G7 1971
Greene, Warwick, 1879-1929.
Letters of Warwick Greene, 1915-1928. Edited by Richard W. Hale. Freeport, N.Y., Books for Libraries Press [1971] xxiv, 309 p.
77-179522   901.9   0836966511
Greene, Warwick, -- 1879-1929.   World War, 1914-1918 -- Personal narratives, American. Baltic States -- Description and travel.

D570.9.M37 1976
Marshall, George C. 1880-1959.
Memoirs of my services in the World War, 1917-1918/ George C. Marshall; with a foreword and notes by James L. Collins, Jr. Boston: Houghton Mifflin, 1976. xiv, 268 p.
76-010834   940.4/81/73   0395207258
Marshall, George C. -- (George Catlett), -- 1880-1959.   World War, 1914-1918 -- Personal narratives, American. World War, 1914-1918 -- Regimental histories -- United States.

D570.9.S84
Swan, Carroll Judson, 1879-
My company, by Carroll J. Swan, captain, Company D, 101st engineers, 26th division, U. S. A. ... Boston, Houghton Mifflin company, 1918. x p. 1 l. 2
18-022661
World War, 1914-1918 -- Personal narratives.

D580 World War I (1914-1918)
— Naval operations
— General works.
Freedom of the seas

D580.H34 1994
Halpern, Paul G., 1937-
A naval history of World War I/ Paul G. Halpern. Annapolis, Md.: Naval Institute Press, c1994. xiii, 591 p.
93-024265   940.4/5   0870212664
World War, 1914-1918 -- Naval operations.

D580.H35 1987
Halpern, Paul G., 1937-
The naval war in the Mediterranean, 1914-1918/ by Paul G. Halpern. Annapolis, Md.: Naval Institute Press, 1987. xix, 631 p.
86-062238   940.4/5   0870214489
World War, 1914-1918 -- Naval operations. World War, 1939-1945 -- Campaigns -- Mediterranean Sea.

D581-582 World War I (1914-1918)
— Naval operations
— Anglo-German

D581.H56 1983
Hough, Richard Alexander, 1922-
The Great War at sea, 1914-1918/ Richard Hough. Oxford; Oxford University Press, 1983. xii, 353 p.
84-106046   940.4/5941   0192158716
World War, 1914-1918 -- Naval operations, British.

D582.J8.C63 1977
Costello, John.
Jutland, 1916/ John Costello and Terry Hughes. New York: Holt, Rinehart and Winston, 1977, c1976. 230 p.
76-015599   940.4/56   0030184665
Jutland, Battle of, 1916.

D582.J8.G68 1996
Gordon, G. A. H.
The rules of the game: Jutland and British naval command/ Andrew Gordon. Annapolis, Md.: Naval Institute Press, c1996. xii, 708 p.
96-069418   940.4/5941   155750718X
Jutland, Battle of, 1916. World War, 1914-1918 - - Naval operations.   Great Britain -- History, Naval -- 20th century.

D582.J8.Y38 2000
Yates, Keith, 1928-
Flawed victory: Jutland, 1916/ Keith Yates. Annapolis, Md.: Naval Institute Press, c2000. xviii, 314 p.
99-053217   940.4/56   1557509816
Jutland, Battle of, 1916.

D589 World War I (1914-1918)
— Naval operations — Other, A-Z

D589.U6.J65 1998
Jones, Jerry W., 1964-
U.S. battleship operations in World War I/ Jerry W. Jones. Annapolis, Md.: Naval Institute Press, c1998. ix, 170 p.
97-046092   940.4/5973   1557504113
World War, 1914-1918 -- Naval operations, American.   United States -- History, Naval -- 20th century.

D592 World War I (1914-1918)
— Submarine operations
— German

D592.L8.B34
Bailey, Thomas Andrew, 1902-
The Lusitania disaster: an episode in modern warfare and diplomacy/ Thomas A. Bailey and Paul B. Ryan. New York: Free Press, [1975] xv, 383 p.
75-002806   940.4/514   0029012406
World War, 1914-1918 -- Naval operations.

D600 World War I (1914-1918)
— Aerial operations
— General works

D600.K46 1991
Kennett, Lee B.
The first air war, 1914-1918/ Lee Kennett. New York: Free Press, c1991. xii, 275 p.
90-043632   940.4/4   0029173019
World War, 1914-1918 -- Aerial operations.

D600.M565 1993
Morrow, John Howard, 1944-
The Great War in the air: military aviation from 1909 to 1921/ John H. Morrow, Jr. Washington: Smithsonian Institution Press, c1993. xx, 458 p.
92-017437   940.4/4   1560982381
World War, 1914-1918 -- Aerial operations.

D602 World War I (1914-1918)
— Aerial operations — English

D602.J66
Jones, Neville.
The origins of strategic bombing; a study of the development of British air strategic thought and practice up to 1918. London, Kimber, 1973. 240 p.
74-164725   940.4/49/42   0718300939
World War, 1914-1918 -- Aerial operations, British. Bombing, Aerial -- History.

D602.R54 1996
Rogers, Bogart.
A Yankee ace in the RAF: the World War I letters of Captain Bogart Rogers/ edited by John H. Morrow & Earl Rogers. Lawrence, Kan.: University Press of Kansas, 1996. ix, 264 p.
96-007191   940.4/4941   0700607986
Rogers, Bogart -- Correspondence. World War, 1914-1918 -- Personal narratives, American. World War, 1914-1918 -- Aerial operations, British. Fighter pilots -- United States -- Correspondence.

D604 World War I (1914-1918)
— Aerial operations — German

D604.M64 1982
Morrow, John Howard, 1944-
German air power in World War I/ John H. Morrow, Jr. Lincoln: University of Nebraska Press, c1982. xii, 267 p.
81-011588   940.54/4943   0803230761
World War, 1914-1918 -- Aerial operations, German. Aeronautics, Military -- Germany -- History -- 20th century.

D606 World War I (1914-1918)
— Aerial operations — United States

D606.C66 1996
Cooke, James J.
The U.S. Air Service in the Great War, 1917-1919/ James J. Cooke. Westport, Conn.: Praeger, 1996. x, 248 p.
95-034093   940.4/4973   0275948625
World War, 1914-1918 -- Aerial operations, American.

D606.M5
Mitchell, William, 1879-1936.
Memoirs of World War I: "from start to finish of our greatest war." New York, Random House [1960] 312 p.
60-005548   940.44973
World War, 1914-1918 -- Aerial operations, American.

D610 World War I (1914-1918)
— Diplomatic history — General works

D610.K39 2000
Kawamura, Noriko, 1955-
Turbulence in the Pacific: Japanese-U.S. relations during World War I/ Noriko Kawamura. Westport, Conn.: Praeger, 2000. xii, 173 p.
99-055034   940.3/2   0275968537
World War, 1914-1918 -- Diplomatic history. United States -- Foreign relations -- Japan. Japan -- Foreign relations -- United States.

D611 World War I (1914-1918)
— Diplomatic history — General special

D611.C35
Calder, Kenneth J.
Britain and the origins of the new Europe, 1914-1918/ Kenneth J. Calder. Cambridge [Eng.]; Cambridge University Press, 1976. viii, 268 p.
75-012161   940.3/22/41   0521208971
World War, 1914-1918 -- Diplomatic history. World War, 1914-1918 -- Great Britain. Minorities -- Europe, Eastern. Great Britain -- Foreign relations -- 1910-1936.

D613 World War I (1914-1918)
— Diplomatic history — Peace efforts during the war

D613.G62 2000
Goemans, H. E. 1957-
War and punishment: the causes of war termination and the First World War/ H.E. Goemans. Princeton, N.J.: Princeton University Press, c2000. x, 355 p.
00-036693   940.4/39   0691049432
Peace. World War, 1914-1918 -- Armistices. Peace treaties.

D618-621 World War I (1914-1918)
— Diplomatic history — Individual regions or countries

D618.A42 1988
Albert, Bill.
South America and the First World War: the impact of the war on Brazil, Argentina, Peru, and Chile/ Bill Albert with the assistance of Paul Henderson. Cambridge; Cambridge University Press, 1988. x, 388 p.
87-014310   330.98/0033   0521346509
World War, 1914-1918 -- South America. World War, 1914-1918 -- Influence.

D619.F34 1985
Ferrell, Robert H.
Woodrow Wilson and World War I, 1917-1921/ Robert H. Ferrell. New York: Harper & Row, c1985. xii, 346 p.
84-048160   940.3/73   0060112298
Wilson, Woodrow -- 1856-1924. World War, 1914-1918 -- United States. World War, 1914-1918 -- Diplomatic history. United States -- Politics and government -- 1913-1921.

D619.L347 1970
Lansing, Robert, 1864-1928.
War memoirs of Robert Lansing, Secretary of State. Westport, Conn., Greenwood Press [1970] 383 p.
78-110853   940.3/22/73   0837145201
World War, 1914-1918 -- United States. Neutrality -- United States. United States -- Foreign relations -- 1913-1921.

D619.M383
May, Ernest R.
The World War and American isolation, 1914-1917. Cambridge, Harvard University Press, 1959. viii, 482 p.
58-012971   940.32
World War, 1914-1918 -- Diplomatic history. United States -- Foreign relations -- 1913-1921.

D619.S435 1967
Seymour, Charles, 1885-1963.
American neutrality, 1914-1917; essays on the causes of American intervention in the World War. [Hamden, Conn.] Archon Books, 1967, [c1935] vii, 187 p.
67-017250   940.3/2
World War, 1914-1918 -- United States. Neutrality -- United States. United States -- Foreign relations -- 1913-1921.

D621.F8.S75 1982
Stevenson, D. 1954-
French war aims against Germany, 1914-1919/ D. Stevenson. Oxford; Clarendon Press, 1982. xiv, 283 p.
82-001121   940.3/2   0198225741
World War, 1914-1918 -- Diplomatic history. France -- Foreign relations -- Germany. Germany -- Foreign relations -- France.

D621.J3.D53 1999
Dickinson, Frederick R., 1961-
War and national reinvention: Japan in the Great War, 1914-1919/ Frederick R. Dickinson. Cambridge, Mass.: Harvard University Asia Center: 1999. xviii, 363 p.
99-023508   940.3/2252   0674946553
World War, 1914-1918 -- Diplomatic history. World War, 1914-1918 -- Japan. Japan -- Foreign relations -- 1912-1945.

D627 World War I (1914-1918)
— Special topics — Prisoners and prisons

D627.G3.O3
O'Brien, Pat, d. 1920.
Outwitting the Hun; my escape from a German prison camp, by Lieut. Pat O'Brien. New York Harper & brothers [c1918] 283 p.
18-007366
World War, 1914-1918 -- Prisoners and prisons, German.

D627.R8.O43 1995
Olcen, Mehmet Arif, 1893-1958.
Vetluga memoir: a Turkish prisoner of war in Russia, 1916-1918/ by Mehmet Arif Olcen; introduction and epilogue by Ali Nejat Olcen; translated and edited by Gary Leiser. Gainesville: University Press of Florida, c1995. xi, 246 p.
94-048881   940.4/7247/092   0813013534
Olcen, Mehmet Arif, -- 1893-1958. World War, 1914-1918 -- Personal narratives, Turkish. Prisoners of war -- Turkey -- Biography. Prisoners of war -- Russia -- Biography.

D630 World War I (1914-1918)
— Special topics — Biography, A-Z

D630.C8.A36
Cutler, G. Ripley.
Of battles long ago: memoirs of an American ambulance driver in World War I/ G. Ripley Cutler; edited and with an introd. by Charles H. Knickerbocker. Hicksville, N.Y.: Exposition Press, c1979. 280 p.
79-050656   940.4/753   0682493961
Cutler, G. Ripley. World War, 1914-1918 -- Medical care. World War, 1914-1918 -- France. World War, 1914-1918 -- Personal narratives, American.

D632 World War I (1914-1918) — Special topics — Press. Censorship. Publicity

D632.T46 1987
Thompson, John A.
Reformers and war: American progressive publicists and the First World War/ John A. Thompson. Cambridge [Cambridgeshire]: Cambridge University Press, 1987. xi, 300 p.
86-026329   973.91   052125289X
World War, 1914-1918 -- Public opinion. Press -- United States -- History -- 20th century. Reformers -- United States -- History -- 20th century. United States -- Politics and government -- 1901-1953. United States -- Foreign relations -- 20th century.

D635 World War I (1914-1918) — Special topics — Economic aspects. Commerce, finance, postal service, etc. (General)

D635.B87 1985
Burk, Kathleen.
Britain, America and the sinews of war, 1914-1918/ Kathleen Burk. Boston; G. Allen & Unwin, 1985. x, 286 p.
84-009262   940.3/1   0049400762
World War, 1914-1918 -- Economic aspects -- United States. World War, 1914-1918 -- Economic aspects -- Great Britain. United States -- Foreign economic relations -- Great Britain. Great Britain -- Foreign economic relations -- United States.

D635.O38 1989
Offer, Avner.
The First World War, an agrarian interpretation/ Avner Offer. Oxford [England]: Clarendon Press; 1989. xix, 449 p.
89-003190   940.53/113   0198219466
World War, 1914-1918 -- Economic aspects. World War, 1914-1918 -- Causes. Agriculture -- Economic aspects -- Europe -- History -- 20th century.

D637 World War I (1914-1918) — Special topics — Relief work. Charities. Protection. Refugees

D637.H6 1959
Hoover, Herbert, 1874-1964.
An American epic. Chicago, H. Regnery Co., 1959-1964. 4 v.
59-013696   361.53
International relief. World War, 1914-1918 -- Civilian relief. World War, 1939-1945 -- Civilian relief.

D639 World War I (1914-1918) — Special topics — Other special topics, A-Z

D639.C38.C74 1995
Crerar, Duff, 1955-
Padres in no man's land: Canadian chaplains in the Great War/ Duff Crerar. Montreal; McGill-Queen's Press, c1995. x, 424 p.
95-181165   940.4/78/0922   0773512306
World War, 1914-1918 -- Personal narratives, Canadian. World War, 1914-1918 -- Chaplains -- Canada. Chaplains, Military -- Canada -- Biography.

D639.P7.A93 2000
Cornwall, Mark.
The undermining of Austria-Hungary: the battle for hearts and minds/ Mark Cornwall. New York: St. Martin's Press, c2000. xvi, 485 p.
99-059429   940.4/887436   0312231512
World War, 1914-1918 -- Austria -- Propaganda. World War, 1914-1918 -- Austria. World War, 1914-1918 -- Public opinion. Austria -- Foreign relations -- 1867-1918. Hungary -- History -- 1867-1918.

D639.P7.G396 2000
Welch, David.
Germany, propaganda and total war, 1914-1918: the sins of omission/ David Welch. New Brunswick, N.J.: Rutgers University Press, 2000. ix, 355 p.
99-043944   940.4/887   0813527988
Propaganda, German -- Germany -- History -- 20th century. World War, 1914-1918 -- Propaganda. World War, 1914-1918 -- Germany -- Propaganda.

D639.P7.G775 1992
Messinger, Gary S., 1943-
British propaganda and the state in the First World War/ Gary S. Messinger. Manchester; Manchester University Press; c1992. x, 292 p.
92-007433   940.4/88641   0719030145
World War, 1914-1918 -- Propaganda. Propaganda, British -- History -- 20th century. Great Britain -- Politics and government -- 1910-1936.

D639.P7.R85 1995
Jahn, Hubertus.
Patriotic culture in Russia during World War I/ Hubertus F. Jahn. Ithaca: Cornell University Press, 1995. xii, 229 p.
95-008512   940.3/47   080143131X
World War, 1914-1918 -- Russia. World War, 1914-1918 -- Propaganda. World War, 1914-1918 -- Theater and the war.

D639.P7.U67 1996
Ross, Stewart Halsey.
Propaganda for war: how the United States was conditioned to fight the Great War of 1914-1918/ by Stewart Halsey Ross. Jefferson, N.C.: McFarland, c1996. ix, 341 p.
95-025927   940.54/88673   0786401117
World War, 1914-1918 -- Propaganda. Propaganda, American -- History -- 20th century. World War, 1914-1918 -- United States. United States -- Politics and government -- 1913-1921.

D639.P77.K84 1997
Kuhlman, Erika A., 1961-
Petticoats and white feathers: gender conformity, race, the Progressive peace movement, and the debate over war, 1895-1919/ Erika A. Kuhlman. Westport, Conn.: Greenwood Press, 1997. xiv, 146 p.
97-002225   940.3/16   031330341X
World War, 1914-1918 -- Protest movements -- United States. World War, 1939-1945 -- Women -- United States. Feminists -- United States -- Political activity. United States -- Politics and government -- 1913-1921.

D639.P88.F743 1996
Hanna, Martha.
The mobilization of intellect: French scholars and writers during the Great War/ Martha Hanna. Cambridge, Mass.: Harvard University Press, 1996. ix, 292 p.
95-042544   940.4/0944   0674577558
World War, 1914-1918 -- France. France -- Intellectual life -- 20th century. World War, 1914-1918 -- Public opinion.

D639.W7.D38 2000
Darrow, Margaret H., 1950-
French women and the First World War: war stories of the home front/ Margaret H. Darrow. Oxford; Berg, 2000. ix, 341 p.
1859733611
World War, 1914-1918 -- Women -- France. World War, 1914-1918 -- France -- Participation, Female. Women -- France -- History -- 20th century.

D639.W7.G38 1997
Gavin, Lettie, 1922-
American women in World War I: they also served/ Lettie Gavin. Niwot, Colo.: Univesity Press of Colorado, c1997. xi, 295 p.
96-038466   940.4/0082   087081432X
World War, 1914-1918 -- Women -- United States. Women -- United States -- History -- 20th century.

D639.W7.L48 1999
Lines of fire: women writers of World War I/ edited by Margaret R. Higonnet. New York, N.Y.: Plume, c1999. p. cm.
98-019253   940.3/082   0452281466
World War, 1914-1918 -- Women.

D640 World War I (1914-1918) — Personal narratives and other accounts

D640.A2.B75 1999
Brittain, Vera, 1893-1970.
Letters from a lost generation: the First World War letters of Vera Brittain and four friends, Roland Leighton, Edward Brittain, Victor Richardson, Geoffrey Thurlow/ edited by Alan Bishop and Mark Bostridge. Boston: Northeastern University Press, 1999. xix, 427 p.
98-042383   940.4/8141   1555533795
Brittain, Vera, -- 1893-1970 -- Correspondence. Brittain, Vera, -- 1893-1970 -- Friends and associates. World War, 1914-1918 -- Personal narratives, British. Women authors, English -- 20th century -- Correspondence. Pacifists -- Great Britain -- Correspondence.

D640.A2.D86 1995
Dungan, Myles.
Irish voices from the Great War/ Myles Dungan.
Dublin, Ireland; Irish Academic Press, c1995.
219 p.
96-125253   940.4/81415   0716525739
World War, 1914-1918 -- Personal narratives,
Irish.

D640.A2.G35 1998
Gallagher, Jean, 1962-
The world wars through the female gaze/ Jean
Gallagher. Carbondale: Southern Illinois
University Press, 1998. xii, 191 p.
97-048874   940.4/8173   0809322080
World War, 1914-1918 -- Personal narratives,
American. World War, 1914-1918 -- Pictorial
works. World War, 1939-1945 -- Personal
narratives, American.

D640.B581713
Bloch, Marc Leopold Benjamin, 1886-1944.
Memoirs of war, 1914-15/ Marc Bloch; translated
and with an introd. by Carole Fink. Ithaca, N.Y.:
Cornell University Press, c1980. 177 p.
79-006849   940.4/81/44   080141220X
Bloch, Marc Leopold Benjamin, -- 1886-1944.
World War, 1914-1918 -- Personal narratives,
French.

D640.B5833 1956
Blunden, Edmund, 1896-1974.
Undertones of war; with a new pref. by the author.
London, Oxford University Press, 1956. xvi, 366 p.
56-059214   940.48142
World War, 1914-1918 -- Personal narratives,
English. World War, 1914-1918 -- Poetry.

D640.S3415
Sassoon, Siegfried, 1886-1967.
Memoirs of an infantry officer.   New York,
Coward, McCann, inc., 1930. 3 p.
30-025630   940.481
World War, 1914-1918 -- Personal narratives,
English.

D640.W5
Wharton, Edith, 1862-1937.
Fighting France, from Dunkerque to Belfort, by
Edith Wharton ... New York, C. Scribner's Sons,
1915. 238 p.
15-025358   0837177596
World War, 1914-1918 -- Personal narratives.

D640.W578 1994
Wilder, Amos Niven, 1895-
Armageddon revisited: a World War I journal/
Amos N. Wilder. New Haven: Yale University
Press, c1994. xv, 168 p.
93-033296   940.4/8173   0300055609
Wilder, Amos Niven, -- 1895- Soldiers -- United
States -- Biography. World War, 1914-1918 --
Personal narratives, American.

D641 World War I
(1914-1918)
— Armistice of Compiegne,
1918

D641.K4
Keynes, John Maynard, 1883-1946.
Two memoirs: Dr. Melchior, a defeated enemy,
and My early beliefs. Introduced by David Garnett.
New York, A. M. Kelley, 1949. 106 p.
51-000051   940.3141
Melchior, Carl, -- 1871-1933. World War, 1914-
1918 -- Armistices. World War, 1914-1918 -- Food
question -- Germany.

D641.L68 1996
Lowry, Bullitt, 1936-
Armistice 1918/ by Bullitt Lowry. Kent, Ohio:
Kent State University Press, c1996. xv, 245 p.
96-007600   940.4/39   0873385535
World War, 1914-1918 -- Armistices.

D642-643 World War I (1914-1918)
— Peace
— Sources and documents

D642.P3 1920
The deliberations of the Council of Four (March
24-June 28, 1919)/ notes of the official interpreter,
Paul Mantoux; translated and edited by Arthur S.
Link, with the assistance of Manfred F. Boemeke.
Princeton, N.J.: Princeton University Press, c1992.
2 v.
90-028089   940.3/141   0691047936
World War, 1914-1918 -- Peace -- Sources.
World War, 1914-1918 -- Diplomatic history --
Sources.

D643.A7.B3
Bailey, Thomas Andrew, 1902-
Woodrow Wilson and the lost peace, by Thomas A.
Bailey. New York, The Macmillan company, 1944.
xii p.
44-006237   940.3141
Wilson, Woodrow, -- 1856-1924.   World War,
1914-1918 -- United States.

D643.A7.B3
Bailey, Thomas Andrew, 1902-
Woodrow Wilson and the great betrayal/ by
Thomas A. Bailey. Chicago: Quadrangle Books,
Inc., 1963, c1945. xii, 429 p.
Wilson, Woodrow, -- 1856-1924.   World War,
1914-1918 -- United States.   United States --
Politics and government -- 1913-1921.

D643.A7.H7
Hoover, Herbert, 1874-1964.
America's first crusade [by] Herbert Hoover. New
York, C. Scribner's sons, 1942. viii p.
42-000183   940.3141
World War, 1914-1918 -- United States.

D644 World War I (1914-1918)
— Peace — General works

D644.E5 1972
Elcock, H. J.
Portrait of a decision: the Council of Four and the
Treaty of Versailles [by] Howard Elcock. London,
Eyre Methuen, 1972. xiii, 386 p.
73-156447   940.3/141   0413283704
Paris. Peace Conference, 1919. Treaty of
Versailles (1919)

D644.G7
Greene, Theodore P., 1921-
Wilson at Versailles. Boston, Heath [1957] 114 p.
57-001944   940.3/141
Wilson, Woodrow, -- 1856-1924.

D644.L3 1971
Lansing, Robert, 1864-1928.
The peace negotiations; a personal narrative.
Westport, Conn., Greenwood Press [1971] vi,
328 p.
74-110852   940.3/142   0837145198
Wilson, Woodrow, -- 1856-1924.

D644.L55 1972
Lloyd George, David, 1863-1945.
Memoirs of the Peace Conference. New York, H.
Fertig, 1972. 2 v.
70-080566   940.3/141
World War, 1914-1918 -- Peace.

D644.M37 1976
Marks, Sally.
The illusion of peace: international relations in
Europe, 1918-1933/ Sally Marks. New York: St.
Martin's Press, 1976. 184 p.
76-011281   327.4
World War, 1914-1918 -- Peace. World War,
1939-1945 -- Causes.

D644.N36 1965
Nicolson, Harold George, 1886-1968.
Peacemaking, 1919, by Harold Nicolson. New
York, Grosset & Dunlap [1965] vii, 378 p.
65-013213   940.3141
World War, 1914-1918 -- Peace.

D644.S46
Seymour, Charles, 1885-1963.
Geography, justice, and politics at the Paris
Conference of 1919.   New York, American
Geographical Society, 1951. iv, 24 p.
51-008380   940.31412
World War, 1939-1945 -- Territorial questions.

D644.S478 1991
Sharp, Alan.
The Versailles settlement: peacemaking in Paris,
1919/ Alan Sharp. New York: St. Martin's Press,
1991. xi, 243 p.
90-022402   940.3/142   0312060491
World War, 1914-1918 -- Peace. World War,
1914-1918 -- Reparations.

D645 World War I (1914-1918) — Peace — General special

D645.A42 1987
Ambrosius, Lloyd E.
Woodrow Wilson and the American diplomatic tradition: the treaty fight in perspective/ Lloyd E. Ambrosius. Cambridge [Cambridgeshire]; Cambridge University Press, 1987. xvii, 323 p.
86-033347 940.3/142 0521334535
Wilson, Woodrow, -- 1856-1924. World War, 1914-1918 -- Peace. United States -- Foreign relations -- 1913-1921.

D645.K54 1995
Kleine-Ahlbrandt, W. Laird
The burden of victory: France, Britain, and the enforcement of the Versaille peace, 1919-1925/ Wm. Laird Kleine-Ahlbrandt. Lanham, Md.: University Press of America, c1995. xiii, 342 p.
95-033189 940.3/141 0761800689
World War, 1914-1918 -- Peace. France -- Foreign relations -- Great Britain. Great Britain -- Foreign relations -- France.

D645.M66 1994
Moore, Sara.
Peace without victory for the Allies, 1918-1932/ by Sara Moore; foreword by Forrest Capie. Oxford; Berg, 1994. xi, 383 p.
94-007230 940.3/12 1859730264
World War, 1914-1918 -- Peace. World politics -- 1900-1945. Economic history -- 1918-1945.

D645.W34 1986
Walworth, Arthur, 1903-
Wilson and his peacemakers: American diplomacy at the Paris Peace Conference, 1919/ Arthur Walworth. New York: Norton, c1986. xiii, 618 p.
83-019491 940.3/141 0393018679
Wilson, Woodrow, -- 1856-1924. World War, 1914-1918 -- Peace. World War, 1914-1918 -- Diplomatic history. United States -- Foreign relations -- Europe. Europe -- Foreign relations -- United States. United States -- Foreign relations -- 1913-1921.

D648-650 World War I (1914-1918) — Peace — Special topics

D648.T72
Trachtenberg, Marc, 1946-
Reparation in world politics: France and European economic diplomacy, 1916-1923/ Marc Trachtenberg. New York: Columbia University Press, 1980. x, 423 p.
79-026898 940.3/1422 023104786X
World War, 1914-1918 -- Reparations. World War, 1914-1918 -- Germany. France -- Foreign economic relations.

D650.M5.K5
King, Jere Clemens.
Foch versus Clemenceau; France and German dismemberment, 1918-1919. Cambridge, Harvard University Press, 1960. vi, 137 p.
60-011557 944.08
Clemenceau, Georges, -- 1841-1929. Foch, Ferdinand, -- 1851-1929. World War, 1914-1918 -- Territorial questions -- Rhine River and Valley.

D651 World War I (1914-1918) — Peace — Individual regions or countries, A-Z

D651.A4.D54 1990
Digre, Brian Kenneth.
Imperialism's new clothes: the repartition of tropical Africa, 1914-1919/ Brian Digre. New York: P. Lang, c1990. xiii, 225 p.
89-028908 940.3/1424 0820411205
World War, 1914-1918 -- Territorial questions -- Africa. Africa -- Politics and government -- To 1945. World War, 1914-1918 -- Africa. Africa -- Colonization.

D651.G5.H5 1968
Hirst, Francis Wrigley, 1873-1953.
The consequences of the war to Great Britain. New York, Greenwood Press [1968] xx, 311 p.
68-057610 942.082
World War, 1914-1918 -- Great Britain.

D651.H7.M15
Macartney, C. A. 1895-1978.
Hungary and her successors; the treaty of Trianon and its consequences 1919-1937, by C. A. Macartney. London, Oxford university press 1937. xxi, 504 p.
38-030825 943.9
Minorities. World War, 1914-1918 -- Territorial questions -- Hungary. Hungary -- Nationality. Hungary -- Boundaries.

D651.R8.T5
Thompson, John M.
Russia, Bolshevism, and the Versailles peace [by] John M. Thompson. Princeton, N.J., Princeton University Press, 1966 [i.e. 19 vii, 429 p.
66-017712 940.3/141
World War, 1914-1918 -- Soviet Union. World War, 1914-1918 -- Peace. Communism -- Soviet Union.

D659 World War I (1914-1918) — Reconstruction. Post-war period — Individual countries

D659.G3.A7 1972
Angell, James W. 1898-1986.
The recovery of Germany, by James W. Angell. Westport, Conn., Greenwood Press [1972, c1932] xix, 442 p.
75-138197 330.943/08 0837155509
Reconstruction (1914-1939) -- Germany. Germany -- Economic conditions -- 1918-1945.

D663 World War I (1914-1918) — Celebrations. Memorials. Monuments — General works

D663.K56 1998
King, Alex
Memorials of the great war in Britain: the symbolism and politics of remembrance/ Alex King. Oxford; Berg, 1998 xi, 274 p.
98-211640 940.4/6541 1859739830
World War, 1914-1918 -- Monuments -- Great Britain. War memorials -- Great Britain. World War, 1914-1918 -- Great Britain.

D720 Period between world wars (1919-1939) — General works

D720.G3 1950
Gathorne-Hardy, Geoffrey Malcolm, 1878-
A short history of international affairs, 1920-1939. London, Oxford University Press, 1950. xi, 540 p.
51-002789 909.82
World politics.

D720.L34 1990
Large, David Clay.
Between two fires: Europe's path in the 1930s/ David Clay Large. New York: Norton, c1990. 425 p.
89-003125 940.5 0393027511
Europe -- History -- 1918-1945.

D720.N3 1963
Namier, Lewis Bernstein, 1888-1960.
Europe in decay; a study in disintegration, 1936-1940. Gloucester, Mass.: P. Smith, 1963. 329 p.
63-004320 940.52
World War, 1939-1945 -- Causes. Europe -- History -- 1918-1945.

D723 Period between world wars (1919-1939) — General special

D723.L43 1987
Lee, Stephen J., 1945-
The European dictatorships, 1918-1945/ Stephen J. Lee. London; Methuen, 1987. xv, 343 p.
86-031171 940.5 0416422705
Totalitarianism. Totalitarianism. Dictators. Europe -- Politics and government -- 1918-1945. Europe -- Politics and government -- 1918-1945.

D723.N48 1988
Neutral Europe between war and revolution, 1917-23/ edited by Hans A. Schmitt. Charlottesville: University Press of Virginia, 1988. ix, 257 p.
87-028724 940.3/14 0813911532
Neutrality -- Europe. World War, 1914-1918 -- Influence.

D726.5 Period between world wars (1919-1939) — European social life and customs. Civilization — Fascism

D726.5.C35 1980
Carsten, F. L.
The rise of fascism/ F.L. Carsten. Berkeley: University of California Press, 1980, c1967. 279 p.
80-051592 320.5/33/094 0520043073
Fascism -- Europe. Europe -- History -- 20th century.

D727 Period between world wars (1919-1939) — Political and diplomatic history

D727.B654 2000
Brendon, Piers.
The dark valley: a panorama of the 1930s/ Piers Brendon. New York: Knopf: 2000. xviii, 795 p.
00-034918   940.5/2   0375408819
World politics, 1933-1945. National socialism. Europe -- History -- 1918-1945. Japan -- History -- 1926-1945. Soviet Union -- History -- 1925-1953.

D727.B655 1999
Brody, J. Kenneth.
The avoidable war/ J. Kenneth Brody. New Brunswick, N.J.: Transaction Publishers, c1999-c2000. 2 v.
98-049011   940.5   156000374X
World War, 1939-1945 -- Causes. World War, 1939-1945 -- Diplomatic history. Europe -- Politics and government -- 1918-1945.

D727.C5 1971
Chamberlain, Neville, 1869-1940.
In search of peace. Freeport, N.Y., Books for Libraries Press [1971] viii, 309 p.
77-156627   942.084   0836922743
Peace. Great Britain -- Foreign relations -- 1936-1945. Europe -- Politics and government -- 1918-1945.

D727.C54 1971
Churchill, Winston, 1874-1965.
Step by step, 1936-1939. Freeport, N.Y., Books for Libraries Press [1971, c1939] xii, 323 p.
72-156631   940.5/2   0836923103
Europe -- Politics and government -- 1918-1945. Great Britain -- Foreign relations -- 1936-1945.

D727.G745 2000
Grossman, Mark.
Encyclopedia of the interwar years: from 1919 to 1939/ Mark Grossman. New York, NY: Facts On File, Inc., c2000. xv, 400 p.
99-085998   909.82/2/03   0816035768
History, Modern -- 20th century -- Encyclopedias.

D727.K516 1988
Kitchen, Martin.
Europe between the wars: a political history/ Martin Kitchen. London; Longman, 1988. vii, 350 p.
87-003227   940.5/1   0582017416
Europe -- Politics and government -- 1918-1945.

D727.L37 2000
Lee, Stephen J., 1945-
European dictatorships, 1918-1945/ Stephen J. Lee. London; aNew York: Routledge, 2000. viii, 340 p.
99-059922   940.5   0415230454
Dictators -- Europe. Europe -- Politics and government -- 1918-1945.

D727.L385 1998
Leibovitz, Clement.
In our time: the Chamberlain-Hitler collusion/ Clement Leibovitz and Alvin Finkel; preface by Christopher Hitchens. New York: Monthly Review Press, c1998. 319 p.
97-039461   940.5/2   0853459983
World War, 1939-1945 -- Causes. World War, 1939-1945 -- Diplomatic history.

D727.M87 1984
Murray, Williamson.
The change in the European balance of power, 1938-1939: the path to ruin/ Williamson Murray. Princeton, N.J.: Princeton University Press, c1984. xix, 494 p.
83-043085   940.5/2   0691054134
World War, 1939-1945 -- Causes. Balance of power. Europe -- Politics and government -- 1918-1945.

D727.R6
Robbins, Keith.
Munich 1938. London, Cassell, 1968. 398 p.
68-108772   940.531/2   0304931292
Czechoslovakia -- History -- 1918-1938. Germany -- Foreign relations -- 1933-1945. Europe -- Politics and government -- 1918-1945.

D727.T37 1979
Taylor, Telford.
Munich: the price of peace/ by Telford Taylor. Garden City, N.Y.: Doubleday, 1979. xvi, 1084 p.
73-022794   940.53/12   0385020538
World War, 1939-1945 -- Causes.

D734 World War II (1939-1945) — Congresses, conferences, etc.

D734.A1.U57 1976
United States.
The Conferences at Malta and Yalta, 1945. Westport, Conn.: Greenwood Press, 1976. lxxviii, 1032
76-000125   940.53/14   0837187788
World War, 1939-1945 -- Sources.

D734.B4 1945ad
Feis, Herbert, 1893-1972.
Between war and peace; the Potsdam Conference. Princeton, N.J., Princeton University Press, 1960. viii, 367 p.
60-012230   940.5314
Potsdam Conference (1945)

D734.C7 1970
Stettinius, Edward R. 1900-1949.
Roosevelt and the Russians; the Yalta Conference. Edited by Walter Johnson. Westport, Conn., Greenwood Press [1970, c1949] xvi, 367 p.
75-100179   940.531   0837129761
Roosevelt, Franklin D. -- (Franklin Delano), -- 1882-1945.

D734.I55 1958c
European resistance movements, 1939-1945. New York, Pergamon Press, 1960. xvii, 410 p.
59-014494   940.534
World War, 1939-1945 -- Underground movements -- Congresses.

D735 World War II (1939-1945) — Sources and documents

D735.L3
Langsam, Walter Consuelo, 1906-
Historic documents of World War II. Princeton, N. J., Van Nostrand [1958] 192 p.
58-014435
World War, 1939-1945 -- Sources.

D735.W65
World War II, policy and strategy: selected documents with commentary/ Hans-Adolf Jacobsen and Arthur L. Smith, Jr. Santa Barbara, Calif.: Clio Books, c1979. xiii, 505 p.
79-011507   940.53/1   0874362911
World War, 1939-1945 -- Sources.

D736 World War II (1939-1945) — Biography — Collective

D736.A63 1996
Ancell, R. Manning, 1942-
The biographical dictionary of World War II generals and flag officers: the U.S. Armed Forces/ R. Manning Ancell with Christine M. Miller. Westport, Conn.: Greenwood Press, 1996. xii, 706 p.
95-050450   940.53/092/20   0313295468
World War, 1939-1945 -- Biography -- Dictionaries. Generals -- United States -- Biography -- Dictionaries. Admirals -- United States -- Biography -- Dictionaries. United States -- Armed Forces -- Biography -- Dictionaries.

D736.K43 1978
Keegan, John, 1934-
Who was who in World War II/ edited by John Keegan. New York: T. Y. Crowell, 1978. 224 p.
77-095149   940.53/092/2   0690017537
World War, 1939-1945 -- Biography.

D740 World War II (1939-1945) — Dictionaries

D740.S57
The Simon and Schuster encyclopedia of World War II/ edited by Thomas Parrish, chief consultant editor, S. L. A. Marshall. New York: Simon and Schuster, c1978. 767 p.
78-009590   940.53/03   0671242776
World War, 1939-1945 -- Encyclopedias.

D740.S65 1982
Snyder, Louis Leo, 1907-
Louis L. Snyder's Historical guide to World War II/ Louis L. Snyder. Westport, Conn.: Greenwood Press, 1982. xii, 838 p.
81-013433   940.53/03/21   0313232164
World War, 1939-1945 -- Dictionaries.

D740.W47 1990
Wheal, Elizabeth-Anne.
A dictionary of the Second World War/ Elizabeth-Anne Wheal, Stephen Pope, and James Taylor. New York: P. Bedrick Books, 1990. xvi, 541 p.
90-000312   940.53/03   0872263371
World War, 1939-1945 -- Dictionaries.

D740.W66 2000
World War II: a visual encyclopedia/ [general editor, John Keegan]. London: PRC Pub.; 2000. 512 p.
00-712462   940.53/03   1855858789
World War, 1939-1945 -- Encyclopedias.

D740.W67 1999
World War II in Europe: an encyclopedia/ editor, David T. Zabecki; assistant editors, Carl O. Schuster, Paul J. Rose, William H. Van Husen. New York: Garland Pub., 1999. 2 v.
98-027981   940.53   0824070291
World War, 1939-1945 -- Europe -- Encyclopedias.

D741 World War II (1939-1945) — Causes. Origins. Aims — General works

D741.L26
Lafore, Laurence Davis.
The end of glory; an interpretation of the origins of World War II [by] Laurence Lafore. Philadelphia, J. B. Lippincott Co. [1970] 280 p.
72-088739 940.53/12
World War, 1939-1945 -- Causes.

D741.L29 1991
Lamb, Richard.
The drift to war, 1922-1939/ Richard Lamb. New York: St. Martin's Press, 1991. xii, 372 p.
90-028087 909.82/2 0312058586
World War, 1939-1945 -- Causes.   Europe -- Politics and government -- 1918-1945. Great Britain -- Foreign relations -- 1910-1936. Great Britain -- Foreign relations -- 1936-1945.

D741.O85 1990
Overy, R. J.
The road to war/ Richard Overy with Andrew Wheatcroft. New York: Random House, [c1990] xiii, 364 p.
89-010435 940.53/11 0394582608
World War, 1939-1945 -- Causes.

D741.R53 1995
Roberts, Geoffrey K.
The Soviet Union and the origins of the Second World War: Russo-German relations and the road to war, 1933-1941/ Geoffrey Roberts. New York: St. Martin's Press, 1995. x, 192 p.
94-046862 327.47043/09/043 0312126034
World War, 1939-1945 -- Causes.   Russia -- Relations -- Germany. Germany -- Relations -- Russia.

D741.S64 1987
Smith, Gene.
The dark summer: an intimate history of the events that led to World War II/ Gene Smith. New York: Macmillan; c1987. xi, 314 p.
87-007897 940.53/112 0026119706
World War, 1939-1945 -- Causes.   Europe -- Politics and government -- 1918-1945.

D741.T34 1962
Taylor, A. J. P. 1906-
The origins of the Second World War. New York, Atheneum, 1968 [c1961] 296 p.
62-007543 940.5311
World War, 1939-1945 -- Causes.

D741.W36 1989
Watt, Donald Cameron.
How war came: the immediate origins of the Second World War, 1938-1939/ Donald Cameron Watt. New York: Pantheon Books, 1989. p. cm.
89-008802 940.53/11.220 039457916X
World War, 1939-1945--Causes.

D742 World War II (1939-1945) — Causes. Origins. Aims — By region or country, A-Z

D742.C5.S85 1993
Sun, You-Li, 1955-
China and the origins of the Pacific War, 1931-1941/ Youli Sun. New York: St. Martin's Press, 1993. xi, 244 p.
92-036305 940.53/11/0951 0312090102
World War, 1939-1945 -- Causes. World War, 1939-1945 -- China. World War, 1939-1945 -- Japan. China -- Foreign relations -- Japan. Japan -- Foreign relations -- China. China -- Foreign relations -- 1912-1949.

D742.E852
Prazmowska, Anita.
Eastern Europe and the origins of the Second World War/ Anita J. Prazmowska. New York: St. Martin's Press, 2000. x, 278 p.
00-020996 940.53/112 0312233523
World War, 1939-1945 -- Causes.   Europe, Eastern -- Politics and government -- 1918-1945.

D742.F7.Y68 1996
Young, Robert J., 1942-
France and the origins of the Second World War/ Robert J. Young. New York: St. Martin's Press, 1996. 191 p.
96-010410 940.53/11 0312161859
World War, 1939-1945 -- Causes.   France -- Politics and government -- 1914-1940.

D742.J3.S38
Schroeder, Paul W.
The Axis alliance and Japanese-American relations, 1941. Ithaca, N. Y., Published for the American Historical Associatio [1958] ix, 246 p.
58-002112 940.5324
Anti-comintern pact. World War, 1939-1945 -- Causes.   Japan -- Foreign relations -- Foreign relations -- United States. United States -- Foreign relations -- Japan.

D742.U5.M44
Melosi, Martin V., 1947-
The shadow of Pearl Harbor: political controversy over the surprise attack, 1941-1946/ by Martin V. Melosi. College Station: Texas A & M University Press, c1977. 183 p.
77-023578 940.53/75 0890960313
World War, 1939-1945 -- Causes. World War, 1939-1945 -- United States. Pearl Harbor (Hawaii), Attack on, 1941. United States -- Politics and government -- 1933-1945.

D743 World War II (1939-1945) — General works

D743.A57 1962a
Alexander of Tunis, Harold Rupert Leofric George Alexander 1891-1969.
The Alexander memoirs, 1940-1945. Edited by John North. New York, McGraw-Hill [c1962] xiii, 209 p.
63-012437 940.542
World War, 1939-1945 -- Campaigns.

D743.B73
Bryant, Arthur, 1899-
Triumph in the west; a history of the war years based on the diaries of Field-Marshal Lord Alanbrooke, chief of the Imperial General Staff. Garden City, N.Y., Doubleday, 1959. xviii, 438 p.
59-013960 940.53
World War, 1939-1945.

D743.C24 1989
Calvocoressi, Peter.
Total war: the causes and courses of the Second World War/ Peter Calvocoressi, Guy Wint, and John Pritchard.Rev. 2nd ed. New York: Pantheon Books, c1989. xxviii, 1315 p.
88-043278 940.53.219 0394578112
World War, 1939-1945.

D743.C47
Churchill, Winston, 1874-1965.
The Second World War/ by Winston S. Churchill. Boston: Houghton Mifflin Co.: 1948-1953. 6 v.
48-002880 940.53
World War, 1939-1945. World War, 1939-1945 -- Great Britain.

D743.C555 2000
Command decisions/ edited with introductory essay by Kent Roberts Greenfield; the authors: Martin Blumenson ... [et al.] Washington, D.C.: Center of Military History, United States Army: 2000. viii, 565 p.
00-327837 940.54/2
World War, 1939-1945 -- Campaigns. Strategy.

D743.E35 1990
Eisenhower, Dwight D. 1890-1969.
Crusade in Europe/ Dwight D. Eisenhower. New York: Doubleday, [1990], c1948 xiv, 559 p.
90-037598 940.54/1 0385416199
Eisenhower, Dwight D. -- (Dwight David), -- 1890-1969.   World War, 1939-1945 -- Campaigns. World War, 1939-1945 -- Personal narratives, American. Presidents -- United States -- Biography.

D743.E43 1990
Ellis, John, 1945-
Brute force: allied strategy and tactics in the Second World War/ John Ellis. New York: Viking, 1990. xxii, 643 p.
90-050047 940.54/012 0670807737
World War, 1939-1945 -- Campaigns. Strategy.

D743.G666
Greenfield, Kent Roberts, 1893-1967.
American strategy in World War II: a reconsideration. Baltimore, Johns Hopkins Press, 1963. viii, 145 p.
63-019554 940.54012
World War, 1939-1945. Strategy.

D743.J313 1965
Jacobsen, Hans Adolf,
Decisive battles of World War II; the German view. Edited by H. A. Jacobsen and J. Rohwer. Introd. by Cyril Falls. Translated from the German by Edward Fitzgerald. New York, Putnam [1965] 509 p.
64-013541 940.54
World War, 1939-1945.

D743.L514 1971
Liddell Hart, Basil Henry, 1895-1970.
History of the Second World War. New York, Putnam [1971, c1970] xvi, 768 p.
79-136796 940.53
World War, 1939-1945.

D743.M74
Morison, Samuel Eliot, 1887-1976.
Strategy and compromise. Boston, Little, Brown
[1958] 120 p.
58-006030   940.542
World War, 1939-1945 -- Campaigns.

D743.M75 1996
Moskin, J. Robert.
Mr. Truman's war: the final victories of World War
II and the birth of the postwar world / J. Robert
Moskin. New York: Random House, c1996. xvii,
411 p.
95-046449   940.54/25   067940936X
Truman, Harry S., -- 1884-1972.   World War,
1939-1945 -- United States. World War, 1939-
1945.

D743.O76 1986
Orwell, George, 1903-1950.
Orwell, the war commentaries/ edited with an
introduction by W.J. West. New York: Pantheon
Books, [1986] 253 p.
86-005057   940.53   0394553373
World War, 1939-1945.

D743.O94 1996
Overy, R. J.
Why the allies won/ Richard Overy. New York:
W.W. Norton, 1996. xiv, 396 p.
95-052444   940.53   0393039250
World War, 1939-1945. Strategy.

D743.P3
Patton, George S. 1885-1945
War as I knew it. Annotated by Colonel Paul D.
Harkins. Boston, Houghton Mifflin Co., 1947. xix,
425 p.
47-006664   940.542
World War, 1939-1945 -- Campaigns -- Africa,
North. World War, 1939-1945 -- Campaigns --
Western. World War, 1939-1945 -- Personal
narratives, American.

D743.W4
Wedemeyer, Albert C. 1896-
Wedemeyer reports!   New York, Holt [1958]
497 p.
58-014458   940.53
World War, 1939-1945.

D743.W424 1994
Weinberg, Gerhard L.
A world at arms: a global history of World War II/
Gerhard L. Weinberg. Cambridge [Eng.];
Cambridge University Press, 1994. xix, 1178 p.
92-037637   940.53.220   0521443172
World War, 1939-1945.

D743.W524 1990
Willmott, H. P.
The great crusade: a new complete history of the
Second World War/ H.P. Willmott. New York:
Free Press, 1990, c1989. xi, 499 p.
90-035738   940.53   0029347157
World War, 1939-1945.

D743.W68 1968
Wright, Gordon, 1912-
The ordeal of total war, 1939-1945. New York,
Harper & Row [1968] xv, 315 p.
68-028221   940.53
World War, 1939-1945.

D743.2 World War II (1939-1945) — Pictorial works

D743.2.D69 1990
Douglas, Roy, 1924-
The World War, 1939-1943 [i.e. 1945]: the
cartoonists' vision/ Roy Douglas. London;
Routledge, 1990. xii, 300 p.
89-006395   940.53/0207   0415030498
World War, 1939-1945 -- Caricatures and
cartoons. Wit and humor, Pictorial.

D743.23 World War II (1939-1945) — Motion pictures about the war

D743.23.B74 1988
Britain and the cinema in the Second World War/
edited by Philip M. Taylor. New York: St. Martin's
Press, 1988. x, 210 p.
87-027017   302.2/343/0941   0312016050
World War, 1939-1945 -- Motion pictures and
the war. Motion pictures -- Great Britain --
History.

D743.23.D63 1993
Doherty, Thomas Patrick.
Projections of war: Hollywood, American culture,
and World War II/ Thomas Doherty. New York:
Columbia University Press, c1993. x, 364 p.
93-020420   791.43/658   0231082444
World War, 1939-1945 -- Motion pictures and
the war. Motion pictures -- United States --
History.

D743.23.R38 2001
Rattigan, Neil, 1946-
This is England: British film and the People's War,
1939-1945/ Neil Rattigan. Madison [N.J.]:
Fairleigh Dickinson University Press; c2001.
355 p.
00-042956   940.53   0838638627
World War, 1939-1945 -- Motion pictures and
the war. Motion pictures -- Great Britain -- History
-- 20th cventury.

D743.23.S55 1996
Shull, Michael S., 1949-
Hollywood war films, 1937-1945: an exhaustive
filmography of American feature-length motion
pictures relating to World War II/ [compiled by]
Michael S. Shull and David Edward Wilt.
Jefferson, N.C.: McFarland & Co., 1996. xi, 482 p.
96-004799   940.53   0786401451
World War, 1939-1945 -- Motion pictures and
the war. World War, 1939-1945 -- Film catalogs.
War films -- United States.

D743.23.W67 1996
World War II, film, and history/ edited by John
Whiteclay Chambers II, David Culbert. New York:
Oxford University Press, 1996. xv, 187 p.
95-049890   791.43/658   0195099664
World War, 1939-1945 -- Motion pictures and
the war.

D743.25 World War II (1939-1945) — Posters

D743.25.B57 1998
Bird, William L.
Design for victory: World War II posters on the
American home front/ William L. Bird, Jr. and
Harry R. Rubenstein. New York: Princeton
Architectural Press, 1998. p. cm.
97-048361   940.53/022/2   1568981406
World War, 1939-1945 -- Posters. Posters,
American.

D743.42 World War II (1939-1945) — Historiography

D743.42.K42 1996
Keegan, John, 1934-
The battle for history: re-fighting World War II/
John Keegan. New York: Vintage Books, 1996.
128 p.
95-024899   940.53/072   0679767436
World War, 1939-1945 -- Historiography.

D743.42.W67 1997
World War II in Europe, Africa, and the Americas,
with general sources: a handbook of literature and
research/ edited by Loyd E. Lee; foreword by Mark
A. Stoler; Robin Higham, advisory editor.
Westport, Conn.: Greenwood Press, 1997. xix,
525 p.
96-037044   940.53/072   0313293252
World War, 1939-1945 -- Historiography.
History, Modern -- 1945- -- Historiography.

D743.5 World War II (1939-1945) — Outlines, syllabi, tables, etc.

D743.5.C52 1990
Chronology and index of the Second World War,
1938-1945/ compiled by the Royal Institute of
International Affairs. Westport, Conn.: Meckler,
c1990. 446 p.
89-048664   940.53/02/02   088736568X
World War, 1939-1945 -- Chronology.

D743.5.P57 1996
Polmar, Norman.
World War II: the encyclopedia of the war years,
1941-1945/ Norman Polmar, Thomas B. Allen.
New York: Random House, c1996. xix, 940 p.
96-029215   940.53/02/02   0679770399
World War, 1939-1945 -- Chronology. World
War, 1939-1945 -- United States -- Chronology.
World War, 1939-1945 -- Encyclopedias.

D743.9 World War II (1939-1945) — Pamphlets, addresses, sermons, etc.

D743.9.C295 1948
Camus, Albert, 1913-1960.
Lettres a un ami allemand; avec une pref. inedite.
[Paris] Gallimard [1948] 86 p.
49-024178   940.5304
World War, 1939-1945.

D743.9.H68
Hoover, Herbert, 1874-1964.
Addresses upon the American road, 1941-1945/ by
Herbert Hoover. New York, D. Van Nostrand
Company, inc., 1946. xi, 442 p.
46-008550   940.5373
World War, 1939-1945 World War, 1939-1945 --
Peace. World War, 1939-1945 -- Food supply.
United States -- Economic policy.

D743.9.M287
Marshall, S. L. A. 1900-1977.
Battle at Best. With a foreword by J.F.C. Fuller.
Illustrated by Garver Miller. New York, Morrow,
1963 [c1964] xii, 272 p.
63-020046   940.542
World War, 1939-1945 -- Anecdotes. World War,
1939-1945 -- Personal narratives.

D744-744.7 World War II
(1939-1945)
— General special

D744.E45 1993
Ellis, John, 1945-
World War II: a statistical survey: the essential
facts and figures for all the combatants/ John Ellis.
New York, NY: Facts on File, c1993. 315 p.
93-010627   940.53   0816029717
World War, 1939-1945 -- Statistics.

D744.4.G35 1996
Garrett, Stephen A., 1939-
Conscience and power: an examination of dirty
hands and political leadership/ Stephen A. Garrett.
New York: St. Martin's Press, 1996. x, 198 p.
95-051501   940.53/1   0312159080
World War, 1939-1945 -- Moral and ethical
aspects. Political leadership -- Moral and ethical
aspects -- Czechoslovakia -- Case studies. Political
leadership -- Moral and ethical aspects -- France -
- Case studies.

D744.5.U6.S58 1997
Sittser, Gerald Lawson, 1950-
A cautious patriotism: the American churches &
the Second World War/ Gerald L. Sittser. Chapel
Hill: University of North Carolina Press, c1997. x,
317 p.
96-035005   940.54/78   0807823333
World War, 1939-1945 -- Religious aspects. War
-- Religious aspects -- Christianity. World War,
1939-1945 -- Influence. United States -- Church
history -- 20th century.

D744.55.B45 1998
Beidler, Philip D.
The Good War's greatest hits: World War II and
American remembering/ by Philip D. Beidler.
Athens: University of Georgia, c1998. x, 220 p.
97-051434   791.43/658   0820320013
World War, 1939-1945 -- Psychological aspects.
World War, 1939-1945 -- Motion pictures and the
war. World War, 1939-1945 -- Literature and the
war.

D744.55.W45 2001
Weiner, Amir, 1961-
Making sense of war: the Second World War and
the fate of the Bolshevik Revolution/ Amir Weiner.
Princeton: Princeton University Press, c2001. xv,
416 p.
00-044125   940.53/1   0691057028
World War, 1939-1945 -- Psychological aspects.
World War, 1939-1945 -- Soviet Union. World
War, 1939-1945 -- Social aspects -- Soviet Union.
Vinnytsia Region (Ukraine) -- History -- 20th
century.

D744.7.H3.B35 1992
Bailey, Beth L., 1957-
The first strange place: the alchemy of race and sex
in World War II Hawaii/ Beth Bailey, David
Farber. New York: Free Press, c1992. ix, 270 p.
92-036559   940.53/969   0029012228
World War, 1939-1945 -- Social aspects --
Hawaii. World War, 1939-1945 -- Women --
Hawaii.   Hawaii -- Race relations. Hawaii --
Social conditions.

D745.2 World War II (1939-1945)
— Satire, caricature, etc.
— English

D745.2.M34 1968
Mauldin, Bill, 1921-
Up front. Text and pictures by Bill Mauldin.
Foreword by David Halberstam. New York, Norton
[1968] x, 228 p.
68-024264   741.5973
World War, 1939-1945 -- Caricatures and
cartoons. American wit and humor, Pictorial.

D748 World War II (1939-1945) —
Diplomatic history.
General relations (towards war)
— General works

D748.C37 1999
Carley, Michael Jabara, 1945-
1939: the alliance that never was and the coming of
World War II/ Michael Jabara Carley. Chicago:
I.R. Dee, 1999. xxv, 321 p.
99-024873   940.53/112   1566632528
World War, 1939-1945 -- Diplomatic history.
World War, 1939-1945 -- Causes.

D748.D38 1989
Day, David, 1949-
The great betrayal: Britain, Australia & the onset
of the Pacific War, 1939-42/ David Day. New
York: Norton, 1989, c1988. x, 388 p.
88-037238   940.54/0994   039302685X
World War, 1939-1945 -- Diplomatic history.
Australia -- Foreign relations -- Great Britain.
Great Britain -- Foreign relations -- Australia.

D748.D68 1981
Douglas, Roy, 1924-
From war to cold war, 1942-48/ Roy Douglas. New
York: St. Martin's Press, 1981. 224 p.
80-027270   940.53/2   0312308620
World War, 1939-1945 -- Diplomatic history.
World politics -- 1945-1955. United States --
Foreign relations -- Soviet Union. Soviet Union --
Foreign relations -- United States.

D748.F4
Feis, Herbert, 1893-1972.
Churchill, Roosevelt, Stalin; the war they waged
and the peace they sought. Princeton, N.J.,
Princeton University Press, 1957. xi, 692 p.
57-005470   940.5322
World War, 1939-1945 -- Diplomatic history.

D748.N3
Namier, Lewis Bernstein, 1888-1960.
Diplomatic prelude, 1938-1939/ Sir Lewis
Bernstein Namier. London: Macmillan, 1948. xviii,
502 p.
48-018171   940.532
World War, 1939-1945 -- Diplomatic history.
World War, 1939-1945 -- Causes.

D748.W4
Welles, Sumner, 1892-
Seven decisions that shaped history. New York,
Harper [1951] xviii, 236 p.
51-010044   940.532273
World politics. World War, 1939-1945 --
Diplomatic history.

D749 World War II (1939-1945) —
Diplomatic history. General
relations (towards war)
— General special. Neutrality

D749.B4813 1999
Blet, Pierre,
Pius XII and the Second World War: according to
the Archives of the Vatican/ by Pierre Blet;
translated by Lawrence J. Johnson. New York:
Paulist Press, 1999. xv, 304 p.
99-024020   940.53/2545634   0809105039
Pius -- XII, -- Pope, -- 1876-1958. World War,
1939-1945 -- Diplomatic history. World War,
1939-1945 -- Vatican City.

D749.E36 1991
Edmonds, Robin.
The big three: Churchill, Roosevelt, and Stalin in
peace & war/ Robin Edmonds. New York: Norton,
c1991. 608 p.
90-006854   940.53/2   0393028895
Churchill, Winston, -- Sir, -- 1874-1965. Roosevelt,
Franklin D. -- (Franklin Delano), -- 1882-1945.
Stalin, Joseph, -- 1879-1953. World War, 1939-
1945 -- Diplomatic history.

D749.E82 1985
Eubank, Keith.
Summit at Teheran/ Keith Eubank. New York: W.
Morrow, c1985. 528 p.
84-025538   940.53/2   0688043364
World War, 1939-1945 -- Diplomatic history.

D749.G37 1993
Gardner, Lloyd C., 1934-
Spheres of influence: the great powers partition
Europe, from Munich to Yalta/ Lloyd C. Gardner.
Chicago: I.R. Dee, 1993. xvi, 302 p.
92-040147   940.53/142   1566630118
World War, 1939-1945 -- Diplomatic history.
Spheres of influence. Reconstruction (1939-1951)
Europe -- History -- 1945-

D749.N33 1990
Nadeau, Remi A.
Stalin, Churchill, and Roosevelt divide Europe/ Remi Nadeau. New York: Praeger, 1990. xii, 259 p.
90-007413 940.53/2 0275934500
Stalin, Joseph, -- 1879-1953. Churchill, Winston, -- Sir, -- 1874-1965. Roosevelt, Franklin D. -- (Franklin Delano), -- 1882-1945. World War, 1939-1945 -- Diplomatic history. Europe -- Politics and government -- 1918-1945.

D749.P33 1992
Packard, Jerrold M.
Neither friend nor foe: the European neutrals in World War II/ Jerrold M. Packard. New York: Scribner; c1992. xiii, 432 p.
92-005960 940.53/2 0684192489
World War, 1939-1945 -- Diplomatic history. Neutrality -- History -- 20th century.

D749.S25 1985
Sainsbury, Keith.
The turning point: Roosevelt, Stalin, Churchill, and Chiang-Kai-Shek, 1943: the Moscow, Cairo, and Teheran conferences/ Keith Sainsbury. Oxford: Oxford University Press, 1985. 373 p.
84-012237 940.53/2 0192158589
World War, 1939-1945 -- Diplomatic history.

D749.5 World War II (1939-1945) — Diplomatic history. General relations (towards war) — Separate treaties during the war, A-Z

D749.5.R8.B37 1995
Barros, James.
Double deception: Stalin, Hitler, and the invasion of Russia/ James Barros and Richard Gregor. DeKalb: Northern Illinois University Press, 1995. 307 p.
94-011771 940.53/2247 0875801919
World War, 1939-1945 -- Soviet Union -- Diplomatic history. World War, 1939-1945 -- Campaigns -- Soviet Union. Soviet Union -- History -- German occupation, 1941-1944.

D749.5.R8.R43 1988
Read, Anthony.
The deadly embrace: Hitler, Stalin, and the Nazi-Soviet Pact, 1939-1941/ Anthony Read and David Fisher. New York: Norton, 1988. xxi, 687 p.
88-018123 940.53/2 0393025284
World War, 1939-1945 -- Diplomatic history. Germany -- Foreign relations -- Soviet Union. Soviet Union -- Foreign relations -- Germany.

D750-754 World War II (1939-1945) — Diplomatic history. General relations (towards war) — By region or country

D750.B43 1990
Bell, P. M. H. 1930-
John Bull and the Bear: British public opinion, foreign policy, and the Soviet Union, 1941-1945/ P.M.H. Bell. London; E. Arnold; 1990. x, 214 p.
90-000862 940.53/22 0340533072
World War, 1939-1945 -- Diplomatic history. Public opinion -- Great Britain. World War, 1939-1945 -- Progaganda. Soviet Union -- Foreign public opinion, British. Great Britain -- Foreign relations -- Soviet Union. Soviet Union -- Foreign relations -- Great Britain.

D750.B47 1995
Best, Anthony, 1964-
Britain, Japan, and Pearl Harbor: avoiding war in East Asia, 1936-41/ Antony Best. London; Routledge, 1995. xii, 260 p.
94-042457 0415111714
World War, 1939-1945 -- Diplomatic history. World War, 1939-1945 -- Causes. Japan -- Foreign relations -- Great Britain. Great Britain -- Foreign relations -- Japan. Great Britain -- Foreign relations -- East Asia.

D750.C67 1991
Costello, John.
Ten days to destiny: the secret story of the Hess peace initiative and British efforts to strike a deal with Hitler/ John Costello. New York: W. Morrow, c1991. xvi, 600 p.
91-003372 940.53/2 0688103634
Hess, Rudolf, -- 1894-1987. World War, 1939-1945 -- Diplomatic history. World War, 1939-1945 -- Peace. World War, 1939-1945 -- Propaganda. Germany -- Foreign relations -- Great Britain. Great Britain -- Foreign relations -- Germany.

D750.D95 1990
Dykes, Vivian, 1898-1943.
Establishing the Anglo-American alliance: the Second World War diaries of Brigadier Vivian Dykes/ [edited by] Alex Danchev. London; Brassey's, 1990. xi, 241 p.
89-022279 940.54/8141 0080362605
Dykes, Vivian, -- 1898-1943 -- Diaries. World War, 1939-1945 -- Diplomatic history. World War, 1939-1945 -- Personal narratives, British. Generals -- Great Britain -- Diaries. Great Britain -- Military relations -- United States. United States -- Military relations -- Great Britain.

D750.H4
Henderson, Nevile, 1882-1942.
Failure of a mission; Berlin 1937-1939, by the Right Honorable Sir Nevile Henderson. New York, G. P. Putnam's sons [c1940] xi, 334 p.
40-027393 940.531
Henderson, Nevile, -- Sir, -- 1882-1942. World war, 1939-1945 -- Diplomatic history. World War, 1939-1945 -- Personal narratives, British. World War, 1939-1945 -- Germany. Great Britain -- Foreign relations -- Germany. Germany -- Foreign relations -- Great Britain.

D750.K47 1982
Kersaudy, Francois, 1948-
Churchill and De Gaulle/ Francois Kersaudy. New York: Atheneum, 1982, c1981. 476 p.
81-069154 940.53/22/41 0689112653
Churchill, Winston, -- Sir, -- 1874-1965 -- Contributions in diplomacy. Gaulle, Charles de, -- 1890-1970. World War, 1939-1945 -- Diplomatic history. Prime ministers -- Great Britain -- Biography. Presidents -- France -- Biography. Great Britain -- Foreign relations -- France. France -- Foreign relations -- Great Britain.

D750.P68 1995
Prazmowska, Anita.
Britain and Poland, 1939-1943: the betrayed ally/ Anita J. Prazmowska. Cambridge; Cambridge University Press, 1995. xi, 233 p.
94-026412 940.53/2 052140309X
World War, 1939-1945 -- Diplomatic history. Great Britain -- Foreign relations -- Poland. Poland -- Foreign relations -- Great Britain.

D750.W35 2000
Wolton, Suke.
Lord Hailey, the Colonial Office and the politics of race and empire in the Second World War: the loss of white prestige/ Suke Wolton. New York: St. Martin's Press in association with St. Antho 2000. xii, 221 p.
99-086154 940.53/2 0312232144
Hailey, William Malcolm Hailey, -- Baron, -- 1872-1969. World War, 1939-1945 -- Diplomatic history. Race relations -- Political aspects. Great Britain -- Colonies.

D752.A36 1988
Aglion, Raoul.
Roosevelt and de Gaulle: allies in conflict: a personal memoir/ Raoul Aglion. New York: Free Press; c1988. x, 237 p.
87-027187 940.53/22/730944 0029015405
Roosevelt, Franklin D. -- (Franklin Delano), -- 1882-1945. Gaulle, Charles de, -- 1890-1970. Aglion, Raoul. World War, 1939-1945 -- Diplomatic history. World War, 1939-1945 -- Personal narratives, French. Diplomats -- France -- Biography. France -- Foreign relations -- United States. United States -- Foreign relations -- France.

D752.M34 1995
Maguire, G. E.
Anglo-American policy towards the free French/ G.E. Maguire. New York: St. Martin's Press, 1995. x, 210 p.
95-011453 940.53/2 0312127103
World War, 1939-1945 -- Diplomatic history. France -- Foreign relations -- Great Britain. Great Britain -- Foreign relations -- France. United States -- Foreign relations -- France.

D752.8.W45 1996
Weiss, Steve, 1915-
Allies in conlict: Anglo-American strategic negotiations, 1938-44/ Steve Weiss. New York: St. Martin's Press, 1996. x, 213 p.
96-024196 940.53/22 0312164319
World War, 1939-1945 -- Diplomatic history. United States -- Military relations -- Great Britain. Great Britain -- Military relations -- United States.

D753.B23 1992
Bagby, Wesley Marvin, 1922-
The Eagle-Dragon alliance: America's relations with China in World War II/ Wesley M. Bagby. Newark: University of Delaware Press; 1992.. 306 p.
90-050932 940.53/22 0874134188
World War, 1939-1945 -- Diplomatic history. United States -- Foreign relations -- China. China -- Foreign relations -- United States.

D753.B45 1990
Bennett, Edward M. 1927-
Franklin D. Roosevelt and the search for victory: American-Soviet relations, 1939-1945/ Edward M. Bennett. Wilmington, Del.: SR Books, 1990. xxvii, 207 p.
90-008562 940.53/2273 084202364X
World War, 1939-1945 -- Dipolmatic history. United States -- Foreign relations -- Soviet Union. Soviet Union -- Foreign relations -- United States.

D753.D56
Divine, Robert A.,
Causes and consequences of World War II. Edited with an introd. by Robert A. Divine. Chicago, Quadrangle Books, 1969. 375 p.
71-078305 940.532/2/73
World War, 1939-1945 -- Diplomatic history. World War, 1939-1945 -- United States.

D753.F4
Feis, Herbert, 1893-1972.
The road to Pearl Harbor; the coming of the war between the United States and Japan. Princeton, Princeton University Press, 1950. xii, 356 p.
50-009585 940.532273
World War, 1939-1945 -- United States. World War, 1939-1945 -- Japan. United States -- Foreign relations -- Japan. Japan -- Foreign relations -- United States.

D753.H28
Harriman, W. Averell 1891-1986.
Special envoy to Churchill and Stalin, 1941-1946/ by W. Averell Harriman and Elie Abel. New York: Random House, c1975. xii, 595 p.
75-010275 940.53/2 0394482964
Harriman, W. Averell -- (William Averell), -- 1891-1986. World War, 1939-1945 -- Diplomatic history. World War, 1939-1945 -- United States. Statesmen -- United States -- Biography. United States -- Foreign relations -- 1933-1945.

D753.H38 1988
Heinrichs, Waldo H.
Threshold of war: Franklin D. Roosevelt and American entry into World War II/ Waldo Heinrichs. New York: Oxford University Press, 1988. x, 279 p.
88-005303 940.53/2 019504424X
Roosevelt, Franklin D. -- (Franklin Delano), -- 1882-1945. World War, 1939-1945 -- Diplomatic history. World War, 1939-1945 -- United States.

D753.I47 1990
In danger undaunted: the anti-interventionist movement of 1940-1941 as revealed in the papers of the America First Committee/ edited by Justus D. Doenecke. Stanford, Calif.: Hoover Institution Press, c1990. xii, 491 p.
89-035269 940.53/73 0817988416
World War, 1939-1945 -- United States. Neutrality -- United States.

D753.L27 1976
Lash, Joseph P., 1909-
Roosevelt and Churchill, 1939-1941: the partnership that saved the West/ Joseph P. Lash. New York: Norton, c1976. 528 p.
76-018276 940.53/2 0393055949
Roosevelt, Franklin D. -- (Franklin Delano), -- 1882-1945. Churchill, Winston, -- Sir, -- 1874-1965 -- Contributions in diplomacy. World War, 1939-1945 -- Diplomatic history. World War, 1939-1945 -- United States. World War, 1939-1945 -- Great Britain.

D753.P35 1997
Paz Salinas, Maria Emilia.
Strategy, security, and spies: Mexico and the U.S. as allies in World War II/ Maria Emilia Paz. University Park, Pa.: Pennsylvania State University Press, c1997. xii, 264 p.
96-031047 940.53/2 0271016655
World War, 1939-1945 -- Diplomatic history. United States -- Military relations -- Mexico. Mexico -- Military relations -- United States. Mexico -- Politics and government -- 1910-1946.

D753.S485 1995
Shogan, Robert.
Hard bargain: how FDR twisted Churchill's arm, evaded the law, and changed the role of the American presidency/ Robert Shogan. New York: Scribner, c1995. 320 p.
94-045909 940.53/2241 0689121601
Roosevelt, Franklin D. -- (Franklin Delano), -- 1882-1945. Churchill, Winston, -- Sir, -- 1874-1965. World War, 1939-1945 -- Diplomatic history. World War, 1939-1945 -- Equipment and supplies. Destroyers (Warships) -- United States -- History -- 20th century. United States -- Foreign relations -- Great Britain. Great Britain -- Foreign relations -- United States.

D753.S68 2000
Stafford, David.
Roosevelt and Churchill: men of secrets/ David Stafford. Woodstock, N.Y.: Overlook Press, 2000. xxiv, 359 p.
00-055750 941.084/092 1585670685
Roosevelt, Franklin D. -- (Franklin Delano), -- 1882-1945 -- Friends and associates. Churchill, Winston, -- Sir, -- 1874-1965 -- Friends and associates. World War, 1939-1945 -- Diplomatic history. World War, 1939-1945 -- Secret service. Presidents -- United States -- Biography. United States -- Foreign relations -- 1933-1945. United States -- Relations -- Great Britain. Great Britain -- Relations -- United States.

D753.T352513 1994
The final confrontation: Japan's negotiations with the United States, 1941/ James William Morley, editor; David A. Titus, translator. New York: Columbia University Press, c1994. xxxviii, 437 p.
94-001392 940.53/2 0231080247
World War, 1939-1945 -- Diplomatic history. World War, 1939-1945 -- Causes. United States -- Foreign relations -- 1933-1945. Japan -- Foreign relations -- United States. United States -- Foreign relations -- Japan.

D753.2.R9.M37
Martel, Leon.
Lend-lease, loans, and the coming of the Cold War: a study of the implementation of foreign policy/ Leon Martel. Boulder, Colo.: Westview Press, 1979. xix, 304 p.
79-013678 327.73/047 0891584536
Lend-lease operations (1941-1945). World War, 1939-1945 -- Influence. United States -- Foreign relations -- Soviet Union. Soviet Union -- Foreign relations -- United States.

D753.8.C67 1987
Corbett, P. Scott.
Quiet passages: the exchange of civilians between the United States and Japan during the Second World War/ P. Scott Corbett. Kent, Ohio: Kent State University Press, c1987. viii, 226 p.
87-002069 940.53/2 0873383435
World War, 1939-1945 -- Diplomatic history. World War, 1939-1945 -- Japanese Americans. World War, 1939-1945 -- Evacuation of civilians -- United States. United States -- Foreign relations -- Japan. Japan -- Foreign relations -- United States.

D753.8.O38 1999
Okihiro, Gary Y., 1945-
Storied lives: Japanese American students and World War II/ Gary Y. Okihiro; with a contribution by Leslie A. Ito. Seattle: University of Washington Press, c1999. xiv, 182 p.
98-051100 940.53/089/956073 0295977647
World War, 1939-1945 -- Japanese Americans. Japanese American college students -- Social conditions. Japanese American college students -- Economic conditions. United States -- Race relations.

D754.C5.L58 1996
Liu, Xiaoyuan.
A partnership for disorder: China, the United States, and their policies for the postwar disposition of the Japanese empire, 1941-1945/ Liu Xiaoyuan. Cambridge [England]; Cambridge University Press, 1996. xiii, 343 p.
95-045847 940.53/2 0521550998
World War, 1939-1945 -- Diplomatic history. United States -- Foreign relations -- China. China -- Foreign relations -- United States. China -- Foreign relations -- 1912-1949. United States -- Foreign relations -- 1933-1945.

D754.F5.F5 1983
Finland and World War II, 1939-1944/ edited by John H. Wuorinen. Westport, Conn.: Greenwood Press, 1983. iv, 228 p.
83-012616 940.53/4897 0313241333
World War, 1939-1945 -- Finland. World War, 1939-1945 -- Diplomatic history. Finland -- Foreign relations -- Soviet Union. Soviet Union -- Foreign relations -- Finland. Finland -- History -- 1939-

D754.I5.C37 1975
Carroll, Joseph T.
Ireland in the war years/ Joseph T. Carroll. Newton Abbot: David and Charles; 1975. 190 p.
74-016547 940.53/417 0844805653
De Valera, Eamonn, -- 1882-1975. Neutrality -- Ireland. World War, 1939-1945 -- Ireland. Ireland -- History -- 1922-

D754.I5.D64 1999
Doherty, Richard.
Irish men and women in the Second World War/ Richard Doherty. Dublin, Ireland: Four Courts, 1999. 319 p.
00-269237 1851824413
World War, 1939-1945 -- Ireland. Neutrality -- Ireland. World War, 1939-1945 -- Participation, Irish.

D754.R9.W4 1972
Weinberg, Gerhard L.
Germany and the Soviet Union 1939-1941, by Gerhard L. Weinberg. Leiden, E. J. Brill, 1972. vii, 218 p.
72-196908 940.53/2
World War, 1939-1945 -- Diplomatic history. Soviet Union -- Foreign relations -- Germany. Germany -- Foreign relations -- Soviet Union.

D754.S29.S27 1983
Scandinavia during the Second World War/ edited by Henrik S. Nissen; translated by Thomas Munch-Petersen. Minneapolis: University of Minnesota Press; c1983. x, 407 p.
82-002779 940.53/48 0816611106
World War, 1939-1945 -- Scandinavia. Scandinavia -- History -- 20th century.

D754.S65.T6713 1987
Topitsch, Ernst, 1919-
Stalin's war: a radical new theory of the origins of the second world war/ Ernst Topitsch; translated by A. and B.E. Taylor. New York: St. Martin's Press, 1987. 152 p.
87-016332 940.53/2 0312009895
World War, 1939-1945 -- Diplomatic history. Communist strategy. Soviet Union -- Foreign relations -- 1917-1945.

D754.S9.S3813 2000
Switzerland and the Second World War/ edited by Georg Kreis. London; F. Cass, 2000. xvii, 378 p.
99-059213 940.53/494 0714650293
World War, 1939-1945 -- Switzerland. Neutrality.

D754.T4.A43 1993
Aldrich, Richard J. 1961-
The key to the South: Britain, the United States, and Thailand during the approach of the Pacific War, 1929-1942/ Richard J. Aldrich. Kuala Lumpur; Oxford University Press, 1993. xxii, 416 p.
92-042994 940.53/22 0195886127
World War, 1939-1945 -- Diplomatic history. World War, 1939-1945 -- Thailand. Thailand -- Foreign relations -- Great Britain. Great Britain -- Foreign relations -- Thailand. United States -- Foreign relations -- Thailand.

D754.Y9.M37 1990
Martin, David, 1914-
The web of disinformation: Churchill's Yugoslav blunder/ David Martin. San Diego: Harcourt Brace Jovanovich, c1990. xxxiii, 425 p.
90-030029 940.53/2241 0151807043
Churchill, Winston, -- Sir, -- 1874-1965 -- Contributions in diplomacy. Klugmann, James. World War, 1939-1945 -- Diplomatic history. Great Britain -- Foreign relations -- Yugoslavia. Yugoslavia -- Foreign relations -- Great Britain. Yugoslavia -- Politics and government -- 1918-1945.

D755.1-755.7 World War II (1939-1945) — Military operations. The war effort — By period

D755.1.B3813 1968
Beaufre, Andre.
1940; the fall of France. Translated from the French by Desmond Flower. With a pref. by Sir Basil Liddell Hart. New York, Knopf, 1968 [c1967] xxi, 215 p.
67-018628 944.081/0924
World War, 1939-1945 -- Personal narratives, French. World War, 1939-1945 -- France.

D755.7.G55 1995
Gilbert, Martin, 1936-
The day the war ended: May 8, 1945--victory in Europe/ Martin Gilbert. New York: H. Holt, 1995. xxi, 473 p.
94-045809 940.54/21 0805039260
World War, 1939-1945 -- Campaigns -- Western Front. V-E Day, 1945.

D756-769.85 World War II (1939-1945) — Military operations. The war effort — By region

D756.B7
Bradley, Omar Nelson, 1893-1981.
A soldier's story. New York, Holt [1951] xix, 618 p.
51-011294 940.542
Bradley, Omar Nelson, -- 1893-1981. World War, 1939-1945 -- Personal narratives, American. World War, 1939-1945 -- Campaigns -- Western Front.

D756.M27
MacDonald, Charles Brown, 1922-
The mighty endeavor; American armed forces in the European theater in World War II [by] Charles B. MacDonald. New York, Oxford University Press, 1969. 564 p.
70-083047 940.542/1
World War, 1939-1945 -- Campaigns -- Western Front. World War, 1939-1945 -- United States. United States -- History -- 1933-1945.

D756.3.H68 1988
Hoyt, Edwin Palmer.
The GI's war: the story of American soldiers in Europe in World War II/ Edwin P. Hoyt. New York: McGraw-Hill, c1988. xviii, 620 p.
87-029868 940.54/12/73 0070306273
World War, 1939-1945 -- Campaigns -- Europe. World War, 1939-1945 -- Campaigns -- Africa, North. Soldiers -- United States -- History -- 20th century.

D756.5.A7.E4
Eisenhower, John S. D., 1922-
The bitter woods; the dramatic story, told at all echelons, from supreme command to squad leader, of the crisis that shook the Western coalition: Hitler's surprise Ardennes offensives, by John S. D. Eisenhower. New York, Putnam [1969] 506 p.
68-015504 940.542/1
Ardennes, Battle of the, 1944-1945.

D756.5.A7.O74 1997
Orfalea, Gregory, 1949-
Messengers of the lost battalion: the heroic 551st and the turning of the tide at the Battle of the Bulge/ Gregory Orfalea. New York: Free Press, c1997. xxiv, 408 p.
96-043681 940.54/21431 0684828049
Orfalea, Aref, -- d.1985. World War, 1939-1945 -- Regimental histories -- United States. Ardennes, Battle of the, 1944-1945. Soldiers -- United States -- Biography.

D756.5.B7.H67 1989
Hough, Richard Alexander, 1922-
The Battle of Britain: the greatest air battle of World War II/ Richard Hough and Denis Richards. New York; Norton, 1989. xvii, 413 p.
89-012697 940.54/211 039302766X
Britain, Battle of, 1940.

D756.5.B7.T3
Taylor, Telford.
The breaking wave; the Second World War in the summer of 1940. New York, Simon and Schuster [1967] ix, 378 p.
66-020249 940.542/1
Britain, Battle of, 1940.

D756.5.D5.V55 1989
Villa, Brian Loring.
Unauthorized action: Mountbatten and the Dieppe Raid/ Brian Loring Villa. Toronto; Oxford University Press, 1989. xiii, 314 p.
89-213778 940.54/21425 0195406796
Mountbatten of Burma, Louis Mountbatten, -- Earl, -- 1900-1979. World War, 1939-1945 -- Canada. Dieppe Raid, 1942.

D756.5.D8.E93 2000
The evacuation from Dunkirk: Operation Dynamo, 26 May-4 June 1940/ edited with a preface by W.J.R. Gardner. London; F. Cass, 2000. xiv, 210 p.
00-031707 940.54/21428 0714651206
Dunkerque (France), Battle of, 1940. World War, 1939-1945 -- Naval operations, British.

D756.5.N6.B44 1980
Bennett, Ralph Francis.
Ultra in the West: the Normandy campaign, 1944-45/ Ralph Bennett. New York: Scribner, 1980, c1979. xvi, 336 p.
80-050912 940.54/21 0684167042
World War, 1939-1945 -- Campaigns -- France -- Normandy. World War, 1939-1945 -- Cryptography. World War, 1939-1945 -- Secret Service -- Great Britain. Normandy (France) -- History.

D756.5.N6.H345 2001
Hart, R.
Clash of arms: how the allies won in Normandy/ Russell A. Hart. Boulder, Colo.: Lynne Rienner, 2001. xviii, 469 p.
00-042208 940.54/21421 1555879470
World War, 1939-1945 -- Campaigns -- France -- Normandy.

D756.5.N6 L435 2001
Lewis, Adrian R.
Omaha Beach: a flawed victory/ Adrian R. Lewis. Chapel Hill, NC: University of North Carolina Press, 2001. xii, 382 p.
00-046692 940.54/21421 080782609X
Operation Neptune. World War, 1939-1945 -- Campaigns -- France -- Normandy. Normandy (France) -- History, Military -- 20th century.

D756.5.N6.M496 1997
Mitcham, Samuel W.
The Desert Fox in Normandy: Rommel's defense of Fortress Europe/ Samuel W. Mitcham, Jr. Westport, Conn.: Praeger, 1997. xiv, 229 p.
96-049808 940.54/2142 0275954846
Rommel, Erwin, -- 1891-1944. World War, 1939-1945 -- Campaigns -- France -- Normandy. Normandy (France) -- History, Military.

D756.5.N6.R9
Ryan, Cornelius.
The longest day: June 6, 1944. New York, Simon and Schuster, 1959. 350 p.
59-009499 940.5421
World War, 1939-1945 -- Campaigns -- France -- Normandy. Normandy (France) -- History.

D756.5.N6.S85 1997
Sullivan, John J., 1925-
Overlord's eagles: operations of the United States Army Air Forces in the invasion of Normandy in World War II/ by John J. Sullivan. Jefferson, N.C.: McFarland & Co., c1997. xiv, 210 p.
97-001650 940.54/2142 0786402121
World War, 1939-1945 -- Aerial operations, American. World War, 1939-1945 -- Campaigns -- France -- Normandy. Normandy (France) -- History, Military.

D756.5.N6.V65 1994
Voices of D-Day: the story of the Allied invasion, told by those who were there/ edited by Ronald J. Drez. Baton Rouge: Louisiana State University Press, 1994. p. cm.
93-041311   940.54/21442   0807119024
World War, 1939-1945 -- Campaigns -- France -- Normandy. World War, 1939-1945 -- Personal narratives. Normandy (France) -- History, Military.

D757.B27 1991
Bartov, Omer.
Hitler's army: soldiers, Nazis, and war in the Third Reich/ Omer Bartov. New York: Oxford University Press, 1991. xiv, 238 p.
90-048960   940.54/0943   0195068793
National socialism. World War, 1939-1945 -- Atrocities. Germany -- Armed Forces -- History -- 20th century. Germany -- Armed Forces -- Political activity.

D757.G339 2000
Megargee, Geoffrey P., 1959-
Inside Hitler's High Command/ Geoffrey P. Megargee; foreword by Williamson Murray. Lawrence: University Press of Kansas, c2000. xxi, 327 p.
99-056340   940.54/213   0700610154
World War, 1939-1945 -- Campaigns -- Germany. Command of troops -- Germany -- History -- 20th century. Generals -- Germany -- History -- 20th century. Germany -- Armed Forces -- History -- World War, 1939-1945.

D757.G56 1998
Goda, Norman J. W., 1961-
Tomorrow the world: Hitler, Northwest Africa, and the path toward America/ Norman J.W. Goda. College Station: Texas A & M University Press, c1998. xxvi, 307 p.
97-043802   940.54/013   0890968071
Hitler, Adolf, -- 1889-1945.   World War, 1939-1945 -- Germany. Strategy. Germany -- Foreign relations -- 1933-1945.

D757.G813 1952
Guderian, Heinz, 1888-1954.
Panzer leader. Foreword by B.H. Lidell Hart. Translated from the German by Constantine Fitzgibbon. New York, Dutton, 1952. 528 p.
52-007787   940.5343
World War, 1939-1945 -- Personal narratives, German. World War, 1939-1945 -- Germany.

D757.H297 1991
Hancock, Eleanor.
The National Socialist leadership and total war, 1941-5/ Eleanor Hancock. New York: St. Martin's Press, 1991. xix, 332 p.
91-031201   940.53/43   0312072023
World War, 1939-1945 -- Germany. Political leadership -- Germany -- History -- 20th century. National socialism.

D757.K5 1995
Kitchen, Martin.
Nazi Germany at war/ Martin Kitchen. London; Longman, 1995. 329 p.
93-044808   940.53/43   0582073871
World War, 1939-1945 -- Germany. National socialism. Germany -- History -- 1933-1945.

D757.L5 1948a
Liddell Hart, Basil Henry, 1895-
The German generals talk. New York, W. Morrow, 1948. xi, 308 p.
48-004499   940.5354
Generals -- Germany. World War, 1939-1945 -- Campaigns. World War, 1939-1945 -- Germany.

D757.P48 1990
Peterson, Edward N. 1925-
The many faces of defeat: the German people's experience in 1945/ Edward N. Peterson. New York: P. Lang, c1990. 369 p.
90-005829   940.53   0820413518
World War, 1939-1945 -- Germany. Prisoners of war -- Germany -- History -- 20th century. Germany -- Economic conditions -- 1945-1990.

D757.S9.H35 1998
Halbrook, Stephen P.
Target Switzerland: Swiss armed neutrality in World War II/ by Stephen P. Halbrook. Rockville Centre, NY: Sarpedon, c1998. xii, 320 p.
98-205047   940.53/494   1885119534
World War, 1939-1945 -- Switzerland. Neutrality -- Switzerland. Switzerland -- Defenses. Switzerland -- Politics and government -- 20th century.

D757.W545 1990
Wilt, Alan F.
War from the top: German and British military decision making during World War II/ Alan F. Wilt. Bloomington: Indiana University Press, c1990. ix, 390 p.
89-045566   940.54/01   0253364558
World War, 1939-1945 -- Campaigns. World War, 1939-1945 -- Germany. World War, 1939-1945 -- Great Britain.

D757.85.S8
Stein, George H., 1934-
The Waffen SS: Hitler's elite guard at war, 1939-1945/ by George H. Stein. Ithaca, N.Y.: Cornell University Press, c1966, 1977 p xxxiv, 330 p.
66-011049   940.541343   080140407x
World War, 1939-1945 -- Germany.

D757.85.S95
Sydnor, Charles W.
Soldiers of destruction: the SS Death's Head Division, 1933-1945/ Charles W. Sydnor, Jr. Princeton, N.J.: Princeton University Press, c1977. xvi, 371 p.
77-072138   940.54/13/43   0691052557
World War, 1939-1945 -- Regimental histories -- Germany. World War, 1939-1945 -- Campaigns -- France. World War, 1939-1945 -- Campaigns -- Soviet Union. France -- History -- German occupation, 1940-1945. Soviet Union -- History -- German occupation, 1941-1944.

D757.9.B4.L44 1999
Le Tissier, Tony, 1932-
Race for the Reichstag: the 1945 Battle for Berlin/ Tony Le Tissier. London; F. Cass, 1999. xix, 265 p.
99-013500   940.54/213155   0714649295
Berlin, Battle of, 1945.

D757.9.B4.R43 1993
Read, Anthony.
The fall of Berlin/ Anthony Read and David Fisher. New York: W.W. Norton, 1993. 513 p. [8] p.
92-028641   940.54/213   0393034720
Berlin, Battle of, 1945. World War, 1939-1945 -- Germany. National socialism. Germany -- History -- 1933-1945. Berlin (Germany) -- History.

D757.9.B418 2002
Beevor, Antony,
The fall of Berlin, 1945/ Antony Beevor. New York: Viking, c2002. xxxvii, 489 p.
2002-510674   940.54213155.221   0670030414
Berlin, Battle of, Berlin, Germany, 1945. World War, 1939-1945--Germany--Berlin.

D759.A617 2001
Alanbrooke, Alan Brooke,
War diaries, 1939-1945: Field Marshal Lord Alanbrooke/ edited by Alex Danchev and Daniel Todman. Berkeley: University of California Press, c2001. li, 763 p.
2001-033204   0520233018
Alanbrooke, Alan Brooke, Viscount, 1883-1963--Diaries. World War, 1939-1945--Great Britain. Marshals--Great Britain--Diaries.

D759.F76 2000
French, David, 1954-
Raising Churchill's army: the British army and the war against Germany, 1919-1945/ David French. Oxford; Oxford University Press, 2000. xii, 319 p.
99-057301   940.54/1241   0198206410
World War, 1939-1945 -- Great Britain.

D759.J44 1990
Jefferys, Kevin.
The Churchill coalition and wartime politics, 1940-1945/ Kevin Jefferys. Manchester; Manchester University Press; c1991. 242 p.
90-006414   940.53/41   0719025591
Churchill, Winston, -- Sir, -- 1874-1965 -- Military leadership.   World War, 1939-1945 -- Great Britain. Great Britain -- Politics and government -- 1936-1945.

D759.L84 1991
Lukacs, John, 1924-
The duel: 10 May-31 July 1940: the eighty-day struggle between Churchill and Hitler/ John Lukacs. New York: Ticknor & Fields, 1991. 258 p.
90-011263   940.54/21   0899199674
Churchill, Winston, -- Sir, -- 1874-1965. Hitler, Adolf, -- 1889-1945. World War, 1939-1945 -- Germany. World War, 1939-1945 -- Campaigns -- Western Front. World War, 1939-1945 -- Great Britain.

D759.S77 1998
Strawson, John.
Churchill and Hitler: in victory and defeat/ John Strawson. New York: Fromm International Pub. Corp., 1998. xxxi, 540 p.
98-029771   941.084/092   0880642254
Churchill, Winston, -- Sir, -- 1874-1965. Hitler, Adolf, -- 1889-1945. Prime ministers -- Great Britain -- Biography. World War, 1939-1945 -- Great Britain. World War, 1939-1945 -- Germany.

D760.L7.F74 1999
Freedman, Jean R.
Whistling in the dark: memory and culture in wartime London/ Jean R. Freedman. Lexington: University Press of Kentucky, c1999. xiii, 230 p.
98-027439   940.53/421/0922   0813120764
World War, 1939-1945 -- England -- London. World War, 1939-1945 -- Personal narratives, British. London (England) -- History -- 1800-1950.

D760.8.L7.Z54 1995
Ziegler, Philip.
London at war, 1939-1945/ Philip Ziegler. New York: Knopf, c1995. viii, 372 p.
94-047817   942.1084   0679432981
World War, 1939-1945 -- England -- London. London (England) -- History -- 1800-1950.

D760.8.M53.T47 1989
Thoms, David.
War, industry, and society: the Midlands, 1939-45/ David Thoms. London; Routledge, 1989. x, 197 p.
88-036770   942.4/084   041502272X
World War, 1939-1945 -- England -- Midlands. Industries -- England -- Midlands. Midlands (England) -- Social conditions.

D761.B562 1968
Bloch, Marc Leopold Benjamin, 1886-1944.
Strange defeat; a statement of evidence written in 1940. With an introd. by Sir Maurice Powicke and a foreword by Georges Altman. Translated from the French by Gerard Hopkins. New York, Octagon Books, 1968. xxii, 178 p.
68-015797   940.5344
World War, 1939-1945 -- France. World War, 1939-1945 -- Personal narratives, French.

D761.D64 1994
Doubler, Michael D. 1955-
Closing with the enemy: how GIs fought the war in Europe, 1944-1945/ Michael D. Doubler. Lawrence, Kan.: University Press of Kansas, c1994. xiv, 354 p.
94-025067   940.54/21   0700606750
World War, 1939-1945 -- Campaigns -- France. World War, 1939-1945 -- Campaigns -- Germany. World War, 1939-1945 -- United STates.

D761.F65 1988
Footitt, Hilary.
France, 1943-1945/ Hilary Footitt and John Simmonds. New York: Holmes & Meier, 1988. xvi, 319 p.
88-003086   940.53/44   0841911754
World War, 1939-1945 -- France.   France -- History -- German occupation, 1940-1945.

D761.K54 1996
Kiesling, Eugenia C.
Arming against Hitler: France and the limits of military planning/ Eugenia C. Kiesling. Lawrence, Kan.: University Press of Kansas, c1996. xiv, 260 p.
95-053924   940.53/44   0700607641
World War, 1939-1945 -- France. Military art and science -- France. France -- History, Military -- 20th century.

D761.W4
Weigley, Russell Frank.
Eisenhower's lieutenants: the campaign of France and Germany, 1944-1945/ Russell F. Weigley. Bloomington: Indiana University Press, c1981. xviii, 800 p.
80-008175   940.54/21   0253133335
World War, 1939-1945 -- Campaigns -- France. World War, 1939-1945 -- Campaigns -- Germany. World War, 1939-1945 -- United States. France -- History -- German occupation, 1940-1945. Germany -- History -- 1933-1945.

D761.9.A1.T48 1998
Thomas, Martin.
The French empires at war, 1940-45/ Martin Thomas. Manchester; Manchester University Press; 1998. p. cm.
98-010253   940.3/44   0719050340
World War, 1939-1945 -- France. Imperialism. France -- Colonies -- History, Military.

D762.L63.R53 1999
Rickard, John Nelson, 1969-
Patton at bay: the Lorraine campaign, September to December, 1944/ John Nelson Rickard; foreword by Carlo D'Este. Westport, Conn.: Praeger, 1999. xviii, 295 p.
98-036753   940.54/21438/092   0275963543
Patton, George S. -- (George Smith), -- 1885-1945. World War, 1939-1945 -- Campaigns -- France -- Lorraine. Generals -- United States -- Biography. Lorraine (France) -- History, Military.

D762.O42.C37
Carlisle, Olga Andreyev.
Island in time: a memoir of childhood/ Olga Carlisle. New York: Holt, Rinehart, and Winston, c1980. 226 p.
79-009434   940.53/44/64   0030533260
Carlisle, Olga Andreyev -- Childhood and youth. World War, 1939-1945 -- France -- Oleron, ile d'. World War, 1939-1945 -- Personal narratives, French. Poets, Russian -- 20th century -- Biography. Oleron, ile d' (France) -- Biography.

D762.S68.F86 1992
Funk, Arthur Layton, 1914-
Hidden ally: the French resistance, special operations, and the landings in southern France, 1944/ Arthur Layton Funk. New York: Greenwood Press, 1992. xvi, 338 p.
91-030600   940.54/214   0313279950
Operation Dragoon, 1944. World War, 1939-1945 -- Underground movements -- France, Southern.

D763.I82.A55
Blumenson, Martin.
Anzio: the gamble that failed.   Lippincott, 1963. 212 p.
63-011752   940.5421
Anzio Beachhead, 1944. Great battles of history series.

D763.N4.M3 1970
Maass, Walter B.
The Netherlands at war: 1940-1945, by Walter B. Maass. London, Abelard-Schuman [1970] 264 p.
68-014569   940.53492   0200715526
World War, 1939-1945 -- Netherlands.

D763.N4.R9
Ryan, Cornelius.
A bridge too far. New York, Simon and Schuster [1974] 670 p.
74-003253   940.54/21   0671217925
Arnhem, Battle of, 1944.

D764.B47
Bialer, Seweryn,
Stalin and his generals; Soviet military memoirs of World War II. New York, Pegasus [1969] x, 644 p.
67-025506   940.54/0947
Stalin, Joseph, -- 1879-1953.   World War, 1939-1945 -- Soviet Union. World War, 1939-1945 -- Personal narratives, Russian. Generals -- Soviet Union.

D764.E352 1964
Erenburg, Ilia, 1891-1967.
The war: 1941-1945 [by] Ilya Ehrenburg. Translated by Tatiana Shebunina, in collaboration with Yvonne Kapp. London, MacGibbon & Kee, 1964. 198 p.
65-087534
World War, 1939-1945 -- Soviet Union.

D764.E74 1975b vol. 1
Erickson, John, 1929-
The road to Stalingrad/ John Erickson. New York: Harper & Row, [1975] x, 594 p.
74-024657   940.54/21 s   0060111410
Stalingrad, Battle of, 1942-1943.

D764.F6813 1977
The Russian war, 1941-1945/ edited by Daniela Mrazkova and Vladimir Remes; introd. by Harrison Salisbury; pref. and notes by A. J. P. Taylor. New York: Dutton, 1977, c1975. vii, 152 p.
77-001970   940.54/21   0525195602
World War, 1939-1945 -- Campaigns -- Soviet Union -- Pictorial works. News photographers. Soviet Union -- History -- German occupation, 1941-1944 -- Pictorial works.

D764.F845 1997
Fugate, Bryan I., 1943-
Thunder on the Dnepr: Zhukov-Stalin and the defeat of Hitler's Blitzkrieg/ Bryan I. Fugate and Lev Dvoretsky. Novato, CA: Presidio, c1997. xvi, 415 p.
96-051177   940.54/2177   0891415297
Zhukov, Georgii Konstantinovich), -- 1896-1974. Stalin, Joseph, -- 1879-1953. World War, 1939-1945 -- Soviet Union. World War, 1939-1945 -- Campaigns -- Eastern Front.

D764.G556 1998
Glantz, David M.
Stumbling colossus: the Red Army on the eve of World War/ David M. Glantz; maps by Darin Grauberger and George F. McCleary, Jr. Lawrence, Kan.: University Press of Kansas, c1998. xvii, 374 p.
97-033277   940.54/217   0700608796
World War, 1939-1945 -- Campaigns -- Eastern Front. Soviet Union -- History, Military.

D764.G557 1995
Glantz, David M.
When Titans clashed: how the Red Army stopped Hitler/ David M. Glantz, Jonathan M. House. Lawrence, Kan.: University Press of Kansas, c1995. xi, 414 p.
95-024588   947.084   070060717X
World War, 1939-1945 -- Campaigns -- Eastern Front.

D764.G5575 1999
Glantz, David M.
Zhukov's greatest defeat: the Red Army's epic disaster in Operation Mars, 1942/ David M. Glantz; German translations by Mary E. Glantz; maps by Darin Grauberger. Lawrence, Kan.: University Press of Kansas, c1999. x, 421 p.
98-046835   940.54/217/092   070060944X
Zhukov, Georgii Konstantinovich, -- 1896-1974. World War, 1939-1945 -- Campaigns -- Eastern Front. World War, 1939-1945 -- Soviet Union. Marshals -- Soviet Union -- Biography.

D764.H374 1998
Hayward, Joel S. A.
Stopped at Stalingrad: the Luftwaffe and Hitler's defeat in the east, 1942-1943/ Joel S.A. Hayward. Lawrence, Kan.: University Press of Kansas, c1998. xxiii, 393 p.
97-022541   940.54/21747   0700608761
Hitler, Adolf, -- 1889-1945.   World War, 1939-1945 -- Campaigns -- Eastern Front. Stalingrad, Battle of, 1942-1943. Strategy.

D764.K454 1997
Khaldei, Evgenii, 1917-
Witness to history: the photographs of Yevgeny Khaldei/ biographical essay by Alexander and Alice Nakhimovsky. New York, N.Y.: Aperture, c1997. 94 p.
97-073708   0893817384
Khaldei, Evgenii, -- 1917- War photographers -- Soviet Union -- Biography. World War, 1939-1945 -- Soviet Union -- Pictorial works. World War, 1939-1945 -- Europe, Eastern -- Pictorial works.

D764.M825 1997
Muller, Rolf-Dieter, 1948-
Hitler's war in the East, 1941-1945: a critical assessment/ Rolf-Dieter Muller and Gerd R. Ueberschar; translation of texts by Bruce D. Little. Providence, RI: Berghahn Books, 1997. x, 405 p.
96-044941   940.54/21   1571810684
World War, 1939-1945 -- Campaigns -- Eastern Front. World War, 1939-1945 -- Germany. World War, 1939-1945 -- Soviet Union.

D764.O94 1997
Overy, R. J.
Russia's war: blood upon the snow/ Richard Overy. New York: TV Books: c1997. 431 p.
97-213178   940.54/0947   1575000512
World War, 1939-1945 -- Soviet Union.   Soviet Union -- History -- 1925-1953.

D764.P45 2000
The People's war: responses to World War II in the Soviet Union/ edited by Robert W. Thurston and Bernd Bonwetsch. Urbana: University of Illinois Press, c2000. x, 275 p.
00-008493   947.084/2   0252026004
World War, 1939-1945 -- Soviet Union.

D764.W48 1965
Werth, Alexander,
Russia at war, 1941-1945.   London, Pan, 1965. 984 p.
72-390375   940.5347
World War, 1939-1945--Soviet Union.

D764.Z9313 1997
From peace to war: Germany, Soviet Russia, and the world, 1939-1941/ edited by Bernd Wegner. Providence: Berghahn Books, 1997. vii, 632 p.
96-029084   940.53/47   1571818820
World War, 1939-1945 -- Campaigns -- Soviet Union.   World War, 1939-1945 -- Diplomatic history.

D764.3.L4.S2
Salisbury, Harrison Evans, 1908-
The 900 days; the siege of Leningrad [by] Harrison E. Salisbury. New York, Harper & Row [1969] xi, 635 p.
68-028215   940.542/1
Saint Petersburg (Russia) -- History -- Siege, 1941-1944.

D764.7.D6.G53 1990
Glantz, David M.
From the Don to the Dnepr: Soviet offensive operations, December 1942-August 1943/ David M. Glantz. London, England; F. Cass, 1991. xvi, 430 p.
89-071291   940.54/21777   071463350X
World War, 1939-1945 -- Campaigns -- Russia (Federation) -- Don River Region. World War, 1939-1945 -- Campaigns -- Donets Basin (Ukraine and Russia) Don River Region (Russia) -- History. Donets Basin (Ukraine and Russia) -- History.

D765.O56 1997
Okonski, Walter, 1935-
Wartime Poland, 1939-1945: a select annotated bibliography of books in English/ Walter Okonski. Westport, Conn.: Greenwood Press, 1997. xii, 111 p.
96-033027   016.94053/438   0313300046
World War, 1939-1945 -- Poland -- Bibliography.   Poland -- History -- Occupation, 1939-1945 -- Bibliography.

D765.2.W3.C48
Ciechanowski, Jan M.
The Warsaw Rising of 1944 [by] Jan M. Ciechanowski. [London, Cambridge University Press, 1974. xi, 332 p.
73-079315   940.53/438/4   0521202035
Warsaw (Poland) -- History -- Uprising of 1944.

D765.2.W3.P47 1995
Peszke, Michael Alfred.
Battle for Warsaw, 1939-1944/ Michael Alfred Peszke. Boulder: East European Monographs; 1995. xi, 325 p.
95-061204   940.54/21384   0880333243
World War, 1939-1945 -- Campaigns -- Poland -- Warsaw.   Warsaw (Poland) -- History, Military.

D766.D47 1990
D'Este, Carlo, 1936-
World War II in the Mediterranean, 1942-1945/ by Carlo D'Este; with an introduction by John S.D. Eisenhower. Chapel Hill, N.C.: Algonquin Books of Chapel Hill, 1990. xxii, 218 p.
90-000019   940.54/23   0945575041
World War, 1939-1945 -- Campaigns -- Mediterranean Region.

D766.J66 1996
Jones, Matthew, 1966-
Britain, the United States and the Mediterranean War, 1942-44/ Matthew Jones. Houndmills, Basingstoke, Hampshire: Macmillan Press; 1996. x, 293 p.
95-013256   940.54/21   0333611268
World War, 1939-1945 -- Campaigns -- Mediterranean Region.   Great Britain -- Military relations -- United States. United States -- Military relations -- Great Britain.

D766.4.H55 2000
Hlihor, Constantin.
The Red Army in Romania/ Constantin Hlihor and Ioan Scurtu. Iasi; Portland: Center for Romanian Studies, 2000. 288 p.
00-340784   940.54/09498   9739839258
World War, 1939-1945 -- Occupied territories. World War, 1939-1945 -- Soviet Union. World War, 1939-1945 -- Romania. Romania -- History -- 1914-1944. Romania -- History -- 1944-1989.

D766.7.C7.B44 1994
Beevor, Antony, 1946-
Crete: the battle and the resistance/ Antony Beevor. Boulder: Westview Press, 1994. xiii, 383 p.
93-047914   940.53/4959   0813320798
World War, 1939-1945 -- Campaigns -- Greece -- Crete. World War, 1939-1945 -- Underground movements -- Greece -- Crete.   Crete (Greece) -- History, Military.

D766.7.I7.S74 1988
Stewart, Richard A. 1950-
Sunrise at Abadan: the British and Soviet invasion of Iran, 1941/ Richard A. Stewart. New York: Praeger, 1988. xii, 291 p.
88-009720   940.53/55   0275927938
World War, 1939-1945 -- Campaigns -- Iran. World War, 1939-1945 -- Influence. Great Britain -- Foreign relations -- Iran. Soviet Union -- Foreign relations -- Iran. Iran -- Foreign relations -- Great Britain.

D766.82.C5
Clark, Mark W. 1896-1984.
Calculated risk. New York, Harper [1950] 500 p.
50-010324   940.542
World War, 1939-1945 -- Campaigns -- Africa, North. World War, 1939-1945 -- Campaigns -- Italy.

D766.82.R65
Rommel, Erwin, 1891-1944.
The Rommel papers, edited by B.H. Liddell Hart, with the assistance of Lucie-Maria Rommel, Manfred Rommel, and Fritz Bayerlein. Translated by Paul Findlay. New York, Harcourt, Brace, 1953. xxx, 545 p.
53-005656   940.542
World War, 1939-1945 -- Campaigns -- Africa, North. World War, 1939-1945 -- Campaigns -- Italy.

D766.84.K47 1997
Kerslake, R. T.
Time and the hour: Nigeria, East Africa, and the Second World War/ R.T. Kerslake. London; Radcliffe Press; 1997. xv, 274 p.
97-181188   940.54/23   1860641547
Kerslake, R. T. -- (R. Trevor)   World War, 1939-1945 -- Campaigns -- Africa, Eastern. World War, 1939-1945 -- Personal narratives, British. Colonial administrators -- Nigeria, Northern -- Biography. Nigeria, Northern -- Politics and government -- 20th century.

D766.9.L83 1982b
Lucas, James Sidney.
War in the desert: the Eighth Army at El Alamein/ James Lucas. New York: Beaufort Books, c1982. 284 p.
83-006015   940.54/23   082530153X
El 'Alamein, Battle of, Egypt, 1942. World War, 1939-1945 -- Regimental histories -- Great Britain. World War, 1939-1945 -- Campaigns, -- Africa, North.

D767.C67 1982
Costello, John,
The Pacific War/ John Costello.1st Quill ed. New York: Quill, 1982, c1981. xi, 742 p.
82-015054   940.54/26.219   0688016200
World War, 1939-1945--Pacific Ocean.

D767.C75 1983
Cruickshank, Charles Greig.
SOE in the Far East/ Charles Cruickshank. Oxford; Oxford University Press, 1983. xv, 285 p.
83-235317   940.54/25   0192158732
World War, 1939-1945 -- Campaigns -- Asia, Southeastern. World War, 1939-1945 -- Commando operations -- Asia, Southeastern. Asia, Southeastern -- History -- 1945-

D767.D66 1991
Drea, Edward J., 1944-
MacArthur's ULTRA: codebreaking and the war against Japan, 1942-1945/ Edward J. Drea. Lawrence, Kan.: University Press of Kansas, c1991. p. cm.
91-016842   940.54/26   0700605045
MacArthur, Douglas, -- 1880-1964 -- Military leadership. World War, 1939-1945 -- Cryptography. World War, 1939-1945 -- Military intelligence -- Pacific Area. World War, 1939-1945 -- Campaigns -- Pacific Area. Pacific Area -- History.

D767.F3 1974
Fahey, James J.
Pacific war diary, 1942-1945 [by] James J. Fahey. Westport, Conn., Greenwood Press [1974, c1963] 404 p.
73-021341   940.54/59/73   0837161762
Fahey, James J. -- Diaries.   World War, 1939-1945 -- Naval operations, American. World War, 1939-1945 -- Pacific Ocean.

D767.G75 1998
Griffith, Thomas E.
MacArthur's airman: General George C. Kenney and the war in the southwest Pacific/ Thomas E. Griffith Jr. Lawrence, Kan.: University Press of Kansas, c1998. xiv, 338 p.
98-015696   940.54/4973   0700609091
Kenney, George C. -- (George Churchill), -- 1889-1977.   World War, 1939-1945 -- Aerial operations, American. World War, 1939-1945 -- Personal narratives, American. World War, 1939-1945 -- Campaigns -- Pacific Area.

D767.M67.A3 1988
Mountbatten of Burma, Louis Mountbatten, 1900-1979.
Personal diary of Admiral the Lord Louis Mountbatten, Supreme Allied Commander, South-East Asia, 1943-1946/ edited by Philip Ziegler. London: Collins, 1988. xiii, 357 p.
89-168080   941.082/092   0002176076
Mountbatten of Burma, Louis Mountbatten, -- Earl, -- 1900-1979 -- Diaries.   Admirals -- Great Britain -- Diaries. World War, 1939-1945 -- Personal narratives, British. World War, 1939-1945 -- Asia, Southeastern.

D767.S69 1985
Spector, Ronald H., 1943-
Eagle against the sun: the American war with Japan/ Ronald H. Spector. New York: Free Press, c1985. xvi, 589 p.
84-047888   940.54/26   0029303605
World War, 1939-1945 -- Campaigns -- Pacific Ocean. World War, 1939-1945 -- United States. World War, 1939-1945 -- Japan. United States -- History -- 1933-1945. Japan -- History -- 1912-1945.

D767.W67 1998
World War II in Asia and the Pacific and the war's aftermath, with general themes: a handbook of literature and research/ edited by Loyd E. Lee; foreword by Carol N. Gluck; Robin Higham, advisory editor. Westport, Conn.: Greenwood Press, 1998. xv, 507 p.
98-005348   940.54/25   0313293260
World War, 1939-1945 -- Asia. World War, 1939-1945 -- Pacific Area. World War, 1939-1945 -- Historiography.

D767.W68 2001
World War II in the Pacific: an encyclopedia/ Stanley Sandler, editor. New York: Garland Pub., 2000. p. cm.
00-061773   940.54/25/03   0815318839
World War, 1939-1945 -- Campaigns -- Pacific Ocean -- Encyclopedias.

D767.2.F4 1966
Feis, Herbert, 1893-1972.
The atomic bomb and the end of World War II. Princeton, N.J., Princeton University Press, 1966. vi, 213 p.
66-013312   940.5425
World War, 1939-1945 -- Japan.

D767.2.H29 1978
Havens, Thomas R. H.
Valley of darkness: the Japanese people and World War Two/ Thomas R. H. Havens. New York: Norton, c1978. xi, 280 p.
77-011115   940.53/52   0393056562
World War, 1939-1945 -- Japan.   Japan -- Social life and customs.

D767.2.R44 1997
Rees, David, 1928-
The defeat of Japan/ David Rees. Westport, Conn.: Praeger, 1997. x, 219 p.
97-003687   940.54/25   0275959554
World War, 1939-1945 -- Campaigns -- Pacific Ocean. World politics -- 1933-1945. Pacific Ocean -- History.

D767.2.W67 1998
Wetzler, Peter.
Hirohito and war: imperial tradition and military decision making in prewar Japan/ Peter Wetzler. Honolulu: University of Hawai'i Press, c1998. xi, 294 p.
97-029981   940.54/0952   082481925X
Hirohito, -- Emperor of Japan, -- 1901-   World War, 1939-1945 -- Japan. Military planning -- Japan. Japan -- Politics and government -- 1926-1945. Japan -- Intellectual life -- 20th century.

D767.25.H6.H3
Hachiya, Michihiko, 1903-
Hiroshima diary; the journal of a Japanese physician, August 6-September 30, 1945. Translated and edited by Warner Wells. Chapel Hill, University of North Carolina Press [1955] 238 p.
55-011686   940.544   0807840440
World War, 1939-1945 -- Japan -- Hiroshima-shi. Atomic bomb -- Physiological effect. Nuclear warfare -- Japan. Hiroshima-shi (Japan) -- Sanitary affairs.

D767.25.H6.H348 1996
Harwit, Martin, 1931-
An exhibit denied: lobbying the history of Enola Gay/ Martin Harwit. New York, NY: Copernicus, c1996. xxv, 477 p.
96-018676   940.54/25   0387947973
World War, 1939-1945 -- Japan -- Hiroshima-shi. Atomic bomb -- Moral and ethical aspects. Public history. United States -- Military policy -- Moral and ethical aspects. Hiroshima-shi (Japan) -- History -- Bombardment, 1945 -- Exhibitions.

D767.25.H6.H4 1946c
Hersey, John, 1914-
Hiroshima. New York, A. A. Knopf, 1946. 117 p.
46-011953   940.544
World War, 1939-1945 -- Japan -- Hiroshima-shi. Atomic bomb -- Blast effect. World War, 1939-1945 -- Japan -- Hiroshima-shi. Hiroshima-shi (Japan) -- History -- Bombardment, 1945.

D767.25.H6.H672 1990
Hiroshima: three witnesses/ edited and translated by Richard H. Minear. Princeton, N.J.: Princeton University Press, c1990. xiii, 393 p.
89-010460   940.54/25   0691055734
Hara, Tamiki, -- 1905-1951. Ota, Yoko, -- 1903-1963. Toge, Sankichi, -- 1917-1953. Japanese poetry -- 20th century.   Hiroshima-shi (Japan) -- History -- Bombardment, 1945 -- Personal narratives. Hiroshima-shi (Japan) -- History -- Bombardment, 1945 -- Poetry.

D767.25.H6.L4
Lifton, Robert Jay, 1926-
Death in life; survivors of Hiroshima. New York, Random House [1968, c1967] viii, 594 p.
67-022658   155.9/35
Nuclear warfare -- Psychological aspects. Hiroshima-shi (Japan) -- History -- Bombardment, 1945.

D767.25.H6.M23 1995
Maddox, Robert James.
Weapons for victory: the Hiroshima decision fifty years later/ Robert James Maddox. Columbia: University of Missouri Press, 1995. p. cm.
95-020129   940.54/25   0826210376
Atomic bomb -- History. Nuclear warfare -- Moral and ethical aspects. Hiroshima-shi (Japan) -- History -- Bombardment, 1945. United States -- Military policy. Nagasaki-shi (Japan) -- History -- Bombardment, 1945.

D767.25.H6.Y66 1999
Yoneyama, Lisa, 1959-
Hiroshima traces: time, space, and the dialectics of memory/ Lisa Yoneyama. Berkeley: Los Angeles: 1999. p. cm.
98-031739   940.54/25   0520085868
Hiroshima-shi (Japan) -- History -- Bombardment, 1945.

D767.3.L48 1998
Letcher, John Seymour, 1903-
Good-bye to old Peking: the wartime letters of U.S. Marine Captain John Seymour Letcher, 1937-1939/ edited by Roger B. Jeans & Katie Letcher Lyle. Athens: Ohio University Press, c1998. xx, 242 p.
97-049200   940.54/25   0821412280
Letcher, John Seymour, -- 1903- -- Correspondence.   World War, 1939-1945 -- Personal narratives, American. World War, 1939-1945 -- Campaigns -- China -- Beijing. Marines -- United States -- Correspondence. Beijing (China) -- History.

D767.4.M4
Mellnik, Stephen M. 1907-
Philippine diary, 1939-1945, by Steve Mellnik. Foreword by Carlos P. Romulo. New York, Van Nostrand Reinhold Co. [1969] 316 p.
77-083657   940.542/6
Mellnik, Stephen M. -- (Stephen Michael), -- 1907- -- Diaries.   World War, 1939-1945 -- Campaigns -- Philippines. World War, 1939-1945 -- Prisoners and prisons, Japanese. World War, 1939-1945 -- Personal narratives, American.

D767.4.R62 1991
Rogers, Paul P.
The bitter years: MacArthur and Sutherland/ Paul P. Rogers. New York: Praeger, 1991. xvi, 348 p.
90-036984   940.54/26   0275929191
MacArthur, Douglas, -- 1880-1964. Sutherland, Richard K. Rogers, Paul P. World War, 1939-1945 -- Personal narratives, American. World War, 1939-1945 -- Campaigns -- Philippines. Soldiers -- United States -- Biography.

D767.4.W3
Wainwright, Jonathan Mayhew, 1883-1953.
General Wainwright's story; the account of four years of humiliating defeat, surrender, and captivity/ by General Jonathan M. Wainwright, who paid the price of his country's unpreparedness; edited by Robert Considine. Garden City, N. Y.: Doubleday & co., 1946. 314 p.
46-002757   940.542
Wainwright, Jonathan Mayhew, -- 1883-1953. World War, 1939-1945 -- Philippines -- Bataan (Province). World War, 1939-1945 -- Personal narratives, American. World War, 1939-1945 -- Prisoners and prisons, Japanese.

D767.4.Y69 1992
Young, Donald J., 1930-
The Battle of Bataan: a history of the 90 day siege and eventual surrender of 75,000 Filipino and United States troops to the Japanese in World War II/ by Donald J. Young. Jefferson, N.C.: McFarland, c1992. xiii, 381 p.
92-050326   940.54/25   0899507573
Bataan (Philippines: Province), Battle of, 1942.

D767.6.D58 1971
Dorn, Frank.
Walkout; with Stilwell in Burma.   New York, Crowell [1971] viii, 258 p.
71-158704   940.542/5/0924   0690866178
Dorn, Frank. Stilwell, Joseph Warren, -- 1883-1946. World War, 1939-1945 -- Campaigns -- Burma.

D767.6.S74 1972
Stilwell, Joseph Warren, 1883-1946.
The Stilwell papers. Arr. and edited by Theodore H. White. New York, Schocken Books [1972, c1948] xvi, 357 p.
76-185316   940.54/25/0924
Stilwell, Joseph Warren, -- 1883-1946. World War, 1939-1945 -- Campaigns -- Burma. World War, 1939-1945 -- China. World War, 1939-1945 -- Personal narratives, American.

D767.6.T354 2000
Tamayama, Kazuo.
Tales by Japanese soldiers: of the Burma campaign, 1942-1945/ Kazuo Tamayama and John Nunneley. London: Cassell, 2000. 254 p.
0304355283
World War, 1939-1945 -- Campaigns -- Burma. World War, 1939-1945 -- Personal narratives, Japanese. Burma -- History -- Japanese occupation, 1942-1945.

D767.63.F39 1993
Fay, Peter Ward, 1924-
The forgotten army: India's armed struggle for independence, 1942-1945/ Peter Ward Fay. Ann Arbor: University of Michigan Press, c1993. ix, 573 p.
93-006005   954.03/59   0472101269
World War, 1939-1945 -- India. India -- History -- Autonomy and independence movements.

D767.8.D39 1991
Day, David, 1949-
Reluctant nation: Australia and the Allied defeat of Japan, 1942-45/ David Day. South Melbourne, Australia; Oxford University Press, 1992. x, 366 p.
92-205260   940.54/0994   0195532422
World War, 1939-1945 -- Australia. World War, 1939-1945 -- Japan. World War, 1939-1945 -- Campaigns -- Pacific Area.

D767.8.J62 1996
Johnston, Mark, 1960-
At the front line: experiences of Australian soldiers in World War II/ Mark Johnston. Cambridge [England]; Cambridge University Press, 1996. xx, 261 p.
96-006066   940.54/8194   0521560373
World War, 1939-1945 -- Campaigns. Soldiers -- Australia -- Biography. World War, 1939-1945 -- Personal narratives, Australian.

D767.85.K48 2000
Kia Kaha: New Zealand in the Second World War/ edited by John Crawford. Auckland, N.Z.; Oxford University Press, 2000. xiv, 330 p.
00-364651   940.53/93   0195584384
World War, 1939-1945 -- New Zealand -- Congresses. New Zealand -- History -- 1918-1945 -- Congresses.

D767.9.D86 1998
Dunnigan, James F.
The Pacific war encyclopedia/ James F. Dunnigan and Albert A. Nofi. New York: Facts On File, c1998. 2 v.
97-015634   940.54/099   0816034397
World War, 1939-1945 -- Pacific Area -- Encyclopedias.

D767.9.W42 1988
We shall return!: MacArthur's commanders and the defeat of Japan, 1942-1945/ William M. Leary, editor. Lexington, Ky.: University Press of Kentucky, c1988. xi, 305 p.
88-002731   940.54/26/0924   0813116546
MacArthur, Douglas, -- 1880-1964. World War, 1939-1945 -- Campaigns -- Pacific Area. United States -- Armed Forces -- Biography.

D767.92.P398 1990
Pearl Harbor reexamined: prologue to the Pacific war/ edited by Hilary Conroy and Harry Wray. Honolulu: University of Hawaii Press, c1990. xix, 200 p.
89-037487   940.54/21   0824812352
Pearl Harbor (Hawaii), Attack on, 1941.

D767.92.P7215 1988
Prange, Gordon William, 1910-
December 7, 1941: the day the Japanese attacked Pearl Harbor/ Gordon W. Prange with Donald M. Goldstein and Katherine V. Dillon. New York: McGraw-Hill, c1988. xvi, 493 p.
87-003019   940.54/26   0070506825
Pearl Harbor (Hawaii), Attack on, 1941.

D767.92.R38 1991
Remembering Pearl Harbor: eyewitness accounts by U.S. military men and women/ edited by Robert S. La Forte, Ronald E. Marcello. Wilmington, Del.: SR Books, 1991. xxi, 303 p.
90-040179   940.54/26   0842023712
Pearl Harbor (Hawaii), Attack on, 1941 -- Personal narratives, American.

D767.92.S835 1984
Stephan, John J.
Hawaii under the rising sun: Japan's plans for conquest after Pearl Harbor/ John J. Stephan. Honolulu: University of Hawaii Press, c1984. xii, 228 p.
83-009101   940.54/0952   082480872X
World War, 1939-1945 -- Hawaii. World War, 1939-1945 -- Japan. Japan -- Military policy. Hawaii -- History -- 1900-1959.

D767.95.T316 1998
Taaffe, Stephen R.
MacArthur's jungle war: the 1944 New Guinea campaign/ Stephen R. Taaffe. Lawrence, Kan.: University Press of Kansas, c1998. xiii, 312 p.
97-025228   940.54/26   0700608702
MacArthur, Douglas, -- 1880-1964. World War, 1939-1945 -- Campaigns -- New Guinea.

D767.98.C53 1998
Clemens, Martin, 1915-
Alone on Guadalcanal: a coastwatcher's story/ Martin Clemens. Annapolis, Md.: Naval Institute Press, 1998. xviii, 343 p.
98-034092   940.54/26   155750122X
Clemens, Martin, -- 1915- World War, 1939-1945 -- Campaigns -- Solomon Islands -- Guadalcanal. World War, 1939-1945 -- Personal narratives, British. Military service, Voluntary -- United States.

D767.98.F73 1990
Frank, Richard B.
Guadalcanal/ Richard B. Frank. New York: Random House, c1990. xiv, 800 p.
90-008265   940.54/26   0394588754
Guadalcanal (Solomon Islands), Battle of, 1942-1943.

D767.98.M87 2000
Murray, Williamson.
A war to be won: fighting the Second World War, 1937-1945/ Williamson Murray, Allan R. Millett. Cambridge, Mass.: Belknap Press of Harvard University Press, 2000. xiv, 656 p.
99-086624   940.53   067400163X
World War, 1939-1945.

D767.98.R37 1997
Rasor, Eugene L., 1936-
The Solomon Islands campaign, Guadalcanal to Rabaul: historiography and annotated bibliography/ Eugene L. Rasor. Westport, Conn.: Greenwood Press, 1997. xvi, 146 p.
96-041333   940.54/26   0313300593
World War, 1939-1945 -- Campaigns -- Solomon Islands -- Historiography. World War, 1939-1945 -- Campaigns -- Solomon Islands -- Bibliography.

D767.98.T7 1955
Tregaskis, Richard, 1916-1973.
Guadalcanal diary.   New York: Random House, 1943. 180 p.
55-005820   940.542
World War, 1939-1945 -- Campaigns -- Solomon Islands. World War, 1939-1945 -- Personal narratives, American. U.S. Marine Corps.

D767.99.B68.G35 1991
Gailey, Harry A.
Bougainville, 1943-1945: the forgotten campaign/ Harry A. Gailey. Lexington, Ky.: University Press of Kentucky, c1991. 237 p.
90-028496   940.54/26   0813117488
World War, 1939-1945 -- Campaigns -- Papua New Guinea -- Bougainville Island. Bougainville Island (Papua New Guinea) -- History.

D767.99.I9.A4 1995
Albee, Parker Bishop.
Shadow of Suribachi: raising the flags on Iwo Jima/ Parker Bishop Albee, Jr. and Keller Cushing Freeman. Westport, Conn.: Praeger, 1995. xvii, 174 p.
94-034304   940.54/26   0275950638
Iwo Jima, Battle of, 1945.

D767.99.I9.H38 1988
Hemingway, Albert, 1950-
Ira Hayes, Pima Marine/ by Albert Hemingway. Lanham, MD: University Press of America, c1988. p. cm.
  88-020684 940.54/03 0819171700
Hayes, Ira, -- 1923-1955.   Pima Indians -- Biography. Iwo Jima, Battle of, 1945. Soldiers -- United States -- Biography.

D767.99.I9.M28 1991
Marling, Karal Ann.
Iwo Jima: monuments, memories, and the American hero/ Karal Ann Marling and John Wetenhall. Cambridge, Mass.: Harvard University Press, 1991. 300 p.
  90-042283 940.54/26 0674469801
Iwo Jima, Battle of, 1945. Propaganda, American -- History -- 20th century.

D767.99.W3.C74 1995
Cressman, Robert.
A magnificent fight: the battle for Wake Island/ Robert J. Cressman. Annapolis, Md.: Naval Institute Press, c1995. xiv, 324 p.
  94-032013 940.54/26 1557501408
Wake Island, Battle of, 1941.

D767.99.W3.U78 1997
Urwin, Gregory J. W., 1955-
Facing fearful odds: the siege of Wake Island/ Gregory J.W. Urwin. Lincoln: University of Nebraska Press, c1997. xxiii, 727 p.
  96-054887 940.54/26 0803245556
Wake Island, Battle of, 1941.

D767.99 M53
Poyer, Lin, 1953-
The typhoon of war: Micronesian experiences of the Pacific war/ Lin Poyer, Suzanne Falgout, Laurence Marshall Carucci. Honolulu: University of Hawai'i Press, c2001. xiii, 493 p.
  00-029875 940.54/26 0824821688
World War, 1939-1945 -- Campaigns -- Micronesia (Federated States) World War, 1939-1945 -- Naval operations, American. Micronesia (Federated States) -- History.

D768.15.C62 1992
Coates, Kenneth, 1956-
The Alaska Highway in World War II: the U.S. Army of occupation in Canada's Northwest/ K.S. Coates and W.R. Morrison. Norman: University of Oklahoma Press, c1992. xix, 309 p.
  91-050861 940.53/7191 0806124253
World War, 1939-1945 -- Northwest, Canadian. Alaska Highway -- History. Northwest, Canadian -- History.

D768.18.B39 1988
Baptiste, Fitzroy Andre.
War, cooperation, and conflict: the European possessions in the Caribbean, 1939-1945/ Fitzroy Andre Baptiste. New York: Greenwood Press, 1988. xiv, 351 p.
  87-008643 940.53/3 0313254729
World War, 1939-1945 -- Caribbean Area. World War, 1939-1945 -- Economic aspects -- Caribbean Area.

D769.A533 vol. 1, pt. 1
Greenfield, Kent Roberts, 1893-
The organization of ground combat troops, by Kent Roberts Greenfield, Robert R. Palmer and Bell I. Wiley. Washington, Historical Division, Dept. of the Army, 1947. xvii, 540 p.
  50-014024 355
United States. Army -- Organization. United States. Army -- Mobilization.

D769.A533 vol. 1, pt. 2
Palmer, R. R. 1909-
The procurement and training of ground combat troops, by Robert R. Palmer, Bell I. Wiley and William R. Keast. Washington, Office of the Chief of Military History, Dept. o 1948. xi, 696 p.
  50-013989 355.22
Military education -- United States.

D769.A533 vol. 2, pt. 3
Miller, John, 1915-
Guadalcanal: the first offensive. Washington, Historical Division, Dept. of the Army, 1949. xviii, 413 p.
  50-013988 940.542
World War, 1939-1945 -- Campaigns -- Solomon Islands -- Guadalcanal.

D769.A533 v.2, pt.5
Cannon, M. Hamlin.
Leyte: the return to the Philippines/ by M. Hamlin Cannon. Washington: Office of the Chief of Military History, Dept. o 1954. xvi, 420 p.
  53-061979 940.542
World War, 1939-1945 -- Campaigns -- Philippines -- Leyte.

D769.A533 vol. 3, pt. 1
Cole, Hugh M.
The Lorraine campaign. Washington, Historical Division, Dept. of the Army, 1950. xxi, 657 p.
  50-060957 940.542
World War, 1939-1945 -- Campaigns -- France, Southern.

D769.A533 vol. 3, pt. 2
Harrison, Gordon A.
Cross-channel attack. Washington, Office of the Chief of Military History, Dept. o 1951. xvii, 519 p.
  51-061669 940.542
World War, 1939-1945 -- Campaigns -- France -- Normandy. World War, 1939-1945 -- Amphibious operations.

D769.A533 vol. 8, pt. 4
Dziuban, Stanley W.
Military relations between the United States and Canada, 1939-1945. Washington, Office of the Chief of Military History, Dept. o 1959. xv, 432 p.
  59-060001 940.532
World War, 1939-1945 -- Canada. Canada -- Relations (military) with the United States. -- cm United States -- Relations (military) with Canada. -- cm

D769.A56 1994
Adams, Michael C. C., 1945-
The best war ever: America and World War II/ Michael C.C. Adams. Baltimore: Johns Hopkins University Press, c1994. xvii, 189 p.
  93-004364 940.53/73 080184696X
World War, 1939-1945 -- United States. United States -- History -- 1933-1945.

D769.E55 1997
Eiler, Keith E., 1920-
Mobilizing America: Robert P. Patterson and the war effort, 1940-1945/ Keith E. Eiler. Ithaca: Cornell University Press, 1997. xvi, 588 p.
  97-024827 940.53/73 0801422760
Patterson, Robert Porter, -- 1891-1952. World War, 1939-1945 -- War work -- United States. World War, 1939-1945 -- United States. Cabinet officers -- United States -- Biography.

D769.L4
Leahy, William D.
I was there; the personal story of the Chief of Staff to Presidents Roosevelt and Truman, based on his notes and diaries made at the time. With a foreword by President Truman. New York, Whittlesey House [1950] 527 p.
  50-006546 940.5373
World War, 1939-1945 -- United States. World War, 1939-1945 -- Personal narratives, American.

D769.M34 1999
Mansoor, Peter R., 1960-
The GI offensive in Europe: the triumph of American infantry divisions, 1941-1945/ Peter R. Mansoor. Lawrence, Kan.: University Press of Kansas, c1999. xiv, 346 p.
  98-055249 940.54/1273 070060958X
World War, 1939-1945 -- Campaigns -- Western Front. World War, 1939-1945 -- Regimental histories -- United States.

D769.O64 1993
O'Neill, William L.
A democracy at war: America's fight at home and abroad in World War II/ William L. O'Neill. New York: Free Press; c1993. ix, 480 p.
  93-015677 940.54/0973 0029236789
World War, 1939-1945 -- United States. United States -- History -- 1933-1945.

D769.T42 2000
Takaki, Ronald T., 1939-
Double victory: a multicultural history of America in World War II/ Ronald Takaki. Boston: Little, Brown and Co., c2000. vi, 282 p.
  99-040374 940.53/73 0316831557
World War, 1939-1945 -- United States. Racism -- United States. United States -- Race relations.

D769.1.D64 1997
Doenecke, Justus D.
The battle against intervention, 1939-1941/ by Justus D. Doenecke. Malabar, Fla.: Krieger Pub. Co., 1997. viii, 213 p.
  96-018599 940.54/0973 0894649019
World War, 1939-1945 -- United States. Neutrality -- United States. United States -- Politics and government -- 1933-1945.

D769.1.S76 2000
Stoler, Mark A.
Allies and adversaries: the Joint Chiefs of Staff, the Grand Alliance, and U.S. strategy in World War II/ Mark A. Stoler. Chapel Hill: University of North Carolina Press, c2000. xxii, 380 p.
  00-032589 940.54/012 0807825573
World War, 1939-1945 -- United States. Strategy -- History -- 20th century. Civil-military relations -- United States. United States -- Military relations -- Foreign countries. United States -- Foreign relations -- 1933-1945.

D769.1.W35 1996
Wainstock, Dennis, 1947-
The decision to drop the atomic bomb/ Dennis D. Wainstock. Westport, Conn.: Praeger, 1996. x, 180 p.
  95-042965 940.54/0973 0275954757
Truman, Harry S., -- 1884-1972. World War, 1939-1945 -- Japan. Atomic bomb. World War, 1939-1945 -- United States. United States -- Foreign relations -- 1945-1953.

D769.2.A48 1995
Allen, Thomas B.
Code-name downfall: the secret plan to invade Japan and why Truman dropped the bomb/ Thomas B. Allen and Norman Polmar. New York: Simon & Schuster, 1995. 368 p.
95-010418   940.54/4973   0684804069
World War, 1939-1945 -- United States. World War, 1939-1945 -- Japan. Strategy.

D769.2.M36 1998
McManus, John C., 1965-
The deadly brotherhood: the American combat soldier in World War II/ John C. McManus. Novato, CA: Presidio, c1998. xiv, 353 p.
97-050358   940.54/1273/0922   0891416552
World War, 1939-1945 -- Personal narratives, American. Soldiers -- United States -- Psychology.

D769.2.S34 1998
Schrijvers, Peter, 1963-
The crash of ruin: American combat soldiers in Europe during World War II/ Peter Schrijvers. New York: New York University Press, 1998. xiii, 325 p.
97-014751   940.53/114   081478089X
World War, 1939-1945 -- Campaigns -- Western Front. Soldiers -- United States -- Psychology. World War, 1939-1945 -- Psychological aspects.

D769.31 45th.W45 1998
Whitlock, Flint.
The rock of Anzio: from Sicily to Dachau, a history of the 45th Infantry Division/ Flint Whitlock. Boulder, Colo.: Westview Press, 1998. xvi, 479 p.
98-009185   940.54/1273   0813333997
World War, 1939-1945 -- Regimental histories -- United States.

D769.347.O36 2001
O'Donnell, Patrick K., 1969-
Beyond valor: World War II's Ranger and Airborne veterans reveal the heart of combat/ Patrick K. O'Donnell. New York: Free Press, c2001. xvii, 366 p.
00-061049   940.54/21   0684873842
World War, 1939-1945 -- Commando operations -- United States. World War, 1939-1945 -- Regimental histories -- United States. World War, 1939-1945 -- Campaigns -- Western Front.

D769.45.L67 1995
Lorelli, John A., 1946-
To foreign shores: U.S. amphibious operations in World War II/ John A. Lorelli. Annapolis, Md.: Naval Institute Press, c1995 xix, 362 p.
94-032014   940.54/5   1557505209
World war, 1939-1945 -- Amphibious operations.

D769.8.A6.A67 1984
And justice for all: an oral history of the Japanese American detention camps/ [compiled by] John Tateishi. New York: Random House, c1984. xxvii, 259 p.
82-042823   940.54/72/73   0394539826
Japanese Americans -- Evacuation and relocation, 1942-1945. World War, 1939-1945 -- Personal narratives, American.

D769.8.A6.F49 1997
Fiset, Louis.
Imprisoned apart: the World War II correspondence of an Issei couple/ Louis Fiset. Seattle: University of Washington Press, c1997. xvi, 299 p.
97-029984   940.53/089956   0295976454
Matsushita, Iwao, -- 1892-1979. Matsushita, Hanaye, -- 1898 or 9-1965. Japanese Americans -- Correspondence. Japanese Americans -- Evacuation and relocation, 1942-1945.

D769.8.A6.F66 1990
Fox, Stephen C.
The unknown internment: an oral history of the relocation of Italian Americans during World War II/ Stephen Fox. Boston: Twayne Publishers, c1990. xix, 223 p.
89-078474   940.53/150351073   0805791086
World War, 1939-1945 -- Italian Americans. Italian Americans -- Relocation -- History -- 20th century. Italian Americans -- Interviews.

D769.8.A6.H58 1999
Hirabayashi, Lane Ryo.
The politics of fieldwork: research in an American concentration camp/ Lane Ryo Hirabayashi. Tucson: University of Arizona Press, c1999. xii, 219 p.
98-025489   940.54/7273/0979172   0816518645
World War, 1939-1945 -- Concentration camps -- Arizona -- Poston -- Research. Japanese Americans -- Evacuation and relocation, 1942-1945 -- Research. Poston (Ariz.) -- History -- Research.

D769.8.A6.J345 1987
James, Thomas, 1948-
Exile within: the schooling of Japanese Americans, 1942-1945/ Thomas James. Cambridge, Mass.: Harvard University Press, c1987. viii, 212 p.
86-025792   370/.89956/073   0674275268
Japanese Americans -- Evacuation and relocation, 1942-1945. Japanese Americans -- Education -- History -- 20th century.

D769.8.A6.J36
Japanese American evacuation and resettlement. Berkeley, University of California Press, 1946-54. 3 v.
47-001448   365/.34
Japanese Americans -- Evacuation and relocation, 1942-1945.

D769.8.A6.K73 1997
Krammer, Arnold, 1941-
Undue process: the untold story of America's German alien internees/ Arnold Krammer. London; Rowman & Littlefield, c1997. xi, 209 p.
97-008365   940.53/08931073   0847685187
World War, 1939-1945 -- German Americans. World War, 1939-1945 -- Prisoners and prisons, American.

D769.8.A6.O36 1996
Okihiro, Gary Y., 1945-
Whispered silences: Japanese Americans and World War II/ essay by Gary Y. Okihiro; photographs by Joan Myers. Seattle: University of Washington Press, 1996. 249 p.
95-021895   940.53/1503956073   0295974974
Japanese Americans -- Evacuation and relocation, 1942-1945. World War, 1939-1945 -- Concentration camps -- United States. World War, 1939-1945 -- Personal narratives, American.

D769.8.F7.G47 1996
Holian, Timothy J., 1965-
The German-Americans and World War II: an ethnic experience/ Timothy J. Holian. New York: P. Lang, c1996. xii, 243 p.
95-050143   940.53/150331073   0820430749
World War, 1939-1945 -- German Americans. United States -- Ethnic relations.

D769.85.A21
Newton, Wesley Phillips.
Montgomery in the good war: portrait of a southern city, 1939-1946/ Wesley Phillips Newton; introduction by Allen Cronenberg. Tuscaloosa: University of Alabama Press, c2000. xxix, 321 p.
00-008741   940.53/76147   0817310436
World War, 1939-1945 -- Alabama -- Montgomery. World War, 1939-1945 -- Social aspects -- Alabama -- Montgomery. Montgomery (Ala.) -- History -- 20th century. Montgomery (Ala.) -- Social conditions -- 20th century.

D769.85.T21.N27 1998
Spinney, Robert G.
World War II in Nashville: transformation of the homefront/ Robert G. Spinney. Knoxville: University of Tennessee Press, c1998. xv, 209 p.
97-033759   976.8/55052   157233004X
World War, 1939-1945 -- Tennessee -- Nashville. Nashville (Tenn.) -- History.

D770 World War II (1939-1945)
— Naval operations
— General works.
Battle of the Atlantic

D770.B28 1991
Barnett, Correlli.
Engage the enemy more closely: the Royal Navy in the Second World War/ Correlli Barnett. New York: Norton, 1991. xviii, 1052 p
90-046009   940.54/5941   0393029182
World War, 1939-1945 -- Naval operations, British.

D770.B453 1951
Belot, Raymond de.
The struggle for the Mediterranean, 1939-1945; translated by James A. Field, Jr. Princeton, Princeton University Press, 1951. xix, 287 p.
51-012459   940.545
World War, 1939-1945 -- Mediterranean Sea. World War, 1939-1945 -- Naval operations. World War, 1939-1945 -- Aerial operations.

D770.G37 1999
Gardner, W. J. R.
Decoding history: the battle of the Atlantic and Ultra. Annapolis, Md.: Naval Institute Press, 1999. xvii, 263 p.
99-074458
World War, 1939-1945 -- Campaigns -- Atlantic Ocean.

D770.M49 1995
Miller, Nathan, 1927-
War at sea: a naval history of World War II/ Nathan Miller. New York: Scribner, c1995. 592 p. [16]
95-008484   940.54/5   0684803801
World War, 1939-1945 -- Naval operations.

D770.N6
Norman, Albert, 1914-
Operation Overlord, design and reality; the Allied invasion of Western Europe. Harrisburg, Pa., Military Service Pub. Co. [c1952] xiv, 230 p.
52-009983   940.542
World War, 1939-1945 -- Naval operations. World War, 1939-1945 -- Campaigns -- France. World War, 1939-1945 -- Amphibious operations.

D770.R833
Ruge, Friedrich.
Der Seekrieg; the German Navy's story, 1939-1945. Translated by M. G. Saunders. Annapolis, U.S. Naval Institute [1957] 440 p.
57-014768   940.545
World War, 1939-1945 -- Naval operations.

D770.V28 1988
Van der Vat, Dan.
The Atlantic campaign: World War II's great struggle at sea/ Dan van der Vat; with research by Christine van der Vat. New York: Harper & Row, c1988. xvi, 424 p.
88-045067   940.54/5   0060159677
World War, 1939-1945 -- Campaigns -- Atlantic Ocean. World War, 1939-1945 -- Naval operations.

D771-772 World War II (1939-1945) — Naval operations — Anglo-German

D771.C513 1993
The Churchill war papers/ [compiled by] Martin Gilbert. New York: W.W. Norton, c1993-1995 v. 1-2
92-044367   940.54/5941   0393035220
Churchill, Winston, -- Sir, -- 1874-1965 -- Archives. World War, 1939-1945 -- Sources. World War, 1939-1945 -- Naval operations, British -- Sources.

D771.E95 1999
Evans, Mark Llewellyn.
Great World War II battles in the Arctic/ Mark Llewellyn Evans. Westport, Conn.: Greenwood Press, 1999. 165 p.
98-044594   940.54/5941   0313308926
World War, 1939-1945 -- Naval operations, British. World War, 1939-1945 -- Naval operations, German. World War, 1939-1945 -- Arctic Ocean. Arctic Ocean -- History, Military.

D771.M29 1998
Madsen, Chris, 1968-
The Royal Navy and German naval disarmament, 1942-1947/ Chris Madsen. London; F. Cass, 1998. xx, 277 p.
97-030156   359/.00943/09044   071464823X
Disarmament. Germany -- Military relations -- Great Britain. Great Britain -- Military relations -- Germany.

D771.W38 1958
Wheatley, Ronald.
Operation Sea Lion; German plans for the invasion of England, 1939-1942. Oxford, Clarendon Press, 1958. viii, 201 p.
58-002322   940.542
Operation Sea Lion.

D772.R62.J33 1997
Jackson, Carlton.
Forgotten tragedy: the sinking of HMT Rohna/ Carlton Jackson. Annapolis, Md.: Naval Institute Press, c1997. xvii, 207 p.
96-039333   940.54/21   1557504024
World War, 1939-1945 -- Naval operations, British. World War, 1939-1945 -- Transportation.

D772.3 World War II (1939-1945) — Naval operations — Russian-German

D772.3.L47 1993
Leonov, V. N.
Blood on the shores: Soviet naval commandos in World War II/ Viktor Leonov; translated, with introduction and notes, by James F. Gebhardt. Annapolis, M.D.: Naval Institute Press, c1993. xiv, 212 p.
93-027869   940.54/5947   1557505063
Leonov, V. N. -- (Viktor Nikolaevich) World War, 1939-1945 -- Commando operations. Military scouts -- Soviet Union -- Biography. World War, 1939-1945 -- Naval operations, Russian.

D773-774 World War II (1939-1945) — Naval operations — United States

D773.B53
Riesenberg, Felix, 1913-
Sea war; the story of the U. S. merchant marine in World War II. New York, Rinehart [1956] 320 p.
56-007259   940.545
World War, 1939-1945 -- Naval operations, American. Merchant marine -- United States.

D773.C74 2000
Cressman, Robert.
The official chronology of the U.S. Navy in World War II/ Robert J. Cressman. Annapolis, Md.: Naval Institute Press, 2000. ix, 367 p.
99-039136   940.54/5973/0202   1557501491
World War, 1939-1945 -- Naval operations, American -- Chronology.

D773.M6
Morison, Samuel Eliot
History of United States naval operations in World War II/ by Samuel Eliot Morison. Boston: Little, Brown, 1947-1962. 15 v.
47-001571   940.545973
World War, 1939-1945 -- Naval operations, American.

D773.M62
Morison, Samuel Eliot, 1887-1976.
The two ocean war, a short history of the United States Navy in the Second World War. Boston, Little, Brown [1963] 611 p.
63-008307   940.545973
World War, 1939-1945 -- Naval operations, American.

D773.N495 1999
Newton, Adolph W., 1925-
Better than good: a Black sailor's war, 1943-1945/ Adolph W. Newton, with Winston Eldridge. Annapolis, Md.: Naval Institute Press, c1999. 182 p.
98-038939   940.54/5973/092   1557506493
Newton, Adolph W., -- 1925- World War, 1939-1945 -- Personal narratives, American. World War, 1939-1945 -- Naval operations, American. Afro-American sailors -- Biography.

D773.W48
Willoughby, Malcolm Francis.
The U.S. Coast Guard in World War II. Annapolis, United States Naval Institute [1957] xvii, 347 p.
57-009314   940.545973
World War, 1939-1945 -- Naval operations.

D774.M5.F812
Fuchida, Mitsuo, 1902-
Midway, the battle that doomed Japan: the Japanese Navy's story/ by Mitsuo Fuchida and Masatake Okumiya; Edited by Clarke H. Kawakami and Roger Pineau, with a foreword by Raymond A. Spruance. [Annapolis]: Naval Institute, [1955] 266 p.
55-009027   940.545   0870213725
Midway, Battle of, 1942. World War, 1939-1945 -- Personal narratives, Japanese. World War, 1939-1945 -- Naval operations, Japanese.

D774.M5.P7 1982
Prange, Gordon William, 1910-
Miracle at Midway/ Gordon W. Prange, Donald M. Goldstein and Katherine V. Dillon. New York: McGraw-Hill, c1982. xvii, 469 p.
82-004691   940.54/26   0070506728
Midway, Battle of, 1942.

D777-777.5 World War II (1939-1945) — Naval operations — Japan

D777.U3513 1991
Ugaki, Matome, 1890-1945.
Fading victory: the diary of Admiral Matome Ugaki, 1941-1945/ Masataka Chihaya, translator, with Donald M. Goldstein and Katherine V. Dillon; foreword by Gordon W. Prange. Pittsburgh, Pa.: University of Pittsburgh Press, c1991. xvii, 731 p.
90-012904   940.54/5952/092   0822954621
Ugaki, Matome, -- 1890-1945 -- Diaries. World War, 1939-1945 -- Personal narratives, Japanese. Admirals -- Japan -- Diaries. World War, 1939-1945 -- Naval operations, Japanese.

D777.5.A92.D56 1997
Dingman, Roger,
Ghost of war: the sinking of the Awa Maru and Japanese-American relations, 1945-1995/ Roger Dingman. Annapolis, Md.: Naval Institute Press, c1997. xv, 373 p.
97-025742   940.54/5952   1557501599
World War, 1939-1945 -- Naval operations, Japanese. World War, 1939-1945 -- Naval operations -- Submarine. World War, 1939-1945 -- Naval operations, American. Japan -- Foreign relations -- United States. United States -- Foreign relations -- Japan.

D779 World War II (1939-1945) — Naval operations — Other regions or countries, A-Z

D779.C2.M55 1985
Milner, Marc.
North Atlantic run: the Royal Canadian Navy and the battle for the convoys/ Marc Milner. Annapolis, Md.: Naval Institute Press, c1985. xxiii, 326 p.
85-060967   940.54/5971   0870214500
World War, 1939-1945 -- Naval operations, Canadian. Naval convoys -- Canada -- History -- 20th century. World War, 1939-1945 -- Campaigns -- Atlantic Ocean.

D780 World War II (1939-1945) — Submarine operations — General works

D780.S96 1994
Syrett, David.
The defeat of the German U-boats: the Battle of the Atlantic/ David Syrett. Columbia, S.C.: University of South Carolina Press, c1994. xiv, 344 p.
93-044333   940.54/516/09163   0872499847
World War, 1939-1945 -- Naval operations -- Submarine. World War, 1939-1945 -- Campaigns - - Atlantic Ocean. Anti-submarine warfare -- History.

D781 World War II (1939-1945) — Submarine operations — Germany

D781.B53 1996
Blair, Clay, 1925-
Hitler's U-boat war, 1939-1942/ Clay Blair. New York: Random House, c1996- v. 1-
96-002275   940.54/51
World War, 1939-1945 -- Naval operations -- Submarine. World War, 1939-1945 -- Naval operations, German.

D781.G36 1990
Gannon, Michael, 1927-
Operation Drumbeat: the dramatic true story of Germany's first U-boat attacks along the American coast in World War II/ Michael Gannon. New York: Harper & Row, c1990. xxii, 490 p.
89-046090   940.54/51   0060161558
World War, 1939-1945 -- Naval operations -- Submarine. World War, 1939-1945 -- Naval operations, German. World War, 1939-1945 -- Campaigns -- North Atlantic Ocean. Atlantic Coast (North America) -- History -- 20th century.

D781.M85 1999
Mulligan, Timothy.
Neither sharks nor wolves: the men of Nazi Germany's U-boat arm, 1939-1945/ Timothy P. Mulligan. Annapolis, Md.: Naval Institute Press, c1999. xxv, 340 p.
98-053659   940.54/51   1557505942
World War, 1939-1945 -- Naval operations -- Submarine. World War, 1939-1945 -- Naval operations, German.

D781.W54 1995
Wiggins, Melanie, 1934-
Torpedoes in the Gulf: Galveston and the U-boats, 1942-1943/ Melanie Wiggins. College Station: Texas A&M University Press, c1995. xiii, 265 p.
94-031861   940.54/51   0890966273
World War, 1939-1945 -- Naval operations -- Submarine. World War, 1939-1945 -- Naval operations, German. World War, 1939-1945 -- Campaigns -- Mexico, Gulf of. Galveston (Tex.) -- History.

D785 World War II (1939-1945) — Aerial operations — General works

D785.G3
Nigro, August J., 1934-
Wolfsangel: a German city on trial, 1945-48/ August Nigro. Washington, DC: Brassey's, c2000. p. cm.
00-029251   940.53/43416   1574882457
World War, 1939-1945 -- Germany -- Russelsheim. World War, 1939-1945 -- Prisoners and prisons, German. World War, 1939-1945 -- Atrocities.

D785.G58 1998
Gooderson, Ian.
Air power at the battlefront: allied close air support in Europe, 1943-45/ Ian Gooderson. London; F. Cass, 1998. xviii, 282 p.
97-019029   940.54/4   0714646806
World War, 1939-1945 -- Aerial operations.

D785.M39 1991
McFarland, Stephen Lee, 1950-
To command the sky: the battle for air superiority over Germany, 1942-1944/ Stephen L. McFarland and Wesley Phillips Newton. Washington: Smithsonian Institution Press, c1991. xiii, 328 p.
91-009712   940.54/4   1560980699
World War, 1939-1945 -- Aerial operations.

D785.O9
Overy, R. J.
The air war, 1939-1945/ R.J. Overy. New York: Stein and Day, c1980. xii, 263 p.
80-006200   940.54/4   0812827929
World War, 1939-1945 -- Aerial operations. Military history, Modern -- 20th century.

D785.V47 1968b.
Verrier, Anthony.
The bomber offensive.   New York] Macmillan [1969, c1968] x, 373 p.
76-075410   940.544/2
World War, 1939-1945 -- Aerial operations. Bombardment.

D786 World War II (1939-1945) — Aerial operations — Great Britain

D786.A77 1999
Ash, Eric, 1957-
Sir Frederick Sykes and the air revolution, 1912-1918/ Eric Ash. London; Frank Cass, 1999. xiv, 268 p.
98-022294   940.54/4941   0714648280
Sykes, Frederick Hugh, -- Sir, -- 1877-1954. World War, 1914-1918 -- Aerial operations, British.

D786.B718 1998
British Bombing Survey Unit.
The strategic air war against Germany, 1939-1945: report of the British Bombing Survey Unit/ with forewords by Michael Beetham and John W. Huston; and introductory material by Sebastian Cox. London; F. Cass, 1998. liv, xii, 195 p.
97-022017   940.54/4941   0714647225
World War, 1939-1945 -- Aerial operations, British. Bombing, Aerial -- Germany. Great Britain -- Military policy.

D786.G36 1993
Garrett, Stephen A., 1939-
Ethics and airpower in World War II: the British bombing of German cities/ Stephen A. Garrett. New York: St. Martin's Press, 1993. xvi, 256 p.
92-037119   940.54/4941   0312086830
World War, 1939-1945 -- Aerial operations, British -- Moral and ethical aspects. World War, 1939-1945 -- Moral and ethical aspects -- Germany. Germany -- History -- Bombardment, 1940-1945 -- Moral and ethical aspects. Great Britain -- Military policy -- Moral and ethical aspects.

D786.H318 1995
Harris, Arthur Travers, 1892-
Despatch on war operations, 23rd February, 1942, to 8th May, 1945/ Sir Arthur T. Harris; preface and introduction by Sebastian Cox; and Harris--a German view by Horst Boog. London; F. Cass, 1995. liv, 211 p.
95-033278   940.54/4941   071464692X
Harris, Arthur Travers, -- Sir, -- 1892- World War, 1939-1945 -- Aerial operations, British -- Sources. World War, 1939-1945 -- Campaigns -- Germany -- Sources.

D786.R49 1974
Richards, Denis.
Royal Air Force, 1939-1945/ [by Denis Richards and Hilary St. George Saunders]. London: H. M. S. O., 1974-1975. 3 v.
76-367101   940.54/49/41   0117715921
World War, 1939-1945 -- Aerial operations, British.

D786.T44 1985
Terraine, John.
A time for courage: the Royal Air Force in the European War, 1939-1945/ by John Terraine. New York, N.Y.: Macmillan, c1985. xix, 828 p.
84-017098   940.54/4941   0026169703
World War, 1939-1945 -- Aerial operations, British.

D786.W44 1995
Wells, Mark K., 1953-
Courage and air warfare: the Allied aircrew experience in the Second World War/ Mark K. Wells. Essex, England; F. Cass, c1995 xiv, 240 p.
95-003290   940.54/4941   0714646180
Flight crews -- Great Britain -- History. Flight crews -- United States -- History. World War, 1939-1945 -- Aerial operations, British.

D787 World War II (1939-1945) — Aerial operations — Germany

D787.M5 1960a
Middleton, Drew, 1913-
The sky suspended; the Battle of Britain. London, Secker & Warburg [1960] 255 p.
61-002011
Britain, Battle of, 1940.

D787.M56 1988
Mitcham, Samuel W.
Men of the Luftwaffe/ Samuel W. Mitcham, Jr. Novato, CA: Presidio, c1988. vii, 356 p.
88-006021   940.54/49/43   0891413081
World War, 1939-1945 -- Aerial operations, German.

D788 World War II (1939-1945) — Aerial operations — France

D788.S3 1979
Saint Exupery, Antoine de, 1900-1944.
Pilote de guerre/ Antoine de Saint-Exupery; ill. originales de Romain Slocombe. [Paris?: Bibliotheque des chefs-d'oeuvre, 1979] 228 p.
80-116816   940.54/4944/092
Saint Exupery, Antoine de, -- 1900-1944. World War, 1939-1945 -- Personal narratives, French. World War, 1939-1945 -- Aerial operations, French. Air pilots, Military -- France -- Biography.

D790 World War II (1939-1945) — Aerial operations — United States

D790.C657 1997
Conversino, Mark J.
Fighting with the Soviets: the failure of Operation FRANTIC, 1944-1945/ Mark J. Conversino. Lawrence, Kan.: University Press of Kansas, c1997. xi, 284 p.
96-032956   940.54/4973   0700608087
World War, 1939-1945 -- Aerial operations, American. World War, 1939-1945 -- Aerial operations, Russian. United States -- Relations -- Soviet Union. Soviet Union -- Relations -- United States.

D790.C69 1993
Crane, Conrad C.
Bombs, cities, and civilians: American airpower strategy in World War II/ Conrad C. Crane. Lawrence, Kan.: University Press of Kansas, c1993. xii, 208 p.
92-028141   940.54/4973   0700605746
World War, 1939-1945 -- Aerial operations, American. Bombing, Aerial. World War, 1939-1945 -- Moral and ethical aspects.

D790.D78 1997
Dryden, Charles W.
A-train: memoirs of a Tuskegee Airman/ Charles W. Dryden; with a foreword by Benjamin O. Davis, Jr. Tuscaloosa: University of Alabama Press, c1997. xviii, 421 p.
96-024118   940.54/4973   0817308563
Dryden, Charles W. -- (Charles Walter) World War, 1939-1945 -- Participation, Afro-American. World War, 1939-1945 -- Personal narratives, American. Afro-American air pilots -- Biography. Tuskegee Army Air Field (Ala.)

D790.E95 1997
Ewing, Steve.
Fateful rendezvous: the life of Butch O'Hare/ Steve Ewing and John B. Lundstrom. Annapolis, Md.: Naval Institute Press, c1997. xvi, 358 p.
96-049823   940.54/26/092   1557502471
O'Hare, Edward Henry, -- 1914-1943. World War, 1939-1945 -- Campaigns -- Pacific Area. World War, 1939-1945 -- Naval operations, American. World War, 1939-1945 -- Aerial operations, American.

D790.F584 1991
Ford, Daniel, 1931-
Flying Tigers: Claire Chennault and the American Volunteer Group/ Daniel Ford. Washington: Smithsonian Institution Press, c1991. xiii, 450 p.
90-026953   940.54/4973   1560980117
Chennault, Claire Lee, -- 1893-1958. World War, 1939-1945 -- Aerial operations, American.

D790.G665 1995
Goulter, Christina J. M., 1961-
A forgotten offensive: Royal Air Force Coastal Command's anti-shipping campaign, 1940-1945/ Christina J.M. Goulter. Portland, Or.; Frank Cass, c1995. xxii, 366 p.
95-000938   940.54/4941   0714646172
World War, 1939-1945 -- Aerial operations, British. Merchant marine -- Germany -- History.

D790.H64 2000
Hoffman, Daniel, 1923-
Zone of the interior: a memoir, 1942-1947/ Daniel Hoffman. Baton Rouge: Louisiana State University Press, c2000. xiii, 136 p.
99-050733   940.54/4973/092   0807125687
Hoffman, Daniel, -- 1923- World War, 1939-1945 -- Personal narratives, American. World War, 1939-1945 -- Aerial operations, American. Airmen -- United States -- Biography.

D790.L484 1992
Levine, Alan J.
The strategic bombing of Germany, 1940-1945/ Alan J. Levine. New York: Praeger, 1992. p. cm.
91-045610   940.54/42   0275943194
World War, 1939-1945 -- Aerial operations. Germany -- History -- Bombardment, 1940-1945.

D790.S26 1992
Sandler, Stanley, 1937-
Segregated skies: all-Black combat squadrons of WW II/ Stanley Sandler. Washington, D.C.: Smithsonian Institution Press, c1992. xv, 217 p.
91-039452   940.54/4973   1560981547
World War, 1939-1945 -- Aerial operations, American. World War, 1939-1945 -- Participation, Afro-American.

D790.W378 1996
Werrell, Kenneth P.
Blankets of fire: U.S. bombers over Japan during World War II/ Kenneth P. Werrell. Washington: Smithsonian Institution Press, c1996. xvi, 350 p.
95-024691   940.54/25   1560986654
World War, 1939-1945 -- Aerial operations, American. B-29 bomber. Japan -- History -- Bombardment, 1941-1945.

D792 World War II (1939-1945) — Aerial operations — Other regions or countries, A-Z

D792.J3.I513 1958
Inoguchi, Rikihei.
The divine wind: Japan's Kamikaze Force in World War II/ Rikihei Inoguchi and Tadashi Nakajima, with Roger Pineau; foreword by C.R. Brown. New York: Ballantine Books, c1958. 218 p.
58-013974   940.54/49/52
World War, 1939-1945 -- Aerial operations, Japanese.

D792.J3.O38
Okumiya, Masatake, 1909-
Zero! By Masatake Okumiya and Jiro Horikoshi with Martin Caidin. New York, Dutton, 1956. 424 p.
55-008329   940.544952
World War, 1939-1945 -- Aerial operations, Japanese.

D792.S65.H37 1982
Hardesty, Von, 1939-
Red phoenix: the rise of Soviet air power, 1941-1945/ Von Hardesty. Washington, D.C.: Smithsonian Institution Press, c1982. 288 p.
82-600153   940.54/4947   0874745101
World War, 1939-1945 -- Aerial operations, Soviet. World War, 1939-1945 -- Aerial operations, German.

D792.S65.N64 1994
Noggle, Anne, 1922-
A dance with death: Soviet airwomen in World War II/ text and contemporary portraits by Anne Noggle; introduction by Christine A. White. College Station: Texas A&M University Press, c1994. xiv, 318 p.
94-001301   940.54/4947   089096601X
World War, 1939-1945 -- Aerial operations, Soviet. Women air pilots -- Soviet Union -- History. World War, 1939-1945 -- Participation, Female.

D799 World War II (1939-1945) — Press. Censorship. Publicity. Radio — By region or country, A-Z

D799.I73.O37 1996
O Drisceoil, Donal.
Censorship in Ireland, 1939-1945: neutrality, politics, and society/ Donal O Drisceoil. [Cork]: Cork University Press, [1996] xiv, 352 p.
96-156049   940.53   1859180736
World War, 1939-1945 -- Censorship -- Ireland.

D799.U6.S834 2001
Sweeney, Michael S.
Secrets of victory: the Office of Censorship and the American press and radio in World War II/ Michael S. Sweeney. Chapel Hill, NC: University of North Carolina Press, c2001. 274 p.
00-044721   940.54/88673   0807825980
World War, 1939-1945 -- Censorship -- United States.

D802 World War II (1939-1945) — Occupied territory

D802.A38.F57 1999
Fischer, Bernd Jurgen, 1952-
Albania at war, 1939-1945/ Bernd J. Fischer. West Lafayette, Ind.: Purdue University Press, c1999. xv, 338 p.
98-046675   940.53/4965   1557531412
World War, 1939-1945 -- Albania. Albania -- History -- Axis occupation, 1939-1944.

D802.B4.W37 1993
Warmbrunn, Werner, 1920-
The German occupation of Belgium 1940-1944/ Werner Warmbrunn. New York: P. Lang, c1993. xv, 365 p.
91-035882   940.53/37   0820417734
World War, 1939-1945 -- Belgium. Belgium -- History -- German occupation, 1940-1945.

D802.D4.P45
Petrow, Richard.
The bitter years; the invasion and occupation of Denmark and Norway, April 1940-May 1945. New York, Morrow, 1974. viii, 403 p.
74-009576 940.54/21 0688002757
World War, 1939-1945 -- Campaigns -- Denmark. World War, 1939-1945 -- Campaigns -- Norway. Denmark -- History -- German occupation, 1940-1945. Norway -- History -- German occupation, 1940-1945.

D802.E9.R5613
Rings, Werner.
Life with the enemy: collaboration and resistance in Hitler's Europe, 1939-1945/ Werner Rings; translated from the German by J. Maxwell Brownjohn. Garden City, N.Y.: Doubleday, 1982. vii, 351 p.
80-002980 940.53/4 0385170823
World War, 1939-1945 -- Underground movements -- Europe. Europe -- History -- 1918-1945. Germany -- Foreign relations -- 1933-1945.

D802.E9.W54
Wilkinson, James D., 1943-
The intellectual resistance in Europe/ James D. Wilkinson. Cambridge, Mass.: Harvard University Press, 1981. x, 358 p.
80-024469 940.53/4 0674457757
World War, 1939-1945 -- Underground movements -- Europe. Intellectuals -- Europe. Europe -- Intellectual life -- 20th century.

D802.F8.A92313 1984
Azema, Jean-Pierre.
From Munich to the Liberation, 1938-1944/ Jean-Pierre Azema; translated by Janet Lloyd. Cambridge [Cambridgeshire]; Cambridge University Press; 1984. xxxix, 294 p.
84-005828 940.53/44 0521272386
World War, 1939-1945 -- France.

D802.F8.B6985 2000
Kaplan, Alice Yaeger.
The collaborator: the trial & execution of Robert Brasillach / Alice Kaplan. Chicago: University of Chicago Press, 2000. xvi, 308 p.
99-048291 848/.91209 0226424146
Brasillach, Robert, -- 1909-1945 -- Political and social views. World War, 1939-1945 -- Collaborationists -- France. Fascism and literature -- France -- History -- 20th century. Fascism -- France -- History.

D802.F8 B8613 1996
Burrin, Philippe,
France under the Germans: collaboration and compromise/ Philippe Burrin; translated from the French by Janet Lloyd. New York: New Press; c1996. xii, 530 p
96-069742 940.53/44.221 1565843231
World War, 1939-1945--France. World War, 1939-1945--Collaborationists--France.

D802.F8.D32 2001
Davies, Peter Jonathan, 1966-
France and the Second World War: occupation, collaboration and resistance/ Peter Davies. London; Routledge, 2001. xii, 145 p.
00-036591 944.0816 0415238978
World War, 1939-1945 -- Underground movements -- France. World War, 1939-1945 -- Collaborationists -- France. France -- History -- German occupation, 1940-1945. France -- History -- 1945-

D802.F8.G67
Gordon, Bertram M., 1945-
Collaborationism in France during the Second World War/ Bertram M. Gordon. Ithaca, N.Y.: Cornell University Press, 1980. 393 p.
79-025281 940.53/24/44 0801412633
World War, 1939-1945 -- Collaborationists -- France. France -- History -- German occupation, 1940-1945.

D802.F8.K4
Kedward, H. R.
Resistance in Vichy France: a study of ideas and motivation in the Southern Zone, 1940-1942/ by H. R. Kedward. Oxford [Eng.]; Oxford University Press, 1978. ix, 311 p.
77-030165 940.53/44 0198225296
World War, 1939-1945 -- Underground movements -- France. France -- History -- German occupation, 1940-1945.

D802.F8.K65 1999
Koreman, Megan.
The expectation of justice: France, 1944-1946/ Megan Koreman. Durham, NC: Duke University Press, 1999. p. cm.
99-025936 944.082 0822323524
World War, 1939-1945 -- France. World War, 1939-1945 -- Collaborationists -- France -- Case studies. Social justice -- France -- History -- Case studies. France -- History -- 1945-1958 -- Case studies.

D802.F8.M34 2000
May, Ernest R.
Strange victory: Hitler's conquest of France/ Ernest R. May. New York: Hill and Wang, 2000. viii, 594 p.
99-053619 940.54/214 0809089068
World War, 1939-1945 -- France. France -- History -- German occupation, 1940-1945.

D802.F8.R6213 1996
Rougeyron, Andre.
Agents for escape: inside the French Resistance, 1939-1945/ Andre Rougeyron; translated by Marie-Antoinette McConnell. Baton Rouge: Louisiana State University Press, c1996. xi, 189 p.
95-023387 940.53/44 0807120197
Rougeyron, Andre. World War, 1939-1945 -- Underground movements -- France. World War, 1939-1945 -- Personal narratives, French. Guerrillas -- France -- Biography.

D802.F8.S675 1993
Kedward, H. R.
In search of the maquis: rural resistance in southern France, 1942-1944/ H.R. Kedward. Oxford: Clarendon Press; 1993. xvii, 340 p.
92-023270 940.53/448 0198219318
World War, 1939-1945 -- Underground movements -- France, Southern. France, Southern -- History.

D802.F82.P376
Pryce-Jones, David, 1936-
Paris in the Third Reich: a history of the German occupation, 1940-1944/ by David Pryce-Jones; Michael Rand, picture editor. New York: Holt, Rinehart, and Winston, c1981. x, 294 p.
80-021256 940.53/44 0030456215
World War, 1939-1945 -- France -- Paris. Paris (France) -- History -- 1940-1944.

D802.F82.S21496813 1996
Todorov, Tzvetan, 1939-
A French tragedy: scenes of civil war, summer 1944/ Tzvetan Todorov; translated by Mary Byrd Kelly; translation edited and annotated by Richard J. Golsan. Hanover [N.H.]: Dartmouth College; c1996. xx, 138 p.
96-011603 940.54/8144552 0874517478
Sadrin, Rene. World War, 1939-1945 -- France -- Saint-Amand-Mont-Rond. Mayors -- France -- Saint-Amand-Mont-Rond -- Biography. World War, 1939-1945 -- Personal narratives, French. Saint-Amand-Mont-Rond (France) -- History.

D802.G8.H66 1983
Hondros, John Louis.
Occupation and resistance: the Greek agony, 1941-44/ John Louis Hondros. New York, NY: Pella Pub. Co., 1983. 340 p.
83-062478 940.53/495 0918618193
World War, 1939-1945 -- Underground movements -- Greece. Greece -- History -- Occupation, 1941-1944.

D802.I8.S53 1997
Slaughter, Jane, 1941-
Women and the Italian resistance, 1943-1945/ by Jane Slaughter. Denver, Colo.: Arden Press, 1997. p. cm.
97-004937 940.53/45 0912869135
World War, 1939-1945 -- Underground movements -- Italy. World War, 1939-1945 -- Participation, Female. Women -- Italy -- History -- 20th century.

D802.I8.W55 1988
Wilhelm, Maria.
The other Italy: Italian resistance in World War II/ Maria de Blasio Wilhelm; drawings by Enzo Marino. New York: Norton, c1988. 272 p.
87-031362 940.53/45 0393025683
World War, 1939-1945 -- Underground movements -- Italy.

D802.J3.M37
Martin, Edwin M.
The allied occupation of Japan/ Edwin M. Martin; Pub. under the auspices of the American Institute of Pacific Relations. Stanford: Stanford University Press, 1948. xiv, 155 p.
48-009639 940.5352
Japan -- History -- Allied occupation, 1945-1952.

D802.N7.C64 1997
Cohen, Maynard M. 1920-
A stand against tyranny: Norway's physicians and the Nazis/ Maynard M. Cohen. Detroit, Mich.: Wayne State University Press, 1997. 326 p.
96-014957 940.53/37 081432603X
World War, 1939-1945 -- Underground movements -- Norway. World War, 1939-1945 -- Personal narratives, Norwegian. Physicians -- Norway -- Biography. Norway -- History -- German occupation, 1940-1945.

D802.N7.G5413 1979
Gjelsvik, Tore, 1916-
Norwegian resistance, 1940-1945/ by Tore Gjelsvik; translated from the Norwegian by Thomas Kingston Derry. London: C. Hurst, c1979. x, 224 p.
79-322482 940.53/481
Gjelsvik, Tore, -- 1916- World War, 1939-1945 -- Underground movements -- Norway -- Biography. World War, 1939-1945 -- Personal narratives, Norwegian. Guerrillas -- Norway -- Biography. Norway -- History -- German occupation, 1940-1945.

D802.P52.L896 1996
Lapham, Robert, 1917-
Lapham's raiders: guerrillas in the Philippines,
1942-1945/ Robert Lapham & Bernard Norling.
Lexington: University Press of Kentucky, c1996.
xii, 292 p.
95-020719   940.53/599   0813119499
*Lapham, Robert, -- 1917-   World War, 1939-1945
-- Underground movements -- Philippines -- Luzon.
World War, 1939-1945 -- Personal narratives,
American. Guerrillas -- United States --
Biography. Luzon (Philippines) -- History,
Military.*

D802.P52.L8965 1999
Norling, Bernard, 1924-
The intrepid guerrillas of North Luzon/ Bernard
Norling. Lexington, Ky.: University Press of
Kentucky, c1999. xiv, 284 p.
99-017356   940.53/5991   0813121183
*World War, 1939-1945 -- Underground
movements -- Philippines -- Luzon. Guerrillas --
Philippines -- Luzon -- Biography. Guerrillas --
United States -- Biography. Luzon (Philippines) --
History, Military.*

D802.P62.W3369 1991
Garlinski, Jozef.
The survival of love: memoirs of a resistance
officer/ by Jozef Garlinski. Cambridge, Mass.: B.
Blackwell, 1991. x, 231 p.
90-014548   940.53/4384   0631176594
*Garlinski, Jozef.   World War, 1939-1945 --
Personal narratives, Polish. Soldiers -- Poland --
Biography. World War, 1939-1945 -- Underground
movements -- Poland -- Warsaw. Warsaw (Poland)
-- History.*

D802.S75.G74 1999
Grenkevich, Leonid D.
The Soviet partisan movement, 1941-1944: a
critical historiographical analysis/ Leonid D.
Grenkevich; edited and with a foreword by David
M. Glantz. London; Frank Cass Publishers, 1999.
xv, 368 p.
98-041682   940.53/47   0714648744
*World War, 1939-1945 -- Underground
movements -- Soviet Union. Guerrillas -- Soviet
Union -- History -- 20th century. Soviet Union --
History -- German occupation, 1941-1944.*

D802.S75.M85 1988
Mulligan, Timothy.
The politics of illusion and empire: German
occupation policy in the Soviet Union, 1942-1943/
Timothy Patrick Mulligan. New York: Praeger,
1988. xiv, 206 p.
87-032702   940.53/47   0275928373
*World War, 1939-1945 -- Soviet Union. Military
occupation. Soviet Union -- History -- German
occupation, 1941-1944.*

D802.Y8.D4
Deakin, F. W. 1913-
The embattled mountain [by] F. W. D. Deakin.
New York, Oxford University Press, 1971. xiii,
284 p.
74-169160   940.5342/0924
*Deakin, F. W. -- (Frederick William), -- 1913-
World War, 1939-1945 -- Underground movements
-- Yugoslavia. World War, 1939-1945 -- Personal
narratives, British.*

D802.Y8.T65 1997
Trew, Simon, 1965-
Britain, Mihailovic, and the Chetniks, 1941-42/
Simon Trew. London; St. Martin's Press in
association with King's Co 1997. xiv, 341 p.
97-018290   940.53/497   0312177577
*Mihailovic, Draza, -- 1893-1946.   World War,
1939-1945 -- Underground movements --
Yugoslavia.   Great Britain -- Foreign relations --
Yugoslavia. Yugoslavia -- Foreign relations --
Great Britain. Yugoslavia -- History -- Axis
occupation, 1941-1945.*

D803 World War II (1939-1945) — Atrocities. War crimes — General works

D803.K63 1998
Kochavi, Arieh J.
Prelude to Nuremberg: Allied war crimes policy
and the question of punishment/ Arieh J. Kochavi.
Chapel Hill, N.C.: University of North Carolina
Press, c1998. x, 312 p.
97-047745   940.53/1   080782433X
World War, 1939-1945 -- Atrocities. War crimes.

D803.M365 2000
Margolian, Howard.
Unauthorized entry: the truth about Nazi war
criminals in Canada, 1946-1956/ Howard
Margolian. Toronto; University of Toronto Press,
c2000. viii, 327 p.
00-703123   364.1/38/0971   0802042775
*War criminals -- Canada. War criminals --
Germany. Nazis -- Canada. Canada -- Emigration
and immigration -- Government policy -- History --
20th century.*

D804 World War II (1939-1945) — Atrocities. War crimes — By region or country (committing atrocity), A-Z

D804.G4 B78 1994
Buruma, Ian.
The wages of guilt: memories of war in Germany
and Japan/ Ian Buruma.1st ed. New York: Farrar,
Straus, Giroux, 1994. 330 p.
95-000736   940.54/05.220   0452011566
*World War, 1939-1945--Atrocities. World War,
1939-1945--Germany. World War, 1939-1945--
Japan.*

D804.G4.F2913 1998
Farmer, Sarah Bennett.
Martyred village: commemorating the 1944
massacre at Oradour-sur-Glane/ Sarah Farmer.
Berkeley: University of California Press, c1999.
xvii, 300 p.
98-029646   940.54/05/094466   0520211863
*Oradour-sur-Glane Massacre, 1944. World War,
1939-1945 -- Atrocities. Massacres -- France --
Oradour-sur-Glane. Oradour-sur-Glane (France) -
- History.*

D804.G4.G54 1996
Giziowski, Richard J.
The enigma of General Blaskowitz/ Richard
Giziowski. New York: Hippocrene Books, 1996. p.
cm.
96-042239   940.54/05/0943   0781805031
*Blaskowitz, Johannes von, -- 1883-1948.   War
criminals -- Germany -- Biography. War criminals
-- Polands -- Biography. World War, 1939-1945 --
Atrocities.*

D804.G4.J55 1999
Johnson, Eric A. 1948-
Nazi terror: the Gestapo, Jews, and ordinary
Germans/ Eric A. Johnson. New York: Basic
Books, c1999. xx, 636 p.
00-269061   943.086   0465049060
*World War, 1939-1945 -- Atrocities. Atrocities --
Germany. Holocaust, Jewish (1939-1945) --
Germany.*

D804.G4.M3225 1998
Margolian, Howard.
Conduct unbecoming: the story of the murder of
Canadian prisoners of war in Normandy/ Howard
Margolian. Toronto: University of Toronto Press,
c1998. xiv, 279 p.
98-176842   940.54/7243   0802042139
*World War, 1939-1945 -- Perisoners and
prisons, German. Prisoners of war -- Canada.
Prisoners of war -- Germany. Normandy (France) -
- History, Military.*

D804.G4.M7713 1988
Muller-Hill, Benno, 1933-
Murderous science: elimination by scientific
selection of Jews, Gypsies, and others, Germany
1933-1945/ Benno Muller-Hill; translated by
George Fraser Oxford [Oxfordshire]; Oxford
University Press, 1988 xvi, 208 p.
87-007201   0192615556
*Science and state -- Germany GENOCIDE -
GERMANY - HISTORY - 20TH CENTURY
HUMAN EXPERIMENTATION IN MEDICINE*

D804.G4.N2913 1994
Nazi mass murder: a documentary history of the
use of poison gas/ edited by Eugen Kogon,
Hermann Langbein, and Adalbert Ruckerl; editor's
notes and foreword to the English-language edition
by Pierre Serge Choumoff; translated by Mary
Scott and Caroline Lloyd-Morris. New Haven:
Yale University Press, [1994] c1993 xiii, 289 p.
93-013734   940.54/05   0300054416
*World War, 1939-1945 -- Atrocities. Murder --
Germany. World War, 1939-1945 -- Concentration
camps -- Germany.*

D804.G4.Q47 1995
The quest for the Nazi personality: a psychological
investigation of Nazi war criminals/ Eric A.
Zillmer ... [et al.]. Hillsdale, N.J.: Erlbaum, 1995.
xviii, 254 p.
94-048889   940.54/05   0805818987
*World War, 1939-1945 -- Atrocities --
Psychological aspects. World War, 1939-1945 --
Germany -- Psychological aspects. War criminals -
- Psychology.*

D804.G4.T45 1998
Teschke, John P.
Hitler's legacy: West Germany confronts the
aftermath of the Third Reich/ John P. Teschke.
New York: P. Lang, 1998. 429 p.
98-005312   943.087   0820440264
*National socialism -- Moral and ethical aspects.
War criminals -- Germany -- Psychology. Nazis --
Germany -- Biography. Denazification -- Germany
(East) Germany -- Politics and government --
1945-1990.*

D804.G42.G5
Gilbert, G. M., 1911-
Nuremberg diary. New York, Farrar, Straus, 1947.
471 p.
47-004157   341.4
*Nuremberg Trial of Major German War
Criminals, Nuremberg, Germany, 1945-1946.*

D804 G42.I55
International Military Tribunal.
Trial of the major war criminals before the International Military Tribunal, Nuremberg, 14 November 1945-1 October 1946. Nuremberg,Ger. 1947-49 42 v.
47-031575 341.4 0404536506
Nuremberg Trial of Major German War Criminals, Nuremberg, Germany, 1945-1946. War crimes -- Trials -- Nuremberg -- 1945-1946. War crimes -- Cases.

D804.G42.S64
Smith, Bradley F.
Reaching judgment at Nuremberg/ Bradley F. Smith. New York: Basic Books, c1977. xviii, 349 p.
76-026715 341.6/9 0465068391
Nuremberg Trial of Major German War Criminals, Nuremberg, Germany, 1945-1946.

D804.J33.Y36
Reel, A. Frank
The case of General Yamashita. [by] A. Frank Reel. [Chicago] University of Chicago Press [1949]. vi, 323 p.
49-010326 341.4
Yamashita, Tomobumi, -- 1885-1946.   War crime trials -- Manila, 1946.

D804.S65.L38 1988
Lauck, John H.
Katyn killings: in the record/ by John H. Lauck. Clifton, N.J.: Kingston Press, c1988. xiv, 331 p.
88-080479 940.54/05/094762 0940670305
Katyn Forest Massacre, 1940.

D804.17-804.66 World War II (1939-1945) — Atrocities. War crimes — Holocaust

D804.17.H65 2000
The Holocaust and World War II almanac/ Peggy Saari, Aaron Maurice Saari, editors; Kathleen J. Edgar, Ellice Engdahl, coordinating editors. Detroit: Gale Group, c2001. 3 v.
00-046647 940.53/18 0787650188
Holocaust, Jewish (1939-1945) World War, 1939-1945. Holocaust, Jewish (1939-1945) -- Biography.

D804.175.N49.S25 1996
Saidel, Rochelle G.
Never too late to remember: the politics behind New York City's Holocaust Museum/ Rochelle G. Saidel. New York: Holmes & Meier, 1996. xiii, 290 p.
96-012944 940.53/18/0747471 0841913676
Holocaust, Jewish (1939-1945) -- Museums -- New York (State) -- New York. Jews -- United States -- Politics and government. New York (N.Y.) -- Politics and government -- 1951- New York (State) -- Politics and government -- 1951-

D804.18.H66 1998
The Holocaust and history: the known, the unknown, the disputed, and the reexamined/ edited by Michael Berenbaum and Abraham J. Peck. Bloomington, IN: Indiana University Press, c1998. xv, 836 p.
97-040030 940.53/18 0253333741
Holocaust, Jewish (1939-1945) -- Congresses.

D804.195.F74 1998
Fresh wounds: early narratives of Holocaust survival/ edited by Donald L. Niewyk. Chapel Hill: University of North Carolina Press, c1998. 414 p.
97-017725 940.53/18 0807823937
Holocaust, Jewish (1939-1945) -- Personal narratives. Jews -- Biography.

D804.195.G74 1998
Greenspan, Henry, 1948-
On listening to Holocaust survivors: recounting and life history/ Henry Greenspan; foreword by Robert Coles. Westport, Conn.: Praeger, 1998. xx, 199 p.
98-004944 940.53/18 0275957187
Holocaust, Jewish (1939-1945) -- Personal narratives -- History and criticism. Holocaust survivors -- Interviews -- History and criticism.

D804.195.L46 2000
Lentin, Ronit.
Israel and the daughters of the Shoah: reoccupying the territories of silence/ Ronit Lentin. New York: Berghahn Books, 2000. xiv, 256 p.
00-060886 940.53/18 1571817743
Holocaust, Jewish (1939-1945) -- Personal narratives -- History and criticism. Holocaust, Jewish (1939-1945) -- Influence. Children of Holocaust survivors -- Israel -- Interviews.

D804.195.P37 1998
Patterson, David, 1948-
Sun turned to darkness: memory and recovery in the Holocaust memoir/ David Patterson. Syracuse, N.Y.: Syracuse University Press, 1998. xi, 233 p.
98-024320 940.53/18/092 0815605307
Holocaust, Jewish (1939-1945) -- Personal narratives -- History and criticism. Autobiographical memory.

D804.25.E53 2000
Encyclopedia of the Holocaust/ Schmuel Spector, Robert Rozette, editors. New York: Facts on File, 2000. 528 p.
00-030917 940.53/18/003 0816043337
Holocaust, Jewish (1939-1945) -- Encyclopedias.

D804.25.H66 2001
The Holocaust encyclopedia/ Walter Laqueur, editor; Judith Tydor Baumel, associate editor. New Haven: Yale University Press, c2001. xxxix, 765 p.
00-106567 940.53/18/03 0300084323
Holocaust, Jewish (1939-1945) -- Encyclopedia.

D804.3.A425 1994
Alexander, Edward, 1936-
The Holocaust and the war of ideas/ Edward Alexander. New Brunswick: Transaction Publishers, c1994. ix, 242 p.
93-011119 940.53/18/072 1560001224
Holocaust, Jewish (1939-1945) -- Historiography. Holocaust, Jewish (1939-1945), in literature. Jewish literature -- History and criticism.

D804.3.A45813 1999
Aly, Gotz, 1947-
'Final solution': Nazi population policy and the murder of the European Jews/ Gotz Aly; translated from the German by Belinda Cooper and Allison Brown. London; Arnold; 1999. viii, 305 p.
99-202381 940.53/18 0340677570
Holocaust, Jewish (1939-1945) -- Causes. Germany -- Population policy.

D804.3.B377 1989
Bauman, Zygmunt.
Modernity and the Holocaust/ Zygmunt Bauman. Ithaca, N.Y.: Cornell University Press, 1989. xiv, 224 p.
89-007274 940.53/18 080142397X
Holocaust, Jewish (1939-1945) -- Causes. Genocide -- Sociological aspects. Genocide -- Psychological aspects.

D804.3.B45413 1999
Benz, Wolfgang.
The Holocaust: a German historian examines the genocide/ Wolfgang Benz; translated by Jane Sydenham-Kwiet. New York: Columbia University Press, 1999. xi, 186 p.
98-030726 940.53/18 0231112149
Holocaust, Jewish (1939-1945) Jews -- Germany -- History -- 1933-1945.

D804.3.B463 1998
Bergen, Bernard J.
The banality of evil: Hannah Arendt and "the final solution"/ Bernard J. Bergen. Lanham: Rowman & Littlefield Publishers, c1998. xvii, 169 p.
98-004044 940.53/18 0847692094
Arendt, Hannah -- Views on the Holocaust. Arendt, Hannah. -- Eichmann in Jerusalem. Holocaust, Jewish (1939-1945) -- Causes.

D804.3.B6926 1998
Breaking crystal: writing and memory after Auschwitz/ edited by Efraim Sicher. Urbana: University of Illinois Press, c1998. 378 p.
97-004741 940.53/18 0252022807
Holocaust, Jewish (1939-1945) -- Influence. Holocaust, Jewish (1939-1945), in literature. Israeli literature -- History and criticism.

D804.3.D86 1991
Dwork, Deborah.
Children with a star: Jewish youth in Nazi Europe/ Deborah Dwork. New Haven: Yale University Press, 1991. xlvi, 354 p.
90-023908 940.53/18 0300050542
Holocaust, Jewish (1939-1945) World War, 1939-1945 -- Children. Jewish children in the Holocaust.

D804.3.F45 1995
Feingold, Henry L., 1931-
Bearing witness: how America and its Jews responded to the Holocaust/ Henry L. Feingold. Syracuse, N.Y.: Syracuse University Press, 1995. viii, 322 p.
95-015862 940.53/18 081562669X
Holocaust, Jewish (1939-1945) -- Historiography. Holocaust, Jewish (1939-1945) -- Public opinion. Public opinion -- United States. United States -- Foreign relations -- 1933-1945. United States -- Ethnic relations.

D804.3.F58 1998
Fischel, Jack.
The Holocaust/ Jack R. Fischel. Westport, Conn.: Greenwood Press, 1998. xxxvii, 196 p.
97-029972 940.53/18 0313298793
Holocaust, Jewish (1939-1945) World War, 1939-1945 -- Jewish resistance.

D804.3.F74 1994
Friedlander, Albert H.
Riders towards the dawn: from Holocaust to hope/ Albert H. Friedlander. New York: Continuum, 1994. 328 p.
93-029851 940.53/18 0826406351
Holocaust, Jewish (1939-1945) -- Influence. Holocaust (Jewish theology) Holocaust (Christian theology)

D804.3.G587 1997
Glass, James M.
Life unworthy of life: racial phobia and mass murder in Hitler's Germany/ James M. Glass. New York: Basic Books, c1997. xix, 252 p.
97-020118   940.53/18   0465098444
Holocaust, Jewish (1939-1945) -- Causes. Antisemitism -- Germany. Eugenics -- Germany -- History -- 20th century.

D804.3.G648 1996
Goldhagen, Daniel Jonah.
Hitler's willing executioners: ordinary Germans and the Holocaust/ Daniel Jonah Goldhagen. New York: Knopf: 1996. x, 622 p.
95-038591   940.53/18   0679446958
Holocaust, Jewish (1939-1945) -- Causes. Antisemitism -- Germany. War criminals -- Germany -- Psychology.

D804.3.G662 2000
Good and evil after Auschwitz: ethical implications for today/ edited by Jack Bemporad, John T. Pawlikowski, and Joseph Sievers. Hoboken, NJ: KTAV Pub. House, c2000. xxiii, 330 p.
00-061548   296.3/1174   0881256927
Holocaust, Jewish (1939-1945) -- Moral and ethical aspects -- Congresses. Genocide -- Moral and ethical aspects -- Congresses.

D804.3.H374 1990
Hass, Aaron.
In the shadow of the Holocaust: the second generation/ Aaron Hass. Ithaca: Cornell University Press, 1990. p. cm.
90-002014   940.53/18/019   0801424771
Children of Holocaust survivors -- United States -- Psychology. Children of Holocaust survivors -- United States -- Interviews.

D804.3.H6475 1993
Holocaust literature: a handbook of critical, historical, and literary writings/ edited by Saul S. Friedman; foreword by Dennis Klein. Westport, Conn.: Greenwood Press, 1993. xxx, 677 p.
92-024135   940.53/18   0313262217
Holocaust, Jewish (1939-1945)

D804.3.H6494 1994
Holocaust remembrance: the shapes of memory/ edited by Geoffrey Hartman. Oxford, UK; Blackwell, 1994. xi, 306 p.
92-041095   940.53/18   1557861250
Holocaust, Jewish (1939-1945) -- Historiography. Holocaust, Jewish (1939-1945) -- Influence. Holocaust memorials.

D804.3.H85 2000
Humanity at the limit: the impact of the Holocaust experience on Jews and Christians/ edited by Michael A. Signer. Bloomington: Indiana University Press, c2000. xiv, 461 p.
00-035031   940.53/18   0253337399
Holocaust, Jewish (1939-1945) -- Influence. Judaism -- Relations -- Christianity -- 1945- Christianity and other religions -- Judaism -- 1945-

D804.3.J66 1999
Jones, David H., 1930-
Moral responsibility in the Holocaust: a study in the ethics of character/ David H. Jones. Lanham, Md.: Rowman & Littlefield Publishers, c1999. xi, 257 p.
98-048271   940.53/18   0847692663
Holocaust, Jewish (1939-1945) -- Moral and ethical aspects.

D804.3.K378 1994
Katz, Steven T., 1944-
The holocaust in historical context/ Steven T. Katz. New York: Oxford University Press, 1994- v. 1
91-033049   940.53/18   0195072200
Holocaust, Jewish (1939-1945) Persecution -- History. Genocide.

D804.3.L357 1999
Lang, Berel.
The future of the Holocaust: between history and memory/ Berel Lang. Ithaca, NY: Cornell University Press, 1999. xiv, 198 p.
99-020088   940.53/18   0801435889
Holocaust, Jewish (1939-1945) -- Causes. Holocaust, Jewish (1939-1945) -- Influence. National socialism.

D804.3.L36 1991
Langer, Lawrence L.
Holocaust testimonies: the ruins of memory/ Lawrence L. Langer. New Haven: Yale University Press, c1991. xix, 216 p.
90-044768   940.53/18   0300049668
Holocaust, Jewish (1939-1945) -- Personal narratives -- History and criticism. Holocaust survivors -- Psychology.

D804.3.M35 1988
Maier, Charles S.
The unmasterable past: History, holocaust, and German national identity/ Charles S. Maier. Cambridge, Mass.: Harvard University Press, 1988. xi, 227 p.
88-011690   940.53/15/03924   0674929756
Holocaust, Jewish (1939-1945) -- Historiography. Historians -- Germany (West) Germany -- History -- 20th century -- Historiography.

D804.3.M37 1987
Marrus, Michael Robert.
The Holocaust in history/ Michael R. Marrus. Hanover, NH: Published for Brandeis University Press by Unive 1987. xv, 267 p.
87-006291   940.53/15/039240072   0874514258
Holocaust, Jewish (1939-1945) -- Historiography.

D804.3.N54 2000
Niewyk, Donald L., 1940-
The Columbia guide to the Holocaust/ Donald Niewyk and Francis Nicosia. New York: Columbia University Press, c2000. vii, 473 p.
00-024979   940.53/18   0231112009
Holocaust, Jewish (1939-1945) Holocaust, Jewish (1939-1945) -- Encyclopedias. Holocaust, Jewish (1939-1945) -- Bibliography.

D804.3.R54 1997
Ring, Jennifer, 1948-
The political consequences of thinking: gender and Judaism in the work of Hannah Arendt/ Jennifer Ring. Albany, N.Y.: State University of New York Press, c1997. xiii, 358 p.
96-047278   940.53/18   0791434834
Arendt, Hannah. -- Eichmann in Jerusalem. Arendt, Hannah. -- Jews as pariah. World War, 1939-1945 -- Jews -- Rescue -- Palestine. Holocaust, Jewish (1939-1945) -- Public opinion. Public opinion -- Israel. Israel -- Politics and government.

D804.3.S54 1993
Shaw, Stanford J. 1930-
Turkey and the Holocaust: Turkey's role in rescuing Turkish and European Jewry from Nazi persecution, 1933-1945/ Stanford J. Shaw. New York: New York University Press, 1993. xiii, 423 p.
92-000354   940.53/18   0814779603
Holocaust, Jewish (1939-1945) World War, 1939-1945 -- Jews -- Rescue -- Turkey. Jews -- Turkey -- History -- 20th century. Turkey -- Ethnic relations.

D804.3.S75 1990
Steinberg, Jonathan.
All or nothing: the Axis and the Holocaust, 1941-1943/ Jonathan Steinberg. London; Routledge, 1990. xiv, 320 p.
89-070241   940.53/18/09496   0415047579
Holocaust, Jewish (1939-1945) -- Balkan Peninsula. Holocaust, Jewish (1939-1945) -- France. World War, 1939-1945 -- Jews -- Rescue -- Italy. Italy -- Foreign relations -- Germany. Germany -- Foreign relations -- Italy.

D804.3.T6313 1996
Todorov, Tzvetan, 1939-
Facing the extreme: moral life in the concentration camps/ Tzvetan Todorov; translated by Arthur Denner and Abigail Pollak. New York: Metropolitan Books, 1996. 307 p.
95-032056   940.53/18   0805042636
Holocaust, Jewish (1939-1945) -- Moral and ethical aspects. Concentration camps -- Moral and ethical aspects. Totalitarianism -- Moral and ethical aspects.

D804.3.Y3413 1990
Yahil, Leni.
The Holocaust: the fate of European Jewry, 1932-1945/ Leni Yahil; translated from the Hebrew by Ina Friedman and Haya Galai. New York: Oxford University Press, 1990. xviii, 808 p.
89-037750   940.53/18   019504522X
Holocaust, Jewish (1939-1945) Jews -- Germany -- History -- 1933-1945. Germany -- Ethnic relations.

D804.32.Z45 1998
Zelizer, Barbie.
Remembering to forget: Holocaust memory through the camera's eye/ Barbie Zelizer. Chicago: University of Chicago Press, 1998. viii, 292 p.
98-018164   940.53/18   0226979725
Holocaust, Jewish (1939-1945) -- Pictorial works. Holocaust, Jewish (1939-1945) -- Press coverage. World War, 1939-1945 -- Concentration camps -- Liberation -- Europe -- Pictorial works.

D804.33.L43 2001
Learning about the Holocaust: a student's guide/ Ronald M. Smelser, editor in chief. New York: Macmillan Reference USA, c2001. 4 v.
00-062517   940.53/18   0028655362
Holocaust, Jewish (1939-1945) -- Study and teaching (Secondary)

D804.33.N49 1996
New perspectives on the Holocaust: a guide for teachers and scholars/ edited by Rochelle L. Millen with Timothy A. Bennett ... [et al.]. New York: New York University Press, c1996. xxii, 382 p.
96-010023   940.53/18   0814755399
Holocaust, Jewish (1939-1945) -- Study and teaching. Holocaust, Jewish (1939-1945) -- Causes. Holocaust (Jewish theology)

D804.348.B37 2000
Bartov, Omer.
Mirrors of destruction: war, genocide, and modern identity/ Omer Bartov. Oxford; Oxford University Press, 2000. viii, 302 p.
99-039974   940.53/18/072   0195077237
Holocaust, Jewish (1939-1945) -- Historiography. Genocide. Ethnicity. France -- History -- 20th century -- Historiography.

D804.348.B39 2001
Bauer, Yehuda.
Rethinking the Holocaust/ Yehuda Bauer. New Haven: Yale University Press, c2001. xvi, 335 p.
00-043308   940.53/18/072   0300082568
Holocaust, Jewish (1939-1945) -- Historiography. Holocaust, Jewish (1939-1945) -- Influence.

D804.348.I8 1996
Is the Holocaust unique?: perspectives on comparative genocide/ edited with an introd. by Alan S. Rosenbaum; with a foreword by Israel W. Charny. Boulder, Colo.: Westview Press, 1996. xix, 222 p.
96-033949   940.53/18/072   0813326419
Holocaust, Jewish (1939-1945) -- Historiography. Genocide.

D804.348.L33 1998
LaCapra, Dominick, 1939-
History and memory after Auschwitz/ Dominick LaCapra. Ithaca, NY: Cornell University Press, 1998. ix, 214 p.
97-041845   940.53/18   0801434963
Holocaust, Jewish (1939-1945) -- Historiography. Holocaust, Jewish (1939-1945) -- Psychological aspects. Holocaust, Jewish (1939-1945) -- Influence.

D804.35.L57 1993
Lipstadt, Deborah E.
Denying the Holocaust: the growing assault on truth and memory/ Deborah E. Lipstadt. New York: Free Press, c1993. 278 p.
90-009952   940.53/18   0029192358
Holocaust, Jewish (1939-1945) -- Historiography. Holocaust, Jewish (1939-1945) -- Errors, inventions, etc. Antisemitism -- History -- 20th century.

D804.355.S54 2000
Shermer, Michael.
Denying history: who says the Holocaust never happened and why do they say it?/ Michael Shermer & Alex Grobman; foreword by Arthur Hertzberg. Berkeley: University of California Press, c2000. xviii, 312 p.
00-028690   940.53/18   0520216121
Holocaust denial.

D804.44.W67 1996
The world reacts to the Holocaust/ David S. Wyman, editor; Charles H. Rosenzveig, project director. Baltimore: Johns Hopkins university Press, 1996. xxiii, 981 p.
96-015395   940.53/18   0801849691
Holocaust, Jewish (1939-1945) -- Public opinion. Holocaust, Jewish (1939-1945) -- Influence.

D804.45.U55.N68 1999
Novick, Peter, 1934-
The Holocaust in American life/ Peter Novick. Boston: Houghton Mifflin, 1999. 373 p.
99-020074   943.54/840090   0395840090
Holocaust, Jewish (1939-1945) -- Foreign public opinion, American. Holocaust, Jewish (1939-1945) -- Influence. Holocaust, Jewish (1939-1945) -- Historiography.

D804.47.S57 1998
Sisters in sorrow: voices of care in the Holocaust/ Roger A. Ritvo and Diane M. Plotkin; foreword by Harry James Cargas. College Station, TX: Texas A&M Univ. Press, c1998. xviii, 314 p.
97-046013   940.53/18/082   0890968101
Jewish women in the Holocaust. Holocaust, Jewish (1939-1945) -- Personal narratives. World War, 1939-1945 -- Medical care.

D804.47.W66 1998
Women in the Holocaust/ edited by Dalia Ofer and Lenore J. Weitzman. New Haven, CT: Yale University Press, c1998. vii, 402 p.
97-046011   940.53/18/082   0300073542
Jewish women in the Holocaust.

D804.5.G85.L49 2000
Lewy, Guenter, 1923-
The Nazi persecution of the gypsies/ Guenter Lewy. New York: Oxford University Press, 2000. ix, 306 p.
98-052545   940.53/18/08991497   0195125568
Gypsies -- Nazi persecution. World War, 1939-1945 -- Atrocities. Gypsies -- Germany -- History -- 20th century.

D804.6.F3813 1999
Favez, Jean-Claude.
The Red Cross and the Holocaust/ Jean-Claude Favez; edited and translated by John and Beryl Fletcher. Cambridge, U.K.; Cambridge University Press, 1999. xxxii, 353 p.
99-011233   362.87/81/08992404   052141587X
World War, 1939-1945 -- Jews -- Rescue. Holocaust, Jewish (1939-1945)

D804.6.Z87 2000
Zuroff, Efraim.
The response of Orthodox Jewry in the United States to the Holocaust: the activities of the Vaad ha-Hatzala Rescue Committee, 1939-1945/ by Efraim Zuroff. New York: Michael Scharf Publication Trust of the Yeshiva c2000. xxiv, 316 p.
99-052401   940.53/18   0881256668
World War, 1939-1945 -- Jews -- Rescue. Holocaust, Jewish (1939-1945)

D804.65.P35 2000
Paldiel, Mordecai.
Saving the Jews: amazing stories of men and women who defied the "final solution"/ Mordecai Paldiel. Rockville, Md.: Schreiber, c2000. 338 p.
00-056350   940.53/18   1887563555
Righteous Gentiles in the Holocaust. World War, 1939-1945 -- Jews -- Rescue. Holocaust, Jewish (1939-1945)

D804.66.S84
Sugihara, Seishiro, 1941-
Chiune Sugihara and Japan's Foreign Ministry, between incompetence and culpability. Seishiro Sugihara; translated by Norman Hu. Lanham, MD: United Press of America, 2001.
01-027033   362.87/81//092   0761819711
Sugihara, Chiune, -- 1900-1986. Righteous Gentiles in the Holocaust -- Biography. World War, 1939-1945 -- Causes. United States -- Foreign relations -- Japan. Japan -- Foreign relations -- United States.

D804.66.S84.L48 1996
Levine, Hillel.
In search of Sugihara: the elusive Japanese diplomat who risked his life to rescue 10,000 Jews from the Holocaust/ by Hillel Levine. New York, N.Y.: Free Press, 1996. viii, 323 p.
96-042108   362.87/81/092   0684832518
Sugihara, Chiune, -- 1900-1986. Righteous Gentiles in the Holocaust -- Biography. Diplomats -- Japan -- Biography. Jews -- Persecutions -- Lithuania -- Kaunas.

D805-805.5 World War II (1939-1945) — Prisoners and prisons

D805.A2.B57 1992
Bird, Tom, 1956-
American POWs of World War II: forgotten men tell their stories/ Tom Bird. Westport, Conn.; Praeger, 1
992. xxix, 149 p.
91-046991   940.54/72/0922   0275937070
World War, 1939-1945 -- Prisoners and prisons. World War, 1939-1945 -- Personal narratives, American. World War, 1939-1945 -- Psychological aspects.

D805.A2.G49 1988
Gill, Anton.
The journey back from hell: an oral history: conversations with concentration camp survivors/ Anton Gill. New York: Morrow, c1988. xvi, 494 p.
88-038663   940.53/18   0688088473
World War, 1939-1945 -- Concentration camps -- Europe. World War, 1939-1945 -- Prisoners and prisons, German. Holocaust survivors -- Interviews.

D805.A2.H67 1991
Horner, Helmut, 1916-1990.
A German odyssey: the journal of a German prisoner of war/ Helmut Horner; translated and edited by Allan Kent Powell. Golden, Colo.: Fulcrum Pub., c1991. xiii, 394 p.
90-085221   940.54/72   1555910777
Horner, Helmut, -- 1916-1990. Prisoners of war -- Germany -- Biography. World War, 1939-1945 -- Prisoners and prisons. World War, 1939-1945 -- Personal narratives, German.

D805.A78.B54 1995
Biggs, Chester M., 1921-
Behind the barbed wire: memoir of a World War II U.S. marine captured in North China in 1941 and imprisoned by the Japanese until 1945/ by Chester M. Biggs, Jr. Jefferson, N.C.: McFarland, c1995. vii, 224 p.
94-032415   940.54/7252/092   089950972X
Biggs, Chester M., -- 1921- World War, 1939-1945 -- Prisoners and prisons, Japanese. Prisoners of war -- Asia -- Biography.

D805.B9.B85 1993
Building the death railway: the ordeal of American POWs in Burma, 1942-1945/ edited by Robert S. La Forte & Ronald E. Marcello. Wilmington, Del.: Scholarly Resources, 1993. xxiii, 300 p.
92-027641   940.54/7252/09591   084202428X
World War, 1939-1945 -- Concentration camps -- Burma. World War, 1939-1945 -- Conscript labor. World War, 1939-1945 -- Prisoners and prisons, Japanese.

D805.G3.B45613 1997
Beon, Yves.
Planet Dora: a memoir of the Holocaust and the birth of the space age/ Yves Beon; edited with an introduction by Michael J. Neufeld; translated by Yves Beon and Richard L. Fague. Boulder: WestviewPress, 1997. 250 p.
96-029626   940.53/18/0943224   0813332729
V-1 bomb. V-2 rocket. World War, 1939-1945 -- Prisoners and prisons, German. Dora (Germany: Concentration camp)

D805.G3.B7746 1995
The Buchenwald report/ translated, edited, and with an introduction by David A. Hackett; foreword by Frederick A. Praeger. Boulder: Westview Press, c1995. xviii, 397 p.
94-039714   940.53/1743226   0813317770
Holocaust, Jewish (1939-1945) -- Germany -- Personal narratives.

D805.G3.G45 1998
George, Alexandra, 1952-
Escape from "Ward six": Russia facing past and present/ Alexandra George. Lanham: University Press of America, c1998. xxiv, 760 p.
98-015624   947   0761811397
Russia (Federation) -- Civilization. Russia (Federation) -- Social conditions -- 1991-

D805.G3.M6143 2000
Morrison, Jack G. 1937-
Ravensbruck: everyday life in a women's concentration camp, 1939-45/ Jack G. Morrison. Princeton: Wiener, 2000. p. cm.
99-085963   940.53/1743157   1558762183
World War, 1939-1945 -- Prisoners and prisons, German. Women prisoners -- Germany.

D805.G3.R35 1953
Reid, P. R. 1910-
The Colditz story. Philadelphia, Lippincott, 1953 [c1952] 288 p.
52-013728   940.54/72/43094321
Reid, P. R. -- (Patrick Robert), -- 1910- World War, 1939-1945 -- Prisoners and prisons, German. World War, 1939-1945 -- Personal narratives, British. Prisoners of war -- Germany -- Biography.

D805.G3.R46 2000
Richard, Oscar.
Kriegie: an American POW in Germany/ Oscar G. Richard, III. Baton Rouge: Louisiana State University Press, c2000. x, 130 p.
99-088025   940.53/7243   0807125628
Richard, Oscar. World War, 1939-1945 -- Prisoners and prisons, German. World War, 1939-1945 -- Personal narratives, American. Prisoners of war -- Germany -- Biography.

D805.I55.T3613 1996
Tanaka, Toshiyuki, 1949-
Hidden horrors: Japanese war crimes in World War II/ Yuki Tanaka; with a foreword by John W. Dower. Boulder, Colo.: Westview Press, 1996. xix, 267 p.
96-017735   940.54/05   0813327172
World War, 1939-1945 -- Indonesia -- Prisoners and prisons, Japanese. Australians -- Indonesia -- Crimes against. Japan -- Armed Forces -- Asia, Southeastern -- Attitude.

D805.J3.G54 1994
Giles, Donald T., 1898-1983.
Captive of the Rising Sun: the POW memoirs of rear admiral Donald T. Giles, USN/ edited, and with additional material provided by Donald T. Giles, Jr. Annapolis, Md.: Naval Institute Press, c1994. xv, 232 p.
93-037042   940.54/7252   1557503206
Giles, Donald T., -- 1898-1983. World War, 1939-1945 -- Prisoners and prisons, Japanese. Prisoners of war -- Japan -- Biography. Prisoners of war -- United States -- Biography.

D805.J3 H58 2001
Holmes, Linda Goetz.
Unjust enrichment: how Japan's companies built postwar fortunes using American POWs/ Linda Goetz Holmes. Mechanicsburg, PA: Stackpole Books, c2001. xxii, 202 p.
00-058375   940.54/7252   0811718441
World War, 1939-1945 -- Prisoners and prisons, Japanese. Industries -- Japan -- History -- 20th century. Prisoners of war -- Japan.

D805.L49 2000
Levine, Alan J.
Captivity, flight, and survival in World War II/ by Alan J. Levine. Westport, CT: Praeger, 2000. x, 258 p.
99-086095   940.54/72   027596955X
World War, 1939-1945 -- Prisoners and prisons. Escapes -- History -- 20th century.

D805.M38.P55 2000
Pike, David Wingeate.
Spaniards in the Holocaust: Mauthausen, the horror on the Danube/ David Wingeate Pike. London; Routledge, 2000. xxiv, 442 p.
99-059439   940.54/7243/094362   0415227801
World War, 1939-1945 -- Prisoners and prisons, German. Prisoners of war -- Spain.

D805.P7.C8713 1989
Czech, Danuta.
Auschwitz chronicle, 1939-1945/ Danuta Czech. New York: H. Holt, c1990. xxi, 855 p.
89-035351   940.53/174386   0805009388
Holocaust, Jewish (1939-1945)

D805.P7.D37
The Death camp Treblinka: a documentary/ edited by Alexander Donat; [cover design by Eric Gluckman]. New York: Holocaust Library: [distributed by Schocken Boo c1979. 320 p.
79-053471   940.53/1503/924   0896040097
Holocaust, Jewish (1939-1945) -- Personal narratives.

D805.P7.D41613 1995
Delbo, Charlotte.
Auschwitz and after/ Charlotte Delbo; translated by Rosette C. Lamont; with an introduction by Lawrence L. Langer. New Haven: Yale University Press, c1995. xviii, 354 p.
94-038669   940.53/174386   0300062087
Delbo, Charlotte. World War, 1939-1945 -- Personal narratives, French. Political prisoners -- France -- Biography.

D805.P7.D87 1988
Durand, Arthur A., 1944-
Stalag Luft III: the secret story/ Arthur A. Durand. Baton Rouge: Louisiana State University Press, c1988. xiii, 412 p.
87-033871   940.54/72/43094381   0807113522
World War, 1939-1945 -- Prisoners and prisons, German.

D805.P7.N3413 1989
Nahon, Marco, 1895-
Birkenau: the camp of death/ Marco Nahon; translated from the French by Jacqueline Havaux Bowers; edited and with an introduction by Steven Bowman. Tuscaloosa: University of Alabama Press, c1989. xvii, 149 p.
89-004661   940.54/72/43094386   0817304495
Nahon, Marco, -- 1895- Jews -- Persecutions -- Greece. Holocaust, Jewish (1939-1945) -- Greece -- Personal narratives. Brzezinka (Poland: Concentration camp) Greece -- Ethnic relations.

D805.U5.C29 1997
Carlson, Lewis H.
We were each other's prisoners: an oral history of World War II American and German prisoners of war/ Lewis H. Carlson. New York: Basic Books, c1997. xxvii, 258 p.
96-039116   940.54/7243   0465091202
World War, 1939-1945 -- Prisoners and prisons, American. World War, 1939-1945 -- Prisoners and prisons, German. Prisoners of war -- United States.

D805.U5.E35 1992
Eisenhower and the German POWs: facts against falsehood/ edited by Gunter Bischof and Stephen E. Ambrose. Baton Rouge: Louisiana State University Press, c1992. xvii, 258 p.
92-003908   940.54/7244   0807117587
Eisenhower, Dwight D. -- (Dwight David), -- 1890-1969 -- Congresses. Prisoners of war -- Germany -- History -- 20th century -- Congresses. World War, 1939-1945 -- Prisoners and prisons, American -- Congresses.

D805.U5.F69 2000
Fox, Stephen, 1938-
America's invisible gulag: a biography of German American internment & exclusion in World War II: memory and history/ Stephen Fox. New York: Peter Lang, c2000. xxiv, 379 p.
99-055725   940.53/08931   0820449148
World War, 1939-1945 -- German Americans -- Biography. World War, 1939-1945 -- Prisoners and prisons, American. Oral history.

D805.U5.R63 1995
Robin, Ron Theodore.
The barbed-wire college: reeducating German POWs in the United States during World War II/ Ron Robin. Princeton, N.J.: Princeton University Pres, c1995. x, 217 p.
94-021161   940.54/7273   0691037000
World War, 1939-1945 -- Prisoners and prisons, American. World War, 1939-1945 -- Education and the war. World War, 1939-1945 -- United States.

D805.U6.K57 1988
Koop, Allen V., 1944-
Stark decency: German prisoners of war in a New England village/ Allen V. Koop. Hanover, NH: University Press of New England, c1988. xii, 136 p.
88-005550   940.54/72/73097421   0874514584
World War, 1939-1945 -- Prisoners and prisons, American. Prisoners of war -- New Hampshire -- Stark. Prisoners of war -- Germany. Stark (N.H.) -- History.

D805.5.A96.O54 1998
Olere, David, 1902-1985.
Witness: images of Auschwitz/ David Olere & Alexandre Oler. N. Richland Hills, Tex.: WestWind Press, c1998. 112 p.
98-025406   940.53/174386   094103769X
Holocaust, Jewish (1939-1945) -- Pictorial works.

D805.5.D33.D33 1998
Dachau 29 April 1945: the Rainbow liberation memoirs/ edited by Sam Dann. Lubbock, Tex.: Texas Tech University Press, 1998. xx, 266 p.
98-013755   940.54/1273   0896723917
World War, 1939-1945 -- Personal narratives, American.

D807 World War II (1939-1945) — Medical and sanitary services. Hospitals. Red Cross — By region or country, A-Z

D807.C2.C66 1990
Copp, J. T.
Battle exhaustion: soldiers and psychiatrists in the Canadian Army, 1939-1945/ Terry Copp, Bill McAndrew. Montreal; McGill-Queen's University Press, c1990. x, 249 p.
91-163155   940.54/7571   0773507744
World War, 1939-1945 -- Medical care -- Canada. World War, 1939-1945 -- Psychological aspects. War neuroses.

D807.U5.J33 2000
Jackson, Kathi, 1951-
They called them angels: American military nurses of World War II/ Kathi Jackson. Westport, Conn.: Praeger, 2000. xx, 211 p.
99-059563   940.54/7573   0275968995
World War, 1939-1945 -- Medical care -- United States. Nurses -- United States -- History -- 20th century.

D807.U6.C685 1994
Cowdrey, Albert E.
Fighting for life: American military medicine in World War II/ Albert E. Cowdrey. New York: Free Press; c1994. viii, 392 p.
94-008280   940.54/7573   0029068355
World War, 1939-1945 -- Medical care -- United States. Medicine, Military -- United States -- History -- 20th century.

D807.U6.M357 1999
Mangerich, Agnes Jensen, 1914-
Albanian escape: the true story of U.S. Army nurses behind enemy lines/ Agnes Jensen Mangerich; as told to Evelyn M. Monahan and Rosemary L. Neidel. Lexington, Ky.: University Press of Kentucky, c1999. xiii, 220 p.
98-048348   940.54/7573/092   0813121094
World War, 1939-1945 -- Medical care -- United States. Flight nursing -- United States. Nurses -- United States -- History -- 20th century.

D808 World War II (1939-1945) — Relief work. Charities. Protection. Refugees. Displaced persons — General works

D808.M45 1998
Melton, Judith M., 1941-
The face of exile: autobiographical journeys/ by Judith M. Melton. Iowa City: University of Iowa Press, c1998. xx, 225 p.
98-024440   940.53/086/91   0877456496
World War, 1939-1945 -- Refugees -- Europe. World War, 1939-1945 -- Personal narratives.

D808.W96 1988
Wyman, Mark.
DP: Europe's displaced persons, 1945-1951/ Mark Wyman. Philadelphia: Balch Institute Press; c1988. 257 p.
88-070152   940.53/159   0944190049
World War, 1939-1945 -- Refugees.

D809 World War II (1939-1945) — Relief work. Charities. Protection. Refugees. Displaced persons — By region or country, A-Z

D809.E8.L44 1999
Lagrou, Pieter.
The legacy of Nazi occupation: patriotic memory and national recovery in Western Europe, 1945-1965/ Pieter Lagrou. Cambridge, UK; Cambridge University Press, 1999. p. cm.
99-024431   940.55   0521651808
Reconstruction (1939-1951) -- Europe. Memory. Europe -- History -- 1945-

D809.F7.G57
Gold, Mary Jayne.
Crossroads Marseilles, 1940/ by Mary Jayne Gold. Garden City, N.Y.: Doubleday, 1980. xviii, 412 p.
79-008551   940.53/159   0385156189
Gold, Mary Jayne. Fry, Varian. World War, 1939-1945 -- Refugees. World War, 1939-1945 -- Personal narratives, American. World War, 1939-1945 -- France.

D809.G3.M33 1997
McClelland, Grigor.
Embers of war: letters from a Quaker relief worker in war-torn Germany/ Grigor McClelland. London; British Academic Press; 1997. 230 p.
98-187150   943/.008286   1860643124
McClelland, Grigor -- Correspondence. McClelland, Grigor. Quakers -- Great Britain -- Biography. Quakers -- Germany -- History -- 20th century. Reconstruction (1939-1951) -- Germany. Germany -- History -- 1945-1955.

D809.U5.M37 1999
Marino, Andy.
A quiet American: the secret war of Varian Fry/ Andy Marino. New York: St. Martin's Press, 1999. xi, 403 p.
99-022064   940.54/8173   031220356X
Fry, Varian. Righteous Gentiles in the Holocaust -- France -- Biography. World War, 1939-1945 -- Jews -- Rescue -- France. World War, 1939-1945 -- Personal narratives, American.

D810 World War II (1939-1945) — Other special topics, A-Z

D810.A53.K64 1995
Kohlhoff, Dean.
When the wind was a river: Aleut evacuation in World War II/ Dean Kohlhoff. Seattle: University of Washington Press in association wi c1995. xvi, 234 p.
95-017676   940.53/1503971   0295974036
Aleuts. World War, 1939-1945 -- Alaska. World War, 1939-1945 -- Atrocities.

D810.C38.G66 1998
Goodwin, Bridget.
Keen as mustard: Britain's horrific chemical warfare experiments in Australia/ Bridget Goodwin. St Lucia, Qld., Australia: University of Queensland Press, 1998. 361 p.
98-217406   358/.34/072041   0702229415
World War, 1939-1945 -- Chemical warfare -- Australia. Human experimentation in medicine -- Great Britain. Human experimentation in medicine -- Australia.

D810.C4.D347 1997
Dear poppa: the World War II Berman family letters/ compiled by Ruth Berman; edited by Judy Barrett Litoff. St. Paul: Minnesota Historical Society Press, c1997. xxii, 314 p.
97-006447   940.53/161/092273   0873513576
Berman, Reuben -- Correspondence. Berman family -- Correspondence. World War, 1939-1945 -- Children -- United States -- Correspondence. Children and war -- United States. Youth -- United States -- Correspondence. United States -- Social life and customs -- 1918-1945.

D810.C4.W45 2000
Werner, Emmy E.
Through the eyes of innocents: children witness World War II/ Emmy E. Werner. Boulder, CO: Westview Press, 2000. xiv, 271 p.
99-042028   0813335353
World War, 1939-1945 -- Children. Children -- History -- 20th century.

D810.C6.R95 2000
Rychlak, Ronald J.
Hitler, the war, and the pope/ Ronald J. Rychlak. Huntington, Ind.: Our Sunday Visitor, c2000. xiv, 470 p.
00-105755   940.54/78   0879732172
Pius -- XII, -- Pope, -- 1876-1958. World War, 1939-1945 -- Religious aspects -- Catholic Church.

D810.C698.H53 1995
Hicks, George L.
The comfort women: Japan's brutal regime of enforced prostitution in the Second World War/ George Hicks. New York: W.W. Norton & Co., 1995. 303 p.
95-002162   940.54/05/082095   0393038076
Comfort women -- Asia -- History. Service, Compulsory non-military -- Asia. World War, 1939-1945 -- Women -- Asia.

D810.C698.Y6713 2000
Yoshimi, Yoshiaki, 1946-
Comfort women: sexual slavery in the Japanese military during World War II / Yoshimi Yoshiaki; translated by Suzanne O'Brien. New York: Columbia University Press, c2000. 253 p.
00-030305   940.54/05/082095   023112032X
Comfort women -- Asia. World War, 1939-1945 -- Women -- Asia.

D810.C8.L4813 2001
Levin, Itamar.
His majesty's enemies: Great Britain's war against Holocaust victims and survivors/ Itamar Levin; translated by Natasha Dornberg and Judith Yalon-Fortus; foreword by Avraham Hirschson. Westport, Conn.: Praeger, 2001. xviii, 238 p.
00-032371   940.53/18   0275968162
World War, 1939-1945 -- Confiscations and contributions -- Great Britain. Holocaust, Jewish (1939-1945) -- Economic aspects -- Great Britain. Jews -- Claims.

D810.C82.E45 1991
Eller, Cynthia.
Conscientious objectors and the Second World War: moral and religious arguments in support of pacifism/ Cynthia Eller. New York: Praeger, 1991. viii, 218 p.
90-021594   940.53/162   0275938050
World War, 1939-1945 -- Conscientious objectors -- United States. World War, 1939-1945 -- Moral and ethical aspects. Pacifism.

D810.C82.F73 1996
Frazer, Heather T.
We have just begun to not fight: an oral history of conscientious objectors in civilian public service during World war II/ Heather T. Frazer and John O'Sullivan. New York: Twayne Publishers; c1996. xxv, 268 p.
95-020068   940.53/162/0973   0805791345
World War, 1939-1945 -- Conscientious objectors -- United States. Service, Compulsory nonmilitary -- United States. Oral history.

D810.C82.G66 1997
Goossen, Rachel Waltner.
Women against the good war: conscientious objection and gender on the American home front, 1941-1947/ Rachel Waltner Goossen. Chapel Hill: University of North Carolina Press, c1997. xii, 180 p.
97-009885   940.53/162   080782366X
World War, 1939-1945 -- Conscientious objectors -- United States. World War, 1939-1945 -- Moral and ethical aspects. World War, 1939-1945 -- Women -- United States.

D810.C88.A48 2000
Alvarez, David J.
Secret messages: codebreaking and American diplomacy, 1930-1945/ David Alvarez. Lawrence, KS: University Press of Kansas, 2000. xi, 292 p.
99-049798   940.54/8673   0700610138
World War, 1939-1945 -- Cryptography. Cryptography -- United States -- History -- 20th century. World War, 1939-1945 -- Diplomatic history. United States -- Foreign relations -- 1933-1945.

D810.C88.D46 1997
Denniston, Robin.
Churchill's secret war: diplomatic decrypts, the Foreign Office and Turkey, 1942-44/ Robin Denniston. Thrupp, Stroud, Gloucestershire: Sutton Publishing; 1997. xv, 208 p.
97-155547   940.54/8641   031216582X
Churchill, Winston, -- Sir, -- 1874-1965.   World War, 1939-1945 -- Cryptography. World War, 1939-1945 -- Secret Service -- Great Britain. World War, 1939-1945 -- Electronic intelligence -- Great Britain. Turkey -- History -- 1918-1960. Turkey -- Politics and government -- 1918-1960.

D810.C88.J66 1978
Jones, R. V. 1911-
The wizard war: British scientific intelligence, 1939-1945/ R. V. Jones. New York: Coward, McCann & Geoghegan, 1978. xx, 556 p.
77-017984   940.54/86/41   0698108965
Jones, R. V. -- (Reginald Victor), -- 1911- World War, 1939-1945 -- Cryptography. World War, 1939-1945 -- Secret service -- Great Britain. World War, 1939-1945 -- Personal narratives, British.

D810.C88.K34 1991
Kahn, David, 1930-
Seizing the enigma: the race to break the German U-boat codes, 1939-1943/ David Kahn. Boston: Houghton Mifflin Co., 1991. xii, 336 p.
90-025128   940.54/85   0395427398
World War, 1939-1945 -- Cryptography. World War, 1939-1945 -- Naval operations, German. World War, 1939-1945 -- Naval operations -- Submarine.

D810.C88.L48
Lewin, Ronald.
The American magic: codes, ciphers, and the defeat of Japan/ Ronald Lewin. New York: Farrar Straus Giroux, c1982. xv, 332 p.
81-015099   940.54/86/73   0374104174
World War, 1939-1945 -- Cryptography. World War, 1939-1945 -- Secret service -- United States. World War, 1939-1945 -- Pacific Ocean. Japan -- History -- 1912-1945.

D810.C88.P73 1995
Prados, John.
Combined fleet decoded: the secret history of American intelligence and the Japanese Navy in World War II/ John Prados. New York: Random House, c1995. xxvi, 832 p.
94-020784   940.54/8673   0679437010
World War, 1939-1945 -- Military intelligence -- United States. World War, 1939-1945 -- Cryptography. World War, 1939-1945 -- Naval operations, Japanese.

D810.G9.T4813 1998
Thurner, Erika.
National Socialism and Gypsies in Austria/ Erika Thurner; edited and translated by Gilya Gerda Schmidt; with a foreword by Michael Berenbaum Tuscaloosa: University of Alabama Press, c1998. xx, 218 p.
98-008880   940.54/7243/094363   0817309241
Gypsies -- Nazi persecution -- Austria. World War, 1939-1945 -- Concentration camps -- Austria. World War, 1939-1945 -- Atrocities.

D810.I5.F73 1999
Franco, Jere Bishop, 1948-
Crossing the pond: the native American effort in World War II/ Jere Bishop Franco. Denton, Tex.: University of North Texas Press, 1999. xvii, 232 p.
98-044928   940.54/03   1574410652
World War, 1939-1945 -- Participation, Indian. Indians of North America -- History -- 20th century.

D810.I5.T69 2000
Townsend, Kenneth William, 1951-
World War II and the American Indian/ Kenneth William Townsend. Albuquerque: University of New Mexico Press, c2000. x, 272 p.
99-050786   940.53/089/97   0826320384
World War, 1939-1945 -- Indians. Indiand of North America -- Cultural assimilation. Indians of North America -- Ethnic identity.

D810.J4.B77
Browning, Christopher R.
The final solution and the German Foreign Office: a study of Referat D III of Abteilung Deutschland, 1940-43/ by Christopher R. Browning. New York: Holmes & Meier, 1978. 276 p.
78-008996   940.53/15/03924]   0841904030
Holocaust, Jewish (1939-1945)

D810.J4.D33
Dawidowicz, Lucy S.
The war against the Jews, 1933-1945/ Lucy S. Dawidowicz. New York: Holt, Rinehart and Winston, [1975] xviii, 460 p.
74-015470   940.53/15/03924   003013661X
Holocaust, Jewish (1939-1945) Antisemitism -- Germany.

D810.J4.F5413 1984
Fleming, Gerald.
Hitler and the final solution/ Gerald Fleming; with an introduction by Saul Friedlander. Berkeley: University of California Press, c1984. xxxvi, 219 p.
83-024352   940.53/15/03924   0520051033
Hitler, Adolf, -- 1889-1945 -- Views on Jews. Holocaust, Jewish (1939-1945) Germany -- Ethnic relations.

D810.J4.F55
Flender, Harold.
Rescue in Denmark/ by Harold Flender. New York: Simon and Schuster, 1963. 281 p.
63-009272   940.5404
World War, 1939-1945 -- Jews -- Rescue. Jews -- Denmark. Denmark -- History -- German occupation, 1940-1945.

D810.J4.F715
Frank, Anne, 1929-1945.
The diary of a young girl; translated from the Dutch by B. M. Mooyaart-Doubleday, with an introd. by Eleanor Roosevelt. Garden City, N.Y., Doubleday, 1952. 285 p.
52-006355   940.53492
Frank, Anne, -- 1929-1945 -- Diaries. Holocaust, Jewish (1939-1945) -- Netherlands -- Amsterdam -- Personal narratives. Jewish girls -- Netherlands -- Amsterdam -- Diaries. Jews -- Persecutions -- Netherlands -- Amsterdam. Amsterdam (Netherlands) -- Ethnic relations.

D810.J4.H5 1985b
Hilberg, Raul, 1926-
The destruction of the European Jews/ Raul Hilberg. New York: Holmes & Meier, 1985. 3 v. (1,273 p.)
83-018369   940.53/15/03924   084190832X
Holocaust, Jewish (1939-1945) Germany -- Politics and government -- 1933-1945.

D810.J4.H655 vol. 1
Legalizing the Holocaust: the early phase, 1933-1939/ introduction by John Mendelsohn. New York: Garland, 1982. lii, 212 p.
81-080309   940.53/15/03924 s   082404875X
Jews -- Legal status, laws, etc. -- Germany -- History -- Sources.

D810.J4.H655 vol. 2
Legalizing the Holocaust, the later phase, 1939-1943/ introduction by John Mendelsohn. New York: Garland Pub.,, 1982. 355 p.
81-080310   940.53/15/03924 s   0824048768
Jews -- Germany -- History -- 1933-1945 -- Sources. Holocaust, Jewish (1939-1945) -- Sources. Germany -- Ethnic relations -- Sources.

D810.J4.H655 vol. 3
The Crystal Night Pogrom/ introduction by John Mendelsohn. New York: Garland, 1982. 402 p.
81-080311   940.53/15/03924 s   0824048776
Kristallnacht, 1938 -- Sources. Germany -- Ethnic relations -- Sources.

D810.J4.H655 vol. 7
Jewish emigration: the S.S. St. Louis affair and other cases/ introduction by John Mendelsohn. New York: Garland Pub., 1982. 270 p.
81-080315   940.53/15/03924 s   0824048814
Jews -- Germany -- Migrations -- Sources. Germany -- Emigration and immigration -- Sources. Cuba -- Emigration and immigration -- Sources.

D810.J4.H655 vol. 8
Deportation of the Jews to the east: Stettin, 1940, to Hungary, 1944/ introduction by John Mendelsohn. New York: Garland, 1982. 254 p.
81-080316   940.53/15/03924 s   0824048822
Holocaust, Jewish (1939-1945) -- Sources.

D810.J4.H655 vol. 16
Rescue to Switzerland: the Musy and Saly Mayer affairs/ introduction by Sybil Milton. New York: Garland Pub., 1982. 219 p.
81-080324   940.53/15/03924 s   0824048903
Mayer, Saly, -- 1882-1950.   World War, 1939-1945 -- Jews -- Rescue -- Switzerland -- Sources. Refugees, Jewish -- Switzerland -- Sources. Jews -- Switzerland -- Politics and government -- Sources. Switzerland -- Ethnic relations -- Sources.

D810.J4.K68413 1984
Krakowski, Shmuel.
The war of the doomed: Jewish armed resistance in Poland, 1942-1944/ Shmuel Krakowski; foreword by Yehuda Bauer; translated from the Hebrew by Orah Blaustein. New York: Holmes and Meier, 1984. xii, 340 p.
83-018537   940.53/15/03924   0841908516
World War, 1939-1945 -- Jewish resistance -- Poland. Jews -- Persecutions -- Poland. Holocaust, Jewish (1939-1945) -- Poland. Poland -- History -- Occupation, 1939-1945. Poland -- Ethnic relations.

D810.J4.L267 1990
Lang, Berel.
Act and idea in the Nazi genocide/ Berel Lang. Chicago: University of Chicago Press, 1990. xxii, 258 p.
89-037320   940.53/18   0226468682
Holocaust, Jewish (1939-1945) -- Moral and ethical aspects. Genocide -- Moral and ethical aspects.

D810.J4.L278 1980b
Laqueur, Walter, 1921-
The terrible secret: suppression of the truth about Hitler's "final solution"/ Walter Laqueur. Boston: Little, Brown, c1980. 262 p.
80-026613   943.086   0316514748
Holocaust, Jewish (1939-1945) -- Censorship.

D810.J4.P477 1979
Perl, William R.
The four-front war: from the Holocaust to the Promised Land/ by William R. Perl. New York: Crown Publishers, c1979. viii, 376 p.
79-016255   940.53/1503/924   0517538377
Perl, William R. Holocaust, Jewish (1939-1945) -- Personal narratives. World War, 1939-1945 -- Jews -- Rescue. Palestine -- Emigration and immigration.

D810.J4.T7
Trunk, Isaiah.
Jewish responses to Nazi persecution: collective and individual behavior in extremis/ Isaiah Trunk. New York: Stein and Day, c1979. xii, 371 p.
78-006378   940.53/1503/924   0812825004
Holocaust, Jewish (1939-1945) World War, 1939-1945 -- Personal narratives, Jewish.

D810.J4.Y58 1988
Young, James Edward.
Writing and rewriting the Holocaust: narrative and the consequences of interpretation/ James E. Young. Bloomington: Indiana University Press, c1988. viii, 243 p.
87-035791   940.53/15/039240072   0253367166
Holocaust, Jewish (1939-1945) -- Historiography. Holocaust, Jewish (1939-1945) -- Personal narratives -- History and criticism. Holocaust, Jewish (1939-1945), in literature.

D810.J4.Z8413
Zuker-Bujanowska, Liliana, 1928-
Liliana's journal/ Warsaw 1939-1945/ Liliana Zuker-Bujanowska. New York: Dial Press, c1980. viii, 162 p.
80-000139   943.8/053/0924   080374997X
Zuker-Bujanowska, Liliana, -- 1928- -- Diaries. Holocaust, Jewish (1939-1945) -- Poland -- Warsaw -- Personal narratives. Jews -- Poland -- Warsaw -- Diaries. Warsaw (Poland) -- Biography.

D810.L36 2000
Lanker, Brian.
They drew fire: combat artists of World War II/ Brian Lanker, Nicole Newnham. New York: TV Books, c2000. xi, 180 p.
99-086620   704.9/4994054   1575000857
World War, 1939-1945 -- Art and the war. Artists -- United States -- History -- 20th century.

D810.L64.O36 1994
Ohl, John Kennedy, 1942-
Supplying the troops: General Somervell and American logistics in WWII/ John Kennedy Ohl. DeKalb: Northern Illinois University Press, 1994. x, 331 p.
93-039869   355.4/11/092   0875801854
Somervell, Brehon Burke, -- 1892-1955.   World War, 1939-1945 -- Logistics -- United States.

D810.L642.U653 1994
Waddell, Steve R.
United States Army logistics: the Normandy Campaign/ Steve R. Waddell. Westport, Conn.: Greenwood Press, 1994. xvii, 190 p.
93-049615   940.54/2142   0313290547
World War, 1939-1945 -- Logistics -- United States. World War, 1939-1945 -- Campaigns -- France -- Normandy.

D810.N4.B82
Buchanan, Albert Russell, 1906-
Black Americans in World War II/ A. Russell Buchanan. Santa Barbara, Calif.: Clio Books, c1977. ix, 148 p.
76-053577   940.54/03   0874362276
World War, 1939-1945 -- Afro-Americans. United States -- Race relations.

D810.N4.M38 1983
McGuire, Phillip, 1944-
Taps for a Jim Crow army: letters from black soldiers in World War II/ Phillip McGuire; with a foreword by Benjamin Quarles. Santa Barbara, Calif.: ABC-Clio, c1983. li, 278 p.
82-022689   940.54/03   0874360412
World War, 1939-1945 -- Personal narratives, American. Afro-American soldiers -- Correspondence. World War, 1939-1945 -- Participation, Afro-American. United States -- Armed Forces -- Military life. United States -- Armed Forces -- Afro-Americans.

D810.N4.M67 2000
Morehouse, Maggi M., 1953-
Fighting in the Jim Crow Army: black men and women remember World War II/ Maggi M. Morehouse. Lanham: Rowman & Littlefield, c2000. xviii, 247 p.
00-055257   940.54/03   0847691934
World War, 1939-1945 -- Afro-Americans.

D810.N4.S6 1988
Smith, Graham
When Jim Crow met John Bull: Black American soldiers in World War II Britain/ Graham Smith. New York: St. Martin's Press, 1988, c1987. 265 p.
87-038113   940.53/150396073   0312015968
World War, 1939-1945 -- Participation, Afro-American. Afro-American soldiers -- Great Britain. Racism -- Great Britain. Great Britain -- History -- George VI, 1936-1952.

D810.P7.G318 1997
Bergmeier, H. J. P.
Hitler's airwaves: the inside story of Nazi radio broadcasting and propaganda swing/ Horst J.P. Bergmeier, Rainer E. Lotz. New Haven: Yale University Press, c1997. xiv, 368 p.
96-036617   940.54/88743   0300067097
World War, 1939-1945 -- Propaganda. Radio in propaganda -- Germany. Propaganda, German.

D810.P7.G7216
Balfour, Michael Leonard Graham, 1908-
Propaganda in war, 1939-1945: organisations, policies, and publics, in Britain and Germany/ Michael Balfour. London; Routledge & Kegan Paul, 1979. xvii, 520 p.
79-040304   940.54/88   0710001932
World War, 1939-1945 -- Propaganda. Propaganda, British -- History -- 20th century. Propaganda, German -- History -- 20th century.

D810.P7.G7238 1990
Cole, Robert, 1939-
Britain and the war of words in neutral Europe, 1939-45: the art of the possible/ Robert Cole. New York: St. Martin's Press, 1990. xi, 242 p.
89-034297   940.54/88641   0312035381
World War, 1939-1945 -- Propaganda. Propaganda, Anti-German. Propaganda, British -- History -- 20th century.

D810.P7.G726 2000
Doherty, M. A.
Nazi wireless propaganda: Lord Haw-Haw and British public opinion in the Second World War/ M.A. Doherty. Edinburgh: Edinburgh University Press, c2000. 256 p.
940.5488743   0748613706
Joyce, William, -- 1906-1946.   Propaganda, German. Public opinion -- Britain -- History -- 20th century. Radio in propaganda -- Germany.

D810.P7.G765 1996
Nicholas, Sian.
The echo of war: home front propaganda and the wartime BBC, 1939-45/ Sian Nicholas. Manchester; Manchester Univerity Press; 1996. x, 307 p.
95-032668   940.54/88641   0719046084
Propaganda, British -- History -- 20th century. World War, 1939-1945 -- Propaganda. Radio in propaganda -- Great Britain.

D810.P7.U365 1989
Fussell, Paul, 1924-
Wartime: understanding and behavior in the Second World War/ Paul Fussell. New York: Oxford University Press, 1989. x, 330 p.
89-002875 940.54/886/73 0195037979
World War, 1939-1945 -- United States -- Psychological aspects. World War, 1939-1945 -- Great Britain -- Psychological aspects. World War, 1939-1945 -- Propaganda.

D810.P7.U395 1996
Laurie, Clayton D. 1954-
The propaganda warriors: America's crusade against Nazi Germany/ Clayton D. Laurie. Lawrence, Kan.: University Press of Kansas, c1996. xvi, 335 p.
95-026321 940.54/88673 070060765X
World War, 1939-1945 -- Propaganda. Propaganda, American. Propaganda, Anti-German.

D810.P7.U5 1998
Gilmore, Allison B., 1959-
You can't fight tanks with bayonets: psychological warfare against the Japanese Army in the Southwest Pacific/ Allison B. Gilmore. Lincoln, Neb.: University of Nebraska Press, c1998. xiv, 226 p.
97-029975 940.54/8673 0803221673
World War, 1939-1945 -- Propaganda. World War, 1939-1945 -- Psychological aspects. Propaganda, American -- History -- 20th century.

D810.P7.U53 1989
Soley, Lawrence C.
Radio warfare: OSS and CIA subversive propaganda/ Lawrence C. Soley. New York: Praeger, 1989. x, 249 p.
88-025187 940.54/886/73 0275930513
World War, 1939-1945 -- Propaganda. Propaganda, American. Radio broadcasting -- United States.

D810.P76.S4613 1993
Semelin, Jacques.
Unarmed against Hitler: civilian resistance in Europe, 1939-1943/ Jacques Semelin; translated by Suzan Husserl-Kapit; foreword by Stanley Hoffmann. Westport, Conn.: Praeger, c1993. xii, 198 p.
92-032669 940.53/161 027593960X
World War, 1939-1945 -- Protest movements -- Europe. Passive resistance -- Europe -- History -- 20th century. Nonviolence -- History -- 20th century. Europe -- Politics and government -- 20th century.

D810.P85.U53 1997
Chappell, John D. 1961-
Before the bomb: how America approached the end of the Pacific War/ John D. Chappell. Lexington, Ky.: University Press of Kentucky, 1997. 246 p.
96-031070 940.53 0813119871
World War, 1939-1945 -- Public opinion. World War, 1939-1945 -- United States. Public opinion -- United States -- History -- 20th century.

D810.R33.B77 1999
Brown, Louis, 1929-
A radar history of World War II: technical and military imperatives/ Louis Brown. Bristol; Institute of Physics Pub., 1999. xvi, 563 p.
99-038978 0750306599
World War, 1939-1945 -- Radar.

D810.S2.H37 2000
Hartcup, Guy.
The effect of science on the second World War/ Guy Hartcup. New York: St. Martin's Press, 2000. p. cm.
99-054609 940.53 0312228333
World War, 1939-1945 -- Science.

D810.S2.R53 1994
Richards, Pamela Spence, 1941-
Scientific information in wartime: the Allied-German rivalry, 1939-1945/ Pamela Spence Richards. Westport, Conn.: Greenwood Press, 1994. xii, 177 p.
93-025050 940.54/8 0313290628
World War, 1939-1945 -- Science. World War, 1939-1945 -- Military intelligence.

D810.S2.Z56 1996
Zimmerman, David, 1959-
Top secret exchange: the Tizard mission and the scientific war/ David Zimmerman. Stroud, Gloucestershire: Alan Sutton Pub.; 1996. xii, 252 p.
97-117938 940.54/86 0750912421
Tizard, Henry Thomas, -- Sir, -- 1885-1959. World War, 1939-1945 -- Science. Technical assistance, British -- United States. Technical assistance, American -- Great Britain.

D810.S7.A482 2000
Aldrich, Richard J. 1961-
Intelligence and the war against Japan: Britain, America and the politics of secret service/ Richard J. Aldrich. Cambridge; Cambridge University Press, 2000. xxiv, 500 p.
99-029697 940.54/8641 0521641861
World War, 1939-1945 -- Secret service -- Great Britain. World War, 1939-1945 -- Secret service -- United States. World War, 1939-1945 -- Asia.

D810.S7.A559 1997
Alvarez, David J.
Nothing sacred: Nazi espionage against the Vatican, 1939-1945/ David Alvarez and Robert A. Graham. London; F. Cass, 1997. xiv, 190 p.
97-011657 940.54/8743 0714647446
World War, 1939-1945 -- Secret service -- Germany. World War, 1939-1945 -- Vatican City.

D810.S7.B35 1998
Bath, Alan Harris.
Tracking the axis enemy: the triumph of Anglo-American naval intelligence/ Alan Harris Bath. Lawrence, KS: University Press of Kansas, c1998. xii, 308 p.
98-018726 940.54/8673 0700609172
World War, 1939-1945 -- Secret service -- United States. World War, 1939-1945 -- Secret service -- Great Britain. Military intelligence -- United States -- History -- 20th century.

D810.S7.D78 1996
Dulles, Allen Welsh, 1893-1969.
From Hitler's doorstep: the wartime intelligence reports of Allen Dulles, 1942-1945/ edited with commentary by Neal H. Petersen. University Park, Pa.: Pennsylvania State University Press, c1996. x, 684 p.
95-034966 940.54/8673 0271014857
Dulles, Allen Welsh, -- 1893-1969. World War, 1939-1945 -- Sources. World War, 1939-1945 -- Secret service -- United States.

D810.S7.G552 1990
Glantz, David M.
Soviet military intelligence in war/ David M. Glantz. London, England; Frank Cass, 1990. xv, 422 p.
90-033240 940.54/8647 0714633747
World War, 1939-1945 -- Military intelligence -- Soviet Union. World War, 1939-1945 -- Campaigns.

D810.S7.K25
Kahn, David, 1930-
Hitler's spies: German military intelligence in World War II/ David Kahn. New York: Macmillan, c1978. xiii, 671 p.
77-025271 940.54/87/43 0025606107
World War, 1939-1945 -- Secret service -- Germany. Military intelligence -- Germany -- History -- 20th century. Germany -- History -- 1933-1945.

D810.S7.K33 1989
Katz, Barry M.
Foreign intelligence: research and analysis in the Office of Strategic Services, 1942-1945/ Barry M. Katz. Cambridge, Mass.: Harvard University Press, 1989. xv, 251 p.
89-031278 940.54/86/73 0674308255
World War, 1939-1945 -- Military intelligence -- United States. World War, 1939-1945 -- Secret service -- United States.

D810.S7.L49 1988
Listening to the enemy: key documents on the role of communications intelligence in the war with Japan/ edited with an introduction and notes by Ronald H. Spector. Wilmington, Del.: Scholarly Resources Inc., 1988. xii, 285 p.
87-009478 940.54/86/73 0842022759
World War, 1939-1945 -- Military intelligence -- United States. World War, 1939-1945 -- Cryptography. World War, 1939-1945 -- Japan.

D810.S7.M254 1998
Mahl, Thomas E., 1943-
Desperate deception: British covert operations in the United States, 1939-44/ Thomas E. Mahl. Washington [D.C.]: Brassey's, c1998. xiv, 257 p.
97-019550 940.54/8641 1574880802
World War, 1939-1945 -- Secret service -- Great Britain. World War, 1939-1945 -- Secret service -- United States.

D810.S7.M274 1998
Marshall, Charles F., 1915-
A ramble through my war: Anzio and other joys/ Charles F. Marshall. Baton Rouge: Louisiana State University Press, c1998. x, 300 p.
98-024711 940.54/8673 0807122823
Marshall, Charles F., -- 1915- World War, 1939-1945 -- Secret service -- United States. World War, 1939-1945 -- Personal narratives, American. Intelligence officers -- United States -- Biography.

D810.S7.M375 1998
McIntosh, Elizabeth P., 1915-
Sisterhood of spies: the women of the OSS/ Elizabeth P. McIntosh. Annapolis, Md.: Naval Institute Press, c1998. xiv, 282 p.
97-044242 940.54/8673/092 1557505985
McIntosh, Elizabeth P., -- 1915- World War, 1939-1945 -- Secret service -- United States. World War, 1939-1945 -- Personal narratives, American. Women spies -- United States -- Biography.

D810.S7.S428 1996
Sexton, Donal J.
Signals intelligence in World War II: a research guide/ compiled by Donal J. Sexton, Jr. Westport, Conn.: Greenwood Press, 1996. xl, 163 p.
96-006348   016.94054/85   0313283044
World War, 1939-1945 -- Electronic intelligence -- Bibliography. World War, 1939-1945 -- Cryptography -- Bibliography. Military intelligence -- History -- 20th century -- Bibliography.

D810.S7.S5544 1996
Smith, Bradley F.
Sharing secrets with Stalin: how the Allies traded intelligence, 1941-1945/ Bradley F. Smith. [Lawrence, Kan.]: University Press of Kansas, c1996. xix, 307 p.
96-002395   940.54/85   0700608001
World War, 1939-1945 -- Secret Service. Military intelligence -- History -- 20th century.

D810.S7.Y82 1996
Yu, Maochun, 1962-
OSS in China: prelude to Cold War/ Maochun Yu. New Haven: Yale University Press, c1996. xxii, 340 p.
96-022593   940.54/8673   0300066988
World War, 1939-1945 -- Secret Service -- United States. World War, 1939-1945 -- Secret Service -- China. World War, 1939-1945 -- China.

D810.T8.L36 1990
Lane, Tony, 1937-
The merchant seamen's war/ Tony Lane. Manchester; Manchester University Press; c1990. viii, 287 p.
90-006285   940.54/59   0719023971
Merchant marine -- Great Britain -- History -- 20th century. World War, 1939-1945 -- Transportation. Naval convoys -- History -- 20th century.

D810.W7.B45 1998
Bentley, Amy, 1962-
Eating for victory: food rationing and the politics of domesticity/ Amy Bentley. Urbana: University of Illinois Press, c1998. xiii, 238 p.
97-045471   940.53/082   0252024192
World War, 1939-1945 -- Women -- United States. Women -- United States -- History -- 20th century. Homemakers -- United States -- History -- 20th century.

D810.W7.F57 1991
Fishman, Sarah, 1957-
We will wait: wives of French prisoners of war, 1940-1945/ Sarah Fishman. New Haven: Yale University Press, c1991. xxii, 253 p.
91-004010   944.081/6/082   0300047746
World War, 1939-1945 -- Women -- France. Wives -- France -- History -- 20th century. Prisoners of war -- France.

D810.W7.M44 1997
Merryman, Molly.
Clipped wings: the rise and fall of the Women Airforce Service Pilots (WASPs) of World War II/ Molly Merryman. New York: New York University Press, c1998. xi, 239 p.
97-021217   940.54/4973   0814755674
World War, 1939-1945 -- Participation, Female. Women air pilots -- United States -- History. World War, 1939-1945 -- Aerial operations, American.

D810.W7.R8
Rupp, Leila J., 1950-
Mobilizing women for war: German and American propaganda, 1939-1945/ Leila J. Rupp. Princeton, N.J.: Princeton University Press, 1978. xii, 243 p.
77-085562   940.54/88   0691046492
World War, 1939-1945 -- Women -- United States. World War, 1939-1945 -- Propaganda. Women -- United States -- Social conditions.

D810.W7.S84 1998
Summerfield, Penny.
Reconstructing women's wartime lives: discourse and subjectivity in oral histories of the Second World War/ Penny Summerfield. Manchester, UK; Manchester University Press; 1998. xiii, 338 p.
98-222088   071904460X
World War, 1939-1945 -- Women -- Great Britain. Women -- Great Britain -- History -- 20th century. World War, 1939-1945 -- War work -- Great Britain.

D810.W7.V57 1996
Virden, Jenel.
Good-bye, Piccadilly: British war brides in America/ Jenel Virden. Urbana: University of Illinois Press, c1996. xii, 177 p.
95-004415   940.53/15042   0252022254
World War, 1939-1945 -- Women -- Great Britain. War brides -- Great Britain -- History -- 20th century. Women immigrants -- United States -- History -- 20th century.

D811-811.5 World War II (1939-1945)
— Personal narratives and other accounts

D811.A2.C62 1992
Cook, Haruko Taya.
Japan at war: an oral history/ Haruko Taya Cook and Theodore F. Cook. New York: New Press: 1992. xiii, 479 p.
92-053731   940.53/52/0922   1565840143
World War, 1939-1945 -- Personal narratives, Japanese. World War, 1939-1945 -- Japan. Oral history. Japan -- History -- 1926-1945.

D811.A646 1999
Aquila, Philip L., d.1994.
Home front soldier: the story of a G.I. and his Italian-American family during World War II/ Richard Aquila. Albany: State University of New York Press, c1999. xi, 280 p.
98-004321   940.54/8173   0791440753
Aquila, Philip L., -- d. 1994 -- Correspondence. World War, 1939-1945 -- Personal narratives, American. Soldiers -- United States -- Correspondence. Italian Americans -- Correspondence. Buffalo (N.Y.) -- Social life and customs.

D811.H648 1990
Hoffman, Alice M., 1929-
Archives of memory: a soldier recalls World War II/ Alice M. & Howard S. Hoffman. Lexington, Ky.: University Press of Kentucky, c1990. xv, 199 p.
90-012759   940.54/21/092   0813117186
Hoffman, Howard S., -- 1925- World War, 1939-1945 -- Campaigns -- Western Front. Soldiers -- United States -- Biography. World War, 1939-1945 -- Personal narratives, American.

D811.M684 1992
Mowat, Farley.
My father's son: memories of war and peace/ Farley Mowat. Boston: Houghton Mifflin, c1992. x, 340 p.
92-031729   940.54/8171   0395650291
Mowat, Farley -- Correspondence. Soldiers -- Canada -- Correspondence. World War, 1939-1945 -- Personal narratives, Canadian.

D811.S3228 1997
Sano, Iwao Peter, 1924-
One thousand days in Siberia: the Odyssey of a Japanese-American POW/ Iwao Peter Sano. Lincoln: University of Nebraska Press, c1997. xvii, 210 p.
96-054629   940.54/8252   080324262X
Sano, Iwao Peter, -- 1924- World War, 1939-1945 -- Personal narratives, Japanese. World War, 1939-1945 -- Personal narratives, American. World War, 1939-1945 -- Japanese Americans.

D811.W45
White, William Lindsay, 1900-1973.
They were expendable [by] W. L. White. New York, Harcourt, Brace and company [1942] vii, 209 p.
42-036303   940.542
World War, 1939-1945 -- Personal narratives, American. World War, 1939-1945 -- Campaigns -- Philippines.

D811.5.B82 1991
Bruce, David Kirkpatrick Este.
OSS against the Reich: the World War II diaries of Colonel David K.E. Bruce/ edited by Nelson Douglas Lankford. Kent, Ohio: Kent State University Press, c1991. xii, 257 p.
90-047719   940.54/8173/092   087338427X
Bruce, David Kirkpatrick Este -- Diaries. World War, 1939-1945 -- Personal narratives, American. Intelligence officers -- United States -- Diaries.

D811.5.H429
Henderson, Aileen Kilgore, 1921-
Stateside soldier: life in the Women's Army Corps, 1944 1945/ Aileen Kilgore Henderson. Columbia: University of South Carolina Press, c2001. 252 p.
00-011631   940.54/8173/092   157003396X
Henderson, Aileen Kilgore, -- 1921- World War, 1939-1945 -- Personal narratives, American. Women soldiers -- United States -- Diaries.

D811.5.K54313 1999
Kiyosawa, Kiyoshi, 1890-1945.
A diary of darkness: the wartime diary of Kiyosawa Kiyoshi/ foreword by Marius Jansen; edited with an introduction by Eugene Soviak; translated by Eugene Soviak and Kamiyama Tamie. Princeton, N.J.: Princeton University Press, c1999. xx, 391 p.
98-020063   940.54/8252   069100143X
Kiyosawa, Kiyoshi, -- 1890-1945. World War, 1939-1945 -- Personal narratives, Japanese. Journalists -- Japan -- Diaries.

D811.5.M44
Middleton, Drew, 1913-
Our share of night, a personal narrative of the war years, by Drew Middleton. New York, The Viking press, 1946. 380 p.
46-007613   940.548173
World war, 1939-1945 -- Personal narratives, American.

D811.5.O885 1993
Owings, Alison.
Frauen: German women recall the Third Reich/ by Alison Owings. New Brunswick, N.J.: Rutgers University Press, c1993. xxxix, 494 p.
92-042097   943.086/082   0813519926
World War, 1939-1945 -- Personal narratives, German. World War, 1939-1945 -- Women -- Germany. Women -- Germany -- Interviews.

D811.5.P92
Pyle, Ernie, 1900-1945.
Here is your war/ Ernie Pyle; drawings by Carol Johnson. New York: Henry Holt, 1943. 304 p.
43-015418   940.54/23
Pyle, Ernie, -- 1900-1945. World War, 1939-1945 -- Personal narratives, American. World War, 1939-1945 -- Campaigns -- Tunisia. War correspondents -- United States -- Biography.

D811.5.S5 1941
Shirer, William L. 1904-
Berlin diary; the journal of a foreign correspondent, 1934-1941 [by] William L. Shirer. New York, A. A. Knopf, 1941. 3 p.
41-009746   940.5343
Hitler, Adolf, -- 1889-1945. Shirer, William L. -- (William Lawrence), -- 1904- -- Diaries. World War, 1939-1945 -- Personal narratives, American. World War, 1939-1945 -- Germany. Europe -- Politics and government -- 1918-1945. Germany -- Politics and government -- 1933-1945.

D811.5.T78
Trumbull, Robert.
Nine who survived Hiroshima and Nagasaki; personal experiences of nine men who lived through the atomic bombings. New York, Dutton, 1957. 148 p.
56-008323   940.544
Atomic bomb. World War, 1939-1945 -- Personal narratives, Japanese.

D814.8 World War II (1939-1945) — Peace — Treaties with Axis powers

D814.8.C54 1980
Cohen, Bernard Cecil,
The political process and foreign policy: the making of the Japanese peace settlement/ by Bernard C. Cohen. Westport, Conn.: Greenwood Press, 1980, c1957. x, 293 p.
80-019832   353.0089.219   0313227152
World War, 1939-1945--Peace. World War, 1939-1945--Japan.

D815 World War II (1939-1945) — Peace — General works

D815.A7
Armstrong, Anne, 1924-
Unconditional surrender; the impact of the Casablanca policy upon World War II. New Brunswick, N.J., Rutgers University Press [1961] 304 p.
61-010253   940.54/012
World War, 1939-1945 -- Peace. Anti-Nazi movement. Capitulations, Military.

D816 World War II (1939-1945) — Peace — General special

D816.O24 1971
O'Connor, Raymond Gish.
Diplomacy for victory; FDR and unconditional surrender [by] Raymond G. O'Connor. New York, Norton [1971] xiii, 143 p.
70-155986   940.532/2/73   0393054411
World War, 1939-1945 -- Peace. World War, 1939-1945 -- Diplomatic history. United States -- Foreign relations -- 1933-1945.

D819 World War II (1939-1945) — Peace — Indemnity and reparation

D819.G3.T56 1997
Timm, Angelika.
Jewish claims against East Germany: moral obligations and pragmatic policy/ Angelika Timm. Budapest: Central European University Press, c1997. xi, 291 p.
99-218710   940.53/18   9639116041
Restitution and indemnification claims (1933-) - - Germany (East) Holocaust, Jewish (1939-1945) - - Reparations. Antisemitism -- Germany (East) Germany (East) -- Foreign relations -- Israel. Israel -- Foreign relations -- Germany (East)

D821 World War II (1939-1945) — Peace — By country, groups of countries, etc., A-Z

D821.G4.B3
Backer, John H., 1902-
The decision to divide Germany: American foreign policy in transition/ John H. Backer. Durham, N.C.: Duke University Press, 1978. x, 212 p.
77-084614   940.53/14   0822303914
World War, 1939-1945 -- Peace. World War, 1939-1945 -- Germany. World War, 1939-1945 -- Reparations. United States -- Foreign relations -- Germany. Germany -- Foreign relations -- United States.

D821.G4.K85
Kuklick, Bruce, 1941-
American policy and the division of Germany; the clash with Russia over reparations. Ithaca [N.Y.] Cornell University Press [1972] viii, 286 p.
78-038121   940.53/14   0801407109
World War, 1939-1945 -- Germany. World War, 1939-1945 -- Peace. World War, 1939-1945 -- Reparations.

D821.J3.B8 1954
Butow, Robert J. C. 1924-
Japan's decision to surrender. Foreword by Edwin O. Reischauer. Stanford, Stanford University Press, 1954. xi, 259 p.
54-008145   940.5314
World War, 1939-1945 -- Japan.

D821.U6.S54 1988
Sigal, Leon V.
Fighting to a finish: the politics of war termination in the United States and Japan, 1945/ Leon V. Sigal. Ithaca: Cornell University Press, 1988. xii, 335 p.
87-024876   940.53/2   0801420865
World War, 1939-1945 -- Peace. World War, 1939-1945 -- Diplomatic history. United States -- Foreign relations -- Japan. Japan -- Foreign relations -- United States. United States -- Politics and government -- 1933-1945.

D829 World War II (1939-1945) — Reconstruction — By region or country

D829.E2.D46 1987
Dennis, Peter, 1945-
Troubled days of peace: Mountbatten and South East Asia Command, 1945-46/ Peter Dennis. New York: St. Martin's Press, 1987. xi, 270 p.
87-012753   950/.424   0312009208
Mountbatten of Burma, Louis Mountbatten, -- Earl, -- 1900-1979. Reconstruction (1939-1951) -- East Asia. World War, 1939-1945 -- East Asia.

D829.G3.J315
Jaspers, Karl, 1883-1969.
The question of German guilt, tr. by E. B. Ashton [pseud.] New York, Dial Press, 1947 [i.e. 19 123 p.
48-005014   940.5314443
Reconstruction (1939-1951) -- Germany.

D829.G3.R38 1989
Reconstruction in post-war Germany: British occupation policy and the Western zones, 1945-55/ edited by Ian D. Turner. Oxford, UK; Berg; 1989. xvii, 421 p.
88-023452   940.53/41   0854960961
Reconstruction (1939-1951) -- Germany. World War, 1939-1945 -- Occupied territories. Great Britain -- Foreign relations -- Germany. Germany -- Foreign relations -- Great Britain.

D839.2 Post-war history (1945-   ) — Congresses. Conferences, etc.

D839.2.A17 1998
1968, the world transformed/ edited by Carole Fink, Philipp Gassert, and Detlef Junker. Cambridge, UK; Cambridge University Press, 1998. xi, 490 p.
98-023253   909.82   0521641411
World politics -- 1965-1975 -- Congresses.

D839.3 Post-war history (1945-   ) — Sources and documents

D839.3.I56 vol.4, no.43
Mezerik, A. G. 1901-
The Algerian-French conflict: international impacts, UN action. [New York] 1958. 39 p.
61-019841   965.04
Algeria -- History -- 1945-1962.

D839.7 Post-war history (1945-   ) — Biography — Individual, A-Z

D839.7.H3.L3
Lash, Joseph P., 1909-
Dag Hammarskjold, custodian of the brushfire peace. Garden City, N.Y., Doubleday, 1961. 304 p.
61-012546   923.2485
Hammarskjold, Dag, -- 1905-1961.

D839.7.T5.A35
Thant, U, 1909-1974 1909-1974.
View from the UN/ U Thant. Garden City, N.Y.:
Doubleday, 1978. xix, 508 p.
76-057517   341.23/3/0924   0385115415
Thant, -- U, -- 1909-1974.   Statesmen -- Burma --
Biography.

D840 Post-war history
(1945-   ) — General works

D840.K4
Kennan, George Frost, 1904-
Russia, the atom and the West. New York, Harper
[1958] ix, 116 p.
58-008078   909.82
World politics -- 1955-1965.   Soviet Union --
Foreign relations.

D840.L8 1966
Lukacs, John, 1924-
A new history of the cold war, by John Lukacs.
Garden City, N.Y., Anchor Books, 1966. xii,
426 p.
66-021017   909.82
History, Modern -- 1945- Cold War.

D840.M23 1989
Manchester, William Raymond, 1922-
In our time: the world as seen by Magnum
photographers/ William Manchester; essays by
Jean LaCouture and Fred Ritchin. New York:
American Federation of Arts in association with
c1989. 456 p.
89-032440   909.82   0393027678
History, Modern -- 1945- -- Pictorial works.

D840.N62 1998
Reviewing the Cold War: approaches,
interpretations, and theory/ Nobel Symposium;
edited by Odd Arne Westad. London; F. Cass,
2000. 382 p.
00-031449   327.73047/09/045   0714650722
Cold War. World politics -- 1945- United States
-- Foreign relations -- Soviet Union. Soviet Union -
- Foreign relations -- United States.

D842 Post-war history
(1945-   ) — General special

D842.B46 1997
Bercovitch, Jacob.
International conflict: a chronological encyclopedia
of conflicts and their management, 1945-1995/
Jacob Bercovitch and Richard Jackson.
Washington, D.C.: Congressional Quarterly,
c1997. xxviii, 372 p.
97-030556   909.82/5/0202   156802195X
Conflict management -- History -- 20th century --
Encyclopedias.   World politics -- 1945- --
Encyclopedias.

D842.C64 1992
Connaughton, R. M. 1942-
Military intervention in the 1990s: a new logic of
war/ Richard Connaughton; foreword by Sir Harry
Hinsley. London; Routledge, [1992] xvi, 198 p.
92-007938   341.5/84   0415065240
Intervention (International law) World politics --
1945-

D842.C7 1963
Crozier, Brian.
The morning after: a study of independence. New
York, Oxford University Press, 1963. 299 p.
63-025468   320.157
States, New.

D842.E83 1994
Esman, Milton J. 1918-
Ethnic politics/ Milton J. Esman. Ithaca: Cornell
University Press, 1994. 277 p.
94-014440   909.82   0801430100
World politics -- 1945- Ethnic relations.

D842.J47 1998
Jessup, John E.
An encyclopedic dictionary of conflict and conflict
resolution, 1945-1996/ John E. Jessup. Westport,
Conn.: Greenwood Press, 1998. x, 887 p.
97-040852   903   0313281122
Military history, Modern -- 20th century --
Dictionaries. Conflict management -- History --
20th century -- Dictionaries. Political violence --
History -- 20th century -- Dictionaries.

D842.N38 1982
The New history, the 1980s and beyond: studies in
interdisciplinary history/ edited by Theodore K.
Rabb and Robert I. Rotberg; contributors, Peter H.
Smith ... [et al.]. Princeton, N.J.: Princeton
University Press, c1982. 332 p.
82-047634   909.82/8/072   0691053707
History, Modern -- 1945- -- Historiography.
Historiography.

D842.S4413 1995
Senarclens, Pierre de.
From Yalta to the Iron Curtain: the great powers
and the origins of the cold war/ Pierre de
Senarclens; translated from the French by Amanda
Pingree. Oxford; Berg, 1995. x, 290 p.
94-049070   940.53/141/0947717   0854968091
Cold War. Great powers.

D842.T69 1999
Townson, Duncan.
A dictionary of contemporary history, 1945 to the
present/ Duncan Townson. Oxford, Oxfordshire;
Blackwell Publishers, 1999. p. cm.
98-021835   909.82/5   0631200169
History, Modern -- 1945- -- Dictionaries.

D842.U35 1995
Uekert, Brenda K.
Rivers of blood: a comparative study of
government massacres/ Brenda K. Uekert.
Westport, Conn.: Praeger, 1995. xii, 240 p.
95-006946   909.82   0275951650
Massacres -- History -- 20th century -- Case
studies.

D842.W28 1994
Walker, Martin, 1947-
The Cold War: a history/ Martin Walker. New
York: H. Holt, 1994. xvi, 392 p.
94-005152   909.82   0805031901
World politics -- 1945- Cold War.

D843-847.2 Post-war history
(1945-   ) — 1945-1965
— Political and diplomatic history

D843.A668 1994
Arms, Thomas S.
Encyclopedia of the Cold War/ Thomas S. Arms.
New York, NY: Facts on File, c1994. xii, 628 p.
90-026899   909.82   0816019754
Cold War -- Encyclopedias. World politics --
1945- -- Encyclopedias.

D843.A683 1968
Aron, Raymond, 1905-
On war. Translated from the French by Terence
Kilmartin. New York, W. W. Norton [1968] ix,
143 p.
68-002039   909.82
World politics -- 1955-1965. War.

D843.B2 1991
BBC world service glossary of current affairs/
compiled by BBC Monitoring; editor, Tim Guyse
Williams; contributors, Jackie Bishop ... [et al.].
Chicago: St. James Press, c1991. vi, 813 p.
93-185603   1558621083
World politics -- 1945- -- Dictionaries.

D843.B25
Ball, George W.
The discipline of power; essentials of a modern
world structure, by George W. Ball. Boston, Little,
Brown [1968] 363 p.
67-028228   327
World politics -- 1945-

D843.C25 1996
Calvocoressi, Peter.
World politics since 1945/ Peter Calvocoressi.
London; Longman, 1996. xvii, 878 p.
96-021988   909.82   0582277965
World politics -- 1945-

D843.C5285 1995
Church, Clive H.
Continuity and change in contemporary Europe/
Clive H. Church, Gisela Hendriks. Aldershot,
U.K.; Edward Elgar, c1995. xviii, 290 p.
95-019494   940.55   1852784202
Europe -- Politics and government -- 1945-
Europe -- Economic conditions -- 1945-

D843.C53
Churchill, Winston Leonard Spencer, 1874-
1965.
The sinews of peace, post-war speeches; ed. by
Randolph S. Churchill. Boston, Houghton Mifflin
Co. [1949] 256 p.
49-009229   940.55
World politics -- 1945-1955.   Great Britain --
Politics and government -- 1945-

D843.C57737 2000
Cold War respite: the Geneva Summit of 1955/
edited by Gunter Bischof and Saki Dockrill. Baton
Rouge: Louisiana University Press, 2000. xii,
319 p.
00-028739   327.1/09/045   0807123706
Eisenhower, Dwight D. -- (Dwight David), -- 1890-
1969 -- Congresses.   World politics -- 1945-1955 -
- Congresses. Summit meetings -- Switzerland --
Geneva -- Congresses.   United States -- Foreign
relations -- Soviet Union -- Congresses. Soviet
Union -- Foreign relations -- United States --
Congresses. United States -- Foreign relations --
1945-1989 -- Congresses.

D843.E46 1999
Encyclopedia of conflicts since World War II/ editor, James Ciment; contributors, Kenneth L. Hill, David MacMichael, Carl Skutsch. Armonk, NY: Sharpe Reference, c1999. 4 v.
98-028374   909.82   0765680041
World politics -- 1945- -- Encyclopedias. Military history, Modern -- 20th century -- Encyclopedias. Summit meetings -- Encyclopedias.

D843.G26
Gaitskell, Hugh, 1906-1963.
The challenge of coexistence. Cambridge, Harvard University Press, 1957. 114 p.
57-009075   909.82
International cooperation. World politics -- 1955-1965.

D843.G2813 1971b
Gaulle, Charles de, 1890-1970.
Memoirs of hope: renewal and endeavor. Translated by Terence Kilmartin. New York, Simon and Schuster [1971] 392 p.
76-163103   944.083/0924   0671211188
World politics -- 1945-

D843.H439 1995
Herring, Eric.
Danger and opportunity: explaining international crisis outcomes/ Eric Herring. Manchester [England]; Manchester University Press: Distributed exclusi 1995. xiv, 306 p.
95-003507   327/.09/045   0719042925
World politics -- 1945- International relations.

D843.I486 1993
Innovative leaders in international politics/ edited by Gabriel Sheffer. Albany: State University of New York Press, c1993. xviii, 294 p.
92-028117   303.3/4   0791415198
World politics -- 1945- Political leadership.

D843.J3714
Jaspers, Karl, 1883-1969.
The future of mankind. Translated by E. B. Ashton. [Chicago] University of Chicago Press [1961] 342 p.
60-007237   909.82
World politics -- 1955-1965. Atomic bomb.

D843.L287 1997
Latham, Robert, 1956-
The liberal moment: modernity, security, and the making of postwar international order/ Robert Latham. New York: Columbia University Press, c1997. xiv, 281 p.
96-053164   320.51/3   0231107560
Liberalism -- Europe -- History -- 20th century. Cold War. Europe -- Politics and government -- 1945-

D843.L8413 1999
Lundestad, Geir, 1945-
East, West, North, South: developments in international relations since 1945/ Geir Lundestad; translated from the Norwegian by Gail Adams Kvam. New York: Oxford University Press, 1999. p. cm.
98-055967   909.82/5   0198782381
World politics -- 1945-

D843.N52 1993
Nijman, Jan.
The geopolitics of power and conflict: superpowers in the international system, 1945-1992/ Jan Nijman. London; Belhaven Press; 1993. xiii, 160 p.
93-022649   327.1/01   1852932775
World politics -- 1945- Geopolitics.

D843.N62 1998
Cook, Chris, 1945-
The Facts on File world political almanac: from 1945 to the present/ by Chris Cook. New York: Facts on File, c2001. vii, 600 p.
00-044222   909.82   0816042950
World politics -- 1945-

D843.R623 1997
Robertson, Charles L., 1927-
International politics since World War II: a short history/ Charles L. Robertson. Armonk, N.Y.: M.E. Sharpe, c1997. xiv, 383 p.
96-046431   909.82/5   0765600269
World politics -- 1945-

D843.S3365 1997
Schwartz, Richard Alan, 1951-
The Cold War reference guide: a general history and annotated chronology with selected biographies/ by Richard Alan Schwartz. Jefferson, N.C.: McFarland, c1997. vi, 321 p.
96-038573   902/.02   0786401737
World politics -- 1945- Cold War. Chronology, Historical.

D843.S547 2000
Smith, Joseph, 1945-
Historical dictionary of the Cold War/ Joseph Smith and Simon Davis. Lanham, Md.: Scarecrow Press, 2000. xi, 329 p.
99-041659   909.82/5/03   0810837099
Cold War -- Dictionaries. World politics -- 1945- -- Dictionaries.

D843.W524 1996
Witnesses to the end of the Cold War/ edited by William C. Wohlforth. Baltimore: Johns Hopkins University Press, c1996. xvi, 344 p.
96-013719   327.73047   0801853826
Cold War -- Congresses. World politics -- 1945- -- Congresses. United States -- Foreign relations -- Soviet Union -- Congresses. Soviet Union -- Foreign relations -- United States -- Congresses.

D843.W636 1990
World fact file/ edited by Roger East and the staff of CIRCA Reference; contributing editors, Roger East ... [et al.]. New York: Facts on File, c1990. 607 p.
90-014069   909.82   0816025223
World politics -- 1945- -- Handbooks, manuals, etc. World history -- Handbooks, manuals, etc. Economic history -- 1945- -- Handbooks, manuals, etc.

D843.Y68 1996
Young, John W., 1957-
Winston Churchill's last campaign: Britain and the Cold War, 1951-5/ John W. Young. Oxford; Clarendon Press, 1996. viii, 358 p.
96-166558   940.55/5   0198203675
Churchill, Winston, -- Sir, -- 1874-1965 -- Contributions in diplomacy. Cold War. World politics -- 1945-1955.

D844.R89 1963b
Russell, Bertrand, 1872-1970.
Unarmed victory. London, Allen & Unwin [1963] 155 p.
70-201519   327/.1
World politics -- 1955-1965. Military bases, Soviet -- Cuba. Sino-Indian Border Dispute, 1957-

D844.S47
Shulman, Marshall Darrow.
Beyond the cold war, by Marshall D. Shulman. New Haven, Yale University Press, 1966. vi, 111 p.
65-022338   327
World politics -- 1965-1975. Soviet Union -- Foreign relations -- 1953-1975.

D845.K5
Kissinger, Henry, 1923-
The troubled partnership; a re-appraisal of the Atlantic alliance, by Henry A. Kissinger. New York, Published for the Council on Foreign Relations b [1965] xiv, 266 p.
65-017493   327.4073
North Atlantic Treaty Organization.

D845.T48 1997
Thomas, Ian Q. R.
The promise of alliance: NATO and the political imagination/ Ian Q.R. Thomas. Lanham: Rowman & Littlefield, c1997. xii, 304 p.
97-014246   355/.031/091/821   0847685802
World politics -- 1989- North Atlantic Treaty Organization.

D845.2.N19 1989
NATO at forty: change, continuity, & prospects/ edited by James R. Golden ... [et al.]. Boulder: Westview Press, 1989. xvii, 318 p.
89-032848   355/.031/091821   0813309433
North Atlantic Treaty Organization -- History.

D847.B7 1967
Brzezinski, Zbigniew K., 1928-
The Soviet bloc, unity and conflict, by Zbigniew K. Brzezinski. Cambridge, Harvard University Press, 1967. xviii, 599 p.
67-012531   909.82
Communist countries.

D847.K82 1990
Kurian, George Thomas.
Encyclopedia of the Second World/ by George Thomas Kurian; John J. Karch, associate editor. New York: Facts on File, c1991. x, 614 p.
90-040370   909/.09724   0816012326
Communist countries -- Encyclopedias.

D847.2.R45 1971
Remington, Robin Alison.
The Warsaw pact; case studies in Communist conflict resolution. Cambridge, Mass., MIT Press [1971] xix, 268 p.
76-148971   355.03/1   0262180502
Warsaw pact, 1955.

D848 Post-war history (1945-   ) — 1965-1989 — General works

D848.C38 1988
Caute, David.
The year of the barricades: a journey through 1968/ David Caute. New York: Harper & Row, c1988. xiv, 514 p.
87-045605   909.82   0060158700
History, Modern -- 1945- Radicalism -- History -- 20th century. Insurgency -- History -- 20th century.

D848.M45 1995
Meltzer, Ellen.
Day by day, the eighties/ Ellen Meltzer and Marc Aronson. New York: Facts on File, 1995. 2 v.
94-026632   909.82/02/02   0816015929
Nineteen eighties -- Chronology.

D848.R48 1991
Revolutions of the late twentieth century/ edited by Jack A. Goldstone, Ted Robert Gurr, Farrokh Moshiri. Boulder: Westview Press, 1991. xii, 395 p.
91-017945 909.82 0813375975
History, Modern -- 1945- Revolutions.

D849 Post-war history (1945-   ) — 1965-1989
— Political and diplomatic history

D849.F685 1990
Europe transformed: documents on the end of the Cold War/ edited by Lawrence Freedman. New York: St. Martin's Press, 1990. x, 516 p.
90-008611 940.55 0312052251
Cold War -- History -- Sources. World politics -- 1985-1995 -- Sources. Europe -- Politics and government -- 1945- -- Sources.

D849.G53 1993
Gibbs, Brian H.
Empirical knowledge on world politics: a summary of quantitative research, 1970-1991/ Brian H. Gibbs and J. David Singer. Westport, Conn.: Greenwood Press, 1993. 453 p.
93-025478 320.94 0313272271
Europe -- Politics and government -- 1945- -- Abstracts.

D849.L425 1994
Lebow, Richard Ned.
We all lost the Cold War/ Richard Ned Lebow and Janice Gross Stein. Princeton, N.J.: Princeton University Press, c1994. xiv, 542 p.
93-014206 327.73047 0691033080
Cold War. Cuban Missile Crisis, 1962. Israel-Arab conflicts. Soviet Union -- Foreign relations -- United States. United States -- Foreign relations -- Soviet Union.

D849.L45 1989
Leighton, Marian Kirsch.
The deceptive lure of detente/ Marian Leighton. New York: St. Martin's Press, 1989. 260 p.
88-031581 327.73047 0312028016
World politics -- 1975-1985. World politics -- 1985-1995. Detente.

D849.M72
Morris, Jan, 1926-
Destinations: essays from Rolling stone/ by Jan Morris. New York: Oxford University Press, 1980. 242 p.
79-028492 320.9/047 0195027086
Morris, Jan, -- 1926- Voyages and travels -- 1951-1980. World politics -- 1975-1985.

D849.N39 1991
Naylor, Thomas H.
The Cold War legacy/ Thomas H. Naylor. Lexington, Mass.: Lexington Books, 1991. xiv, 237 p.
90-021842 327/.09/048 066924984X
World politics -- 1985-1995. Cold War.

D849.N5 1991
New thinking & old realities: America, Europe, and Russia/ Michael T. Clark and Simon Serfaty, editors. Washington: Seven Locks Press, c1991. x, 232 p.
90-008999 909.82/8 0932020909
World politics -- 1985-1995. Europe -- Politics and government -- 1945-

D849.W46 1990
The West and the Soviet Union: politics and policy/ edited by Gregory Flynn with Richard E. Greene; foreword by Thomas L. Hughes. New York: St. Martin's Press in association with the Carne 1990. xiv, 266 p.
89-027906 909.82/8 0312040970
World politics -- 1985-1995 -- Congresses. Soviet Union -- Foreign relations -- 1985-1991 -- Congresses.

D860 Post-war history (1945-   ) — 1989-
— Political and diplomatic history

D860.A38 1993
After the Cold War/ international institutions and state strategies in Europe, 1989-1991/ edited by Robert O. Keohane, Joseph S. Nye, Stanley Hoffmann. Cambridge, Mass.: Harvard University Press, 1993. x, 481 p.
92-035682 320.94 0674008634
International agencies -- Europe. Europe -- Politics and government -- 1989-

D860.B3813 1994
Baudrillard, Jean.
The illusion of the end/ Jean Baudrillard; translated by Chris Turner. Stanford, Calif.: Stanford University Press, 1994. viii, 123 p.
94-067802 0804725004
World politics -- 1989- Political sociology. End of the world -- Political aspects.

D860.B79 1993
Brzezinski, Zbigniew K., 1928-
Out of control: global turmoil on the eve of the twenty-first century/ Zbigniew Brzezinski. New York: Scribner; c1993. xv, 240 p.
92-044621 909.82/9 0684196301
World politics -- 1989- Communism -- History -- 20th century. Post-communism. United States -- Foreign relations -- 1993-

D860.B89 1998
Buzan, Barry.
The arms dynamic in world politics/ Barry Buzan & Eric Herring. Boulder: Lynne Rienner, 1998. xiii, 325 p.
97-048486 320.9/04 1555875734
World politics -- 1989- Armaments -- Political aspects.

D860.D46 1992
Denitch, Bogdan Denis.
After the flood: world politics and democracy in the wake of communism/ Bogdan Denitch. [Middletown, Conn.]: Wesleyan University Press; c1992. xiv, 176 p.
92-053858 320/.09/04 0819552488
World politics -- 1989- Post-communism.

D860.D58 1992
Dismantling communism: common causes and regional variations/ edited by Gilbert Rozman with Seizaburo Sato and Gerald Segal. Washington, D.C.: Woodrow Wilson Center Press; 1992. x, 405 p.
92-015892 320.947 0943875358
Post-communism. World politics -- 1985-1995. Communist countries -- Politics and government. Communist countries -- Economic policy.

D860.E93 1999
Evangelista, Matthew, 1958-
Unarmed forces: the transnational movement to end the Cold War/ Matthew Evangelista. Ithaca, NY: Cornell University Press, 1999. ix, 406 p.
98-051376 327.1/74/09045 0801436281
World politics -- 1989- Cold War.

D860.G8413 1995
Guehenno, Jean-Marie, 1949-
The end of the nation-state/ Jean-Marie Guehenno; translated by Victoria Elliott. Minneapolis: University of Minnesota Press, c1995. xiii, 145 p.
95-013430 909.82/9 081662660X
National state. World politics -- 1989- Democracy.

D860.H33 1997
Haas, Ernst B.
Nationalism, liberalism, and progress/ Ernst B. Haas. Ithaca, N.Y.: Cornell University Press, 1997- v. 1
96-048439 320.54 0801431085
World politics -- 1989- Nationalism -- History -- 20th century. Liberalism -- History -- 20th century.

D860.H365 1996
Hanson, Jim M.
The next cold war?: American alternatives for the twenty-first century/ Jim Hanson. Westport, Conn.: Praeger, 1996. ix, 191 p.
95-040581 327/.09/04 0275954730
World politics -- 1989- Cold War. Twenty-first century -- Forecasts. United States -- Foreign relations -- 1989-

D860.I55 2001
Inoguchi, Takashi.
Global change: a Japanese perspective/ Takashi Inoguchi. Houndmills, Basingstoke, Hampshire; Palgrave, 2001. x, 287 p.
00-040460 909.82 0333719204
World politics -- 1989- United States -- Foreign relations -- 1989- Japan -- Foreign relations -- 1989-

D860.I87 1997
Issues in world politics/ Brian White, Richard Little, and Michael Smith, editors. New York: St. Martin's Press, 1997. xvi, 297 p.
97-009650 909.82/4 0312175477
World politics -- 1989-

D860.L55 2000
Lipschutz, Ronnie D.
After authority: war, peace, and global politics in the 21st century/ Ronnie D. Lipschutz. Albany: State University of New York Press, c2000. xi, 242 p.
99-038551 909.82/9 0791445615
World politics -- 1989- War. Peace.

D860.M55 1998
Minahan, James.
Miniature empires: a historical dictionary of the newly independent states/ James Minahan. Westport, Conn.: Greenwood Press, 1998. xvi, 340 p.
98-013979 940.55/9 0313306109
New independent states -- Dictionaries.

D860.M56 1996
Minahan, James.
Nations without states: a historical dictionary of contemporary national movements/ James Minahan; foreword by Leonard W. Doob. Westport, Conn.: Greenwood Press, 1996. xxiv, 692 p.
95-006626   909.82/9/03   0313283540
World politics -- 1989- Nationalism -- History -- 20th century.

D860.N47 1997
Niche diplomacy: middle powers after the Cold War/ edited by Andrew F. Cooper. Houndmills, Basingstoke, Hampshire: Macmillan; 1997. viii, 221 p.
97-008584   327.1/72   0312176228
World politics -- 1989-

D860.R655 1997
The roles of the United States, Russia, and China in the new world order/ edited by Hafeez Malik. New York: St. Martin's, 1997. xix, 333 p.
96-002607   327/.09/049   0312128967
World politics -- 1989- United States -- Foreign relations -- 1989- Soviet Union -- Foreign relations -- 1985-1991. China -- Foreign relations -- 1976-

D860.R87 1997
Rusi, Alpo.
Dangerous peace: new rivalry in world politics/ Alpo M. Rusi. Boulder, Colo.: Westview Press, 1997. x, 194 p.
97-013206   909.82/9   0813322588
World politics -- 1989- Geopolitics.

D860.S75 1998
Statecraft and security: the Cold War and beyond/ edited by Ken Booth. Cambridge, UK; Cambridge University Press, 1998. xiii, 358 p.
97-040985   909.82   0521474531
World politics -- 1989- Cold War -- Influence.

D883 Developing countries — General works

D883.A77 1991
Arnold, Guy.
Wars in the Third World since 1945/ Guy Arnold. London; Cassell, 1991. xxv, 579 p.
92-164345   0304316717
Developing countries -- History, Military.

D883.D4525 1990
Politics in developing countries: comparing experiences with democracy/ edited by Larry Diamond, Juan J. Linz, Seymour Martin Lipset. Boulder, Colo.: L. Rienner Publishers, 1990. viii, 503 p.
90-031540   320.9173/4   1555872123
Developing countries -- Politics and government.

D883.D453 1992
The Democratic revolution: struggles for freedom and pluralism in the developing world/ edited by Larry Diamond. New York, N.Y.: Freedom House; 1992. xix, 254 p.
91-020648   909/.09724082   0932088694
Democracy. Developing countries -- Politics and government.

D883.H33 1992
Hadjor, Kofi Buenor.
Dictionary of Third World terms/ Kofi Buenor Hadjor. London; I.B. Tauris, c1992. 303 p.
91-068011   1850433461
Developing countries -- Dictionaries.

D883.M39 1997
Mason, Michael
Development and disorder: a history of the Third World since 1945/ Mike Mason. Hanover [N.H.]: University Press of New England, c1997. x, 516 p.
97-010706   909/.09724   0874518296
Developing countries -- History.

D883.N49 1990
The New insurgencies: anticommunist guerrillas in the Third World/ [edited by] Michael Radu; with contributions by Anthony Arnold ... [et al.]. New Brunswick, N.J.: Transaction Publishers, c1990. 306 p.
89-035249   303.6/4   0887383076
Anti-communist movements -- Developing countries. Guerrillas -- Developing countries -- History -- 20th century. Developing countries -- Politics and government.

D883.O36 1992
Odom, William E.
On internal war: American and Soviet approaches to Third World clients and insurgents/ William E. Odom. Durham [N.C.]: Duke University Press, 1992. viii, 271 p.
91-018572   909.82   0822311828
Insurgency -- Developing countries -- History -- 20th century. World politics -- 1945- Developing countries -- Politics and government. Developing countries -- Foreign relations -- Soviet Union. Soviet Union -- Foreign relations -- Developing countries.

D883.S16 1998
San Juan, E. 1938-
Beyond postcolonial theory/ E. San Juan. New York: St. Martin's Press, 1998. x, 325 p.
97-019890   909/.09724   0312174268
Postcolonialism. Developing countries.

D883.S79 1994
Sturgill, Claude C., 1933-
The military history of the Third World since 1945: a reference guide/ Claude C. Sturgill. Westport, Conn.: Greenwood Press, 1994. xiii, 237 p.
93-035391   355/.009172/4   0313281521
Military history, Modern -- 20th century. Developing countries -- History, Military.

D887 Developing countries — Foreign and general relations — General works

D887.S87 1990
Superpower competition and crisis prevention in the Third World/ edited by Roy Allison and Phil Williams. Cambridge; Cambridge University Press, 1990. xii, 281 p.
89-031512   327/.091724   0521362806
Developing countries -- Foreign relations.

D887.T45 1991
Third World security in the post-cold war era/ edited by Thomas G. Weiss, Meryl A. Kessler. Boulder: Lynne Rienner Publishers, 1991. xii, 183 p.
91-003672   327/.09172/4   1555872646
National security -- Developing countries. World politics -- 1985-1995.

D888 Developing countries — Foreign and general relations — Relations with individual countries, A-Z

D888.S6.P39 1992
Payne, Richard J., 1949-
The Third World and South Africa: post-apartheid challenges/ Richard J. Payne. Westport, Conn.: Greenwood Press, 1992. xiv, 208 p.
92-008847   327.680172/4   031328542X
Economic sanctions -- South Africa. Apartheid -- South Africa. Developing countries -- Foreign relations -- South Africa. South Africa -- Foreign relations -- Developing countries.

D888.S65.D855 1990
Duncan, W. Raymond 1936-
Moscow and the Third World under Gorbachev/ W. Raymond Duncan and Carolyn McGiffert Ekedahl. Boulder: Westview Press, 1990. xvi, 260 p.
89-078300   327.4701724   0813305187
Gorbachev, Mikhail Sergeevich, -- 1931- Soviet Union -- Foreign relations -- Developing countries. Soviet Union -- Foreign relations -- 1985-1991. Developing countries -- Foreign relations -- Soviet Union.

D888.S65.G66 1991
Goodman, Melvin A. 1938-
Gorbachev's retreat: the Third World/ Melvin A. Goodman. New York: Praeger, 1991. xii, 206 p.
90-023421   327.4701724   0275936961
Developing countries -- Foreign relations -- Soviet Union. Soviet Union -- Foreign relations -- Developing countries. Soviet Union -- Foreign relations -- 1985-1991.

D888.S65.G67 1990
Gorbachev's new thinking and Third World conflicts/ edited by Jiri Valenta and Frank Cibulka. New Brunswick, N.J.: Transaction Publishers, c1990. xxiii, 352 p.
89-033635   327.470172/4   0887382126
Gorbachev, Mikhail Sergeevich, -- 1931- Perestroika. Soviet Union -- Foreign relations -- 1985-1991. Developing countries -- Foreign relations -- Soviet Union. Soviet Union -- Foreign relations -- Developing countries.

D888.S65.L55 1989
The Limits of Soviet power in the developing world/ edited by Edward A. Kolodziej and Roger E. Kanet. Baltimore: Johns Hopkins University Press, 1989. xx, 531 p.
88-011716   327.4701724   0801837626
Developing countries -- Foreign relations -- Soviet Union. Soviet Union -- Foreign relations -- Developing countries. Soviet Union -- Foreign relations -- 1975-

D888.S65.R83 1988
Rubinstein, Alvin Z.
Moscow's Third World strategy/ Alvin Z. Rubinstein. Princeton, N.J.: Princeton University Press, c1988. xi, 329 p.
88-015097   327.4701724   0691077908
Developing countries -- Foreign relations -- Soviet Union. Soviet Union -- Foreign relations -- Developing countries. Soviet Union -- Foreign relations -- 1975-

D888.S65.U79 1990
The USSR and Marxist revolutions in the Third
World/ edited by Mark N. Katz. [Washington,
D.C.]: Woodrow Wilson International Center for
Scholars 1990. ix, 153 p.
90-040405　327.470172/4　0521392659
*Revolutions -- Developing countries. Communism
-- Developing countries. Soviet Union -- Foreign
relations -- Developing countries. Developing
countries -- Foreign relations -- Soviet Union.
Soviet Union -- Foreign relations -- 1985-1991.*

D888.U6.B55 1990
Bills, Scott L.
Empire and cold war: the roots of US-Third World
antagonism, 1945-47/ Scott L. Bills. New York: St.
Martin's Press, 1990. xii, 280 p.
89-037559　327.730172/4　0312036418
*Cold War. United States -- Foreign relations --
Developing countries. Developing countries --
Foreign relations -- United States.*

D888.U6.B73 1989
Brands, H. W.
The specter of neutralism: the United States and
the emergence of the Third World, 1947-1960/
H.W. Brands. New York: Columbia University
Press, c1989. vii, 372 p.
89-024002　327.730172/4　023107168X
*Nonalignment -- Developing countries. United
States -- Foreign relations -- Developing countries.
Developing countries -- Foreign relations -- United
States.*

D888.U6.O43 1993
Ollapally, Deepa Mary.
Confronting conflict: domestic factors and U.S.
policymaking in the Third World/ Deepa Mary
Ollapally. Westport, Conn.: Greenwood Press,
1993. x, 217 p.
92-045073　327.730172/4　0313288240
*Developing countries -- Foreign relations --
United States. United States -- Foreign relations --
Developing countries. Soviet Union -- Foreign
relations -- United States.*

D919-923 Europe — Description and travel — By period

D919.F963 1992
Fuller, Margaret, 1810-1850.
"These sad but glorious days": dispatches from
Europe, 1846-1850/ Margaret Fuller; edited by
Larry J. Reynolds and Susan Belasco Smith. New
Haven: Yale University Press, c1991. xiii, 338 p.
91-013159　914.04/83　0300050380
*Fuller, Margaret, -- 1810-1850 -- Journeys --
Europe. Europe -- History -- 1848-1849.
Europe -- Description and travel.*

D921.B515 1927
Belloc, Hilaire, 1870-1953.
Towns of destiny, by Hilaire Belloc; illustrated by
Edmond L. Warre. New York, R.M. McBride &
company, 1927. viii, 238 p.
27-024256　914
*Cities and towns -- Europe. Cities and towns --
Africa, North.*

D923.G46 1983
A Geography of Europe: problems and prospects/
edited by George W. Hoffman; contributors,
Christopher Shane Davies ... [et al.]. New York:
Wiley, c1983. xv, 647 p.
83-006964　914　0471897086
Europe -- Geography.

D973 Europe — Description and travel — By region

D973.A2.B7
Braudel, Fernand.
La Mediterranee et le monde Mediterraneen a
lepoque de Philippe II. Paris, Colin, 1949. xv,
1160 p.
50-001586
*Physical geography -- Mediterranean region.
Mediterranean Region -- History.*

D973.F69 1993
Fox, Robert,
The inner sea: the Mediterranean and its people/
Robert Fox. New York: Alfred A. Knopf, 1993.
xiii, 575 p.
92-053166　909/.09822.220　0394574524
*Fox, Robert, 1945- --Journeys--Mediterranean
Region.*

D1051-1065 Europe — History — 1945-1989

D1051.L28 1992
Laqueur, Walter, 1921-
Europe in our time: a history, 1945-1992/ Walter
Laqueur. New York: Viking, 1992. xxii, 617 p.
91-016752　940.5　0670835072
Europe -- History -- 1945-

D1051.L5 1963
Lichtheim, George, 1912-
The new Europe: today, and tomorrow. New York,
Praeger [1963] xv, 232 p.
63-011152　940.55
Europe -- History -- 1945-

D1051.T46 2000
Thody, Philip Malcolm Waller, 1928-
Europe since 1945/ Philip Thody. London;
Routledge, 2000. viii, 328 p.
99-043702　940.55　0415207118
Europe -- History -- 1945-

D1051.U785 1997
Urwin, Derek W.
A political history of Western Europe since 1945/
Derek W. Urwin. London; Longman, 1997. xii,
361 p.
96-035274　940.55　0582253748
*Europe -- Politics and government -- 1945- --
Juvenile literature. Europe -- Politics and
government -- 1945-*

D1051.W4
White, Theodore Harold, 1915-
Fire in the ashes: Europe in mid-century. New
York, Sloane, 1953. 405 p.
53-010166　940.55
*Europe -- Politics and government -- 1945-
United States -- Foreign relations -- 1945-1953.*

D1053.H525 1991
Hinds, Lynn Boyd.
The cold war as rhetoric: the beginnings, 1945-
1950/ Lynn Boyd Hinds, Theodore Otto Windt, Jr.
New York: Praeger, 1991. xxiv, 272 p.
91-000445　327/.09/045　0275935787
Cold War. World politics -- 1945-

D1053.K35 1990
Kaldor, Mary.
The imaginary war: understanding the East-West
conflict/ Mary Kaldor. Oxford, OX, UK;
Blackwell, 1990. viii, 290 p.
90-000494　327　1557861803
*Cold War. Detente. Europe -- Politics and
government -- 1945-*

D1053.Y68 1991
Young, John W., 1957-
Cold War Europe, 1945-89: a political history/
John W. Young. London; E. Arnold; 1991. xx,
236 p.
91-009615　940.55　0340551429
*Cold War. Europe -- Politics and government --
1945-*

D1055.L8
Lukacs, John A.
Decline and rise of Europe; a study in recent
history, with particular emphasis on the
development of a European consciousness, by John
Lukacs. Garden City, N.Y., Doubleday, 1965. xii,
295 p.
65-010638　914
European federation. Europe -- Civilization.

D1056.A43 2000
Alcock, Antony Evelyn.
A history of the protection of regional cultural
minorities in Europe: from the Edict of Nantes to
the present day/ Antony Alcock. Basingstoke,
Hampshire, England; St. Martin's Press, 2000. xi,
279 p.
00-030889　305.8/0094　0312235569
*Minorities -- Europe -- History. Minorities --
Government policy -- Europe -- History. Self-
determination, National -- Europe -- History.
Europe -- Ethnic relations -- Government policy.
Europe -- Ethnic relations. Europe -- History --
Autonomy and independence movements.*

D1056.N37
Nations without a State: ethnic minorities in
Western Europe/ edited by Charles R. Foster. New
York, N.Y.: Praeger, 1980. ix, 215 p.
80-020900　323.1/4　0030568072
*Minorities -- Europe. Nationalism -- Europe.
Europe -- Ethnic relations.*

D1056.2.B55
Philipson, Robert.
The identity question: Blacks and Jews in Europe
and America/ Robert Philipson. Jackson:
University Press of Mississippi, c2000. xxi, 254 p.
00-035196　305.89604　1578062926
*Blacks -- Europe -- Social conditions. Jews --
Europe -- Social conditions. Blacks -- United
States -- Social conditions. Europe -- Ethnic
relations. United States -- Ethnic relations.*

D1056.2.M87.M855 1996
Muslim communities in the new Europe/ edited by
Gerd Nonneman, Tim Niblock, Bogdan
Szajkowski. Reading, Berkshire, UK: Ithaca Press,
c1996. ix, 346 p.
96-156596　305.6/97104/09049　0863721923
*Muslims -- Europe. Minorities -- Europe.
Europe -- Ethnic relations. Europe -- Social
conditions -- 20th century.*

D1058.G8 1962
Gunther, John, 1901-1970.
Inside Europe today. New York, Harper, 1962.
390 p.
62-009889　940.55
*Europe -- Politics and government -- 1945-
Europe -- Politics and government -- 1945-*

D1058.K35 2000
Kelly, Saul, 1957-
Cold War in the desert: Britain, the United States, and the Italian colonies, 1945-52/ Saul Kelly. New York: St. Martin's Press, 2000. ix, 207 p.
99-054822 909.82/4 0312231563
World politics -- 1945-1955.   Italy -- Colonies -- Africa -- History -- 20th century.

D1058.L25
Laqueur, Walter, 1921-
A continent astray: Europe, 1970-1978/ Walter Laqueur. New York: Oxford University Press, 1979. vii, 293 p.
78-012021 309.1/4/055 0195025105
*Europe -- Politics and government -- 1945-
Europe -- Economic conditions -- 1945-*

D1058.P54 1997
Piening, Christopher, 1945-
Global Europe: the European Union in world affairs/ Christopher Piening. Boulder, Colo.: L. Rienner Publishers, 1997. xii, 252 p.
97-000043 327.4 1555876943
European Union.   European Union countries -- Foreign relations.

D1058.T718 1999
Trachtenberg, Marc, 1946-
A constructed peace: the making of the European settlement, 1945-1963/ Marc Trachtenberg. Princeton, N.J.: Princeton University Press, c1999. xv, 424 p.
98-034874 327/.094/09045 0691001839
Peace.   Nuclear weapons -- International cooperation.   Europe -- Politics and government -- 1945- Europe -- Foreign relations -- United States. United States -- Foreign relations -- Europe.

D1058.T724 1999
Transatlantic tensions: the United States, Europe, and problem countries/ Richard N. Haass, editor. Washington, D.C.: Brookings Institution Press, c1999. x, 251 p.
99-006238 327.1/09182/109045 0815733526
Terrorism -- History -- 20th century. Human rights -- History -- 20th century. Europe, Western -- Foreign relations -- United States. United States -- Foreign relations -- Europe, Western. Europe, Western -- Foreign relations -- 20th century.

D1060.F55
Florinsky, Michael T., 1894-
Integrated Europe? New York, Macmillan, 1955. 182 p.
55-013682 940.55
European federation.

D1065.E85
Smith, Mark, 1965 July 1-
NATO enlargement during the Cold War: strategy and system in the Western alliance/ Mark Smith. Houndmills, Basingstoke, Hampshire; Palgrave, 2000. x, 207 p.
00-033352 355/.031091821 0312236069
*Security, International. World politics -- 1945-
Europe -- Foreign relations -- United States. United States -- Foreign relations -- Europe.*

D1065.E852.I5 1992
In from the cold: Germany, Russia, and the future of Europe/ edited by Vladimir Baranovsky and Hans-Joachim Spanger; foreword by Eduard Shevardnadze. Boulder [Colo.]: Westview Press, 1992. xxv, 321 p.
92-027253 327.4047 0813386241
Europe -- Foreign relations -- Europe, Eastern. Europe, Eastern -- Foreign relations -- Europe. Europe, Eastern -- Politics and government -- 1989-

D1065.G3.C36 1989
Campbell, Edwina S., 1950-
Germany's past and Europe's future: the challenges of West German foreign policy/ Edwina S. Campbell. Washington: Pergamon-Brassey's, c1989. xxix, 236 p.
89-030654 327.4304 0080367372
Europe -- Foreign relations -- Germany (West) Germany (West) -- Foreign relations -- Europe. Germany (West) -- Politics and government -- 1982-1990.

D1065.G7.B45 1996
Beloff, Max Beloff, 1913-
Britain and European union: dialogue of the deaf/ Lord Beloff. Great Britain: Macmillan Press Ltd.; 1996. vii, 172 p.
96-006786 327.4104 0312161573
European Union countries -- Foreign relations -- Great Britain. Great Britain -- Foreign relations -- European Union countries.

D1065.G7.D63 1991
Dockrill, Saki.
Britain's policy for West German rearmament, 1950-1955/ Saki Dockrill. Cambridge [England]; Cambridge University Press, 1991. xiii, 209 p.
90-033132 327.41043 0521381118
Europe -- Military relations -- Great Britain. Great Britain -- Military relations -- Europe. Germany (West) -- Defenses.

D1065.M628.A44 1997
Allies divided: transatlantic policies for the greater Middle East/ editors, Robert D. Blackwill, Michael Sturmer. Cambridge, Mass.: MIT Press, c1997. viii, 325 p.
97-021781 327.56 0262522446
International cooperation.   United States -- Foreign relations -- Middle East. Middle East -- Foreign relations -- Europe. Middle East -- Foreign relations -- United States.

D1065.R9.R864 1997
Russia and Europe: the emerging security agenda/ edited by Vladimir Baranovsky. Stockholm: Sipri; 1997. xviii, 582 p.
97-180593 327.4704 0198292015
National security -- Russia (Federation) National security -- Europe. Russia (Federation) -- Foreign relations -- Europe. Europe -- Foreign relations -- Russia (Federation) Russia (Federation) -- Foreign relations -- Former Soviet republics.

D1065.S6.B47 1992
Berridge, Geoff.
South Africa, the colonial powers and "African defence": the rise and fall of the white entente, 1948-60/ G.R. Berridge. New York: St. Martin's Press, 1992. xiii, 234 p.
92-018426 327.6804 0312085923
South Africa -- Military relations -- Europe. Europe -- Military relations -- South Africa. South Africa -- Foreign relations -- 1948-1961.

D1065.S65.K46 1995
Kennedy-Pipe, Caroline, 1961-
Stalin's cold war: Soviet strategies in Europe, 1943 to 1956/ Caroline Kennedy-Pipe. Manchester; Manchester University Press; c1995. 218 p.
94-036785 327.47/009/044 0719042011
World politics -- 1945-1955.   Europe -- Foreign relations -- Soviet Union. Soviet Union -- Foreign relations -- United States. United States -- Foreign relations -- Soviet Union.

D1065.S65.V35 1991
Van Oudenaren, John.
Detente in Europe: the Soviet Union and the West since 1953/ John Van Oudenaren. Durham: Duke University Press, 1991. xi, 490 p.
90-025033 327.4704 0822311410
Detente. World politics -- 1945- Europe -- Foreign relations -- Soviet Union. Soviet Union -- Foreign relations -- Europe.

D1065.U5.A788 1997
America and Europe: a partnership for a new era/ David C. Gompert and F. Stephen Larrabee, editors. Cambridge; Cambridge University Press, 1997. xv, 276 p.
96-029483 327.4073 0521591074
Europe -- Foreign relations -- United States. United States -- Foreign relations -- Europe.

D1065.U5.B67 1997
Bronstone, Adam, 1969-
European Union--United States security relations: transatlantic tensions and the theory of international relations/ Adam Bronstone. New York: St. Martin's Press, 1997. x, 282 p.
97-009627 327.7304 0333691369
National security -- European Union countries. United States -- Foreign relations -- European Union countries. European Union countries -- Foreign relations -- United States.

D1065.U5.D86 1994
Duignan, Peter.
The USA and the new Europe, 1945-1993/ Peter Duignan and L.H. Gann. Oxford, UK; B. Blackwell, 1994. x, 357 p.
93-017859 327.7304 1557865183
Europe -- Foreign relations -- United States. United States -- Foreign relations -- Europe. Europe -- Politics and government -- 1945-

D1065.U5.H275 1994
Harper, John Lamberton.
American visions of Europe: Franklin D. Roosevelt, George F. Kennan, and Dean G. Acheson/ John Lamberton Harper. Cambridge; Cambridge University Press, 1994. xi, 378 p.
93-037535 327.7304 0521454832
Roosevelt, Franklin D. -- (Franklin Delano), -- 1882-1945. Kennan, George Frost, -- 1904- Acheson, Dean, -- 1893-1971. United States -- Foreign relations -- Europe.   United States -- Foreign relations -- 20th century. Europe -- Foreign relations -- United States.

D1065.U5.H88 1997
Hutchings, Robert L., 1946-
American diplomacy and the end of the Cold War: an insider's account of U.S. policy in Europe, 1989-1992/ Robert L. Hutchings. Washington, D.C.: Woodrow Wilson Center Press; c1997. xviii, 456 p.
96-048308 327.7304 0801856205
Europe -- Foreign relations -- United States. United States -- Foreign relations -- Europe. Europe -- Politics and government -- 1989-

D1065.U5.J59 1999
John F. Kennedy and Europe/ edited by Douglas Brinkley and Richard T. Griffiths; with a foreword by Theodore Sorensen. Baton Rouge: Louisiana State University Press, c1999. xviii, 349 p.
98-056145 327.7304 0807123323
Kennedy, John F. -- (John Fitzgerald), -- 1917-1963.   United States -- Foreign relations -- Europe. United States -- Politics and government -- 1961-1963. United States -- Foreign relations -- 1961-1963.

D1065.U5.P388 1997
Pells, Richard H.
Not like us: how Europeans have loved, hated, and transformed American culture since World War II/ Richard Pells. New York, NY: Basic Books, 1997. xviii, 444 p.
96-038183   303.48/27304   0465001645
  Popular culture -- Europe.   United States -- Relations -- Europe. Europe -- Civilization -- American influences. Europe -- Relations -- United States.

D1065.U5.S39 1997
Serfaty, Simon.
Stay the course: European unity and Atlantic solidarity/ Simon Serfaty; foreword by Alexander M. Haig, Jr. Westport, Conn.: Praeger, 1997. xii, 115 p.
96-054065   327.7304   0275959325
  European Union. Europe -- Strategic aspects. Europe -- Foreign relations -- United States. United States -- Foreign relations -- Europe. Europe -- Foreign relations -- 1989-

D1065.U5.S413
Servan-Schreiber, Jean Jacques.
The American challenge [by] J. J. Servan-Schreiber. With a foreword by Arthur Schlesinger, Jr. Translated from the French by Ronald Steel. New York, Atheneum, 1968. xviii, 291 p.
68-019793   332.67/373/04
  Investments, American -- Europe. Industrial management -- United States. Industrial management -- Europe.

D2003-2009 Europe — History — 1989-

D2003.H35 2001
Halliday, Fred.
The world at 2000: perils and promises/ Fred Halliday. New York: Palgrave, 2000. p. cm.
 00-062604   909.83   0333945344
  World politics -- 21st century. Globalization. Democracy.

D2009.B83 1993
Buchan, David, 1947-
Europe: the strange superpower/ David Buchan. Aldershot, Hants, England; Dartmouth, c1993. vii, 181 p.
93-024949   320.94   1855214415
  Europe -- Politics and government -- 1989-

D2009.D4613 1997
Democracy and corruption in Europe/ edited by Donatella Della Porta and Yves Meny. London; Pinter, 1997. viii, 208 p.
96-018572   320.94   1855673665
  Political corruption -- Europe -- History -- 20th century.   Europe -- Politics and government -- 1945- Europe -- Politics and government -- 1989-

D2009.E49 1998
Emerson, Michael.
Redrawing the map of Europe/ Michael Emerson. New York, N.Y.: St. Martin's Press, 1998. xxx, 268 p.
98-021461   940.55/9   0312216971
  Europe -- Politics and government -- 1989-

D2009.E87 1991
Europe from below: an East-West dialogue/ edited by Mary Kaldor. London; Verso, 1991. ix, 223 p.
90-049015   320.94   0860913058
  Europe -- Politics and government -- 1989-

D2009.E8765 1998
Europe: the cold divide/ edited by Fergus Carr. Houndmills, Great Britain: Macmillan Press; 1998. xii, 208 p.
97-028028   940.55   0312210248
  Europe -- Politics and government -- 1989-

D2009.G37 1999
Garton Ash, Timothy.
History of the present: essays, sketches, and dispatches from Europe in the 1990s/ Timothy Garton Ash. New York: Random House, c1999. xxi, 405 p.
00-062553   940.55/9   0375503536
  Europe -- Politics and government -- 1989- Europe, Eastern -- Politics and government -- 1989- Europe, Eastern -- Ethnic relations.

D2009.G47 1991
Germany and Europe in transition/ edited by Adam Daniel Rotfeld and Walther Stutzle. Oxford [England]; Oxford University Press, 1991. x, 237 p.
90-019695   940.55   0198291469
  Europe -- Politics and government -- 1989- Sources. Germany (East) -- Politics and government -- 1989-1990 -- Sources. Germany (West) -- Politics and government -- 1982-1990 -- Sources.

D2009.G83 1991
Gucht, Karel de, 1954-
Time and tide wait for no man: the changing European geopolitical landscape/ Karel de Gucht and Stephan Keukeleire; foreword by Valery Giscard d'Estaing. New York: Praeger, 1991. x, 242 p.
91-009196   320.1/2   0275940624
  Geopolitics -- Europe.   Europe -- Politics and government -- 1989-

D2009.H65 2000
Holmes, Douglas R., 1949-
Integral Europe: fast-capitalism, multiculturalism, neofascism/ Douglas R. Holmes. Princeton, N.J.: Princeton University Press, c2000. xiii, 253 p.
00-036686   940.55   0691033889
  Political culture -- Europe -- History -- 20th century. Political anthropology -- Europe. Political socialization -- Europe -- History -- 20th century. Europe -- Economic conditions -- 1945-

D2009.N5 1997
Newhouse, John.
Europe adrift/ John Newhouse. New York: Pantheon Books, c1997. xi, 339 p.
97-002943   320.94   0679433708
  European Union. Europe -- Economic policy. Europe -- Politics and government -- 1989-

D2009.P65 1991
Political power and social change: the United States faces a united Europe/ edited by Norman J. Ornstein and Mark Perlman. Washington, D.C.: AEI Press; 1991. xii, 206 p.
91-021074   327.7304   0844737577
  European federation. Europe -- Economic conditions -- 1945- Europe -- Politics and government -- 1989- Europe -- Social conditions -- 20th century.

D2009.S54 2000
Shore, Cris, 1959-
Building Europe: the cultural politics of European integration/ Cris Shore. London; Routledge, 2000. xii, 258 p.
99-054929   306.2/094   0415180147
  European Union. Nationalism -- Europe. Europe -- Politics and government -- 1989-

D2009.Z54 1998
Zielonka, Jan, 1955-
Explaining Euro-paralysis: why Europe is unable to act in international politics/ Jan Zielonka. Houndmills, Basingstoke, Hampshire: Macmillan Press; c1998. viii, 266 p.
98-015288   327.4   0312214634
  Europe -- Politics and government -- 1989- Europe -- Foreign relations -- 1989-

DA History of Great Britain

DA1 Historiography — General works

DA1.B875 1970
Butterfield, Herbert, 1900-
The Englishman and his history, by H. Butterfield. With a new pref. by the author. [Hamden, Conn.] Archon Books, 1970. x, 142 p.
76-121754   942/.0072/042   0208009930
  Great Britain -- Historiography. Great Britain -- Politics and government.

DA1.F36 1999
The familiar past?: archaeologies of later historical Britain/ edited by Sarah Tarlow and Susie West. London; Routledge, 1999. xiv, 294 p.
98-008227   936.1   0415188059
  Excavations (Archaeology) -- Great Britain. Great Britain -- Historiography. Great Britain -- Antiquities.

DA1.F45 1996
Feske, Victor.
From Belloc to Churchill: private scholars, public culture, and the crisis of British liberalism, 1900-1939/ Victor Feske. Chapel Hill: University of North Carolina Press, c1996. xii, 304 p.
96-010260   941/.0072041   0807822957
  Churchill, Winston, -- Sir, -- 1874-1965. Belloc, Hilaire, -- 1870-1953. Historiography -- Great Britain -- History -- 20th century. Liberalism -- Great Britain -- History -- 20th century. Great Britain -- Intellectual life -- 20th century. Great Britain -- Politics and government -- 1901-1936. Great Britain -- Historiography -- History -- 20th century.

DA1.H53 1996
Hicks, Philip Stephen, 1958-
Neo-classical history and English culture: from Clarendon to Hume/ Philip Hicks. New York: St. Martin's Press, 1996. viii, 289 p.
96-025840   941.06/007202   0312160917
  Clarendon, Edward Hyde, -- Earl of, -- 1609-1674. Hume, David, -- 1711-1776. Historiography -- Great Britain -- History -- 17th century. Classicism -- England. Historiography -- Great Britain -- History -- 18th century. England -- Civilization -- 18th century. Great Britain -- Historiography. England -- Civilization -- Classical influences.

DA1.L66 2000
Looser, Devoney, 1967-
British women writers and the writing of history, 1670-1820/ Devoney Looser. Baltimore: Johns Hopkins University Press, 2000. xi, 272 p.
00-008475   941/.007/2   0801864488
  Historiography -- Great Britain -- History -- 18th century. English prose literature -- Women authors -- History and criticism. English prose literature -- 18th century -- History and criticism. Great Britain -- Historiography.

DA1.M58 2000
Mitchell, Rosemary.
Picturing the past: English history in text and image, 1830-1870/ Rosemary Mitchell. Oxford; Clarendon Prss, 2000. xi, 314 p.
99-089337   941/.007/2   0198208448
Historiography -- Great Britain -- History -- 19th century. Illustrated books -- Great Britain -- History -- 19th century. Illustration of books -- 19th century -- Great Britain. Great Britain -- Historiography.

DA1.W45 1962
West, John, 1926-
Village records. London, Macmillan: 1962. xvi, 208 p.
63-003320
Great Britain -- History, Local -- Sources. Great Britain -- Historiography. Chaddesley Corbett, England -- History -- Sources.

DA1.W665 2000
Woolf, D. R.
Reading history in early modern England/ D.R. Woolf. Cambridge [England]; Cambridge University Press, 2000. xvi, 360 p.
00-023593   941/.007/2   0521780462
Historiography -- Great Britain -- History -- 16th century. Historiography -- Great Britain -- History -- 17th century. Books and reading -- England -- History -- 16th century. Great Britain -- History -- Stuarts, 1603-1714 -- Historiography. Great Britain -- Historiography. Great Britain -- History -- Tudors, 1485-1603 -- Historiography.

DA3 Historiography — Biography of historians

DA3.H29.W43 1997
Weaver, Stewart Angas.
The Hammonds: a marriage in history/ Stewart A. Weaver. Stanford, Calif.: Stanford University Press, c1997. viii, 349 p.
97-025431   941.082/092   0804732426
Hammond, J. L. -- (John Lawrence), -- 1872-1949. Hammond, Barbara Bradby, -- 1873-1962. Agricultural laborers -- Great Britain -- Historiography. Industrial revolution -- Great Britain -- Historiography. Working class -- Great Britain -- Historiography. Great Britain -- Social conditions -- Historiography.

DA3.M3.A4 1974
Macaulay, Thomas Babington Macaulay, 1800-1859.
The letters of Thomas Babington Macaulay, edited by Thomas Pinney. [London] Cambridge University Press, 1974-1981. 6 v.
73-075860   828/.8/09   0521211263
Macaulay, Thomas Babington Macaulay, -- Baron, -- 1800-1859 -- Correspondence. Historians -- Great Britain -- Correspondence.

DA3.M3.H27
Hamburger, Joseph, 1922-
Macaulay and the Whig tradition/ Joseph Hamburger. Chicago: University of Chicago Press, 1976. 274 p.
75-027892   941.081/092/4   0226314723
Macaulay, Thomas Babington Macaulay, -- Baron, -- 1800-1859. Historians -- Great Britain -- Biography. Statesmen -- Great Britain -- Biography. Great Britain -- Politics and government -- 19th century.

DA3.P53.B69 1991
Bowden, Mark.
The life and archaeological work of Lieutenant-General Augustus Henry Lane Fox Pitt Rivers, DCL, FRS, FSA/ Mark Bowden. Cambridge; Cambridge University Press, 1991. p. cm.
90-045313   941.081/092   0521400775
Pitt-Rivers, Augustus Henry Lane-Fox, -- 1827-1900. Archaeology -- Great Britain -- History -- 19th century. Archaeologists -- Great Britain -- Biography. Generals -- Great Britain -- Biography. Great Britain -- Antiquities.

DA3.P69.B47 1996
Berg, Maxine, 1950-
A woman in history, Eileen Power, 1889-1940/ Maxine Berg. Cambridge [England]; Cambridge University Press, 1996. xv, 292 p.
95-034779   940.1/092   0521402786
Power, Eileen Edna, -- 1889-1940. Women historians -- Great Britain -- Biography. Medievalists -- Great Britain -- Biography. Middle Ages -- Historiography. Great Britain -- Historiography. Europe -- Historiography.

DA3.T36.A37 1983
Taylor, A. J. P. 1906-
A personal history/ A.J.P. Taylor. New York: Atheneum, 1983. 278 p.
83-045086   907/.2024   0689114125
Taylor, A. J. P. -- (Alan John Percivale), -- 1906- Historians -- Great Britain -- Biography.

DA3.T36.C65 1993
Cole, Robert, 1939-
A.J.P. Taylor: the traitor within the gates/ Robert Cole. New York: St. Martin's Press, 1993. xi, 285 p.
93-013506   907/.202   0312100663
Taylor, A. J. P. -- (Alan John Percivale), -- 1906- Great Britain -- Historiography. Europe -- Historiography.

DA3.T68.M37 1989
McNeill, William Hardy, 1917-
Arnold J. Toynbee, a life/ William H. McNeill. New York: Oxford University Press, 1989. viii, 346 p.
88-023188   907/.2024   0195058631
Toynbee, Arnold Joseph, -- 1889-1975. Historians -- Great Britain -- Biography.

DA3.T7.C36 1992
Cannadine, David, 1950-
G.M. Trevelyan: a life in history/ David Cannadine. London: HarperCollinsPublishers, 1992. xvi, 288 p.
91-222887   0002158728
Trevelyan, George Macaulay, -- 1876-1962. Historians -- Great Britain -- Biography. Great Britain -- Intellectual life -- 20th century.

DA13 British Empire. Commonwealth of Nations. The Commonwealth — Historical geography

DA13.D3
Darby, H. C. 1909-
An historical geography of England before A.D. 1800; fourteen studies, edited by H.C. Darby ... Cambridge [Eng.] The University Press, 1936. xii, 566 p.
36-018359   911.42
Great Britain -- Historical geography. Great Britain -- History.

DA16 British Empire. Commonwealth of Nations. The Commonwealth — History

DA16.C252
The Cambridge history of the British Empire. Cambridge [Eng.] University Press, 1963. v.
63-024285
Great Britain -- History. Great Britain -- Colonies -- History. Rhodesia (South Africa) -- History.

DA16.C28 2001
Cannadine, David,
Ornamentalism: how the British saw their empire/ David Cannadine. Oxford; Oxford University Press, c2001. xxiv, 263 p.
2001-021407   941.08.221   0195146603
Great Britain--Colonies--History. Public opinion--Great Britain--History. Social classes--Great Britain--Colonies--History.

DA16.C32
Carrington, Charles, 1897-
The British overseas: exploits of a nation of shopkeepers, by C. E. Carrington. London, Cambridge U.P., 1968- v.
68-023176   325.3/42   052109514X
Great Britain -- Colonies -- History.

DA16.C34 1995
Carruthers, Susan L.
Winning hearts and minds: British governments, the media, and colonial counter-insurgency, 1944-1960/ Susan L. Carruthers. London; Leicester University Press, 1995. xi, 307 p.
95-007954   325/.3141   071850027X
Counterinsurgency -- Great Britain -- Colonies -- History -- 20th century. Public opinion -- Great Britain -- Colonies -- History -- 20th century. Insurgency -- Great Britain -- Colonies -- History -- 20th century. Great Britain -- Colonies -- History -- 20th century.

DA16.C47
Churchill, Winston, 1874-1965.
A history of the English-speaking peoples. New York, Dodd, Mead, 1956-58. 4 v.
56-006868   942
English-speaking countries -- History. Great Britain -- History.

DA16.G736
Grierson, Edward, 1914-
The imperial dream: the British Commonwealth and Empire, 1775-1969. London, Collins, 1972. 320 p.
72-180114   909/.09/71242   0002114119
Great Britain -- Colonies. Commonwealth countries -- History.

DA16.J88 1997
Judd, Denis, 1938-
Empire: the British imperial experience from 1765 to the present/ Denis Judd. New York: BasicBooks, [1997], c1996 xxvi, 518 p.
97-012368   941   0465019528
Imperialism -- History. Great Britain -- Colonies -- History -- 20th century. Great Britain -- Colonies -- History -- 18th century. Great Britain -- Colonies -- History -- 19th century.

DA16.L8684 1990
Low, D. A. 1927-
Eclipse of empire/ D.A. Low. Cambridge;
Cambridge University Press, 1991. xvi, 375 p.
89-022286 325/.341 0521383293
*Decolonization -- History. Commonwealth
countries -- History. Great Britain -- Colonies --
History.*

DA16.M245 1995
The man on the spot: essays on British Empire
history/ edited by Roger D. Long. Westport, Conn.:
Greenwood Press, 1995. x, 246 p.
95-009667 941 0313295247
Great Britain -- Colonies -- History.

DA16.M37 1995
McClintock, Anne, 1954-
Imperial leather: race, gender, and sexuality in the
colonial contest/ Anne McClintock. New York:
Routledge, 1995. xi, 449 p.
94-007593 305.3/0941 0415908892
*Sex role -- Great Britain -- Colonies -- History.
Sex -- Great Britain -- Colonies -- History. Man-
woman relationships -- Great Britain -- Colonies --
History. Great Britain -- Colonies -- Race
relations. Great Britain -- Colonies -- History --
20th century. Great Britain -- Colonies -- History -
- 19th century.*

DA16.O74 1996
Orde, Anne.
The eclipse of Great Britain: the United States and
British imperial decline, 1895-1956/ Anne Orde.
New York: St. Martin's Press, 1996. viii, 262 p.
96-007160 909/.0971241082 0312161409
*Imperialism -- History -- 20th century. Great
Britain -- Colonies -- History -- 20th century.
Great Britain -- Foreign relations -- United States.
United States -- Foreign relations -- Great Britain.*

DA16.O95 1998
The Oxford history of the British Empire/ Wm.
Roger Louis,   editor-in-chief. Oxford; Oxford
University Press, 1998-1999. 5 v.
97-036299 909/.0971241.221 019820566X
Imperialism--History.

DA16.P67
Porter, Bernard.
The lion's share: a short history of British
imperialism, 1850-1970/ Bernard Porter. London;
Longman, 1975. xiii, 408 p.
75-016224 941.08 0582481031
*Imperialism -- History. Great Britain -- Foreign
relations -- 20th century. Great Britain -- Colonies
-- History -- 19th century. Great Britain -- Foreign
relations -- 1837-1901.*

DA16.R93 1997
Ryan, James R.
Picturing empire: photography and the
visualization of the British Empire/ James R. Ryan.
Chicago: University of Chicago Press, 1997. 272 p.
97-026401 941.08 0226732339
*Photography -- Great Britain -- Colonies --
History. Imperialism -- Historiography. Great
Britain -- Colonies -- Historiography. Great
Britain -- Colonies -- History -- Pictorial works.*

DA16.S45 1971
Seeley, John Robert, 1834-1895.
The expansion of England. Edited and with an
introd. by John Gross. Chicago, University of
Chicago Press [1971] xxvii, 248 p.
73-152225 909/.09/71242 0226744280
*Great Britain -- Colonies. Great Britain --
History -- 18th century. India -- Politics and
government -- 1765-1947.*

DA16.S84 1996
Stewart, John, 1952-
The British Empire: an encyclopedia of the
Crown's holdings, 1493 through 1995/ by John
Stewart. Jefferson, NC: McFarland & Co., c1996.
xiv, 370 p.
96-005205 941/.003 078640177X
*Great Britain -- Colonies -- History --
Encyclopedias. Great Britain -- Foreign relations -
- Encyclopedias.*

DA17 British Empire. Commonwealth of Nations. The Commonwealth — Biography and memoirs — Individual, A-Z

DA17.C87.L38 1995
Lavin, Deborah.
From empire to international commonwealth: a
biography ofLionel Curtis/ Deborah Lavin. Oxford
[England]: Clarendon Press; 1995. x, 373 p.
95-001819 941.082 0198126166
*Curtis, Lionel, -- 1872-1955. Political scientists --
Great Britain -- Biography. Internationalists --
Great Britain -- Biography. International relations
-- History -- 20th century. Commonwealth
countries -- History -- 20th century -- Biography.
Great Britain -- Colonies -- History -- 20th century
-- Biography.*

DA17.H3.C45 1992
Cell, John Whitson.
Hailey: a study in British imperialism, 1872-1969/
John W. Cell. Cambridge [England]; Cambridge
University Press, 1992. xv, 332 p.
91-022678 325/.341/092 0521411076
*Hailey, William Malcolm Hailey, -- Baron, --
1872-1969.   Colonial administrators -- Great
Britain -- Biography. Colonial administrators --
Africa -- Biography. Colonial administrators --
India -- Biography. Great Britain -- Colonies --
Administration -- History -- 20th century.*

DA17.L56.C48 1987
Charmley, John, 1955-
Lord Lloyd and the decline of the British Empire/
John Charmley. New York: St. Martin's Press,
1987. x, 294 p.
87-020704 941.082 031201306X
*Lloyd of Dolobran, George Ambrose Lloyd, --
Baron, -- 1879-1941.   Colonial administrators --
Great Britain -- Biography.   Great Britain --
Colonies -- Administration -- History -- 20th
century. Great Britain -- Colonies -- History --
20th century.*

DA18 British Empire. Commonwealth of Nations. The Commonwealth — Political history. Imperial federation — General works

DA18.H714 1993
Howe, Stephen, 1958-
Anticolonialism in British politics: the left and the
end of Empire, 1918-1964/ Stephen Howe. Oxford:
Clarendon Press; 1993. xvi, 373 p.
93-010369 325/.341/0904 019820423X
*Decolonization -- Public opinion -- History --
20th century. Imperialism -- Public opinion --
History -- 20th century. Public opinion -- Great
Britain. Great Britain -- Colonies -- Public opinion
-- History -- 20th century. Great Britain -- Politics
and government -- 20th century.*

DA18.W52 1969
Winks, Robin W.,
The age of imperialism, edited by Robin W.
Winks. Englewood Cliffs, N.J., Prentice-Hall
[1969] viii, 184 p.
75-079441 321/.03/08 0130185493
Imperial federation. Imperialism.

DA26 England — Collections — Other collections

DA26.E55
English historical documents. General editor:
David C. Douglas. London, Eyre & Spottiswoode,
1968-   [v.
55-032265
Great Britain -- History -- Sources.

DA27 England — Collections — Collected works of individual authors

DA27.R78
Rowse, A. L. 1903-
The English spirit, essays in history and literature,
by A.L. Rowse ... London, Macmillan & Co. Ltd.,
1944. x, 275 p.
45-001603 942.004
*English literature -- History and criticism.
Great Britain -- History.*

DA27.5 England — General works

DA27.5.G37 1993
Gascoigne, Bamber.
Encyclopedia of Britain/ Bamber Gascoigne. New
York: Macmillan Pub., 1993. 720 p.
93-001881 941/.003 0028971426
Great Britain -- Encyclopedias.

DA27.5.U38 2000
UK today: essential facts in an ever changing
world/ edited by Barry Turner. New York: St.
Martin's Press, 2000. xviii, 544 p.
00-031110 941 0312229925
*Great Britain -- Handbooks, manuals, etc.
Great Britain -- Statistics.*

DA28-28.4 England — History — Biography (Collective)

DA28.D525 1993
The Dictionary of national biography. edited by
C.S. Nicholls; consultant editors, G.H.L. Le May
... [et al.]. Oxford [England]; Oxford University
Press, 1994. xxi, 768 p.
92-009744 920.041 0198652119
Great Britain -- Biography -- Dictionaries.

DA28.H57 2000
The History today who's who in British history/
edited by Juliet Gardiner. London: Collins &
Brown: 2000. 870 p.
2001-334480 920.041 1855857715
*Great Britain -- Biography -- Dictionaries.
Great Britain -- History -- Dictionaries.*

DA28.W616 1998
Who's who in British history: beginnings to 1901/
general editor, Geoffrey Treasure; authors and
contributors, Ian Dawson ... [et al.]. London;
Fitzroy Dearborn Publishers, c1998. 2 v.
98-162133   920.041   1884964907
Great Britain -- Biography -- Dictionaries.
Great Britain -- History.

DA28.1.B7 1963
Brooke, Christopher Nugent Lawrence.
The Saxon & Norman kings.   London, B.T.
Batsford [c1963] 232 p.
63-018127
Great Britain -- History -- Norman period,
1066-1154. Great Britain -- Kings and rulers.
Great Britain -- History -- Anglo Saxon period,
449-1066.

DA28.1.W523 1998
Williamson, David.
The National Portrait Gallery history of the kings
and queens of England/ David Williamson.
London: National Portrait Gallery, c1998. 176 p.
99-221635   941/.009/9   1855142287
Monarchy -- Great Britain -- History. Queens --
Great Britain -- Biography. Queens -- Great
Britain -- Portraits. Great Britain -- Kings and
rulers -- Biography. Great Britain -- Kings and
rulers -- Portraits.

DA28.35.C45.R59
Rowse, A. L. 1903-
The Churchills: from the death of Marlborough to
the present. New York, Harper [1958] 430 p.
58-001688   929.7203
Churchill family.

DA28.35.C45.R6
Rowse, A. L. 1903-
The early Churchills, an English family. New
York, Harper [1956] 378 p.
56-008760   929.7203
Churchill, Winston, -- Sir, -- 1874-1965. Churchill,
Winston, -- Sir, -- 1620?-1688. Marlborough,
Sarah Jennings Churchill, -- Duchess of, -- 1660-
1744.

DA28.35.N67.R63 1983
Robinson, John Martin.
The Dukes of Norfolk: a quincentennial history/
John Martin Robinson. Oxford [Oxfordshire];
Oxford University Press, 1982, c1983. xiii, 264 p.
82-008002   942/.009/92   0192158694
Norfolk, Dukes of. Howard family.   Nobility --
Great Britain -- History.

DA28.4.B56 1998
Biographical dictionary of British prime ministers/
edited by Robert Eccleshall and Graham Walker.
London; Routledge, 1998. xiv, 428 p.
98-011039   941/.0099   0415108306
Prime ministers -- Great Britain -- Biography --
Dictionaries.   Great Britain -- Politics and
government -- Dictionaries.

DA28.4.E54 1995
Englefield, Dermot J. T.
Facts about the British prime ministers: a
compilation of biographical and historical
information/ Dermot Englefield, Janet Seaton,
Isobel White; foreword by Prime Minister John
Major. New York: H.W. Wilson Co., 1995. xxx,
439 p.
94-033988   941/.0099   0824208633
Prime ministers -- Great Britain -- Biography.
Prime ministers.   Great Britain -- Politics and
government.   Great Britain -- Politics and
government.

DA30 England — History — General works

DA30.C6
Clark, G. N. 1890-
English history: a survey, George Clark. Oxford,
Clarendon Press, 1971. xix, 567 p.
70-595865   942   0198223390
Great Britain -- History.

DA30.D355 1999
Davies, Norman.
The Isles: a history/ Norman Davies. Oxford;
Oxford University Press, c1999. xlii, 1222 p.
99-029052   941   0195134427
Great Britain -- History. Great Britain --
Civilization -- European influences. Ireland --
Civilization -- European influences.

DA30.H92 1975
Hume, David, 1711-1776.
The history of England: from the invasion of Julius
Caesar to the Revolution in 1688/ David Hume;
abridged and with an introd. by Rodney W. Kilcup.
Chicago: University of Chicago Press, 1975. lvi,
392 p.
74-016685   942   0226360652
Great Britain -- History.

DA30.P4 vol. 4
Myers, A. R. 1912-1980.
England in the late Middle Ages. Harmondsworth,
Middlesex, Penguin Books [1956] 263 p.
67-004045
Great Britain -- History -- 13th century.

DA30.P7622 vol. 2
Adams, George Burton, 1851-1925.
The history of England, from the Norman Conquest
to the death of John, 1066-1216. London, New
York, Longmans, Green, 1905. New York, AMS
Press, 1969. x, 473 p.
79-005634   942
Great Britain -- History -- Medieval period,
1066-1485.

DA30.P762 vol. 1
Hodgkin, Thomas, 1831-1913.
The history of England, from the earliest times to
the Norman Conquest.   New York, Greenwood
Press [1969] xxi, 528 p.
69-013933   942.01
Constitutional history, Medieval.   Great Britain
-- History -- To 1066.

DA32 England — History — Compends

DA32.T7487 1946
Trevelyan, George Macaulay, 1876-1962.
English social history; a survey of six centuries,
Chaucer to Queen Victoria, by G. M. Trevelyan ...
London, Longmans, Green and Co. [1946] xii,
628 p.
46-007694   942
Great Britain -- History. Great Britain --
Social conditions.

DA32.T749 1973
Trevelyan, George Macaulay, 1876-1962.
History of England/ [by] G. M. Trevelyan. London:
Longman, 1973. xxxiii, 913 p.
75-310626   941   0582484715
Great Britain -- History.

DA34 England — History — Dictionaries. Chronological tables, outlines, etc.

DA34.C28 1985
The Cambridge historical encyclopedia of Great
Britain and Ireland/ editor, Christopher Haigh.
Cambridge   [Cambridgeshire];   Cambridge
University Press, 1985. 392 p.
85-047568   941/.003/21   0521255597
Great Britain -- History -- Dictionaries.
Ireland -- History -- Dictionaries.

DA34.H64 1997
The Columbia companion to British history/ edited
by Juliet Gardiner & Neil Wenborn. New York:
Columbia University Press, 1997. iii, 840 p.
96-023774   941/.003   0231107927
Great Britain -- History -- Encyclopedias.

DA34.O93 1997
The Oxford companion to British history/ edited by
John Cannon.   Oxford [England];   Oxford
University Press, 1997. xii, 1044 p.
97-027598   941/.003   0198661762
Great Britain -- History -- Encyclopedias.

DA34.P36 1997
Panton, Kenneth J. 1945-
Historical dictionary of the United Kingdom/
Kenneth J. Panton and Keith A. Cowland. Lanham,
Md.: Scarecrow Press, 1997-1998. 2 v.
96-023996   941.003   0810831503
Great Britain -- History -- Dictionaries.

DA40-125 England — History — General special

DA40.C29 1988
Cannon, John Ashton.
The Oxford illustrated history of the British
monarchy/ John Cannon and Ralph Griffiths.
Oxford [England]; Oxford University Press, 1988.
ix, 727 p.
88-005172   941   0198227868
Monarchy -- Great Britain -- History.   Great
Britain -- Politics and government. Great Britain --
Kings and rulers -- Biography. Great Britain --
Social conditions.

DA42.S85 1976
Strang, William Strang, 1893-
Britain in world affairs: the fluctuation in power
and influence from Henry VIII to Elizabeth II/ by
Lord William Strang. Westport, Conn.: Greenwood
Press, 1976, c1961. 426 p.
75-032463   327.41   0837185424
Great Britain -- Foreign relations.

DA45.T3 1958
Taylor, A. J. P. 1906-
The trouble makers; dissent over foreign policy,
1792-1939.   Bloomington, Indiana University
Press, 1958. 207 p.
58-009370   327.42
Great Britain -- Foreign relations -- 20th
century. Great Britain -- Foreign relations -- 19th
century.

DA45.W35 1970
Ward, Adolphus William, 1837-1924,
The Cambridge history of British foreign policy, 1783-1919. Edited by A. W. Ward and G. P. Gooch. New York, Octagon Books, 1970. 3 v.
70-119436   327.42
World politics.   Great Britain -- Foreign relations.

DA45.W53
Wiener, Joel H.,
Great Britain: foreign policy and the span of empire, 1689-1971; a documentary history. Edited with commentaries by Joel H. Wiener. Introd.: J. H. Plumb. New York, Chelsea House Publishers [1972] 4 v.
78-179375   327.42   0070797307
Great Britain -- Colonies -- History -- Sources. Great Britain -- Foreign relations -- Sources. Commonwealth countries -- History -- Sources.

DA47.H6
Horn, David Bayne, 1901-
Great Britain and Europe in the eighteenth century. Oxford, Clarendon P., 1967. xi, 411 p.
67-088613   327.4/042
Great Britain -- Foreign relations -- Europe. Europe -- Foreign relations -- Great Britain. Great Britain -- Foreign relations -- 18th century.

DA47.1.D63 1999
Dockrill, M. L.
British establishment perspectives on France, 1936-40/ Michael Dockrill. New York: St. Martin's Press, 1999. xiii, 212 p.
98-003710   327.41044   0312215444
Public opinion -- Great Britain -- History -- 20th century. World War, 1939-1945 -- Great Britain. World War, 1939-1945 -- France. Foreign public opinion, British. France -- Foreign relations -- Great Britain. Great Britain -- Foreign relations -- France.

DA47.1.H47 1998
Herman, John.
The Paris Embassy of Sir Eric Phipps: Anglo-French relations and the Foreign Office, 1937-1939/ John Herman. Brighton [U.K.]; Sussex Academic Press, 1998. viii, 276 p.
98-029477   327.41044   1902210042
Phipps, Eric, -- Sir, -- b. 1875. British -- France -- Paris -- History -- 20th century. France -- Foreign relations -- Great Britain. France -- Foreign relations -- 1914-1940. Great Britain -- Foreign relations -- France.

DA47.1.P47 1995
Pereboom, Maarten L., 1962-
Democracies at the turning point: Britain, France, and the end of the postwar order, 1928-1933/ Maarten L. Pereboom. New York: P. Lang, c1995. x, 239 p.
94-013004   940.5/1   0820425354
World War, 1914-1918 -- Influence. World politics -- 1919-1932. France -- Foreign relations -- Great Britain. France -- Foreign relations -- 1914-1940. Great Britain -- Foreign relations -- France.

DA47.2.C59 1989
Cockett, Richard.
Twilight of truth: Chamberlain, appeasement, and the manipulation of the press/ Richard Cockett. New York: St. Martin's Press, 1989. x, 229 p.
89-004108   327.41043   0312031408
Chamberlain, Neville, -- 1869-1940 -- Views on Germany. Government and the press -- Great Britain -- History -- 20th century. Great Britain -- Politics and government -- 1936-1945. Germany -- Foreign relations -- Great Britain. Great Britain -- Foreign relations -- Germany.

DA47.2.D47 1990
Deighton, Anne, 1949-
The impossible peace: Britain, the division of Germany and the origins of the cold war/ Anne Deighton. Oxford: Clarendon Press; 1990. viii, 283 p.
89-049374   327/.09/044   0198273320
World politics -- 1945-1955. Cold War. Germany -- Foreign relations -- Great Britain. Great Britain -- Foreign relations -- 1945- Great Britain -- Foreign relations -- Germany.

DA47.2.G5 1963a
Gilbert, Martin, 1936-
The appeasers, by Martin Gilbert and Richard Gott. Boston [Houghton Mifflin, 1963. 444 p.
63-009079   327.42043
Chamberlain, Neville, -- 1869-1940.   Germany -- Foreign relations -- Great Britain. Great Britain -- Foreign relations -- 1936-1945. Great Britain -- Foreign relations -- Germany.

DA47.2.H84 2000
Huffman, Joseph P., 1959-
The social politics of medieval diplomacy: Anglo-German relations (1066-1307)/ Joseph P. Huffman. Ann Arbor: University of Michigan Press, c2000. x, 361 p.
99-051933   327.41043   0472110616
Great Britain -- Foreign relations -- Germany. Germany -- Foreign relations -- Great Britain. Great Britain -- Foreign relations -- 1066-1485.

DA47.2.K44
Kennedy, Paul M., 1945-
The rise of the Anglo-German antagonism, 1860-1914/ Paul M. Kennedy. London; Allen & Unwin, 1980. xiv, 604 p.
80-040461   327.41043   0049400606
Great Britain -- Foreign relations -- Germany. Germany -- Foreign relations -- Great Britain.

DA47.2.M19 1998
Maiolo, Joseph A.
The Royal Navy and Nazi Germany, 1933-39: a study in appeasement and the origins of the Second World War/ Joseph A. Maiolo. New York: St. Martin's Press, 1998. xii, 259 p.
98-012708   327.41043   0312214561
World War, 1939-1945 -- Causes. Great Britain -- Foreign relations -- 1910-1936. Great Britain -- History, Naval -- 20th century. Germany -- Foreign relations -- Great Britain.

DA47.2.M26 1998
McDonough, Frank.
Neville Chamberlain, appeasement, and the British road to war/ Frank McDonough. Manchester; Manchester University Press; 1998. ix, 196 p.
97-015519   327.41043/09/043   0719048311
Chamberlain, Neville, -- 1869-1940 -- Views on Germany.   World War, 1939-1945 -- Causes. World politics -- 1900-1945. Great Britain -- Foreign relations -- Germany. Great Britain -- Politics and government -- 1936-1945. Great Britain -- Foreign relations -- 1936-1945.

DA47.2.N49 1997
Newton, Douglas J.
British policy and the Weimar Republic, 1918-1919/ Douglas Newton. Oxford [England]: Clarendon Press; 1997. x, 481 p.
96-052310   327.41043   0198203144
Great Britain -- Relations -- Germany. Great Britain -- Foreign relations -- 1910-1936. Germany -- Foreign relations -- 1918-1933.

DA47.2.S85 2000
Strobl, Gerwin.
The Germanic isle: Nazi perceptions of Britain/ Gerwin Strobl. New York: Cambridge University Press, 2000. p. cm.
99-086657   327.43041/09/043   0521782651
Public opinion -- Germany -- History -- 20th century. Great Britain -- Foreign public opinion, German. Great Britain -- Foreign relations -- 1936-1945. Great Britain -- Foreign relations -- Germany.

DA47.65.C37 2000
Carlton, David, 1938-
Churchill and the Soviet Union/ David Carlton. Manchester [England]; Manchester University Press: 2000. 234 p.
99-042908   327.43041/09/041   0719041066
Churchill, Winston, -- Sir, -- 1874-1965 -- Views on Soviet Union.   Soviet Union -- Foreign relations -- Great Britain. Great Britain -- Foreign relations -- Soviet Union. Great Britain -- Foreign relations -- 20th century.

DA47.65.F65 2000
Folly, Martin H., 1957-
Churchill, Whitehall, and the Soviet Union, 1940-45/ Martin H. Folly. New York: St. Martin's Press, 2000. p. cm.
99-055576   327.41047   0312231148
Churchill, Winston, -- Sir, -- 1874-1965 -- Views on Soviet Union.   Soviet Union -- Foreign relations -- Great Britain. Great Britain -- Foreign relations -- 1936-1945. Soviet Union -- Foreign relations -- 1917-1945.

DA47.65.K44 1990
Keeble, Curtis.
Britain and the Soviet Union, 1917-89/ Sir Curtis Keeble. New York: St. Martin's Press, 1990. xiv, 387 p.
89-036456   327.41047   0312036167
Great Britain -- Foreign relations -- Soviet Union. Soviet Union -- Foreign relations -- Great Britain. Great Britain -- Foreign relations -- 20th century.

DA47.65.N45 1995
Neilson, Keith.
Britain and the last tsar: British policy and Russia, 1894-1917/ Keith Neilson. Oxford: Clarendon Press; 1995. xv, 408 p.
95-020059   327.41047   0198204701
Great Britain -- Foreign relations -- Russia. Great Britain -- Foreign relations -- 1901-1936. Great Britain -- Foreign relations -- 1837-1901.

DA47.8.D86 2000
Dunthorn, David J.
Britain and the Spanish anti-Franco opposition, 1940-1950/ David J. Dunthorn. Houndmills, Basingstoke, Hampshire [England]; Palgrave, 2000. ix, 236 p.
00-040456   327.41046   0333917960
Franco, Francisco, -- 1892-1975 -- Adversaries. Public opinion -- Great Britain -- History -- 20th century. Government, Resistance to -- Spain -- History -- 20th century. Spain -- Foreign public opinion, British -- History -- 20th century. Great Britain -- Foreign relations -- 1936-1945. Great Britain -- Foreign relations -- 1945-1964.

DA47.9.C5.P4913 1992
Peyrefitte, Alain, 1925-
The immobile empire/ Alain Peyrefitte; translated from the French by Jon Rothschild. New York: Knopf: 1992. xxxiii, 630 p.
92-000329   327.41051   0394586549
Macartney, George Macartney, -- Earl, -- 1737-1806. British -- Travel -- China -- History -- 18th century. Great Britain -- Foreign relations -- China. Great Britain -- Foreign relations -- 1789-1820. China -- Foreign relations -- Great Britain.

DA47.9.C6.T36 1992
Tang, James Tuck-Hong, 1957-
Britain's encounter with revolutionary China, 1949-54/ James Tuck-Hong Tang. New York: St. Martin's Press, 1992. xiii, 264 p.
92-009434   327.41051   0312075928
Great Britain -- Foreign relations -- China. China -- Foreign relations -- Great Britain. Great Britain -- Foreign relations -- 1945-

DA47.9.I72.S56 1994
Silverfarb, Daniel, 1943-
The twilight of British ascendancy in the Middle East: a case study of Iraq, 1941-1950/ Daniel Silverfarb. New York: St. Martin's Press, 1994. xiii, 306 p.
93-049550   327.410567/09/044   0312120907
Great Britain -- Foreign relations -- Iraq. Iraq -- History -- Hashemite Kingdom, 1921-1958. Great Britain -- Foreign relations -- 1936-1945.

DA47.9.I77.H86 2001
Huneidi, Sahar.
A broken trust: Herbert Samuel, Zionism and the Palestinians 1920-1925/ Sahar Huneidi; foreword by Walid Khalidi. London: I.B. Tauris, 2001. xviii, 348 p.
01-270137   1860641725
Samuel, Herbert Louis Samuel, -- Viscount, -- 1870-1963. Zionism. Jews -- Palestine -- History -- 20th century. Palestine -- History -- 1917-1948. Great Britain -- Foreign relations -- Palestine. Palestine -- Foreign relations -- Great Britain.

DA47.9.I77.K58
Knox, D. Edward, 1940-
The making of a new Eastern Question: British Palestine policy and the origins of Israel, 1917-1925/ by D. Edward Knox. Washington, D.C.: Catholic University of America Press, c1981. vi, 219 p.
80-021879   327.4105694   0813205557
Great Britain -- Foreign relations -- Palestine. Palestine -- Foreign relations -- Great Britain. Great Britain -- Foreign relations -- 1910-1936.

DA47.9.I8.G38 1996
Gat, Moshe.
Britain and Italy, 1943-1949: the decline of British influence/ Moshe Gat. Brighton: Sussex Academic Press; 1996. ix, 230 p.
96-127596   327.41045   1898723222
Great Britain -- Foreign relations -- Italy. Italy -- Foreign relations -- Great Britain. Great Britain -- History -- George VI, 1936-1952.

DA47.9.J6.P86 1994
Pundik, Ron.
The struggle for sovereignty: relations between Great Britain and Jordan, 1946-1951/ Ron Pundik. Oxford, UK; B. Blackwell, 1994. xi, 363 p.
93-036480   327.4105695   0631192956
Great Britain -- Foreign relations -- Jordan. Great Britain -- Foreign relations -- 1945- Jordan -- Foreign relations -- Great Britain.

DA47.9.P8.S76 1994
Stone, Glyn.
The oldest ally: Britain and the Portuguese connection, 1936-1941/ Glyn Stone. [London]: Royal Historical Society; 1994. ix, 228 p.
94-007840   327.469073/09/043   0861932277
Great Britain -- Foreign relations -- Portugal. Great Britain -- Foreign relations -- 1936-1945. Portugal -- Foreign relations -- Great Britain.

DA50.B23 1990
Babington, Anthony.
Military intervention in Britain: from the Gordon riots to the Gibralter incident/ Anthony Babington. London; Routledge, 1991 x, 242 p.
89-010924   322/.5/0941   0415071488
Civil-military relations -- Great Britain -- History. Law enforcement -- Great Britain -- History. Riots -- Great Britain -- History. Great Britain -- History, Military.

DA59.A24 1988
Abels, Richard Philip, 1951-
Lordship and military obligation in Anglo-Saxon England/ Richard P. Abels. Berkeley: University of California Press, c1988. xii, 313 p.
87-010787   942.01   0520057945
Land tenure -- England -- History -- To 1500. Feudalism -- England -- History -- To 1500. Anglo-Saxons. Great Britain -- History -- Anglo-Saxon period, 449-1066. Great Britain -- History, Military -- 449-1066.

DA59.E94 1997
Evans, Stephen S. 1954-
The lords of battle: image and reality of the comitatus in Dark-Age Britain/ Stephen S. Evans. Woodbridge, Suffolk, UK; Boydell Press, 1997. viii, 169 p.
96-035358   355.02/0942/09021   0851156789
Military art and science -- Great Britain -- History -- Medieval, 500-1500. Epic poetry, English (Old) -- History and criticism. Welsh literature -- To 1550 -- History and criticism. Wales -- History -- To 1063. Great Britain -- Antiquities, Celtic. Great Britain -- History, Military -- 449-1066.

DA60.M67 1994
Morillo, Stephen.
Warfare under the Anglo-Norman kings, 1066-1135/ Stephen Morillo. Woodbridge, Suffolk, UK; Boydell Press, 1994. xii, 207 p.
94-018931   942.02   0851155553
Military art and science -- England -- History -- Medieval, 500-1500. Normans -- England -- Kings and rulers. Knights and knighthood -- England. Great Britain -- History -- Norman period, 1066-1154. Great Britain -- History, Military -- 1066-1485.

DA60.S77 1996
Strickland, Matthew, 1962-
War and chivalry: the conduct and perception of war in England and Normandy, 1066-1217/ Matthew Strickland. New York: Cambridge University Press, 1996. xxii, 387 p.
95-044002   942.02   052144392X
Knights and knighthood -- France -- Normandy -- History -- To 1500. Knights and knighthood -- England -- History -- To 1500. Chivalry -- England -- History -- To 1500. Great Britain -- History -- Norman period, 1066-1154. Great Britain -- History, Military -- 1066-1485. Great Britain -- History -- Angevin period, 1154-1216.

DA60.W37 2000
War and society in medieval and early modern Britain/ edited by Diana Dunn. Liverpool: Liverpool University Press, 2000. vi, 213 p.
2001-339967   0853238758
Military art and science -- Great Britain -- History. War and society -- Great Britain -- History. Great Britain -- History, Military -- 1485-1603. Great Britain -- History, Military -- 1603-1714. Great Britain -- History, Military -- 1066-1485.

DA65.H37 1992
Harvey, A. D.
Collision of empires: Britain in three world wars, 1793-1945/ A.D. Harvey. London; Hambledon Press, 1992. xvi, 784 p.
92-020950   941   1852850787
Anglo-French War, 1793-1802. Napoleonic Wars, 1800-1815. World War, 1914-1918. Great Britain -- History, Military.

DA66.L46 2001
Lenman, Bruce.
England's colonial wars, 1550-1688: conflicts, empire, and national identity/ Bruce P. Lenman. Harlow, England; Longman, 2001. x, 310 p.
01-272728   0582062969
Great Britain -- History, Military -- 1485-1603. Great Britain -- History, Military -- 1603-1714. Great Britain -- Colonies -- History -- 16th century.

DA67.B57 1999
Black, Jeremy.
Britain as a military power, 1688-1815/ Jeremy Black. London: UCL Press, 1999. viii, 332 p.
00-503584   185728772X
Great Britain -- History, Military -- 18th century. Great Britain -- History, Military -- 19th century. Great Britain -- History, Military -- 1603-1714.

DA67.L46 2001
Lenman, Bruce.
Britain's colonial wars, 1688-1783/ Bruce P. Lenman. Harlow, England; Longman, 2001. x, 284 p.
00-046177   941.07   058242402X
Great Britain -- History, Military -- 18th century. United States -- History -- Revolution, 1775-1783 -- British forces. Great Britain -- Colonies -- History -- 18th century.

DA67.1.G76.N45 1996
Nelson, Paul David, 1941-
Sir Charles Grey, First Earl Grey: royal soldier, family patriarch/ Paul David Nelson. Madison [N.J.]: Fairleigh Dickinson University Press, c1996. 253 p.
95-026341   941.07/3/092   083863673X
Grey, Charles Grey, -- Earl of, -- 1729-1807. Generals -- Great Britain -- Biography. United States -- History -- Revolution, 1775-1783 -- British forces. Great Britain -- History, Military -- 18th century -- Biography. West Indies -- History, Military.

DA68.C66 1997
Cookson, J. E.
The British armed nation, 1793-1815/ J.E. Cookson. Oxford: Clarendon Press; 1997. vi, 286 p.
96-044824   941.07/3   0198206585
Great Britain -- History, Military -- 19th century. Great Britain -- History, Military -- 18th century.

DA68.M94 1996
Myerly, Scott Hughes.
British military spectacle: from the Napoleonic Wars through the Crimea/ Scott Hughes Myerly. Cambridge, Mass.: Harvard University Press, 1996. x, 293 p.
96-017260   355.1/7/094109034   0674082494
Rites and ceremonies -- Great Britain -- History -- 19th century. Napoleonic Wars, 1800-1815. Crimean War, 1853-1856. Great Britain -- History, Military -- 19th century.

DA68.12.W4.L62
Longford, Elizabeth (Harman) Pakenham, 1906-
Wellington [by] Elizabeth Longford. New York, Harper & Row [1970-73, c19 2 v.
75-095973   942.07/092/4   0060126698
Wellington, Arthur Wellesley, -- Duke of, -- 1769-1852. Prime ministers -- Great Britain -- Biography. Generals -- Great Britain -- Biography. Great Britain -- History, Military -- 19th century.

DA68.32.B2.J43 1990
Jeal, Tim.
The boy-man: the life of Lord Baden-Powell/ Tim Jeal. New York: Morrow, c1990. xxi, 670 p.
89-013452   355/.0092   0688048994
Baden-Powell of Gilwell, Robert Stephenson Smyth Baden-Powell, -- Baron, -- 1857-1941. Generals -- Great Britain -- Biography. Boy Scouts -- Great Britain -- Biography.

DA68.32.G6.C46 1979
Chenevix Trench, Charles, 1914-
The road to Khartoum: a life of General Charles Gordon/ Charles Chenevix Trench. New York: Norton, 1979, c1978. 320 p.
78-021043   962.4/03/0924   0393012379
Gordon, Charles George, -- 1833-1885. Generals -- Great Britain -- Biography. Colonial administrators -- Africa -- Biography. Egypt -- History -- British occupation, 1882-1936. Sudan -- History -- 1862-1899.

DA68.32.K6.M3 1968
Magnus, Philip Montefiore, 1906-
Kitchener: portrait of an imperialist [by] Philip Magnus. Harmondsworth, Penguin, 1968. 485 p.
72-366576   942.08/0924
Kitchener, Horatio Herbert Kitchener, -- Earl, -- 1850-1916 -- Views on imperialism. Imperialism -- Government policy -- Great Britain. Statesmen -- Great Britain -- Biography. Marshals -- Great Britain -- Biography. Great Britain -- History, Military -- 19th century.

DA69.M33 1995
Mackenzie, S. P.
The home guard: a military and political history/ S.P. Mackenzie. Oxford; Oxford University Press, 1995. xiv, 262 p.
94-043350   941.084   0198205775
World War, 1939-1945 -- War work -- Great Britain. Great Britain -- History, Military -- 20th century. Great Britain -- Politics and government -- 20th century. Great Britain -- Militia -- History.

DA69.3.A55.F7
Fraser, David, 1920-
Alanbrooke/ David Fraser; with a prologue and epilogue by Arthur Bryant. New York: Atheneum, 1982. 604 p.
81-069156   941.085/092/4   068911267X
Alanbrooke, Alan Francis Brooke, -- Viscount, -- 1883- Generals -- Great Britain -- Biography.

DA69.3.H3
De Groot, Gerard J., 1955-
Douglas Haig, 1861-1928/ by Gerard J. de Groot. London: Unwin Hyman, 1988. xi, 441 p.
88-006045   355.3/32/0924   0044401922
Haig, Douglas, -- Sir, -- 1861-1928. Generals -- Great Britain -- Biography.

DA69.3.I8.A3
Ismay, Hastings Lionel Ismay, 1887-1965.
Memoirs. Viking, 1960. 1 v.
60-014086   940.53
Churchill, Winston, -- Sir, -- 1874-1965. World War, 1939-1945.

DA69.3.M56.H355 1983
Hamilton, Nigel.
Master of the battlefield: Monty's war years, 1942-1944/ Nigel Hamilton. New York: McGraw-Hill, c1983. xxxi, 863 p.
83-011252   941.082/092/4   0070258066
Montgomery of Alamein, Bernard Law Montgomery, -- Viscount, -- 1887-1976. Generals -- Great Britain -- Biography.

DA70.R56 1998
Rodger, N. A. M., 1949-
The safeguard of the sea: a naval history of Britain, 660-1649/ N.A.M. Rodger. New York: W.W. Norton, 1998- v. [1]
97-052403   359/.00941   039304579X
Great Britain -- History, Naval.

DA85.H37 1995
Harding, Richard, 1953-
The evolution of the sailing navy, 1509-1815/ Richard Harding. New York: St. Martin's Press, 1995. ix, 181 p.
94-031972   359/.00941   0312124074
Sailing ships -- Great Britain -- History -- 17th century. Sailing ships -- Great Britain -- History -- 18th century. Sailing ships -- Great Britain -- History -- 16th century. Great Britain -- History, Naval.

DA86.A74 1991
Andrews, Kenneth R.
Ships, money, and politics: seafaring and naval enterprise in the reign of Charles I/ Kenneth R. Andrews. Cambridge; Cambridge University Press, 1991. ix, 240 p.
90-040407   359/.00941   052140116X
Merchant marine -- Great Britain -- History -- 17th century. Seafaring life -- Great Britain -- History -- 17th century. Shipping -- Great Britain -- History -- 17th century. Great Britain -- Politics and government -- 1625-1649. Great Britain -- History, Naval -- Stuarts, 1603-1714. Great Britain -- History -- Charles I, 1625-1649.

DA86.L6 2000
Loades, D. M.
England's maritime empire: seapower, commerce, and policy, 1490-1690/ David Loades. Harlow, England; Longman, 2000. xi, 277 p.
00-028193   359/.00941/09031   0582356288
Great Britain -- History, Naval -- Tudors, 1485-1603. Great Britain -- History, Naval -- Stuarts, 1603-1714. England -- Commerce -- History -- 16th century.

DA86.22.D7.K45 1998
Kelsey, Harry, 1929-
Sir Francis Drake: the Queen's pirate/ Harry Kelsey. New Haven: Yale University Press, c1998. xviii, 566 p.
97-040312   942.05/5/092   0300071825
Drake, Francis, -- Sir, -- 1540?-1596. Admirals -- Great Britain -- Biography. Pirates -- Great Britain -- Biography. Explorers -- America -- Biography. Great Britain -- History, Naval -- Tudors, 1485-1603.

DA86.22.R2.S86
Strathmann, Ernest Albert, 1906-
Sir Walter Ralegh, a study in Elizabethan skepticism. New York, Columbia University Press, 1951. ix, 292 p.
51-010319   923.942   0374976406
Raleigh, Walter, -- Sir, -- 1552?-1618. Skepticism.

DA87.1.B6.K46 1989
Kennedy, Gavin.
Captain Bligh: the man and his mutinies/ Gavin Kennedy. London: Duckworth, 1989. xiii, 321 p.
89-125112   0715622315
Bligh, William, -- 1754-1817. Admirals -- Great Britain -- Biography. Governors -- Australia -- New South Wales -- Biography. Mutiny -- Great Britain -- History -- 18th century.

DA87.1.N4.H53 1994
Hibbert, Christopher, 1924-
Nelson: a personal history/ Christopher Hibbert. Reading, Mass.: Addison-Wesley, c1994. xvii, 472 p.
94-039545   940.2/7/092   0201624575
Nelson, Horatio Nelson, -- Viscount, -- 1758-1805. Admirals -- Great Britain -- Biography. Great Britain -- History, Naval -- 18th century. Great Britain -- History, Naval -- 19th century.

DA87.1.N4 P57 1988
Pocock, Tom.
Horatio Nelson/ Tom Pocock. New York: Knopf, 1988. xx, 367 p.
87-046188   940.2/7/0924. 219   0394570561
Nelson, Horatio Nelson, Viscount, 1758-1805. Admirals--Great Britain--Biography.

DA88.B37
Bartlett, C. J. 1931-
Great Britain and sea power: 1815-1853/ by C.J. Bartlett. Oxford: Clarendon Press, 1963. xviii, 364 p.
63-001585   942.074
Sea-power. Great Britain -- History, Naval -- 19th century. Great Britain -- Foreign relations -- 19th century.

DA88.B44 1997
Beeler, John F. 1956-
British naval policy in the Gladstone-Disraeli era, 1866-1880/ John F. Beeler. Stanford, Calif.: Stanford University Press, 1997. xviii, 354 p.
97-033038 359/.00941/09034 0804729816
Gladstone, W. E. -- (William Ewart), -- 1809-1898 -- Views on military policy. Disraeli, Benjamin, -- Earl of Beaconsfield, -- 1804-1881 -- Views on military policy. Great Britain -- History, Naval -- 19th century. Great Britain -- History -- Victoria, 1837-1901. Great Britain -- Military policy.

DA88.H36 1993
Hamilton, C. I.
Anglo-French naval rivalry, 1840-1870/ C.I. Hamilton. Oxford: Clarendon Press; 1993. xiii, 359 p.
93-021761 359/.00941/09034 019820261X
Great Britain -- History, Naval -- 19th century. Great Britain -- Foreign relations -- 1837-1901. Great Britain -- Foreign relations -- France.

DA88.1.C58.M67 1997
Morriss, Roger.
Cockburn and the British Navy in transition: Admiral Sir George Cockburn, 1772-1853/ Roger Morriss. Columbia: University of South Carolina Press, c1997. xiii, 338 p.
97-033915 941.081/092 157003253X
Cockburn, George, -- Sir, -- 1772-1853. Admirals -- Great Britain -- Biography. Great Britain -- History, Naval -- 19th century.

DA88.5 1805.S36 1990
Schom, Alan.
Trafalgar: countdown to battle, 1803-1805/ Alan Schom. New York: Atheneum: 1990. ix, 421 p.
90-000776 940.2/7 0689120559
Trafalgar, Battle of, 1805. Napoleonic Wars, 1800-1815.

DA89.1.F5.M3
Mackay, Ruddock F.
Fisher of Kilverstone, by Ruddock F. Mackay. Oxford, Clarendon Press, 1973. xvi, 539 p.
74-158694 359.3/2/20924 0198224095
Fisher, John Arbuthnot Fisher, -- Baron, -- 1841-1920.

DA89.1.M59.H68
Hough, Richard Alexander, 1922-
Mountbatten/ Richard Hough. New York: Random House, c1981. xv, 302 p.
80-006023 941.082/092/4 039451162X
Mountbatten of Burma, Louis Mountbatten, -- Earl, -- 1900-1979. Admirals -- Great Britain -- Biography. Viceroys -- India -- Biography.

DA89.1.M59 Z54
Ziegler, Philip.
Mountbatten: the official biography/ Philip Ziegler; with a new foreword. London: Phoenix, 2001. xiv, 786 p.
2002-391961 941.082092.221 1842122967
Mountbatten of Burma, Louis Mountbatten, Earl, 1900-1979. British--India--History--20th century. Admirals--Great Britain--Biography. Viceroys--India--Biography.

DA89.5.O47 1990
Omissi, David E., 1960-
Air power and colonial control: the Royal Air Force, 1919-1939/ David E. Omissi. Manchester [England]; Manchester University Press; c1990. xvi, 260 p.
90-040817 358.4/00941/09171241 0719029600
Aeronautics in police work -- Great Britain -- Colonies -- History -- 20th century. Great Britain -- Colonies -- Administration -- History -- 20th century. Great Britain -- History, Military -- 20th century.

DA90.C93 1990
Crossley, David W.
Post-medieval archaeology in Britain/ David Crossley. London; Leicester University Press, 1990. ix, 328 p.
89-029601 942.05 0718512855
Historic sites -- Great Britain. Excavations (Archaeology) -- Great Britain. Great Britain -- Antiquities. Great Britain -- History -- Tudors, 1485-1603. Great Britain -- History -- Stuarts, 1603-1714.

DA90.M28 1988
McCarthy, Michael R.
Medieval pottery in Britain, AD 900-1600/ Michael R. McCarthy and Catherine M. Brooks. [Leicester]: Leicester University Press, 1988. xx, 521 p.
88-177932 738.3/0941/0902 0718512545
Pottery, Medieval -- Great Britain. Great Britain -- Antiquities.

DA90.O86 1992
Ottaway, Patrick.
Archaeology in British towns: from the Emperor Claudius to the Black Death/ Patrick Ottaway. London; Routledge, 1992. xvi, 249 p.
91-041071 936.1 0415000688
Excavations (Archaeology) -- Great Britain. Cities and towns -- Great Britain -- History. Urban archaeology -- Great Britain. Great Britain -- Antiquities.

DA93.A8.P68
Powell, Anthony, 1905-
John Aubrey and his friends. New York, C. Scribner's Sons, 1948. 335 p.
49-008658 928.2
Aubrey, John, -- 1626-1697.

DA110.B36
Barker, Ernest, 1874-1960,
The character of England. Oxford, Clarendon Press, 1947. xii, 595 p.
48-000017 914.2
National characteristics, English. Great Britain. Great Britain -- Civilization.

DA110.G86 2000
Gunn, Simon.
The public culture of the Victorian middle class: ritual and authority and the English industrial city, 1840-1914/ Simon Gunn. Manchester; Manchester University Press; 2000. x, 207 p.
0719057159
Popular culture -- England -- History -- 19th century. Popular culture -- England -- History -- 20th century. Middle class -- England -- History -- 19th century. England -- Civilization -- 19th century. England -- Civilization -- 20th century. England -- Social life and customs -- 19th century.

DA110.P34 1999
Passerini, Luisa.
Europe in love, love in Europe: imagination and politics between the wars/ Luisa Passerini. Washington Square, New York: New York University Press, 1999. viii, 358 p.
98-055135 941 0814766986
Love -- Great Britain -- History -- 20th century. English literature -- European influences. Love -- Europe -- History -- 20th century. Great Britain -- Relations -- Europe. Europe -- Relations -- Great Britain. Great Britain -- Intellectual life -- 20th century.

DA110.P58
Plumb, J. H. 1911-
Studies in social history; a tribute to G. M. Trevelyan. London, Longmans, Green [1955] xv, 287 p.
56-001916 914.004 83691063X
Great Britain -- Social life and customs.

DA118.E48 1992
Elton, G. R.
The English/ Geoffrey Elton. Oxford, UK; Blackwell, 1992. xiii, 248 p.
92-019106 942 0631176810
National characteristics, English. England -- Civilization.

DA118.L33 2000
Langford, Paul.
Englishness identified: manners and character, 1650-1850/ Paul Langford; illustrated by Martin Rowson. Oxford; Oxford University Press, 2000. x, 389 p.
99-041373 306/.0942 019820681X
National characteristics, English -- History. National characteristics, English, in literature. England -- Social life and customs -- 17th century. England -- Social life and customs -- 19th century. England -- Social life and customs -- 18th century.

DA122.J8.J6 1962
Jolliffe, John Edward Austin, 1891-
Pre-feudal England: the Jutes. [London] F. Cass [1962] viii, 122 p.
63-000549 942.01
Land tenure -- Great Britain -- History. Jutes. Manors -- Great Britain. Kent (England) -- History. Great Britain -- Anglo-Saxon period, 449-1066.

DA125.A1.A77 2001
Alibhai-Brown, Yasmin.
Imagining the new Britain/ Yasmin Alibhai-Brown. New York: Routledge, 2001. p. cm.
01-019467 305.8/00941 0415931126
Multiculturalism -- Great Britain. Ethnic groups -- Great Britain. Great Britain -- Ethnic relations. Great Britain -- Civilization.

DA125.A1.G6 1991
Goulbourne, Harry.
Ethnicity and nationalism in post-imperial Britain/ Harry Goulbourne. Cambridge; Cambridge University Press, 1991. xiv, 271 p.
90-020422 305.8/00941 0521400848
Nationalism -- Great Britain -- History -- 20th century. Great Britain -- Ethnic relations -- History -- 20th century. Great Britain -- Politics and government -- 1979-1997.

DA125.A1.G69 1998
Green, Jeffrey, 1944-
Black Edwardians: Black people in Britain, 1901-1914/ Jeffrey Green. London; Frank Cass, 1998. xxi, 279 p.
98-016242   941/.00496   071464871X
Blacks -- Great Britain -- History -- 20th century. Great Britain -- History -- Edward VII, 1901-1910. Great Britain -- History -- George V, 1910-1936.

DA125.A1.K44 1983
Kerridge, Roy.
Real wicked, guy: a view of Black Britain/ Roy Kerridge. Oxford, England: B. Blackwell, 1983. 210 p.
83-184760   305.8/00941   0631132392
Minorities -- Great Britain. Immigrants -- Great Britain. Great Britain -- Race relations.

DA125.A1.R335 1993
Racial violence in Britain 1840-1950/ edited by Panikos Panayi. Leicester: Leicester University Press; 1993. x, 174 p.
92-036259   305.8/00941   0718513975
Racism -- Great Britain -- History -- 19th century. Racism -- Great Britain -- History -- 20th century. Violence -- Great Britain -- History -- 19th century. Great Britain -- Ethnic relations. Great Britain -- Race relations.

DA125.A1.S597 1994
Smith, Anna Marie.
New Right discourse on race and sexuality: Britain, 1968-1990/ Anna Marie Smith. Cambridge [England]; Cambridge University Press, 1994. xii, 285 p.
93-042801   305.8/00941/09045   052145297X
Sexual orientation -- Public opinion -- Great Britain. Homosexuality -- Public opinion -- Great Britain. Public opinion -- Great Britain -- History -- 20th century. Great Britain -- Race relations -- Public opinion. Great Britain -- Politics and government -- 1979-1997.

DA125.A1.S62 1989
Solomos, John.
Race and racism in contemporary Britain/ John Solomos. Houndmills, Basingstoke, Hampshire: Macmillan Education, 1989. xiv, 209 p.
90-122599   305.8/00941   0333421426
Racism -- Great Britain -- History -- 20th century. Blacks -- Great Britain -- Politics and government. Blacks -- Great Britain -- Social conditions. Great Britain -- Race relations.

DA125.A1.W448 2000
Wheeler, Roxann.
The complexion of race: categories of difference in eighteenth-century British culture/ Roxann Wheeler. Philadelphia: University of Pennsylvania Press, c2000. 371 p.
00-025539   305.8/00941/09033   081223541X
Race awareness -- Great Britain -- History -- 18th century. English fiction -- 18th century -- History and criticism. Difference (Psychology) -- History -- 18th century. Great Britain -- Social conditions -- 18th century. Great Britain -- Civilization -- 18th century. Great Britain -- Race relations -- History -- 18th century.

DA125.G4.P36 1990
Panayi, Panikos.
The enemy in our midst: Germans in Britain during the First World War/ Panikos Panayi. New York: Berg; 1991. xii, 312 p.
89-018464   941/.00431   0854963081
Germans -- Great Britain -- History -- 20th century. World War, 1914-1918 -- Great Britain. Great Britain -- Ethnic relations.

DA125.H84.C66 1991
Cottret, Bernard.
The Huguenots in England: immigration and settlement, c. 1550-1700/ Bernard Cottret; translated by Peregrine and Adriana Stevenson with an afterword by Emmanuel Le Roy Ladurie. Cambridge [England]; Cambridge University Press; 1991. xii, 317 p.
90-043066   941/.008/8245   0521333881
Huguenots -- England -- History. Immigrants -- England -- History -- 17th century. Immigrants -- England -- History -- 16th century.

DA125.I7.I72 2000
The Irish diaspora/ edited by Andy Bielenberg. Harlow, England; Longman, 2000. p. cm.
99-053717   941/.0049162   0582369983
Irish -- Great Britain -- History. Irish -- Commonwealth countries -- History. Irish Americans -- History. Ireland -- Emigration and immigration.

DA125.I7.N43 1998
Neal, Frank, 1932-
Black 47: Britain and the famine Irish/ Frank Neal. Houndmills, Basingstoke, Hampshire: MacMillan; 1998. xv, 292 p.
97-016913   941/.0049162   0312176627
Irish -- Great Britain -- History -- 19th century. Famines -- Ireland -- History -- 19th century. Ireland -- Emigration and immigration -- History -- 19th century. Great Britain -- History -- Victoria, 1837-1901. Great Britain -- Emigration and immigration -- History -- 19th century.

DA125.N4.A35 1998
Adi, Hakim.
West Africans in Britain, 1900-1960: nationalism, Pan-Africanism, and communism/ Hakim Adi. London: Lawrence & Wishart, [1998] 224 p.
98-185891   941/.00496066   0853158487
West Africans -- Great Britain -- Politics and government. Students, Black -- Great Britain -- History -- 20th century. Students, Black -- Great Britain -- Political activity. Great Britain -- Race relations.

DA125.N4.M94 1996
Myers, Norma.
Reconstructing the Black past: Blacks in Britain, c. 1780-1830/ Norma Myers. London; F. Cass, c1996. ix, 157 p.
96-006900   941/.00496   0714645753
Blacks -- Great Britain -- History -- 19th century. Blacks -- Great Britain -- History -- 18th century. Great Britain -- Race relations -- History.

DA125.N4.P37 1998
Parsons, Neil.
King Khama, Emperor Joe, and the great white queen: Victorian Britain through African eyes/ Neil Parsons. Chicago, IL: University of Chicago Press, 1998. xviii, 322 p.
97-037111   327.4106883   0226647447
Chamberlain, Joseph, -- 1836-1914 -- Views on Africa. Khama, -- African chief, -- ca. 1830-1923. Africans -- Travel -- Great Britain -- History -- 19th century. Public opinion -- Great Britain -- History -- 19th century. Great Britain -- History -- Victoria, 1837-1901. Botswana -- Foreign relations -- Great Britain. Great Britain -- Foreign relations -- Botswana.

DA125.N4.S65 1988
Solomos, John.
Black youth, racism and the state: the politics of ideology and policy/ John Solomos. Cambridge [Cambridgeshire]; Cambridge University Press, 1988. 284 p.
88-003524   305.8/96041   0521360196
Blacks -- Great Britain -- Politics and government. Youth, Black -- Great Britain -- Social conditions. Youth, Black -- Great Britain -- Economic conditions. Great Britain -- Race relations.

DA125.N4.S65 1995
Solomos, John.
Race, politics, and social change/ John Solomos and Les Back. London; Routledge, 1995. xiii, 232 p.
94-035566   320.941/089/96   0415085772
Blacks -- Great Britain -- Politics and government. Blacks -- Great Britain -- Social conditions. Great Britain -- Race relations.

DA125.Q34.V36 1991
Vann, Richard T.
Friends in life and death: the British and Irish Quakers in the demographic transition, 1650-1900/ Richard T. Vann and David Eversley. Cambridge; Cambridge University Press, 1992. xix, 281 p.
90-021802   941/.0088286   0521392012
Quakers -- Great Britain -- History. Demographic transition -- Great Britain. Demographic transition -- Ireland.

DA125.S57.B87 1998
Burton, Antoinette M., 1961-
At the heart of the Empire: Indians and the colonial encounter in late-Victorian Britain/ Antoinette Burton. Berkeley: University of California Press, c1998. xv, 278 p.
96-029617   305.891/411041/09034   0520209583
Malabari, Behramji M. -- (Behramji Merwanji), -- 1853-1912 -- Journeys -- Great Britain. Ramabai Sarasvati, -- Pandita, -- 1858-1922 -- Journeys -- Great Britain. Sorabji, Cornelia -- Journeys -- Great Britain. East Indians -- Great Britain -- History -- 19th century. Imperialism -- History -- 19th century. Great Britain -- Relations -- India. Great Britain -- History -- Victoria, 1837-1901. Great Britain -- Social life and customs -- 19th century. India -- Relations -- Great Britain.

DA129-260 England — History
— By period
— Early to medieval to 1485

DA129.M43 1998
Medieval England: an encyclopedia/ editors: Paul E. Szarmach, M. Teresa Tavormina, Joel T. Rosenthal. New York: Garland Pub., 1998. lxiv, 882 p.
97-035523   942   0824057864
Great Britain -- History -- Medieval period, 1066-1485 -- Encyclopedias. Great Britain -- History -- Anglo-Saxon period, 449-1066 -- Encyclopedias. England -- Civilization -- 1066-1485 -- Encyclopedias.

DA130.P34 1994
Patterson, Annabel M.
Reading Holinshed's Chronicles/ Annabel Patterson. Chicago: University of Chicago Press, 1994. xviii, 339 p.
93-047629   941   0226649113
Holinshed, Raphael, -- d. 1580? -- Chronicles of England, Scotlande, and Irelande. Historiography -- England -- History -- 16th century. Great Britain -- History -- To 1485 -- Historiography. Great Britain -- History -- Tudors, 1485-1603 -- Historiography.

DA130.P65 1958
Poole, Austin Lane, 1889-1963,
Medieval England. Oxford, Clarendon Press, 1958. 2 v.
58-004429   942
Great Britain -- History -- Anglo-Saxon period, 449-1066. Great Britain -- History -- Medieval period, 1066-1485. Great Britain -- Civilization.

DA130.S44 2000
Schama, Simon.
A history of Britain: at the edge of the world?: 3000 BC-AD 1603/ Simon Schama. New York: Hyperion, c2000. 416 p.
00-061442   941   0786866756
Great Britain -- History -- To 1485. Great Britain -- History -- Tudors, 1485-1603.

DA130.T38 1999
Taufer, Alison.
Holinshed's Chronicles/ Alison Taufer. New York: Twayne Publishers, c1999. xviii, 164 p.
99-038404   941   0805745815
Holinshed, Raphael, -- d. 1580? -- Chronicles of England, Scotlande, and Irelande. Historiography -- England -- History -- 16th century. Great Britain -- History -- To 1485 -- Historiography. Great Britain -- History -- Tudors, 1485-1603 -- Historiography.

DA135.B59
Hunter Blair, Peter, 1912-1982.
Roman Britain and early England, 55 B.C.-A.D. 871./ Peter Hunter Blair. Edinburgh; T. Nelson, 1963. xii, 292 p.
63-024835   942.01   0393003612
Great Britain -- History -- To 1066.

DA135.M15 1982
MacDougall, Hugh A.
Racial myth in English history: Trojans, Teutons, and Anglo-Saxons/ Hugh A. MacDougall. Montreal: Harvest House; 1982. ix, 146 p.
81-069941   942.01   087451228X
Geoffrey, -- of Monmouth, Bishop of St. Asaph, -- 1100?-1154. Anglo-Saxon race. English -- Origin. Middle Ages -- Historiography. Great Britain -- History -- To 1066 -- Historiography.

DA140.G49.C87 1994
Curley, Michael J., 1942-
Geoffrey of Monmouth/ Michael J. Curley. New York: Twayne Publishers; c1994. xiv, 181 p.
94-014513   936.2/007202   0805770550
Geoffrey, -- of Monmouth, Bishop of St. Asaph, -- 1100?-1154. -- Historia regum Britanniae. Arthur, -- King. Arthurian romances -- Sources. Britons -- Kings and rulers. Britons -- Historiography. Great Britain -- History -- To 1066 -- Historiography.

DA140.L33 1979b
Laing, Lloyd Robert.
Celtic Britain/ Lloyd Laing. New York: Scribner, c1979. xi, 190 p.
78-066127   936.1   0684162253
Celts -- Great Britain. Britons. Great Britain -- Antiquities, Celtic. Great Britain -- History -- To 1066.

DA140.S72 1998
Snyder, Christopher A.
An age of tyrants: Britain and the Britons, A.D. 400-600/ Christopher A. Snyder. University Park: Pennsylvania State University Press, c1998. xix, 403 p.
97-018784   936.1   0271017422
Excavations (Archaeology) -- Great Britain. Great Britain -- History -- To 1066 -- Sources. Britons -- History. Great Britain -- Civilization -- To 1066. Great Britain -- Antiquities, Celtic.

DA141.C74 2000
Creighton, John, 1964-
Coins and power in late Iron Age Britain/ John Creighton. Cambridge UK; Cambridge University Press, 2000. xiv, 249 p.
00-710524   936.1/01   0521772079
Cunobelinus, -- King of the Britons, -- d. 43? Power (Social sciences) -- Great Britain -- History -- To 500. Coinage -- Great Britain -- History -- To 500. Coins, Celtic -- Great Britain. Great Britain -- History -- To 55 B.C.

DA142.H3
Hawkins, Gerald S.
Stonehenge decoded [by] Gerald S. Hawkins in collaboration with John B. White. Garden City, N.Y., Doubleday, 1965. viii, 202 p.
65-019933   913.36
Megalithic monuments -- England -- Wiltshire. Man, Prehistoric -- England -- Wiltshire. Astronomy, Ancient. Wiltshire (England) -- Antiquities. Stonehenge (England)

DA142.N67 1997
North, John David.
Stonehenge: a new interpretation of prehistoric man and the cosmos/ John North. New York: Free Press, 1997. p. cm.
97-031439   936.2/319   0684845121
Megalithic monuments -- England -- Wiltshire. Man, Prehistoric -- England -- Wiltshire. Astronomy, Ancient. Wiltshire (England) -- Antiquities. Stonehenge (England)

DA145.B94 1991
Burnham, Barry C.
The small towns of Roman Britain/ Barry C. Burnham and John Wacher. Berkeley: University of California Press, c1990. xii, 388 p.
90-041007   936.2   0520073037
Cities and towns, Ancient -- Great Britain. Excavations (Archaeology) -- Great Britain. Romans -- Great Britain -- History. Great Britain -- Antiquities, Roman. Great Britain -- History -- Roman period, 55 B.C.-449 A.D.

DA145.C37 1995
Casey, P. J.
Carausius and Allectus: the British usurpers/ P.J. Casey; with translations of the texts by R.S.O. Tomlin. New Haven: Yale University Press, 1995, c1994. 213 p.
94-060726   936.1   0300060629
Carausius, -- d. 293. Allectus, -- d. 296. Numismatics, Roman -- Great Britain. Romans -- Great Britain -- History. Great Britain -- Antiquities, Roman. Great Britain -- History -- Roman period, 55 B.C.-449 A.D.

DA145.C57 1969
Collingwood, R. G. 1889-1943.
The archaeology of Roman Britain [by] R. G. Collingwood and Ian Richmond; with a chapter by B. R. Hartley on Samian ware. London, Methuen, 1969. xxv, 350 p.
79-407851   913.3/6   041627580X
Romans -- Great Britain. Great Britain -- Antiquities, Roman.

DA145.D36 1997
Dark, K. R.
The landscape of Roman Britain/ Ken Dark and Petra Dark. Stroud, Gloucestershire: Sutton, 1997. 186 p.
97-148332   936.1/04   0750909641
Land settlement pattersn -- Great Britain. Landscape archaeology -- Great Britain. Romans - - Great Britain. Great Britain -- Antiquities, Roman. Great Britain -- History -- Roman period, 55 B.C.-449 A.D. -- Historiography.

DA145.F8 1987
Frere, Sheppard Sunderland.
Britannia: a history of Roman Britain/ Sheppard Frere. London; Routledge & Kegan Paul, 1987. xvi, 423 p.
87-004951   936.2/04   0710212151
Romans -- Great Britain. Great Britain -- History -- Roman period, 55 B.C.-449 A.D. Great Britain -- Antiquities, Roman.

DA145.J665 1996
Jones, Michael E. 1952-
The end of Roman Britain/ Michael E. Jones. Ithaca: Cornell Univerity Press, 1996. ix, 323 p.
95-052873   936.1/04   0801427894
Romans -- Great Britain -- History. Anglo-Saxons. Great Britain -- History -- Invasions. Great Britain -- History -- Roman period, 55 B.C.-449 A.D. Rome -- History -- Germanic Invasions, 3rd-6th centuries.

DA145.M34
Margary, Ivan Donald.
Roman roads in Britain. London, Phoenix House [1955- v.
55-007628
Roads, Roman -- Great Britain.

DA145.M5 1990
Millett, Martin.
The romanization of Britain: an essay in archaeological interpretation/ Martin Millett. Cambridge [England]; Cambridge University Press, 1990. xvi, 255 p.
89-035682   936.1   0521360846
Excavations (Archaeology) -- Great Britain. Romans -- Great Britain -- History. Great Britain -- Antiquities, Roman. Great Britain -- History -- Roman period, 55 B.C.-449 A.D.

DA145.P67 1992
Potter, T. W.
Roman Britain/ T.W. Potter and Catherine Johns. Berkeley: University of California Press, c1992. 239 p.
92-025283   936.2/04   0520081684
Great Britain -- Antiquities, Roman. Romans -- Great Britain. Great Britain -- History -- Roman period, 55 B.C.-449 A.D.

DA145.S26
Salway, Peter.
Roman Britain/ by Peter Salway. Oxford: Clarendon Press; 1981. xviii, 824 p.
80-041811   936.1/04   019821717X
Great Britain -- History -- Roman period, 55 B.C.-449 A.D.

DA145.W124 2000
Wacher, J. S.
A portrait of Roman Britain/ John Wacher.
London; Routledge, 2000. 139 p.
99-048121 936.1/04 0415033217
*Romans -- Great Britain. Great Britain --
Antiquities, Roman. Great Britain -- History --
Roman period, 55 B.C.-449 A.D.*

DA145.W13 1975
Wacher, J. S.
The towns of Roman Britain/ John Wacher.
Berkeley: University of California Press, 1975,
c1974. 460 p.
73-091663 936.1 0520026691
*Cities and towns, Ancient -- Great Britain.
Romans -- Great Britain. Great Britain --
Antiquities, Roman. Great Britain -- History --
Roman period, 55 B.C.-449 A.D.*

DA145.2.F55 1989
Fletcher, R. A.
Who's who in Roman Britain and Anglo-Saxon
England/ Richard Fletcher. Chicago: St. James
Press, c1989. xix, 245 p.
90-063659 942.01/092/2 1558621318
*Biography -- Middle Ages, 500-1500 --
Biography. Romans -- Great Britain -- Biography.
Anglo-Saxons -- Biography. Great Britain --
History -- Roman period, 55 B.C.-449 A.D. --
Biography. Great Britain -- History -- Anglo Saxon
period, 449-1066 -- Biography.*

DA150.A6 1983b
The Anglo-Saxon chronicle: a collaborative
edition/ general editors, David Dumville & Simon
Keynes. Cambridge [Cambridgeshire]: D.S.
Brewer; 1983-1996 v. 1, 4, 6, 1
83-017130 942.01 085991125X
*Great Britain -- History -- Anglo-Saxon period,
449-1066.*

DA150.G483.H54 1994
Higham, N. J.
The English conquest: Gildas and Britain in the
fifth century/ N.J. Higham. Manchester;
Manchester University Press; c1994. viii, 220 p.
93-045583 942.01/4 0719040795
*Gildas, -- 516?-570? -- Liber querulus de excidio
Britanniae. Civilization, Ancient --
Historiography. Anglo-Saxons -- Historiography.
Britons -- Historiography. Great Britain -- History
-- Anglo-Saxon period, 449-1066. Great Britain --
History -- Anglo-Saxon period, 449-1066 --
Historiography.*

DA152.A7267 2000
Anglo-Saxon history: basic readings/ edited by
David A.E. Pelteret. New York: Garland Pub.,
2000. xxx, 450 p.
00-023328 942.01 0815331401
*Anglo-Saxons. Great Britain -- History --
Anglo-Saxon period, 449-1066.*

DA152.B58 1998
The Blackwell encyclopedia of Anglo-Saxon
England/ edited by Michael Lapidge; with John
Blair, Simon Keynes, and Donald Scragg. Malden,
Mass.: Blackwell, 1998. p. cm.
98-020814 942.01 0631155651
*Great Britain -- History -- Anglo-Saxon period,
449-1066 -- Encyclopedias. England -- Civilization
-- To 1066 -- Encyclopedias.*

DA152.H53 1995
Higham, N. J.
An English empire: Bede and the early Anglo-
Saxon kings/ N.J. Higham. Manchester;
Manchester University Press; 1995. viii, 269 p.
94-023921 942.01 0719044235
*Bede, -- the Venerable, Saint, -- 673-735. Anglo-
Saxons -- Kings and rulers. Monarchy -- England.
Great Britain -- Politics and government -- 449-
1066.*

DA152.H533 1997
Higham, N. J.
The convert kings: power and religious affiliation
in early Anglo-Saxon England/ N.J. Higham.
Manchester, UK; Manchester University Press:
1997. x, 293 p.
96-052281 942.01 0719048273
*Anglo-Saxons -- Kings and rulers -- Religious
aspects. Christianity and politics -- England --
History. Power (Social sciences) -- England --
History. Great Britain -- Politics and government -
- 449-1066. England -- Church history -- 449-
1066.*

DA152.H59 1989
Hodges, Richard.
The Anglo-Saxon achievement: archaeology & the
beginnings of English society/ Richard Hodges.
Ithaca, N.Y.: Cornell University Press, 1989. xi,
212 p.
89-033422 942.01 0801423988
*Social history -- Medieval, 500-1500.
Excavations (Archaeology) -- England.
Civilization, Anglo-Saxon. Great Britain -- History
-- Anglo-Saxon period, 449-1066. England --
Antiquities. England -- Social conditions -- To
1066.*

DA152.J65 1996
John, Eric.
Reassessing Anglo-Saxon England/ Eric John.
Manchester; Manchester University Press; 1996.
xii, 204 p.
96-002687 941.01 0719048672
*Civilization, Anglo-Saxon. Civilization,
Medieval. Anglo-Saxons. England -- Civilization --
To 1066. Great Britain -- History -- Anglo-Saxon
period, 449-1066.*

DA152.M97 1986
Myres, J. N. L.
The English settlements/ by J.N.L. Myres. Oxford
[Oxfordshire]: Clarendon Press; 1986. xxviii,
248 p.
85-015538 942.01 0198217196
*Social history -- Medieval, 500-1500. Land
settlement -- England -- History. Anglo-Saxons.
Great Britain -- History -- Anglo Saxon period,
449-1066.*

DA152.O75 1989
The Origins of Anglo-Saxon kingdoms/ edited by
Steven Bassett. London; Leicester University
Press, 1989. xii, 300 p.
89-008009 942.01 0718513177
*Anglo-Saxons -- Kings and rulers -- Congresses.
Monarchy -- England -- Congresses. Great Britain
-- History -- Anglo-Saxon period, 449-1066 --
Congresses. Great Britain -- Politics and
government -- 449-1066 -- Congresses.*

DA152.Y673 1995
Yorke, Barbara, 1951-
Wessex in the early Middle Ages/ Barbara Yorke.
London; Leicester University Press, 1995. xiii,
367 p.
95-014446 942/.01 0718513142
*Anglo-Saxons -- England -- Wessex -- History.
Wessex (England) -- History. Great Britain --
History -- Anglo-Saxon period, 449-1066.*

DA152.2.H86 1977
Hunter Blair, Peter, 1912-1982.
An introduction to Anglo-Saxon England/ Peter
Hunter Blair. Cambridge [Eng.]; Cambridge
University Press, 1977. xv, 379 p.
77-071404 942.01 0521216508.
*Anglo-Saxons. Great Britain -- History --
Anglo-Saxon period, 449-1066.*

DA152.5.A7.B78 1999
Bruce, Christopher W.
The Arthurian name dictionary/ Christopher W.
Bruce. New York: Garland, 1999. x, [1], 504 p.
98-037750 942.01/4 0815328656
*Arthur, -- King -- Dictionaries. Britons -- Kings
and rulers -- Folklore -- Dictionaries. Names,
Geographical -- Dictionaries. Arthurian romances
-- Dictionaries. Great Britain -- History -- To 1066
-- Legends -- Dictionaries. Great Britain --
Antiquities, Celtic -- Legends -- Dictionaries.*

DA153.A88 1966
Asser, John, d. 909
Life of King Alfred. Translated with introd. and
notes by L. C. Jane. New York, Cooper Square
Publishers, 1966. lix, 173 p.
66-027658 942.01/0924
*Alfred, -- King of England, -- 849-899. Anglo-
Saxons -- England -- Wessex -- Kings and rulers --
Biography. Great Britain -- Kings and rulers --
Biography. Great Britain -- History -- Alfred, 871-
899.*

DA154.8.C57 1994
Clarke, Peter A.
The English nobility under Edward the Confessor/
Peter A. Clarke. Oxford: Clarendon Press; 1994.
xi, 386 p.
93-027129 942.01/9 0198204426
*Land tenure -- England -- History. Nobility --
England -- History. Anglo-Saxons. Great Britain --
History -- Edward, the Confessor, 1042-1066.*

DA154.8.V5
The life of King Edward, who rests at Westminster.
Attributed to a monk of St. Bertin. Edited and
translated with introd. and notes by Frank Barlow.
London, Nelson [1962] lxxxii, 81, 8
62-006101 923.142
*Edward, -- King of England, -- ca. 1003-1066.
Great Britain -- History -- Anglo-Saxon period
449-1066.*

DA155.C38 1998
Carver, M. O. H.
Sutton Hoo: burial ground of kings?/ Martin
Carver. Philadelphia, Penn.: University of
Pennsylvania Press, 1998. xii, 195 p.
98-016434 936.2/646 0812234553
*Anglo-Saxons -- Kings and rulers -- Death and
burial. Excavations (Archaeology) -- England --
Suffolk. Ships, Medieval -- England -- Suffolk.
Suffolk (England) -- Antiquities. East Anglia
(England) -- Kings and rulers -- Death and burial.
Sutton Hoo Ship Burial (England)*

DA158.H34 2000
Hadley, D. M. 1967-
The Northern Danelaw: its social structure, c. 800-1100/ D.M. Hadley. London; Leicester University Press, 2000. x, 374 p.
99-087413   333.3/22/0942809021   0718500148
Land tenure -- England, Northern -- History -- To 1500. Peasantry -- England, Northern -- History -- To 1500. Vikings -- England, Northern. England, Northern -- Social conditions. Great Britain -- History -- Invasions. Great Britain -- History -- Anglo-Saxon period, 449-1066.

DA160.R45 1994
The reign of Cnut: King of England, Denmark and Norway/ edited by Alexander R. Rumble. London: Leicester University Press; 1994. xvii, 341 p.
94-016870   942.02   0838636055
Canute -- I, -- King of England, -- 995?-1035. Danes -- England -- History.   Great Britain -- Kings and rulers -- Biography. Denmark -- Kings and rulers -- Biography. Norway -- Kings and rulers -- Biography.

DA160.S73 1997
Stafford, Pauline.
Queen Emma and Queen Edith: queenship and women's power in eleventh-century England/ Pauline Stafford. Oxford, UK; Blackwell Publishers, 1997. xi, 371 p.
96-038246   942.01/9/0922   0631166793
Emma, -- Queen, consort of Canute I, King of England, -- d. 1052. Edith, -- Queen, consort of Edward, King of England, -- ca. 1020-1075. Women -- England -- History -- Middle Ages, 500-1500. Power (Social sciences) -- England -- History. Queens -- Great Britain -- Biography. Great Britain -- Kings and rulers -- Succession. Great Britain -- History -- Anglo Saxon period, 449-1066.

DA161.D48 1999
DeVries, Kelly, 1956-
The Norwegian invasion of England in 1066/ Kelly DeVries. Woodbridge, Suffolk; Boydell Press, 1999. xii, 322 p.
99-037405   942.02/1   0851157637
Harold, -- King of England, -- 1022?-1066. Harald -- III Hardradi, -- King of Norway, -- 1015-1066. Stamford Bridge, Battle of, 1066. Great Britain -- History, Military -- 449-1066. Great Britain -- History -- Invasions. Norway -- History, Military.

DA175.H34 2001
Hagger, Mark S.
The fortunes of a Norman family: the de Verduns in England, Ireland and Wales, 1066-1316/ Mark S. Hagger. Dublin; Four Courts Press, c2001. 286 p.
1851825967
De Verdun family.   Normans -- Great Britain -- History -- To 1500. Normans -- Ireland -- History -- To 1500. Great Britain -- History -- Medieval period, 1066-1485. Great Britain -- Social life and customs -- 1066-1485. Ireland -- History -- To 1603.

DA175.W36 1987
Warren, W. L. 1929-
The governance of Norman and Angevin England, 1086-1272/ W.L. Warren. Stanford, Calif.: Stanford University Press, 1987. xv, 237 p.
85-061473   942.02   0804713073
Anjou, House of.   Normans -- England -- History -- To 1500. Constitutional history, Medieval. Great Britain -- Politics and government -- 1066-1485. Great Britain -- History -- Angevin period, 1154-1216. Great Britain -- History -- Norman period, 1066-1154.

DA176.B3 1956
Barrow, G. W. S.
Feudal Britain; the completion of the medieval kingdoms, 1066-1314. London, E. Arnold [1956] 452 p.
57-000112   942.02
Feudalism -- Great Britain.   Great Britain -- Politics and government -- 1066-1485.

DA176.B44 1972
Beresford, M. W. 1920-
Deserted medieval villages: studies. Edited by Maurice Beresford and John G. Hurst. New York, St. Martin's Press [1972, c1971] xviii, 340 p.
75-190102   914.2/03
Extinct cities -- Great Britain. Excavations (Archaeology) -- Great Britain. Villages -- Great Britain -- History. Great Britain -- History -- Medieval period, 1066-1485. Great Britain -- Antiquities.

DA176.T94 1988
Tyerman, Christopher.
England and the Crusades, 1095-1588/ Christopher Tyerman. Chicago: University of Chicago Press, 1988. xvi, 492 p.
87-030252   942   0226820122
Crusades.   Great Britain -- History -- Tudors, 1485-1603. Great Britain -- History -- Medieval period, 1066-1485. England -- Church history -- 1066-1485.

DA176.W66 1988
Wood, Charles T.
Joan of Arc and Richard III: sex, saints, and government in the Middle Ages/ Charles T. Wood. New York: Oxford University Press, 1988. ix, 269 p.
87-035023   942.04   0195040600
Joan, -- of Arc, Saint, -- 1412-1431. Richard -- III, -- King of England, -- 1452-1485. Monarchy -- Great Britain -- History -- To 1500. Monarchy -- France -- History -- To 1500. Sex -- Political aspects -- History -- To 1500. France -- Politics and government -- 1328-1589. France -- Politics and government -- 987-1328. Great Britain -- Politics and government -- 1066-1485.

DA177.H53 1991
Hicks, M. A.
Who's who in late medieval England, 1272-1485/ Michael A. Hicks. Chicago: St. James Press, c1991. xxv, 382 p.
90-064267   1558621350
Biography -- Middle Ages, 500-1500 -- Dictionaries.   Great Britain -- History -- Lancaster and York, 1399-1485 -- Biography. Great Britain -- History -- Medieval period, 1066-1485 -- Biography. Great Britain -- History -- Plantagenets, 1154-1399 -- Biography.

DA185.B27 1974
Barnie, John.
War in medieval English society; social values in the Hundred Years War, 1337-99. Ithaca, N.Y., Cornell University Press [1974] xiii, 204 p.
74-002687   914.2/03/37   0801408652
Hundred Years' War, 1339-1453 -- Public opinion. War and society -- England -- History -- To 1500. Public opinion -- England -- History -- To 1500. England -- Civilization -- 1066-1485.

DA185.C87 1968
Coulton, G. G. 1858-1947,
Social life in Britain from the conquest to the Reformation. New York, Barnes & Noble [1968] xx, 566 p.
68-023758   914.2/03
Social history -- Medieval, 500-1500. Reformation -- Great Britain.   Great Britain -- Social life and customs -- 1066-1485.

DA185.M47 1988
Mertes, Kate.
The English noble household, 1250-1600: good governance and politic rule/ Kate Mertes. Oxford, OX, UK; B. Blackwell, 1988. 235 p.
87-025356   942   0631153195
Nobility -- Great Britain -- History. Households -- England -- History. England -- Social life and customs -- 1066-1485. Great Britain -- History -- Medieval period, 1066-1485. Great Britain -- History -- Tudors, 1485-1603.

DA190.D7.D656 1985
Domesday book: a reassessment/ edited by Peter Sawyer. London; E. Arnold, 1985. x, 182 p.
86-103554   333.3/22/0942   0713164409
Real property -- England -- History -- To 1500. Land tenure -- England -- History -- To 1500. Manuscripts, Medieval -- England. England -- Economic conditions -- 1066-1485. Great Britain -- History -- Norman period, 1066-1154.

DA190.D7.G28
Galbraith, V. H. 1889-
Domesday book: its place in administrative history/ by V. H. Galbraith. Oxford [Eng.]: Clarendon Press, 1974. xxxv, 193 p.
75-308915   333.3/22/0942   0198224249
Land tenure -- England.   England -- Rural conditions.

DA190.D7.R64 2000
Roffe, David.
Domesday: the inquest and the book/ David Roffe. Oxford, [U.K.]; Oxford University Press, 2000. xix, 282 p.
99-056324   942.02   0198208472
Real property -- England -- History -- To 1500. Land tenure -- England -- History -- To 1500. Manuscripts, Medieval -- England. England -- Economic conditions -- 1066-1485. Great Britain -- History -- Norman period, 1066-1154.

DA195.B28 2000
Bartlett, Robert, 1950-
England under the Norman and Angevin kings, 1075-1225/ Robert Bartlett. Oxford [England]: Clarendon Press; 2000. xxx, 772 p.
99-016108   942.02   0198227418
Anjou, House of. Normans -- England -- History -- To 1500.   England -- Civilization -- 1066-1485. Great Britain -- History -- Norman period, 1066-1154. Great Britain -- History -- Angevin period, 1154-1216.

DA195.G74 1997
Green, Judith A.
The aristocracy of Norman England/ Judith A. Green. Cambridge, U.K.; Cambridge University Press, 1997. xv, 497 p.
96-043682   940.1   0521335094
Aristocracy (Political science) -- England -- History. Social history -- Medieval, 500-1500. Normans -- England. Great Britain -- Politics and government -- 1066-1154.

DA195.H83 1994
Hudson, John.
Land, law, and lordship in Anglo-Norman England/ John Hudson. Oxford: Clarendon Press; 1994. ix, 320 p.
93-013962   333.3/22/094209021   019820437X
Land tenure -- England -- History -- To 1500. Feudal law -- England -- History -- To 1500. Feudalism -- England -- History -- To 1500. Great Britain -- History -- Norman period, 1066-1154.

DA195.W55 1995
Williams, Ann, 1937-
The English and the Norman conquest/ Ann Williams. Woodbridge, Suffolk, UK; Boydell Press, 1995. xiii, 264 p.
95-009715   941.02   085115588X
National characteristics, English -- History -- To 1500. Normans -- England -- History -- To 1500. Civilization, Anglo-Saxon. Great Britain -- History -- Norman period, 1066-1154.

DA197.F57 1991
Fleming, Robin.
Kings and lords in Conquest England/ Robin Fleming. Cambridge; Cambridge University Press, 1991. xxi, 257 p.
90-001565   942.02/1   0521393094
Land tenure -- England -- History -- To 1500. Nobility -- England -- History -- To 1500. Normans -- England -- History. Great Britain -- Kings and rulers. Great Britain -- History -- William I, 1066-1087. Great Britain -- History -- Canute, 1017-1035.

DA197.G65 1994
Golding, Brian.
Conquest and colonisation: the Normans in Britain, 1066-1100/ Brian Golding. New York, N.Y.: St. Martin's Press, 1994. xiv, 227 p.
93-047458   942.02/1   031212127X
Normans -- Great Britain.   Great Britain -- History -- William II, Rufus, 1087-1100. Great Britain -- History -- William I, 1066-1087.

DA205.N838 1969b
Norgate, Kate.
England under the Angevin kings.   New York, Haskell House, 1969. 2 v.
68-025255   942/.03   0838301843
Anjou, House of.   England -- Civilization -- 1066-1485. Great Britain -- History -- Angevin period, 1154-1216.

DA206.W48 1999
White, G. J.
Restoration and reform, 1153-1165: recovery from civil war in England/ Graeme J. White. Cambridge, UK; Cambridge University Press, 2000. xvii, 248 p.
99-019516   942.03/1   0521554594
Great Britain -- Politics and government -- 1154-1189. Great Britain -- History -- Henry II, 1154-1189. Great Britain -- History -- Stephen, 1135-1154.

DA207.G48 1979
Gillingham, John.
Richard the Lionheart/ John Gillingham. New York: Times Books, [1979] c1978. 318 p.
78-063599   942.03/2/0924   0812908023
Richard -- I, -- King of England, -- 1157-1199. Great Britain -- History -- Richard I, 1189-1199. Great Britain -- Kings and rulers -- Biography.

DA208.W33 1978b
Warren, W. L. 1929-
King John/ W. L. Warren. Berkeley: University of California Press, c1978. xi, 350 p.
77-020332   942.03/3/0924   0520036107.
John, -- King of England, -- 1167?-1216.   Great Britain -- History -- John, 1199-1216. Great Britain -- Kings and rulers -- Biography.

DA209.E6.K45 1950
Kelly, Amy Ruth, 1878-
Eleanor of Aquitaine and the four kings. Cambridge, Harvard University Press, 1950. xii, 431 p.
50-006545   923.142
Eleanor, -- of Aquitaine, Queen, consort of Henry II, King of England, -- 1122?-1204.   Queens -- Great Britain -- Biography.   Great Britain -- History -- Plantagenets, 1154-1399.

DA209.G5.B37 1982
Bartlett, Robert, 1950-
Gerald of Wales, 1146-1223/ Robert Bartlett. Oxford: Clarendon Press; 1982. 246 p.
82-145750   942.9/007/2024   0198218923
Giraldus, -- Cambrensis, -- 1146?-1223?   Wales -- History -- To 1536 -- Historiography.

DA225.H37 1993
Harding, Alan.
England in the thirteenth century/ Alan Harding. Cambridge [England]; Cambridge University Press, 1993. xiv, 351 p.
92-030603   942.03/4   0521302749
Great Britain -- History -- 13th century. England -- Civilization -- 1066-1485.

DA225.L56 1988
Lloyd, S. D.
English society and the crusade, 1216-1307/ Simon Lloyd. Oxford: Clarendon Press; 1988. xiii, 329 p.
88-001088   940.1/84   0198229496
Crusades -- Later, 13th, 14th, and 15th centuries. Social history -- Medieval, 500-1500.   Great Britain -- History -- 13th century. England -- Social conditions -- 1066-1485. Great Britain -- History -- Edward I, 1272-1307.

DA225.M34 1959
McKisack, May.
The fourteenth century, 1307-1399/ by May McKisack. Oxford: Clarendon Press; c1959. xix, 598 p.
59-016710   942.03/7
Great Britain -- History -- 14th century.

DA228.E44.H69 1998
Howell, Margaret.
Eleanor of Provence: queenship in thirteenth-century England/ Margaret Howell. Oxford, UK; Blackwell Publishers, 1998. xxii, 349 p.
97-006679   941.03/4/092   0631172866
Eleanor of Provence, -- Queen, consort of Henry III, King of England, -- 1223 or 4-1291. Queens -- Great Britain -- Biography.   Great Britain -- History -- Henry III, 1216-1272.

DA228.M7.M33 1994
Maddicott, John Robert.
Simon De Montfort/ J.R. Maddicott. Cambridge; Cambridge University Press, 1994. xxiii, 404 p.
93-033224   942.03/4/092   0521374936
Montfort, Simon de, -- Earl of Leicester, -- 1208?-1265.   Revolutionaries -- Great Britain -- Biography. Nobility -- Great Britain -- Biography. Great Britain -- History -- Barons' War, 1263-1267.

DA229.P37 1995
Parsons, John Carmi, 1947-
Eleanor of Castile: queen and society in thirteenth-century England/ John Carmi Parsons. New York: St. Martin's Press, 1995. xix, 364 p.
94-031086   942.03/5/092   0312086490
Eleanor, -- Queen, consort of Edward I, King of England, -- d. 1290.   Queens -- Great Britain -- Biography.   England -- Social life and customs -- 1066-1485. Great Britain -- History -- Edward I, 1272-1307.

DA229.P72 1988
Prestwich, Michael.
Edward I/ Michael Prestwich. Berkeley: University of California Press, 1988. xv, 618 p.
88-005759   942.03/5/0924   0520062663
Edward -- I, -- King of England, -- 1239-1307. Great Britain -- History -- Edward I, 1272-1307. Great Britain -- Kings and rulers -- Biography.

DA229.R33 2000
Raban, Sandra.
England under Edward I and Edward II/ Sandra Raban. Malden, MA: Blackwell Publishers, 2000. p. cm.
00-023643   942.03/5/092   0631203575
Great Britain -- History -- Edward I, 1272-1307. Great Britain -- History -- Edward II, 1307-1327.

DA233.O74 1990
Ormrod, W. M., 1957-
The reign of Edward III: crown and political society in England, 1327-1377/ W.M. Ormrod. New Haven: Yale University Press, 1990. xiii, 280 p.
90-038270   942.03/7   0300048750
Edward -- III, -- King of England, -- 1312-1377. Great Britain -- Politics and government -- 1327-1377.

DA233.R64 2000
Rogers, Clifford J.
War cruel and sharp: English strategy under Edward III, 1327-1360/ Clifford J. Rogers. Woodbridge, Suffolk, UK; Boydell Press, 2000. xviii, 458 p.
00-042922   944/.025   0851158048
Edward -- III, -- King of England, -- 1312-1377 -- Military leadership.   Military art and science -- England -- History -- Medieval, 500-1500.   Great Britain -- History -- Edward III, 1327-1377. Great Britain -- History, Military -- 1066-1485.

DA234.B37
Barber, Richard W.
Edward, Prince of Wales and Aquitaine: a biography of the Black Prince/ Richard Barber. New York: Scribner, c1978. 298 p.
78-054019   942.03/7/0924   0684158647
Edward, -- Prince of Wales, -- 1330-1376. Princes -- Great Britain -- Biography.   Great Britain -- History -- Edward III, 1327-1377.

DA235.F79 1996
Fryde, E. B.
Peasants and landlords in later Medieval England/ E.B. Fryde. New York: St. Martin's Press, 1996. xi, 371 p.
96-023198   942.04   0312163703
Tyler's Insurrection, 1381. Peasant uprisings -- England -- History. Landlord and tenant -- England -- History. Great Britain -- History -- 14th century. Great Britain -- History -- Richard II, 1377-1399. Great Britain -- History -- Lancaster and York, 1399-1485.

DA235.S26 1997
Saul, Nigel.
Richard II/ Nigel Saul. New Haven: Yale
University Press, c1997. xiv, 514 p.
96-036062   942.03/8/092   0300070039
Richard -- II, -- King of England, -- 1367-1400.
Great Britain -- History -- Richard II, 1377-1399.
Great Britain -- Kings and rulers -- Biography.

DA240.B4 1968
Bennett, H. S. 1889-
The Pastons and their England: studies in an age of
transition, by H. S. Bennett. London, Cambridge
U.P., 1968. xvi, 271 p.
68-023175   914.2/03/4   0521095131
Paston family -- Correspondence. Social history -
- Medieval, 500-1500. Norfolk (England) -- Social
life and customs. England -- Social life and
customs -- 1066-1485. Great Britain -- History --
Lancaster and York, 1399-1485.

DA240.P32 1971
Paston letters: selected and edited with an
introduction/ notes and glossary by Norman Davis;
critical comment by Horace Walpole, Virginia
Woolf and others. Oxford, Clarendon Press, 1971.
xxx, 165 p.
72-181315   914.2/03/408   0198710240
Paston family -- Correspondence. Social history -
- Medieval, 500-1500 -- Sources.   England --
Social life and customs -- 1066-1485 -- Sources.
Great Britain -- History -- Lancaster and York,
1399-1485 -- Sources.

DA240.R53 1990
Richmond, Colin.
The Paston family in the fifteenth century: the first
phase/ Colin Richmond. Cambridge [England];
Cambridge University Press, 1990. xxi, 269 p.
89-025147   942   0521385024
Paston family -- Correspondence.   Paston letters.
Great Britain -- History -- Henry VII, 1485-1509.
Norfolk (England) -- Social life and customs.
England -- Social life and customs -- 1066-1485.

DA245.A24 2001
Aberth, John, 1963-
From the brink of the apocalypse: confronting
famine, war, plague, and death in the later middle
ages/ John Aberth. New York: Routledge , 2001.
xii, 304 p.
00-038263   942.04   0415927153
Apocalyptic literature -- History and criticism.
Disasters -- England -- History -- To 1500.
Famines -- England -- History -- To 1500. England
-- Civilization -- 1066-1485. Great Britain --
History -- 14th century. Great Britain -- History --
Lancaster and York, 1399-1485.

DA245.B43 1989
Bean, J. M. W.
From lord to patron: lordship in late medieval
England/ J.M.W. Bean. Manchester, UK:
Manchester University Press, c1989. xii, 279 p.
89-004777   942.03   0719028558
Patronage, Political -- England -- History. Social
history -- Medieval, 500-1500. Feudalism --
England -- History. Great Britain -- Politics and
government -- 1154-1399. Great Britain -- Politics
and government -- 1399-1485. England -- Social
conditions -- 1066-1485.

DA245.F52 1994
Fifteenth-Century attitudes: perceptions of society
in late medieval England/ edited by Rosemary
Horrox.   Cambridge   [England];   Cambridge
University Press, 1994. xii, 244 p.
94-005622   942.04   0521404835
Great Britain -- History -- Lancaster and York,
1399-1485. England -- Social conditions -- 1066-
1485.

DA245.S77 1998
Strohm, Paul, 1938-
England's empty throne: usurpation and the
language of legitimation, 1399-1422/ Paul Strohm.
New Haven: Yale Unversity Press, c1998. xiv,
274 p.
98-004399   942.04/1   0300075448
Richard -- II, -- King of England, -- 1367-1400 --
Death and burial.   Lollards.   Great Britain --
History -- Henry IV, 1399-1413. Great Britain --
History -- Henry V, 1413-1422. Great Britain --
Kings and rulers -- Succession.

DA250.R76
Ross, Charles Derek.
The Wars of the Roses: a concise history/ Charles
Ross. London: Thames and Hudson, 1976. 190 p.
76-374627   942.04   0500250499
Great Britain -- History -- Wars of the Roses,
1455-1485. Great Britain -- History, Military --
1066-1485.

DA255.B48 1994
Bevan, Bryan.
Henry IV/ Bryan Bevan. New York: St. Martin's
Press, 1994. ix, 166 p.
94-241055   942.04/1/092   0312116969
Henry -- IV, -- King of England, -- 1367-1413.
Great Britain -- History -- Henry IV, 1399-1413.
Great Britain -- Kings and rulers -- Biography.

DA256.A4 1992
Allmand, C. T.
Henry V/ Christopher Allmand. Berkeley:
University of California Press, c1992. xiv, 480 p.
92-029108   942.04/2/092   0520082931
Henry -- V, -- King of England, -- 1387-1422.
Great Britain -- History -- Henry V, 1413-1422.
Great Britain -- Kings and rulers -- Biography.

DA256.W8 1968
Wylie, James Hamilton, 1844-1914.
The reign of Henry the Fifth.   New York,
Greenwood Press, 1968. 3 v.
69-010175   942.04/2
Great Britain -- History -- Henry v, 1413-1422.

DA257.W38 1996
Watts, John Lovett.
Henry VI and the politics of kingship/ John Lovett
Watts. New York: Cambridge University Press,
1996. xvii, 399 p.
95-038634   320.942/09/024   0521420393
Henry -- VI, -- King of England, -- 1421-1471.
Monarchy -- Great Britain -- History.   Great
Britain -- Kings and rulers -- Biography. Great
Britain -- Politics and government -- 1399-1485.
Great Britain -- History -- Henry VI, 1422-1461.

DA258.R67
Ross, Charles Derek.
Edward IV/ Charles Ross. Berkeley: University of
California Press, 1974. xvi, 479 p.
74-079771   942.04/4/0924   0520027817
Great Britain -- Politics and government --
1461-1483.

DA260.H65 1989
Horrox, Rosemary.
Richard III: a study of service/ Rosemary Horrox.
Cambridge; Cambridge University Press, 1989. x,
358 p.
88-022899   942.04/6/0924   0521334284
Richard -- III, -- King of England, -- 1452-1485.
Great Britain -- Kings and rulers -- Biography.
Great Britain -- History -- Richard III, 1483-1485.

DA260.P65 1991
Pollard, A. J.
Richard III and the princes in the Tower/ A.J.
Pollard. New York: St. Martin's Press, 1991. xviii,
260 p.
91-003934   942.05/092   0312067151
Richard -- III, -- King of England, -- 1452-1485.
Edward -- V, -- King of England, -- 1470-1483 --
Death and burial.   Richard, -- Duke of York, --
1473-1483 -- Death and burial. Princes -- Great
Britain -- Biography. Murder -- England -- History
-- To 1500. Great Britain -- History -- Richard III,
1483-1485 -- Historiography. Great Britain --
Kings and rulers -- Biography.

DA300-592 England — History — By period — Modern, 1485-

DA300.J66 2000
Jones, Whitney R. D. 1924-
The tree of commonwealth, 1450-1793/ Whitney
R.D. Jones. Madison, [N.J.]: Fairleigh Dickinson
University Press; c2000. 394 p.
99-049988   941   0838638376
Democracy -- Great Britain -- History.   Great
Britain -- Politics and government -- 1603-1714.
Great Britain -- Politics and government -- 18th
century. Great Britain -- Politics and government -
- 1485-1603.

DA300.L58 1984
Lloyd, Trevor Owen.
The British Empire, 1558-1983/ T.O. Lloyd. New
York: Oxford University Press, 1984. xvi, 430 p.
83-019481   909/.0971241   0198730241
Great Britain -- History -- Modern period,
1485- Great Britain -- Colonies -- History. Great
Britain -- Colonies -- Administration.

DA314.F47
Ferguson, Arthur B.
Clio unbound: perception of the social and cultural
past in Renaissance England/ Arthur B. Ferguson.
Durham, N.C.: Duke University Press, 1979. xv,
443 p.
78-067198   907/.2042   0822304171
Renaissance -- England -- Historiography.
Great Britain -- History -- Early Stuarts, 1603-
1649 -- Historiography. Great Britain -- History --
Medieval period, 1066-1485 -- Historiography.
Great Britain -- History -- Tudors, 1485-1603 --
Historiography.

DA315.E54 1995
Ellis, Steven G., 1950-
Tudor frontiers and noble power: the making of the
British state/ Steven G. Ellis. Oxford: Clarendon
Press; 1995. xxi, 303 p.
94-049540   942.05   0198201338
Tudor, House of. Nobility -- Great Britain --
History -- 16th century. Power (Social sciences) --
Great Britain -- History -- 16th century. Great
Britain -- Politics and government -- 1485-1603.

DA315.E6 1974
Elton, G. R.
England under the Tudors/ by G. R. Elton. London: Methuen, 1974. xi, 522 p.
74-185525   942.05   0416787207
Tudor, House of.   England -- Civilization -- 16th century. Great Britain -- History -- Tudors, 1485-1603.

DA315.G89 1988
Guy, J. A.
Tudor England/ John Guy. Oxford [Oxfordshire]; Oxford University Press, 1988. xiii, 582 p.
88-005371   942.05   0198730888
Tudor, House of.   England -- Civilization -- 16th century. Great Britain -- History -- Tudors, 1485-1603.

DA315.H28 1993
Haigh, Christopher.
English reformations: religion, politics, and society under the Tudors/ Christopher Haigh. Oxford: Clarendon Press; 1993. ix, 367 p.
92-021515   942.05   0198221630
Reformation -- England. Great Britain -- Social conditions. Great Britain -- Church history -- 16th century. Great Britain -- History -- Tudors, 1485-1603.

DA315.H46 2000
Hindle, Steve, 1965-
The state and social change in early modern England, c. 1550-1640/ Steve Hindle. New York: St. Martin's Press, 2000. xi, 338 p.
99-043173   942.05   0312229186
Social change -- England -- History -- 16th century. Social change -- England -- History -- 17th century. Great Britain -- Politics and government -- 1485-1603. Great Britain -- Politics and government -- 1603-1649. England -- Social conditions -- 16th century.

DA315.L578 1997
Loades, D. M.
Tudor government: structures of authority in the Sixteenth Century/ David Loades. Oxford, UK; Blackwell Publishers, 1997. x, 296 p.
96-054621   320.942/09/031   0631191569
Power (Social sciences) -- England -- History -- 16th century. Church and state -- England -- History -- 16th century. Authority -- History -- 16th century. Great Britain -- Politics and government -- 1485-1603.

DA315.M36 1988
Manning, Roger B.
Village revolts: social protest and popular disturbances in England, 1509-1640/ Roger B. Manning. Oxford [Oxfordshire]: Clarendon Press; 1988. xiii, 354 p.
87-022050   942.05   0198201168
Riots -- England -- History. Social movements -- England -- History. Villages -- England -- History. Great Britain -- History -- Tudors, 1485-1603. Great Britain -- History -- Early Stuarts, 1603-1649.

DA315.T58 1998
Tittler, Robert.
The Reformation and the towns in England: politics and political culture, c. 1540-1640/ Robert Tittler. Oxford; Clarendon Press, 1998. x, 395 p.
97-047540   942.05   0198207182
City and town life -- England -- History -- 16th century. City and town life -- England -- History -- 17th century. Political culture -- England -- History -- 16th century. Great Britain -- Politics and government -- 1603-1649. Great Britain -- Politics and government -- 1485-1603.

DA317.R68 1990
Routh, C. R. N.
Who's who in Tudor England/ C.R.N. Routh; revised by Peter Holmes. Chicago: St. James Press, c1990. xiii, 476 p.
90-063661   942.05/092/2   1558621334
Great Britain -- History -- Tudors, 1485-1603 -- Biography -- Dictionaries. England -- Civilization -- 16th century -- Dictionaries. England -- Biography -- Dictionaries.

DA317.1.W45 1996
Weir, Alison.
The children of Henry VIII/ Alison Weir.1st American ed. New York: Ballantine Books, 1996. xiv, 385 p. [8] p. of plates
96-014849   942.052/092/2. 220   0345391187
Henry VIII, King of England, 1491-1547--Family. Edward VI, King of England, 1537-1553. Grey, Jane, Lady, 1537-1554. Queens--Great Britain--Biography.

DA317.8.C8.M34 1996
MacCulloch, Diarmaid.
Thomas Cranmer: a life/ Diarmaid MacCulloch New Haven, CT: Yale University Press, c1996. xii, 692 p.
95-049593   283/.092   0300066880
Cranmer, Thomas, -- 1489-1556. Statesmen -- Great Britain -- Biography. Theologians -- England -- Biography. Bishops -- England -- Biography. Great Britain -- History -- Tudors, 1485-1603 -- Biography. Great Britain -- Politics and government -- 1509-1547. Great Britain -- Church history -- 16th century.

DA317.8.P6
Mayer, Thomas F., 1937-
Reginald Pole: prince and prophet/ Thomas F. Mayer. Cambridge, UK; Cambridge University Press, 2000. xv, 468 p.
99-088997   282/.092   0521371880
Pole, Reginald, -- 1500-1558. Church and state -- England -- History -- 16th century. Cardinals -- Biography. Great Britain -- History -- Henry VIII, 1509-1547 -- Biography. England -- Church history -- 16th century. Great Britain -- History -- Mary I, 1553-1558 -- Biography.

DA320.C65 1989
Collins, Stephen L.
From divine cosmos to sovereign state: an intellectual history of consciousness and the idea of order in Renaissance England/ Stephen L. Collins. New York: Oxford University Press, 1989. viii, 235 p.
88-004225   941.05   019505458X
Philosophy, English -- 16th century. Philosophy, English -- 17th century. Cosmology -- History. Great Britain -- Politics and government -- 1485-1603. Great Britain -- Politics and government -- 1603-1649. Great Britain -- Intellectual life -- 16th century.

DA320.C94 1997
Cressy, David.
Birth, marriage, and death: ritual, religion, and the life-cycle in Tudor and Stuart England/ David Cressy. Oxford [Eng.]; Oxford University Press, 1997. xv, 641 p.
97-182367   942.05   0198201680
Rites and ceremonies -- England -- History -- 17th century. Funeral rites and ceremonies -- England -- History. Marriage customs and rites -- England -- History. England -- Social life and customs -- 17th century. England -- Social life and customs -- 16th century.

DA320.H286 2000
Hazard, Mary E.
Elizabethan silent language/ Mary E. Hazard. Lincoln: University of Nebraska Press, c2000. xii, 345 p.
99-048632   302.2/0942/09031   0803223978
Communication -- Social aspects -- England -- History -- 16th century. Language and culture -- England -- History -- 16th century. Art and literature -- England -- History -- 16th century. Great Britain -- History -- Elizabeth, 1558-1603. England -- Civilization -- 16th century.

DA320.H87 1994
Hutton, Ronald.
The rise and fall of merry England: the ritual year, 1400-1700/ Ronald Hutton. Oxford; Oxford University Press, 1994. xi, 366 p.
93-043092   942   0198203632
Rites and ceremonies -- England -- History. Social history -- Medieval, 500-1500. Popular culture -- England -- History. England -- Social life and customs -- 16th century. England -- Social life and customs -- 17th century. England -- Social life and customs -- 1066-1485.

DA320.O74 1994
Orlin, Lena Cowen.
Private matters and public culture in post-Reformation England/ Lena Cowen Orlin. Ithaca: Cornell University Press, 1994. xiii, 309 p.
94-001035   941.06   0801428580
Domestic drama, English -- History and criticism. Patriarchy -- England -- History -- 16th century. Property -- England -- History -- 16th century. England -- Social life and customs -- 16th century.

DA320.R49 1999
Renaissance culture and the everyday/ edited by Patricia Fumerton and Simon Hunt. Philadelphia: University of Pennsylvania Press, c1999. vi, 366 p.
98-035173   942   0812234545
Renaissance -- England. Renaissance. Europe -- Social life and customs. England -- Social life and customs -- 16th century. England -- Social life and customs -- 17th century.

DA320.W7
Wright, Louis B. 1899-
Life and letters in Tudor and Stuart England, edited by Louis B. Wright and Virginia A. LaMar. Ithaca, N.Y., Published for the Folger Shakespeare Library by [1962] vii, 528 p.
62-021552   942.05
Great Britain -- History -- Tudors, 1485-1603. Great Britain -- History -- Stuarts, 1603-1714. England -- Civilization.

DA325.G86 1995
Gunn, S. J.
Early Tudor government, 1485-1558/ S.J. Gunn. New York: St. Martin's Press, 1995. p. cm.
94-034078   320.942   0312124937
Great Britain -- Politics and government -- 1485-1603.

DA330.A43 1980
Alexander, Michael Van Cleave, 1937-
The first of the Tudors: a study of Henry VII and his reign/ by Michael Van Cleave Alexander. Totowa, N.J.: Rowman and Littlefield, c1980. x, 280 p.
79-028135   942.05/1/0924   0847662594
Henry -- VII, -- King of England, -- 1457-1509. Great Britain -- History -- Henry VII, 1485-1509. Great Britain -- Kings and rulers -- Biography.

DA330.T4 1971
Temperley, Gladys.
Henry VII. With an introd. by James T. Shotwell. Westport, Conn., Greenwood Press [1971] xiv, 453 p.
75-110871 942.05/1/0924 0837145503
Henry -- VII, -- King of England, -- 1457-1509.
Great Britain -- History -- Henry VII, 1485-1509.

DA330.8.R5.J66 1992
Jones, Michael K.
The King's mother: Lady Margaret Beaufort, Countess of Richmond and Derby/ Michael K. Jones, Malcolm G. Underwood. Cambridge [England]; Cambridge University Press, 1992. xv, 322 p.
90-025937 942.04/092 052134512X
Beaufort, Margaret, -- Countess of Richmond and Derby, -- 1443-1509. Henry -- VII, -- King of England, -- 1457-1509 -- Family. Tudor, House of. Nobility -- Great Britain -- Biography. Great Britain -- History -- Wars of the Roses, 1455-1485 -- Biography. Great Britain -- History -- Henry VII, 1485-1509 -- Biography.

DA330.8.S55.B46 1987
Bennett, Michael J. 1949-
Lambert Simnel and the Battle of Stoke/ Michael Bennett. New York: St. Martin's Press, 1987. vii, 157 p.
87-014666 942.05/1 0312012136
Simnel, Lambert. Stoke, Battle of, England, 1487. Impostors and imposture -- Great Britain -- Biography. Great Britain -- History -- Henry VII, 1485-1509.

DA332.E496
Elton, G. R.
Policy and police; the enforcement of the Reformation in the age of Thomas Cromwell [by] G. R. Elton. Cambridge [Eng.] University Press, 1972. xi, 446 p.
79-172831 942.05/2 0521083834
Cromwell, Thomas, -- Earl of Essex, -- 1485?-1540. Reformation -- England. Treason -- England. Great Britain -- Politics and government -- 1509-1547. England -- Church history -- 16th century.

DA332.E497 1977
Elton, G. R.
Reform and Reformation--England, 1509-1558/ G. R. Elton. Cambridge, Mass.: Harvard University Press, 1977. vi, 423 p.
77-006464 941.05/092/2 0674752457
Reformation -- England. Great Britain -- History -- Edward VI, 1547-1553. Great Britain -- History -- Mary I, 1553-1558. England -- Church history -- 16th century.

DA332.E74 1997
Erickson, Carolly,
Great Harry/ Carolly Erickson. New York: St. Martin's Press, 1997. p. cm.
97-022175 942.05.221 0312168586
Henry -- VIII, King of England, 1491-1547.

DA332.R48 1993
Rex, Richard.
Henry VIII and the English Reformation/ Richard Rex. New York: St. Martin's Press, 1993. ix, 205 p.
92-025105 942.05/2 0312086652
Henry -- VIII, -- King of England, -- 1491-1547. Reformation -- England. England -- Church history -- 16th century. Great Britain -- History -- Henry VIII, 1509-1547.

DA332.S25 1968b
Scarisbrick, J. J.
Henry VIII, by J. J. Scarisbrick. Berkeley, University of California Press, 1968. xiv, 561 p.
68-010995 942.05/2/0924
Henry -- VIII, -- King of England, -- 1491-1547. Great Britain -- History -- Henry VIII, 1509-1547. Great Britain -- Kings and rulers -- Biography.

DA332.W45 2001
Weir, Alison.
Henry VIII: the king and his court/ Alison Weir.1st American ed. New York: Ballantine Books, 2001. viii, 632 p. [16] p. of plates
2001-116042 942.05/2/092. 221 0345436598
Henry -- VIII, King of England, 1491-1547.

DA333.A2 W45 1991
Weir, Alison.
The six wives of Henry VIII/ Alison Weir.1st American ed. New York: Grove Weidenfeld, 1991. xii, 643 p.
91-029522 942.05/2/092. 220 0802114970
Henry -- VIII, King of England, 1491-1547--Marriage. Marriages of royalty and nobility--Great Britain--History--16th Queens--Great Britain--Biography. Wives--Great Britain--Biography.

DA333.A6.M3 1942
Mattingly, Garrett, 1900-1962.
Catherine of Aragon, by Garrett Mattingly. London, J. Cape [1942] 343 p.
42-020687 923.142
Catharine, -- of Aragon, Queen, consort of Henry VIII, King of England, -- 1485-1536. Queens -- Great Britain -- Biography. Great Britain -- History -- Henry VIII, 1509-1547 -- Biography.

DA333.B6.W37 1989
Warnicke, Retha M.
The rise and fall of Anne Boleyn: family politics at the court of Henry VIII/ Retha M. Warnicke. New York: Cambridge University Press, 1989. xi, 326 p.
88-037708 942.05/2/0924 0521370000
Anne Boleyn, -- Queen, consort of Henry VIII, King of England, -- 1507-1536. Queens -- Great Britain -- Biography. Great Britain -- Politics and government -- 1509-1547.

DA333.C54.W37 2000
Warnicke, Retha M.
The marrying of Anne of Cleves: royal protocol in early modern England/ Retha M. Warnicke. New York: Cambridge University Press, 2000. xiv, 343 p.
99-030163 392.5/086/210942 0521770378
Anne, -- of Cleves, Queen, consort of Henry VIII, King of England, -- 1515-1557 -- Marriage. Henry -- VIII, -- King of England, -- 1491-1547 -- Marriage. Marriage customs and rites -- England -- History -- 16th century. Marriages of royalty and nobility -- Great Britain -- History -- 16th century. Queens -- Great Britain -- Biography. Great Britain -- History -- Henry VIII, 1509-1547.

DA333.P3.J36 1999
James, Susan E., 1945-
Kateryn Parr: the making of a queen/ Susan E. James. Aldershot, Hants; Ashgate, 1999. x, 467 p.
98-043404 942.05/2/092 1840146834
Catharine Parr, -- Queen, consort of Henry VIII, King of England, -- 1512-1548. Queens -- Great Britain -- Biography. Great Britain -- History -- Henry VIII, 1509-1547 -- Biography.

DA334.A1.R52 1983
Ridley, Jasper Godwin.
Statesman and saint: Cardinal Wolsey, Sir Thomas More, and the politics of Henry VIII/ Jasper Ridley. New York: Viking Press, 1983, c1982. 338 p.
82-070122 942.05/2/0922 0670489050
Wolsey, Thomas, -- 1475?-1530. More, Thomas, -- Sir, Saint, -- 1478-1535. Statesmen -- Great Britain -- Biography. Cardinals -- England -- Biography. Christian martyrs -- England -- Biography. Great Britain -- History -- Henry VIII, 1509-1547. Great Britain -- Church history -- 16th century.

DA334.M8.A64 1998
Ackroyd, Peter, 1949-
The life of Thomas More/ Peter Ackroyd. New York: Nan A. Talese, 1998. x, 447 p.
98-024333 942.05/2/092 0385477090
More, Thomas, -- Sir, Saint, -- 1478-1535. Christian martyrs -- England -- Biography. Statesmen -- Great Britain -- Biography. Humanists -- England -- Biography. Great Britain -- Politics and government -- 1509-1547. Great Britain -- History -- Henry VIII, 1509-1547 -- Biography.

DA334.M8.G88 2000
Guy, J. A.
Thomas More/ John Guy. London: Arnold; 2000. xviii, 251 p.
00-711136 942.05/2/092 0340731389
More, Thomas, -- Sir, Saint, -- 1478-1535. Christian martyrs -- England -- Biography. Statesmen -- Great Britain -- Biography. Humanists -- England -- Biography. Great Britain -- Politics and government -- 1509-1547. Great Britain -- History -- Henry VIII, 1509-1547 -- Biography.

DA334.M8.M275 1984
Marius, Richard.
Thomas More: a biography/ Richard Marius. New York: Knopf: 1984. xxiv, 562 p.
84-047645 942.05/2/0924 0394459822
More, Thomas, -- Sir, Saint, -- 1478-1535. Statesmen -- Great Britain -- Biography. Christian martyrs -- England -- Biography. Humanists -- England -- Biography. Great Britain -- History -- Henry VIII, 1509-1547 -- Biography.

DA334.W8.C29 1991
Cardinal Wolsey: church, state, and art/ edited by S.J. Gunn and P.G. Lindley. Cambridge; Cambridge University Press, 1991. xvi, 329 p.
90-037890 942.05/2/092 0521375681
Wolsey, Thomas, -- 1475?-1530. Statesmen -- Great Britain -- Biography. Art patrons -- England -- Biography. Cardinals -- England -- Biography. Great Britain -- History -- Henry VIII, 1509-1547 -- Biography. Great Britain -- Politics and government -- 1509-1547. Great Britain -- Church history -- 16th century.

DA335.L5.L572 1983
The Lisle letters: an abridgement/ edited by Muriel St. Clare Byrne; selected and arranged by Bridget Boland; foreword by Hugh Trevor-Roper. Chicago: University of Chicago Press, 1983. xxvi, 436 p.
82-015914 942.05 0226088006
Lisle, Arthur Plantagenet, -- Viscount, -- 1480?-1542. Statesmen -- Great Britain -- Correspondence. England -- Social life and customs -- 16th century -- Sources.

DA337.H55 1988b
Hill, C. P.
Who's who in Stuart Britain/ C.P. Hill. Chicago, Ill.: St. James Press, c1988. xiv, 466 p.
90-063660   941.06/092/2   1558621326
Great Britain -- History -- Stuarts, 1603-1714 - - Biography -- Dictionaries.

DA339.B87 1996
Bush, M. L.
The pilgrimage of grace: a study of the rebel armies of October 1536/ Michael Bush. Manchester; Manchester University Press; 1996. xviii, 445 p.
95-001037   942.05/2   0719046963
Insurgency -- England, Northern -- History -- 16th century. Pilgrimage of Grace, 1536-1537. Great Britain -- History, Military -- 1485-1603. Great Britain -- History -- Henry VIII, 1509-1547.

DA340.L5794 1992
Loades, D. M.
The mid-Tudor crisis, 1545-1565/ David Loades. New York: St. Martin's Press, 1992. 215 p.
92-008291   942.05/3   031208370X
Tudor, House of.   Great Britain -- History -- Mary I, 1553-1558. Great Britain -- History -- Tudors, 1485-1603. Great Britain -- History -- Edward VI, 1547-1553.

DA345.J59
Jordan, W. K. 1902-
Edward VI: the threshold of power; the dominance of the Duke of Northumberland, by W. K. Jordan. London, Allen & Unwin [1970] 565 p.
78-556152   942.05/3   0049420836
Somerset, Edward Seymour, -- Duke of, -- 1506?-1552. Northumberland, John Dudley, -- Duke of, -- 1502-1553.   Great Britain -- History -- Edward VI, 1547-1553.

DA345.J6
Jordan, W. K. 1902-
Edward VI: the young King; the protectorship of the Duke of Somerset, by W. K. Jordan. London, Allen & Unwin, 1968. 544 p.
74-369313   942.05/3   0049420720
Somerset, Edward Seymour, -- Duke of, -- 1506?-1552.   Great Britain -- History -- Edward VI, 1547-1553.

DA345.L36 1977
Land, Stephen K.
Kett's rebellion: the Norfolk rising of 1549/ Stephen K. Land. Ipswich [Eng.]: Boydell Press; 1977. 165 p.
78-307172   942.05/3   087471995X
Kett's Rebellion, 1549.   Norfolk (England) -- History. Great Britain -- History -- Edward VI, 1547-1553.

DA345.1.N6.L63 1996
Loades, D. M.
John Dudley, Duke of Northumberland, 1504-1553/ David Loades. Oxford [England]: Clarendon Press; 1996. xi, 333 p.
97-108604   942.05/3/092   0198201931
Northumberland, John Dudley, -- Duke of, -- 1502-1553. Dudley family. Nobility -- Great Britain -- Biography. Statesmen -- Great Britain -- Biography.   Great Britain -- Politics and government -- 1485-1603.

DA347.E74 1998
Erickson, Carolly,
Bloody Mary/ Carolly Erickson. New York: St. Martin's Griffin, 1998. p. cm.
98-016069   942.05/4/092. 221   0312187068
Mary -- I,   Queen of England,   1516-1558. Queens--Great Britain--Biography.

DA347.L579 1989
Loades, D. M.
Mary Tudor: a life/ David Loades. Oxford, UK; Basil Blackwell, c1989 xiii, 410 p.
89-007163   942.05/4/092   0631154531
Mary -- I, -- Queen of England, -- 1516-1558. Queens -- Great Britain -- Biography.   Great Britain -- History -- Mary I, 1553-1558.

DA347.L58 1979
Loades, D. M.
The reign of Mary Tudor: politics, government, and religion in England, 1553-1558/ D. M. Loades. New York: St. Martin's Press, 1979. xii, 516 p.
79-016479   942.05/4/0924   031267029X
Mary -- I, -- Queen of England, -- 1516-1558. Tudor, House of.   England -- Church history -- 16th century. Great Britain -- Politics and government -- 1553-1558.

DA350.A25 2000
Elizabeth I, Queen of England, 1533-1603 1533-1603.
Elizabeth I: collected works/ edited by Leah S. Marcus, Janel Mueller, and Mary Beth Rose. Chicago: University of Chicago Press, 2000. p. cm.
99-028794   942.05/5/092   0226504646
Elizabeth -- I, -- Queen of England, -- 1533-1603 -- Correspondence.   Queens -- Great Britain -- Correspondence.   Great Britain -- History -- Elizabeth, 1558-1603 -- Sources.

DA350.A84 1988
Ashley, Leonard R. N.
Elizabethan popular culture/ Leonard R.N. Ashley. Bowling Green, Ohio: Bowling Green State University Popular Press, c1988. 316 p.
88-071063   942.05   0879724269
Popular culture -- England -- History -- 16th century -- Sources.   Great Britain -- History -- Elizabeth, 1558-1603 -- Sources. England -- Social life and customs -- 16th century -- Sources.

DA355.A84 1984
Ashton, Robert, 1924-
Reformation and revolution, 1558-1660/ Robert Ashton. London; Granada, 1984. xx, 503 p.
83-197192   942.05/5   0246106662
Great Britain -- History -- Elizabeth, 1558-1603. Great Britain -- History -- Stuarts, 1603-1714.

DA355.E74 1997
Erickson, Carolly,
The first Elizabeth/ Carolly Erickson. New York: St. Martin's Press, 1997. p. cm.
97-022176   942.05/5/092. 221   031216842X
Elizabeth -- I, Queen of England, 1533-1603. Queens--Great Britain--Biography.

DA355.J65 1993
Jones, Norman L. 1951-
The birth of the Elizabethan Age: England in the 1560s/ Norman Jones. Oxford, UK; B. Blackwell, 1993. xii, 300 p.
93-001116   942.05   063116796X
Great Britain -- History -- Elizabeth, 1558-1603. England -- Civilization -- 16th century.

DA355.L458 1994
Levin, Carole, 1948-
The heart and stomach of a king: Elizabeth I and the politics of sex and power/ Carole Levin. Philadelphia: University of Pennsylvania Press, c1994. x, 243 p.
94-007315   942.05/5/092   0812232526
Elizabeth -- I, -- Queen of England, -- 1533-1603. Sex role -- Political aspects -- Great Britain -- History -- 16th century. Queens -- Great Britain -- Biography. Power (Social sciences) Great Britain - - History -- Elizabeth, 1558-1603.

DA355.M25 1992
MacCaffrey, Wallace T.
Elizabeth I: war and politics, 1588-1603/ Volume III by Wallace T. MacCaffrey. Princeton, N.J.: Princeton University Press, 1992. xv, 592 p.
91-033656   942.05/5   0691031886
Elizabeth -- I, -- Queen of England, -- 1533-1603. Great Britain -- History, Military -- 1485-1603. Great Britain -- History -- Elizabeth, 1558-1603. Great Britain -- Politics and government -- 1558-1603.

DA355.M26
MacCaffrey, Wallace T.
Queen Elizabeth and the making of policy, 1572-1588/ Vol. II by Wallace T. MacCaffrey. Princeton, N.J.: Princeton University Press, 1981. 530 p.
80-008564   942.05/5   0691053243
Elizabeth -- I, -- Queen of England, -- 1533-1603. Great Britain -- Politics and government -- 1558-1603.

DA355.M27
MacCaffrey, Wallace T.
The shaping of the Elizabethan regime,/ Vol. I by Wallace MacCaffrey. Princeton, N.J., Princeton University Press, 1968. xiv, 501 p.
68-027409   942.05/5
Great Britain -- History -- Elizabeth, 1558-1603.

DA355.R53 1988
Ridley, Jasper Godwin.
Elizabeth I: the shrewdness of virtue/ Jasper Ridley. New York, N.Y.: Viking, 1988, c1987. 391 p.
87-040273   942.05/5/0924   0670815268
Elizabeth -- I, -- Queen of England, -- 1533-1603. Queens -- Great Britain -- Biography.   Great Britain -- History -- Elizabeth, 1558-1603.

DA355.R67 1955a
Rowse, A. L. 1903-
The expansion of Elizabethan England. London, Macmillan; 1955. xiii, 449 p.
56-000171   942.055
Great Britain -- Foreign relations -- 1558-1603. Great Britain -- Politics and government -- 1558-1603.

DA355.S8 1928b
Strachey, Lytton, 1880-1932.
Elizabeth and Essex, a tragic history by Lytton Strachey. New York, Harcourt, Brace and company [1928] 296 p.
28-026937
Elizabeth -- I, -- Queen of England, -- 1533-1603. Essex, Robert Devereux, -- Earl of, -- 1566-1601. Queens -- Great Britain -- Biography.   Great Britain -- Court and courtiers -- Biography. Great Britain -- History -- Elizabeth, 1558-1603.

DA355.W36 1998
Weir, Alison.
The life of Elizabeth I/ Alison Weir.1st American
ed. New York: Ballantine, 1998. 532 p.
98-034917 942.05/5/092. 221 0345405331
*Elizabeth -- I, Queen of England, 1533-1603.
Queens--Great Britain--Biography.*

DA355.W39
Wernham, R. B. 1906-
The making of Elizabethan foreign policy, 1558-
1603/ R. B. Wernham. Berkeley: University of
California Press, c1980. vii, 109 p.
80-010425 327.42 0520039661
*Great Britain -- Foreign relations -- 1485-
1603. Great Britain -- History -- Elizabeth, 1558-
1603.*

DA355.W4835 1995
Williams, Penry.
The later Tudors: England, 1547-1603/ Penry
Williams. Oxford: Clarendon Press; 1995. xxi,
606 p.
95-008886 942.05 0198228201
*Tudor, House of. Great Britain -- History --
Tudors, 1485-1603. England -- Civilization -- 16th
century. Great Britain -- History -- Elizabeth,
1558-1603.*

DA356.C3 1968
Campbell, Mildred, 1897-
The English yeoman under Elizabeth and the early
Stuarts, by Mildred Campbell. New York, A. M.
Kelley, 1968. xiii, 453 p.
68-004919 914.2/03/55
*Yeomanry (Social class) Country life -- England.
Agriculture -- England -- History. Great Britain --
Social life and customs -- 16th century. Great
Britain -- Social life and customs -- 17th century.*

DA356.C56 1999
Cole, Mary Hill, 1957-
The portable queen: Elizabeth I and the politics of
ceremony/ Mary Hill Cole. Amherst: University of
Massachusetts Press, c1999. x, 277 p.
99-027676 942.05/5/092 1558492143
*Elizabeth -- I, -- Queen of England, -- 1533-1603.
Rites and ceremonies -- England -- History -- 16th
century. Visits of state -- England -- History -- 16th
century. Royal visitors -- England -- History --
16th century. Great Britain -- Politics and
government -- 1558-1603. England -- Social life
and customs -- 16th century. Great Britain -- Court
and courtiers -- History -- 16th century.*

DA356.H37 1992
Hartley, T. E.
Elizabeth's parliaments: queen, lords, and
commons, 1559-1601/ T.E. Hartley. Manchester;
Manchester University Press: c1992. 184 p.
91-037905 942.05/5 0719032164
*Elizabeth -- I, -- Queen of England, -- 1533-1603.
Great Britain -- Politics and government -- 1558-
1603.*

DA356.R65 1951
Rowse, A. L. 1903-
The England of Elizabeth; the structure of society.
New York, Macmillan, 1951 [c1950] xv, 546 p.
51-004102 942.055
*Great Britain -- History -- Elizabeth, 1558-
1603.*

DA356.S8
Stone, Lawrence.
The crisis of the aristocracy, 1558-1641. Oxford,
Clarendon Press, 1979, c1965. xxiv, 841 p.
65-003206 914.2
*Upper class -- Great Britain. Nobility -- Great
Britain. Great Britain -- Civilization -- 16th cent.*

DA356.W47 1984
Wernham, R. B. 1906-
After the Armada: Elizabethan England and the
struggle for Western Europe, 1588-1595/ R.B.
Wernham. Oxford [Oxfordshire]: Clarendon Press;
1984. xxi, 613 p.
83-008281 940.2/32 0198227531
*Armada, 1588. Great Britain -- Politics and
government -- 1558-1603. Great Britain -- History
-- Elizabeth, 1558-1603. Great Britain -- Foreign
relations -- Europe.*

DA357.W34 1999
Wagner, J. A.
Historical dictionary of the Elizabethan world:
Britain, Ireland, Europe, and America/ by John A.
Wagner. Phoenix, Ariz.: Oryx Press, 1999. xxxix,
392 p.
99-031109 942.05/5/03 1573562009
*Great Britain -- History -- Elizabeth, 1558-
1603 -- Encyclopedias. America -- Discovery and
exploration -- English -- Encyclopedias. Ireland --
History -- 1558-1603 -- Encyclopedias.*

DA358.E8.H28 1999
Hammer, Paul E. J.
The polarisation of Elizabethan politics: the
political career of Robert Devereux, 2nd Earl of
Essex, 1585-1597/ Paul E.J. Hammer. Cambridge;
Cambridge University Press, 1999. xviii, 446 p.
98-035139 942.05/5/092 0521434858
*Essex, Robert Devereux, -- Earl of, -- 1566-1601.
Politicians -- Great Britain -- Biography. Great
Britain -- Politics and government -- 1558-1603.
Great Britain -- Court and courtiers -- Biography.
Great Britain -- History -- Elizabeth, 1558-1603 --
Biography.*

DA358.E8.L3
Lacey, Robert.
Robert, Earl of Essex. New York, Atheneum,
1971. xiii, 338 p.
70-139313 942.05/5/0924
*Essex, Robert Devereux, -- Earl of, -- 1566-1601.
Great Britain -- History -- Elizabeth, 1558-1603 --
Biography. Great Britain -- Court and courtiers --
Biography.*

DA358.S2.H35 1989
Haynes, Alan.
Robert Cecil, Earl of Salisbury, 1563-1612: servant
of two sovereigns/ Alan Haynes. London: P. Owen,
1989. 239 p.
89-051003 0720607167
*Salisbury, Robert Cecil, -- Earl of, -- 1563-1612.
Statesmen -- Great Britain -- Biography. Nobility -
- Great Britain -- Biography. Great Britain --
History -- Elizabeth, 1558-1603. Great Britain --
History -- James I, 1603-1625.*

DA358.S5.O8 1972
Osborn, James Marshall.
Young Philip Sidney, 1572-1577 [by] James M.
Osborn. New Haven, Published for the Elizabethan
Club [by] Yale Uni 1972. xxiv, 565 p.
77-151584 942.05/5/0924 0300014430
*Sidney, Philip, -- Sir, -- 1554-1586 -- Childhood
and youth. Poets, English -- Early modern, 1500-
1700 -- Biography. Great Britain -- Court and
courtiers -- Biography.*

DA358.W2.R42 1978
Read, Conyers, 1881-1959.
Mr. Secretary Walsingham and the policy of Queen
Elizabeth/ by Conyers Read. [New York: AMS
Press], 1978. 3 v.
75-041223 942.05/5/0922 0404134904
*Walsingham, Francis, -- Sir, -- 1530?-1590.
Elizabeth -- I, -- Queen of England, -- 1533-1603.
Great Britain -- Politics and government -- 1558-
1603.*

DA360.E54 1991
England, Spain, and the Gran Armada 1585-1604:
essays from the Anglo-Spanish conferences,
London and Madrid, 1988/ edited by M.J.
Rodriguez-Salgado and Simon Adams. Savage,
Md.: Barnes & Noble Books, 1990. xv, 308 p.
91-000506 942.05/5 0389209554
*Armada, 1588 -- Congresses. Spain -- History,
Naval -- 16th century -- Congresses. Spain --
History -- Philip II, 1556-1598 -- Congresses.
Great Britain -- History, Naval -- Tudors, 1485-
1603 -- Congresses.*

DA360.F43 1988
Fernandez-Armesto, Felipe.
The Spanish Armada: the experience of war in
1588/ Felipe Fernandez-Armesto. Oxford
[Oxfordshire]; Oxford University Press, 1988. x,
300 p.
87-022914 946/.04 0198229267
*Armada, 1588. Spain -- History -- Philip II,
1556-1598. Great Britain -- History, Naval --
Tudors, 1485-1603.*

DA360.M3
Mattingly, Garrett, 1900-1962.
The Armada. Boston, Houghton Mifflin, 1959.
443 p.
59-008861 942.055
*Armada, 1588. Spain -- History, Naval -- 16th
century. Spain -- History -- Philip II, 1556-1598.
Great Britain -- History -- Elizabeth, 1558-1603.*

DA360.R37 1993
Rasor, Eugene L., 1936-
The Spanish Armada of 1588: historiography and
annotated bibliography/ Eugene L. Rasor.
Westport, Conn.: Greenwood Press, 1993. xviii,
277 p.
92-031759 942.05/5 0313283036
*Armada, 1588 -- Historiography. Armada, 1588 -
- Bibliography. Great Britain -- History, Naval --
Tudors, 1485-1603 -- Bibliography. Spain --
History, Naval -- 16th century -- Historiography.
Spain -- History, Naval -- 16th century --
Bibliography.*

DA360.W37 1994
Wernham, R. B. 1906-
The return of the armadas: the last years of the
Elizabethan war against Spain, 1595-1603/ R.B.
Wernham. Oxford: Clarendon Press; 1994. xiv,
452 p.
93-024130 942.05/5 0198204434
*Great Britain -- History -- Elizabeth, 1558-
1603. Spain -- History, Naval -- 16th century.
Spain -- History, Naval -- 17th century.*

DA375.A8
Ashley, Maurice, 1907-
England in the seventeenth century. London;
Penguin Books, [1952]. 266 p.
53-005282
Great Britain -- History -- Stuarts, 1603-1714.

DA375.C74 1980
Coward, Barry.
The Stuart age: a history of England 1603-1714/ Barry Coward. London; Longman, 1980. xii, 493 p.
79-042887 941.06 0582482798
  Great Britain -- History -- Stuarts, 1603-1714. England -- Civilization -- 17th century.

DA375.H5
Hill, Christopher, 1912-
The century of revolution, 1603-1714. Edinburgh, T. Nelson [1961] 340 p.
61-066046 942.06
  Great Britain -- History -- Stuarts, 1603-1714.

DA375.H54 1985
Hill, Christopher, 1912-
The collected essays of Christopher Hill/ Christopher Hill. Amherst: University of Massachusetts Press, 1985-1986. 3 v.
84-016446 082 0870234676
  English literature -- Early modern, 1500-1700 -- History and criticism. Literature and society -- Great Britain. Great Britain -- History -- Stuarts, 1603-1714. Great Britain -- Intellectual life -- 17th century.

DA375.H57 1996
Historical dictionary of Stuart England, 1603-1689/ Ronald H. Fritze and William B. Robison, editors-in-chief; Walter Sutton, assistant editor. Westport, Conn.: Greenwood Press, 1996. xix, 611 p.
94-039244 941.06/03 0313283915
  Great Britain -- History -- Stuarts, 1603-1714 -- Dictionaries.

DA375.K4 1977
Kenyon, J. P. 1927-
The Stuarts: a study in English kingship/ [by] J. P. Kenyon. London: Severn House: [Distributed by Hutchinson], 1977. 223 p.
78-303149 941.06/092/2 0727800973
  Stuart, -- House of.   Great Britain -- History -- Stuarts, 1603-1714.

DA375.L35 1995
Lang, Timothy.
The Victorians and the Stuart heritage: interpretations of a discordant past/ Timothy Lang. Cambridge; Cambridge University Press, 1995. xiv, 233 p.
94-031974 941.06/072041 0521474647
  Historiography -- Great Britain -- History -- 19th century. Great Britain -- History -- Stuarts, 1603-1714 -- Historiography. Great Britain -- Intellectual life -- 19th century. Great Britain -- History -- Victoria, 1837-1901.

DA375.L48 1987
Levack, Brian P.
The formation of the British state: England, Scotland, and the Union, 1603-1707/ Brian P. Levack. Oxford [Oxfordshire]: Clarendon Press; 1987. viii, 260 p.
87-012299 941.06 0198201133
  Great Britain -- History -- Stuarts, 1603-1714. Scotland -- History -- Stuarts, to the Union, 1371-1707. England -- Foreign relations -- Scotland.

DA375.R6
Roberts, Clayton.
The growth of responsible government in Stuart England. Cambridge, Cambridge U.P., 1966. xii, 467 p.
66-011033 320.942
  Ministerial responsibility -- Great Britain. Great Britain -- Politics and government -- 1603-1714. Great Britain -- Constitutional history.

DA375.S39 2000
Scott, Jonathan, 1958-
England's troubles: seventeenth-century English political instability in European context/ Jonathan Scott. Cambridge, UK; Cambridge University Press, 2000. xii, 546 p.
99-038436 941.06 0521411920
  Great Britain -- Politics and government -- 1603-1714. Great Britain -- Politics and government -- 1642-1660. England -- Civilization -- European influences.

DA375.S55 2000
Sharpe, Kevin
Reading revolutions: the politics of reading in early modern England/ Kevin Sharpe. New Haven, CT: Yale University Press, c2000. xiv, 358 p.
99-089405 941.06/3 0300081529
  Politics and literature -- Great Britain -- History -- 17th century. Books and reading -- Great Britain -- History -- 17th century. Books and reading -- Political aspects -- Great Britain. Great Britain -- History -- Puritan Revolution, 1642-1660. Great Britain -- Politics and government -- 1603-1714.

DA375.T7 1949
Trevelyan, George Macaulay, 1876-1962.
England under the Stuarts. New York, Putnam, 1949. xiii, 466 p.
50-014448
  Great Britain -- History -- Stuarts, 1603-1714.

DA378.B3.C6 1963
Coleman, D. C. 1920-
Sir John Banks, baronet and businessman; a study of business, politics, and society in later Stuart England. Oxford, Clarendon Press, 1963. ix, 215 p.
63-024910 923.342
  Banks, John, -- Sir, bart., -- 1627-1699.

DA380.H47
Hill, Christopher, 1912-
Change and continuity in seventeenth-century England/ Christopher Hill. London: Weidenfeld and Nicolson, [1974] xiv, 370 p.
75-305460 941.06 0297768220
  England -- Civilization -- 17th century. Great Britain -- History -- Stuarts, 1603-1714.

DA380.H48
Hill, Christopher, 1912-
Intellectual origins of the English revolution. Oxford, Clarendon Press, 1965. ix, 333 p.
65-003182 942.06
  Great Britain -- History -- Puritan Revolution, 1642-1660. Great Britain -- Intellectual life -- 17th century.

DA380.H5
Hill, Christopher.
Puritanism and revolution; studies in interpretation of the English Revolution of the 17th century. London, Secker & Warburg, 1958. 402 p.
59-000890 942.062
  Great Britain -- Social conditions. Great Britain -- History -- Puritan Revolution, 1642-1660.

DA380.H52 1964
Hill, Christopher, 1912-
Society and Puritanism in pre-Revolutionary England. New York, Schocken Books [1964] 520 p.
64-013350 942.062
  Puritans -- Great Britain.   Great Britain -- History -- Civil War, 1642-1649 -- Causes. Great Britain -- Social conditions.

DA380.S53 1983
Shapiro, Barbara J.
Probability and certainty in seventeenth-century England: a study of the relationships between natural science, religion, history, law, and literature/ Barbara J. Shapiro. Princeton, N.J.: Princeton University Press, c1983. x, 347 p.
82-061385 001.2 0691053790
  Knowledge, Theory of -- History -- 17th century. England -- Intellectual life -- 17th century.

DA380.S93 2001
Swann, Marjorie.
Curiosities and texts: the culture of collecting in early modern England/ Marjorie Swann. Philadelphia: University of Pennsylvania Press, c2001. p. cm.
01-027021 942.06 0812236106
  Collectors and collecting -- England -- History -- 17th century. English literature -- Early modern, 1500-1700 -- History and criticism. Curiosities and wonders -- England -- History -- 17th century. England -- Civilization -- 17th century.

DA390.D3 1959
Davies, Godfrey, 1892-1957.
The early Stuarts: 1603-1660. Oxford: Clarendon Press, 1959. xxii, 458 p.
59-001862 942.06
  Great Britain -- History -- James I, 1603-1625. Great Britain -- History -- Charles I, 1625-1649. Great Britain -- History -- Commonwealth and Protectorate, 1649-1660.

DA390.E8
Eusden, John Dykstra.
Puritans, lawyers, and politics in early seventeenth-century England. New Haven, Yale University Press, 1958. xii, 238 p.
58-005457 942.06
  Puritans. Church and state in Great Britain. Common law -- History.

DA390.H57 1986
Hirst, Derek.
Authority and conflict: England, 1603-1658/ Derek Hirst. Cambridge, Mass.: Harvard University Press, 1986. viii, 390 p.
85-024957 941.06 0674052900
  Great Britain -- History -- Early Stuarts, 1603-1649. Great Britain -- History -- Commonwealth and Protectorate, 1649-1660. England -- Social conditions -- 17th century.

DA390.P43 1990
Peck, Linda Levy.
Court patronage and corruption in early Stuart England/ Linda Levy Peck. Boston; Unwin Hyman, 1990. xii, 319 p.
90-012481 306.2/0941/09032 0049421956
  Patronage, Political -- Great Britain -- History -- 17th century. Political corruption -- Great Britain -- History -- 17th century. Great Britain -- Politics and government -- 1603-1649. Great Britain -- Court and courtiers -- History -- 17th century. England -- Social conditions -- 17th century.

DA390.W37 1991
War and government in Britain: 1598-1650/ Mark Charles Fissel editor. Manchester; Manchester University Press; c1991. ix, 293 p.
90-021943 941.06/1 0719028876
  Great Britain -- Politics and government -- 1603-1649. Great Britain -- Politics and government -- 1558-1603. Great Britain -- History, Military -- 1603-1714.

DA391.A4
Akrigg, G. P. V.
Jacobean pageant; or, The court of King James I. Cambridge, Harvard University Press, 1962. xi, 431 p.
62-005508 942.061
Great Britain -- History -- James I, 1603-1625. Great Britain -- Court and courtiers -- History -- 17th century.

DA391.B46 1999
Bergeron, David Moore.
King James & letters of homoerotic desire/ David M. Bergeron. Iowa City: University of Iowa Press, c1999. viii, 251 p.
98-048368 941.06/1/092 0877456690
James -- I, -- King of England, -- 1566-1625 -- Correspondence. James -- I, -- King of England, -- 1566-1625 -- Sexual behavior. Homosexuality, Male -- Scotland -- History -- 16th century -- Sources. Homosexuality, Male -- Great Britain -- History -- 17th century -- Sources. Letter writing -- Great Britain -- History -- 17th century. Great Britain -- Kings and rulers -- Correspondence.

DA391.B47 1991
Bergeron, David Moore.
Royal family, royal lovers: King James of England and Scotland/ David M. Bergeron. Columbia: University of Missouri Press, c1991. x, 222 p.
91-009282 941.06/1/092 0826207839
James -- I, -- King of England, -- 1566-1625. Stuart, House of. Scotland -- History -- James VI, 1567-1625. Great Britain -- Kings and rulers -- Biography. Scotland -- Kings and rulers -- Biography.

DA391.J35 1984
James I, King of England, 1566-1625 1566-1625.
Letters of King James VI & I/ edited, with an introduction, by G.P.V. Akrigg. Berkeley: University of California Press, c1984. xxii, 546 p.
82-020135 941.06/1/0924 0520047079
James -- I, -- King of England, -- 1566-1625. Great Britain -- History -- James I, 1603-1625 -- Sources. Scotland -- History -- James VI, 1567-1625 -- Sources. Great Britain -- Kings and rulers -- Correspondence.

DA391.L43 1990
Lee, Maurice.
Great Britain's Solomon: James VI and I in his three kingdoms/ Maurice Lee, Jr. Urbana: University of Illinois Press, c1990. xvi, 332 p.
89-020143 941.06/1/092 0252016866
James -- I, -- King of England, -- 1566-1625. Great Britain -- History -- James I, 1603-1625. Great Britain -- Kings and rulers -- Biography.

DA391.Y68 2000
Young, Michael B.
King James and the history of homosexuality/ Michael B. Young. New York: New York University Press, 2000. ix, 221 p.
99-025169 941.06/1/092 0814796931
James -- I, -- King of England, -- 1566-1625 -- Sexual behavior. Homosexuality, Male -- Great Britain -- History -- 16th century. Homosexuality, Male -- Great Britain -- History -- 17th century. Homosexuality, Male -- Scotland -- History. Great Britain -- History -- James I, 1603-1625. Scotland -- History -- James VI, 1567-1625. Great Britain -- Kings and rulers -- Biography.

DA391.1.B9.L63 1981
Lockyer, Roger.
Buckingham, the life and political career of George Villiers, first Duke of Buckingham, 1592-1628/ by Roger Lockyer. London; Longman, 1981. xix, 506 p.
80-040578 942.06/2/0924 0582502969
Buckingham, George Villiers, -- Duke of, -- 1592-1628. Politicians -- Great Britain -- Biography. Great Britain -- Politics and government -- 1603-1649. Great Britain -- Court and courtiers -- Biography.

DA391.1.S3.R33 1998
Rabb, Theodore K.
Jacobean gentleman: Sir Edwin Sandys, 1561-1629/ Theodore K. Rabb. Princeton, N.J.: Princeton University Press, c1998. xii, 412 p.
97-044316 941.06/1/092 0691026947
Sandys, Edwin, -- Sir, -- 1561-1629. Legislators -- Great Britain -- Biography. Great Britain -- History -- James I, 1603-1625 -- Biography. Great Britain -- Politics and government -- 1603-1625.

DA392.N53 1991
Nicholls, Mark, 1959-
Investigating Gunpowder plot/ Mark Nicholls. Manchester [England]; Manchester University Press: 1991. vii, 254 p.
90-020286 941.06/1 0719032253
Gunpowder Plot, 1605. Great Britain -- History -- James I, 1603-1625.

DA395.C66 1987
Cope, Esther S.
Politics without parliaments, 1629-1640/ Esther S. Cope. London; Allen & Unwin, 1987. xiii, 252 p.
86-010935 941.06/3 0049410202
Great Britain -- Politics and government -- 1625-1649.

DA395.R87 1991
Russell, Conrad.
The fall of the British monarchies, 1637-1642/ Conrad Russell. Oxford: Clarendon Press; 1991. xix, 550 p.
90-041302 941.06/2 019822754X
Charles -- I, -- King of England, -- 1600-1649. Monarchy -- Great Britain -- History -- 17th century. Scotland -- Politics and government -- 1625-1649. Great Britain -- Politics and government -- 1625-1649. Ireland -- Politics and government -- 17th century.

DA395.Z3 1970
Zagorin, Perez.
The court and the country; the beginning of the English Revolution. New York, Atheneum, 1970 [c1969] xiv, 366 p.
72-104129 320.9/42
Great Britain -- History -- Charles I, 1625-1649. Great Britain -- Social conditions -- 17th century.

DA396.A2.A84 1987
Ashley, Maurice, 1907-
Charles I and Oliver Cromwell: a study in contrasts and comparisons/ Maurice Ashley. London; Methuen, 1987. 243 p.
87-207169 941.06/2/092 0413162702
Charles -- I, -- King of England, -- 1600-1649. Cromwell, Oliver, -- 1599-1658. Heads of state -- Great Britain -- Biography. Generals -- Great Britain -- Biography. Great Britain -- History -- Stuarts, 1603-1714 -- Biography. Great Britain -- Kings and rulers -- Biography.

DA396.A2.R28 1989
Reeve, L. J.
Charles I and the road to personal rule/ L.J. Reeve. Cambridge [England]; Cambridge University Press, 1989. xi, 325 p.
89-000723 941.06/2/0924 0521361842
Charles -- I, -- King of England, -- 1600-1649. Great Britain -- Politics and government -- 1625-1649.

DA396.A2.S48 1992
Sharpe, Kevin
The personal rule of Charles I/ Kevin Sharpe. New Haven: Yale University Press, 1992. xxiii, 983 p.
92-016271 941.06/2 0300056885
Charles -- I, -- King of England, -- 1600-1649. Great Britain -- Politics and government -- 1625-1649.

DA396.L3.C37 1987
Carlton, Charles, 1941-
Archbishop William Laud/ Charles Carlton. London; Routledge & Kegan Paul, 1987. x, 272 p.
87-023322 283/.092/4 0710204639
Laud, William, -- 1573-1645. Statesmen -- Great Britain -- Biography. Great Britain -- History -- Charles I, 1625-1649. Great Britain -- Church history -- 17th century.

DA396.S8.W4 1970
Wedgwood, C. V. 1910-
Strafford, 1593-1641, by C. V. Wedgwood. Westport, Conn., Greenwood Press [1970] 366 p.
76-110882 942.06/2/0924 083714566X
Strafford, Thomas Wentworth -- 1st Earl of, -- 1593-1641. Statesmen -- Great Britain -- Biography. Trials (Treason) -- Great Britain. Ireland -- Politics and government -- 17th century. Great Britain -- History -- Charles I, 1625-1649 -- Biography. Great Britain -- Politics and government -- 1603-1649.

DA397.D43 1970
D'Ewes, Simonds, 1602-1650.
The journal of Sir Simonds D'Ewes; from the first recess of the Long Parliament to the withdrawal of King Charles from London. Edited by Willson Havelock Coates. [Hamden, Conn.] Archon Books, 1970 [c1942] xliv, 459 p.
71-122400 942.06/2/0924 0208009485
Great Britain -- Politics and government -- 1625-1649.

DA400.C6125
Clarendon, Edward Hyde, 1609-1674.
Selections from The history of the Rebellion and Civil Wars, and The life, by himself. Edited by G. Huehns. London, Oxford University Press [1955] xlv, 492 p.
55-001428 942.062
Great Britain -- History -- Puritan Revolution, 1642-1660. Great Britain -- History -- Charles II, 1660-1685.

DA400.H3 1964
Haller, William, b. 1885.
The Leveller tracts, 1647-1653. Edited by William Haller and Godfrey Davies. Gloucester, Mass., P. Smith, 1964 [c1944] vi, 481 p.
64-004072 942.063
Lilburne, John, -- 1614?-1657. Levellers. Great Britain -- History -- Puritan Revolution, 1642-1660 -- Sources. Great Britain -- Politics and government -- 1642-1660.

DA400.H63.K73 1990
Kraynak, Robert P., 1949-
History and modernity in the thought of Thomas Hobbes/ Robert P. Kraynak. Ithaca, N.Y.: Cornell University Press, 1990. vii, 224 p.
90-036301   941.06/2   0801424275
Hobbes, Thomas, -- 1588-1679. -- Behemoth. Hobbes, Thomas, -- 1588-1679 -- Views on modern history. Historiography -- Great Britain -- History -- 17th century. Great Britain -- History -- Civil War, 1642-1649 -- Historiography. Great Britain -- History -- Puritan Revolution, 1642-1660 -- Historiography.

DA403.M33 1996
MacLachlan, Alastair.
The rise and fall of revolutionary England: an essay on the fabrication of seventeenth-century history/ Alastair MacLachlan. New York: St. Martin's Press, 1996. viii, 431 p.
95-031667   941.06   031212841X
England -- Civilization -- 17th century -- Historiography. Great Britain -- History -- Stuarts, 1603-1714 -- Historiography. Great Britain -- History -- Puritan Revolution, 1642-1660 -- Historiography.

DA403.R53 1977b
Richardson, R. C.
The debate on the English Revolution/ R. C. Richardson. New York: St. Martin's Press, 1977. xi, 195 p.
77-073803   941.06/07/2   0312188900
Great Britain -- History -- Puritan Revolution, 1642-1660 -- Historiography.

DA405.B343 2000
Bennett, Martyn.
The civil wars experienced: Britain and Ireland, 1638-1661/ Martyn Bennett. London; Routledge, 2000. xxvi, 277 p.
99-033248   941.06   0415159016
Great Britain -- History -- Puritan Revolution, 1642-1660. Great Britain -- History -- Civil War, 1642-1649. Great Britain -- History -- Charles I, 1625-1649.

DA405.B344 2000
Bennett, Martyn.
Historical dictionary of the British and Irish Civil Wars, 1637-1660/ Martyn Bennett. Lanham, Md.: Scarecrow Press, 2000. xxi, 253 p.
99-026024   941.06/2   0810836610
Great Britain -- History -- Puritan Revolution, 1642-1660 -- Dictionaries. Great Britain -- History -- Charles I, 1625-1649 -- Dictionaries. Ireland -- History -- 1649-1660 -- Dictionaries.

DA405.C58 1998
The civil wars: a military history of England, Scotland, and Ireland 1638-1660/ edited by John Kenyon and Jane Ohlmeyer; consultant editor, John Morrill. Oxford; Oxford University Press, 1998. xxiv, 391 p.
98-019829   941.06   019866222X
Great Britain -- History -- Puritan Revolution, 1642-1660. Great Britain -- History -- Civil War, 1642-1649. Great Britain -- History, Military -- 1603-1714.

DA405.F7
Frank, Joseph, 1916-
The Levellers; a history of the writings of three seventeenth-century social democrats: John Lilburne, Richard Overton, William Walwyn. Cambridge, Harvard University Press, 1955. viii, 345 p.
55-010971   942.062
Lilburne, John, -- 1614?-1657. Walwyn, William, -- 1600-1681. Overton, Richard, -- fl. 1646. Levellers.

DA405.G46 1991
Gentles, I. J.
The new model army in England, Ireland, and Scotland, 1645-1653/ Ian Gentles. Oxford, UK; Blackwell, 1992. xi, 584 p.
90-028320   941.06/2   0631158693
Great Britain -- History, Military -- 1603-1714. Great Britain -- History -- Puritan Revolution, 1642-1660.

DA405.H49 1984
Hill, Christopher, 1912-
The experience of defeat: Milton and some contemporaries/ Christopher Hill. N.Y., N.Y.: Viking, 1984. 342 p.
83-040211   941.06   0670302082
Milton, John, -- 1608-1674 -- Political and social views. Religious thought -- England. Religious thought -- 17th century. England -- Intellectual life -- 17th century. Great Britain -- History -- Puritan Revolution, 1642-1660 -- Influence.

DA405.W42 vol. 1
Wedgwood, C. V. 1910-
The King's peace, 1637-1641.   New York, Macmillan, 1955. 510 p.
55-003603   942.062
Great Britain -- History -- Charles I, 1625-1649.

DA405.W42 vol. 2
Wedgwood, C. V. 1910-
King's war: 1641-1647/ Macmillan, 1959. 702 p.
59-007446
Great Britain -- History -- Civil War, 1642-1649.

DA407.A1.A8
Ashley, Maurice, 1907-
Cromwell's generals. London, Cape [1954] 256 p.
54-001644   942.064
Cromwell, Oliver, -- 1599-1658 -- Military leadership. Generals -- Great Britain. Great Britain -- History -- Commonwealth and Protectorate, 1649-1660. Great Britain -- History, Military -- 17th century.

DA407.S5.H3
Haley, Kenneth Harold Dobson.
The first Earl of Shaftesbury, by K. H. D. Haley. Oxford, Clarendon P., 1968. xii, 767 p.
68-111124   942.06/6/0924   0198213697
Shaftesbury, Anthony Ashley Cooper, -- Earl of, -- 1621-1683.

DA407.S6.S43 1988
Scott, Jonathan, 1958-
Algernon Sidney and the English republic, 1623-1677/ Jonathan Scott. Cambridge [Cambridgeshire]; Cambridge University Press, 1988. xii, 258 p.
87-033391   941.06/6/0924   0521352908
Sidney, Algernon, -- 1622-1683. Politicians -- Great Britain -- Biography. Political scientists -- Great Britain -- Biography. Great Britain -- History -- Puritan Revolution, 1642-1660. Great Britain -- History -- Charles II, 1660-1685. Great Britain -- Politics and government -- 1603-1714.

DA407.W35.A2 1989
Walwyn, William, b. 1600.
The writings of William Walwyn/ edited by Jack R. McMichael and Barbara Taft; foreword by Christopher Hill. Athens: University of Georgia Press, c1989. xvi, 584 p.
87-018162   941.06   0820310174
Levellers. Medicine -- Great Britain -- History -- 17th century -- Sources. Great Britain -- Politics and government -- 1642-1660 -- Sources. Great Britain -- Church history -- 17th century -- Sources.

DA413.F85 1997
Fukuda, Arihiro.
Sovereignty and the sword: Harrington, Hobbes, and mixed government in the English civil wars/ Arihiro Fukuda. Oxford; Clarendon Press, 1997. xii, 175 p.
97-000429   941.06/2   0198206836
Harrington, James, -- 1611-1677. -- Commonwealth of Oceana. Hobbes, Thomas, -- 1588-1679. -- Leviathan. Political science -- Great Britain -- History -- 17th century. Great Britain -- History -- Civil War, 1642-1649 -- Historiography. Great Britain -- Politics and government -- 1642-1649 -- Historiography.

DA415.A79 1994
Ashton, Robert, 1924-
Counter-revolution: the second civil war and its origins, 1646-8/ Robert Ashton. New Haven, Conn.: Yale University Press, 1994. xxi, 520 p.
94-019546   941.06/2   0300061145
Counterrevolutionaries -- Great Britain -- History -- 17th century. Great Britain -- History -- Civil War, 1642-1649.

DA415.B35 1997
Bennett, Martyn.
The civil wars in Britain and Ireland, 1638-1651/ Martyn Bennett. Oxford, UK; Blackwell Publishers, 1997. xiii, 446 p.
95-038662   941.06/2   0631191542
Great Britain -- History -- Civil War, 1642-1649. Great Britain -- History -- Commonwealth and Protectorate, 1649-1660. Ireland -- History -- 1625-1649.

DA415.C3 1992
Carlton, Charles, 1941-
Going to the wars: the experience of the British civil wars, 1638-1651/ Charles Carlton. London; Routledge, 1992. xii, 428 p.
92-000295   941.06   0415032822
Great Britain -- History -- Civil War, 1642-1649. Great Britain -- History -- Charles I, 1625-1649. Great Britain -- History -- Commonwealth and Protectorate, 1649-1660.

DA415.H53 1993
Hibbert, Christopher, 1924-
Cavaliers & roundheads: the English Civil War, 1642-1649/ Christopher Hibbert. New York: C. Scribner's Sons, c1993. xiv, 337 p.
92-042669   941.06/2   0684195577
Royalists -- Great Britain -- History -- 17th century. Roundheads. Great Britain -- History -- Civil War, 1642-1649.

DA415.K44 2000
Kennedy, D. E., 1928-
The English Revolution, 1642-1649/ D.E. Kennedy. New York: St. Martin's Press, 2000. p. cm.
99-055928   942.06/2   031223063X
Great Britain -- History -- Civil War, 1642-1649.

DA415.K45 1988
Kenyon, J. P. 1927-
The civil wars of England/ by J.P. Kenyon. New York: Knopf, 1988. viii, 272 p.
87-046108 941.06/2 0394552598
Great Britain -- History -- Civil War, 1642-1649.

DA415.L48 1997
Lindley, Keith.
Popular politics and religion in Civil War London/ Keith Lindley. Aldershot, England: Scolar Press; c1997. xiii, 442 p.
96-034695 941.06/2 1859283438
Popular culture -- England -- London -- History - 17th century. Populism -- England -- London -- History -- 17th century. Religious thought -- England -- London. London (England) -- Politics and government. London (England) -- History -- 17th century. Great Britain -- History -- Civil War, 1642-1649.

DA415.R78 1990
Russell, Conrad.
The causes of the English Civil War/ Conrad Russell. Oxford: Clarendon Press; c1990. xv, 236 p.
90-030543 941.06/2 0198221428
Great Britain -- History -- Civil War, 1642-1649 -- Causes.

DA415.S26 1989
Sanderson, John
"But the people's creatures": the philosophical basis of the English Civil War/ John Sanderson. Manchester; Manchester University Press; c1989. viii, 240 p.
88-008519 941.06/2 0719027659
Political science -- Great Britain -- Philosophy -- History -- 17th century. Philosophy, English -- 17th century. Great Britain -- History -- Civil War, 1642-1649 -- Causes. Great Britain -- Politics and government -- 1642-1649.

DA415.S62 1994
Smith, David L. 1963-
Constitutional royalism and the search for settlement, c. 1640-1649/ David L. Smith. Cambridge; Cambridge University Press, 1994. xvi, 371 p.
93-034969 941.06/2 0521410568
Monarchy -- Great Britain -- History -- 17th century. Constitutional history -- Great Britain. Great Britain -- Politics and government -- 1642-1649. Great Britain -- Politics and government -- 1625-1649.

DA415.W63 1987
Woolrych, Austin, 1918-
Soldiers and statesmen: the General Council of the Army and its debates, 1647-1648/ Austin Woolrych. Oxford: Clarendon Press; 1987. xi, 361 p.
86-031209 941.06/2 0198227523
Great Britain -- Politics and government -- 1642-1649.

DA425.B8 1997
Britnell, R. H.
The closing of the Middle Ages?: England, 1471-1529/ Richard Britnell. Oxford; Blackwell, 1997. viii, 286 p.
96-051565 942.04 0631165983
Middle Ages. Great Britain -- History -- Henry VIII, 1509-1547. Great Britain -- History -- Henry VII, 1485-1509. England -- Civilization.

DA425.C24 1989
Capp, B. S.
Cromwell's navy: the fleet and the English Revolution, 1648-1660/ Bernard Capp. Oxford [England]: Clarendon Press; 1989. xii, 420 p.
88-038180 941.06/3 019820115X
Cromwell, Oliver, -- 1599-1658. Great Britain -- History -- Commonwealth and Protectorate, 1649-1660. Great Britain -- History -- Puritan Revolution, 1642-1660. Great Britain -- History, Naval -- Stuarts, 1603-1714.

DA425.D39 1969
Davies, Godfrey, 1892-1957.
The restoration of Charles II, 1658-1660. London, Oxford U.P., 1969. viii, 383 p.
73-413014 942.06/5
Charles -- II, -- King of England, -- 1630-1685. Great Britain -- History -- Commonwealth and Protectorate 1649-1660.

DA425.P56 1996
Pincus, Steven C. A.
Protestantism and patriotism: ideologies and the making of English foreign policy, 1650-1668/ Steven C.A. Pincus. Cambridge [England]; Cambridge University Press, 1996. xii, 506 p.
95-007666 327.41 0521434874
Christianity and politics -- Protestant churches -- History -- 17th century. Protestant churches -- England -- History -- 17th century. Patriotism -- England -- History -- 17th century. Great Britain -- Foreign relations -- 1649-1660. Great Britain -- Foreign relations -- 1660-1688.

DA425.V46 1995
Venning, Timothy.
Cromwellian foreign policy/ Timothy Venning. New York: St. Martin's Press, 1995. xiv, 324 p.
94-034686 327.41 0333633881
Cromwell, Oliver, -- 1599-1658. Great Britain -- Foreign relations -- 1649-1660.

DA425.W59 1982
Woolrych, Austin, 1918-
Commonwealth to protectorate/ by Austin Woolrych. Oxford: Clarendon Press; 1982. xii, 446 p.
82-167677 941.06/3 0198226594
Great Britain -- Politics and government -- 1649-1660.

DA426.A78 1958
Ashley, Maurice, 1907-
Oliver Cromwell and the Puritan Revolution, by Maurice Ashley. London, English Universities Press [1958] 192 p.
70-018565 942.06/4/0924
Cromwell, Oliver, -- 1599-1658. Great Britain -- History -- Puritan Revolution, 1642-1660.

DA426.G38 1996
Gaunt, Peter.
Oliver Cromwell/ Peter Gaunt. Oxford [England]; Blackwell Publishers with the Historical Associa 1996. viii, 263 p.
95-020324 941.06/4/092 0631183566
Cromwell, Oliver, -- 1599-1658. Heads of state -- Great Britain -- Biography. Generals -- Great Britain -- Biography. Great Britain -- History -- Puritan Revolution, 1642-1660 -- Biography.

DA426.H49 1970b
Hill, Christopher, 1912-
God's Englishman; Oliver Cromwell and the English Revolution [by] Christopher Hill. New York, Dial Press, 1970. 324 p.
75-111450 942.06/4/0924
Cromwell, Oliver, -- 1599-1658. Great Britain -- History -- Puritan Revolution, 1642-1660.

DA426.W4
Wedgwood, C. V. 1910-
Oliver Cromwell. New York, Macmillan [1956] 144 p.
57-005972
Cromwell, Oliver, -- 1599-1658. -- cn   Great Britain -- History -- Puritan Revolution, 1642-1660. -- cm

DA427.K66 2000
Knoppers, Laura Lunger.
Constructing Cromwell: ceremony, portrait, and print, 1645-1661/ Laura Lunger Knoppers. Cambridge, U.K.; Cambridge University Press, 2000. xiii, 249 p.
99-016228 941.06/4/092 0521662613
Cromwell, Oliver, -- 1599-1658 -- Public opinion. Cromwell, Oliver, -- 1599-1658 -- In literature. Cromwell, Oliver, -- 1599-1658 -- Portraits. Political satire, English -- History and criticism. Heads of state -- Public opinion -- Great Britain. English literature -- Early modern, 1500-1700 -- History and criticism. Great Britain -- History -- Restoration, 1660-1688. Great Britain -- History -- Commonwealth and Protectorate, 1649-1660 -- Historiography.

DA435.B53 1991
Black, Jeremy.
A system of ambition?: British foreign policy, 1660-1793/ Jeremy Black. London; Longman, 1991. xiv, 279 p.
90-042971 327.41 0582080142
Great Britain -- Foreign relations -- 1660-1714. Great Britain -- Foreign relations -- 1714-1837.

DA435.J66
Jones, J. R. 1925-
Country and court: England, 1658-1714/ J. R. Jones. Cambridge, Mass.: Harvard University Press, 1978. 377 p.
78-005362 942.06 0674175255
Great Britain -- History -- Commonwealth and Protectorate, 1649-1660. Great Britain -- History -- 1660-1714.

DA435.M14 1953
Macaulay, Thomas Babington Macaulay, 1800-1859.
History of England from the accession of James II. Introd. by Douglas Jerrold. London, Dent; 4 v.
53-011664 942.067
Great Britain -- History -- William and Mary, 1689-1702. Great Britain -- History -- James II, 1685-1688.

DA435.W37 2000
Weil, Rachel Judith.
Political passions: gender, the family, and political argument in England, 1680-1714/ Rachel Weil. New York: Manchester University Press, 2000. p. cm.
00-020196 941.06 0719056225
Women in politics -- Great Britain -- History -- 17th century. Women in politics -- Great Britain -- History -- 18th century. Family -- Great Britain -- History -- 17th century. Great Britain -- Politics and government -- 1660-1714.

DA435.Z66 1999
Zook, Melinda S.
Radical Whigs and conspiratorial politics in late Stuart England/ Melinda S. Zook. University Park: Pennsylvania State University Press, c1999. xxi, 234 p.
98-041057   320.942/09/032   0271018569
Political science -- England -- History -- 17th century. Conspiracies -- England -- History -- 17th century. Radicalism -- England -- History -- 17th century. Great Britain -- History -- Revolution of 1688 -- Causes. Great Britain -- Politics and government -- 1660-1688. Great Britain -- Kings and rulers -- Succession.

DA437.W4.F87 1998
Furdell, Elizabeth Lane.
James Welwood: physician to the Glorious Revolution/ Elizabeth Lane Furdell. Conshohocken, PA: Combined Pub., c1998. 288 p.
00-708604   941.06/092   1580970052
Welwood, James, -- 1652-1727. Pamphleteers -- Great Britain -- Biography. Physicians -- Great Britain -- Biography. Great Britain -- History -- George I, 1714-1727 -- Biography. Great Britain -- History -- Revolution of 1688 -- Historiography. Great Britain -- History -- 1660-1714 -- Biography.

DA445.H24 1987
Harris, Tim, 1958-
London crowds in the reign of Charles II: propaganda and politics from the Restoration until the exclusion crisis/ Tim Harris. Cambridge [Cambridgeshire]; Cambridge University Press, 1987. xiv, 264 p.
87-014651   941/.06/6   0521326230
Propaganda, British -- History -- 17th century. Crowds. Political participation -- England -- London -- History -- 17th century. Great Britain -- History -- Charles II, 1660-1685. Great Britain -- Politics and government -- 1660-1688. London (England) -- History -- 17th century.

DA445.O5 1979
Ogg, David, 1887-1965.
England in the reign of Charles II/ by David Ogg. Westport, Conn.: Greenwood Press, 1979, c1955. 2 v.
78-011572   942.06/6   0313210381
Great Britain -- History -- Charles II, 1660-1685.

DA445.S42 1989
Seaward, Paul.
The Cavalier Parliament and the reconstruction of the Old Regime, 1661-1667/ Paul Seaward. Cambridge [England]; Cambridge University Press, 1989. xii, 359 p.
88-015603   941.06/6   0521340306
Royalists -- Great Britain -- History -- 17th century. Great Britain -- Politics and government -- 1660-1688.

DA445.S68 2000
Spurr, John.
England in the 1670s: this masquerading age/ John Spurr. Malden, MA: Blackwell Publishers, 2000. xvii, 350 p.
00-037897   941.06/6   0631192565
Great Britain -- History -- Charles II, 1660-1685. England -- Civilization -- 17th century.

DA446.H93 1989
Hutton, Ronald.
Charles the Second, King of England, Scotland, and Ireland/ Ronald Hutton. Oxford [England]: Clarendon Press; 1989. xii, 554 p.
89-034059   941.06/6/092   0198229119
Charles -- II, -- King of England, -- 1630-1685. Great Britain -- Kings and rulers -- Biography. Great Britain -- History -- Charles II, 1660-1685.

DA447.A3.A8 1957
Aubrey, John, 1626-1697.
Brief lives. Edited from the original manuscripts and with a life of John Aubrey by Oliver Lawson Dick. Foreword by Edmund Wilson. Ann Arbor, University of Michigan Press [1957] cvi, 341 p.
57-013981   920.042
Aubrey, John, -- 1626-1697.   Great Britain -- Biography.

DA447.C6.H37 1983
Harris, R. W.
Clarendon and the English Revolution/ R.W. Harris. Stanford, Calif.: Stanford University Press, 1983. 456 p.
83-040092   941.06/092/4   0804712166
Clarendon, Edward Hyde, -- Earl of, -- 1609-1674. Statesmen -- Great Britain -- Biography. Historians -- Great Britain -- Biography. Great Britain -- Politics and government -- 1625-1649. Great Britain -- Politics and government -- 1649-1660. Great Britain -- Politics and government -- 1660-1688.

DA447.C6.O45 1988
Ollard, Richard Lawrence.
Clarendon and his friends/ by Richard Ollard. New York: Atheneum, 1988, c1987. xv, 367 p.
87-019502   941.06/092/4   0689117310
Clarendon, Edward Hyde, -- Earl of, -- 1609-1674. Clarendon, Edward Hyde, -- Earl of, -- 1609-1674 -- Friends and associates. Statesmen -- Great Britain -- Biography. Historians -- Great Britain -- Biography. Great Britain -- History -- Stuarts, 1603-1714 -- Biography.

DA447.E9.A44
Evelyn, John, 1620-1706.
Diary. Now first printed in full from the mss. belonging to John Evelyn,   Oxford, Clarendon Press, 1955. 6 v.
56-013545
Great Britain -- History -- Stuarts, 1603-1714. Great Britain -- Court and courtiers.

DA447.H2.A2 1989
Halifax, George Savile, 1633-1695.
The works of George Savile, Marquis of Halifax/ edited by Mark N. Brown: in three volumes. Oxford [Oxfordshire]: Clarendon Press; 1989. 3 v.
86-023914   082   0198127529

DA447.P4.A4 1970
Pepys, Samuel, 1633-1703.
The diary of Samuel Pepys. A new and complete transcription edited by Robert Latham and William Matthews. Contributing editors: William A. Armstrong [and others] Berkeley, University of California Press [1970]-1983 v. 1-10
70-096950   914.2/03/6   0520015754
Pepys, Samuel, -- 1633-1703 -- Diaries. Authors, English -- Early modern, 1500-1700 -- Diaries. Statesmen -- Great Britain -- Diaries. Great Britain -- Politics and government -- 1660-1688. Great Britain -- Social life and customs -- 17th century.

DA447.P4.C66 2001
Coote, Stephen.
Samuel Pepys: a life/ Stephen Coote. New York: Palgrave for St. Martin's Press, 2001. xiii, 386 p.
2001-271668   941.06/092   0312239297
Pepys, Samuel, -- 1633-1703. Statesmen -- Great Britain -- Biography. Authors, English -- Early modern, 1500-1700 -- Biography. English diaries -- History and criticism. Great Britain -- Social life and customs -- 17th century. Great Britain -- History -- Stuarts, 1603-1714 -- Biography.

DA447.P4.H4
Heath, Helen Truesdell
The letters of Samuel Pepys and his family circle. Oxford, Clarendon Press, 1955. xl, 253 p.
55-001764
Pepys, Samuel, -- 1633-1703.

DA448.G7 1992
Greaves, Richard L.
Secrets of the kingdom: British radicals from the Popish Plot to the Revolution of 1688-1689/ Richard L. Greaves. Stanford, Calif.: Stanford University Press, 1992. xvii, 465 p.
91-044781   941.06/7   0804720525
Radicalism -- Great Britain -- History -- 17th century. Popish Plot, 1678. Great Britain -- History -- Revolution of 1688. Great Britain -- Politics and government -- 1660-1688.

DA448.G75 1986
Greaves, Richard L.
Deliver us from evil: the radical underground in Britain, 1660-1663/ Richard L. Greaves. New York: Oxford University Press, 1986. x, 291 p.
85-018772   941.06/6.219   0195039858
Radicalism--Great   Britain--History--17th century. Subversive activities--Great Britain--History--17th century.

DA448.G754 1990
Greaves, Richard L.
Enemies under his feet: radicals and nonconformists in Britain, 1664-1677/ Richard L. Greaves. Stanford, Calif.: Stanford University Press, 1990. xii, 324 p.
89-021991   941.06/6   0804717753
Radicalism -- Great Britain -- History -- 17th century. Dissenters, Religious -- Great Britain -- History -- 17th century. Subversive activities -- Great Britain -- History -- 17th century. Great Britain -- Politics and government -- 1660-1688.

DA448.K45 1972
Kenyon, J. P. 1927-
The Popish Plot [by] John Kenyon. New York, St. Martin's Press [1972] 300 p.
72-076795   942.06/6
Popish Plot, 1678.

DA448.K62 1994
Knights, Mark.
Politics and opinion in crisis, 1678-81/ Mark Knights. Cambridge [England]; Cambridge University Press, 1994. xv, 424 p.
93-042095   941.06/6   0521418046
Public opinion -- Great Britain -- History -- 17th century. Great Britain -- Kings and rulers -- Succession -- Public opinion. Great Britain -- Politics and government -- 1660-1688.

DA448.9.E17 1978
Earle, Peter, 1937-
Monmouth's rebels: the road to Sedgemoor 1685/ Peter Earle. New York: St. Martin's Press, 1978, c1977. xi, 236 p.
77-084928   942.06/7   0312545126
Monmouth's Rebellion, 1685.

DA450.A83 1977
Ashley, Maurice, 1907-
James II/ Maurice Ashley. Minneapolis: University of Minnesota Press, 1977. 342 p.
78-103953   942.06/7/0924   0816608261
James -- II, -- King of England, -- 1633-1701.
Great Britain -- History -- James II, 1685-1688.
Great Britain -- Kings and rulers -- Biography.

DA450.C35 2000
Callow, John.
The making of King James II: the formative years of a fallen king/ John Callow. Stroud, Gloucestershire: Sutton, 2000. ix, 373 p.
01-326374   0750923989
James -- II, -- King of England, -- 1633-1701.
Great Britain -- History -- Restoration, 1660-1688.
Great Britain -- Kings and rulers -- Biography.

DA452.A54 1991
The Anglo-Dutch moment: essays on the Glorious Revolution and its world impact/ edited by Jonathan I. Israel. Cambridge [England]; Cambridge University Press, 1991. xv, 502 p.
90-036082   941.06/7   0521390753
Civilization, Western -- Dutch influences. Dutch -- Great Britain -- History -- 17th century. Revolutions -- History -- 17th century. Great Britain -- History -- Revolution of 1688. Great Britain -- History -- Revolution of 1688 -- Influence. Great Britain -- History -- William and Mary, 1689-1702.

DA452.C63 1996
Claydon, Tony.
William III and the godly revolution/ Tony Claydon. Cambridge; Cambridge University Press, 1996. xiv, 272 p.
95-014567   941.06/8   0521473292
William -- III, -- King of England, -- 1650-1702. James -- II, -- King of England, -- 1633-1701. Great Britain -- Kings and rulers -- Succession. Great Britain -- History -- Revolution of 1688 -- Propaganda. Great Britain -- Politics and government -- 1689-1702.

DA452.S3
Schwoerer, Lois G.
The Declaration of Rights, 1689/ Lois G. Schwoerer. Baltimore: Johns Hopkins University Press, c1981. xvi, 391 p.
81-002942   342.41/085   0801824303
Great Britain -- Politics and government -- 1660-1688.

DA452.S69 1988
Speck, W. A. 1938-
Reluctant revolutionaries: Englishmen and the revolution of 1688/ W.A. Speck. Oxford [England]; Oxford University Press, 1988. viii, 267 p.
88-002741   941.06/7   019822768X
Great Britain -- History -- Revolution of 1688.
Great Britain -- History -- James II, 1685-1688.

DA460.J66 1988
Jones, D. W., 1941-
War and economy in the age of William III and Marlborough/ D.W. Jones. Oxford, UK; B. Blackwell, 1988. xviii, 351 p.
88-010522   941.06/8   0631160698
Marlborough, John Churchill, -- Duke of, -- 1650-1722. Grand Alliance, War of the, 1689-1697 -- Economic aspects -- Great Britain. Great Britain -- History -- William and Mary, 1689-1702. Great Britain -- History, Military -- 1603-1714. Great Britain -- History, Military -- 18th century.

DA462.A3 W27 2003
Waller, Maureen.
Ungrateful daughters: the Stuart princesses who stole their father's crown/ Maureen Waller.1st U.S. ed. New York: St. Martin's Press, 2003. p. cm.
2002-031879   947.06/8.221   031230711X
Mary -- II, Queen of England, 1662-1694. James -- II, King of England, 1633-1701--Family. Anne, Queen of Great Britain, 1665-1714. Queens--Great Britain--Biography.

DA462.M3.A
Ashley, Maurice, 1907-
Marlborough.   New York: Macmillan, [1956]. 144 p.
58-003932
Marlborough, John Churchill, -- Duke of, -- 1650-1722.

DA462.M3.C45 1947
Churchill, Winston S.
Marlborough; his life and times.   London: George G. Harrap & Co., Ltd., (1947) 1966. 2 v.
48-019354   923.542
Marlborough, John Churchill, -- First duke of, -- 1650-1722. Great Britain -- History -- Stuarts, 1603-1714. Great Britain -- History -- 1714-1837.

DA470.D73 2000
Drayton, Richard Harry.
Nature's government: science, imperial Britain, and the 'Improvement' of the World/ Richard Drayton. New Haven: Yale University Press, c2000. xxi, 346 p.
99-059158   325/.341/009033   0300059760
Imperialism -- History. Botany, Economic -- Political aspects -- Great Britain. Botany -- Great Britain -- History. Great Britain -- History -- 18th century. Great Britain -- History -- 19th century.

DA470.W48
Wiener, Joel H.
Great Britain: the lion at home; a documentary history of domestic policy, 1689-1973. Editor: Joel H. Wiener. New York, Chelsea House Publishers, 1974. 4 v.
74-007447   942   0835207765
Great Britain -- History -- 18th century -- Sources. Great Britain -- History -- 19th century -- Sources. Great Britain -- History -- 20th century -- Sources.

DA480.B72 1990
Bradley, James E., 1944-
Religion, revolution, and English radicalism: nonconformity in eighteenth-century politics and society/ James E. Bradley. Cambridge [England]; Cambridge University Press, c1990. xxi, 473 p.
90-033078   941.07   0521380103(ha
Dissenters, Religious -- Political activity -- England -- History -- 18th century. Religion and politics -- England -- History -- 18th century. Radicalism -- England -- History -- 18th century. Great Britain -- Politics and government -- 18th century. England -- Church history -- 18th century.

DA480.B75 1997
Britain in the Hanoverian age, 1714-1837: an encyclopedia/ editor, Gerald Newman; associate editors, Leslie Ellen Brown ... [et al.]. New York: Garland Pub., 1997. xxv, 871 p.
97-016840   941.07   0815303963
Great Britain -- History -- 1714-1837 -- Encyclopedias.

DA480.D53 1995
Dickinson, H. T.
The politics of the people in eighteenth-century Britain/ H.T. Dickinson. New York: St. Martin's Press, 1995. x, 346 p.
94-034276   320.941   0312124562
Popular culture -- Great Britain -- History -- 18th century. Great Britain -- Politics and government -- 18th century.

DA480.H45 1996
Hill, Brian W.
The early parties and politics in Britain, 1688-1832/ Brian Hill. New York: St. Martin's Press, 1996. vi, 246 p.
96-004612   320.941/09/033   0312159137
Political parties -- Great Britain -- History -- 18th century. Political parties -- Great Britain -- History -- 19th century. Political parties -- Great Britain -- History -- 17th century. Great Britain -- Politics and government -- 18th century. Great Britain -- Politics and government -- 1689-1702. Great Britain -- Politics and government -- 1800-1837.

DA480.L27 1991
Langford, Paul.
Public life and the propertied Englishman, 1689-1798/ Paul Langford. Oxford: Clarendon Press; 1991. xiii, 608 p.
90-041689   941.07   0198201494
Middle class -- England -- Political activity -- History -- 18th century. Middle class -- England -- Political activity -- History -- 17th century. Great Britain -- Politics and government -- 18th century. Great Britain -- Politics and government -- 1689-1702.

DA480.L462
Lecky, William Edward Hartpole, 1838-1903.
A history of England in the eighteenth century. New York, D. Appleton, 1892-[93] New York, AMS Press [1968] 7 v.
68-057226   942.07/1
Great Britain -- History -- 18th century. Great Britain -- Social life and customs -- 18th century.

DA480.M627 1994
Miller, Peter N., 1964-
Defining the common good: empire, religion, and philosophy in eighteenth-century Britain/ Peter N. Miller. Cambridge; Cambridge University Press, 1994. xii, 472 p.
93-019862   941.07   0521442591
Political science -- Great Britain -- History -- 18th century. Imperialism -- History -- 18th century. Philosophy, British -- 18th century. Great Britain -- Church history -- 18th century. Great Britain -- Politics and government -- 18th century.

DA480.N3 1970
Namier, Lewis Bernstein, 1888-1960.
Crossroads of power; essays on eighteenth-century England. Freeport, N.Y., Books for Libraries Press [1970, c1962] viii, 234 p.
77-119604   942.07/08   0836916905
Great Britain -- History -- 18th century.

DA480.O38 1997
O'Gorman, Frank.
The long eighteenth century: British political and social history, 1688-1832/ Frank O'Gorman. London; Arnold; 1997. xvi, 415 p.
97-014187   941.07   034056752X
Great Britain -- Politics and government -- 18th century. Great Britain -- Politics and government -- 1800-1837. Great Britain -- Politics and government -- 1689-1702.

DA480.P55 1975
Plumb, J. H. 1911-
The first four Georges/ J. H. Plumb. Boston: Little, Brown, 1975, c1956. 208 p.
74-012150   942.07/092/2
Great Britain -- History -- 1714-1837. Great Britain -- Kings and rulers -- Biography.

DA480.P56 1979
Plumb, J. H. 1911-
Men and centuries/ J. H. Plumb. Westport, Conn.: Greenwood Press, [1979] c1963. 294 p.
78-026300   941   0313208689
English literature -- History and criticism. Great Britain -- History -- 18th century. Africa -- Discovery and exploration -- English.

DA483.P6.W5 1966a
Williams, Basil, 1867-1950.
The life of William Pitt, earl of Chatham. New York, Octagon Books, 1966. 2 v.
66-030301   942.07/3/0924
Pitt, William, -- Earl of Chatham, -- 1708-1778. Statesmen -- Great Britain -- Biography. Great Britain -- Politics and government -- 18th century.

DA483.W2.A499
Walpole, Horace, 1717-1797.
Letters,/ selected by W.S. Lewis, with an introd. by R.W. Ketton-Cremer. London, Folio Society, 1951. 283 p.
52-001184   928.2
Walpole, Horace, -- 1717-1797.

DA483.W2.K4 1966
Ketton-Cremer, Robert Wyndham, 1906-
Horace Walpole; a biography, by R. W. Ketton-Cremer. Ithaca, N. Y., Cornell University Press [1966, c1964] xv, 317 p.
66-011431
Walpole, Horace, -- 1717-1797.

DA485.C65 1992
Colley, Linda.
Britons: forging the nation, 1707-1837/ Linda Colley. New Haven: Yale University Press, 1992. x, 429 p.
92-013256   941.07   0300057377
National characteristics, British -- History. Nationalism -- Great Britain -- History. Great Britain -- Civilization -- 18th century. Great Britain -- Civilization -- 17th century.

DA485.C78 1990
Cruickshank, Dan.
Life in the Georgian city/ Dan Cruickshank and Neil Burton. London; Viking, 1990. xv, 288 p.
89-052085   0670812668
City and town life -- Great Britain -- History -- 18th century. Cities and towns -- Great Britain -- History -- 18th century. Architecture, Georgian -- Great Britain. Great Britain -- Social life and customs -- 18th century.

DA485.E18 2000
Eagles, Robin, 1971-
Francophilia in English society, 1748-1815/ Robin Eagles. New York: St. Martin's Press, 2000. x, 229 p.
00-030894   303.48/242044/09033   0333764846
British -- France -- History -- 18th century. British -- France -- History -- 19th century. France -- History -- Revolution, 1789-1799 -- Refugees. Great Britain -- Civilization -- French influences. England -- Social life and customs -- 19th century.

DA485.J37
Jarrett, Derek.
England in the age of Hogarth/ Derek Jarrett. New York: Viking Press, 1974. 256 p.
74-005538   942.07   0670296244
Hogarth, William, -- 1697-1764.   England -- Civilization -- 18th century.

DA485.P54 1997
Pittock, Murray.
Inventing and resisting Britain: cultural identities in Britain and Ireland, 1685-1789/ Murray G.H. Pittock. New York: St. Martin's Press, 1997. ix, 189
96-041005   941.07   0312165765
National characteristics, British -- History -- 18th century. National characteristics, British -- History -- 17th century. National characteristics, Irish -- History -- 18th century. Great Britain -- Civilization -- 18th century. Scotland -- History -- 18th century. England -- Civilization -- 18th century.

DA485.T77
Turberville, Arthur Stanley, 1888-1945.
Johnson's England; an account of the life & manners of his age, edited by A. S. Turberville. Oxford, Clarendon press 1933. 2 v.
34-000592   914.2
Johnson, Samuel, -- 1709-1784.   Great Britain -- History -- 18th cent. Great Britain -- Intellectual life. Great Britain -- Civilization.

DA486.R43 1983
Reed, Michael A.
The Georgian triumph, 1700-1830/ Michael Reed. London; Routledge & Kegan Paul, 1983. xvi, 240 p.
82-016640   941.07   0710094140
Landscape -- Great Britain -- History -- 18th century. Landscape -- Great Britain -- History -- 19th century. Great Britain -- History -- 18th century. Great Britain -- History -- 1800-1837. Great Britain -- Historical geography.

DA495.B83 1993
Bucholz, R. O., 1958-
The Augustan court: Queen Anne and the decline of court culture/ R.O. Bucholz. Stanford, Calif.: Stanford University Press, 1993. xvi, 418 p.
92-000440   941.06/9/092   0804720800
Great Britain -- History -- Anne, 1702-1714. Great Britain -- Court and courtiers -- History -- 18th century.

DA495.S73 1994
Speck, W. A. 1938-
The birth of Britain: a new nation, 1700-1710/ W.A. Speck. Oxford, England, UK; Blackwell, 1994. xiv, 235 p.
93-045877   941.06/9
Great Britain -- History -- Anne, 1702-1714. Great Britain -- History -- William and Mary, 1689-1702.

DA495.T7
Trevelyan, George Macaulay, 1876-1962.
England under Queen Anne ... by George Macaulay Trevelyan ... London, Longmans, Green and co., 1930-34. 3 v.
30-023326   942.069
Spanish Succession, War of, 1701-1714. Great Britain -- History -- Anne, 1702-1714.

DA498.A3 1979
Addison, Joseph, 1672-1719.
The freeholder/ Joseph Addison; edited with an introd. and notes by James Leheny. Oxford: Clarendon Press; 1979. xi, 283 p.
78-041130   320.9/41/071   0198124945
Great Britain -- Politics and government -- 1714-1727.

DA498.B53 1985
Black, Jeremy.
British foreign policy in the age of Walpole/ Jeremy Black. Edinburgh: J. Donald; c1985. xi, 202 p.
85-213381   941.07/1   0859761266
Walpole, Robert, -- Earl of Orford, -- 1676-1745. Great Britain -- Foreign relations -- 1714-1727. Great Britain -- Foreign relations -- 1727-1760.

DA498.C66 1988
Cook, Chris, 1945-
British historical facts, 1688-1760/ Chris Cook and John Stevenson. New York: St. Martin's Press, 1988. viii, 252 p.
88-007047   941.07   0312021062
Great Britain -- History -- 18th century. Great Britain -- History -- 1689-1714. Great Britain -- History -- Revolution of 1688.

DA498.R63 1989
Rogers, Nicholas.
Whigs and cities: popular politics in the age of Walpole and Pitt/ Nicholas Rogers. Oxford: Clarendon Press; 1989. xi, 440 p.
89-037415   320.941/09/033   0198217854
Walpole, Robert, -- Earl of Orford, -- 1676-1745. Pitt, William, -- Earl of Chatham, -- 1708-1778. Populism -- Great Britain -- History -- 18th century. Working class -- Great Britain -- Political activity -- History -- 18th century. Cities and towns -- Great Britain -- History -- 18th century. Great Britain -- Politics and government -- 1714-1760. London (England) -- Politics and government.

DA498.S68
Speck, W. A. 1938-
Stability and strife: England, 1714-1760/ W. A. Speck. Cambridge, Mass.: Harvard University Press, 1977. 311 p.
77-022773   942.07/2   0674833473
Great Britain -- Politics and government -- 1714-1760.

DA501.A2.H4
Hatton, Ragnhild Marie.
George I, elector and king/ Ragnhild Hatton. Cambridge, Mass.: Harvard University Press, 1978. 416 p.
77-015058   941.07/1/0924   0674349350
George -- I, -- King of Great Britain, -- 1660-1727. Great Britain -- Kings and rulers -- Biography. Great Britain -- History -- George I, 1714-1727.

DA501.B6.K7 1968
Kramnick, Isaac.
Bolingbroke and his circle; the politics of nostalgia in the age of Walpole. Cambridge, Mass., Harvard University Press, 1968. xiii, 321 p.
68-015639   942.07/1
Bolingbroke, Henry St. John, -- Viscount, -- 1678-1751. Bolingbroke, Henry St. John, -- Viscount, -- 1678-1751 -- Friends and associates. Nostalgia -- Political aspects -- Great Britain. Great Britain -- Intellectual life -- 18th century. Great Britain -- Politics and government -- 1714-1760.

DA501.C5.S52 1971
Shellabarger, Samuel, 1888-1954.
Lord Chesterfield and his world. New York, Biblo and Tannen, 1971 [c1951] 456 p.
72-156737   942.07/1/0924   0819602728
Chesterfield, Philip Dormer Stanhope, -- Earl of, -- 1694-1773. Authors, English -- 18th century -- Biography. Statesmen -- Great Britain -- Biography. Great Britain -- Civilization -- 18th century. Great Britain -- Politics and government -- 18th century.

DA501.G73.J64 1997
Johnson, Allen S.
A prologue to revolution: the political career of George Grenville (1712-1770)/ Allen S. Johnson. Lanham, MD: University Press of America, c1997. xi, 353 p.
96-044589   941.07/092   0761806008
Grenville, George, -- 1712-1770. Prime ministers -- Great Britain -- Biography. Great Britain -- Politics and government -- 1727-1760. Great Britain -- Politics and government -- 1760-1789. United States -- History -- Revolution, 1775-1783 -- Causes.

DA501.H47.H34 1974
Halsband, Robert, 1914-
Lord Hervey; eighteenth-century courtier. New York, Oxford University Press, 1974 [c1973] xiv, 380 p.
73-087774   942.07/2/0924   0195017315
Hervey, John Hervey, -- Baron, -- 1696-1743. Great Britain -- Court and courtiers -- History -- 18th century. Great Britain -- Court and courtiers -- Biography.

DA501.M7.H3
Halsband, Robert, 1914-
The life of Lady Mary Wortley Montagu. Oxford, Clarendon Press, 1956 [i.e.195 313 p.
56-014373   928.2
Montagu, Mary Wortley, -- Lady, -- 1689-1762.

DA501.M7.L68 1994
Lowenthal, Cynthia.
Lady Mary Wortley Montagu and the eighteenth-century familiar letter/ Cynthia Lowenthal. Athens: University of Georgia Press, c1994. x, 261 p.
92-041757   826/.5   0820315451
Montagu, Mary Wortley, -- Lady, -- 1689-1762 -- Correspondence. Women authors, English -- 18th century -- Correspondence. Diplomats' spouses -- Great Britain -- Correspondence. English letters -- History and criticism.

DA501.W2.P52
Plumb, J. H. 1911-
Sir Robert Walpole. Boston, Houghton, Mifflin, 1956-61. 2 v.
56-011765   923.242
Walpole, Robert, -- Earl of Orford, -- 1676-1745.

DA501.W2.W67 1998
Woodfine, Philip.
Britannia's glories: the Walpole ministry and the 1739 war with Spain/ Philip Woodfine. Woodbridge, Suffolk, UK; Royal Historical Society/Boydell Press, 1998. 279 p.
97-037250   946/.055   0861932307
Walpole, Robert, -- Earl of Orford, -- 1676-1745. Anglo-Spanish War, 1739-1748. Great Britain -- Foreign relations -- Spain. Spain -- Foreign relations -- Great Britain. Great Britain -- Politics and government -- 1714-1760.

DA505.B975 1968
Butterfield, Herbert, 1900-
George III, Lord North, and the people, 1779-80, by H. Butterfield. New York, Russell & Russell [1968] 407 p.
68-010907   942.07/3
George -- III, -- King of Great Britain, -- 1738-1820. North, Frederick, -- Lord, -- 1732-1792. Great Britain -- Politics and government -- 1760-1789.

DA505.C36 1990
Carretta, Vincent.
George III and the satirists from Hogarth to Byron/ Vincent Carretta. Athens: University of Georgia Press, c1990. xviii, 389 p.
89-004778   942.07/3   0820311464
George -- III, -- King of Great Britain, -- 1738-1820 -- Humor. Political satire, English -- History and criticism. English wit and humor, Pictorial. Great Britain -- Politics and government -- 1760-1820 -- Humor. Great Britain -- Politics and government -- 1760-1820 -- Caricatures and cartoons.

DA505.C48 1982
Christie, Ian R.
Wars and revolutions: Britain 1760-1815/ Ian R. Christie. Cambridge, Mass.: Harvard University Press, 1982. 359 p.
82-003009   941.07/3   0674947606
Great Britain -- Politics and government -- 1760-1820. Great Britain -- Foreign relations -- France. France -- Foreign relations -- Great Britain.

DA505.D47 2001
Derry, John W.
Politics in the age of Fox, Pitt, and Liverpool/ John W. Derry. New York: Palgrave, 2001. p. cm.
00-065212   941.07/3   0333946367
Fox, Charles James, -- 1749-1806. Pitt, William, -- 1759-1806. Liverpool, Robert Banks Jenkinson, -- Earl of, -- 1770-1828. Great Britain -- Politics and government -- 1800-1837. Great Britain -- Politics and government -- 1760-1820.

DA505.W38
Watson, John Steven.
The reign of George III: 1760-1815. Oxford: Clarendon Press, c1960. 637 p.
60-050916   942.073
Great Britain -- History -- George III, 1760-1820.

DA506.A1.Q4
Quennell, Peter, 1905-
...The profane virtues; four studies of the eighteenth century. New York, The Viking press, 1945. 6 p. . 220 p.
45-005993   928.2
Wilkes, John, -- 1727-1797. Boswell, James, -- 1740-1795. Gibbon, Edward, -- 1737-1794.

DA506.A2.H53 1998
Hibbert, Christopher, 1924-
George III: a personal history/ Christopher Hibbert. New York: Basic Books, c1998. xiii, 463 p.
99-182008   941.07/3/092   0465027237
George -- III, -- King of Great Britain, -- 1738-1820. Great Britain -- History -- George III, 1760-1820. Great Britain -- Kings and rulers -- Biography.

DA506.B85 1960
Burke, Edmund, 1729-1797.
Selected works/ Edmund Burke; edited by W.J. Bate. New York: Modern Library, c1960. viii, 536 p.
60-007687
Great Britain -- Politics and government -- 1760-1820.

DA506.B9.C65
Courtney, C. P.
Montesquieu and Burke. Oxford, Blackwell, 1963. xv, 204 p.
65-004028
Burke, Edmund, -- 1729-1797. Montesquieu, Charles de Secondat, -- baron de, -- 1689-1755. Political science -- History -- Great Britain. Great Britain -- Politics and government -- 1760-1820.

DA506.F7.T87 1921
Trevelyan, George Otto, 1838-1928.
George the Third and Charles Fox, the concluding part of The American revolution, by the Right Hon. George Otto Trevelyan. New York, Longmans, Green, and Co., 1921-27. 2 v.
36-012866   942.073
George -- III, -- King of Great Britain, -- 1738-1820. Fox, Charles James, -- 1749-1806. Great Britain -- History -- George III, 1760-1820. Great Britain -- Politics and government -- 1760-1820. United States -- History -- Revolution, 1775-1783.

DA506.W2.A13 1963
Walpole, Horace,
Horace Walpole: memoirs and portraits/ edited by M. Hodgart. New York: Macmillan, 1963. 264 p.
63-017297   942.073
Walpole, Horace, -- Earl of Orford, 4th. Great Britain -- History -- George II, 1727-1760. Great Britain -- History -- George III, 1760-1820.

DA510.B67
Brewer, John, 1947-
Party ideology and popular politics at the accession of George III/ John Brewer. Cambridge; Cambridge University Press, 1976. ix, 382 p.
76-014773   320.9/41/073   0521210496
Political parties -- Great Britain -- History -- 18th century. Populism -- Great Britain -- History -- 18th century. Great Britain -- Politics and government -- 1760-1789.

DA510.C73 2000
Conway, Stephen, 1957-
The British Isles and the War of American Independence/ Stephen Conway. Oxford, [England]; Oxford University Press, 2000. vii, 407 p.
99-045407   941.07/3   0198206593
National characteristics, British -- History -- 18th century. Nationalism -- Great Britain -- History -- 18th century. Great Britain -- History -- George III, 1760-1820. United States -- History -- Revolution, 1775-1783 -- Influence. Great Britain -- Civilization -- American influences.

DA510.G68 2000
Gould, Eliga H.
The persistence of empire: British political culture in the age of the American Revolution/ Eliga H. Gould. Chapel Hill, N.C.: Published for the Omohundro Institute of Early A c2000. xxiv, 262 p.
99-034607   941.07/3   0807825298
Great Britain -- Politics and government -- 1760-1789. United States -- History -- Revolution, 1775-1783. Great Britain -- Colonies -- History -- 18th century.

DA510.S26 1990
Scott, H. M. 1946-
British foreign policy in the age of the American Revolution/ H.M. Scott. Oxford [England]: Clarendon Press; 1990. xiii, 377 p.
90-006886   327.41/009/033   0198201958
Great Britain -- Foreign relations -- 1760-1789. United States -- History -- Revolution, 1775-1783.

DA512.W6.R8
Rude, George F. E.
Wilkes and liberty; a social study of 1763 to 1774. Oxford, Clarendon Press, 1962. xvi, 240 p.
62-001596   923.242
Wilkes, John, -- 1727-1797.   Great Britain -- Politics and government -- 1760-1789.

DA512.W6.T55 1996
Thomas, Peter David Garner.
John Wilkes, a friend to liberty/ Peter D.G. Thomas. New York: Clarendon Press, 1996. vi, 280 p.
95-036715   941.07/3/092   0198205449
Wilkes, John, -- 1727-1797.   Radicalism -- Great Britain -- History -- 18th century. Politicians -- Great Britain -- Biography. Liberty. Great Britain -- Politics and government -- 1760-1789.

DA520.G6 1979
Goodwin, Albert.
The friends of liberty: the English democratic movement in the age of the French revolution/ Albert Goodwin. Cambridge, Mass.: Harvard University Press, 1979. 594 p.
78-015673   320.9/41/073   0674323394
Radicalism -- Great Britain.   Great Britain -- Politics and government -- 1789-1820.

DA520.M67 1998
Morris, Marilyn, 1957-
The British monarchy and the French Revolution/ Marilyn Morris. New Haven: Yale University Press, c1998. viii, 229 p.
97-016330   320.441/09/033   0300071442
George -- III, -- King of Great Britain, -- 1738-1820.   Monarchy -- Great Britain -- History -- 18th century. Monarchy -- Great Britain -- History -- 19th century.   Great Britain -- Politics and government -- 1789-1820. France -- History -- Revolution, 1789-1799 -- Influence. Great Britain -- Civilization -- French influences.

DA521.C65
Cobbett, William, 1763-1835.
A history of the last hundred days of English freedom, by William Cobbett; with an introduction, "Main events of Cobbett's life", and a biographical index, London, The Labour publishing company, limited, and G. A 1921. 3 p.
22-000278
Great Britain -- Politics and government -- 1800-1837.

DA522.C2.T3 1968
Temperley, Harold William Vazeille, 1879-1939.
Life of Canning. New York: Haskell House, 1968. 293 p.
68-025269   942.07/4/0924
Canning, George, -- 1770-1827.   Statesmen -- Great Britain -- Biography.   Great Britain -- Politics and government -- 1789-1820. Great Britain -- Politics and government -- 1820-1830.

DA522.C5.D93 1992
Dyck, Ian.
William Cobbett and rural popular culture/ Ian Dyck. Cambridge [England]; Cambridge University Press, 1992. xvi, 312 p.
91-017636   941.07/3/092   052141394X
Cobbett, William, -- 1763-1835 -- Contributions in popular culture.   Popular culture -- Great Britain -- Historiography. Agricultural laborers -- Great Britain -- Historiography. Great Britain -- Rural conditions -- Historiography. Great Britain -- History -- 1800-1837 -- Historiography. Great Britain -- History -- 1789-1820 -- Historiography.

DA522.C5.O8
Osborne, John Walter, 1927-
William Cobbett: his thoughts and his times, by John W. Osborne. New Brunswick, N.J., Rutgers University Press [1966] x, 272 p.
66-018874   070.0924
Cobbett, William, -- 1763-1835.

DA522.D5.F68 2000
Foreman, Amanda, 1968-
Georgiana, Duchess of Devonshire/ Amanda Foreman. New York: Random House, [2000]. xx, 454 p.
99-023580   941.07/092   0375502947
Devonshire, Georgiana Spencer Cavendish, -- Duchess of, -- 1757-1806.   Women politicians -- Great Britain -- Biography. Nobility -- Great Britain -- Biography. Great Britain -- Social life and customs -- 18th century. Great Britain -- Politics and government -- 1789-1820.

DA522.L7.G37 1984
Gash, Norman.
Lord Liverpool: the life and political career of Robert Banks Jenkinson, Second Earl of Liverpool, 1770-1828/ Norman Gash. Cambridge, Mass.: Harvard University Press, 1984. xvii, 265 p.
84-012842   942.07/4/0924   0674539109
Liverpool, Robert Banks Jenkinson, -- Earl of, -- 1770-1828.   Prime ministers -- Great Britain -- Biography.   Great Britain -- Politics and government -- 1800-1837.

DA522.L8.D47 1976
Derry, John W.
Castlereagh/ John W. Derry. New York: St. Martin's Press, 1976. viii, 247 p.
75-029820   941.07/3/0924
Castlereagh, Robert Stewart, -- Viscount, -- 1769-1822.   Statesmen -- Great Britain -- Biography. Ireland -- Politics and government -- 1760-1820. Great Britain -- Politics and government -- 1789-1820.

DA522.P6.M33 1984
Mackesy, Piers.
War without victory: the downfall of Pitt, 1799-1802/ Piers Mackesy. Oxford: Clardendon Press; 1984. xi, 248 p.
84-232979   941.07/3   0198224958
Pitt, William, -- 1759-1806. Melville, Henry Dundas, -- Viscount, -- 1742-1811.   Second Coalition, War of the, 1798-1801.   Great Britain -- Politics and government -- 1789-1820.

DA522.P6.M65 1997
Mori, Jennifer.
William Pitt and the French Revolution, 1785-1795/ Jennifer Mori. New York: St. Martin's Press, 1997. xi, 305 p.
97-010963   327.41044/09/033   0312173083
Pitt, William, -- 1759-1806.   Great Britain -- Politics and government -- 1760-1820. France -- History -- Revolution, 1789-1799 -- Influence. Great Britain -- Foreign relations -- France.

DA522.W6.P64 1978
Pollock, John Charles.
Wilberforce/ John Pollock. New York: St. Martin's Press, 1978, c1977. xvi, 368 p.
77-086525   326/.092/4   0312879423
Wilberforce, William, -- 1759-1833.   Legislators -- Great Britain -- Biography. Abolitionists -- Great Britain -- Biography. Philanthropists -- Great Britain -- Biography. Great Britain -- Politics and government -- 1760-1820. Great Britain -- Politics and government -- 1820-1830.

DA529.E53 1992
The Encyclopedia of romanticism: culture in Britain, 1780s-1830s/ Laura Dabundo, editor; Pamela Olinto, Greg Rider, Gail Roos, editorial assistants. New York: Garland Pub., 1992. xviii, 662 p.
92-002682   941.07/3   0824069978
Romanticism -- Great Britain -- Encyclopedias. Great Britain -- Civilization -- 18th century -- Encyclopedias. Great Britain -- Civilization -- 19th century -- Encyclopedias.

DA530.B68
Briggs, Asa, 1921-
The age of improvement/ by Asa Briggs. London; Longmans, Green, c1959. xii, 547 p.
59-000816
Great Britain -- History -- George III, 1760-1820. Great Britain -- History -- 19th century.

DA530.C5 1989
Clarke, John 1947-
British diplomacy and foreign policy, 1782-1865: the national interest/ John Clarke. London; Unwin Hyman, 1989. 350 p.
88-017295   327.41   0044450400
Great Britain -- Foreign relations -- 19th century. Great Britain -- Foreign relations -- 1760-1820.

DA530.H446 1982
Harrison, Brian Howard.
Peaceable kingdom: stability and change in modern Britain/ by Brian Harrison. Oxford: Clarendon Press; 1982. 493 p.
82-006400   306/.0941   0198226039
Great Britain -- Politics and government -- 19th century. Great Britain -- Politics and government -- 20th century. Great Britain -- Politics and government -- 1760-1820.

DA530.H447 1975b
Hayes, Paul M.
The nineteenth century, 1814-80/ Paul Hayes. New York: St. Martin's Press, 1975. xi, 334 p.
75-010760   327.41
Great Britain -- Foreign relations -- 19th century.

DA530.N56 2000
The nineteenth century: the British Isles, 1815-1901/ edited by Colin Matthew. Oxford; Oxford University Press, c2000. xiv, 342 p.
00-711765   941.081   0198731442
Great Britain -- History -- 19th century.

DA530.P66 2000
Poole, Steve.
The politics of regicide in England, 1760-1850: troublesome subjects/ Steve Poole. Manchester; Manchester University Press; viii, 232 p.
941.07   0719050359
Monarchy -- Great Britain -- History -- 18th century. Monarchy -- Great Britain -- History -- 19th century. Great Britain -- History -- 18th century. Great Britain -- History -- 19th century.

DA530.W57 2000
Women in British politics, 1760-1860: the power of the petticoat/ edited by Kathryn Gleadle and Sarah Richardson. New York: St. Martin's Press, 2000. xii, 179 p.
00-022313   941/.0082   0312233566
Women in politics -- Great Britain -- History -- 19th century. Women in politics -- Great Britain -- History -- 18th century. Great Britain -- Politics and government -- 19th century. Great Britain -- Politics and government -- 1760-1820.

DA530.W58 1982
Wood, Anthony.
Nineteenth century Britain, 1815-1914/ Anthony Wood. Harlow, Essex, UK: Longman, 1982. viii, 470 p.
82-222946   941.081   0582353106
Great Britain -- History -- 19th century. Great Britain -- History -- Edward VII, 1901-1910. Great Britain -- History -- George V, 1910-1936.

DA530.W6 1962
Woodward, E. L. 1890-
The age of reform, 1815-1870. Oxford, Clarendon Press, 1962. xix, 681 p.
62-004675   942.07   0-19-821711-0
Great Britain -- Politics and government -- 19th century. Great Britain -- History -- 19th century. Great Britain -- Social conditions.

DA531.2.G7
Graubard, Stephen Richards.
Burke, Disraeli and Churchill; the politics of perseverance.   Cambridge, Harvard University Press, 1961. 262 p.
61-006349   923.242
Disraeli, Benjamin, -- Earl of Beaconsfield, -- 1804-1881. Churchill, Winston, -- Sir, -- 1874-1965. Burke, Edmund, -- 1729-1797.

DA533.A574 1991
Anderson, Patricia
The printed image and the transformation of popular culture, 1790-1860/ Patricia Anderson. Oxford: Clarendon Press; 1991. x, 211 p.
91-002828   302.23/2   019811236X
Popular culture -- Great Britain -- History -- 19th century. Working class -- Great Britain -- Books and reading -- History -- 19th century. Women -- Great Britain -- Books and reading -- History -- 19th century.

DA533.B33 1998
Bailey, Peter, 1937-
Popular culture and performance in the Victorian city/ Peter Bailey. Cambridge, UK; Cambridge University Press, 1998. x, 258 p.
99-174955   941.08   052157417X
City and town life -- Great Britain -- History -- 19th century. Popular culture -- Great Britain -- History -- 19th century. Performing arts -- Great Britain -- History -- 19th century. Great Britain -- Social life and customs -- 19th century.

DA533.H48 1982
Heyck, Thomas William, 1938-
The transformation of intellectual life in Victorian England/ T.W. Heyck. New York: St. Martin's Press, 1982. 262 p.
82-000840   305.5/52/0942   0312814275
England -- Intellectual life -- 19th century.

DA533.H55
Himmelfarb, Gertrude.
Victorian minds.   New York, Knopf, 1968. xiii, 392 p.
67-018617   942.081
Great Britain -- Intellectual life -- 19th century. Great Britain -- History -- Victoria, 1837-1901.

DA533.H74 1998
Homans, Margaret, 1952-
Royal representations: Queen Victoria and British culture, 1837-1876/ Margaret Homans. Chicago: University of Chicago Press, 1998. xxxvii, 283 p.
98-019836   941.081   0226351130
Victoria, -- Queen of Great Britain, -- 1819-1901. Monarchy -- Great Britain -- History -- 19th century. Queens -- Great Britain -- Biography. Queens in literature. Great Britain -- History -- Victoria, 1837-1901. Great Britain -- Civilization -- 19th century.

DA533.H85
Houghton, Walter Edwards, 1904-
The Victorian frame of mind, 1830-1870.   New Haven, Published for Wellesley College by Yale Universi 1957. 467 p.
57-006339   942.081
Great Britain -- Intellectual life -- 19th century. Great Britain -- History -- Victoria, 1837-1901.

DA533.K55
Kitson Clark, G. S. R. 1900-1975.
The making of Victorian England/ G. Kitson Clark. Cambridge, Mass.: Harvard University Press, 1962. xiii, 312 p.
62-051827   914.2
Great Britain -- Civilization.

DA533.M75 2001
Morgan, Marjorie.
National identities and travel in Victorian Britain/ Marjorie Morgan. Houndmills, Basingstoke, Hampshire; Palgrave, 2001. x, 271 p.
00-041511   941.081   0333719999
National characteristics, British -- History -- 19th century. Travelers -- Great Britain -- History -- 19th century. British -- Europe -- History -- 19th century. Great Britain -- Civilization -- 19th century. Great Britain -- History -- Victoria, 1837-1901. Great Britain -- Description and travel.

DA533.P455 1987
Pemble, John.
The Mediterranean passion: Victorians and Edwardians in the South/ John Pemble. Oxford [Oxfordshire]: Clarendon Press; 1987. viii, 312 p.
86-033183   941.08   0198201001
British -- Travel -- Mediterranean Region -- History. Travelers -- Mediterranean Region -- Biography. British -- Travel -- Mediterranean Region -- History. Mediterranean Region -- Description and travel. Great Britain -- Civilization -- Mediterranean influences. Great Britain -- Civilization -- 19th century.

DA533.P66 1995
Poovey, Mary.
Making a social body: British cultural formation, 1830-1864/ Mary Poovey. Chicago: University of Chicago Press, 1995. x, 255 p.
95-004153   941.081   0226675238
National characteristics, British -- History -- 19th century. Arts, Modern -- 19th century -- Great Britain. Arts, British. Great Britain -- History -- Victoria, 1837-1901. Great Britain -- Civilization -- 19th century. Great Britain -- Social conditions -- 19th century.

DA533.R37
Read, Donald.
England, 1868-1914: the age of urban democracy/ by Donald Read. London; Longman, 1979. xiv, 530 p.
78-041034   942.081   058248278X
Great Britain -- History -- Victoria, 1837-1901. Great Britain -- History -- Edward VII, 1901-1910. England -- Civilization -- 19th century.

DA533.W59
Wiener, Martin J.
English culture and the decline of the industrial spirit, 1850-1980/ Martin J. Wiener. Cambridge; Cambridge University Press, 1981. xi, 217 p.
80-022684   942.08   0521234182
Industries -- Social aspects -- England. England -- Civilization -- 20th century. England -- Civilization -- 19th century.

DA535.B35 1998
Bailey, Brian J.
The Luddite Rebellion/ Brian Bailey. New York: New York University Press, c1998. xvii, 182 p.
98-006214   941.07/3   0814713351
Sabotage in the workplace -- England -- History -- 19th century. Textile workers -- England -- History -- 19th century. Riots -- England -- History -- 19th century. Great Britain -- History -- 1789-1820.

DA535.G37
Gash, Norman.
Aristocracy and people: Britain, 1815-1865/ Norman Gash. Cambridge, Mass.: Harvard University Press, 1979. 375 p.
79-013638   309.1/41/07   0674044908
Nobility -- Great Britain -- History. Upper class -- Great Britain -- History. Great Britain -- Social life and customs -- 19th century. Great Britain -- Politics and government -- 1800-1837. Great Britain -- Politics and government -- 1837-1901.

DA535.W45 1973
White, Reginald James.
Waterloo to Peterloo, by R. J. White. New York, Russell & Russell [1973, c1957] ix, 202 p.
72-090571   309.1/42/073   084621718X
Great Britain -- History -- 1800-1837. Great Britain -- Social conditions -- 19th century.

DA536.A88.M67 1990
Moss, D. J. 1938-
Thomas Attwood: the biography of a radical/ David J. Moss. Montreal; McGill-Queen's University Press, c1990. 377 p.
90-162482   941.07/092   0773507086
Attwood, Thomas, -- 1783-1856. Politicians -- Great Britain -- Biography. Economists -- Great Britain -- Biography. Bankers -- Great Britain -- Biography. Great Britain -- Politics and government -- 1837-1901. Great Britain -- Politics and government -- 1800-1837. Birmingham (England) -- Biography.

DA536.C3.W6 1971
Woodham Smith, Cecil Blanche Fitz Gerald, 1896-
The reason why, by Cecil Woodham-Smith. New York, McGraw-Hill [1971, c1953] 287 p.
72-155886   942.081/0924   0070716706
Cardigan, James Thomas Brudenell, -- Earl of, -- 1797-1868. Lucan, George Charles Bingham, -- Earl of, -- 1800-1888. Balaklava (Ukraine), Battle of, 1854.

DA536.C6.R4 1968
Read, Donald.
Cobden and Bright: a Victorian political partnership. New York, St. Martin's Press, 1968 [c1967] ix, 275 p.
68-015436   942.081/0922
Cobden, Richard, -- 1804-1865. Bright, John, -- 1811-1889.   Great Britain -- Politics and government -- 1837-1901.

DA536.G84.S65 1990
Smith, E. A.
Lord Grey, 1764-1845/ E.A. Smith. Oxford [England]: Clarendon Press; 1990. viii, 338 p.
89-027446   941.07/5/092   019820163X
Grey, Charles Grey, -- Earl, -- 1764-1845.   Prime ministers -- Great Britain -- Biography.   Great Britain -- Politics and government -- 1800-1837. Great Britain -- Politics and government -- 1789-1820.

DA536.M15.A35
Macaulay, Thomas Babington Macaulay, 1800-1859.
Speeches by Lord Macaulay, with his Minute on Indian education; selected, with an introduction and notes, by G. M. Young. London, Oxford University Press, H. Milford [1935] xxii p.
36-027128   824.83

DA536.M15.K5
Knowles, David, 1896-
Lord Macaulay, 1800-1859.   Cambridge [Eng.] University Press, 1960. 30 p.
60-002407   928.2
Macaulay, Thomas Babington Macaulay, -- Baron, -- 1800-1859.

DA536.M5.C5 1954
Cecil, David, 1902-
Melbourne.   Indianapolis, Bobbs-Merrill [1954] 450 p.
54-009486   923.242
Melbourne, William Lamb, -- Viscount, -- 1779-1848. Lamb, Caroline, -- Lady, -- 1785-1828. Victoria, -- Queen of Great Britain, -- 1819-1901.

DA536.M5.M58 1997
Mitchell, L. G.
Lord Melbourne, 1779-1848/ L.G. Mitchell. Oxford; Oxford University Press, 1997. xviii, 349 p.
97-177477   941.07/5/092   0198205929
Melbourne, William Lamb, -- 2d Viscount, -- 1779-1848.   Prime ministers -- Great Britain -- Biography.   Great Britain -- Politics and government -- 1830-1837. Great Britain -- Politics and government -- 1837-1901.

DA536.P2.B68 1982
Bourne, Kenneth.
Palmerston, the early years, 1784-1841/ by Kenneth Bourne. New York: Macmillan, c1982. xiv, 749 p.
81-018582   941.081/092/4   0029037409
Palmerston, Henry John Temple, -- Viscount, -- 1784-1865.   Prime ministers -- Great Britain -- Biography.   Great Britain -- Foreign relations -- 1837-1901.   Great Britain -- Politics and government -- 1837-1901.

DA536.P2.S74 1991
Steele, E. D.
Palmerston and liberalism, 1855-1865/ E.D. Steele. Cambridge [England]; Cambridge University Press, 1991. xiii, 467 p.
90-040491   941.081/092   0521400457
Palmerston, Henry John Temple, -- Viscount, -- 1784-1865.   Liberalism -- Great Britain -- History -- 19th century.   Great Britain -- Politics and government -- 1837-1901.

DA536.P3.G3
Gash, Norman.
Mr. Secretary Peel; the life of Sir Robert Peel to 1830. Cambridge, Harvard University Press, 1961. xiv, 693 p.
61-009686   923.242
Peel, Robert, -- Sir, -- 1788-1850.

DA538.A1 H53 1975
Hibbert, Christopher,
George IV, regent and king, 1811-1830/ Christopher Hibbert.1st U.S. ed. New York: Harper & Row, [1975] c1973. xiv, 430 p.
75-313668   941.07/4/0924.   0060118865
George -- IV, King of Great Britain, 1762-1830.

DA538.A1.R5
Richardson, Joanna.
The disastrous marriage; a study of George IV and Caroline of Brunswick.   London, Cape [1960] 255 p.
61-000982   942.074
George -- IV, -- King of Great Britain, -- 1762-1830. Caroline Amelia Elizabeth, -- Queen, consort of George IV, King of Great Britain, -- 1768-1821.

DA539.N48 1990
Newbould, Ian.
Whiggery and reform, 1830-41: the politics of government/ Ian Newbould. Stanford, Calif.: Stanford University Press, 1990. x, 401 p.
89-062180   941.08   0804717591
Great Britain -- Politics and government -- 1830-1837.   Great Britain -- Politics and government -- 1837-1901.

DA541.F54.W43 1987
Weaver, Stewart Angas.
John Fielden and the politics of popular radicalism, 1832-1847/ Stewart Angas Weaver. Oxford: Clarendon Press; 1987. ix, 320 p.
87-005517   941.081/092/4   0198229275
Fielden, John, -- 1784-1849.   Radicalism -- Great Britain -- History -- 19th century. Populism -- Great Britain -- History -- 19th century. Industrialists -- Great Britain -- Biography. Great Britain -- Politics and government -- 1837-1901. Great Britain -- Politics and government -- 1830-1837.

DA550.B68 1970
Bourne, Kenneth.
The foreign policy of Victorian England, 1830-1902. Oxford, Clarendon P., 1970. xii, 531 p.
75-543411   327.42   0198730071
Great Britain -- Foreign relations -- 1837-1901. Great Britain -- History -- Victoria, 1837-1901 -- Sources.

DA550.B75 1989
Briggs, Asa, 1921-
Victorian things/ Asa Briggs. Chicago, IL: University of Chicago Press, 1989, c1988. p. cm.
88-030633   941.081   0226074838
Popular culture -- Great Britain -- History -- 19th century. Material culture -- Great Britain -- History -- 19th century. Great Britain -- History -- Victoria, 1837-1901.

DA550.B8
Burn, William Laurence.
The age of equipoise; a study of the mid-Victorian generation. New York, Norton [1964] 340 p.
64-002007   914.2
Great Britain -- History -- Victoria, 1837-1901. Great Britain -- Civilization.

DA550.C62 1991
Collini, Stefan, 1947-
Public moralists: political thought and intellectual life in Britain, 1850-1930/ Stefan Collini. Oxford: Clarendon Press; 1991. 383 p.
91-011490   941.08   0198201737
Political science -- Great Britain -- History -- 19th century. Political science -- Great Britain -- History -- 20th century. Intellectuals -- Great Britain -- Attitudes -- History. Great Britain -- Intellectual life -- 19th century. Great Britain -- Intellectual life -- 20th century.

DA550.E9 1968b
Evans, R. J.
The Victorian Age, 1815-1914 [by] R. J. Evans. New York, St. Martin's Press, 1968. ix, 357 p.
68-024273   942.081
Great Britain -- History -- Victoria, 1837-1901.

DA550.G68 1988
Gould, Peter C.
Early Green politics: back to nature, back to the land, and socialism in Britain, 1880-1900/ Peter C. Gould. Brighton, Sussex: Harvester Press; 1988. x, 225 p.
87-036074   941.081   0312019521
Socialism -- Great Britain -- History -- 19th century. Radicalism -- Great Britain -- History -- 19th century. Nature conservation -- Political aspects -- Great Britain -- History -- 19th century. Great Britain -- Politics and government -- 1837-1901. Great Britain -- Rural conditions -- 19th century.

DA550.J45 1994
Jenkins, T. A. 1958-
The Liberal ascendancy, 1830-1886/ T.A. Jenkins. New York: St. Martin's Press, 1994. xi, 252 p.
94-001160   941.081   0312121679
Liberalism -- Great Britain -- History -- 19th century. Great Britain -- Politics and government -- 1830-1837. Great Britain -- Politics and government -- 1837-1901.

DA550.J65
Jones, Wilbur Devereux.
The Peelites, 1846-1857, by Wilbur Devereux Jones [and] Arvel B. Erickson. [Columbus] Ohio State University Press [1972] xii, 259 p.
79-157717   942.081   0814201628
Peel, Robert, -- Sir, -- 1788-1850.   Great Britain -- Politics and government -- 1837-1901.

DA550.M28 2001
Machin, G. I. T.
The rise of democracy in Britain, 1830-1918/ Ian Machin. New York: St. Martin's Press, 2000. p. cm.
00-040448   320.941/09/034   0312235445
Democracy -- Great Britain -- History -- 19th century. Democracy -- Great Britain -- History -- 20th century.   Great Britain -- Politics and government -- 1837-1901. Great Britain -- Politics and government -- 1830-1837. Great Britain -- Politics and government -- 1901-1936.

DA550.N49 1997
Newsome, David, 1929-
The Victorian world picture: perceptions and introspections in an age of change/ David Newsome. New Brunswick, N.J.: Rutgers University Press, 1997. x, 310 p.
97-015588 941.081/072 0813524547
Historiography -- Great Britain -- History -- 19th century. Social change -- Historiography. World history -- Historiography. Great Britain -- Intellectual life -- 19th century. Great Britain -- Relations -- Foreign countries -- Historiography. Great Britain -- History -- Victoria, 1837-1901 -- Historiography.

DA550.P28 1993
Parry, J. P. 1957-
The rise and fall of liberal government in Victorian Britain/ Jonathan Parry. New Haven: Yale University Press, 1993. viii, 383 p.
93-005937 941.081 0300057792
Liberalism -- Great Britain -- History -- 19th century. Great Britain -- Politics and government -- 1837-1901.

DA550.S3 2000
Schlossberg, Herbert.
The silent revolution and the making of Victorian England/ Herbert Schlossberg. Columbus: Ohio State University Press, c2000. x, 405 p.
99-056104 941.081 0814208436
Religion and sociology -- Great Britain -- History -- 19th century. Evangelicalism -- Great Britain -- History -- 19th century. Great Britain -- History -- Victoria, 1837-1901. Great Britain -- Church history -- 19th century. Great Britain -- Civilization -- 19th century.

DA550.T53 1988
Thompson, F. M. L.
The rise of respectable society: a social history of Victorian Britain, 1830-1900/ F.M.L. Thompson. Cambridge, Mass.: Harvard University Press, 1988. 382 p.
88-014802 941.081 0674772857
Gentry -- Great Britain -- History -- 19th century. Great Britain -- History -- Victoria, 1837-1901. Great Britain -- Social life and customs -- 19th century.

DA550.V53 1988
Victorian Britain: an encyclopedia/ Sally Mitchell, editor ... [et al.]. New York: Garland Pub., 1988. xxi, 986 p.
87-029947 941.081/03/21 0824015134
Great Britain -- History -- Victoria, 1837-1901 -- Dictionaries. Great Britain -- Civilization -- 19th century -- Dictionaries.

DA554.B4
Benson, E. F. 1867-1940.
Queen Victoria, by E. F. Benson ... London, Longmans, Green and Co., 1935. 406 p.
35-027133 923.142
Victoria, -- Queen of Great Britain, -- 1819-1901.

DA554.H5 2000
Hibbert, Christopher, 1924-
Queen Victoria: a personal history/ Christopher Hibbert. New York: Basic Books, c2000. xviii, 557 p.
2001-269136 941.081/092 0465067611
Victoria, -- Queen of Great Britain, -- 1819-1901. Queens -- Great Britain -- Biography. Great Britain -- History -- Victoria, 1837-1901.

DA554.M86 1996
Munich, Adrienne.
Queen Victoria's secrets/ Adrienne Munich. New York: Columbia University Press, c1996. xx, 254 p.
95-043737 941.081 0231104804
Victoria, -- Queen of Great Britain, -- 1819-1901. Women -- Great Britain -- History -- 19th century. Queens -- Great Britain -- Biography. Great Britain -- Social life and customs -- 19th century. Great Britain -- History -- Victoria, 1837-1901.

DA554.S7 1969
Strachey, Lytton, 1880-1932.
Queen Victoria, by Lytton Strachey. London, Chatto & Windus, 1969. 257 p.
72-435370 942.081/0924 0701111313
Victoria, -- Queen of Great Britain, -- 1819-1901. Queens -- Great Britain -- Biography. Great Britain -- History -- Victoria, 1837-1901.

DA555.C48 1991
Charlot, Monica.
Victoria: the young queen/ Monica Charlot. Oxford, UK; Blackwell, 1991. vii, 492 p.
90-024757 941.081/092 0631174370
Victoria, -- Queen of Great Britain, -- 1819-1901 - - Childhood and youth. Queens -- Great Britain -- Biography. Great Britain -- History -- Victoria, 1837-1901.

DA559.7.F29 1987
Faber, Richard, 1924-
Young England/ Richard Faber. London; Faber and Faber, 1987. xii, 276 p.
88-672089 057114831X
Young England movement. Great Britain -- Politics and government -- 1837-1901. Great Britain -- Intellectual life -- 19th century.

DA559.7.G35
Gash, Norman.
Reaction and reconstruction in English politics, 1832-1852. Oxford, Clarendon Press, 1965. 227 p.
66-000609
Great Britain -- Politics and government -- 1837-1901. Great Britain -- Politics and government -- 1830-1837.

DA559.7.H7 1967
Hovell, Mark, 1888-1916.
The Chartist movement. Edited and completed with a memoir by T. F. Tout. New York, A. M. Kelley, 1967. xxxvii, 327 p.
67-004890 329.9/42
Chartism.

DA560.A18 1993
The 1890s: an encyclopedia of British literature, art, and culture/ edited by G.A. Cevasco. New York: Garland, 1993. xxi, 714 p.
92-042341 941.081/03 0824025857
English literature -- 19th century -- Encyclopedias. Art, Modern -- 19th century -- Great Britain -- Encyclopedias. Great Britain -- History -- Victoria, 1837-1901 -- Encyclopedias. Great Britain -- Civilization -- 19th century -- Encyclopedias.

DA560.B53 1992
Biagini, Eugenio F.
Liberty, retrenchment, and reform: popular liberalism in the Age of Gladstone, 1860-1880/ Eugenio F. Biagini. Cambridge; Cambridge University Press, 1992. xii, 476 p.
91-019673 941.081 0521403154
Gladstone, W. E. -- (William Ewart), -- 1809-1898. Liberalism -- Great Britain -- History -- 19th century. Great Britain -- Politics and government -- 1837-1901.

DA560.B84 1970
Briggs, Asa, 1921-
Victorian people; a reassessment of persons and themes, 1851-67. [Chicago] University of Chicago Press [1970] ix, 312 p.
71-016973 914.2/03/810922 0226074900
Great Britain -- History -- Victoria, 1837-1901. Great Britain -- Biography.

DA560.F48 1985
Feuchtwanger, E. J.
Democracy and empire: Britain, 1865-1914/ E.J. Feuchtwanger. London: E. Arnold, 1985. 408 p.
85-173115 941.081 0713161612
Great Britain -- Politics and government -- 1837-1901. Great Britain -- Politics and government -- 1901-1936.

DA560.H58 1998
Hoppen, K. Theodore, 1941-
The mid-Victorian generation, 1846-1886/ K. Theodore Hoppen. Oxford: Clarendon Press; 1998. xviii, 787 p.
97-018126 941.081 0198228341
Great Britain -- History -- Victoria, 1837-1901.

DA560.L29 1998
Lawrence, Jon.
Speaking for the people: party, language, and popular politics in England, 1867-1914/ Jon Lawrence. Cambridge, United Kingdom; Cambridge University Press, 1998. xiii, 289 p.
97-030166 324/.0941/09034 052147034X
English language -- Political aspects -- Great Britain. Political parties -- Great Britain -- History. Popular culture -- Great Britain -- History. Great Britain -- Politics and government - - 1901-1936. Great Britain -- Politics and government -- 1837-1901.

DA560.P79 1982
Pugh, Martin.
The making of modern British politics, 1867-1939/ Martin Pugh. New York: St. Martin's Press, 1982. xi, 337 p.
81-023292 941.08 0312507011
Political parties -- Great Britain -- History. Great Britain -- Politics and government -- 1837-1901. Great Britain -- Politics and government -- 1901-1936. Great Britain -- Politics and government -- 1936-1945.

DA560.S39 1993
Searle, G. R.
Entrepreneurial politics in mid-Victorian Britain/ G.R. Searle. New York: Oxford University Press, 1993. viii, 346 p.
92-028432 941.081 0198203578
Middle class -- Great Britain -- Political activity -- History -- 19th century. Entrepreneurship -- Great Britain -- History -- 19th century. Great Britain -- Politics and government -- 1837-1901.

DA560.S44 1992
Shannon, Richard.
The age of Disraeli, 1868-1881: the rise of Tory democracy/ Richard Shannon. London; Longman, 1992. vii, 445 p.
91-037163 324.24104/09/034 0582507138
Disraeli, Benjamin, -- Earl of Beaconsfield, -- 1804-1881. Great Britain -- Politics and government -- 1837-1901.

DA560.T38 1995
Taylor, Miles.
The decline of British radicalism, 1847-1860/
Miles Taylor. Oxford [England]: Clarendon Press;
1995. x, 422 p.
94-003537   941.081   0198204825
*Racicalism -- Great Britain -- History -- 19th
century. Great Britain -- Politics and government
-- 1837-1901.*

DA560.W3 1996
Wellhofer, E. Spencer, 1941-
Democracy, capitalism, and empire in late
Victorian Britain, 1885-1910/ E. Spencer
Wellhofer. Houndmills, Basingstoke, Hampshire:
Macmillan Press; 1996. xiv, 264 p.
95-043678   941.081   0333643135
*Capitalism -- Great Britain -- History -- 19th
century. Democracy -- Great Britain -- History --
19th century. Great Britain -- Politics and
government -- 1901-1910. Great Britain -- Politics
and government -- 1837-1901. Great Britain --
Colonies -- History -- 19th century.*

DA562.W55 1989
Wilson, A. N. 1950-
Eminent Victorians/ A.N. Wilson. London: BBC
Books, 1989. 240 p.
91-182934   941.081/092/2   0563207191
*Great Britain -- History -- Victoria, 1837-1901
-- Biography.*

DA563.4.C76 1997
Crosby, Travis L., 1936-
The two Mr. Gladstones: a study in psychology and
history/ Travis L. Crosby. New Haven: Yale
University Press, c1997. x, 287 p.
96-026547   941.081/092   0300068271
*Gladstone, W. E. -- (William Ewart), -- 1809-1898
-- Psychology. Prime ministers -- Great Britain --
Psychology. Political psychology. Great Britain --
Politics and government -- 1837-1901.*

DA563.4.J45 1997
Jenkins, Roy.
Gladstone: a biography/ Roy Jenkins. New York:
Random House, 1997. 698 p.
96-049632   941.081/092   0679451447
*Gladstone, W. E. -- (William Ewart), -- 1809-1898.
Prime ministers -- Great Britain -- Biography.
Great Britain -- Politics and government -- 1837-
1901.*

DA563.4.K5 1966
Knaplund, Paul, 1885-1964
Gladstone and Britain's imperial policy. [Hamden,
Conn.] Archon Books, 1966. 256 p.
67-000124   325.342
*Gladstone, W. E. -- (William Ewart), -- 1809-1898
-- Views on imperialism. Imperialism -- History --
19th century. Imperialism -- Government policy --
Great Britain. Great Britain -- Colonies -- History
-- 19th century.*

DA563.4.S5 1984
Shannon, Richard.
Gladstone/ Richard Shannon. Chapel Hill:
University of North Carolina Press, 1984-1999. 2
v.
83-019860   941.081/092/4   0807815918
*Gladstone, W. E. -- (William Ewart), -- 1809-1898.
Prime ministers -- Great Britain -- Biography.
Great Britain -- Politics and government -- 1837-
1901.*

DA563.5.J46 1988
Jenkins, T. A. 1958-
Gladstone, Whiggery, and the Liberal Party, 1874-
1886/ T.A. Jenkins. Oxford: Clarendon Press;
1988. vi, 328 p.
87-028113   941.081   019820129X
*Gladstone, W. E. -- (William Ewart), -- 1809-1898.
Great Britain -- Politics and government -- 1837-
1901.*

DA564.B3.B6 1967
Blake, Robert, 1916-
Disraeli. New York, St. Martin's Press [1967,
c1966] xxiv, 819 p.
67-011837   942.081/0924
*Disraeli, Benjamin, -- Earl of Beaconsfield, --
1804-1881. Prime ministers -- Great Britain --
Biography. Great Britain -- History -- Victoria,
1837-1901.*

DA564.B3.F48 2000
Feuchtwanger, E. J.
Disraeli/ Edgar Feuchtwanger. London: Arnold;
2000. xii, 244 p.
00-712703   941.081/092   0340719095
*Disraeli, Benjamin, -- Earl of Beaconsfield, --
1804-1881. Prime ministers -- Great Britain --
Biography. Great Britain -- Politics and
government -- 1837-1901.*

DA564.B3.H52 1978b
Hibbert, Christopher, 1924-
Disraeli and his world/ Christopher Hibbert. New
York: Scribner, c1978. 128 p.
78-059111   941.081/092/4   0684159155
*Disraeli, Benjamin, -- Earl of Beaconsfield, --
1804-1881. Prime ministers -- Great Britain --
Biography. Great Britain -- Politics and
government -- 1837-1901.*

DA564.B3.R53 1995
Ridley, Jane.
Young Disraeli, 1804-1846/ Jane Ridley. New
York: Crown Publishers, c1995. x, 406 p.
94-025543   941.081/092   0517586436
*Disraeli, Benjamin, -- Earl of Beaconsfield, --
1804-1881. Prime ministers -- Great Britain --
Biography.*

DA564.B3.S65 1996
Smith, Paul, 1937-
Disraeli: a brief life/ Paul Smith. Cambridge;
Cambridge University Press, c1996. x, 246 p.
95-051407   941.081/092   0521381509
*Disraeli, Benjamin, -- Earl of Beaconsfield, --
1804-1881. Prime ministers -- Great Britain --
Biography. Jews -- Great Britain -- Biography.
Romanticism -- Great Britain. Great Britain --
History -- Victoria, 1837-1901.*

DA564.R7.J3 1963
Rhodes James, Robert, 1933-
Rosebery, a biography of Archibald Philip, fifth
earl of Rosebery. London, Weidenfeld and
Nicolson [1963] xiv, 534 p.
63-024262
*Rosebery, Archibald Philip Primrose, -- Earl of, --
1847-1929.*

DA565.B8.T8 1971
Trevelyan, George Macaulay, 1876-1962.
The life of John Bright. Westport, Conn.,
Greenwood Press [1971] x, [1], 480 p.
72-110873   942.081/0924   083714552X
*Bright, John, -- 1811-1889. Great Britain --
Politics and government -- 19th century.*

DA565.C15.W54 1974
Wilson, John, 1924-
CB: a life of Sir Henry Campbell-Bannerman.
New York, St. Martin's Press [1974, c1973] 717 p.
73-085379   942.082/092/4
Campbell-Bannerman, Henry, -- Sir, -- 1836-1908.

DA565.C4.A32
Chamberlain, Joseph, 1836-1914.
A political memoir, 1880-92. Edited from the
original manuscript by C. H. D. Howard. London,
Batchworth Press [1953] xx, 340 p.
53-002236   942.081
*Great Britain -- Politics and government --
1837-1901.*

DA565.C4.B45 1996
Bell, Peter, 1949-
Chamberlain, Germany and Japan, 1933-4/ Peter
Bell. New York: St. Martin's Press, 1996. xii,
240 p.
95-053264   941.084   0312158831
*Chamberlain, Neville, -- 1869-1940 -- Views on
foreign relations. World politics -- 1933-1945.
Great Britain -- Foreign relations -- 1910-1936.
Great Britain -- Foreign relations -- Germany.
Germany -- Foreign relations -- Great Britain.*

DA565.C4.M35 1994
Marsh, Peter T.
Joseph Chamberlain: entrepreneur in politics/ Peter
T. Marsh. New Haven: Yale University Press,
1994. xvii, 725 p.
93-047209   941.081/092   0300058012
*Chamberlain, Joseph, -- 1836-1914. Statesmen --
Great Britain -- Biography. Industrialists -- Great
Britain -- Biography. Great Britain -- Politics and
government -- 1837-1901. Great Britain -- Politics
and government -- 1901-1910.*

DA565.C6.C6 1952
Churchill, Winston, 1874-1965.
Lord Randolph Churchill. London, Odhams Press.
1952. 840 p.
52-032352   923.242
*Churchill, Randolph Henry Spencer, -- Lord, --
1849-1895.*

DA565.C6.M3
Martin, Ralph G., 1920-
Jennie: the life of Lady Randolph Churchill, by
Ralph G. Martin. Englewood Cliffs, N.J., Prentice-
Hall [1969-71] 2 v.
68-054197   942.081/0924
*Churchill, Randolph Spencer, -- Lady, -- 1854-
1921.*

DA565.D4.J33 1994
Jackson, Patrick, 1929-
The last of the Whigs: a political biography of
Lord Hartington, later eighth Duke of Devonshire
(1833-1908)/ Patrick Jackson. Rutherford:
Fairleigh Dickinson University Press; c1994.
398 p.
92-055030   941.081/092   0838635148
*Devonshire, Spencer Compton Cavendish, -- Duke
of, -- 1833-1908. Statesmen -- Great Britain --
Biography. Great Britain -- Politics and
government -- 1837-1901. Great Britain -- Politics
and government -- 1901-1910.*

DA565.D6.N53 1995
Nicholls, David, 1948-
The lost prime minister: a life of Sir Charles Dilke/ David Nicholls. London; Hambledon Press, 1995. xxix, 386 p.
95-006072   941.081/092   1852851252
Dilke, Charles Wentworth, -- Sir, -- 1843-1911. Radicalism -- Great Britain -- History -- 19th century. Politicians -- Great Britain -- Biography. Great Britain -- Politics and government -- 1837-1901.

DA565.H75.M35 1989
McKercher, B. J. C., 1950-
Esme Howard: a diplomatic biography/ B.J.C. McKercher. Cambridge [England]; Cambridge University Press, 1989. xiv, 482 p.
88-027440   327.2/0924   052132257X
Howard of Penrith, Esme Howard, -- Baron, -- 1863-1939.   Diplomats -- Great Britain -- Biography.   Great Britain -- Foreign relations -- 1901-1936.

DA565.M75.M87 2000
Murray, Scott W., 1962-
Liberal diplomacy and German unification: the early career of Robert Morier/ by Scott W. Murray. Westport, Conn.: Praeger, 2000. xxii, 277 p.
99-059653   327.41/043/092   0275967301
Morier, Robert, -- Sir, -- 1826-1893. Diplomats -- Great Britain -- Biography. Constitutional history -- Germany -- Prussia. Free trade -- Great Britain. Great Britain -- Foreign relations -- 19th century. Germany -- Foreign relations -- Great Britain. Great Britain -- Foreign relations -- Germany.

DA565.M78.K66
Koss, Stephen E.
John Morley at the India Office, 1905-1910, by Stephen E. Koss. New Haven, Yale University Press, 1969. viii, 231 p.
72-081423   325.3/1/0924
Morley, John, -- 1838-1923.   India -- Politics and government -- 1765-1947. Great Britain -- Colonies.

DA565.R825.U72 1999
Urbach, Karina.
Bismarck's favourite Englishman: Lord Odo Russell's mission to Berlin/ Karina Urbach. London; I.B. Tauris, 1999. vii, 279 p.
   1860644384
Russell, Odo, -- Sir, -- 1829-1884. Bismarck, Otto, -- Furst von, -- 1815-1898. Diplomats -- Great Britain -- Biography.   Europe -- Politics and government -- 1871-1918. Great Britain -- Foreign relations -- Germany. Germany -- Foreign relations -- Great Britain.

DA566.C545 1997
Clarke, P. F.
Hope and glory: Britain, 1900-1990/ Peter Clarke. London; Penguin Books, 1997. x, 454 p.
98-100813   941.082   0140148302
Great Britain -- History -- 20th century.

DA566.S4
Seaman, L. C. B.
Post-Victorian Britain: 1902-1951/ L.C.B. Seaman. London: Methuen, 1966. xi, 531 p.
66-071853   942.082
Great Britain -- History -- 20th century.

DA566.T38 1965
Taylor, A. J. P. 1906-
English history: 1914-1945.   Oxford University Press, 1965. 708 p.
65-027513   942.082
Great Britain -- History -- 20th century.

DA566.T835 1995
Twentieth-century Britain: an encyclopedia/ editor, F.M. Leventhal. New York: Garland Pub., 1995. xxxviii, 902 p.
95-030749   941.082/03   0824072057
Great Britain -- History -- 20th century -- Encyclopedias. Great Britain -- Civilization -- 20th century -- Encyclopedias.

DA566.W55
Wingfield-Stratford, Esme Cecil, 1882-
Before the lamps went out, by Esme Wingfield-Stratford ... London, Hodder & Stoughton Limited [1945] 255 p.
46-003228   942.08
Great Britain -- Social life and customs. Great Britain -- History -- 20th century.

DA566.2.C67 1993
Cook, Chris, 1945-
The St. Martin's guide to sources in contemporary British history/ compiled for the British Library of Political and Economic Science by Chris Cook and David Waller. New York: St. Martin's Press, 1993- v. 1-
93-011678   016.941/085   0312103034
Archives -- Great Britain -- Directories.   Great Britain -- History -- Elizabeth II, 1952- -- Sources -- Directories. Great Britain -- History -- Elizabeth II, 1952- -- Archival resources -- Directories. Great Britain -- History -- 20th century -- Sources -- Directories.

DA566.4.A665 1991
Annan, Noel Gilroy Annan, 1916-
Our age: English intellectuals between the World Wars--a group portrait/ Noel Annan. New York: Random House, c1990. x, 479 p.
90-052887   941.085   0394542959
Great Britain -- Intellectual life -- 20th century.

DA566.4.H39 1996
Haseler, Stephen, 1942-
The English tribe: identity, nation, and Europe/ Stephen Haseler. Houndmills, Basingstoke, Hampshire: Macmillan Press; 1996. ix, 201 p.
95-051722   305.8/00941/09045   0312160046
National characteristics, English. Group identity -- England -- History -- 20th century. Nationalism -- England -- History -- 20th century. England -- Civilization -- 20th century. England -- Relations -- Europe. Europe -- Relations -- England.

DA566.4.M357 1968
Marwick, Arthur, 1936-
Britain in the century of total war; war, peace, and social change, 1900-1967. Boston, Little, Brown [1968] 511 p.
68-017276   942.082
History, Modern -- 20th century.   Great Britain -- Civilization -- 20th century.

DA566.4.W48
Williams, Raymond.
The long revolution/ by Raymond Williams. New York: Columbia University Press, 1961. xiv, 369 p.
61-006336
Great Britain -- Intellectual life. Great Britain -- Intellectual life -- 20th century.

DA566.7.B29 1989
Bartlett, C. J. 1931-
British foreign policy in the twentieth century/ C.J. Bartlett. New York: St. Martin's Press, 1989. lx, 144 p.
88-034583   327.41   031202844X
Great Britain -- Foreign relations -- 20th century.

DA566.7.B442
Beloff, Max Beloff, 1913-
Imperial sunset. New York, Knopf, 1970-1989. 2 v.
69-011480   327.42   0911378928
Great Britain -- Foreign relations -- 20th century.

DA566.7.B446 1984
Beloff, Max Beloff, 1913-
Wars and welfare: Britain, 1914-1945/ Max Beloff. London; E. Arnold, 1984. vi, 281 p.
84-116530   941.083   0713161639
Great Britain -- Politics and government -- 20th century.

DA566.7.C53 1938a
Churchill, Winston, 1874-1965.
While England slept; a survey of world affairs, 1932-1938, by Winston S. Churchill. With a preface and notes by Randolph S. Churchill. New York, G.P. Putnam's Sons, 1938. xii, 404 p.
38-027899   942.08
Disarmament. Security, International.   Great Britain -- Foreign relations -- 20th century. Europe -- Politics and government -- 1918-1945. Germany -- Politics and government -- 1933-1945.

DA566.7.C64 1999
Copsey, Nigel, 1967-
Anti-fascism in Britain/ Nigel Copsey. New York: St. Martin's Press, 1999. p. cm.
99-033827   320.53/3/09410904   0312227655
Anti-fascist movements -- Great Britain -- History -- 20th century. Fascism -- Great Britain -- History -- 20th century. Great Britain -- Politics and government -- 20th century.

DA566.7.E53 2000
Encyclopedia of British and Irish political organizations: parties, groups, and movements of the twentieth century/ Peter Barberis ... [et al.]. London; Pinter, 2000. vii, 562 p.
98-052555   320.941/09/04   1855672642
Political parties -- Great Britain -- History -- 20th century -- Encyclopedias. Political parties -- Ireland -- History -- 20th century -- Encyclopedias. Pressure groups -- Great Britain -- History -- 20th century -- Encyclopedias. Great Britain -- Politics and government -- 20th century -- Encyclopedias. Ireland -- Politics and government -- 20th century -- Encyclopedias.

DA566.7.E93 1996
Evans, Brendan, 1944-
From Salisbury to Major: continuity and change in conservative politics/ Brendan Evans and Andrew Taylor. Manchester; Manchester University Press; 1996. vii, 288 p.
95-030846   324.24104/09/04   0719042909
Salisbury, Robert Cecil, -- marquess of, -- 1830-1903. Major, John Roy, -- 1943- Conservatism -- Great Britain -- History -- 20th century Great Britain -- Politics and government -- 20th century.

DA566.7.R547 1994
Robbins, Keith.
Politicians, diplomacy, and war in modern British history/ Keith Robbins. London; Hambledon Press, c1994. xi, 306 p.
94-002354   941   1852851112
Bryce, James Bryce, -- Viscount, -- 1838-1922. Bright, John, -- 1811-1889.   Great Britain -- Politics and government -- 1837-1901. Great Britain -- Politics and government -- 1901-1910. Great Britain -- Foreign relations.

DA566.7.T55 1995
Thurlow, Richard C.
The secret state: British internal security in the twentieth century/ Richard Thurlow. Oxford, UK; Blackwell, 1995. xiii, 458 p.
94-006153   941.082   0631160663
Internal security -- Great Britain -- History -- 20th century. Official secrets -- Great Britain -- History -- 20th century. Great Britain -- Politics and government -- 20th century.

DA566.9.A1.B57 1990
The Blackwell biographical dictionary of British political life in the twentieth century/ edited by Keith Robbins. Oxford, OX, UK; Blackwell Reference, 1990. xii, 449 p.
89-048260   920.041   0631157689
Politicians -- Great Britain -- Biography -- Dictionaries. Great Britain -- Politics and government -- 20th century -- Dictionaries. Great Britain -- Biography -- Dictionaries.

DA566.9.B15.B34 1988
Ball, Stuart, 1956-
Baldwin and the Conservative Party: the crisis of 1929-1931/ Stuart Ball. New Haven: Yale University Press, 1988. xix, 266 p.
87-022504   941.083/092/4   0300039611
Baldwin, Stanley Baldwin, -- Earl, -- 1867-1947. Depressions -- 1929 -- Great Britain. Great Britain -- Politics and government -- 1910-1936.

DA566.9.B15.W56 1999
Williamson, Philip, 1953-
Stanley Baldwin: conservative leadership and national values/ Philip Williamson. Cambridge; Cambridge University Press, 1999. xvi, 378 p.
98-043633   941.083/092   0521432278
Baldwin, Stanley Baldwin, -- Earl, -- 1867-1947. Conservatism -- Great Britain -- History -- 20th century. Prime ministers -- Great Britain -- Biography. Great Britain -- Politics and government -- 1910-1936.

DA566.9.B2.T66 1997
Tomes, Jason.
Balfour and foreign policy: the international thought of conservative statesman/ Jason Tomes. Cambridge; Cambridge University Press, 1997. ix, 323 p.
96-019709   327.41   0521581184
Balfour, Arthur James Balfour, -- Earl of, -- 1848-1930 -- Views on foreign relations. Conservatism -- Great Britain -- History -- 20th century. Great Britain -- Foreign relations -- 1901-1936. Great Britain -- Foreign relations -- 1837-1901. Great Britain -- Intellectual life.

DA566.9.B37.C49 1993
Chisholm, Anne.
Lord Beaverbrook: a life/ by Anne Chisholm and Michael Davie. New York: Knopf: 1993. ix, 589 p.
92-054282   941.082/092   0394568796
Beaverbrook, Max Aitken, -- Baron, -- 1879-1964. Newspaper publishing -- Great Britain -- History -- 20th century. Publishers and publishing -- Great Britain -- Biography. Politicians -- Great Britain -- Biography. Great Britain -- Politics and government -- 20th century.

DA566.9.B56.A3 1996
Bonham Carter, Violet, 1887-1969.
Lantern slides: the diaries and letters of Violet Bonham Carter, 1904-1914/ edited by Mark Bonham Carter & Mark Pottle. London: Weidenfeld & Nicolson, 1996. xxviii, 461 p.
96-208311   941.082/3/092   0297816497
Bonham Carter, Violet, -- 1887-1969 -- Diaries. Asquith, H. H. -- (Herbert Henry), -- 1852-1928 -- Family. Bonham Carter, Violet, -- 1887-1969 -- Correspondence. Women in politics -- Great Britain -- Biography. Great Britain -- Politics and government -- 1901-1936 -- Sources. Great Britain -- Social life and customs -- 20th century -- Sources.

DA566.9.C43.G73 1997
Grayson, Richard S., 1969-
Austen Chamberlain and the commitment to Europe: British foreign policy, 1924-29/ Richard S. Grayson. London; Frank Cass, 1997. xviii, 318 p.
97-010824   327.41   0714647586
Chamberlain, Austen, -- Sir, -- 1863-1937. Great Britain -- Foreign relations -- 1910-1936. Great Britain -- Foreign relations -- Europe. Europe -- Foreign relations -- Great Britain.

DA566.9.C44.A3
Chandos, Oliver Lyttelton, 1893-
The memoirs of Lord Chandos: an unexpected view from the summit/ by Oliver Lyttelton, Viscount Chandos. New York: New American Library, 1963. xvi, 430 p.
63-021512   923.242
Chandos, Oliver Lyttelton, -- 1st viscount, -- 1893- Great Britain -- History -- 20th century.

DA566.9.C5.A375 1961
Churchill, Winston, 1874-1965.
The unwritten alliance: speeches 1953-1959. Edited by Randolph S. Churchill. London, Cassell [1961] xi, 332 p.
63-006468
Great Britain -- Politics and government -- 1945- Great Britain -- Relations (general) with the United States. United States -- Relations (general) with Great Britain.

DA566.9.C5.A4 1997
Churchill, Winston, 1874-1965.
Winston Churchill and Emery Reves: correspondence, 1937-1964/ edited with an introduction and notes by Martin Gilbert. Austin, TX: University of Texas Press, 1997. viii, 397 p.
97-014310   941.084/092   0292712014
Churchill, Winston, -- Sir, -- 1874-1965 -- Correspondence. Reves, Emery, -- 1904- Correspondence. Literary agents -- Europe -- Correspondence. Prime ministers -- Great Britain -- Correspondence.

DA566.9.C5.A63 1993
Addison, Paul, 1943-
Churchill on the home front, 1900-1955/ Paul Addison. London: Pimlico, 1993. xi, 493 p.
94-192295   941.081/092   0712658262
Churchill, Winston, -- Sir, -- 1874-1965. Prime ministers -- Great Britain -- Biography. Great Britain -- Politics and government -- 20th century.

DA566.9.C5.G463 1982
Gilbert, Martin, 1936-
Winston Churchill, the wilderness years/ Martin Gilbert. Boston: Houghton Mifflin, 1982. 279 p.
82-009279   941.082/092/4   0395318696
Churchill, Winston, -- Sir, -- 1874-1965. Prime ministers -- Great Britain -- Biography. Great Britain -- Politics and government -- 1910-1936. Great Britain -- Politics and government -- 1936-1945.

DA566.9.C5 J46 2001
Jenkins, Roy.
Churchill: a biography/ Roy Jenkins.1st ed. New York: Farrar, Straus and Giroux, 2001. xxi, 1002 p.
2001-040560   941.084/092. 221   0374123543
Churchill, Winston, Sir, 1874-1965. Prime ministers--Great Britain--Biography.

DA566.9.C5.M26 1983
Manchester, William Raymond, 1922-
The last lion, Winston Spencer Churchill/ by William Manchester. Boston: Little, Brown, c1983-c1988 v. 1-2
82-024972   941.084/092/4   0316545031
Churchill, Winston, -- Sir, -- 1874-1965. Great Britain -- Politics and government -- 20th century. Great Britain -- Foreign relations -- 20th century.

DA566.9.C525.G55 1999
Gillies, Donald.
Radical diplomat: the life of Archibald Clark Kerr, Lord Inverchapel, 1882-1951/ Donald Gillies. London; I.B. Tauris Publishers; 1999. x, 256 p.
1860642969
Clark Kerr, Archibald John Kerr, -- Baron Inverchapel, -- 1882-1951. Clark Kerr, Archibald John Kerr, -- Baron Inverchapel, -- 1882-1951 -- Biography. Diplomats -- Great Britain -- Biography. World War, 1939-1945 -- Diplomatic history. Great Britain -- Foreign relations -- 1936-1945.

DA566.9.C64.A3
Cooper, Duff, 1890-1954.
Old men forget: the autobiography of Duff Cooper (Viscount Norwich) London: Hart-Davis, 1953. 399 p.
54-004615
Cooper, Duff, -- Viscount Norwich, -- 1890-1954. Statesmen -- Great Britain -- Biography. Great Britain -- Politics and government -- 20th century.

DA566.9.C76.W58 1997
Witherell, Larry L., 1949-
Rebel on the right: Henry Page Croft and the crisis of British Conservatism, 1903-1914/ Larry L. Witherell. Newark: University of Delaware Press; c1997. 291 p.
97-013256   941.084/092   0874136229
Croft, Henry Page, -- 1881-1947. Conservatism -- Great Britain -- History -- 20th century. Great Britain -- Politics and government -- 1910-1936. Great Britain -- Politics and government -- 1901-1910.

DA566.9.E28.A36
Eden, Anthony, 1897-
Facing the dictators; the memoirs of Anthony Eden, earl of Avon. Boston, Houghton Mifflin, 1962. 746 p.
62-018265   941.085/5/0924
Eden, Anthony, -- Earl of Avon, -- 1897- -- Views on foreign relations. Great Britain -- Foreign relations -- 1936-1945. Great Britain -- Foreign relations -- 1910-1936.

DA566.9.E28.D88 1997
Dutton, David, 1947-
Anthony Eden: a life and reputation/ David Dutton. London; Arnold: c1997. xiv, 576 p.
96-009223   941.082/092   0340561688
Eden, Anthony, -- Earl of Avon, -- 1897- Prime ministers -- Great Britain -- Biography. Great Britain -- Politics and government -- 20th century.

DA566.9.E28.R48 1987
Rhodes James, Robert, 1933-
Anthony Eden/ Robert Rhodes James. New York:
McGraw-Hill, 1987, c1986. xiv, 665 p.
87-002940 941.085/5/0924 0070322856
*Eden, Anthony, -- Earl of Avon, -- 1897- Great
Britain -- Politics and government -- 1936-1945.
Great Britain -- Politics and government -- 1945-
1964. Great Britain -- Foreign relations -- 1936-
1945.*

DA566.9.G3.B75 1996
Brivati, Brian.
Hugh Gaitskell/ Brian Brivati. London: Richard
Cohen Books, 1996. xix, 492 p.
96-214415 941.08/092 1860660738
*Gaitskell, Hugh, -- 1906-1963. Politicians --
Great Britain -- Biography. Great Britain --
Politics and government -- 1945-1964. Great
Britain -- Politics and government -- 1936-1945.*

DA566.9.G3.W54
Williams, Philip Maynard.
Hugh Gaitskell: a political biography/ Philip M.
Williams. London: J. Cape, 1979. xx, 1007 p.
79-322770 941.0855/092/4 022401451X
*Gaitskell, Hugh, -- 1906-1963. Politicians --
Great Britain -- Biography. Great Britain --
Politics and government -- 1936-1945. Great
Britain -- Politics and government -- 1945-1964.*

DA566.9.H27.K6
Koss, Stephen E.
Lord Haldane; scapegoat for liberalism [by]
Stephen E. Koss. New York, Columbia University
Press, 1969. ix, 263 p.
69-019460 942.083/0924
*Haldane, R. B. Haldane -- (Richard Burdon
Haldane), -- Viscount, -- 1856-1928. Statesmen --
Great Britain -- Biography. Liberalism -- Great
Britain -- History. Great Britain -- Politics and
government -- 1901-1936. Great Britain -- Politics
and government -- 1837-1901.*

DA566.9.L5.B4
Beaverbrook, Max Aitken, 1879-1964.
The decline and fall of Lloyd George. New York,
Duell, Sloan and Pearce [1963] 320 p.
63-014328 923.242
*Lloyd George, David, -- 1863-1945. Great
Britain -- History -- 1910-1936.*

DA566.9.L5.G56 1987
Gilbert, Bentley B., 1924-
David Lloyd George: a political life/ Bentley
Brinkerhoff Gilbert. Columbus: Ohio State
University Press, c1987-c1992 v. 1-2
86-033211 941.083/092 0814204325
*Lloyd George, David, -- 1863-1945. Prime
ministers -- Great Britain -- Biography. Great
Britain -- Politics and government -- 1837-1901.
Great Britain -- Politics and government -- 1901-
1936.*

DA566.9.L5.G78 1978b
Grigg, John, 1924-
Lloyd George, the people's champion, 1902-1911/
John Grigg. Berkeley: University of California
Press, c1978. 391 p.
77-091762 941.083/092/4 0520036344
*Lloyd George, David, -- 1863-1945. Prime
ministers -- Great Britain -- Biography. Great
Britain -- Politics and government -- 1901-1910.*

DA566.9.L5.W76 1991
Wrigley, Chris.
Lloyd George and the challenge of Labour: the
post-war coalition, 1918-1922/ Chris Wrigley. New
York: St. Martin's Press, 1991. viii, 326 p.
90-039708 941.083/092 0312019696
*Lloyd George, David, -- 1863-1945. Coalition
governments -- Great Britain -- History -- 20th
century. Labour Party (Great Britain) -- History.
Great Britain -- Politics and government -- 1910-
1936.*

DA566.9.M25.M37
Marquand, David.
Ramsay MacDonald/ David Marquand. London: J.
Cape, 1977. xvi, 903 p.
77-358953 942.083/092/4 0224012959
*MacDonald, James Ramsay, -- 1866-1937. Prime
ministers -- Great Britain -- Biography. Great
Britain -- Politics and government -- 1910-1936.*

DA566.9.M33.A27 1971b
Macmillan, Harold, 1894-
Riding the storm, 1956-1959. New York, Harper
& Row [1971] viii, 786 p.
79-156535 942.085/0924 0060127749
*Macmillan, Harold, -- 1894- Great Britain --
Politics and government -- 1945-1964. Great
Britain -- Foreign relations -- 1945-*

DA566.9.M33.A28 1969
Macmillan, Harold, 1894-
Tides of fortune, 1945-1955. New York, Harper &
Row [1969] xxii, 729 p.
78-083609 942.085/0924
*   Great Britain -- Politics and government --
20th century. Great Britain -- Foreign relations --
20th century.*

DA566.9.M33.G4 1998
Gearson, John P. S., 1963-
Harold Macmillan and the Berlin Wall crisis, 1958-
62: the limits of interests and force/ John P. S.
Gearson. New York, N.Y.: St. Martin's Press,
1998. xiii, 281 p.
97-005095 327.41043 0312174004
*Macmillan, Harold, -- 1894- Berlin Wall, Berlin,
Germany, 1961-1989. Berlin (Germany) --
Politics and government -- 1945-1990. Great
Britain -- Foreign relations -- Germany. Germany
-- Foreign relations -- Great Britain.*

DA566.9.M33.H6 1989
Horne, Alistair.
Harold Macmillan/ Alistair Horne. New York,
N.Y.: A.A. Knopf: Viking, 1989- v. 1
88-040341 941.085/5/0924 0670805025
*Macmillan, Harold, -- 1894- Prime ministers --
Great Britain -- Biography. Great Britain --
Politics and government -- 1945-1964. Great
Britain -- Politics and government -- 20th century.*

DA566.9.M63.D37 1975
Darroch, Sandra Jobson.
Ottoline: the life of Lady Ottoline Morrell/ Sandra
Jobson Darroch. New York: Coward, McCann &
Geoghegan, 1975. 317 p.
74-016641 941.083/0924 0698106342
*Morrell, Ottoline Violet Anne Cavendish-Bentinck,
-- Lady, -- 1873-1938. Women intellectuals --
Great Britain -- Biography. England --
Intellectual life -- 20th century.*

DA566.9.O7.J42
Jenkins, Roy.
Asquith; portrait of a man and an era. New York,
Chilmark Press [c1964] 572 p.
65-014596 923.242
Asquith, H. H. -- (Herbert Henry), -- 1852-1928.

DA566.9.O7.K67 1976b
Koss, Stephen E.
Asquith/ Stephen Koss. New York: St. Martin's
Press, 1976. x, 310 p.
76-020200 941.083/092/4
*Asquith, H. H. -- (Herbert Henry), -- 1852-1928.
Prime ministers -- Great Britain -- Biography.
Great Britain -- Politics and government -- 1901-
1936. Great Britain -- Politics and government --
1837-1901.*

DA566.9.O8.A52 1963
Asquith, Margot, 1864-1945.
The autobiography of Margot Asquith/ Edited with
an introduction by Mark Bonham Carter.
Houghton Mifflin Co., c1962. 342 p.
63-007202 920.7
Asquith, Margot, -- 1864-1945.

DA566.9.W4.W4
Wedgwood, C. V. 1910-
The last of the radicals, Josiah Wedgwood, M.P.
London, Cape [1951] 252 p.
51-013163 923.242
*Wedgwood, Josiah Clement Wedgwood, -- Baron, -
- 1872-1943.*

DA567.S24
St. Aubyn, Giles.
Edward VII, Prince and King/ Giles St. Aubyn.
New York: Atheneum, 1979. 555 p.
78-063294 941.082/3/0924 0689109377
*Edward -- VII, -- King of Great Britain, -- 1841-
1910. Great Britain -- History -- Victoria, 1837-
1901. Great Britain -- History -- Edward VII,
1901-1910. Great Britain -- Kings and rulers --
Biography.*

DA570.S4 1971b
Searle, G. R.
The quest for national efficiency: a study in British
politics and political thought, 1899-1914 [by] G. R.
Searle. Berkeley, University of California Press,
1971. x, 286 p.
75-126758 320.9/42/082 0520017943
*   Great Britain -- Politics and government --
1901-1936. Great Britain -- Politics and
government -- 1837-1901.*

DA570.S47 1997
Short, Brian, 1944-
Land and society in Edwardian Britain/ Brian
Short. Cambridge, U.K.; Cambridge University
Press, 1997. xvii, 378 p.
96-013963 941.082/3 0521570352
*   Landscape -- Great Britain -- History -- 20th
century. Land use -- Great Britain -- History --
20th century. Great Britain -- History -- Edward
VII, 1901-1910. Great Britain -- Historical
geography.*

DA570.W53 1991
Williams, Rhodri, 1959-
Defending the Empire: the Conservative Party and
British defence policy, 1899-1915/ Rhodri
Williams. New Haven, Conn.: Yale University
Press, 1991. x, 306 p.
90-050944 320.941 0300050488
*   Great Britain -- Colonies -- Administration --
History -- 20th century. Great Britain -- Politics
and government -- 1901-1936. Great Britain --
Military policy.*

DA574.A1.M33 1975b
Macmillan, Harold, 1894-
The past masters: politics and politicians, 1906-1939/ Harold Macmillan. New York: Harper & Row, c1975. 240 p.
75-029880   354/.41/000922   0060128143
Macmillan, Harold, -- 1894- Statesmen -- Great Britain -- Biography. Great Britain -- Politics and government -- 1901-1936.

DA574.A8.M87 1999
Musolf, Karen J., 1937-
From Plymouth to Parliament: a rhetorical history of Nancy Astor's 1919 campaign/ Karen J. Musolf. New York: St. Martin's Press, c1999. xi, 244 p.
98-041946   941.082/092   0312213646
Astor, Nancy Witcher Langhorne Astor, -- Viscountess, -- 1879-1964.   Rhetoric -- Political aspects -- Great Britain -- History -- 20th century. Women legislators -- Great Britain -- Biography. Americans -- Great Britain -- Biography. Great Britain -- Politics and government -- 1910-1936.

DA574.M6.A35 1972
Mosley, Oswald, 1896-
My life.   New Rochelle, N.Y., Arlington House [1972, c1968] 521 p.
78-179718   942.084/0924   0870001604
Mosley, Oswald, -- Sir, -- 1896- Mosley, Oswald, -- Sir, -- 1896- Politicians -- Great Britain -- Biography. Fascists -- Great Britain -- Biography. Fascism -- Great Britain. Great Britain -- Politics and government -- 20th century.

DA574.M6.M67 1991
Mosley, Nicholas, 1923-
Rules of the game; Beyond the pale: memoirs of Sir Oswald Mosley and family/ Nicholas Mosley. Elmwood Park, IL, USA: Dalkey Archives Press, c1991. x, 596 p.
90-014042   941.082/092   0916583759
Mosley, Oswald, -- Sir, -- 1896- Mosley, Cynthia, -- Lady, -- 1898-1933. Politicians -- Great Britain -- Biography. Fascism -- Great Britain -- History -- 20th century.   Great Britain -- Politics and government -- 20th century.

DA574.M6.S55
Skidelsky, Robert Jacob Alexander, 1939-
Oswald Mosley [by] Robert Skidelsky. New York, Holt, Rinehart and Winston [c1975] 578 p.
74-006941   942.084/092/4   0030865808
Mosley, Oswald, -- Sir, -- 1896- Statesmen -- Great Britain -- Biography.

DA576.B45
Bettey, J. H.
English historical documents, 1906-1939: a selection edited by J. H. Bettey. London, Routledge & K. Paul, 1967. x, 198 p.
67-109889   942.083/08   710060246
Great Britain -- History -- 20th century -- Sources.

DA576.B53 1985
Blake, Robert, 1916-
The decline of power, 1915-1964/ Robert Blake. New York: Oxford University Press, 1985. x, 462 p.
85-004909   941.082   0195204808
Great Britain -- Politics and government -- 1910-1936. Great Britain -- Politics and government -- 1936-1945. Great Britain -- Politics and government -- 1945-1964.

DA576.D3 1997
Dangerfield, George,
The strange death of Liberal England/ George Dangerfield; [new foreword by Peter Stansky]. Stanford, CA: Stanford University Press, 1997. 364 p.
96-070279   941.083.221   0804729301
Liberalism--Great   Britain--History--20th century.

DA576.E95 2000
Ewing, K. D.
The struggle for civil liberties: political freedom and the rule of law in Britain, 1914-1945/ K.D. Ewing and C. Gearty. Oxford; Oxford University Press, 2000. xvii, 451 p.
99-047701   941.083   0198256655
Civil rights -- Great Britain -- History -- 20th century. Law -- Great Britain -- History -- 20th century. Great Britain -- Politics and government -- 1901-1936. Great Britain -- Politics and government -- 1936-1945.

DA576.F74 1995
French, David, 1954-
The strategy of the Lloyd George coalition, 1916-1918/ David French. Oxford [England]: Clarendon Press; 1995. vi, 332 p.
94-049330   940.3/41   0198205597
Lloyd George, David, -- 1863-1945.   Coalition governments -- Great Britain -- History -- 20th century.   Great Britain -- Politics and government -- 1901-1936.

DA577.B34 1968
Beaverbrook, Max Aitken, 1879-1964.
Men and power, 1917-1918.   [Hamden, Conn.] Archon Books, 1968 [c1956] 447 p.
68-007599   320.9/42
World War, 1914-1918 -- Great Britain.   Great Britain -- Politics and government -- 1910-1936.

DA577.M37
Marwick, Arthur, 1936-
The deluge; British society and the First World War. Boston, Little, Brown [1966, c1965] 336 p.
66-010818   914.20383
World War, 1914-1918 -- Great Britain. Reconstruction (1914-1939) -- Great Britain. Great Britain -- Social conditions -- 20th century.

DA577.T86 1992
Turner, John, 1949 May 18-
British politics and the Great War: coalition and conflict, 1915-1918/ John Turner. New Haven: Yale University Press, 1992. xi, 511 p.
90-050994   941.083   0300050461
World War, 1914-1918 -- Great Britain. Great Britain -- Politics and government -- 1910-1936.

DA578.A3 1993
Adams, R. J. Q. 1943-
British politics and foreign policy in the age of appeasement, 1935-39/ R.J.Q. Adams. Stanford, Calif.: Stanford University Press, 1993. xii, 192 p.
92-080809   0804721009
Great Britain -- Politics and government -- 1936-1945.   Great Britain -- Politics and government -- 1910-1936. Great Britain -- Foreign relations -- 1936-1945.

DA578.K4 1962
Kennedy, John F. 1917-1963.
Why England slept.   Garden City, N. Y., Doubleday, [1962, c1961] 200 p.
62-004326   942.083
Disarmament.   Great Britain -- Politics and government -- 1910-1936. Great Britain -- Politics and government -- 1936-1945.

DA578.L33 1990
Laybourn, Keith.
Britain on the breadline: a social and political history of Britain between the wars/ Keith Laybourn. Gloucester [England]; A. Sutton, 1990. x, 222 p.
90-031518   941.082   086299490X
Great Britain -- Politics and government -- 1910-1936. Great Britain -- Politics and government -- 1936-1945. Great Britain -- Social conditions -- 20th century.

DA578.L45 1990
Lewis, Terrance L., 1958-
A climate for appeasement/ Terrance L. Lewis. New York: P. Lang, c1991. x, 263 p.
90-006166   941.083   0820413143
Peace movements -- Great Britain -- History -- 20th century. Public opinion -- Great Britain -- History -- 20th century. World War, 1914-1918 -- Literature and the war. Great Britain -- Politics and government -- 1936-1945. Great Britain -- Foreign relations -- 1936-1945. Great Britain -- Foreign relations -- Germany.

DA578.L77 1999
Lucas, John, 1937-
The radical twenties: writing, politics, and culture/ New Brunswick, NJ: Rutgers University Press, 1999. p. cm.
98-052817   941.082   0813526817
Politics and literature -- Great Britain -- History -- 20th century. English literature -- 20th century -- History and criticism. Radicalism -- Great Britain -- History -- 20th century. Great Britain -- Civilization -- 20th century. Great Britain -- Politics and government -- 1910-1936.

DA578.P65 1993
Post, Gaines, 1937-
Dilemmas of appeasement: British deterrence and defense, 1934-1937/ Gaines Post, Jr. Ithaca: Cornell University Press, 1993. xiii, 363 p.
92-027606   327.41/009/043   0801427487
World War, 1939-1945 -- Causes. Great Britain -- Politics and government -- 1910-1936. Great Britain -- History, Military -- 20th century. Great Britain -- Foreign relations -- 1936-1945.

DA578.R68
Rowse, A. L. 1903-
Appeasement; a study in political decline, 1933-1939. New York, Norton [1961] 123 p.
61-017123   942.084
Great Britain -- Politics and government -- 20th century.

DA580.B538 1988
Bloch, Michael.
The secret file of the Duke of Windsor/ Michael Bloch. New York: Harper & Row, c1988. xvi, 326 p.
88-039284   941.084/092/4
Windsor, Edward, -- Duke of, -- 1894-1972. Great Britain -- Kings and rulers -- Biography. Great Britain -- History -- Edward VIII, 1936.

DA585.A8.B77 1995
Brookshire, Jerry H.
Clement Attlee/ Jerry H. Brookshire. Manchester; Manchester University Press; 1995. ix, 257 p.
95-030848   941.085/4/092   071903244X
Attlee, C. R. -- (Clement Richard), -- 1883-1967. Prime ministers -- Great Britain -- Biography. Great Britain -- Politics and government -- 20th century.

DA585.A8.P43 1997
Pearce, R. D.
Attlee/ Robert Pearce. London; Longman, 1997. vii, 206 p.
96-044365   941.085/4/092   0582256917
Attlee, C. R. -- (Clement Richard), -- 1883-1967. Prime ministers -- Great Britain -- Biography. Great Britain -- Politics and government -- 20th century.

DA585.B38.F62
Foot, Michael, 1913-
Aneurin Bevan, a biography.   New York, Atheneum, 1963- v.
63-017846   942/.084/092/4   0689105878
Bevan, Aneurin, -- 1897-1960. Socialists -- Great Britain -- Biography. Statesmen -- Great Britain -- Biography. Wales -- Politics and government -- 20th century. Wales -- Biography.

DA585.B4.W44 1993
Weiler, Peter, 1942-
Ernest Bevin/ Peter Weiler. Manchester, UK; Manchester University Press; c1993. x, 232 p.
92-002494   941.085/092   0719021782
Bevin, Ernest, -- 1881-1951. Statesmen -- Great Britain -- Biography. Labor leaders -- Great Britain -- Biography. Great Britain -- Foreign relations -- 1945-

DA585.C5.C48 1990
Charmley, John, 1955-
Chamberlain and the lost peace/ John Charmley. Chicago: I.R. Dee, 1990. xiv, 257 p.
90-032618   941.084   0929587332
Chamberlain, Neville, -- 1869-1940 -- Views on Germany. World War, 1939-1945 -- Causes. Great Britain -- Foreign relations -- 1936-1945. Great Britain -- Foreign relations -- Germany. Germany -- Foreign relations -- Great Britain.

DA585.C5.F4 1970
Feiling, Keith Grahame, 1884-
The life of Neville Chamberlain, by Keith Feiling. Hamden, Conn., Archon Books, 1970. xi, 477 p.
75-095598   942.084/0924
Chamberlain, Neville, -- 1869-1940. Prime ministers -- Great Britain -- Biography. Great Britain -- Politics and government -- 1936-1945.

DA585.J6.W4
West, Rebecca, 1892-
The meaning of treason. New York, Viking Press, 1947. 307 p.
47-011976   942.084
Joyce, William, -- 1906-1946. Amery, John, -- 1911 or 12-1945. Trials (Treason) -- Great Britain.

DA585.M6.M67 1991
Morgan, Janet P.
Edwina Mountbatten: a life of her own/ Janet Morgan. New York: Scribner: 1991. xv, 489 p.
91-000546   941.082/092   0684193469
Mountbatten of Burma, Edwina Ashley Mountbatten, -- Countess, -- 1901-1960. Mountbatten of Burma, Louis Mountbatten, -- Earl, -- 1900-1979 -- Marriage. Statesmen's spouses -- Great Britain -- Biography.

DA586.H48 1991
Hill, Christopher, 1948-
Cabinet decisions on foreign policy: the British experience, October 1938-June 1941/ Christopher Hill. Cambridge [England]; Cambridge University Press, 1991. xx, 359 p.
90-041804   327.41   0521391954
Cabinet system -- Great Britain -- History -- 20th century.   Great Britain -- Foreign relations -- 1936-1945.

DA586.N49 1996
Newton, Scott, 1956-
Profits of peace: the political economy of Anglo-German appeasement/ Scott Newton. Oxford [England]: Clarendon Press, 1996. 217 p.
95-030149   327.41043/09/043   0198202121
Great Britain -- Politics and government -- 1936-1945. Great Britain -- Economic conditions -- 20th century. Great Britain -- Foreign relations -- 1936-1945.

DA586.R46 1999
Renton, Dave, 1972-
Fascism, anti-fascism, and Britain in the 1940s/ Dave Renton. New York: St. Martin, 1999. p. cm.
99-015878   941.085   0312225016
Fascism -- Great Britain -- History -- 20th century. Anti-fascist movements -- Great Britain -- History -- 20th century. Great Britain -- Politics and government -- 1936-1945. Great Britain -- Politics and government -- 1945-1964.

DA587.C28 1969b
Calder, Angus.
The people's war; Britain, 1939-1945. New York, Pantheon Books [1969] 656 p.
67-019178   940.5342
World War, 1939-1945 -- Great Britain.

DA588.C57 1951
Churchill, Winston, 1874-1965.
In the balance; speeches 1949 and 1950. Edited by Randolph S. Churchill. London, Cassell [1951] x, 456 p.
52-001448
World politics -- 1945- European federation. Great Britain -- Politics and government -- 1945-1964. Great Britain -- Foreign relations -- 1936-1945.

DA588.H46 1994
Hennessy, Peter, 1947-
Never again: Britain, 1945-1951/ Peter Hennessy. New York: Pantheon Books, c1993. xvi, 544 p.
93-048430   941.085/4   0679433635
World War, 1939-1945 -- Great Britain -- Influence. Great Britain -- History -- George VI, 1936-1952.

DA588.M637 1984
Morgan, Kenneth O.
Labour in power, 1945-1951/ by Kenneth O. Morgan. Oxford: Clarendon Press, 1984. xviii, 546 p.
83-019290   941.085/4   0192158651
Attlee, C. R. -- (Clement Richard), -- 1883-1967. Great Britain -- Social policy. Great Britain -- Foreign relations -- 1945- Great Britain -- Politics and government -- 1945-1964.

DA589.4.E53 1999
Encyclopedia of contemporary British culture/ edited by Peter Childs and Mike Storry. London; Routledge, 1999. xxvii, 628 p.
98-032205   306/.0941/0904   0415147263
Great Britain -- Civilization -- 20th century -- Encyclopedias. Great Britain -- History -- Elizabeth II, 1952- -- Encyclopedias.

DA589.4.V45 1994
Veldman, Meredith.
Fantasy, the bomb, and the greening of Britain: romantic protest, 1945-1980/ Meredith Veldman. Cambridge [England]; Cambridge University Press, 1994. xiii, 325 p.
93-012772   941.085   0521440602
Literature and society -- Great Britain -- History -- 20th century. Antinuclear movement -- Great Britain -- History -- 20th century. Fantasy literature, English -- History and criticism. Great Britain -- Civilization -- 1945-

DA589.7.B78 1984
Bruce-Gardyne, Jock.
Mrs. Thatcher's first administration: the prophets confounded/ Jock Bruce-Gardyne. New York: St. Martin's Press, 1984. xi, 199 p.
84-011528   941.085/7   0312551401
Thatcher, Margaret.   Great Britain -- Politics and government -- 1979-1997.

DA589.7.C69 1998
Coxall, W. N.
British politics since the war/ Bill Coxall and Lynton Robins.   Houndmills, Basingstoke [England]: Macmillan; 1998. xiii, 322 p.
97-035661   941.085   0312211082
World War, 1939-1945 -- Influence.   Great Britain -- Politics and government -- 1945-

DA589.7.J44 1997
Jefferys, Kevin.
Retreat from new Jerusalem: British politics, 1951-64/ Kevin Jefferys. New York: St. Martin's Press, 1997. 243 p.
96-034939   320.941/09/045   0312165382
Great Britain -- Politics and government -- 1945-1964.

DA589.7.M37 1999
Marsh, David, 1946-
Postwar British politics in perspective/ David Marsh ... [et al.]. Cambridge [England]: Polity Press; 1999. p. cm.
98-047771   320.941/09/045   0745620299
World War, 1939-1945 -- Great Britain -- Influence.   Great Britain -- Politics and government -- 1945-

DA589.7.M39 1991
Mayer, Frank A., 1942-
The opposition years: Winston S. Churchill and the Conservative Party, 1945-1951/ Frank A. Mayer. New York: P. Lang, c1992. 187 p.
91-004348   941.084   0820416614
Churchill, Winston, -- Sir, -- 1874-1965. Conservatism -- Great Britain -- History -- 20th century. Great Britain -- Politics and government -- 1945-1964.

DA589.7.R53 1990
Riddell, Peter.
The Thatcher decade: how Britain has changed during the 1980s/ Peter Riddell. New York: B. Blackwell, 1989. x, 236 p.
89-031770   941.085/8   0631162747
Thatcher, Margaret.   Great Britain -- Politics and government -- 1979-1997.

DA589.7.S25 1982
Sampson, Anthony.
The changing anatomy of Britain/ Anthony Sampson. New York: Random House, c1982. xv, 476 p.
82-042811   941.085   0394531434
Elite (Social sciences) -- Great Britain.   Great Britain -- Politics and government -- 1979-1997. Great Britain -- Economic conditions -- 1979-1997.

DA589.8.B45 1997
Bell, P. M. H. 1930-
France and Britain 1940-1994: the long separation/
P.M.H. Bell. New York: Longman, 1997. p. cm.
96-028654   327.41044   0582289203
World War, 1939-1945 -- Diplomatic history.
Great Britain -- Foreign relations -- 1936-1945.
Great Britain -- Foreign relations -- 1945- Great
Britain -- Foreign relations -- France.

DA589.8.B57 1993
Blackwell, Michael.
Clinging to grandeur: British attitudes and foreign
policy in the aftermath of the Second World War/
Michael Blackwell. Westport, Conn.: Greenwood
Press, 1993. 196 p.
92-030012   327.41   0313286167
Statesmen -- Great Britain -- Attitudes. National
characteristics, British. World War, 1939-1945 --
Influence. Great Britain -- Foreign relations --
1945-

DA589.8.S53 1997
Sharp, Paul, 1953-
Thatcher's diplomacy: the revival of British foreign
policy/ Paul Sharp. New York: St. Martin's Press,
1997. xviii, 269 p.
96-028748   327.41/009/048   0333658426
Thatcher, Margaret -- Views on foreign relations.
Great Britain -- Foreign relations -- 1945-

DA589.8.S56 2000
Shore, Peter, 1924-
Separate ways: the heart of Europe/ Peter Shore.
London: Duckworth, 2000. xi, 244 p.
320.941   0715629727
European Union -- Great Britain. Great Britain
-- Relations -- Europe. Europe -- Relations --
Great Britain. Great Britain -- Relations --
Foreign countries.

DA591.A45
Taylor, John A., 1942-
Diana, self-interest, and British national identity/
John A. Taylor. Westport, Conn.: Praeger, 2000. x,
168 p.
99-059652   941.085/092   027596826X
Diana, -- Princess of Wales, -- 1961- -- Influence.
National characteristics, British -- History -- 20th
century. Self-interest -- Great Britain -- History --
20th century. Nationalism -- Great Britain --
History -- 20th century. Great Britain --
Civilization -- 20th century.

DA591.C36.A3 1989
Carrington, Peter Alexander Rupert Carington,
1919-
Reflecting on things past: the memoirs of Peter
Lord Carrington. New York: Harper & Row,
[1989], c1988 x, 406 p.
88-045542   941.082/092/4   0060390905
Carrington, Peter Alexander Rupert Carington,
Baron, -- 1919- Statesmen -- Great Britain --
Biography.   Great Britain -- Politics and
government -- 1945- Europe -- Defenses -- History
-- 20th century.

DA591.H38.A3 1990
Healey, Denis.
The time of my life/ Denis Healey. New York:
W.W. Norton, 1990, c1989. xiv, 606 p.
89-077173   941.085092   0393028755
Healey, Denis.   Statesmen -- Great Britain --
Biography.   Great Britain -- Politics and
government -- 1945-

DA591.J46.A3 1991
Jenkins, Roy.
A life at the center: memoirs of a radical reformer/
Roy Jenkins. New York: Random House, c1991.
xviii, 585 p.
92-050544   941.085/6/092   0679413111
Jenkins, Roy.   Statesmen -- Great Britain --
Biography.   Great Britain -- Politics and
government -- 1945-

DA591.T47.J46 1988
Jenkins, Peter.
Mrs. Thatcher's revolution: the ending of the
socialist era/ Peter Jenkins. Cambridge, Mass.:
Harvard University Press, 1988. xxxvi, 417 p.
88-007231   941.085/8/0924   0674588320
Thatcher, Margaret. Socialism -- Great Britain --
History -- 20th century. Conservatism -- Great
Britain -- History -- 20th century. Great Britain --
Politics and government -- 1979-1997.

DA591.T47.K38 1987
Kavanagh, Dennis.
Thatcherism and British politics: the end of
consensus?/   Dennis   Kavanagh.   Oxford
[Oxfordshire]; Oxford University Press, 1987. viii,
334 p.
86-023725   941.085/7   0198275226
Thatcher, Margaret.   Conservatism -- Great
Britain -- History -- 20th century.   Great Britain --
Politics and government -- 1945-

DA591.T47 T476 1993
Thatcher, Margaret.
The Downing Street years/ Margaret Thatcher.1st
ed. New York, NY: HarperCollins, c1993. xiv,
914 p.
93-239539   941.085/7.220   0060170565
Thatcher, Margaret.   Women prime ministers--
Great Britain--Biography.

DA591.T47 Y68 1989
Young, Hugo.
The Iron Lady: a biography of Margaret Thatcher/
Hugo Young.1st American ed. New York: Farrar
Strauss Giroux, 1989. xii, 569 p.
89-011875   941.085/8/092.220   0374226512
Thatcher, Margaret.   Women prime ministers--
Great Britain--Biography.

DA591.W5.M67 1992
Morgan, Austen, 1949-
Harold Wilson/ Austen Morgan. London: Pluto
Press, 1992. xv, 625 p.
92-002730   941.085/6/092   0745306357
Wilson, Harold, -- Sir, -- 1916- Prime ministers --
Great Britain -- Biography.   Great Britain --
Politics and government -- 1945-1964.

DA592.B7415 1998
Britain in the nineties: the politics of paradox/
edited by Hugh Berrington. London; Frank Cass,
1998. 231 p.
98-016038   320.941/09/049   0714648809
Great Britain -- Politics and government --
1979-1997. Great Britain -- Politics and
government -- 1997-

DA592.M67 1990
Morgan, Kenneth O.
The people's peace: British history, 1945-1989/
Kenneth O. Morgan. Oxford; Oxford University
Press, 1990. xiii, 558 p.
89-077325   941.085   0198227647
Great Britain -- History -- Elizabeth II, 1952-
Great Britain -- History -- George VI, 1936-1952.

DA592.P45 1997
Pelling, Henry.
Churchill's peacetime ministry, 1951-55/ Henry
Pelling. New York: St. Martin's Press, 1997. ix,
216 p.
96-002994   941.085/5   0312162715
Churchill, Winston, -- Sir, -- 1874-1965.   Great
Britain -- Politics and government -- 1945-1964.

DA592.R65
Royal Institute of International Affairs.
British foreign policy: some relevant documents,
January 1950-April 1955. London, [1955] viii,
127 p.
56-000165   327.42
Great Britain -- Foreign relations -- 1945-

DA592.S23 1972
Sampson, Anthony.
The new anatomy of Britain. New York, Stein and
Day [1972, c1971] xviii, 773 p.
78-186150   309.1/42/085   0812814568
Great Britain -- Civilization -- 1945- Great
Britain -- Politics and government -- 1964-1979.

DA600 England — Historical geography

DA600.C664 1988
The Countryside of medieval England/ edited by
Grenville Astill and Annie Grant; illustrations
drawn by Brian Williams. Oxford, UK; B.
Blackwell, 1988. xi, 282 p.
87-035521   942/.009734   0631150919
Social history -- Medieval, 500-1500. Land use,
Rural -- England -- History. Country life --
England -- History. England -- Social life and
customs -- 1066-1485. England -- Historical
geography. England -- Rural conditions.

DA600.H6 1970
Hoskins, W. G. 1908-
The making of the English landscape [by] W. G.
Hoskins. [Harmondsworth, Eng.] Penguin Books
[1970] 325 p.
77-021107   911/.42   0140210350
England -- Historical geography.

DA600.M295 2000
Mayhew, Robert J. 1971-
Enlightenment geography: the political languages
of British geography, 1650-1850/ Robert J.
Mayhew. New York: St. Martin's Press, 2000. viii,
324 p.
00-027247   911/.41   0312234759
Geography -- Great Britain -- History. Political
geography -- History. Enlightenment -- Great
Britain. Great Britain -- Intellectual life. Great
Britain -- Politics and government. Great Britain --
Historical geography.

DA610-631 England — Description and travel — By period

DA610.D23
Darby, H. C. 1909-
Domesday England/ by H. C. Darby. Cambridge
[Eng.]; Cambridge University Press, 1977. xiii,
416 p.
76-011485   911/.42   052121307X
Geography, Medieval -- Sources.   England --
Historical geography.

DA630.J27 1969
James, Henry, 1843-1916.
English hours. With illus. by Joseph Pennell. New York, Horizon Press [1969, c1968] xxxiv, 336 p.
68-055315   914.2/04/81
James, Henry, -- 1843-1916 -- Journeys -- England.   England -- Description and travel.

DA630.P7 1984
Priestley, J. B. 1894-
English journey/ J.B. Priestley. Chicago: University of Chicago Press, c1984. 320 p.
83-040619   914.2/0483   0226682129
Priestley, J. B. -- (John Boynton), -- 1894- Journeys -- England. Priestley, J. B. -- (John Boynton), -- 1894-   England -- Description and travel.

DA631.B34
Banks, F. R.
English villages. Photos. by Edwin Smith. London, B.T. Batsford [c1963] 224 p.
64-002119
Villages -- England.   England -- Description and travel.

DA640 England — Gazetteers. Dictionaries, etc.

DA640.D27
Darby, H. C. 1909-
Domesday gazetteer/ by H. C. Darby and G. R. Versey. Cambridge [Eng.]; Cambridge University Press, 1975. viii, 544 p.
75-019532   914.2/003   0521206669
Geography, Medieval -- Sources.   England -- Gazetteers.

DA645 England — Place names

DA645.M55 1991
Mills, A. D.
A dictionary of English place names/ A.D. Mills. Oxford [England]; Oxford University Press, 1991. xxxi, 388 p.
90-028522   914.2/003   0198691564
Names, Geographical -- England. English language -- Etymology -- Names -- Dictionaries. England -- History, Local -- Dictionaries.

DA650 England — Guidebooks

DA650.W287 1998
Ward, Paul, 1964-
Red flag and Union Jack: Englishness, patriotism, and the British left, 1881-1924/ Paul Ward. Rochester, NY: Royal Historical Society/Boydell Press, c1998. viii, 232 p.
98-036316   941.08   0861932390
Patriotism -- Great Britain -- History -- 19th century. Patriotism -- Great Britain -- History -- 20th century. Socialism -- Great Britain -- History -- 19th century. Great Britain -- Politics and government -- 1837-1901. Soviet Union -- History -- Revolution, 1917-1921 -- Influence. Great Britain -- Politics and government -- 1901-1936.

DA655 England — Preservation of historic monuments, etc.

DA655.P74 1993
Prentice, Richard
Tourism and heritage attractions/ Richard Prentice. London; Routledge, 1993. xv, 253 p.
92-019910   363.6/9/0941   041508525X
Historic sites -- Conservation and restoration -- Great Britain. Cultural property, Protection of -- Great Britain. Historical museums -- Great Britain.

DA660 England — Castles, halls, cathedrals, etc. — General works

DA660.P48 1995
Pettifer, Adrian, 1959-
English castles: a guide by counties/ Adrian Pettifer. Woodbridge, Suffolk, UK; Boydell Press, 1995. xxii, 344 p.
95-022530   914.204/859   0851156002
Castles -- England -- Guidebooks.

DA660.P68 1990
Pounds, Norman John Greville.
The medieval castle in England and Wales: a social and political history/ N.J.G. Pounds. Cambridge [England]; Cambridge University Press, 1990. xvii, 357 p.
89-077363   942   0521383498
Castles -- England -- History. Castles -- Wales -- History.   England -- Social conditions -- 1066-1485. Great Britain -- Politics and government -- 1066-1485. Wales -- History -- 1063-1536.

DA670 England — Local history and description — Counties, regions, etc., A-Z

DA670.B695.W55 1997
Williamson, Tom.
The Norfolk broads: a landscape history/ Tom Williamson. Manchester; Manchester University Press, 1997. p. cm.
96-051935   914.26/17   0719048001
Landscape -- England -- Broads, The -- History. Land use -- England -- Broads, The -- History. Landscape -- England -- Norfolk -- History. Broads, The (England) -- Historical geography. Norfolk (England) -- Historical geography.

DA670.C8.J27 1999
Jaggard, Edwin, 1942-
Cornwall politics in the age of reform, 1790-1885/ Edwin Jaggard. Woodbridge, Suffolk; Boydell Press, 1999. xi, 238 p.
99-036470   942.3/7081   0861932439
Elections -- England -- Cornwall (County) -- History -- 19th century.   Cornwall (England: County) -- Politics and government.

DA670.C8.R6 1969b
Rowse, A. L. 1903-
Tudor Cornwall; portrait of a society, by A. L. Rowse. New York, C. Scribner [1969] 462 p.
69-017046   914.23/7/035
Cornwall (England: County) -- History. Great Britain -- History -- Tudors, 1485-1603. England -- Social conditions -- 16th century.

DA670.E7.P66 1991
Poos, Lawrence R.
A rural society after the Black Death: Essex, 1350-1525/ L.R. Poos. Cambridge [England]; Cambridge University Press, 1991. xv, 330 p.
90-002692   942.6/7   0521382602
Social history -- Medieval, 500-1500. Black death -- England -- Essex -- History. England -- Social conditions -- 1066-1485. England -- Social conditions -- 16th century. Essex (England) -- History.

DA670.G5.R65 1992
Rollison, David, 1945-
The local origins of modern society: Gloucestershire 1500-1800/ David Rollison. London; Routledge, 1992. xvi, 319 p.
91-041500   942.4/1   0415070007
Gloucestershire (England) -- History. Gloucestershire (England) -- Social conditions.

DA670.H4.D64 1995
Dohar, William J.
The Black Death and pastoral leadership: the Diocese of Hereford in the fourteenth century/ William J. Dohar. Philadelphia: University of Pennsylvania Press, c1995. xvi, 198 p.
94-033224   942.4/4   0812232623
Church work with the sick -- England -- Herefordshire -- History. Medicine, Medieval -- England -- Herefordshire -- History. Black death -- England -- Herefordshire -- History. Herefordshire (England) -- Church history. Herefordshire (England) -- History.

DA670.K3.C494 1977
Clark, Peter, 1944-
English provincial society from the Reformation to the Revolution: religion, politics, and society in Kent, 1500-1640/ Peter Clark. Rutherford [N.J.]: Fairleigh Dickinson University Press, c1977. xiii, 504 p.
76-053900   942.2/3/05   0838620752
Reformation -- Kent (England)   Kent (England) -- Politics and government. Kent (England) -- Church history.

DA670.L19.C5 3rd ser. vol. 34
Morgan, Philip.
War and society in medieval Cheshire, 1277-1403/ Philip Morgan. Manchester, UK: Published for the Chetham Society by Manchester 1987. 254 p.
87-011044   942.7/14 s   0719013429
Feudalism -- England -- Cheshire -- History -- To 1500.   Great Britain -- History, Military -- 1066-1485. Cheshire (England) -- History, Military. Cheshire (England) -- History.

DA670.M64.B43 1988
Beckett, J. V.
The East Midlands from AD 1000/ J.V. Beckett. London; Longman, 1988. xix, 393 p.
87-002985   942.4   0582492696
Midlands (England) -- History.

DA670.M64.G45 1992
Gelling, Margaret.
The West Midlands in the early Middle Ages/ Margaret Gelling. Leicester; Leicester University Press; 1992. ix, 221 p.
92-015239   942.4   0718511700
Britons -- England -- Midlands. Romans -- England -- Midlands. Midlands (England) -- History. Anglo-Saxons -- England -- Midlands. Midlands (England) -- Antiquities.

DA670.N73.M87 1990
Musgrove, Frank.
The north of England: a history from Roman times to the present/ Frank Musgrove. Oxford, UK; B. Blackwell, 1990. vii, 374 p.
90-000416   942.7   0631162739
England, Northern -- History.

DA670.S29.R57 1997
Rippon, Stephen, 1968-
The Severn estuary: landscape evolution and wetland reclamation/ Stephen Rippon. London; Leicester University Press, 1997. xii, 318 p.
96-027923   911/.424   0718500695
Landscape archaeology -- Severn River Estuary (England and Wales) Wetlands -- Severn River Estuary (England and Wales) Severn River Estuary (England and Wales) -- Historical geography.

DA670.W48.C86 1993
Cunliffe, Barry W.
Wessex to AD 1000/ Barry Cunliffe. London; Longman, 1993. xvii, 388 p.
92-012638   942.3   0582492793
Prehistoric peoples -- England -- Wessex. Land settlement -- England -- Wessex. England -- Civilization -- To 1066. Wessex (England) -- History. Wessex (England) -- Antiquities.

DA670.Y4.D35 1994
Dalton, Paul.
Conquest, anarchy, and lordship: Yorkshire, 1066-1154/ Paul Dalton. Cambridge [England]; Cambridge University Press, 1994. xxii, 345 p.
93-013985   942.8/102   0521450985
Land tenure -- England -- Yorkshire -- History. Feudalism -- England -- Yorkshire -- History. Normans -- England -- Yorkshire -- History. Yorkshire (England) -- Politics and government. Great Britain -- History -- Norman period, 1066-1154.

DA677-684 England — London — History, antiquities, description

DA677.P67 1995
Porter, Roy, 1946-
London, a social history/ Roy Porter. Cambridge, Mass.: Harvard University Press, 1995. xv, 431 p.
94-033025   942.1   0674538382
London (England) -- History. London (England) -- Social conditions. London (England) -- Social life and customs.

DA677.P7 1962a
Pritchett, V. S. 1900-
London perceived. Photos. by Evelyn Hofer. London] Chatto & Windus [1962] 116 p.
62-058202
London.

DA677.S54 1998
Sheppard, F. H. W. 1921-
London: a history/ Francis Sheppard. Oxford; Oxford University Press, 1998. xv, 442 p.
98-007999   942.1   0198229224
London (England) -- History.

DA680.A74 1991
Archer, Ian W.
The pursuit of stability: social relations in Elizabethan London/ Ian W. Archer. Cambridge [England]; Cambridge University Press, 1991. xvi, 307 p.
90-033136   942.1/2055   0521373158
London (England) -- History -- 16th century. Great Britain -- History -- Elizabeth, 1558-1603. London (England) -- Social conditions.

DA680.M9
Myers, A. R. 1912-1980.
London in the age of Chaucer, by A. R. Myers. Norman, University of Oklahoma Press [1972] xi, 236 p.
73-177342   914.21/03/3   0806109971
London (England) -- History -- To 1500.

DA682.O33 1998
Ogborn, Miles.
Spaces of modernity: London's geographies, 1680-1780/ Miles Ogborn. New York: Guilford Press, c1998. xi, 340 p.
98-013000   942.1/07   1572303433
Architecture, Modern -- 17th-18th centuries -- England -- London. Public spaces -- England -- London -- History. London (England) -- History -- 17th century. London (England) -- Historical geography. London (England) -- History -- 18th century.

DA682.R8
Rude, George F. E.
Hanoverian London, 1714-1808 [by] George Rude. Berkeley, University of California, 1971. xvi, 271 p.
69-010590   914.21/03/7   0520017781
London (England) -- History -- 18th century.

DA682.S38 1983
Schwartz, Richard B.
Daily life in Johnson's London/ Richard B. Schwartz. Madison, Wis.: University of Wisconsin Press, 1983. xix, 196 p.
83-050080   942.107   0299094944
Johnson, Samuel, -- 1709-1784 -- Homes and haunts -- England -- London. London (England) -- Description and travel. London (England) -- Social life and customs -- 18th century.

DA683.L88 1992
London--world city, 1800-1840/ edited by Celina Fox. New Haven: Yale University Press in association with the Mu 1992. 624 p.
92-050447   942.1/081   0300052847
London (England) -- History -- 1800-1950 -- Exhibitions.

DA683.N425 2000
Nead, Lynda.
Victorian Babylon: people, streets and images in nineteenth-century London/ Lynda Nead. New Haven: Yale University Press, c2000. viii, 251 p.
00-031037   942.1/2   0300085052
City and town life -- England -- London -- History -- 19th century. Gas-lighting -- England -- London -- History -- 19th century. Streets -- England -- London -- History -- 19th century. London (England) -- History -- 1800-1950. Great Britain -- History -- Victoria, 1837-1901. London (England) -- Social conditions.

DA684.P293 1996
Paterson, John, 1923-
Edwardians: London life and letters, 1901-1914/ John Paterson. Chicago: I.R. Dee, 1996. 330 p.
95-045742   942.1082/3   1566631017
London (England) -- Social life and customs -- 20th century -- Sources. London (England) -- Intellectual life -- 20th century -- Sources. Great Britain -- History -- Edward VII, 1901-1910 -- Sources.

DA685 England — London — Parishes, boroughs, streets, etc., A-Z

DA685.B65.B45 1995
Bell, Quentin.
Bloomsbury recalled/ Quentin Bell. New York: Columbia University Press, 1995. 234 p.
95-045907   942.1/42   0231105649
Bell, Quentin -- Family. Intellectuals -- England -- London -- Biography. Artists -- England -- London -- Biography. Authors, English -- England -- London -- Biography. Bloomsbury (London, England) -- Intellectual life -- 20th century.

DA685.B65.C39 1990
Caws, Mary Ann.
Women of Bloomsbury: Virginia, Vanessa, and Carrington/ Mary Ann Caws. New York: Routledge, 1990. xvi, 218 p.
89-024273   942.1/42   0415901340
Woolf, Virginia, -- 1882-1941. Bell, Vanessa, -- 1879-1961. Carrington, Dora de Houghton, -- 1893-1932. Women -- England -- Bloomsbury (London) -- Biography. Bloomsbury group. Art and literature -- England -- History -- 20th century. Bloomsbury (London, England) -- Intellectual life. London (England) -- Biography.

DA685.B65.S73 1996
Stansky, Peter.
On or about December 1910: early Bloomsbury and its intimate world/ Peter Stansky. Cambridge, Mass.: Harvard University Press, 1996. viii, 289 p.
96-017588   820.9/00912   0674636058
Woolf, Virginia, -- 1882-1941 -- Friends and associates. Authors, English -- England -- London -- Biography. Intellectuals -- England -- London -- Biography. Artists -- England -- London -- Biography. Bloomsbury (London, England) -- Intellectual life -- 20th century. Bloomsbury (London, England) -- Biography.

DA685.E1.L56 1996
Linehan, Thomas P.
East London for Mosley: the British Union of Fascists in east London and south-west Essex, 1933-40/ Thomas P. Linehan. London; Frank Cass, 1996. xx, 316 p.
96-018660   320.94267   0714642681
Mosley, Oswald, -- Sir, -- 1896- Fascism -- England -- London -- History -- 20th century. Fascism -- England -- Essex -- History -- 20th century. Great Britain -- Politics and government -- 1936-1945. Essex (England) -- Politics and government. Great Britain -- Politics and government -- 1910-1936.

DA685.H28.M39 1991
McIntosh, Marjorie Keniston.
A community transformed: the manor and liberty of Havering, 1500-1620/ Marjorie Keniston McIntosh. Cambridge, [England]; Cambridge University Press, 1991. xviii, 489 p.
90-002315   942.1/74   0521381428
Manors -- England -- London -- History. Community organization -- England -- London -- History. London (England) -- History -- 17th century. Havering (London, England) -- History. London (England) -- History -- 16th century.

DA685.S7.C37 1996
Carlin, Martha.
Medieval Southwark/ Martha Carlin. London; Hambledon Press, 1996. xxiii, 351 p.
95-047679   942.1/64   1852851163
Architecture, Medieval -- England -- London. Southwark (London, England) -- History. London (England) -- History -- To 1500.

DA685.W5.R67 1989
Rosser, Gervase.
Medieval Westminster, 1200-1540/ Gervase Rosser. Oxford: Clarendon Press; 1989. xvii, 425 p.
89-009399   942.1/32   0198201567
Westminster (London, England) -- History. London (England) -- History -- To 1500. England -- Civilization -- 1066-1485.

DA687 England — London — Institutions

DA687.L22
Yorke, James.
Lancaster House: London's greatest town house/ James Yorke. London: Merrell; c2001. 192 p.
   1858941261
Architecture, Domestic -- England -- London -- History. Great Britain -- History -- House of Lancaster, 1399-1461.

DA687.W5.B56 1995
Binski, Paul.
Westminster Abbey and the Plantagenets: kingship and the representation of power, 1200-1400/ Paul Binski. New Haven: Yale University Press, 1995. viii, 241 p.
94-024291   942.1/3203   0300059809
Plantagenet, House of. Rites and ceremonies -- England -- London -- History. Art -- Political aspects -- England -- London. Architecture and state -- Great Britain. Great Britain -- Politics and government -- 1154-1399. Great Britain -- Kings and rulers.

DA688 England — London — Social life and customs. Culture. Intellectual life

DA688.S58
Sitwell, Sacheverell, 1897-
Morning, noon and night in London. London, Macmillan, 1948. v, 85 p.
49-005398   914.21
Concanen, Alfred, -- 1835-1886.   London -- Social life and customs.

DA690 England — Other cities, towns, etc., A-Z

DA690.B49 1994
Bew, Paul.
Ideology and the Irish question: Ulster unionism and Irish nationalism, 1912-1916/ Paul Bew. Oxford: Clarendon Press; 1994. xix, 165 p.
94-009295   941.5082/1   0198202024
Ulster (Northern Ireland and Ireland) -- Politics and government. Unionism (Irish politics) -- History -- 20th century. Nationalism -- Ireland -- History -- 20th century. Ireland -- Politics and government -- 1910-1921.

DA690.C2.G37 1989
Gascoigne, John,
Cambridge in the age of the Enlightenment: science, religion, and politics from the Restoration to the French Revolution/ John Gascoigne. Cambridge; Cambridge University Press, 1989. xi, 358 p.
88-021413   942.6/5906   0521351391
Religion -- Study and teaching (Higher) -- England -- Cambridge -- History. Political science -- Study and teaching (Higher) -- England -- Cambridge -- History. Science -- Study and teaching (Higher) -- England -- Cambridge -- History. England -- Intellectual life -- 17th century. Cambridge (England) -- Intellectual life. England -- Intellectual life -- 18th century.

DA690.C7.H54 1998
Higgs, Laquita M., 1937-
Godliness and governance in Tudor Colchester/ Laquita M. Higgs. Ann Arbor: University of Michigan Press, c1998. xiii, 434 p.
98-008957   941.05   0472108905
Colchester (England) -- Politics and government. Great Britain -- History -- Tudors, 1485-1603. Colchester (England) -- Church history.

DA690.C75.C56 1991
Coss, Peter R.
Lordship, knighthood, and locality: a study in English society, c. 1180-c. 1280/ Peter Coss. Cambridge, England; Cambridge University Press, 1991. xv, 361 p.
90-002656   942.4/9803   0521402964
Knights and knighthood -- England -- Coventry -- History -- To 1500. Land tenure -- England -- Coventry -- History -- To 1500. Feudalism -- England -- Coventry -- History -- To 1500. Coventry (England) -- History. England -- Social conditions -- 1066-1485.

DA690.C75.T57 1990
Tiratsoo, Nick, 1952-
Reconstruction, affluence, and labour politics: Coventry, 1945-60/ N. Tiratsoo. London; Routledge, 1990. viii, 176 p.
90-032889   942.4/98   041504877X
Reconstruction (1939-1951) -- England -- Coventry. Coventry (England) -- Economic conditions. Coventry (England) -- Politics and government.

DA690.D96.A54 1994
Anglo-Norman Durham: 1093-1193/ edited by David Rollason, Margaret Harvey, Michael Prestwich. Woodbridge, Suffolk, UK; Boydell Press, 1994. xxix, 506 p.
94-018926   942.8/6501   0851153909
Monasticism and religious orders -- England -- Durham. Architecture, Romanesque -- England -- Durham. Manuscripts, Medieval -- England -- Durham. Durham (England) -- History.

DA690.G45
Fortune, Dion.
Glastonbury--Avalon of the heart/ Dion Fortune. York Beach, Me.: Samuel Weiser, 2000. 98, [1] p.
99-055714   936.2/38   1578631572
Occultism -- England -- Glastonbury. Avalon (Legendary place) Christian antiquities -- England -- Glastonbury. Glastonbury (England) -- Antiquities.

DA690.G83
Bold, John.
Greenwich: an architectural history of the Royal Hospital for Seamen and the Queen's House/ John Bold; with contributions by Peter Guillery ... [et al.]; architectural graphics by Andrew Donald; photographs by Derek Kendall. New Haven: Published for The Paul Mellon Centre for Studies c2000. vii, 292 p.
00-042880   942.1/62   0300083971
Architecture -- England -- London. Greenwich (London, England) -- Buildings, structures, etc.

DA690.H17.S63 1994
Smail, John.
The origins of middle-class culture: Halifax, Yorkshire, 1660-1780/ John Smail. Ithaca: Cornell University Press, 1994. xvi, 241 p.
94-020852   942.8/12   0801429900
Middle class -- England -- Halifax -- History. Halifax (England) -- Civilization.

DA690.H702.N35 1988
Nair, Gwyneth.
Highley: the development of a community, 1550-1880/ Gwyneth Nair. Oxford, OX, UK; B. Blackwell, 1988. ix, 264 p.
88-004337   942.4/59   0631153381
Villages -- England -- Shropshire -- Case studies. Rural development -- England -- Highley (Shropshire) -- Case studies. Highley (Shropshire) -- History. Highley (Shropshire) -- Social life and customs. England -- Rural conditions -- Case studies.

DA690.L8.N43 1988
Neal, Frank, 1932-
Sectarian violence: the Liverpool experience, 1819-1914: an aspect of Anglo-Irish history/ Frank Neal. Manchester, U.K.: Manchester University Press; c1988. xi, 272 p.
87-026030   942.7/53081   0719014832
Irish -- England -- Liverpool (England) -- History -- 19th century. Violence -- England -- Liverpool (England) -- History -- 19th century. Liverpool (England) -- Social conditions. Liverpool (England) -- Ethnic relations. Liverpool (England) -- Church history.

DA690.M4.W47 1990
Werbner, Pnina.
The migration process: capital, gifts, and offerings among British Pakistanis/ Pnina Werbner. New York: Berg; 1990. xii, 391 p.
89-035877   305.8/914122042733   0854966250
Pakistanis -- England -- Manchester -- Economic conditions. Pakistanis -- England -- Manchester -- Social life and customs. Gifts -- England -- Manchester.

DA690.R44.M37 1993
Marcombe, David.
English small town life: Retford, 1520-1642/ David Marcombe. [Nottingham]: Dept. of Adult Education, University of Nottingh 1993. xii, 319 p.
94-172692   942.5/21   1850410674
City and town life -- England -- East Retford -- History -- 16th century. City and town life -- England -- East Retford -- History -- 17th century. East Retford (England) -- History.

DA709 Wales — Compends

DA709.M38 1994
May, John.
Reference Wales/ compiled by John May. Cardiff: University of Wales Press, 1994. xi, 356 p.
95-137131 942.9 0708312349
Wales -- Statistics -- Handbooks, manuals, etc. Wales -- Chronology -- Handbooks, manuals, etc.

DA711.5 Wales — Social life and customs. Civilization

DA711.5.T76 1993
Trosset, Carol, 1959-
Welshness performed: Welsh concepts of person and society/ Carol Trosset. Tucson: University of Arizona Press, c1993. x, 183 p.
93-013100 942.9 0816513783
National characteristics, Welsh.   Wales -- Civilization.

DA714 Wales — History — General works

DA714.H58 1981 vol. 4
Jenkins, Geraint H.
The foundations of modern Wales: Wales 1642-1780/ by Geraint H. Jenkins. Oxford [Oxfordshire]; Clarendon Press, 1987. ix, 490 p.
87-012412 942.906 019821734X
Wales -- History -- 1536-1700. Wales -- History -- 18th century.

DA714.H58 1981 vol. 6
Morgan, Kenneth O.
Rebirth of a nation: Wales, 1880-1980/ by Kenneth O. Morgan. New York: Oxford University Press, 1981. xi, 463 p.
80-040337 942.9 0198217366
Wales -- History.

DA714.J585 1984
Jones, Gareth Elwyn.
Modern Wales: a concise history, c. 1485-1979/ Gareth Elwyn Jones. Cambridge [Cambridgeshire]; Cambridge University Press, 1984. xii, 364 p.
84-009590 942.9 0521242320
Wales -- History. Wales -- Economic conditions. Wales -- Social conditions.

DA715-722 Wales — History — By period

DA715.C37 1995
Carr, A. D. 1938-
Medieval Wales/ A.D. Carr. Houndmills, Basingstoke, Hampshire: Macmillan Press; 1995. xviii, 165 p.
94-038197 942.9/03 0312125097
Wales -- History -- 1063-1536.

DA715.D37 1987
Davies, R. R.
Conquest, coexistence, and change Wales, 1063-1415/ by R.R. Davies. Oxford [Oxfordshire]: Clarendon Press; 1987. xv, 530 p.
86-031066 942 0198217323
Wales -- History -- To 1536.

DA715.G75 1994
Griffiths, Ralph Alan.
Conquerors and conquered in medieval Wales/ Ralph A. Griffiths. New York: St. Martin's Press, 1994. x, 374 p.
93-044168 942.9 0312121199
Normans -- Wales -- History.   Wales -- History -- 1063-1284. Wales -- History -- 1284-1536.

DA715.J635 1994
Jones, J. Gwynfor, 1936-
Early modern Wales: c. 1525-1640/ J. Gwynfor Jones. New York: St. Martin's Press, 1994. xv, 270 p.
93-026870 942.905 031210362X
Wales -- History -- 1536-1700. Wales -- History -- 1284-1536.

DA715.M33 1991
Maund, K. L., 1962-
Ireland, Wales, and England in the eleventh century/ K.L. Maund. Woodbridge, Suffolk; Boydell Press, 1991. 238 p.
90-019312 942.01/8 0851155332
Wales -- History -- To 1063. Wales -- History -- 1063-1284. Wales -- Relations -- Ireland.

DA715.W26
Walker, David, 1923-
The Norman conquerors/ David Walker. Swansea: C. Davies, 1977. 109 p.
77-368499 942.9/01 0715403028
Normans -- Wales.   Wales -- History -- 1063-1284.

DA716.G5.D5 1995
Davies, R. R.
The revolt of Owain Glyn Dwr/ R.R. Davies. Oxford, England; Oxford University Press, 1995. xi, 401 p.
95-010826 942.904/1/092 0198205082
Glendower,   Owen,   --   1359?-1416? Revolutionaries -- Wales -- Biography. Nationalism -- Wales -- History. Princes -- Wales -- Biography. Wales -- History -- 1284-1536.

DA716.G5.H46 1996
Henken, Elissa R.
National redeemer: Owain Glyndwr in Welsh tradition/ Elissa R. Henken. Ithaca, N.Y.: Cornell University Press, 1996. x, 250 p.
96-010286 942.9/041/092 0801432685
Glendower, Owen, -- 1359?-1416? Nationalism -- Wales -- Historiography. Revolutionaries -- Wales -- Biography. Princes -- Wales -- Biography. Wales -- History -- 1284-1536 -- Historiography.

DA716.O94.C37 1991
Carr, A. D. 1938-
Owen of Wales: the end of the House of Gwynedd/ A.D. Carr. Cardiff: University of Wales Press, 1991. 140 p.
91-129062 942.903/7/092 0708310648
Owain ap Thomas ap Rhodri, -- ca. 1340-1378. Princes -- Wales -- Biography.   Wales -- History -- 1284-1536 -- Biography.

DA720.E79
Evans, Evan David.
A history of Wales, 1660-1815/ [by] E. D. Evans. Cardiff: University of Wales Press, 1976. x, 267 p.
77-378785 942.9/06 0708306241
Wales -- History -- 1536-1700. Wales -- History -- 18th century.

DA720.T482 1998
Thomas, Peter David Garner.
Politics in eighteenth-century Wales/ Peter D.G. Thomas. Cardiff: University of Wales Press, 1998. xi, 268 p.
98-131561 942.907 0708314449
Wales -- Politics and government. Wales -- History -- 18th century.

DA722.A33 1991
Adamson, David L.
Class, ideology, and the nation: a theory of Welsh nationalism/ David L. Adamson. Cardiff: University of Wales Press, 1991. 223 p.
91-217748   0708310826
Nationalism -- Wales. National characteristics, Welsh. Wales -- Politics and government.

DA722.M617 1995
Morgan, Kenneth O.
Modern Wales: politics, places and people/ Kenneth O. Morgan. Cardiff: University of Wales Press, 1995. xiv, 492 p.
96-157940 942.908 0708313175
Wales -- History -- 19th century. Wales -- History -- 20th century.

DA722.P47
Philip, Alan Butt.
The Welsh question: nationalism in Welsh politics, 1945-1970/ Alan Butt Philip. Cardiff: University of Wales Press, 1975. xv, 367 p.
75-316747 320.9/429/085 0708305377
Nationalism -- Wales.   Wales -- Politics and government -- 20th century.

DA722.P66 1998
Pope, Robert, 1969-
Building Jerusalem: nonconformity, labour, and the social question in Wales, 1906-1939/ by Robert Pope. Cardiff: University of Wales Press, 1998. xiii, 269 p.
98-131567 942.9082 0708314139
Dissenters, Religious -- Wales -- History -- 20th century. Labor movement -- Wales -- History -- 20th century.   Wales -- History -- 20th century. Wales -- Social conditions -- 20th century.

DA722.W355 1991
Wallace, Ryland, 1951-
Organise! organise! organise!: a study of reform agitations in Wales, 1840-1886/ by Ryland Wallace. Cardiff: University of Wales Press, 1991. xvi, 267 p.
91-230731 322.4/4/09429 0708310788
Wales -- Politics and government -- 19th century. Wales -- Social conditions -- 19th century.

DA730 Wales — Description and travel — 1801-1950

DA730.T44 1959
Thomas, Dylan, 1914-1953.
A child's Christmas in Wales. [New York] New Directions [1959, c1954]
59-013174 821.912 0811202038
Christmas -- Wales.   Wales -- Social life and customs.

DA755 Scotland — Sources and documents

DA755.D57
Donaldson, Gordon,
Scottish historical documents [compiled by] Gordon Donaldson. New York, Barnes & Noble [1970] xi, 287 p.
71-021537   941   0389040479
Scotland -- History -- Sources.

DA757.9 Scotland — History — Dictionaries. Chronological tables, outlines, etc.

DA757.9.O94 2001
The Oxford companion to Scottish history/ edited by Michael Lynch. Oxford: Oxford University Press, 2001. xxv, 732 p.
2002-276941   941.1/003.221   0192116967
Scotland -- History -- Encyclopedias.

DA758.3 Scotland — History — Biography (Collective)

DA758.3.S8.P58 1991
Pittock, Murray.
The invention of Scotland: the Stuart myth and the Scottish identity, 1638 to the present/ Murray G.H. Pittock. London; Routledge, 1991. 198 p.
90-024511   941.1   0415055865
Stuart, House of.   Nationalism -- Scotland -- History.   National characteristics, Scottish. Scotland -- Historiography. Scotland -- Kings and rulers.

DA759 Scotland — History — Historiography

DA759.K53 1993
Kidd, Colin.
Subverting Scotland's past: Scottish whig historians and the creation of an Anglo-British identity, 1689-c. 1830/ Colin Kidd. Cambridge [England]; Cambridge University Press, 1993. xiii, 322 p.
92-046708   941.1/0072   052143484X
National characteristics, Scottish -- Historiography. Historiography -- Scotland -- History. Nationalism -- Scotland -- History. Scotland -- Intellectual life -- 18th century. Scotland -- Historiography.

DA760 Scotland — History — General works

DA760.D48 1999
Devine, T. M.
The Scottish nation: a history, 1700-2000/ T.M. Devine.1st American ed. New York: Viking, 1999. xxiii, 695 p.
99-038391   941.1.221   0670888117
National characteristics, Scottish--History. Nationalism--Scotland--History.

DA760.E3 vol. 1
Duncan, A. A. M.
Scotland, the making of the kingdom/ Archibald A. M. Duncan. New York: Barnes & Noble, 1975. xii, 705 p.
75-005386   941.1 s   0064918300
Scotland -- History -- To 1603.

DA760.M58 2002
Mitchison, Rosalind.
A history of Scotland/ Rosalind Mitchison.3rd ed. London; Routledge, 2002. p. cm.
2001-048949   941.1.221   0415278805
Scotland -- History.

DA772-774.5 Scotland — History — General special

DA772.C618 2000
Collins encyclopaedia of Scotland/ edited by John Keay and Julia Keay.Rev. ed. London: HarperCollins, 2000. xvii, 1102 p.
2001-339028   941.1/003.221   0007103530
Scotland -- Civilization -- Encyclopedias. Scotland -- Encyclopedias.

DA772.S32 1989
Scottish society, 1500-1800/ edited by R.A. Houston and I.D. Whyte. Cambridge; Cambridge University Press, 1989. xii, 298 p.
88-005004   941.1   0521325226
Scotland -- Social life and customs. Scotland -- History -- 16th century. Scotland -- History -- 17th century.

DA774.H4
Henderson, Isabel.
The Picts. New York, Praeger [1967] 228 p.
67-015744   914.1/03/1
Picts. Art, Pictish. Scotland -- History -- To 1057.

DA774.5.H37 1998
Harper, Marjory.
Emigration from Scotland between the wars: opportunity or exile?/ Marjory Harper. Manchester; Manchester University Press; 1998. xv, 243 p.
00-302889   071904927X
Scots -- Foreign countries -- History -- 20th century.   Scotland -- Emigration and immigration -- History -- 20th century.

DA774.8-822 Scotland — History — By period

DA774.8.W4
Webster, Bruce.
Scotland from the eleventh century to 1603/ by Bruce Webster. Ithaca, N.Y.: Cornell University Press, 1975. 239 p.
74-019416   941.1/007/2   080140942X
Middle Ages -- Historiography.   Scotland -- History -- To 1603 -- Historiography.

DA775.B37 2000
Barrell, A. D. M.
Medieval Scotland/ A.D.M. Barrell. Cambridge, UK; Cambridge University Press, 2000. x, 296 p.
99-086098   941.1   0521584434
Scotland -- History -- 1057-1603. Scotland -- History -- To 1057.

DA777.H83 1994
Hudson, Benjamin T.
Kings of Celtic Scotland/ Benjamin T. Hudson. Westport, Conn.: Greenwood Press, 1994. xvii, 195 p.
93-049542   936.1/102   0313290873
Celts -- Scotland -- Kings and rulers.   Scotland -- History -- To 1057.

DA777.S68 1984
Smyth, Alfred P.
Warlords and holy men: Scotland, AD 80-1000/ Alfred P. Smyth. London; E. Arnold, 1984. viii, 279 p.
84-120168   941.101   0713163054
Scotland -- History -- To 1057.

DA782.8.S36 1990
Scotland in the reign of Alexander III, 1249-1286/ edited by Norman H. Reid. Edinburgh: John Donald Publishers Ltd., c1990. xiv, 218 p.
91-102260   941.102   0859762181
Alexander -- III, -- King of Scotland, -- 1241-1286 -- Congresses.   Scotland -- History -- Alexander III, 1249-1286 -- Congresses.

DA783.G72 1984
Grant, Alexander.
Independence and nationhood: Scotland, 1306-1469/ Alexander Grant. London; E. Arnold, 1984. 248 p.
84-071796   941.1   0713163097
Nationalism -- Scotland -- History -- To 1500. Middle Ages. Scotland -- History -- 1057-1603. Scotland -- History -- Autonomy and independence movements.

DA783.7.M38 1990
McGladdery, Christine.
James II/ Christine McGladdery. Edinburgh: John Donald Publishers Ltd., c1990. vii, 185 p.
91-129077   941.104/092   0859763048
James -- II, -- King of Scotland, -- 1430-1460. Scotland -- Kings and rulers -- Biography. Scotland -- History -- James II, 1437-1460.

DA784.3.M33.H55 1993
Hill, James Michael.
Fire and sword: Sorley Boy MacDonnell and the rise of Clan Ian Mor, 1538-1590/ J. Michael Hill. London: Athlone Press, 1993. xiii, 321 p.
94-142349   941.1/505/092   0485114372
MacDonnell, Sorley Boy, -- 1505?-1590. Clans -- Scotland -- Highlands -- History -- 16th century. Clans -- Ulster (Northern Ireland and Ireland) -- History -- 16th century. Ulster (Northern Ireland and Ireland) -- Biography. Scotland -- History -- 16th century -- Biography.

DA784.5.F74 1991
Fradenburg, Louise Olga, 1953-
City, marriage, tournament: arts of rule in late medieval Scotland/ Louise Olga Fradenburg. Madison, Wis.: University of Wisconsin Press, c1991. xv, 390 p.
91-012976   941.104   0299129500
James -- III, -- King of Scotland, -- 1451-1488. James -- IV, -- King of Scotland, -- 1473-1513. Stuart, House of. Scottish literature -- To 1700 -- History and criticism. Tournaments, Medieval -- Scotland -- History -- To 1500. Monarchy -- Scotland -- History -- To 1500. Edinburgh (Scotland) -- Intellectual life. Scotland -- Politics and government -- 15th century. Scotland -- Civilization -- 15th century.

DA784.5.M23 1989
Macdougall, Norman.
James IV/ Norman Macdougall. Edinburgh: John Donald Publishers Ltd., c1989. x, 339 p.
90-139378   941.104/092   0859762009
James -- IV, -- King of Scotland, -- 1473-1513. Scotland -- Kings and rulers -- Biography. Scotland -- History -- James IV, 1488-1513.

DA785.G665 1999
Goodare, Julian.
State and society in early modern Scotland/ Julian Goodare. Oxford; Oxford University Press, 1999. xv, 366 p.
   019820762X
Scotland -- Politics and government -- 16th century. Scotland -- Politics and government -- 17th century. Scotland -- History -- 16th century.

DA786.F73 1995
Franklin, David Byrd.
The Scottish regency of the Earl of Arran: a study in the failure of Anglo-Scottish relations/ David Franklin. Lewiston, N.Y.: Edwin Mellen Press, c1995. v, 210 p.
94-041356   941.105/092   0773489711
Arran, James Hamilton, -- Earl of, -- d. 1575. Regency -- Scotland.   Scotland -- Politics and government -- 16th century. England -- Foreign relations -- Scotland. Scotland -- Foreign relations -- England.

DA787.A1.D59
Donaldson, Gordon.
Mary, Queen of Scots/ [by] Gordon Donaldson; with a foreword by A. L. Rowse. London: English Universities Press, 1974. 200 p.
74-186753   941.05/092/4   0340123834
Mary, -- Queen of Scots, -- 1542-1587.   Queens -- Scotland -- Biography.   Scotland -- History -- Mary Stuart, 1542-1567.

DA787.A1.L62 1998
Lewis, Jayne Elizabeth.
Mary Queen of Scots: romance and nation/ Jayne Elizabeth Lewis. London; Routledge, 1998. xii, 259 p.
98-017140   941.105/092   0415114802
Mary, -- Queen of Scots, -- 1542-1587.   Queens -- Scotland -- Biography.   Scotland -- History -- Mary Stuart, 1542-1567.

DA787.A1.M28 1988
Mary Stewart, queen in three kingdoms/ edited by Michael Lynch. Oxford, UK; B. Blackwell, 1988. xvii, 238 p.
87-035448   941.105/092/4   0631152636
Mary, -- Queen of Scots, -- 1542-1587.   Queens -- Scotland -- Biography. Queens -- France -- Biography. Great Britain -- History -- Elizabeth, 1558-1603. Scotland -- History -- Mary Stuart, 1542-1567. France -- History -- Francis II, 1559-1560.

DA787.D3 W45 2003
Weir, Alison.
Mary, Queen of Scots, and the murder of Lord Darnley/ Alison Weir.1st ed. New York: Ballantine Books, 2003. p. cm.
 2002-034467   941.105/092.221   034543658X
Darnley, Henry Stuart, Lord, 1545-1567--Death and burial. Mary, Queen of Scots, 1542-1587--Marriage.   Murder--Scotland--History--16th century. Queens--Scotland--Biography.

DA800.B76 1992
Brown, Keith M.
Kingdom or province?: Scotland and the regal union, 1603-1715/ Keith M. Brown. New York: St. Martin's Press, 1992. xi, 226 p.
92-019659   941.106   0312083874
Scotland -- Politics and government -- 17th century. Scotland -- Politics and government -- 18th century. Scotland -- History -- The Union, 1707.

DA800.M56 1983
Mitchison, Rosalind.
Lordship to patronage: Scotland, 1603-1745/ Rosalind Mitchison. London; E. Arnold, 1983. 198 p.
83-217946   941.106   0713163135
Scotland -- History -- 17th century. Scotland -- History -- 1689-1745.

DA803.15.L43
Lee, Maurice.
Government by pen: Scotland under James VI and I/ Maurice Lee, Jr. Urbana: University of Illinois Press, c1980. xiv, 232 p.
79-016830   941.1/04   0252007654
James -- I, -- King of England, -- 1566-1625. Scotland -- History -- James VI, 1567-1625. Scotland -- Politics and government -- 1371-1707.

DA803.3.D66 1990
Donald, Peter.
An uncounselled king: Charles I and the Scottish troubles, 1637-1641/ Peter Donald. Cambridge; Cambridge University Press, 1990. xv, 351 p.
89-077392   941.106/2   0521372356
Charles -- I, -- King of England, -- 1600-1649. Scotland -- History -- Charles I, 1625-1649.

DA803.3.M33 1991
Macinnes, Allan I.
Charles I and the making of the covenanting movement, 1625-1641/ Allan I. Macinnes. Edinburgh: J. Donald Publishers, c1991. ix, 228 p.
91-156266   941.06/2   0859762955
Covenanters.   Scotland -- History -- Charles I, 1625-1649.

DA803.7.A3.C68
Cowan, Edward J.
Montrose: for covenant and king/ Edward J. Cowan. London: Weidenfeld and Nicolson, c1977. vii, 326 p.
77-365889   942.06/242/092   0297772090
Montrose, James Graham, -- Marquis of, -- 1612-1650.   Royalists -- Scotland -- Biography. Generals -- Scotland -- Biography.   Scotland -- History -- Charles I, 1625-1649 -- Biography.

DA809.D38 2000
Davidson, Neil, 1957-
The origins of Scottish nationhood/ Neil Davidson. London; Pluto Press, 2000. vii, 264 p.
99-089799   941.107   0745316085
Nationalism -- Scotland -- History -- 18th century. National characteristics, Scottish -- History -- 18th century. Scotland -- History -- 18th century. Scotland -- History -- The Union, 1707.

DA812.A43 1993
Allan, David.
Virtue, learning, and the Scottish Enlightenment: ideas of scholarship in early modern history/ David Allan. Edinburgh: Edinburgh University Press, c1993. viii, 276 p.
94-108658   0748604340
Historiography -- Scotland -- History -- 18th century. Philosophy, Scottish -- 18th century. Enlightenment -- Scotland. Scotland -- Intellectual life -- 18th century.

DA813.G53 1988
Gibson, John S.
Playing the Scottish card: the Franco-Jacobite invasion of 1708/ John S. Gibson. Edinburgh: Edinburgh University Press, c1988. x, 169 p.
89-106644   941.106/9   085224567X
Jacobites -- History.   France -- Foreign relations -- Great Britain. Great Britain -- Foreign relations -- France. Scotland -- History -- 18th century.

DA813.M86 1989
Monod, Paul Kleber.
Jacobitism and the English people, 1688-1788/ Paul Kleber Monod. Cambridge; Cambridge University Press, 1989. xvi, 408 p.
88-036743   941.507   0521335345
Jacobites.   England -- Civilization -- 18th century. England -- Civilization -- 17th century. Great Britain -- Politics and government -- 18th century.

DA814.A5.E7 1989
Erickson, Carolly, 1943-
Bonnie Prince Charlie: a biography/ Carolly Erickson. New York: W. Morrow, c1989. 331 p.
88-013438   941.07/2/0924   0688060870
Charles Edward, -- Prince, grandson of James II, King of England, -- 1720-1788.   Jacobite Rebellion, 1745-1746. Princes -- Great Britain -- Biography.   Scotland -- History -- 18th century.

DA814.A5.M37 1988
McLynn, F. J.
Charles Edward Stuart: a tragedy in many acts/ Frank McLynn. London; Routledge, 1988. xii, 640 p.
88-002384   941.07/2/0924   0415002729
Charles Edward, -- Prince, grandson of James II, King of England, -- 1720-1788.   Jacobite Rebellion, 1745-1746. Princes -- Great Britain -- Biography. Scotland -- History -- 18th century.

DA815.M38 1990
McFarland, E. W.
Protestants first: Orangeism in nineteenth century Scotland/ E.W. McFarland. Edinburgh: Edinburgh University Press; c1990. viii, 255 p.
91-164884   305.6   074860202X
Orangemen -- Scotland -- History -- 19th century. Protestants -- Scotland -- Political activity -- History -- 19th century. Scotland -- Politics and government -- 19th century.

DA821.F79 1987
Fry, Michael, 1947-
Patronage and principle: a political history of modern Scotland/ Michael Fry. Aberdeen: Aberdeen University Press, 1987. 299 p.
88-100636   941.108   0080350631
Patronage, Political -- Scotland -- History. Scotland -- Politics and government -- 20th century. Scotland -- Politics and government -- 19th century.

DA822.M3.S36 1995
Sanger, Clyde.
Malcolm MacDonald: bringing an end to empire/ Clyde Sanger. Montreal; McGill-Queen's University Press, c1995. xxi, 498 p.
96-132147   941.082/092   0773513035
MacDonald, Malcolm, -- 1901-   Colonial administrators -- Great Britain -- Biography. Diplomats -- Great Britain -- Biography. Decolonization. Scotland -- Biography. Great Britain -- Colonies -- Administration -- History -- 20th century.

DA850 Scotland — Description and travel — History of travel

DA850.T875 1995
Turnock, David.
The making of the Scottish rural landscape/ David
Turnock. Aldershot, Hants, England: Brookfield,
Vt.: c1995. xiv, 315 p.
94-044740   911/.411   1859280277
*Country life -- Scotland -- History. Landscape --
Scotland -- History. Land use -- Scotland --
History. Scotland -- Geography, Historical.
Scotland -- Rural conditions.*

DA850.W48 1991
Whyte, Ian
The changing Scottish landscape, 1500-1800/ Ian
and Kathleen Whyte. London; Routledge, 1991. x,
251 p.
90-024524   911/.411   0415029929
*Landscape -- Scotland -- History. Land use --
Scotland -- History. Scotland -- Historical
geography.*

DA880 Scotland — Counties, regions, etc., A-Z

DA880.H4.J6 1970
Johnson, Samuel, 1709-1784.
Johnson's Journey to the western islands of
Scotland; and Boswell's Journal of a tour to the
Hebrides with Samuel Johnson, LL.D; edited by R.
W. Chapman. London, Oxford U.P., 1970. xix,
475 p.
75-507901   914.11/7/047   0192810723
*Hebrides (Scotland) -- Description and travel -
- Early works to 1800. Scotland -- Description and
travel -- Early works to 1800.*

DA880.H6.D37 1994
Devine, T. M.
Clanship to crofters' war: the social transformation
of the Scottish Highlands/ T.M. Devine.
Manchester [England]; Manchester University
Press: c1994. viii, 258 p.
93-030886   941.1/507   0719034817
*Highlands (Scotland) -- History. Highlands
(Scotland) -- Social conditions.*

DA880.H6.G64 1987
Grant, I. F.
Periods in highland history/ I.F. Grant, Hugh
Cheape. London: Shepheard-Walwyn; 1987. xiii,
306 p.
87-062815   941.1/5   0856830577
Highlands (Scotland) -- History.

DA880.H7.F5
Finlay, Ian.
Highlands. Batsford, 1963.
64-002146
*Highlands (Scotland) -- Description and travel.
Scotland -- Description and travel.*

DA880.I7.M14 1990
MacArthur, E. Mairi.
Iona: the living memory of a crofting community,
1750-1914/ E. Mairi MacArthur. Edinburgh:
Edinburgh University Press, c1990. vii, 260 p.
91-142294   941.4/23   0748602143
*Crofters -- Scotland -- Iona -- History. Farm life
-- Scotland -- Iona -- History. Oral tradition --
Scotland -- Iona. Iona (Scotland) -- History.*

DA880.P25.L69 1998
Lowe, Christopher.
Coastal erosion and the archaeological assessment
of an eroding shoreline at St Boniface Church,
Papa Westray, Orkney/ Christopher Lowe; with
contributions from Sheila Boardman ... [et al.].
Phoenix Mill, Thrupp, Stroud, Gloucestershire:,
Sutton Publishing; 1998. xvi, 215 p.
99-170743   936.1/32   0750917555
*Excavations (Archaeology) -- Scotland -- Papa
Westray. Coast changes -- Scotland -- Papa
Westray. Papa Westray (Scotland) -- Antiquities.
Orkney (Scotland) -- Antiquities.*

DA880.S6.M26 1997
Macdonald, Sharon.
Reimagining culture: histories, identities, and the
Gaelic renaissance/ Sharon Macdonald. Oxford;
New York: Berg, 1997. xix, 297 p.
98-115323   941.1/82   1859739806
*Scottish Gaelic language -- Social aspects --
Scotland -- Skye, Island of. Community life --
Scotland -- Skye, Island of. Group identity --
Scotland -- Skye, Island of. Skye, Island of
(Scotland) -- Civilization.*

DA890 Scotland — Cities, towns, etc., A-Z

DA890.G5.G43 1994
Glasgow/ edited by T.M. Devine and Gordon
Jackson. Manchester; Manchester University Press:
c1994- xii, 435 p.
93-047156   941.4/43   0719036917
Glasgow (Scotland) -- History.

DA890.M87.G3
Gaskell, Philip.
Morvern transformed: a Highland parish in the
nineteenth century.   London, Cambridge U.P.,
1968 xix, 273 p.
67-024944   941.3/8
*Country life -- Scotland -- Highlands -- History -
- 19th century.*

DA906 Ireland — General works

DA906.E53 2000
Encyclopedia of Ireland: an A-Z guide to its
people, places, history, and culture/ Ciaran Brady,
general editor. New York: Oxford University
Press, c2000. x, 390 p.
00-062393   941.5/003   0195216857
*Ireland -- Encyclopedias. Northern Ireland --
Encyclopedias.*

DA908 Ireland — Historiography — General works

DA908.O46 1998
O'Mahony, Patrick, 1957-
Rethinking Irish history: nationalism, identity, and
deology/ Patrick O'Mahony and Gerard Delanty.
New York: St. Martin's Press, 1998. 222 p.
97-052927   305.8/009415   0312214022
*Nationalism -- Ireland -- Historiography. Group
identity -- Ireland -- Historiography. National
characteristics, Irish -- Historiography. Ireland --
Historiography.*

DA908.7 Ireland — Historiography — Biography of historians

DA908.7.K43
Cunningham, Bernadette.
The world of Geoffrey Keating: history, myth, and
religion in seventeenth-century Ireland/ Bernadette
Cunningham. Dublin; Four Courts Press, c2000.
xv, 263 p.
01-269053   1851825339
*Keating, Geoffrey, -- 1570?-1644?   Celts --
Ireland -- Historiography. Historians -- Ireland --
Biography. Ireland -- History -- 17th century.
Ireland -- History -- 1172-1603 -- Historiography.
Ireland -- History -- To 1172 -- Historiography.*

DA910 Ireland — History — General works

DA910.B67 1982
Bottigheimer, Karl S.
Ireland and the Irish: a short history/ Karl S.
Bottigheimer. New York: Columbia University
Press, 1982. ix, 301 p.
82-004160   941.5   0231046103
Ireland -- History. Ireland -- Civilization.

DA910.D66 1990
Doherty, J. E.
A chronology of Irish history since 1500/ J.E.
Doherty, D.J. Hickey. Savage, Md.: Barnes &
Noble Books, 1990. 395 p.
90-000152   941.5/002/02   0389208957
Ireland -- History -- Chronology.

DA910.T39 1997
Thomas, Colin, 1939-
Historical dictionary of Ireland/ Colin Thomas,
Avril Thomas. Lanham, Md.: Scarecrow Press,
1997. xliv, 263 p.
97-002136   941.5/003   081083300X
*Ireland -- History -- Dictionaries. Ireland --
Chronology.*

DA912 Ireland — History — Compends

DA912.N48
A new history of Ireland/ edited by T.W. Moody,
F.X. Martin, F.J. Byrne. Oxford [England]:
Clarendon Press; 1976-1986 v. 2-6, 8-9
76-376168   941.5   0198217390
Ireland -- History.

DA912.N485 1991
Newman, P. R.
Companion to Irish history, 1603-1921: from the submission of Tyrone to partition/ Peter R. Newman. Oxford [England]; Facts On File, c1991. xi, 244 p.
91-023677   941.5/003   081602572X
Ireland -- History -- Encyclopedias. Ireland -- Biography -- Dictionaries.

DA913 Ireland — History — Addresses, essays, lectures

DA913.C66 1984
The Course of Irish History/ edited by T.W. Moody and F.X. Martin. Cork: Published in association with Radio Telefis Eire 1984. 479 p.
84-237579   941.5   0853427100
Ireland -- History.

DA913.S45 2001
Shaw, Bernard, 1856-1950.
The matter with Ireland/ Bernard Shaw; edited by Dan H. Laurence and David H. Greene. Gainesville: University Press of Florida, 2001. xxvi, 354 p.
01-016182   941.5081   0813018862
Ireland -- History.

DA914-925 Ireland — History — General special

DA914.G47 2000
Geraghty, Tony.
The Irish War: the hidden conflict between the IRA and British Intelligence/ Tony Geraghty. Baltimore: Johns Hopkins University Press, 2000. xxxv, 420 p.
99-087238   941.60824   0801864569
Political violence -- Ireland -- History. Terrorism -- Northern Ireland -- History. Counterinsurgency -- Ireland -- History. Northern Ireland -- History, Military. Ireland -- History, Military.

DA914.M55 1996
A military history of Ireland/ edited by Thomas Bartlett and Keith Jeffery. Cambridge; Cambridge University Press, 1996. xxv, 565 p.
95-006124   355/.009415   0521415993
Ireland -- History, Military.

DA920.B348 1987
Barry, Terence B.
The archaeology of medieval Ireland/ T.B. Barry. London; Methuen, 1987. xvii, 234 p.
87-011210   941.5   0416303609
Excavations (Archaeology) -- Ireland. Archaeology, Medieval. Ireland -- Antiquities. Ireland -- History -- 1172-1603.

DA920.F57 1992
Flanagan, Laurence.
A dictionary of Irish archaeology/ Laurence Flanagan. Savage, Md.: Barnes & Noble Books, 1992. 221 p.
91-028279   936.1/003   0389209724
Excavations (Archaeology) -- Ireland -- Dictionaries. Excavations (Archaeology) -- Northern Ireland -- Dictionaries. Northern Ireland -- Antiquities -- Dictionaries. Ireland -- Antiquities -- Dictionaries.

DA925.A36 1988
Akenson, Donald H.
Small differences: Irish Catholics and Irish Protestants, 1815-1922: an international perspective/ Donald Harman Akenson. Kingston: McGill-Queen's University Press, c1988. xii, 236 p.
88-196583   941.508   0773506365
National characteristics, Irish. Catholics -- Ireland -- History. Protestants -- Ireland -- History. Ireland -- Social life and customs -- 19th century. Ireland -- Social life and customs -- 20th century.

DA925.B47 1998
The Blackwell companion to modern Irish culture/ edited by William J. McCormack. Malden, Mass.: Blackwell Publishers, 1998. p. cm.
98-005572   941.5   0631165258
Ireland -- Civilization -- Handbooks, manuals, etc.

DA925.H88 1987
Hutchinson, John, 1949-
The dynamics of cultural nationalism: the Gaelic revival and the creation of the Irish nation state/ John Hutchinson. London; Allen & Unwin, 1987. viii, 343 p.
86-028844   941.508   0043202047
Nationalism -- Ireland -- History. Civilization, Celtic. National characteristics, Irish. Ireland -- Intellectual life. Ireland -- Politics and government -- 20th century.

DA930-965 Ireland — History — By period

DA930.E38 1990
Edwards, Nancy.
The archaeology of early medieval Ireland/ Nancy Edwards. Philadelphia: University of Pennsylvania Press, 1990. 226 p.
90-040298   941.501   081223085X
Excavations (Archaeology) -- Ireland. Ireland -- Antiquities. Archaeology, Medieval. Ireland -- History -- To 1172.

DA930.R5313 1988
Richter, Michael,
Medieval Ireland: the enduring tradition/ Michael Richter; with a foreword by Proinseas Ni Chatain. New York: St. Martin's Press, 1988. 214 p.
88-015655   941.5   0312023383
Ireland -- History -- To 1603. Ireland -- Church history -- 600-1500.

DA930.5.R53 1999
Richter, Michael, Professor Dr.
Ireland and her neighbours in the seventh century/ Michael Richter. New York: St. Martin's Press, 1999. 256 p.
98-037332   941.501   0312220758
Manuscripts, Latin (Medieval and modern) -- Ireland. Seventh century. Ireland -- Civilization -- European influences. Europe -- Civilization -- Irish influences. Ireland -- Relations -- Europe.

DA931.F74 2001
Freeman, Philip, 1961-
Ireland and the classical world/ Philip Freeman. Austin: University of Texas Press, 2001. xvi, 148 p.
00-027762   303.48/23615038   0292725183
Irish language -- Foreign elements -- Latin. Latin language -- Influence on Irish. Greece -- Relations -- Ireland. Ireland -- Antiquities, Roman. Ireland -- Relations -- Rome. Rome -- Relations -- Ireland.

DA931.R34 1994
Raftery, Barry.
Pagan Celtic Ireland: the enigma of the Irish Iron Age/ Barry Raftery. London; Thames and Hudson, c1994. 240 p.
93-061274   936.1/02   0500050724
Fortification, Prehistoric -- Ireland. Romans -- Ireland -- History. Celts -- Ireland -- History. Ireland -- Antiquities, Roman. Ireland -- Antiquities, Celtic.

DA935.B14 1963
Bagwell, Richard, 1840-1918.
Ireland under the Tudors; with a succinct account of the earlier history. [London] Holland Press [c1963] 3 v.
67-009028
Ireland -- History -- 16th century.

DA935.B69 1994
Brady, Ciaran.
The chief governors: the rise and fall of reform government in Tudor Ireland, 1536-1588/ Ciaran Brady. Cambridge; Cambridge University Press, 1994. xviii, 322 p.
93-043767   941.505   0521461766
Tudor, House of. British -- Ireland -- History -- 16th century. Ireland -- Politics and government -- 1172-1603. Great Britain -- Politics and government -- 1485-1603.

DA935.E58 1985
Ellis, Steven G., 1950-
Tudor Ireland: crown, community, and the conflict of cultures, 1470-1603/ Steven G. Ellis. London; Longman, 1985. x, 388 p.
84-027874   941.505   0582493412
Culture conflict -- Ireland -- History -- 16th century. British -- Ireland -- History -- 16th century. Ireland -- History -- 1172-1603. Great Britain -- History -- Tudors,1485-1603.

DA935.L46 1995
Lennon, Colm.
Sixteenth-century Ireland: the incomplete conquest/ Colm Lennon. New York: St. Martin's Press, c1995. 390 p.
94-032460   941.505   0312124627
Ireland -- History -- 16th century.

DA935.M22
MacCurtain, Margaret.
Tudor and Stuart Ireland [by] Margaret MacCurtain. [Dublin] Gill and Macmillan [c1972] 211 p.
74-173300   941.55
Stuart, House of. Tudor, House of. Ireland -- History -- 16th century. Ireland -- History -- 17th century.

DA935.P35 1994
Palmer, William, 1951-
The problem of Ireland in Tudor foreign policy, 1485-1603/ William Palmer. Woodbridge, Suffolk; Boydell Press, 1994. 161 p.
94-034484   941.505   0851155626
British -- Ireland -- History -- 16th century. Great Britain -- Foreign relations -- 1485-1603. Great Britain -- Foreign relations -- Europe. Europe -- Foreign relations -- Great Britain.

DA937.F3 1970
Falls, Cyril, 1888-1971.
Elizabeth's Irish wars, by Cyril Falls. New York, Barnes & Noble [1970] 362 p.
72-013225   941.5/5   0389039616
British -- Ireland -- History -- 16th century. Great Britain -- History, Military -- 1485-1603. Great Britain -- History -- Elizabeth, 1558-1603. Ireland -- History -- 1558-1603.

DA938.F67 1988
Foster, R. F. 1949-
Modern Ireland, 1600-1972/ R.F. Foster. New York, N.Y.: Penguin Books, 1989, c1988. xiii, 688 p.
89-118698   941.5   0713990104
Ireland -- History -- 1691- Ireland -- History -- 17th century.

DA938.O37 1971
O'Farrell, Patrick James.
Ireland's English question; Anglo-Irish relations 1534-1970 [by] Patrick O'Farrell. New York, Schocken Books [1971] 336 p.
75-159481   327.415/042
Irish question.   Ireland -- Politics and government.

DA940.F59 1989
Fitzpatrick, Brendan.
Seventeenth-century Ireland: the war of religions/ Brendan Fitzpatrick. Totowa, N.J.: Barnes & Noble Books, 1989. 291 p.
88-023589   941.506   0389208140
Ireland -- History -- 17th century.

DA940.J36 1995
James, Francis Godwin, 1913-
Lords of the ascendancy: the Irish House of Lords and its members, 1600-1800/ Francis G. James. Washington, DC: Catholic University of America Press, c1995. 248 p.
95-011179   305.5/223/0941509032   0813208408
Ireland -- Politics and government -- 17th century. Legislators -- Ireland -- Biography. Nobility -- Ireland -- History. Ireland -- Politics and government -- 18th century.

DA940.5.C7.C36 1982
Canny, Nicholas P.
The upstart earl: a study of the social and mental world of Richard Boyle, first Earl of Cork, 1566-1643/   Nicholas   Canny.   Cambridge [Cambridgeshire]; Cambridge University Press, 1982. xii, 211 p.
81-021687   941.506/092/4   0521244161
Cork, Richard Boyle, -- Earl of, -- 1566-1643. Statesmen -- Great Britain -- Biography.   Ireland - - Social life and customs -- 17th century. Ireland -- Social life and customs -- 16th century.

DA940.5.S27.W38 1992
Wauchope, Piers.
Patrick Sarsfield and the Williamite War/ Piers Wauchope. Dublin: Irish Academic Press, c1992. 334 p.
92-173679   0716524767
Sarsfield, Patrick, -- Earl of Lucan, -- d. 1693. Soldiers -- Ireland -- Biography. Generals -- France -- Biography. Ireland -- History -- War of 1689-1691 -- Biography.

DA941.5.C5 1966a
Clarke, Aidan.
The old English in Ireland, 1625-42. Ithaca, N.Y., Cornell University Press [1966] 287 p.
66-015553   941.56
British -- Ireland.   Ireland -- History -- 1625-1649.

DA944.4.B37
Barnard, T. C.
Cromwellian Ireland: English government and reform in Ireland 1649-1660/ by T. C. Barnard. London: Oxford University Press, 1975. ix, 349 p.
75-317054   941.5/06   0198218583
Cromwell, Oliver, -- 1599-1658 -- Views on Ireland.   Land settlement -- Ireland -- History -- 17th century. Protestants -- Ireland -- History -- 17th century. British -- Ireland -- History -- 17th century. Ireland -- History -- 1649-1660.

DA944.4.W48 1999
Wheeler, James Scott.
Cromwell in Ireland/ by James Scott Wheeler. New York: St. Martin's Press, 1999. p. cm.
99-022173   941.506   0312225504
Cromwell, Oliver, -- 1599-1658 -- Military leadership. Cromwell, Oliver, -- 1599-1658 -- Journeys -- Ireland. Cromwell, Oliver, -- 1599-1658 -- Views on Ireland.   Ireland -- History -- 1649-1660.

DA945.K56 1990
Kings in conflict: the revolutionary war in Ireland and its aftermath, 1689-1750/ edited W.A. Maguire. Belfast: Blackstaff Press, 1990. xiv, 203 p.
90-222625   941.506   0856404357
Ireland -- History -- War of 1689-1691. Ireland -- History -- War of 1689-1691 -- Influence. Ireland -- Military relations -- France.

DA947.B37 1992
Bartlett, Thomas.
The fall and rise of the Irish nation: the catholic question, 1690-1830/ Thomas Bartlett. Savage, Md.: Barnes & Noble Books, 1992. xi, 430 p.
91-026241   941.507   0389209740
Church   and   state   --   Ireland.   Catholic emancipation. Catholics -- Ireland. Ireland -- Church history. Ireland -- Politics and government -- 1800-1837. Ireland -- Politics and government -- 18th century.

DA947.B4 1976
Beckett, J. C. 1912-
The Anglo-Irish tradition/ J. C. Beckett. Ithaca, N.Y.: Cornell University Press, 1976. 158 p.
76-020093   941.5/004/21   0801410568
British -- Ireland -- History. Irish question.

DA947.C66 1992
Connolly, S. J.
Religion, law, and power: the making of Protestant Ireland,   1660-1760/   S.J.   Connolly.   Oxford [England]: Clarendon Press; 1992. viii, 346 p.
91-039688   941.06   0198201184
Protestants -- Ireland -- History -- 18th century. Protestants -- Ireland -- History -- 17th century. Ireland -- History -- 18th century. Ireland -- History -- 17th century.

DA947.J35
James, Francis Godwin.
Ireland in the Empire, 1688-1770; a history of Ireland from the Williamite Wars to the eve of the American Revolution. Cambridge, Mass., Harvard University Press, 1973. 356 p.
72-087772   320.9/415/07   0674466268
Ireland -- Politics and government -- 18th century.

DA947.M198
McDowell, R. B. 1913-
Ireland in the age of imperialism and revolution, 1760-1801/   by   R.   B.   McDowell. Oxford: Clarendon Press; 1979. 740 p.
79-040413   941.507   019822480X
Ireland -- History -- 1760-1820.

DA947.M23 1994
McFarland, E. W.
Ireland and Scotland in the age of revolution: planting the green bough/ E.W. McFarland. Edinburgh: Edinburgh University Press, c1994. xii, 272 p.
95-131152   0748605398
Radicalism -- Ireland -- History. Radicalism -- Scotland -- History.   Ireland -- Politics and government -- 1800-1837. Ireland -- Politics and government -- 18th century. Scotland -- Politics and government -- 18th century.

DA947.3.O29 1997
O Ciosain, Niall, 1960-
Print and popular culture in Ireland, 1750-1850/ Niall O Ciosain. New York: St. Martin's Press, 1997. ix, 249 p.
97-005891   941.5   0312174551
Popular literature -- Publishing -- Ireland -- History -- 18th century. Popular literature -- Publishing -- Ireland -- History -- 19th century. Popular culture -- Ireland -- History -- 18th century. Ireland -- Civilization -- 18th century. Ireland -- Civilization -- 19th century.

DA948.A2.B4
Beckett, J. C. 1912-
Protestant dissent in Ireland, 1687-1780. London, Faber and Faber [1948] 161 p.
48-003038   274.15
Dissenters -- Ireland.

DA948.A2.L38 1993
Leighton, C. D. A.
Catholicism in a Protestant kingdom: a study of the Irish Ancien Regime/ C.D.A. Leighton. New York: St. Martin's Press, 1994. x, 218 p.
93-005866   941.507/08822   0312103018
Catholics -- Ireland -- History -- 18th century. Church and state -- Ireland -- History -- 18th century. Ireland -- Church history.

DA948.4.O25 1987
O'Brien, Gerard.
Anglo-Irish politics in the age of Grattan and Pitt/ Gerard O'Brien. Blackrock, Co. Dublin: Irish Academic Press, c1987. 231 p.
88-102003   941.507   0716523779
Grattan, Henry, -- 1746-1820. Pitt, W. M. -- (William Morton), -- 1754 or 5-1836. Irish question.   Ireland -- Politics and government -- 1760-1820. Ireland -- Foreign relations -- Great Britain. Great Britain -- Foreign relations -- Ireland.

DA948.5.M38 1998
McBride, Ian.
Scripture politics: Ulster Presbyterians and Irish radicalism in the late eighteenth century/ I.R. McBride. Oxford: Clarendon Press; 1998. 274 p.
98-003202   941.607   0198206429
Presbyterians -- Ulster (Northern Ireland and Ireland) -- History -- 18th century. Christianity and politics -- Ireland -- History -- 18th century. Radicalism -- Ireland -- History -- 18th century. Ireland -- Politics and government -- 18th century. Ulster (Northern Ireland and Ireland) -- Politics and government. Ireland -- History -- 1760-1820.

DA948.6.T6.E45 1989
Elliott, Marianne, 1948-
Wolfe Tone, prophet of Irish independence/
Marianne Elliott. New Haven: Yale University
Press, 1989. x, 492 p.
89-036283   941.507/092   0300046375
*Tone, Theobald Wolfe, -- 1763-1798. Nationalism
-- Ireland -- History -- 18th century.
Revolutionaries -- Ireland -- Biography.
Republicanism -- Ireland -- History -- 18th
century. Ireland -- History -- Rebellion of 1798 --
Biography. Ireland -- Politics and government --
1760-1820.*

DA949.C48 1998
Chambers, Liam.
Rebellion in Kildare, 1790-1803/ Liam Chambers.
Dublin; Four Courts Press, c1998. 173 p.
98-192066   185182362X
*Insurgency -- Ireland -- Kildare (County) --
History -- 18th century. Insurgency -- Ireland --
Kildare (County) -- History -- 19th century.
Ireland -- History -- Rebellion of 1798. Kildare
(Ireland: County) -- History.*

DA949.P3 1970
Pakenham, Thomas, 1933-
The year of liberty; the story of the great Irish
rebellion of 1798.   Englewood Cliffs, N.J.,
Prentice-Hall [1970, c1969] 416 p.
79-096825   941.5/7   0139718958
Ireland -- History -- Rebellion of 1798.

DA949.5.G46 1999
Geoghegan, Patrick M.
The Irish Act of Union: a study in high politics,
1798-1801/ Patrick M. Geoghegan. New York: St.
Martin's Press, 1999. p. cm.
99-016691   941.507   0312227280
*Ireland -- History -- The Union, 1800. Ireland -
- Politics and government -- 1760-1820.*

DA950.B69 1990
Boyce, David George, 1942-
Nineteenth-century Ireland: the search for stability/
D. George Boyce. Savage, Md.: Barnes & Noble
Books, 1991. ix, 345 p.
90-014420   941.5081   0389209341
Ireland -- History -- 19th century.

DA950.C76 1996
Crossman, Virginia.
Politics, law and order in nineteenth-century
Ireland/ Virginia Crossman. New York: St.
Martin's Press, 1996. 290 p.
96-028747   363.2/3/0941509034   0312164432
*Law enforcement -- Ireland -- History -- 19th
century. Ireland -- Politics and government --
19th century. Ireland -- History -- 19th century.*

DA950.H68 1984
Hoppen, K. Theodore, 1941-
Elections, politics, and society in Ireland, 1832-
1885/ K. Theodore Hoppen. Oxford [Oxfordshire]:
Clarendon Press; 1984. xix, 569 p.
84-004347   324.9415/081   0198226306
*Elections -- Ireland -- History -- 19th century.
Ireland -- Politics and government -- 1837-1901.
Ireland -- Social conditions -- 19th century..*

DA950.I68
Ireland under the Union: varieties of tension:
essays in honour of T. W. Moody/ edited by F. S.
L. Lyons & R. A. J. Hawkins. Oxford: Clarendon
Press; 1980. x, 337 p.
79-040386   941.5081   0198224699
*Moody, T. W. -- (Theodore William), -- 1907- --
Addresses, essays, lectures.   Ireland -- History --
19th century -- Addresses, essays, lectures.*

DA950.K56 2001
Kinzer, Bruce L., 1948-
England's disgrace?: J.S. Mill and the Irish
question/ Bruce L. Kinzer. Toronto; University of
Toronto Press, c2001. x, 292 p.
01-524232   0802048625
*Mill, John Stuart, -- 1806-1873 -- Views on
Ireland. Irish question. Ireland -- Foreign public
opinion, English -- History -- 19th century. Ireland
-- Politics and government -- 19th century.*

DA950.M18 1977
MacDonagh, Oliver.
Ireland: the Union and its aftermath/ Oliver
MacDonagh. London: G. Allen & Unwin, 1977.
176 p.
77-372393   941.508   0049410040
*Ireland -- History -- 19th century. Ireland --
History -- 20th century.*

DA950.O37
O'Farrell, Patrick James.
England and Ireland since 1800/ Patrick O'Farrell.
London: Oxford University Press, 1975. 193 p.
76-351038   327.42/0415   0192158147
*Irish question.   Ireland -- Politics and
government -- 19th century. Ireland -- Politics and
government -- 20th century.*

DA950.1.E24 1999
Eagleton, Terry, 1943-
Scholars and rebels in nineteenth-century Ireland/
Terry Eagleton. Malden, Mass.: Blackwell
Publishers, 1999. p. cm.
99-034968   306/.09418/35   0631214453
*English literature -- Irish authors -- History and
criticism. English literature -- 19th century --
History and criticism. Politics and literature --
Ireland -- History -- 19th century. Dublin (Ireland)
-- Intellectual life -- 19th century. Ireland --
Intellectual life -- 19th century.*

DA950.22.M228 1989
MacDonagh, Oliver.
The emancipist: Daniel O'Connell, 1830-47/
Volume 2 Oliver MacDonagh. New York: St.
Martin's Press, 1989. xi, 372 p.
89-019716   941.5081/092   0312037112
*O'Connell, Daniel, -- 1775-1847.   Nationalists --
Ireland -- Biography. Politicians -- Ireland --
Biography. Catholic emancipation. Ireland --
Politics and government -- 19th century.*

DA950.22.M23 1988
MacDonagh, Oliver.
The hereditary bondsman: Daniel O'Connell, 1775-
1829/ Volume 1 Oliver MacDonagh. New York:
St. Martin's Press, 1988, c1987. viii, 328 p.
87-027770   941.5081/092/4   0312016166
*O'Connell, Daniel, -- 1775-1847.   Nationalists --
Ireland -- Biography. Politicians -- Ireland --
Biography. Catholic emancipation. Ireland --
Politics and government -- 19th century.*

DA950.3.H54 1992
Hinde, Wendy.
Catholic emancipation: a shake to men's minds/
Wendy Hinde. Oxford, UK; Blackwell, 1992.
211 p.
91-029537   941.5081   0631167838
*Catholic emancipation.   Ireland -- History --
1800-1837.*

DA950.7.G72 1999
Gray, Peter, 1965-
Famine, land, and politics: British government and
Irish society, 1843-1850/ Peter Gray. Dublin; Irish
Academic Press, 1999. ix, 384 p.
98-042975   941.5081   071652564X
*Land tenure -- Ireland -- History -- 19th century.
Famines -- Ireland -- History -- 19th century.
Ireland -- Foreign economic relations -- Great
Britain -- History -- 19th century. Great Britain --
Politics and government -- 1837-1901. Ireland --
History -- Famine, 1845-1852.*

DA950.7.J67 1997
Jordan, Thomas Edward.
Ireland and the quality of life: the famine era/
Thomas E. Jordan. Lewiston, N.Y.: Edwin Mellen
Press, c1997. v, 379 p.
97-004174   941.5081   0773486771
*Famines -- Ireland -- History -- 19th century.
Stress (Psychology) -- Ireland -- History -- 19th
century. Quality of life -- Ireland -- History -- 19th
century. Ireland -- Social life and customs -- 19th
century. Ireland -- History -- Famine, 1845-1852.
Ireland -- History -- 1837-1901.*

DA950.7.M67 1995
Morash, Chris, 1963-
Writing the Irish famine/ Christopher Morash.
Oxford: Clarendon Press; 1995. 213 p.
94-048444   941.5081   0198182791
*Famines -- Ireland -- History -- 19th century --
Historiography.   Ireland -- History -- Famine,
1845-1852 -- Historiography.*

DA950.7.O366 1999
O Grada, Cormac.
Black '47 and beyond: the great Irish famine in
history, economy, and memory/ Cormac O Grada.
Princeton, N.J.: Princeton University Press, c1999.
xii, 302 p.
98-027291   941.508   0691015503
*Famines -- Ireland -- History -- 19th century.
Ireland -- History -- 1837-1901. Ireland --
Economic conditions -- 19th century. Ireland --
History -- Famine, 1845-1852.*

DA951.G37 1988
Garvin, Tom.
Nationalist revolutionaries in Ireland, 1858-1928/
Tom Garvin. Oxford [Oxfordshire]: Clarendon
Press; 1988, c1987. xi, 180 p.
87-018540   941.5081   0198201346
*Nationalism -- Ireland -- History.
Revolutionaries -- Ireland. Ireland -- Politics and
government -- 1837-1901. Ireland -- Politics and
government -- 20th century.*

DA951.L94 1971b
Lyons, F. S. L. 1923-
Ireland since the famine [by] F. S. L. Lyons. New
York, Scribner [1971] xiii, 852 p.
78-141708   309.1/415/08   0684103699
*Famines -- Ireland -- History -- Politics and
government -- 20th century. Northern Ireland --
Politics and government. Ireland -- History --
Famine, 1845-1852.*

DA952.D55.O25 1990
O'Cathaoir, Brendan, 1941-
John Blake Dillon, young Irelander/ Brendan
O'Cathaoir. Blackrock, Co., Dublin: Irish
Academic Press, c1990. 211 p.
91-115005   941.5081/092   0716524678
*Dillon, John Blake, -- 1814-1866. Dillon, John
Blake, -- 1814-1866. Nationalists -- Ireland --
Biography. Young Ireland movement. Ireland --
Politics and government -- 1837-1901.*

DA952.S28.J33 1995
Jackson, Alvin.
Colonel Edward Saunderson: land and loyalty in Victorian Ireland/ Alvin Jackson. Oxford [England]: Clarendon Press; 1995. x, 276 p.
94-039702   941.508/092   0198204981
Saunderson, Edward James, -- 1837-1920. Landlord and tenant -- Political aspects -- Ireland -- History -- 19th century. Land tenure -- Political aspects -- Ireland -- History -- 19th century. Gentry -- Ireland -- History -- 19th century. Ireland -- Politics and government -- 1837-1901. Ireland -- History -- 1837-1901 -- Biography.

DA954.O24 1971b
O Broin, Leon, 1902-
Fenian fever; an Anglo-American dilemma. New York, New York University Press, 1971. x, 264 p.
76-165471   941.58   0814761518
Irish Americans. Fenians. Ireland -- History -- 1837-1901.

DA954.R34 1999
Rafferty, Oliver.
The church, the state, and the Fenian threat, 1861-75/ Oliver P. Rafferty. Basingstoke, Hampshire: Macmillan Press; 1999. xviii, 229 p.
98-049491   941.5081   0312220634
Fenians. Church and state -- Ireland -- History -- 19th century. Ireland -- History -- 1837-1901.

DA955.K47 1994
Kerr, Donal, 1927-
A nation of beggars?: priests, people, and politics in famine Ireland, 1846-1852/ Donal A. Kerr. Oxford [England]: Clarendon Press; 1994. 370 p.
94-013314   941.5081   0198200501
Russell, John Russell, -- Earl, -- 1792-1878 -- Views on Ireland. Church and state -- Ireland -- History -- 19th century Protestants -- Ireland -- History -- 19th century. Catholics -- Ireland -- History -- 19th century. Ireland -- Politics and government -- 1837-1901. Ireland -- Church history -- 19th century. Ireland -- History -- Famine, 1845-1852.

DA957.M8 1991
Muenger, Elizabeth A.
The British military dilemma in Ireland: occupation politics, 1886-1914/ Elizabeth A. Muenger. Lawrence, Kan.: University Press of Kansas, c1991. ix, 254 p.
91-011120   322/.5/0941   0700604871
Civil-military relations -- Ireland -- History. Ireland -- Politics and government -- 1901-1910. Ireland -- Politics and government -- 1910-1921. Great Britain -- Military policy.

DA957.O24 1998
O'Day, Alan.
Irish home rule, 1867-1921/ Alan O'Day. Manchester, UK; Manchester University Press: c1998. liii, 346 p.
97-047404   941.508   0719037751
Home rule -- Ireland. Ireland -- Politics and government -- 1901-1910. Ireland -- Politics and government -- 1910-1921. Ireland -- Politics and government -- 1837-1901.

DA957.9.L36 1990
Larkin, Emmet J., 1927-
The Roman Catholic Church and the Home Rule movement in Ireland, 1870-1874/ by Emmet Larkin. Chapel Hill: University of North Carolina Press, c1990. xxi, 416 p.
89-036347   322/.1/0941509034   0807818860
Home rule -- Ireland. Christianity and politics. Ireland -- Politics and government -- 1837-1901.

DA958.D2.M66 1981
Moody, T. W. 1907-
Davitt and Irish revolution, 1846-82/ by T.W. Moody. Oxford: Clarendon Press; 1981. xxiv, 674 p.
82-124277   941.5081/092/4   019822382X
Davitt, Michael, -- 1846-1906. Fenians -- History. Revolutionaries -- Ireland -- Biography. Ireland -- Politics and government -- 1837-1901.

DA958.H4.C35 1996
Callanan, Frank.
T.M. Healy/ Frank Callanan. Cork: Cork University Press, [1996] xxvii, 754 p.
95-237916   941.508   1859180094
Healy, T. M. -- (Timothy Michael), -- 1855-1931. Politicians -- Ireland -- Biography. Ireland -- Politics and government -- 19th century. Ireland -- Politics and government -- 20th century.

DA958.M25.A4 1993
MacBride, Maud Gonne.
The Gonne-Yeats letters 1893-1938/ edited by Anna MacBride White and A. Norman Jeffares. New York: Norton, 1993, c1992. xvi, 544 p.
92-001683   821/.8   0393034453
Yeats, W. B. -- (William Butler), -- 1865-1939 -- Correspondence. MacBride, Maud Gonne -- Correspondence. Feminists -- Ireland -- Correspondence. Revolutionaries -- Ireland -- Correspondence. Poets, Irish -- 20th century -- Correspondence.

DA958.M25.W37 1990
Ward, Margaret.
Maud Gonne: Ireland's Joan of Arc/ Margaret Ward. London; Pandora, 1990. xii, 211 p.
90-195067   0044405839
Gonne, Maud, -- 1866-1953. Women revolutionaries -- Ireland -- Biography. Women politicians -- Ireland -- Biography. Feminists -- Ireland -- Biography. Ireland -- History -- 20th century -- Biography.

DA958.P2.C35 1992
Callanan, Frank.
The Parnell split, 1890-91/ Frank Callanan. Syracuse, N.Y.: Syracuse University Press, c1992. xxiv, 328 p.
92-032592   941.5081/092   0815625979
Parnell, Charles Stewart, -- 1846-1891. Ireland -- Politics and government -- 1837-1901.

DA958.P2.L89
Lyons, F. S. L. 1923-
Charles Stewart Parnell/ F. S. L. Lyons. New York: Oxford University Press, 1977. 704 p.
77-367920   941.5081/092/4   0195199499
Parnell, Charles Stewart, -- 1846-1891. Nationalists -- Ireland -- Biography. Politicians -- Biography. Home rule -- Ireland. Ireland -- Politics and government -- 1837-1901.

DA958.P2.L9
Lyons, F. S. L. 1923-
The fall of Parnell, Toronto, University of Toronto Press, 1960. xii, 362 p.
60-050712
Parnell, Charles Stewart, -- 1846-1891. Ireland -- History -- 1837-1901.

DA958.P24.C67 1991
Cote, Jane McL.
Fanny and Anna Parnell: Ireland's patriot sisters/ Jane McL. Cote. New York: St. Martin's Press, 1991. xix, 331 p.
90-026393   941.5/0922   0312060890
Parnell, Fanny. Parnell, Anna, -- 1852-1911. Parnell, Charles Stewart, -- 1846-1891 -- Family. Nationalists -- Ireland -- Biography. Land reform -- Ireland -- History. Home rule -- Ireland -- History.

DA959.B43 1980
Bell, J. Bowyer, 1931-
The secret army: the IRA, 1916-1979/ J. Bowyer Bell. Cambridge, Mass.: MIT Press, 1980, c1979. xiv, 481 p.
79-090067   941.508   0262021455
Political violence -- Ireland -- History -- 20th century. Ireland -- History -- 20th century. Northern Ireland -- History.

DA959.B69 1988
Boyce, David George, 1942-
The Irish question and British politics, 1868-1986/ D.G. Boyce. New York: St. Martin's Press, 1988. x, 157 p.
88-021140   941.608   0312024789
Irish question. Ireland -- Politics and government -- 1837-1901. Northern Ireland -- Politics and government -- 1969-1994. Great Britain -- Politics and government -- 20th century.

DA959.C68 1993
Coogan, Tim Pat, 1935-
The IRA: a history/ Tim Pat Coogan. Niwot, Colo.: Roberts Rinehart Publishers, c1993. xvii, 510 p.
93-085475   941.60824   187937367X
Ireland -- Politics and government -- 20th century. Northern Ireland -- Politics and government -- 1969-

DA959.K463 1994
Keogh, Dermot.
Twentieth-century Ireland: nation and state/ Dermot Keogh. Dublin: Gill & Macmillan, c1994. xxiii, 504 p.
94-158136   0717116255
Ireland -- Politics and government -- 20th century. Northern Ireland -- Politics and government.

DA959.O5 1983
O'Malley, Padraig.
The uncivil wars: Ireland today/ Padraig O'Malley. Boston: Houghton Mifflin, 1983. xvii, 481 p.
83-010677   941.50824   039534414X
Irish question. Home rule -- Ireland. Ireland -- Politics and government -- 20th century. Northern Ireland -- Politics and government -- 1969-1994.

DA959.W48 1992
White, Robert W. 1958-
Provisional Irish republicans: an oral and interpretive history/ Robert W. White. Westport, Conn.; Greenwood Press, 1993. xiv, 206 p.
92-025806   941.60824   0313285640
Violence -- Northern Ireland -- History. Violence -- Ireland -- History. Ireland -- Politics and government -- 20th century. Northern Ireland -- Politics and government -- 1969-1994.

DA959.1.F355 1998
Fallon, Brian.
An age of innocence: Irish culture, 1930-1960/ Brian Fallon. New York: St. Martin's Press, 1998. 313 p.
98-030040   941.5082   0312219245
Ireland -- Civilization -- 20th century. Ireland -- History -- 1922-

DA959.1.F43 1993
Fennell, Desmond.
Heresy: the battle of ideas in modern Ireland/ Desmond Fennell. Belfast, Northern Ireland: Blackstaff Press; 1993. xiii, 289 p.
93-235216   0856405051
   Ireland -- Intellectual life -- 20th century. Ireland -- Politics and government -- 20th century. Northern Ireland -- Politics and government -- 1969-1994.

DA959.1.N68 1970
Nowlan, Kevin B.,
Ireland in the war years and after 1939-51, edited by Kevin B. Nowlan and T. Desmond Williams. Notre Dame, Ind.] University of Notre Dame Press [1970, c1969] ix, 216 p.
74-098905   941.5/9
   Ireland -- Civilization. Northern Ireland -- History.

DA959.1.W75 2000
Writing in the Irish Republic: literature, culture, politics 1949-1999/ edited by Ray Ryan. New York: St. Martin's Press , 2000. x, 289 p.
00-033267   959.5082   0312231539
   English literature -- Irish authors -- History and criticism. English literature -- 20th century -- History and criticism. Ireland -- Civilization -- 20th century. Ireland -- Politics and government -- 20th century. Ireland -- In literature.

DA960.B48 1987
Bew, Paul.
Conflict and conciliation in Ireland, 1890-1910: Parnellites and radical agrarians/ Paul Bew. Oxford [Oxfordshire]: Clarendon Press; 1987. 241 p.
86-028578   941.5082/1   0198227582
   Parnell, Charles Stewart, -- 1846-1891 -- Influence. Nationalism -- Ireland -- History. Land tenure -- Ireland -- History. Ireland -- Politics and government -- 1901-1910. Ireland -- Politics and government -- 1837-1901.

DA960.H36 1998
Hart, Peter.
The I.R.A. and its enemies: violence and community in Cork, 1916-1923/ Peter Hart. Oxford: Clarendon Press; 1998. xv, 350 p.
98-017246   941.5082/2   0198205376
   Violence -- Ireland -- Cork (County) -- History -- 20th century. Community life -- Ireland -- Cork (County) -- History -- 20th century. Ireland -- History -- Easter Rising, 1916. Cork (Ireland: County) -- History. Ireland -- History -- Civil War, 1922-1923.

DA960.K46 1992
Kendle, John, 1937-
Walter Long, Ireland, and the Union, 1905-1920/ John Kendle. Montreal; McGill-Queen's University Press, c1992. xi, 246 p.
95-114508   941.082/3/092   0773509089
Long, Walter Hume Long, -- Viscount, -- 1854-1920. Irish question. Ireland -- Politics and government -- 1910-1921. Ireland -- Politics and government -- 1901-1910.

DA960.W48 1966a
Williams, Desmond
The Irish struggle, 1916-1926. Toronto, University of Toronto Press [1966] vii, 193 p.
67-072956
   Ireland -- History -- 20th century.

DA962.B43 1960
Bennett, Richard, 1912-
The Black and Tans. Boston, Houghton Mifflin, 1960 [c1959] 228 p.
60-016112   941.59
   Ireland -- History -- 1920-

DA962.D27
Dangerfield, George, 1904-1986.
The damnable question: a study in Anglo-Irish relations/ by George Dangerfield. Boston: Little, Brown, c1976. xiv, 400 p.
76-005456   941.5082/1   0316172006
   Home rule -- Ireland. Irish question. Ireland -- Politics and government -- 1901-1910. Ireland -- Politics and government -- 1910-1921. Great Britain -- Foreign relations -- Ireland.

DA962.H46 1998
Hennessey, Thomas.
Dividing Ireland: World War I and partition/ Thomas Hennessey. London; Routledge, 1998. xxi, 280 p.
98-007697   941.5082/1   0415174201
   Nationalism -- Ulster (Northern Ireland and Ireland) -- History -- 20th century. Nationalism -- Ireland -- History -- 20th century. World War, 1914-1918 -- Influence. Ireland -- History -- Partition, 1921.

DA962.O27 1971
Ó Broin, León,
Dublin Castle and the 1916 rising. [Rev. ed.] New York, New York University Press, 1971. 192 p.
78-138554   941.5/9/0924   081476150X
Nathan, Matthew, Sir, 1862-1939.

DA962.W33
Ward, Alan J.
The Easter Rising: revolution and Irish nationalism/ Alan J. Ward. Arlington Heights, Ill.: AHM Pub. Corp., c1980. vi, 184 p.
79-055729   941.5082/1   0882958038
   Nationalism -- Ireland -- History -- 20th century. Ireland -- Politics and government -- 1910-1921. Ireland -- History -- Easter Rising, 1916.

DA963.B45 2000
Bell, J. Bowyer, 1931-
The IRA, 1968-2000: analysis of a secret army/ J. Bowyer Bell. London: Frank Cass, 2000. xx, 351 p.
00-030340   941.5082   0714650706
   Political violence -- Ireland -- History -- 20th century. Political violence -- Northern Ireland -- History -- 20th century. Ireland -- History -- 1922- Northern Ireland -- History.

DA963.C64
Coogan, Tim Pat, 1935-
Ireland since the rising. New York, Praeger [1966] xii, 355 p.
66-017363   941.59
   Ireland -- History -- 1922-

DA963.D86 1995
Dunphy, Richard.
The making of Fianna Fail power in Ireland, 1923-1948/ Richard Dunphy. Oxford [England]: Clarendon Press; 1995. xvi, 340 p.
94-044524   324.2417/083   0198204744
   Political parties -- Ireland -- History -- 20th century. Ireland -- Politics and government -- 1922-1949.

DA963.E53 1994
English, Richard, 1963-
Radicals and the republic: socialist republicanism in the Irish Free State, 1925-1937/ Richard English. Oxford [England]: Clarendon Press; 1994. viii, 309 p.
94-009430   941.5082/2   019820289X
   Republicanism -- Ireland -- History -- 20th century. Radicalism -- Ireland -- History -- 20th century. Socialism -- Ireland -- History -- 20th century. Ireland -- Politics and government -- 1922-1949.

DA963.G37 1996
Garvin, Tom.
1922, the birth of Irish democracy/ Tom Garvin. New York: St. Martin's Press, 1996. xii, 240 p.
96-009801   941.5082/2   0312164777
   Nationalism -- Ireland -- History -- 20th century, Democracy -- Ireland -- History -- 20th century. Ireland -- Politics and government -- 1922-1949. Ireland -- History -- Civil War, 1922-1923.

DA963.H63 1988
Hopkinson, Michael.
Green against green: the Irish Civil War/ Michael Hopkinson. New York: St. Martin's Press, 1988. xvi, 336 p.
88-018827   941.508   0312024487
   Ireland -- History -- Civil War, 1922-1923. Ireland -- History -- 1910-1921.

DA963.H69 2000
Howe, Stephen, 1958-
Ireland and empire: colonial legacies in Irish history and culture/ Stephen Howe. Oxford; Oxford University Press, 2000. 334 p.
99-045413   941.5082   0198208251
   Public opinion -- Northern Ireland -- History. Imperialism -- Public opinion -- History. Public opinion -- Ireland -- History. Great Britain -- Foreign public opinion, Irish. Ireland -- History -- 20th century.

DA963.I745 2000
Ireland and the Second World War: politics, society and remembrance/ Brian Girvin and Geoffrey Roberts, editors. Dublin; Four Courts Press, c2000. 186 p.
00-703256   940.53/415   1851824820
   World War, 1939-1945 -- Ireland. World War, 1939-1945 -- Participation, Irish. Neutrality -- Ireland. Ireland -- Politics and government -- 1922-1949.

DA963.L44 1989
Lee, Joseph, 1942-
Ireland, 1912-1985: politics and society/ J.J. Lee. Cambridge; Cambridge University Press, 1989. xxi, 754 p.
88-023763   941.5082   0521266483
   Ireland -- History -- 1922- Ireland -- History -- 1910-1921.

DA963.M28 1991
Mansergh, Nicholas.
The unresolved question: the Anglo-Irish settlement and its undoing, 1912-72/ Nicholas Mansergh. New Haven: Yale University Press, 1991. x, 386 p.
91-050587   941.5082   0300050690
   Irish unification question. Irish question. Ireland -- Politics and government -- 20th century. Northern Ireland -- Politics and government -- 1969-1994.

DA963.R44 1999
Regan, John
The Irish counter-revolution, 1921-36: Treatyite politics and settlement in independent Ireland/ John Regan. New York: St. Martin's Press, 1999. p. cm.
99-022263   941.5082/2   0312227272
Counterrevolutionaries -- Ireland -- History -- 20th century. Ireland -- Politics and government -- 1922-1949.

DA963.R93 1994
Ryan, Mark, 1960-
War & peace in Ireland: Britain and the IRA in the new world order/ Mark Ryan. London; Pluto Press, 1994. xi, 173 p.
94-008049   941.50824   0745309232
Violence -- Northern Ireland. Irish question. Violence -- Ireland -- History -- 20th century. Ireland -- Politics and government -- 1949- Northern Ireland -- Politics and government -- 1969-1994. Great Britain -- Foreign relations -- Ireland.

DA963.S625 1995
Smith, M. L. R. 1963-
Fighting for Ireland?: the military strategy of the Irish Republican movement/ M.L.R. Smith. London; Routledge, 1995. xxvii, 265 p.
95-006524   941.60824   0415091616
Insurgency -- Ireland -- History -- 20th century. Violence -- Ireland -- History -- 20th century. Ireland -- History, Military -- 20th century. Northern Ireland -- History, Military -- 1969-

DA963.U46 1990
Understanding contemporary Ireland: state, class, and development in the Republic of Ireland/ Richard Breen ... [et al.]. New York: St. Martin's Press, 1990. xii, 248 p.
89-034362   941.5082   0312035578
Social classes -- Ireland -- History -- 20th century. Ireland -- Politics and government -- 1949- Ireland -- Economic conditions -- 1949- Ireland -- Social conditions.

DA964.A2.O39 1999
O'Halpin, Eunan.
Defending Ireland: the Irish state and its enemies since 1922/ Eunan O'Halpin. Oxford; Oxford University Press, 1999. xvi, 382 p.
98-055137   355/.0330417   0198204264
Ireland -- Politics and government -- 1922- Ireland -- Military policy -- History -- 20th century. Ireland -- Defenses -- History -- 20th century.

DA964.U6.D39 1998
Davis, Troy D., 1962-
Dublin's American policy: Irish-American diplomatic relations, 1945-1952/ Troy D. Davis. Washington, D.C.: Catholic University of America Press, c1998. xvii, 237 p.
97-040218   327.417073/09/045   0813209072
Ireland -- Foreign relations -- 1922- United States -- Foreign relations -- Ireland. Ireland -- Foreign relations -- United States.

DA965.C3.D64 2000
Doerries, Reinhard R.
Prelude to the Easter Rising: Sir Roger Casement in imperial Germany/ Reinhard R. Doerries. London; Frank Cass, c2000. xiv, 233 p.
99-034128   914.304/84   071465003X
Casement, Roger, -- Sir, -- 1864-1916 -- Journeys -- Germany. Irish -- Travel -- Germany -- History -- 20th century. World War, 1914-1918 -- Germany. Ireland -- Foreign relations -- Germany. Germany -- Foreign relations -- Ireland. Ireland -- History -- Easter Rising, 1916 -- Causes.

DA965.C48.A3 1991
Clarke, Kathleen, 1878-1972.
Revolutionary woman: Kathleen Clarke, 1878-1972: an autobiography/ edited by Helen Litton. Dublin: O'Brien Press, 1991. 240 p.
91-151575   941.5082/092   0862782457
Clarke, Kathleen, -- 1878-1972. Revolutionaries -- Ireland -- Biography. Ireland -- History -- Easter Rising, 1916 -- Personal narratives. Ireland -- History -- 20th century -- Biography.

DA965.C7.A68 1994
Anderson, W. K. 1953-
James Connolly and the Irish left/ W.K. Anderson. Dublin: Irish Academic Press; c1994. 200 p.
94-177993   335.4/092   0716525224
Connolly, James, -- 1868-1916 -- Political and social views. Socialism -- Ireland -- History -- 20th century. Socialism -- Ireland -- History -- 19th century. Ireland -- Politics and government -- 1910-1921. Ireland -- Politics and government -- 1837-1901. Ireland -- Politics and government -- 1901-1910.

DA965.C7.G7 1971
Greaves, C. Desmond.
The life and times of James Connolly, by C. Desmond Greaves. New York, International Publishers [1971, c1961] 448 p.
78-188758   335.4/092/4
Connolly, James, -- 1868-1916. Revolutionaries -- Ireland -- Biography. Ireland -- History -- Easter Rising, 1916 -- Biography.

DA965.C7.M67 1988
Morgan, Austen, 1949-
James Connolly: a political biography/ Austen Morgan. Manchester [England]: Manchester University Press; c1988. x, 244 p.
87-031335   335.4/092/4   0719025192
Connolly, James, -- 1868-1916. Revolutionaries -- Ireland -- Biography. Socialists -- Ireland -- Biography. Ireland -- History -- Easter Rising, 1916. Ireland -- Politics and government -- 1901-1910. Ireland -- Politics and government -- 1910-1921.

DA965.C74.A3 1996
Connolly, Joseph, 1885-1961.
Memoirs of Senator Joseph Connolly (1885-1961): a founder of modern Ireland/ edited by J. Anthony Gaughan. Blackrock, Co. Dublin: Irish Academic Press, 1996. 481 p.
96-171471   328.415/092   0716526115
Connolly, Joseph, -- 1885-1961. Legislators -- Ireland -- Biography. Ireland -- Politics and government -- 20th century.

DA965.D4 C66 1995
Coogan, Tim Pat,
Eamon de Valera: the man who was Ireland/ by Tim Pat Coogan.1st U.S. ed. New York: HarperCollins, [1995] xii, 772 p.
94-024515   941.7082/2/092. 220   0060171219
De Valera, Eamonn, 1882-1975. Presidents--Ireland--Biography.

DA965.D4.D868 1991
Dwyer, T. Ryle.
De Valera: the man & the myths/ T. Ryle Dwyer. Dublin, Ireland: Poolbeg, 1991. x, 370 p.
91-169999   941.5082/092   1853711217
De Valera, Eamonn, -- 1882-1975. Presidents -- Ireland -- Biography. Ireland -- Politics and government -- 20th century.

DA965.D4.L6 1971
Longford, Frank Pakenham, 1905-
Eamon de Valera [by] the Earl of Longford & Thomas P. O'Neill. Boston, Houghton Mifflin, 1971, [c1970] xix, 499 p.
77-144076   941.5/9/0924   0395121019
De Valera, Eamonn, -- 1882-1975. Revolutionaries -- Ireland -- Biography. Presidents -- Ireland -- Biography. Ireland -- Politics and government -- 20th century.

DA965.H9.D88 1991
Dunleavy, Janet Egleson.
Douglas Hyde: a maker of modern Ireland/ J.E. Dunleavy and G.W. Dunleavy. Berkeley: University of California Press, c1991. p. cm.
90-040120   941.5082/2/092   0520066847
Hyde, Douglas, -- 1860-1949. Presidents -- Ireland -- Biography. Nationalists -- Ireland -- Biography. Scholars -- Ireland -- Biography. Ireland -- History -- 20th century.

DA965.M84.V35 1992
Valiulis, Maryann Gialanella, 1947-
Portrait of a revolutionary: General Richard Mulcahy and the founding of the Irish Free State/ Maryann Gialanella Valiulis. Lexington: University Press of Kentucky, c1992. xii, 289 p.
92-009800   941.5082/1   0813117917
Mulcahy, Richard, -- 1886-1971. Revolutionaries -- Ireland -- Biography. Statesmen -- Ireland -- Biography. Ireland -- History -- Civil War, 1922-1923 -- Biography. Ireland -- History -- Easter Rising, 1916 -- Biography.

DA965.O553.E54 1998
English, Richard, 1963-
Ernie O'Malley: IRA intellectual/ Richard English. Oxford: Clarendon Press; 1998. xii, 267 p.
98-190991   941.5082/2/092   0198205953
O'Malley, Ernie, -- 1898-1957. Revolutionaries -- Ireland -- Biography. Authors, Irish -- 20th century -- Biography. Ireland -- History -- Civil War, 1922-1923 -- Biography.

DA965.P4.M67 1994
Moran, Sean Farrell, 1951-
Patrick Pearse and the politics of redemption: the mind of the Easter Rising, 1916/ Sean Farrell Moran. Washington, D.C.: Catholic University of America Press, c1994. x, 233 p.
92-026449   941.5082/1   0813207754
Pearse, Padraic, -- 1879-1916. Revolutionaries -- Ireland -- Biography. Ireland -- Politics and government -- 1910-1921. Ireland -- History -- Easter Rising, 1916.

DA965.R63.H67 1997
Horgan, John, 1940-
Mary Robinson: an independent voice/ John Horgan. Dublin: O'Brien Press, 1997. 224 p.
97-213134   941.50824/092   0862785405
Robinson, Mary, -- 1944- Presidents -- Ireland -- Biography. Diplomats -- Ireland -- Biography. Ireland -- Politics and government -- 1949-

DA990 Ireland — Counties, regions, etc., A-Z

DA990.L5.S63 1982
Smyth, Alfred P.
Celtic Leinster: towards an historical geography of early Irish civilization, A.D. 500-1600/ Alfred P. Smyth. Blackrock, County Dublin: Irish Academic Press, c1982. xvi, 197 p.
83-100005   941.8   0716500973
Celts -- Ireland -- Leinster. Leinster (Ireland) -- Historical geography. Ireland -- Civilization.

DA990.M8.E27 1998
Early medieval Munster: archaeology, history, and society/ edited by Michael A. Monk and John Sheehan. Cork: Cork University Press, 1998. [ix], 220 p.
99-192209   941.9   1859181074
Archaeology, Medieval -- Ireland -- Munster. Excavations (Archaeology) -- Ireland -- Munster. Munster (Ireland) -- History. Munster (Ireland) -- Antiquities.

DA990.T5.P69 1993
Power, T. P.
Land, politics, and society in eighteenth-century Tipperary/ Thomas P. Power. Oxford: Clarendon Press; 1993. xiv, 376 p.
93-022481   941.9/2   0198203160
Land tenure -- Ireland -- Tipperary (County) -- History -- 18th century. Tipperary (Ireland: County) -- Politics and government. Tipperary (Ireland: County) -- Social conditions.

DA990.U46.B2254 1992
Bardon, Jonathan, 1941-
A history of Ulster/ Jonathan Bardon. Dundonald, Belfast, Northern Ireland: Blackstaff Press, 1992. x, 914 p.
92-225896   941.6   0856404667
Ulster (Northern Ireland and Ireland) -- History.

DA990.U46.B3593 1999
Bew, Paul.
Northern Ireland: a chronology of the Troubles, 1968-1999/ Paul Bew and Gordon Gillespie. Lanham, Md.: Scarecrow Press, 1999. xxi, 471 p.
99-048569   941.60824   0810837358
Northern Ireland -- History -- 1969-1994 -- Chronology. Northern Ireland -- History -- 1994- -- Chronology.

DA990.U46.B56 1997
Bloomfield, David, 1954-
Peacemaking strategies in Northern Ireland: building complementarity in conflict management theory/ David Bloomfield. New York, N.Y.: St. Martin's Press, 1997. xvi, 240 p.
96-039086   941.60824   0312163460
Conflict management -- Northern Ireland. Political violence -- Northern Ireland. Peace movements -- Northern Ireland. Northern Ireland -- Politics and government -- 1994-

DA990.U46.B675 1994
Bruce, Steve, 1954-
The edge of the union: the Ulster loyalist political vision/ Steve Bruce. Oxford; Oxford University Press, 1994. viii, 176 p.
94-007710   941.60824   0198279752
Protestants -- Ulster (Northern Ireland and Ireland) -- Political activity. Political violence -- Northern Ireland -- History -- 20th century. Northern Ireland -- Politics and government -- 1969-1994.

DA990.U46.B678 1992
Bruce, Steve, 1954-
The red hand: Protestant paramilitaries in Northern Ireland/ Steve Bruce. Oxford; Oxford University Press, 1992. xiv, 311 p.
91-046663   941.60824   0192159615
Paramilitary forces -- Northern Ireland -- History. Protestants -- Northern Ireland -- History. Terrorism -- Northern Ireland -- History. Northern Ireland -- History -- 1969-1994.

DA990.U46.C36 1996
Cash, John Daniel.
Identity, ideology and conflict: the structuration of politics in Northern Ireland/ John Daniel Cash. New York: Cambridge University Press, 1996. x, 230 p.
95-041395   320.9416/01/9   0521550521
Northern Ireland -- Politics and government -- 1969-

DA990.U46.C86 1991
Cunningham, Michael J., 1959-
British government policy in Northern Ireland, 1969-89: its nature and execution/ Michael J. Cunningham. Manchester; Manchester University Press; c1991. 292 p.
90-025518   320.9416   0719025680
Northern Ireland -- Politics and government -- 1969-1994.

DA990.U46.D38 1994
Davis, Richard P.
Mirror hate: the convergent ideology of Northern Ireland paramilitaries, 1966-1992/ Richard Davis. Aldershot, Hants, England; Dartmouth, c1994. vi, 345 p.
94-027123   941.5082   1855215586
Paramilitary forces -- Northern Ireland -- History -- 20th century. Propaganda -- Northern Ireland -- History -- 20th century. Irish unification question. Northern Ireland -- History -- 1969-1994.

DA990.U46.E44 1999
Elliott, Sydney.
Conflict in Northern Ireland: an encyclopedia/ by Sydney Elliott & W.D. Flackes. Santa Barbara, Calif.: ABC-CLIO, 1999. p. cm.
98-043819   941.608/2/04   0874369894
Political violence -- Northern Ireland -- Encyclopedias. Social conflict -- Northern Ireland -- Encyclopedias. Northern Ireland -- History -- Encyclopedias.

DA990.U46.F345 2000
Farrell, Sean, 1966-
Rituals and riots: sectarian violence and political culture in Ulster, 1784-1886/ Sean Farrell. Lexington: University Press of Kentucky, c2000. ix, 252 p.
00-028309   941.6081   081312171X
Violence -- Ulster (Northern Ireland and Ireland) -- History. Riots -- Ulster (Northern Ireland and Ireland) -- History. Ulster (Northern Ireland and Ireland) -- Church history. Ulster (Northern Ireland and Ireland) -- History.

DA990.U46.F39 1999
Fay, Marie-Therese, 1973-
Northern Ireland's troubles: the human costs/ Marie-Therese Fay, Mike Morrissey, and Marie Smyth. London; Pluto Press in association with The Cost fo the 1999. x, 229 p.
98-045434   941.6   0745313795
Political violence -- Social aspects -- Northern Ireland -- History -- 20th century. Political violence -- Economic aspects -- Northern Ireland -- History -- 20th century. Victims of terrorism -- Northern Ireland -- History -- 20th century. Northern Ireland -- History.

DA990.U46.F87 1990
The Future of Northern Ireland/ edited by John McGarry and Brendan O'Leary; with a foreword by Arend Lijphart. Oxford [England]: Clarendon Press; 1990. xx, 376 p.
90-036853   941.50824   0198273290
Northern Ireland -- Politics and government -- 1969-1994.

DA990.U46.G32 1990
Gaffikin, Frank.
Northern Ireland: the Thatcher years/ Michael Morrissey and Frank Gaffikin and Michael Morrissey. London; Zed Books, 1990. 238 p.
89-025027   941.60824   086232906X
Thatcher, Margaret.   Northern Ireland -- Politics and government -- 1969-1994.

DA990.U46.H43 1997
Hennessey, Thomas.
A history of Northern Ireland, 1920-1996/ Thomas Hennessey. New York: St. Martin's Press, 1997. xiv, 347 p.
97-036311   941.60824   0312211120
Northern Ireland -- History -- 1969-1994. Ulster (Northern Ireland and Ireland) -- History.

DA990.U46.H435 2001
Hennessey, Thomas.
The Northern Ireland peace process: ending the troubles?/ Thomas Hennessey. New York: Palgrave, c2001. 256 p.
00-048351   941.60824   0312239491
Peace movements -- Northern Ireland -- History -- 20th century. Northern Ireland -- Politics and government -- 1969-1994. Northern Ireland -- Politics and government -- 1994-

DA990.U46.H854 1996
Hume, John, 1937-
A new Ireland: politics, peace, and reconciliation/ John Hume; foreword by Edward M. Kennedy; introduction by Tom McEnery; edited by Jack Van Zandt and Tom McEnery. Boulder, Colo.: Roberts Rinehart Publishers; c1996. 192 p.
95-072789   941.50824   1570980667
Peace movements -- Northern Ireland. Reconciliation. Northern Ireland -- Politics and government -- 1969-1994.

DA990.U46.H87 1990
Hurley, Mark J. 1919-
Blood on the shamrock: an American ponders Northern Ireland, 1968-1989/ Mark J. Hurley. New York: P. Lang, c1990. 384 p.
89-014409   941.60824   0820412627
Northern Ireland -- History -- 1969-1994.

DA990.U46.L687 1998
Loughlin, James.
The Ulster question since 1945/ James Loughlin. New York: St. Martin's Press, 1998. xvi, 151 p.
98-005558   941.6082   0312214464
Irish unification question. Northern Ireland -- Politics and government. Ireland -- Politics and government -- 1949- Ulster (Northern Ireland and Ireland) -- Politics and government.

DA990.U46.M432 1999
McCall, Cathal, 1966-
Identity in Northern Ireland: communities, politics, and change/ Cathal McCall. New York: St. Martin's Press, 1999. xviii, 230 p.
98-030879   320.9416/09/049   0312218443
Nationalism -- Northern Ireland. Northern Ireland -- Politics and government -- 1994- Northern Ireland -- Relations -- Europe. Europe -- Relations -- Northern Ireland.

DA990.U46.M458 1998
McPhilemy, Sean.
The Committee: political assassination in Northern Ireland/ Sean McPhilemy. Niwot, Colo.: Roberts Rinehart Publishers; c1998. 418 p.
98-065007   941.60824   1570982112
Political violence -- Northern Ireland -- History -- 20th century. Assassination -- Northern Ireland -- History -- 20th century. Northern Ireland -- History -- 1969-1994.

DA990.U46.M78 1999
Mulholland, Marc, 1971-
Northern Ireland at the crossroads: Ulster Unionism in the O'Neill years 1960-9/ Marc Mulholland. New York: St. Martin's Press, 1999. p. cm.
99-046717   941.60824   031222835X
O'Neill, Terence, -- 1914-   Unionism (Irish politics)   Northern Ireland -- Politics and government -- 1969-1994.

DA990.U46.N67 1996
Northern Ireland politics/ edited by Arthur Aughey and Duncan Morrow. London; Longman Pub., 1996. xi, 247 p.
95-045047   320.9416/09/04   0582253462
Northern Ireland -- Politics and government -- 1969-1994. Ulster (Northern Ireland and Ireland) -- Politics and government. Northern Ireland -- Politics and government -- 1994-

DA990.U46.O52 1993
O'Leary, Brendan.
The politics of antagonism: understanding Northern Ireland/ Brendan O'Leary & John McGarry. London; Athlone Press, 1993. xvii, 358 p.
92-026103   941.60824   0485800039
Northern Ireland -- Politics and government -- 1969-1994.

DA990.U46.P355 1998
Parkinson, Alan F.
Ulster loyalism and the British media/ Alan F. Parkinson. Dublin, Ireland; Four Courts Press, c1998. 184 p.
98-191348   1851823921
Public opinion -- Great Britain -- History -- 20th century. Protestants -- Northern Ireland -- Political activity. Mass media and public opinion -- Great Britain. Northern Ireland -- Politics and government.

DA990.U46.P515 2000
Personal accounts from Northern Ireland's troubles: public conflict, private loss/ edited by Marie Smyth and Marie-Therese Fay. London; Pluto Press, 2000. x, 147 p.
99-056756   941.6   0745316190
Victims of terrorism -- Northern Ireland -- History -- 20th century. Political violence -- Northern Ireland -- History -- 20th century. Social conflict -- Northern Ireland -- History -- 20th century. Northern Ireland -- History. Northern Ireland -- Social conditions -- 1969-

DA990.U46.P66 1996
Porter, Norman, 1952-
Rethinking unionism: an alternative vision for Northern Ireland/ Norman Porter. Belfast: Blackstaff Press, 1996. xiv, 252 p.
96-219212   941.60824   085640585X
Unionism (Irish politics)   Northern Ireland -- Politics and government -- 1994- Northern Ireland -- Politics and government -- 1969-1994.

DA990.U46.P86 1990
Purdie, Bob.
Politics in the streets: the origins of the civil rights movement in Northern Ireland/ Bob Purdie. Belfast: Blackstaff Press, 1990. xii, 286 p.
90-224943   0856404373
Civil rights movements -- Northern Ireland -- History -- 20th century.   Northern Ireland -- Politics and government.

DA990.U46.R83 1996
Ruane, Joseph.
The dynamics of conflict in Northern Ireland: power, conflict, and emancipation/ by Joseph Ruane and Jennifer Todd. Cambridge; Cambridge University Press, 1996. xvi, 365 p.
95-052013   941.6   0521560187
Social conflict -- Northern Ireland.   Northern Ireland -- Politics and government.

DA990.U46.S774 1996
Stevenson, Jonathan, 1956-
We wrecked the place: contemplating an end to the Northern Irish troubles/ Jonathan Stevenson. New York: Free Press, c1996. xx, 294 p.
96-018302   320.9416   068482745X
Peace movements -- Northern Ireland. Violence -- Northern Ireland. Irish question. Northern Ireland -- Social conditions. Northern Ireland -- Politics and government.

DA990.U46.T37 1999
Taylor, Peter, 1942-
Loyalists/ Peter Taylor. London: Bloomsbury Pub., 1999. viii, 278 p.
99-197174   941.60824   0747543887
Paramilitary forces -- Northern Ireland -- History -- 20th century. Political violence -- Northern Ireland -- History -- 20th century. Protestantism -- Northern Ireland -- History -- 20th century. Northern Ireland -- History.

DA990.U46.U76 2000
Urquhart, Diane.
Women in Ulster politics, 1890-1940: a history not yet told/ Diane Urquhart. Dublin; Irish Academic Press, 2000. 276 p.
99-089205   320.9/0082/09416   0716526271
Women in politics -- Ulster (Northern Ireland and Ireland) -- History -- 20th century. Women in politics -- Ulster (Northern Ireland and Ireland) -- History -- 19th century. Women -- Ulster (Northern Ireland and Ireland) -- Politics and government. Ulster (Northern Ireland and Ireland) -- Politics and government.

DA990.U46.W488 1995
Wilson, Andrew J., 1962-
Irish-America and the Ulster Conflict, 1968-1995/ Andrew J. Wilson. Washington, D.C.: Catholic University of America Press, c1995. xiii, 322 p.
94-042884   941.60824   0813208289
Public opinion -- United States -- History -- 20th century. Irish Americans -- Attitudes. Irish question. United States -- Foreign relations -- Northern Ireland. Northern Ireland -- Foreign relations -- United States. Northern Ireland -- History -- 1969-1994 -- Foreign public opinion, American.

DA990.U46.W756 1996
Wright, Frank, 1948-
Two lands on one soil: Ulster politics before home rule/ Frank Wright. New York: St. Martin's Press, 1996. xi, 595 p.
95-049971   941.608   0312159242
Ulster (Northern Ireland and Ireland) -- History. Social conflict -- Ulster (Northern Ireland and Ireland) Northern Ireland -- History -- 1969-1994.

DA995 Ireland — Cities, towns, etc., A-Z

DA995.D75.G74 1998
Greaves, Richard L.
Dublin's merchant-Quaker: Anthony Sharp and the Community of Friends, 1643-1707/ Richard L. Greaves. Stanford, Calif.: Stanford University Press, 1998. x, 337 p.
98-003683   941.8/350088286   0804734526
Sharp, Anthony, -- 1643-1707 -- Homes and haunts -- Ireland -- Dublin.   Quakers -- Ireland -- Dublin -- History -- 17th century. Merchants -- Ireland -- Dublin -- Biography. Quakers -- Ireland -- Dublin -- Biography.

DA995.D75.H55 1997
Hill, Jacqueline R.
From patriots to unionists: Dublin civic politics and Irish Protestant patriotism, 1660-1840/ Jacqueline Hill. Oxford; Clarendon Press, 1997. xix, 444 p.
97-212625   941.8/35   0198206356
Patriotism -- Ireland -- Dublin -- History. Unionism (Irish politics) Protestants -- Ireland -- Dublin -- History. Dublin (Ireland) -- Politics and government.

DA995.D75.K3
Kain, Richard Morgan, 1908-
Dublin in the age of William Butler Yeats and James Joyce/ by Richard M. Kain. Norman: University of Oklahoma Press [1962] 216 p.
62-016474   914.183
Irish literature -- History and criticism.   Dublin (Ireland) -- Intellectual life. Dublin (Ireland) -- Politics and government.

DA995.D75.M22 1993
MacLaran, Andrew.
Dublin: the shaping of a capital/ Andrew MacLaran. London; Belhaven Press; 1993. xiii, 242 p.
92-043255   941.8/35   0470220090
Dublin (Ireland) -- History.

DA995.D75.M43 1988
Medieval Dublin excavations, 1962-81. Dublin: Royal Irish Academy, 1988-1997 v. 1-5
89-129197   936.1/835   0901714682
Excavations (Archaeology) -- Ireland -- Dublin. Northmen -- Ireland -- Dublin. Archaeology, Medieval. Dublin (Ireland) -- Antiquities.

DA995.L75.W35 2000
Walsh, Dermot, 1957-
Bloody Sunday and the rule of law in Northern Ireland/ Dermot Walsh. New York: St. Martin's Press, 2000. p. cm.
99-053147   941.6/210824   0312230583
Demonstrations -- Northern Ireland -- Londonderry -- History -- 20th century. Political violence -- Northern Ireland -- Londonderry -- History -- 20th century. Massacres -- Northern Ireland -- Londonderry -- History -- 20th century. Northern Ireland -- History -- 1969-1994. Londonderry (Northern Ireland) -- History.

DA995.T46.G85 1995
Gulliver, P. H.
Merchants and shopkeepers: a historical anthropology of an Irish market town, 1200-1991/ P.H. Gulliver and Marilyn Silverman. Toronto; University of Toronto Press, c1995. ix, 440 p.
95-211277   941.8/9   0802006442
Market towns -- Ireland -- Kilkenny -- History. Thomastown (Kilkenny, Ireland) -- Social conditions. Thomastown (Kilkenny, Ireland) -- History.

DAW History of Central Europe

DAW1009 General works

DAW1009.C46 2000
Central Europe profiled: essential facts on society, business, and politics in central Europe/ edited by Barry Turner. New York: St. Martin's Press, 2000. p. cm.
99-053354   943   0312229941
Central Europe.

DAW1047 History — By period — 1500-1815

DAW1047.W55 2000
Wilson, Peter H.
Absolutism in central Europe/ Peter H. Wilson. London; Routledge, 2000. 173 p.
99-085981   320.943   0415233518
Despotism -- Europe, Central. Europe, Central -- Politics and government.

DAW1051 History — By period — 1989-

DAW1051.A47 1999
America's new allies: Poland, Hungary, and the Czech Republic in NATO/ edited by Andrew A. Michta. Seattle; University of Washington Press, c1999. 214 p.
99-035704   355/.031091821   0295979062
National security -- Europe, Central. Europe, Central -- Foreign relations. Europe, Central -- Military policy. Poland -- Foreign relations -- 1989-

DB35-886 History of Austria

DB35 History — Dictionaries. Chronological tables, outlines, etc.

DB35.F53 1999
Fichtner, Paula S.
Historical dictionary of Austria/ Paula Sutter Fichtner. Lanham, Md.: Scarecrow Press, 1999. xxvi, 301 p.
99-010714   943.6/003   0810836394
Austria -- History -- Dictionaries.

DB36.3 History — Biography (Collective) — Houses, noble families, etc., A-Z

DB36.3.H3 B4713 1994
Bérenger, Jean,
A history of the Habsburg empire/ Jean Bérenger; translated by C.A. Simpson. London; Longman, 1994- v. <1 >
93-007777   943.6.220   0582090105
Habsburg, House of.

DB36.3.H3.I54 1994
Ingrao, Charles W.
The Habsburg monarchy, 1618-1815/ Charles Ingrao. Cambridge [England]; Cambridge University Press, 1994. xiii, 262 p.
93-017030   943.6/03   052138009X
Habsburg, House of.   Austria -- History -- 1519-1740. Austria -- History -- 1740-1789. Austria -- History -- 1789-1815.

DB48 History — Political and diplomatic history. Foreign and general relations — 20th century. The Austrian question

DB48.G4 1963
Gehl, Jurgen.
Austria, Germany, and the Anschluss, 1931-1938. Foreword by Alan Bullock. London, Oxford University Press, 1963. x, 212 p.
63-025360   943.605
Anschluss movement, 1918-1938.   Austria -- Foreign relations -- Germany. Germany -- Foreign relations -- Austria.

DB48.S5
Seton-Watson, R. W. 1879-1951.
The southern Slav question and the Habsburg Monarchy/ by R. W. Seton-Watson. London: Constable & Co., 1911. xii, 463 p.
12-019152
Yugoslavs. Eastern question (Balkan) Austria -- Politics and government -- 1867-1918.

DB65-99.2 History — By period — 1521-

DB65.E9
Evans, Robert John Weston.
The making of the Habsburg monarchy, 1550-1700: an interpretation/ R. J. W. Evans. Oxford: Clarendon Press; 1979. xxiii, 531 p.
79-040616   943.6/03   0198225601
Austria -- History -- 1519-1740.

DB65.5.S73 1994
State and society in early modern Austria/ edited by Charles W. Ingrao. West Lafayette, Ind.: Purdue University Press, c1994. xvi, 339 p.
93-033879   943.6/03   1557530475
Habsburg, House of.   Austria -- Politics and government -- 17th century. Austria -- Politics and government -- 16th century. Holy Roman Empire -- History -- 1517-1648.

DB71.C7 1970
Crankshaw, Edward.
Maria Theresa. New York, Viking Press [1970, c1969] 366 p.
70-094850   943/.053/0924   0670456314
Maria Theresa, -- Empress of Austria, -- 1717-1780.   Austria -- History -- Maria Theresa, 1740-1780.

DB74.B43
Bernard, Paul P.
Joseph II, by Paul P. Bernard. New York, Twayne Publishers [1968] 155 p.
67-025205   943/.057/0924
Joseph -- II, -- Holy Roman Emperor, -- 1741-1790.

DB74.7.P47.B47 1991
Bernard, Paul P.
From the enlightenment to the police state: the public life of Johann Anton Pergen/ Paul P. Bernard. Urbana: University of Illinois Press, c1991. xi, 252 p.
90-038594   363.2/83/092   0252017455
Pergen, Johann Anton, -- 1725-1814. Statesmen -- Austria -- Biography. Secret service -- Austria -- History -- 18th century. Political crimes and offenses -- Austria -- Prevention -- History -- 18th century. Austria -- Politics and government -- 1740-1789. Austria -- Politics and government -- 1789-1815.

DB80.J38 1987
Jelavich, Barbara, 1923-
Modern Austria: empire and republic, 1815-1986/ Barbara Jelavich. Cambridge; Cambridge University Press, 1987. xvii, 346 p.
86-033371   943.6/04   0521303206
Austria -- History -- 1815-1848. Austria -- History -- 1848-1867. Austria -- History -- 1867-1918.

DB80.M3 1969
Macartney, Carlile Aylmer, 1895-
The Habsburg Empire, 1790-1918 [by] C. A. Macartney. New York, Macmillan [1969] xiv, 886 p.
69-012834   943.6/04
Austria -- History -- 1789-1900. Austria -- History -- 1867-1918.

DB80.S58 1989
Sked, Alan, 1947-
The decline and fall of the Habsburg Empire, 1815-1918/ Alan Sked. London; Longman, 1989. vii, 295 p.
88-009003   943.6/04   0582025303
Habsburg, House of.   Austria -- History -- 1848-1867. Austria -- History -- 1867-1918. Austria -- History -- 1815-1848.

DB80.T382
Taylor, A. J. P. 1906-
The Habsburg monarchy, 1809-1918; a history of the Austrian Empire and Austria-Hungary. London, H. Hamilton [1948] 279 p.
49-019763   943.6
Austria -- History -- 1789-1900. Austria -- History -- 20th century.

DB80.8.M57.C
Cecil, Algernon, 1879-1953.
Metternich, 1773-1859; a study of his period and personality. London, Eyre and Spottiswoode [1947] x, 324 p.
48-007443   923.2436
Metternich, Clemens Wenzel Lothar, -- Furst von, -- 1773-1859   Europe -- Politics and government -- 1789-1900.

DB81.B55 1991
Billinger, Robert D., 1944-
Metternich and the German question: states' rights and federal duties, 1820-1834/ Robert D. Billinger, Jr. Newark: University of Delaware Press; c1991. 230 p.
90-050002   943/.073   0874134072
Metternich, Clemens Wenzel Lothar, -- Furst von, -- 1773-1859.   Austria -- Foreign relations -- 1815-1848.   Deutscher Bund (1815-1866) -- History.

DB85.C7 1983
Crankshaw, Edward.
The fall of the House of Habsburg/ by Edward Crankshaw. New York: Penguin, 1983. 459 p.
82-018071   943.6/04   0140064591
Habsburg, House of. Franz Joseph -- I, -- Emperor of Austria, -- 1830-1916.   Austria -- History -- Francis Joseph, 1848-1916.

DB85.J8 1996
Judson, Pieter M.
Exclusive revolutionaries: liberal politics, social experience, and national identity in the Austrian Empire, 1848-1914/ Pieter M. Judson. Ann Arbor: University of Michigan Press, c1996. xi, 304 p.
96-029423   943.604/4   0472107402
Liberalism -- Austria -- History. Nationalism -- Austria -- History. State, The. Austria -- Social conditions. Austria -- Politics and government -- 1848-1918.

DB86.B74 1990
Bridge, F. R.
The Habsburg monarchy among the great powers, 1815-1918/ F.R. Bridge. New York: Berg: 1990. viii, 417 p.
89-028947   943.6/04   0854963073
Austria -- Foreign relations -- 1867-1918.

DB86.K3 1964
Kann, Robert A., 1906-
The multinational empire: nationalism and national reform in the Habsburg monarchy, 1848-1918/ by Robert A. Kann. New York: Octagon Books, 1977, c1950. 2 v.
64-016383   943.6   0324945039
Nationalism -- Austria. Minorities -- Austria. Austria -- History -- 1848-1867. Austria -- History -- 1867-1918. Austria -- Politics and government -- 1848-1918.

DB86.W515 1990
Williamson, Samuel R.
Austria-Hungary and the origins of the First World War/ Samuel R. Williamson, Jr. New York: St. Martin's Press, 1991. xviii, 272 p.
90-041895   943.6/044   0312052391
World War, 1914-1918 -- Causes. Austria -- History -- 1867-1918.

DB89.F7.D4
Dedijer, Vladimir.
The road to Sarajevo. New York, Simon and Schuster [1966] 550 p. illus.
65-024282   943.604
Franz Ferdinand, -- Archduke of Austria, -- 1863-1914 -- Assassination.   Austria -- Politics and government -- 1867-1918.

DB91.J3 1961
Jaszi, Oazkar, 1875-1957.
The dissolution of the Habsburg Monarchy. [Chicago] University of Chicago Press [1961, c1929] 482 p.
61-019632   943.604
Habsburg, House of.   Nationalism -- Austria. Austria -- History -- 1867-1918. Austria -- Social conditions. Austria -- Foreign relations -- 1867-1918.

DB91.S72 1971
Stadler, Karl R.
Austria, by Karl R. Stadler. New York, Praeger [1971] 346 p.
69-012307   943.6/05
Austria -- History -- 20th century.

DB91.2.W3413 1994
Wagnleitner, Reinhold, 1949-
Coca-colonization and the Cold War: the cultural mission of the United States in Austria after the Second World War/ Reinhold Wagnleitner; translated by Diana M. Wolf. Chapel Hill: University of North Carolina Press, c1994. xv, 367 p.
93-038431   303.48//2436073   0807821497
Propaganda, American -- Austria.   Austria -- Intellectual life -- 20th century. United States -- Relations -- Austria. Austria -- Civilization -- American influences.

DB97.A17 1991
1938-- and the consequences: questions and responses: interviews/ by Elfriede Schmidt; translated by Peter J. Lyth. Riverside, Calif.: Ariadne Press, c1992. 381 p.
91-025375   943.605/1   0929497341
Anschluss movement, 1918-1938 -- Sources. Antisemitism -- Austria -- History -- 20th century -- Sources. Interviews. Austria -- History -- Anschluss, 1938 -- Sources.

DB97.C65 1989
Conquering the past: Austrian Nazism yesterday & today/ edited by F. Parkinson. Detroit: Wayne State University Press, 1989. 345 p.
88-031328   324.436/038   0814320546
National socialism.   Austria -- Politics and government -- 20th century.

DB97.K5513 1988
Kindermann, Gottfried Karl, 1926-
Hitler's defeat in Austria, 1933-1934: Europe's first containment of Nazi expansionism/ Gottfried-Karl Kindermann; translated by Sonia Brough and David Taylor. Boulder, Colo.: Westview Press, 1988. xxvii, 234 p.
87-025426   943.6/051   0813305942
Hitler, Adolf, -- 1889-1945.   Austria -- Politics and government -- 1918-1938. Austria -- Foreign relations -- Germany. Germany -- Foreign relations -- Austria.

DB99.B87 2000
Bukey, Evan Burr, 1940-
Hitler's Austria: popular sentiment in the Nazi era, 1938-1945/ Evan Burr Bukey. Chapel Hill, N.C.: University of North Carolina Press, c2000. xvi, 320 p.
99-021475   943.605/22   0807825166
Hitler, Adolf, -- 1889-1945.   National socialism -- Austria. Antisemitism -- Austria. Austria -- History -- Anschluss, 1938.

DB99.L89
Luza, Radomir.
Austro-German relations in the Anschluss era/ Radomir Luza. Princeton, N.J.: Princeton University Press, [1975] xvi, 438 p.
74-025619   943.6/05   0691075689
Schirach, Baldur von, -- 1907-   Nationalism -- Germany.   Austria -- Politics and government -- 1918-1938. Austria -- History -- 1938-1945. Austria -- History -- Anschluss, 1938.

DB99.2.F58 1990
Fitzmaurice, John.
Austrian politics and society today: in defence of Austria/ John Fitzmaurice; foreword by Bruno Kreisky. New York: St. Martin's Press, 1990. xviii, 191 p.
90-032409   943.605/3   0312047061
Austria -- Politics and government -- 1945- Austria -- Civilization -- 20th century.

DB99.2.M58 1992
Mitten, Richard.
The politics of antisemitic prejudice: the Waldheim phenomenon in Austria/ Richard Mitten. Boulder: Westview Press, 1992. ix, 260 p.
92-014286   943.605   0813376300
Waldheim, Kurt.   Antisemitism -- Austria -- History -- 20th century.   Austria -- Politics and government -- 1945-

DB99.2.P47 2000
Pick, Hella.
Guilty victim: Austria from the Holocaust to Haider/ Hella Pick. London; I.B. Tauris, c2000. xv, 246 p.
00-711856   943.605/3   1860646182
Memory -- Political aspects -- Austria. National socialism -- Historiography. Political culture -- Austria. Austria -- Foreign relations -- 1955- Austria -- Politics and government -- 1945-

DB99.2.S85 1990
Sully, Melanie A.
A contemporary history of Austria/ Melanie A. Sully. London; Routledge, 1990. xiii, 179 p.
89-049329   943.605/3   0415019281
Austria -- Politics and government -- 1945-

DB205-217 Local history and description — Provinces, regions, etc. — Czechoslovakia

DB205.B68 1971
Bradley, J. F. N. 1930-
Czechoslovakia: a short history, by J. F. N. Bradley. Edinburgh, Edinburgh University Press, 1971. iii-xii, 212 p.
78-159593   943.7   0852241933
Czechoslovakia -- History.

DB205.S4 1965
Seton-Watson, R. W. 1879-1951.
A history of the Czechs and Slovaks, by R.W. Seton-Watson. Hamden, Conn., Archon Books, 1965. 413 p.
65-016973   943.7
Bohemia (Czech Republic) -- History. Slovak Republic (Czechoslovakia) -- History. Czechoslovakia -- History.

DB208.K3
Kaminsky, Howard, 1924-
A history of the Hussite revolution. Berkeley, University of California Press, 1967. xv, 580 p.
67-012608   943.7/02
Hussites.

DB215.H54
A History of the Czechoslovak Republic, 1918-1948. Edited by Victor S. Mamatey and Radomir Luza. Princeton, N.J., Princeton University Press [1973] xi, 534 p.
79-039791   943.7/03   0691052050
Czechoslovakia -- History.

DB215.K588
Korbel, Josef.
Twentieth-century Czechoslovakia: the meanings of its history/ Josef Korbel. New York: Columbia University Press, 1977. xii, 346 p.
76-054250   943.7/03   0231037244
Czechoslovakia -- History.

DB215.Z55 1975
Zinner, Paul E.
Communist strategy and tactics in Czechoslovakia, 1918-48/ Paul E. Zinner. Westport, Conn.: Greenwood Press, 1975, c1963. xi, 264 p.
75-032464   943.7/03   0837185505
Czechoslovakia -- Politics and government. Komunistická strana ̑Ceskoslovenska. Czechoslovakia -- History -- Coup d'état, 1948.

DB215.3.M38
Mastny, Vojtech, 1936-
The Czechs under Nazi rule; the failure of national resistance, 1939-1942. New York, Columbia University Press, 1971. xiii, 274 p.
72-132065   943.7/03   0231033036
Czechoslovakia -- History -- 1938-1945. Bohemia and Moravia (Protectorate, 1939-1945) -- Politics and government.

DB215.5.B83
Busek, Vratislav
Czechoslovakia. Vratislav Busek and Nicolas Spulber, editors. New York, Published for the Mid-European Studies Center of [1957] xvii, 520 p.
57-009333   943.7
Czechoslovakia.

DB215.5.G5
Golan, Galia.
The Czechoslovak reform movement; communism in crisis, 1962-1968. Cambridge [Eng.] University Press, 1971. viii, 349 p.
76-163059   309.1/437/04
Czechoslovakia -- Politics and government -- 1945-1992. Czechoslovakia -- Intellectual life -- 1945-1992.

DB215.5.K68
Korbel, Josef.
The communist subversion of Czechoslovakia, 1938-1948; the failure of coexistence. Princeton, N.J., Princeton University Press, 1959. 258 p.
59-011080   943.703
Communism--Czechoslovakia.

DB215.5.K87
Kusin, Vladimir V.
The intellectual origins of the Prague spring; the development of reformist ideas in Czechoslovakia, 1956-1967, by Vladimir V. Kusin. Cambridge [Eng.] University Press, 1971. v, 153 p.
73-155582   320.9/437/04   0521081246
Czechoslovakia -- Politics and government -- 1945-1992. Czechoslovakia -- History -- Intervention, 1968.

DB217.B3.A4 1971
Benes, Edvard, 1884-1948.
My war memoirs, by Eduard Benes. Translated from the Czech by Paul Selver. Westport, Conn., Greenwood Press [1971] 512 p.
70-114467   943.7/03/0924   0837147638
Benes, Edvard, -- 1884-1948.   World War, 1914-1918 -- Czechoslovakia.

DB217.M3.S4 1940
Selver, Paul, 1888-
Masaryk, a biography by Paul Selver; introd. by Jan Masaryk. London, M. Joseph [1940] 326 p.
40-013000   923.1437
Masaryk, Tomas Garrigue, -- Pres. Czechoslovak Republic, -- 1850-1937.

DB679 Local history and description — Provinces, regions, etc. — Slovakia

DB679.M513 1963
Mikus, Joseph A.
Slovakia, a political history: 1918-1950. Milwaukee, Marquette University Press, 1963. xxxiii, 392 p.
63-013803   943.735
Slovak Socialist Republic (Czechoslovakia) -- Politics and government. Czechoslovakia -- Politics and government.

DB739 Local history and description — Provinces, regions, etc. — Transylvania

DB739.H57
Hitchins, Keith, 1931-
The Rumanian national movement in Transylvania, 1780-1849. Cambridge, Harvard University Press, 1969. xi, 316 p.
69-012724   320.1/58/094984
Transylvania (Romania) -- Politics and government.

DB844 Local history and description — Vienna — Biography

DB844.L8.G44 1990
Geehr, Richard S.
Karl Lueger: mayor of fin de siecle Vienna/ Richard S. Geehr. Detroit: Wayne State University Press, 1990. 408 p.
89-034449   943.6/13044/092   0814320775
Lueger, Karl, -- 1844-1910.   Mayors -- Austria -- Vienna -- Biography.   Vienna (Austria) -- Civilization. Vienna (Austria) -- Politics and government.

DB851 Local history and description — Vienna — Social life and customs. Civilization. Intellectual life

DB851.S42 1979
Schorske, Carl E.
Fin-de-siecle Vienna: politics and culture/ Carl E. Schorske. New York: Knopf: distributed by Random House, 1979. xxx, 378 p.
79-002155   943.6/1304   0394505964
Vienna (Austria) -- Intellectual life -- Addresses, essays, lectures. Austria -- Politics and government -- 1867-1918 -- Addresses, essays, lectures.

DB853-854 Local history and description — Vienna — History and description

DB853.S65 1993
Spielman, John P. 1930-
The city & the crown: Vienna and the imperial court, 1600-1740/ John P. Spielman. West Lafayette, Ind.: Purdue University Press, c1993. ix, 264 p.
91-034379   943.6/13   1557530211
Vienna (Austria) -- History. Austria -- Court and courtiers.

DB854.B67 1995
Boyer, John W.
Culture and political crisis in Vienna: Christian socialism in power, 1897-1918/ John W. Boyer. Chicago: University of Chicago Press, 1995. xvi, 702 p.
94-036240   320.9436/13/09034   0226069605
Radicalism -- Austria -- Vienna. Socialism, Christian -- Austria -- Vienna. Austria -- Politics and government -- 1867-1918. Vienna (Austria) -- Cultural policy. Vienna (Austria) -- Politics and government.

DB886 History of Liechtenstein — General works

DB886.M45 1993
Meier, Regula A., 1929-
Liechtenstein/ Regula A. Meier, compiler. Oxford, England; Clio Press, c1993. xx, 123 p.
94-160591   016.94364/8   1851092013
Liechtenstein -- Bibliography.

DB904-958.3 History of Hungary

DB904 Gazetteers. Dictionaries, etc.

DB904.V37 1997
Vardy, Steven Bela, 1935-
Historical dictionary of Hungary/ Steven Bela Vardy. Lanham, Md.: Scarecrow Press, 1997. xx, 813 p.
96-043058   943.9/003   0810832542
Hungary -- History -- Dictionaries -- English.

DB906 General works

DB906.M3413 1999
A companion to Hungarian studies/ edited by
Laszlo Kosa. Budapest: Akademiai Kiado, 1999.
509 p.
2001-382537   943.9   9630576775
Hungary -- Handbooks, manuals, etc.

DB925.1 History — Compends

DB925.1.K57 2002
Kontler, László.
A history of Hungary: millennium in Central
Europe/ László Kontler. New York: Palgrave
Macmillan, 2002. p. cm.
2002-075298   943.9.221   1403903166
Hungary -- History.

DB925.1.M6413 2001
Molnár, Miklós,
A concise history of Hungary/ Miklós Molnár;
translated by Anna Magyar. Cambridge, U.K.;
Cambridge University Press, c2001. xviii, 370 p.
00-041408   943.9.221   0521667364
Hungary -- History.

DB925.3 History — Addresses, essays, lectures

DB925.3.H57 1990
A History of Hungary/ Peter F. Sugar, general
editor; Peter Hanak, associate editor; Tibor Frank,
editorial assistant. Bloomington: Indiana
University Press, c1990. xiv, 432 p.
88-046215   943.9   0253355788
Hungary -- History.

DB933-945 History — By period 1792-1918. 19th century

DB933.F74 2000
Freifeld, Alice.
Nationalism and the crowd in liberal Hungary,
1848-1914/ Alice Freifeld. Washington, D.C.:
Woodrow Wilson Center Press; c2000. xii, 398 p.
00-008814   943.9/042   0801864623
*Nationalism -- Hungary -- History -- 19th
century. Nationalism -- Hungary -- History -- 20th
century. Liberalism -- Hungary -- History -- 19th
century.*

DB937.D42
Deak, Istvan.
The lawful revolution: Louis Kossuth and the
Hungarians, 1848-1849/ Istvan Deak. New York:
Columbia University Press, 1979. xxi, 415 p.
78-022063   943.9/04/0924   0231046022
*Kossuth, Lajos, -- 1802-1894.   Statesmen --
Hungary -- Biography.   Hungary -- History --
Uprising of 1848-1849.*

DB945.H5613 1988
Hoensch, Jorg K.
A history of modern Hungary: 1867-1986/ Jorg K.
Hoensch; translated by Kim Traynor. London;
Longman, 1988. xiii, 320 p.
87-004170   943.9/05   0582014840
*Hungary -- History -- 1867-1918. Hungary --
History -- 20th century.*

DB955-958.3 History — By period — 20th century

DB955.N37
Nagy-Talavera, Nicholas M., 1929-
The Green Shirts and the others; a history of
Fascism in Hungary and Rumania, by Nicholas M.
Nagy-Talavera. Stanford, Calif., Hoover Institution
Press, Stanford University [1970] xii, 427 p.
74-098136   943.9/05   0817918515
*Szalasi Ferenc, -- 1897-1946. Codreanu, Corneliu
Zelea, -- 1899-1938.   Hungary -- Politics and
government -- 1918-1945. Romania -- Politics and
government -- 1914-1944.*

DB955.6.H67.S25 1994
Sakmyster, Thomas L.
Hungary's admiral on horseback: Miklos Horthy,
1918-1944/ Thomas Sakmyster. Boulder: East
European Monographs; 1994. x, 476 p.
94-061021
*Horthy, Miklos, -- nagybanyai, -- 1868-1957.
Admirals -- Hungary -- Biography. Regents --
Hungary -- Biography.   Hungary -- Politics and
government -- 1918-1945.*

DB956.B37 1993
Barany, Zoltan D.
Soldiers and politics in Eastern Europe, 1945-90:
the case of Hungary/ Zoltan D. Barany. New York,
N.Y.: St. Martin's Press, 1993. xi, 243 p.
93-016624   943.905   0312097220
*Civil-military relations -- Hungary.   Hungary --
Politics and government -- 1945-1989.*

DB956.C7913 1997
Csanadi, Maria.
Party states and their legacies in post-communist
transformation/ Maria Csanadi. Cheltenham, UK;
E. Elgar, c1997. xlvii, 386 p.
97-025009   320.9439/09/045   1858986451
*Communism -- Hungary.   Hungary -- Politics
and government -- 1945-1989.*

DB956.R66 1996
Roman, Eric, 1926-
Hungary and the victor powers, 1945-1950/ Eric
Roman. New York: St. Martin's Press, 1996. x,
342 p.
95-052046   943.905/3   0312158912
*Hungary -- History -- 1945-1989. Hungary --
Foreign relations -- 1945-1989.*

DB956.Z5
Zinner, Paul E.
Revolution in Hungary.   New York, Columbia
University Press, 1962. xi, 380 p.
62-017062   943.9105
*Communism -- Hungary.   Hungary -- History --
Revolution, 1956. Hungary -- Politics and
government -- 1945-1989.*

DB957 .A1713 1996
The Hungarian Revolution of 1956: reform, revolt,
and repression, 1953-1963/ edited by György
Litván; English version edited and translated by
János M. Bak, Lyman H. Legters. London;
Longman, 1996. xv, 221 p.
95-045648   943.905/2 20   0582215048
*Csongrád Megye (Hungary) -- Newspapers. Szeged
(Hungary) -- Newspapers.*

DB957.F47 1989
Felkay, Andrew.
Hungary and the USSR, 1956-1988: Kadar's
political leadership/ Andrew Felkay. New York:
Greenwood Press, 1989. x, 334 p.
88-021358   327.439047   0313259828
*Kadar, Janos, -- 1912-   Hungary -- Politics and
government -- 1945-1989. Hungary -- Foreign
relations -- Soviet Union. Soviet Union -- Foreign
relations -- Hungary.*

DB957.L3 1970
Lasky, Melvin J.,
The Hungarian revolution; a white book. The story
of the October uprising as recorded in documents,
dispatches, eye-witness accounts, and world-wide
reactions. Edited by Melvin J. Lasky. Freeport,
N.Y., Books for Libraries Press [1970, c1957]
318 p.
70-119936   943.9/105   0836953797
Hungary -- History -- Revolution, 1956.

DB957.L6
Lomax, William.
Hungary 1956/ [by] Bill Lomax. London: Allen
and Busby, 1976. 222 p.
77-362753   943.9/05   0850311888
Hungary -- History -- Revolution, 1956.

DB958.3.L38 1995
Lawful revolution in Hungary, 1989-94/ Bela K.
Kiraly, editor, Andras Bozoki, associate editor.
Boulder, Colo.: Social Science Monographs; 1995.
xv, 519 p.
95-072957   0880333421
Hungary -- Politics and government -- 1989-

DB2005-2848 History of Czechoslovakia

DB2005 Collected works (nonserial) — Several authors

DB2005.B64 1998
Bohemia in history/ edited by Mikulas Teich.
Cambridge, U.K.; Cambridge University Press,
1998. xiv, 389 p.
97-023902   943.71   0521431557
Bohemia (Czech Republic) -- History.

DB2063 History — General works — 1977-

DB2063.S28 1998
Sayer, Derek.
The coasts of Bohemia: a Czech history/ Derek
Sayer; translations from the Czech by Alena Sayer.
Princeton, N.J.: Princeton University Press, c1998.
xv, 442 p.
97-041418   943.71   0691057605
*Bohemia (Czech Republic) -- History. Czech
Republic -- History.*

DB2078 History — Foreign and general relations — Relations with individual regions or countries, A-Z

DB2078.G3.L85 1996
Lukes, Igor.
Czechoslovakia between Stalin and Hitler: the diplomacy of Edvard Benes in the 1930s/ Igor Lukes. New York: Oxford University Press, 1996. xii, 318 p.
95-009284   327.437043/09/043   0195102665
Benes, Edvard, -- 1884-1948   Czechoslovakia -- Foreign relations -- Germany. Germany -- Foreign relations -- Czechoslovakia. Czechoslovakia -- Foreign relations -- Soviet Union.

DB2187.5-2244.7 History — By period — Czechoslovak Republic, 1918-1992

DB2187.5.C94 1989
Czechoslovakia: crossroads and crises, 1918-88/ edited by Norman Stone and Eduard Strouhal. New York: St. Martin's Press, 1989. xviii, 336 p.
89-006068   943.7/03   0312032013
Czechoslovakia -- History.

DB2188.7.C73 1991
Crane, John O., d. 1982.
Czechoslovakia: anvil of the Cold War/ John O. Crane and Sylvia Crane; foreword by Corliss Lamont. New York: Praeger, 1991. xxvi, 352 p.
90-039146   943.7/03   0275935779
Czechoslovakia -- Politics and government.

DB2188.7.K73 1996
Krejci, Jaroslav, 1916-
Czechoslovakia, 1918-92: a laboratory for social change/ Jaroslav Krejci and Pavel Machonin. New York: St. Martin's Press in asociation with St. Antony 1996. xviii, 266 p.
95-052408   943.7/03   031212693X
Social   change   --   Czechoslovakia. Czechoslovakia -- Politics and government -- 20th century.

DB2191.M38.S58 1994
Skilling, H. Gordon 1912-
T.G. Masaryk: against the current, 1882-1914/ H. Gordon   Skilling.   University   Park,   Pa.: Pennsylvania State University Press, 1994. xv, 248 p.
93-029636   943.7/032/092   0271010428
Masaryk, T. G. -- (Tomas Garrigue), -- 1850-1937 -- Political and social views.

DB2216.R4613 1989
Renner, Hans.
A history of Czechoslovakia since 1945/ Hans Renner; [translated from the Dutch by Evelien Hurst-Buist]. London; Routledge, 1989. xi, 200 p.
89-006040   943.7/04   0415003636
Czechoslovakia -- History -- 1945-1992.

DB2218.7.M9 1981
Myant, M. R.
Socialism and democracy in Czechoslovakia, 1945-1948/ M.R. Myant. Cambridge; Cambridge University Press, 1981. ix, 302 p.
80-041951   943.7/042   0521236681
Czechoslovakia -- Politics and government -- 1945-1992.

DB2222.K37x 1987b
Kaplan, Karel.
The short march: the Communist takeover in Czechoslovakia, 1945-1948 / Karel Kaplan. London: C. Hurst, c1987. xiv, 207 p.
87-673445   0905838963
Communism--Czechoslovakia--History.

DB2228.7.W47 1992
Wheaton, Bernard.
The Velvet Revolution: Czechoslovakia, 1988-1991/ Bernard Wheaton and Zdenek Kavan. Boulder: Westview Press, 1992. xvi, 255 p.
92-008442   943.704/3   0813312035
Czechoslovakia -- Politics and government -- 1968-1989. Czechoslovakia -- Politics and government -- 1989-1992.

DB2238.H38.A5 1997
Havel, Vaclav.
The art of the impossible: politics as morality in practice: speeches and writings, 1990-1996/ by Vaclav Havel; translated from the Czech by Paul Wilson and others. New York: Knopf: 1997. xix, 273 p.
96-052262   943.7105/092   0679451064
Political ethics. Citizenship -- Moral and ethical aspects. Post-communism. Czech Republic -- Politics and government -- Moral and ethical aspects.

DB2238.7.H65 1996
Holy, Ladislav.
The little Czech and the Great Czech Nation: national   identity   and   the   post-communist transformation   of   society/   Ladislav   Holy. Cambridge; Cambridge University Press, 1996. x, 226 p.
95-048157   943.7105   0521554691
National characteristics, Czech. Social change -- Czech Republic. Czech Republic -- Politics and government.

DB2238.7.L44 1996
Leff, Carol Skalnik.
The Czech and Slovak republics: nation versus state/ Carol Skalnik Leff. Boulder, Colo.: Westview Press, 1996. xvii, 295 p.
96-012080   320.9437   0813329213
Post-communism -- Czech Republic. Post-communism -- Slovakia. Communism -- Czechoslovakia. Czechoslovakia -- Politics and government -- 1945-1992. Czech Republic -- Politics and government. Slovakia -- Politics and government.

DB2241.H38.A513 1990
Havel, Vaclav.
Disturbing the peace: a conversation with Karel Hvizdala/ Vaclav Havel; translated from the Czech and with an introduction by Paul Wilson. New York: Knopf: 1990. xvii, 228 p.
90-052609   943.704/3/092   0394584414
Havel, Vaclav -- Interviews.   Presidents -- Czechoslovakia -- Interviews. Dramatists, Czech -- 20th   century   --   Interviews.   Playwriting. Czechoslovakia -- Politics and government -- 1968-1989.

DB2241.H38.A5 1991b
Havel, Vaclav.
Open letters: selected writings, 1965-1990/ by Vaclav Havel; selected and edited by Paul Wilson. New York: Knopf: 1991. xiv, 415 p.
90-053561   943.704/3   0679400273
Czechoslovakia -- Politics and government -- 1968-1989.

DB2241.H38.C75 1999
Critical essays on Vaclav Havel/ edited by Marketa Goetz-Stankiewicz and Phyllis Carey. New York: G.K. Hall: c1999. xii, 297 p.
98-054637   943.704/3/092   078388463X
Havel, Vaclav.   Presidents -- Czechoslovakia -- Biography.   Presidents -- Czech Republic -- Biography. Dramatists, Czech -- 20th century -- Biography.

DB2244.7.S44 2000
Shepherd, Robin H. E., 1968-
Czechoslovakia: the velvet revolution and beyond/ Robin H.E. Shepherd. Houndsmills: Macmillan Press Ltd.; 2000. ix, 204 p.
99-051860   943.705   0312230680
Czech Republic -- Politics and government -- 1993- Czech Republic -- Economic conditions. Slovakia -- Politics and government -- 1993-

DB2711 Slovakia — General works

DB2711.L86 2000
Lunt, Susie.
Slovakia/ Susie Lunt and Zora Milenkovic, compilers. -- Oxford, England; Clio Press, c2000. xvii, 186 p.
   016.94373   1851092811
Slovakia -- Bibliography.

DB2742 Slovakia — Ethnography — Individual elements in the population, A-Z

DB2742.R8.M3413 1993
Magocsi, Paul R.
The Rusyns of Slovakia: an historical survey/ Paul Robert Magocsi. [Boulder]: East European Monographs; 1993. 185 p.
93-071875   0880332786
Ruthenians -- Slovakia -- History.

DB2744 Slovakia — History — Dictionaries. Chronological tables, outlines, etc.

DB2744.K57 1999
Kirschbaum, Stanislav J.
Historical dictionary of Slovakia/ Stanislav J. Kirschbaum. Lanham, Md.: Scarecrow Press, 1999. lxxxvi, 213 p
98-022754   943.73/003   0810835061
Slovakia -- History -- Dictionaries.

DB2763 Slovakia — History — General works

DB2763.K57 1995
Kirschbaum, Stanislav J.
A history of Slovakia: the struggle for survival/ Stanislav J. Kirschbaum. New York: St. Martin's Press, 1995. xvi, 350 p.
94-022501   943.7/3   0312104030
Slovakia -- History.

DB2763.T66 2001
Toma, Peter A.
Slovakia: from Samo to Dzurinda/ Peter A. Toma and Duˆsan Kováˆc. Stanford, CA: Hoover Institution Press, 2001. xxxi, 432 p.
00-054246   943.73.221   0817999523
Slovakia -- History.

DB2848 Slovakia — History — By period

DB2848.G65 1999
Goldman, Minton F.
Slovakia since independence: a struggle for democracy/ Minton F. Goldman. Westport, Conn.: Praeger, 1999. xi, 247 p.
98-015656   327.4373   0275961893
Slovakia -- Politics and government -- 1993- Slovakia -- Foreign relations -- 1993-

DC History of France

DC20 Pictorial works

DC20.A2 1936
Adams, Henry, 1838-1918.
Mont-Saint-Michel and Chartres [by] Henry Adams. With an introduction by Ralph Adams Cram. Boston, Houghton Mifflin company, 1936. xiv, p.
36-027246   914.4
Civilization, Medieval.   Le Mont-Saint-Michel (France)

DC20.5 Historical geography

DC20.5.B7313 1988
Braudel, Fernand.
The identity of France/ Fernand Braudel; translated from the French by Sian Reynolds. New York: Harper & Row, c1988- v.
88-045566   911/.44   0060160217
Human geography -- France.   France -- Historical geography. France -- Description and travel.

DC20.5.P5813 1993
Planhol, Xavier de.
An historical geography of France/ Xavier de Planhol; with the collaboration of Paul Claval; translated by Janet Lloyd. Cambridge; Cambridge University Press; 1994. xxiii, 563 p.
92-045912   911/.44   0521322081
Human geography -- France.   France -- Historical geography.

DC33 Social life and customs. Civilization. Intellectual life — General works

DC33.A87 1996
Auslander, Leora.
Taste and power: furnishing Modern France/ Leora Auslander. Berkeley: University of California Press, c1996. xv, 495 p.
95-000715   944   0520088948
Furniture -- Styles -- Social aspects -- France. Social change -- France. Politics and culture -- France. France -- Civilization. France -- Politics and government -- 1789-

DC33.D33
Davis, Natalie Zemon, 1928-
Society and culture in early modern France: eight essays/ by Natalie Zemon Davis. Stanford, Calif.: Stanford University Press, 1975. xviii, 362 p.
74-082777   944/.027   0804708681
France -- Civilization.

DC33.J66 1994
Jones, Colin, 1947-
The Cambridge illustrated history of France/ Colin Jones. Cambridge; Cambridge University Press, 1994. 352 p.
94-019310   944   0521432944
France -- Civilization.

DC33.W37 1991
Weber, Eugen Joseph, 1925-
My France: politics, culture, myth/ Eugen Weber. Cambridge, Mass.: Belknap Press of Harvard University Press, 1991. 412 p.
90-035780   944   0674595750
Politics and culture -- France -- History. France -- Civilization. France -- Politics and government -- 20th century.

DC33.2 Social life and customs. Civilization. Intellectual life — By period — Early to medieval

DC33.2.B413 1991
Beaune, Colette.
The birth of an ideology: myths and symbols of nation in late-medieval France/ Colette Beaune; translated by Susan Ross Huston; edited by Fredric L. Cheyette. Berkeley: University of California Press, c1991. vii, 427 p.
90-024687   944/.02   0520059417
France -- Social life and customs -- 1328-1600. France -- History -- Medieval period, 987-1515. France -- Church history -- 987-1515.

DC33.2.B59 1998
Bouchard, Constance Brittain.
Strong of body, brave and noble: chivalry and society in medieval France/ Constance Brittain Bouchard. Ithaca: Cornell University Press, 1998. xii, 198 p.
97-038906   944/.02   0801430976
Nobility -- France -- History -- To 1500. Chivalry -- France -- History -- To 1500. France -- Civilization -- 1000-1328.

DC33.2.D7513 1991
Duby, Georges.
France in the Middle Ages 987-1460: from Hugh Capet to Joan of Arc/ Georges Duby; translated by Juliet Vale. Oxford, UK; B. Blackwell, 1991. xv, 331 p.
91-007753   944/.02   063117026X
Hugh Capet, -- King of France, -- ca. 938-996. Joan, -- of Arc, Saint, -- 1412-1431.   France -- Church history -- 987-1515. France -- Civilization. France -- History -- Medieval period, 987-1515.

DC33.2.H83 1985
Huizinga, Johan, 1872-1945.
The waning of the Middle Ages: a study of the forms of life, thought, and art in France and the Netherlands in the XIVth and XVth centuries/ by J. Huizinga. New York: St. Martin's Press, [1985], c1924 viii, 328 p.
84-009980   944   0312855400
Civilization, Medieval.   France -- Civilization -- 1328-1600. Netherlands -- Civilization.

DC33.2.M44 1995
Medieval France: an encyclopedia/ William W. Kibler ... [et al.], editors. New York: Garland Pub., 1995. xxvi, 1047 p.
95-002617   944/.003   0824044444
France -- Civilization -- Encyclopedias.

DC33.2.P68 1989
Power, culture, and religion in France, c. 1350-c. 1550/ edited by Christopher Allmand. Woodbridge, Suffolk; Boydell Press, 1989. xiii, 163 p.
88-007932   944.219   0851155146
Politics and culture--France--History--Congresses. Reformation--France--Congresses.

DC33.2.R5413
Riche, Pierre.
Daily life in the world of Charlemagne/ Pierre Riche; translated by Jo Ann McNamara. [Philadelphia]: University of Pennsylvania Press, 1978. xvi, 336 p.
78-053330   944/.01   0812210964
France -- Civilization -- 700-1000.

DC33.2.W66 1998
Woolf, Greg.
Becoming Roman: the origins of provincial civilization in Gaul/ Greg Woolf. Cambridge, U.K.; Cambridge University Press, 1998. xv, 296 p.
97-047263   944   0521414458
Romans -- Gaul. Cities and towns, Ancient. Rome -- History -- Empire, 30 B.C.-284 A.D. Gaul -- Civilization -- Roman influences. Rome -- Provinces -- Administration.

DC33.3 Social life and customs. Civilization. Intellectual life — By period — Renaissance period. 16th century

DC33.3.C45 1997
Changing identities in early modern France/ Michael Wolfe, editor; with a foreword by Natalie Zemon Davis. Durham: Duke University Press, 1997. x, 410 p.
96-033335   944/.025.220   0822319136
French--Identity.   Social   classes--France. Renaissance--France.

DC33.3.F4 1977
Febvre, Lucien Paul Victor, 1878-1956.
Life in Renaissance France/ Lucien Febvre; edited
and translated by Marian Rothstein. Cambridge,
Mass.: Harvard University Press, 1977. xx, 163 p.
77-007454 944/.02 0674531752
*Renaissance -- France.   France -- Civilization --
1328-1600.*

DC33.3.G36 1995
Garrisson, Janine.
A history of sixteenth-century France, 1483-1598:
Renaissance, Reformation, and rebellion/ Janine
Garrisson; translated by Richard Rex. New York:
St. Martin's Press, 1995. x, 438 p.
94-047567 944/.028 0312126123
*Renaissance -- France. Reformation -- France.
France -- Civilization -- 1328-1600. France --
History -- Wars of the Huguenots, 1562-1598.*

DC33.3.K44
Kelley, Donald R., 1931-
The beginning of ideology: consciousness and
society in the French Reformation/ Donald R.
Kelley. Cambridge [Eng.]; Cambridge University
Press, 1981. xv, 351 p.
80-041237 944/.028 0521235049
*Reformation -- France.   France -- History --
16th century. France -- Civilization -- 1328-1600.*

DC33.3.M39 2000
McGowan, Margaret M.
The vision of Rome in late Renaissance France/
Margaret M. McGowan. New Haven: Yale
University Press, c2000. xiii, 461 p.
00-033556 944 0300085354
*Renaissance -- France.   France -- Civilization --
1328-1600 -- Roman influences. France --
Antiquities, Roman.*

DC33.3.R64 1996
Roelker, Nancy L.
One king, one faith: the Parlement of Paris and the
religious reformations of the sixteenth century/
Nancy Lyman Roelker. Berkeley: University of
California Press, c1996. xi, 543 p.
94-040396 944/.029 0520086260
*Monarchy -- France -- History -- 16th century.
Reformation -- France. Religion and politics --
France -- History -- 16th century.   France --
Civilization -- 1328-1600. France -- History --
Wars of the Huguenots, 1562-1598.*

DC33.3.S44 1998
Sedgwick, Alexander, 1930-
The travails of conscience: the Arnauld family and
the Ancien Regime/ Alexander Sedgwick.
Cambridge, Mass.: Harvard University Press, 1998.
x, 297 p.
97-042556 929/.2/0944 0674905679
*Arnauld family.   Despotism -- France -- Religious
aspects. Religion and politics -- France -- History.
Fronde. Royalists -- France -- Biography. France -
- History -- Wars of the Huguenots, 1562-1598.
France -- Genealogy.*

DC33.4 Social life and customs. Civilization. Intellectual life — By period — 17th-18th centuries

DC33.4.G62 1994
Gordon, Daniel, 1961-
Citizens without sovereignty: equality and
sociability in French thought, 1670-1789/ Daniel
Gordon. Princeton, N.J.: Princeton University
Press, c1994. viii, 270 p.
94-005876 001.1/0944 0691056994
*Enlightenment. Despotism -- France -- Social
aspects. French language -- Social aspects --
France. France -- Intellectual life.*

DC33.4.P385 1997
Pasco, Allan H.
Sick heroes: French society and literature in the
romantic age, 1750-1850/ Allan H. Pasco. Exeter,
Devon, UK: University of Exeter Press, 1997. xvii,
250 p.
98-150513 944 0859895491
*French fiction -- 18th century. French fiction --
19th century. Romanticism -- France. France --
Social life and customs -- 18th century. France --
Social life and customs -- 19th century. France --
Civilization -- 18th century.*

DC33.4.S55 1996
Smith, Jay M., 1961-
The culture of merit: nobility, royal service, and
the making of absolute monarchy in France, 1600-
1789/ Jay M. Smith. Ann Arbor: University of
Michigan Press, c1996. vii, 305 p.
96-009992 944/.033 0472096389
*Louis -- XIV, -- King of France, -- 1638-1715 --
Influence.   Monarchy -- France -- Moral and
ethical aspects.   France -- Civilization -- 17th
century. France -- Kings and rulers -- Conduct of
life. France -- Civilization -- 18th century.*

DC33.5 Social life and customs. Civilization. Intellectual life — By period — 1789-1830

DC33.5.C6713 1998
Corbin, Alain.
Village bells: sound and meaning in the nineteenth-
century French countryside/ Alain Corbin;
translated by Martin Thom. New York: Columbia
University Press, c1998. xx, 416 p.
98-013799 944/.08 0231104502
*Church bells -- France -- History -- 19th century.
Country life -- France -- History -- 19th century.
France -- Social life and customs -- 19th century.*

DC33.5.F73 1984
The French romantics/ edited by D.G. Charlton.
Cambridge [Cambridgeshire]; Cambridge
University Press, 1984. 2 v.
83-021010 944.06 0521244137
*Romanticism -- France -- History. Arts -- France
-- History -- 19th century. France -- Civilization --
1789-1830. France -- Civilization -- 1830-1900.*

DC33.5.H46 1987
Hemmings, F. W. J. 1920-
Culture and society in France, 1789-1848/ F.W.J.
Hemmings. [New York]: P. Lang, 1987. ix, 342 p.
87-133670 700/.944 0820405396
*France -- Civilization -- 1789-1830. France --
Civilization -- 1830-1900.*

DC33.5.M34 1988
Mansel, Philip, 1951-
The court of France, 1789-1830/ Philip Mansel.
Cambridge [England]; Cambridge University
Press, 1988. xi, 224 p.
88-005010 944/.00880621 0521309956
*France -- Civilization -- 1789-1830. France --
Court and courtiers. France -- Kings and rulers.*

DC33.6 Social life and customs. Civilization. Intellectual life — By period — 1831-1900

DC33.6.D28 1999
Datta, Venita, 1961-
Birth of a national icon: the literary avant-garde
and the origins of the intellectual in France/ Venita
Datta. Albany, NY: State University of New York
Press, c1999. xi, 327 p.
98-039033 944.081/2/08631 0791442071
*Social change -- France. Avant-garde
(Aesthetics) -- France. Intellectuals -- France --
Political activity -- History -- 19th century. France
-- Intellectual life -- 19th century -- Political
aspects.*

DC33.6.M33 2000
Mathews, Timothy.
Literature, art and the pursuit of decay in
twentieth-century France/ Timothy Mathews.
Cambridge, UK; Cambridge University Press,
2000. xi, 232 p.
00-029262 944.081 0521419700
France -- Intellectual life -- 20th century.

DC33.6.W43 1986
Weber, Eugen Joseph, 1925-
France, fin de siecle/ Eugen Weber. Cambridge,
Mass.: Belknap Press, 1986. x, 294 p.
85-030569 944.06 0674318129
France -- Civilization -- 1830-1900.

DC33.7 Social life and customs. Civilization. Intellectual life — By period — 1901-

DC33.7.C597 1994
Corbett, James, 1942-
Through French windows: an introduction to
France in the nineties/ James Corbett. Ann Arbor:
University of Michigan Press, c1994. x, 415 p.
93-041808 944.083/9 0472094696
*France -- Civilization -- 20th century. France -
- Cultural policy -- History -- 20th century. France
-- Politics and government -- 1981-1995.*

DC33.7.E53 1998
Encyclopedia of contemporary French culture/
edited by Alex Hughes and Keith Reader. London;
Routledge, 1998. xxii, 618 p.
97-031879 944.08/03 0415131863
*Popular culture -- France -- Encyclopedias.
France -- Civilization -- 1945- -- Encyclopedias.*

DC33.7.F726 1995
French culture, 1900-1975/ edited by Catharine
Savage Brosman; associate editors, Tom Conley ...
[et al.]. Detroit: Gale Research, c1995. xl, 449 p.
94-044385 306/.0944/0904 0810384825
*Popular culture -- France -- History -- 20th
century -- Dictionaries. Intellectuals -- France --
Biography -- Dictionaries.   France -- Civilization -
- 20th century -- Dictionaries.*

DC33.7.H29 1991
Handbook of French popular culture/ edited by
Pierre L. Horn. New York: Greenwood Press,
1991. x, 307 p.
90-023170   306.4/0944   0313261210
   *Popular culture -- France -- History -- 20th
century.*

DC33.7.J83 1998
Judt, Tony.
The burden of responsibility: Blum, Camus, Aron,
and the French twentieth century/ Tony Judt.
Chicago: University of Chicago Press, 1998. viii,
196 p.
98-022269   944.08/092/2   0226414183
   *Blum, Leon, -- 1872-1950 -- Contributions in
ethics.   Camus,   Albert,   --   1913-1960   --
Contributions in ethics. Aron, Raymond, -- 1905-
- Contributions in ethics. Intellectuals -- France --
Political activity -- History -- 20th century.
France -- Intellectual life -- 20th century --
Political aspects.*

DC33.7.J84 1992
Judt, Tony.
Past imperfect: French intellectuals, 1944-1956/
Tony Judt. Berkeley: University of California
Press, c1992. x, 348 p.
91-042870   944.082   0520079213
   *Intellectuals -- France -- Political activity --
History -- 20th century. Communism and
intellectuals -- France -- History -- 20th century.
France -- Intellectual life -- 20th century.*

DC33.7.L43 1992
Lebovics, Herman.
True France: the wars over cultural identity, 1900-
1945/ Herman Lebovics. Ithaca: Cornell University
Press, 1992. xix, 221 p.
91-044697   944.081   0801426871
   *Politics and culture -- France -- History -- 20th
century.   France -- Civilization -- 20th century.
France -- Colonies -- History -- 20th century.
France -- Cultural policy -- History -- 20th
century.*

DC33.7.M285 2000
Mathy, Jean-Philippe.
French resistance: the French-American culture
wars/   Jean-Philippe   Mathy.   Minneapolis:
University of Minnesota Press, 2000. p. cm.
99-057336   303.48/244073   0816634424
   *Politics and culture.   United States --
Intellectual life -- French influences. United States
-- Relations -- France. France -- Relations --
United States.*

DC33.7.N63 1996
Northcutt, Wayne.
The regions of France: a reference guide to history
and culture/ Wayne Northcutt. Westport, Conn.:
Greenwood Press, 1996. x, 310 p.
96-005806   944.083   031329223X
   *Popular   culture   --   France   --   Regions.
Decentralization in government -- France --
History -- 20th century. France -- Civilization --
1945-*

DC33.7.R397 1997
Rearick, Charles, 1942-
The French in love and war: popular culture in the
era of the World Wars/ Charles Rearick. New
Haven: Yale University Press, c1997. x, 321 p.
96-050287   306/.0944   0300064330
   *Popular culture -- France -- History -- 20th
century. National characteristics, French. France
-- Civilization -- 20th century.*

DC33.7.R65 1995
Ross, Kristin.
Fast cars, clean bodies: decolonization and the
reordering of French culture/ Kristin Ross.
Cambridge, Mass.: MIT Press, c1995. x, 261 p.
94-017815   944.083   0262181614
   *Decolonization -- France -- History -- 20th
century. Technology -- Social aspects -- France --
History -- 20th century. Popular culture -- France
-- History -- 20th century. France -- Civilization --
American influences. France -- Civilization --
1945-*

DC33.7.S76 1992
Stoekl, Allan.
Agonies of the intellectual: commitment,
subjectivity, and the performative in the twentieth-
century French tradition/ Allan Stoekl. Lincoln:
University of Nebraska Press, 1992. 384 p.
91-017143   001.1/0944   0803242158
   *Philosophy, Modern -- 20th century.   France --
Intellectual life -- 20th century.*

DC34 Ethnography — General works

DC34.F6
Flanner, Janet, 1892-
An American in Paris; profile of an interlude
between two wars, by Janet Flanner. New York,
Simon and Schuster [c1940] 415 p.
40-007616   914.4
   National characteristics, French.

DC34.L413 1994
Le Wita, Beatrix.
French bourgeois culture/ Beatrix Le Wita;
translated from the French by J.A. Underwood.
Cambridge; New York: 1994. x, 168 p.
93-029766   944   0521440998
   *National characteristics, French. Middle class --
France -- Social life and customs.*

DC34.L5 1995
Lehning, James R., 1947-
Peasant and French: cultural contact in rural France
during the nineteenth century/ James R. Lehning.
Cambridge   [England];   Cambridge   University
Press, 1995. xii, 239 p.
94-022859   944.06   052146210X
   *National characteristics, French. Nationalism --
France -- History -- 19th century. Peasantry --
France -- Political activity. France -- Cultural
policy -- History -- 19th century.*

DC34.5 Ethnography — Individual elements in the population, A-Z

DC34.5.A4.M33 1997
MacMaster, Neil, 1945-
Colonial migrants and racism: Algerians in France,
1900-62/ Neil MacMaster. New York: St. Martin's
Press, 1997. vii, 307 p.
96-032471   305.892/765044/0904   0333644662
   *Algerians -- France -- History -- 20th century.
Immigrants -- Government policy -- France.
Racism -- France. Algeria -- Emigration and
immigration -- History -- 20th century. France --
Emigration and immigration -- History -- 20th
century. Algeria -- History -- Revolution, 1954-
1962 -- Influence.*

DC35 History — Dictionaries. Chronological tables, outlines, etc.

DC35.H35 2000
Haine, W. Scott.
The history of France/ W. Scott Haine. Westport,
Conn.: Greenwood Press, 2000. xviii, 260 p.
99-055229   944   0313303282
   *France -- History. France -- History --
Chronology.*

DC35.R39 1998
Raymond, Gino.
Historical dictionary of France/ Gino Raymond.
Lanham, Md.: Scarecrow Press, 1998. xxviii,
347 p.
98-006671   944/.003   0810834677
   France -- History -- Dictionaries.

DC36.7 History — Biography (Collective) — Queens, princesses, etc.

DC36.7.M38 2001
Matarasso, Pauline Maud.
Queen's mate: three women of power in France on
the eve of the   Renaissance/ Pauline Matarasso.
Aldershot; Ashgate, c2001. xiii, 317 p.
00-068242   944/.027/092. 221   0754603210
   *Anne, of France, 1461-1522. Anne, of Brittany,
Consort of Louis XII, King of France, 1476-1514.
Louise, de Savoie, duchesse d'Angoulême, 1476-
1531.*

DC36.9 History — Historiography — General works

DC36.9.B5713 2001
Birnbaum, Pierre.
The idea of France/ Pierre Birnbaum; translated by
M.B. DeBevoise.1st American ed. New York: Hill
and Wang, 2001. xii, 370 p.
00-063430   944.221   0809046504
   *Church   and   state--France--History--20th
century. Decentralization in government--France.*

DC36.9.B6413 1998
Boer, Pim den.
History as a profession: the study of history in
France 1818-1914/ Pim den Boer; translated by
Arnold J. Pomerans. Princeton, N.J.: Princeton
University Press, c1998. xv, 470 p.
97-039415   907/.2044   0691033390
   *History -- Study and teaching -- France. France
-- History -- 19th century -- Historiography.*

DC36.9.L24 2000
LaCapra, Dominick, 1939-
History and reading: Tocqueville, Foucault, French
studies/ Dominick LaCapra. Toronto; University of
Toronto Press, c2000. 235 p.
00-363249   944/.007/2   0802043941
   *Tocqueville, Alexis de, -- 1805-1859. -- Ancien
regime et la revolution. Foucault, Michel. -- Folie
et deraison. Tocqueville, Alexis de, -- 1805-1859. -
- Ancien regime et la revolution. Litterature et
histoire. Histoire -- Methodologie. Literature and
history. France -- Study and teaching. France --
Historiography. France -- Etude et enseignement.*

DC36.9.L37213 1979
Le Roy Ladurie, Emmanuel.
The territory of the historian/ Emmanuel Le Roy Ladurie; translated from the French by Ben and Sian Reynolds. Chicago: University of Chicago Press, 1979. viii, 345 p.
78-031362 944/.0072 0226473279
France -- Historiography.

DC36.9.L37213 1981
Le Roy Ladurie, Emmanuel.
The mind and method of the historian/ Emmanuel Le Roy Ladurie; translated by Sian Reynolds and Ben Reynolds. Chicago: University of Chicago Press, c1981. v, 310 p.
81-000449 944/.0072 0226473260
France -- Historiography.

DC36.9.S76
Stoianovich, Traian.
French historical method: the Annales paradigm/ by Traian Stoianovich; with a foreword by Fernand Braudel. Ithaca, N.Y.: Cornell University Press, 1976. 260 p.
75-036996 907/.2 080140861X
France -- Historiography.

DC36.98 History — Historiography — Biography of historians

DC36.98.B58.E44 1988
Ellis, Harold A.
Boulainvilliers and the French monarchy: aristocratic politics in early eighteenth-century France/ Harold A. Ellis. Ithaca: Cornell University Press, 1988. xii, 283 p.
87-047971 944/.033/0924 0801421306
Boulainvilliers, Henri, -- comte de, -- 1658-1722. Historians -- France -- Biography. Monarchy -- France -- History -- 18th century -- Historiography. France -- History -- Louis XIV, 1643-1715 -- Historiography.

DC36.98.M5.M54 1990
Mitzman, Arthur, 1931-
Michelet, historian: rebirth and romanticism in Nineteenth-Century France/ Arthur Mitzman. New Haven: Yale University Press, c1990. xxv, 339 p.
89-027244 944/.007202
Michelet, Jules, -- 1798-1874. Historians -- France -- Biography. Romanticism -- France -- History -- 19th century. France -- History -- 19th century.

DC36.98.T63.J3713 1988
Jardin, Andre, 1912-
Tocqueville: a biography/ Andre Jardin; translated from the French by Lydia Davis with Robert Hemenway. New York: Farrar Straus Giroux, c1988. 550 p.
88-010255 944/.072024 0374278369
Tocqueville, Alexis de, -- 1805-1859. Tocqueville, Alexis de, -- 1805-1859 -- Journeys -- North America. Historians -- France -- Biography. France -- Politics and government -- 1848-1870. United States -- Description and travel. France -- Politics and government -- 1830-1848.

DC36.98.T63.M36 1994
Mancini, Matthew J.
Alexis de Tocqueville/ Matthew Mancini. New York: Twayne Publishers; c1994. xiv, 163 p.
93-036335 944/.007202 0805743057
Tocqueville, Alexis de, -- 1805-1859. Tocqueville, Alexis de, -- 1805-1859 -- Political and social views. Historians -- France -- Biography.

DC36.98.T63.M57 1996
Mitchell, Harvey.
Individual choice and the structures of history: Alexis de Tocqueville as historian reappraised/ Harvey Mitchell. Cambridge; Cambridge University Press, c1996. xiii, 290 p.
95-033642 944/.007202 0521560918
Tocqueville, Alexis de, -- 1805-1859 -- Philosophy. Tocqueville, Alexis de, -- 1805-1859 -- Political and social views. Historians -- France -- Biography. Revolutions -- Philosophy. Decentralization in government -- France.

DC39 History — Compends

DC39.M372 1957
Maurois, Andre, 1885-1967.
A history of France. Translated from the French by Henry L. Binsse. Additional chapters translated by Gerard Hopkins. New York, Farrar, Straus and Cudahy [c1956] 598 p.
57-010003
France -- History.

DC52 History — Naval history — 17th-18th centuries

DC52.P75 1995
Pritchard, James S., 1939-
Anatomy of a naval disaster: the 1746 French naval expedition to North America/ James Pritchard. Montreal; McGill-Queen's University Press, c1995. xvi, 322 p.
96-154384 944/.034 0773513256
La Rochefoucauld de Roye, Jean-Baptiste-Louis-Frederic de, -- duc d'Anville, -- 1709-1746. France -- History -- Louis XV, 1715-1774. France -- History, Naval -- 18th century. Canada -- History -- 1713-1763 (New France).

DC58 History — Political and diplomatic history. Foreign and general relations — 19th-20th centuries

DC58.J46 1991
Jenkins, Brian, 1944-
Nationalism in France: class and nation since 1789/ Brian Jenkins. Savage, Md.: Barnes & Noble, 1990, c1991. p. cm.
90-001113 320.5/4/0944 0389209430
Nationalism -- France -- History. France -- Politics and government -- 1789-

DC58.R36 1995
Remaking the hexagon: the new France in the new Europe/ edited by Gregory Flynn. Boulder: Westview Press, 1995. x, 277 p.
94-046249 944.083/9 0813389194
National characteristics, French. Europe 1992. Social change -- France -- History -- 20th century. France -- Politics and government -- 1981- France -- Civilization -- Philosophy. France -- Relations -- Europe.

DC59.8 History — General special

DC59.8.G3.C37
Carrias, Eugene.
Le danger allemand (1866-1945) Paris, Presses universitaires de France, 1952. 259 p.
52-040497
Militarism. Germany -- Foreign relations -- France. France -- Foreign relations -- Germany.

DC59.8.G7
Thomas, Martin.
The French North African crisis: colonial breakdown and Anglo-French relations, 1945-62/ Martin Thomas. Houndmills, Basingstoke, Hampshire: Macmillan Press; 2000. xv, 287 p.
00-033268 965/.0461 0333715608
France -- Foreign relations -- Great Britain. Great Britain -- Foreign relations -- France. France -- Foreign relations -- 1945-1958.

DC59.8.N5
Bullard, Alice.
Exile to paradise: savagery and civilization in Paris and the South Pacific, 1790-1900/ Alice Bullard. Stanford, Calif.: Stanford University Press, 2000. 380 p.
00-055640 0804738785
Civilization -- Philosophy. Penal colonies -- New Caledonia -- History -- 19th century. New Caledonia -- Relations -- France. France -- Relations -- New Caledonia. France -- Colonies -- New Caledonia -- History -- 19th century.

DC59.8.U6.K85 1993
Kuisel, Richard F.
Seducing the French: the dilemma of Americanization/ Richard F. Kuisel. Berkeley: University of California Press, c1993. xiii, 296 p.
92-026548 944 0520079620
France -- Civilization -- American influences. France -- Civilization -- 20th century. France -- Relations -- United States.

DC61-108 History — By period — Early to medieval to 1515

DC61.S43 1996
Scott, Walter, 1771-1832.
Tales of a grandfather: the history of France (second series)/ Sir Walter Scott; edited by William Baker and J.H. Alexander. DeKalb: Northern Illinois University Press, 1996. xxxiii, 251 p.
95-047959 944 0875802087
France -- History. France -- Kings and rulers -- History.

DC62.C2.H2
Caesar, Julius.
The Gallic War, and other writings. Translated, with an introd. by Moses Hadas. New York, Modern Library [1957] xix, 363 p.
57-006492 878.1
Caesar, Julius -- Translations into English. Military history, Ancient. Gaul -- History -- Gallic Wars, 58-51 B.C. Rome -- History.

DC62.C2.W36
Caesar, Julius.
War commentaries of Caesar. Translated by Rex Warner. [New York] New American Library [1960] 335 p.
60-009463   944.01
Rome -- History -- Civil War, 49-48 B.C. Gaul -- History -- 58 B.C.-511 A.D.

DC62.D69 1983
Drinkwater, J. F.
Roman Gaul: the three provinces, 58 BC-AD 260/ J.F. Drinkwater. Ithaca, N.Y.: Cornell University Press, 1983. x, 256 p.
83-045143   936.4
Civilization, Ancient. Romans -- France. Gaul -- History -- 58 B.C.-511 A.D.

DC63.K56 1990
King, Anthony.
Roman Gaul and Germany/ Anthony King. [Berkeley]: University of California Press, 1990. 240 p.
89-020546   936.4   0520069897
Romans -- Gaul -- History. Excavations (Archaeology) -- France. Excavations (Archaeology) -- Germany. France -- Antiquities, Roman. Germany -- Antiquities, Roman. Gaul -- History -- 58 B.C.-511 A.D.

DC64.H46 1995
Hen, Yitzak.
Culture and religion in Merovingian Gaul, A.D. 481-751/ by Yitzhak Hen. Leiden; E.J. Brill, 1995. xiii, 308 p.
95-018889   944/.013   9004103473
Merovingians -- France. France -- Civilization -- To 700. France -- Church history -- To 987. France -- History -- To 987.

DC64.J36 1988
James, Edward, 1947-
The Franks/ Edward James. Oxford, UK; B. Blackwell, 1988. 265 p.
87-034153   944   0631148728
Clovis, -- King of the Franks, -- ca. 466-511. Franks -- France -- History. Franks -- History. France -- Church history -- To 987.

DC65.B33 1994
Bachrach, Bernard S., 1939-
The anatomy of a little war: a diplomatic and military history of the Gundovald affair (568-586)/ Bernard S. Bachrach. Boulder: Westview Press, 1994. xx, 283 p.
94-023140   944/.013   0813314925
Gundovald, -- 6th cent. Merovingians -- History, Military. Franks -- History -- To 768.

DC65.G43 1988
Geary, Patrick, J., 1948-
Before France and Germany: the creation and transformation of the Merovingian world/ Patrick J. Geary. New York: Oxford University Press, 1988. xii, 259 p.
87-007927   943/.01   0195044576
Merovingians. France -- History -- To 987. Germany -- History -- To 843.

DC65.J35 1982
James, Edward, 1947-
The origins of France: from Clovis to the Capetians, 500-1000/ Edward James. New York: St. Martin's Press, 1982. xxiii, 253 p.
82-010691   944/.01   0312588623
France -- History -- To 987.

DC65.W3 1982
Wallace-Hadrill, J. M.
The long-haired kings/ J.M. Wallace-Hadrill. Toronto; Published by University of Toronto Press in asso c1982. 261 p.
82-188926   944/.01   0802065007
Merovingians. France -- History -- To 987. France -- Kings and rulers.

DC65.W48 1994
Wood, I. N. 1950-
The Merovingian kingdoms, 450-751/ Ian Wood. London; Longman, 1994. xii, 395 p.
92-046027   940/.013   0582218780
Merovingians. France -- History -- To 987. France -- Church history -- To 987. France -- Kings and rulers -- History.

DC70.A2.A713 1991
The annals of St-Bertin/ translated and annotated by Janet L. Nelson. Manchester; Manchester University Press; c1991. x, 267 p.
91-004030   944   0719034256
France -- History -- To 987 -- Sources.

DC70.B84 1991
Bullough, Donald A.
Carolingian renewal: sources and heritage/ D.A. Bullough. Manchester [England]; Manchester University Press; c1991. viii, 343 p.
90-020283   944/.014   0719033543
Carolingians. France -- Civilization -- 700-1000. England -- Civilization -- To 1066.

DC70.H313
Halphen, Louis, 1880-1950.
Charlemagne and the Carolingian Empire/ by Louis Halphen; translated by Giselle de Nie. Amsterdam; North-Holland Pub. Co., 1977. xx, 366 p.
76-003514   944/.01   0720490073
Carolingians. France -- History -- To 987.

DC70.R5313 1993
Riche, Pierre.
The Carolingians: a family who forged Europe/ Pierre Riche; translated from the French by Michael Idomir Allen. Philadelphia: University of Pennsylvania Press, c1993. xix, 398 p.
91-303532   944/.01   0812213424
Carolingians. Middle Ages -- History. Civilization, Medieval. France -- History -- To 987. Europe -- History -- 476-1492. France -- Kings and rulers.

DC73.A2.R39 1976
The Reign of Charlemagne: documents on Carolingian government and administration/ [compiled by] H. R. Loyn and John Percival. New York: St. Martin's Press, 1976, c1975. ix, 164 p.
75-032935   944/.01
Charlemagne, -- Emperor, -- 742-814 -- Sources. Constitutional history, Medieval -- Sources. Carolingians -- Sources. France -- History -- To 987 -- Sources.

DC73.C65 1998
Collins, Roger, 1949-
Charlemagne/ Roger Collins. Toronto: University of Toronto Press, 1998. xv, 234 p.
98-229698   944/.014   0802044166
Charlemagne, -- Emperor, -- 742-814. Charlemagne, -- Emperor, -- 742-814. Civilization, Medieval. Civilisation medievale. France -- Histoire -- Jusqu'a 987. Saint Empire romain germanique -- Histoire -- Jusqu'a 1517. Holy Roman Empire -- History -- To 1517.

DC73.D88 1994
Dutton, Paul Edward, 1952-
The politics of dreaming in the Carolingian empire/ Paul Edward Dutton. Lincoln: University of Nebraska Press, c1994. xii, 329 p.
93-038615   944/.014   080321653X
Charlemagne, -- Emperor, -- 742-814 -- Influence. Dream interpretation -- Political aspects. Carolingians. Political poetry, Latin (Medieval and modern) -- France -- History and criticism. France -- Politics and government -- To 987 -- Sources.

DC73.H29 1995
Halphen, Louis, 1880-1950.
Charlemagne et l'empire carolingien/ Louis Halphen; postface de Pierre Riche. Paris: A. Michel, c1995. 550 p.
96-200387   944/.014   2226077634
Charlemagne, -- Emperor, -- 742-814. Holy Roman Empire -- Kings and rulers -- Biography. Civilization, Medieval. Carolingians -- Influence. France -- Kings and rulers -- Biography. France -- History -- To 987.

DC73.32.T8 1960
Einhard, ca. 770-840 ca. 770-840.
The life of Charlemagne. With a foreword by Sidney Painter. [Translated by Samuel Epes Turner. Ann Arbor] University of Michigan Press [1960] 74 p.
60-016107   923.14
Charlemagne, -- Emperor, -- 742-814. Holy Roman Empire -- Kings and rulers -- Biography. France -- Kings and rulers -- Biography.

DC74.C45 1989
Charlemagne's heir: new perspectives on the reign of Louis the Pious (814-840)/ edited by Peter Godman and Roger Collins. Oxford [England]; Clarendon Press, 1990. xx, 738 p.
89-071055   944/.014/092   0198219946
Louis -- I, -- Emperor, -- 778-840. Charlemagne, -- Emperor, -- 742-814 -- Family. France -- Civilization -- 700-1000. France -- Kings and rulers -- Biography.

DC82.F313
Fawtier, Robert, 1885-
The Capetian kings of France; monarchy & nation, 987-1328. Translated into English by Lionel Butler and R. J. Adam. London, Macmillan; 1960. 242 p.
60-001438   944.021
France -- History -- Capetians, 987-1328.

DC82.P6513 1990
Poly, Jean-Pierre, 1941-
The feudal transformation: 900-1200/ Jean-Pierre Poly, Eric Bournazel; translated by Caroline Higgitt. New York: Holmes & Meier, 1991. xvii, 404 p.
90-042094   944/.02   0841911673
Middle Ages -- History. Feudalism -- France -- History. France -- History -- Capetians, 987-1328.

DC83.3.S93
Sumption, Jonathan.
The Albigensian Crusade/ Jonathan Sumption. London; Faber, 1978. 269 p.
78-318324   272/.3   0571110649
Albigenses. Heresies, Christian -- France -- Languedoc -- History -- Middle Ages, 600-1500. France -- Church history -- 987-1515. France -- History -- 13th century. Languedoc (France) -- History.

DC90.B35 1986
Baldwin, John W.
The government of Philip Augustus: foundations of French royal power in the Middle Ages/ John W. Baldwin. Berkeley: University of California Press, c1986. xxi, 611 p.
84-023930 944/.023/0924.219 0520052722
Philip -- II, King of France, 1165-1223. Constitutional history, Medieval.

DC90.D813 1990
Duby, Georges.
The legend of Bouvines: war, religion, and culture in the Middle Ages/ Georges Duby; translated by Catherine Tihanyi. Berkeley: University of California Press, 1990. 234 p.
89-035224 944/.023 0520062388
Philip -- II, -- King of France, -- 1165-1223. Bouvines, Battle of, 1214. France -- History -- Philip II Augustus, 1180-1223 -- Historiography.

DC91.R5313 1992
Richard, Jean, 1921 Feb. 7--
Saint Louis: Crusader King of France/ Jean Richard; edited and abridged by Simon Lloyd; translatd by Jean Birrell. Cambridge; Cambridge University Press, c1992. xxix, 354 p.
91-002621 944/.023/092 0521381568
Louis -- IX, -- King of France, -- 1214-1270. Christian saints -- France -- Biography. France -- History -- Louis IX, 1226-1270. France -- Kings and rulers -- Biography.

DC92.S83
Strayer, Joseph Reese, 1904-
The reign of Philip the Fair/ by Joseph R. Strayer. Princeton, N.J.: Princeton University Press, c1980. xvi, 450 p.
79-003232 944/.024/0924 0691053022
Philip -- IV, -- King of France, -- 1268-1314. France -- History -- Philip IV, 1285-1314. France -- Kings and rulers -- Biography.

DC95.6.P68 1995
Potter, David, 1948-
A history of France, 1460-1560: the emergence of a nation state/ David Potter. New York: St. Martin's Press, 1995. xvi, 438 p.
94-032239 944/.02 0312124805
Louis -- XI, -- King of France, -- 1423-1483 -- Influence. Monarchy -- France -- History. National state. France -- History -- House of Valois, 1328-1589 -- Historiography. France -- History -- 16th century. France -- History -- 15th century.

DC96.C87 1993
Curry, Anne.
The Hundred Years War/ Anne Curry. New York: St. Martin's Press, 1993. xiv, 192 p.
92-037357 944/.025 0312091427
Hundred Years' War, 1339-1453. France -- History, Military -- 1328-1589. France -- Kings and rulers -- Genealogy. France -- Foreign relations -- Great Britain.

DC96.S86 1991
Sumption, Jonathan.
The Hundred Years War: trial by battle/ Jonathan Sumption. Philadelphia: University of Pennsylvania Press, 1991. xi, 659 p.
91-025816 944/.025 0812231473
Hundred Years' War, 1339-1453. France -- History -- House of Valois, 1328-1589. Great Britain -- History -- Medieval period, 1066-1485. France -- History, Military -- 1328-1589.

DC96.V34 1990
Vale, M. G. A.
The Angevin legacy and the Hundred Years War, 1250-1340/ Malcolm Vale. Oxford; Blackwell, 1990. xi, 317 p.
89-000934 944/.025 0631132430
Hundred Years' War, 1339-1453 -- Causes. France -- Foreign relations -- Great Britain. Great Britain -- Foreign relations -- France. France -- Politics and government -- 987-1328.

DC96.5.W75 1998
Wright, Nicholas.
Knights and peasants: the Hundred Years War in the French countryside/ Nicholas Wright. Woodbridge, Suffolk, UK; Boydell Press, 1998. x, 144 p.
97-040647 944/.025 0851155359
Hundred Years' War, 1339-1453 -- Social aspects -- France. Peasantry -- France -- Social conditions. Chivalry -- France -- History.

DC97.C54.H46 1996
Henneman, John Bell, 1935-
Olivier de Clisson and political society in France under Charles V and Charles VI/ John Bell Henneman. Philadelphia: University of Pennsylvania Press, c1996. xiv, 341 p.
96-011190 944/.025/092 0812233530
Clisson, Olivier de, -- 1336-1407. Nobility -- France -- Brittany -- Biography. Soldiers -- France -- Biography. Hundred Years War, 1339-1453 -- Biography. France -- Politics and government -- 1328-1589. France -- Relations -- England. England -- Relations -- France.

DC103.G47 1981
Gies, Frances.
Joan of Arc: the legend and the reality/ Frances Gies. New York: Harper & Row, c1981. 306 p.
80-007900 944/.026/0924 0690019424
Joan, -- of Arc, Saint, -- 1412-1431. Christian saints -- France -- Biography.

DC103.L96 1977
Lucie-Smith, Edward.
Joan of Arc/ Edward Lucie-Smith. New York: Norton, 1977, c1976. xiv, 239 p.
77-009509 944/.026/0924 0393075206
Joan, -- of Arc, Saint, -- 1412-1431. Christian saints -- France -- Biography.

DC103.W27 1981
Warner, Marina, 1946-
Joan of Arc: the image of female heroism/ Marina Warner. New York: Knopf, 1981. xxvi, 349 p.
80-002720 944/.026/0924 0394411455
Joan, -- of Arc, Saint, -- 1412-1431. Christian saints -- France -- Biography.

DC104.F73 2000
Fraioli, Deborah A., 1942-
Joan of Arc: the early debate/ Deborah A. Fraioli. Woodbridge, Suffolk, UK; Boydell Press, 2000. x, 235 p.
99-038918 944/.026/092 0851155723
Joan, -- of Arc, Saint, -- 1412-1431 -- In literature. Christian women saints -- France -- Biography -- Sources. Trust in God -- Christianity. France -- History -- Charles VII, 1422-1461 -- Historiography. France -- History -- Medieval period, 987-1515 -- Sources.

DC106.L3513 1994
Le Roy Ladurie, Emmanuel.
The royal French state, 1460-1610/ Emmanuel Le Roy Ladurie; translated by Juliet Vale. Oxford, UK; Blackwell Publishers, 1994. x, 320 p.
93-014144 944/.028 0631170278
Louis -- XI, -- King of France, -- 1423-1483 -- Influence. Henry -- IV, -- King of France, -- 1553-1610 -- Influence. Renaissance -- France. Reformation -- France. Nationalism -- France. France -- History -- Bourbons, 1589-1789. France -- History -- House of Valois, 1328-1589.

DC108.B38 1994
Baumgartner, Frederic J.
Louis XII/ by Frederic J. Baumgartner. New York: St. Martin's Press, 1994. xiii, 319 p.
94-004477 944/.027 0312120729
Louis -- XII, -- King of France, -- 1462-1515. France -- Kings and rulers -- Biography. France -- History -- Louis XII, 1498-1515.

DC110-138 History — By period — Modern, 1515-

DC110.B723 1998
Briggs, Robin.
Early modern France, 1560-1715/ Robin Briggs.2nd ed. Oxford; Oxford University Press, 1998. xi, 241 p.
97-015348 944/.028.221 0192892843
France -- History -- 16th century. France -- History -- 17th century.

DC110.C575 1995
Collins, James B.
The state in early modern France/ James B. Collins. Cambridge; Cambridge University Press, 1995. xxxiv, 280 p.
94-033992 944/.03.220 0521387248
Monarchy--France--History.

DC110.K64 2001
Knecht, R. J.
The rise and fall of Renaissance France, 1483-1610/ Robert Knecht.2nd ed. Malden, MA: Blackwell, 2001. p. cm.
00-069804 944/.028.221 0631227296
France -- History -- House of Valois, 1328-1589. France -- History -- Bourbons, 1589-1789.

DC111.H45 1991
Heller, Henry.
Iron and blood: civil wars in sixteenth-century France/ Henry Heller. Montreal; McGill-Queen's University Press, c1991. xiv, 191 p.
91-177910 944/.028 0773508163
France -- History -- 16th century. France -- Social conditions -- 16th century.

DC111.R43 2002
Renaissance and Reformation France, 1500-1648/ edited by Mack P. Holt. Oxford; Oxford University Press, 2002. p. cm.
2002-030746 944/.028.221 0198731655
Renaissance--France. Reformation--France.

DC111.3.H65 1995
Holt, Mack P.
The French wars of religion, 1562-1629/ Mack P. Holt. Cambridge [England]; Cambridge University Press, xiv, 239 p.
95-002277 944/.029.220 0521358736
Reformation--France. Religion and politics--France. Huguenots--France--History--17th century.

DC111.3.K55 2000
Knecht, R. J.
The French civil wars, 1562-1598/ R.J. Knecht. Harlow, Essex, England; Pearson Education, 2000. p. cm.
00-026013   944/.029   0582095492
France -- History -- Wars of the Huguenots, 1562-1598.

DC111.5.M3 1994
Major, J. Russell
From Renaissance monarchy to absolute monarchy: French kings, nobles, & estates/ J. Russell Major. Baltimore: Johns Hopkins University Press, c1994. xxi, 444 p.
93-047260   944/.025.221   0801847761
Renaissance--France.   Monarchy--France. Nobility--France.

DC112.B6.P58 1993
Pitts, Vincent J. 1947-
The man who sacked Rome: Charles de Bourbon, constable of France (1490-1527)/ Vincent J. Pitts. New York: P. Lang, c1993. x, 614 p.
93-018629   944/.025   0820424560
Bourbon, Charles, -- duc de, -- 1490-1527 -- Military leadership. Bourbon, House of. Nobility - - France -- Biography.   France -- History -- Francis I, 1515-1547. Rome (Italy) -- History -- Siege, 1527.

DC113.K58
Knecht, R. J.
Francis I/ R.J. Knecht. Cambridge; Cambridge University Press, 1982. xv, 480 p.
81-012197   944/.028/0924   0521243440
Francis -- I, -- King of France, -- 1494-1547. France -- History -- Francis I, 1515-1547. France -- Kings and rulers -- Biography.

DC114.B38 1988
Baumgartner, Frederic J.
Henry II, King of France 1547-1559/ Frederic J. Baumgartner. Durham: Duke University Press, 1988. xiv, 358 p.
87-019955   944/.028   0822307952
Henry -- II, -- King of France, -- 1519-1559. France -- History -- Henry II, 1547-1559. France - - Kings and rulers -- Biography.

DC116.5.S25 1975b
Salmon, J. H. M. 1925-
Society in crisis: France in the sixteenth century/ J. H. M. Salmon. New York: St. Martin's Press, 1975. 383 p.
75-005141   944/.028
Church and state -- France.   France -- History - - Wars of the Huguenots, 1562-1598. France -- Social conditions.

DC116.5.W66 1996
Wood, James B., 1946-
The king's army: warfare, soldiers, and society during the wars of religion in France, 1562-1576/ James B. Wood. Cambridge [England]; New York: 1996. xvi, 349 p.
95-040713   944/.029   0521550033
Charles -- IX, -- King of France, -- 1550-1574 -- Military leadership. Henry -- III, -- King of France, -- 1551-1589 -- Military leadership. France -- History -- Wars of the Huguenots, 1562-1598.

DC118.K56 1988
Kingdon, Robert McCune, 1927-
Myths about the St. Bartholomew's Day massacres, 1572-1576/ Robert M. Kingdon. Cambridge, Mass.: Harvard University Press, 1988. vi, 269 p.
87-013540   944/.029   0674598318
Saint Bartholomew's Day, Massacre of, France, 1572. Huguenots -- France -- History -- 16th century.   France -- History -- Errors, inventions, etc. France -- History -- Wars of the Huguenots, 1562-1598.

DC119.8.H44 1959
Heritier, Jean, 1892-
Catherine de Medicis/ Jean Heritier. Paris: A. Fayard, c1959. 626 p.
60-033887
Catherine de Medicis, -- Queen, consort of Henry II, King of France, -- 1519-1589.   Queens -- France -- Biography.

DC119.8.K64 1998
Knecht, R. J.
Catherine De' Medici/ R.J. Knecht. London; Longman, 1998. xiv, 340 p.
97-037451   944/.028/092. 221   0582082420
Catherine de Médicis, Queen, consort of Henry II, King of France,   Queens--France--Biography. Mothers of kings and rulers--France--Biography.

DC121.L4713 1996
Le Roy Ladurie, Emmanuel.
The Ancien Regime: a history of France, 1610-1774/ Emmanuel Le Roy Ladurie; translated by Mark Greengrass. Oxford, OX, UK; Blackwell Publishers, 1996. vii, 586 p.
95-043602   944/.03   0631170286
France -- History -- 17th century. France -- History -- 18th century. France -- Civilization -- 17th century.

DC121.3.B49213 1990
Berce, Yves Marie.
History of peasant revolts: the social origins of rebellion in early modern France/ Yves-Marie Berce; translated by Amanda Whitmore. Ithaca, N.Y.: Cornell University Press, 1990. x, 359 p.
90-053182   944/.03   0801425441
Peasant uprisings -- France.   France -- History - - Bourbons, 1589-1789.   France -- Social conditions -- 16th century.   France -- Social conditions -- 17th century.

DC121.3.B49613 1996
Berce, Yves Marie.
The birth of absolutism: a history of France, 1598-1661/ Yves-Marie Berce; translated by Richard Rex New York: St. Martin's Press, 1996. viii, 262 p.
95-031745   944/.033   0312158009
Monarchy -- France -- History -- 17th century. Religion and politics -- France -- History -- 17th century. Fronde. France -- History -- 17th century.

DC121.7.D48 1993
Dewald, Jonathan.
Aristocratic experience and the origins of modern culture: France, 1570-1715/ Jonathan Dewald. Berkeley: University of California Press, c1993. xii, 231 p.
92-006572   944/.03   0520078373
Nobility -- France -- Intellectual life. Aristocracy (Social class) in literature. Social evolution. France -- Civilization -- 17th century.

DC121.8.P4
Miller, Peter N., 1964-
Peiresc's Europe: learning and virtue in the seventeenth century/ Peter N. Miller. New Haven: Yale University Press, c2000. xv, 234 p.
00-036505   944/.032/092   0300082525
Peiresc, Nicolas Claude Fabri de, -- 1580-1637. Humanists -- France -- Biography. Statesmen -- France -- Biography. France -- Intellectual life -- 17th century. Europe -- Intellectual life -- 17th century.

DC122.B88 1984
Buisseret, David.
Henry IV/ David Buisseret. London; G. Allen & Unwin, 1984. xiv, 235 p.
83-022464   944/.031/0924   0049440128
Henry -- IV, -- King of France, -- 1553-1610. France -- History -- Henry IV, 1589-1610. France -- Kings and rulers -- Biography.

DC123.B66 1988
Bonney, Richard.
Society and government in France under Richelieu and Mazarin, 1624-61/ Richard Bonney. New York: St. Martin's Press, 1988. xiv, 247 p.
87-020290   944/.32   0312013035
Richelieu, Armand Jean du Plessis, -- duc de. -- 1585-1642.   Mazarin, Jules, -- 1602-1661. France -- Politics and government -- 1610-1643. France -- Politics and government -- 1643-1715.

DC123.T313 1975
Tapie, Victor Lucien, 1900-1974.
France in the age of Louis XIII and Richelieu [by] Victor-L. Tapie. Translated and edited by D. McN. Lockie. With a foreword by A. G. Dickens. New York, Praeger [1975] xix, 622 p.
74-008919   944/.032   0275525309
France -- History -- Louis XIII, 1610-1643.

DC123.3.R3 1963
Ranum, Orest A.
Richelieu and the councillors of Louis XIII, a study of the secretaries of state and superintendents of finance in the ministry of Richelieu, 1635-1642. Oxford [Eng.] Clarendon Press, 1963. vi, 211 p.
63-003603   944.632
Richelieu, Armand Jean du Plessis, -- duc de, -- 1585-1642.   France -- Politics and government - - 1610-1643.

DC123.3.S39 1990
Sawyer, Jeffrey K.
Printed poison: pamphlet propaganda, faction politics, and the public sphere in early seventeenth-century France/ Jeffrey K. Sawyer. Berkeley: University of California Press, c1990. xx, 178 p.
89-049051   944/.032   0520068831
Public opinion -- France -- History -- 17th century. Despotism -- France -- History -- 17th century. Pamphleteers -- France -- Political activity -- History -- 17th century. France -- History -- Louis XIII, 1610-1643 -- Pamphlets.

DC123.8.M66 1989
Moote, A. Lloyd
Louis XIII, the Just/ A. Lloyd Moote. Berkeley: University of California Press, c1989. xiv, 401 p.
88-017344   944/.032/0924   0520064852
Louis -- XIII, -- King of France, -- 1601-1643. France -- Kings and rulers -- Biography. France -- History -- Louis XIII, 1610-1643.

DC123.9.L5.H8 1959
Huxley, Aldous, 1894-1963.
Grey eminence/ Aldous Huxley. New York: Meridian Books, 1959, c1941. 342 p.
59-012139   922.244
Joseph, -- pere, -- 1577-1638.

DC123.9.R5.B4 1930
Belloc, Hilaire, 1870-1953.
Richelieu/ by Hilaire Belloc. London: E. Benn, 1930. 311 p.
30-012076   923.2
Richelieu, Armand Jean du Plessis, -- duc de, -- 1585-1642.   France -- History -- Louis XIII, 1610-1643.

DC123.9.R5.B44 1991
Bergin, Joseph, 1948-
The rise of Richelieu/ Joseph Bergin. New Haven: Yale University Press, 1991. xiii, 282 p.
90-050943   944/.032/092   0300049927
Richelieu, Armand Jean du Plessis, -- duc de, -- 1581-1642.   Statesmen -- France -- Biography. Cardinals -- France -- Biography. Political ethics -- France -- History -- 17th century. France -- History -- Louis XIII, 1610-1643.

DC123.9.R5.C5
Church, William Farr, 1912-
Richelieu and reason of state, by William F. Church. Princeton, N.J., Princeton University Press [1973, c1972] 554 p.
76-181518   944/.032/0924   0691051992
Richelieu, Armand Jean du Plessis, -- duc de, -- 1585-1642.   France -- Politics and government -- 1610-1643.

DC123.9.R5 K54 1991
Knecht, R. J.
Richelieu/ Robert Knecht. London [England]; Longman, 1991 ix, 259 p.
90-042972   944/.032/092. 220   0582557100
Richelieu, Armand Jean du Plessis, duc de, 1585-1642. Statesmen--France--Biography. Cardinals--France--Biography.

DC123.9.R5.L48 2000
Levi, Anthony.
Cardinal Richelieu and the making of France/ Anthony Levi. New York: Carroll & Graf, 2000. 327 p.
01-267748   944/.032/092   078670778X
Richelieu, Armand Jean du Plessis, -- duc de, -- 1585-1642.   Statesmen -- France -- Biography. Cardinals -- France -- Biography. France -- History -- Louis XIII, 1610-1643.

DC123.9.R5.W4
Wedgwood, C. V. 1910-
Richelieu and the French monarchy/ by C.V. Wedgwood. London: Published by Hodder & Stoughton for the English 1949. ix, 204 p.
49-049380   923.244
Richelieu, Armand Jean du Plessis, -- duc de, -- 1585-1642.

DC124.4.R36 1993
Ranum, Orest A.
The Fronde: a French revolution, 1648-1652/ Orest Ranum. New York: W.W. Norton, c1993. 386 p.
93-006816   944/.033   0393035506
Fronde. Taxation -- France -- History -- 17th century. France -- History -- Louis XIV, 1643-1715. Bordeaux (France) -- History -- Uprising, 1652-1653.

DC126.B45 1997
Beik, William, 1941-
Urban protest in seventeenth-century France: the culture of retribution/ William Beik. Cambridge; Cambridge University Press, 1997. xiii, 283 p.
96-002951   944/.033   0521573084
City and town life -- France -- History -- 17th century. Protest movements -- France -- History -- 17th century. Social conflict -- France -- History -- 17th century. France -- History -- 17th century.

DC126.L4613 2001
Le Roy Ladurie, Emmanuel.
Saint-Simon and the court of Louis XIV/ Emmanuel Le Roy Ladurie, with the collaboration of Jean-Franois Fitou;   translated by Arthur Goldhammer. Chicago: University of Chicago Press, 2001. ix, 432 p.
00-013227   944/.033.221   0226473201
Saint-Simon, Louis de Rouvroy, duc de, 1675-1755. Mémoires.

DC126.M43 1988
Mettam, Roger.
Power and faction in Louis XIV's France/ Roger Mettam. Oxford, UK; B. Blackwell, 1988. viii, 343 p.
87-011442   944/.033   0631156674
Louis -- XIV, -- King of France, -- 1638-1715. Monarchy -- France -- History -- 17th century. France -- Politics and government -- 1643-1715.

DC127.3.L68 1976
Louis XIV and Europe/ edited by Ragnhild Hatton. Columbus: Ohio State University Press, 1976. xiii, 311 p.
75-045334   320.9/44/033   0814202543
France -- Foreign relations -- 1643-1715. France -- Politics and government -- 1643-1715.

DC128.S86 1992
Sun king: the ascendancy of French culture during the reign of Louis XIV/ edited by David Lee Rubin. Washington: Folger Shakespeare Library; c1992. 242 p.
90-055041   944/.033   0918016940
Louis -- XIV, -- King of France, -- 1638-1715 -- Influence -- Congresses. Louis -- XIV, -- King of France, -- 1638-1715 -- Art patronage -- Congresses. Science and state -- France -- History -- 17th century -- Congresses. Arts, French -- Congresses. France -- Civilization -- 18th century -- Congresses. France -- Civilization -- 17th century -- Congresses. France -- Court and courtiers -- Congresses.

DC128.5.B87 1992
Burke, Peter.
The fabrication of Louis XIV/ Peter Burke. New Haven: Yale University Press, 1992. xi, 242 p.
91-011899   944/.033   0300051530
Louis -- XIV, -- King of France, -- 1638-1715 -- Public opinion. Government publicity -- France -- History -- 17th century. Public opinion -- France -- History -- 17th century.   France -- Kings and rulers -- Public opinion.

DC128.5.Z36 1997
Zanger, Abby E.
Scenes from the marriage of Louis XIV: nuptial fictions and the making of absolutist power/ Abby E. Zanger. Stanford, Calif.: Stanford University Press, 1997. xv, 244 p.
97-018467   944/.033/092   0804729778
Louis -- XIV, -- King of France, -- 1638-1715 -- Marriage. Marie Therese, -- Queen, consort of Louis XIV, King of France, -- 1638-1683 -- Marriage. Symbolism in politics -- France -- Public opinion. Public opinion -- France. Marriages of royalty and nobility in literature.

DC129.B375 1987
Bernier, Olivier.
Louis XIV: a royal life/ Olivier Bernier. Garden City, N.Y.: Doubleday, 1987. 373 p.
87-005445   944/.033/0924   0385197853
Louis -- XIV, -- King of France, -- 1638-1715. France -- History -- Louis XIV, 1643-1715. France -- Kings and rulers -- Biography. France -- Court and courtiers -- History -- 17th century.

DC129.G613 1970b
Goubert, Pierre.
Louis XIV and twenty million Frenchmen; translated [from the French] by Anne Carter. London, Allen Lane, 1970. 350 p.
76-498058   944/.033   0713901039
Louis -- XIV, -- King of France, -- 1638-1715. France -- History -- Louis XIV, 1643-1715

DC129.W6 1968
Wolf, John Baptist, 1907-
Louis XIV, by John B. Wolf. New York, Norton [1968] xix, 678 p.
67-020618   944/.033/0924
Louis -- XIV, -- King of France, -- 1638-1715.

DC130.M4.T73 1995
Treasure, G. R. R.
Mazarin: the crisis of absolutism in France/ Geoffrey Treasure. London; Routledge, 1995. xv, 413 p.
95-011451   944/.033/092   0415014573
Mazarin, Jules, -- 1602-1661.   Statesmen -- France -- Biography. Despotism -- France -- History -- 17th century. Fronde. France -- History -- Louis XIV, 1643-1715.

DC130.M8
Pitts, Vincent J. 1947-
La Grande Mademoiselle at the Court of France: 1627-1693/ Vincent J. Pitts. Baltimore; Johns Hopkins University Press, c2000. xiv, 367 p.
00-008266   944/.03/092   0801864666
Montpensier, Anne-Marie-Louise d'Orleans, -- duchesse de, -- 1627-1693.   France -- Court and courtiers -- History -- 17th century. France -- History -- Louis XIV, 1643-1715.

DC130.O73.B37 1989
Barker, Nancy Nichols.
Brother to the Sun King--Philippe, Duke of Orleans/ Nancy Nichols Barker. Baltimore: Johns Hopkins University Press, c1989. xvi, 317 p.
88-046061   944/.033/0924   080183791X
Orleans, Philippe, -- duc d', -- 1640-1701 -- Family. Louis -- XIV, -- King of France, -- 1638-1715 -- Family. Princes -- France -- Biography. France -- History -- Louis XIV, 1643-1715.

DC130.S2.A1992
Saint-Simon, Louis de Rouvroy, 1675-1755.
Historical memoirs of the duc de Saint-Simon; a shortened version. Edited and translated by Lucy Norton, with an introd. by D. W. Brogan. New York, McGraw-Hill [1968-72. v. 3 v.
67-024825   944/.033/0924   007054459X
Saint-Simon, Louis de Rouvroy, -- duc de, -- 1675-1755. Saint-Simon, Louis de Rouvroy, -- duc de, -- 1675-1755.   France -- History -- Louis XIV, 1643-1715. France -- History -- Regency, 1715-1723. France -- Court and courtiers.

DC131.B4 1967
Behrens, C. B. A.
The ancien regime [by] C. B. A. Behrens. New York] Harcourt, Brace & World [1967] 215 p.
67-011707   944/.034
France -- History -- Louis XV, 1715-1774. France -- History -- Louis XVI, 1774-1793. Europe -- History -- 18th century.

DC131.9.D85.A3413 1984
Du Pont de Nemours, Pierre Samuel, 1739-1817.
The autobiography of Du Pont de Nemours/ translated, and with an introduction by Elizabeth Fox-Genovese. Wilmington, Del.: Scholarly Resources, c1984. xviii, 298 p.
84-010645 944.04/092/4
Du Pont de Nemours, Pierre Samuel, -- 1739-1817. Du Pont family. Intellectuals -- France -- Biography. France -- History -- 18th century.

DC133.3.D37 1982
Darnton, Robert.
The literary underground of the Old Regime/ Robert Darnton. Cambridge, Mass.: Harvard University Press, 1982. ix, 258 p.
82-002918 944.04/2 0674536568
Underground literature -- France. France -- History -- Revolution, 1789-1799 -- Causes and character.

DC133.3.K8
Kunstler, Charles, 1887-
La vie quotidienne sous Louis XV. [Paris] Hachette c1953, 348 p.
54-031355
France -- Social life and customs.

DC133.4.F3713 1995
Farge, Arlette.
Subversive words: public opinion in eighteenth-century France/ Arlette Farge; translated by Rosemary Morris. University Park, Pa.: Pennsylvania State University Press, 1995. ix, 219 p.
95-114539 944/.034 0271014318
Public opinion -- France -- History -- 18th century. Communication in politics -- France -- History -- 18th century. Political participation -- France -- History -- 18th century.

DC133.4.G73 2000
Graham, Lisa Jane, 1963-
If the king only knew: seditious speech in the Reign of Louis XV/ Lisa Jane Graham. Charlottesville; University Press of Virginia, 2000. xi, 324 p.
99-046302 944/.034/092 0813919274
Louis -- XV, -- King of France, -- 1710-1774 -- Public opinion. Sedition -- France -- History -- 18th century -- Archival resources. Public opinion -- France -- History. France -- Politics and government -- 18th century -- Historiography.

DC133.4.P43 1996
Peabody, Sue.
There are no slaves in France: the political culture of race and slavery in the Ancien Regime/ Sue Peabody. New York: Oxford University Press, 1996. x, 210 p.
95-039056 305.896/044/09033 0195101987
Racism -- France -- History -- 18th century. Blacks -- Legal status, laws, etc. -- France -- History -- 18th century. Political culture -- France -- History -- 18th century. France -- Race relations -- History -- 18th century.

DC133.4.R64 1995
Rogister, John.
Louis XV and the Parlement of Paris, 1737-1755/ John Rogister. Cambridge; Cambridge University Press, 1995. xxv, 288 p.
94-010668 944/.034 0521403952
Louis -- XV, -- King of France, -- 1710-1774. Despotism -- France -- History -- 18th century. France -- Politics and government -- 1715-1774 -- Religious aspects.

DC135.C58.W66 1995
Woodbridge, John D., 1941-
Revolt in prerevolutionary France: the Prince de Conti's conspiracy against Louis XV, 1755-1757/ John D. Woodbridge. Baltimore: Johns Hopkins University Press, 1995. xvii, 242 p.
94-021460 944/.034 0801849454
Conti, Louis Francois de Bourbon, -- prince de, -- 1717-1776. Louis -- XV, -- King of France, -- 1710-1774 -- Assassination attempt, 1757. Offenses against heads of state -- France. Nobility -- France -- Biography.

DC136.5.B3413 1997
Baecque, Antoine de.
The body politic: corporeal metaphor in revolutionary France, 1770-1800/ Antoine de Baecque; translated by Charlotte Mandell. Stanford, Calif.: Stanford University Press, 1997. xvi, 363 p.
96-044516 944/.035 0804728151
Louis -- XVI, -- King of France, -- 1754-1793 -- Death and burial -- Symbolic aspects. Body, Human -- Symbolic aspects -- France. France -- Politics and government -- 18th century -- Historiography. France -- History -- Revolution, 1789-1799 -- Art and the revolution.

DC137.H37 1993
Hardman, John.
Louis XVI/ John Hardman. New Haven: Yale University Press, 1993. viii, 264 p.
92-013117 944/.035/092 0300057199
Louis -- XVI, -- King of France, -- 1754-1793. France -- Kings and rulers -- Biography. France -- History -- Louis XVI, 1774-1793. France -- History -- Revolution, 1789-1799.

DC137.08.J68
Jordan, David P., 1939-
The king's trial: the French Revolution vs. Louis XVI/ David P. Jordan. Berkeley: University of California Press, c1979. xx, 275 p.
78-054797 944/.035/0924 0520036840
Louis -- XVI, -- King of France, -- 1754-1793. France -- History -- Revolution, 1789-1799. France -- Kings and rulers -- Biography.

DC137.08.W34
Walzer, Michael,
Regicide and revolution; speeches at the trial of Louis XVI. Edited with an introd. by Michael Walzer. Translated by Marian Rothstein. [London, Cambridge University Press [1974] vii, 219 p.
73-094370 944/.035/0924 0521203708
Louis -- XVI, -- King of France, -- 1754-1793. Monarchy -- France. Regicides. France -- History -- Revolution, 1789-1799.

DC137.1.E77 1991
Erickson, Carolly, 1943-
To the scaffold: the life of Marie Antoinette/ Carolly Erickson. New York: W. Morrow and Co., c1991. 384 p.
90-045488 944/.035/092 0688073018
Marie Antoinette, -- Queen, consort of Louis XVI, King of France, -- 1755-1793. Queens -- France -- Biography. France -- History -- Louis XVI, 1774-1793.

DC137.1.L4813 2000
Lever, Evelyne.
Marie Antoinette: the last queen of France/ by Evelyne Lever; translated from the French by Catherine Temerson. New York: Farrar, Straus and Giroux, 2000. viii, 357 p.
00-028763 944/.035/092 0374199388
Marie Antoinette, -- Queen, consort of Louis XVI, King of France, -- 1755-1793. Queens -- France -- Biography. France -- History -- Louis XVI, 1774-1793.

DC137.1.S47 1981
Seward, Desmond, 1935-
Marie Antoinette/ Desmond Seward. New York: St. Martin's Press, c1981. 297 p.
81-021442 944/.035/0924 0312514670
Marie Antoinette, -- Queen, consort of Louis XVI, King of France, -- 1755-1793. Queens -- France -- Biography.

DC137.1.T5613 1997
Thomas, Chantal.
The wicked queen: the origins of the myth of Marie-Antoinette/ by Chantal Thomas; translated by Julie Rose. New York: Zone Books, 1999. 255 p.
96-050157 944/.035/092 0942299396
Marie Antoinette, -- Queen, consort of Louis XVI, King of France, -- 1755-1793. Queens -- France -- Biography. France -- History -- Revolution, 1789-1799 -- Pamphlets.

DC138.C4813 1991
Chartier, Roger, 1945-
The cultural origins of the French Revolution/ Roger Chartier; translated by Lydia G. Cochrane. Durham, N.C.: Duke University Press, 1991. xix, 238 p.
90-024404 944.04 0822309939
Politics and culture -- France -- History -- 18th century. Enlightenment -- France. Violence -- France -- History -- 18th century. France -- History -- Revolution, 1789-1799 -- Causes.

DC138.E3613
Egret, Jean.
The French prerevolution, 1787-1788/ Jean Egret; translated by Wesley D. Camp; introd. by J. F. Bosher. Chicago: University of Chicago Press, c1977. xxii, 314 p.
77-078576 944/.035 0226191427
France -- History -- Revolution, 1789-1799 -- Causes. France -- History -- Louis XVI, 1774-1793.

DC138.F813
Furet, Francois, 1927-
Interpreting the French Revolution/ Francois Furet; translated by Elborg Forster. Cambridge; Cambridge University Press; 1981. x, 204 p.
80-042290 944.04 052123574X
Cochin, Augustin, -- 1876-1916. Tocqueville, Alexis de, -- 1805-1859. France -- History -- Revolution, 1789-1799 -- Causes and character. France -- History -- Revolution, 1789-1799 -- Historiography.

DC138.M46 1990
Merrick, Jeffrey.
The desacralization of the French monarchy in the eighteenth century/ Jeffrey W. Merrick. Baton Rouge: Louisiana State University Press, c1990. xiv, 196 p.
89-013491 944.04 0807115371
Monarchy -- France -- History -- 18th century. Divine right of kings -- France -- History -- 18th century. Religion and politics -- France -- History -- 18th century. France -- History -- Revolution, 1789-1799 -- Causes.

DC138.S76 1994
Stone, Bailey, 1946-
The genesis of the French Revolution: a global-historical interpretation/ Bailey Stone. Cambridge [England]; Cambridge University Press, 1994. vii, 268 p.
93-001002   944.04   0521445566
Enlightenment. World politics -- To 1900. France -- History -- Revolution, 1789-1799 -- Causes. France -- History -- Revolution, 1789-1799 -- Influence.

DC138.S94 2000
Swenson, James.
On Jean-Jacques Rousseau: considered as one of the first authors of the Revolution/ James Swenson. Stanford, Calif.: Stanford University Press, 2000. xiii, 320 p.
99-039445   944.04   0804735557
Rousseau, Jean-Jacques, -- 1712-1778 -- Criticism and interpretation. Rousseau, Jean-Jacques, -- 1712-1778 -- Political and social views. Politics and literature -- France -- History -- 18th century. France -- History -- Revolution, 1789-1799 -- Historiography. France -- History -- Revolution, 1789-1799 -- Literature and the revolution.

DC138.T6313 1998
Tocqueville, Alexis de,
The Old Regime and the Revolution/ Alexis de Tocqueville; edited and with an introduction and critical apparatus by François Furet and Françoise Mélonio; translated by Alan S. Kahan. Chicago: University of Chicago Press, c1998-c2001. 2 v.
97-043814   944.04.221   0226805336
France -- History -- Revolution, 1789-1799 -- Causes.

DC138.T6344.H4
Herr, Richard.
Tocqueville and the old regime. Princeton, N.J., Princeton University Press, 1962. 142 p.
62-007404   944.04
Tocqueville, Alexis de, -- 1805-1859. -- L'ancien regime et la revolution.

DC141-249 History — By period — Revolutionary and Napoleonic period, 1789-1815

DC141.G5 1971
Gilchrist, John Thomas, comp.
The press in the French Revolution; a selection of documents taken from the press of the Revolution for the years 1789-1794 [compiled by] J. Gilchrist [and] W. J. Murray. [New York] St. Martin's Press [1971] xvi, 335 p.
77-150256   944.04
France -- History -- Revolution, 1789-1799 -- Sources.

DC141.R6
Roberts, J. M. 1928-
French Revolution documents. Editors: J.M. Roberts and R.C. Cobb. New York, Barnes & Noble, 1966- v.
66-006974
France -- History -- Revolution -- Sources. -- cm

DC141.3.A4.S53 1998
Shapiro, Gilbert.
Revolutionary demands: a content analysis of the Cahiers de doleances of 1789/ Gilbert Shapiro and John Markoff; with contributions by Timothy Tackett and Philip Dawson; foreword by Charles Tilly. Stanford, Calif.: Stanford University Press, 1998. xxxi, 684 p.
98-011257   944.04   0804726698
France -- History -- Revolution, 1789-1799 -- Sources. France -- History -- Revolution, 1789-1799 -- Databases.

DC143.C6
Cobban, Alfred.
Aspects of the French Revolution. New York, G. Braziller [1968] 328 p.
68-024195   944.04/08
France -- History -- Revolution, 1789-1799 -- Addresses, essays, lectures.

DC145.Y35 1993
Yalom, Marilyn.
Blood sisters: the French Revolution in women's memory/ Marilyn Yalom. New York: Basic Books, c1993. xi, 308 p.
92-054518   944.04/082   0465092632
Autobiography -- Women authors. French prose literature -- Women authors. France -- History -- Revolution, 1789-1799 -- Personal narratives, French. France -- History -- Revolution, 1789-1799 -- Women.

DC146.B756
Ballard, John R., 1957-
Continuity during the storm: Boissy d'Anglas and the era of the French Revolution/ John R. Ballard. Westport, Conn.: Greenwood Press, 2000. xi, 203 p.
99-462064   944.04/092   0313315086
Boissy d'Anglas, Francois-Antoine, -- comte de, -- 1756-1826. Revolutionaries -- France -- Biography. Legislators -- France -- Biography. France -- History -- Revolution, 1789-1799.

DC146.D2.H35 1978
Hampson, Norman.
Danton/ Norman Hampson. New York: Holmes & Meier Publishers, 1978. x, 182 p.
78-009817   944.04/092/4   0841904081
Danton, Georges Jacques, -- 1759-1794. Revolutionaries -- France -- Biography. France -- History -- Revolution, 1789-1799.

DC146.L2.G59
Gottschalk, Louis Reichenthal, 1899-1975.
Lafayette between the American and the French Revolution (1783-1789) Chicago, University of Chicago Press [1950] xi, 461 p.
50-005286   923.544
Lafayette, Marie Joseph Paul Yves Roch Gilbert Du Motier, -- marquis de, -- 1757-1834.

DC146.L2.G6
Gottschalk, Louis Reichenthal, 1899-1975.
Lafayette comes to America/ by Louis Gottschalk. Chicago, Ill.: University of Chicago Press, 1935. xiii, 184 p.
35-015130   923.544
Lafayette, Marie Joseph Paul Yves Roch Gilbert Du Motier, -- marquis de, -- 1757-1834. United States -- History -- Revolution, 1775-1783 -- Participation, French.

DC146.L2.K73 1996
Kramer, Lloyd S.
Lafayette in two worlds: public cultures and personal identities in an age of revolutions/ Lloyd Kramer. Chapel Hill, N.C.: University of North Carolina Press, c1996. xii, 354 p.
95-021113   973.3/24   0807822582
Lafayette, Marie Joseph Paul Yves Roch Gilbert Du Motier, -- marquis de, -- 1757-1834 -- Influence. Lafayette, Marie Joseph Paul Yves Roch Gilbert Du Motier, -- marquis de, -- 1757-1834 -- Relations with intellectuals. Generals -- France -- Biography. Generals -- United States -- Biography. Statesmen -- France -- Biography. United States -- History -- Revolution, 1775-1783 -- Participation, French. France -- Politics and government -- 1789-1900. France -- History -- July Revolution, 1830.

DC146.L2.N44 1991
Neely, Sylvia.
Lafayette and the liberal ideal, 1814-1824: politics and conspiracy in an age of reaction/ Sylvia Neely. Carbondale: Southern Illinois University Press, c1991. viii, 390 p.
90-025649   944.04/0920   0809317338
Lafayette, Marie Joseph Paul Yves Roch Gilbert Du Motier, -- marquis de, -- 1757-1834 -- Influence. Statesmen -- France -- Biography. France -- Politics and government -- 1814-1830.

DC146.M3.C57 1997
Conner, Clifford D., 1941-
Jean Paul Marat: scientist and revolutionary/ Clifford D. Conner. Atlantic Highlands, N.J.: Humanities Press, 1997. xiii, 285 p.
96-023026   944.04/092   0391039970
Marat, Jean Paul, -- 1743-1793. Scientists -- France -- Biography. Revolutionaries -- France -- Biography. Jacobins -- France -- Biography. France -- History -- Revolution, 1789-1799.

DC146.M7.L95 1990
Luttrell, Barbara.
Mirabeau/ Barbara Luttrell. Carbondale: Southern Illinois University Press, c1990. ix, 307 p.
90-039621   944.04/1/092   0809317052
Mirabeau, Honore-Gabriel de Riquetti, -- comte de, -- 1749-1791 -- Political and social views. Revolutionaries -- France -- Biography. France -- History -- Revolution, 1789-1791.

DC146.R6 H27 1999
Hardman, John.
Robespierre/ John Hardman. London; Longman, 1999. p. cm.
98-043327   944.04/092.221   0582287146
Robespierre, Maximilien, 1758-1794. Revolutionaries--France--Biography.

DC146.R6.J67 1985
Jordan, David P., 1939-
The revolutionary career of Maximilien Robespierre/ David P. Jordan. New York: Free Press, c1985. xii, 308 p.
85-001871   944.04   002916530X
Robespierre, Maximilien, -- 1758-1794 -- Political and social views. Revolutionaries -- France -- Biography. France -- History -- Revolution, 1789-1799.

DC146.R6.R83 1976
Rude, George F. E.
Robespierre: portrait of a Revolutionary Democrat/ George Rude. New York: Viking Press, 1976, c1975. 254 p.
75-002448   944.04/1/0924   0670601284
Robespierre, Maximilien, -- 1758-1794.

DC146.S135.H36 1991
Hampson, Norman.
Saint-Just/ Norman Hampson. Oxford, UK;
Blackwell, 1991. 245 p.
90-039891 944.04/092 063116233X
*Saint-Just, -- 1767-1794. Revolutionaries --
France -- Biography. France -- History --
Revolution, 1789-1799.*

DC146.S7.A25 2000
**Staël, Madame de (Anne-Louise-Germaine)
1766-1817.**
Ten years of exile/ Germaine de Stael; translated
by Avriel H. Goldberger. DeKalb: Northern Illinois
University Press, 2000. lvi, 271 p.
99-023994 944.04/092 0875802559
*Stael, -- Madame de -- (Anne-Louise-Germaine), --
1766-1817 -- Exile. Women authors, French --
19th century -- Biography. Women intellectuals --
France -- Biography. France -- History --
Consulate and First Empire, 1799-1815.*

DC146.S7.A6
Andrews, Wayne.
Germaine: a portrait of Madame de Stael/ Wayne
Andrews. New York: Atheneum, 1963. viii, 237 p.
63-017856 928.4
*Stael, -- Madame de -- (Anne-Louise-Germaine), --
1766-1817.*

DC147.C47
Chandler, David G.
Dictionary of the Napoleonic Wars/ David G.
Chandler; [maps and diagrs. drawn by Sheila
Waters and Hazel Watson from sketches prepared
by the author]. New York: Macmillan, c1979.
xxxvi, 570 p.
79-014124 944.04/03 0025236709
Napoleonic Wars, 1800-1815.

DC147.8.D69
Doyle, William, 1942-
Origins of the French revolution/ by William
Doyle. Oxford; Oxford University Press, 1980.
247 p.
80-040740 944.04/072 0198730209
*France -- History -- Revolution, 1789-1799 --
Historiography. France -- History -- Revolution,
1789-1799 -- Causes and character.*

DC147.8.O77 1990
Orr, Linda, 1943-
Headless history: nineteenth-century French
historiography of the Revolution/ Linda Orr.
Ithaca: Cornell University Press, 1990. xiii, 185 p.
89-022140 944.04/072 0801423791
*Historiography -- France -- History -- 19th
century. French literature -- 19th century --
History and criticism. Literature and revolutions.
France -- History -- Revolution, 1789-1799 --
Historiography. France -- Intellectual life -- 19th
century. France -- History -- Revolution, 1789-
1799 -- Influence.*

DC147.8.R37 1992
Representing the French Revolution: literature,
historiography, and art/ edited by James A.W.
Heffernan. Hanover, NH: Dartmouth College:
c1992. xv, 286 p.
91-050816 944.04 0874515653
*Public opinion -- Great Britain. France --
History -- Revolution, 1789-1799 -- Literature and
the revolution. France -- History -- Revolution,
1789-1799 -- Art and the revolution. France --
History -- Revolution, 1789-1799 -- Foreign public
opinion, British.*

DC148.B69 1988
Bosher, J. F.
The French Revolution/ J.F. Bosher. New York:
W.W. Norton, c1988. lxi, 353 p.
87-031224 944.04 0393025888
*France -- History -- Revolution, 1789-1799.
France -- History -- Revolution, 1789-1799 --
Influence.*

DC148.C388 2001
Censer, Jack Richard.
Liberty, equality, fraternity: exploring the French
Revolution/ Jack R. Censer and Lynn Hunt.
University Park, Pa.: Pennsylvania State University
Press, c2001. xiii, 212 p.
00-033653 944.04 0271020873
France -- History -- Revolution, 1789-1799.

DC148.D5313 1989
A critical dictionary of the French Revolution/
edited by Francois Furet and Mona Ozouf;
translated by Arthur Goldhammer. Cambridge,
Mass.: Belknap Press of Harvard University Press,
1989. xxii, 1063 p.
89-030656 944.04 0674177282
*France -- History -- Revolution, 1789-1799.
France -- History -- Revolution, 1789-1799 --
Historiography.*

DC148.D69 1989
Doyle, William, 1942-
The Oxford history of the French Revolution/ by
William Doyle. Oxford [England]: Clarendon
Press; 1989. x, 466 p.
88-037235 944.04/03/21 0198227817
*France -- History -- Revolution, 1789-1799.
Europe -- History -- 1789-1815.*

DC148.F7 1983 vol. 2
Bouloiseau, Marc.
The Jacobin Republic, 1792-1794/ Marc
Bouloiseau; translated by Jonathan Mandelbaum.
Cambridge [Cambridgeshire]; Cambridge
University Press; 1983. xvi, 251 p.
83-005293 944.04 s 0521247268
France -- History -- Revolution, 1789-1799.

DC148.F7 1984 vol. 3
Woronoff, Denis, 1939-
The Thermidorean regime and the directory, 1794-
1799/ Denis Woronoff; translated by Julian
Jackson. Cambridge [Cambridgeshire]; Cambridge
University Press; 1984. xxi, 207 p.
83-007672 944.04 052124725X
*France -- Politics and government -- 1789-
1799.*

DC148.F724 1991
The French Revolution in culture and society/
edited by David G. Troyansky, Alfred Cismaru,
and Norwood Andrews, Jr. New York: Greenwood
Press, 1991. xvii, 221 p.
90-047326 944.04 0313274282
*Politics and culture -- France -- History -- 18th
century. France -- History -- Revolution, 1789-
1799 -- Influence. France -- History -- Revolution,
1789-1799 -- Social aspects.*

DC148.F8713 1992
Furet, Francois, 1927-
Revolutionary France, 1770-1880/ Francois Furet;
translated by Antonia Nevill. Oxford, UK;
Blackwell, 1992. 630 p.
91-047098 944.04 0631170294
*France -- History -- Revolution, 1789-1799.
France -- History -- 19th century. France --
History -- Revolution, 1789-1799 -- Influence.*

DC148.H26
Hampson, Norman.
A social history of the French Revolution/ by
Norman Hampson. London: Routledge and K.
Paul; 1965, c1963. viii, 278 p.
64-001533
*Social classes -- France. France -- History --
Revolution, 1789-1799.*

DC148.H86 1992
Hunt, Lynn Avery.
The family romance of the French Revolution/
Lynn Hunt. Berkeley: University of California
Press, c1992 xvi, 213 p.
91-026852 944.04 0520077415
*Louis -- XVI, -- King of France, -- 1754-1793 --
Death and burial. Symbolism in politics -- France
-- History -- 18th century. Regicides. Family --
France -- History -- 18th century. France --
History -- Revolution, 1789-1799 -- Psychological
aspects.*

DC148.L413
Lefebvre, Georges, 1874-1959.
The French Revolution. Translated from the French
by Elizabeth Moss Evanson. London, Routledge &
K. Paul; 1962-64. 2 v.
64-011939 944.04
France -- History -- Revolution, 1789-1799.

DC148.R83 1988
Rude, George F. E.
The French Revolution/ George Rude. New York,
N.Y.: Weidenfeld & Nicolson, c1988. p. cm.
88-010707 944.04/072 1555841503
*France -- History -- 1789-1815. France --
History -- Revolution, 1789-1799 --
Historiography.*

DC148.S43 1989
Schama, Simon.
Citizens: a chronicle of the French Revolution/
Simon Schama. New York: Knopf: 1989. xx,
948 p.
88-045320 944.04 0394559487
France -- History -- Revolution, 1789-1799.

DC148.S5613 1975
Soboul, Albert.
The French Revolution, 1787-1799; from the
storming of the Bastille to Napoleon. Translated
from the French by Alan Forrest & Colin Jones.
New York, Random House [1975, c1974] 638 p.
74-008159 944.04 0394473922
France -- History -- Revolution, 1789-1799.

DC148.S985 1974b
Sydenham, M. J.
The first French republic, 1792-1804 [by] M. J.
Sydenham. Berkeley, University of California
Press, 1973 [i.e. 19 xi, 360 p.
73-085796 944.04 0520025776
*France -- History -- Revolution, 1789-1799.
France -- History -- Consulate and First Empire,
1799-1815.*

DC148.T683
Tocqueville, Alexis de, 1805-1859.
The European revolution & correspondence with
Gobineau/ Alexis de Tocqueville; introduced,
edited, and translated by John Lukacs. Garden
City, N.Y., Doubleday, 1959. xi, 340 p.
59-006275
*France -- History -- Revolution, 1789-1799.
Europe -- History -- 1789-1900.*

DC150.M32 1998
Margerison, Kenneth.
Pamphlets & public opinion: the campaign for a union of orders in the early French Revolution/ Kenneth Margerison. West Lafayette, Ind.: Purdue University Press, c1998. xiii, 258 p.
97-014474 944.04 1557531099
Public opinion -- France.   France -- History -- Revolution, 1789-1799 -- Pamphlets. France -- Politics and government -- 1789-1799 -- Public opinion.

DC151.A58 1997
Alder, Ken.
Engineering the Revolution: arms and Enlightenment in France, 1763-1815/ Ken Alder. Princeton, N.J.: Princeton University Press, c1997. xvi, 476 p.
96-025139 944.04 0691026718
Artillery -- Technological innovations -- France -- History -- 18th century. Military engineers -- France -- Political activity -- History -- 18th century. Enlightenment -- France -- Influence. France -- History -- Revolution, 1789-1799 -- Influence. France -- Politics and government -- 1789-1815. France -- History, Military -- 1789-1815.

DC151.B4313 1988
Bertaud, Jean Paul.
The army of the French Revolution: from citizen-soldiers to instrument of power/ Jean-Paul Bertaud; translated by R.R. Palmer. Princeton, N.J.: Princeton University Press, c1988. xvi, 382 p.
88-015098 944.04 0691055378
France -- History, Military -- 1789-1815. France -- History -- Revolution, 1789-1799 -- Influence.

DC151.F6713 1989
Forrest, Alan I.
Conscripts and deserters: the army and French society during the Revolution and Empire/ Alan Forrest. New York: Oxford University Press, 1989. viii, 294 p.
88-034568 944.04 0195059379
Napoleonic Wars, 1800-1815 -- Desertions -- France. Napoleonic Wars, 1800-1815 -- Draft resisters -- France. France -- History, Military -- 1789-1815.

DC151.F68 1990
Forrest, Alan I.
The soldiers of the French Revolution/ Alan Forrest. Durham: Duke University Press, 1990. xx, 224 p.
89-035875 944.04 0822309092
Soldiers -- France -- History -- 18th century. France -- History, Military -- 1789-1815.

DC151.H32 1990
Haythornthwaite, Philip J.
The Napoleonic source book/ Philip J. Haythornthwaite. New York: Facts on File, c1990. 414 p.
90-003392 940.2/7 0816025479
Napoleon -- I, -- Emperor of the French, -- 1769-1821 -- Military leadership -- Sources. Napoleonic Wars, 1800-1815 -- Campaigns -- Sources. Europe -- History -- 1789-1815 -- Sources. France -- History, Military -- 1789-1815 -- Sources.

DC151.M9 1998
Muir, Rory, 1962-
Tactics and the experience of battle in the age of Napoleon/ Rory Muir. New Haven, Conn.: Yale University Press, c1998. x, 342 p.
97-044386 940.2/7 0300073852
Napoleonic Wars, 1800-1815 -- Campaigns. Military art and science -- France -- History -- 19th century. Tactics.

DC151.P67 1999
Pope, Stephen.
Dictionary of the Napoleonic wars/ Stephen Pope. New York: Facts on File, 1999. 572 p.
99-048829 940.2/7 0816042438
Napoleonic Wars, 1800-1815 -- Dictionaries. France -- History, Military -- 1789-1815 -- Dictionaries.

DC152.E44 1988
Elting, John Robert.
Swords around a throne: Napoleon's Grande Armée/ John R. Elting. New York: Free Press, c1988. xiv, 769 p.
88-000348 355/.00944 0029095018
Napoleonic Wars, 1800-1815 -- Regimental histories -- France. France -- History, Military -- 1789-1815.

DC153.C66 1995
Cormack, William S.
Revolution and political conflict in the French Navy, 1789-1794/ William S. Cormack. Cambridge; Cambridge University Press, 1995. xiii, 343 p.
94-017249 944.04/1 0521472091
France -- History, Naval -- 18th century. France -- History -- Revolution, 1789-1799 -- Influence. Toulon (France) -- History -- Siege, 1793.

DC155.B76 1995
Brown, Howard G.
War, revolution, and the bureaucratic state: politics and army administration in France, 1791-1799/ Howard G. Brown. Oxford: Clarendon Press; 1995. ix, 361 p.
94-045315 944.04/2 0198205422
Civil-military relations -- France -- History -- 18th century. Organizational change -- France -- History -- 18th century. Public administration -- France -- History. France -- History -- Revolution, 1789-1799 -- Influence.

DC155.F74 1987
The French Revolution and the creation of modern political culture. Oxford; Pergamon Press, 1987-1994. 4 v.
87-016080 944.04 0080342582
Political science -- Europe -- History -- Congresses. Political culture -- Europe -- History -- 19th century -- Congresses. France -- Politics and government -- 1789-1900 -- Congresses. Europe -- Politics and government -- 1789-1900 -- Congresses. France -- History -- Revolution, 1789-1799 -- Influence -- Congresses.

DC155.S23 1990
Sa'adah, Anne.
The shaping of liberal politics in revolutionary France: a comparative perspective/ Anne Sa'adah. Princeton, N.J.: Princeton University Press, c1990. xiv, 248 p.
90-030700 320.5/1/0944 0691078246
Liberalism -- France -- History -- 18th century. Jacobins -- France -- History -- 18th century. France -- Politics and government -- 1789-1799.

DC155.W65 1994
Woloch, Isser, 1937-
The new regime: transformations of the French civic order, 1789-1820s/ Isser Woloch. New York: W.W. Norton, c1994. 536 p.
93-001917 944.04 0393035913
France -- Politics and government -- 1789-1799. Social change -- Political aspects. France -- Politics and government -- 19th century.

DC158.2.M3
McManners, John.
The French Revolution and the Church. London, S.P.C.K. for the Church Historical Society, 1969. xiv, 161 p.
70-465912 322/.1/0944 0281023352
France -- History -- Revolution, 1789-1799 -- Religious aspects -- Catholic Church. France -- Church history -- 18th century.

DC158.2.V36 1996
Van Kley, Dale K., 1941-
The religious origins of the French Revolution: from Calvin to the civil constitution, 1560-1791/ Dale K. Van Kley. New Haven, CT: Yale University Press, c1996. x, 390 p.
95-047072 944.04 0300064780
Christianity and politics -- History. Secularism -- France -- History -- 18th century. Church and state -- France -- History -- 18th century. France -- History -- Revolution, 1789-1799 -- Religious aspects. France -- Church history -- 18th century.

DC158.8.A53 2000
Andrews, Stuart.
The British periodical press and the French Revolution, 1789-99/ Stuart Andrews. Houndmills, Basingstoke, Hampshire [England]; Palgrave, 2000. xi, 280 p.
00-033321 944.04 0333738519
Press and politics -- Great Britain -- History -- 18th century. English newspapers -- History -- 18th century. Public opinion -- Great Britain -- History -- 18th century. France -- History -- Revolution, 1789-1799 -- Journalists. France -- History -- Revolution, 1789-1799 -- Foreign public opinion, British. Great Britain -- Politics and government -- 1789-1820.

DC158.8.C6 1968
Cobban, Alfred.
The social interpretation of the French Revolution. London, Cambridge U.P., 1968. xii, 178 p.
71-474746 944.04 0521095484
France -- History -- Revolution, 1789-1799. France -- Social conditions -- 18th century.

DC158.8.D37 1990
Darnton, Robert.
The kiss of Lamourette: reflections in cultural history/ Robert Darnton. New York: Norton, c1990. xxi, 393 p.
89-009431 944.04 0393027538
Civilization, Modern -- 20th century. Books and reading. France -- History -- Revolution, 1789-1799 -- Influence.

DC158.8.E57 1996
Elson Roessler, Shirley, 1942-
Out of the shadows: women and politics in the French Revolution, 1789-95/ Shirley Elson Roessler. New York: P. Lang, c1996. x, 275 p.
94-040970 944.04/082 0820425656
Women in politics -- France -- History -- 18th century. Women revolutionaries -- France -- History -- 18th century. Women's rights -- France -- History -- 18th century. France -- History -- Revolution, 1789-1799 -- Women.

DC158.8.G88 1992
Gutwirth, Madelyn.
The twilight of the goddesses: women and representation in the French revolutionary era/ Madelyn Gutwirth. New Brunswick, N.J.: Rutgers University Press, c1992. xxi, 440 p.
91-030118 944.04 0813517990
Women's rights -- France -- History -- 18th century. Sex discrimination -- France -- History -- 18th century. Women in popular culture -- France -- History -- 18th century. France -- History -- Revolution, 1789-1799 -- Women.

DC158.8.H86 1984
Hunt, Lynn Avery.
Politics, culture, and class in the French Revolution/ Lynn Hunt. Berkeley: University of California Press, c1984. xv, 251 p.
83-027528 306/.2/0944 0520052048
Politics and culture -- France -- History -- 18th century. Social classes -- France -- History -- 18th century. France -- History -- Revolution, 1789-1799 -- Social aspects.

DC158.8.K38 1985
Kates, Gary, 1952-
The Cercle social, the Girondins, and the French Revolution/ Gary Kates. Princeton, N.J.: Princeton University Press, c1985. xiv, 325 p.
84-042890 944/.3604 0691054401
Girondists. France -- History -- Revolution, 1789-1799.

DC158.8.K46 1989
Kennedy, Emmet.
A cultural history of the French Revolution/ Emmet Kennedy. New Haven: Yale University Press, c1989. xxviii, 463 p.
88-039966 944.04 0300044267
Politics and culture -- France -- History -- 18th century. France -- Cultural policy -- History -- 18th century. France -- History -- Revolution, 1789-1799 -- Influence. France -- History -- Revolution, 1789-1799 -- Social aspects.

DC158.8.R366 2000
Rapport, Michael.
Nationality and citizenship in revolutionary France: the treatment of foreigners 1789-1799/ Michael Rapport. Oxford; Clarendon, 2000. viii, 382 p.
00-710272 944.04 0198208456
Immigrants -- France -- History -- 1789-1793. France -- History -- 1789-1793.

DC158.8.R62
Roberts, J. M. 1928-
The French Revolution/ J. M. Roberts. Oxford [Eng.]; Oxford University Press, 1978. ix, 176 p.
78-040193 944.04 0192890697
France -- History -- Revolution, 1789-1799 -- Causes.

DC158.8.R8
Rude, George F. E.
The crowd in the French Revolution. Oxford, Clarendon Press, 1959. viii, 267 p.
59-001108 944.04
Crowds -- France. France -- History -- Revolution, 1789-1799 -- Economic aspects.

DC158.8.S613
Soboul, Albert.
The Parisian sans-culottes and the French Revolution, 1793-4. [English translation by Gwynne Lewis] Oxford, Clarendon Press, 1964. 280 p.
64-005298 914.4
Sansculottes. France -- History -- Reign of Terror, 1793-1794.

DC159.O9613 1988
Ozouf, Mona.
Festivals and the French Revolution/ Mona Ozouf; translated by Alan Sheridan. Cambridge, Mass.: Harvard University Press, 1988. xviii, 378 p.
87-014958 944.04 0674298837
Festivals -- France -- History -- 18th century. France -- Social life and customs -- 1789-1815. France -- History -- Revolution, 1789-1799.

DC159.R6 1960
Robiquet, Jean, 1874-
La vie quotidienne au temps de la revolution. [Paris] Hachette [1960, c1938] 256 p.
39-014318 944.04
France -- Social life and customs. France -- History -- Revolution.

DC160.K36 1995
Kaplan, Steven L.
Farewell, Revolution: the historians' feud: France, 1789/1989/ Steven Laurence Kaplan. Ithaca: Cornell University Press, 1995. xiii, 234 p.
94-044202 944.04 080143145X
French Revolution Bicentennial, 1989. Historiography -- France -- History -- 20th century. France -- History -- Revolution, 1789-1799 -- Centennial celebrations, etc. France -- History -- Revolution, 1789-1799 -- Influence. Historians -- France -- Attitudes.

DC161.C3 1934
Carlyle, Thomas, 1795-1881.
The French revolution; a history, by Thomas Carlyle. New York, The Modern library [1934] xxxi, 748 p.
34-027104 944.04
France -- History -- Revolution, 1789-1799. France -- History -- Louis XVI, 1774-1793.

DC161.M51532
Michelet, Jules, 1798-1874.
History of the French Revolution. Histoire de la Revolution francaise. Translated by Keith Botsford. Text and notes by Gerald Walter. Wynnewood, Pa., Livingston Pub. Co., 1972- v.
78-178737 944.04 0870980386
France -- History -- Revolution, 1789-1799. France -- History -- Revolution, 1789-1799 -- Causes.

DC163.J64 1988
Jones, P. M.
The peasantry in the French Revolution/ P.M. Jones. Cambridge [Cambridgeshire]; Cambridge University Press, 1988. xvi, 306 p.
88-007337 944.04 052133070X
Peasantry -- France -- History -- 18th century. Land tenure -- France -- History -- 18th century. France -- History -- Revolution, 1789-1799 -- Causes. France -- Economic conditions -- 18th century.

DC163.L413 1973
Lefebvre, Georges, 1874-1959.
The Great Fear of 1789; rural panic in revolutionary France. Introd. by George Rude. Translated from the French by Joan White. New York, Pantheon Books [1973] xvi, 234 p.
72-012379 944.04/1 0394484944
Peasantry -- France -- History -- 18th century. France -- History -- Revolution, 1789. France -- History -- Revolution, 1789-1799 -- Causes. France -- Economic conditions.

DC165.F57 1994
Fitzsimmons, Michael P., 1949-
The remaking of France: the National Assembly and the Constitution of 1791/ Michael P. Fitzsimmons. Cambridge [England]; Cambridge University Press, 1994. xvi, 273 p.
93-035732 944.04/1 0521454077
Nationalism -- France -- History -- 18th century. Political participation -- France -- History -- 18th century. France -- Politics and government -- 1789-1799 -- Citizen participation.

DC165.H35 1988
Hampson, Norman.
Prelude to terror: the Constituent Assembly and the failure of consensus, 1789-1791/ Norman Hampson. Oxford, UK; B. Blackwell, 1988. xiv, 199 p.
87-035576 944.04/1 0631152377
France -- History -- Revolution, 1789-1791. France -- Politics and government -- 1789-1799.

DC165.T33 1996
Tackett, Timothy, 1945-
Becoming a revolutionary: the deputies of the French National Assembly and the emergence of a revolutionary culture (1789-1790)/ Timothy Tackett. Princeton, N.J.: Princeton University Press, c1996. xvi, 355 p.
95-038122 944.04 0691043841
Political culture -- France -- History -- 18th century. Legislators -- France -- Attitudes. Enlightenment -- France -- Influence. France -- History -- Revolution, 1789-1799 -- Causes.

DC167.5.L8713 1997
Lusebrink, Hans-Jurgen.
The Bastille: a history of a symbol of despotism and freedom/ Hans-Jurgen Lusebrink and Rolf Reichardt; translated by Norbert Schurer. Durham: Duke University Press, 1997. xv, 304 p.
96-051990 944.04 0822318946
Liberty -- History. Symbolism in politics -- France. France -- History -- Revolution, 1789-1799 -- Influence.

DC170.A53 2000
Andress, David, 1969-
Massacre at the Champ de Mars: popular dissent and political culture in the French Revolution/ David Andress. Suffolk, UK; Royal Historical Society: 2000. x, 239 p.
00-031088 944.04 0861932471
Louis -- XVI, -- King of France, -- 1754-1793 -- Flight to Varennes, 1791. Bailly, Jean Sylvain, -- 1736-1793 -- Death and burial. France -- History -- 1789-1793 -- Atrocities.

DC177.P3 1970
Palmer, R. R. 1909-
Twelve who ruled: the year of the terror in the French Revolution/ by R.R. Palmer. -- Princeton: Princeton University Press, 1969. 417 p.
63-000003 944.04 0691007616
France -- History -- Reign of Terror, 1793-1794.

DC178.F44 1987
Feher, Ferenc, 1933-
The frozen revolution: an essay on Jacobinism/ Ferenc Feher. Cambridge [Cambridgeshire]; Cambridge University Press; 1987. viii, 178 p.
87-002976 944.04 052134283X
Jacobins -- France -- History. France -- History -- Revolution, 1789-1799 -- Societies, etc. France -- History -- Revolution, 1789-1799 -- Influence.

DC178.H54 1998
Higonnet, Patrice L. R.
Goodness beyond virtue: Jacobins during the French Revolution/ Patrice Higonnet. Cambridge, Mass.: Harvard University Press, 1998. 397 p.
98-010187 944.04 0674470613
Jacobins -- France. France -- History -- Revolution, 1789-1799 -- Societies, etc.

DC178.K45 2000
Kennedy, Michael L.
The Jacobin clubs in the French Revolution, 1793-1795/ Michael L. Kennedy. New York; Berghahn Books, 2000. 312 p.
99-025697 944.004/3 1571811869
Jacobins -- France. France -- History -- Revolution, 1789-1799 -- Societies, etc. France -- History -- Reign of Terror, 1793-1794.

DC183.5.M35 2000
Mayer, Arno J.
The furies: violence and terror in the French and Russian Revolutions/ Arno J. Mayer. Princeton, N.J.: Princeton University Press, 2000. xvii, 716 p.
99-045096 944.04 0691048975
Political violence -- France. Political violence -- Soviet Union. Terror -- Soviet Union. Soviet Union -- History -- Revolution, 1917-1921 -- Influence. France -- History -- Reign of Terror, 1793-1794. France -- History -- Revolution, 1789-1799 -- Influence.

DC183.5.S58 1994
Slavin, Morris, 1913-
The Hebertistes to the guillotine: anatomy of a "conspiracy" in revolutionary France/ Morris Slavin. Baton Rouge: Louisiana State University Press, c1994. xvii, 280 p.
93-045300 944.04 0807118389
Hebert, Jacques-Rene, -- 1757-1794 -- Death and burial. Revolutionaries -- France -- Death. Guillotine. France -- Politics and government -- 1789-1799. France -- History -- Revolution, 1789-1799 -- Societies, etc.

DC184.C613 1987
Cobb, Richard, 1917-
The people's armies: the armees revolutionnaires, instrument of the terror in the departments, April 1793 to floreal year II/ Richard Cobb; translated by Marianne Elliott. New Haven: Yale University Press, 1987. xiv, 776 p.
87-010641 944.04/2 0300027281
France -- History -- Revolution, 1789-1799.

DC186.L9
Lyons, Martyn.
France under the directory/ Martyn Lyons. Cambridge [Eng.]; Cambridge University Press, 1975. x, 259 p.
76-351309 944.04/5 0521207851.
France -- History -- Directory, 1795-1799.

DC187.8.R67 1978
Rose, R. B.
Gracchus Babeuf: the first revolutionary Communist/ R. B. Rose. Stanford, Calif.: Stanford University Press, 1978. viii, 434 p.
76-054099 944.04/092/4 0804709491
Babeuf, Gracchus, -- 1760-1797. Revolutionaries -- France -- Biography.

DC194.S52 1993
Shapiro, Barry M.
Revolutionary justice in Paris, 1789-1790/ Barry M. Shapiro. Cambridge [England]; Cambridge University Press, 1993. xvii, 302 p.
92-010280 944.04/1 0521415985
Humanitarianism -- Political aspects. Conspiracies -- France -- Paris -- History -- 18th century. Justice, Administration of -- France -- Paris -- History -- 18th century. Paris (France) -- History -- 1789-1799.

DC195.A625.F67 1996
Forrest, Alan I.
The Revolution in provincial France: Aquitaine, 1789-1799/ Alan Forrest. Oxford: Clarendon Press; 1996. vi, 377 p.
96-005762 944/.7 019820616X
Aquitaine (France) -- History. France -- History -- Revolution, 1789-1799.

DC195.B6.F67
Forrest, Alan I.
Society and politics in revolutionary Bordeaux/ by Alan Forrest. London; Oxford University Press, 1975. 300 p.
75-322598 944/.71 0198218591
Bordeaux (France) -- Politics and government. Bordeaux (France) -- Social conditions. France -- History -- Revolution, 1789-1799.

DC195.C2.H36 1989
Hanson, Paul R., 1952-
Provincial politics in the French Revolution: Caen and Limoges, 1789-1794/ Paul R. Hanson. Baton Rouge: Louisiana State University Press, c1989. xviii, 273 p.
89-008156 944/.22 0807115207
Caen (France) -- Politics and government. Limoges (France) -- Politics and government. France -- History -- Revolution, 1789-1799.

DC195.L9.E36 1990
Edmonds, W. D.
Jacobinism and the revolt of Lyon, 1789-1793/ W.D. Edmonds. Oxford [England]: Clarendon Press; 1990. xi, 349 p.
89-025477 944.04 0198227493
Jacobins -- France -- Lyon -- History -- 18th century. France -- History -- Revolution, 1789-1799. Lyon (France) -- History.

DC195.S56.R36 1991
Ramsay, Clay.
The ideology of the Great Fear: the Soissonnais in 1789/ Clay Ramsay. Baltimore: Johns Hopkins University Press, c1992. xxxi, 311 p.
91-017665 944/.345 0801841976
Rumor -- France -- Soissons Region. Fear -- France -- Soissons Region -- History -- 18th century. Peasant uprisings -- France -- Soissons Region -- History -- 18th century. France -- History -- Revolution, 1789. Soissons Region (France) -- History. Soissons Region (France) -- Militia -- History.

DC195.T8.H86
Hunt, Lynn Avery.
Revolution and urban politics in Provincial France: Troyes and Reims, 1786-1790/ Lynn Avery Hunt. Stanford, Calif.: Stanford University Press, 1978. viii, 187 p.
76-048016 944.04/1 0804709408
France -- History -- Revolution, 1789-1799. Troyes (France) -- Politics and government. Reims (France) -- Politics and government.

DC201.B4713
Bergeron, Louis, 1929-
France under Napoleon/ by Louis Bergeron; translated by R.R. Palmer. Princeton, N.J.: Princeton University Press, c1981. xiv, 230 p.
81-004549 944.05 0691053332
France -- History -- Consulate and First Empire, 1799-1815.

DC201.D4
Deutsch, Harold C.
The genesis of Napoleonic imperialism, by Harold C. Deutsch. Cambridge, Harvard University Press; 1938. xxi, 460 p.
38-002656 327.44
Napoleon -- I, -- Emperor of the French, -- 1769-1821. Imperialism. France -- History -- Consulate and First Empire, 1799-1815.

DC201.L96 1994
Lyons, Martyn.
Napoleon Bonaparte and the legacy of the French Revolution/ Martyn Lyons. New York: St. Martin's Press, 1994. xiv, 344 p.
93-044280 944.05/092 0312121229
Napoleon -- I, -- Emperor of the French, -- 1769-1821. Napoleonic Wars, 1800-1815. France -- History -- Consulate and First Empire, 1799-1815. France -- History -- Revolution, 1789-1799 -- Influence.

DC203.C9 1972
Cronin, Vincent.
Napoleon Bonaparte; an intimate biography. New York, Morrow, 1972 [c1971] 480 p.
72-166356 944.05/092/4
Napoleon -- I, -- Emperor of the French, -- 1769-1821.

DC203.T53 1952a
Thompson, J. M. 1878-1956.
Napoleon Bonapate. New York, Oxford University Press, 1952. ix, 463 p.
52-009576 923.144
Napoleon -- I, -- Emperor of the French, -- 1769-1821.

DC203.9.C647 1987
Connelly, Owen, 1929-
Blundering to glory: Napoleon's military campaigns/ Owen Connelly. Wilmington, Del.: Scholarly Resources, 1987. x, 250 p.
87-009507 940.2/7 0842022317
Napoleon -- I, -- Emperor of the French, -- 1769-1821 -- Military leadership. Napoleonic Wars, 1800-1815 -- Campaigns. Military art and science -- France -- History -- 18th century. Military art and science -- France -- History -- 19th century.

DC203.9.W785 2001
Woloch, Isser, 1937-
Napoleon and his collaborators: the making of a dictatorship/ Isser Woloch. New York: W.W. Norton, c2001. xv, 281 p.
00-062230 944.05/092 0393050092
Napoleon -- I, -- Emperor of the French -- 1769-1821 -- Friends and associates. Dictatorship -- France. France -- Politics and government -- 1789-1815. France -- Officials and employees -- Biography.

DC213.H6
Napoleon I, Emperor of the French, 1769-1821. 1769-1821.
Letters and documents. Selected and translated by John Eldred Howard. New York, Oxford University Press, 1961- v.
61-004572 923.144

DC214.H4 1969
Napoleon I, Emperor of the French, 1769-1821. 1769-1821.
The mind of Napoleon; a selection from his written and spoken words, edited and translated by J. Christopher Herold. New York, Columbia University Press, [1969, c1955] xxxix, 322 p.
55-009068   308.1

DC216.1.K55
Knapton, Ernest John.
Empress Josephine/ Ernest John Knapton. Cambridge, Mass.: Harvard University Press, 1963. xiii, 359 p.
63-017203   923.144
Josephine, -- Empress, consort of Napoleon I, Emperor of the French, -- 1763-1814.

DC225.L55 1973
Lloyd, Christopher, 1906-
The Nile Campaign: Nelson and Napoleon in Egypt. Newton Abbot, David and Charles; 1973. 120 p.
73-159590   940.2/7   0064843372
Nelson, Horatio Nelson, -- Viscount, -- 1758-1805. Napoleonic Wars, 1800-1815 -- Campaigns -- Egypt. Egypt -- History -- French occupation, 1798-1801.

DC226.6.P362.G35 1993
Gallaher, John G.
Napoleon's Irish legion/ John G. Gallaher. Carbondale [Ill.]: Southern Illinois University Press, c1993. xi, 281 p.
92-018518   940.2/7   0809318253
Napoleonic Wars, 1800-1815 -- Participation, Irish. France -- History, Military -- 1789-1815. Ireland -- History, Military.

DC226.6.P362.H34 1992
Hall, Christopher D. 1950-
British strategy in the Napoleonic war, 1803-15/ Christopher D. Hall. Manchester; Manchester University Press; c1992. xii, 239 p.
91-036489   940.2/7   0719036062
Napoleonic Wars, 1800-1815 -- Participation, British. Strategy -- History -- 19th century. Great Britain -- History, Military -- 1789-1820. France -- History, Military -- 1789-1815.

DC227.F57 1992
Flayhart, William H., 1944-
Counterpoint to Trafalgar: the Anglo-Russian invasion of Naples, 1805-1806/ William Henry Flayhart III. Columbia: University of South Carolina Press, c1992. xi, 198 p.
92-009696   940.2/7   0872498247
Napoleonic Wars, 1800-1815 -- Campaigns -- Italy. Trafalgar, Battle of, 1805. France -- Foreign relations -- Europe. Europe -- Foreign relations -- France. Europe -- History, Military -- 1789-1815.

DC232.M85 1996
Muir, Rory, 1962-
Britain and the defeat of Napoleon, 1807-1815/ Rory Muir. New Haven: Yale University Press, 1996. xiv, 466 p.
95-032097   940.2/7   0300064438
Wellington, Arthur Wellesley, -- Duke of, -- 1769-1852 -- Military leadership. Peninsular War, 1807-1814 -- Campaigns -- Participation, British. Waterloo, Battle of, 1815. Military art and science. Great Britain -- Foreign relations -- 1800-1837.

DC234.A76 1990
Arnold, James R.
Crisis on the Danube: Napoleon's Austrian campaign of 1809/ James R. Arnold. New York: Paragon House, 1990. xiii, 286 p.
89-072195   940.2/7   1557781370
Napoleonic Wars, 1800-1815 -- Campaigns -- Austria. Napoleonic Wars, 1800-1815 -- Campaigns -- Germany -- Bavaria. Napoleonic Wars, 1800-1815 -- Diplomatic history. France -- History, Military.

DC234.A77 1995
Arnold, James R.
Napoleon conquers Austria: the 1809 campaign for Vienna/ James R. Arnold. Westport, Conn.: Praeger, 1995. vi, 247 p.
94-044177   940.2/7   0275946940
Napoleon -- I, -- Emperor of the French, -- 1769-1821 -- Military leadership. Napoleonic Wars, 1800-1815 -- Campaigns -- Austria -- Vienna. France -- History, Military. Vienna (Austria) -- History, Military.

DC234.8.E67 1994
Epstein, Robert M.
Napoleon's last victory and the emergence of modern war/ Robert M. Epstein; foreword by Russell F. Weigley. Lawrence, Kan.: University Press of Kansas, c1994. xv, 215 p.
93-038243   940.2/7   0700606645
Napoleon -- I, -- Emperor of the French, -- 1769-1821 -- Military leadership. Wagram, Battle of, 1809. Napoleonic Wars, 1800-1815 -- Campaigns -- Austria. Military art and science -- France -- History -- 19th century.

DC235.R43 1990
Riehn, Richard K., 1928-
1812: Napoleon's Russian campaign/ Richard K. Riehn. New York: McGraw-Hill, c1990. ix, 525 p.
89-028432   940.2/7   0070527318
Napoleon -- I, -- Emperor of the French, -- 1769-1821 -- Military leadership. Napoleonic Wars, 1800-1815 -- Campaigns -- Russia. Russia -- History, Military -- 1801-1917.

DC235.T32 1971
Tarle, Evgenii Viktorovich, 1874-1955.
Napoleon's invasion of Russia, 1812 [by] Eugene Tarle. New York, Octagon Books, 1971 [c1942] 422 p.
77-120670   940.2/7
Napoleon -- I, -- Emperor of the French, -- 1769-1821 -- Invasion of Russia, 1812.

DC236.R55 2000
Riley, J. P.
Napoleon and the World War of 1813: lessons in coalition warfighting/ J.P. Riley. London; F. Cass, 2000. xiv, 480 p.
99-016266   940.2/7   0714648930
Napoleon -- I, -- Emperor of the French, -- 1769-1821 -- Military leadership. Napoleonic Wars, 1800-1815 -- Diplomatic history. Wars of Liberation, 1813-1814. France -- Foreign relations -- 1792-1815. France -- Colonies -- North America.

DC238.M32 1982
MacKenzie, Norman Ian.
The escape from Elba: the fall and flight of Napoleon, 1814-1815/ Norman MacKenzie. New York: Oxford University Press, 1982. xv, 299 p.
81-018672   944.05   0192158635
Napoleon, -- I, -- Emperor of the French, -- 1769-1821 -- Elba and the Hundred Days, 1814-1815.

DC239.A44 1991
Alexander, R. S., 1954-
Bonapartism and revolutionary tradition in France: the federes of 1815/ R.S. Alexander. Cambridge [England]; Cambridge University Press, 1991. xii, 314 p.
90-001856   944.05   0521361125
Napoleon -- I, -- Emperor of the French, -- 1769-1821 -- Elba and the Hundred Days, 1814-1815. France -- History -- Consulate and First Empire, 1799-1815.

DC239.S36 1992
Schom, Alan.
One hundred days: Napoleon's road to Waterloo/ Alan Schom. New York: Atheneum: 1992. xv, 398 p.
92-004249   944.05   0689120974
Napoleon -- I, -- Emperor of the French, -- 1769-1821 -- Elba and the Hundred Days, 1814-1815. Waterloo, Battle of, 1815.

DC249.N5 1946
Nicolson, Harold George, 1886-1968.
The Congress of Vienna, a study in allied unity: 1812-1822, by Harold Nicolson. London, Constable & co. ltd. [1946] xiii, 312 p.
46-021112   940.27
Europe -- Politics -- 1789-1815.

DC251-354.8 History — By period — 19th century

DC251.B8 1969
Bury, J. P. T. 1908-
France, 1814-1940 [by] J. P. T. Bury. London, Methuen, 1969. xii, 348 p.
77-374947   944   0416122604
France -- History -- 1789-1900. France -- History -- Third Republic, 1870-1940.

DC252.A46 1993
Aminzade, Ronald, 1949-
Ballots and barricades: class formation and republican politics in France, 1830-1871/ Ronald Aminzade. Princeton, N.J.: Princeton University Press, c1993. xiv, 321 p.
93-018279   944.06   0691094799
Social history. Republicanism -- France -- History -- 19th century. Revolutions -- France -- History -- 19th century. Rouen (France) -- Social conditions. France -- Politics and government -- 19th century. Toulouse (France) -- Social conditions.

DC252.P53 1995
Pilbeam, Pamela M., 1941-
Republicanism in nineteenth-century France, 1814-1871/ Pamela M. Pilbeam. New York: St. Martin's Press, 1995. xii, 370 p.
94-030651   944.06   0312124201
Republicanism -- France -- History -- 19th century. Revolutions -- France -- History -- 19th century. France -- Politics and government -- 1789-1900.

DC252.R38 1997
Reddy, William M.
The invisible code: honor and sentiment in postrevolutionary France, 1814-1848/ William M. Reddy. Berkeley: University of California Press, c1997. xv, 258 p.
96-021675   944.04   0520205367
Honor -- France -- History -- 19th century. Women and democracy -- France -- History -- 19th century. France -- Social conditions -- 19th century. France -- History -- Revolution, 1789-1799 -- Influence.

DC255.C4.A43 1961a
Chateaubriand, Francois-Rene, 1768-1848.
The memoirs of Chateaubriand. Selected, translated, and with an introd., by Robert Baldick. New York, Knopf, 1961. xxii, 394 p.
61-017387   928.4
Chateaubriand, Francois-Rene, -- vicomte de, -- 1768-1848.

DC255.G8.J6
Johnson, Douglas W. J.
Guizot; aspects of French history, 1787-1874. London, Routledge & K. Paul, 1963. ix, 469 p.
63-005018
Guizot, -- M., -- 1787-1874.

DC255.S5.B47
Bertocci, Philip A., 1940-
Jules Simon: Republican anticlericalism and cultural politics in France, 1848-1886/ Philip A. Bertocci. Columbia: University of Missouri Press, 1978. vi, 247 p.
77-014668   320.5   082620239X
Simon, Jules, -- 1814-1896.   Anti-clericalism -- France.   France -- Politics and government -- 19th century.

DC255.T3.B7
Brinton, Crane, 1898-1968.
The lives of Talleyrand. New York, W. W. Norton & company, inc. [c1936] 316 p.
36-022597
Talleyrand-Perigord, Charles Maurice de, -- prince de Benevent, -- 1754-1838.

DC256.H57 1987
Historical dictionary of France from the 1815 restoration to the Second Empire/ edited by Edgar Leon Newman; Robert Lawrence Simpson, assistant editor. New York: Greenwood Press, c1987. 2 v.
85-017728   944.06/03/21   0313227519
France -- History -- Restoration, 1814-1830 -- Dictionaries. France -- History -- Louis Philip, 1830-1848 -- Dictionaries. France -- History -- Second Republic, 1848-1852 -- Dictionaries.

DC256.8.K76 2000
Kroen, Sheryl, 1961-
Politics and theater: the crisis of legitimacy in restoration France, 1815-1830/ Sheryl Kroen. Berkeley: University of California Press, c2000. xiv, 394 p.
99-048330   944.06   0520222148
Moliere, 1622-1673. -- Tartuffe -- Influence. Legitimacy of governments -- France. Monarchy -- France -- History -- 19th century. Democracy -- France -- History -- 19th century. France -- History -- Restoration, 1814-1830 -- Political aspects. France -- History -- July Revolution, 1830 -- Theater and the revolution.

DC256.8.S66 1987
Spitzer, Alan B. 1925-
The French generation of 1820/ Alan B. Spitzer. Princeton, N.J.: Princeton University Press, c1987. xvi, 335 p.
86-025471   944.06   0691054967
Generations -- France -- History -- 19th century. France -- History -- Restoration, 1814-1830. France -- Intellectual life -- 19th century. France -- Social conditions -- 19th century.

DC261.P56
Pinkney, David H.
The French revolution of 1830, by David H. Pinkney. [Princeton] N.J., Princeton University Press [1972] ix, 397 p.
72-039051   944.07   0691052026
France -- History -- July Revolution, 1830.

DC266.5.C68 1988
Collingham, H. A. C., 1947-1986.
The July monarchy: a political history of France, 1830-1848/ H.A.C. Collingham; with R.S. Alexander. London; Longman, 1988. xii, 468 p.
87-024490   944.06   0582021863
France -- Politics and government -- 1830-1848.

DC270.T652 1949
Tocqueville, Alexis de, 1805-1859.
Recollections. Translated by Alexander Teixeira de Mattos. Edited with many additions from the original text and an introd. by J. P. Mayer. New York, Columbia University Press, 1949. xxvi, 331 p.
49-050219   944.07
Tocqueville, Alexis de, -- 1805-1859.   Historians -- France -- Biography.   France -- History -- February Revolution, 1848.

DC270.T6559.S47 1988
Shiner, L. E. 1934-
The secret mirror: literary form and history in Tocqueville's Recollections/ L.E. Shiner. Ithaca: Cornell University Press, 1988. xvii, 224 p.
88-003679   944.07/092/4   0801421500
Tocqueville, Alexis de, -- 1805-1859. -- Souvenirs. Tocqueville, Alexis de, -- 1805-1859 -- Literary art. Autobiography. Literature and history -- France. France -- History -- February Revolution, 1848 -- Historiography.

DC271.L9.S74 1984
Stewart, Mary Lynn, 1945-
The artisan republic: revolution, reaction, and resistance in Lyon, 1848-1851/ Mary Lynn Stewart-McDougall. Kingston: McGill-Queen's University Press; 1984. xix, 211 p.
85-167713   944/.582307   0773504265
Lyon (France) -- History. France -- History -- February Revolution, 1848. France -- History -- Second Republic, 1848-1852.

DC272.A3513 1983
Agulhon, Maurice.
The Republican experiment, 1848-1852/ Maurice Agulhon; translated by Janet Lloyd. Cambridge [Cambridgeshire]; Cambridge University Press; 1983. xiv, 211 p.
82-023461   944.07   0521248299
France -- History -- Second Republic, 1848-1852.

DC272.5.M42
Merriman, John M.
The agony of the Republic: the repression of the left in revolutionary France, 1848-1851/ John M. Merriman. New Haven: Yale University Press, 1978. xxxvi, 298 p.
77-010434   320.9/44/07   0300021518
Radicalism -- France -- History.   France -- Politics and government -- 1848-1852.

DC273.6.J46
Jennings, Lawrence C.
France and Europe in 1848: a study of French foreign affairs in time of crisis, [by] Lawrence C. Jennings. Oxford, Clarendon Press, 1973. ix, 280 p.
73-173775   327.44/04   0198225148
France -- History -- Second Republic, 1848-1852. France -- Foreign relations -- Europe. Europe -- Foreign relations -- France.

DC274.M35
Marx, Karl, 1818-1883.
The eighteenth Brumaire of Louis Bonaparte, by Karl Marx; with explanatory notes. New York, International Publishers [1935] 128 p.
38-012871   944.07
France -- History -- Coup d'etat, 1851. France -- Politics and government -- 1848-1852. France -- History -- February Revolution, 1848.

DC276.5.B34 2000
Baguley, David.
Napoleon III and his regime: an extravaganza/ David Baguley. Baton Rouge: Louisiana State University Press, 2000. xxii, 425 p.
00-040573   944.07   0807126241
Napoleon -- III, -- Emperor of the French, -- 1808-1873 -- In literature. Napoleon -- III, -- Emperor of the French, -- 1808-1873 -- In art. Symbolism in politics.   France -- History -- Second Empire, 1852-1870 -- Sources.

DC276.5.C35
Campbell, Stuart L., 1938-
The Second Empire revisited: a study in French historiography/ Stuart L. Campbell. New Brunswick, N.J.: Rutgers University Press, c1978. xv, 231 p.
77-020247   944.07/07/2   0813508568
France -- History -- Second Empire, 1852-1870 -- Historiography.

DC277.E27 1983
Echard, William E., 1931-
Napoleon III and the Concert of Europe/ William E. Echard. Baton Rouge: Louisiana State University Press, c1983. xiv, 327 p.
82-012660   944.07   0807110566
Napoleon -- III, -- Emperor of the French, -- 1808-1873. Concert of Europe. France -- Foreign relations -- 1848-1870.

DC277.H39 1998
Hazareesingh, Sudhir.
From subject to citizen: the Second Empire and the emergence of modern French democracy/ Sudhir Hazareesingh. Princeton, N.J.: Princeton University Press, c1998. xiii, 393 p.
97-044318   944.07   0691016992
Political culture -- France -- History -- 19th century. Democracy -- France -- History -- 19th century. France -- History -- Second Empire, 1852-1870.

DC278.T78 1997
Truesdell, Matthew.
Spectacular politics: Louis-Napoleon Bonaparte and the Fete imperiale, 1849-1870/ Matthew Truesdell. New York: Oxford University Press, 1997. x, 238 p.
96-027986   944.07   019510689X
Napoleon -- III, -- Emperor of the French, -- 1808-1873 -- Influence. Symbolism in politics. Mass media and public opinion -- France -- History -- 19th century. Rites and ceremonies -- France -- History -- 19th century. France -- Cultural policy. France -- Politics and government -- 1848-1870 -- Social aspects.

DC280.C6
Corley, T. A. B. 1923-
Democratic despot; a life of Napoleon III. London, Barrie and Rockliff [1961] xi, 402 p.
61-066635
Napoleon -- III, -- Emperor of the French, -- 1808-1873.

DC280.S6 1968
Simpson, F. A. b. 1883.
The rise of Louis Napoleon, by F. A. Simpson. London, Cass, 1968. xvii, 400 p.
77-403534   944.07/0924
Napoleon -- III, -- Emperor of the French, -- 1808-1873. Napoleon -- III, -- Emperor of the French, -- 1808-1873 -- Bibliography.   France -- Politics and government -- 1830-1848. Europe -- Politics and government -- 1815-1848.

DC280.4.G6
Gooch, G. P. 1873-1968.
The Second Empire. [London] Longmans, [1960] 324 p.
60-003451   944.07
Napoleon -- III, -- Emperor of the French, -- 1808-1873.   France -- History -- Second Empire, 1852-1870.

DC280.5.H3.C5 1957
Chapman, Joan Margaret.
The life and times of Baron Haussmann; Paris in the second empire [by] J. M. and Brian Chapman. London, Weidenfeld and Nicolson [1957] 262 p.
57-059325
Haussmann, Georges Eugene, -- baron, -- 1809-1891.   City planning -- Paris.   Paris (France) -- City planning.

DC280.5.M67.C6713 1992
Corbin, Alain.
The village of cannibals: rage and murder in France, 1870/ Alain Corbin; translated by Arthur Goldhammer.   Cambridge,   Mass.:   Harvard University Press, 1992. 164 p.
91-033028   944/.72   067493900X
Moneys, Alain de, -- d. 1870 -- Assassination. Franco-Prussian War, 1870-1871 -- Atrocities. Nobility -- France -- Hautefaye -- Biography. Hautefaye (France) -- History.

DC292.S7
Steefel, Lawrence Dinkelspiel, 1894-
Bismarck, the Hohenzollern candidacy, and the origins of the Franco-German War of 1870. Cambridge, Harvard University Press, 1962. xi, 281 p.
62-013271   943.082
Bismarck, Otto, -- Furst von, -- 1815-1898. Franco-Prussian War, 1870-1871 -- Causes.

DC304.5.W55 1993
Williams, Roger Lawrence, 1923-
Napoleon III and the Stoeffel Affair/ Roger L. Williams Worland, Wyo.: High Plains Pub. Co., c1993. xv, 219 p.
93-077109   1881019039
Napoleon -- III, -- Emperor of the French, -- 1808-1873 -- Military leadership. Stoffel, Eugene-Georges-Henri-Celeste, -- baron, -- 1821-1907. Bazaine, Achille Francois, -- 1811-1888 -- Trials, litigation, etc. Trials (Treason) -- France -- Versailles. Franco-Prussian War, 1870-1871 -- Psychological aspects. France -- History, Military -- 19th century. France -- Politics and government -- 1870-1940.

DC312.M3 1940
Marx, Karl, 1818-1883.
The civil war in France/ Karl Marx; with an introd. by Frederick Engles. New York: International publishers, c1940. 96 p.
40-035820
Paris (France) -- Siege, 1870-1871. Paris (France) -- History -- Commune, 1871.

DC316.C47 1994
Christiansen, Rupert.
Paris Babylon: the story of the Paris Commune/ Rupert Christiansen. New York, N.Y., U.S.A.: Viking, c1994. ix, 434 p.
94-032711   944.081/2   067083131X
Franco-Prussian War, 1870-1871 -- Influence. Paris (France) -- Moral conditions -- History -- 19th century. Paris (France) -- History -- Commune, 1871 -- Causes.

DC317.T66 1981
Tombs, Robert.
The war against Paris, 1871/ Robert Tombs. Cambridge; Cambridge University Press, 1981. xii, 256 p.
80-042024   944/.36081   0521235510
Paris (France) -- History -- Commune, 1871. France -- History, Military -- 19th century.

DC325.M55 2000
Milner, John, 1946-
Art, war and revolution in France, 1870-1871: myth, reportage and reality/ John Milner. New Haven: Yale University Press, c2000. xi, 243 p.
00-023891   943.082   0300084072
Franco-Prussian War, 1870-1871 -- Influence. Franco-Prussian War, 1870-1871 -- Art and the war. Propaganda, Anti-German -- France. Paris (France) -- History -- Commune, 1871 -- Press coverage.

DC330.Z44
Zeldin, Theodore, 1933-
France, 1848-1945, by Theodore Zeldin. Oxford, Clarendon Press, 1973-77. 2 v.
73-180595   944.081   0198221045
France -- Civilization -- 1830-1900. France -- Civilization -- 1901-1945.

DC335.A3813 1993
Agulhon, Maurice.
The French Republic, 1879-1992/ Maurice Agulhon; translated by Antonia Nevill. Oxford, UK; B. Blackwell, 1993. vii, 582 p.
92-045622   944.08   0631170316
France -- History -- Third Republic, 1870-1940. France -- History -- 20th century. France -- Politics and government -- 1870-1940.

DC335.B75 1966
Brogan, D. W. 1900-1974.
The development of modern France, 1870-1939 [by] D. W. Brogan. New York, Harper & Row [1966] 2 v.
66-002183   944.08
France -- History -- Third Republic, 1870-1940. France -- Politics and government -- 1870-1940.

DC335.S4
Sedgwick, Alexander, 1930-
The Third French Republic, 1870-1914.   New York, Crowell [c1968] x, 148 p.
68-013384   944.081
France -- History -- Third Republic, 1870-1940.

DC335.S66 2000
Sowerwine, Charles,
France since 1870: culture, politics and society/ Charles Sowerwine. New York: St. Martin's Press, 2000. p. cm.
00-034522   944.081.221   033365837X
France -- History -- Third Republic, 1870-1940. France -- Politics and government -- 20th century. France -- History, Military -- 20th century.

DC337.J6
Joll, James.
The decline of the Third Republic.   New York, Praeger [1959] 127 p.
59-007824
France -- History -- Third Republic, 1870-1940.

DC338.S48 1968
Shattuck, Roger.
The banquet years; the origins of the avant garde in France, 1885 to World War I: Alfred Jarry, Henri Rousseau, Erik Satie [and] Guillaume Apollinaire. New York, Vintage Books [1968] xiv, 397 p.
68-012411   914.4/03/810922
Jarry, Alfred, -- 1873-1907. Rousseau, Henri Julien Felix, -- 1844-1910. Satie, Erik, -- 1866-1925.   France -- Intellectual life.

DC340.K26 1992
Kale, Steven D., 1957-
Legitimism and the reconstruction of French society, 1852-1883/ Steven D. Kale. Baton Rouge: Louisiana State University Press, c1992. xviii, 374 p.
92-009297   944.06   0807117277
Royalists -- France -- History -- 19th century. France -- Social conditions -- 19th century. France -- Politics and government -- 19th century. France -- Kings and rulers -- Succession.

DC340.L6
Locke, Robert R., 1932-
French legitimists and the politics of moral order in the early Third Republic [by] Robert R. Locke. Princeton, N.J., Princeton University Press [1974] x, 321 p.
73-017404   320.9/44/081   0691052158
Right and left (Political science)   France -- Politics and government -- 1870-1940.

DC340.N67 1995
Nord, Philip G., 1950-
The republican moment: struggles for democracy in nineteenth-century France/ Philip Nord. Cambridge, Mass.: Harvard University Press, 1995. 321 p.
95-010445   944.07   0674762711
Republicanism -- France -- History -- 19th century. Middle class -- France -- Political activity. Elite (Social sciences) -- France -- Attitudes. France -- Politics and government -- 1870-1940. France -- History -- Third Republic, 1870-1940.

DC341.K44 1983
Keiger, John F. V.
France and the origins of the first World War/ John F.V. Keiger. New York: St. Martin's Press, 1983. vii, 201 p.
83-008660   327.73   0312302924
World War, 1914-1918 -- Causes.   France -- Foreign relations -- 1870-1940.

DC342.B56 1990
Biographical dictionary of French political leaders since 1870/ edited by David S. Bell, Douglas Johnson, Peter Morris. New York: Simon & Schuster, c1990. xxix, 463 p.
90-009662   944.08/092/2   0130846902
Politicians -- France -- Biography -- Dictionaries. France -- Politics and government -- 1870-1940 -- Dictionaries. France -- Politics and government -- 20th century -- Dictionaries.

DC342.8.C32.E8
Eubank, Keith.
Paul Cambon; master diplomatist. Norman, University of Oklahoma Press [1960] xiii, 221 p.
60-013479 923.244
Cambon, Paul, -- 1843-1924. France -- Foreign relations -- 1870-1940.

DC342.8.C6.B7
Bruun, Geoffrey, 1898-
Clemenceau, by Geoffrey Bruun. Cambridge, Mass., Harvard University Press, 1943. x, 225 p.
43-003445 923.244
Clemenceau, Georges, -- 1841-1929. -- cn. France -- History -- Third Republic, 1870-1940.

DC342.8.C6.N43 1991
Newhall, David S.
Clemenceau: a life at war/ David S. Newhall. Lewiston, N.Y., USA: E. Mellen Press, c1991. xv, 682 p.
90-020994 944.081/4/092 0889467854
Clemenceau, Georges, -- 1841-1929. Heads of state -- France -- Biography. France -- Politics and government -- 1870-1940.

DC342.8.C6W34 1976
Watson, David Robin.
Georges Clemenceau: a political biography/ David Robin Watson. New York: David McKay, [1976, c1974] 463 p.
76-028607 0679507035
Clemenceau, Georges, -- 1841-1929.

DC342.8.J4.G63
Goldberg, Harvey, 1923-1987.
The life of Jean Jaures. Madison, University of Wisconsin Press, 1962. 590 p.
62-007216 923.244
Jaures, Jean, -- 1859-1914. Socialism in France.

DC342.8.P35.S76 1996
Stone, Judith F., 1946-
Sons of the Revolution: radical democrats in France, 1862-1914/ Judith F. Stone. Baton Rouge: Louisiana State University Press, c1996. xii, 434 p.
95-032092 944.08/092 0807120200
Pelletan, Camille, -- 1846-1915 -- Influence. Republicanism -- France -- History -- 19th century. Legislators -- France -- Biography. France -- History -- Third Republic, 1870-1940.

DC342.8.P4.L67 1985
Lottman, Herbert R.
Petain, hero or traitor: the untold story/ Herbert R. Lottman. New York: W. Morrow, c1985. 444 p.
84-221511 944.081/092/4 0688037569
Petain, Philippe, -- 1856-1951. Heads of state -- France -- Biography. Marshals -- France -- Biography. France -- Politics and government -- 1914-1940. France -- Politics and government -- 1940-1945.

DC354.D88 1987
The Dreyfus affair: art, truth, and justice/ edited by Norman L. Kleeblatt. Berkeley: University of California Press, c1987. xxxiii, 315 p.
87-016241 944.06 0520059395
Dreyfus, Alfred, -- 1859-1935 -- Exhibitions. Antisemitism -- France -- History -- 19th century -- Exhibitions. Treason -- France -- History -- 19th century -- Exhibitions. Artists -- France -- Political activity -- History -- 19th century -- Exhibitions. France -- Politics and government -- 1870-1940 -- Exhibitions. France -- Intellectual life -- 19th century -- Exhibitions.

DC354.H63
Hoffman, Robert Louis, 1937-
More than a trial: the struggle over Captain Dreyfus/ Robert L. Hoffman. New York: Free Press; c1980. viii, 247 p.
80-000642 944.081/092/4 0029147700
Dreyfus, Alfred, -- 1859-1935.

DC354.8.Z6513 1996
Zola, Emile, 1840-1902.
The Dreyfus affair: "J'accuse" and other writings/ Emile Zola; edited by Alain Pages; translated by Eleanor Levieux. New Haven, Conn.: Yale University Press, c1996. xxxvi, 208 p.
96-001735 944/.0812/092 0300066899
Dreyfus, Alfred, -- 1859-1935 -- Trials, litigation, etc. -- Sources. Zola, Emile, -- 1840-1902 -- Correspondence. Trials (Treason) -- France -- Sources. Antisemitism -- France. Press and politics -- France.

DC363-424 History — By period — 20th century

DC363.W66 1999
Wood, Nancy.
Vectors of memory: legacies of trauma in postwar Europe/ Nancy Wood. Oxford; Berg, 1999. vii, 204 p.
    1859732895
Memory (Philosophy) Nationalism -- France. Nationalism -- Germany. France -- History -- 20th century. Germany -- History -- 20th century.

DC365.H8
Hughes, H. Stuart 1916-
The obstructed path; French social thought in the years of desperation, 1930-1960 [by] H. Stuart Hughes. New York, Harper & Row [1968] xi, 304 p.
67-028807 914.4/03/8
France -- Intellectual life -- 20th century.

DC369.A33 1995
Adamthwaite, Anthony P.
Grandeur and misery: France's bid for power in Europe, 1914-1940/ Anthony Adamthwaite. London; Arnold; 1995. xx, 276 p.
95-016078 944.081 034064530X
World War, 1914-1918 -- France -- Influence. Reconstruction (1914-1939) -- France. France -- Politics and government -- 1914-1940. Europe -- Politics and government -- 1918-1945. France -- Foreign relations -- 1914-1940.

DC369.A48
Albrecht-Carrie, Rene, 1904-
France, Europe and the two world wars. New York, Harper [1961] 346 p.
60-015808 940 .5
France -- Foreign relations -- 1870-1940. Europe -- Politics -- 20th century.

DC369.F97 1998
Fysh, Peter.
The politics of racism in France/ Peter Fysh and Jim Wolfreys. New York: St. Martin's Press, 1998. xiv, 240 p.
98-023545 305.8/00944 0312217226
Racism -- France -- History -- 20th century. Immigrants -- France -- History -- 20th century. France -- Politics and government -- 20th century.

DC369.H36 1993
Hayne, M. B.
The French Foreign Office and the origins of the First World War, 1898-1914/ M.B. Hayne. Oxford: Clarendon Press; 1993. 328 p.
92-021914 327.44 0198202709
World War, 1914-1918 -- Causes. Foreign ministers -- France -- History -- 20th century. France -- Foreign relations -- 1870-1940.

DC369.L27 1988
Larkin, Maurice.
France since the Popular Front: government and people, 1936-1986/ Maurice Larkin. Oxford [England]: Clarendon Press; 1988. xix, 435 p.
88-002742 944.08 0198730349
France -- Politics and government -- 1914-1940. France -- Politics and government -- 1940-1945. France -- Politics and government -- 1945-

DC369.M525 1994
Miller, Michael Barry, 1945-
Shanghai on the Metro: spies, intrigue, and the French between the wars/ Michael B. Miller. Berkeley: University of California Press, c1994. xiv, 448 p.
93-034114 944.081 0520085191
Intelligence Service -- France -- History -- 20th century. Espionage -- France -- History -- 20th century. France -- History -- 1914-1940. France -- Foreign relations -- 1914-1940.

DC369.M593
Moraze, Charles, 1913-
The French and the Republic. Translated by Jean-Jacques Demorest. Ithaca, N.Y., Cornell University Press [1958] 214 p.
58-059444 944.08
France -- Politics and government -- 20th century.

DC369.W36
Weber, Eugen Joseph, 1925-
Action francaise; royalism and reaction in twentieth century France. Stanford, Calif., Stanford University Press, 1962. 594 p.
62-015267
France -- Politics and government -- 1870-1940.

DC369.W5613 1998
Winock, Michel.
Nationalism, anti-semitism, and fascism in France/ Michel Winock; translated by Jane Marie Todd. Stanford, Calif.: Stanford University Press, 1998. 351 p.
98-011298 944.081 0804732868
Nationalism -- France. Antisemitism -- France. Nationalists -- France -- Biography. France -- Politics and government -- 20th century.

DC373.B35.Y68 1991
Young, Robert J., 1942-
Power and pleasure: Louis Barthou and the Third French Republic/ Robert J. Young. Montreal; McGill-Queen's University Press, c1991. xv, 330 p.
92-242799 0773508635
Barthou, Louis, -- 1862-1934 Statesmen -- France -- Biography. France -- Politics and government -- 1870-1940.

DC373.B5.C6
Colton, Joel G., 1918-
Leon Blum, humanist in politics [by] Joel Colton. New York: Knopf, 1966. xiv, 512 p.
65-018764 944.08150924
Blum, Leon, -- 1872-1950. Statesmen -- France -- Biography.

DC373.B5.L3313 1982
Lacouture, Jean.
Leon Blum/ by Jean Lacouture; translated by
George Holoch. New York, N.Y.: Holmes &
Meier, 1982. xii, 571 p.
81-020083   944.081/5/0924   0841907765
*Blum, Leon, -- 1872-1950.   Statesmen -- France --
Biography.   France -- Politics and government --
20th century.*

DC373.C25.B47 1992
Berenson, Edward, 1949-
The trial of Madame Caillaux/ Edward Berenson.
Berkeley: University of California Press, c1992.
xii, 296 p.
91-002689   364.1/523/092   0520073479
*Caillaux, Henriette. Caillaux, Joseph, -- 1863-
1944. Calmette, Gaston, -- 1858-1914 --
Assassination. Statesmen's spouses -- France --
Biography. Sex discrimination -- France -- History
-- 20th century. Press and politics -- France --
History -- 20th century. France -- Politics and
government -- 1870-1940.*

DC373.G3.A25
Gaulle, Charles de, 1890-1970.
De Gaulle: implacable ally [edited by] Roy C.
Macridis. With a special introd. by Maurice
Duverger. New York, Harper & Row [1966] xxxv,
248 p.
66-012560   944.080924
*Gaulle, Charles de, -- 1890-1970. Gaulle, Charles
de, -- 1890-1970.   France -- Politics and
government -- 20th century. France -- Foreign
relations -- 1945-*

DC373.G3.G67 1962
Grinnell-Milne, Duncan William.
The triumph of integrity; a portrait of Charles de
Gaulle. New York, Macmillan, 1962. 334 p.
62-009294   923.144
*Gaulle, Charles de, -- 1890-1970.   France --
Politics and government -- 1940-1945.*

DC373.G3.L2513
Lacouture, Jean.
De Gaulle. Translated by Francis K. Price. [New
York] New American Library [1966] 215 p.
66-024425   944.080924
Gaulle, Charles de, -- 1890-1970.

DC373.G3.W4
Werth, Alexander, 1901-
De Gaulle; a political biography.   New York,
Simon and Schuster [1966] 416 p.
66-021828   944.080924
*Gaulle, Charles de, -- 1890-1970.   France --
Politics and government -- 20th century.*

DC373.L35.C6
Cole, Hubert.
Laval, a biography.   New York, Putnam [1963]
314 p.
63-009657   923.244

DC373.V3.D68 1992
Douglas, Allen, 1949-
From fascism to libertarian communism: Georges
Valois against the Third Republic/ Allen Douglas.
Berkeley: University of California Press, c1992.
xix, 328 p.
92-015114   944.081/092   0520076788
*Valois, Georges, -- 1878-1945.   Right and left
(Political science) Politicians -- France --
Biography. France -- Politics and government --
20th century.*

DC385.K45 1997
Keiger, John F. V.
Raymond Poincare/ J.F.V. Keiger. Cambridge;
Cambridge University Press, 1997. x, 413 p.
96-026316   944.081/092   0521573874
*Poincare, Raymond, -- 1860-1934.   Presidents --
France -- Biography.   France -- Politics and
government -- 1870-1940.*

DC385.W7 1967
Wright, Gordon, 1912-
Raymond Poincare and the French presidency.
New York, Octagon Books, 1967 [c1942] ix,
271 p.
67-018792   944.081/0924
*Poincare, Raymond, -- 1860-1934.   France --
Presidents. France -- Politics and government --
1914-1940.*

DC389.G68
Greene, Nathanael, 1935-
From Versailles to Vichy: the Third French
Republic, 1919-1940. New York, Crowell [1970]
x, 160 p.
70-013854   944.081/5
*France -- Politics and government -- 1914-
1940.*

DC389.R433
Reynaud, Paul, 1878-1966.
In the thick of the fight, 1930-1945. Translated by
James D. Lambert. New York, Simon and Schuster
[1955] 684 p.
55-004907   944.08
*World War, 1939-1945 -- France.   France --
History -- 1914-1940.*

DC389.W35 1994
Weber, Eugen Joseph, 1925-
The hollow years: France in the 1930s/ Eugen
Weber. New York: Norton, c1994. xii, 352 p.
94-018612   944.081   0393036715
*Reconstruction   (1914-1939)   --   France.
Depressions -- 1929 -- France. World War, 1914-
1918 -- Influence. Germany -- Relations -- France.
France -- Relations -- Germany. France -- History
-- 1914-1940.*

DC393.M55.F37 1990
Farrar, Marjorie Milbank.
Principled pragmatist: the political career of
Alexandre Millerand/ Marjorie Milbank Farrar.
New York: Berg: 1991. xi, 432 p.
89-018016   944.0815092   085496665X
*Millerand, Alexandre, -- 1859-1943. Presidents --
France -- Biography. Socialists -- France --
Biography. France -- Politics and government --
1870-1940.*

DC396.F74 1999
French colonial empire and the Popular Front: hope
and disillusion/ edited by Tony Chafer and
Amanda Sackur. New York: St. Martin's Press,
1999. xvii, 264 p.
98-037554   909/.0971244081   0312218265
*Decolonization -- France -- Influence. France --
Politics and government -- 20th century. France --
Colonies -- History.*

DC396.J335 1988
Jackson, Julian, 1954-
The Popular Front in France: defending
democracy, 1934-38/ Julian Jackson. Cambridge
[Cambridgeshire]; Cambridge University Press,
1988. xv, 353 p.
87-017204   944.081/5   0521320887
*Popular fronts -- France -- History -- 20th
century.   France -- Politics and government --
1914-1940.*

DC396.L22513 1995
Lacaze, Yvon.
France and Munich: a study of decision making in
international affairs/ by Yvon Lacaze. Boulder
[Colo.]: East European Monographs; 1995. 366 p.
95-061584   940.53/12   0880333294
*World War, 1939-1945 -- Causes. World War,
1939-1945 -- Diplomatic history.   France --
Foreign relations -- 1914-1940. Europe -- Politics
and government -- 1918-1945.*

DC396.M5 1964
Micaud, Charles Antoine, 1910-
The French right and Nazi Germany, 1933-1939; a
study of public opinion, by Charles A Micaud.
New York, Octagon Books, 1964 [c1943] x, 255 p.
64-024855   327.43044
*Public opinion -- France.   France -- Politics and
government -- 1914-1940.*

DC396.S66 1995
Soucy, Robert, 1933-
French fascism: the second wave, 1933-1939/
Robert Soucy. New Haven: Yale University Press,
c1995. xii, 352 p.
94-030025   320.5/33/0944   0300059965
*Fascism -- France -- History.   France -- Politics
and government -- 1914-1940.*

DC396.W42 1966
Werth, Alexander, 1901-
The twilight of France, 1933-1940. Edited with an
introd. by D. W. Brogan. New York, H. Fertig,
1966 [c1942] xxii, 368 p.
66-024358   944.0815
*World War, 1939-1945 -- France.   France --
Politics and government -- 1914-1940. France --
Foreign relations -- 1914-1940.*

DC397.A71343 1969
Aron, Robert, 1898-
The Vichy regime, 1940-44. In collaboration with
Georgette Elgey. Translated by Humphrey Hare.
Boston, Beacon Press [1969] viii, 536 p.
70-089958   944.081/6
*France -- History -- German occupation, 1940-
1945.*

DC397.G59 2000
Golsan, Richard Joseph, 1952-
Vichy's afterlife: history and counterhistory in
postwar France/ Richard J. Golsan. Lincoln:
University of Nebraska Press, c2000. xi, 232 p.
00-024203   944/.597   0803270941
*Historians -- France -- Attitudes. War crime
trials -- France -- Public opinion. Public opinion --
France. Vichy (France) -- Politics and government
-- Moral and ethical aspects. France -- History --
German occupation, 1940-1945 -- Historiography.*

DC397.H32 1995
Halls, W. D.
Politics, society and Christianity in Vichy France/
W.D. Halls. Oxford; Berg, 1995. xi, 419 p.
95-100269   944.081   185973071X
*World   War,   1939-1945   --   Underground
movements -- France. Christians -- France --
Attitudes. Youth movement -- France -- History --
20th century. France -- History -- German
occupation, 1940-1945. France -- Politics and
government -- 1940-1945. Vichy (France) --
Cultural policy.*

DC397.H58 1998
Historical dictionary of World War II France: the Occupation, Vichy, and the Resistance, 1938-1946/ edited by Bertram M. Gordon. Westport, Conn.: Greenwood Press, 1998. xxvi, 432 p.
97-018190   940.53/44   0313294216
World War, 1939-1945 -- Underground movements -- France -- Dictionaries. World War, 1939-1945 -- France -- Colonies -- Dictionaries. France -- History -- German occupation, 1940-1945 -- Dictionaries.

DC397.H83
Huddleston, Sisley, 1883-1952.
France: the tragic years, 1939-1947; an eyewitness account of war, occupation, and liberation. New York, Devin-Adair, 1955. 360 p.
54-010820   *944.081
Terrorism. France -- History -- 1945- France -- History -- German occupation, 1940-1945.

DC397.J18 2001
Jackson, Julian,
France: the dark years, 1940-1944/ Julian Jackson. Oxford; Oxford University Press, 2001. xix, 660 p.
2001-275045   944.081/6.221   0198207069
World War, 1939-1945--France.

DC397.M413
Mendes-France, Pierre, 1907-
The pursuit of freedom.   London, Longmans, Green [1956] vii, 256 p.
57-002876
World War, 1939-1945 -- France World War, 1939-1945 -- Prisoners and prisons, French France -- Politics and government -- 1940-1945. -- cm

DC397.M53
Michel, Henri, 1907-
Les courants de pensee de la Resistance. Paris, Presses universitaires de France, 1962. 842 p.
64-033359
France -- Politics and government -- 1940-1945.

DC397.P37
Paxton, Robert O.
Vichy France: old guard and new order, 1940-1944 [by] Robert O. Paxton. New York, Knopf; distributed by Random House, 1972. 399 p.
74-171140   320.9/44/0816   0394473604
France -- Politics and government -- 1940-1945. France -- History -- German occupation, 1940-1945.

DC397.P595 1998
Pollard, Miranda.
Reign of virtue: mobilizing gender in Vichy France/ Miranda Pollard. Chicago, Ill.: The University of Chicago Press, 1998. xxi, 285 p.
98-013332   944.081/6   0226673499
Petain, Philippe, -- 1856-1951 -- Influence. World War, 1939-1945 -- Women -- Abuse of -- France. Women's rights -- Government policy -- France -- Vichy. France -- History -- German occupation, 1940-1945.

DC397.R7314 1991
Rousso, Henry, 1954-
The Vichy syndrome: history and memory in France since 1944/ Henry Rousso; translated by Arthur Goldhammer. Cambridge, Mass.: Harvard University Press, 1991. xii, 384 p.
90-020006   944.082   0674935381
Petain, Philippe, -- 1856-1951 -- Influence. World War, 1939-1945 -- France. France -- Politics and government -- 1945- France -- History -- German occupation, 1940-1945.

DC397.S47 1989
Shennan, Andrew.
Rethinking France: plans for renewal, 1940-1946/ Andrew Shennan. Oxford: Clarendon Press; 1989. xii, 332 p.
89-009294   944.081/6   019827520X
Political planning -- France -- History -- 20th century. Reconstruction (1939-1951) -- France. France -- Politics and government -- 1940-1945. France -- Politics and government -- 1945-1958. France -- Civilization -- Philosophy.

DC401.H57 1992
Historical dictionary of the French Fourth and Fifth Republics, 1946-1991/ Wayne Northcutt, editor-in-chief. New York: Greenwood Press, 1992. xv, 527 p.
91-017387   944.082   0313263566
France -- History -- 1945- -- Dictionaries.

DC401.R62
Romains, Jules, 1885-1972.
A Frenchman examines his conscience. Translated by Cornelia Schaeffer. [London] Deutsch [1955] 118 p.
55-012549   944.082
National characteristics, French.   France -- Politics and government -- 1945-

DC401.S6
Smith, Tony, 1942-
The French stake in Algeria, 1945-1962/ Tony Smith. Ithaca, N.Y.: Cornell University Press, 1978. 199 p.
78-007713   944.082   0801411254
France -- Politics and government -- 1945-1958. France -- Politics and government -- 1958- France -- Colonies.

DC404.A7
Aron, Raymond, 1905-
Le grand schisme. [Paris] Gallimard [1948] 346 p.
48-023952   944.082
World politics -- 1945- France -- Politics and government -- 1945-

DC404.C3
Camus, Albert, 1913-1960.
Actuelles: chroniques, 1944-1948/   Paris: Gallimard, 1950. 270 p.
50-012742   944.082
French language -- Non-fiction.   France -- Politics and government -- 1945-

DC404.F74 1990
French and British foreign policies in transition: the challenge of adjustment/ edited by Francoise de La Serre, Jacques Leruez, and Helen Wallace. New York: Berg Publishers for the Royal Institute of Inter 1990. xv, 261 p.
89-017946   327.41   0854965971
World politics -- 1945- France -- Foreign relations -- 1945- Great Britain -- Foreign relations -- 1945- France -- Foreign relations -- Great Britain.

DC404.H53 1998
Hitchcock, William I.
France restored: Cold War diplomacy and the quest for leadership in Europe, 1944-1954/ William I. Hitchcock, foreword by John Lewis Gaddis. Chapel Hill: University of North Carolina Press, c1998. xii, 291 p.
97-051123   327.44   0807824283
Reconstruction (1939-1951) -- France. Political leadership -- France. World politics -- 1945-1955. France -- Foreign relations -- Germany. Germany -- Foreign relations -- France. France -- Foreign relations -- 1945-

DC404.R5413 1987
Rioux, Jean-Pierre, 1939-
The Fourth Republic, 1944-1958/ Jean-Pierre Rioux; translated by Godfrey Rogers. Cambridge [Cambridgeshire]; Cambridge University Press; 1987. xv, 531 p.
86-028403   944.082   0521252385
France -- Politics and government -- 1945-1958. France -- History -- 1945-

DC404.V56 1995
Vinen, Richard.
Bourgeois politics in France, 1945-1951/ Richard Vinen. Cambridge; Cambridge University Press, 1995. xiii, 300 p.
94-021349   944.082   0521474515
France -- Politics and government -- 1945-

DC404.W3513 1991
Wall, Irwin M.
The United States and the making of postwar France, 1945-1954/ Irwin M. Wall. Cambridge; Cambridge University Press, 1991. x, 324 p.
90-047868   327.44073   0521402174
France -- Foreign relations -- United States. United States -- Foreign relations -- France. France -- Politics and government -- 1945-1958.

DC404.Y68 1990
Young, John W., 1957-
France, the Cold War, and the Western alliance, 1944-49: French foreign policy and post-war Europe/ John W. Young. New York: St. Martin's Press, 1990. 309 p.
89-029481   327.44   0312041934
Cold War.   France -- Foreign relations -- Europe. Europe -- Foreign relations -- France. France -- Foreign relations -- 1945-

DC407.M4.L3213 1984
Lacouture, Jean.
Pierre Mendes France/ Jean Lacouture; translated by George Holoch. New York: Holmes & Meier, 1984. viii, 486 p.
84-010912   944.082/092/4   0841908567
Mendes-France, Pierre, -- 1907- Statesmen -- France -- Biography. Prime ministers -- France -- Biography. France -- Politics and government -- 1945-1958. France -- Politics and government -- 1958-

DC412.C51413 1971b
Charlot, Jean.
The Gaullist phenomenon: the Gaullist movement in the Fifth Republic. Translated by Monica Charlot and Marianne Neighbour. New York, Praeger [1971] 205 p.
70-165527   320.9/44/083
Gaullism.   France -- Politics and government -- 1958-

DC412.S8
Sulzberger, C. L. 1912-
Test: De Gaulle and Algeria. New York, Harcourt, Brace & World [1962] 228 p.
62-019028   944.082
Gaulle, Charles de, -- 1890-1970.   France -- Politics and government -- 1958- Algeria -- History -- 1945-1962.

DC412.W4
Werth, Alexander, 1901-
The De Gaulle revolution. London, R. Hale [1960] 404 p.
61-002661   944.082
Gaulle, Charles de, -- 1890-1970.   France -- Politics and government -- 1958-

DC414.A73 1999
Atack, Margaret.
May 68 in French fiction and film: rethinking society, rethinking representation/ Margaret Atack. Oxford; Oxford University Press, 1999. viii, 182 p.
00-698470   843/.91409358   0198715145
Riots -- France -- Paris. Riots in literature. France -- Intellectual life -- 20th century.

DC417.G67 1995
Gordon, Philip H., 1962-
France, Germany, and the Western Alliance/ Philip H. Gordon. Boulder: Westview Press, 1995. 127 p.
94-040322   327.4   0813325552
World politics -- 1945- Security, International. Germany -- Foreign relations -- France. France -- Foreign relations -- 1945- France -- Foreign relations -- Germany.

DC417.H38 1991
Hauss, Charles.
Politics in Gaullist France: coping with chaos/ Charles Hauss. New York: Praeger, 1991. xiv, 181 p.
90-037788   320.944   0275937348
France -- Politics and government -- 1958-

DC417.P55 1993
Phillips, Peggy A., 1952-
Republican France: divided loyalties/ Peggy Anne Phillips. Westport, Conn.: Greenwood Press, 1993. xxiii, 168 p.
92-045075   944.083   0313275033
Riots -- France -- Paris -- Influence. Radicalism -- France -- History -- 20th century. Algeria -- History -- Revolution, 1954-1962 -- Influence. France -- Politics and government -- 1958- France -- Race relations -- History -- 20th century.

DC417.T485 1999
Thody, Philip Malcolm Waller, 1928-
The Fifth French Republic/ Philip Thody. London; Routledge, 1999. p. cm.
98-007696   944.083   0415187532
Presidents -- France -- Influence. Anti-Americanism -- France. France -- Politics and government -- 1958- France -- Foreign relations -- 1958-

DC420.G67 1993
Gordon, Philip H., 1962-
A certain idea of France: French security policy and the Gaullist legacy/ Philip H. Gordon. Princeton, N.J.: Princeton University Press, c1993. xix, 255 p.
92-023532   944.083/6   0691086478
Gaulle, Charles de, -- 1890-1970 -- Influence. Gaulle, Charles de, -- 1890-1970 -- Military leadership. Cold War. France -- Military policy. France -- Relations -- Europe. Europe -- Relations -- France.

DC420.L313 1990
Lacouture, Jean.
De Gaulle/ Jean Lacouture. New York: Norton, 1990-1992. 2 v.
90-037997   944.083/6/092   039302699X
Gaulle, Charles de, -- 1890-1970. Heads of state -- France -- Biography. Generals -- France -- Biography. World War, 1939-1945 -- Diplomatic history.

DC420.M325 1996
Mahoney, Daniel J.
De Gaulle: statesmanship, grandeur, and modern democracy/ Daniel J. Mahoney; foreword by Pierre Manent. Westport, Conn.: Praeger, 1996. xiii, 188 p.
95-050530   944.083/6/092   0275949222
Gaulle, Charles de, -- 1890-1970 -- Philosophy. Gaulle, Charles de, -- 1890-1970 -- Views on France. Gaulle, Charles de, -- 1890-1970 -- Political and social views.

DC421.B4713 2000
Berstein, Serge.
The Pompidou years, 1969-1974/ Serge Berstein and Jean-Pierre Rioux; translated by Christopher Woodall. Cambridge, U.K.; Cambridge University Press, 2000. xx, 273 p.
99-023268   944.083/7/092   0521580617
Pompidou, Georges, -- 1911-1974. Presidents -- France -- Biography. France -- Politics and government -- 1969-1974.

DC423.B4 1995
Baumann-Reynolds, Sally.
Francois Mitterrand: the making of a Socialist prince in Republican France/ Sally Baumann-Reynolds. Westport, Conn.: Praeger, 1995. xiii, 200 p.
94-037201   944.083/8/092   0275948870
Mitterrand, Francois, -- 1916- Mitterrand, Francois, -- 1916- -- Political and social views. Presidents -- France -- Biography. Political leadership -- France -- History -- 20th century. Socialism -- France -- History -- 20th century. France -- Politics and government -- 20th century.

DC423.E44 1999
Eling, Kim, 1970-
The politics of cultural policy in France/ Kim Eling. New York, N.Y.: St. Martin's Press, 1999. xvi, 226 p.
98-043275   306/.0944   0312219741
Mitterrand, Francois, -- 1916- -- Influence. Art patronage -- France. Art and state -- France. France -- Politics and government -- 1981-1995. France -- Cultural policy.

DC423.F724 1996
France: from the Cold War to the new world order/ edited by Tony Chafer and Brian Jenkins. Houndmills, Basingstoke, Hampshire: Macmillan Press; 1996. xi, 245 p.
95-031041   944.083/9   033363666X
Cold War. Peaceful change (International relations) European Union -- France. France -- Politics and government -- 1981-1995.

DC423.F745 1997
French presidentialism and the election of 1995/ edited by John Gaffney, Lorna Milne. Aldershot; Ashgate, c1997. xii, 305 p.
97-022278   324.944/0839   1855215675
Public opinion -- France. Mass media and public opinion -- France. Presidents -- France -- Election -- 1995. France -- Social conditions -- 1945- France -- Politics and government -- 1981-1995 -- Public opinion.

DC423.F748 1998
Friend, Julius Weis.
The long presidency: France in the Mitterrand years, 1981-1995/ Julius W. Friend. Boulder, Col.: Westview Press, c1998. xii, 308 p.
97-031017   944.083/8/092   0813328500
Mitterrand, Francois, -- 1916- -- Influence. Socialism -- France -- History -- 20th century. France -- Politics and government -- 1981-1995. Europe -- Politics and government -- 1945-

DC423.M578 1998
The Mitterrand years: legacy and evaluation/ edited by Mairi Maclean. New York, N.Y.: St. Martin's Press, 1998. xv, 336 p.
97-013392   944.083/9/092   0312210825
Mitterrand, Francois, -- 1916- -- Influence -- Congresses. Twenty first century -- Forecasts -- Congresses. France -- Cultural policy -- Congresses. France -- Politics and government -- 1981-1995 -- Congresses.

DC423.M672 1997
Morray, J. P. 1916-
Grand disillusion: Francois Mitterrand and the French left/ Joseph P. Morray. Westport, Conn.: Praeger, 1997. 168 p.
96-032466   944.08   0275957357
Mitterrand, Francois, -- 1916- -- Political and social views. Presidents -- France -- Biography. Socialism -- France -- History -- 20th century. France -- Politics and government -- 1981-1995.

DC423.N67 1992
Northcutt, Wayne.
Mitterrand: a political biography/ Wayne Northcutt. New York: Holmes & Meier, 1992. xvi, 399 p.
91-029986   944.083/8/092   0841912955
Mitterrand, Francois, -- 1916- -- Influence. Presidents -- France -- Biography. Socialists -- France -- Biography. Political leadership -- France -- History -- 20th century. France -- Politics and government -- 20th century.

DC423.S556 1996
Simmons, Harvey G. 1935-
The French National Front: the extremist challenge to democracy/ Harvey G. Simmons. Boulder, Colo.: Westview Press, 1996. x, 285 p.
96-009105   944.083   0813328918
Le Pen, Jean-Marie, -- 1928- -- Influence. Fascism -- France -- History -- 20th century. Racism -- France -- History -- 20th century. France -- Politics and government -- 1981-1995.

DC423.S565 1988
Singer, Daniel, 1926-
Is socialism doomed?: the meaning of Mitterrand/ Daniel Singer. New York: Oxford University Press, 1988. vi, 324 p.
87-020356   944.083/8   019504925X
Mitterrand, Francois, -- 1916- -- Influence. Socialism -- France -- History -- 20th century. France -- Economic policy -- 20th century. France -- Politics and government -- 1981-1995. France -- Economic conditions -- 1945-

DC424.C485 1996
Chirac's challenge: liberalization, Europeanization, and malaise in France/ edited by John T.S. Keeller and Martin A. Schain. New York: St. Martin's Press, 1996. x, 406 p.
96-036044   944.083/9   0312122705
Chirac, Jacques, -- 1932- -- Political and social views. European Union -- France. Political leadership -- France. France -- Social conditions. France -- Politics and government -- 1995-

DC424.G89 1998
Guyomarch, Alain.
France in the European union/ Alain Guyomarch, Howard Machin and Ella Ritchie. New York: St. Martin's Press, 1998. xvi, 267 p.
97-041069   944.081   0312212674
European Union -- France. Social history. France -- Foreign relations -- 1945- France -- Politics and government -- 20th century.

DC611 Local history and description — Regions, provinces, departments, etc., A-Z

DC611.A606.B23 1993
Bachrach, Bernard S., 1939-
Fulk Nerra, the neo-Roman consul, 987-1040: a political biography of the Angevin count/ Bernard S. Bachrach. Berkeley: University of California Press, c1993. xvi, 392 p.
93-013891   944/.021/092   0520079965
Fulk -- III Nerra, -- Count of Anjou, -- ca. 970-1040. Anjou, House of.   France -- Kings and rulers -- Biography. Anjou (France) -- Biography. France -- Civilization -- Roman influences.

DC611.A607
Jessee, W. Scott, 1949-
Robert the Burgundian and the counts of Anjou, ca. 1025-1098/ W. Scott Jessee. Washington, D.C.: Catholic University Press of America, c2000. x, 206 p.
99-048573   944/.1802/092   0813209730
Robert, -- the Burgundian, -- d. 1098.   Nobility -- France -- Anjou -- Biography.   France -- History -- Medieval period, 987-1515 -- Sources. Anjou (France) -- History -- Sources.

DC611.B313.G3 1970
Gallop, Rodney, 1901-1948.
A book of the Basques. Illustrated with a map and drawings by Marjorie Gallop. Reno, University of Nevada Press, 1970. xv, 298 p.
76-137133   914.66/03   087417029X
Basques.

DC611.B5783.S4413 1991
Segalen, Martine.
Fifteen generations of Bretons: kinship and society in lower Brittany, 1720-1980/ Martine Segalen; translated from the French by J.A. Underwood. Cambridge; Cambridge University Press; 1991. xiv, 323 p.
90-032222   944/.1   0521333695
Family -- France -- Bigouden -- History. Peasantry -- France -- Bigouden -- Social conditions. Bigouden (France) -- Social life and customs. Bigouden (France) -- Social conditions.

DC611.B7747.C4437 1997
Small, Graeme, 1963-
George Chastelain and the shaping of Valois Burgundy: political and historical culture at court in the fifteenth century/ Graeme Small. Woodbridge, Suffolk, UK; Royal Historical Society: 1997. 302 p.
97-016769   944/.4025   0861932374
Chastellain, Georges, -- 1405?-1475 -- Chronique. Political culture -- France -- Burgundy -- History -- 15th century.   Burgundy (France) -- Historiography. Burgundy (France) -- Court and courtiers -- History -- 15th century. Burgundy (France) -- History -- House of Valois, 1363-1477.

DC611.B78.C263 1963
Calmette, Joseph, 1873-1952.
The golden age of Burgundy; the magnificent dukes and their courts. Translated from the French by Doreen Weightman. New York, W.W. Norton [1963, c1962] 371 p.
63-009876   944.4
Philip, -- Duke of Burgundy, -- 1342-1404. John, -- Duke of Burgundy, -- 1371-1419. Charles, -- Duke of Burgundy, -- 1433-1477.

DC611.B78.V35 1979
Vaughan, Richard, 1927-
Philip the bold: the formation of the Burgundian state/ Richard Vaughan. London; Longman, 1979. xvi, 278 p.
78-040794   944/.4/025   0582490480
Philip, -- Duke of Burgundy, -- 1342-1404. Burgundy (France) -- History -- House of Valois, 1363-1477.

DC611.B781.W4 1989
Weightman, Christine B.
Margaret of York, Duchess of Burgundy, 1446-1503/ Christine Weightman. New York: St. Martin's Press, 1989. x, 244 p.
89-032024   944/.4027/092   0312031041
Charles, -- Duke of Burgundy, -- 1433-1477 -- Marriage. Margaret, -- of York, Duchess, Consort of Charles the Bold, Duke of Burgundy, -- 1446-1503. Wives -- France -- Biography. Burgundy (France) -- Kings and rulers -- Biography. Burgundy (France) -- History -- House of Valois, 1363-1477. Great Britain -- History -- House of York, 1461-1485.

DC611.B854.G35 1991
Galliou, Patrick.
The Bretons/ Patrick Galliou and Michael Jones. Oxford, UK; B. Blackwell, 1991. xvi, 334 p.
90-024758   944/.1   0631164065
Bretons -- History.   Brittany (France) -- History.

DC611.B854.J66 1988
Jones, Michael
The creation of Brittany: a late medieval state/ Michael Jones. London; Hambledon Press, 1988. xiv, 435 p.
87-018153   944/.1   090762880X
Brittany (France) -- History. France -- History -- Medieval period, 987-1515.

DC611.B856.S65 1992
Smith, Julia M. H.
Province and empire: Brittany and the Carolingians/ Julia M.H. Smith. Cambridge [England]; Cambridge University Press, 1992. xx, 237 p.
91-014286   944/.1   0521382858
Carolingians.   France -- History -- To 987. Brittany (France) -- History.

DC611.B9173.H4413
Helias, Pierre Jakez.
The horse of pride: life in a Breton village/ Pierre-Jakez Helias; translated and abridged by June Guicharnaud; foreword by Laurence Wylie. New Haven: Yale University Press, 1978. xvii, 351 p.
78-006929   944/.11   0300020368
Helias, Pierre Jakez.   Brittany (France) -- Social life and customs. Brittany (France) -- Biography.

DC611.C811.B75
Boswell, James, 1740-1795.
The journal of a tour to Corsica: & memoirs of Pascal Paoli, by James Boswell...ed., with an introduction, by S. C. Roberts. Cambridge [Eng.] The University press, 1929 [1923] xvii, 110 p.
24-000762
Paoli, Pascal, -- 1725-1807.   Corsica (France)

DC611.F498.F67 1993
Ford, Caroline C., 1956-
Creating the nation in provincial France: religion and political identity in Brittany/ Caroline Ford. Princeton, N.J.: Princeton University Press, c1993. xii, 255 p.
92-020828   944/.11   0691056676
Acculturation -- France -- Finistere -- Political aspects. Politics and culture -- France -- Finistere. Nationalism -- France -- Finistere. Finistere (France) -- Politics and government. France -- Politics and government -- 1789-

DC611.G217.Z37 1995
Zaretsky, Robert, 1955-
Nimes at war: religion, politics, and public opinion in the Gard, 1938-1944/ Robert Zaretsky. University Park, Pa.: Pennsylvania State University Press, c1995. xi, 276 p.
93-041182   944/.830815   0271013265
Conservatism -- France -- Gard. Communism and Christianity -- France -- Gard. Antisemitism -- France -- Gard. France -- History -- 1914-1940. France -- History -- German occupation, 1940-1945. Gard (France) -- History.

DC611.N856.S43 1988
Searle, Eleanor.
Predatory kinship and the creation of Norman power, 840-1066/ Eleanor Searle. Berkeley: University of California Press, c1988. xi, 356 p.
88-004808   944/.02   0520062760
Normans -- France -- Normandy -- Politics and government.   Normandy (France) -- History -- To 1515.

DC611.N856.S56 1997
Shopkow, Leah.
History and community: Norman historical writing in the eleventh and twelfth centuries/ Leah Shopkow. Washington, D.C.: Catholic University of America Press, c1997. xv, 327 p.
96-032081   944/.2   0813208823
Normandy, Dukes of.   Middle Ages -- Historiography. Historians -- France -- Normandy -- Influence. Great Britain -- Relations -- France. France -- Relations -- Great Britain. Normandy (France) -- Genealogy.

DC611.N894.C37 1998
Carroll, Stuart, 1965-
Noble power during the French wars of religion: the Guise affinity and the Catholic cause in Normandy/ Stuart Carroll. Cambridge, U.K.; Cambridge University Press, 1998. xv, 298 p.
97-038680   944/.2   0521624045
Guise, House of. Nobility -- France -- Normandy -- Political activity.   France -- History -- Wars of the Huguenots, 1562-1598. Normandy (France) -- History -- Religious aspects.

DC611.P588.P68 1993
Potter, David, 1948-
War and government in the French provinces: Picardy, 1470-1560/ David Potter. Cambridge [England]; Cambridge University Press, 1993. xv, 393 p.
92-011887   944/.26   0521431891
Nobility -- France -- Picardy -- History -- 16th century.   France -- Politics and government -- 16th century. France -- Military policy. Picardy (France) -- History.

DC611.P985.S24 1989
Sahlins, Peter.
Boundaries: the making of France and Spain in the Pyreneens/ Peter Sahlins. Berkeley: University of California Press, c1989. xxi, 351 p.
89-004711   946/.52   0520065387
Self-determination, National -- Cerdana (Spain and France) -- History. Pyrenees (France and Spain) -- History. Cerdana (Spain and France) -- History. Catalonia (Spain) -- History.

DC611.V357.W9 1964b
Wylie, Laurence William, 1909-
Village in the Vaucluse, by Laurence Wylie. Cambridge, Harvard University Press, 1964. xviii, 377 p.
64-023470   914.49/2
Vaucluse (France: Dept.) -- Social life and customs.

DC650.5 Local history and description — Alsace-Lorraine — History

DC650.5.G66 1998
Goodfellow, Samuel Huston.
Between the swastika and the Cross of Lorraine: fascisms in interwar Alsace/ Samuel Huston Goodfellow. DeKalb: Northern Illinois University Press, c1999. viii, 230 p.
98-008822   335.6/0944/383   0875802389
Fascism -- France -- Alsace. Alsace (France) -- Politics and government. France -- Politics and government -- 1914-1940.

DC707 Local history and description — Paris — General works. Description and travel. Pictorial works

DC707.A45
Alsop, Susan Mary.
To Marietta from Paris, 1945-1960/ by Susan Mary Alsop. Garden City, N.Y.: Doubleday, 1975. xi, 370 p.
74-033628   944/.36/0820924   0385097743
Alsop, Susan Mary.   Paris (France)

DC707.A823
Atget, Eugene, 1856-1927.
A vision of Paris. The photographs of Eugene Atget; the words of Marcel Proust. Edited with an introd. by Arthur D. Trottenberg. New York, Macmillan, 1963. 211 p.
62-019417   914.436
Paris (France) -- History -- Pictorial works.

DC715 Local history and description — Paris — Social life and customs. Culture. Civilization

DC715.E2 1965
Easton, Malcolm.
Artists and writers in Paris; the Bohemian idea, 1803-1867. New York, St Martin's Press, 1964 [i. e. viii, 205 p.
64-024268   709.4436
Bohemianism. Artists in literature. French fiction -- 19th century -- History and criticism. Paris (France) -- Intellectual life.

DC715.F3713 1993
Farge, Arlette.
Fragile lives: violence, power and solidarity in eighteenth-century Paris/ Arlette Farge; translated by Carol Shelton. Cambridge, Mass.: Harvard University Press, 1993. 314 p.
93-016756   944/.36   067431638X
Paris (France) -- Social life and customs -- 18th century.

DC715.R6413 1987
Roche, Daniel.
The people of Paris: an essay in popular culture in the 18th century/ Daniel Roche; translated by Marie Evans in association with Gwynne Lewis. Berkeley: University of California Press, 1987. 277 p.
86-024506   306/.094436   0520058577
Popular culture -- France -- Paris -- History -- 18th century.   Paris (France) -- Social life and customs -- 18th century.

DC715.S39 1998
Schwartz, Vanessa R.
Spectacular realities: early mass culture in fin-de-siecle Paris/ Vanessa R. Schwartz. Berkeley: University of California Press, c1998. xiii, 230 p.
97-002201   944.06   0520209591
Popular culture -- France -- Paris -- History -- 19th century. Leisure industry -- France -- Paris. Spectacular, The -- Government policy -- France -- Paris. France -- Civilization -- 19th century.

DC715.W26 2000
Walz, Robin, 1957-
Pulp surrealism: insolent popular culture in early twentieth-century Paris/ Robin Walz. Berkeley: University of California Press, c2000. xii, 206 p.
99-034874   306/.0944/3610904   0520216199
Popular culture -- France -- Paris -- History -- 20th century. Surrealism (Literature) French literature -- 20th century -- History and criticism. Paris (France) -- Intellectual life -- 20th century.

DC718 Local history and description — Paris — Ethnography

DC718.A36.S76 1996
Stovall, Tyler Edward.
Paris noir: African Americans in the City of Light/ Tyler Stovall. Boston: Houghton Mifflin, 1996. xvi, 366 p.
96-024566   944/.3600496073   0395683998
Afro-Americans -- France -- Paris -- History -- 20th century. Toleration -- France -- Paris -- History -- 20th century. Liberty. Paris (France) -- Intellectual life -- 20th century. Paris (France) -- Race relations -- History -- 20th century.

DC719 Local history and description — Paris — Political history

DC719.D54 1991
Diefendorf, Barbara B.,
Beneath the cross: Catholics and Huguenots in sixteenth-century Paris / Barbara B. Diefendorf. New York: Oxford University Press, 1991. 272 p.
90-020737   944/.361029.220   0195070135
Religious   fanaticism--Paris--History--16th century. Religious   tolerance--France--Paris--History--16th century.

DC725-737 Local history and description — Paris — History

DC725.T48 1991
Thompson, Guy Llewelyn.
Paris and its people under English rule: the Anglo-Burgundian Regime, 1420-1436/ Guy Llewelyn Thompson. Oxford: Clarendon Press; 1991. xiii, 276 p.
90-007836   944/.025   0198221592
Hundred Years War, 1339-1453 -- Occupied territories. Paris (France) -- History -- To 1515. Great Britain -- History -- Henry VI, 1422-1461. Paris (France) -- Social conditions.

DC729.I84 1986
Isherwood, Robert M., 1935-
Farce and fantasy: popular entertainment in eighteenth-century Paris/ Robert M. Isherwood. New York: Oxford University Press, 1986. ix, 324 p.
85-003072   790/.0944/36   0195036484
Performing arts -- France -- Paris -- History -- 18th century. Music-halls (Variety-theaters, cabarets, etc.) -- France -- Paris -- History -- 18th century. Paris (France) -- Social life and customs -- 18th century.

DC729.T76 1996
Trout, Andrew P.
City on the Seine: Paris in the time of Richelieu and Louis XIV/ Andrew Trout. New York: St. Martin's Press, 1996. x, 275 p.
95-052596   944/.361033   0312129335
Richelieu, Armand Jean du Plessis, -- duc de, -- 1585-1642 -- Contributions in urban renewal. Louis -- XIV, -- King of France, -- 1638-1715 -- Contributions in architecture. Urban transportation -- France -- Seine River -- History -- 17th century. Paris (France) -- History -- Louis XIV, 1643-1715. Paris (France) -- History -- Louis XIII, 1610-1643.

DC731.G6313 1998
Godineau, Dominique.
The women of Paris and their French Revolution/ Dominique Godineau; translated by Katherine Streip. Berkeley: University of California Press, c1998. xxii, 415 p.
96-031744   944/.36104/082   0520067185
Working class women -- France -- Paris -- History -- 18th century. Women -- France -- Paris -- Social conditions. Women in public life -- France -- Paris -- History -- 18th century. Paris (France) -- History -- 1789-1799 -- Women.

DC733.B45 1974
Bezucha, Robert J.
The Lyon uprising of 1834: social and political conflict in the early July monarchy/ Robert J. Bezucha. Cambridge, Mass.: Harvard University Press, 1974. xv, 271 p.
74-075780   944.06/3   0674539656
Lyon (France) -- History -- Insurrection, 1834.

DC733.P59
Pinkney, David H.
Napoleon III and the rebuilding of Paris. Princeton, N.J., Princeton University Press, 1958. xi, 245 p.
58-006108   944.07   0691051364
Napoleon -- III, -- Emperor of the French, -- 1808-1873. City planning -- France. Paris (France) -- City planning. Paris (France) -- Public works.

DC735.J3
James, Henry, 1843-1916.
Parisian sketches; letters to the New York tribune, 1875-1876. Edited with an introd. by Leon Edel and Ilse Dusoir Lind. [New York] New York University Press, 1957. xxxvii, 262 p.
57-007914   914.436
Paris (France) -- Description and travel.

DC737.F55
Flanner, Janet, 1892-
Paris journal [by] Janet Flanner (Genet) Edited by William Shawn. New York, Atheneum, 1965- v.
65-025903   944.082
France -- Politics and government -- 1945- Paris (France) -- History -- 1944- Paris (France) -- Intellectual life.

DC752 Local history and description — Paris — Sections, districts, etc.

DC752.M7.J8413
Jullian, Philippe.
Montmartre/ Philippe Jullian; translated by Anne Carter. Oxford: Phaidon; 1977. 206 p.
76-005353   944/.362   0714817120
Montmartre (Paris, France)

DC801 Local history and description — Other cities, towns, etc., A-Z

DC801.A677
Lambert, of Ardres, b. ca. 1140 b. ca. 1140.
The history of the counts of Guines and lords of Ardres/ Lambert of Ardres; translated with an introduction by Leah Shopkow. Philadelphia: University of Pennsylvania Press, c2001. 279 p.
00-044311   929.7/4   0812235681
Guines, Counts of. Ardres family. Nobility -- France -- Ardres -- History -- To 1500. Ardres (France) -- Genealogy.

DC801.B693.A34
Ackerman, Evelyn Bernette.
Village on the Seine: tradition and change in Bonnieres, 1815-1914/ Evelyn Bernette Ackerman. Ithaca, N.Y.: Cornell University Press, 1978. 185 p.
78-058071   944/.36   0801411785
Bonnieres-sur-Seine, France -- History. Bonnieres-sur-Seine, France -- Social conditions. Bonnieres-sur-Seine, France -- Economic conditions.

DC801.B853.C2713 1991
Carles, Emilie, 1900-
A life of her own: a countrywoman in twentieth-century France/ by Emilie Carles, as told to Robert Destanque; translated with an introduction and afterword by Avriel H. Goldberger. New Brunswick: Rutgers University Press, c1991. xix, 271 p.
90-041861   944/.97   0813516412
Carles, Emilie -- 1900- Teachers -- France -- Briançonnais -- Biography. Farmers -- France -- Briançonnais -- Biography. Pacifists -- France -- Briançonnais -- Biography. Briançonnais (France) -- Biography. France -- History -- 20th century.

DC801.C287.M46 1994
Mentzer, Raymond A.
Blood & belief: family survival and confessional identity among the provincial Huguenot nobility/ Raymond A. Mentzer, Jr. West Lafayette, Ind.: Purdue University Press, c1994. viii, 272 p.
93-025955   944/.85   1557530416
Lacger family. Nobility -- France -- Castres -- Biography. Huguenots -- France -- Castres -- Biography. Castres (France) -- Religious life and customs. Castres (France) -- Genealogy.

DC801.C43.W9
Wylie, Laurence William, 1909-
Chanzeaux, a village in Anjou. Edited by Laurence Wylie. Cambridge, Mass., Harvard University Press, 1966. xx, 383 p.
66-018258   914.4/18
Chanzeaux, France.

DC801.C657.W35 1995
Wallace, Peter George, 1952-
Communities and conflict in early modern Colmar, 1575-1730/ Peter G. Wallace. Atlantic Highlands, N.J.: Humanities Press, 1995. xiv, 299 p.
93-006916   944/.3833   0391038222
Reformation -- France -- Colmar Region. Middle class -- France -- Colmar -- Registers. Urbanization -- Social aspects -- France -- Colmar. Colmar Region (France) -- History. Colmar (France) -- Church history.

DC801.L967.P37 1997
Passmore, Kevin.
From liberalism to fascism: the Right in a French province, 1928-1939/ Kevin Passmore. Cambridge, U.K.; Cambridge University Press, 1997. xvii, 333 p.
96-043847   944/.58230815   0521580188
Fascism -- France -- Lyon Region -- History -- 20th century. France -- History -- 1914-1940. Lyon Region (France) -- Politics and government.

DC801.M37.H63 1999
Hodge, A. Trevor.
Ancient Greek France/ A. Trevor Hodge. Philadelphia, Pa.: University of Pennsylvania Press, 1999. viii, 312 p.
98-047415   936.4   0812234820
Greeks -- France -- Marseille Region -- History. Cities and towns, Ancient -- Mediterranean Region -- History. Gaul -- Civilization -- Greek influences. Marseille Region (France) -- Civilization -- Greek influences.

DC801.M65.H36 1995
Halsall, Guy.
Settlement and social organization: the Merovingian region of Metz/ Guy Halsall. Cambridge [England]; Cambridge University Press, 1995. xx, 307 p.
94-031106   936.4   0521442567
Merovingians -- France -- Metz Region. Excavations (Archaeology) -- France -- Metz Region. Metz Region (France) -- Antiquities. Metz Region (France) -- History. Metz Region (France) -- Social conditions.

DC801.M753.L4713 1978b
Le Roy Ladurie, Emmanuel.
Montaillou: the promised land of error/ Emmanuel Le Roy Ladurie; translated by Barbara Bray. New York: G. Braziller, 1978. xvii, 383 p.
77-006124   944/.88   0807608750
Montaillou (France) -- History. Montaillou (France) -- Social life and customs. Montaillou (France) -- Religious life and customs.

DC801.M76.D37 1989
Darrow, Margaret H., 1950-
Revolution in the house: family, class, and inheritance in southern France, 1775-1825/ Margaret H. Darrow. Princeton, N.J.: Princeton University Press, c1989. xiv, 279 p.
89-004028   944/.75   0691055629
Family -- France -- Montauban (Tarn-et-Garonne) -- History. Inheritance and succession -- France -- Montauban (Tarn-et-Garonne) -- History. Montauban (Tarn-et-Garonne, France) -- History. France -- History -- Revolution, 1789-1799 -- Influence.

DC801.R75.L4713
Le Roy Ladurie, Emmanuel.
Carnival in Romans/ Emmanuel LeRoy Ladurie; translated from the French by Mary Feeney. New York: G. Braziller, 1979. xvi, 426 p.
79-052163   944/.98   0807609285
Romans, France (Drome) -- History. France -- History -- Wars of the Huguenots, 1562-1598.

DC801.R86 B46
Benedict, Philip.
Rouen during the Wars of Religion/ Philip Benedict. Cambridge [Eng.]; Cambridge University Press, 1981. xx, 297 p.
79-041364   944/.25   0521228182
Rouen (France) -- History. France -- History -- Wars of the Huguenots, 1562-1598.

DC801.S577.C47 1982
Chrisman, Miriam Usher.
Lay culture, learned culture: books and social change in Strasbourg, 1480-1599/ Miriam Usher Chrisman. New Haven: Yale University Press, c1982. xxx, 401 p.
82-002771   001.1/0944/3835   0300025300
Printing -- France -- Strasbourg -- History. Strasbourg (France) -- Intellectual life. Strasbourg (France) -- Imprints.

DC801.T726.S36 1989
Schneider, Robert Alan.
Public life in Toulouse, 1463-1789: from municipal republic to cosmopolitan city/ Robert A. Schneider. Ithaca: Cornell University Press, 1989. xiii, 395 p.
89-042880   944/.862   0801421918
Local government -- France -- History. Urbanization -- France -- Toulouse -- History -- 18th century. Popular culture -- France -- Toulouse -- History. Toulouse (France) -- History.

DC801.T87.R63 1996
Roberts, Penny.
A city in conflict: Troyes during the French wars of religion/ Penny Roberts. Manchester; Manchester University Press; 1996. x, 228 p.
95-023334   944/.331   0719046947
Reformation -- France -- Troyes. France -- History -- Wars of the Huguenots, 1562-1598. Troyes (France) -- History. Troyes (France) -- Church history -- 16th century.

DD History of Germany

DD3 Sources and documents. Collections

DD3.S55
Snyder, Louis Leo, 1907-
Documents of German history. New Brunswick, N.J., Rutgers University Press, 1958. xxiii, 619 p.
57-010968   943.0082
Germany -- History -- Sources.

DD5 Collected works — Individual authors

DD5.G66 1969
Gooch, G. P. 1873-1968.
Studies in German history. New York, Russell & Russell [1969] vii, 515 p.
70-075465   943
Germany -- History -- Addresses, essays, lectures.

DD14 Gazetteers. Dictionaries, etc.

DD14.M64 1998
Modern Germany: an encyclopedia of history, people, and culture, 1871-1990/ editors, Dieter K. Buse, Juergen C. Doerr. New York: Garland Pub., 1998. 2 v.
97-013829   943.08   0815305036
Germany -- History -- 1871- -- Encyclopedias. Germany -- Intellectual life -- Encyclopedias. Germany -- Civilization -- Encyclopedias.

DD20 Monumental and picturesque. Pictorial works

DD20.N48 2000
Neumann, Klaus, 1958-
Shifting memories: the Nazi past in the new Germany/ Klaus Neumann. Ann Arbor: University of Michigan Press, c2000. x, 333 p.
00-009466   943.086/072   0472111477
Memorials -- Germany. Memory -- Social aspects -- Germany. Memory -- Political aspects -- Germany. Germany -- History -- 1933-1945 -- Historiography.

DD43 Description and travel — 1946-

DD43.S65
Spender, Stephen, 1909-
European witness. New York, Reynal & Hitchcock [1946] 246 p.
46-008643   914.3
Germany -- Intellectual life. Germany -- Description and travel. France -- Intellectual life.

DD61 Social life and customs. Civilization. Intellectual life — General works

DD61.G47 1955
Germany, a companion to German studies/ edited by Jethro Bithell. London: Methuen, 1955. xii, 578 p.
55-003335   914.3
National characteristics, German. German literature -- History and criticism. Art, German. Germany -- Civilization. Germany -- History.

DD64 Social life and customs. Civilization. Intellectual life — By period — Medieval

DD64.B8613 1991
Bumke, Joachim.
Courtly culture: literature and society in the high Middle Ages/ Joachim Bumke; translated by Thomas Dunlap. Berkeley: University of California Press, c1991. ix, 770 p.
90-039790   943/.02/08621   0520066340
Chivalry. German literature -- Middle High German, 1050-1500 -- History and criticism. Literature and society -- Germany -- History. Germany -- Court and courtiers -- History.

DD65 Social life and customs. Civilization. Intellectual life — By period — 1517-1789. Early modern

DD65.D8513 1992
Dulmen, Richard van.
The society of the Enlightenment: the rise of the middle class and Enlightenment culture in Germany/ Richard van Dulmen; translated by Anthony Williams. New York: St. Martin's Press, 1992. 231 p.
92-229650
Learned institutions and societies -- Germany -- History -- 18th century. Enlightenment -- Germany. Social classes -- Germany -- History -- 18th century. Germany -- Intellectual life -- 18th century.

DD67 Social life and customs. Civilization. Intellectual life — By period — 1871-

DD67.K67 1998
Koshar, Rudy.
Germany's transient pasts: preservation and national memory in the twentieth century/ by Rudy Koshar. Chapel Hill: University of North Carolina Press, c1998. p. cm.
97-036877   363.6/9/0943   0807823988
Historic preservation -- Germany -- History -- 20th century. Group identity -- Germany -- History -- 20th century. Architecture and state -- Germany -- History -- 20th century. Germany -- Cultural policy.

DD74 Ethnography — General works

DD74.P27 2000
Panayi, Panikos.
Ethnic minorities in nineteenth and twentieth century Germany: Jews, gypsies, Poles, Turks and others/ Panikos Panayi. New York: Longman, 2000. xvi, 288 p.
00-038443   305.8/00943   0582267609
Minorities -- Germany -- History -- 19th century. Minorities -- Germany -- History -- 20th century. Germany -- Ethnic relations.

DD76 Ethnography — National characteristics, etc.

DD76.E7 1966
Ergang, Robert Reinhold, 1898-
Herder and the foundations of German nationalism. New York, Octagon Books, 1966 [c1931] 288 p.
66-019732   193
Herder, Johann Gottfried, -- 1744-1803. Nationalism -- Germany.

DD76.J36 1989
James, Harold.
A German identity: 1770-1990/ Harold James. New York: Routledge, c1989. xii, 240 p.
89-003515   943   0415901804
Nationalism -- Germany -- History. Ethnicity -- Germany. German reunification question (1949-1990) Germany -- Economic conditions. Germany -- Social conditions.

DD76.S72 1961
Stern, Fritz Richard, 1926-
The politics of cultural despair; a study in the rise of the Germanic ideology. Berkeley, University of California Press, 1961. 367 p.
61-007517   943
Lagarde, Paul de, -- 1827-1891. Langbehn, Julius, -- 1851-1907. Moeller van den Bruck, Arthur, -- 1876-1925. Nationalism -- Germany. National socialism.

DD84 History — Dictionaries. Chronological tables, outlines, etc.

DD84.T48 1994
Thompson, Wayne C., 1943-
Historical dictionary of Germany/ by Wayne C. Thompson, Susan L. Thompson, Juliet S. Thompson. Metuchen, N.J.: Scarecrow Press, 1994. xvi, 637 p.
94-005673   943/.003   0810828693
Germany -- History -- Dictionaries.

DD86 History — Historiography — General works

DD86.C73 2000
Crane, Susan A.
Collecting and historical consciousness in early nineteenth-century Germany/ Susan A. Crane. Ithaca, NY: Cornell University Press, 2000. xv, 195 p.
00-037681   943/.0072   0801437520
Historical research -- Germany -- History -- 19th century. Nationalism -- Germany -- History -- 19th century. Germany -- Intellectual life -- History -- 19th century. Germany -- Historiography.

DD86.I34 1983
Iggers, Georg G.
The German conception of history: the national tradition of historical thought from Herder to the present/ by Georg G. Iggers. Middletown, Conn.: Wesleyan University Press; 1983. xvi, 388 p.
83-001337   943/.0072   0819560804
Germany -- Historiography.

DD89 History — 1801-

DD89.B27 1966
Barraclough, Geoffrey, 1908-
The origins of modern Germany, by G. Barraclough. Oxford, B. Blackwell, 1966. xi, 481 p.
68-007947 943
　Germany -- History.

DD89.H3513 1968
Heer, Friedrich, 1916-
The Holy Roman Empire. Translated by Janet Sondheimer. New York, Praeger [1968] xiv, 309 p.
68-030935 943
　Germany -- History. Austria -- History. Holy Roman Empire -- History.

DD90 History — Compends

DD90.T87 1999
Turk, Eleanor L., 1935-
The history of Germany/ Eleanor L. Turk. Westport, Conn.: Greenwood Press, 1999. p. cm.
98-035258 943 031330274X
　Germany -- History. Germany -- Economic conditions -- 20th century. Germany -- Politics and government -- 20th century.

DD112-120 History — General special — Political and diplomatic history

DD112.K82
Krieger, Leonard.
The German idea of freedom: history of a political tradition/ Leonard Krieger. Boston: Beacon Press, c1957. xii, 540 p.
57-009088 943
　Liberalism. Nationalism -- Germany. Germany -- Politics and government.

DD114.A76 1991
Arnold, Benjamin.
Princes and territories in medieval Germany/ Benjamin Arnold. Cambridge [England]; Cambridge University Press, 1991. xiv, 314 p.
90-033134 943 0521390850
　Constitutional history, Medieval. Nobility -- Germany -- History -- To 1500. Germany -- Politics and government -- To 1517.

DD117.B8
Bulow, Bernhard, 1849-1929.
Imperial Germany, by Prince Bernhard von Bulow, tr. by Marie A. Lewenz, M.A.; with frontispiece. New York, Dodd, Mead and Company, 1914. 342 p.
14-005975
　Germany -- Politics and government. Germany -- Foreign relations.

DD120.S65.N45 1997
Nekrich, A. M.
Pariahs, partners, predators: German-Soviet relations, 1922-1941/ Aleksandr M. Nekrich; edited and translated by Gregory L. Freeze; with a foreword by Adam B. Ulam. New York: Columbia University Press, c1997. xiv, 308 p.
96-029605 327.43047/09/042 0231106769
　Germany -- Foreign relations -- Soviet Union. Soviet Union -- Foreign relations -- Germany.

DD120.S7
Bowen, Wayne H., 1968-
Spaniards and Nazi Germany: collaboration in the new order/ Wayne H. Bowen. Columbia, Mo: University of Missouri Press, c2000. xii, 250 p.
00-056785 327.46043 0826213006
　World War, 1939-1945. Fascism. Germany -- Foreign relations -- 1933-1945. Spain -- Foreign relations -- 1939-1975. Germany -- Foreign relations -- Spain.

DD126-174 History — By period — Early and medieval to 1519

DD126.B35
Barraclough, Geoffrey, 1908-
Mediaeval Germany, 911-1250; essays by German historians, translated with an introduction by Geoffrey Barraclough. Oxford, B. Blackwell, 1938. 2 v.
39-018883 943.02
　Constitutional history -- Germany. Constitutional history, Medieval. Church and state -- Germany. Germany -- History -- 843-1273.

DD126.M43 2001
Medieval Germany/ edited by John M. Jeep. New York: Garland Pub., 2001. p. cm.
00-061780 943/.02/03 0824076443
　Civilization, Medieval -- Encyclopedias. Germany -- History -- 1273-1517 -- Encyclopedias. Netherlands -- History -- To 1384 -- Encyclopedias. Netherlands -- History -- House of Burgundy, 1384-1477 -- Encyclopedias.

DD129.G7
Uneasy allies: British-German relations and European integration since 1945/ edited by Klaus Larres with Elizabeth Meehan. New York: Oxford University Press, 2000. xvi, 344 p.
99-057192 337.41043 0198293836
　European Union. Great Britain -- Relations -- Germany. Germany -- Relations -- Great Britain. Europe -- Economic integration.

DD130.B76 2001
Brown, Warren, 1963-
Unjust seizure: conflict, interest, and authority in an early medieval society/ Warren Brown. Ithaca: Cornell University Press, 2001. xvi, 224 p.
00-011427 940.1 0801437903
　Carolingians. Property -- Europe -- History. Power (Social sciences) -- Europe -- History. Germany -- Religious life and customs -- Middle Ages, 843-1517. Germany -- History -- Saxon House, 919-1024. Bavaria (Germany) -- History -- To 1180.

DD141.F8313 1986
Fuhrmann, Horst.
Germany in the High Middle Ages, c. 1050-1200/ Horst Fuhrmann; translated by Timothy Reuter. Cambridge [Cambridgeshire]; Cambridge University Press, 1986. vii, 209 p.
85-029988 943/.023 0521266386
　Germany -- History -- 843-1273.

DD143.R68 1999
Robinson, I. S. 1947 Feb. 11-
Henry IV of Germany, 1056-1106/ I.S. Robinson. Cambridge; Cambridge University Press, 1999. vii, 408 p.
00-700442 943/.023/092 0521651131
　Henry -- IV, -- Holy Roman Emperor, -- 1050-1106. Constitutional history -- Holy Roman Empire. Constitutional history -- Holy Roman Empire. Holy Roman Empire -- History -- Henry IV, 1056-1106. Germany -- Kings and rulers -- Biography. Holy Roman Empire -- Kings and rulers -- Biography.

DD143.W46 1999
Weinfurter, Stefan.
The Salian century: main currents in an age of transition/ Stefan Weinfurter; translated by Barbara M. Bowlus; foreword by Charles R. Bowlus. Philadelphia, Pa.: University of Pennsylvania Press,c 1999. xiv, 233 p.
99-025597 943/.023 0812235088
　Franconian House. Germany -- History -- Franconian House, 1024-1125. Holy Roman Empire -- History -- Franconian House, 1024-1125.

DD147.5.H5.J6713 1986
Jordan, Karl.
Henry the Lion: a biography/ Karl Jordan; translated by P.S. Falla. Oxford: Clarendon Press; 1986. 268 p.
86-005165 943/.21024/0924 0198219695
　Henry, -- Duke of Saxony, -- 1129-1195. Princes -- Germany -- Biography. Germany -- History -- Frederick I, 1152-1190.

DD151.V34
Van Cleve, Thomas Curtis, 1888-
The Emperor Frederick II of Hohenstaufen, immutator mundi. Oxford, Clarendon Press, 1972. xx, 607 p.
73-150754 943/.025/0924 019822513X
　Frederick -- II, -- Holy Roman Emperor, -- 1194-1250. Holy Roman Empire -- Kings and rulers -- Biography. Naples (Kingdom) -- Kings and rulers -- Biography.

DD156.D83 1983
Du Boulay, F. R. H.
Germany in the later Middle Ages/ by F.R.H. Du Boulay. London: Athlone Press, 1983. xii, 260 p.
84-672301 0485112205
　Germany -- History -- 1273-1517.

DD174.B46 1982
Benecke, Gerhard.
Maximilian I (1459-1519): an analytical biography/ Gerhard Benecke. London; Routledge & Kegan Paul, 1982. xiii, 205 p.
82-000608 943/.029/0924 0710090234
　Maximilian -- I, -- Holy Roman Emperor, -- 1459-1519. Holy Roman Empire -- Kings and rulers -- Biography. Germany -- History -- Maximilian I, 1493-1519.

DD174.S87
Strauss, Gerald, 1922-
Manifestations of discontent in Germany on the eve of the Reformation; a collection of documents selected, translated, and introduced, by Gerald Strauss. Bloomington, Indiana University Press [1971] xxiii, 247 p.
75-135014 943/.03 0253336708
　Reformation -- Germany. Germany -- History -- Frederick III, 1440-1493 -- Sources. Germany -- History -- Maximilian I, 1493-1519 -- Sources. Germany -- Church history -- 16th century -- Sources.

DD175-257.4 History — By period — Modern, 1519-

DD175.G34 1991
Gagliardo, John G.
Germany under the old regime, 1600-1790/ John G. Gagliardo. London; Longman, 1991. ix, 453 p.
90-046361   943   0582491053
Germany -- History -- 17th century. Germany -- History -- 18th century.

DD175.H84 1992
Hughes, Michael.
Early modern Germany, 1477-1806/ Michael Hughes. Philadelphia: University of Pennsylvania Press, 1992. xix, 219 p.
91-041377   943/.028   0812231821
Germany -- History -- 1517-1871. Germany -- History -- Frederick III, 1440-1493. Germany -- History -- Maximilian I, 1493-1519.

DD175.R3313 1988
Raff, Diether, 1931-
A history of Germany: from the medieval empire to the present / Diether Raff; translated by Bruce Little. Oxford, Oxfordshire, UK; Berg: 1988. viii, 507 p.
88-008613   943   0854962352
Germany -- History -- 1789-1900. Germany -- History -- 20th century.

DD179.R62 1988
Rodriguez-Salgado, M. J.
The changing face of empire: Charles V, Philip II, and Habsburg authority, 1551-1559/ M.J. Rodriguez-Salgado. Cambridge [Cambridgeshire]; Cambridge University Press, 1988. xvi, 375 p.
87-032647   943/.031   052130346X
Charles -- V, -- Holy Roman Emperor, -- 1500-1558. Philip -- II, -- King of Spain, -- 1527-1598. Holy Roman Empire -- History -- Charles V, 1519-1556.

DD182.B613
Blickle, Peter.
The Revolution of 1525: the German Peasants' War from a new perspective/ Peter Blickle; translated by Thomas A. Brady, Jr., and H.C. Erik Midelfort. Baltimore: Johns Hopkins University Press, c1981. xxvi, 246 p.
81-047603   943/.031   0801824729
Peasants' War, 1524-1525.

DD182.E52 1967
Engels, Friedrich, 1820-1895.
The German revolutions: The Peasant War in Germany, and Germany: revolution and counter-revolution. Edited and with an introd. by Leonard Krieger. Chicago, University of Chicago Press [1967] xlvii, 246 p.
67-015314   943/.008   0226208680
Communism -- Germany. Peasants' War, 1524-1525. Germany -- Social conditions. Austria -- History -- Revolution, 1848-1849. Germany -- History -- Revolution, 1848-1849.

DD193.B7
Bruford, Walter Horace, 1894-
Germany in the eighteenth century. Cambridge [Eng.] The University Press 1968 xii, 354 p.
35-007429
German literature -- 18th century -- History and criticism. Germany -- Social life and customs. Germany -- Politics and government -- 18th century. Germany -- Economic conditions.

DD193.5 .M37 1996
Marchand, Suzanne L.,
Down from Olympus: archaeology and philhellenism in Germany, 1750-1970/ Suzanne L. Marchand. Princeton, N.J.: Princeton University Press, c1996. xxiv, 400 p.
95-053324   938/.0072043 20   0691043930
Germany -- Intellectual life -- 18th century. Germany -- Intellectual life -- 19th century. Germany -- Intellectual life -- 20th century. Archaeology--Germany--History. Enlightenment--Germany. Art, Greek--Influence. Neoclassicism (Art) -- Germany. Civilization, Classical.

DD197.M413
Meinecke, Friedrich, 1862-1954.
The age of German liberation, 1795-1815/ Friedrich Meinecke; edited with an introd. by Peter Paret; [translated by Peter Paret and Helmuth Fischer]. Berkeley: University of California Press, c1977. xxiii, 131 p.
74-079767   943/.06   0520027922
Germany -- History -- 1789-1900. Prussia (Germany) -- History -- 1740-1815.

DD203.B59 1998
Blackbourn, David, 1949-
The long nineteenth century: a history of Germany, 1780-1918/ David Blackbourn. New York: Oxford University Press, 1998. xxiv, 578 p.
97-029535   943/.07   0195076710
Germany -- History -- 1789-1900. Germany -- History -- 1871-1918. Germany -- Intellectual life -- 19th century.

DD203.M2713
Mann, Golo, 1909-
The history of Germany since 1789. Translated from the German by Marian Jackson. New York, Praeger [1968] xii, 547 p.
67-024685   943
Germany -- History -- 1789-1900. Germany -- History -- 20th century.

DD203.N5513 1996
Nipperdey, Thomas.
Germany from Napoleon to Bismarck, 1800-1866/ Thomas Nipperdey; translated by Daniel Nolan. Princeton, NJ: Princeton University Press, c1996. viii, 760 p.
95-004498   943/.07   069102636X
Germany -- History -- 1789-1900.

DD203.S48 1989
Sheehan, James J.
German history, 1770-1866/ by James J. Sheehan. Oxford [England]: Clarendon Press; 1989. xvii, 969 p.
89-023023   943   0198221207
Germany -- History -- 1740-1806. Germany -- History -- 1806-1815. Germany -- History -- 1815-1866.

DD203.T3 1946
Taylor, A. J. P. 1906-
The course of German history; a survey of the development of Germany since 1815, by A. J. P. Taylor. New York, Coward-McCann, inc. [1946] 230 p.
46-004974   943.07
Germany -- History -- 1789-1900. Germany -- History -- 20th century.

DD204.B475 1997
Berger, Stefan.
The search for normality: national identity and historical consciousness in Germany since 1800/ Stefan Berger. Providence: Berghahn Books, 1997. xi, 307 p.
96-053355   907/.2043   1571818634
Conservatism -- Germany -- History -- 19th century. Germany -- Historiography. Nationalism -- Germany.

DD204.B5213 1984
Blackbourn, David, 1949-
The peculiarities of German history: bourgeois society and politics in nineteenth-century Germany/ David Blackbourn and Geoff Eley. Oxford [Oxfordshire]; Oxford University Press, 1984. viii, 300 p.
84-010051   943/.07   0198730586
Germany -- History -- 1789-1900 -- Historiography.

DD204.S3413 1990
Schulze, Hagen.
The course of German nationalism: from Frederick the Great to Bismarck, 1763-1867/ Hagen Schulze; translated by Sarah Hanbury-Tenison. Cambridge; Cambridge University Press, 1991. xii, 174 p.
89-077388   943   0521373794
Nationalism -- Germany -- History -- 19th century. Germany -- History -- 1789-1900. Germany -- History -- 1848-1870.

DD204.S53
Sheehan, James J.
German liberalism in the nineteenth century/ James J. Sheehan. Chicago: University of Chicago Press, 1978. 411 p.
77-025971   320.5/12/0943   0226752070
Liberalism -- Germany. Germany -- Politics and government -- 19th century.

DD204.S57 1995
Smith, Helmut Walser, 1962-
German nationalism and religious conflict: culture, ideology, politics, 1870-1914/ Helmut Walser Smith. Princeton, N.J.: Princeton University Press, c1995. xiii, 271 p.
94-016983   320.5/4/0943   0691036241
Nationalism -- Germany -- History -- 19th century. Kulturkampf -- Germany. Church and state -- Germany. Germany -- Politics and government -- 1871-1918.

DD204.S58 1991
Smith, Woodruff D.
Politics and the sciences of culture in Germany, 1840-1920/ Woodruff D. Smith. New York: Oxford University Press, 1991. ix, 298 p.
90-042623   001.1/0943/09034   0195065360
Politics and culture -- Germany -- History -- 19th century. Learning and scholarship -- Germany -- History -- 20th century. Germany -- Intellectual life -- 19th century.

DD207.S5413 1998
Siemann, Wolfram.
The German revolution of 1848-49/ Wolfram Siemann; translated by Christiane Banerji. New York: St. Martin's Press, 1998. xv, 260 p.
98-021100   943/.076   0312216947
Germany -- History -- Revolution, 1848-1849.

DD210.B613
Bohme, Helmut, 1936-
The foundation of the German Empire: select documents; edited by Helmut Bohme; translated [from the German] by Agatha Ramm. London, Oxford University Press, 1971. xxi, 271 p.
79-030796   943/.07   0198730128
Germany -- History -- 1848-1870 -- Sources

DD210.E48 1986
Eley, Geoff, 1949-
From unification to Nazism: reinterpreting the German past/ Geoff Eley. Boston: Allen & Unwin, 1986. 290 p.
85-011183   943.08   0049430386
Germany -- History -- 1848-1870. Germany -- History -- 1871-

DD210.H25
Hamerow, Theodore S.
The social foundations of German unification, 1858-1871 [by] Theodore S. Hamerow. Princeton, N.J., Princeton University Press, 1969-72. 2 v.
75-075241   320.9/43/07   0691051747
Bismarck, Otto, -- Furst von, -- 1815-1898. Germany -- Politics and government -- 1848-1870. Germany -- Economic conditions -- 19th century. Germany -- Social conditions.

DD217.S5
Simon, Walter Michael, 1922-
Germany in the age of Bismarck, by W. M. Simon. London, George Allen and Unwin; 1968. x, 246 p.
68-117995   943.08/3
Bismarck, Otto, -- Furst von, -- 1815-1898. Germany -- History -- 1848-1870 -- Sources. Germany -- History -- 1871-1918 -- Sources.

DD218.A2 1966
Bismarck, Otto, 1815-1898.
The memoirs; being the reflections and reminiscences of Otto, Prince von Bismarck, written and dictated by himself after his retirement from office/ Bismarck. Translated from the German under the supervision of A. J. Butler. New York: Howard Fertig, 1966. 2 v.
66-024343   943.080924
Bismarck, Otto, -- Furst von, -- 1815-1898. Europe -- Politics -- 1789-1900. Germany -- History -- 1789-1900. Prussia (Germany) -- Politics and government -- 1815-1870.

DD218.C7
Crankshaw, Edward.
Bismarck/ Edward Crankshaw. New York: Viking Press, 1981. x, 451 p.
80-029171   943.08/092/4   067016982X
Bismarck, Otto, -- Furst von, -- 1815-1898. Statesmen -- Germany -- Biography. Germany -- Politics and government -- 1871-1888. Prussia (Germany) -- Politics and government -- 1815-1870.

DD218.P44 1990
Pflanze, Otto.
Bismarck and the development of Germany/ Otto Pflanze. Princeton, N.J.: Princeton University Press, c1990. 3 v.
89-011004   943/.07   0691055874
Bismarck, Otto, -- Furst von, -- 1815-1866. Germany -- History -- 1815-1866. Germany -- History -- 1866-1871.

DD218.T33 1955a
Taylor, A. J. P. 1906-
Bismarck, the man and the statesman. New York, Knopf, 1955. 286 p.
55-010649   923.243
Bismarck, Otto, -- Furst von, -- 1815-1898. Statesmen -- Germany -- Biography.

DD219.H6.R5
Rich, Norman.
Friedrich von Holstein, politics and diplomacy in the era of Bismarck and Wilhelm II. Cambridge [Eng.] University Press, 1965. 2 v.
64-021565   943.08
Holstein, Friedrich von, -- 1837-1909.   Germany -- Foreign relations -- 1871-1918. Germany -- Politics and government -- 1871-1918.

DD219.M7.F75 1995
Friedrich, Otto, 1929-
Blood and iron: from Bismarck to Hitler the von Moltke family's impact on German history/ Otto Friedrich. New York, NY: HarperCollins, c1995. xiii, 434 p.
95-038436   943.08/092/2   0060168668
Moltke family. Moltke, Helmuth, -- Graf von, -- 1800-1891. Moltke, Helmuth James, -- Graf von, -- 1907-1945. Germany -- History -- 1933-1945. Germany -- History -- 1918-1933. Germany -- History, Military -- 19th century.

DD220.C34
Calleo, David P., 1934-
The German problem reconsidered: Germany and the world order, 1870 to the present/ David Calleo. Cambridge; Cambridge University Press, 1978. xi, 239 p.
78-009683   943.08   0521223091
World politics -- 19th century. World politics -- 20th century. Germany -- History -- 1871-1918. Germany -- History -- 20th century. Germany -- History -- Philosophy.

DD220.C72 1978b
Craig, Gordon Alexander, 1913-
Germany, 1866-1945/ by Gordon A. Craig. New York: Oxford University Press, 1978. xv, 825 p.
78-058471   943.08   0198221134
Germany -- History -- 1866-1871. Germany -- History -- 1871-1918. Germany -- History -- 1918-1933.

DD220.I635 1996
Imperial Germany: a historiographical companion/ edited by Roger Chickering. Westport, Conn.: Greenwood Press, 1996. vi, 538 p.
95-036431   943.08   0313276412
Historiography -- Germany. Germany -- History -- 1871-1918. Germany -- Historiography. Germany -- Social conditions -- 1871-1918.

DD220.M5613 1995
Mommsen, Wolfgang J., 1930-
Imperial Germany 1867-1918: politics, culture, and society in an authoritarian state/ Wolfgang J. Mommsen; translated by Richard Deveson. London; Arnold: 1995. xi, 304 p.
95-031744   943.08   0340645342
Political culture -- Germany. Germany -- Politics and government -- 1871-1918. Germany -- Politics and government -- 1866-1871. Germany -- Cultural policy.

DD220.W48 1986
Williamson, D. G.
Bismarck and Germany, 1862-1890/ D.G. Williamson. London; Longman, 1986. v, 138 p.
85-019714   943.08   0582354137
Bismarck, Otto, -- Furst von, -- 1815-1898. Germany -- History -- 1871-1918. Germany -- History -- 1848-1870.

DD221.E48 1990
Elections, parties, and political traditions: social foundations of German parties and party systems, 1867-1987/ edited by Karl Rohe. New York: Berg: 1990. xii, 244 p.
89-018033   320.943   0854966196
Political parties -- Germany -- History. Elections -- Germany -- History. Germany -- Politics and government -- 1870-

DD221.H5713 1989
Hildebrand, Klaus.
German foreign policy from Bismarck to Adenauer: the limits of statecraft/ Klaus Hildebrand; translated by Louise Willmot. London; Unwin Hyman, 1989. x, 261 p.
89-005693   327.43/09/034   0044450702
Bismarck, Otto, -- Furst von, -- 1815-1898. Adenauer, Konrad, -- 1876-1967. Germany -- Foreign relations -- 1871- Germany (West) -- Foreign relations.

DD221.S38 2000
Seligmann, Matthew S., 1967-
Germany from Reich to Republic 1871-1918: politics, hierarchy and elites/ Matthew S. Seligmann & Roderick R. McLean. New York: St. Martin's Press, 2000. p. cm.
99-088127   943.08   0312232926
Bismarck, Otto, -- Furst von, -- 1815-1898. William -- II, -- German Emperor, -- 1859-1941. Constitutional history -- Germany. Political culture -- Germany. Imperialism. Germany -- Politics and government -- 1871-1918. Germany -- Foreign relations -- 1871-1918.

DD221.5.E8 1990
Escape into war?: the foreign policy of imperial Germany/ edited by Gregor Schollgen. Oxford, UK; Berg: 1990. xi, 185 p.
90-000345   327.43   0854962751
Germany -- Foreign relations -- 1871-1918.

DD222.K67 2000
Koshar, Rudy.
From monuments to traces: artifacts of German memory, 1870-1990/ Rudy Koshar. Berkeley: University of California Press, c2000. xvi, 352 p.
99-088549   943.08   0520217683
War memorials -- Germany. National monuments -- Germany. Symbolism in politics -- Germany. Germany -- History -- 20th century -- Historiography. Germany -- History -- 1871-1918 -- Historiography.

DD224.K65 1995
Kollander, Patricia.
Frederick III: Germany's liberal emperor/ Patricia Kollander. Westport, Conn.: Greenwood Press, 1995. xvii, 215 p.
94-039268   943/.07/092   0313294836
Frederick -- III, -- German Emperor, -- 1831-1888. Liberalism -- Germany -- History -- 19th century. Conservatism -- Germany -- History -- 19th century. Germany -- Kings and rulers -- Biography. Germany -- Politics and government -- 1871-1918.

DD228.K812 1954
Kurenberg, Joachim von, 1892-1954.
The Kaiser; a life of Wilhelm II, last Emperor of Germany. Translated by H. T. Russel and Herta Hagen. London, Cassell [1954] 370 p.
55-001352   923.143
William -- II, -- German Emperor, -- 1859-1941. Germany -- History -- William II, 1888-1918.

DD228.P33
Pachter, Henry Maximilian, 1907-
Modern Germany: a social, cultural, and political
history/ Henry M. Pachter. Boulder, Colo.:
Westview Press, 1978. xi, 415 p.
78-002030   943.08/4   0891581669
Germany -- History -- William II, 1888-1918.
Germany -- History -- 20th century.

DD228.5.E45
Eley, Geoff, 1949-
Reshaping the German right: radical nationalism
and political change after Bismarck/ Geoff Eley.
New Haven: Yale University Press, 1980. xii,
387 p.
79-020711   320.9/43/084   0300023863
Nationalism -- Germany -- History.   Germany --
Politics and government -- 1888-1918.

DD228.5.F5513
Fischer, Fritz, 1908-
War of illusions: German policies from 1911 to
1914/ by Fritz Fischer; with a foreword by Sir Alan
Bullock; translated from the German by Marian
Jackson. New York: Norton, [1975] xiii, 578 p.
74-034142   327.43   0393054802
World War, 1914-1918 -- Causes.   Germany --
Politics and government -- 1888-1918. Germany --
Foreign relations -- 1888-1918.

DD228.5.R38 2000
Repp, Kevin.
Reformers, critics, and the paths of German
modernity: anti-politics and the search for
alternatives, 1890-1914/ Kevin Repp. Cambridge,
Mass.: Harvard University Press, 2000. x, 358 p.
00-020603   943.08/4   0674000579
Political culture -- Germany -- History -- 19th
century. Social reformers -- Germany -- History --
19th century. Germany -- Politics and government
-- 19th century. Germany -- Social policy -- 19th
century. Germany -- Intellectual life -- 19th
century.

DD228.8.B38 1973b
Berghahn, Volker Rolf.
Germany and the approach of war in 1914 [by] V.
R. Berghahn. New York, St. Martin's Press [1973]
260 p.
73-086664   940.3/112
Bethmann Hollweg, Theobald von, -- 1856-1921.
World War, 1914-1918 -- Germany.   Germany --
Politics and government -- 1888-1918.

DD228.8.L8 1969
Lutz, Ralph Haswell, 1886-1968,
Fall of the German Empire, 1914-1918.
Translations by David G. Rempel and Gertrude
Rendtorff. New York, Octagon Books, 1969
[c1932] 2 v.
71-089977   943.08/4
World War, 1914-1918 -- Germany. World War,
1914-1918 -- Sources. World War, 1914-1918 --
Diplomatic history. Germany -- History -- William
II, 1888-1918 -- Sources. Germany -- History --
Revolution, 1918 -- Sources. Germany -- Politics
and government -- 1888-1918.

DD229.A45
William II, German Emperor, 1859-1941 1859-
1941.
The Kaiser's memoirs, Wilhelm II, emperor of
Germany, 1888-1918; English translation by
Thomas R. Ybarra.   New York; Harper 1922.
365 p.
22-021224
William -- II, -- German Emperor, -- 1859-1941.
World War, 1914-1918 World War, 1914-1918 --
Causes. World politics. Germany -- Politics and
government -- 1888-1918. Europe -- History --
1871-1918.

DD229.C4 1989
Cecil, Lamar.
Wilhelm II/ Lamar Cecil. Chapel Hill: University
of North Carolina Press, c1989-1996. 2 v.
 88-027798   943.08/4/0924   0807818283
William -- II, -- German Emperor, -- 1859-1941.
Germany -- Kings and rulers -- Biography.
Germany -- History -- William II, 1888-1918.

DD229.C53 2000
Clark, Christopher M.
Kaiser Wilhelm II/ Christopher M. Clark. Harlow,
England; Longman, 2000. xvi, 271 p.
00-030939   943.08/4/092   0582245591
William -- II, -- German Emperor, -- 1859-1941.
Germany -- Politics and government -- 1888-1918.
Germany -- Kings and rulers -- Biography.

DD229.K54 1991
Kohut, Thomas August.
Wilhelm II and the Germans: a study in leadership/
Thomas A. Kohut. New York: Oxford University
Press, 1991. ix, 331 p.
90-042490   943.08/4/092   0195061721
Wilhelm -- II, -- German Emperor, -- 1859-1941 --
Psychology.   Leadership.   Germany -- Politics
and government -- 1871-1933. Germany -- Kings
and rulers -- Psychology.

DD229.R6412813 1998
Rohl, John C. G.
Young Wilhelm: the Kaiser's early life, 1859-1888/
John C.G. Rohl; translated by Jeremy Gaines and
Rebecca Wallach. Cambridge, U.K.; Cambridge
University Press, 1998. xxv, 979 p.
98-012909   943.08/3/092   0521497523
William -- II, -- German Emperor, -- 1859-1941.
Germany -- Kings and rulers -- Biography.
Germany -- History -- William I, 1871-1888.

DD229.R6413 1994
Rohl, John C. G.
The Kaiser and his court: Wilhelm II and the
government of Germany/ John C.G. Rohl;
translated from the German by Terence F. Cole.
Cambridge; Cambridge University Press, 1994. xi,
275 p.
94-000006   943.08/4/092   0521402239
William -- II, -- German Emperor, -- 1859-1941.
William -- II, -- German Emperor, -- 1859-1941 --
Views on Jews.   Germany -- Kings and rulers --
Biography. Germany -- Politics and government --
1888-1918.

DD229.W25 1998
Waite, Robert G. L. 1919-
Kaiser and Fuhrer: a comparative study of
personality and politics/ Robert G.L. Waite.
Toronto; University of Toronto Press, c1998. xiii,
511 p.
98-208146   943.08/4/092   080204185X
William -- II, -- German Emperor, -- 1859-1941 --
Psychology. Hitler, Adolf, -- 1889-1945 --
Psychology.   Heads of state -- Germany --
Psychology.   Germany -- Kings and rulers --
Psychology.

DD231.B8.L47 1990
Lerman, Katharine Anne.
The Chancellor as courtier: Bernhard von Bulow
and the governance of Germany, 1900-1909/
Katharine Anne Lerman. Cambridge [England];
Cambridge University Press, 1990. xiii, 350 p.
89-034312   943.08/092   052138155X
Bulow, Bernhard, -- Furst von, -- 1849-1929.
Statesmen -- Germany -- Biography.   Germany --
Politics and government -- 1888-1918.

DD231.H5.W5 1967
Wheeler-Bennett, John Wheeler, 1902-1975.
Hindenburg, The Wooden Titan. New York, St.
Martin's, 1967 507 p.
67-015778   943.085/0924
hindenburg, paul von, -- 1847-1934 -- biography
Germany -- History -- 20th century.

DD231.R17.A313
Raeder, Erich, 1876-1960.
My life; translated from the German by Henry W.
Drexel. Annapolis, United States Naval Institute,
1960. 430 p.
60-009236   923.543
Raeder, Erich, -- 1876-1960.   Germany --
History, Naval -- 20th century.

DD231.R3.K43 1969
Kessler, Harry, 1868-1937.
Walther Rathenau; his life and work. [Translated
by W. D. Robson-Scott and Lawrence Hyde, and
rev. by the author, with notes and additions for
English readers] New York, H. Fertig, 1969
[c1928] 400 p.
68-009663   943.085/0924
Rathenau, Walther, -- 1867-1922.   Germany --
History -- 20th century.

DD231.S83.B7
Bretton, Henry L., 1916-
Stresemann and the revision of Versailles; a fight
for reason.   Stanford, Stanford University Press
[1953] xii, 199 p.
53-006446   940.3141
Stresemann, Gustav, -- 1878-1929.

DD231.T5.A3513 1970
Tirpitz, Alfred von, 1849-1930.
My memoirs. New York, AMS Press [1970] 2 v.
 77-111779   940.4/512/0924   0404064647
Tirpitz, Alfred von, -- 1849-1930. Tirpitz, Alfred
von, -- 1849-1930.   World War, 1914-1918 --
Naval operations, German. Admirals -- Germany --
Biography. World War, 1914-1918 -- Germany.

DD231.T5.S34 1998
Scheck, Raffael, 1960-
Alfred von Tirpitz and German right-wing politics,
1914-1930/ Raffael Scheck. Atlantic Highlands,
N.J.: Humanities Press, 1998. xxii, 261 p.
97-013616   359/.0092   039104043X
Tirpitz, Alfred von, -- 1849-1930.   Admirals --
Germany -- Biography. Conservatism -- Germany -
- History Nationalism -- Germany -- History.
Germany -- Politics and government -- 1888-1918.
Germany -- Politics and government -- 1918-1933.

DD232.P35
Passant, Ernest James.
A short history of Germany, 1815-1945. Economic
sections by W. O. Henderson, and with
contributions by C. J. Child and D. C. Watt.
Cambridge [Eng.] University Press, 1959. 255 p.
59-001749   943.08
Germany -- History -- 1789-1900. Germany --
History -- 20th century.

DD237.E913
Eyck, Erich, 1878-1964.
A History of the Weimar Republic. Translated by Harlan P. Hanson and Robert G. L. Waite. Cambridge, Harvard University Press, 1962-1963. 2 v.
  62-017219   9453.085
  Germany -- History -- 1918-1933.

DD237.M5713 1996
Mommsen, Hans.
The rise and fall of Weimar democracy/ Hans Mommsen; translated by Elborg Forster & Larry Eugene Jones. Chapel Hill, NC: University of North Carolina Press, c1996. xv, 604 p.
  95-008902   943.085   0807822493
  Germany -- History -- 1918-1933.

DD238.F74 1998
Fritzsche, Peter, 1959-
Germans into Nazis/ Peter Fritzsche. Cambridge, Mass.: Harvard University Press, 1998. v, 269 p.
  97-023453   943.085   067435091X
  Nationalism -- Germany -- 20th century. World War, 1914-1918 -- Social aspects -- Germany. National socialism. Germany -- Politics and government -- 1918-1933. Germany -- Politics and government -- 1933-1945. Germany -- Social conditions -- 1918-1933.

DD238.H45 1984
Herf, Jeffrey, 1947-
Reactionary modernism: technology, culture, and politics in Weimar and the Third Reich/ Jeffrey Herf. Cambridge [Cambridgeshire]; Cambridge University Press, 1984. xii, 251 p.
  84-003227   943.086   0521265665
  Enlightenment -- Germany. Germany -- History -- 1918-1933. Germany -- Intellectual life -- 20th century.

DD238.L43
Lebovics, Herman.
Social conservatism and the middle classes in Germany, 1914-1933. Princeton, N.J., Princeton University Press, 1969. xi, 248 p.
  68-056316   320.5/2
  Conservatism -- Germany. Middle class -- Germany. Germany -- Politics and government -- 1888-1918. Germany -- Politics and government -- 1918-1933.

DD238.W34
Waite, Robert George Leeson, 1919-
Vanguard of nazism; the Free Corps movement in post-war Germany, 1918-1923. Cambridge, Harvard University Press, 1952. xii, 344 p.
  52-005045   943.085
  Germany. -- Heer. -- Freikorps. Germany -- History -- 1918-1933.

DD238.W55 1990
Williamson, D. G.
The British in Germany, 1918-1930: the reluctant occupiers/ David G. Williamson. New York: Berg: 1991. xv, 374 p.
  90-037546   943.085   085496584X
  Military government -- Germany -- History -- 20th century. Military government -- Great Britain -- History -- 20th century. British -- Germany -- History -- 20th century. Germany -- History -- Allied occupation, 1918-1930. Rhineland (Germany) -- History.

DD239.B37 1988
Barnouw, Dagmar.
Weimar intellectuals and the threat of modernity/ Dagmar Barnouw. Bloomington: Indiana University Press, c1988. 344 p.
  87-045246   830/.9/355   0253364272
  Ideology. Civilization, Modern -- 20th century. Germany -- Intellectual life -- 20th century.

DD239.B713 1990
Bloch, Ernst, 1885-1977.
Heritage of our times/ Ernst Bloch; translated by Neville and Stephen Plaice. Berkeley: University of California Press, 1991. xiv, 377 p.
  90-011013   943.08   0520070577
  National socialism. Middle class -- Germany -- History. Germany -- Social conditions -- 1918-1933. Germany -- Social conditions -- 1933-1945. Germany -- Civilization -- 20th century.

DD239.G38
Gay, Peter, 1923-
Weimar culture: the outsider as insider.   New York, Harper & Row [1968] xv, 205 p.
  68-029572   001.2/0943
  Germany -- Intellectual life -- 20th century. Germany -- Politics and government -- 1918-1933.

DD239.L3 1974b
Laqueur, Walter, 1921-
Weimar: a cultural history, 1918-1933/ Walter Laqueur. New York: Putnam, 1974. 308 p.
  74-016605   943.085   0399114491
  Germany -- Politics and government -- 1918-1933. Germany -- Intellectual life -- 20th century.

DD239.S74 1999
Stern, Fritz Richard, 1926-
Einstein's German world/ Fritz Stern. Princeton, NJ: Princeton University Press, c1999. 335 p.
  99-020128   943.087   069105939X
  Einstein, Albert, -- 1879-1955. Political persecution -- Germany -- History -- 20th century. Technology transfer. Antisemitism -- Germany. Germany -- Intellectual life -- History -- 20th century.

DD240.B35 2000
Bendersky, Joseph W., 1946-
A history of Nazi Germany: 1919-1945/ Joseph W. Bendersky. Chicago, Ill.: Burnham, [2000] x, 244 p.
  99-047007   943.085   083041567X
  Hitler, Adolf, -- 1889-1945. National socialism. Germany -- Politics and government -- 1918-1933. Germany -- Politics and government -- 1933-1945.

DD240.B63 1996
Bookbinder, Paul.
Weimar Germany: the republic of the reasonable/ Paul Bookbinder. Manchester; Manchester University Press; 1996. vii, 275 p.
  95-047914   320.943   0719042860
  Germany -- Politics and government -- 1918-1933. Germany -- Intellectual life -- 20th century. Germany -- Social conditions -- 1918-1933.

DD240.F46 1993
Feuchtwanger, E. J.
From Weimar to Hitler: Germany, 1918-33/ E.J. Feuchtwanger. New York: St. Martin's Press, 1993. ix, 376 p.
  92-044734   943.085   0312095880
  National socialism. Germany -- Politics and government -- 1918-1933.

DD240.F85 1992
Fulbrook, Mary, 1951-
The divided nation: a history of Germany, 1918-1990/ Mary Fulbrook. New York: Oxford University Press, 1992. 405 p.
  92-007981   943.087   0195075706
  Germany -- Politics and government -- 20th century.

DD240.T36 1983
Taylor, Simon.
Germany, 1918-1933: revolution, counter-revolution and the rise of Hitler/ Simon Taylor. London: Duckworth, 1983. 131 p.
  82-237174   943.085   0715616897
  Germany -- Politics and government -- 1918-1933.

DD240.T8
Turner, Henry Ashby.
Stresemann and the politics of the Weimar Republic. Princeton, N.J., Princeton University Press, 1963. v, 287 p.
  63-010002   943.085
  Stresemann, Gustav, -- 1879-1929. Germany -- Politics and government -- 1918-1933.

DD240.W76 1996
Woods, Roger, 1949-
The conservative revolution in the Weimar Republic/ Roger Woods. Houndmills, Basingstoke, Hampshire: Macmillan Press; 1996. ix, 173 p.
  95-042058   943.085   033365014X
  Conservatism -- Germany. Nationalism -- Germany. Germany -- Politics and government -- 1918-1933.

DD241.R8.H5 1953
Hilger, Gustav.
The incompatible allies; a memoir-history of German-Soviet relations, 1918-1941 [by] Gustav Hilger [and] Alfred G. Meyer. New York, Macmillan, 1953. xiii, 350 p.
  53-012899   327.430947
  Diplomats -- Correspondence, reminiscences, etc. Germany -- Foreign relations -- Soviet Union. Soviet Union -- Foreign relations -- Germany.

DD243.B35 1990
Baird, Jay W.
To die for Germany: heroes in the Nazi pantheon/ Jay W. Baird. Bloomington: Indiana University Press, c1990. xvii, 329 p.
  89-045189   943.086/0922   025331125X
  Heroes -- Mythology -- Germany. Germany -- Biography. Germany -- History -- 1933-1945 -- Biography. Germany -- Intellectual life -- 20th century.

DD243.K5613 2000
Knopp, Guido, 1948-
Hitler's henchmen/ Guido Knopp; translated by Angus McGeoch. Phoenix Mill [England]: Sutton, 2000. v, 330 p.
  01-326373   364.1/38/092243   0750925876
  Hitler, Adolf, -- 1889-1945. Nazis -- Germany -- Biography. National socialism. Germany -- History -- 1933-1945.

DD244.S64 1993
Stachura, Peter D.
Political leaders in Weimar Germany: a biographical study/ Peter D. Stachura. New York: Harvester Wheatsheaf, 1993. viii, 230 p.
  92-030716   920.043   0130203300
  Politicians -- Germany -- Biography. Germany -- Politics and government -- 1918-1933.

DD247.B7.P38 1998
Patch, William L., 1953-
Heinrich Bruning and the dissolution of the Weimar Republic/ William L. Patch, Jr. Cambridge, UK; Cambridge University Press, 1998. ix, 358 p.
97-043388   943.085/092   0521624223
Bruning, Heinrich, -- 1885-1970. Statesmen -- Germany -- Biography. Political parties -- Germany -- History. National socialism. Germany -- Politics and government -- 1918-1933.

DD247.G6.A25 1970
Goebbels, Joseph, 1897-1945.
The Goebbels diaries, 1942-1943. Edited, translated, and with an introd. by Louis P. Lochner. Westport, Conn., Greenwood Press [1970, c1948] ix, 566 p.
74-108391   943.086/0924   0837138159
Goebbels, Joseph, -- 1897-1945. Goebbels, Joseph, -- 1897-1945 -- Diaries. Nazis -- Diaries. Germany -- Politics and government -- 1933-1945.

DD247.G6.A2913 1983
Goebbels, Joseph, 1897-1945.
The Goebbels diaries, 1939-1941/ translated and edited by Fred Taylor. New York: Putnam, 1983, c1982. xiii, 490 p.
82-018574   943.086   0399127631
Goebbels, Joseph, -- 1897-1945 -- Diaries. Statesmen -- Germany -- Diaries. World War, 1939-1945 -- Germany. Propaganda, German. Germany -- Politics and government -- 1933-1945.

DD247.G67.M67
Mosley, Leonard, 1913-
The Reich Marshal; a biography of Hermann Goering. Garden City, N.Y., Doubleday, 1974. xi, 394 p.
73-020825   943.086/092/4   0385049617
Goring, Hermann, -- 1893-1946.

DD247.H33.A315
Hassell, Ulrich von, 1881-1944.
The Von Hassell diaries, 1938-1944: The story of the forces against Hitler inside Germany, as recorded/ by Ambassador Ulrich von Hassell, a leader of the movement; with an introduction by Allen Welsh Dulles. Garden City, N.Y.: Doubleday, 1947. xiv, 400 p.
47-011273   943.086
World War, 1939-1945 -- Germany. Germany -- Politics and government -- 1933-1945.

DD247.H5.A33 1940
Hitler, Adolf, 1889-1945.
... Mien kampf, complete and unabridged, fully annotated. Editorial sponsors: John Chamberlain, Sidney B. Fay [and others] New York, Reynal & Hitchcock, 1940. xxxvi, 1003 p
40-031074   923.143
Germany -- Politics and government -- 20th cent.

DD247.H5.A57513 1990
Hitler, Adolf, 1889-1945.
Speeches and proclamations, 1932-1945/ Hitler; [edited by] Max Domarus; [translated from the German by Mary Fran Gilbert]. Wauconda, IL, U.S.A.: Bolchazy-Carducci, c1990-c1997 v. 1-3
89-017737   943.086   086516228X
Germany -- Politics and government -- 1933-1945 -- Sources.

DD247.H5.A664553
Hitler, Adolf, 1889-1945.
The testament of Adolf Hitler; the Hitler-Bormann documents, February-April 1945, edited by Francois Genoud. Translated from the German by R.H.Stevens. With an introd. by H.R.Trevor-Roper. London, Cassell [1961,c1960] 115 p.
65-007281
World War, 1939-1945 -- Germany. National socialism. Germany -- Politics and government -- 1933-1945.

DD247.H5.A685 1953a
Hitler, Adolf, 1889-1945.
Secret conversations, 1941-1944 [translated by Norman Cameron and R. H. Stevens] With an introductory essay on The mind of Adolf Hitler, by H. R. Trevor-Roper. New York, Farrar, Straus and Young [1953] xxx, 597 p.
53-009116   923.143

DD247.H5.B79 1992
Bullock, Alan, 1914-
Hitler and Stalin: parallel lives/ Alan Bullock. New York: Knopf: 1992. xviii, 1081 p
91-052711   943.086/092   0394586018
Hitler, Adolf, -- 1889-1945. Stalin, Joseph, -- 1879-1953. Heads of state -- Europe -- Biography. Germany -- History -- 1933-1945. Soviet Union -- History -- 1925-1953.

DD247.H5.B85 1960
Bullock, Alan Louis Charles,
Hitler, a study in tyranny. New York, Harper [1960] 776 p.
60-013434   923.143
Hitler, Adolf, -- 1889-1945. -- ram. Hitler, Adolf, -- 1889-1945.

DD247.H5.C325 1978
Carr, William, 1921-
Hitler: a study in personality and politics/ William Carr. London: Edward Arnold, 1978. x, 200 p.
80-465328   943.086/092/4   0713161418
Hitler, Adolf, -- 1889-1945. Heads of state -- Germany -- Biography. Germany -- History -- 1933-1945.

DD247.H5.D384 1996
Davidson, Eugene, 1902-
The unmaking of Adolf Hitler/ Eugene Davidson. Columbia: University of Missouri Press, c1996. ix, 519 p.
95-053092   943.086   0826210457
Hitler, Adolf, -- 1889-1945. National socialism. Heads of state -- Germany -- Biography. Germany -- Politics and government -- 1933-1945.

DD247.H5.F4713
Fest, Joachim C., 1926-
Hitler [by] Joachim C. Fest. Translated from the German by Richard and Clara Winston. New York, Harcourt Brace Jovanovich [1974] xiii, 844 p.
73-018154   943.086/092/4   0151416508
Hitler, Adolf, -- 1889-1945.

DD247.H5.F54 1989
Flood, Charles Bracelen.
Hitler, the path to power/ Charles Bracelen Flood. Boston: Houghton Mifflin, 1989. x, 686 p.
88-039547   943.086/092/4   0395353122
Hitler, Adolf, -- 1889-1945. Heads of state -- Germany -- Biography. Germany -- Politics and government -- 1918-1933.

DD247.H5.H26513
Haffner, Sebastian.
The meaning of Hitler/ Sebastian Haffner; translated by Ewald Osers. London: Weidenfeld and Nicolson, c1979. 165 p.
79-319187   943.086/092/4   0297775723
Hitler, Adolf, -- 1889-1945. Heads of state -- Germany -- Biography.

DD247.H5.H369
Hesse, Fritz, 1898-
Hitler and the English. Edited and translated from the German by F. A. Voigt. London, A. Wingate [1954] 218 p.
55-043965   327.430942
Hitler, Adolf, -- 1889-1945. World War, 1939-1945 -- Germany. Great Britain -- Foreign relations -- Germany. Germany -- Foreign relations -- Great Britain.

DD247.H5.K46 2001
Kershaw, Ian.
Hitler/ Ian Kershaw. New York: W.W. Norton, 1999-2000. 2 v.
98-029569   943.086/092   0393046710
Hitler, Adolf, -- 1889-1945. Heads of state -- Germany -- Biography. National socialism -- History. Antisemitism -- Austria. Germany -- Politics and government -- 1933-1945. Germany -- Politics and government -- 1918-1933.

DD247.H5.K73 2000
Kohler, Joachim, 1952-
Wagner's Hitler: the prophet and his disciple/ J oachim Kohler; translated and introduced by Ronal Taylor. Cambridge, UK: Polity Press; 2000. p. cm.
99-058487   943.086/092   0745622399
Hitler, Adolf, -- 1889-1945 -- Political and social views. Wagner, Richard, -- 1813-1883 -- Influence. Antisemitism -- Germany. Holocaust, Jewish (1939-1945) -- Causes.

DD247.H5.K813 1955
Kubizek, August.
The young Hitler I knew. Translated from the German by E.V. Anderson; with an introd. by H.R. Trevor-Roper. Boston, Houghton Mifflin, 1955 [c1954] xv, 298 p.
55-005301   923.143
Hitler, Adolf, -- 1889-1945.

DD247.H5.N53 2000
Nicholls, David, 1949-
Adolf Hitler: a biographical companion/ David Nicholls. Santa Barbara, Calif.: ABC-CLIO, c2000. xxx, 357 p.
00-010198   943.086/092   0874369657
Hitler, Adolf, -- 1889-1945. Heads of state -- Germany -- Biography. National socialism. Germany -- Politics and government -- 1933-1945.

DD247.H5.S347 1992
Schwaab, Edleff H.
Hitler's mind: a plunge into madness/ Edleff H. Schwaab; foreword by Peter H. Wolff. New York: Praeger, 1992. xxxvii, 202 p.
91-026390   943.086/092   0275941329
Hitler, Adolf, -- 1889-1945 -- Psychology. Heads of state -- Germany -- Psychology. Germany -- Politics and government -- 1933-1945.

DD247.H5.T52 1997
Thomsett, Michael C.
The German opposition to Hitler: the resistance, the underground, and assassination plots, 1938-1945/ Michael C. Thomsett. Jefferson, N.C.: McFarland, c1997. vii, 278 p.
97-018933   943.086/092   0786403721
Hitler, Adolf, -- 1889-1945 -- Assassination attempts. Heads of state -- Germany -- Biography. Anti-Nazi movement -- Germany. Germany -- Politics and government -- 1933-1945.

DD247.H5.T7 1971
Trevor-Roper, H. R. 1914-
The last days of Hitler [by] H. R. Trevor-Roper. London, Macmillan, 1971. lxiii, 286 p.
72-176406   943.086/092/4   0333075277
Hitler, Adolf, -- 1889-1945.

DD247.H5.V48 1998
Victor, George.
Hitler: the pathology of evil/ George Victor. Washington, D.C.: Brassey's, c1998. ix, 262 p.
97-035632   943.085/092   1574881329
Hitler, Adolf, -- 1889-1945 -- Psychology. Heads of state -- Germany -- Biography. Heads of state -- Germany -- Psychology. National socialism -- Psychological aspects. Germany -- Politics and government -- 1933-1945.

DD247.M6.A413 1990
Moltke, Helmuth James, 1907-1945.
Letters to Freya: 1939-1945/ Helmuth James von Moltke; edited and translated from the German by Beate Ruhm von Oppen. New York: Knopf, 1990. 441 p.
89-045268   943.086/092   0394579232
Moltke, Helmuth James, -- Graf von, -- 1907-1945 -- Correspondence. Moltke, Freya von -- Correspondence. Nationalists -- Germany -- Correspondence. Anti-Nazi movement -- Germany. World War, 1939-1945 -- Personal narratives, German.

DD247.P3.R65 1996
Rolfs, Richard W.
The sorcerer's apprentice: the life of Franz von Papen/ Richard W. Rolfs. Lanham: University Press of America, c1996. xiii, 470 p.
95-043733   327.2/092   0761801626
Papen, Franz von, -- 1879-1969. Diplomats -- Germany -- Biography. Conservatism -- Germany -- History. Germany -- Foreign relations -- 20th century. Germany -- Politics and government -- 1918-1933. Germany -- Politics and government -- 1933-1945.

DD247.P38.G613 1964
Gorlitz, Walter, 1913-
Paulus and Stalingrad: a life of Field-Marshal Friedrich Paulus, with notes, correspondence, and documents from his papers/ by Walter Goerlitz; with a preface by Ernst Alexander Paulus; translated by R. H. Stevens. New York: Citadel Press, 1963. xvi, 301 p.
63-021199
Paulus, Friedrich   Stalingrad, Battle of, 1942-1943.

DD247.R57.Y68 1951
Young, Desmond.
Rommel, the desert fox: foreword by Sir Claude Auchinleck. New York, Harper [1951, c1950] xvii, 264 p.
51-009112   923.543
Rommel, Erwin, -- 1891-1944. Marshals -- Germany -- Biography. World War, 1939-1945 -- Germany. World War, 1939-1945 -- Campaigns -- Africa, North.

DD247.S342.H6413 1995
Hoffmann, Peter, 1930-
Stauffenberg: a family history, 1905-1944/ Peter Hoffmann. Cambridge [England]; Cambridge University Press, 1995. xvii, 424 p.
94-031228   943.08   0521453070
Schenk von Stauffenberg, Klaus Philipp, -- Graf, -- 1907-1944. Schenk von Stauffenberg, Klaus Philipp, -- Graf, -- 1907-1944 -- Family. Hitler, Adolf, -- 1889-1945 -- Assassination attempt, 1944 (July 20) Revolutionaries -- Germany -- Biography. Anti-Nazi movement -- Germany -- Biography.

DD247.S384.A3 1991
Schumann, Willy, 1927-
Being present: growing up in Hitler's Germany/ Willy Schumann. Kent, Ohio: Kent State University Press, c1991. xi, 212 p.
91-009996   943.086/092   0873384474
Schumann, Willy, -- 1927- National socialism. Children -- Germany -- Biography. Youth -- Germany -- Biography. Germany -- History -- 1933-1945.

DD247.S63.A313 1970
Speer, Albert, 1905-
Inside the Third Reich: memoirs, Translated from the German by Richard and Clara Winston. Introd. by Eugene Davidson. [New York] Macmillan [1970] xviii, 596 p.
70-119132   943.086/0924
Speer, Albert, -- 1905- Hitler, Adolf, -- 1889-1945. Architects -- Germany -- Biography. Nazis -- Biography. Germany -- Politics and government -- 1933-1945.

DD247.S63.S47 1995
Sereny, Gitta.
Albert Speer: his battle with truth/ Gitta Sereny. New York: Knopf, 1995. xiv, 757 p.
94-019764   943.086/092   0394529154
Speer, Albert, -- 1905- Nazis -- Biography. War criminals -- Germany -- Biography. Germany -- Politics and government -- 1933-1945.

DD247.T7.S95 1969
Sykes, Christopher, 1907-
Tormented loyalty; the story of a German aristocrat who defied Hitler. New York, Harper & Row [1969] 477 p.
69-015266   943.086/0924
Trott zu Solz, Adam von, -- 1909-1944. Hitler, Adolf, -- 1889-1945 -- Assassination attempt, 1944 (July 20) Anti-Nazi movement.

DD247.T766.M33 1992
MacDonogh, Giles, 1955-
A good German: Adam von Trott zu Solz/ Giles MacDonogh. Woodstock, N.Y.: Overlook Press, 1992. x, 358 p.
91-037266   943.086/092   0879514493
Trott zu Solz, Adam von, -- 1909-1944. Anti-Nazi movement -- Germany -- Biography.

DD249.A78 1972
Angress, Werner T.
Stillborn revolution; the Communist bid for power in Germany, 1921-1923, by Werner T. Angress. Port Washington, N.Y., Kennikat Press [1972, c1963] 2 v.
79-159080   943.085   0804616221
Communism -- Germany. Germany -- Politics and government -- 1918-1933.

DD253.R38
Rauschning, Hermann, 1887-
The revolution of nihilism; warning to the West, by Hermann Rauschning. New York, Alliance Book Corporation, [c1939] xvii, 300 p.
39-021141   943.085
Germany -- Politics and government -- 1933-1945.

DD253.25.B76 1996
Brustein, William.
The logic of evil: the social origins of the Nazi Party, 1925-1933/ William Brustein. New Haven: Yale University Press, c1996. xiv, 235 p.
95-047263   943.086   0300065337
National socialism. Political parties -- Germany -- History -- 20th century. Germany -- Social conditions -- 1918-1933. Germany -- Politics and government -- 1933-1945. Germany -- Economic conditions -- 1918-1945.

DD253.25.O7
Orlow, Dietrich.
The history of the Nazi Party.   [Pittsburgh] University of Pittsburgh Press [1969-73] 2 v.
69-020026   329.9/43   0822931834
Nationalsozialistische Deutsche Arbeiter-Partei -- History.

DD253.5.R4 1989
Rempel, Gerhard.
Hitler's children: the Hitler Youth and the SS/ Gerhard Rempel. Chapel Hill: Univeristy of North Carolina Press, c1989. xii, 354 p.
88-028036   943.086   0807818410
Hitler-Jugend. Waffen-SS. Nationalsozialistische Deutsche Arbeiter-Partei. Schutzstaffel.

DD253.6.H613 1970
Hohne, Heinz, 1926-
The Order of the Death's Head; the story of Hitler's S.S. Translated from the German by Richard Barry. New York, Coward-McCann [1970, c1969] xii, 690 p.
69-019032   943.086
Nationalsozialistische Deutsche Arbeiter-Partei. Schutzstaffel.

DD253.7.C36 1998
Campbell, Bruce, 1955-
The SA generals and the rise of Nazism/ Bruce Campbell. Lexington, Ky.: University Press of Kentucky, c1998. ix, 278 p.
98-005266   943.085   0813120470
National socialism. Generals -- Germany -- Biography. Germany -- Politics and government -- 1918-1933. Germany -- Military policy.

DD256.3.B27 1988
Balfour, Michael Leonard Graham, 1908-
Withstanding Hitler in Germany, 1933-45/ Michael Balfour. London; Routledge, 1988. xxii, 310 p.
88-000331   943.086   0415006171
Anti-Nazi movement. National socialism -- Psychological aspects. Germany -- Biography.

DD256.3.H59513 1988
Hoffmann, Peter, 1930-
German resistance to Hitler/ Peter Hoffmann. Cambridge, Mass.: Harvard University Press, 1988. 169 p.
87-015038   943.086/092/4   0674350855
Hitler, Adolf, -- 1889-1945 -- Assassination attempt, 1944 (July 20) Anti-Nazi movement.

DD256.3.V673 1992
Von Klemperer, Klemens, 1916-
German resistance against Hitler: the search for allies abroad, 1938-1945/ Klemens Von Klemperer. Oxford: Clarendon Press; 1993. xvi, 487 p.
91-034961   943.086   0198219407
Anti-Nazi movement -- Germany. World War, 1939-1945 -- Diplomatic history. Germany -- Foreign relations -- 1933-1945.

DD256.5.A58
Allen, William Sheridan.
The Nazi seizure of power; the experience of a single German town, 1930-1935.   Chicago, Quadrangle Books, 1965. xi, 345 p.
65-010378   943.086
Local government -- Germany -- Case studies. National socialism.   Germany -- Politics and government -- 1918-1933.

DD256.5.B32 1992
Bankier, David.
The Germans and the final solution: public opinion under Nazism/ David Banker. Oxford, UK; B. Blackwell, 1992. vii, 206 p.
91-017503   943.086   0631179682
Antisemitism -- Germany. Holocaust, Jewish (1939-1945) -- Public opinion. Public opinion -- Germany. Germany -- History -- 1933-1945.

DD256.5.B674
Bramsted, Ernest Kohn.
Goebbels and National Socialist propaganda, 1925-1945, by Ernest K. Bramsted. [East Lansing] Michigan State University Press, 1965. xxxvii, 488 p.
64-019392   301.15230943
Goebbels, Joseph, -- 1897-1945.   Propaganda, German. World War, 1939-1945 -- Propaganda.

DD256.5.B94 2000
Burleigh, Michael, 1955-
The Third Reich: a new history/ Michael Burleigh. New York: Hill and Wang, 2000. p. cm.
00-031838   943.086   0809093251
Germany -- History -- 1933-1945.

DD256.5.D43413 1990
Germany and the Second World War/ edited by the Militaergeschichtliches Forschungsamt (Research Institute for Military History). Oxford: Clarendon Press; 1990-1995 v. 1-3
90-007135   943.086   019822866X
World War, 1939-1945 -- Germany.   Germany -- History -- 1933-1945.

DD256.5.E92 1989
Evans, Richard J.
In Hitler's shadow: West German historians and the attempt to escape from the Nazi past/ Richard J. Evans. New York: Pantheon Books, c1989. x, 196 p.
88-043239   943.086   0394576861
Historiography -- Germany (West)   Germany -- History -- 1933-1945 -- Historiography.

DD256.5.F55 1995
Fischer, Klaus P., 1942-
Nazi Germany: a new history/ Klaus P. Fischer. New York: Continuum, c1995. viii, 734 p.
94-041796   943.086   0826407978
Hitler, Adolf, -- 1889-1945.   National socialism. Germany -- History -- 1933-1945.

DD256.5.F73354 1987
Freeman, Michael J., 1950-
Atlas of Nazi Germany/ Michael Freeman; consulting editor, Tim Mason. New York: Macmillan, c1987. 205 p.
87-012261   943.086/022/3   0029106818
Germany -- Historical geography. Germany -- Historical geography -- Maps. Germany -- History -- 1933-1945.

DD256.5.F7335713 1993
Frei, Norbert.
National socialist rule in Germany: the Fuhrer State 1933 -1945/ Norbert Frei; translated by Simon B. Steyne. Oxford, UK: Blackwell, 1993. viii, 276 p.
92-023312   943.086   0631168583
National socialism.   Germany -- Politics and government -- 1933-1945.

DD256.5.F739 1995
Friedlander, Henry, 1930-
The origins of Nazi genocide: from euthanasia to the final solution/ Henry Friedlander. Chapel Hill: University of North Carolina Press, c1995. xxiii, 421 p.
94-040941   943.086   0807822086
National socialism -- Moral and ethical aspects. Euthanasia -- Political aspects -- Germany -- History -- 20th century. Medical ethics -- Germany -- History -- 20th century. Germany -- Politics and government -- 1933-1945.

DD256.5.G52
Gisevius, Hans Bernd, 1904-
To the bitter end/ Translated from the German by Richard and Clara Winston. Boston: Houghton Mifflin, 1947. xv, 632 p.
47-005861   943.086
Germany -- Politics and government -- 1933-1945.

DD256.5.G76313 1991
The encyclopedia of the Third Reich/ edited by Christian Zentner and Friedemann Bedurftig; English translation edited by Amy Hackett. New York: Macmillan; c1991. 2 v.
90-049885   943.086/03   0028975006
Germany -- History -- 1933-1945 -- Encyclopedias.

DD256.5.K46513 1987
Kershaw, Ian.
The "Hitler myth": image and reality in the Third Reich/ Ian Kershaw. Oxford: Clarendon Press; c1987. xii, 297 p.
86-028583   943.086   0198219644
Hitler, Adolf, -- 1889-1945.   Public opinion -- Germany. Propaganda, German -- History -- 20th century. Germany -- Politics and government -- 1933-1945.

DD256.5.K47 1985
Kershaw, Ian.
The Nazi dictatorship: problems and perspectives of interpretation/ Ian Kershaw. London; E. Arnold, 1985. viii, 164 p.
85-175474   321.9/4/0943   0713164085
National socialism -- History.   Germany -- Politics and government -- 1933-1945.

DD256.5.L51313 1997
Encyclopedia of German resistance to the Nazi movement/ edited by Wolfgang Benz and Walter H. Pehle; translated by Lance W. Garmer. New York: Continuum, 1997. xi, 354 p.
96-020003   943.086/03   0826409458
Anti-Nazi   movement   --   Germany   -- Encyclopedias.   National   socialism   -- Encyclopedias.   Germany   --   Politics   and government -- 1933-1945 -- Encyclopedias.

DD256.5.M383 1968
Mau, Hermann.
German history, 1933-1945; an assessment by German historians, by Hermann Mau and Helmut Krausnick. [Translated from the German by Andrew and Eva Wilson] London, O. Wolff, 1968 [c1959]
60-000425   943.086
Germany -- History -- 1933-1945. -- cm

DD256.5.M75 1990
Muhlberger, Detlef.
Hitler's followers: studies in the sociology of the Nazi movement/ Detlef Muhlberger. London; Routledge, 1991. xii, 276 p.
90-008455   320.5/33/0943   0415008026
National socialism -- Social aspects.

DD256.5.N59 1975
Noakes, Jeremy.
Documents on Nazism, 1919-1945/ introduced and edited by Jeremy Noakes and Geoffrey Pridham. New York: Viking Press, 1975, c1974. 704 p.
74-005514   943.086   0670275840
National socialism -- History -- Sources. Germany -- History -- 1933-1945 -- Sources.

DD256.5.R473
Rich, Norman.
Hitler's war aims. New York, Norton [1973- v.
78-116108   943.086/092/4   0393054543
Hitler, Adolf, -- 1889-1945.   World War, 1939-1945 -- Occupied territories. National socialism. World War, 1939-1945 -- Germany. Germany -- Foreign relations -- 1933-1945.

DD256.5.S3356 1997
Schmitt, Hans A.
Quakers and Nazis: inner light in outer darkness/ Hans A. Schmitt. Columbia: University of Missouri Press, c1997. xiii, 296 p.
97-018914   289.6/43/09043   0826211348
National socialism and religion. Quakers -- Germany -- History -- 20th century. Society of Friends -- Germany -- History -- 20th century. Germany -- History -- 1933-1945. Germany -- Church history -- 1933-1945.

DD256.5.S48
Shirer, William L. 1904-
The rise and fall of the Third Reich; a history of Nazi Germany. New York, Simon and Schuster, 1960. 1245 p.
60-006729   943.086
Hitler, Adolf, -- 1889-1945.   World War, 1939-1945 -- Germany.   Germany -- History -- 1933-1945.

DD256.5.S5813 1997
Sofsky, Wolfgang.
The order of terror: the concentration camp/ Wolfgang Sofsky; translated by William Templer. Princeton, N.J.: Princeton University Press, c1997. viii, 356 p.
96-019212   940.54/7243   069104354X
World War, 1939-1945 -- Concentration camps -- Germany. Concentration camps -- Psychological aspects. Concentration camps -- Germany -- History.

DD256.5.T283 1987
Taylor, James, 1931-
The Third Reich almanac/ James Taylor and Warren Shaw. New York: World Almanac, c1987. 392 p.
88-000256 943.086/03/21 0886873630
National socialism -- Dictionaries. Germany -- History -- 1933-1945 -- Dictionaries.

DD256.5.W4324 1993
Welch, David.
The Third Reich: politics and propaganda/ David Welch. London; Routledge, 1993. xiii, 203 p.
92-026236 943.086 0415090334
National socialism. Propaganda, German -- History -- 20th century. World War, 1939-1945 -- Propaganda. National socialism -- Public opinion. Germany -- History -- 1933-1945.

DD256.5.W464 1995
When truth was treason: German youth against Hitler: the story of the Helmuth Hubener Group/ based on the narrative of Karl-Heinz Schnibbe with documents and notes; compiled, translated and edited by Blair R. Holmes and Alan F. Keele; foreword by Klaus J. Hansen. Urbana: University of Illinois Press, c1995. xxix, 425 p.
95-003567 943.086 0252022017
Schnibbe, Karl-Heinz.   Anti-Nazi movement -- Germany. Mormons -- Germany -- Biography. Germany -- Politics and government -- 1933-1945.

DD256.5.W49 1982
Williamson, D. G.
The Third Reich/ D.G. Williamson. Harlow, Essex, UK: Longman, 1982. iv, 108 p.
82-237970 943.086 0582353068
Germany -- History -- 1933-1945.

DD256.6.M85 2000
Muller, Jan-Werner, 1970-
Another country: German intellectuals, unification, and national identity/ Jan-Werner Muller. New Haven: Yale University Press, c2000. 310 p.
00-031054 943.087 0300083882
Intellectuals -- Germany -- Political activity. Nationalism -- Germany -- History -- 20th century. Political culture -- Germany -- History -- 20th century. Germany -- Cultural policy.

DD256.7.L43 2001
LeBor, Adam.
Seduced by Hitler: the choices of a nation and the ethics of survival/ by Adam LeBor and Roger Boyes. Naperville, Ill.: Sourcebooks, 2001. xi, 356 p.
00-066162 943.086 1570717427
National socialism -- Moral and ethical aspects. Informers -- Germany -- History -- 20th century. Military occupation. Germany -- Politics and government -- 1933-1945.

DD257.B34 1992
Balfour, Michael Leonard Graham, 1908-
Germany: the tides of power/ Michael Balfour. London; Routledge, 1992. vii, 271 p.
91-041075 320.943 0415067871
Germany -- Politics and government -- 1945- Germany -- Politics and government. Germany (West) -- Politics and government.

DD257.C55
Clay, Lucius D. 1897-1978.
Decision in Germany.   Garden City, N. Y.: Doubleday , 1950. xiv, 522 p.
50-005813 943.086
Germany -- History -- 1945-

DD257.C64 1990
Coping with the past: Germany and Austria after 1945/ edited by Kathy Harms, Lutz R. Reuter, and Volker Durr. Madison, Wis.: Pub. for Monatshefte by the Univ of Wisconsin Press, c1990. ix, 269 p.
90-013031 943.087 0299970728
World War, 1939-1945 -- Influence -- Congresses. Holocaust, Jewish (1939-1945) -- Germany -- Influence -- Congresses. Holocaust, Jewish (1939-1945) -- Austria -- Influence -- Congresses. Austria -- Politics and government -- 1945- -- Congresses. Germany -- Politics and government -- 1945-1990 -- Congresses.

DD257.M26 1993
McAdams, A. James.
Germany divided: from the wall to reunification/ A. James McAdams. Princeton, N.J.: Princeton University Press, c1993. xvii, 250 p.
92-015654 943.087 0691078920
Germany -- Politics and government -- 1945-1990. Germany -- Politics and government -- 1990- Germany (East) -- Foreign relations -- Germany (West)

DD257.S66 1997
Standifer, Leon C.
Binding up the wounds: an American soldier in occupied Germany, 1945-1946/ Leon C. Standifer. Baton Rouge: Louisiana State University Press, c1997. xvii, 209 p.
96-038212 940.55/4 0807120944
Standifer, Leon.   Soldiers -- United States -- Biography.   Reconstruction   (1939-1951) -- Biography. Military government -- Germany.

DD257.2.G5
Gimbel, John, 1922-
The American occupation of Germany; politics and the military, 1945-1949. Stanford, Calif., Stanford University Press, 1968. xiv, 335 p.
68-026778 355.02/8/0943
Economic Assistance, American -- History. Berlin (Germany) -- Blockade, 1948-1949. Germany -- History -- 1945-1955.

DD257.2.V33 2001
Vaccaro, Tony, 1922-
Entering Germany: 1944-1949/ Tony Vaccaro. Koln: Taschen, c2001. 187 p.
01-405656 3822859087
World War, 1939-1945 -- Destruction and pillage -- Germany -- Pictorial works. War photographers -- United States. War photography -- Germany. Germany -- Pictorial works.

DD257.2.W54 1989
Willett, Ralph.
The Americanization of Germany, 1945-1949/ Ralph Willett. London; Routledge, 1989. xi, 151 p.
88-028654 943.087 0415002877
Popular culture -- Germany -- History -- 20th century.   Germany -- Civilization -- American influences. Germany -- Civilization -- 20th century.

DD257.2.W55
Willis, F. Roy 1930-
The French in Germany, 1945-1949. Stanford, Calif., Stanford University Press, 1962. viii, 308 p.
61-016886 943.087
Germany (Territory under Allied occupation, 1945-1955: French Zone) Germany -- History -- 1945-1955.

DD257.25.B336 1996
Barnouw, Dagmar.
Germany 1945: views of war and violence/ Dagmar Barnouw. Bloomington, Inu.: Indiana University Press, c1996. xviii, 255 p.
96-011185 943.087 0253330467
Reconstruction (1939-1951) -- Germany. World War, 1939-1945 -- Germany. Germany -- History - - 1945-1955.

DD257.25.G45 1987
Germany between East and West/ edited by Edwina Moreton. Cambridge [Cambridgeshire]; Cambridge University Press, 1987. viii, 185 p.
87-006337 943.087 0521342775
German reunification question (1949-1990) World politics -- 1975-1985. World politics -- 1985-1995.

DD257.25.N55 1988
Ninkovich, Frank A., 1944-
Germany and the United States: the transformation of the German question since 1945/ Frank Ninkovich. Boston: Twayne Publishers, c1988. xv, 201 p.
87-028176 943.087 0805779035
German reunification question (1949-1990) Germany -- Foreign relations -- United States. United States -- Foreign relations -- Germany.

DD257.25.N58 2001
Niven, William John, 1956-
Dividing and uniting Germany/ Bill Niven and J.K.A. Thomaneck London; Routledge, 2000. p. cm.
00-032319 943.087 0415183286
German reunification question (1949-1990) Regionalism -- Germany.   Germany -- History -- Unification, 1990 -- Social aspects.

DD257.25.V47 1991
Verheyen, Dirk.
The German question: a cultural, historical, and geopolitical exploration/ by Dirk Verheyen. Boulder: Westview Press, 1991. xii, 228 p.
91-014449 943.087 0813383595
German reunification question (1949-1990)

DD257.4.G75
Great Britain. Foreign Office
Selected documents on Germany and the question of Berlin, 1944-1961. London, H. M. Stationery Off., 1961. xiii, 483 p.
62-001298
German reunification question (1949-1990) Berlin question, (1945-   ) Germany -- History -- 1945-1955.

DD257.4.N44
Nettl, J. P.
The Eastern Zone and Soviet policy in Germany, 1945-50. London, Oxford University Press, 1951. xix, 324 p.
51-014125 943.086
Germany. Germany (East) -- Economic conditions.

DD257.4.P43
Peterson, Edward Norman.
The American occupation of Germany: retreat to victory/ Edward N. Peterson. Detroit: Wayne State University Press, 1977, c1978. 376 p.
77-028965 940.53/144/0943 0814315887
Germany -- History -- 1945-1955. Berlin (Germany) -- Politics and government -- 1945-1990.

DD258.7 West Germany — History — General works

DD258.7.B35 1982
Balfour, Michael Leonard Graham, 1908-
West Germany: a contemporary history/ Michael Balfour. New York: St. Martin's Press, 1982. 307 p.
81-021293   943.087   0312862970
Germany (West) -- History. Germany (West) -- Politics and government.

DD258.7.B37 1989
Bark, Dennis L.
A history of West Germany/ [Dennis L. Bark and David R. Gress]. Oxford, UK; Blackwell, 1989- v. 1
88-038212   943.087   0631167870
Germany (West) -- History.

DD258.75 West Germany — History — Politics and government

DD258.75.F43 1989
The Federal Republic of Germany at forty/ edited by Peter H. Merkl. New York: New York University Press, c1989. xii, 505 p.
89-032630   943   0814754457
Germany (West) -- Politics and government.

DD258.8-258.85 West Germany — History — Foreign and general relations

DD258.8.H37 1989
Hanrieder, Wolfram F.
Germany, America, Europe: forty years of German foreign policy/ Wolfram F. Hanrieder. New Haven: Yale University Press, c1989. xviii, 509 p.
88-030356   327.43   0300040229
Germany (West) -- Foreign relations.

DD258.85.S6.P58 1992
Pittman, Avril.
From Ostpolitik to reunification: West German-Soviet political relations since 1974/ Avril Pittman. Cambridge [England]; Cambridge University Press, 1992. xix, 226 p.
91-000880   327.43047   0521401666
Germany (West) -- Foreign relations -- Soviet Union. Soviet Union -- Foreign relations -- Germany (West) Soviet Union -- Foreign relations -- 1975-1985.

DD259-262 West Germany — History — By period

DD259.C7 1982
Craig, Gordon Alexander, 1913-
The Germans/ Gordon A. Craig. New York: Putnam, c1982. 350 p.
81-008650   943   0399124365
Germany (West) -- History.

DD259.P74 1979
Prittie, Terence, 1913-
The velvet chancellors: a history of post-war Germany/ Terence Prittie. London: Muller, 1979. xii, 286 p.
80-464210   943.087   0584104618
Germany (West) -- History. Germany -- History -- 1945-1990.

DD259.4.G653
Grass, Gunter, 1927-
Speak out; speeches, open letters, commentaries. Translated by Ralph Manheim. Introd. by Michael Harrington. New York, Harcourt, Brace & World [1969] xii, 142 p.
69-012035   320.9/43
Germany (West) -- Politics and government -- Addresses, essays, lectures.

DD259.4.M36 1989
McGhee, George Crews, 1912-
At the creation of a new Germany: from Adenauer to Brandt: an ambassador's account/ George McGhee; foreword by John J. McCloy. New Haven: Yale University Press, c1989. xxiv, 289 p.
88-010829   303.4/8243/073   0300042507
McGhee, George Crews, -- 1912- Adenauer, Konrad, -- 1876-1967. Brandt, Willy -- 1913- Diplomats -- United States -- Biography. Diplomats -- Germany (West) -- Biography. Germany (West) -- Politics and government. Germany (West) -- Relations -- United States. United States -- Relations -- Germany (West)

DD259.5.M47 1995
Merritt, Richard L.
Democracy imposed: U.S. occupation policy and the German public, 1945-1949/ Richard L. Merritt. New Haven: Yale University Press, c1995. xxi, 452 p.
95-004263   327.43073   0300060378
Military government -- Germany -- History -- 20th century. Germany -- Foreign relations -- United States. United States -- Foreign relations -- Germany. Germany -- History -- 1945-1955.

DD259.7.A3.A333
Adenauer, Konrad, 1876-1967.
Memoirs/ Translated by Beate Ruhm von Oppen. H. Regnery Co., c1966- v.
65-026906   943.0870924
Adenauer, Konrad, -- 1876-1967. World politics -- 1945- Germany -- Politics and government -- 1945-1990. Germany (West) -- Politics and government.

DD259.7.A3.H5
Hiscocks, Richard.
The Adenauer era. Philadelphia, Lippincott [1966] x, 312 p.
66-023243   943.0870924
Adenauer, Konrad, -- 1876-1967. Germany (West) -- Politics and government. Germany (West) -- Social conditions.

DD259.7.A3.W413
Weymar, Paul.
Adenauer, his authorized biography. Translated from the German by Peter de Mendelssohn. New York, Dutton, 1957. 509 p.
56-006313   923.243
Adenauer, Konrad, -- 1876-1967.

DD259.7.B7.P74 1974b
Prittie, Terence, 1913-
Willy Brandt; portrait of a statesman [by] Terence Prittie. New York, Schocken Books [1974] 356 p.
74-009229   943.087/092/4   0805235612
Brandt, Willy, -- 1913-

DD260.4.D58 1989
The dividing Rhine: politics and society in contemporary France and Germany/ edited by John Trumpbour. Oxford; Berg; 1989. viii, 208 p.
89-006568   306/.0943   0854965890
Germany (West) -- Politics and government. Germany (West) -- Social conditions. France -- Politics and government -- 1945-

DD260.5.R67 1987
Rosolowsky, Diane.
West Germany's foreign policy: the impact of the Social Democrats and the Greens/ Diane Rosolowsky. New York: Greenwood Press, 1987. x, 155 p.
87-012017   327.43   0313256721
Germany (West) -- Foreign relations. Germany (West) -- Politics and government -- 1982-1990.

DD260.65.G47.A3 1998
Genscher, Hans Dietrich.
Rebuilding a house divided: a memoir by the architect of Germany's reunification/ Hans-Dietrich Genscher; translated from the German by Thomas Thornton. New York: Broadway Books, c1998. xi, 580 p.
97-011772   943.086   0553067125
Genscher, Hans Dietrich. Foreign ministers -- Germany -- Biography. German reunification question (1949-1990) Germany -- Foreign relations -- 1945- Germany (West) -- Politics and government.

DD260.65.W45.W442 1999
Weizsacker, Richard, 1920-
From Weimar to the Wall: my life in German politics/ Richard von Weizsacker; translated from the German by Ruth Hein. New York: Broadway Books, c1999. 422p.
98-050156   943.087/092   0767903013
Weizsacker, Richard, -- Freiherr von, -- 1920- Presidents -- Germany -- Biography. National socialism. Germany -- Politics and government -- 20th century.

DD260.8.B7413 1992
Brandt, Willy, 1913-
My life in politics/ Willy Brandt. London; Hamish Hamilton, 1992. xxv, 498 p.
92-224956   0241130735
Brandt, Willy, -- 1913- Heads of state -- Germany (West) -- Biography. Germany (West) -- Politics and government.

DD260.85.S3613 1989
Schmidt, Helmut, 1918 Dec. 23-
Men and powers: a political retrospective/ Helmut Schmidt; translated from the German by Ruth Hein. New York: Random House, c1989. xx, 410 p.
88-043219   943.087/7/092   0394569946
Schmidt, Helmut, -- 1918 Dec. 23- Heads of state -- Germany (West) -- Biography. Germany (West) -- Politics and government -- 1982-1990. Germany (West) -- Foreign relations.

DD262.L48 1991
Lewis, Rand C.
A Nazi legacy: right-wing extremism in postwar Germany/ Rand C. Lewis. New York: Praeger, 1991. xvi, 184 p.
90-024277   943.087   0275938530
Fascism -- Germany (West) Right and left (Political science) Germany (West) -- Politics and government -- 1982-1990.

DD262.P7813 1996
Pruys, Karl Hugo, 1938-
Kohl, genius of the present: a biography of Helmut Kohl/ edited [sic] by Karl Hugo Pruys; translated by Kathleen Bunten. Chicago: Edition Q, c1996. xiv, 402 p.
96-023379   943.087/8/092   1883695104
Kohl, Helmut, -- 1930- Heads of state -- Germany -- Biography. Germany -- Politics and government -- 1982-1990. Germany -- History -- Unification, 1990.

DD283 East Germany — History — Political history

DD283.D46 1988
Dennis, Mike, 1940-
German Democratic Republic: politics, economics, and society/ Mike Dennis. London; Pinter Publishers, 1988. xxi, 223 p.
87-032889 943.1087 0861874137
  Germany (East) -- Politics and government. Germany (East) -- Social conditions. Germany (East) -- Economic conditions.

DD283.E27 1988
East Germany in comparative perspective/ edited by David Childs, Thomas A. Baylis, Marilyn Rueschemeyer. London; Routledge, 1989. xvi, 238 p.
88-031913 943.1 0415004969
  Germany (East) -- Politics and government. Germany (East) -- Social conditions. Germany (East) -- Economic conditions.

DD283.F85 1995
Fulbrook, Mary, 1951-
Anatomy of a dictatorship: inside the GDR, 1949-1989/ Mary Fulbrook. New York: Oxford University Press, 1995. xii, 307 p.
95-030139 943.1087 0198203128
  Germany (East) -- Politics and government. Germany (East) -- History. Germany -- History -- 1945-1990.

DD285-289.5 East Germany — History — By period

DD285.N35 1995
Naimark, Norman M.
The Russians in Germany: a history of the Soviet Zone of occupation, 1945-1949/ Norman M. Naimark. Cambridge, Mass.: Belknap Press of Harvard University Press, 1995. p. cm.
95-007725 943.087/4 0674784057
  Communism and culture -- Germany (East) Germany (East) -- Economic policy. Germany (East) -- Politics and government. Germany (East) -- Social policy.

DD285.P48 1999
Peterson, Edward N. 1925-
Russian commands and German resistance: the Soviet Occupation, 1945-1949/ Edward N. Peterson. New York: P. Lang, c1999. 510 p.
98-004812 943/.10874 0820439487
  Military occupation. Russians -- Germany (East) Opposition (Political science) -- Germany (East) Germany (East) -- Politics and government.

DD286.3.A53 2000
Andress, Reinhard, 1957-
Protokolliteratur in der DDR: der dokumentierte Alltag/ Reinhard Andress. New York: P. Lang, c2000. ix, 220 p.
99-019439 943/.1087 0820444928
  Protocol-books -- Germany (East) Oral history. Germany (East) -- Biography -- History and criticism.

DD286.4.D46 2000
Dennis, Mike, 1940-
The rise and fall of the German Democratic Republic, 1945-1990/ Mike Dennis. Harlow, England; Longman, 2000. p. cm.
00-045311 943/.1087 0582245613
  Protest movements -- Germany (East) Political culture -- Germany (East) Germany (East) -- Politics and government. Germany -- History -- Unification, 1990. Germany (East) -- Social conditions.

DD286.5.L6713 1998
Loth, Wilfried.
Stalin's unwanted child: the Soviet Union, the German question, and the founding of the GDR/ Wilfried Loth; translated by Robert F. Hogg. New York: St. Martin's Press, 1998. xiii, 234 p.
97-038375 327.431047 0312210280
  Military government -- Germany (East) Military occupation. Germany (East) -- Politics and government. Germany (East) -- Foreign relations -- Soviet Union. Soviet Union -- Foreign relations -- Germany (East)

DD289.D27 1991
Darnton, Robert.
Berlin journal, 1989-1990/ Robert Darnton. New York: Norton, c1991. 352 p.
90-019745 943.1087/8 0393029700
  Anti-communist movements -- Germany (East) Berlin (Germany) -- History -- 1945-1990. Germany (East) -- Politics and government -- 1989-1990.

DD289.G44 1992
Gedmin, Jeffrey.
The hidden hand: Gorbachev and the collapse of East Germany/ Jeffrey Gedmin. Washington, D.C.: AEI Press; 1992. ix, 169 p.
92-002764 327.470431 0844737941
  Gorbachev, Mikhail Sergeevich, -- 1931- Perestroika -- Germany (East) Soviet Union -- Foreign relations -- Germany (East) Germany (East) -- Politics and government. Germany (East) -- Foreign relations -- Soviet Union.

DD289.M47 1993
Merkl, Peter H.
German unification in the European context/ Peter H. Merkl; with a contribution by Gert-Joachim Glaessner. University Park, Pa.: Pennsylvania State University Press, c1993. xiv, 448 p.
92-031665 943.087/9 0271009225
  Germany -- History -- Unification, 1990. Germany -- Relations -- Europe. Europe -- Relations -- Germany.

DD289.5.A38 1998
After the wall: Eastern Germany since 1989/ edited by Patricia J. Smith. Boulder, Colo.: Westview Press, 1998. xvi, 350 p.
98-022540 943.087/9 0813332095
  Xenophobia -- Germany (East) Political culture -- Germany (East) Germany (East) -- Politics and government -- 1989-1990. Germany -- History -- Unification, 1990. Germany -- Economic conditions -- 1990-

DD289.5.B47 1999
Berdahl, Daphne, 1964-
Where the world ended: re-unification and identity in the German borderland/ Daphne Berdahl. Berkeley, Calif.: University of California Press, c1999. xiii, 294 p.
98-007099 341.4/2 0520214765
  Ethnology -- Germany -- Case studies. Social change -- Germany -- Kella. Germany (East) -- Boundaries -- Case studies. Kella (Germany) -- Case studies. Kella (Germany) -- Social life and customs -- 20th century.

DD290.22 Reunified Germany, 1990- — Sources and documents

DD290.22.D4813 1994b
Uniting Germany: documents and debates, 1944-1993/ edited by Konrad H. Jarausch and Volker Gransow; translated by Allison Brown and Belinda Cooper. Providence: Berghahn Books, 1994. xxx, 282 p.
94-020694 943.087 1571810102
  German reunification question (1949-1990) -- Sources Germany -- History -- Unification, 1990 -- Sources.

DD290.25 Reunified Germany, 1990- — General works

DD290.25.D84 1998
Duffield, John S.
World power forsaken: political culture, international institutions, and German security policy after unification/ John S. Duffield. Stanford, Calif.: Stanford University Press, c1998. xvi, 385 p.
97-039359 320.943 0804733651
  Political culture -- Germany. National security -- Germany. World politics -- 1989- Germany -- Politics and government -- 1990-

DD290.25.G37 1993
Garton Ash, Timothy.
In Europe's name: Germany and the divided continent/ Timothy Garton Ash. New York: Random House, c1993. 680 p.
93-005477 943.087/9 0394557115
  German reunification question (1949-1990) Germany -- History -- Unification, 1990. Germany -- Politics and government -- 1945-1990. Germany -- Relations -- Europe.

DD290.25.G57 1992
Glaessner, Gert-Joachim, 1944-
The unification process in Germany: from dictatorship to democracy/ Gert-Joachim Glaessner; translated from the German by Colin B. Grant. New York: St. Martin's Press, c1992. viii, 248 p.
92-016646 943.087/9 0312085702
  Germany -- History -- Unification, 1990.

DD290.25.J37 1994
Jarausch, Konrad Hugo.
The rush to German unity/ Konrad H. Jarausch.
New York: Oxford University Press, 1994. xvii,
280 p.
93-000625   943.087   0195072758
*German reunification question (1949-1990)
Opposition (Political science) -- Germany (East)
Germany (East) -- Social conditions. Germany
(East) -- Politics and government -- 1989-1990.
Germany -- History -- Unification, 1990.*

DD290.29 Reunified Germany, 1990- — Political history

DD290.29.B34 1999
Banchoff, Thomas F., 1964-
The German problem transformed: institutions,
politics, and foreign policy, 1945-1995/ Thomas
Banchoff. Ann Arbor: University of Michigan
Press, c1999. x, 217 p.
98-058102   327.43   047211008X
*Germany -- Politics and government -- 1990-
Germany (West) -- Foreign relations -- Europe,
Eastern. Europe, Eastern -- Foreign relations --
Germany (West)*

DD290.29.G495 1997
Germany reunified: a five- and fifty-year
retrospective/ edited by Peter M. Daly ... [et al.].
New York: P. Lang, c1997. xviii, 256 p.
97-011728   943.087/9   0820438030
*Art and state -- Germany. Art and state --
Germany (East) Mass media -- Germany. Germany
-- Cultural policy. Germany -- History --
Unification, 1990. Germany -- Intellectual life --
20th century.*

DD290.29.H46 2000
Heneghan, Tom.
Unchained eagle: Germany after the wall. Harlow;
Reuters, 2000. xvi, 245 p.
  943.0   0273650122
Germany -- History -- 1990-

DD290.29.M37 1997
Markovits, Andrei S.
The German predicament: memory and power in
the new Europe/ Andrei S. Markovits and Simon
Reich. Ithaca, N.Y.: Cornell University Press,
1997. xv, 248 p.
96-042943   320.943   0801428025
*Political culture -- Germany.   Germany --
Relations -- Europe. Europe -- Relations --
Germany. Germany -- Politics and government --
1990-*

DD290.29.M49 2001
McAdams, A. James.
Judging the past in unified Germany/ A. James
McAdams. Cambridge, UK; Cambridge University
Press, 2001. xix, 244 p.
00-064185   943.08   0521802083
*Justice, Administration of -- Germany (East)
Restitution and indemnification claims (1933-) --
Germany (East) Justice and politics -- Germany.
Germany (East) -- Politics and government.
Germany -- History -- Unification, 1990.*

DD290.29.M87 1998
Mushaben, Joyce Marie, 1952-
From post-war to post-wall generations: changing
attitudes towards the national question and NATO
in the Federal Republic of Germany/ Joyce Marie
Mushaben. Boulder, Colo.: Westview Press, 1998.
xiv, 420 p.
97-031491   943.087   0813311527
*National characteristics, German. National
security -- Germany -- Public opinion. Political
culture -- Germany. Germany -- Military policy --
Public opinion. Germany -- History -- Unification,
1990. Germany -- Foreign relations -- 1990-*

DD290.29.S73 1998
Staab, Andreas, 1965-
National identity in eastern Germany: inner
unification or continued separation?/ Andreas
Staab. Westport, Conn.: Praeger, 1998. 180 p.
97-035135   943.087/9/019   027596177X
*Political participation -- Germany -- History --
20th century. Political culture -- Germany.
Political culture -- Germany (East) Germany
(East) -- Politics and government -- 1989-1990.*

DD290.29.Z45 1995
Zelikow, Philip, 1954-
Germany unified and Europe transformed: a study
in statecraft/ Philip Zelikow, Condoleezza Rice.
Cambridge, Mass.: Harvard University Press, 1995.
xvi, 493 p.
95-012187   943.087/9   0674353242
*European federation.   Germany -- Politics and
government -- 1990-   Europe -- Politics and
government -- 1989-   Germany -- History --
Unification, 1990.*

DD290.3 Reunified Germany, 1990- — Foreign and general relations

DD290.3.N49 1992
The New Germany and the new Europe/ Paul B.
Stares, editor. Washington, D.C.: Brookings
Institution, c1992. xiv, 406 p.
92-026403   327.43   0815781385
*European cooperation.   Germany -- Relations --
Europe. Europe -- Relations -- Germany. Europe --
Politics and government -- 1989-*

DD290.3.O89 2000
Otte, Max, 1964-
A rising middle power?: German foreign policy in
transformation, 1989-1999/ by Max Otte and
Jurgen Greve. New York: St. Martin's Press,
2000. p. cm.
99-055259   943.087/9   0312226535
*Germany -- History -- Unification, 1990.
Germany -- Foreign relations -- 1945- Germany --
Foreign relations -- 1990-*

DD290.3.T36 1997
Tamed power: Germany in Europe/ edited by Peter
J. Katzenstein. Ithaca, N.Y.: Cornell University
Press, 1997. xiv, 314 p.
97-030056   303.48/24304   0801434297
*European Union -- Germany.   Europe --
Relations -- Germany. Germany -- Relations --
Europe. Europe -- Economic integration.*

DD290.33 Reunified Germany, 1990- — Biography and memoirs — Individual, A-Z

DD290.33.L34
Lafontaine, Oskar, 1943-
The heart beats on the left/ Oskar Lafontaine;
translated by Ronald Taylor. Cambridge [England]:
Polity; 2000. xiv, 219 p.
00-039956   943/.420878/092   0745625819
*Lafontaine, Oskar, -- 1943- Schroder, Gerhard, --
1944- Politicians -- Germany -- Biography.
Germany -- Politics and government -- 1990-*

DD347 Prussia — History — General works

DD347.C3
Carsten, F. L.
The origins of Prussia. Oxford, Clarendon Press,
1954. 309 p.
54-004860
Prussia (Germany) -- History.

DD347.L45 2000
Levinger, Matthew Bernard, 1960-
Enlightened nationalism: the transformation of
Prussian political culture, 1806-1848/ Matthew
Levinger. Oxford; Oxford University Press, 2000.
xiv, 317 p.
99-032583   943/.07   0195131851
*Political culture -- Germany -- Prussia -- History
-- 19th century. Nationalism -- Germany -- Prussia
-- History -- 19th century. Enlightenment --
Germany -- Prussia. Prussia (Germany) --
Historiography.*

DD397-453 Prussia — History — By period

DD397.R25 1969
Ranke, Leopold von, 1795-1886.
Memoirs of the House of Brandenburg and history
of Prussia during the seventeenth and eighteenth
centuries. Translated from the German by Sir
Alexr. and Lady Duff Gordon. New York, Haskell
House Publishers, 1969. 3 v.
68-025278   943/.05   0838301681
*Prussia (Germany) -- History -- Frederick
William I, 1713-1740. Prussia (Germany) --
History -- Frederick II, 1740-1786.*

DD404.G32 1942
Gaxotte, Pierre.
Frederick the Great/ by Pierre Gaxotte; translated
by R. A. Bell. New Haven: Yale University Press,
1942. 420 p.
42-002150
*Frederick William -- I, -- King of Prussia, -- 1688-
1740. -- cn. Frederick -- II, -- King of Prussia, --
1712-1786. -- In   Prussia (Germany) -- History -
- Frederick II, 1740-1786.*

DD404.S28 1983
Schieder, Theodor.
Friedrich der Grosse: ein Konigtum der
Widerspruche/ Theodor Schieder. Frankfurt am
Main: Propylaen Verlag, 1983. 538 p.
84-103994   943/.053/0924   354907638X
*Frederick -- II, -- King of Prussia, -- 1712-1786.
Prussia (Germany) -- Kings and rulers --
Biography. Prussia (Germany) -- History --
Frederick II, 1740-1786.*

DD404.S57 1963a
Simon, Edith.
The making of Frederick the Great. Boston, Little, Brown [1963] 296 p.
63-008963   923.143
Frederick -- II, -- King of Prussia, -- 1712-1786.

DD419.B45 1992
Beiser, Frederick C., 1949-
Enlightenment, revolution, and romanticism: the genesis of modern German political thought, 1790-1800/ Frederick C. Beiser. Cambridge, Mass.: Harvard University Press, 1992. xiii, 434 p.
91-040026   320.5/0943   0674257278
Liberalism -- Germany. Romanticism -- Germany. Conservatism -- Germany. Germany -- Politics and government -- 1740-1806.

DD419.B47 1988
Berdahl, Robert M.
The politics of the Prussian nobility: the development of a conservative ideology, 1770-1848/ Robert M. Berdahl. Princeton, N.J.: Princeton University Press, c1988. xiii, 384 p.
88-017616   943   069105536X
Conservatism -- Germany -- Prussia. Nobility -- Germany -- Prussia. Prussia (Germany) -- Politics and government -- 1740-1815. Prussia (Germany) -- Politics and government -- 1806-1848.

DD420.S56 1997
Simms, Brendan.
The impact of Napoleon: Prussian high politics, foreign policy and the crisis of the executive, 1797-1806/ Brendan Simms. Cambridge [England]; Cambridge University Press, 1997. xiii, 390 p.
96-006483   943/.073   0521453607
Napoleon -- I, -- Emperor of the French, -- 1769-1821. Prussia (Germany) -- History -- Frederick William III, 1797-1840. Prussia (Germany) -- Foreign relations -- 1786-1806.

DD422.C5.P33
Paret, Peter.
Clausewitz and the state/ Peter Paret. New York: Oxford University Press, 1976. viii, 467 p.
75-016901   943/.06/0924   0195019881
Clausewitz, Carl von, -- 1780-1831. Intellectuals -- Germany -- Biography. Nobility -- Germany -- Biography. State, The.

DD422.H8.S93
Sweet, Paul Robinson, 1907-
Wilhelm von Humboldt: a biography/ by Paul R. Sweet. Columbus: Ohio State University Press, c1978-c1980. 2 v.
77-026654   943/.06/0924   0814202748
Humboldt, Wilhelm, -- Freiherr von, -- 1767-1835. Statesmen -- Germany -- Biography.

DD424.8.B37 1995
Barclay, David E., 1948-
Frederick William IV and the Prussian monarchy, 1840-1861/ David E. Barclay. Oxford: Clarendon Press; 1995. xiii, 335 p.
95-031078   943/.076/092   0198204302
Frederick William -- IV, -- King of Prussia, -- 1795-1861. Monarchy -- Germany -- Prussia -- History. Prussia (Germany) -- Kings and rulers -- Biography. Prussia (Germany) -- History -- Frederick William IV, 1840-1861.

DD438.W39 1996
Wawro, Geoffrey.
The Austro-Prussian War: Austria's war with Prussia and Italy in 1866/ Geoffrey Wawro. Cambridge [England]; Cambridge University Press, 1996. xiii, 313 p.
95-050529   943/.076   0521560594
Austro-Prussian War, 1866. Custozza, Battle of, 1866. Koniggratz, Battle of, 1866. Italy -- Politics and government -- 1849-1870. Germany -- Politics and government -- 1848-1870. Austria -- Politics and government -- 1848-1918.

DD453.B37 1995
Baranowski, Shelley.
The sanctity of rural life: nobility, Protestantism, and Nazism in Weimar Prussia/ Shelley Baranowski. New York: Oxford University Press, 1995. x, 267 p.
94-019307   943.085   0195068815
Church and state -- Germany -- Prussia -- History. Conservatism -- Germany -- Prussia -- History. National socialism -- Germany -- Prussia. Prussia (Germany) -- Church history. Prussia (Germany) -- Social conditions. Agriculture and state -- Germany -- Prussia.

DD453.O76 1991
Orlow, Dietrich.
Weimar Prussia, 1925-1933: the illusion of strength/ Dietrich Orlow. Pittsburgh, Pa.: University of Pittsburgh Press, c1991. 368 p.
91-008117   943.085   0822936844
Prussia (Germany) -- History -- 1918-1933.

DD491 Prussia — Local history and description

DD491.S68.S8
Steefel, Lawrence Dinkelspiel, 1894-
The Schleswig-Holstein question, by Lawrence D. Steefel. Cambridge, Harvard University Press; 1932. xii, 400 p.
32-009250   943.51
Schleswig-Holstein question.

DD801 Local history and description — States, provinces, regions, etc., A-Z

DD801.B42.D68 1992
Dorondo, D. R., 1957-
Bavaria and German federalism: Reich to republic, 1918-33, 1945-49/ D.R. Dorondo. London: Macmillan; 1992. xix, 165 p.
91-027965   320.943   0333538250
Federal government -- Germany (West) Bavaria (Germany) -- Politics and government -- 1945-Bavaria (Germany) -- Politics and government -- 1918-1945.

DD801.B64.H3813 1998
Heilbronner, Oded.
Catholicism, political culture, and the countryside: a social history of the Nazi Party in south Germany/ Oded Heilbronner. Ann Arbor: University of Michigan Press, c1998. xiii, 317 p.
98-008996   324.243/038/09434609042   0472109103
National socialism -- Germany -- Black Forest Region. Nationalsozialistische Deutsche Arbeiter-Partei. Catholics -- Germany -- Black Forest Region -- Political activity.

DD801.B64.L84 1997
Luebke, David Martin, 1960-
His majesty's rebels: communities, factions, and rural revolt in the Black Forest, 1725-1745/ David Martin Luebke. Ithaca, N.Y.: Cornell University Press, 1997. xiii, 270 p.
97-000720   943/.46   0801433460
Black Forest (Germany) -- History. Black Forest (Germany) -- Rural conditions. Black Forest (Germany) -- Economic conditions.

DD801.F566.Z57 1997
Zmora, Hillay, 1964-
State and nobility in early modern Germany: the knightly feud in Franconia, 1440-1567/ Hillay Zmora. Cambridge, U.K.; Cambridge University Press, 1997. xiii, 232 p.
97-001834   943.7/33   0521561795
Nobility -- Germany -- Franconia -- History. Knights and knighthood -- Germany -- Franconia -- History. Feudal law -- Germany -- Franconia. Franconia (Germany) -- Politics and government.

DD801.H57.I54 1987
Ingrao, Charles W.
The Hessian mercenary state: ideas, institutions, and reform under Frederick II, 1760-1785/ Charles W. Ingrao. Cambridge [Cambridgeshire]; Cambridge University Press, 1987. xi, 240 p.
86-008274   943/.41053   0521327563
Frederick -- II, -- Landgrave of Hesse-Kassel, -- 1720-1785. Hesse (Germany) -- History -- 1567-1806.

DD801.H57.T39 1994
Taylor, Peter K. 1950-
Indentured to liberty: peasant life and the Hessian military state, 1688-1815/ Peter K. Taylor. Ithaca, NY: Cornell University Press, c1994. xvi, 275 p.
93-041906   943/.41   0801429161
Peasantry -- Germany -- Hesse. Finance, Public -- Germany -- Hesse -- History -- 18th century. German mercenaries -- History -- 18th century. Hesse (Germany) -- Armed Forces -- History -- 18th century. Hesse (Germany) -- History. Hesse (Germany) -- Rural conditions.

DD801.H57.T47 1995
Theibault, John, 1957-
German villages in crisis: rural life in Hesse-Kassel and the Thirty Years' War, 1580-1720/ John Theibault. Atlantic Highlands, N.J.: Humanities Press, 1995. xi, 237 p.
93-028755   943/.412041   0391038397
Villages -- Germany -- Hesse -- History -- 17th century. Thirty Years' War, 1618-1648 -- Social aspects -- Germany -- Hesse. Hesse (Germany) -- Social life and customs. Germany -- History -- 1517-1648. Hesse (Germany) -- Rural conditions.

DD801.P448.A67 1990
Applegate, Celia.
A nation of provincials: the German idea of Heimat/ Celia Applegate. Berkeley: University of California Press, c1990. xi, 273 p.
89-020522   943/.435004   0520063945
Ethnicity -- Germany -- Palatinate. Ethnology -- Germany -- Palatinate. Palatinate (Germany) -- Ethnic relations.

DD801.R682.O86 1993
Osmond, Jonathan, 1953-
Rural protest in the Weimar Republic: the free peasantry in the Rhineland and Bavaria/ Jonathan Osmond. New York, N.Y.: St. Martin's Press, 1993. xiv, 224 p.
92-025187   943/.3085/08624   0312086237
Peasantry -- Germany -- Rhineland -- History -- 20th century. Peasantry -- Germany -- Bavaria -- History -- 20th century. Rhineland (German) -- History. Bavaria (Germany) -- History. Rhineland (Germany) -- Rural conditions.

DD801.R682.S64 1991
Sperber, Jonathan, 1952-
Rhineland radicals: the democratic movement and the revolution of 1848-1849/ Jonathan Sperber. Princeton, N.J.: Princeton University Press, c1991. xvi, 528 p.
91-000127   943/.4   069103172X
Rhineland (Germany) -- History. Germany -- History -- Revolution, 1848-1849.

DD801.R76.I56 2000
Innes, Matthew.
State and society in the early Middle Ages: the middle Rhine valley, 400-1000/ Matthew Innes. Cambridge, UK; Cambridge University Press, 2000. xvi, 316 p.
99-033218   306.2/09434   0521594553
Political culture -- Rhine River Valley -- History -- To 1500. Cities and towns, Medieval -- Rhine River Valley. Elite (Social sciences) -- Rhine River Valley -- History. Rhine River Valley -- Social conditions. Germany -- History -- To 843. France -- Social conditions -- To 987.

DD801.S13.F74
Freymond, Jacques.
The Saar conflict, 1945-1955. With a foreword by John Goormaghtigh. London, Stevens; [1960] xxviii, 395 p.
60-008716   943.427
Saar Valley -- History.

DD801.S352.L36 1997
Lapp, Benjamin, 1958-
Revolution from the right: politics, class, and the rise of Nazism in Saxony, 1919-1933/ Benjamin Lapp. Atlantic Highlands, NJ: Humanities Press, 1997. xv, 248 p.
96-052073   320.943/21/09041   0391040278
Conservatism -- Germany -- Saxony. National socialism -- Germany -- Saxony. Right and left (Political science) -- Germany -- Saxony. Saxony (Germany) -- Politics and government. Germany -- Politics and government -- 1918-1933.

DD801.W76.W55 1995
Wilson, Peter H.
War, state, and society in Wurttemberg, 1677-1793/ Peter H. Wilson. Cambridge; Cambridge University Press, 1995. xvii, 294 p.
94-016546   943/.47   0521473020
Social classes -- Germany -- Wurttemberg -- History -- 18th century. Wurttemberg (Germany) -- Politics and government. Wurttemberg (Germany) -- History, Military. Holy Roman Empire -- History -- 1648-1804.

DD801.W765.C66 1997
Confino, Alon.
The nation as a local metaphor: Wurttemberg, imperial Germany, and national memory, 1871-1918/ Alon Confino. Chapel Hill: University of North Carolina Press, c1997. xiii, 280 p.
96-052039   320.54/0943/47   0807823597
Nationalism -- Germany -- Wurttemberg. National characteristics, German. Wurttemberg (Germany) -- Politics and government. Germany -- Politics and government -- 1871-1918.

DD857 Local history and description — Berlin — Biography

DD857.A2.H34 1995
Hafner, Katie.
The house at the bridge: a story of modern Germany/ Katie Hafner. New York: Scribner, c1995. 256 p.
94-033580   920.043157   0684194007
Jews -- Persecutions -- Germany -- Berlin -- History. Berlin Wall, Berlin Germany, 1961-1989. Berlin (Germany) -- Ethnic relations. Berlin (Germany) -- Biography. Berlin (Germany) -- Politics and government -- 1945-1990.

DD857.B7.A3
Brandt, Willy, 1913-
My road to Berlin/ by Willy Brandt, as told to Leo Lania. Doubleday, 1960. 287 p.
60-010666   923.243
Brandt, Willy, -- 1913- Mayors -- Germany -- Berlin -- Biography.   Berlin (Germany) -- Biography. Berlin (Germany) -- History -- 1945-1990.

DD860 Local history and description — Berlin — General works. Description

DD860.L37 2000
Large, David Clay.
Berlin/ David Clay Large. New York: Basic Books, c2000. xxvii, 706 p.
00-034280   943/.155   046502646X
Berlin (Germany) -- History. Berlin (Germany) -- Description and travel. Berlin (Germany) -- Social life and customs.

DD860.W24 1993
Wallace, Ian, 1942-
Berlin/ Ian Wallace, Compiler. Oxford, Eng.; Clio Press, c1993. xx, 160 p.
94-124908   016.943155   1851091424
Berlin (Germany) -- Bibliography.

DD866 Local history and description — Berlin — Social life and customs. Civilization. Intellectual life

DD866.E44 1988
Elkins, T. H.
Berlin: the spatial structure of a divided city/ T.H. Elkins with B. Hofmeister. London; Methuen, 1988. xvi, 274 p.
87-021722   943.1/55   0416922201
Berlin (Germany) -- History. Berlin (Germany) -- Geography.

DD866.S3513 1998
Schivelbusch, Wolfgang, 1941-
In a cold crater: cultural and intellectual life in Berlin, 1945-1948/ Wolfgang Schivelbusch; translated by Kelly Barry. Berkeley: University of California Press, c1998. xiii, 230 p.
97-040067   943/.155   0520203666
Intellectuals -- Germany -- Berlin -- History -- 20th century. Berlin (Germany) -- Social life and customs. Berlin (Germany) -- Intellectual life.

DD881 Local history and description — Berlin — History and description

DD881.D3
Davison, W. Phillips 1918-
The Berlin blockade; a study in cold war politics. Princeton, N. J., Princeton University Press, 1958. 423p.
58-006103   943.15
Berlin (Germany) -- History -- 1945-1990.

DD881.R5 1998
Richie, Alexandra.
Faust's metropolis: a history of Berlin/ Alexandra Richie. New York: Carroll & Graf, 1998. xxviii, 1139 p.
98-016802   943/.155   0786705108
Berlin (Germany) -- History.

DD881.S46 1983
Shlaim, Avi.
The United States and the Berlin Blockade, 1948-1949: a study in crisis decision-making/ Avi Shlaim. Berkeley: University of California Press, c1983. xiii, 463 p.
81-019636   943.1/550874   0520043855
Berlin (Germany) -- History -- Blockade, 1948-1949. United States -- Foreign relations -- Soviet Union -- Decision making. Soviet Union -- Foreign relations -- United States -- Decision making.

DD881.T87 1997
Tusa, Ann.
The last division: a history of Berlin, 1945-1989/ Ann Tusa. Reading, Mass.: Addison-Wesley, c1997. xi, 431 p.
96-041763   943.1/55087   0201143992
Military government -- Germany -- Berlin. Berlin Wall, Berlin, Germany, 1961-1989. Berlin (Germany) -- History -- 1945-1990.

DD901 Local history and description — Other cities, towns, etc., A-Z — General

DD901.D283.K5
Kimmich, Christoph M.
The free city; Danzig and German foreign policy, 1919-1934, by Christoph M. Kimmich. New Haven, Yale University Press, 1968. 196 p.
68-027758   320.9/438/2
Stresemann, Gustav, -- 1878-1929.   Gdansk (Poland) -- Politics and government. Germany -- Foreign relations -- 1918-1933.

DD901.F78.P35 1999
Palmowski, Jan.
Urban liberalism in imperial Germany: Frankfurt am Main, 1866-1914/ Jan Palmowski. Oxford; Oxford University Press, 1999. xiv, 391 p.
98-042428   320.51/0943/416409434
0198207506
Liberalism -- Germany -- Frankfurt am Main -- History -- 19th century. Middle class -- Germany -- Frankfurt am Main -- History -- 19th century. Political parties -- Germany -- Frankfurt am Main -- History -- 19th century. Frankfurt am Main (Germany) -- Politics and government.

DD901.H28.M42 1998
McElligott, Anthony, 1955-
Contested city: municipal politics and the rise of Nazism in Altona, 1917-1937/ Anthony McElligott. Ann Arbor: University of Michigan Press, c1998. xii, 334 p.
98-019712   320.943/515   0472109294
National socialism -- Germany -- Hamburg. Political parties -- Germany -- Hamburg. Municipal government -- Germany -- Hamburg. Hamburg (Germany) -- Politics and government. Hamburg-Altona (Hamburg, Germany) -- Politics and government.

DD901.M83.L36 1997
Large, David Clay.
Where ghosts walked: Munich's road to the Third Reich/ David Clay Large. New York: W.W. Norton, c1997. xxv, 406 p.
97-004263   943/.364   039303836X
National socialism -- Germany -- Munich. Conservatism -- Germany -- Munich. Munich (Germany) -- Social conditions. Munich (Germany) -- Intellectual life.

DD901.O2397.R56 1992
Rinderle, Walter, 1940-
The Nazi impact on a German village/ Walter Rinderle and Bernard Norling. Lexington: University Press of Kentucky, c1993. 276 p.
92-010030   943/.4626   0813117941
National socialism -- Germany -- Oberschopfheim. Oberschopfheim (Germany) -- History.

DD901.S87.F6
Ford, Franklin L. 1920-
Strasbourg in transition, 1648-1789. Cambridge, Harvard University Press, 1958. xvii, 321 p.
58-007247   943.445
Strasbourg (France) -- History. Strassburg (Germany) -- History.

DE History of the Greco-Roman World

DE5 Dictionaries. Encyclopedias

DE5.L29 1999
Late antiquity: a guide to the postclassical world/ G.W. Bowersock, Peter Brown, Oleg Grabar, editors. Cambridge, Mass.; Belknap Press of Harvard University Press, 1999. xiii, 780 p.
99-025639   938/.003   0674511735
Classical dictionaries.

DE5.O9 1999
The Oxford classical dictionary/ edited by Simon Hornblower and Antony Spawforth.3rd ed. Oxford; Oxford University Press, c1999. lv, 1640 p.
2001-271109   938/.003.221   0195216938
Classical dictionaries.

DE7 Biography (Collective)

DE7.H39 2000
Hazel, John.
Who's who in the Greek world/ John Hazel. London; Routledge, 2000. x, 285 p.
99-046943   920.038   0415124972
Classical biography -- Dictionaries. Greece -- Biography -- Dictionaries. Middle East -- Biography -- Dictionaries. Mediterranean Region -- History -- To 476.

DE8 Historiography — General works

DE8.F55 1986
Finley, M. I. 1912-
Ancient history: evidence and models/ M.I. Finley. New York, N.Y., U.S.A.: Viking, 1986, c1985. 131 p.
85-040616   938/.0072   0670809705
History -- Research. Greece -- Historiography. Rome -- Historiography.

DE8.F67 1983
Fornara, Charles W.
The nature of history in ancient Greece and Rome/ Charles William Fornara. Berkeley: University of California Press, c1983. xiv, 215 p.
82-021888   949.5/0072   0520049101
Historiography -- Greece. Historiography -- Rome. Greece -- Historiography. Rome -- Historiography.

DE9 Historiography — Biography of historians and archaeologists

DE9.A1
Medwid, Linda M., 1952-
The makers of classical archaeology: a reference work/ Linda M. Medwid. Amherst, N.Y.: Humanity Books, 2000. 352 p.
99-462362   930.1/092/2   1573928267
Classicists -- Biography. Archaeology -- Biography. Classical antiquities -- Bio-bibliography.

DE9.T54.F56 1994
Flower, Michael A.
Theopompus of Chios: history and rhetoric in the fourth century B.C./ Michael Attyah Flower. Oxford [England]: Clarendon Press; 1994. xii, 252 p.
94-013786   938/.09/092   0198140797
Theopompus, -- of Chios. Historians -- Greece -- Biography. Historiography -- Greece. Greece -- History -- To 146 B.C. -- Historiography.

DE59 Antiquities. Civilization. Culture — Works, 1801- — General works

DE59.E93 1999
The eye expanded: life and the arts in Greco-Roman antiquity/ edited by Frances B. Titchener and Richard F. Moorton. Berkeley: University of California Press, c1999. xiii, 294 p.
98-041403   938   0520210298
Civilization, Western -- Classical influences. Rome -- Civilization. Greece -- Civilization.

DE59.G74 1989
Green, Peter, 1924-
Classical bearings: interpreting ancient history and culture/ Peter Green. New York, N.Y.: Thames and Hudson, 1989. 328 p.
89-050628   938   050025107X
Civilization, Classical.

DE59.O94 1986
The Oxford history of the classical world/ edited by John Boardman, Jasper Griffin, Oswyn Murray. Oxford [Oxfordshire]; Oxford University Press, 1986. vii, 882 p.
85-021774   938   0198721129
Civilization, Classical.

DE60 Antiquities. Civilization. Culture — Works, 1801- — General special

DE60.D97 1998
Dyson, Stephen L.
Ancient marbles to American shores: classical archaeology in the United States/ Stephen L. Dyson. Philadelphia: University of Pennsylvania Press, c1998. xiv, 323 p.
98-021208   938   0812234464
Classical antiquities. Archaeology -- United States -- History -- 20th century. Archaeological museums and collections -- United States -- Influence.

DE61 Antiquities. Civilization. Culture — Works, 1801- — Special topics, A-Z

DE61.B87.M67 1992
Morris, Ian, 1960-
Death-ritual and social structure in classical antiquity/ Ian Morris. Cambridge; Cambridge University Press, 1992. xvii, 264 p.
91-330669   393/.0938   0521374650
Burial -- Rome. Civilization, Classical. Burial -- Greece.

DE61.S43.W33 1998
Wachsmann, Shelley.
Seagoing ships & seamanship in the Bronze Age Levant/ Shelley Wachsmann; foreword by George F. Bass. College Station: Texas A&M University Press; c1998. xii, 417 p.
96-049815   910/.9163/80901   0890967091
Underwater archaeology -- Mediterranean Region. Bronze age -- Mediterranean Region. Seafaring life -- Mediterranean Region. Mediterranean Region -- Antiquities.

DE61.Y68.K55 1991
Kleijwegt, Marc.
Ancient youth: the ambiguity of youth and the absence of adolescence in Greco-Roman society/ by Marc Kleijwegt. Amsterdam: J.C. Gieben, 1991. xvi, 401 p.
91-185568   9050630634
Youth -- Rome. Youth -- Greece.

DE73.2 Ethnography — Individual elements in the population, A-Z

DE73.2.S4.S26
Sandars, N. K.
The sea peoples: warriors of the ancient Mediterranean, 1250-1150 B.C./ N. K. Sandars. London: Thames and Hudson, c1978. 224 p.
77-083798   939.1   050002085X
Sea Peoples. Mediterranean region -- History -- To 476.

DE86 History — By period — Ancient to 476. Greco-Roman era

DE86.G738 1990
Green, Peter, 1924-
Alexander to Actium: the historical evolution of the Hellenistic age/ Peter Green. Berkeley: University of California Press, c1990. xxiii, 970 p.
86-004339   938   0520056116
Hellenism. Greece -- History -- Macedonian Hegemony, 323-281 B.C. Greece -- History -- 281-146 B.C. Mediterranean Region -- History -- To 476.

DE94 History — By period — 476-1517

DE94.F47 1987
Fernandez-Armesto, Felipe.
Before Columbus: exploration and colonization from the Mediterranean to the Atlantic, 1229-1492/ Felipe Fernandez-Armesto. Philadelphia: University of Pennsylvania Press, 1987. x, 283 p.
87-010764   909/.09822   0812280830
Atlantic Coast (Africa) -- History. Mediterranean Region -- History. Atlantic Coast (Europe) -- History.

DF History of Greece

DF12 Ancient Greece — Sources and documents. Collections. Classical authors

DF12.C7 1983
Crawford, Michael H. 1939-
Archaic and Classical Greece: a selection of ancient sources in translation/ Michael Crawford, David Whitehead. Cambridge [Cambridgeshire, England]; Cambridge University Press, 1983. xxiii, 634 p.
82-004355   938   0521227755
Greece -- History -- To 146 B.C. -- Sources.

DF16 Ancient Greece — Dictionaries

DF16.S23 1995
Sacks, David.
Encyclopedia of the ancient Greek world/ David Sacks; historical consultant Oswyn Murray, original drawings by Margaret Bunson. New York: Facts on File, c1995. xiii, 306 p.
94-033229   938   0816023239
Greece -- Civilization -- To 146 B.C. -- Dictionaries.

DF27 Ancient Greece — Geography. Travel — General works

DF27.P383.A73 1996
Arafat, K. W.
Pausanias' Greece: ancient artists and Roman rulers/ K.W. Arafat. Cambridge; Cambridge University Press, 1996. xvi, 246 p.
95-032378   938   0521553407
Pausanias -- Knowledge -- Greece. Emperors -- Rome. Rome -- Civilization. Greece -- Antiquities. Rome -- Kings and rulers.

DF27.P4 1913
Pausanias.
Pausanias's Description of Greece, tr. with a commentary, by J. G. Frazer. London, Macmillan and co., limited, 1913. 6 v.
13-007360
Greece -- Antiquities. Greece -- Description and travel.

DF77 Ancient Greece — Antiquities. Civilization. Culture — General works

DF77.A595 1999
Ancient Greece: a political, social, and cultural history/ by Sarah B. Pomeroy, Stanley M. Burstein, Walter Donlan, Jennifer Tolbert Roberts. New York: Oxford University Press, 1999. xxix, 512 p.
98-014544   938   0195097424
Hellenism. Greece -- Civilization -- To 146 B.C.

DF77.B9445
Burn, A. R. 1902-
Minoans, Philistines, and Greeks, B.C. 1400-900, by A.R. Burn ... London, K. Paul, Trench, Trubner & Co., ltd.; 1930. xv, p.
30-028579   913.38
Homer. Civilization, Homeric. Philistines. Etruscans. Crete (Greece) -- Antiquities.

DF77 .C63 1994
Classical Greece: ancient histories and modern archaeologies/ edited by Ian Morris. Cambridge [England]; Cambridge University Press, xiv, 244 p.
93-006625   938/.0072 20   0521456789
Greece -- Antiquities. Greece -- Civilization -- To 146 B.C. Archaeology and history--Greece.

DF77.E35 1973
Ehrenberg, Victor, 1891-
From Solon to Socrates; Greek history and civilization during the sixth and fifth centuries B.C. London, Methuen [distributed by Barnes & Noble, New York 1973] xvii, 505 p.
73-180774   913.38/03   0416776108
Greece -- Civilization -- To 146 B.C. Greece -- History -- To 146 B.C.

DF77.F53 1970
Finley, M. I. 1912-
Early Greece; the Bronze and archaic ages [by] M. I. Finley. New York, Norton [1970] 155 p.
78-095884   913.38/03/11   0393054101
Bronze Age -- Greece. Civilization, Homeric. Greece -- History -- Geometric period, ca. 900-700 B.C. Greece -- History -- Age of Tyrants, 7th-6th centuries B.C. Greece -- Antiquities.

DF77.F75 1980
Frost, Frank J., 1929-
Greek society/ Frank J. Frost. Lexington, Mass.: Heath, c1980. xv, 215 p.
79-089480   938   066902452X
Greece -- Civilization -- To 146 B.C.

DF77.H5464 1993
Hellenistic history and culture/ edited and with an introduction by Peter Green. Berkeley: University of California Press, c1993. xvi, 293 p.
91-031398   938   0520075641
Hellenism.

DF77.L43
Levi, Peter.
Atlas of the Greek world/ by Peter Levi. New York, N.Y.: Facts on File, c1980. 239 p.
81-122477   938   0871964481
Greece -- Civilization -- To 146 B.C. Greece -- Maps.

DF77.M82 1993
Murray, Oswyn.
Early Greece/ Oswyn Murray.2nd ed. Cambridge, Mass.: Harvard University Press, 1993. 353 p.
93-015040   938.220   067422132X
Greece -- Civilization -- To 146 B.C.

DF77.S49 1987
Snodgrass, Anthony M.
An archaeology of Greece: the present state and future scope of a discipline/ Anthony M. Snodgrass. Berkeley: University of California Press, c1987. xv, 218 p.
86-019702   938   0520058550
Archaeology -- Greece. Greece -- Antiquities.

DF78-85 Ancient Greece — Antiquities. Civilization. Culture — Public and political antiquities

DF78.A65 1988
The Archaeology of the Olympics: the Olympics and other festivals in antiquity/ edited by Wendy J. Raschke. Madison, Wis.: University of Wisconsin Press, 1988. xiii, 297 p.
87-040150   938   0299113302
Games -- Greece. Greece -- Antiquities.

DF78.B398 1987
Bernal, Martin.
Black Athena: the Afroasiatic roots of classical civilization/ Martin Bernal. New Brunswick, N.J.: Rutgers University Press, 1987-1991 v. 1-2
87-016408   949.5   081351276X
Greece -- Civilization -- Egyptian influences. Greece -- Civilization -- Phoenician influences. Greece -- Civilization -- To 146 B.C.

DF78.B8513 1992
Burkert, Walter, 1931-
The orientalizing revolution: Near Eastern influence on Greek culture in the early archaic age/ Walter Burkert; translated by Walter Burkert and Margaret E. Pinder. Cambridge, Mass.: Harvard University Press, c1992. 225 p.
92-008923   938   0674643631
Greece -- Civilization -- To 146 B.C. Greece -- Civilization -- Middle Eastern influences.

DF78.D4613
Detienne, Marcel.
Cunning intelligence in Greek culture and society/ Marcel Detienne and Jean-Pierre Vernant; translated from the French by Janet Lloyd. Hassocks [Eng.]: Harvester Press; c1978. 337 p.
80-154770   938   0391007408
Philosophy, Ancient. Reasoning.   Greece -- Intellectual life -- To 146 B.C.

DF78.F5513 1965
Flaceliere, Robert, 1904-
Daily life in Greece at the time of Pericles. Translated from the French by Peter Green. New York, Macmillan, 1965. xvi, 310 p.
65-013591   913.8
Greece -- Social life and customs.

DF78.G28 1990
Garland, Robert.
The Greek way of life: from conception to old age/ Robert Garland. Ithaca, N.Y.: Cornell University Press, c1990. xiii, 376 p.
89-042955   306/.09495   080142335X
Life cycle, Human.   Greece -- Social life and customs.

DF78.G5313
Gernet, Louis, 1882-
The anthropology of ancient Greece/ Louis Gernet; translated by John Hamilton and Blaise Nagy. Baltimore: Johns Hopkins University Press, c1981. xiii, 378 p.
81-047598   938   0801821126
Mythology, Greek. Philosophy, Ancient. Greece -- Civilization -- To 146 B.C. Greece -- Religion.

DF78.M6
Momigliano, Arnaldo.
Alien wisdom: the limits of Hellenization/ Arnaldo Momigliano. Cambridge; Cambridge University Press, 1975. 174 p.
75-010237   938   0521208769
Greece -- Civilization -- To 146 B.C.

DF78 .M635 1999
Morris, Ian,
Archaeology as cultural history: words and things in Iron Age Greece / Ian Morris. Malden, Mass: Blackwall, 1999. p. cm.
99-019855   938 21   0631196021
Greece -- Civilization. Greece -- Antiquities. Iron age--Greece.   Archaeology--Social aspects--Greece.

DF78.S2813 2000
Greek thought: a guide to classical knowledge/ edited by Jacques Brunschwig and Geoffrey E.R. Lloyd, with the collaboration of Pierre Pellegrin; translated under the direction of Catherine Porter. Cambridge, Mass.: Belknap Press of Harvard University Press, 2000. xv, 1024 p.
00-036032   938   067400261X
Intellectuals -- Greece -- Biography. Thought and thinking. Greece -- Intellectual life -- To 146 B.C. Greece -- Politics and government -- To 146 B.C.

DF78.S67 1991
Sourvinou-Inwood, Christiane.
"Reading" Greek culture: texts and images, rituals and myths/ Christiane Sourvinou-Inwood. Oxford [England]: Clarendon Press; 1991. vi, 315 p.
90-021986   938   0198147503
Greece -- Civilization -- To 146 B.C.

DF78.T53 2000
Thornton, Bruce S.
Greek ways: how the Greeks created western civilization/ Bruce S. Thornton. San Francisco: Encounter Books, 2000. 242 p.
00-039376   949.5   1893554031
Civilization, Modern -- Greek influences. Sexual ethics -- Greece.   Greece -- Civilization -- Influence.

DF78.V4813 1982
Vernant, Jean Pierre.
The origins of Greek thought/ Jean-Pierre Vernant. Ithaca, N.Y.: Cornell University Press, 1982. 144 p.
81-015247   938   0801410045
Philosophy, Ancient.   Greece -- Civilization -- To 146 B.C.

DF82.P64 1988
Powell, Anton.
Athens and Sparta: constructing Greek political and social history from 478 BC/ Anton Powell. Portland, Or.: Areopagitica Press, 1988. 423 p.
88-003390   938/.5   0918400090
Greece -- Politics and government -- To 146 B.C. Greece -- Social conditions -- To 146 B.C. Athens (Greece) -- Politics and government.

DF82.W47 1986
Whitehead, David,
The demes of Attica, 508/7-ca. 250 B.C.: a political and social study/ by David Whitehead. Princeton, N.J.: Princeton University Press, c1986. xxvii, 485 p.
85-042709   938   0691094128
Local government -- Greece -- Attike.   Greece -- Politics and government -- To 146 B.C. Attike (Greece) -- Politics and government. Attike (Greece) -- Social conditions.

DF85.D46 1990
Demand, Nancy H.
Urban relocation in archaic and classical Greece: flight and consolidation/ by Nancy H. Demand. Norman: University of Oklahoma Press, c1990. xi, 257 p.
89-040737   938   0806122781
Synoecism.

DF85.J615
Jones, A. H. M. 1904-1970.
The Greek city from Alexander to Justinian, by A. H. M. Jones ... Oxford, The Clarendon press, 1940. x, 393 p.
40-029459   352.038
Cities and towns, Ancient -- Greece. Cities and towns -- Greece. Municipal government -- Greece.

DF85.J6 1971
Jones, A. H. M.   1904-1970.
The cities of the eastern Roman provinces. Rev. by Michael Avi-Yonah [and others] Oxford [Eng.] Clarendon Press, 1971. xvii, 595 p.
74-025037   938/.009/732
Cities and towns, Ancient. Hellenism.   Rome -- Provinces -- Administration. Greece -- Colonies.

DF85.M35 1994
Malkin, Irad.
Myth and territory in the Spartan Mediterranean/ Irad Malkin. Cambridge [England]; Cambridge University Press, 1994. xvii, 278 p.
93-030357   938/.9   0521411831
Cities and towns, Ancient -- Mediterranean Region. Mythology, Greek. Greeks -- Colonization -- Mediterranean Region. Sparta (Extinct city) -- Colonies.

DF91-101 Ancient Greece — Antiquities. Civilization. Culture — Private antiquities

DF91.D4
De Ste. Croix, G. E. M. (Geoffrey Ernest Maurice)
The class struggle in the ancient Greek world: from the archaic age to the Arab conquests/ G.E.M. de Ste. Croix. Ithaca, N.Y.: Cornell University Press, 1981. xi, 732 p.
81-066650   305.5/09495   0801414423
Social classes -- Greece -- History. Slavery -- Greece -- History.   Greece -- Social life and customs. Greece -- Social conditions.

DF93.S5313 1990
Sissa, Giulia, 1954-
Greek virginity/ Giulia Sissa; translated by Arthur Goldhammer. Cambridge, Mass.: Harvard University Press, 1990. 240 p.
89-015466   305.4/00938   0674363205
Women -- Greece. Virginity -- Greece. Human body -- Mythology -- Greece.

DF93.S55
Slater, Philip Elliot.
The glory of Hera; Greek mythology and the Greek family, by Philip E. Slater. Boston, Beacon Press [1968] xxvi, 513 p.
68-024373   301.42/7   0807057959
Mythology, Greek. Women -- Greece. Family -- Greece.

DF99.N48 1999
Nevett, Lisa C.
House and society in the ancient Greek world/ Lisa C. Nevett. Cambridge; Cambridge University Press, 1999. xi, 220 p.
98-038089   306/.0938   005216439X
Dwellings -- Social aspects -- Greece. Social archaeology -- Greece.   Greece -- Social conditions -- To 146 B.C.

DF101.M67 1987
Morris, Ian, 1960-
Burial and ancient society: the rise of the Greek city-state/   Ian   Morris.   Cambridge [Cambridgeshire]; Cambridge University Press, 1987. ix, 262 p.
86-032719   938   052132680X
Funeral rites and ceremonies -- Greece. City-states -- Greece. Tombs -- Greece. Greece -- Antiquities.

DF105 Ancient Greece — Antiquities. Civilization. Culture — Agriculture

DF105.G35 1991a
Gallant, Thomas W.
Risk and survival in ancient Greece: reconstructing the rural domestic economy/ Thomas W. Gallant. Stanford, Calif.: Stanford University Press, 1991. xvi, 267 p.
90-070905   338.1/0938   0804718571
Agriculture -- Economic aspects -- Greece -- History. Risk management -- Greece -- History.

DF123 Ancient Greece — Antiquities. Civilization. Culture — Religious antiquities

DF123.N45 1992
Neils, Jenifer, 1950-
Goddess and polis: the Panathenaic Festival in ancient Athens: [exhibition]/ Jenifer Neils with contributions by E.J.W. Barber ... [et al.]. Hanover, N.H.: Hood Museum of Art, Dartmouth College; 1992. 227 p.
92-017660   938/.5/007473   0691036128
Panathenaia -- Exhibitions. Arts, Greek -- Exhibitions. Greece -- Antiquities -- Exhibitions.

DF123.P37
Parke, H. W. 1903-
Festivals of the Athenians/ H. W. Parke. Ithaca, N.Y.: Cornell University Press, 1977. 208 p.
76-012819   394.2/69385   0801410541
Festivals -- Greece. Festivals -- Greece -- Athens. Athens (Greece) -- Social life and customs. Greece -- Religious life and customs. Greece -- Social life and customs.

DF130 Ancient Greece — Antiquities. Civilization. Culture — Art antiquities

DF130.P44 1993
Pedley, John Griffiths.
Greek art and archaeology/ John Griffiths Pedley. New York: H.N. Abrams, 1993. 367 p.
92-009707   938   0810933691
Art, Greek. Greece -- Antiquities.

DF135 Ancient Greece — Ethnology — General works

DF135.H33 1997
Hall, Jonathan M.
Ethnic Identity in Greek antiquity/ Jonathan M. Hall. Cambridge; Cambridge University Press, 1997. xviii, 228 p.
96-009563   305.8/00938   052158017X
Minorities -- Greece -- Ethnic identity. Greece -- Ethnic relations. Greece -- Civilization -- To 146 B.C.

DF209.5-212 Ancient Greece — History — Historiography

DF209.5.H65 1951
Hill, George Francis, 1867-1948.
Sources for Greek history: between the Persian and Peloponnesian wars/ collected and arranged by G. F. Hill. Oxford: Clarendon Press, 1951. xx, 426 p.
52-006068   938.04
Greece -- History -- Sources.

DF211.G75 1994
Greek historiography/ edited by Simon Hornblower. Oxford: Clarendon Press; 1994. xii, 286 p.
93-045956   938/.0072   019814931X
Historiography -- Greece. Greece -- History -- To 146 B.C. -- Historiography.

DF211.S47 1997
Shrimpton, Gordon Spencer.
History and memory in Ancient Greece/ Gordon S. Shrimpton; with an appendix on Herodotus' source citations by G.S. Shrimpton and K.M. Gillis. Montreal; McGill-Queen's University Press, c1997. xvii, 318 p.
97-219419   938/.0072   0773510214
Historians -- Greece. Knowledge, Theory of. Greece -- Historiography.

DF212.C35.A67 1999
Allen, Susan Heuck, 1952-
Finding the walls of Troy: Frank Calvert and Heinrich Schliemann at Hisarlik/ Susan Heuck Allen. Berkeley: University of California Press, c1999. xiii, 409 p.
98-013101   930.1/092   0520208684
Calvert, Frank, -- 1828-1908 -- Contributions in archaeology. Schliemann, Heinrich, -- 1822-1890 -- Professional ethics. Archaeologists -- Great Britain -- Biography. Consuls -- Turkey -- Biography. Archaeologists -- Germany -- Biography. Troy (Extinct city)

DF212.E82.M33 2000
MacGillivray, J. A.
Minotaur: Sir Arthur Evans and the archaeology of the Minoan myth/ Joseph Alexander MacGillivray. New York: Hill and Wang, 2000. viii, 373 p.
00-033606   939/.18   0809030357
Evans, Arthur, -- Sir, -- 1851-1941. Excavations (Archaeology) -- Greece -- Crete. Minoans. Archaeologists -- Great Britain -- Biography. Crete (Greece) -- Antiquities. Knossos (Extinct city)

DF214 Ancient Greece — History — General works

DF214.D37 1993
Davies, John Kenyon.
Democracy and classical Greece/ J.K. Davies.2nd ed. Cambridge, Mass.: Harvard University Press, 1993. x, 308 p.
93-000795   938.220   0674196074
Greece -- History -- To 146 B.C.

DF214.D4 1963
De Selincourt, Aubrey, 1894-1962.
The world of Herodotus. Boston, Little, Brown [1963, c1962] 392 p.
62-017957   938
Greece -- History. Greece -- Civilization -- To 146 B.C. Greece -- History -- Persian Wars, 500-449 B.C.

DF214.G78 1988
Grant, Michael, 1914-
The rise of the Greeks/ Michael Grant. New York: C. Scribner's Sons, 1988, c1987. xv, 391 p.
87-034741   938/.02   0684185369
Greece -- History -- To 146 B.C.

DF214.H28 1986
Hammond, N. G. L. 1907-
A history of Greece to 322 B.C./ by N.G.L. Hammond. Oxford [Oxfordshire]: Clarendon Press; 1986. xxi, 691 p.
86-005222   938   0198730969
Greece -- History -- To 146 B.C.

DF214.S45
Sealey, Raphael.
A history of the Greek city states, ca. 700-338 B.C./ Raphael Sealey. Berkeley: University of California Press, c1976. xxi, 516 p.
75-027934   938
City-states -- Greece -- History. Greece -- History -- To 146 B.C.

DF220-235.48 Ancient Greece — History — By period

DF220.C43
Chadwick, John, 1920-
The Mycenaean world/ John Chadwick. Cambridge [Eng.]; Cambridge University Press, 1976. xvii, 201 p.
75-036021   938/.01   0521210771.
Civilization, Mycenaean.

DF220.C58 1977
Coldstream, J. N. 1927-
Geometric Greece/ J. N. Coldstream; [maps by Kenneth Clarke]. New York: St. Martin's Press, 1977. 405 p.
77-078085   938   0312323654
Civilization, Homeric. Greece -- Civilization -- To 146 B.C. Greece -- Antiquities. Greece -- History -- Geometric period, ca. 900-700 B.C.

DF220.D44 1972
Desborough, V. R. d'A.
The Greek dark ages [by] V. R. d'A. Desborough. New York, St. Martin's Press [1972] 388 p.
79-180736   913.38/03/1
Civilization, Aegean.

DF220.D49 1994
Dickinson, O. T. P. K.
The Aegean Bronze age/ Oliver Dickinson. Cambridge: Cambridge University Press, 1994. xxii, 342 p.
93-002666   939/.1   0521242800
Civilization, Aegean. Bronze age -- Aegean Sea Region. Aegean Sea Region -- Antiquities.

DF220.D73 1988
Drews, Robert.
The coming of the Greeks: Indo-European conquests in the Aegean and the Near East/ Robert Drews. Princeton, N.J.: Princeton University Press, c1988. xviii, 257 p.
88-015104   938   069103592X
Greeks -- Origin. Bronze age -- Greece. Indo-Europeans -- Origin.

DF220.H65
Hooker, J. T.
Mycenaean Greece/ J. T. Hooker. London; Routledge & K. Paul, 1976. xiii, 316 p.
77-353999   938/.01   0710083793
Civilization, Mycenaean.

DF220.P3 1965
Palmer, Leonard Robert, 1906-
Mycenaeans and Minoans: Aegean prehistory in the light of the Linear B tablets/ Leonard R. Palmer. New York: Knopf, c1965. 369 p.
64-019093   913.3918031
   Civilization, Mycenaean.   Crete (Greece) -- Antiquities.

DF220.V4
Vermeule, Emily.
Greece in the bronze age. Chicago, University of Chicago Press [1964] xix, 406 p.
64-023427   913.38
   Bronze age -- Greece. Civilization, Mycenaean.

DF220.3.C37 1991
Castleden, Rodney.
Minoans: life in Bronze Age Crete/ Rodney Castleden; illustrated by the author. London; Routledge, 1990. xi, 210 p.
90-032407   939/.18   0415040701
   Minoans -- Social life and customs.   Crete (Greece) -- Social life and customs.

DF221.C8.C37 1990
Castleden, Rodney.
The Knossos labyrinth: a new view of the "Palace of Minos" at Knosos/ Rodney Castleden; illustrated by the author. London; Routledge, 1990. xi, 205 p.
89-006234   938   0415033152
   Knossos (Extinct city) Crete (Greece) -- Antiquities. Greece -- Antiquities.

DF221.C8.E75
Evans, Arthur, 1851-1941.
The palace of Minos; a comparative account of the successive stages of the early Cretan civilization as illustrated by the discoveries at Knossos, by Sir Arthur Evans ... London, Macmillan and Co., limited, 1921-35. 4 v. in 6
22-006622
   Crete (Greece) -- Antiquities. Greece -- Civilization.

DF221.C8.W54 1977b
Willetts, R. F., 1915-
The civilization of ancient Crete/ R. F. Willetts. Berkeley: University of California Press, 1977, c1976. 279 p.
76-055575   939.1/8   0520034066
   Crete (Greece) -- Civilization.

DF221.M9.M93
Mylonas, George E. 1898-
Mycenae and the Mycenaean Age, by George E. Mylonas. Princeton, N.J., Princeton University Press, 1966. xvi, 251 p.
65-017154   913.391031
   Civilization, Mycenaean.   Mycenae (Extinct city)

DF221.T38.D68 1983
Doumas, Christos.
Thera, Pompeii of the ancient Aegean: excavations at Akrotiri, 1967-79/ Christos G. Doumas. New York, N.Y.: Thames and Hudson, 1983. 168 p.
81-086685   939/.15   0500390169
   Excavations (Archaeology) -- Greece -- Thera Island. Excavations (Archaeology) -- Greece -- Akroterion. Thera Island (Greece) -- Antiquities. Akroterion (Greece) -- Antiquities. Greece -- Antiquities.

DF221.T38.F67 1997
Forsyth, Phyllis Young.
Thera in the Bronze Age/ Phyllis Young Forsyth. New York: P. Lang, c1997. 201 p.
97-013093   939/.15   0820437883
   Bronze Age -- Greece -- Thera Island. Volcanoes -- Greece -- Thera Island. Akroterion (Greece) -- Antiquities. Thera Island (Greece) -- Antiquities.

DF221.5.N48 1997
New light on a dark age: exploring the culture of geometric Greece/ edited by Susan Langdon. Columbia, Mo.: University of Missouri Press, c1997. xii, 247 p.
96-043443   938/.01   0826210996
   Civilization, Homeric -- Congresses. Cults -- Greece -- Congresses. Greece -- Antiquities -- Congresses. Greece -- History -- Geometric period, ca. 900-700 B.C. -- Congresses.

DF222.A6
Andrewes, Antony, 1910-
The Greek tyrants.   London: Hutchinson's University Library, 1960, c1956. 167 p.
56-008629
   Dictators.   Greece -- History.

DF222.S66
Snodgrass, Anthony M.
Archaic Greece: the age of experiment/ Anthony Snodgrass. London: J.M. Dent, 1980. 236 p.
82-464126   938/.01   0460043382
   Greece -- History -- To 146 B.C.

DF222.2.K87 1999
Kurke, Leslie.
Coins, bodies, games, and gold: the politics of meaning in archaic Greece/ Leslie Kurke. Princeton, NJ: Princeton University Press, c1999. xxi, 384 p.
99-012205   938   069101731X
   Meaning (Psychology) -- Greece. Coins, Greek -- Greece -- History. Greece -- Antiquities. Greece -- Civilization -- To 146 B.C. Greece -- Social conditions -- To 146 B.C.

DF225.G88 1969
Grundy, George Beardoe, 1861-1948.
The great Persian War and its preliminaries; a study of the evidence, literary and topographical. New York, AMS Press [1969] xiii, 591 p.
71-084875   938/.03
   Greece -- History -- Persian Wars, 500-449 B.C.

DF227.B3 1993
Badian, E.
From Plataea to Potidaea: studies in the history and historiography of the Pentecontaetia/ E. Badian. Baltimore: Johns Hopkins University Press, c1993. xii, 264 p.
92-017327   938/.04   0801844312
   Greece -- History -- Athenian supremacy, 479-431 B.C.

DF227.F54 1991
Figueira, Thomas J.
Athens and Aigina in the age of imperial colonization/ Thomas J. Figueira. Baltimore: Johns Hopkins University Press, c1991. xii, 274 p.
91-022167   938/.04   0801842964
   Greece -- History -- Athenian supremacy, 479-431 B.C. Athens (Greece) -- History. Aegina Island (Greece) -- History.

DF227.H67 1983
Hornblower, Simon.
The Greek world, 479-323 BC/ Simon Hornblower. London; Methuen, 1983. xi, 354 p.
83-013062   938   0416749909
   Greece -- History -- Athenian Supremacy, 479-431 B.C. Greece -- History -- Peloponnesian War, 431-404 B.C. Greece -- History -- Spartan and Theban Supremacies, 404-362 B.C.

DF227.M44 1979
Meiggs, Russell.
The Athenian empire/ Russell Meiggs. Oxford: Clarendon Press; 1979, c1972. xvi, 620 p.
80-456017   938/.04   0198148437
   Greece -- History -- Athenian supremacy, 479-431 B.C. Athens (Greece) -- History. Greece -- History -- Peloponnesian War, 431-404 B.C.

DF227.5.M56 1997
Miller, Margaret Christina.
Athens and Persia in the fifth century B.C.: a study in cultural receptivity/ Margaret C. Miller. Cambridge; Cambridge University Press, 1997. xiv, 331 p.
96-021496   0521495989
   Greece -- History -- Athenian supremacy, 479-431 B.C. Athens (Greece) -- Relations -- Iran. Iran -- Relations -- Greece -- Athens.

DF228.A8.H46 1995
Henry, Madeleine Mary, 1949-
Prisoner of history: Aspasia of Miletus and her biographical tradition/ Madeleine M. Henry. New York: Oxford University Press, 1995. 201 p.
94-001250   938/.504/092   0195087127
   Aspasia. Pericles, -- 499-429 B.C. Mistresses -- Greece -- Athens -- Biography. Women in politics -- Greece -- Athens -- Biography. Greece -- History -- Athenian supremacy, 479-431 B.C.

DF229.D55 1995
Dillery, John, 1961-
Xenophon and the history of his times/ John Dillery. London; Routledge, 1995. xii, 337 p.
94-030021   938/.007202   041509139X
   Xenophon -- Political and social views. Xenophon. -- Hellenica. Imperialism. History -- Philosophy. Greece -- History -- Peloponnesian War, 431-404 B.C. Greece -- History -- Spartan and Theban Supremacies, 404-362 B.C.

DF229.T5.C7 1951
Thucydides.
Complete writings: The Peloponnesian war. The unabridged Crawley translation with an introd. by John H. Finley, Jr. New York, Modern Library [1951] xxi, 516 p.
51-002474   888.2   0394309510
   Greece -- History -- Peloponnesian War, 431-404 B.C.

DF229.T5.J6 1972
Thucydides.
History of the Peloponnesian War. Translated by Rex Warner, with an introd. and notes by M. I. Finley. Harmondsworth, Eng., Penguin Books [1972] 648 p.
73-174843   938/.05   0140440399
   Greece -- History -- Peloponnesian War, 431-404 B.C.

DF229.T6.H65 1991
Hornblower, Simon.
A commentary on Thucydides/ Simon Hornblower. Oxford: Clarendon Press; 1991-1996 v. 1-2
91-003432   938/.007202   0198148801
   Thucydides. -- History of the Peloponnesian War. Greece -- History -- Peloponnesian War, 431-404 B.C. -- Historiography.

DF229.T6.H67 1987
Hornblower, Simon.
Thucydides/ Simon Hornblower. Baltimore: Johns Hopkins University Press, 1987. ix, 230 p.
87-004213   938/.0072024   0801835291
Thucydides. -- History of the Peloponnesian War. Greece -- Intellectual life -- To 146 B.C. Greece -- Historiography.

DF229.T6.R64 1998
Rood, Tim.
Thucydides: narrative and explanation/ Tim Rood. Oxford; Clarendon Press, c1998. xi, 339 p.
98-007982   938/.05/092   0198152566
Thucydides -- Criticism and interpretation. Thucydides. -- History of the Peloponnesian War -- Criticism, Textual.   Greece -- History -- Peloponnesian War, 431-404 B.C.

DF229.2.K3
Kagan, Donald.
The outbreak of the Peloponnesian War. Ithaca [N.Y.] Cornell University Press [1969] xvi, 420 p.
69-018212   938/.05   0801405017
Greece -- History -- Peloponnesian War, 431-404 B.C.

DF229.37.K34 1987
Kagan, Donald.
The fall of the Athenian Empire/ Donald Kagan. Ithaca, N.Y.: Cornell University Press, 1987. xviii, 455 p.
86-032946   938/.05   0801419352
Greece -- History -- Peloponnesian War, 431-404 B.C. Athens (Greece) -- History.

DF230.A4.F67 1989
Forde, Steven, 1954-
The ambition to rule: Alcibiades and the politics of imperialism in Thucydides/ Steven Forde. Ithaca: Cornell University Press, 1989. viii, 216 p.
88-047919   938/.05/0924   0801421381
Alcibiades. Thucydides. -- History of the Peloponnesian War. Statesmen -- Greece -- Athens -- Biography. Generals -- Greece -- Athens -- Biography. Greece -- History -- Peloponnesian War, 431-404 B.C. -- Historiography.

DF231.4.H35
Hamilton, Charles D. 1940-
Sparta's bitter victories: politics and diplomacy in the Corinthian War/ Charles D. Hamilton. Ithaca, N.Y.: Cornell University Press, 1979. 346 p.
78-058045   938/.06   0801411580
Greece -- History -- Corinthian War, 395-386 B.C. Greece -- History -- Peloponnesian War, 431-404 B.C. -- Influence. Sparta (Extinct city) -- History.

DF232.A33.H36 1991
Hamilton, Charles D. 1940-
Agesilaus and the failure of Spartan hegemony/ Charles D. Hamilton. Ithaca: Cornell University Press, 1991. xix, 280 p.
90-055738   938/.906/092   0801425409
Agesilaus -- II, -- King of Sparta.   Sparta (Extinct city) -- History. Greece -- History -- Spartan and Theban Supremacies, 404-362 B.C. Sparta (Extinct city) -- Kings and rulers -- Biography.

DF233.E4
Ellis, John R.
Philip II and Macedonian imperialism/ [by] J. R. Ellis. London: Thames and Hudson, 1976. 312 p.
76-380632   938/.1/070924   0500400288
Philip -- II, -- King of Macedonia, -- 382-336 B.C. Greece -- History -- To 146 B.C. Macedonia -- History. Greece -- Kings and rulers -- Biography.

DF233.2.C37 2000
Carney, Elizabeth Donnelly, 1947-
Women and monarchy in Macedonia/ Elizabeth Donnelly Carney. Norman: University of Oklahoma Press, c2000. xiii, 369 p.
99-037790   938/.1/0082   0806132124
Queens -- Macedonia -- Biography. Women in public life -- Macedonia -- Biography. Women -- Macedonia -- History.

DF233.8.A66.T74 1992
Trevett, Jeremy.
Apollodoros, the son of Pasion/ Jeremy Trevett. Oxford [England]: Clarendon Press; 1992. xiv, 209 p.
92-013297   938/.506/092   0198147902
Apollodoros, -- db. ca. 394 B.C.   Politicians -- Greece -- Athens -- Biography. Orators -- Greece -- Athens -- Biography. Athens (Greece) -- History.

DF233.8.P59.H35 1994
Hammond, N. G. L. 1907-
Philip of Macedon/ N.G.L. Hammond. Baltimore: Johns Hopkins University Press, c1994. 235 p.
94-001067   938/.07/092   0801849276
Philip -- II, -- King of Macedonia, -- 382-336 B.C. Chaeronea, Battle of, 338 B.C.   Greece -- Kings and rulers -- Biography. Greece -- History -- Macedonian Expansion, 359-323 B.C. Macedonia -- Kings and rulers -- Biography.

DF234.A7513 1976
Arrian.
Arrian/ with an English translation by P. A. Brunt. Cambridge, Mass.: Harvard University Press, 1976-1983. 2 v.
76-367911   938/.07/0924   0674992601
Alexander, -- the Great, -- 356-323 B.C.   Iran -- History -- To 640. India -- Description and travel -- Early works to 1800.

DF234.A773.B67
Bosworth, A. B.
A historical commentary on Arrian's History of Alexander/ by A. B. Bosworth. Oxford: Clarendon Press; 1980-1995 v. 1-2
79-040885   938/.07   0198148283
Arrian. -- Anabasis. Alexander, -- the Great, -- 356-323 B.C. -- Campaigns.

DF234.B66 1988
Bosworth, A. B.
Conquest and empire: the reign of Alexander the Great/ A.B. Bosworth. Cambridge [England]; Cambridge University Press, 1988. xiii, 330 p.
87-035499   938/.07/0924   0521343208
Alexander, -- the Great, -- 356-323 B.C. Generals -- Greece -- Biography.   Greece -- Kings and rulers -- Biography. Greece -- History -- Macedonian Expansion, 359-323 B.C.

DF234.G68 1974
Green, Peter, 1924-
Alexander of Macedon, 356-323 B.C.; a historical biography. Harmondsworth, Penguin, 1974. xxxi, 617 p.
74-166969   938/.07/0924   0140216901
Alexander, -- the Great, -- 356-323 B.C. Generals -- Greece -- Biography.   Greece -- History -- Macedonian Expansion, 359-323 B.C. Greece -- Kings and rulers -- Biography.

DF234.O27 1992
O'Brien, John Maxwell, 1939-
Alexander the Great: the invisible enemy: a biography/ John Maxwell O'Brien. London; Routledge, 1992. xx, 336 p.
91-037212   938/.07/092   0415072549
Alexander, -- the Great, -- 356-323 B.C. -- Alcohol use. Generals -- Greece -- Biography. Greece -- History -- Macedonian Expansion, 359-323 B.C. Greece -- Kings and rulers -- Biography.

DF234.2.B67 1988
Bosworth, A. B.
From Arrian to Alexander: studies in historical interpretation/ A.B. Bosworth. Oxford: Clarendon Press; 1988. x, 225 p.
87-007038   938/.07/072   0198148631
Alexander, -- the Great, -- 356-323 B.C. Arrian. Greece -- History -- Macedonian Expansion, 359-323 B.C. -- Historiography.

DF234.2.F73 1996
Fraser, P. M.
Cities of Alexander the Great/ P.M. Fraser. Oxford: Clarendon Press; 1996. xi, 259 p.
95-019063   938/.07   0198150067
Alexander, -- the Great, -- 356-323 B.C. -- Contributions in city planning. Cities and towns, Ancient.   Greece -- History -- Macedonian Expansion, 359-323 B.C.

DF234.6.B67 1996
Bosworth, A. B.
Alexander and the East: the tragedy of triumph/ A.B. Bosworth. Oxford: Clarendon Press; 1996. xvi, 218 p.
96-021705   938/.07   0198149913
Alexander, -- the Great, -- 356-323 B.C. -- Military leadership. Massacres -- Asia -- History. Massacres -- Mexico -- History. Greece -- History -- Macedonian Expansion, 359-323 B.C. -- Campaigns -- Asia. Mexico -- History -- Conquest, 1519-1540.

DF235.A1.H44 1981
The Hellenistic world from Alexander to the Roman conquest: a selection of ancient sources in translation/ M.M. Austin. Cambridge; Cambridge University Press, 1981. xv, 488 p.
81-006136   938/.08   0521228298
Greece -- History -- Macedonian Hegemony, 323-281 B.C. -- Sources. Greece -- History -- 281-146 B.C. -- Sources.

DF235.S54 2000
Shipley, Graham.
The Greek world after Alexander, 323-30 B.C./ Graham Shipley. London; Routledge, 2000. xxxi, 568 p.
99-036098   938/.08   0415046173
Alexander, -- the Great, -- 356-323 B.C. -- Influence. Hellenism -- Historiography. Greece -- Civilization -- To 146 B.C. -- Historiography. Rome -- History -- Republic, 265-30 B.C. -- Historiography. Mediterranean Region -- Civilization -- Greek influences.

DF235.W3 1982
Walbank, F. W. 1909-
The Hellenistic world/ F.W. Walbank. Cambridge, Mass.: Harvard University Press, 1982, c1981. 287 p.
81-020050   938/.08   0674387252
Hellenism. Greece -- Civilization -- To 146 B.C. Mediterranean Region -- Civilization.

DF235.48.A57.B55 1990
Billows, Richard A.
Antigonos the One-eyed and the creation of the
Hellenistic state/ Richard A. Billows. Berkeley:
University of California Press, c1990. xix, 515 p.
89-004677 938/.108/0924 0520063783
*Antigonus -- I, -- King of Macedonia, -- 382-301
B.C. Macedonia -- History -- Diadochi, 323-276
B.C. Greece -- History -- Macedonian Hegemony,
323-281 B.C. Macedonia -- Kings and rulers --
Bibliography.*

DF235.48.L97.L86 1992
Lund, Helen S. 1959-
Lysimachus: a study in early Hellenistic kingship/
Helen S. Lund. London; Routledge, 1992. xii,
287 p.
92-002796 938/.08/092 0415070619
*Lysimachus, -- King of Thrace, -- ca. 361-281 B.C.
Greece -- History -- Macedonian Hegemony, 323-
281 B.C. Macedonia -- History -- Diadochi, 323-
276 B.C. Thrace -- Kings and rulers -- Biography.*

DF251 Ancient Greece — Local
history and description —
Territories, colonies, regions, etc.
(in combinations)

DF251.B6 1980
Boardman, John, 1927-
The Greeks overseas: their early colonies and
trade/ John Boardman. New York: Thames and
Hudson, 1980. 288 p.
79-066132 938/.02 0500250693
Greece -- Colonies -- History.

DF251.C37 1995
Cargill, Jack.
Athenian settlements of the fourth century B.C./ by
Jack Cargill. Leiden; E.J. Brill, 1995. xxvii, 487 p.
95-007098 325/.338 9004099913
*Greeks -- Colonization -- History. Greece --
Colonies -- History.*

DF261 Ancient Greece — Local
history and description — Separate
states, territories, islands, etc., A-Z

DF261.A2.S36 2000
Scholten, Joseph B., 1957-
The politics of plunder: Aitolians and their koinon
in the early Hellenistic era, 279-217 B.C./ Joseph
B. Scholten. Berkeley: University of California
Press, c2000. xxvi, 339 p.
96-026732 949.5/1 0520201876
Hellenism. Aetolia (Greece) -- History.

DF261.C65.S24 1984
Salmon, J. B.
Wealthy Corinth: a history of the city to 338 BC/
J.B. Salmon. Oxford: Clarendon Press; 1984. xviii,
464 p.
83-004138 938/.7 019814833X
Corinth (Greece) -- History.

DF261.C8.A35 1992
The aerial atlas of ancient Crete/ edited by J.
Wilson Myers, Eleanor Emlen Myers, and Gerald
Cadogan; geomorphology by John A. Gifford; with
contributions by Stylianos Alexiou ... [et al.].
Berkeley: University of California Press, c1992.
xix, 318 p.
91-020649 914.99/8/0222 0520073827
*Crete (Greece) -- Antiquities. Crete (Greece) --
Aerial photographs. Crete (Greece) -- Pictorial
works.*

DF261.C8.W49
Willetts, R. F., 1915-
Ancient Crete; a social history from early times
until the Roman occupation, by R.F. Willetts.
London, Routledge and K. Paul [1965] ix, 197 p.
66-000483 939.18
Crete (Greece) -- History.

DF261.D35.F6
Fontenrose, Joseph Eddy, 1903-
The Delphic oracle, its responses and operations,
with a catalogue of responses/ Joseph Fontenrose.
Berkeley: University of California Press, c1978.
xviii, 476 p.
76-047969 292/.3/2 0520033604
*Delphian oracle. Apollo (Greek deity) -- Cult --
Greece -- Delphi (Extinct city) Oracles, Greek.
Delphi (Extinct city) -- History.*

DF261.D35.M57 1990
Morgan, Catherine.
Athletes and oracles: the transformation of
Olympia and Delphi in the eighth century BC/
Catherine Morgan. Cambridge [England];
Cambridge University Press, 1990. xi, 324 p.
89-000504 938/.8 0521374510
*Temples -- Greece -- Delphi (Extinct city)
Olympia (Greece: Ancient sanctuary) Delphi
(Extinct city) Greece -- Antiquities.*

DF261.E4.M88
Mylonas, George E. 1898-
Eleusis and the Eleusinian mysteries. Princeton,
N.J., Princeton University Press, 1961. xx, 346 p.
61-007421 292.65
Eleusinian mysteries. Eleusis (Greece)

DF261.M2.B67 1990
Borza, Eugene N.
In the shadow of Olympus: the emergence of
Macedon/ Eugene N. Borza. Princeton, N.J.:
Princeton University Press, 1990. xvii, 333 p.
89-028210 938/.1 0691055491
Macedonia -- History -- To 168 B.C.

DF261.M2.E7713 1990
Errington, R. M.
A history of Macedonia/ R. Malcolm Errington;
translated by Catherine Errington. Berkeley:
University of California Press, c1990. x, 320 p.
89-020193 938/.1 0520063198
Macedonia -- History -- To 168 B.C.

DF261.M2.H35 1989
Hammond, N. G. L. 1907-
The Macedonian State: origins, institutions, and
history/ N.G.L. Hammond. Oxford [England]:
Clarendon Press: 1989. xx, 413 p.
89-008575 938/.1 0198148836
Macedonia -- History -- To 168 B.C.

DF261.M45.S26 1998
Sandy Pylos: an archaeological history from Nestor
to Navarino/ edited by Jack L. Davis; with
contributions by Susan E. Alcock ... [et al.].
Austin: University of Texas Press, 1998. xliii,
342 p.
97-040652 949.5/22 0292715943
*Excavations (Archaeology) -- Greece --
Messenia. Navarino, Battle of, 1827. Messenia
(Greece) -- Antiquities. Messenia (Greece) --
History.*

DF261.N45.N45 1990
Nemea: a guide to the site and museum/ edited by
Stephen G. Miller; with contributions by Ana M.
Abraldes ... [et al.]. Berkeley: University of
California Press, c1990. xiii, 214 p.
89-004942 938/.6 0520065905
*Nemea Site (Greece) -- Guidebooks. Greece --
Antiquities -- Guidebooks.*

DF261.O5.D713 1968
Drees, Ludwig.
Olympia: gods, artists and athletes; English
translation [from the German] by Gerald Onn. New
York, Praeger [1968] 193 p.
68-008255 913.8/6 269670157
*Art -- Greece. Olympics. Olympia (Greece:
Ancient sanctuary).*

DF261.S8 C37 2001
Cartledge, Paul.
Sparta and Lakonia: a regional history, 1300-362
B.C./ Paul Cartledge.2nd ed. New York:
Routledge, 2001. p. cm.
2001-034888 938.9.221 0415262763
*Sparta (Extinct city) -- History. Lakōonia (Greece)
-- History.*

DF261.S8.C373 1989
Cartledge, Paul.
Hellenistic and Roman Sparta, a tale of two cities/
Paul Cartledge and Antony Spawforth. London;
Routledge, 1989. xiii, 304 p.
88-032138 938/.9 0415032903
Sparta (Extinct city) -- History.

DF275-287 Ancient Greece —
Local history and description
— Athens

DF275 .C28 2001
Camp, John McK.
The archaeology of Athens/ John M. Camp. New
Haven: Yale University Press, c2001. xii, 340 p.
2001-002711 938/.5 21 0300081979
*Athens (Greece) -- Antiquities. Excavations
(Archaeology)--Greece--Athens. Historic sites--
Greece--Athens.*

DF275.L36 1993
Lambert, S. D., 1960-
The phratries of Attica/ S.D. Lambert. Ann Arbor:
University of Michigan Press, c1993. xi, 424 p.
92-041140 306.2/0938/5 0472103881
*Citizenship -- Greece -- Athens. Kinship --
Greece -- Athens. Clans -- Greece -- Athens.
Athens (Greece) -- Religious life and customs.
Athens (Greece) -- Social life and customs.*

DF275.O33 1998
Ober, Josiah.
Political dissent in democratic Athens: intellectual
critics of popular rule/ Josiah Ober. Princeton,
N.J.: Princeton University Press, c1998. xiv, 417 p.
98-007110 937 s 0691001227
*Democracy -- Greece -- Athens --
Historiography. Dissenters -- Greece -- Athens --
Political activity. Athens (Greece) -- Intellectual
life -- Political aspects.*

DF277.F68 1990
Fornara, Charles W.
Athens from Cleisthenes to Pericles/ Charles W.
Fornara and Loren J. Samons II. Berkeley:
University of California Press, c1991. xvii, 199 p.
90-011166 938/.504 0520069234
Athens (Greece) -- Politics and government.

DF277.S315 1993
Sealey, Raphael.
Demosthenes and his time: a study in defeat/ Raphael Sealey. New York: Oxford University Press, 1993. x, 340 p.
92-018540 938/.5 0195079280
Demosthenes.   Greece -- Politics and government -- To 146 B.C. Athens (Greece) -- Politics and government.

DF285.F4 1969
Ferguson, William Scott, 1875-1954.
Hellenistic Athens; an historical essay. New York, H. Fertig, 1969. xviii, 487 p.
68-009652 938
Athens (Greece) -- History.

DF285.H313 1997
Habicht, Christian.
Athens from Alexander to Antony/ Christian Habicht; translated by Deborah Lucas Schneider. Cambridge, Mass.: Harvard University Press, 1997. viii, 406 p.
97-005180 938/.5 0674051114
Hellenism.   Athens (Greece) -- History.

DF287.A2.H87 1999
Hurwit, Jeffrey M., 1949-
The Athenian Acropolis: history, mythology, and archaeology from the Neolithic era to the present/ Jeffrey M. Hurwit. Cambridge, UK; Cambridge University Press, 1999. xv, 384 p.
98-003713 938/.5 0521417864
Monuments -- Conservation and restoration -- Greece -- Athens. Excavations (Archaeology) -- Greece -- Athens.   Acropolis (Athens, Greece) -- History. Athens (Greece) -- Civilization.

DF287.P4.G37 1987
Garland, Robert.
The Piraeus: from the fifth to the first century B.C./ Robert Garland. Ithaca, N.Y.: Cornell University Press, 1987. viii, 280 p.
87-047596 938/.8 0801420415
Piraeus (Greece)

DF503 Medieval Greece. Byzantine Empire, 323-1453 — Sources and documents — General works

DF503.B983 1984
Byzantium: church, society, and civilization seen through contemporary eyes/ [compiled by] Deno John Geanakoplos. Chicago: University of Chicago Press, 1984. xxxix, 485 p.
83-004806 949.5 0226284603
Byzantine Empire -- History -- Sources.

DF505.7 Medieval Greece. Byzantine Empire, 323-1453 — Historiography — Biography of historians, area studies specialists, archaeologists, etc.

DF505.7.P7.C35 1985
Cameron, Averil.
Procopius and the sixth century/ Averil Cameron. Berkeley: University of California Press, c1985. xiii, 297 p.
84-028020 907/.2024 0520055179
Procopius.   Byzantine Empire -- Intellectual life. Byzantine Empire -- History -- Justinian I, 527-565 -- Historiography.

DF521 Medieval Greece. Byzantine Empire, 323-1453 — Social life and customs. Civilization. Intellectual life — General works

DF521.M36 1980
Mango, Cyril A.
Byzantium, the empire of New Rome/ Cyril Mango. New York: Scribner, c1980. xiii, 334 p.
80-005870 949.5 0684167689
Byzantine Empire -- Civilization.

DF521.O93 1991
The Oxford dictionary of Byzantium/ Alexander P. Kazhdan, editor in chief; Alice-Mary Talbot, executive editor; Anthony Cutler, editor for art history; Timothy E. Gregory, editor for archaeology and historical geography; Nancy P. Sevcenko, associate editor. New York: Oxford University Press, 1991. 3 v.
90-023208 949.5/03/03 0195046528
Byzantine   Empire --   Civilization -- Dictionaries.

DF531 Medieval Greece. Byzantine Empire, 323-1453 — Social life and customs. Civilization. Intellectual life — General special

DF531.D42
Diehl, Charles, 1859-1944.
Byzantium: greatness and decline. Translated from the French by Naomi Walford. With introd. and bibliography by Peter Charanis. New Brunswick, N.J., Rutgers University Press, 1957. xviii, 366 p.
57-006223 949.5
Byzantine Empire -- History. Byzantine Empire -- Civilization.

DF531.F69 1993
Fowden, Garth.
Empire to commonwealth: consequences of monotheism in late antiquity/ Garth Fowden. Princeton, N.J.: Princeton University Press, c1993. xvii, 205 p.
92-037903 949.5/01 0691069891
Religion and civilization. Monotheism. Rome -- Civilization -- Christian influences. Byzantine Empire -- Civilization. Islamic Empire -- Civilization.

DF531.R8 1956
Runciman, Steven, 1903-
Byzantine   civilization.   Cleveland,   World Publishing company 1961. 255 p.
56-006570 949.5
Byzantine Empire -- Civilization.

DF543 Medieval Greece. Byzantine Empire, 323-1453 — Military history

DF543.L53 1990
Liebeschuetz, J. H. W. G.
Barbarians and bishops: army, church, and state in the age of Arcadius and Chrysostom/ J.H.W.G. Liebeschuetz. Oxford: Clarendon Press; 1990, c1989. xiv, 312 p.
89-037625 949.5/01 0198148860
John Chrysostom, -- Saint, -- d. 407 -- Adversaries. German   mercenaries --   Byzantine   Empire. Byzantine Empire -- History -- Arcadius, 395-408.

DF545 Medieval Greece. Byzantine Empire, 323-1453 — Political history

DF545.V78
Vryonis, Speros, 1928-
The decline of medieval Hellenism in Asia Minor and the process of Islamization from the eleventh through the fifteenth century [by] Speros Vryonis, Jr. Berkeley, University of California Press, 1971. xvii, 532 p.
75-094984 913.3/95/03 0520015975
Civilization, Islamic. Hellenism -- History -- To 1500.   Turkey -- History -- To 1453. Byzantine Empire -- Civilization -- 1081-1453. Byzantine Empire -- History -- 1081-1453.

DF547 Medieval Greece. Byzantine Empire, 323-1453 — Foreign and general relations — Relations with individual regions or countries, A-Z

DF547.I8.N53 1988
Nicol, Donald MacGillivray.
Byzantium and Venice: a study in diplomatic and cultural relations/ Donald M. Nicol. Cambridge; Cambridge University Press, 1988. x, 465 p.
88-005019 327.495045/31 0521341574
Byzantine Empire -- Relations -- Italy -- Venice. Venice (Italy) -- Relations -- Byzantine Empire.

DF547.L37.L5413 1993
Lilie, Ralph-Johannes.
Byzantium and the crusader states, 1096-1204 / by Ralph-Johannes Lilie; translated by J.C. Morris and Jean E. Ridings. Oxford: Clarendon Press; 1993. ix, 342 p.
93-017966 949.5/03 0198204078
Crusades.   Latin Orient -- Foreign relations -- Byzantine Empire. Byzantine Empire -- Foreign relations -- 1081-1453. Byzantine Empire -- Foreign relations -- Latin Orient.

DF552 Medieval Greece. Byzantine Empire, 323-1453 — History — General works

DF552.O25 1971b
Obolensky, Dimitri, 1918-
The Byzantine commonwealth; Eastern Europe, 500-1453. New York, Praeger Publishers [1971] xiv, 445 p.
73-137892 914.95/03
Byzantine Empire. Byzantine Empire -- Civilization. Balkan Peninsula -- Civilization -- Byzantine influences.

DF552.R67 2001
Rosser, John H. 1942-
Historical dictionary of Byzantium/ John H. Rosser. Lanham, Md.: Scarecrow Press, 2001. xli, 479 p.
00-053334 949.5/02 0810839792
Byzantine Empire -- History -- Dictionaries.

DF552.5 Medieval Greece. Byzantine Empire, 323-1453 — History — Compends

DF552.5.O8153 1969
Ostrogorski, Georgije.
History of the Byzantine state [by] George Ostrogorsky. Translated from the German by Joan Hussey. With a foreword by Peter Charanis. New Brunswick, N.J., Rutgers University Press, 1969. xl, 624 p.
71-083571   949.5   0813505992
Byzantine Empire -- History.

DF553-581 Medieval Greece. Byzantine Empire, 323-1453 — History — Eastern Empire, 323/476-1057

DF553.N67 1989
Norwich, John Julius, 1929-
Byzantium/ John Julius Norwich. New York: Knopf: 1989-1996. 3 v.
88-045508   949.5   0394537785
Byzantine Empire -- History.

DF555.G73 1998
Grant, Michael, 1914-
From Rome to Byzantium: the fifth century A.D./ Michael Grant. London; Routledge, 1998. xiii, 203 p.
97-014796   938   0415147530
Fifth century, A.D. Byzantine Empire -- History -- To 527. Rome -- History -- 284-476.

DF555.W55 1999
Williams, Stephen, 1942-
The Rome that did not fall: the survival of the East in the fifth century/ Stephen Williams and Gerard Friell. London; Routledge, 1999. p. cm.
98-022745   949.5/013   0415154030
Emperors -- Rome. Emperors -- Byzantine Empire. Byzantine Empire -- History -- To 527. Rome -- History -- Empire, 284-476. Rome -- History -- Germanic Invasions, 3rd-6th centuries.

DF556.W45 1996
Whittow, Mark, 1957-
The making of Byzantium, 600-1025/ Mark Whittow. Berkeley: University of California Press, c1996. xxv, 477 p.
95-044924   949.5   0520204964
Byzantine Empire -- Church history. Byzantine Empire -- History -- 527-1081.

DF571.H35 1990
Haldon, John F.
Byzantium in the seventh century: the transformation of a culture/ J.F. Haldon. Cambridge [England]; Cambridge University Press, 1990. xxiii, 486 p.
89-017309   949.5/01   0521264928
Byzantine Empire -- Civilization -- 527-1081.

DF572.M34 1991
Maas, Michael, 1951-
John Lydus and the Roman past: antiquarianism and politics in the age of Justinian/ Michael Maas. London; Routledge, 1992. ix, 207 p.
91-009119   949.5/01/092   0415060214
Lydus, Johannes Laurentius, -- 490-ca. 565. Byzantine Empire -- History -- Justinian I, 527-565. Byzantine Empire -- Civilization -- Roman influences.

DF572.P999 1967
Procopius.
History of the wars, Secret history, and Buildings/ Newly translated, edited, abridged, and with an introd. by Averil Cameron. New York: Twayne Publishers, [1967] xii, 351 p.
67-028144   949.501
Byzantine Empire -- History -- Justinian I, 525-565.

DF572.U73 1979
Ure, P. N. 1879-1950.
Justinian and his age/ P. N. Ure. Westport, Conn.: Greenwood Press, 1979. 262 p.
78-031752   949.5/01/0924   0313209162
Justinian -- I, -- Emperor of the East, -- 483?-565. Byzantine Empire -- History -- Justinian I, 527-565.

DF572.8.E5.G37 1999
Garland, Lynda, 1955-
Byzantine empresses: women and power in Byzantium, AD 527-1204/ Lynda Garland. London; Routledge, 1999. xix, 343 p.
98-023383   949.5/0099   0415146887
Empresses -- Byzantine Empire -- Biography. Leadership in women -- Byzantine Empire -- History. Byzantine Empire -- History -- 1081-1453. Byzantine Empire -- History -- 527-1081.

DF581.T73 1988
Treadgold, Warren T.
The Byzantine revival, 780-842/ Warren Treadgold. Stanford, Calif.: Stanford University Press, 1988. xv, 504 p.
87-037392   949.5/02   0804714622
Byzantine Empire -- History -- 527-1081.

DF605-645 Medieval Greece. Byzantine Empire, 323-1453 — History — 1057-1453

DF605.C6 1967a
Comnena, Anna, b. 1083.
The Alexiad of the Princess Anna Comnena, being the history of the reign of her father, Alexius I, Emperor of the Romans, 1081-1118 A.D. Translated by Elizabeth A. S. Dawes. New York, Barnes & Noble [1967] viii, 439 p.
67-005910   949.5/03/0924
Alexius -- I Comnenus, -- Emperor of the East, -- 1048-1118. Middle Ages -- Sources. Byzantine Empire -- History -- Alexius I Comnenus, 1081-1118.

DF607.M34 1993
Magdalino, Paul.
The empire of Manuel I Komnenos, 1143-1180/ Paul Magdalino. Cambridge [England]; Cambridge University Press, 1993. xix, 557 p.
92-013501   949.5/03   0521305713
Manuel -- I Comnenus, -- Emperor of the East, -- ca. 1120-1180. Byzantine Empire -- History -- Manuel I Comnenus, 1143-1180.

DF609.L63 1995
Lock, Peter, 1949-
The Franks in the Aegean, 1204-1500/ Peter Lock. London; Longman, 1995. xiii, 400 p.
94-039822   949.5/02   0582051401
Franks -- Aegean Sea Region -- History. Crusades -- Later, 13th, 14th, and 15th centuries. Civilization, Aegean -- Foreign influences. Byzantine Empire -- History -- 1081-1453.

DF631.B313 1970
Vakalopoulos, Apostolos E. 1909-
Origins of the Greek nation; the Byzantine period, 1204-1461, by Apostolos E. Vacalopoulos. New Brunswick, N.J., Rutgers University Press [1970] xxviii, 401 p.
75-119511   949.5/04   081350659X
Greece -- History -- 323-1453. Greece -- Civilization.

DF633.3.N53 1994
Nicol, Donald MacGillivray.
The Byzantine lady: ten portraits, 1250-1500/ Donald M. Nicol. Cambridge; Cambridge University Press, 1994. x, 143 p.
93-035728   949.5/04/0922   0521455316
Women -- Byzantine Empire -- History -- Middle Ages, 500-1500. Upper class -- Byzantine Empire -- Biography. Social history -- Medieval, 500-1500. Byzantine Empire -- Civilization -- 1081-1453.

DF635.G4
Geanakoplos, Deno John.
Emperor Michael Palaeologus and the West, 1258-1282; a study in Byzantine-Latin relations. Cambridge, Harvard University Press, 1959. xii, 434 p.
59-007652   949.504
Michael Palaeologus, -- VIII, -- Emperor of the East, -- 1234-1282.   Byzantine Empire -- Foreign relations.

DF645.P4813
Phrantzes, Georgios, b. 1401.
The fall of the Byzantine Empire: a chronicle/ by George Sphrantzes, 1401-1477; translated by Marios Philippides. Amherst: University of Massachusetts Press, 1980. 174 p.
79-005498   949.5/04   0870232908
Byzantine Empire -- History -- John VIII Palaeologus, 1425-1448. Byzantine Empire -- History -- Constantine XI Dragases, 1448-1453. Istanbul (Turkey) -- History -- Siege, 1453.

DF717 Modern Greece — General works. Compends

DF717.K68 1987
Kourvetaris, George A.
A profile of modern Greece, in search of identity/ Yorgos A. Kourvetaris and Betty A. Dobratz. Oxford [Oxfordshire]; Clarendon Press, 1987. ix, 266 p.
87-015404   949.5   019827551X
Greece.

DF721 Modern Greece — Description and travel — 1453-1820

DF721.B53 1993
Biddle, Nicholas, 1786-1844.
Nicholas Biddle in Greece: the journals and letters of 1806/ edited by R.A. McNeal. University Park, Pa.: Pennsylvania State University Press, c1993. viii, 243 p.
92-035459   949.5/05   0271009144
Greece -- Description and travel.

DF721.S76 1987
Stoneman, Richard.
Land of lost gods: the search for classical Greece/ Richard Stoneman. Norman: University of Oklahoma Press, c1987. xvii, 346 p.
86-040529   914.95/04   0806120525
Travelers -- Greece -- History. Travelers -- Turkey -- History. Greece -- Antiquities. Turkey -- Description and travel. Greece -- Description and travel.

DF741 Modern Greece — Social life and customs. Civilization. Culture

DF741.G73 1985
The Greek world: classical, Byzantine, and modern/ texts by Robert Browning ... et al.; edited by Robert Browning. London: Thames and Hudson, c1985. 328 p.
86-158583   949.5   0500250928
Greece -- Civilization.

DF757 Modern Greece — History — General works

DF757.C56
Clogg, Richard, 1939-
A short history of modern Greece/ Richard Clogg. Cambridge: Cambridge University Press, 1979. viii, 241 p.
78-072083   949.5   0521224799
Greece -- History -- 1453-

DF757.E53 2000
Encyclopedia of Greece and the Hellenic tradition/ editor, Graham Speake. London; Fitzroy Dearborn, c2000. 2 v.
01-267772   938/.003   1579581412
Greece -- History -- Encyclopedias.

DF757 .W6 1991
Woodhouse, C. M.
Modern Greece: a short history/ C.M. Woodhouse. 5th ed., Rev. London; Faber and Faber, 1991. 379 p.
91-217212   0571161227
Greece -- History -- 1453-1821. Greece -- History -- 1821- Byzantine Empire -- History.

DF787 Modern Greece — History — Political and diplomatic history

DF787.T8.B33 1990
Bahcheli, Tozun.
Greek-Turkish relations since 1955/ Tozun Bahcheli. Boulder: Westview Press, 1990. xv, 216 p.
86-032612   327.4950561   0813372356
Greece -- Foreign relations -- Turkey. Turkey -- Foreign relations -- Greece. Greece -- Foreign relations -- 20th century.

DF787.T8.G726 1990
The Greek-Turkish conflict in the 1990s: domestic and external influences/ edited by Dimitri Constas. New York: St. Martin's Press, 1991. xv, 279 p.
90-035540   327.4950561   0312048874
Greece -- Foreign relations -- Turkey. Turkey -- Foreign relations -- Greece. Greece -- Foreign relations -- 1974-

DF787.U5.C37 1988
Cassimatis, Louis P.
American influence in Greece, 1917-1929/ Louis P. Cassimatis. Kent, Ohio: Kent State University Press, c1988. xiii, 300 p.
88-003012   303.4/8273/0495   0873383575
Greece -- Relations -- United States. United States -- Relations -- Greece. Greece -- History -- 1917-1944.

DF801-854 Modern Greece — History — By period

DF801.M68 1976b
The Movement for Greek independence, 1770-1821: a collection of documents/ edited and translated with an introd. by Richard Clogg. New York: Barnes & Noble, 1976. xxiii, 232 p.
75-044747   949.5/05   0064912167
Greece -- History -- 1453-1821 -- Sources.

DF802.C57 2002
Clogg, Richard,
A concise history of Greece/ Richard Clogg. Cambridge, England; Cambridge University Press, 2002. xv, 291 p.
2002-725551   949.5.220   0521808723
Greece -- History -- 1821-

DF802.V47 1995
Veremes, Thanos.
Historical dictionary of Greece/ by Thanos M. Veremis and Mark Dragoumis. Metuchen, N.J.: Scarecrow Press, 1995. xvii, 258 p.
94-014447   949.5   081082888X
Greece -- History -- 1821- -- Dictionaries.

DF823.P4
Petropulos, John Anthony.
Politics and statecraft in the kingdom of Greece, 1833-1843. Princeton, N.J., Princeton University Press, 1968. xix, 646 p.
66-021837   329.9/495
Greece -- Politics and government -- 19th century.

DF836.K37.W66 1982
Woodhouse, C. M. 1917-
Karamanlis, the restorer of Greek democracy/ C.M. Woodhouse. Oxford: Clarendon Press; c1982. vi, 297 p.
82-006393   949.5/07/0924   0198225849
Karamanlis, Konstantinos, -- 1907- Statesmen -- Greece -- Biography. Presidents -- Greece -- Biography. Greece -- History -- 1950-1967. Greece -- History -- 1974-

DF845.S4 1973
Smith, Michael Llewellyn, 1939-
Ionian vision; Greece in Asia Minor, 1919-1922. New York, St. Martin's Press [1973] 401 p.
73-080083   949.5/06
Greco-Turkish War, 1921-1922. Greeks -- Turkey. Greece -- Politics and government -- 1917-1935.

DF849.I2
Iatrides, John O.
Revolt in Athens; the Greek Communist "Second Round," 1944-1945, by John O. Iatrides. With a foreword by William Hardy McNeill. Princeton, N.J., Princeton University Press [1972] xiv, 340 p.
76-039052   320.9/495/07   0691052034
World War, 1939-1945 -- Underground movements -- Greece. Greece -- Politics and government -- 1935-1967.

DF849.52.C56 1995
Close, David
The origins of the Greek civil war/ David H. Close. London; Longman, 1995. xiv, 248 p.
94-039794   949.507/4   0582064724
Greece -- Politics and government -- 1935-1967. Greece -- History -- Civil War,1944-1949 -- Diplomatic history. Greece -- History -- Civil War, 1944-1949 -- Causes.

DF849.58.M48.V37 1998
Vatikiotis, P. J. 1928-
Popular autocracy in Greece, 1936-41: a political biography of general Ioannis Metaxas/ P.J. Vatikiotis. London; Frank Cass, 1998. xi, 223 p.
97-039080   949.507   0714648698
Metaxas, Ioannis, -- 1871-1941. Dictators -- Greece -- Biography. Generals -- Greece -- Biography. Greece -- History -- 1917-1944. Greece -- Politics and government -- 1935-1967.

DF852.C56
Clogg, Richard, 1939-
Greece under military rule; edited by Richard Clogg and George Yannopoulos. London, Secker & Warburg [1972] xxii, 272 p.
73-150404   309.1/495/07   0436102552
Greece -- Politics and government -- 1967-1974.

DF852.P34
Papandreou, Andreas George.
Democracy at gunpoint: the Greek front [by] Andreas Papandreou. Garden City, N.Y., Doubleday, 1970. xv, 365 p.
73-101714   949.5/07
Greece -- Politics and government -- 1935-1967.

DF854.G74 1988
Greece under socialism: a NATO ally adrift/ edited by Nikolaos A. Stavrou; introduction by Matthew Nimetz. New Rochelle, N.Y.: A.D. Caratzas, c1988. xiv, 428 p.
88-028985   949.5/076   089241460X
Greece -- Politics and government -- 1974-

DF901 Modern Greece — Local history and description — Regions, provinces, islands, etc., A-Z

DF901.A69.J35 1994
Jameson, Michael H.
A Greek countryside: the southern Argolid from prehistory to the present day/ Michael H. Jameson, Curtis N. Runnels, Tjeerd H. van Andel; with a register of sites by Curtis N. Runnels and Mark H. Munn. Stanford, Calif.: Stanford University Press, 1994. xviii, 654 p.
93-017456   949.5/2   0804716080
Human geography -- Greece -- Argolis Peninsula. Argolis Peninsula (Greece) -- History. Argolis Peninsula (Greece) -- Geography. Argolis Peninsula (Greece) -- Antiquities.

DF901.A75.K37 1997
Karakasidou, Anastasia N.
Fields of wheat, hills of blood: passages to nationhood in Greek Macedonia, 1870-1990/ Anastasia N. Karakasidou. Chicago: University of Chicago Press, 1997. xxiii, 334 p.
96-034475   949.5/607   0226424936
Ethnohistory -- Greece -- Assiros Region. Nationalism -- Greece -- Macedonia. Assiros Region (Greece) -- History.

DF901.C83
McKee, Sally.
Uncommon dominion: Venetian Crete and the myth of ethnic purity/ Sally McKee. Philadelphia: University of Pennsylvania Press, c2000. xiii, 272 p.
00-028658   305.8/009495/90902   0812235622
Ethnicity -- Greece -- Crete -- History. Crete (Greece) -- Ethnic relations -- History. Crete (Greece) -- History -- Venetian rule, 1204-1669.

DF901.C83.G74 2000
Greene, Molly, 1959-
A shared world: Christians and Muslims in the early modern Mediterranean/ Molly Greene. Princeton, N.J.: Princeton University Press, c2000. xii, 228 p.
99-041888   949.5/905   0691008981
Crete (Greece) -- History -- Venetian rule, 1204-1669 -- Influence. Crete (Greece) -- History -- Turkish rule, 1669-1898. Middle East -- Civilization -- Religious aspects.

DF901.K25.S88 1998
Sutton, David E.
Memories cast in stone: the relevance of the past in everyday life/ David E. Sutton. Oxford; Berg, 1998. xi, 241 p.
98-211638   949.5/87   1859739482
Kalymnos Island (Greece) -- History. Kalymnos Island (Greece) -- Social life and customs.

DF920-923 Modern Greece — Local history and description — Athens

DF920.F38 1993
Faubion, James D., 1957-
Modern Greek lessons: a primer in historical constructivism/ James D. Faubion. Princeton, N. J.: Princeton University Press, c1993. xxiv, 307 p.
93-015480   949.5/12   069109473X
Athens (Greece) -- Civilization.

DF923.M35 1992
Mackenzie, Molly.
Turkish Athens: the forgotten centuries 1456-1832/ Molly Mackenzie. Reading, Berkshire, Great Britain: Ithaca Press, 1992. 148 p.
949.5/1205   0863721435
Athens (Greece) -- History.

DF951 Modern Greece — Local history and description — Other cities, towns, etc., A-Z

DF951.R4.H47 1991
Herzfeld, Michael, 1947-
A place in history: social and monumental time in a Cretan town/ Michael Herzfeld. Princeton, N.J.: Princeton University Press, c1991. xvi, 305 p.
90-028755   949.9/8   069109456X
Rethymnon (Greece) -- History.

DG History of Italy

DG13 Ancient Italy. Rome to 476 — Sources and documents. Collections. Classical authors

DG13.L4
Lewis, Naphtali,
Roman civilization; selected readings, edited with an introd. and notes, by Naphtali Lewis & Meyer Reinhold. New York, Columbia University Press, 1951-1955. 2 v.
51-014589   937
Rome -- Civilization. Rome -- History -- Sources.

DG16 Ancient Italy. Rome to 476 — Dictionaries

DG16.P685
Platner, Samuel Ball, 1863-1921.
A topographical dictionary of ancient Rome, by Samuel Ball Platner, completed and revised by Thomas Ashby. London, Oxford university press, H.Milford, 1929. xxiii, 608 p.
30-010804   913.376
Rome (Italy) -- Antiquities. Rome (Italy) -- Description and travel.

DG28 Ancient Italy. Rome to 476 — Geography. Description and travel — General works

DG28.O36 1993
O'Connor, Colin.
Roman bridges/ Colin O'Connor, with photographs, sketches, and diagrams by the author. Cambridge; Cambridge University Press, 1993. xvi, 235 p.
92-030900   388.1/32/0937   0521393264
Bridges -- Rome. Roads, Roman. Aqueducts -- Rome Rome -- Antiquities.

DG55-59 Ancient Italy. Rome to 476 — Local history and description — Regions, provinces, etc.

DG55.M3.D8 1968
Dunbabin, T. J.
The western Greeks; the history of Sicily and South Italy from the foundation of the Greek colonies to 480 B.C., by T. J. Dunbabin. Oxford, Clarendon P., 1968. ix, 504 p.
77-353250   913.3/7/8031
Greece -- Colonies. Magna Grecia -- History.

DG55.S9.C38 1990
Caven, Brian, 1921-
Dionysius I: war-lord of Sicily/ Brian Caven. New Haven: Yale University Press, 1990. xii, 272 p.
89-050651   937/.803/092   0300045077
Dionysius -- I, -- ca. 430-367 B.C.   Syracuse (Italy) -- Kings and rulers -- Biography. Sicily (Italy) -- History -- To 800.

DG59.A2.A64 2000
Ando, Clifford, 1969-
Imperial ideology and provincial loyalty in the Roman Empire/ Clifford Ando. Berkeley: University of California Press, c2000. xxi, 494 p.
99-041499   937/.06   0520220676
Allegiance -- Rome. Political stability -- Rome. Rome -- Provinces -- Administration. Rome -- Cultural policy -- Influence. Rome -- History -- Empire, 30 B.C.-476 A.D. -- Influence.

DG59.A2.D97 1985
Dyson, Stephen L.
The creation of the Roman frontier/ Stephen L. Dyson. Princeton, N.J.: Princeton University Press, c1985. xii, 324 p.
84-042881   937   0691035776
Rome -- Provinces -- History. Rome -- Colonies -- History. Rome -- Boundaries -- History.

DG59.A2.E44 1996
Elton, Hugh.
Frontiers of the Roman Empire/ Hugh Elton. Bloomington: Indiana University Press, c1996. ix, 150 p.
95-047958   937/.06   0253331110
Rome -- Boundaries -- Social aspects. Rome -- Boundaries -- Economic aspects.

DG59.A2.W5513 1994
Whittaker, C. R.
Frontiers of the Roman Empire: a social and economic study/ C.R. Whittaker. Baltimore: Johns Hopkins University Press, c1994. xvi, 341 p.
93-031342   937/.06   0801846773
Boundaries. Rome -- Boundaries -- History.

DG59.D3.C63 1988
Cichorius, Conrad, 1863-
Trajan's Column: a new edition of the Cichorius plates/ introduction, commentary, and notes by Frank Lepper and Sheppard Frere. Gloucester, UK; Alan Sutton, 1988. xviii, 339 p.
88-177924   937/.07   0862994675
Trajan, -- Emperor of Rome, -- 53-117 -- Monuments -- Italy -- Rome.   Dacian War, 1st, 101-102. Dacian War, 2nd, 105-106. Trajan's Column (Rome, Italy) Rome (Italy) -- Antiquities. Italy -- Antiquities.

DG63-68 Ancient Italy. Rome to 476 — Local history and description — Rome (City) to 476

DG63.H57 1994
Holloway, R. Ross, 1934-
The archaeology of early Rome and Latium/ R. Ross Holloway. London; Routledge, 1994. xx, 203 p.
93-011279   937/.6   0415080657
Excavations (Archaeology) -- Italy -- Rome. Excavations (Archaeology) -- Italy -- Lazio. Rome (Italy) -- Antiquities. Lazio (Italy) -- Antiquities.

DG63.K7 1983
Krautheimer, Richard, 1897-
Three Christian capitals: topography and politics/ Richard Krautheimer. Berkeley: University of California Press, c1983. xiv, 167 p.
81-013148   937/.08   0520045416
Christian antiquities -- Italy -- Rome. Christian antiquities -- Turkey -- Istanbul. Christian antiquities -- Italy -- Milan. Milan (Italy) -- Description and travel. Rome (Italy) -- Description and travel. Istanbul (Turkey) -- Description and travel.

DG63.R54 1992
Ridley, Ronald T., 1940-
The eagle and the spade: archaeology in Rome during the Napoleonic Era/ Ronald T. Ridley. Cambridge; Cambridge University Press, 1992. xxviii, 328 p.
90-043070   937/.6   0521401917
Excavations (Archaeology) -- Italy -- Rome -- History -- 19th century.   Rome (Italy) -- Antiquities -- Conservation and restoration -- History -- 19th century.

DG65.G7313 1997
Grandazzi, Alexandre.
The foundation of Rome: myth and history/ Alexandre Grandazzi; translated by Jane Marie Todd. Ithaca: Cornell University Press, 1997. x, 236 p.
97-017341   937   080143114X
Mythology, Roman. Archaeology and history -- Italy -- Rome. Excavations (Archaeology) -- Italy -- Rome. Rome (Italy) -- Antiquities. Rome (Italy) -- History -- To 476. Rome -- History -- To 510 B.C. -- Historiography.

DG68.R5 1992
Richardson, Lawrence.
A new topographical dictionary of ancient Rome/ L. Richardson, Jr. Baltimore: Johns Hopkins University Press, c1992. xxxiv, 458 p.
91-045046   913.7/003   0801843006
Rome (Italy) -- Buildings, structures, etc. -- Dictionaries.

DG70 Ancient Italy.
Rome to 476
— Local history and description
— Other cities, towns, etc., A-Z

DG70.O8.M4 1973
Meiggs, Russell.
Roman Ostia/ by Russell Meiggs. Oxford [Eng.]: Clarendon Press, 1973. xix, 622 p.
74-182367   913.37/6   0198148100
Ostia (Extinct city)

DG70.P3.P42 1990
Pedley, John Griffiths.
Paestum, Greeks and Romans in southern Italy/ John Griffiths Pedley. New York, N.Y.: Thames and Hudson, 1990. 184 p.
89-051868   937/.7   0500390274
Greeks -- Italy -- Paestum (Extinct city) Romans -- Italy -- Paestum (Extinct city) Paestum (Extinct city)

DG70.P7.J29
Jashemski, Wilhelmina Mary Feemster, 1910-
The gardens of Pompeii: Herculaneum and the villas destroyed by Vesuvius/ Wilhelmina F. Jashemski; photos., drawings, and plans, Stanley A. Jashemski. New Rochelle, N.Y.: Caratzas Bros., 1979. x, 372 p.
79-051383   937/.7   0892410965
Gardens -- Italy -- Pompeii (Extinct city) Horticulture -- Italy -- Pompeii (Extinct city) Gardens in art. Pompeii (Extinct city)

DG70.P7.L55 1997
Ling, Roger.
The insula of the Menander at Pompeii/ Roger Ling; with contributions by Paul Arthur ... [et al.]. Oxford: Clarendon Press; 1997- v. 1
96-034438   937/.7   0198134096
Excavations (Archaeology) -- Italy -- Pompeii (Extinct city)   Pompeii (Extinct city) -- Buildings, structures, etc.

DG70.P7.W33 1994
Wallace-Hadrill, Andrew.
Houses and society in Pompeii and Herculaneum/ Andrew Wallace-Hadrill. Princeton, N.J.: Princeton University Press, c1994. xviii, 244 p.
93-017828   307.3/3616/09377   0691069875
Material culture -- Italy -- Pompeii (Extinct city) Material culture -- Italy -- Herculaneum (Extinct city) Architecture, Domestic -- Italy -- Pompeii (Extinct city) Pompeii (Extinct city) -- Social life and customs. Herculaneum (Extinct city) -- Social life and customs. Pompeii (Extinct city) -- Buildings, structures, etc.

DG70.P7.Z3613 1998
Zanker, Paul.
Pompeii: public and private life/ Paul Zanker; translated by Deborah Lucas Schneider. Cambridge, Mass.: Harvard University Press, 1998. ix, 251 p.
98-024720   937/.7   0674689666
Cities and towns, Ancient -- Rome. City planning -- Rome. Politics and culture -- Rome. Pompeii (Extinct city) Pompeii (Extinct city) -- Social life and customs.

DG77 Ancient Italy.
Rome to 476
— Antiquities. Civilization.
Culture — General works

DG77.A35 1994
Adkins, Lesley.
Handbook to life in ancient Rome/ Lesley Adkins and Roy A. Adkins. New York, NY: Facts on File, c1994. xi, 404 p.
93-011213   937   0816027552
Rome -- Civilization. Rome -- Social life and customs.

DG77.C597 1982
Cornell, Tim.
Atlas of the Roman world/ by Tim Cornell and John Matthews. New York: Facts on File, c1982. 240 p.
81-019591   937/.02   0871966522
Rome -- Civilization. Rome -- Maps.

DG77.G78 1992
Gruen, Erich S.
Culture and national identity in Republican Rome/ Erich S. Gruen. Ithaca, N.Y.: Cornell University Press, 1992. xiii, 347 p.
92-052756   937   0801427592
Rome -- Civilization. Rome -- Civilization -- Greek influences.

DG78 Ancient Italy.
Rome to 476 — Antiquities.
Civilization. Culture
— General special

DG78.B37 1993
Barton, Carlin A., 1948-
The sorrows of the ancient Romans: the gladiator and the monster/ Carlin A. Barton. Princeton, N.J.: Princeton University Press, c1993. 210 p.
92-013603   937   069105696X
National characteristics, Roman.

DG78.C32
Carcopino, Jerome, 1881-1970.
Daily life in ancient Rome; the people and the city at the height of the empire, by Jerome Carcopino, edited with bibliography and notes by Henry T. Rowell. Translated from the French by E. O. Lorimer. New Haven, Yale university press, 1940. xv, 342 p.
40-034290   937.6
Rome -- Social life and customs. Rome (Italy) -- History -- To 476.

DG78.D8713 1993
Dupont, Florence.
Daily life in ancient Rome/ Florence Dupont; translated by Christopher Woodall. Oxford, UK; Blackwell, 1993. xi, 314 p.
92-011082   937/.02   0631178775
Rome -- Social life and customs.

DG81-89 Ancient Italy.
Rome to 476
— Antiquities. Civilization.
Culture —
Public and political antiquities

DG81.T38
Taylor, Lily Ross, 1886-
Party politics in the age of Caesar. Berkeley, University of Calif. Press, 1949. viii, 255 p.
49-002564   937.05
Political parties -- Rome. Rome -- Politics and government -- 265-30 B.C.

DG82.C67 1996
Corbeill, Anthony, 1960-
Controlling laughter: political humor in the late Roman Republic/ Anthony Corbeill. Princeton, N.J.: Princeton University Press, c1996. x, 251 p.
96-000868   320.937   0691027390
Political oratory -- Rome. Political ethics -- Rome. Politics and culture -- Rome. Rome -- Politics and government -- Humor.

DG82.S8613
Storoni Mazzolani, Lidia.
The idea of the city in Roman thought: from walled city to spiritual commonwealth. Translated by S. O'Donnell. Bloomington, Indiana University Press [1970] 288 p.
79-108947   913.37/03   0253139805
Cities and towns, Ancient -- Rome. Rome -- Civilization.

DG83.3.G413 1969b
Gelzer, Matthias, 1886-1974.
The Roman nobility. Translated with an introd. by Robin Seager. New York, Barnes & Noble, 1969. xiv, 164 p.
68-059641   929.7/5
Nobility -- Rome.

DG83.5.A1.B73
Broughton, T. Robert S. 1900-
The magistrates of the Roman Republic, by T. Robert S. Broughton with the collaboration of Marcia L. Patterson. New York, American Philological Association, 1951-52. 2 v.
51-006071   937.02
Magistrates, Roman.   Rome -- Officials and employees. Rome -- History -- Republic, 510-30 B.C.

DG89.M13
MacMullen, Ramsay, 1928-
Soldier and civilian in the later Roman Empire.
Cambridge, Harvard University Press, 1963. vii,
217 p.
63-007591   355.10937
*Rome (Italy) -- Army -- Military life. Rome
(Italy) -- Social life and customs.*

DG89.R675 1998
Roth, Jonathan, 1955-
The logistics of the Roman army at war (264 B.C.-
A.D. 235)/ by Jonathan P. Roth. Leiden; Brill,
1999. xxi, 399 p.
98-042368   355.4/11/0937   9004112715
*Logistics. Rome -- Army -- Transportation --
Equipment and supplies. Rome -- Army -- Supplies
and stores. Rome -- History, Military -- 265-30
B.C.*

DG91-103 Ancient Italy.
Rome to 476 —
Antiquities. Civilization. Culture
— Private antiquities

DG91.W54 1989
Wiedemann, Thomas E. J.
Adults and children in the Roman Empire/ Thomas
Wiedemann. New Haven: Yale University Press,
1989. xii, 221 p.
88-051383   305.23/0937   0300043805
Children -- Rome.

DG97.Y45 1992
Yegul, Fikret K., 1941-
Baths and bathing in classical antiquity/ Fikret
Yegul. New York, N.Y.: Architectural History
Foundation; c1992. ix, 501 p.
91-024855   391/.64   0262240351
*Baths -- Rome -- History. Hygiene -- History.
Public baths -- Rome. Rome -- Antiquities.*

DG103.F56 1996
Flower, Harriet I.
Ancestor masks and aristocratic power in Roman
culture/ Harriet I. Flower. Oxford: Clarendon
Press; 1996. xvii, 411 p.
96-042045   393/.9   0198150180
*Funeral rites and ceremonies -- Rome. Masks --
Rome. Nobility -- Rome.*

DG103.T69
Toynbee, J. M. C. d. 1985.
Death and burial in the Roman world [by] J. M. C.
Toynbee. Ithaca, N.Y., Cornell University Press
[1971] 336 p.
77-120603   393/.0937   0801405939
*Funeral rites and ceremonies -- Rome. Tombs --
Rome. Rome -- Social life and customs.*

DG124 Ancient Italy.
Rome to 476 — Antiquities.
Civilization. Culture —
Religious antiquities

DG124.M33
MacCormack, Sabine.
Art and ceremony in late antiquity/ Sabine G.
MacCormack. Berkeley: University of California
Press, c1981. xvi, 417 p.
78-062864   937/.06   0520037790
*Emperor worship -- Rome. Rites and ceremonies
-- Rome. Emperors -- Rome -- Succession. Rome --
History -- Empire, 284-476.*

DG190 Ancient Italy.
Rome to 476 — Ethnography

DG190.T48 1989
Thompson, Lloyd A.
Romans and Blacks/ Lloyd A. Thompson. Norman:
University of Oklahoma Press, 1989. xii, 253 p.
88-040549   305.8/96/037   0806122013
Blacks -- Rome.

DG203 Ancient Italy.
Rome to 476 — History
— Biography (Collective)

DG203.H39 2001
Hazel, John.
Who's who in the Roman world/ John Hazel.
London; Routledge, 2001. xii, 367 p.
    920.037   0415224101
Rome -- Biography. Rome -- History.

DG205-206 Ancient Italy.
Rome to 476 — History
— Historiography

DG205.P53 1988
Plass, Paul, 1933-
Wit and the writing of history: the rhetoric of
historiography in imperial Rome/ Paul Plass.
Madison, Wis.: University of Wisconsin Press,
c1988. x, 182 p.
88-040193   937/.0072   0299118002
*Historiography -- Rome. Latin wit and humor.
Rome -- Historiography.*

DG206.G5.C7 1989
Craddock, Patricia B.
Edward Gibbon, luminous historian, 1772-1794/
Patricia B. Craddock. Baltimore: Johns Hopkins
University Press, c1989. xv, 432 p.
88-045416   937/.0072024   0801837200
*Gibbon, Edward, -- 1737-1794. Gibbon, Edward, -
- 1737-1794. -- History of the decline and fall of
the Roman Empire.   Historiography -- Great
Britain -- History -- 18th century. Historians --
Great Britain -- Biography.   Rome -- History --
Empire, 30 B.C.-476 A.D. -- Historiography.
Byzantine Empire -- Historiography.*

DG207-209 Ancient Italy.
Rome to 476 — History
— General works

DG207.L583.F45 1998
Feldherr, Andrew, 1963-
Spectacle and society in Livy's history/ Andrew
Feldherr. Berkeley: University of California Press,
c1998. xiv, 251 p.
97-036872   937   0520210263
*Livy. -- Ab urbe condita. Livy -- Criticism and
interpretation.   Rome -- History. Rome --
Historiography.*

DG207.L583.M5 1995
Miles, Gary B.
Livy: reconstructing early Rome/ Gary B. Miles.
Ithaca: Cornell University Press, 1995. xi, 251 p.
94-043821   937   0801430607
*Livy. -- Ab urbe condita. Livy -- Criticism and
interpretation -- History.   Rome -- History. Rome
-- Historiography.*

DG207.T2.C45
Tacitus, Cornelius.
The complete works of Tacitus: The annals. The
history. The life of Cnaeus Julius Agricola.
Germany and its tribes. A dialogue on oratory.
Translated form the Latin by Alfred John Church
and William Jackson Brodribb; edited, and with an
introduction, by Moses Hadas. New York, The
Modern library [1942] xxv, 773 p.
42-036137   878.6
*Tacitus, Cornelius -- Translations into English.
Rome -- History.*

DG209.J652
Jones, A. H. M. 1904-1970,
A history of Rome through the fifth century, edited
by A. H. M. Jones. New York, Walker [1968- v.
68-013332   937
Rome -- History.

DG209.S95 1979
Syme, Ronald, 1903-
Roman papers/ Ronald Syme; edited by E. Badian.
Oxford: Clarendon Press; 1979-1991 v. 1-7
79-040437   937/.06   0198143672
Rome -- History.

DG210 Ancient Italy.
Rome to 476 — History
— Compends. Textbooks

DG210.S8 1953
Starr, Chester G., 1914-
The emergence of Rome as ruler of the Western
World.   Ithaca, Cornell University Press, 1953.
122 p.
53-002022   937
Rome -- History.

DG211 Ancient Italy.
Rome to 476 — History
— General special

DG211.L5
Lintott, A. W.
Violence in republican Rome, by A. W. Lintott.
Oxford, Clarendon P., 1968. xi, 234 p.
78-363006   362   0198142676
*Violence -- Rome. Criminal law (Roman law)
Rome -- History -- Republic, 510-30 B.C.*

DG221-330 Ancient Italy.
Rome to 476 — History
— By period

DG221.P34513 1990
Pallottino, Massimo.
A history of earliest Italy/ Massimo Pallottino;
translated by Martin Ryle and Kate Soper. Ann
Arbor: University of Michigan Press, c1991. x,
206 p.
89-035606   937   0472100971
*Italic peoples -- History.   Italy -- History -- To
476.*

DG221.5.S24 1982
Salmon, Edward Togo.
The making of Roman Italy/ E.T. Salmon. Ithaca,
N.Y.: Cornell University Press, 1982. xi, 212 p.
81-068745   937   0801414385
*Italic peoples -- History. Italic peoples --
Cultural assimilation. Italy -- History -- To 476.
Rome -- History -- Republic, 510-30 B.C.*

DG223.B345 1998
Barker, Graeme.
The Etruscans/ Graeme Barker and Tom Rasmussen. Oxford; Blackwell Publishers, 1998. xii, 379 p.
97-016462   937/.5   0631177159
Etruscans.

DG223.P283 1975
Pallottino, Massimo.
The Etruscans. Translated by J. Cremona. Edited by David Ridgway. Bloomington, Indiana University Press [1975] 316 p.
74-006082   913.37/5/03   0253320801
Etruscans.

DG225.C44.E44 1998
Ellis, Peter Berresford.
Celt and Roman: the Celts of Italy/ Peter Berresford Ellis. New York: St. Martin's Press, 1998. xi, 288 p.
98-004886   937/.009416   0312214197
Celts -- Rome -- History. Civilization, Celtic. Rome -- History -- Republic, 510-30 B.C. -- Historiography.

DG231.D95 1991
Dyson, Stephen L.
Community and society in Roman Italy/ Stephen L. Dyson. Baltimore: Johns Hopkins University Press, c1992. xii, 383 p.
91-020070   937   0801841755
Cities and towns, Ancient -- Italy. Italy -- Rural conditions. Italy -- Antiquities, Roman. Italy -- History -- To 476.

DG231.S35 1969
Scullard, H. H. 1903-
A history of the Roman world from 753 to 146 B.C., by Howard H. Scullard. London, Methuen, 1969. xiv, 480 p.
70-384646   913.3/7/031   0416436609
Rome -- History -- To 510 B.C. Rome -- History -- Republic, 510-30 B.C.

DG231.3.H3
Harris, William V.
War and imperialism in Republican Rome, 327-70 B.C./ by William V. Harris. Oxford: Clarendon Press; 1979. 293 p.
78-040490   937/.02   0198148275
War. Imperialism. Rome -- History -- Republic, 510-30 B.C. Rome -- Foreign relations -- 510-30 B.C.

DG233.G33 1991
Gabba, Emilio.
Dionysius and The history of archaic Rome/ Emilio Gabba. Berkeley: University of California Press, c1991. xviii, 253 p.
90-011138   937   0520073029
Dionysius, -- of Halicarnassus. -- Antiquitates romanae.   Rome -- History -- To 510 B.C. -- Historiography. Rome -- History -- Republic, 510-265 B.C. -- Historiography.

DG233.2.S63 1996
Smith, Christopher John, 1965-
Early Rome and Latium: economy and society c. 1000 to 500 BC/ Christopher John Smith. Oxford: Clarendon Press; 1996. viii, 290 p.
95-022082   937/.601   0198150318
Excavations (Archaeology) -- Italy -- Lazio. Lazio (Italy) -- History. Rome -- History -- To 510 B.C. Lazio (Italy) -- antiquities.

DG241.J34 1997
Jaeger, Mary, 1960-
Livy's written Rome/ Mary Jaeger. Ann Arbor: University of Michigan Press, c1997. xii, 205 p.
97-021070   937/.02   0472107895
Livy. -- Ab urbe condita.   Rome -- History -- Republic, 265-30 B.C.

DG241.2.G78 1984
Gruen, Erich S.
The Hellenistic world and the coming of Rome/ Erich S. Gruen. Berkeley: University of California Press, c1984. 2 v.
82-008581   937/.02   0520045696
Hellenism. Imperialism.   Rome -- History -- Republic, 265-30 B.C. Greece -- History -- 281-146 B.C.

DG241.2.M38 1997
Matz, David.
An ancient Rome chronology, 264-27 B.C./ by David Matz. Jefferson, N.C.: McFarland & Co., c1997. vii, 228 p.
96-046861   937/.04/0202   0786401613
Rome -- History -- 265-30 B.C. -- Chronology.

DG242.G65 2000
Goldsworthy, Adrian Keith.
The Punic wars/ Adrian Goldsworthy. London: Cassell, 2000. 412 p.
01-334818   0304352845
Punic wars.

DG249.L3513 1998
Lancel, Serge.
Hannibal/ Serge Lancel; translated by Antonia Nevill. Malden, Mass.: Blackwell, 1998. p. cm.
97-037371   937/.04/092   0631206310
Hannibal, -- 247-182 B.C.   Generals -- Tunisia -- Carthage (Extinct city) -- Biography.   Carthage (Extinct city) -- History, Military. Rome -- History -- Republic, 265-30 B.C.

DG250.L58213
Livy.
Rome and the Mediterranean: books XXXI-XLV of The history of Rome from its foundation/ [by] Livy; translated [from the Latin] by Henry Bettenson; with an introduction by A. H. McDonald. Harmondsworth: Penguin, 1976. 699 p.
76-378574   937/.02   0140443185
Bettenson, Henry Scowcroft.   Rome -- History -- Republic, 265-30 B.C.

DG250.S3
Scullard, H. H. 1903-
Roman politics, 220-150 B.C. Oxford, Clarendon Press, 1951. xvi, 325 p.
51-010700   937.04
Rome -- Politics and government -- 265-30 B.C.

DG254.G3132
Gabba, Emilio.
Republican Rome, the army, and the allies/ Emilio Gabba; translated by P. J. Cuff. Berkeley: University of California Press, 1976. ix, 272 p.
76-014307   937/.05   0520032594
Rome -- Politics and government -- 265-30 B.C. Rome -- Army -- History.

DG254.G8 1960
Greenidge, A. H. J. 1865-1906.
Sources for Roman history, 133-70 B.C., collected and arr. by A. H. J. Greenidge and A. M. Clay. Oxford, Clarendon Press, 1960. viii, 318 p.
60-002011   937.02
Rome -- History -- Republic, 510-30 B.C. -- Sources.

DG254.L36 1994
Langguth, A. J. 1933-
A noise of war: Caesar, Pompey, Octavian, and the struggle for Rome/ A.J. Langguth. New York: Simon & Schuster, c1994. 384 p.
93-039196   937/.05   0671708295
Rome -- History -- Republic, 265-30 B.C.

DG254.S35 1970
Scullard, H. H. 1903-
From the Gracchi to Nero: a history of Rome from 133 B.C. to A.D. 68, by H. H. Scullard. London, Methuen, 1970. xv, 484 p.
71-560931   937/.05   0416077501
Rome -- History -- Republic, 265-30 B.C. Rome -- History -- The five Julii, 30 B.C.-68 A.D.

DG254.S9 2002
Syme, Ronald,
The Roman revolution/ by Ronald Syme. Oxford; Oxford University Press, 2002. xi, 568 p.
2002-725567   937/.05 21   0192803204
Rome -- Politics and government -- 265-30 B.C. Rome -- Politics and government -- 30 B.C.-68 A.D.

DG254.2.M55 1998
Millar, Fergus.
The crowd in Rome in the late Republic/ Fergus Millar. Ann Arbor: University of Michigan Press, 1998. xvi, 236 p.
97-050351   937/.05   0472108921
Crowds -- Rome -- History. Collective behavior. Rome -- Politics and government -- 265-30 B.C.

DG254.2.S4
Seager, Robin,
The crisis of the Roman republic: studies in political and social history; selected and introduced by Robin Seager. Cambridge, Heffer; 1969. xiii, 218 p.
73-427018   309.1/37   0852700245
Rome -- Politics and government -- 265-30 B.C.

DG258.R38
Rawson, Beryl.
The politics of friendship: Pompey and Cicero/ [by] Beryl Rawson. Sydney: Sydney University Press, 1978. vi, 217 p.
78-320651   937/.05/0924   0424068001
Pompey, -- the Great, -- 106-48 B.C. Cicero, Marcus Tullius. Statesmen -- Rome -- Biography. Generals -- Rome -- Biography. Rome -- History -- Republic, 265-30 B.C.

DG260.C5.B27 1972
Bailey, D. R. Shackleton 1917-
Cicero [by] D. R. Shackleton Bailey. New York, Scribner [1972, c1971] xii, 290 p.
78-176156   937/.05/0924   0684126834
Cicero, Marcus Tullius.   Rome -- History -- Republic, 265-30 B.C.

DG260.C5.F8413 1992
Fuhrmann, Manfred.
Cicero and the Roman Republic/ Manfred Fuhrmann; translated by W.E. Yuill. Oxford, UK; B. Blackwell, 1992. viii, 249 p.
91-041486   937/.05/092   0631178791
Cicero, Marcus Tullius.   Orators -- Rome -- Biography. Statesmen -- Rome -- Biography. Rome -- Politics and government -- 265-30 B.C.

DG260.C5.R38 1983
Rawson, Elizabeth.
Cicero: a portrait/ Elizabeth Rawson. Ithaca, N.Y.:
Cornell University Press, 1983, c1975. xvi, 341 p.
83-070178   937/.05/0924   0801416280
*Cicero, Marcus Tullius.   Statesmen -- Rome --
Biography. Orators -- Rome -- Biography. Rome --
History -- Republic, 265-30 B.C.*

DG260.C53.M57
Mitchell, Thomas N., 1939-
Cicero, the ascending years/ Thomas N. Mitchell.
New Haven: Yale University Press, 1979. xii,
259 p.
78-031188   937/.05/0924   0300022778
*Cicero, Marcus Tullius.   Statesmen -- Rome --
Biography. Orators -- Rome -- Biography.*

DG260.C53.M58 1991
Mitchell, Thomas N., 1939-
Cicero, the senior statesman/ Thomas N. Mitchell.
New Haven: Yale University Press, c1991. x,
345 p.
90-038157   937/.05/092   0300047797
*Cicero, Marcus Tullius.   Statesmen -- Rome --
Biography. Orators -- Rome -- Biography. Rome --
Politics and government -- 265-30 B.C.*

DG260.C63.T37 1999
Tatum, W. Jeffrey.
The patrician tribune: Publius Clodius Pulcher/ by
W. Jeffrey Tatum. Chapel Hill: The University of
North Carolina Press, 1999. p. cm.
98-037096   937/.06/092   0807824801
*Clodius, Publius -- ca. 93-52 B.C.   Politicians --
Rome -- Biography.   Rome -- Politics and
government -- 265-30 B.C.*

DG260.L8.K43 1992
Keaveney, Arthur.
Lucullus: a life/ Arthur Keaveney. London;
Routledge, 1992. x, 275 p.
91-040530   937/.05/092   0415032199
*Lucullus, -- ca. 117 B.C.-ca. 56 B.C.   Generals --
Rome -- Biography. Statesmen -- Rome --
Biography. Rome -- History -- Republic, 265-30
B.C.*

DG261.M3713 1995
Meier, Christian, 1929-
Caesar/ Christian Meier; translated from the
German by David McLintock. New York:
BasicBooks/HarperCollins, [1995]. 513 p. 16 p.
95-030003   937/.05/092   0465008941
*Caesar, Julius.   Statesmen -- Rome -- Biography.
Generals -- Rome -- Biography. Rome -- History --
Republic, 265-30 B.C.*

DG270.B86 2002
Bunson, Matthew.
Encyclopedia of the Roman empire/ Matthew
Bunson.Rev. ed. New York: Facts On File, c2002.
xviii, 636 p.
2001-053253   937/.06.221   0816045623
*Rome -- History -- Empire, 30 B.C.-476 A.D. --
Encyclopedias.*

DG270.H45
Henderson, Bernard W. 1872-1929.
Five Roman emperors: Vespasian, Titus, Domitian,
Nerva, Trajan, A.D. 69-117, by Bernard W.
Henderson. Cambridge [Eng.] The University
press, 1927. xiii, 357 p.
28-005894
*Emperors -- Rome.   Rome -- History -- Empire,
30 B.C.-476 A.D.*

DG270.M33 1988
MacMullen, Ramsay, 1928-
Corruption and the decline of Rome/ Ramsay
MacMullen. New Haven: Yale University Press,
c1988. xii, 319 p.
88-000096   937/.06   0300043139
*Power (Social sciences)   Rome -- Politics and
government -- 30 B.C.-284 A.D.*

DG271.B78 1990
Brunt, P. A.
Roman imperial themes/ P.A. Brunt. Oxford:
Clarendon Press; 1990. 551 p.
89-037458   937/.06   0198144768
Rome -- History -- Empire, 30 B.C.-476 A.D.

DG271.R6 1957
Rostovtsev, Mikhail Ivanovich, 1870-1952
The social and economic history of the Roman
Empire/ by M. Rostovtzeff. -- Oxford: Clarendon
Press, 1966. 2 v.
58-000362   937.06
*Rome -- Economic conditions. Rome -- History
-- Empire, 30 B.C.-476 A.D. Rome -- Social
conditions*

DG273.M33 2000
MacMullen, Ramsay, 1928-
Romanization in the time of Augustus/ Ramsay
MacMullen. New Haven: Yale University Press,
c2000. xi, 222 p.
00-028108   937/.07   0300082541
*Acculturation -- Rome.   Rome -- History --
Augustus, 30 B.C.-14 A.D. Rome -- Provinces --
Administration. Rome -- Civilization.*

DG274.S28 1995
Scarre, Christopher.
Chronicle of the Roman emperors: the reign-by-
reign record of the rulers of Imperial Rome/ Chris
Scarre. London; Thames and Hudson, c1995.
240 p.
95-060277   937/.06/0922   0500050775
*Emperors -- Rome -- Biography.   Rome --
History -- Empire, 30 B.C.-476 A.D.*

DG274.S32 1976
Lives of the later Caesars: the first part of the
Augustan history: with newly compiled Lives of
Nerva and Trajan/ translated and introduced by
Anthony Birley. Harmondsworth, Eng.; Penguin
Books, 1976. 336 p.
76-373411   937/.07/0922   0140443088
*Emperors -- Rome -- Biography.   Rome --
History -- Empire, 30 B.C.-284 A.D.*

DG275.R65 1988
The Roman Empire: Augustus to Hadrian/ edited
and translated by Robert K. Sherk. Cambridge
[Cambridgeshire]; Cambridge University Press,
1988. xxii, 302 p.
87-024204   937/.07   0521330254
*Rome -- History -- Empire, 30 B.C.-284 A.D. --
Sources.*

DG276.G36 1987
Garnsey, Peter.
The Roman Empire: economy, society, and culture/
Peter Garnsey & Richard Saller. Berkeley:
University of California Press, 1987. 231 p.
86-025029   937/.07   0520060660
Rome -- History -- Empire, 30 B.C.-284 A.D.

DG276.5.C26 1984
Campbell, J. B.
The Emperor and the Roman Army, 31 BC-AD
235/ J.B. Campbell. Oxford [Oxfordshire]:
Clarendon Press; 1984. xix, 468 p.
83-019353   322/.5/0937   0198148348
*Emperors -- Rome -- Duties.   Rome -- Army --
Political activity. Rome -- Army -- Organization.
Rome -- Politics and government -- 30 B.C.-284
A.D.*

DG277.S7.T5 1957
Suetonius, ca. 69-ca. 122 ca. 69-ca. 12
The twelve Caesars. Translated by Robert Graves.
[Harmondsworth, Middlesex, Penguin Books
[1957] 315 p.
57-009665   937.07
*Emperors -- Rome -- Biography.   Rome --
History -- The five Julii, 30 B.C.-68 A.D. Rome --
History -- Flavians, 69-96.*

DG279.B43 1990
Between republic and empire: interpretations of
Augustus and his principate/ edited by Kurt A.
Raaflaub and Mark Toher; with contributions by
G.W. Bowersock ... [et al.]. Berkeley: University
of California Press, c1990. xxi, 495 p.
89-004788   937/.07/0924   0520066766
*Augustus, -- Emperor of Rome, -- 63 B.C.-14 A.D.
Emperors -- Rome -- Biography. Rome -- History
-- Augustus, 30 B.C.-14 A.D.*

DG279.G17 1996
Galinsky, Karl, 1942-
Augustan culture: an interpretive introduction/ Karl
Galinsky. Princeton, N.J.: Princeton University
Press, c1996. xi, 474 p.
95-033469   937/.07   069104435X
*Rome -- History -- Augustus, 30 B.C.-14 A.D.
Rome -- Civilization.*

DG279.S68 1998
Southern, Pat.
Augustus/ Pat Southern. London; Routledge, 1998.
xv, 271 p.
97-047532   937/.07/092   0415166314
*Augustus, -- Emperor of Rome, -- 63 B.C.-14 A.D.
Emperors -- Rome -- Biography. Rome -- History
-- Augustus, 30 B.C.-14 A.D.*

DG281.R65 2001
Roller, Matthew B., 1966-
Constructing autocracy: aristocrats and emperors in
Julio-Claudian Rome/ Matthew B. Roller.
Princeton: Princeton University Press, c2001. x,
319 p.
00-056511   937/.07   069105021X
*Aristocracy (Political science) -- Rome.
Emperors -- Rome. Class consciousness -- Rome.
Rome -- History -- The five Julii, 30 B.C.-68 A.D.*

DG281.W66 1998
Woodman, A. J. 1945-
Tacitus reviewed/ A.J. Woodman. Oxford:
Clarendon Press; 1998. xii, 255 p.
98-027415   937/.07   0198152582
*Tacitus, Cornelius. -- Annales.   Rome -- History
-- The five Julii, 30 B.C.-68 A.D. Rome --
Historiography.*

DG282.6.B37 1996
Barrett, Anthony, 1941-
Agrippina: sex, power, and politics in the early
Empire/ Anthony A. Barrett. New Haven: Yale
University Press, 1996. xxi, 330 p.
96-060318   937/.07/092   0300065981
*Agrippina, -- Minor, -- 15-59.   Empresses -- Rome
-- Biography.   Rome -- History -- The five Julii, 30
B.C.-68 A.D.*

DG283.B37 1990
Barrett, Anthony, 1941-
Caligula: the corruption of power/ Anthony A. Barrett. New Haven: Yale University Press, 1990. xxvi, 334 p.
89-051310   937/.07/092   0300046537
Caligula, -- Emperor of Rome, -- 12-41. Emperors -- Rome -- Biography.   Rome -- History -- Caligula, 37-41.

DG284.L47 1990
Levick, Barbara.
Claudius/ Barbara Levick. New Haven: Yale University Press, 1990. xvi, 256 p.
89-051800   937/.07/092   0300047347
Claudius, -- Emperor of Rome, -- 10 B.C.-54 A.D. Roman emperors -- Biography.   Rome -- History -- Claudius, 41-54.

DG284.M62 1962
Momigliano, Arnaldo.
Claudius, the Emperor and his achievement. Translated by W. D. Hogarth. With a new bibliography, 1942-59. New York, Barnes & Noble [1962] 143 p.
62-053113   923.137
Claudius, -- Emperor of Rome, -- 10 B.C.-54 A.D.

DG286.A84 1999
Ash, Rhiannon.
Ordering anarchy: armies and leaders in Tacitus' Histories / Rhiannon Ash. Ann Arbor, Mich.: University of Michigan Press, c1999. ix, 246 p.
99-047172   937/.07/092   0472111132
Tacitus, Cornelius. -- Historiae -- Technique. Generals -- Rome -- Biography. Emperors -- Rome -- Biography. Rome -- Army -- History -- Civil War, 68-69. Rome -- History -- Flavians, 69-96 -- Historiography.

DG286.M3
McCrum, Michael.
Select documents of the principates of the Flavian emperors, including the year of revolution, A.D. 68-96, collected by M. McCrum and A. G. Woodhead. Cambridge [Eng.] University Press, 1961. xii, 160 p.
61-003772   937.07
Rome -- History -- Flavians, 69-96 -- Sources.

DG291.S68 1997
Southern, Pat.
Domitian: tragic tyrant/ Pat Southern. London; Routledge , 1997. viii, 164 p.
97-002760   937/.07/092   0415165253
Domitian, -- Emperor of Rome, -- 51-96. Emperors -- Rome -- Biography. Rome -- History -- Domitian, 81-96.

DG292.G73 1994
Grant, Michael, 1914-
The Antonines: the Roman empire in transition/ Michael Grant. London; Routledge, 1994. viii, 210 p.
94-000597   937/.07   0415107547
Emperors -- Rome. Rome -- Civilization. Rome -- History -- Antonines, 96-192.

DG294.B46 1997
Bennett, Julian.
Trajan, optimus princeps: a life and times/ Julian Bennett. Bloomington: Indiana University Press, c1997. xvii, 317 p.
96-031094   937/.07/092   0253332168
Trajan, -- Emperor of Rome, -- 53-117. Emperors -- Rome -- Biography. Rome -- History -- Trajan, 98-117.

DG295.B57 1997
Birley, Anthony Richard.
Hadrian: the restless emperor/ Anthony R. Birley. London; Routledge, 1997. xvii, 399 p.
96-049232   937/.07/092   041516544X
Hadrian, -- Emperor of Rome, -- 76-138. Emperors -- Rome -- Biography. Hadrian's Wall (England) Rome -- History -- Hadrian, 117-138. Roman Forum (Rome, Italy)

DG295.B62 2000
Boatwright, Mary Taliaferro.
Hadrian and the cities of the Roman empire/ Mary T. Boatwright. Princeton, N.J.: Princeton University Press, c2000. xviii, 243 p.
99-041096   937.07/092   0691048894
Hadrian, -- Emperor of Rome, -- 76-138 -- Influence.   Emperors -- Rome -- Biography. Patron and client -- Rome. Cities and towns -- Rome -- Administration. Rome -- History -- Empire, 30 B.C.-284 A.D.

DG295.B63 1987
Boatwright, Mary Taliaferro.
Hadrian and the city of Rome/ Mary Taliaferro Boatwright. Princeton, N.J.: Princeton University Press, 1987. xx, 312 p.
86-030440   937/.07   0691035881
Hadrian, -- Emperor of Rome, -- 76-138.   Rome (Italy) -- History -- To 476. Rome -- History -- Hadrian, 117-138.

DG297 .B5 2000
Birley, Anthony Richard.
Marcus Aurelius, a biography/ Anthony Birley. Rev. ed. London: Routledge, c2000. 320 p.
00-711200   937/.07/092.B 21   0415171253
Marcus Aurelius, Emperor of Rome, 121-180. Emperors--Rome--Biography.

DG297.F3 1975
Farquharson, A. S. L. 1871-1942.
Marcus Aurelius: his life and his world/ by A. S. L. Farquharson; edited by D. A. Rees. Westport, Conn.: Greenwood Press, 1975. vi, 154 p.
75-011854   937/.07/0924   0837181399
Marcus Aurelius, -- Emperor of Rome, -- 121-180.

DG298.G73 1996
Grant, Michael, 1914-
The Severans: the changed Roman Empire/ Michael Grant. London; Routledge, 1996. xvi, 117 p.
95-045816   937/.07   0415127726
Rome -- History -- Severans, 193-235.

DG306.M3
MacMullen, Ramsay, 1928-
Roman government's response to crisis, A.D. 235-337/ Ramsay MacMullen. New Haven: Yale University Press, 1976. ix, 308 p.
75-043324   937/.07   0300020082
Rome -- History -- Maximinus, 235-238. Rome -- Politics and government -- 30 B.C.-284 A.D.

DG308.W37 1999
Watson, Alaric, 1958-
Aurelian and the third century/ Alaric Watson. London; Routledge, 1999. xvi, 303 p.
98-023382   937/.07/092   0415072484
Aurelian, -- Emperor of Rome, -- ca. 215-275. Emperors -- Rome -- Biography. Rome -- History -- Aurelian, 270-275.

DG311.B98 1958
Bury, J. B. 1861-1927.
History of the later Roman Empire from the death of Theodosius I. to the death of Justinian. New York, Dover Publications [1958] 2 v.
58-011273   937.08
Rome -- History -- Empire, 284-476. Byzantine Empire -- History.

DG311.G6.J67
Jordan, David P., 1939-
Gibbon and his Roman Empire [by] David P. Jordan. Urbana, University of Illinois Press [1971] xv, 245 p.
78-141515   937.06   0252001524
Gibbon, Edward, -- 1737-1794. -- History of the decline and fall of the Roman Empire.   Rome -- History -- Empire, 30 B.C.-476 A.D. -- Historiography.   Byzantine Empire -- Historiography.

DG311.J6 1964
Jones, A. H. M. 1904-1970.
The later Roman Empire, 284-602; a social, economic and administrative survey by A. H. M. Jones. Norman, University of Oklahoma Press [1964] 2 v.
64-020762   913.7
Byzantine Empire -- History. Rome -- History -- Empire, 284-476.

DG311.J62 1966a
Jones, A. H. M. 1904-1970.
The decline of the ancient world [by] A. H. M. Jones. New York, Holt, Rinehart and Winston [1966] viii, 414 p.
66-015446   937.08
Rome -- History -- Empire, 284-476. Byzantine Empire -- History -- To 527.

DG311.S35 2000
Schiavone, Aldo.
The end of the past: ancient Rome and the modern West/ Aldo Schiavone; translated by Margery J. Schneider. Cambridge, Mass.; Harvard University Press, 2000. viii, 278 p.
99-057780   937/.06   0674000625
Civilization, Western -- Roman influences. Rome -- History -- Empire, 30 B.C.-476 A.D. Europe -- History -- 476-1492 -- Economic aspects.

DG312.L44 1993
Lee, A. D.
Information and frontiers: Roman foreign relations in late antiquity/ A.D. Lee. Cambridge [England]; Cambridge University Press, 1993. xxii, 213 p.
92-034199   327.37/009/015   052139256X
Rome -- Foreign relations -- 284-476.

DG312.P38 1987
Pelikan, Jaroslav Jan, 1923-
The excellent empire: the fall of Rome and the triumph of the church/ Jaroslav Pelikan. San Francisco: Harper & Row, c1987. xiii, 133 p.
87-045194   937/.09   0062546368
Gibbon, Edward, -- 1737-1794. -- History of the decline and fall of the Roman Empire.   Church history -- Primitive and early church, ca. 30-600. Fathers of the church. Rome -- History -- Empire, 284-476.

DG312.W3
Walbank, F. W. 1909-
The decline of the Roman Empire in the West. London, Cobbett Press, 1946. xii, 97 p.
47-005029   937.06
Rome -- History -- Empire, 30 B.C.-476 A.D. Rome -- Economic conditions. Rome -- Social conditions.

DG312.W6613 1997
Wolfram, Herwig.
The Roman Empire and its Germanic peoples/ Herwig Wolfram; translated by Thomas Dunlap. Berkeley, Calif.: University of California Press, c1997. xx, 361 p.
96-039741   937/.09   0520085116
Germanic peoples -- Rome. Rome -- History -- Germanic Invasions, 3rd-6th centuries -- Historiography. Rome -- History -- Germanic Invasions, 3rd-6th centuries.

DG312.5.S5.H37 1994
Harries, Jill.
Sidonius Apollinaris and the fall of Rome, AD 407-485/ Jill Harries. Oxford: Clarendon Press; 1994. xii, 292 p.
94-025064   937/.09/092   0198144725
Sidonius Apollinaris, -- Saint, -- 431 or 2-ca. 487 -- Views on Rome. Bishops -- France -- Clermont-Ferrand -- Biography. Christian saints -- Biography. Legislators -- Rome -- Biography. Gaul -- History -- 58 B.C.-511. Rome -- History -- Empire, 284-476.

DG315.B35
Barnes, Timothy David.
Constantine and Eusebius/ Timothy D. Barnes. Cambridge, Mass.: Harvard University Press, 1981. vi, 458 p.
81-004248   937/.08/0922   0674165306
Constantine -- I, -- Emperor of Rome, -- d. 337. Eusebius, -- of Caesarea, Bishop of Caesarea, -- ca. 260-ca. 340. Church history -- Primitive and early church, ca. 30-600.   Rome -- History -- Constantine I, the Great, 306-337.

DG315.C65 1998
Constantine: history, historiography, and legend/ edited by Samuel N.C. Lieu and Dominic Montserrat. London; Routledge, 1998. xix, 238 p.
97-045571   937/.08/092   0415107474
Constantine -- I, -- Emperor of Rome, -- d. 337. Emperors -- Rome -- Biography. Religion and state -- Rome -- History. Legends, Christian -- Rome. Rome -- History -- Constantine I, the Great, 306-337 -- Historiography.

DG316.B37 1998
Barnes, Timothy David.
Ammianus Marcellinus and the representation of historical reality/ Timothy D. Barnes. Ithaca, N.Y.: Cornell University Press, 1998. xiv, 290 p.
98-019791   937/.007/202   0801435269
Ammianus Marcellinus. -- Rerum gestarum libri. Historiography -- Rome.   Rome -- History -- Empire, 284-476 -- Historiography.

DG316.7.M38 1989
Matthews, John
The Roman empire of Ammianus/ John Matthews. Baltimore: Johns Hopkins University Press, 1989. xiv, 608 p.
89-045756   937/.08   0801839653
Ammianus Marcellinus. -- Rerum gestarum libri. Rome -- History -- Empire, 284-476 -- Historiography.

DG317.B76 1976
Browning, Robert, 1914-
The Emperor Julian/ Robert Browning. Berkeley: University of California Press, c1976. xii, 256 p.
75-013159   937/.08/0924   0520030346
Julian, -- Emperor of Rome, -- 331-363.

DG319.G63
Goffart, Walter A.
Barbarians and Romans, A.D. 418-584: the techniques of accommodation/ by Walter Goffart. Princeton, N.J.: Princeton University Press, c1980. xv, 278 p.
80-007522   940.1/2   0691053030
Acculturation -- Rome. Rome -- Emigration and immigration. Rome -- History -- Germanic Invasions, 3rd-6th centuries.

DG319.M37
Matthews, John
Western aristocracies and imperial court, A.D. 364-425/ by John Matthews. Oxford: Clarendon Press, 1975. xiv, 427 p.
75-309538   322.4/3/0937   0198148178
Church history -- Primitive and early church, ca. 30-600.   Rome -- Court and courtiers. Rome -- History -- Empire, 284-476.

DG322.H64 1982
Holum, Kenneth G.
Theodosian empresses: women and imperial dominion in late antiquity/ Kenneth G. Holum. Berkeley: University of California Press, c1982. xiv, 258 p.
81-043690   937/.02   0520041623
Empresses -- Rome -- Biography. Nobility -- Rome -- Biography.   Rome -- History -- Theodosians, 379-455.

DG330.P3313 1987
Pacatus Drepanius, Latinus, 4th cent.
Panegyric to the Emperor Theodosius/ Pacatus; translated with an introduction by C.E.V. Nixon. Liverpool: Liverpool University Press; 1987. 122 p.
88-103035   937/.08/0924   0853230765
Theodosius -- I, -- Emperor of Rome, -- 347-395. Roman emperors -- Biography.   Rome -- History -- Theodosius I, the Great, 379-395.

DG330.W55 1995
Williams, Stephen, 1942-
Theodosius: the empire at bay/ Stephen Williams and Gerard Friell. New Haven: Yale University Press, 1995, c1994. 238 p.
94-060725   937/.08/092   0300061730
Theodosius -- I, -- Emperor of Rome, -- 347-395. Roman emperors -- Biography.   Rome -- History -- Theodosius I, the Great, 379-395.

DG428 Medieval and modern Italy, 476-
— Description and travel — 1901-1918

DG428.J3 1959
James, Henry, 1843-1916.
Italian hours.   New York, Grove Press [1959] 376 p.
59-005420   914.5
James, Henry, -- 1843-1916 -- Journeys -- Italy. Authors, American -- 19th century -- Journeys -- Italy. Italy -- Description and travel.

DG441 Medieval and modern Italy, 476-
— Social life and customs. Civilization — General works

DG441.F67 1990
Forgacs, David.
Italian culture in the industrial era, 1880-1980: cultural industries, politics, and the public/ David Forgacs. Manchester; Manchester University Press; c1990. 231 p.
89-038180   945.09   0719028124
Popular culture -- Italy -- History -- 20th century. Popular culture -- Italy -- History -- 19th century. Politics and culture -- Italy. Italy -- Politics and government -- 20th century.

DG441.O48
Olschki, Leonardo, 1885-
The genius of Italy.   Ithaca, N.Y. Cornell University Press [1954, c1949] 481 p.
54-012760   914.5
Italy -- History.

DG443 Medieval and modern Italy, 476-
— Social life and customs. Civilization — Early through 1400

DG443.B42 1981
Becker, Marvin B.
Medieval Italy: constraints and creativity/ Marvin B. Becker. Bloomington: Indiana University Press, c1981. ix, 242 p.
80-008376   945   0253152941
Italy -- Civilization -- 476-1268. Italy -- Religious life and customs.

DG445 Medieval and modern Italy, 476-
— Social life and customs. Civilization — 1401-1600. Renaissance

DG445.B85 1999
Burke, Peter.
The Italian Renaissance: culture and society in Italy/ Peter Burke.2. ed. Princeton, N.J.: Princeton University Press, 1999. p. cm.
98-048379   0691006784
Renaissance--Italy. Arts, Italian. Art patronage--Italy.

DG450 Medieval and modern Italy, 476-
— Social life and customs. Civilization — 1816-1945

DG450.E53 2000
Encyclopedia of contemporary Italian culture/ edited by Gino Moliterno. London; Routledge, 2000. xxiv, 677 p.
99-038356   945.09/03   0415145848
Italy -- Civilization -- 20th century -- Encyclopedias.

DG453 Medieval and modern Italy, 476-
— Social life and customs. Civilization — Italian culture in foreign countries

DG453.G33 2000
Gabaccia, Donna R., 1949-
Italy's many diasporas/ Donna R. Gabaccia. Seattle: University of Washington Press, 2000. xv, 264 p.
99-042484 909/.0451 0295979178
Italians -- Foreign countries. Italy -- Emigration and immigration.

DG455 Medieval and modern Italy, 476-
— Ethnography — General works

DG455.O96 2000
The outsider: prejudice and politics in Italy/ Paul M. Sniderman ... [et al.] Princeton, N.J.: Princeton University Press c2000. x, 218 p.
99-089723 303.3/8751 0691048398
Racism -- Italy. Culture conflict -- Italy. Italy -- Race relations. Italy -- Emigration and immigration. Italy -- Ethnic relations.

DG465-465.7 Medieval and modern Italy, 476-
— History — Historiography

DG465.C62
Cochrane, Eric W.
Historians and historiography in the Italian Renaissance/ Eric Cochrane. Chicago: University of Chicago Press, 1981. xx, 649 p.
80-016097 945/.0072 0226111520
Historiography -- History. Renaissance -- Italy. Humanism. Italy -- History, Local. Italy -- Historiography. Italy -- History -- 1492-1559.

DG465.7.G56.Z56 1995
Zimmermann, T. C. Price, 1934-
Paolo Giovio: the historian and the crisis of sixteenth-century Italy/ T.C. Price Zimmermann. Princeton, N.J.: Princeton University Press, 1995. xii, 391 p.
95-004302 945/.07/092 0691043787
Giovio, Paolo, -- 1483-1552. Biographers -- Italy -- Biography. Bishops -- Italy -- Biography. Historians -- Italy -- Biography. Italy -- History -- 1492-1559 -- Historiography.

DG467 Medieval and modern Italy, 476-
— History — General works

DG467.L67 1980 vol. 6
Hearder, Harry.
Italy in the age of the Risorgimento, 1790-1870/ Harry Hearder. London; Longman, 1983. x, 325 p.
82-023974 945/.08 0582491460
Italy -- History -- 1789-1870.

DG483.5-494 Medieval and modern Italy, 476-
— History — General special

DG483.5.H36 1998
Hanlon, Gregory, 1953-
The twilight of a military tradition: Italian aristocrats and European conflicts, 1560-1800/ Gregory Hanlon. New York: Holmes & Meier, 1998. xii, 371 p.
97-026922 945/.0086/21 0841913870
Aristocracy (Social class) -- Italy -- History. Italy -- History, Military -- 1789-1815. Italy -- History, Military -- 1559-1789. Europe -- History, Military -- 1492-1648.

DG484.G66 1989
Gooch, John.
Army, state, and society in Italy, 1870-1915/ John Gooch. New York: St. Martin's Press, 1989. xiv, 219 p.
88-023368 945.09 0312025238
Italy -- History -- 1870-1914. Italy -- History, Military -- 1870-1914.

DG494.M37 1979
Martines, Lauro.
Power and imagination: city-states in Renaissance Italy/ by Lauro Martines. New York: Knopf, 1979. ix, 368 p.
78-011666 945 0394501128
Cities and towns -- Italy -- History. City-states -- Italy -- History. Renaissance -- Italy. Italy -- Civilization -- 476-1268. Italy -- Civilization -- 1268-1559. Italy -- Politics and government -- 1268-1559.

DG504-581 Medieval and modern Italy, 476-
— History — By period

DG504.A56 1997
Amory, Patrick, 1965-
Ethnography and the barbarians: the Goths in Italy, A.D. 489-554/ Patrick Amory. Cambridge; Cambridge University Press, 1997. p. cm.
96-002952 945/.01
Goths -- Italy -- History. Italy -- History -- 476-774.

DG504.T46 1982
Thompson, E. A.
Romans and barbarians: the decline of the western empire/ E.A. Thompson. Madison: University of Wisconsin Press, 1982. ix, 329 p.
81-050828 945/.01 029908700X
Rome -- History -- Germanic Invasions, 3rd-6th centuries.

DG530.P84 1973b
Pullan, Brian S.
A history of early Renaissance Italy: from the mid-thirteenth to the mid-fifteenth century [by] Brian Pullan. New York, St. Martin's Press [1973, c1972] 386 p.
72-093030 914.5/03/5
Renaissance -- Italy. Italy -- Civilization -- 1268-1559. Italy -- History -- 1268-1492.

DG533.B85 1958
Burckhardt, Jacob, 1818-1897.
The civilization of the Renaissance in Italy. [Translation by S. G. C. Middlemore] New York, Harper [1959] 2 v.
58-010149 945.05
Renaissance -- Italy. Italy -- Civilization.

DG533.H39 1977
Hay, Denys.
The Italian Renaissance in its historical background/ by Denys Hay. Cambridge, [Eng.]; Cambridge University Press, 1977, c1976. xvi, 228 p.
76-008293 945/.05 0521213215.
Renaissance -- Italy.

DG535.B6
Bowsky, William M.
Henry VII in Italy; the conflict of empire and city-state, 1310-1313. Lincoln, University of Nebraska Press, 1960. xii, 301 p.
60-007325 945.05
Heinrich -- VII, -- Emperor of Germany, -- 1269?-1313. City-states -- Italy -- History. Renaissance -- Italy. Italy -- History -- 1268-1492.

DG537.M34 1974
Mallett, Michael Edward.
Mercenaries and their masters; warfare in renaissance Italy [by] Michael Mallett. Totowa, N.J., Rowman and Littlefield [1974] 284 p.
74-154444 355.3/1 0874714478
Condottieri. Renaissance -- Italy. Italy -- History -- 1268-1492. Italy -- History, Military.

DG539.G813 1984
Guicciardini, Francesco, 1483-1540.
The history of Italy/ by Francesco Guicciardini; translated, edited, with notes and an introduction by Sidney Alexander. Princeton, N.J.: Princeton University Press, 1984, c1969. xxvii, 457 p.
83-043221 945/.06 0691054177
Italy -- History -- 1492-1559.

DG540.H36 2000
Hanlon, Gregory.
Early modern Italy, 1550-1800: three seasons in European history/ Gregory Hanlon. New York: St. Martin's Press, 2000. xv, 444 p.
99-055573 945/.07 0312231792
Italy -- History -- 16th century. Italy -- History -- 17th century. Italy -- History -- 18th century.

DG545.V4513 1989
Venturi, Franco.
The end of the Old Regime in Europe, 1768-1776: the first crisis/ Franco Venturi; translated by R. Burr Litchfield. Princeton, N.J.: Princeton University Press, c1989. xxiii, 453 p.
88-039914 940.2/53 0691055645
Italy -- History -- 18th century. Europe -- History -- 18th century.

DG551.T36
Tannenbaum, Edward R.
Modern Italy; a topical history since 1861. Edited by Edward R. Tannenbaum and Emiliana P. Noether. New York, New York University Press, 1974. xxix, 395 p.
73-020031 309.1/45/09 081478156X
Italy -- History -- 19th century. Italy -- History -- 20th century.

DG552.M25 1989
Mack Smith, Denis, 1920-
Italy and its monarchy/ Denis Mack Smith. New Haven: Yale University Press, c1989. xi, 402 p.
89-051311 945 0300046618
Italy -- Politics and government -- 1849-1870. Italy -- Politics and government -- 1870-1914. Italy -- Politics and government -- 1914-1945.

DG552.M26
Mack Smith, Denis, 1920-
The making of Italy, 1796-1870. New York,
Walker [1968] viii, 428 p.
68-013331 945/.08/08
  Italy -- History -- 19th century -- Sources.

DG552.5.L68
Lovett, Clara Maria, 1939-
The democratic movement in Italy, 1830-1876/
Clara M. Lovett. Cambridge, Mass.: Harvard
University Press, 1982. x, 285 p.
81-006403 945.08 0674196457
  Liberalism -- Italy -- History -- 19th century.
Revolutionaries -- Italy -- Biography. Italy --
Politics and government -- 1815-1870.

DG552.5.M3
Mack Smith, Denis, 1920-
Victor Emanuel, Cavour and the Risorgimento.
London, Oxford University Press, 1971. xviii,
381 p.
74-031860 945/.08/0922 0192125508
Cavour, Camillo Benso, -- conte di, -- 1810-1861.
Victor Emmanuel -- II, -- King of Italy, -- 1820-
1878.   Italy -- History -- 1849-1870.

DG552.8.C25.L68
Lovett, Clara Maria, 1939-
Carlo Cattaneo and the politics of the
Risorgimento, 1820-1860. The Hague, Nijhoff,
1972 [1973] x, 138 p.
73-164298 320.9/45/08 9024712831
Cattaneo, Carlo, -- 1801-1869.   Italy -- Politics
and government -- 1815-1870.

DG552.8.C3.M17 1985
Mack Smith, Denis, 1920-
Cavour/ Denis Mack-Smith. New York: Knopf,
1985. xiii, 294 p.
84-048815 945/.08/0924 0394538854
Cavour, Camillo Benso, -- conte di, -- 1810-1861.
Statesmen -- Italy -- Biography.   Italy -- History --
1849-1870.

DG552.8.M292
Mazzini, Giuseppe, 1805-1872.
Mazzini's letters/ translated from the Italian by
Alice de Rosen Jervis, with an introduction and
notes by Bolton King. London; J. M. Dent & sons
ltd. [1930]. xvi, 211 p.
30-024139
Mazzini, Giuseppe, 1805-1872. Italy -- History --
19th century. Italy -- Politics and government --
19th century.

DG552.8.M3.S34 1997
Sarti, Roland, 1937-
Mazzini: a life for the religion of politics/ Roland
Sarti. Westport, Conn: Praeger, 1997. x, 249 p.
96-037112 945.08 0275950808
Mazzini, Giuseppe, -- 1805-1872.   Revolutionaries
-- Italy -- Biography.   Statesmen -- Italy --
Biography.   Italy -- Politics and government --
1815-1870.

DG554.M3 1985
Mack Smith, Denis,
Cavour and Garibaldi, 1860: a study in political
conflict/ by D. Mack Smith. Cambridge
[Cambridgeshire]; Cambridge University Press,
xvii, 458 p.
84-046028 945/.08.219 0521316375
Cavour, Camillo Benso, conte di, 1810-1861.
Garibaldi, Giuseppe, 1807-1882.

DG555 .C55 1996
Clark, Martin,
Modern Italy, 1871-1995/ Martin Clark. 2nd ed.
London; Longman, 1996. xiii, 474 p.
95-053742 945/.09 20 0582051266
Italy -- History -- 1870-1914. Italy -- History --
20th century.

DG555.G53 1999
Gilbert, Mark, 1961-
Historical dictionary of modern Italy/ Mark F.
Gilbert and K. Robert Nilsson. Lanham, Md.:
Scarecrow Press, 1999. xxxvi, 463 p.
98-041159 945/.08/03 0810835843
  Italy -- History -- 1870-1914 -- Dictionaries.
Italy -- History -- 20th century -- Dictionaries.

DG564.C43 1996
Chabod, Federico.
Italian foreign policy: the statecraft of the
founders/ Federico Chabod; translated by William
McCuaig. Princeton, N.J.: Princeton University
Press, c1996. xlvi, 593 p.
95-000489 327.45 0691044511
  Italy -- Foreign relations -- 1870-1914.

DG568.5.B66 1983
Bosworth, R. J. B.
Italy and the approach of the First World War/
Richard Bosworth. New York: St. Martin's Press,
1983. viii, 174 p.
82-016841 945.08 0312439245
  World War, 1914-1918 -- Italy. World War,
1914-1918 -- Causes.   Italy -- Politics and
government -- 1870-1914.   Italy -- Foreign
relations -- 1870-1914.

DG571.B444 1997
Berezin, Mabel.
Making the fascist self: the political culture of
interwar Italy/ Mabel Berezin. Ithaca, [N.Y.]:
Cornell University Press, 1997. xv, 267 p.
96-053410 306.2/0945/09041 0801432022
Mussolini, Benito, -- 1883-1945 -- Influence.
Fascism -- Italy -- History. Fascism and culture --
Italy -- History. Symbolism in politics -- Italy --
History. Italy -- Politics and government -- 1922-
1945.

DG571.F2 1997
Falasca-Zamponi, Simonetta, 1957-
Fascist spectacle: the aesthetics of power in
Mussolini's Italy/ Simonetta Falasca-Zamponi.
Berkeley: University of California Press, c1997. xi,
303 p.
96-028827 320.5/33/0945 0520206231
Fascism -- Italy. Fascism and culture -- Italy.
Aesthetics, Italian -- 20th century. Italy -- Politics
and government -- 1922-1945.

DG571.G3913 1996
Gentile, Emilio, 1946-
The sacralization of politics in fascist Italy/ Emilio
Gentile; translated by Keith Botsford. Cambridge,
Mass.: Harvard University Press, 1996. xi, 208 p.
96-005074 945.091 0674784758
  Fascism and the Catholic Church -- Italy.
Fascism -- Italy. Italy -- Politics and government -
- 1922-1945.

DG571.K34 2000
Kallis, Aristotle A., 1970-
Fascist ideology: territory and expansionism in
Italy and Germany, 1922-1945/ Aristotle A. Kallis.
London Routledge, 2000. ix, 286 p.
99-087416 320.53/3/0943 0415216117
  Fascism -- Italy -- History. Nationalism -- Italy --
History -- 20th century. National socialism --
Germany -- History. Germany -- Foreign relations
-- 1933-1945. Italy -- Foreign relations -- 1922-
1945.

DG571.K63 2000
Knox, MacGregor.
Common destiny: dictatorship, foreign policy, and
war in Fascist Italy and Nazi Germany/ MacGregor
Knox. Cambridge, UK; Cambridge University
Press, 2000. xiv, 262 p.
99-016896 943.08 0521582083
  Fascism -- Italy -- History. National socialism --
History. Italy -- Politics and government -- 1922-
1945. Italy -- Foreign relations -- 1922-1945.
Germany -- Foreign relations -- 1933-1945.

DG571.M22
Mack Smith, Denis, 1920-
Mussolini's Roman Empire/ Denis Mack Smith.
New York: Viking Press, 1976. xii, 322 p.
75-046618 945.091/092/4 0670496529
Mussolini, Benito, -- 1883-1945.   Italy --
Politics and government -- 1922-1945.

DG571.M255 1998
Mallett, Robert, 1961-
The Italian Navy and Fascist expansionism, 1935-
40/ Robert Mallett. London; Frank Cass, 1998. xiv,
240 p.
98-022477 359/.00945/09043 0714648787
  Sea-power -- Italy -- History -- 20th century.
Fascism -- Italy. Italo-Ethiopian War, 1935-1936 -
- Naval operations. Italy -- History, Naval -- 20th
century.

DG571.M6422 1995
Morgan, Philip, 1948-
Italian fascism, 1919-1945/ Philip Morgan. New
York: St. Martin's Press, 1995. xi, 209 p.
94-029898 945.091 0312123213
  Fascism -- Italy -- History -- 20th century.   Italy
-- Politics and government -- 1914-1945.

DG571.M764 1968
Mussolini, Benito, 1883-1945.
Fascism; doctrine and institutions. New York, H.
Fertig, 1968. 313 p.
68-009636 321.9/4/0945
  Fascism -- Italy.

DG571.16.B67 1998
Bosworth, R. J. B.
The Italian dictatorship: problems and perspectives
in the interpretation of Mussolini and fascism/
R.J.B. Bosworth. London; Arnold, 1998. x, 269 p.
98-014742 945.09/072 0340677287
Mussolini, Benito, -- 1883-1945.   Fascism -- Italy
-- Historiography. Historiography -- Italy --
History -- 20th century.   Italy -- Politics and
government -- 1922-1945 -- Historiography.

DG572.D56 1991
Domenico, Roy Palmer.
Italian fascists on trial, 1943-1948/ Roy Palmer
Domenico. Chapel Hill: University of North
Carolina Press, c1991. xvii, 295 p.
91-050251 945.091 0807820067
  Fascism -- Italy -- History -- 20th century. Anti-
fascist movements -- Italy -- History -- 20th
century. Italy -- Politics and government -- 1943-
1947. Italy -- Politics and government -- 1945-

DG575.B3.S44 1987
Segre, Claudio G.
Italo Balbo: a Fascist life/ Claudio G. Segr`e.
Berkeley: University of California Press, c1987.
xvi, 466 p.
86-016108   945.091/092/4   0520058666
*Balbo, Italo, -- 1896-1940.   Cabinet officers --
Italy -- Biography. Air pilots -- Italy -- Biography.
Fascism -- Italy -- History -- 20th century. Italy --
Politics and government -- 1914-1945.*

DG575.C52.A32
Ciano, Galeazzo, 1903-1944.
Ciano's diary, 1939-1943. Edited, with an
introduction, by Malcolm Muggeridge. Foreword
by Sumner Welles. London, W. Heinemann [1948]
xxii, 575 p.
47-028173
*World War, 1939-1945 -- Italy.   Italy -- Foreign
relations -- 1922-1945.*

DG575.G5.D4
De Grand, Alexander J., 1938-
The hunchback's tailor: Giovanni Giolitti and
liberal Italy from the challenge of mass politics to
the rise of fascism, 1882-1922/ Alexander De
Grand. Westport, Conn.: Praeger, 2001. x, 294 p.
00-025126   945.09   027596874X
*Giolitti, Giovanni, -- 1842-1928.   Liberalism --
Italy -- History -- 19th century. Liberalism -- Italy
-- History -- 20th century.   Italy -- Politics and
government -- 1870-1914. Italy -- Politics and
government -- 1914-1922.*

DG575.M8.A2 1970
Mussolini, Benito, 1883-1945.
My autobiography. With a foreword by Richard
Washburn Child. Westport, Conn., Greenwood
Press [1970] xix, 318 p.
78-109803   945.091/0924   0837142946
Italy -- Politics and government -- 1914-1945.

DG575.M8.M223 1982
Mack Smith, Denis, 1920-
Mussolini/ Denis Mack Smith. New York: Knopf,
1982. xiv, 429 p.
81-048127   945.091/092/4   0394506944
*Mussolini, Benito, -- 1883-1945.   Fascism -- Italy
-- History. Heads of state -- Italy -- Biography.
Italy -- Politics and government -- 1922-1945.*

DG575.M8.M835313 1974
Mussolini, Rachele, 1892-
Mussolini: an intimate biography by his widow,
Rachele Mussolini, as told to Albert Zarca. New
York, Morrow, 1974. vi, 291 p.
74-001129   945.091/092/4   0688002668
Mussolini, Benito, -- 1883-1945.

DG577.5.H83 1979
Hughes, H. Stuart 1916-
The United States and Italy/ H. Stuart Hughes.
Cambridge, Mass.: Harvard University Press, 1979.
xiii, 324 p.
79-063706   945.092   0674925459
*Italy -- Politics and government -- 1945-1976.
Italy -- Politics and government -- 1976- Italy --
Economic conditions -- 1945-*

DG577.5.L86 1990
Lumley, Robert, 1951-
States of emergency: cultures of revolt in Italy
from 1968 to 1978/ Robert Lumley. London;
Verso, 1990. xii, 377 p.
89-070705   945.092/6   086091254X
*Students -- Italy -- Political activity -- History --
20th century. Working class -- Italy -- Political
activity -- History -- 20th century.   Social
movements -- Italy -- History -- 20th century. Italy
-- Politics and government -- 1976-1994. Italy --
Politics and government -- 1945-1976. Italy --
Social conditions -- 1945-1976.*

DG581.B84 1998
Bufacchi, Vittorio, 1957-
Italy since 1989: events and interpretations/
Vittorio Bufacchi and Simon Burgess. New York:
St. Martin's Press, c1998. xiv, 275 p.
97-024013   320.945/09/049   0312210507
*Berlusconi, Silvio, -- 1936- Dini, Lamberto.
Political corruption -- Italy. Italy -- Politics and
government -- 1994- Italy -- Politics and
government -- 1976-1994.*

DG581.B87 1998
Burnett, Stanton H.
The Italian guillotine: Operation Clean Hands and
the overthrow of Italy's First Republic/ Stanton H.
Burnett and Luca Mantovani. Lanham: Rowman &
Littlefield Publishers, 1998. xii, 332 p.
98-012811   320.945/09/049   0847688771
*Italy -- Politics and government -- 1976-1994.
Italy -- Politics and government -- 1994- Political
corruption -- Italy -- History -- 20th century.*

DG581.E63 1993
The End of post-war politics in Italy: the landmark
1992 elections/ edited by Gianfranco Pasquino and
Patrick McCarthy. Boulder: Westview Press, 1993.
ix, 187 p.
93-020826   945.092/9   0813386284
*Elections -- Italy. Political parties -- Italy.   Italy
-- Politics and government -- 1976-1994.*

DG618.6 Northern Italy — Piedmont. Savoy — History

DG618.6.B76 1997
Broers, Michael.
Napoleonic imperialism and the Savoyard
monarchy, 1773-1821: state building in Piedmont/
Michael Broers. Lewiston [N.Y.]: Edwin Mellen
Press, c1997. xii, 582 p.
97-020840   945/.108   0773486097
*Napoleon -- I, -- Emperor of the French, -- 1769-
1821 -- Influence. Savoy, House of -- Influence.
Imperialism -- Historiography.   Piedmont
(Principality) -- History -- Annexation to France.
Piedmont (Principality) -- Politics and
government.*

DG637 Northern Italy — Genoa — History

DG637.E67 1996
Epstein, Steven, 1952-
Genoa & the Genoese, 958-1528/ Steven A.
Epstein. Chapel Hill, N.C.: University of North
Carolina Press, c1996. xx, 396 p.
95-026585   945/.182   0807822914
*Genoa (Italy) -- History -- To 1339. Genoa
(Italy) -- History -- 1339-1528.*

DG675.6 Northern Italy — Venice — Social life and customs

DG675.6.B7 1996
Brown, Patricia Fortini, 1936-
Venice & antiquity: the Venetian sense of the past/
Patricia Fortini Brown. New Haven: Yale
University Press, c1996. xii, 361 p.
96-003196   945/.31   0300067003
*Art and history -- Italy -- Venice. Art, Italian --
Italy -- Venice -- Foreign influences. Art, Italian --
Classical influences. Venice (Italy) -- Civilization -
- Classical influences. Venice (Italy) -- Civilization
-- Foreign influences. Venice (Italy) -- History --
697-1508.*

DG675.6.D38 1994
Davis, Robert C. 1948-
The war of the fists: popular culture and public
violence in late Renaissance Venice/ Robert C.
Davis. New York: Oxford University Press, 1994.
vi, 232 p.
93-020591   945/.31   0195084039
*Violence -- Italy -- Venice -- History -- 17th
century. Battles -- Italy -- Venice -- History -- 17th
century. Bridges -- Italy -- Venice -- History -- 17th
century. Venice (Italy) -- Social life and customs.*

DG677.99-678.55 Northern Italy — Venice — History

DG677.99.M37.K56 1994
King, Margaret L., 1947-
The death of the child Valerio Marcello/ Margaret
L. King. Chicago: University of Chicago Press,
1994. xviii, 484 p.
93-044666   945/.3105/0922   0226436195
*Marcello, Jacopo Antonio, -- ca. 1400-ca. 1464.
Marcello, Valerio, -- 1452-1461 -- Death and
burial. Nobility -- Italy -- Venice -- Biography.
Consolation. Mourning customs -- Italy. Venice
(Italy) -- History -- 15th century.*

DG678.24.C66.G54 1993
Gleason, Elisabeth G.
Gasparo Contarini: Venice, Rome, and reform/
Elisabeth G. Gleason. Berkeley: University of
California Press, c1993. xvii, 335 p.
92-025925   945/.31   0520080572
*Contarini, Gasparo, -- 1483-1542.   Statesmen --
Italy -- Venice -- Biography.   Venice (Italy) --
Foreign relations.*

DG678.55.G56
Ginsborg, Paul.
Daniele Manin and the Venetian revolution of
1848-49/ Paul Ginsborg. Cambridge; Cambridge
University Press, 1979. xiv, 417 p.
78-056180   945/.31   0521220777
*Manin, Daniele, -- 1804-1857.   Venice (Italy) --
History -- 1848-1849.*

DG734.2 Central Italy — Tuscany. Florence — Description and travel

DG734.2.M36 1959
McCarthy, Mary, 1912-
The stones of Florence. Harcourt, Brace, 1959. 1 v.
59-010257   945/.51
Florence (Italy) -- Description and travel.

DG735.6 Central Italy — Tuscany. Florence — Social life and customs. Civilization

DG735.6.A33 1993
Adamson, Walter L.
Avant-garde Florence: from modernism to fascism/ Walter L. Adamson. Cambridge, Mass.: Harvard University Press, 1993. x, 338 p.
93-008062   945/.51   067405525X
Modernism (Art) -- Italy -- Florence. Fascism and culture -- Italy -- Florence. Avant-garde (Aesthetics) -- Italy -- Florence. Florence (Italy) -- Intellectual life.

DG737-738.7 Central Italy — Tuscany. Florence — History

DG737.A2.B813 2001
Bruni, Leonardo, 1369-1444.
History of the Florentine people/ Leonardo Bruni; edited and translated by James Hankins. Cambridge, Mass.: Harvard University Press, 2001- v. 1
00-053490   945/.51   0674005066
Florence (Italy) -- History -- To 1421.

DG737.A2.M4 1960
Machiavelli, Niccolo, 1469-1527.
History of Florence and of the affairs of Italy, from the earliest times to the death of Lorenzo the Magnificent/ Niccolo Machiavelli. Introd. to the Torchbook ed. by Felix Gilbert. New York: Harper & Brothers, c1960. xxv, 417 p.
60-051391   945.51
Florence (Italy) -- History.

DG737.26.B7 1962
Brucker, Gene A.
Florentine politics and society, 1343-1378. Princeton, N.J., Princeton University Press, 1962. xiii, 431 p.
62-007035   945.41
Florence (Italy) -- Politics and government.

DG737.4.F59 2000
Florentine Tuscany: structures and practices of power/ edited by William J. Connell and Andrea Zorzi. Cambridge, UK; Cambridge University Press, 2000. xii, 357 p.
99-033441   945/.505   0521591112hb
Tuscany (Italy) -- Politics and government -- 1434-1737. Tuscany (Italy) -- Politics and government -- To 1434. Tuscany (Italy) -- Economic conditions -- 1434-1737.

DG737.42.H34
Hale, J. R. 1923-
Florence and the Medici: the pattern of control/ J. R. Hale. [London]: Thames and Hudson, c1977. 208 p.
78-306330   945/.51   0500250596
Medici, House of. Florence (Italy) -- History -- 1421-1737. Florence (Italy) -- Kings and rulers -- Biography.

DG737.5.G813 1970
Guicciardini, Francesco, 1483-1540.
The history of Florence. Translation, introd., and notes, by Mario Domandi. New York, Harper & Row [1970] xlvii, 327 p.
79-104704   945/.51
Renaissance -- Italy -- Florence. Florence (Italy) -- History -- 1421-1737.

DG737.55.G63 1998
Godman, Peter.
From Poliziano to Machiavelli: Florentine humanism in the high Renaissance/ Peter Godman. Princeton, N.J.: Princeton University Press, c1998. xiv, 366 p.
97-044320   945/.51   0691017468
Humanism -- Italy -- Florence -- History. Renaissance -- Italy -- Florence. Italian literature -- Italy -- Florence -- History and criticism. Florence (Italy) -- History -- 1421-1737.

DG737.55.M3
Martines, Lauro.
The social world of the Florentine humanists, 1390-1460. Princeton, N. J., Princeton University Press, 1963. x, 419 p.
63-007073   914.551
Humanists. Florence (Italy) -- Social life and customs. Florence (Italy) -- Intellectual life.

DG737.8.C57 1991
Clarke, Paula C.
The Soderini and the Medici: power and patronage in fifteenth-century Florence/ Paula C. Clarke. Oxford: Clarendon Press; 1991. ix, 293 p.
90-049433   320.945/51/09024   0198229925
Soderini, Niccolo, -- 1401-1474. Soderini, Tommaso, -- 1403-1485. Medici, House of. Florence (Italy) -- Politics and government -- 1421-1737.

DG737.97.P58 1994
Polizzotto, Lorenzo.
The elect nation: the Savonarolan movement in Florence, 1494-1545/ Lorenzo Polizzotto. Oxford: Clarendon Press; 1994. xiv, 488 p.
93-031942   945/.5106   0199206007
Savonarola, Girolamo, -- 1452-1498 -- Political and social views. Savonarola, Girolamo, -- 1452-1498 -- Influence. Piagnoni (Savonarolan movement) Florence (Italy) -- Politics and government -- 1421-1737.

DG738.14.M2.A4 1996
Machiavelli, Niccolo, 1469-1527.
Machiavelli and his friends: their personal correspondence/ [Niccolo Machiavelli]; translated and edited by James B. Atkinson and David Sices. Dekalb, Ill.: Northern Illinois University Press, 1996. xxix, 621 p.
96-003106   945/.06/092   0875802109
Machiavelli, Niccolo, -- 1469-1527 -- Correspondence. Intellectuals -- Italy -- Correspondence. Statesmen -- Italy -- Correspondence. Authors, Italian -- 16th century -- Correspondence. Florence (Italy) -- Politics and government -- 1421-1737.

DG738.14.M2.R513
Ridolfi, Roberto, 1895-
The life of Niccolo Machiavelli. Translated from the Italian by Cecil Grayson. [Chicago] University of Chicago Press [1963] 337 p.
62-015048   923.245
Machiavelli, Niccolo, -- 1469-1527.

DG738.14.M2.V74 2000
Viroli, Maurizio.
Niccolo's smile: a biography of Machiavelli/ Maurizio Viroli; translated from the Italian by Antony Shugaar. New York: Farrar, Straus and Giroux, 2000. xv, 271 p.
00-029380   945/.5106/092   0374221871
Machiavelli, Niccolo, -- 1469-1527. Statesmen -- Italy -- Florence -- Biography. Intellectuals -- Italy -- Florence -- Biography. Authors, Italian -- 16th century -- Biography. Florence (Italy) -- Politics and government -- 1421-1737.

DG738.14.P37.P45 1987
Phillips, Mark, 1946-
The memoir of Marco Parenti: a life in Medici Florence/ Mark Phillips. Princeton, N.J.: Princeton University Press, 1987. xiv, 283 p.
87-045533   945/.51   0691055025
Parenti, Marco. Strozzi family. Medici, House of. Florence (Italy) -- History -- 1421-1737. Florence (Italy) -- Biography.

DG738.7.S64 1989
Snowden, Frank M. 1946-
The fascist revolution in Tuscany, 1919-1922/ Frank M. Snowden. Cambridge [England]; Cambridge University Press, 1989. xi, 295 p.
88-035278   945/.5   0521361176
Fascism -- Italy -- Tuscany -- History -- 20th century. Tuscany (Italy) -- Politics and government.

DG797-799 Central Italy — Papal States (States of the Church). Holy See. Vatican City — History

DG797.P37 1972b
Partner, Peter.
The lands of St. Peter; the Papal State in the Middle Ages and the early Renaissance. Berkeley, University of California Press, 1972. xvii, 471 p.
73-182793   945/.6   0520021819
Papal States -- History -- To 962. Papal States -- History -- 962-1309.

DG797.8.R68 1998
Rowland, Ingrid D.
The culture of the High Renaissance: ancients and moderns in sixteenth-century Rome/ Ingrid D. Rowland. Cambridge, U.K.; Cambridge University Press, 1998. xiv, 384 p.
97-029765   945/.06   0521581451
Renaissance -- Italy -- Rome. Arts, Italian -- Italy -- Rome. Rome (Italy) -- Civilization -- 16th century. Rome (Italy) -- Civilization -- Classical influences.

DG799.H3 1968
Halperin, Samuel William.
Italy and the Vatican at war; a study of their relations from the outbreak of the Franco-Prussian War to the death of Pius IX, by S. William Halperin. New York, Greenwood Press [1968, c1939] xvii, 483 p.
68-057606   322/.1/0945
Roman question. Church and state -- Italy.

DG805 Central Italy — Rome (Modern city) — Description

DG805.B5715
Stendhal, 1783-1842 1783-1842.
A Roman journal, by Stendhal [pseud.] Edited and translated by Haakon Chevalier. New York, Orion Press; distributed by Crown Publishers [c1957] xxiii, 354 p.
57-013279   914.56
Rome (Italy)

DG811-812.12 Central Italy — Rome (Modern city) — History

DG811.K7
Krautheimer, Richard, 1897-
Rome, profile of a city, 312-1308/ by Richard Krautheimer. Princeton, N.J.: Princeton University Press, 1980. xvi, 389 p.
78-070304   945/.632   069103947X
Church history -- Primitive and early church, ca. 30-600. Church history -- Middle Ages, 600-1500. Historic buildings -- Italy -- Rome. Rome (Italy) -- History -- 476-1420. Rome (Italy) -- History -- To 476. Rome (Italy) -- Buildings, structures, etc.

DG812.P37
Partner, Peter.
Renaissance Rome, 1500-1559: a portrait of a society/ Peter Partner. Berkeley: University of California Press, c1976. 241 p.
75-013154   945/.632/06   0520030265
Papacy -- History -- 1447-1565. Renaissance -- Italy -- Rome. Rome (Italy) -- Economic conditions. Rome (Italy) -- History -- 1420-1798. Rome (Italy) -- Social life and customs.

DG812.12.G68 1998
Gouwens, Kenneth.
Remembering the Renaissance: humanist narratives of the sack of Rome/ by Kenneth Gouwens. Leiden; Brill, 1998. xix, 232 p.
98-002822   945/.63207   9004109692
Humanists -- Italy -- Rome. Humanism in literature. Papacy -- History -- 1447-1565. Rome (Italy) -- History -- Siege, 1527.

DG827 Southern Italy — History — By period

DG827.K74 1992
Kreutz, Barbara M.
Before the Normans: Southern Italy in the ninth and tenth centuries/ Barbara M. Kreutz. Philadelphia: University of Pennsylvania Press, c1991. xxxi, 228 p.
91-029118   945/.702   0812231015
Italy, Southern -- History -- 535-1268. Italy, Southern -- Social conditions.

DG847.14-848.1 Southern Italy — Naples. Kingdom of the Two Sicilies — History

DG847.14.W65 1995
Wolf, Kenneth Baxter, 1957-
Making history: the Normans and their historians in eleventh-century Italy/ Kenneth Baxter Wolf. Philadelphia: University of Pennsylvania Press, c1995. xiii, 192 p.
94-044633   945/.03   0812232984
Normans -- Italy -- Historiography. Normans -- Italy -- Sicily -- Historiography. Italy, Southern -- History -- 535-1268 -- Historiography. Mediterranean Region -- Historiography.

DG847.17.B46 1987
Bentley, Jerry H., 1949-
Politics and culture in Renaissance Naples/ Jerry H. Bentley. Princeton, N.J.: Princeton University Press, 1987. xi, 327 p.
87-945511   945/.7   0691054983
Renaissance -- Italy -- Naples (Kingdom) Humanism -- Italy -- Naples (Kingdom) -- History. Political science -- Italy -- Naples (Kingdom) -- History. Naples (Kingdom) -- Civilization.

DG848.1.A88 1992
Astarita, Tommaso.
The continuity of feudal power: the Caracciolo di Brienza in Spanish Naples/ Tommaso Astarita. Cambridge; Cambridge University Press, 1992. x, 281 p.
91-003024   945/.7   0521404746
Caracciolo family. Feudalism -- Italy -- Naples (Kingdom) -- History. Naples (Kingdom) -- History -- Spanish rule, 1442-1707.

DG867.215-869.2 Southern Italy — Sicily — History

DG867.215.R64
Loud, G. A.
The age of Robert Guiscard: southern Italy and the Norman conquest/ G.A. Loud. New York: Longman, 2000. p. cm.
00-042126   945/.8   0582045282
Robert Guiscard -- Duke of Apulia, Calabria, and Sicily, -- ca. 1015-1085. Nobility -- Italy -- Sicily -- Biography. Nobility -- Italy -- Naples (Kingdom) -- Biography. Sicily -- History -- 1016-1194. Naples (Kingdom) -- History -- 1016-1268.

DG867.28.R8
Runciman, Steven, 1903-
The Sicilian Vespers; a history of the Mediterranean world in the later thirteenth century. Cambridge [Eng.] University Press, 1958. xiii, 355 p.
58-002158   945.8
Sicily (Italy) -- History -- 1194-1282. Mediterranean Region -- History.

DG868.44.R53 1998
Riall, Lucy, 1962-
Sicily and the unification of Italy: liberal policy and local power, 1859-1866/ Lucy Riall. Oxford: Clarendon Press; 1998. viii, 252 p.
97-018125   945/.808   0198206801
Liberalism -- Italy -- History -- 19th century. Decentralization in government -- Italy -- History -- 19th century. Sicily (Italy) -- Politics and government -- 1815-1870. Italy -- Politics and government -- 1849-1870.

DG869.2.F56 1998
Finkelstein, Monte S., 1950-
Separatism, the allies and the mafia: the struggle for Sicilian independence, 1943-1948/ Monte S. Finkelstein. Bethlehem, [PA]: Lehigh University Press, c1998. 289 p.
98-013534   945.091   0934223513
Mafia -- Italy -- Sicily. Sicily (Italy) -- Politics and government -- 1870-1945. Sicily (Italy) -- Politics and government -- 1945- Italy -- History -- Allied occupation, 1943-1947.

DG975 Cities (other than metropolitan), provinces, etc., A-Z

DG975.F42.T86 1996
Tuohy, Thomas.
Herculean Ferrara: Ercole d'Este, 1471-1505, and the invention of a ducal capital/ Thomas Tuohy. Cambridge; Cambridge University Press, 1996. xxxi, 534 p.
96-185795   945/.4   0521464714
Ercole -- I d'Este, -- Duke of Ferrara, Modena, and Reggio, -- 1431-1505. Este family. Ercole -- I d'Este, -- Duke of Ferrara, Modena and Reggio, -- 1431-1505. Art patronage -- Italy -- Ferrara. Ferrara (Italy) -- Genealogy. Ferrara (Italy) -- History. Ferrara (Italy) -- Buildings, structures, etc. -- Sources.

DG975.L82.B73 1995
Bratchel, M. E.
Lucca, 1430-1494: the reconstruction of an Italian city-republic/ M.E. Bratchel. Oxford [England]: Clarendon Press; 1995. viii, 346 p.
94-028693   945/.5305   0198204841
Lucca (Italy) -- History.

DG975.L95.Z3813 1997
Zavattini, Cesare, 1902-
Un paese: portrait of an Italian village/ text by Cesare Zavattini; photographs by Paul Strand; [English translation by Marguerite Shore]. New York: Aperture, c1997. 104 p.
96-080073   945.4   0893817007
Luzzara (Italy) Luzzara (Italy) -- Pictorial works.

DG975.P15.K64 1998
Kohl, Benjamin G.
Padua under the Carrara, 1318-1405/ Benjamin G. Kohl. Baltimore: Johns Hopkins University Press, 1998. xxvi, 466 p.
97-030172   945/.32   0801857031
Carrara family. Cities and towns -- Renaissance -- Italy -- Padua. Padua (Italy) -- Kings and rulers -- History. Padua (Italy) -- Foreign relations. Padua (Italy) -- History.

DG975.P65.H4,
Herlihy, David.
Medieval and Renaissance Pistoia; the social history of an Italian town, 1200-1430. New Haven, Yale University Press, 1967. xviii, 297 p.
67-013437   914.5/52/03
Pistoia (Italy) -- Social conditions. Pistoia (Italy) -- History.

DG975.S5.B68 1981
Bowsky, William M.
A medieval Italian commune: Siena under the
Nine, 1287-1355/ William M. Bowsky. Berkeley:
University of California Press, c1981. xxii, 327 p.
80-021234 945/.5804 0520042565
 *Siena (Italy) -- History -- Rule of the Nine,
1287-1355.*

DG975.S5.C25 1998
Caferro, William.
Mercenary companies and the decline of Siena/
William Caferro. Baltimore: The Johns Hopkins
University Press, 1998. xx, 251 p.
97-038339 945/.58 0801857880
 *Mercenary troops -- Italy -- Siena -- History.
Armies -- Italy -- Siena -- History. Condottieri --
History. Siena (Italy) -- History.*

DG975.S5.W35 1991
Waley, Daniel Philip.
Siena and the Sienese in the thirteenth century/
Daniel Waley. Cambridge; Cambridge University
Press, 1991. xxii, 220 p.
90-020127 945/.58 052140312X
 *Siena (Italy) -- History. Siena (Italy) -- Social
life and customs -- Sources. Siena (Italy) -- Social
life and customs.*

DG975.U3.M85 1993
Muir, Edward, 1946-
Mad blood stirring: vendetta & factions in Friuli
during the Renaissance/ Edward Muir. Baltimore:
Johns Hopkins University Press, c1993. xxx, 390 p.
92-015211 945/.391 0801844460
*Savorgnan family. Delle Torre family. Massacres -
- Italy -- Udine. Vendetta -- Italy -- Friuli --
History -- 16th century. Friuli (Italy) -- History.
Udine (Italy) -- History.*

DG975.V38.C67 1993
Cosgrove, Denis E.
The Palladian landscape: geographical change and
its cultural representations in sixteenth-century
Italy/ Denis Cosgrove. University Park, Pa.: Penn
State University Press, 1993. xv, 270 p.
92-033774 945/.3 027100942X
*Palladio, Andrea -- 1508-1580.   Human
geography -- Italy -- Veneto. Landscape
assessment -- Italy -- Veneto. Architecture,
Renaissance -- Italy -- Veneto. Veneto (Italy) --
Civilization.*

DG975.V7.G78 1988
Grubb, James S., 1952-
Firstborn of Venice: Vicenza in the early
Renaissance state/ James S. Grubb. Baltimore:
Johns Hopkins University Press, c1988. xx, 238 p.
87-033878 945/.31 0801836131
 *Renaissance -- Italy -- Vicenza. Renaissance --
Italy -- Venice. City-states -- Italy -- History.
Vicenza (Italy) -- History. Venice (Italy) -- History
-- 697-1508.*

DH186.5 History of the Low
Countries — By period
— Wars of independence,
1555-1648

DH186.5.G37 1992
Gelderen, Martin van.
The political thought of the Dutch revolt, 1555-
1590/ Martin van Gelderen. Cambridge [England];
Cambridge University Press, 1992. xi, 332 p.
91-045932 949.2/03 0521392047
 *Netherlands -- Politics and government --
1556-1648.*

DH186.5.P283
Parker, Geoffrey, 1943-
The Dutch revolt/ Geoffrey Parker. Ithaca, N.Y.:
Cornell University Press, 1977. 327 p.
77-077553 949.2/03 080141136X
 *Netherlands -- History -- Wars of
Independence, 1556-1648.*

DH491 Ethnography —
General works

DH491.F48 1992
The Flemish movement: a documentary history,
1780-1990/ edited by Theo Hermans; co-editors,
Louis Vos, Lode Wils. London; Athlone Press,
1992. xii, 476 p.
91-022810 949.3 0485113686
 *Flemish movement -- History -- Sources. Dutch
language -- Political aspects -- Belgium.*

DH491.N325 1998
Nationalism in Belgium: shifting identities, 1780-
1995/ edited by Kas Deprez and Louis Vos. New
York, N.Y.: St. Martin's Press, 1998. xvi, 281 p.
97-038683 949.3 0312212496
 *Nationalism -- Belgium -- History. Belgium --
Politics and government. Belgium -- Civilization --
19th century. Belgium -- Civilization -- 20th
century.*

DH511 History of Belgium —
Dictionaries. Chronological
tables, outlines, etc.

DH511.S73 1999
Stallaerts, Robert.
Historical dictionary of Belgium/ Robert Stallaerts.
Lanham, Md.: Scarecrow Press, 1999. xxviii,
303 p.
98-049221 949.3/003 0810836033
 Belgium -- History -- Dictionaries.

DH620 History — By period —
1794-1909

DH620.K67
Kossmann, E. H. 1922-
The low countries, 1780-1940/ by E. H. Kossmann.
Oxford [Eng.]: Clarendon Press; 1978. ix, 784 p.
77-030291 949.3 0198221088
 *Belgium -- History. Netherlands -- History --
1714-1795. Netherlands -- History -- 19th century.*

DJ History of
Netherlands (Holland)

DJ158-202 History — By period —
1555-1795. United Provinces

DJ158.R693 1988
Rowen, Herbert Harvey.
The princes of Orange: the stadholders in the
Dutch Republic/ Herbert H. Rowen. Cambridge
[Cambridgeshire]; Cambridge University Press,
1988. xi, 253 p.
87-018323 949.2/04 0521345251
*Orange-Nassau, House of.   Netherlands --
Politics and government -- 1556-1648. Netherlands
-- Politics and government -- 1648-1795.
Netherlands -- Kings and rulers -- History.*

DJ202.D44 1992
The Dutch Republic in the eighteenth century:
decline, Enlightenment, and revolution/ edited by
Margaret C. Jacob and Wijnand W. Mijnhardt.
Ithaca: Cornell University Press, 1992. ix, 365 p.
91-055551 949.2./04 0801426243
 *Civilization, Modern -- 18th century.
Enlightenment -- Netherlands. Netherlands --
History -- 1714-1795.*

DJ261 History — By period
— 19th-20th centuries

DJ261.K8413 1990
Kuitenbrouwer, M.
The Netherlands and the rise of modern
imperialism: colonies and foreign policy, 1870-
1902/ Maarten Kuitenbrouwer; translated from the
Dutch by Hugh Beyer. New York: Berg; 1991. vii,
407 p.
90-036901 949.2/06 0854966811
 *Netherlands -- Foreign relations -- 1830-1898.
Netherlands -- Foreign relations -- 1898-1948.
Netherlands -- Colonies.*

DJ401 Local history and
description — Provinces,
regions, islands, etc., A-Z

DJ401.H6.P75 1994
Price, J. L.
Holland and the Dutch Republic in the seventeenth
century: the politics of particularism/ J.L. Price.
Oxford [England]: Clarendon Press; 1994. 312 p.
93-027130 949.2/3 0198203837
 *Holland (Netherlands: Province) -- History.
Holland (Netherlands: Province) -- Politics and
government. Netherlands -- History -- Wars of
Independence, 1556-1648.*

DJ401.H64.T73 1990
Tracy, James D.
Holland under Habsburg rule, 1506-1566: the
formation of a body politic/ James D. Tracy.
Berkeley: University of California Press, c1990. ix,
330 p.
90-010856 949.2/02 0520068823
 *Holland (Netherlands: Province) -- History.
Netherlands -- History -- House of Habsburg,
1477-1556. Netherlands -- History -- Wars of
Independence, 1556-1648.*

DJK History of Eastern
Europe (General)

DJK4 Collected works
(nonserial)
— Several authors

DJK4 .S93 vol. 3.JK46
Sedlar, Jean W.
East Central Europe in the Middle Ages, 1000-
1500/ Jean W. Sedlar. Seattle: University of
Washington Press, c1994. xiii, 556 p.
93-017820 947 20 0295972912
*Europe, Eastern -- History. Europe, Central --
History.*

DJK4.S93 vol. 4.K4188
Stone, Daniel,
The Polish-Lithuanian state, 1386-1795/ Daniel Stone. Seattle: University of Washington Press, c2001. xii, 374 p.
00-051179 943 s.a943.8/0221 0295980931
Poland -- History -- To 1795.

DJK4.S93 vol. 5
Sugar, Peter F.
Southeastern Europe under Ottoman rule, 1354-1804/ by Peter F. Sugar. Seattle: University of Washington Press, c1977. xvii, 365 p.
76-007799 949 s 0295954434
Turks -- Balkan Peninsula. Balkan Peninsula -- History.

DJK4.S93 vol. 6
Kann, Robert A., 1906-
The peoples of the Eastern Habsburg lands, 1526-1918/ by Robert A. Kann and Zdenek V. David. Seattle: University of Washington Press, c1984. xvi, 543 p.
83-021629 943 s 0295960957
Europe, Eastern -- History. Europe, Central -- History. Austria -- History.

DJK4.S93 vol. 7.K4349
Wandycz, Piotr Stefan.
The lands of partitioned Poland, 1795-1918, by Piotr S. Wandycz. Seattle, University of Washington Press [1974] xvii, 431 p.
74-008311 949 s.a943.8 19 0295953519
Europe, Eastern -- History.

DJK4.S93 vol. 8
Jelavich, Charles.
The establishment of the Balkan national states, 1804-1920/ Charles and Barbara Jelavich. Seattle: University of Washington Press, c1977. xv, 358 p.
76-049162 949 s 0295954442
Eastern question (Balkan) Balkan Peninsula -- Politics and government -- 19th century. Balkan Peninsula -- Politics and government -- 20th century.

DJK4.S93 vol. 9
Rothschild, Joseph.
East Central Europe between the two World Wars. Seattle, University of Washington Press [1974] xvii, 420 p.
74-008327 949 s 0295953500
Europe, Eastern -- History.

DJK36 History — Study and teaching. Slavic studies — By region or country, A-Z

DJK36.S85 1997
Stokes, Gale, 1933-
Three eras of political change in Eastern Europe/ Gale Stokes. New York: Oxford University Press, 1997. xiii, 240 p.
96-033655 947 0195104811
Europe, Eastern -- History. Yugoslavia -- History.

DJK38 History — General works — 1801-

DJK38.B458 1997
Berend, T. Ivan 1930-
Decades of crisis: Central and Eastern Europe before World War II/ Ivan T. Berend. Berkeley, Calif.: University of California Press, c1998. xxiv, 437 p.
97-039432 947/.009/04 0520206177
Europe, Eastern -- History -- 20th century. Europe, Central -- History.

DJK42 History — Political history

DJK42.C65 1991
The Columbia history of Eastern Europe in the twentieth century/ edited by Joseph Held. New York: Columbia University Press, c1992. lxix, 435 p.
91-029132 909/.09717082 0231076967
Europe, Eastern -- History -- 20th century.

DJK45 History — Foreign and general relations — Relations with individual countries, A-Z

DJK45.S65.D38 1988
Dawisha, Karen.
Eastern Europe, Gorbachev, and reform: the great challenge/ Karen Dawisha. Cambridge [England]; Cambridge University Press, 1988. xiii, 268 p.
87-037376 327/.0947 0521355605
Gorbachev, Mikhail Sergeevich, -- 1931- Europe, Eastern -- Foreign relations -- Soviet Union. Soviet Union -- Foreign relations -- Europe, Eastern. Europe, Eastern -- Politics and government -- 1945-1989.

DJK45.S65.G37 1990
Gati, Charles.
The bloc that failed: Soviet-East European relations in transition/ Charles Gati. Bloomington: Indiana University Press, c1990. xiv, 226 p.
89-036971 327.47 0253325315
Soviet Union -- Foreign relations -- Europe, Eastern. Europe, Eastern -- Foreign relations -- 1945-1989. Europe, Eastern -- Foreign relations -- Soviet Union.

DJK45.S65.S69 1994
The Soviet Union in Eastern Europe, 1945-89/ edited by Odd Arne Westad, Sven Holtsmark, Iver B. Neumann. New York: St. Martin's Press, 1994. viii, 234 p.
93-008746 303.48/247 0333602307
Europe, Eastern -- Relations -- Soviet Union. Soviet Union -- Relations -- Europe, Eastern. Europe, Eastern -- Politics and government -- 1945-1989.

DJK49-51 History — By period — 20th century

DJK49.E17 1995
Eastern European nationalism in the twentieth century/ Peter F. Sugar, editor Lanham, Md.: American University Press, c1995. 456 p.
95-004255 320.5/4 187938339X
Nationalism -- Europe, Eastern. Europe, Eastern -- Politics and government -- 20th century.

DJK50.B77 1988
Brown, J. F. 1928-
Eastern Europe and communist rule/ J.F. Brown. Durham: Duke University Press, 1988. xii, 562 p.
87-030572 947 082230810X
Europe, Eastern -- History -- 1945-1989. Communist countries -- History.

DJK50.B78 1991
Brown, J. F. 1928-
Surge to freedom: the end of Communist rule in Eastern Europe/ J.F. Brown. Durham: Duke University Press, 1991. x, 338 p.
90-044883 947.084 0822311453
Europe, Eastern -- History -- 1945-1989.

DJK50.F76 1991
From Stalinism to pluralism: a documentary history of Eastern Europe since 1945/ edited by Gale Stokes. New York: Oxford University Press, 1991. xi, 267 p.
90-034250 947 0195063813
Europe, Eastern -- History -- 1945-1989 -- Sources.

DJK50.G35 1990
Garton Ash, Timothy.
The magic lantern: the revolution of '89 witnessed in Warsaw, Budapest, Berlin, and Prague/ Timothy Garton Ash. New York: Random House, 1990. 156 p.
90-053147 947.085 0394588843
Garton Ash, Timothy. Europe, Eastern -- History -- 1945-1989.

DJK50.H43 1994
Held, Joseph.
Dictionary of East European history since 1945/ Joseph Held. Westport, Conn.: Greenwood Press, 1994. x, 509 p.
93-035840 947.08/03 0313265194
Europe, Eastern -- History -- 1945- -- Dictionaries.

DJK50.L437 1997
The legacy of the Soviet bloc/ edited by Jane Shapiro Zacek and Ilpyong J. Kim. Gainesville: University Press of Florida, c1997. viii, 280 p.
96-016351 320.947 0813014751
Post-communism -- Europe, Eastern. Europe, Eastern -- Foreign relations -- 1989- Europe, Eastern -- Politics and government -- 1945-

DJK50.M38 1992
Mason, David S. 1947-
Revolution in East-Central Europe: the rise and fall of Communism and the Cold War/ David S. Mason. Boulder: Westview Press, 1992. xiv, 216 p.
92-005339 947 0813313406
Communism -- Europe, Eastern. Europe, Eastern -- Politics and government -- 1945-

DJK50.R67 1989
Rothschild, Joseph.
Return to diversity: a political history of East Central Europe since World War II/ Joseph Rothschild. New York: Oxford University Press, 1989. x, 257 p.
88-001505 949 0195045742
Europe, Eastern -- History -- 1945-1989.

DJK50.S75 1993
Stokes, Gale, 1933-
The walls came tumbling down: the collapse of communism in Eastern Europe/ Gale Stokes. New York; Oxford University Press, 1993. viii, 319 p.
92-044862 940/.09717 0195066448
Europe, Eastern -- History -- 1945-

DJK50 .T57 1992
Tismaneanu, Vladimir.
Reinventing politics: Eastern Europe from Stalin to Havel/ Vladimir Tismaneanu. New York: Free Press; xvii, 312 p.
91-042878 947 20 0029326052
Europe, Eastern -- Politics and government -- 1945-

DJK51.B74 2001
Brown, J. F. 1928-
The grooves of change: Eastern Europe at the turn of the millennium/ J.F. Brown. Durham, NC: Duke University Press, 2001. p. cm.
00-047655 947.085 0822326523
Europe, Eastern -- History -- 1989-

DJK51.B75 1994
Brown, J. F. 1928-
Hopes and shadows: Eastern Europe after communism/ J.F. Brown. Durham: Duke University Press, 1994. xi, 367 p.
93-047347 947 0822314460
Europe, Eastern -- Politics and government -- 1989-

DJK51.C67 1997
The Consolidation of democracy in East-Central Europe/ edited by Karen Dawisha and Bruce Parrott. Cambridge, U.K.; Cambridge University Press, 1997. xx, 389 p.
97-178526 320.947 0521590647
Democracy -- Europe, Eastern. Post-communism -- Europe, Eastern. Democratization -- Europe, Eastern. Europe, Eastern -- Politics and government -- 1989-

DJK51.C68 1995
Contemporary nationalism in East Central Europe/ edited by Paul Latawski. New York, N.Y.: St. Martin's Press, 1995. xiii, 200 p.
94-016291 320.5/4/0947 0312122764
Nationalism -- Europe, Eastern. Europe, Eastern -- Politics and government -- 1989-

DJK51.E265 1992
Eastern Europe in revolution/ edited by Ivo Banac. Ithaca, N.Y.: Cornell University Press, 1992. x, 255 p.
91-057903 943/.0009717 0801427118
Europe, Eastern -- Politics and government -- 1989-

DJK51.G654 1997
Goldman, Minton F.
Revolution and change in Central and Eastern Europe: political, economic, and social challenges/ Minton F. Goldman; with a foreword by Karl W. Ryavec. Armonk, N.Y.: M.E. Sharpe, c1997. xiv, 497 p.
95-052512 940/.09717 1563247577
Post-communism -- Europe, Eastern. Yugoslav War, 1991-1995. Europe, Eastern -- Politics and government -- 1989- Europe, Eastern -- Economic conditions -- 1989- Europe, Eastern -- Social conditions -- 1989-

DJK51.L85 1996
Lukic, Reneo.
Europe from the Balkans to the Urals: the disintegration of Yugoslavia and the Soviet Union/ Reneo Lukic and Allen Lynch. Solna, Sweden: SIPRI; 1996. xvii, 436 p.
96-024364 320.947 0198292007
World politics -- 1989- Soviet Union -- Politics and government -- 1985-1991. Yugoslavia -- Politics and government -- 1980-1992. Europe, Eastern -- Politics and government -- 1989-

DJK51.P684 1997
Postcommunist presidents/ edited by Ray Taras. Cambridge; Cambridge University Press, 1997. ix, 250 p.
96-050024 320.447 0521582822
Presidents -- Europe, Eastern. Presidents -- Former Soviet republics. Post-communism -- Europe, Eastern. Europe, Eastern -- Politics and government -- 1989- Former Soviet republics -- Politics and government.

DJK51.R476 1999
The Revolutions of 1989/ edited by Vladimir Tismaneanu. London; Routledge, 1999. x, 270 p.
98-034372 947/.009/048 21 041516950X
Europe, Eastern -- Politics and government -- 1989-

DJK61 Local history and description — Black Sea region

DJK61.P65 2001
Politics of the Black Sea: dynamics of cooperation and conflict/ edited by Tunc Aybak. London; I.B. Tauris, 2001. xiii, 272 p.
2001-270083 327/.09163/89 1860644546
Black Sea Coast -- Foreign relations. Black Sea Coast -- Politics and government. Black Sea Coast -- Economic conditions.

DK History of Russia. Soviet Union. Former Soviet Republics

DK1.5 Societies. Serials — Commonwealth of Independent States

DK1.5.R876 1996
Russia and the Commonwealth of Independent States: documents, data, and analysis/ Zbigniew Brzezinski, Paige Sullivan, editors; The center for strategic and international studies. Armonk, N.Y.: M.E. Sharpe, c1997. xxi, 866 p.
96-018164 947.086 1563246376
Commonwealth of Independent States.

DK3 Sources and documents

DK3.D55 1974
Dmytryshyn, Basil, 1925-
Imperial Russia; a source book, 1700-1917. Hinsdale, Ill., Dryden Press [1974] xi, 497 p.
73-004179 947 0030892376
Soviet Union -- History -- Sources.

DK14 Gazetteers. Dictionaries, etc.

DK14.C35 1994
The Cambridge encyclopedia of Russia and the former Soviet Union/ edited by Archie Brown, Michael Kaser, and Gerald S. Smith; associate editor, Patricia Brown. Cambridge [Cambridgeshire]; Cambridge University Press, 1994. xi, 604 p.
94-024668 947/.003 0521355931
Russia -- Encyclopedias. Soviet Union -- Encyclopedias. Former Soviet republics -- Encyclopedias.

DK14.P39 2001
Paxton, John.
Imperial Russia: a reference handbook/ John Paxton. New York: Palgrave, 2001. xiv, 257 p.
00-026867 947 0312234805
Russia -- Handbooks, manuals, etc.

DK17 General works

DK17.S64 1986
The Soviet Union and Eastern Europe/ edited by George Schopflin. New York, N.Y.: Facts on file, c1986. xvii, 637 p.
85-025403 947 0816012601
Soviet Union. Europe, Eastern.

DK17.S655
The Soviet Union since Stalin/ edited by Stephen F. Cohen, Alexander Rabinowitch, and Robert Sharlet. Bloomington: Indiana University Press, c1980. viii, 342 p.
79-003092 947.084/2 0253322723
Soviet Union -- Congresses.

DK26 Description and travel — 1856-1900

DK26.D8 1961
Dumas, Alexandre, 1802-1870.
Adventures in Czarist Russia. Translated and edited by Alma Elizabeth Murch. Philadelphia Chilton Co., Book Division [1961] 208 p.
61-005758 914.7
Soviet Union -- Description and travel.

DK32 Social life and customs. Civilization — General works

DK32.C523
Cherniavsky, Michael.
Tsar and people; studies in Russian myths. New Haven, Yale University Press, 1961. 258 p.
61-014431 914.7
National characteristics, Russian.

DK32.E6 1998
Entertaining tsarist Russia: tales, songs, plays, movies, jokes, ads, and images from Russian urban life, 1779-1917/ edited by James von Geldern and Louise McReynolds. Bloomington: Indiana University Press, c1998. xxvii, 394 p.
97-052597   306/.0947/09034   0253334071
Popular culture -- Russia. Russian literature -- 18th century. Russian literature -- 19th century. Russia -- Civilization -- 18th century. Russia -- Civilization -- 1801-1917.

DK32.M18 1999
Malia, Martin E.
Russia under western eyes: from the Bronze Horseman to the Lenin Mausoleum/ Martin Malia. Cambridge, MA: The Belnap Press of Harvard University Press, 1999. xii, 514 p.
98-039769   947   0674781201
Russia -- Civilization. Soviet Union -- Civilization. Russia -- Foreign public opinion.

DK32.M4 1955
Masaryk, T. G. 1850-1937.
The spirit of Russia; studies in history, literature and philosophy. Translated from the German original by Eden and Cedar Paul, with additional chapters and bibliographies by Jan Slavik; the former translated and the latter condensed and translated by W. R. & Z. Lee. London, G. Allen & Unwin; [1955] 2 v.
55-008662   947
Dostoyevsky, Fyodor, -- 1821-1881.   Philosophy, Russian. Russian literature -- History and criticism. Soviet Union -- History.

DK32.M62 1998
Milner-Gulland, R. R.
Cultural atlas of Russia and the former Soviet Union/ by Robin Milner-Gulland with Nikolai Dejevsky. New York: Checkmark Books, 1998. p. cm.
98-029263   947   0816038155
Art, Russian. Art, Soviet.   Former Soviet republics -- Civilization. Former Soviet republics -- Maps.

DK32.M626 1997
Milner-Gulland, R. R.
The Russians/ Robin Milner-Gulland. Oxford, UK; Blackwell, 1997. p. cm.
96-051542   947   0631188053
National characteristics, Russian.   Russia -- History -- To 1533. Russia -- History -- 1533-1613. Russia -- History -- 1613-1689.

DK32.7 Social life and customs. Civilization — Intellectual life

DK32.7.B5
Billington, James H.
The icon and the axe; an interpretive history of Russian culture, by James H. Billington. New York, Knopf, 1966. xviii, 786 p.
66-018687   914.703
Soviet Union -- Intellectual life.

DK32.7.P49
Pipes, Richard.
The Russian intelligentsia. New York, Columbia University Press, 1961. 234 p.
61-006160   914.7
Intellectuals. Soviet Union -- Intellectual life.

DK32.7.P512 1967
Plekhanov, Georgii Valentinovich, 1856-1918.
History of Russian social thought. Translated from the Russian by Boris M. Bekkar and others. New York, H. Fertig, 1967. 224 p.
66-025858   914.7/03
Soviet Union -- Social conditions. Soviet Union -- Civilization.

DK33 Ethnography — General works

DK33.F68 1997
Fowkes, Ben.
The disintegration of the Soviet Union: a study in the rise and triumph of nationalism/ Ben Fowkes. New York: St. Martin's Press, 1997. xii, 273 p.
96-034181   305.8/00947   0312161964
Nationalism -- Soviet Union. Minorities -- Soviet Union. Soviet Union -- Ethnic relations.

DK33.H35 1975
Handbook of major Soviet nationalities/ Zev Katz, editor; Rosemarie Rogers, associate editor; Frederic Harned, assistant editor. New York: Free Press, [1975] xiv, 481 p.
74-010458   914.7/06   0029170907
Ethnology -- Soviet Union. Soviet Union.

DK33.K4527 1995
Khazanov, Anatoly M. 1937-
After the USSR: ethnicity, nationalism and politics in the Commonwealth of Independent States/ Anatoly M. Khazanov. Madison, Wis.: The University of Wisconsin Press, c1995. xxi, 311 p.
95-005696   305.8/00947   0299148904
Minorities -- Former Soviet republics. Ethnology -- Former Soviet republics. Nationalism -- Former Soviet republics. Former Soviet republics -- Politics and government. Former Soviet republics -- Ethnic relations.

DK33.N26 1990
Nahaylo, Bohdan.
Soviet disunion: a history of the nationalities problem in the USSR/ Bohdan Nahaylo and Victor Swoboda. New York: Free Press, 1990. xvi, 432 p.
89-071502   947/.004   0029224012
Ethnology -- Soviet Union. Soviet Union -- History. Soviet Union -- Ethnic relations.

DK33.N294 1990
The Nationalities factor in Soviet politics and society/ edited by Lubomyr Hajda, Mark Beissinger. Boulder, Colo.: Westview Press, 1990. vii, 331 p.
89-070469   305.8/00947   0813376890
Nationalism -- Soviet Union. Minorities -- Soviet Union. Soviet Union -- Politics and government -- 1985-1991. Soviet Union -- Ethnic relations.

DK33.P65 1992
The Post Soviet nations: perspectives on the demise of the USSR/ Alexander J. Motyl, editor. New York: Columbia University Press, c1992. xi, 322 p.
92-017109   947.085/4   0231078943
Nationalism -- Soviet Union. Minorities -- Soviet Union. Soviet Union -- Ethnic relations. Soviet Union -- Politics and government -- 1985-1991.

DK33.R36 2000
Rancour-Laferriere, Daniel.
Russian nationalism from an interdisciplinary perspective: imagining Russia/ Daniel Rancour-Laferriere. Lewiston, N.Y.: E. Mellen Press, c2000. xx, 349 p.
00-058237   320.54/0947   0773476717
Russians -- Ethnic identity. Nationalism -- Russia. Nationalism -- Russia (Federation)

DK33.T54 1997
Tishkov, Valerii Aleksandrovich.
Ethnicity, nationalism and conflict in and after the Soviet Union: the mind aflame/ Valery Tishkov. London; Sage, 1997. xv, 334 p.
96-071477   305.8/00947   0761951849
Nationalism -- Soviet Union. Minorities -- Soviet Union. Nationalism -- Former Soviet republics. Soviet Union -- Ethnic relations. Former Soviet republics -- Ethnic relations.

DK34 Ethnography — Individual elements in the population, A-Z

DK34.B7.C76 1997
Cross, Anthony Glenn.
By the banks of the Neva: chapters from the lives and careers of the British in eighteenth-century Russia/ Anthony Cross. Cambridge; Cambridge University Press, 1997. xv, 474 p.
96-003825   947/.00421   0521552931
British -- Russia.   Russia -- History -- 1689-1801.

DK34.C57
Jaimoukha, Amjad M.
The Circassians: a handbook/ Amjad Jaimoukha. New York: Palgrave, 2001. 384 p.
00-065254   947.5/00499624   0312239947
Circassians.

DK34.G3.L66 1988
Long, James W., 1942-
From privileged to dispossessed: the Volga Germans, 1860-1917/ James W. Long. Lincoln: University of Nebraska Press, c1988. xv, 337 p.
88-001144   947/.800431   0803228813
Germans -- Russia (Federation) -- Volga River Region -- History.

DK34.M8.B46 1986
Bennigsen, Alexandre.
Muslims of the Soviet empire: a guide/ Alexandre Bennigsen, S. Enders Wimbush. Bloomington: Indiana University Press, c1986. xvi, 294 p.
86-015343   947/.00882971   0253339588
Muslims -- Soviet Union. Islam -- Soviet Union.

DK34.M8.R87 2000
Russian American relations: Islamic and Turkic dimensions in the Volga-Ural basin/ edited by Hafeez Malik. Houndsmills: Macmillan Press Ltd.; 2000. xv, 314 p.
00-021896   947/.00882971   0312231687
Muslims -- Russia -- History. Muslims -- Soviet Union -- History. Muslims -- Russia (Federation) -- History. Russia (Federation) -- Relations -- United States. United States -- Relations -- Russia (Federation)

DK34.N4.G65 1999
Golovnev, A. V.
Siberian survival: the Nenets and their story/ Andrei V. Golovnev and Gail Osherenko. Ithaca, NY: Cornell University Press, 1999. xiii, 176 p.
98-048118   957/.3   0801436311
Nentsy -- History. Nentsy -- Government relations. Nentsy -- Social life and customs. IAmal Peninsula (Russia) -- Politics and government. IAmal Peninsula (Russia) -- Social life and customs.

DK34.T8.Z4
Zenkovsky, Serge A.
Pan-Turkism and Islam in Russia.   Cambridge, Harvard University Press, 1960. 345 p.
60-005399   947
Turks -- Soviet Union. Minorities -- Soviet Union. Mohammedans in Russia.

DK35.5 Russians in foreign countries (General)

DK35.5.C48 1996
Chinn, Jeff.
Russians as the new minority: ethnicity and nationalism in the Soviet successor states/ Jeff Chinn, Robert Kaiser. Boulder, Colo.: Westview Press, 1996. xii, 308 p.
96-006849   947   0813322499
Russians -- Former Soviet republics. Nationalism -- Former Soviet republics.   Former Soviet republics -- Ethnic relations.

DK35.5.H37 1994
Hardeman, Hilde.
Coming to terms with the Soviet regime: the "Changing signposts" movement among Russian emigres in the early 1920s/ Hilde Hardeman. DeKalb: Northern Illinois University Press, 1994. x, 319 p.
94-007871   947.084/1   0875801870
Russians -- Foreign countries -- Politics and government. Russians -- Foreign countries -- Intellectual life.   Soviet Union -- History -- Revolution, 1917-1921. Soviet Union -- Politics and government -- 1917-1936.

DK35.5.R34 1990
Raeff, Marc.
Russia abroad: a cultural history of the Russian emigration, 1919-1939/ Marc Raeff. New York: Oxford University Press, 1990. viii, 239 p.
89-034887   305.8/917104/09042   0195056833
Russians -- Foreign countries. Russians -- Intellectual life. Political refugees -- Soviet Union. Soviet Union -- History -- Revolution, 1917-1921 -- Refugees.

DK35.5.R39 2000
Raymond, Boris, 1925-
The Russian diaspora, 1917-1941/ Boris Raymond and David R. Jones. Lanham, MD: Scarecrow, 2000. p. cm.
00-024822   305.89171/0092/2   0810837862
Russians -- Foreign countries -- Biography. Soviet Union -- Emigration and immigration.

DK36 History — Dictionaries. Chronological tables, outlines, etc.

DK36.M55 1976
The Modern encyclopedia of Russian and Soviet history/ edited by Joseph L. Wieczynski. Gulf Breeze, Fla.: Academic International Press, 1976-1996 v. 1-59
75-011091   947/.003   0875690645
Russia -- History -- Dictionaries. Former Soviet republics -- History -- Dictionaries.

DK36.P39 1993
Paxton, John.
Encyclopedia of Russian history: from the Christianization of Kiev to the break-up of the U.S.S.R./ John Paxton. Santa Barbara, Calif.: ABC-CLIO, c1993. x, 483 p.
93-029564   947/.003   0874366909
Kievan Rus -- Encyclopedias. Russia -- Encyclopedias. Soviet Union -- Encyclopedias.

DK36.R39 1998
Raymond, Boris, 1925-
Historical dictionary of Russia/ Boris Raymond and Paul Duffy. Lanham, Md.: Scarecrow Press, c1998. xxxiv, 411 p.
97-022659   947/.003   0810833573
Russia -- History -- Dictionaries. Soviet Union -- History -- Dictionaries. Russia (Federation) -- History -- 1991- -- Dictionaries.

DK37.2 History — Biography (Collective) — Women

DK37.2.I5 2000
In the shadow of revolution: life stories of Russian women from 1917 to the second World War/ edited by Sheila Fitzpatrick and Yuri Slezkine; translated by Yuri Slezkine. Princeton, NJ: Princeton University Press, c2000. viii, 443 p.
99-054904   947.084/082   0691019487
Women -- Soviet Union -- Biography. Soviet Union -- History -- 1917-1936. Soviet Union -- History -- 1925-1953.

DK38 History — Historiography — General works

DK38.B5 1962
Rewriting Russian history: Soviet interpretations of Russia's past/ edited by Cyril E. Black. New York: Vintage Books, 1962. xv, 431 p.
63-001520   947
Soviet Union -- History -- Historiography.

DK38.C45
Christoff, Peter K.
An introduction to nineteenth-century Russian Slavophilism: a study in ideas/ by Peter K. Christoff. 's-Gravenhage: Mouton, 1961-c1991. 4 v.
63-045564   947.08   0813380804
Civilization, Slavic -- Historiography. Slavophilism. Historiography -- Russia -- History -- 19th century.

DK38.C64 1996
Cohen, Ariel.
Russian imperialism: development and crisis/ Ariel Cohen. Westport, Conn.: Praeger, 1996. xiv, 180 p.
95-043730   947/.0072   0275953378
Imperialism.   Soviet Union -- Historiography. Former Soviet republics -- Historiography. Russia -- Historiography.

DK38.M2725 2001
Markwick, Roger D.
Rewriting history in soviet Russia: the politics of revisionist historiography, 1956-1974/ Roger D. Markwick; foreword by Donald J. Raleigh. New York: Palgrave, 2001. xx, 327 p.
00-048337   947/.0072   0333792092
Soviet Union -- Historiography.

DK38.S68 1989
Soviet historians and perestroika: the first phase/ edited by Donald J. Raleigh. Armonk, N.Y.: M.E. Sharpe, c1989. xvi, 291 p.
89-010724   947/.0072   0873325540
Perestroika. Historians -- Soviet Union. Soviet Union -- Politics and government -- 1985-1991. Soviet Union -- Intellectual life. Soviet Union -- Historiography.

DK38.V4413
Vernadsky, George, 1887-1973.
Russian historiography: a history/ by George Vernadsky; edited by Sergei Pushkarev; translated by Nickolas Lupinin. Belmont, Mass.: Nordland Pub. Co., c1978. iv, 575 p.
77-095207   947/.007/2   0913124257
Soviet Union -- Historiography.

DK38.7 History — Historiography — Biography of historians, area studies specialists, archaeologists, etc.

DK38.7.K53.B97 1995
Byrnes, Robert Francis.
V.O. Kliuchevskii, historian of Russia/ Robert F. Byrnes. Bloomington: Indiana University Press, c1995. xxi, 301 p.
95-018202   947/.007202   025332940X
Kliuchevskii, V. O. -- (Vasilii Osipovich), -- 1841-1911.   Historians -- Russia -- Biography. Russia -- History.

DK40 History — General works — 1801-

DK40.A25 1995
Acton, Edward.
Russia: the tsarist and Soviet legacy/ Edward Acton. 2nd ed. London; Longman, 1995. xiv, 401 p.
94-011457   947.220   0582089220
Russia -- History.

DK40.D84
Dukes, Paul, 1934-
A history of Russia: medieval, modern, and contemporary. New York, McGraw-Hill [1974] xi, 361 p.
74-001154   947   0070180326
Civilization, Medieval.   Soviet Union -- History. Russia -- History.

DK40.H66 2001
Hosking, Geoffrey A.
Russia and the Russians: a history/ Geoffrey Hosking. Cambridge, MA: Belknap Press of Harvard University Press, 2001. xiii, 718 p.
00-065085   947   0674004736
Russia -- History. Soviet Union -- History. Russia (Federation) -- History -- 1991-

DK40.L55 2001
Lieven, D. C. B.
Empire: the Russian Empire and its rivals/ Dominic Lieven. New Haven, Conn.: Yale University Press, 2001. 486 p.
01-276500   947   0300088590
Imperialism -- History -- Case studies. Soviet Union -- History. Europe -- Politics and government -- 1789-1900. Russia -- History.

DK40.M67 1997
Moss, Walter.
A history of Russia/ Walter G. Moss. New York: McGraw-Hill, c1997. 2 v.
96-034845   947   0070434808
Russia -- History. Soviet Union -- History.

DK40.P47 1974b
Pipes, Richard.
Russia under the old regime/ Richard Pipes. New York: Scribner, c1974. xxii, 360 p.
74-032567   947   0684140411
Russia -- History.

DK40.R5 1984
Riasanovsky, Nicholas Valentine, 1923-
A history of Russia/ Nicholas V. Riasanovsky. New York: Oxford University Press, 1984. xx, 695 p.
83-004116   947   0195033612
Soviet Union -- History.

DK40.S6213
Solovev, Sergei Mikhailovich, 1820-1879.
History of Russia. Gulf Breeze, FL: Academic International Press, 1976-1999 v. 5, 7-10, 1
75-011085   947   0875690661
Russia -- History.

DK40.V4 1933
Vernadsky, George, 1887-1973.
A history of Russia, by George Vernadsky ... with a preface by Michael Ivanovich Rostovtzeff. New Haven, Yale university press; [1933] xix, 413 p.
34-011827   947
Soviet Union -- History.

DK41 History — Elementary textbooks

DK41.C44 1956
Charques, Richard Denis, 1899-
A short history of Russia. New York, Dutton, 1956. 284 p.
56-010700   947
Soviet Union -- History.

DK41.M39 1962
Mazour, Anatole Gregory, 1900-
Russia, tsarist and communist.   Princeton, N.J., Van Nostrand [1962] 995 p.
62-004431   947
Soviet Union -- History.

DK49 History — General special — Philosophy of Russian/Soviet history

DK49.D86 2000
Duncan, Peter J. S., 1953-
Russian messianism: third Rome, holy revolution, communism and after/ Peter J.S. Duncan. London; Routledge, 2000. xiii, 235 p.
99-059925   947/.001   0415152054
Russia -- History -- Philosophy. Soviet Union -- History -- Philosophy. Russia (Federation) -- History -- Philosophy.

DK49.G6713 2000
Gorbachev, Mikhail Sergeevich, 1931-
Gorbachev: on my country and the world/ [Mikhail Gorbachev]; translated from Russian by George Shriver. New York: Columbia University Press, c2000. 300 p.
99-031273   947.085/01   0231115148
Gorbachev, Mikhail Sergeevich, -- 1931- -- Political and social views. World politics -- 1989- Soviet Union -- History -- Philosophy. Russia (Federation) -- History -- 1991- -- Philosophy.

DK49.H68 1997
Hosking, Geoffrey A.
Russia: people and empire, 1552-1917/ Geoffrey Hosking. Cambridge, Mass.: Harvard University Press, 1997. xxviii, 548 p.
97-005069   947/.04   067478118X
National characteristics, Russian.   Russia -- History -- 1613-1917 -- Philosophy. Russia -- History -- 1533-1613 -- Philosophy.

DK52.5-54 History — General special — Military history

DK52.5.D83
Duffy, Christopher, 1936-
Russia's military way to the West: origins and nature of Russian military power, 1700-1800/ Christopher Duffy. London: Routledge & Kegan Paul, 1981. xiii, 256 p.
82-100403   947   0710007973
Russia -- History, Military -- To 1801.

DK54.O36 1998
Odom, William E.
The collapse of the Soviet military/ William E. Odom. New Haven, CT: Yale University Press, c1998. xiii, 523 p.
98-017588   355/.00947   0300074697
Soviet Union -- History, Military.

DK61 History — General special — Political history

DK61.G74 1994
Green, Barbara B.
The dynamics of Russian politics: a short history/ Barbara B. Green. Westport, Conn.: Greenwoood Press, 1994. viii, 236 p.
93-028042   947   0313288860
Communism -- Soviet Union.   Soviet Union -- Politics and government. Russia -- Politics and government.

DK63.3-69 History — General special — Foreign and general relations

DK63.3.D32
Dallin, Alexander.
Soviet conduct in world affairs; a selection of readings. New York, Columbia University Press, 1960. 318 p.
59-015509   327.47
Soviet Union -- Foreign relations -- 1917-1945. Soviet Union -- Foreign relations -- 1945-1991.

DK63.3.D33
Dallin, David J., 1889-1962.
Soviet foreign policy after Stalin.   Philadelphia, Lippincott, 1961 [c1960] xii, 543 p.
60-014257   327.47
Soviet Union -- Foreign relations -- 1953-1975.

DK63.3.K38
Kennan, George Frost, 1904-
Russia and the West under Lenin and Stalin. Boston, Little, Brown [1961] 411 p.
61-009292   327.47
Soviet Union -- Foreign relations -- 1917-1945.

DK63.3.S368
Shulman, Marshall Darrow.
Stalin's foreign policy reappraised.   Cambridge, Harvard University Press, 1963. vi, 320 p.
63-013816   327.47
Soviet Union -- Foreign relations -- 1945-1991.

DK66.J4 1974
Jelavich, Barbara, 1923-
St. Petersburg and Moscow: tsarist and Soviet foreign policy, 1814-1974 [by] Barbara Jelavich. Bloomington, Indiana University Press [1974] xii, 480 p.
73-016537   327.47   0253350506
Soviet Union -- Foreign relations -- History.

DK67.4.J4
Jelavich, Charles.
Tsarist Russia and Balkan nationalism; Russian influence in the internal affairs of Bulgaria and Serbia, 1879-1886.   Berkeley, University of California Press, 1958. x, 304 p.
58-012830
Soviet Union -- Foreign relations -- Bulgaria. Soviet Union -- Foreign relations -- Serbia. Serbia -- Foreign relations -- Soviet Union.

DK67.5.G3.L25 1991
Laird, Robbin F. 1946-
The Soviets, Germany, and the new Europe/ Robbin F. Laird. Boulder: Westview Press, 1991. 212 p.
91-024783   327.47043   0813380480
Soviet Union -- Foreign relations -- Germany. Germany -- Foreign relations -- Soviet Union. Soviet Union -- Foreign relations -- 1985-1991.

DK67.5.G3.S77 1999
Stent, Angela.
Russia and Germany reborn: unification, the Soviet collapse, and the new Europe/ Angela E. Stent. Princeton, NJ: Princeton University Press, c1999. xviii, 300 p.
98-003532   327.47043   0691059659
National security -- Europe. World politics -- 1989- Russia (Federation) -- Foreign relations -- Germany. Germany -- Foreign relations -- Russia (Federation) Germany -- History -- Unification, 1990.

DK67.5.R6.V47 1992
Verona, Sergiu.
Military occupation and diplomacy: Soviet troops in Romania, 1944-1958/ Sergiu Verona; foreword by J.F. Brown. Durham: Duke University Press, 1992. xii, 211 p.
91-026601 327.470498 0822311712
Soviet Union -- Foreign relations -- Romania. Romania -- Foreign relations -- Soviet Union. Soviet Union -- Armed Forces -- Romania.

DK67.5 .U38
Szporluk, Roman.
Russia, Ukraine, and the breakup of the Soviet Union/ Roman Szporluk. Stanford, CA: Hoover Institution Press, 2000. xlix, 437 p.
99-050309 947.085/4 0817995420
Nationalism -- Russia (Federation) Nationalism - - Ukraine. Russia (Federation) -- Relations -- Ukraine. Ukraine -- Relations -- Russia (Federation) Ukraine -- History -- 1944-1991.

DK68.7.A6.S66 1989
The Soviet withdrawal from Afghanistan/ edited by Amin Saikal and William Maley. Cambridge; Cambridge University Press, 1989. 177 p.
89-031506 958.104/5 0521375886
Soviet Union -- Foreign relations -- Afghanistan. Afghanistan -- Foreign relations -- Soviet Union. Soviet Union -- Foreign relations -- 1985-1991.

DK68.7.C5.B75 1998
Brothers in arms: the rise and fall of the Sino-Soviet alliance, 1945-1963/ edited by Odd Arne Westad. Washington, D. C.: Woodrow Wilson Center Press: 1998. p. cm.
98-042422 327.51047 0804734844
Soviet Union -- Foreign relations -- China. China -- Foreign relations -- Soviet Union.

DK68.7.C5.D58 1992
Dittmer, Lowell.
Sino-Soviet normalization and its international implications, 1945-1990/ Lowell Dittmer. Seattle: University of Washington Press, c1992. viii, 373 p.
91-015770 327.47051 0295971185
Soviet Union -- Foreign relations -- China. China -- Foreign relations -- Soviet Union. Soviet Union -- Foreign relations -- 1945-1991.

DK68.7.G28.G88 2000
Gvosdev, Nikolas K., 1969-
Imperial policies and perspectives towards Georgia, 1760-1819/ Nikolas K. Gvosdev. Houndmills, Basingstoke, Hampshire [England]: Macmillan Press; 2000. xxi, 197 p.
99-048655 327.4704758 0333748433
Potemkin, Grigorii Aleksandrovich, -- kniaz, -- 1739-1791. TSitsianov, Pavel Dmitrievich, -- kniaz, -- 1754-1806. Russia -- Foreign relations -- 1689-1801. Russia -- Foreign relations -- 1801-1825. Georgia (Republic) -- Foreign relations -- To 1801.

DK68.7.G3.C69 1996
Cox, David, 1956-
Retreating from the cold war: Germany, Russia, and the withdrawal of the Western Group of Forces/ David Cox. Washington Square, New York: New York University Press, 1996. xiii, 185 p.
95-039395 327.47043/09/048 0814715281
Germany -- Military relations -- Soviet Union. Soviet Union -- Military relations -- Germany. Soviet Union -- History -- 1985-1991.

DK68.7.I7.R44 1995
Regional power rivalries in the new Eurasia: Russia, Turkey, and Iran/ edited by Alvin Z. Rubinstein and Oles M. Smolansky. Armonk N.Y.: M.E. Sharpe, c1995. xii, 290 p.
95-006805 303.48/247055 1563246228
Former Soviet republics -- Relations -- Iran. Iran -- Relations -- Former Soviet republics. Former Soviet republics -- Relations -- Turkey.

DK68.7.I7.S56 1991
Smolansky, Oles M.
The USSR and Iraq: the Soviet quest for influence/ Oles M. Smolansky with Bettie M. Smolansky. Durham, NC: Duke University Press, c1991. xi, 346 p.
90-048597 327.470567 082231116X
Iraq -- Foreign relations -- Soviet Union. Soviet Union -- Foreign relations -- Iraq. Soviet Union -- Foreign relations -- 1953-1975. Soviet Union -- Foreign relations -- 1975-1985.

DK68.7.J3 K56 2000
Kimura, Hiroshi, 1936-
Japanese-Russian relations under Brezhnev and Andropov/ Hiroshi Kimura. Armonk, N.Y.: M.E. Sharpe, c2000. xxi, 335 p.
99-086081 327.52047/09/047 0765605856
National security -- Soviet Union. National security -- Japan. Soviet Union -- Foreign relations -- 1945-1991. Japan -- Foreign relations -- 1945-1989. Soviet Union -- Foreign relations -- Japan.

DK68.7.T9.R83 1982
Rubinstein, Alvin Z.
Soviet policy toward Turkey, Iran, and Afghanistan: the dynamics of influence/ Alvin Z. Rubinstein. New York, N.Y.: Praeger, 1982. xiii, 200 p.
82-007513 327.4705 0030525063
Soviet Union -- Foreign relations -- Turkey. Turkey -- Foreign relations -- Soviet Union. Soviet Union -- Foreign relations -- Iran.

DK69.B3
Barghoorn, Frederick Charles, 1911-
The Soviet image of the United States; a study in distortion. New York, Harcourt, Brace [1950] xviii, 297 p.
50-010897 327.470973
Propaganda, Russian. Public opinion -- Soviet Union. Soviet Union -- Foreign relations -- United States. United States -- Foreign relations -- Soviet Union.

DK72-111 History — By period — Early to 1613

DK72.V4
Vernadsky, George, 1887-1973.
The origins of Russia. Oxford, Clarendon Press, 1959. x, 354 p.
59-001228 947.01
Russia -- History -- To 1533.

DK90.H28 1985
Halperin, Charles J.
Russia and the Golden Horde: the Mongol impact on medieval Russian history/ Charles J. Halperin. Bloomington: Indiana University Press, c1985. ix, 180 p.
84-048254 947/.03 0253350336
Golden Horde. Russia -- History -- 1237-1480.

DK90.O86 1998
Ostrowski, Donald G.
Muscovy and the Mongols: cross-cultural influences on the steppe frontier, 1304-1589/ Donald Ostrowski. Cambridge; Cambridge University Press, 1998. xvi, 329 p.
97-021385 947/.03 052159085X
Mongols -- Russia. Russia -- History -- 1237-1480. Russia -- History -- Period of Consolidation, 1462-1605. Russia -- Foreign influences.

DK106.G7 1968
Graham, Stephen, 1884-
Ivan the Terrible; life of Ivan IV of Russia. [Hamden, Conn.] Archon Books, 1968. x, 335 p.
68-008020 947/.04/0924 0208006834
Ivan -- IV, -- the Terrible, Czar of Russia, -- 1530-1584. Russia -- History -- Ivan IV, 1533-1584.

DK106.P5513
Platonov, S. F. 1860-1933.
Ivan the Terrible [by] S. F. Platonov. Edited and translated by Joseph L. Wieczynski. With In search of Ivan the Terrible, by Richard Hellie. [Gulf Breeze, Fla.] Academic International Press, 1974. xxxviii, 166 p.
77-176468 947/.04/0924 0875690548
Ivan -- IV, -- the Terrible, Czar of Russia, -- 1530-1584. Russia -- History -- Ivan IV, 1533-1584.

DK109.P513
Platonov, S. F. 1860-1933.
Boris Godunov, Tsar of Russia. Translated from the Russian by L. Rex Pyles. With an introductory essay S. F. Platonov: Eminence and obscurity, by John T. Alexander. [Gulf Breeze, Fla.] Academic International Press, 1973. xlii, 230 p.
73-176467 947/.04/0924 0875690246
Boris Fyodorovich Godunov, -- Czar of Russia -- 1551 or 2-1605. Russia -- History -- Boris Fyodorovich Godunov, 1598-1605.

DK111.D86 2001
Dunning, Chester S. L., 1949-
Russia's first civil war: the Time of Troubles and the founding of the Romanov dynasty/ Chester S.L. Dunning. University Park, Penn.: Pennsylvania State University Press, 2001. xiii, 657 p.
00-028817 947/.045 0271020741
Russia -- History -- Time of Troubles, 1598-1613.

DK113.2-264.8 History — By period — House of Romanov, 1613-1917

DK113.2.D84
Dukes, Paul, 1934-
The making of Russian absolutism, 1613-1801/ Paul Dukes. London; Longman, 1982. 197 p.
81-008333 947 058248684X
Russia -- Politics and government -- 1613-1689. Russia -- Politics and government -- 1689-1801.

DK114.K573
Kliuchevskii, V. O. 1841-1911.
A course in Russian history: the seventeenth century, by V. O. Kliuchevsky. Translated from the Russian by Natalie Duddington. Introd. by Alfred J. Rieber. Chicago, Quadrangle Books [1968] xl, 400 p.
68-026442 947/.04
Russia -- History -- Time of Troubles, 1598-1613. Russia -- History -- 1613-1689.

DK118.L66 1984
Longworth, Philip, 1933-
Alexis, tsar of all the Russias/ Philip Longworth.
New York: F. Watts, 1984. xiii, 305 p.
84-050633   947/.048/0924   0531097706
Aleksei Mikhailovich, -- Czar of Russia, -- 1629-
1676.   Russia -- Kings and rulers -- Biography.

DK127.L43 1991
LeDonne, John P., 1935-
Absolutism and ruling class: the formation of the
Russian political order, 1700-1825/ John P.
LeDonne. New York: Oxford University Press,
1991. xvii, 376 p.
90-020057   306.2/0947   019506805X
Despotism. Political leadership -- Russia --
History -- 18th century. Political leadership --
Russia -- History -- 19th century. Russia -- Politics
and government -- 1801-1825. Russia -- Politics
and government -- 1689-1801.

DK131.H84 1998
Hughes, Lindsey, 1949-
Russia in the age of Peter the Great/ Lindsey
Hughes. New Haven, Conn.: Yale University Press,
c1998. xxix, 602 p.
98-018667   947/.05   0300075391
Peter -- I, -- Emperor of Russia, -- 1672-1725.
Russia -- History -- Peter I, 1689-1725.

DK131.K553
Kliuchevskii, Vasilii Osipovich.
Peter the Great. St. Martin's Pr., 1958.
59-001544   923.147
Russia -- History -- 1672-1725, Peter 1st. Peter
the Great, Emperor of Russia, 1st. Soviet Union --
Civilization.

DK131.M28
Massie, Robert K., 1929-
Peter the Great, his life and world/ Robert K.
Massie. New York: Knopf, 1980. xii, 909 p.
80-007635   947.05/092/4   0394500326
Peter -- I, -- Emperor of Russia, -- 1672-1725.
Russia -- History -- Peter I, 1689-1725. Russia --
Kings and rulers -- Biography.

DK132.R53 1985
Riasanovsky, Nicholas Valentine, 1923-
The image of Peter the Great in Russian history
and thought/ Nicholas V. Riasanovsky. New York:
Oxford University Press, 1985. ix, 331 p.
83-025157   947/.05/0924   0195034562
Peter -- I, -- Emperor of Russia, -- 1672-1725 --
Influence. Peter -- I, -- Emperor of Russia, -- 1672-
1725 -- In literature. Peter -- I, -- Emperor of
Russia, -- 1672-1725 -- Psychology.   Russia --
Intellectual life.

DK170.A58 1989
Alexander, John T.
Catherine the Great: life and legend/ John T.
Alexander. New York: Oxford University Press,
1989. xii, 418 p.
88-010122   947/.063/0924   0195052366
Catherine -- II, -- Empress of Russia, -- 1729-1796.
Russia -- Kings and rulers -- Biography. Russia --
History -- Catherine II, 1762-1796.

DK171.D44 1990
De Madariaga, Isabel, 1919-
Catherine the Great: a short history/ Isabel De
Madariaga. New Haven: Yale University Press,
1990. viii, 240 p.
90-043666   947/.063/092   0300048459
Catherine -- II, -- Empress of Russia, -- 1729-1796.
Russia -- History -- Catherine II, 1729-1796.

DK171.D45
De Madariaga, Isabel, 1919-
Russia in the age of Catherine the Great/ Isabel de
Madariaga. New Haven: Yale University Press,
c1981. xii, 698 p.
80-021993   947/.063   0300025157
Catherine -- II, -- Empress of Russia, -- 1729-1796.
Russia -- History -- Catherine II, 1729-1796.

DK186.2.R34 1988
Ragsdale, Hugh.
Tsar Paul and the question of madness: an essay in
history and psychology/ Hugh Ragsdale. New
York: Greenwood Press, 1988. xviii, 266 p.
88-024677   947/.071/0924   0313266085
Paul -- I, -- Emperor of Russia, -- 1754-1801 --
Mental health.   Russia -- Kings and rulers --
Biography. Russia -- History -- Paul I, 1796-1801.

DK189.C66 1976
Crankshaw, Edward.
The shadow of the winter palace: Russia's drift to
revolution, 1825-1917/ Edward Crankshaw. New
York: Viking Press, 1976. 429 p.
76-010636   947/.07   0670637823
Romanov, House of.   Russia -- History --
Nicholas II, 1894-1917. Russia -- History -- 1801-
1917.

DK189.K7 1970
Kornilov, A. A. 1862-1925.
Modern Russian history; from the age of Catherine
the Great to the end of the nineteenth century,
Translated from the Russian by Alexander S. Kaun.
With a bibliography by John S. Curtiss. New York,
Russell & Russell [1970, c1944] 310 p.
74-102513   947/.07
Russia -- History -- 1801-1917. Russia --
History -- Catherine II, 1762-1796.

DK189.M68 1992
Mosse, Werner Eugen.
Perestroika under the tsars/ W.E. Mosse. London;
I.B. Tauris & Co.: 1992. xii, 298 p.
91-068023   1850435197
Perestroika.   Soviet Union -- Politics and
government -- 1801-1917.

DK189.P813
Pushkarev, S. G. b. 1888.
The emergence of modern Russia, 1801-1917.
Translated by Robert H. McNeal and Tova Yedlin.
New York, Holt, Rinehart and Winston [1963]
512 p.
63-008819   947.07
Soviet Union -- History -- 1801-1917. Russia --
History -- 1904-1914.

DK189 .S44 1988
Seton-Watson, Hugh.
The Russian empire, 1801-1917/ by Hugh Seton-
Watson. Oxford [England]: Clarendon Press; xx,
813 p.
87-031165   947.08 19   0198221525
Russia -- History -- 1801-1917. Russia -- History --
Nicholas II, 1894-1917.

DK189.V413
Venturi, Franco.
Roots of revolution; a history of the populist and
socialist movements in nineteenth century Russia.
Translated from the Italian by Francis Haskell.
New York, Alfred A. Knopf, [c1960] xxxvi, 850 p.
59-005423   947.08
Populism -- Soviet Union.

DK189.2.B4613 1979
Berdiaev, Nikolai, 1874-1948.
The Russian idea/ Nicolas Berdyaev. Westport,
Conn.: Greenwood Press, 1979. 255 p.
78-032021   947/.07   0313209685
Soviet Union -- Intellectual life -- 1801-1917.

DK189.2.K45 1998
Kelly, Aileen.
Toward another shore: Russian thinkers between
necessity and chance/ Aileen M. Kelly. New
Haven, Conn.: Yale University Press, c1998.
400 p.
97-047188   947
Intellectuals -- Russia. Intellectuals -- Soviet
Union.   Russia -- Intellectual life -- 1801-1917.
Soviet Union -- Intellectual life.

DK189.2.R87 1996
Russia--women--culture/ edited by Helena Goscilo
and Beth Holmgren. Bloomington: Indiana
University Press, c1996. xiv, 386 p.
95-038295   947/.07   025333019X
Women -- Russia. Women -- Soviet Union.
Russia -- Civilization -- 1801-1917. Soviet Union --
Civilization.

DK189.2.S45 2000
Self and story in Russian history/ edited by Laura
Engelstein and Stephanie Sandler. Ithaca: Cornell
University Press, c2000. ix, 363 p.
00-008839   947/.07   0801437911
Russia -- Intellectual life -- 1801-1917.

DK191.P348
Palmer, Alan Warwick.
Alexander I: Tsar of war and peace [by] Alan
Palmer. New York, Harper & Row [1974] xviii,
487 p.
74-001844   947/.07/0924   0060132647
Alexander -- I, -- Emperor of Russia, -- 1777-1825.
Russia -- History -- Alexander I, 1801-1825.

DK194.M3 1997
Martin, Alexander M.
Romantics, reformers, reactionaries: Russian
conservative thought and politics in the reign of
Alexander I/ Alexander M. Martin. DeKalb, Ill.:
Northern Illinois University Press, 1997. x, 294 p.
96-053558   947/.072   0875802265
Conservatism -- Russia -- History.   Russia --
History -- Alexander I, 1801-1825.

DK197.L6 1954
Lobanov-Rostovsky, Andrei, 1892-
Russia and Europe, 1825-1878/ by A. Lobanov-
Rostovsky. Ann Arbor, Mich.: G. Wahr Pub. Co.,
1954. 330 p.
55-001181   940.28
Russia -- Foreign relations -- 1801-1917.
Europe -- Politics and government -- 1789-1900.
Soviet Union -- Foreign relations -- Europe.

DK197.L6 1968
Lobanov-Rostovsky, Andrei, 1892-
Russia and Europe, 1789-1825, by Andrei A.
Lobanov-Rostovsky. New York, Greenwood Press,
1968 [c1947] xviii, 448 p.
68-030825   327.47
Russia -- Foreign relations -- 1801-1825.

DK209.6.H4.A32
Herzen, Aleksandr, 1812-1870.
The memoirs of Alexander Herzen, parts I and II,
translated from the Russian by J. D. Duff. New
Haven, Yale university press; [etc., etc.] 1923. xvi,
384 p.
23-013462   928.917

DK209.6.H4.A33
Herzen, Aleksandr, 1812-1870.
My past and thoughts, the memoirs of Alexander Herzen; the authorised translation; translated from the Russian by Constance Garnett. London, Chatto & Windus, 1924-27. 6 v.
24-017707

DK209.6.H4.M3
Malia, Martin E.
Alexander Herzen and the birth of Russian socialism, 1812-1855. Cambridge, Harvard University Press, 1961. ix, 486 p.
61-006425   335.0947
Herzen, Aleksandr, -- 1812-1870.   Socialism in Russia.

DK210.L56
Lincoln, W. Bruce.
Nicholas I, emperor and autocrat of all the Russias/ W. Bruce Lincoln. Bloomington: Indiana University Press, c1978. 424 p.
77-015764   947/.073/0924   0253340594
Nicholas -- I, -- Emperor of Russia, -- 1796-1855. Russia -- Kings and rulers -- Biography. Russia -- History -- Nicholas I, 1825-1855.

DK210.P713
Presniakov, A. E. 1870-1929.
Emperor Nicholas I of Russia, the apogee of autocracy, 1825-1855 [by] A.E. Presniakov. Edited and translated by Judith C. Zacek. With Nicholas I and the course of Russian history, by Nicholas V. Riasanovsky. [Gulf Breeze, Fla.] Academic International Press, 1974. xl, 102 p.
74-176053   320.9/47/07   087569053X
Nicholas -- I, -- Emperor of Russia, -- 1796-1855. Russia -- History -- Nicholas I, 1825-1855.

DK210.R5
Riasanovsky, Nicholas Valentine, 1923-
Nicholas I and official nationality in Russia, 1825-1855/ Nicholas V. Riasanovsky. Berkeley: University of California Press, c1959. viii, 296 p.
59-011316   947.07
Nicholas -- I, -- Emperor of Russia, -- 1796-1855. Nationalism -- Soviet Union.

DK214.E34 1999
Edgerton, Robert B., 1931-
Death or glory: the legacy of the Crimean War/ Robert B. Edgerton. Boulder, CO: Westview Press, 1999. ix, 288 p.
98-052878   947/.0738   0813335701
Crimean War, 1853-1856.

DK215.H27 1999
Harris, Stephen M., 1965-
British military intelligence in the Crimean War, 1854-1856/ Stephen M. Harris. London; Frank Cass, 1999. xxiv, 182 p.
98-035867   947/.07388   0714646717
Crimean War, 1853-1856 -- Military intelligence -- Great Britain. Military intelligence -- Great Britain -- History -- 19th century.

DK215.R53 1985
Rich, Norman.
Why the Crimean War?: a cautionary tale/ Norman Rich. Hanover [N.H.]: Published for Brown University by University Press 1985. xix, 258 p.
84-040593   947/.073   0874513286
Crimean War, 1853-1856 -- Diplomatic history. Crimean War, 1853-1856 -- Causes.

DK219.3.H55 2000
Hillyar, Anna, 1957-
Revolutionary women in Russia, 1870-1917: a study in collective biography/ Anna Hillyar and Jane McDermid. Manchester: Manchester University Press: 2000. 232 p.
00-020182   947.08   0719048370
Women revolutionaries -- Soviet Union -- Biography. Radicalism -- Russia -- History -- 19th century. Radicalism -- Russia -- History -- 20th century. Russia -- History -- 1801-1917.

DK219.3.L3
Lampert, Evgenii, 1913-
Sons against fathers; studies in Russian radicalism and revolution [by] E. Lampert. Oxford, Clarendon Press, 1965. vi, 405 p.
65-002412
Dobroliubov, N. A. -- (Nikolai Aleksandrovich), -- 1836-1861. Pisarev, D. I. -- (Dmitrii Ivanovich), -- 1840-1868. Chernyshevsky, Nikolay Gavrilovich, -- 1828-1889. Revolutions -- Soviet Union.

DK220.B48 1991
Between tsar and people: educated society and the quest for public identity in late imperial Russia/ edited by Edith W. Clowes, Samuel D. Kassow, and James L. West. Princeton, N.J.: Princeton University Press, c1991. ix, 383 p.
90-009079   947.08/1   0691031533
Intellectuals -- Russia -- History -- 19th century. Middle class -- Russia -- History -- 19th century. Russia -- History -- Nicholas II, 1894-1917. Russia -- History -- Alexander II, 1855-1881. Russia -- History -- Alexander III, 1881-1894.

DK220.L56 1990
Lincoln, W. Bruce.
The great reforms: autocracy, bureaucracy, and the politics of change in Imperial Russia/ W. Bruce Lincoln. DeKalb, Ill.: Northern Illinois University Press, 1990. xxi, 281 p.
90-007186   947.08   0875801552
Russia -- Politics and government -- 1855-1881. Russia -- Politics and government -- 1881-1894. Russia -- Politics and government -- 1894-1917.

DK220.M6 1992
Mosse, Werner Eugen.
Alexander II and the modernization of Russia/ W.E. Mosse. London; I.B. Tauris & Co.: 1992. 191 p.
91-068022   947.08/1/092   1850435138
Alexander -- II, -- Emperor of Russia, -- 1818-1881. Russia -- Kings and rulers -- Biography. Russia -- History -- Alexander II, 1855-1881.

DK221.U38 1977
Ulam, Adam Bruno, 1922-
In the name of the people: prophets and conspirators in prerevolutionary Russia/ Adam B. Ulam. New York: Viking Press, 1977. xii, 418 p.
76-042221   947.08   0670396915
Revolutionaries -- Russia -- Biography. Russia -- Intellectual life -- 1801-1917. Russia -- Politics and government -- 1855-1881.

DK221.Z313
Zaionchkovskii, Petr Andreevich.
The Russian autocracy in crisis, 1878-1882/ Peter A. Zaionchkovsky; edited, translated, and with a new introd. by Gary M. Hamburg. Gulf Breeze, FL: Academic International Press, 1979. xiii, 375 p.
79-110846   320.9/47/08   0875690319
Russia -- Politics and government -- 1855-1881.

DK223.S4
Seton-Watson, Hugh.
The decline of imperial Russia, 1855-1914. With 8 maps. New York, F. A. Praeger [1952] 406 p.
52-007488   947.08
Russia -- History -- 1801-1917.

DK240.L56 1983
Lincoln, W. Bruce.
In war's dark shadow: the Russians before the Great War/ W. Bruce Lincoln. New York: Dial Press, c1983. xvi, 557 p.
82-022152   947.08   0385274092
Russia -- History -- Alexander III, 1881-1894. Russia -- History -- Nicholas II, 1894-1917. Soviet Union -- History -- Revolution, 1917-1921 -- Causes.

DK241.R63 1983
Rogger, Hans.
Russia in the age of modernisation and revolution, 1881-1917/ Hans Rogger. London; Longman, 1983. viii, 323 p.
83-000714   947.08/2   0582489113
Russia -- History -- Alexander III, 1881-1894. Russia -- History -- Nicholas II, 1894-1917. Soviet Union -- History -- Revolution, 1917-1921 -- Causes.

DK246.K64 1985
Kort, Michael, 1944-
The Soviet colossus: a history of the USSR/ Michael Kort. New York: Scribner, c1985. xiii, 318 p.
84-020253   947/.08   0684181789
Soviet Union -- History. Russia -- History -- Nicholas II, 1894-1917.

DK246.T65 1981
Treadgold, Donald W., 1922-
Twentieth century Russia/ Donald W. Treadgold. Boston: Houghton Mifflin, c1981. xiii, 555 p.
80-050983   947.084   0395307589
Soviet Union -- History -- 20th century.

DK246.U4
Ulam, Adam Bruno, 1922-
The Bolsheviks; the intellectual and political history of the triumph of communism in Russia [by] Adam B. Ulam. New York, Macmillan [1965] ix, 598 p.
65-018463   335.430947
Lenin, Vladimir Ilich, -- 1870-1924.   Communism -- Soviet Union -- History.

DK246 .V58 1993
Von Laue, Theodore H.
Why Lenin? Why Stalin? Why Gorbachev?: the rise and fall of the Soviet system/ Theodore H. Von Laue. 3rd ed. New York, NY: HarperCollins College Publishers, c1993. xii, 194 p.
92-015870   947.084 20   0065011112
Soviet Union -- History -- 20th century. Soviet Union -- Politics and government -- 1985-1991.

DK253.L54 1989
Lieven, D. C. B.
Russia's rulers under the old regime/ Dominic Lieven. New Haven: Yale University Press, 1989. xxii, 407 p.
88-038155   947.08/092/2   0300043716
Nicholas -- II, -- Emperor of Russia, -- 1868-1918 -- Friends and associates. Nobility -- Russia -- History -- 19th century. Elite (Social sciences) -- Russia. Russia -- Politics and government -- 1894-1917. Russia -- Kings and rulers -- Biography.

DK254.A5.A3 1997
Alexandra, 1872-1918.
The last diary of Tsaritsa Alexandra/ introduction by Robert K. Massie; edited by Vladimir A. Kozlov and Vladimir M. Khrustalev; notes edited by Alexandra Raskina; notes, chronology, glossary, and afterword translated by Laura E. Wolfson; preparation of the diary, notes, and appendixes New Haven: Yale University Press, c1997. lx, 222 p.
97-015675   947.08/3/092   0300072120
Alexandra, -- Empress, consort of Nicholas II, Emperor of Russia, -- 1872-1918 -- Diaries. Alexandra, -- Empress, consort of Nicholas II, Emperor of Russia, -- 1872-1918 -- Last years. Empresses -- Russia -- Diaries. Russia -- History -- Nicholas II, 1894-1917. Soviet Union -- History -- Revolution, 1917-1921.

DK254.C57.O36 1988
O'Connor, Timothy Edward.
Diplomacy and revolution: G.V. Chicherin and Soviet foreign affairs, 1918-1930/ Timothy Edward O'Connor. Ames: Iowa State University Press, 1988. xx, 250 p.
87-016785   327.47/0092/4   0813803675
Chicherin, Georgii Vasilevich, -- 1872-1936. Diplomats -- Soviet Union -- Biography. Soviet Union -- Foreign relations -- 1917-1945.

DK254.K52.C66 1989
Conquest, Robert.
Stalin and the Kirov murder/ Robert Conquest. New York: Oxford University Press, 1989. xiv, 164 p.
88-011994   947.084/2/0924   0195055799
Kirov, Sergei Mironovich, -- 1886-1934 -- Assassination. Stalin, Joseph, -- 1879-1953. Terrorism -- Soviet Union. Soviet Union -- Politics and government -- 1917-1936.

DK254.L3.A254 1973
Lenin, Vladimir Ilich, 1870-1924.
The essentials of Lenin. Westport, Conn., Hyperion Press [1973] 2 v.
73-000847   335.43/092/4   0883550431
Socialism. Soviet Union -- Politics and government -- 1917-1936.

DK254.L4.F53
Fischer, Louis, 1896-1970.
The life of Lenin. New York, Harper & Row [1964] viii, 703 p.
64-014385   923.247
Lenin, Vladimir Ilich, -- 1870-1924.

DK254.L4.S4323 2000
Service, Robert.
Lenin--a biography/ Robert Service. Cambridge, MA: Harvard University Press, 2000. xxv, 561 p.
00-021394   947.084/1/092   0674003306
Lenin, Vladimir Ilich, -- 1870-1924. Heads of state -- Soviet Union -- Biography. Revolutionaries -- Russia -- Biography. Russia -- Politics and government -- 1894-1917. Soviet Union -- Politics and government -- 1917-1936.

DK254.L4.S4324 1985
Service, Robert.
Lenin, a political life/ Robert Service. Bloomington: Indiana University Press, c1985-c1995. 3 v.
84-043044   947.084/1/0924   0253333245
Lenin, Vladimir Ilich, -- 1870-1924. Heads of state -- Soviet Union -- Biography. Revolutionaries -- Russia -- Biography. Russia -- Politics and government -- 1894-1917. Soviet Union -- Politics and government -- 1917-1936.

DK254.L4.S75 1942
Stalin, Joseph, 1879-1953.
Leninism; selected writings by Joseph Stalin. New York, International Publishers [1942] 479 p.
42-024314   947.084
Lenin, Vladimir Ilich, -- 1870-1924. Communism -- Soviet Union. Proletariat. Soviet Union -- Politics and government -- 1917-1936.

DK254.L4.T7 1971
Trotsky, Leon, 1879-1940.
Lenin; notes for a biographer [by] Leon Trotsky. With an introd. by Bertram D. Wolfe. Translated from the Russian and annotated by Tamara Deutscher. New York, G. P. Putnam's Sons [c1971] 224 p.
75-136807   947.084/1/0924
Lenin, Vladimir Ilich, -- 1870-1924.

DK254.L4 V587 1994
Volkogonov, Dmitriæi Antonovich.
Lenin: a new biography/ Dmitri Volkogonov; translated and edited by Harold Shukman. New York: Free Press, c1994. xxxix, 529 p.
94-031752   947.084/1/092.B 20   0029334357
Lenin, Vladimir Il§ich, 1870-1924. Soviet Union -- History -- 1917-1936. Heads of state--Soviet Union--Biography.

DK254.L4.W6 1964
Wolfe, Bertram David, 1896-1977.
Three who made a revolution; a biographical history. New York, Dial Press, 1964. viii, 659 p.
64-003227   947.08
Lenin, Vladimir Ilich, -- 1870-1924. Trotsky, Leon, -- 1879-1940. Stalin, Joseph, -- 1879-1953.

DK254.L46.T85 1983
Tumarkin, Nina.
Lenin lives!: the Lenin cult in Soviet Russia/ Nina Tumarkin. Cambridge, Mass.: Harvard University Press, 1983. xiii, 315 p.
82-015665   947.084/1/092   0674524306
Lenin, Vladimir Ilich, -- 1870-1924 -- Influence. Statesmen -- Soviet Union -- Biography. Soviet Union -- History.

DK254.M52.S76 1996
Stockdale, Melissa Kirschke.
Paul Miliukov and the quest for a liberal Russia, 1880-1918/ Melissa Kirschke Stockdale. Ithaca, [N.Y.]: Cornell University Press, 1996. xix, 379 p.
96-027319   947.08/3/092   0801432480
Miliukov, P. N. -- (Pavel Nikolaevich), -- 1859-1943. Statesmen -- Russia -- Biography. Historians -- Russia -- Biography. Russia -- Politics and government -- 1894-1917.

DK254.R3.M69 1997
Moynahan, Brian, 1941-
Rasputin: the saint who sinned/ Brian Moynahan. New York: Random House, c1997. xii, 400 p.
97-005025   947.08/3/092   0679419306
Rasputin, Grigori Efimovich, -- ca. 1870-1916. Russia -- Court and courtiers -- Biography. Russia -- History -- Nicholas II, 1894-1917.

DK254.S595
Ascher, Abraham, 1928-
P.A. Stolypin: the search for stability in late Imperial Russia/ Abraham Ascher. Stanford, CA: Stanford University Press, 2001. xii, 468 p.
00-063520   947.08/3/092   0804739773
Stolypin, Petr Arkadevich, -- 1862-1911. Statesmen -- Russia -- Biography. Russia -- Politics and government -- 1904-1914.

DK254.S595.W35 1998
Waldron, Peter.
Between two revolutions: Stolypin and the politics of renewal in Russia/ Peter Waldron. Dekalb: Northern Illinois University Press, c1998. viii, 220 p.
97-040255   947.08/3/092   0875802354
Stolypin, Petr Arkadevich, -- 1862-1911. Statesmen -- Russia -- Biography. Russia -- Politics and government -- 1904-1914.

DK254.S597.P5
Pipes, Richard.
Struve, liberal on the left, 1870-1905. Cambridge, Mass., Harvard University Press, 1970. xiii, 415 p.
77-131463   947.08   0674845951
Struve, Petr Berngardovich, -- 1870-1944.

DK254.S597 P52
Pipes, Richard.
Struve, liberal on the right, 1905-1944/ Richard Pipes. Cambridge: Harvard University Press, 1980. xix, 526 p.
79-016145   947.08   0674846001
Struve, Petr Berngardovich, 1870-1944. Intellectuals--Soviet Union--Biography. Politicians--Soviet Union--Biography. Economists--Soviet Union--Biography.

DK254.T6.A25 1963
Trotsky, Leon, 1879-1940.
Basic writings. Edited and introduced by Irving Howe. New York, Random House [c1963] 427 p.
63-016157
Communism. Soviet Union -- Politics and government.

DK254.T6.A48
Trotsky, Leon, 1879-1940.
My life: an attempt at an autobiography.   C. Scribner's sons, 1930. 599 p.
30-012073
Trotsky, Leon, -- 1879-1940. Russia -- Politics and government -- 1894-1917. Soviet Union -- Politics and government -- 1917-1936.

DK254.T6.D4
Deutscher, Isaac, 1907-1967.
The prophet armed: Trotsky, 1879-1921. New York, Oxford University Press, 1954. viii, 540 p.
54-005291   947.083*
Trotsky, Leon, -- 1879-1940.

DK254.T6.D415
Deutscher, Isaac, 1907-1967.
The prophet outcast: Trotsky, 1929-1940. London, Oxford University Press, 1963. xv, 543 p.
63-024133   923.247
Trotsky, Leon, -- 1879-1940.

DK254.T6.D42
Deutscher, Isaac, 1907-
The prophet unarmed: Trotsky, 1921-1929. London, Oxford University Press, 1959. 490 p.
59-003695   923.247
Trotsky, Leon, -- 1879-1940.

DK254.T6.T49 2000
Thatcher, Ian D.
Leon Trotsky and World War One: August 1914-February 1917/ Ian D. Thatcher. Houndsmills: Macmillan Press Ltd.; 2000. vii, 262 p.
00-027151   947.084/092   0312234872
Trotsky, Leon, -- 1879-1940 -- Views on World War, 1914-1918. Trotsky, Leon, -- 1879-1940 -- Contributions in literature. World War, 1914-1918 -- Press coverage -- Russia.

DK254.T6.V6513 1996
Volkogonov, Dmitrii Antonovich.
Trotsky: the eternal revolutionary/ Dmitri Volkogonov; translated and edited by Harold Shukman. New York: The Free Press, c1996. xxxvi, 524 p.
95-042315 947.084/092 0684822938
Trotsky, Leon, -- 1879-1940. Revolutionaries -- Soviet Union -- Biography. Soviet Union -- Politics and government -- 1917-1936.

DK255 .V4413 1994
Vekhi = Landmarks: a collection of articles about the Russian intelligentsia/ Nikolai Berdiaev ... et al.; translated and edited by Marshall S. Shatz and Judith E. Zimmerman; with a foreword by Marc Raeff. Armonk, NY: M.E. Sharpe, c1994. xxxviii, 187 p.
94-026039 001.1/0947 20 1563243911
Russia -- Intellectual life -- 1801-1917. Intellectuals--Russia.

DK258.C3713 2000
Carrere d'Encausse, Helene.
Nicholas II: the interrupted transition/ Helene Carrere d'Encausse; translated by George Holoch.. New York: Holmes & Meier Publishers, c2000. xiii, 321 p.
99-048898 947.08/3/092 0841913978
Nicholas -- II, -- Emperor of Russia, -- 1868-1918. Russia -- Kings and rulers -- Biography. Russia -- History -- Nicholas II, 1894-1917.

DK258.L46 1994
Lieven, D. C. B.
Nicholas II: twilight of the Empire/ Dominic Lieven. 1st U.S. ed. New York: St. Martin's Press, 1994. xii, 292 p.
93-037269 947.08/3/092. 220 031210510X
Nicholas II, Emperor of Russia, 1868-1918. Emperors--Russia--Biography.

DK258.N458 1999
Nicholas II, Emperor of Russia, 1868-1918 1868-1918.
The complete wartime correspondence of Tsar Nicholas II and the Empress Alexandra: April 1914-March 1917/ edited by Joseph T. Fuhrmann. Westport, Conn.: Greenwood Press, 1999. 773 p.
97-018193 947.08/3/092 0313305110
Nicholas -- II, -- Emperor of Russia, -- 1868-1918 -- Correspondence. Alexandra, -- Empress, consort of Nicholas II, Emperor of Russia, -- 1872-1918 -- Correspondence. Russia -- Kings and rulers -- Correspondence. Russia -- History -- Nicholas II, 1894-1917 -- Sources.

DK258.S74 1995
Steinberg, Mark D., 1953-
The fall of the Romanovs: political dreams and personal struggles in a time of revolution/ Mark D. Steinberg and Vladimir M. Khrustalev; Russian documents translated by Elizabeth Tucker. New Haven, CT: Yale University Press, c1995. xviii, 444 p.
95-000477 947.08/3/0922 0300065574
Nicholas -- II, -- Emperor of Russia, -- 1868-1918 -- Last years -- Sources. Alexandra, -- Empress, consort of Nicholas II, Emperor of Russia, -- 1872-1918 -- Last years -- Sources. Russia -- History -- Nicholas II, 1894-1917 -- Sources. Russia -- Kings and rulers -- Biography -- Sources. Soviet Union -- History -- Revolution, 1917-1921 -- Sources.

DK258.V44 1990
Verner, Andrew M., 1949-
The crisis of Russian autocracy: Nicholas II and the 1905 Revolution/ Andrew M. Verner. Princeton, N.J.: Princeton University Press, c1990. x, 372 p.
89-010710 947.08/3 0691047731
Nicholas -- II, -- Emperor of Russia, -- 1868-1918. Russia -- Kings and rulers -- Biography. Russia -- History -- Revolution, 1905-1907.

DK260.C37 1965
Charques, Richard Denis, 1899-
The twilight of Imperial Russia/ Richard Charques. London: Phoenix House, c1958, 1965 p 256 p.
60-000282
Russia -- History -- Nicholas II, 1894-1917.

DK260.F54 1997
Figes, Orlando.
A people's tragedy: the Russian Revolution, 1891-1924/ Orlando Figes. New York: Viking, 1997. p. cm.
96-036761 947.08/3 0670859168
Russia -- History -- Nicholas II, 1894-1917. Soviet Union -- History -- Revolution, 1917-1921. Soviet Union -- History -- 1917-1936.

DK262.L53 1986
Lincoln, W. Bruce.
Passage through Armageddon: the Russians in war and revolution, 1914-1918/ W. Bruce Lincoln. New York: Simon and Schuster, c1986. 637 p.
86-003696 947.08/3 0671557092
World War, 1914-1918 -- Russia. Russia -- History -- Nicholas II, 1894-1917. Soviet Union -- History -- Revolution, 1917-1921 -- Causes. Soviet Union -- History -- Revolution, 1917-1921.

DK262.O413
Oldenburg, S. S.
Last tsar: Nicholas II, his reign & his Russia/ S. S. Oldenburg; translated by Leonid I. Mihalap and Patrick J. Rollins; edited by Patrick J. Rollins; with Searching for the last tsar by Patrick J. Rollins. Gulf Breeze, Fla.: Academic International Press, 1975-1978. 4 v.
76-351188 947.08/092/4 0875690637
Nicholas -- II, -- Emperor of Russia, -- 1868-1918. Russia -- History -- Nicholas II, 1894-1917.

DK262.R87 1999
Russia under the last tsar: opposition and subversion, 1894-1917/ edited by Anna Geifman. Malden, MA: Blackwell Publishers, 1999. viii, 310 p.
99-011162 947.08/3 1557869944
Government, Resistance to -- Russia. Russia -- Politics and government -- 1894-1917.

DK263.A9 1988
Ascher, Abraham, 1928-
The Revolution of 1905/ Abraham Ascher. Stanford, Calif.: Stanford University Press, 1988-1992. 2 v.
87-026657 947.08/3 0804714363
Russia -- History -- Revolution, 1905-1907.

DK264.2.O3.W45 1993
Weinberg, Robert.
The revolution of 1905 in Odessa: blood on the steps/ Robert Weinberg. Bloomington: Indiana University Press, c1993. xvi, 302 p.
92-023096 947/.717 0253363810
Labor movement -- Ukraine -- Odesa -- History. Jews -- Persecutions -- Ukraine -- Odesa. Odesa (Ukraine) -- History. Ukraine -- History -- Revolution, 1905-1907. Odesa (Ukraine) -- Ethnic relations.

DK264.8.S5 1969
Smith, Clarence Jay.
The Russian struggle for power, 1914-1917; a study of Russian foreign policy during the First World War, by C. Jay Smith, Jr. New York, Greenwood Press [1969, c1956] xv, 553 p.
75-090709 327.47 0837122821
World War, 1914-1918 -- Russia. Russia -- Foreign relations -- 1894-1917.

DK265-265.9 History — By period — Revolution, 1917-1921

DK265.A135 1967aa
Revolutionary Russia [by] Oskar Anweiler [and others] Edited by Richard Pipes. Cambridge, Mass., Harvard University Press, 1968. x, 365 p.
68-015641 947.084/1
Soviet Union -- History -- Revolution, 1917-1921. Soviet Union -- History -- Congresses.

DK265.A553.A28 1990
Acton, Edward.
Rethinking the Russian Revolution/ Edward Acton. London; E. Arnold; 1990. 229 p.
90-000865 947.084/1/072 0713166096
Soviet Union -- History -- Revolution, 1917-1921 -- Historiography.

DK265.B54 1988
The Blackwell encyclopedia of the Russian Revolution/ edited by Harold Shukman. Oxford, UK; B. Blackwell, 1988. xiv, 418 p.
88-010360 947.084/1 0631152385
Soviet Union -- History -- Revolution, 1917-1921 -- Encyclopedias.

DK265.B633133 1997
The Bolsheviks in Russian society: the revolution and the civil wars/ edited by Vladimir N. Brovkin. New Haven, Conn.: Yale University Press, c1997. 333 p.
96-047127 947.084 0300067062
Soviet Union -- History -- Revolution, 1917-1921.

DK265.C43
Chamberlin, William Henry, 1897-1969.
The Russian revolution, 1917-1921, by William Henry Chamberlin . New York, The Macmillan company, 1935. 2 v.
35-007577
Soviet Union -- History -- Revolution, 1917-1921.

DK265.D27
Daniels, Robert Vincent.
Red October; the Bolshevik Revolution of 1917 [by] Robert V. Daniels. New York, Scribner [1967] xiv, 269 p.
67-024060 947.084/1
Soviet Union -- History -- Revolution, 1917-1921.

DK265.F48 1982
Fitzpatrick, Sheila.
The Russian Revolution/ Sheila Fitzpatrick. Oxford [Oxfordshire]; Oxford University Press, 1982. vi, 181 p.
82-003611 947.084/1 0192191624
Soviet Union -- History -- Revolution, 1917-1921.

DK265.K33 1964
Kautsky, Karl, 1854-1938.
The dictatorship of the proletariat. Introd. by John H. Kautsky. [Translated by H. J. Stenning. Ann Arbor] University of Michigan Press [1964] xxxvii, 149 p.
64-055366   335.413
   Communism -- Soviet Union Dictatorship of the proletariat. Democracy.

DK265.M3153 2000
Marples, David R.
Lenin's revolution: Russia, 1917-1921/ David R. Marples. Harlow, England; Longman, 2000. xv, 156 p.
00-040535   947.084/1   058231917X
   Soviet Union -- History -- Revolution, 1917-1921.

DK265.M375
Medvedev, Roy Aleksandrovich, 1925-
The October Revolution/ Roy A. Medvedev; translated by George Saunders; foreword by Harrison E. Salisbury. New York: Columbia University Press, 1979. xix, 240 p.
79-009854   947.084   0231045905
   Soviet Union -- History -- Revolution, 1917-1921.

DK265.P474 1990
Pipes, Richard.
The Russian Revolution/ Richard Pipes. New York: Knopf, 1990. xxiv, 944 p.
89-035129   947.084/1   0394502418
   Soviet Union -- History -- Revolution, 1917-1921. Russia -- History -- Nicholas II, 1894-1917.

DK265 .P4742 1995
Pipes, Richard.
A concise history of the Russian Revolution/ Richard Pipes. 1st ed. New York: Knopf, 1995. xvii, 431 p.
95-003127   947.084/1 20   0679422773
Soviet Union -- History -- Revolution, 1917-1921. Russia -- History -- Nicholas II, 1894-1917.

DK265.R3718 1996
Read, Christopher, 1946-
From Tsar to Soviets: the Russian people and their revolution, 1917-21/ Christopher Read. New York: Oxford University Press, 1996. vi, 330 p.
96-138387   947.084/1   0195212428
   Soviet Union -- History -- Revolution, 1917-1921.

DK265.R38 1967
Reed, John, 1887-1920.
Ten days that shook the world. With a foreword by V. I. Lenin, a pref. by N. K. Krupskaya, and a new introd. by John Howard Lawson. New York, International Publishers [1967] l, 395 p.
67-027252   947.084/1   0717802000
   Soviet Union -- History -- Revolution, 1917-1921.

DK265.S668
Stalin, Joseph, 1879-1953.
The October revolution; a collection of articles and speeches by Joseph Stalin. New York, International publishers [1934] 168 p.
35-006324   947.084
   Communism -- Soviet Union   Soviet Union -- History -- Revolution, 1917-1921.

DK265.T773 1957
Trotsky, Leon, 1879-1940.
The history of the Russian Revolution. Translated from the Russian by Max Eastman. Ann Arbor, University of Michigan Press [1974,c1932] 3 v. in 1
 57-013948   947/084
   Soviet Union -- History -- Revolution, 1917-1921.

DK265.W24 2000
Wade, Rex A.
The Russian Revolution, 1917/ Rex A. Wade. Cambridge; Cambridge University Press, 2000. xvii, 337 p.
99-056317   947.084/1   0521415489
   Soviet Union -- History -- Revolution, 1917-1921.

DK265.19.B813 1987
Burdzhalov, E. N. 1906-1985.
Russia's second revolution: the February 1917 uprising in Petrograd/ by E.N. Burdzhalov; translated and edited by Donald J. Raleigh. Bloomington: Indiana University Press, c1987. xxii, 388 p.
86-045955   947.084/1   0253204402
   Russia -- History -- February Revolution, 1917. Saint Petersburg (Russia) -- History -- 1917-

DK265.2.K453
Kenez, Peter.
Civil War in South Russia, 1919-1920: the defeat of the Whites/ Peter Kenez. Berkeley: Published for the Hoover Institution on War, Rev c1977. xviii, 378 p.
76-047998   947.084/1   0520033469
   Soviet Union -- History -- Revolution, 1917-1921. Soviet Union, Southern -- History.

DK265.4.S66 1996
Somin, Ilya.
Stillborn crusade: the tragic failure of Western intervention in the Russian Civil War, 1918-1920/ Ilya Somin. New Brunswick, N.J., U.S.A.: Transaction Publishers, c1996. viii, 236 p.
96-013273   947.084/1   1560002743
   Soviet Union -- History -- Allied intervention, 1918-1920.

DK265.42.U5.F64 1995
Foglesong, David S.
America's secret war against Bolshevism: U.S. intervention in the Russian Civil War, 1917-1920/ David S. Foglesong. Chapel Hill: University of North Carolina Press, c1995. x, 386 p.
94-049528   947.084/1   0807822280
   Soviet Union -- History -- Allied intervention, 1918-1920. United States -- Foreign relations -- 1913-1921.

DK265.7.B3 1988
Babine, Alexis Vasilevich, 1866-1930.
A Russian civil war diary: Alexis Babine in Saratov, 1917-1922/ Donald J. Raleigh, editor. Durham: Duke University Press, 1988. xxiv, 240 p.
88-003967   947.084   0822308355
Babine, Alexis Vasilevich, -- 1866-1930 -- Diaries. College teachers -- Soviet Union -- Diaries. Librarians -- Soviet Union -- Diaries. Soviet Union -- History -- Revolution, 1917-1921 -- Personal narratives. Saratov (Russia) -- History.

DK265.7.J83 1998
Judson, William V. 1865-1923.
Russia in war and revolution: General William V. Judson's accounts from Petrograd, 1917-1918/ edited by Neil V. Salzman. Kent, Ohio: Kent State University Press, c1998. xxxiv, 334 p.
97-035946   947.084/1   0873385977
Judson, William V. -- (William Voorhees), -- 1865-1923.   United States -- Foreign relations -- Soviet Union. Soviet Union -- Foreign relations -- United States. United States -- Foreign relations -- 1913-1921.

DK265.7.L6
Lockhart, Robert Hamilton Bruce, 1887-1970.
The two revolutions, an eye-witness study of Russia, 1917.   London, Phoenix House [1957] 116 p.
57-001720
   Soviet Union -- History -- Revolution, 1917-1921 -- Personal narratives.

DK265.7.S8813 1984
Sukhanov, N. N. 1882-1940.
The Russian revolution, 1917: a personal record/ by N.N Sukhanov; edited, abridged, and translated by Joel Carmichael from Zapiski o revolutsii; with new addendum by the editor. Princeton, N.J.: Princeton University Press, c1984. xl, 691 p.
83-043102   947.084/1   0691054061
Sukhanov, N. N. -- (Nikolai Nikolaevich), -- 1882-1940.   Journalists -- Soviet Union -- Biography. Editors -- Soviet Union -- Biography. Soviet Union -- History -- Revolution, 1917-1921 -- Personal narratives.

DK265.8.L4.R27 1976
Rabinowitch, Alexander.
The Bolsheviks come to power: the revolution of 1917 in Petrograd/ Alexander Rabinowitch. New York: W. W. Norton, c1976. xxxiii, 393 p.
76-020756   947/.45/0841   0393055868
Lenin, Vladimir Ilich, -- 1870-1924.   Saint Petersburg (Russia) -- History -- Revolution, 1917-1921. Soviet Union -- History -- Revolution, 1917-1921.

DK265.8.S5.S59 1996
Smele, Jon.
Civil war in Siberia: the anti-Bolshevik government of Admiral Kolchak, 1918-1920/ Jonathan D. Smele. Cambridge; Cambridge University Press, 1996. xix, 759 p.
96-014039   957.08   0521573351
Kolchak, Aleksandr Vasiliyevich, -- 1873-1920. Siberia (Russia) -- History -- Revolution, 1917-1921.

DK265.8.U4.A6
Adams, Arthur E.
Bolsheviks in the Ukraine; the second campaign, 1918-1919.   New Haven, Yale University Press, 1963. 440 p.
63-007930   947.71
   Ukraine -- History -- Revolution, 1917-1921.

DK265.9.D45.P37 1989
Party, state, and society in the Russian Civil War: explorations in social history/ edited by Diane P. Koenker, William G. Rosenberg, and Ronald Grigor Suny. Bloomington: Indiana University Press, c1989. xiv, 450 p.
88-046042   947.084/1   0253332621
Socialism -- Soviet Union -- History.   Soviet Union -- Social conditions. Soviet Union -- History -- Revolution, 1917-1921.

DK265.9.I5.C3 1973
Carr, Edward Hallett, 1892-
The Soviet impact on the Western World. New York, H. Fertig, 1973 [c1947] xii, 113 p.
73-080532   335.43
Communism.   Soviet Union -- History --
Revolution, 1917-1921 -- Influence.

DK265.9.M45.L54 1997
Liebich, Andre, 1948-
From the other shore: Russian social democracy after 1921/ Andre Liebich. Cambridge, Mass.: Harvard University Press, 1997. xi, 476 p.
96-041417   947.084   0674325176
Mensheviks -- History. Socialist parties -- Soviet
Union -- History.

DK266-293 History — By period — Soviet regime, 1918-1991

DK266.A33.C64 1985
Cohen, Stephen F.
Rethinking the Soviet experience: politics and history since 1917/ Stephen F. Cohen. New York: Oxford University Press, 1985. xiii, 222 p.
84-000749   947/.0072   0195034686
Soviet Union -- Historiography. Soviet Union --
Study and teaching -- History.

DK266.A33.H35 2000
Halfin, Igal.
From darkness to light: class, consciousness, and salvation in revolutionary Russia/ Igal Halfin. Pittsburgh, Pa.: University of Pittsburgh Press, c2000. xii, 474 p.
99-006970   947.084   082294104X
History -- Philosophy. Philosophy, Marxist --
Russia. Philosophy, Marxist -- Soviet Union. Soviet
Union -- History -- 1917-1936 -- Historiography.
Soviet Union -- History -- 1917-1936 --
Philosophy.

DK266.C263
Carr, Edward Hallett, 1892-
A history of Soviet Russia. New York, Macmillan, 1951 [c1950]- v.
51-001610   947.084
Soviet Union -- History.

DK266.C47513 1993
Chuev, Feliks Ivanovich, 1941-
Molotov remembers: inside Kremlin politics: conversations with Felix Chuev/ edited with an introduction and notes by Albert Resis. Chicago: I.R. Dee, 1993. xxiii, 438 p.
93-011253   320.947   1566630274
Molotov, Vyacheslav Mikhaylovich, -- 1890- --
Interviews.   Soviet Union -- Foreign relations.
Soviet Union -- Politics and government.

DK266.D28 1997
Davies, R. W. 1925-
Soviet history in the Yeltsin era/ R.W. Davies. New York: St. Martin's Press, 1997. viii, 264 p.
96-029714   947.084/07/2047   0312173725
Historiography -- Russia (Federation)   Soviet
Union -- Historiography.

DK266.D39 1990
De Mowbray, Stephen.
A chronology of Soviet history/ by Stephen de Mowbray. Boston, MA: G.K. Hall, c1990- xiii, 386 p.
89-071644   947.084/02/02   0816118205
Soviet Union -- History -- 1917- -- Chronology.

DK266.F37 1990
Farber, Samuel, 1939-
Before Stalinism: the rise and fall of Soviet democracy/ Samuel Farber. London; Verso, 1990. xiii, 288 p.
90-042082   947.084   0860913155
Communism -- Soviet Union -- History.
Democracy. Soviet Union -- History. Soviet Union
-- History -- Revolution, 1917-1921.

DK266 .H58 1993
Hosking, Geoffrey A.
The first socialist society: a history of the Soviet Union from within/ Geoffrey Hosking. 2nd enl. ed. Cambridge, Mass.: Harvard University Press, 1993. 570 p. [8] p. of plates
92-037806   947 20   0674304438
Soviet Union -- History.

DK266.H59 1988
Hough, Jerry F., 1935-
Russia and the West: Gorbachev and the politics of reform/ Jerry Hough. New York: Simon and Schuster, c1988. 301 p.
87-028891   327.47073   0671618393
Gorbachev, Mikhail Sergeevich, -- 1931-   Soviet
Union -- Politics and government. Soviet Union --
Foreign relations -- United States. United States --
Foreign relations -- Soviet Union.

DK266.M354
McCauley, Martin.
The Soviet Union since 1917/ Martin McCauley. London; Longman, 1981. xiv, 290 p.
80-041827   947.084   0582489792
Soviet Union -- History.

DK266.N22 1997
Naiman, Eric, 1958-
Sex in public: the incarnation of early Soviet ideology/ Eric Naiman. Princeton, N.J.: Princeton University Press, c1997. x, 307 p.
96-043642   947.084   0691026262
Communism and sex -- Soviet Union.   Soviet
Union -- History -- 1917-1936.

DK266.P53 1964
Pipes, Richard.
The formation of the Soviet Union; Communism and nationalism, 1917-1923. Cambridge, Harvard University Press, 1964. xii, 365 p.
64-021284   947.0841   0674309502
Soviet Union -- History -- 1917-1936.

DK266.R384 2001
Read, Christopher, 1946-
The making and breaking of the Soviet system: an interpretation/ Christopher Read. Houndmills, Basingstoke, Hampshire; Palgrave, 2001. x, 250 p.
00-048296   947   0333731522
Soviet Union -- History.

DK266.R82 1991
Russia in the era of NEP: explorations in Soviet society and culture/ edited by Sheila Fitzpatrick, Alexander Rabinowitch, and Richard Stites. Bloomington: Indiana University Press, c1991. viii, 344 p.
90-025044   947.084   0253322243
Soviet Union -- Politics and government --
1917-1936. Soviet Union -- Intellectual life --
1917-1970. Soviet Union -- Economic policy --
1917-1928.

DK266.S495 1998
Service, Robert.
A history of twentieth-century Russia/ Robert Service. Cambridge, Mass.: Harvard University Press, 1998. xxxiii, 653 p.
97-037440   947.086   0674403479
Soviet Union -- History. Russia (Federation) --
History -- 1991-

DK266.S5276 1992
Siegelbaum, Lewis H.
Soviet state and society between revolutions, 1918-1929/ Lewis H. Siegelbaum. Cambridge [England]; Cambridge University Press, 1992. xiii, 284 p.
91-032336   947.084/1   0521362156
Soviet Union -- History -- 1917-1936.

DK266.U49 1974
Ulam, Adam Bruno, 1922-
Expansion and coexistence: Soviet foreign policy, 1917-73 [by] Adam B. Ulam. New York, Praeger [1974] viii, 797 p.
73-008181   327.47
Soviet Union -- Foreign relations.

DK266.3.B58 1997
Bonnell, Victoria E.
Iconography of power: Soviet political posters under Lenin and Stalin/ Victoria E. Bonnell. Berkeley: University of California Press, c1997. xxii, 363 p.
96-036252   947.084   0520087127
Political posters, Russian.   Soviet Union --
Politics and government -- 1936-1953 -- Posters.
Soviet Union -- Politics and government -- 1917-
1936 -- Posters.

DK266.3.S54 1996
Smith, Kathleen E.
Remembering Stalin's victims: popular memory and the end of the USSR/ Kathleen E. Smith. Ithaca, NY: Cornell University Press, 1996. xv, 220 p.
95-041397   947.084   0801431948
Political rehabilitation -- Soviet Union.
Dissenters -- Soviet Union. Post-communism --
Former Soviet republics. Soviet Union -- Politics
and government. Political rehabilitation -- Former
Soviet republics.

DK266.3.S86 1993
Suny, Ronald Grigor.
The revenge of the past: nationalism, revolution, and the collapse of the Soviet Union/ Ronald Grigor Suny. Stanford, Calif.: Stanford University Press, c1993. xix, 200 p.
93-010373   320.5/4/0947   0804721343
Nationalism -- Soviet Union.   Soviet Union --
History.

DK266.4.S75 1989
Stites, Richard.
Revolutionary dreams: utopian vision and experimental life in the Russian Revolution/ Richard Stites. New York: Oxford University Press, 1989. xii, 307 p.
88-005263   947.084   0195055365
Utopias.   Soviet Union -- Intellectual life. Soviet
Union -- History -- Revolution, 1917-1921.

DK266.45.D66 1998
Donaldson, Robert H.
The foreign policy of Russia: changing systems, enduring interests/ by Robert H. Donaldson, Joseph L. Nogee. Armonk, N.Y.: M.E. Sharpe, 1998. ix, 322 p.
98-014390   327.47   0765600463
Soviet Union -- Foreign relations. Russia
(Federation) -- Foreign relations.

DK266.45.G65 1994
Goldgeier, James M.
Leadership style and Soviet foreign policy: Stalin, Khrushchev, Brezhnev, Gorbachev/ James M. Goldgeier. Baltimore: Johns Hopkins University Press, c1994. x, 169 p.
94-000330   327.47   0801848660
   Soviet Union -- Foreign relations -- 1945-1991. Soviet Union -- Politics and government -- 1945-1991.

DK266.45.K46 1998
Kennedy-Pipe, Caroline, 1961-
Russia and the world, 1917-1991/ Caroline Kennedy-Pipe. London; Arnold, 1998. ix, 229 p.
98-019853   327.47   0340652047
   Soviet Union -- Foreign relations.

DK266.5.B57 1994
Blank, Stephen, 1950-
The Sorcerer as apprentice: Stalin as commissar of nationalities, 1917-1924/ Stephen Blank. Westport, Conn.: Greenwood Press, 1994. 295 p.
93-018148   320.947   0313286833
   Stalin, Joseph, -- 1879-1953.   Soviet Union -- Cultural policy. Minorities -- Government policy -- Soviet Union.   Soviet Union -- Politics and government -- 1917-1936.

DK267.B585513 1992
Boffa, Giuseppe.
The Stalin phenomenon/ Giuseppe Boffa; translated by Nicholas Fersen. Ithaca: Cornell University Press, 1992. xii, 205 p.
91-000813   947.084/2   080142576X
Stalin, Joseph, -- 1879-1953.   Soviet Union -- Politics and government.

DK267.H596 1984
Hochman, Jiri.
The Soviet Union and the failure of collective security, 1934-1938/ Jiri Hochman. Ithaca: Cornell University Press, 1984. 253 p.
84-045149   327.47   0801416558
   Security, International. World politics -- 1933-1945. Soviet Union -- Foreign relations -- 1917-1945.

DK267.H597 1994
Hochschild, Adam.
The unquiet ghost: Russians remember Stalin/ Adam Hochschild. New York, N.Y., U.S.A.: Viking, 1994. xxvii, 304 p.
93-027473   947.084   0670840912
Stalin, Joseph, -- 1879-1953.   Soviet Union -- History -- 1925-1953.

DK267.K38 1995
Keep, John L. H.
Last of the empires: a history of the Soviet Union, 1945-1991/ John L.H. Keep. Oxford; Oxford University Press, 1995. viii, 477 p.
94-037237   947.084   0192192558
   Soviet Union -- History.

DK267.L36 1990
Laqueur, Walter, 1921-
Stalin: the glasnost revelations/ Walter Laqueur. New York: Scribner's, c1990. xi, 382 p.
90-032253   947.084/2   0684192039
Stalin, Joseph, -- 1879-1953.   Soviet Union -- Politics and government -- 1936-1953.

DK267.M3567 1996
Mastny, Vojtech, 1936-
The Cold War and Soviet insecurity: the Stalin years/ Vojtech Mastny. New York: Oxford University Press, 1996. xi, 285 p.
95-049341   947.084/2   0195106164
   National security -- Soviet Union.   Soviet Union -- Politics and government -- 1936-1953.

DK267.M41413
Medvedev, Roy Aleksandrovich, 1925-
Let history judge: the origins and consequences of Stalinism [by] Roy A. Medvedev. Translated by Colleen Taylor. Edited by David Joravsky and by Georges Haupt. New York, Knopf, 1971. xxxiv, 566 p.
70-031702   947.084/2   0394446453
Stalin, Joseph, -- 1879-1953.   Political atrocities -- Soviet Union.   Soviet Union -- Politics and government -- 1917-1936. Soviet Union -- Politics and government -- 1936-1953.

DK267.S17 1961
Salisbury, Harrison Evans, 1908-
Moscow journal; the end of Stalin.   [Chicago] University of Chicago Press [1961] 449 p.
61-016621   947.0842
   Soviet Union -- History -- 1925-1953 -- Chronology.

DK267.S69386 2000
Stalinism as a way of life: a narrative in documents/ Lewis Siegelbaum and Andrei Sokolov; documents compiled by Ludmila Kosheleva ... [et al.]; text preparation and commentary by Lewis Siegelbaum, Andrei Sokolov, and Sergei Zhuravlev; translated from the Russian by Thomas Hoisington and Steven Shabad. New Haven, CT: Yale University Press, c2000. xvii, 460 p.
00-032074   947.084   0300084803
   Soviet Union -- History -- 1925-1953 -- Sources.

DK267.T52 1996
Thurston, Robert W.
Life and terror in Stalin's Russia, 1934-1941/ Robert W. Thurston. New Haven: Yale University Press, c1996. xxi, 296 p.
95-041333   947.084/2   0300064012
Stalin, Joseph, -- 1879-1953.   Political purges -- Soviet Union. Totalitarianism.   Soviet Union -- Politics and government -- 1936-1953.

DK267.T73
Trotsky, Leon, 1879-1940.
The revolution betrayed. What is the Soviet Union and where is it going? Translated by Max Eastman. Garden City, N.Y., Doubleday, Doran & Company, inc., 1937. vii p. 1 .
37-027208   947.084
   Soviet Union -- Politics and government -- 1917-1936. Soviet Union -- Economic conditions -- 1917-1945. Soviet Union -- Social conditions.

DK267.Z78 1996
Zubok, V. M.
Inside the Kremlin's cold war: from Stalin to Khrushchev/   Vladislav   Zubok,   Constantine Pleshakov. Cambridge, Mass.: Harvard University Press, 1996. xv, 346 p.
95-026457   327.47   0674455312
   Cold War.   Soviet Union -- Foreign relations -- 1945-1991.

DK268.A1.V5813 1998
Volkogonov, Dmitrii Antonovich.
Autopsy for an empire: the seven leaders who built the Soviet regime/ Dmitri Volkogonov; edited and translated by Harold Shukman. New York: Free Press, c1998. xxvii, 572 p.
98-010287   947.084/0922   0684834200
   Heads of state -- Soviet Union -- Biography. Statesmen -- Soviet Union -- Biography. Soviet Union -- History.

DK268.A54.A3 1997
Andreev-Khomiakov, Gennady.
Bitter waters: life and work in Stalin's Russia/ by Gennady Andreev-Khomiakov; translated by Ann E. Healy. Boulder, Colo.: Westview Press, 1997. p. cm.
96-053092   947.084/2/092   0813323908
Andreev-Khomiakov, Gennady.   Political prisoners -- Soviet Union -- Biography. Political persecution -- Soviet Union.   Soviet Union -- History -- 1925-1953.

DK268.B384.K58 1993
Knight, Amy W., 1946-
Beria, Stalin's first lieutenant/ Amy Knight. Princeton, N.J.: Princeton University Press, c1993. xvi, 312 p.
93-003937   947.084/2/092   0691032572
Beriia, L. P. -- (Lavrentii Pavlovich), -- 1899-1953.   Politicians -- Soviet Union -- Biography. Internal security -- Soviet Union. Georgia (Republic) -- Politics and government. Soviet Union -- Politics and government -- 1936-1953.

DK268.B76.C63 1973
Cohen, Stephen F.
Bukharin and the Bolshevik Revolution; a political biography, 1888-1938 [by] Stephen F. Cohen. New York, A. A. Knopf; [distributed by Random House] 1973. xix, 495 p.
73-007288   947.084/092/4   0394460146
Bukharin, Nikolai Ivanovich, -- 1888-1938. Statesmen -- Soviet Union -- Biography. Revolutionaries -- Soviet Union -- Biography. Soviet Union -- Politics and government -- 1917-1936. Soviet Union -- Economic policy -- 1917-1928.

DK268.B76.N4913 1993
Larina, Anna.
This I cannot forget: the memoirs of Nikolai Bukharin's widow/ Anna Larina; introduction by Stephen F. Cohen; translated from the Russian by Gary Kern. New York: W.W. Norton & Co., c1993. 384 p.
91-012739   947.084/092   0393030253
Larina, Anna. Bukharin, Nikolai Ivanovich, -- 1888-1938.   Revolutionaries -- Soviet Union -- Biography. Wives -- Soviet Union -- Biography. Soviet Union -- Politics and government -- 1917-1936.

DK268.G47.A3413 1981
Ginzburg, Evgeniia Semenovna.
Within the whirlwind/ Eugenia Ginzburg; translated by Ian Boland; introduction by Heinrich Boll. New York: Harcourt Brace Jovanovich, c1981. xix, 423 p.
80-008748   365.6/092/4   0151975175
Ginzburg, Evgeniia Semenovna.   Political prisoners -- Soviet Union -- Biography.   Soviet Union -- Social conditions.

DK268.K5 K58 1999
Knight, Amy W.,
Who killed Kirov?: the Kremlin's greatest mystery/ Amy Knight. 1st ed. New York: Hill and Wang, 1999. xiv, 331 p.
98-048989 947.084/1/092.B 21 0809064049
Kirov, Sergeœi Mironovich, 1886-1934. Revolutionaries--Soviet Union--Biography.

DK268.L46.A3 2000
Likhachev, Dmitrii Sergeevich.
Reflections on the Russian soul: a memoir/ Dmitry S. Likhachev. Hungary; Central European University Press, 2000. xvii, 296 p.
00-031502 947.086/092 9639116467
Likhachev, Dmitrii Sergeevich. Intellectuals -- Soviet Union -- Biography. Intellectuals -- Russia (Federation) -- Biography. Soviet Union -- Intellectual life. Russia (Federation) -- Intellectual life -- 1991-

DK268.S75.A34 1970
Stalin, Joseph, 1879-1953.
Selected writings. Westport, Conn., Greenwood Press [1970] 479 p.
78-109976 335.43 0837144825
Communism -- Soviet Union. Soviet Union -- Politics and government.

DK268.S8.A4 1995
Stalin's letters to Molotov, 1925-1936/ edited by Lars T. Lih, Oleg V. Naumov, and Oleg V. Khlevniuk; Russian consulting scholars, L. Kosheleva ... [et al.]; translated from the Russian by Catherine A. Fitzpatrick; foreword by Robert C. Tucker. New Haven: Yale University Press, c1995. xviii, 276 p.
94-044050 947.084/2/092 0300062117
Stalin, Joseph, -- 1879-1953 -- Correspondence. Molotov, Vyacheslav Mikhaylovich, -- 1890- -- Correspondence. Heads of state -- Soviet Union -- Correspondence. Soviet Union -- Politics and government -- 1917-1936.

DK268.S8.B69 2001
Brackman, Roman, 1931-
The secret file of Joseph Stalin: a hidden life/ Roman Brackman. London; Frank Cass, c2001. xx, 466 p.
00-050861 947.084 0714650501
Stalin, Joseph, -- 1879-1953. Heads of state -- Soviet Union -- Biography. Russia -- History -- Nicholas II, 1894-1917. Soviet Union -- Politics and government -- 1917-1936. Soviet Union -- Politics and government -- 1936-1953.

DK268.S8.C65 1991
Conquest, Robert.
Stalin: breaker of nations/ Robert Conquest. New York, N.Y., U.S.A.: Viking, 1991. xvii, 346 p.
91-028782 947.084/2/092 0670840890
Stalin, Joseph, -- 1879-1953. Statesmen -- Soviet Union -- Biography. Soviet Union -- Politics and government.

DK268.S8.D48 1967
Deutscher, Isaac, 1907-1967.
Stalin; a political biography. New York, Oxford University Press, 1967, [c1966] xvi, 661 p.
67-004373 947.084/2/0924
Stalin, Joseph, -- 1879-1953.

DK268.S8.S48 1987
Slusser, Robert M.
Stalin in October: the man who missed the revolution/ Robert M. Slusser. Baltimore: Johns Hopkins University Press, c1987. xi, 281 p.
87-003666 947.084/2/0924 0801834570
Stalin, Joseph, -- 1879-1953. Revolutionaries -- Soviet Union -- Biography. Soviet Union -- History -- Revolution, 1917-1921.

DK268.S8.T7 1968
Trotsky, Leon, 1879-1940.
Stalin: an appraisal of the man and his influence, by Leon Trotsky; edited and translated from the Russian by Charles Malamuth. London, MacGibbon & Kee, 1968. xv, 516 p.
77-386055 947.084/2/0924 0261620762
Stalin, Joseph, -- 1879-1953.

DK268.S8.T85 1973
Tucker, Robert C.
Stalin as revolutionary, 1879-1929; a study in history and personality [by] Robert C. Tucker. New York, Norton [1973] xx, 519 p.
73-006541 947.084/2/0924 039305487X
Stalin, Joseph, -- 1879-1953.

DK268.S8 T86 1990
Tucker, Robert C.
Stalin in power: the revolution from above, 1928-1941/ Robert C. Tucker. New York: Norton, c1990. xix, 707 p.
89-078047 947.084/2/092.220 039302881X
Stalin, Joseph, 1879-1953. Heads of state--Soviet Union--Biography.

DK268.S8.U4 1973
Ulam, Adam Bruno, 1922-
Stalin; the man and his era [by] Adam B. Ulam. New York, Viking Press [1973] 760 p.
73-006226 947.084/2/0924 0670666831
Stalin, Joseph, -- 1879-1953. Heads of state -- Soviet Union -- Biography. Revolutionaries -- Soviet Union -- Biography. Soviet Union -- History -- 1925-1953.

DK268.S8.V5613 1991
Volkogonov, Dmitrii Antonovich.
Stalin: triumph and tragedy/ Dmitri Volkogonov; edited and translated from the Russian by Harold Shukman. New York: Grove Weidenfeld, 1991. xxvii, 642 p.
91-019468 947.084/2/092 0802111653
Stalin, Joseph, -- 1879-1953. Heads of state -- Soviet Union -- Biography. Soviet Union -- History.

DK268.3.G513
Ginzburg, Evgeniia Semenovna.
Journey into the whirlwind. Translated by Paul Stevenson and Max Hayward. New York, Harcourt, Brace & World [1967] 418 p.
67-026000 947.084/2/0924
Political prisoners -- Soviet Union -- Biography. Soviet Union -- Social conditions.

DK268.3.K86 1963
Kulski, Wladyslaw Wszebor, 1903-
The Soviet regime; communism in practice. Syracuse, N.Y.] Syracuse University Press, 1963. xii, 444 p.
63-021982 947.084
Communism -- Soviet Union. Soviet Union -- Intellectual life. Soviet Union -- Social conditions - - 1945-1991.

DK268.3.R83 1998
Ruder, Cynthia Ann, 1956-
Making history for Stalin: the story of the Belomor Canal/ Cynthia A. Ruder. Gainesville: University Press of Florida, 1998. xvi, 248 p.
97-024059 947.084 0813015677
Russian literature -- 20th century -- History and criticism. Socialist realism in literature. White Sea-Baltic Canal (Russia) -- History. White Sea-Baltic Canal (Russia) in literature. Soviet Union -- Social life and customs -- 1917-1970.

DK273.G3
Gallagher, Matthew P.
The Soviet history of World War II: myths, memories, and realities. New York, Praeger [1963] 205 p.
63-009908 940.5347
World War, 1939-1945 -- Soviet Union. World War, 1939-1945 -- Historiography. Soviet Union - - Historiography.

DK273.R33 1995
Raack, R. C.
Stalin's drive to the West, 1938-1945: the origins of the Cold War/ R.C. Raack. Stanford, Calif.: Stanford University Press, 1995. viii, 265 p.
95-004990 947.084/2 0804724156
Stalin, Joseph, -- 1879-1953. World War, 1939-1945 -- Diplomatic history. World War, 1939-1945 -- Soviet Union. Soviet Union -- Foreign relations -- 1917-1945. Europe -- Politics and government -- 1918-1945.

DK273.R78 1995
Culture and entertainment in wartime Russia/ edited by Richard Stites. Bloomington: Indiana University Press, c1995. vi, 215 p.
94-027315 947.084/2 025335403X
Popular culture -- Soviet Union. World War, 1939-1945 -- Soviet Union. Soviet Union -- Intellectual life -- 1917-1970.

DK274.B77 1998
Brudny, Yitzhak M.
Reinventing Russia: Russian nationalism and the Soviet state, 1953-1991/ Yitzhak M. Brudny. Cambridge, Mass.: Harvard University Press, 1998. x, 352 p.
98-023969 947.085 0674754085
Nationalism -- Soviet Union. Soviet Union -- Politics and government -- 1985-1991. Soviet Union -- Politics and government -- 1953-1985.

DK274.C62
Conquest, Robert.
Power and policy in the U.S.S.R.; the study of Soviet dynastics. New York, St. Martin's Press, 1961. x, 485 p.
61-015941 947.0842
Soviet Union -- Politics and government -- 1945-1991.

DK274.C63
Conquest, Robert.
Russia after Khrushchev. New York, Praeger [1965] viii, 267 p.
65-015645 947.085
Soviet Union -- Politics and government -- 1953-1985.

DK274.C69
Crankshaw, Edward.
Khrushchev's Russia. Baltimore, Penguin Books [1959] 183 p.
60-023715 914.7
Khrushchev, Nikita Sergeevich, -- 1894-1971. Soviet Union -- Politics and government -- 1953-1985.

DK274.D28
Dallin, Alexander.
Soviet politics since Khrushchev, edited by Alexander Dallin and Thomas B. Larson. Englewood Cliffs, N.J., Prentice-Hall [1968] viii, 181 p.
68-014468   300/.947
Soviet Union -- Politics and government -- 1953-1985.

DK274.H68
Hough, Jerry F., 1935-
Soviet leadership in transition/ Jerry F. Hough. Washington, D.C.: Brookings Institution, c1980. xi, 175 p.
80-067873   947.085   0815737424
Soviet Union -- Politics and government -- 1953-1985.

DK274.M3513
Medvedev, Roy Aleksandrovich, 1925-
On Soviet dissent/ Roy Medvedev; interviews with Piero Ostellino; translated from the Italian by William A. Packer; edited by George Saunders. New York: Columbia University Press, 1980. 158 p.
79-027877   323.1/47   0231048122
Medvedev, Roy Aleksandrovich, -- 1925- Dissenters -- Soviet Union.   Soviet Union -- Politics and government -- 1953-1985.

DK274.S276 1975
Sakharov, Andrei, 1921-
My country and the world/ Andrei D. Sakharov; translated by Guy V. Daniels. New York: Knopf: distributed by Random House, 1975. xvi, 109 p.
75-024963   320.9/47/085   039440226X
Disarmament. World politics -- 1975-1985. Soviet Union -- Politics and government -- 1953-1985. Soviet Union -- Foreign relations -- 1975- United States -- Foreign relations -- 1974-1977.

DK274.S277 1974
Sakharov, Andrei, 1921-
Sakharov speaks [by] Andrei D. Sakharov. Edited and with a foreword by Harrison E. Salisbury. New York, A. A. Knopf, 1974. vi, 245 p.
73-021154   323.4/0947   0394492090
Sakharov, Andrei, -- 1921- Civilization, Modern -- 1950- Soviet Union -- Politics and government -- 1953-1985.

DK274.U4 1983
Ulam, Adam Bruno, 1922-
Dangerous relations: the Soviet Union in world politics, 1970-1982/ Adam B. Ulam. New York: Oxford University Press, 1983. vi, 325 p.
82-014261   327.47   0195032373
Detente. World politics -- 1965-1975. World politics -- 1975-1985. Soviet Union -- Foreign relations -- 1953-1975. Soviet Union -- Foreign relations -- 1975-

DK274.W4 1962
Werth, Alexander, 1901-
Russia under Khrushchev. New York, Hill and Wang [c1961] 352 p.
62-011998
Khrushchev, Nikita Sergeevich, -- 1894-1971. Soviet Union -- Politics and government -- 1953-1985. Soviet Union -- Foreign relations -- 1945-1991.

DK274.3.K47 1987
Khrushchev and Khrushchevism/ edited by Martin McCauley. Bloomington: Indiana University Press, c1987. xii, 243 p.
86-033896   947.085/2   0253331420
Khrushchev, Nikita Sergeevich, -- 1894-1971. Soviet Union -- Politics and government -- 1953-1985.

DK274.3.S63 1990
Soldiers and the Soviet state: civil-military relations from Brezhnev to Gorbachev/ Timothy J. Colton and Thane Gustafson, editors. Princeton, N.J.: Princeton University Press, c1990. xiii, 370 p.
90-008104   322/.5/0947   0691087637
Civil supremacy over the military -- Soviet Union. Soviet Union -- Politics and government -- 1985-1991. Soviet Union -- Military policy. Soviet Union -- Politics and government -- 1953-1985.

DK275.B73.A3 1995
Brezhneva, Luba, 1943-
The world I left behind: pieces of a past/ Luba Brezhneva; translated by Geoffrey Polk. New York: Random House, c1995. 947.085/3/092 0679439110
94-041088
Brezhneva, Luba, -- 1943- Brezhnev family. Brezhnev, Leonid Ilich, -- 1906- -- Family. Soviet Union -- Politics and government -- 1953-1985.

DK275.C45.Z46 1989
Zemtsov, Ilya.
Chernenko: the last Bolshevik: the Soviet Union on the eve of Perestroika/ Ilya Zemtsov. New Brunswick, N.J., U.S.A.: Transaction Publishers, c1989. xv, 308 p.
88-019993   947.085/092/4   0887382606
Chernenko, K. U. -- (Konstantin Ustinovich), -- 1911- Heads of state -- Soviet Union -- Biography.   Soviet Union -- Politics and government -- 1953-1985.

DK275.D63.A3 1995
Dobrynin, Anatoliy Fedorovich, 1919-
In confidence: Moscow's ambassador to America's six Cold War presidents (1962-1986)/ Anatoly Dobrynin. New York: Times Books, Random House, c1995. xiii, 672 p.
95-011611   327.2/092   0812923286
Dobrynin, Anatoliy Fedorovich, -- 1919- Ambassadors -- Soviet Union -- Biography. United States -- Foreign relations -- Soviet Union. Soviet Union -- Foreign relations -- United States. United States -- Foreign relations -- 20th century.

DK275.K5.A326
Khrushchev, Nikita Sergeevich, 1894-1971.
Khrushchev remembers; the last testament. Translated and edited by Strobe Talbott. With a foreword by Edward Crankshaw and an introd. by Jerrold L. Schecter. Boston, Little, Brown [1974] xxxi, 602 p.
74-004095   947.085/092/4
Khrushchev, Nikita Sergeevich, -- 1894-1971. Soviet Union -- Politics and government -- 1953-1985.

DK275.K5.A36
Khrushchev, Nikita Sergeevich, 1894-1971.
Khrushchev speaks; selected speeches, articles, and press conferences, 1949-1961. Edited, with commentary, by Thomas P. Whitney. Ann Arbor, University of Michigan Press [1963] 466 p.
63-008075

DK275.K5.K4874213 2000
Khrushchev, Sergei.
Nikita Khrushchev: creation of a superpower/ Sergei N. Khrushchev; translated by Shirley Benson; foreword by William Taubman; annotations by William C. Wohlforth. University Park, Pa.: Pennsylvania State University Press, c2000. xviii, 765 p.
98-054931   947.08   0271019271
Khrushchev, Nikita Sergeevich, -- 1894-1971. Khrushchev, Sergei. Heads of state -- Soviet Union -- Biography. World politics -- 1945- Soviet Union -- Politics and government -- 1953-1985.

DK275.K5 T38 2003
Taubman, William.
Khrushchev: the man and his era/ William Taubman. 1st ed. New York: Norton, c2003. xx, 876 p.
2002-026404   947.085/2/092.B 21   0393051447
Khrushchev, Nikita Sergeevich, 1894-1971. Heads of state--Soviet Union--Biography.

DK275.K5.T66 1995
Tompson, William J.
Khrushchev--a political life/ William J. Tompson. New York: St. Martin's Press, 1995. ix, 341 p.
94-019567   947.085/2   0312123655
Khrushchev, Nikita Sergeevich, -- 1894-1971. Heads of state -- Soviet Union -- Biography. Soviet Union -- Politics and government -- 1953-1985.

DK276.I5
Inkeles, Alex, 1920-
The Soviet citizen; daily life in a totalitarian society, by Alex Inkeles and Raymond A. Bauer with the assistance of David Gleicher and Irving Roscow. New York, Atheneum, 1968 [c1959] xx, 533 p.
59-009277   914.7
Soviet Union -- Social conditions -- 1945-1991. Soviet Union -- Politics and government -- 1953-1985.

DK276.S48 1990
Shlapentokh, Vladimir.
Soviet intellectuals and political power: the post-Stalin era/ Vladimir Shlapentokh. Princeton, N.J.: Princeton University Press, c1990. xiv, 330 p.
90-036648   947.084   0691094594
Soviet Union -- Intellectual life. Soviet Union -- Politics and government -- 1953-1985. Soviet Union -- Politics and government -- 1985-1991.

DK282.S63 1991
Sodaro, Michael J.
Moscow, Germany, and the West from Khrushchev to Gorbachev/ Michael J. Sodaro. Ithaca: Cornell University Press, 1990. xiv, 423 p.
90-084233   327.47043   0801425298
Soviet Union -- Foreign relations -- Germany. Germany -- Foreign relations -- Soviet Union. Soviet Union -- Foreign relations -- 1953-1975.

DK286.L37 1990
Laqueur, Walter, 1921-
Soviet Union 2000: reform or revolution?/ Walter Laqueur with John Erickson ... [et al.]. New York: St. Martin's Press, c1990. xx, 201 p.
89-077845   947.085/4   0312044259
Soviet Union -- Politics and government -- 1985-1991.

DK286.L48 1988
Lewin, Moshe, 1921-
The Gorbachev phenomenon: a historical interpretation/ Moshe Lewin. Berkeley: University of California Press, c1988. xii, 176 p.
87-022162   947.085   0520062574
Gorbachev, Mikhail Sergeevich, -- 1931-Perestroika. Soviet Union -- History -- 1953-

DK286.5.G64 1989
Gorbachev and glasnost: viewpoints from the Soviet press/ edited by Isaac J. Tarasulo. Wilmington, Del.: SR Books, 1989. xxvi, 363 p.
89-010510   947.085/4   0842023372
Glasnost. Soviet Union -- Politics and government -- 1985-1991.

DK286.5.H67 1992
Hosking, Geoffrey A.
The road to post-Communism: independent political movements in the Soviet Union, 1985-1991/ Geoffrey A. Hosking, Jonathan Aves, and Peter J.S. Duncan. London; Pinter Publishers: 1992. 236 p.
92-014811   322/.0947/09048   1855670801
Nationalism -- Soviet Union -- Republics. Post-communism -- Soviet Union. Soviet Union -- Politics and government -- 1985-1991. Soviet Union -- History -- Autonomy and independence movements.

DK287.C64 1989
Cohen, Stephen F.
Voices of glasnost: conversations with Gorbachev's reformers/ by Stephen F. Cohen and Katrina vanden Heuvel. New York: Norton, c1989. p. cm.
89-032441   947   0393026256
Glasnost. Interviews -- Soviet Union.

DK288.B76 1996
Brown, Archie, 1938-
The Gorbachev factor/ Archie Brown. Oxford, England; Oxford University Press, 1996. xv, 406 p.
95-049061   947.085/4/092   0198273444
Gorbachev, Mikhail Sergeevich, -- 1931-   Soviet Union -- Politics and government -- 1985-1991.

DK288.C3713 1993
Carrere d'Encausse, Helene.
The end of the Soviet empire: the triumph of the nations/ Helene Carrere d'Encausse; translated by Franklin Philip. New York: BasicBooks, c1993. xii, 292 p.
91-059006   947.085/4   0465098126
Soviet Union -- Politics and government -- 1985-1991.

DK288.C74 1991
The Crisis of Leninism and the decline of the left: the revolutions of 1989/ edited by Daniel Chirot. Seattle: University of Washington Press, c1991. xv, 245 p.
91-011289   909.82/9   029597110X
Soviet Union -- Politics and government -- 1985-1991 -- Congresses. China -- Politics and government -- 1976- -- Congresses. Europe, Eastern -- Politics and government -- 1989- -- Congresses.

DK288.D34 1998
D'Agostino, Anthony, 1937-
Gorbachev's revolution/ Anthony D'Agostino. New York: New York University Press, 1998. ix, 384 p.
97-030236   947.085/4   0814718981
Soviet Union -- Politics and government -- 1985-1991.

DK288.D45 1998
DeLuca, Anthony R.
Politics, diplomacy, and the media: Gorbachev's legacy in the West/ Anthony R. DeLuca. Westport, Conn.: Praeger, 1998. x, 165 p.
98-004931   947.085   0275959686
Gorbachev, Mikhail Sergeevich, -- 1931-Communication in politics -- Soviet Union. Public relations and politics -- Soviet Union. Mass media and public opinion -- Soviet Union. Soviet Union -- Politics and government -- 1985-1991.

DK288.D865 1993
Dunlop, John B.
The rise of Russia and the fall of the Soviet empire/ John B. Dunlop. Princeton, N.J.: Princeton University Press, c1993. xi, 360 p.
93-001648   947.085   0691078750
Soviet Union -- Politics and government -- 1985-1991. Russia (Federation) -- Politics and government.

DK288.E35 1989
Eklof, Ben, 1946-
Soviet briefing: Gorbachev and the reform period/ Ben Eklof. Boulder: Westview Press, 1989. xi, 195 p.
88-020575   947.085/4   0813307929
Soviet Union -- Politics and government -- 1985-1991. Soviet Union -- Social conditions -- 1970-1991.

DK288.G59 1991
Goldman, Marshall I.
What went wrong with Perestroika/ Marshall I. Goldman. New York: Norton, c1991. 258 p.
91-016281   947.085/4   0393030717
Gorbachev, Mikhail Sergeevich, -- 1931-Perestroika. Soviet Union -- Politics and government -- 1985-1991.

DK288.H67 1990
Hosking, Geoffrey A.
The awakening of the Soviet Union/ Geoffrey Hosking. Cambridge, Mass.: Harvard University Press, 1990. viii, 182 p.
89-038876   947.085   0674055500
Perestroika. Soviet Union -- Politics and government -- 1985-1991. Soviet Union -- Intellectual life -- 1970-1991. Soviet Union -- Social life and customs -- 1970-1991.

DK288.K57 1991
Kirkpatrick, Jeane J.
The withering away of the totalitarian state-- and other surprises/ Jeane J. Kirkpatrick. Washington, D.C.: AEI Press; 1990. xi, 317 p.
90-019951   947.085/4   0844737275
Totalitarianism. Soviet Union -- Foreign relations -- 1985-1991. Soviet Union -- Politics and government -- 1985-1991.

DK288.K85 1992
Kull, Steven.
Burying Lenin: the revolution in Soviet ideology and foreign policy/ Steven Kull. Boulder: Westview Press, 1992. xvi, 219 p.
91-045077   327.47   0813315018
Perestroika. Soviet Union -- Foreign relations -- 1985-1991. Soviet Union -- Politics and government -- 1985-1991.

DK288.L36 1990
Lane, David Stuart.
Soviet society under perestroika/ David Lane. Boston: Unwin Hyman, 1990. xv, 401 p.
89-024916   306.2/0947   0044451660
Perestroika. Soviet Union -- Social conditions -- 1970-1991. Soviet Union -- Politics and government -- 1985-1991.

DK288.M386 1995
Matlock, Jack F.
Autopsy on an empire: the American ambassador's account of the collapse of the Soviet Union/ Jack F. Matlock, Jr. New York: Random House, c1995. viii, 836 p.
95-013833   327.47073   0679413766
Soviet Union -- Politics and government -- 1985-1991. Soviet Union -- Foreign relations -- United States. United States -- Foreign relations -- Soviet Union.

DK288.M42 1992
McAuley, Mary.
Soviet politics 1917-1991/ Mary McAuley. Oxford; Oxford University Press, 1992. 132 p.
92-007517   947.084   0198780664
Soviet Union -- Politics and government.

DK288.M88 1997
Murrell, G. D. G.
Russia's transition to democracy: an internal political history, 1989-1996/ G.D.G. Murrell; foreword by Brian Fall. Brighton; Sussex Academic Press, 1997. xii, 276 p.
97-123517   947.085   1898723575
Democratization -- Soviet Union. Democratization -- Russia (Federation) Soviet Union -- Politics and government -- 1985-1991. Russia (Federation) -- Politics and government -- 1991-

DK288.N37 1990
The Nationalities question in the Soviet Union/ edited by Graham Smith. London; Longman, 1990. ix, 389 p.
90-034756   320.947   0582039533
Nationalism -- Soviet Union. Perestroika. Soviet Union -- Politics and government -- 1985-1991.

DK288.R46 1993
Remnick, David.
Lenin's tomb: the last days of the Soviet Empire/ David Remnick. New York: Random House, c1993. xii, 576 p.
92-056841   947.085/4   0679423761
Soviet Union -- Politics and government -- 1985-1991.

DK288.S59 1990
Smith, Hedrick.
The new Russians/ Hedrick Smith. New York: Random House, 1990. xxxi, 621 p.
90-053127   947.085   0394581903
Gorbachev, Mikhail Sergeevich, -- 1931-Perestroika. Soviet Union -- Politics and government -- 1985-1991. Soviet Union -- Social conditions -- 1970-1991.

DK288.T43 1988
Teague, Elizabeth.
Solidarity and the Soviet worker: the impact of the Polish events of 1980 on Soviet internal politics/ Elizabeth Teague. London; Croom Helm; c1988. 378 p.
87-031036   947.085/3   0709943504
Public opinion -- Soviet Union. Working class -- Soviet Union -- History -- 20th century. Soviet Union -- Politics and government -- 1985-1991. Poland -- Politics and government -- 1980-1989. Soviet Union -- Politics and government -- 1953-1985.

DK288.W46 1991
White, Stephen, 1945-
Gorbachev and after/ Stephen White. Cambridge; Cambridge University Press, c1991. ix, 310 p.
91-217741   947.085/4   0521413796
Gorbachev, Mikhail Sergeevich, -- 1931-   Soviet Union -- Politics and government -- 1985-

DK288.Z37 1990
Zaslavskaia, T. I.
The second socialist revolution: an alternative Soviet strategy/ Tatyana Zaslavskaya; foreword by Teodor Shanin; translated by Susan M. Davies with Jenny Warren. Bloomington: Indiana University Press, c1990. xx, 241 p.
90-034127   947.085/4   025336860X
Perestroika. Soviet Union -- Economic policy -- 1986-1991. Soviet Union -- Social conditions -- 1970-1991. Soviet Union -- Politics and government -- 1985-1991.

DK289.G675 1987
Gorbachev, Mikhail Sergeevich, 1931-
Perestroika: new thinking for our country and the world/ Mikhail Gorbachev. Cambridge [Cambridgeshire]; Harper & Row, c1987. p. cm.
87-046197   327/.09/048
World politics -- 1985-1995. Perestroika. Soviet Union -- Foreign relations -- 1975- Soviet Union -- Politics and government -- 1985-1991.

DK289.S686 1987
The Soviet Union in transition/ edited by Kinya Niiseki; contributors, Seweryn Bialer ... [et al.]. Boulder, Colo.: Westview Press, 1987. ix, 243 p.
86-032611   327.47   0813373751
Soviet Union -- Foreign relations -- 1975- Soviet Union -- Economic policy -- 1981-1985. Soviet Union -- Politics and government -- 1953-1985.

DK290.3.G67.A3 1996
Gorbachev, Mikhail Sergeevich, 1931-
Memoirs/ Mikhail Gorbachev. New York: Doubleday, 1996. xxix, 769 p.
96-041308   947.085/4/092   0385480199
Gorbachev, Mikhail Sergeevich, -- 1931- Heads of state -- Soviet Union -- Biography. Soviet Union -- History -- 1985-1991.

DK290.3.G67.G7313 1995
Grachev, A. S.
Final days: the inside story of the collapse of the Soviet Union/ Andrei S. Grachev; with a foreword by Archie Brown; translated by Margo Milne. Boulder, Colo.: Westview Press, c1995. xviii, 222 p.
95-016424   947.085/4/092   0813322065
Gorbachev, Mikhail Sergeevich, -- 1931- Presidents -- Soviet Union -- Biography. Soviet Union -- Politics and government -- 1985-1991.

DK290.3.S54.E38 1997
Ekedahl, Carolyn McGiffert.
The wars of Eduard Shevardnadze/ Carolyn McGiffert Ekedahl and Melvin A. Goodman. University Park, Pa.: Pennsylvania State University Press, c1997. xxiii, 331 p.
96-019615   947.085/4/092   0271016043
Shevardnadze, Eduard Amvrosievich. Statesmen -- Soviet Union -- Biography. Soviet Union -- Foreign relations -- 1985-1991.

DK290.3.Y45
Yeltsin, Boris Nikolayevich, 1931-
Midnight diaries/ Boris Yeltsin; translated by Catherine A. Fitzpatrick. New York: PublicAffairs, c2000. xxiii, 398 p.
00-062624   947.086/092   1586480111
Yeltsin, Boris Nikolayevich, -- 1931- Heads of state -- Russia (Federation) -- Biography. Russia (Federation) -- Politics and government -- 1991-

DK292.R86 1994
Russia at the barricades: eyewitness accounts of the August 1991 coup/ edited by Victoria E. Bonnell, Ann Cooper, and Gregory Freidin. Armonk, N.Y.: M.E. Sharpe, c1994. xx, 371 p.
93-027944   947.085/4/0922   1563242710
Soviet Union -- History -- Attempted coup, 1991 -- Personal narratives. Soviet Union -- History -- Attempted coup, 1991 -- Sources.

DK293.C656 1998
Commonwealth and independence in post-Soviet Eurasia/ edited by Bruno Coppieters, Alexei Zverev and Dmitri Trenin. London; F. Cass, c1998. 224 p.
97-049408   947.086   0714648817
Former Soviet republics -- Politics and government. Former Soviet republics -- Ethnic realtions.

DK293.D38 1994
Dawisha, Karen.
Russia and the new states of Eurasia: the politics of upheaval/ Karen Dawisha and Bruce Parrott. Cambridge [England]; Cambridge University Press, 1994. xvii, 437 p.
93-020994   947.086   0521452627
Former Soviet republics -- Politics and government.

DK293.N387 1998
Nations abroad: diaspora politics and international relations in the former Soviet Union/ edited by Charles King and Neil J. Melvin. Boulder, Colo.: Westview Press, 1998. p. cm.
98-026641   305.8/00947   081339015X
Ethnology -- Former Soviet republics -- Political aspects. Former Soviet republics -- Ethnic relations -- Political aspects. Former Soviet Republics -- Foreign relations.

DK293.W43 1996
Webber, Mark.
The international politics of Russia and the successor states/ Mark Webber. Manchester; Manchester University Press, 1996. xvii, 366 p.
95-004960   947.085/4   0719039606
National security -- Former Soviet republics. World politics -- 1989- Former Soviet republics -- Economic conditions. Soviet Union -- Politics and government -- 1985-1991. Former Soviet republics -- Foreign relations.

DK411-443 Poland

DK411.M5
Milosz, Czeslaw.
The captive mind; translated from the Polish by Jane Zielonko. New York, Knopf, 1953. 251 p.
52-012209   914.38
Communism -- Poland. Poland -- Intellectual life.

DK414.S45
Sharp, Samuel L 1908-
Poland, white eagle on a red field. Cambridge, Harvard University Press, 1953. vii, 338 p.
53-006034   943.8
Poland -- History.

DK434.K33 1972
Kaplan, Herbert H.
The first partition of Poland [by] Herbert H. Kaplan. New York, Columbia University Press, 1962. [New York, AMS Press, 1972] xvi, 215 p.
76-171548   943.8/02   0404036368
Poland -- History -- First partition, 1772.

DK434.L7 1969
Lord, Robert Howard, 1885-1954.
The second partition of Poland; a study in diplomatic history. New York, AMS Press [1969] xxx, 586 p.
73-101268   943.8/02
Poland -- History -- Second partition, 1793.

DK437.L48 1969
Leslie, R. F.
Reform and insurrection in Russian Poland, 1856-1865. Westport, Conn., Greenwood Press [1969, c1963] ix, 272 p.
72-091767   943.8/03   0837124158
Poland -- History -- 1830-1864.

DK440.5.P5.A42
Pilsudski, Jozef, 1867-1935.
Joseph Pilsudski; the memories of a Polish revolutionary and soldier, translated and edited by D. R. Gillie. London, Faber & Faber [1931] x, 377 p.
31-015807   923.5438
Socialism in Poland. World War, 1914-1918 -- Poland. Poland -- Politics and government.

DK443.S7 1975
Staar, Richard Felix, 1923-
Poland, 1944-1962: the Sovietization of a captive people/ Richard F. Staar. Westport, Conn.: Greenwood Press, 1975, c1962. xviii, 300 p.
75-001297   943.8/05   0837180082
Communism -- Poland. Poland -- History -- 1945-1980.

DK458-459.5 Finland

DK458.W8 1931a
Wuorinen, John Henry.
Nationalism in modern Finland, by John H. Wuorinen. New York, Columbia University Press, 1931. x, 302 p.
31-033686   947.1
Finland -- History. Finland -- Nationality. Finland -- Politics and government.

DK459.K57 1979
Kirby, D. G.
Finland in the twentieth century/ by D.G. Kirby. Minneapolis: University of Minnesota Press, c1979. x, 253 p.
79-011651   948.97/03   0816608954
Finland -- Politics and government -- 20th century.

DK459.5.J33
Jakobson, Max.
The diplomacy of the winter war; an account of the Russo-Finnish War, 1939-1940. Cambridge, Mass., Harvard University Press, 1961. 281 p.
61-005578
Russo-Finnish War, 1939-1940 -- Diplomatic history.

DK459.5.T312
Tanner, Vaino, 1881-1966.
The winter war: Finland against Russia, 1939-1940. Stanford, Calif., Stanford University Press [1957] 274 p.
57-005904   947.1
Russo-Finnish War, 1939-1940.

DK502.7 Local history and description — Baltic States — General works

DK502.7.B3437 1996
The Baltic states after independence/ Ole Norgaard ... [et al.] Cheltenham, England; E. Elgar, c1996. x, 231 p.
95-040193   947/.4   1858983037
Post-communism -- Baltic States. Democracy -- Baltic States. Baltic States -- Politics and government -- 1991- Baltic States -- Economic conditions. Baltic States -- Social conditions.

DK502.7.B344 1994
The Baltic States: the national self-determination of Estonia, Latvia, and Lithuania/ edited by Graham Smith. New York: St. Martin's Press, 1994. xii, 214 p.
93-045834   947/.4   0312120605
Nationalism -- Baltic States. Baltic States -- History -- Autonomy and independence movements.

DK502.7.K57 1995
Kirby, D. G.
The Baltic world, 1772-1993: Europe's northern periphery in an age of change/ David Kirby. London; Longman, 1995. viii, 472 p.
94-022617   947/.407   058200408X
Baltic States -- History.

DK502.7.L54 1993
Lieven, Anatol.
The Baltic revolution: Estonia, Latvia, Lithuania, and the path to independence/ Anatol Lieven. New Haven: Yale University Press, 1993. xxv, 454 p.
92-047282   947/.4   0300055528
Baltic States -- History.

DK502.7.T68 1990
Toward independence: the Baltic popular movements/ edited by Jan Arveds Trapans. Boulder: Westview Press, 1991. [vii], 166 p.
90-023124   947/.4   0813381444
Nationalism -- Baltic States -- Congresses. Baltic States -- History -- Autonomy and independence movements -- Congresses. Soviet Union -- History -- Autonomy and independence movements -- Congresses.

DK502.715 Local history and description — Baltic States — Foreign and general relations

DK502.715.B67 1998
Bordering Russia: theory and prospects for Europe's Baltic Rim/ edited by Hans Mouritzen. Aldershot; Ashgate, c1998. xii, 322 p.
97-039119   327.479047   185521959X
European Union. World politics -- 1989- Russia (Federation) -- Foreign relations -- Finland. Finland -- Foreign relations -- Russia (Federation) Russia (Federation) -- Foreign relations -- Poland.

DK502.74 Local history and description — Baltic States — By period

DK502.74.E39 1999
Eksteins, Modris.
Walking since daybreak: a story of Eastern Europe, World War II, and the heart of our century/ Modris Eksteins. Boston: Houghton Mifflin Co., 1999. xiv, 258 p.
99-017856   947.9   0395937477
Eksteins, Modris.   Baltic States -- History -- 1940-1991.

DK503.54 Local history and description — Estonia — History

DK503.54 .R38 2001
Raun, Toivo U.
Estonia and the Estonians/ Toivo U. Raun. Updated 2nd ed. Stanford, Calif.: Hoover Institution Press, Stanford University, xix, 366 p.
2002-279856   947.98 21   0817928529
Estonia -- History. Estonia -- History -- Autonomy and independence movements.

DK503.54.T33 1993
Taagepera, Rein.
Estonia: return to independence/ Rein Taagepera. Boulder: Westview Press, 1993. xv, 268 p.
92-021376   947/.41   0813311993
Estonia -- History.

DK504.37 Local history and description — Latvia — History

DK504.37.P58 1997
Plakans, Andrejs.
Historical dictionary of Latvia/ Andrejs Plakans. Lanham, Md.: Scarecrow Press, 1997. xxvi, 193 p.
96-049234   947.96/003   0810832925
Latvia -- History -- Dictionaries.

DK505.37-505.85 Local history and description — Lithuania — History

DK505.37.S89 1997
Suziedelis, Saulius, 1945-
Historical dictionary of Lithuania/ Saulius Suziedelis. Lanham, MD: Scarecrow Press, 1997. p. cm.
97-012398   947.93/003   0810833352
Lithuania -- History -- Dictionaries.

DK505.54.V37 1997
Vardys, Vytas Stanley, 1924-
Lithuania: the rebel nation/ V. Stanley Vardys and Judith B. Sedaitis. Boulder, Colo.: Westview Press, 1997. xi, 242 p.
96-042556   947/.5   0813383080
Lithuania -- History.

DK505.74.E38 1998
Eidintas, A.
Lithuania in European politics: the years of first republic, 1918-1940/ Alfonsas Eidintas, Vytautas Zalys; [introduction and afterword by Alfred Erich Senn]; edited by Edvardas Tuskenis. New York: St. Martin's Press, 1998. 250 p.
97-003589   947.93084   031217232X
Lithuania -- History -- 1918-1945.

DK505.74.S46 1990
Senn, Alfred Erich.
Lithuania awakening/ Alfred Erich Senn. Berkeley: University of California Press, c1990. 294 p.
90-032503   947/.5084   0520071700
Nationalism -- Lithuania -- History -- 20th century.   Lithuania -- History -- 1945-1991. Lithuania -- History -- 1918-1945.

DK505.8.A84 1999
Ashbourne, Alexandra, 1971-
Lithuania: the rebirth of a nation, 1991-1994/ Alexandra Ashbourne. Lanham, Md.: Lexington Books, c1999. xii, 219 p.
99-020819   947.9308/6   0739100270
Lithuania -- History -- 1991-

DK505.85.L36
Landsbergis, Vytautas.
Lithuania, independent again: the autobiography of Vytautas Landsbergis/ prepared for an English-speaking audience by Anthony Packer and Eimutis Sova. Seattle: University of Washington Press, 2000. xii, 388 p.
00-691032   0295979593
Landsbergis, Vytautas. Statesmen -- Lithuania -- Biography. Lithuania -- Politics and government -- 1945-1991. Lithuania -- Politics and government -- 1991-

DK507.37-507.73 Local history and description — Belarus. Byelorussian — History

DK507.37.Z37 1998
Zaprudnik, Jan.
Historical dictionary of Belarus/ Jan Zaprudnik. Lanham, Md.: Scarecrow Press, 1998. xxxvii, 299 p.
97-041119   947.8   0810834499
Belarus -- History -- Dictionaries.

DK507.54.Z37 1993
Zaprudnik, Jan.
Belarus: at a crossroads in history/ Jan Zaprudnik. Boulder: Westview Press, c1993. xxi, 278 p.
92-042923   947/.65   0813313392
Belarus -- History.

DK507.73.M37 1996
Marples, David R.
Belarus: from Soviet rule to nuclear catastrophe/ David R. Marples. New York: St. Martin's Press, 1996. xxi, 179 p.
96-033782   947/.65084   0312161816
Chernobyl Nuclear Accident, Chornobyl, Ukraine, 1986.   Belarus -- History -- 1991- Belarus -- History -- 1917-1991.

DK508.45-508.848 Local history and description — Ukraine — History

DK508.45.W55 2000
Wilson, Andrew, 1961-
The Ukrainians: unexpected nation/ Andrew Wilson. New Haven: Yale University Press, c2000. xviii, 366 p.
00-033565   947.7   0300083556
Ukraine -- History.

DK508.5.H683 1970
Hrushevskyi, Mykhailo, 1866-1934.
A history of Ukraine, by Michael Hrushevsky. Edited by O. J. Frederiksen. Pref. by George Vernadsky. Published for the Ukrainian National Association. [Hamden, Conn.] Archon Books, 1970 [c1941] xviii, 629 p.
72-120370   947.7/1   0208009671
Ukraine -- History. Kievan Rus -- History.

DK508.51.M34 1996
Magocsi, Paul R.
A history of Ukraine/ Paul Robert Magocsi. Seattle: University of Washington Press, c1996. xxi, 784 p.
96-020027   947/.71   0295975806
Ukraine -- History. Kievan Rus -- History.

DK508.51.S93 2000
Subtelny, Orest.
Ukraine: a history/ Orest Subtelny. 3rd ed. Toronto; University of Toronto Press, 2000. xvi, 736 p.
2001-268184   947.7.221   0802083900
Ukraine -- History.

DK508.57.R9.L54 1999
Lieven, Anatol.
Ukraine & Russia: a fraternal rivalry/ Anatol Lieven. Washington, DC: United States Institute of Peace Press, 1999. xvi, 182 p.
99-012974   303.48/2477047   1878379879
Nationalism -- Ukraine. Nationalism -- Russia (Federation) Ukraine -- Relations -- Russia (Federation) Russia (Federation) -- Relations -- Ukraine.

DK508.57.R9.S65 2001
Solchanyk, Roman.
Ukraine and Russia: the post-Soviet transition/ Roman Solchanyk. Lanham, MD: Rowman & Littlefield Publishers, c2001. xii, 237 p.
00-059058   327.477047   0742510174
Ukraine -- Foreign relations -- Russia (Federation) Russia (Federation) -- Foreign relations -- Ukraine. Ukraine -- Foreign relations -- 1991-

DK508.84.K89 1994
Kuzio, Taras.
Ukraine: Perestroika to independence/ Taras Kuzio and Andrew Wilson; foreword by Norman Stone. New York: St. Martin's Press, 1994. xiv, 260 p.
92-020998   947/.71   0312086520
Nationalism -- Ukraine. Perestroika -- Ukraine. Ukraine -- History -- Autonomy and independence movements.

DK508.848.W55 1996
Wilson, Andrew, 1961-
Ukrainian nationalism in the 1990s: a minority faith/ Andrew Wilson. Cambridge [Eng.]; Cambridge University Press, 1996. xvii, 300 p.
96-028278   320.5/4/094771   0521482852
Nationalism -- Ukraine. Ukraine -- Politics and government -- 1991- Ukraine -- Ethnic relations -- Political aspects.

DK509 Local history and description — Southern Soviet Union

DK509.G65 1994
Goldenberg, Suzanne, 1962-
Pride of small nations: the Caucasus and post-Soviet disorder/ Suzanne Goldenberg. London; Zed Books, c1994. xv, 233 p.
95-101718   947.9   1856492370
Caucasus -- History.

DK509.H88 1994
Hunter, Shireen.
The transcaucasia in transition: nation-building and conflict/ Shireen T. Hunter. Washington, D.C.: Center for Strategic and International Studies,i c1994. xiii, 223 p.
94-014614   947/.9   0892062479
Transcaucasia -- Politics and government.

DK509.37-509.54 Local history and description — Moldova. Moldavian S.S.R. Bessarabia — History

DK509.37.B74 2000
Brezianu, Andrei.
Historical dictionary of the Republic of Moldova/ Andrei Brezianu. Lanham, Md.: Scarecrow Press, 2000. lxi, 274 p.
99-051306   947.6   081083734X
Moldova -- History -- Dictionaries.

DK509.54 .K56 2000
King, Charles,
The Moldovans: Romania, Russia, and the politics of culture/ Charles King. Stanford, CA: Hoover Institution Press, c2000. xxix, 303 p.
99-041906   947.6 21   081799792X
Moldova -- History.

DK510.33-510.36 Local history and description — Russia (Federation). Russian S.F.S.R. — Ethnography

DK510.33.D73 1998
Draitser, Emil, 1937-
Taking penguins to the movies: ethnic humor in Russia/ Emil A. Draitser. Detroit: Wayne State University Press, 1998. 199 p.
97-044214   305.8/00947   0814323278
Russian wit and humor. Joking -- Russia (Federation) Russia (Federation) -- Ethnic relations.

DK510.33.F35 2000
The fall of an empire, the birth of a nation: national identities in Russia/ edited by Chris J. Chulos and Timo Piirainen. Aldershot, England; Ashgate, c2000. vii, 227 p.
99-076159   1855219026
Ethnicity -- Russia (Federation) Nationalism -- Russia (Federation) Russia (Federation) -- Ethnic relations. Russia (Federation) -- Politics and government -- 1991-

DK510.33.M36 1997
Managing conflict in the former Soviet Union: Russian and American perspectives/ editors, Alexei Arbatov ... [et al.]. Cambridge, Mass.: MIT Press, c1997. xv, 556 p.
97-011343   327.47   0262510936
Russia (Federation) -- Ethnic relations -- Government policy. United States -- Ethnic relations -- Government policy.

DK510.36.K65 1995
Kolsto, Pal.
Russians in the former Soviet republics/ Paul Kolstoe; with a contribution by Andrei Edemsky. Bloomington: Indiana University Press, c1995. xii, 340 p.
95-005773   323.1/09171/247   0253329175
Russians -- Former Soviet republics. Former Soviet republics -- Ethnic relations.

DK510.36.N18 1994
The new Russian diaspora: Russian minorities in the former Soviet republics/ edited by Vladimir Shlapentokh, Munir Sendich, and Emil Payin. Armonk, N.Y.: M.E. Sharpe, c1994. xxv, 221 p.
94-000727   305.891/71047   1563243350
Russians -- Former Soviet republics. Immigrants -- Russia (Federation) Former Soviet republics -- Emigration and immigration.

DK510.555-510.766 Local history and description — Russia (Federation). Russian S.F.S.R. — History

DK510.555.A45 1998
Allensworth, Wayne, 1959-
The Russian question: nationalism, modernization, and post-Communist Russia/ Wayne Allensworth. Lanham, Md.: Rowman & Littlefield, c1998. xiii, 351 p.
98-024157   320.947/09/049   0847690024
Nationalism -- Russia (Federation) Patriotism -- Russia (Federation) Post-communism -- Russia (Federation) Russia (Federation) -- History -- Philosophy.

DK510.762.C66 1999
Consuming Russia: popular culture, sex, and society since Gorbachev/ edited by Adele Marie Baker. Durham, [N.C.]: Duke University Press, 1999. p. cm.
98-050856   947.086   0822322811
Popular culture -- Russia (Federation) Sex -- Russia (Federation) Russia (Federation) -- Civilization.

DK510.762.M4 1996
McDaniel, Tim.
The Agony of the Russian idea/ Tim McDaniel. Princeton, N.J.: Princeton University Press, c1996. x, 201 p.
95-053191   947.08   0691027862
Post-communism -- Russia (Federation) Political culture -- Russia (Federation) -- History. Public opinion -- Russia (Federation) Russia (Federation) -- Politics and government. Russia (Federation) -- Social conditions. Soviet Union -- Social conditions.

DK510.763.R43 2001
Reddaway, Peter.
The tragedy of Russia's reforms: market bolshevism against democracy/ Peter Reddaway and Dmitri Glinski. Washington, D.C.: United States Institute of Peace Press, 2001. xvi, 745 p.
00-020482 947.086 1929223072
Post-communism -- Russia (Federation) Russia (Federation) -- Politics and government -- 1991- Russia (Federation) -- Social conditions -- 1991- Russia (Federation) -- Social policy.

DK510.763.R46 1997
Remnick, David.
Resurrection: the struggle for a new Russia/ David Remnick. New York: Random House, c1997. xiii, 398 p.
96-047360 947.086 067942377X
Russia (Federation) -- Politics and government -- 1991-

DK510.763.R859 2001
Russia in the new century: stability or disorder?/ edited by Victoria E. Bonnell and George W. Breslauer. Boulder, Colo.: Westview Press, c2001. xii, 380 p.
00-043310 947.086 0813390419
Nationalism -- Russia (Federation) Post-communism -- Russia (Federation) Russia (Federation) -- Social conditions -- 1991- Russia (Federation) -- Politics and government -- 1991- Russia (Federation) -- Economic conditions -- 1991-

DK510.763.R872 2001
Russia's fate through Russian eyes: voices of the new generation/ edited by Heyward Isham; with Natan M. Shklyar; with an introduction by Jack F. Matlock. Boulder, CO: Westview Press, c2001. xviii, 429 p.
00-046224 947.086 0813338662
Russia (Federation) -- Politics and government -- 1991- Russia (Federation) -- Economic conditions -- 1991- Russia (Federation) -- Social conditions -- 1991-

DK510.763.T78 1997
Truscott, Peter.
Russia first: breaking with the West/ Peter Truscott. London; I.B. Tauris, 1997. p. cm.
97-038382 947.086 1860641997
Russia (Federation) -- Politics and government -- 1991-

DK510.764.B69 1997
Bowker, Mike.
Russian foreign policy and the end of the Cold War/ Mike Bowker. Aldershot, Hants, England; Dartmouth Pub. Co., c1997. ix, 297 p.
96-039521 327.47 185521461X
World politics -- 1989- Cold War. Soviet Union -- Foreign relations -- 1985-1991. Russia (Federation) -- Foreign relations.

DK510.764.B87 1996
Buszynski, Leszek.
Russian foreign policy after the Cold War/ Leszek Buszynski. Westport, Conn: Praeger, 1996. xiv, 243 p.
96-000551 327.47 0275955850
Russia (Federation) -- Foreign relations.

DK510.766.Z48.K37 1995
Kartsev, Vladimir Petrovich.
!Zhirinovsky!/ Vladimir Kartsev with Todd Bludeau. New York: Columbia University Press, c1995. xii, 198 p.
95-000960 947.086/092 0231102100
Zhirinovskii, Vladimir, -- 1946- Politicians -- Russia (Federation) -- Biography. Russia (Federation) -- Politics and government -- 1991-

DK511-651 Local history and description — Russia (Federation). Russian S.F.S.R. — Local history and description of European Russian S.F.S.R.

DK511.B3.M57 1983
Misiunas, Romuald J.
The Baltic States, years of dependence, 1940-1980/ by Romuald J. Misiunas and Rein Taagepera. Berkeley: University of California Press, c1983. xvi, 333 p.
82-004727 947/.40842 0520046250
Baltic States -- History -- 1940-1991.

DK511.B3.R3413
Rauch, Georg von.
The Baltic States: the years of independence; Estonia, Latvia, Lithuania, 1917-1940, by Georg von Rauch. Translated from the German by Gerald Onn. Berkeley, University of California Press [1974] xv, 265 p.
73-086849 947/.4/084 0520026004
Baltic States -- History.

DK511.C2.K27 2000
Karny, Yo'av.
Highlanders: a journey to the Caucasus in quest of memory/ Yo'av Karny. New York: Farrar, Straus and Giroux, 2000. xxvi, 436 p.
99-086037 305.8/009475 0374226024
Ethnicity -- Russia (Federation) -- Caucasus, Northern. Minorities -- Russia (Federation) -- Caucasus, Northern. Islam -- Russia (Federation) -- Caucasus, Northern. Caucasus, Northern (Russia) -- Ethnic relations. Caucasus, Northern (Russia) -- History -- Autonomy and independence movements. Russia -- Ethnic relations.

DK511.C37.D86 1998
Dunlop, John B.
Russia confronts Chechnya: roots of a separatist conflict/ John B. Dunlop. Cambridge; Cambridge University Press, 1998. xi, 234 p.
97-051840 947.5/2 052163184X
Chechnia (Russia) -- History. Chechnia (Russia) -- History -- Civil War, 1994-1996 -- Causes.

DK511.C37.K597 1999
Knezys, Stasys.
The war in Chechnya/ Stasys Knezys and Romanas Sedlickas. College Station, TX: Texas A&M University Press, 1999. xiv, 359 p.
98-053500 947.5/2 089096856X
Chechnia (Russia) -- History -- Civil War, 1994-

DK511.C37.L54 1998
Lieven, Anatol.
Chechnya: tombstone of Russian power/ Anatol Lieven; with photographs by Heidi Bradner. New Haven: Yale University Press, c1998. xii, 436 p.
98-084479 947.5/2 0300073984
Chechnia (Russia) -- History -- Civil War, 1994-1996.

DK511.C37.R87 1998
Russia and Chechnia: the permanent crisis: essays on Russo-Chechen relations/ edited by Ben Fowkes. New York: St. Martin's Press, 1998. viii, 188 p.
97-037269 947.5/2 0312211279
Chechnia (Russia) -- Relations -- Russia (Federation) Russia (Federation) -- Relations -- Chechnia (Russia) Chechnia (Russia) -- History -- Autonomy and independence movements.

DK511.C37.S44 2001
Seely, Robert.
Russo-Chechen conflict, 1800-2000: a deadly embrace/ Robert Seely. Portland, OR: Frank Cass, c2001. xi, 333 p.
00-034546 947.5/2 0714649929
Chechnia (Russia) -- History -- Civil War, 1994-

DK511.C7 F497
Fisher, Alan W.
The Crimean Tatars/ Alan Fisher. Stanford, Calif.: Hoover Institution Press, c1978. xii, 264 p.
76-041085 947/.717/004943 0817966617
Crimea (Ukraine) -- History. Crimean Tatars-- History.

DK511.D7.K87 1998
Kuromiya, Hiroaki.
Freedom and terror in the Donbas: a Ukrainian-Russian borderland, 1870s-1990s/ Hiroaki Kuromiya. Cambridge [England]; Cambridge University Press, 1998. xiv, 357 p.
98-015789 947.7/4 0521622387
Political persecution -- Donets Basin (Ukraine and Russia) Donets Basin (Ukraine and Russia) -- History -- 20th century. Donets Basin (Ukraine and Russia) -- History -- 19th century.

DK511.G4.L3
Lang, David Marshall.
A modern history of Soviet Georgia. New York, Grove Press [1962] 298 p.
62-013057 947.95
Georgian S.S.R. -- History.

DK511.K157.B68 1999
Boterbloem, Kees, 1962-
Life and death under Stalin: Kalinin Province, 1945-1953/ Kees Boterbloem. Montreal; McGill-Queen's University Press, c1999. xxv, 435 p.
00-340568 947/.240842 0773518118
Kaliningradskaia oblast (Russia) -- History -- 20th century.

DK557.V65 1995
Volkov, Solomon.
St. Petersburg: a cultural history/ Solomon Volkov; translated by Antonina W. Bouis. New York: Free Press, c1995. xxiv, 598 p.
95-024116 947/.453 0028740521
Saint Petersburg (Russia) -- Civilization.

DK568.M35 1990
McKean, Robert B.
St. Petersburg between the revolutions: workers and revolutionaries, June 1907-February 1917/ Robert B. McKean. New Haven: Yale University Press, 1990. xv, 606 p.
89-070734 947/.453083 0300047916
Labor movement -- Russia (Federation) -- Saint Petersburg -- History -- 20th century. Revolutionaries -- Russia (Federation) -- Saint Petersburg -- History -- 20th century. Saint Petersburg (Russia) -- History -- To 1917.

DK651.M159.K675 1995
Kotkin, Stephen.
Magnetic mountain: Stalinism as a civilization/
Stephen Kotkin. Berkeley: University of California
Press, c1995. xxv, 639 p.
94-011839   947/.87   0520069080
*Communism -- Soviet Union -- Case studies.
Soviet Union -- Politics and government -- 1917-
1936. Magnitogorsk (Russia) -- History.*

DK651.M159.K68 1991
Kotkin, Stephen.
Steeltown, USSR: Soviet society in the Gorbachev
era/ Stephen Kotkin. Berkeley: University of
California Press, c1991. xxx, 269 p.
90-011310   947/.87   0520073533
*Perestroika -- Russia (Federation) --
Magnitogorsk. Magnitogorsk (Russia) -- Politics
and government. Soviet Union -- Politics and
government -- 1985-1991.*

DK672.9 Local history and description — Georgia (Republic). Georgian S.S.R. Georgian — Description and travel

DK672.9.N38 1998
Nasmyth, Peter.
Georgia: in the mountains of poetry/ Peter
Nasmyth. New York: St. Martin's Press, 1998. xiii,
306 p.
98-017593   947.58   031221524X
*Georgia (Republic) -- Description and travel.
Georgia (Republic) -- History -- 1991-*

DK675.4 Local history and description — Georgia (Republic). Georgian S.S.R. Georgian — History

DK675.4.S86 1988
Suny, Ronald Grigor.
The making of the Georgian nation/ Ronald Grigor
Suny. Bloomington: Indiana University Press in
association with Hoo c1988. xviii, 395 p.
87-021367   947/.95   0253336236
Georgia (Republic) -- History.

DK687.5 Local history and description — Armenia (Republic). Armenian S.S.R. — History

DK687.5.M37 1999
Masih, Joseph R.
Armenia: at the crossroads/ Joseph R. Masih,
Robert O. Krikorian. Amsterdam, The Netherlands:
Harwood Academic Publishers, c1999. xxxiii,
142 p.
905702344X
*Armenia (Republic) -- Economic conditions --
1991- Armenia (Republic) -- Foreign relations.
Armenia (Republic) -- History -- 1991-*

DK695.4-696.6 Local history and description — Azerbaijan. Azerbaijan S.S.R. — History

DK695.4.S95 1995
Swietochowski, Tadeusz, 1934-
Russia and Azerbaijan: a borderland in transition/
Tadeusz Swietochowski. New York: Columbia
University Press, c1995. x, 290 p.
94-048574   327.47055/3   0231070683
*Nationalism -- Azerbaijan -- History.
Nationalism -- Iran -- Azerbaijan -- History.
Azerbaijan -- History. Azerbaijan (Iran) -- History.
Russia -- Relations -- Azerbaijan.*

DK696.6.A48 1992
Altstadt, Audrey L., 1953-
The Azerbaijani Turks: power and identity under
Russian rule/ Audrey L. Altstadt. Stanford, Calif.:
Hoover Institution Press, Stanford University,
c1992. xxiv, 331 p.
91-041684   947/.91   0817991816
*Azerbaijanis -- Social life and customs.
Azerbaijan -- Politics and government.*

DK699 Local history and description — Azerbaijan. Azerbaijan — Local history and description

DK699.N34.C76 1998
Croissant, Michael P., 1971-
The Armenia-Azerbaijan conflict: causes and
implications/ Michael P. Croissant. Westport,
Conn.: Praeger, 1998. xiv, 172 p.
98-005238   947.54   0275962415
*Nagorno-Karabakh Conflict, 1988-1994.
Armenia (Republic) -- Relations -- Azerbaijan.
Azerbaijan -- Relations -- Armenia (Republic)*

DK753 Local history and description — Siberia — General works

DK753.R3713 1996
Rasputin, Valentin Grigorevich.
Siberia, Siberia/ Valentin Rasputin; translated, and
with an introduction by Margaret Winchell and
Gerald Mikkelson; photographs by Boris Dmitriev.
Evanston, Ill.: Northwestern University Press,
c1996. 438 p.
96-007098   957   0810112876
*Ethnopsychology -- Russia (Federation) --
Siberia. Siberia (Russia) -- History. Siberia
(Russia) -- Environmental conditions.*

DK755 Local history and description — Siberia — Description and travel

DK755.K342x
Kennan, George, 1845-1924.
Siberia and the exile system/ Abridged from the 1st
ed. of 1891. With an introd. by George Frost
Kennan. [Chicago] University of Chicago Press
[1958] xix, 243 p.
58-005618   915.7
*Siberia (Russia) -- Description and travel.
Siberia (Russia) -- Exiles.*

DK759 Local history and description — Siberia — Ethnography

DK759.C45
Kerttula, Anna M.
Antler on the sea: the Yup'ik and Chukchi of the
Russian Far East/ Anna M. Kerttula. Ithaca, NY:
Cornell University Press, 2000. xiii, 180 p.
00-034036   957/.7   0801436818
*Chukchi. Yupik Eskimos -- Russia (Federation) --
Chukotskii avtonomnyi okrug. Ethnology -- Russia
(Federation) -- Chukotskii avtonomnyi okrug.
Chukotskii avtonomnyi okrug (Russia) -- Ethnic
relations.*

DK759.K53.B35 1999
Balzer, Marjorie Mandelstam.
The tenacity of ethnicity: a Siberian saga in global
perspective/ Marjorie Mandelstam Balzer.
Princeton, NJ: Princeton University Press, c1999.
xiv, 326 p.
99-022818   957/.004945   0691006741
*Khanty. Ethnology -- Russia (Federation) --
Siberia. Indigenous peoples -- Russia (Federation)
-- Siberia. Siberia (Russia) -- Ethnic relations.*

DK759.K6
Rethmann, Petra, 1964-
Tundra Passages: history and gender in the Russian
Far East/ Petra Rethmann. University Park, Pa.:
Pennsylvania State University Press, c2001. xxiv,
219 p.
00-027429   306/.09577   0271020571
*Koryaks -- Social conditions. Man-woman
relationships -- Russia (Federation) -- Koriakskii
avtonomnyi okrug. Post-communism -- Russia
(Federation) -- Koriakskii avtonomnyi okrug.
Koriakskii avtonomnyi okrug (Russia) -- Social
conditions. Koriakskii avtonomnyi okrug (Russia) -
- Social life and customs.*

DK761-766 Local history and description — Siberia — History

DK761.L56 1994
Lincoln, W. Bruce.
The conquest of a continent: Siberia and the
Russians/ W. Bruce Lincoln. New York: Random
House, c1994. xxii, 500 p.
93-022342   957   067941214X
Siberia (Russia) -- History.

DK761.M68 1998
Mote, Victor L.
Siberia--worlds apart/ Victor L. Mote. Boulder,
CO: Westview Press, 1998. xvi, 239 p.
98-014843   957   0813312981
Siberia (Russia) -- History.

DK766.M36 1991
Marks, Steven G. 1958-
Road to power: the Trans-Siberian railroad and the
colonization of Asian Russia, 1850-1917/ Steven
G. Marks. Ithaca, N.Y.: Cornell University Press,
1991. xxi, 240 p.
90-055734   957.08   0801425336
*Vitte, S. IU. -- (Sergei IUlevich), -- graf, -- 1849-
1915. Russia -- Economic conditions -- 1861-
1917. Siberia (Russia) -- History.*

DK771-781 Local history and description — Siberia — Local history and description

DK771.A3.B37 1999
Bassin, Mark.
Imperial visions: nationalist imagination and geographical expansion in the Russian Far East, 1840-1865/ Mark Bassin. Cambridge; Cambridge University Press, 1999. xiv, 329 p.
98-030355   957/.7   0521391741
Amur River Region (China and Russia) -- History -- 19th century.

DK771.A3.E83 1999
Evans, John L.
Russian expansion on the Amur, 1848-1860: the push to the Pacific/ John L. Evans. Lewiston, N.Y.: Edwin Mellen Press, c1999. iii, 245 p.
98-047706   327.47051   0773482792
Amur River Region (China and Russia) -- History -- 19th century. Russia -- Territorial expansion. Russia -- Foreign relations -- China.

DK771.D3.S74 1994
Stephan, John J.
The Russian Far East: a history/ John J. Stephan. Stanford, Calif.: Stanford University Press, 1994. xxiii, 481 p.
93-042011   950   0804723117
Russian Far East (Russia) -- History.

DK771.K67.B373 1998
Bardach, Janusz.
Man is wolf to man: surviving the gulag/ Janusz Bardach, Kathleen Gleeson. Berkeley, Calif.: University of California Press, c1998. xvi, 392 p.
98-005402   940.54/7247/09577   0520213521
Bardach, Janusz. Political prisoners -- Russia (Federation) -- Kolyma Mountains Region -- Biography. Kolyma Mountains Region -- History -- 20th century.

DK781.D98
Bychkova Jordan, Bella.
Siberian village: land and life in the Sakha Republic/ Bella Bychkova Jordan and Terry G. Jordan-Bychkov. Minneapolis: University of Minnesota Press, 2001. p. cm.
00-013104   957/.5   0816635692
Dzharkhan (Russia) -- Social life and customs. Dzharkhan (Russia) -- History. Sakha (Russia) -- Social life and customs.

DK781.M3 S35 1989
Scott, John,
Behind the Urals: an American worker in Russia's city of steel/ by John Scott. Enl. ed./ prepared by Stephen Kotkin. Bloomington, [Ind.]: Indiana University Press, c1989. xxv, 306 p.
88-046214   947/.87 19   0253351251
Scott, John, 1912-   --Journeys--Russia (Federation)--Magnitogorsk.   Steel industry and trade--Russia (Federation)--Magnitogorsk.

DK857.5-859.56 Local history and description — Soviet Central Asia. West Turkestan — History

DK857.5.A53 1997
Anderson, John,
The international politics of Central Asia/ John Anderson. Manchester, Eng.; Manchester University Press: 1997. x, 225 p.
97-005365   943   0719043727
Asia, Central -- Politics and government. Asia, Central -- Politics and government -- 1991- Asia, Central -- Foreign relations.

DK858.P5
Pierce, Richard A.
Russian Central Asia, 1867-1917; a study in colonial rule.   Berkeley, University of California Press, 1960. viii, 359 p.
59-011314
Soviet Union -- History.

DK859.5.C454 1994
Central Asia and the Caucasus after the Soviet Union: domestic and international dynamics/ edited by Mohiaddin Mesbahi. Gainesville: University Press of Florida, c1994. x, 353 p.
94-016204   947/.9086   0813013070
Muslims -- Former Soviet republics. Caucasus -- History. Asia, Central -- History -- 1991- Former Soviet republics -- Ethnic relations.

DK859.5.C66 1997
Conflict, cleavage, and change in Central Asia and the Caucasus/ edited by Karen Dawisha and Bruce Parrott. Cambridge, U.K.; Cambridge University Press, 1997. xviii, 423 p.
96-052478   320.958/09/049   0521592461
Democracy -- Asia, Central. Democracy -- Caucasus. Democratization -- Asia, Central. Asia, Central -- Politics and government -- 1991- Caucasus -- Politics and government.

DK859.5.H34 1995
Haghayeghi, Mehrdad.
Islam and politics in Central Asia/ Mehrdad Haghayeghi. New York: St. Martin's Press, 1995. p. cm.
94-030960   320.958   0312096224
Islam and politics -- Asia, Central. Islam -- Asia, Central -- History -- 20th century. Asia, Central -- Politics and government -- 1991- Asia, Central -- Ethnic relations.

DK859.5.H86 1996
Hunter, Shireen.
Central Asia since independence/ Shireen T. Hunter; forword by Marie Bennigsen Broxup. Westport, Conn.: Praeger, 1996. xx, 220 p.
96-010165   958   0275955389
Asia, Central -- History -- 1991-

DK859.5.O43 1996
Olcott, Martha Brill, 1949-
Central Asia's new states: independence, foreign policy, and regional security/ Martha Brill Olcott. Washington, D.C.: United States Institute of Peace Press, 1996. xv, 202 p.
95-030153   958   1878379518
Asia, Central -- Politics and government -- 1991-

DK859.56.G57 1999
Glenn, John, 1963-
The Soviet legacy in Central Asia/ John Glenn. New York: St. Martin's Press, 1999. p. cm.
98-055307   320.54/0958/09048   0312222181
National security -- Asia, Central. Nationalism -- Asia, Central. Asia, Central -- Politics and government -- 1991- Asia, Central -- Ethnic relations.

DK908.6-908.867 Local history and description — Kazakhstan. Kazakh S.S.R. — History

DK908.6 .O43 1995
Olcott, Martha Brill,
The Kazakhs/ Martha Brill Olcott. 2nd ed. Stanford, Calif.: Hoover Institution Press, Stanford University xxiii, 388 p.
95-019311   958/.45 20   0817993525
Kazakstan -- History.

DK908.867
George, Alexandra, 1952-
Journey into Kazakhstan: the true face of the Nazarbayev regime/ Alexandra George. Lanham, MD: University Press of America, 2001. p. cm.
01-018115   958.45086   0761819649
Kazakhstan -- Politics and government -- 1991-

DK928.85 Local history and description — Tajikistan. Tajik S.S.R. Tadzhikistan — History

DK928.85.T3313 1997
Tajikistan: the trials of independence/ edited by Mohammad-Reza Djalili, Frederic Grare and Shirin Akiner. New York: St. Martin's Press, 1997. xiii, 248 p.
97-017189   958.608/6   0312161433
Tajikistan -- History.

DK948.62-948.8657 Local history and description — Uzbekistan. Uzbek S.S.R. — History

DK948.62.A45 1990
Allworth, Edward.
The modern Uzbeks: from the fourteenth century to the present: a cultural history/ Edward A. Allworth. Stanford, Calif.: Hoover Institution Press, Stanford University, 1990. xiv, 410 p.
89-019899   958/.7   0817987312
Uzbekistan -- History.

DK948.83.B87 1997
Burton, Audrey.
The Bukharans: a dynastic, diplomatic, and commercial history, 1550-1702/ Audrey Burton. New York: St. Martin's Press, 1997. xx, 664 p.
97-012314   958   0312173873
Khanate of Bukhara -- History.

DK948.86.C75 1991
Critchlow, James.
Nationalism in Uzbekistan: a Soviet Republic's road to sovereignty/ James Critchlow. Boulder: Westview Press, 1991. xviii, 231 p.
91-027668   958/.7   0813384036
Nationalism -- Uzbekistan. Uzbekistan -- History -- Autonomy and independence movements. Soviet Union -- Ethnic relations.

DK948.8657.K3747 1998
Karimov, I. A., 1938-
Uzbekistan on the threshold of the twenty-first century: challenges to stability and progress/ Islam Karimov. New York: St. Martin's Press, 1998. ix, 196 p.
98-014840 958.7086 0312213689
National security -- Uzbekistan.   Uzbekistan -- Economic conditions -- 1991- Uzbekistan -- Politics and government -- 1991-

DK4030-4452 History of Poland

DK4030 Gazetteers. Dictionaries, etc.

DK4030.S26 1994
Sanford, George.
Historical dictionary of Poland/ by George Sanford and Adriana Gozdecka-Sanford. Metuchen, NJ: Scarecrow Press, 1994. xxii, 339 p.
93-043939 943.6/003 0810828189
Poland -- Dictionaries.

DK4040 General works

DK4040.P57 1994
Poland: a country study/ edited by Glenn E. Curtis.3rd ed. Washington, D.C.: Federal Research Division, Library of Congress: xlix, 356 p.
93-046235 943.8.220 0844408271
Poland.

DK4123 History — Dictionaries. Chronological tables, outlines, etc.

DK4123.L47 1996
Lerski, Jerzy J. 1917-
Historical dictionary of Poland, 966-1945/ George J. Lerski; with special editing and emendations by Piotr Wrobel and Richard J. Kozicki; foreword by Aleksander Gieysztor. Westport, Conn.: Greenwood Press, 1996. xviii, 750 p.
94-046940 943.8/003 0313260079
Poland -- History -- Dictionaries.

DK4140 History — General works

DK4140.D38 1982
Davies, Norman.
God's playground, a history of Poland/ by Norman Davies. New York: Columbia University Press, 1982. 2 v.
81-010241 943.8 0231043260
Poland -- History.

DK4140.D385 2001
Davies, Norman,
Heart of Europe: the past in Poland's present/ Norman Davies.New ed. Oxford; Oxford University Press, 2001. 483 p.
2001-278779 943.8.221 0192801260
Poland -- History.

DK4140.H3413 1992
Halecki, Oskar,
A history of Poland/ O. Halecki; with additional material by A. Polansky [i.e. Polonsky] and Thaddeus V. Grommada [i.e. Gromada].New ed. New York: Dorset Press, 1992. xii, 472 p.
93-166910 943.8.220 0880298588
Poland -- History.

DK4140.Z36 1988
Zamoyski, Adam.
The Polish way: a thousand-year history of the Poles and their culture/ Adam Zamoyski. New York: F. Watts, 1988, c1987. ix, 422 p. [12] p. of plates
87-050290 943.8.219 0531150690
Poland -- History.

DK4179.2 History — General special — Political and diplomatic history. Politics and government

DK4179.2.P65 2001
The Polish-Lithuanian monarchy in European context c. 1500-1795/ edited by Richard Butterwick. Houndmills, Basingstoke, Hampshire; Palgrave, xix, 249 p.
00-054533 943.8/02.221 0333773829
Monarchy--Poland.

DK4185 History — General special — Diplomatic history. Foreign and general relations

DK4185.G3 A53 2001
Anderson, Sheldon R., 1951-
A Cold War in the Soviet Bloc: Polish-East German relations: 1945-1962/ Sheldon Anderson. Boulder, Colo.: Westview Press, 2001. xviii, 314 p.
00-063305 327.4380431 0813337836
Poland -- Foreign relations -- Germany (East) Germany (East) -- Foreign relations -- Poland. Poland -- Foreign relations -- 1945-1989.

DK4185.G3 P54 2001
Pickus, David,
Dying with an enlightening fall: Poland in the eyes of German intellectuals, 1764-1800/ David Pickus. Lanham, Md.: Lexington Books, c2001. vii, 291 p.
00-040195 943.8.221 0739101536
Public opinion--Germany.

DK4185.R9 K35 1993
Kamiânski, Andrzej Sulima.
Republic vs. autocracy: Poland-Lithuania and Russia, 1686-1697/ Andrzej Sulima Kamiânski. Cambridge, Mass.: Distributed by Harvard University Press for the 312 p.
92-054346 327.438047.220 0916458490
Poland -- Foreign relations -- Russia. Russia -- Foreign relations -- Poland. Poland -- Foreign relations -- 1572-1763. Russia -- Foreign relations -- 1689-1725. Russia -- Foreign relations -- To 1689. Ukraine -- History -- 1648-1775.

DK4188-4330 History — By period — To 1795

DK4188.R46 1982
A Republic of nobles: studies in Polish history to 1864/ edited and translated by J.K. Fedorowicz, co-editors, Maria Bogucka, Henryk Samsonowicz. Cambridge [Cambridgeshire]; Cambridge University Press, 1982. xvi, 293 p.
81-012284 943.8/02 052124093X
Poland -- History -- To 1795. Poland -- History -- 1795-1864.

DK4249.5.P7913 1997
Przybyszewski, Boleslaw.
Saint Jadwiga, Queen of Poland 1374-1399/ Fr. Boleslaw Przybyszewski; [translated by Bruce MacQueen]. Rome: Postulate for the Canonosation of Blessed Queen Jadwiga; xii, 116 p.
98-102008 943.8/02/092. 221 0948202696
Jadwiga, Queen, consort of Wladyslaw II Jagiello, King of Poland, ca. Queens--Poland--Biography.

DK4312.P3.A3513
Pasek, Jan Chryzostom.
Memoirs of the Polish Baroque: the writings of Jan Chryzostom Pasek, a squire of the Commonwealth of Poland and Lithuania/ edited, translated, with an introduction and notes by Catherine S. Leach; foreword by Wiktor Weintraub. Berkeley: University of California Press, c1976. lxiv, 327 p.
74-077731 943.8/02/0924 0520027523
Pasek, Jan Chryzostom. Gentry -- Poland -- Biography. Poland -- History -- 17th century.

DK4314.5.L84 1991
Lukowski, Jerzy.
Liberty's folly: the Polish-Lithuanian commonwealth in the eighteenth century, 1697-1795/ Jerzy Lukowski. London; Routledge, 1991. xv, 316 p.
91-185495 943.8/02 0415032288
Civilization, Modern -- 18th century. Poland -- Civilization -- To 1795.

DK4330.B88 1998
Butterwick, Richard.
Poland's last king and English culture: Stanislaw August Poniatowski, 1732-1798/ Richard Butterwick. Oxford: Clarendon Press; 1998. xix, 376 p.
97-033338 943.8/025/092 0198207018
Stanislaw -- II August, -- King of Poland, -- 1732-1798.   Poland -- History -- Stanislaus II Augustus, 1764-1795. Poland -- Civilization -- English influences.

DK4358-4385 History — By period — 1795-1918. 19th century (General)

DK4358.W34 1994
Walicki, Andrzej.
Philosophy and romantic nationalism: the case of Poland/ Andrzej Walicki.University of Notre Dame Press ed. Notre Dame, Ind.: University of Notre Dame Press, 1994. 415 p.
94-019333 943.8/03.220 0268038066
Nationalism--Poland. Philosophy, Polish--19th century. Messianism, Political--Poland.

DK4382.C73 1987
Craig, Mary.
Lech Walesa and his Poland/ Mary Craig. New York: Continuum, 1987, c1986. 326 p.
87-006731 943.8/05 0826403905
Walesa, Lech, -- 1943- Poland -- History -- 20th century.

DK4382.D9
Dziewanowski, M. K.
Poland in the twentieth century/ M. K. Dziewanowski. New York: Columbia University Press, 1977. xiii, 309 p.
76-051216 943.8 0231035772
Poland -- History -- 20th century.

DK4382.H57 1983
The History of Poland since 1863/ R.F. Leslie ... [et al.]; edited by R.F. Leslie.1st pbk. ed., with epilogue. Cambridge; Cambridge University Press, 1983. xii, 499 p.
83-234973 943.8.219 0521226457
Poland -- History -- 20th century. Poland -- History -- 1864-1918.

DK4385.B57 1995
Blobaum, Robert.
Rewolucja: Russian Poland, 1904-1907/ Robert E. Blobaum. Ithaca: Cornell University Press, 1995. xx, 300 p.
94-033165 943.8/033 0801430542
Poland -- History -- Revolution, 1905-1907.

DK4402-4415 History — By period — 1918-1945

DK4402.K37 1985
Karski, Jan, 1914-
The Great Powers & Poland, 1919-1945: from Versailles to Yalta/ Jan Karski. Lanham, MD: University Press of America, c1985. xvi, 697 p.
84-022000 943.8/04 0819143987
Poland -- Foreign relations -- 1918-1945. Europe -- Politics and government -- 1918-1945. United States -- Foreign relations -- Poland.

DK4410.G76
Gross, Jan Tomasz.
Polish society under German occupation: the Generalgouvernement, 1939-1944/ Jan Tomasz Gross. Princeton, N.J.: Princeton University Press, c1979. xviii, 343 p.
78-070298 943.8/05 0691093814
Poland -- History -- Occupation, 1939-1945.

DK4410.K4713 1991
Kersten, Krystyna.
The establishment of Communist rule in Poland, 1943-1948/ Krystyna Kersten; translated and annotated by John Micgiel and Michael H. Bernhard; foreword by Jan T. Gross. Berkeley: University of California Press, c1991. xxxiv, 535 p.
90-048639 943.805/3 0520062191
Communism -- Poland. Poland -- Politics and government -- 1945-1980. Poland -- Politics and government -- 1918-1945.

DK4415.G76 2002
Gross, Jan Tomasz.
Revolution from abroad: the Soviet conquest of Poland's western Ukraine and western Belorussia/ Jan T. Gross.Expanded ed./ with a new preface by the author. Princeton: Princeton University Press, 2002. p. cm.
2001-058838 943.8/053.221 0691096031
World War, 1939-1945--Personal narratives, Polish.

DK4430-4442 History — By period — 1945-1989. People's Republic

DK4430.A83 1982
Ascherson, Neal.
The Polish August: the self-limiting revolution/ Neal Ascherson. New York: Viking Press, 1982. 320 p.
81-052150 943.8/05 0670563056
Poland -- History -- 1980-1989.

DK4433.W76 1998
Wrobel, Piotr.
Historical dictionary of Poland, 1945-1996/ Piotr Wrobel; with editing by Anna Wrobel. Westport, Conn.: Greenwood Press, 1998. xx, 423 p.
97-040855 943.805 031329772X
Poland -- History -- 1945- -- Dictionaries.

DK4435.J37.P454 1998
Pelinka, Anton, 1941-
Politics of the lesser evil: leadership, democracy, and Jaruzelski's Poland/ Anton Pelinka. New Brunswick, NJ: Transaction Publishers, 1998. p. cm.
97-051254 943.805/6/092 1560003677
Jaruzelski, W. -- (Wojciech) Democracy. Leadership. Poland -- Politics and government -- 1980-1989.

DK4436.M55 1990
Michta, Andrew A.
Red Eagle: the army in Polish politics, 1944-1988/ Andrew A. Michta. Stanford, Calif.: Hoover Institution Press, c1990. 270 p.
89-019742 943.805 0817988610
Poland -- Politics and government -- 1945-1980. Poland -- Politics and government -- 1980-1989.

DK4437.B48 1990
Between East and West: writings from Kultura/ Robert Kostrzewa, editor. 1st ed. New York: Hill and Wang, 1990. xiv, 273 p.
89-038196 943.805.220 0809029375
Poland -- Intellectual life -- 1945-1989.

DK4438.T67 1987
Toraânska, Teresa.
"Them": Stalin's Polish puppets/ Teresa Toranska; translated from the Polish by Agnieszka Kolakowska; with an introduction by Harry Willetts. 1st U.S. ed. New York: Harper & Row, c1987. 384 p.
86-045364 943.8/05.219 0060156570
Poland -- Politics and government -- 1945-1980. Poland -- Foreign relations -- Soviet Union. Soviet Union -- Foreign relations -- Poland.

DK4440.G64 1982
Goldfarb, Jeffrey C.
On cultural freedom: an exploration of public life in Poland and America/ Jeffrey C. Goldfarb. Chicago: University of Chicago Press, 1982. x, 173 p.
82-008325 303.4/82438/073 0226300994
Politics and culture -- Poland. Politics and culture -- United States. Poland -- Intellectual life -- 1945-1989. United States -- Intellectual life -- 20th century.

DK4440.L47 1988
Lepak, Keith John.
Prelude to Solidarity: Poland and the politics of the Gierek regime/ Keith John Lepak. New York: Columbia University Press, 1988. xvii, 271 p.
88-002834 943.8/05 0231066082
Gierek, Edward, -- 1913- Poland -- Politics and government -- 1945-1980.

DK4440.P58 1983
Poland, genesis of a revolution/ edited by Abraham Brumberg. New York: Random House, c1983. xii, 322 p.
82-040137 943.8/056 0394523237
Poland -- History -- 1945-

DK4442.A53 1985
Andrews, Nicholas G.
Poland 1980-81: Solidarity versus the Party/ by Nicholas G. Andrews. Washington, DC: National Defense University Press, 1985. xii, 351 p.
84-601067 943.8/056.219
Poland -- Politics and government -- 1980-1989. NSZZ "Solidarnoâsâc" (Labor organization)

DK4442.D4 1983
De Weydenthal, Jan B.
The Polish drama, 1980-1982/ Jan B. de Weydenthal, Bruce D. Porter, Kevin Devlin. Lexington, Mass.: Lexington Books, c1983. viii, 351 p.
82-048527 943.8 0669062146
Communism -- Europe. Poland -- History -- 1980-1989.

DK4442.K635 1988
Kolankiewicz, George.
Poland: politics, economics, and society/ George Kolankiewicz and Paul G. Lewis. London; Pinter Publishers, 1988. xx, 210 p.
88-005858 943.8/05 0861874366
Poland -- Politics and government -- 1980-1989. Poland -- Economic conditions -- 1981-1990. Poland -- Social conditions -- 1980-

DK4442.M53 1985
Michnik, Adam.
Letters from prison and other essays/ Adam Michnik; translated by Maya Latynski; foreword by Czeslaw Milosz; introduction by Jonathan Schell. Berkeley: University of California Press, c1985. xlii, 354 p.
85-001196 943.8/056.219 0520053710
Michnik, Adam. Political prisoners--Poland--Correspondence.

DK4442.P645 1991
Polish paradoxes/ edited by Stanislaw Gomulka and Anthony Polonsky. London; Routledge, 1991. vii, 274 p.
89-006318 943.805 0415043751
Poland -- Civilization -- 1945-

DK4442.R33 1990
Rachwald, Arthur R.
In search of Poland: the superpowers' response to Solidarity, 1980-1989/ Arthur R. Rachwald. Stanford, Calif.: Hoover Institution Press, c1990. xii, 149 p.
90-004551 327/.09438 0817989617
Soviet Union -- Foreign relations -- Poland. Poland -- Foreign relations -- Soviet Union. United States -- Foreign relations -- Poland.

DK4442.S72 1984
Staniszkis, Jadwiga.
Poland's self-limiting revolution/ by Jadwiga
Staniszkis; edited by Jan T. Gross. Princeton, N.J.:
Princeton University Press, c1984. xii, 352 p.
82-061387   943.8/055   0691094039
  Poland -- Politics and government -- 1980-
1989. Poland -- Politics and government -- 1945-

DK4446-4452 History — By period — 1989-

DK4446.P65 1991
Poland into the 1990s: economy and society in
transition / edited by George Blazyca and Ryszard
Rapacki. New York: St. Martin's Press, 1991. x,
148 p.
90-048969   943.805/6   0312057466
  Poland -- History -- 1989-

DK4449.M53 1998
Michnik, Adam.
Letters from freedom: post-cold war realities and
perspectives/ Adam Michnik; edited by Irena
Grudziânska Gross; foreword by Ken Jowitt; with
new translations from the Polish by Jane Cave.
Berkeley: University of California Press, c1998.
xxxiii, 348 p.
98-022701   947/.0009/049.221   0520217608
Michnik, Adam--Interviews.

DK4449.M55 1994
Millard, F.
The anatomy of the new Poland: post-Communist
politics in its first phase/ Frances Millard.
Aldershot, Hants, England; E. Elgar, c1994. ix,
260 p.
93-034443   320.9438   1852789247
  Poland -- Politics and government -- 1989-

DK4452.W34.K8713 1993
Kurski, Jaroslaw, 1963-
Lech Walesa: democrat or dictator?/ Jaroslaw
Kurski; translated by Peter Obst. Boulder:
Westview Press, 1993. xx, 178 p.
93-009886   943.8   0813317886
Walesa, Lech, -- 1943- Presidents -- Poland --
Biography.   Poland -- Politics and government --
1989-

DL History of Northern Europe. Scandinavia

DL5 General works

DL5.S38 2000
Scandinavia profiled: essential facts on society,
business, and politics in Scandinavia/ edited by
Barry Turner. New York: St. Martin's Press,
2000. p. cm.
 99-053352   948   0312229933
  Scandinavia -- Handbooks, manuals, etc.

DL5.S44
Scott, Franklin Daniel, 1901-
Scandinavia/ Franklin D. Scott. Cambridge:
Harvard University Press, 1975. x, 330 p.
75-002818   948   0674790006
  Scandinavia.

DL10 Description and travel — 1901-1950

DL10.O373
Ogrizek, Dore, 1899-
Scandinavia: Denmark, Norway, Sweden, Finland,
and Iceland. [Translated by Paddy O'Hanlon and H.
Iredale Nelson] New York, McGraw-Hill Book Co.
[1952] 438 p.
52-010537
  Scandinavia -- Description and travel. Finland
-- Description and travel. Iceland -- Description
and travel.

DL11 Description and travel — 1951-1980

DL11.F84
Fullerton, Brian.
Scandinavia; an introductory geography [by] Brian
Fullerton and Alan F. Williams. New York,
Praeger Publishers [1972] xiv, 374 p.
79-186468   914.8
  Scandinavia -- Geography.

DL30 Social life and customs. Civilization — General works

DL30.F75 1950
Friis, Henning Kristian, 1911-
Scandinavia, between East and West.   Ithaca,
Cornell University Press, 1950. x, 388 p.
50-008531   914.8
  Scandinavia -- Economic conditions.
Scandinavia -- Social conditions. Scandinavia --
Politics.

DL30.M43 1993
Medieval Scandinavia: an encyclopedia/ Phillip
Pulsiano, editor; Kirsten Wolf, co-editor; Paul
Acker, associate editor, Donald K. Fry, associate
editor; advisers, Knut Helle ... [et al.]. New York:
Garland, 1993. xix, 768 p.
92-019300   948/.02/03   0824047877
  Northmen -- Encyclopedias.   Scandinavia --
Civilization -- Encyclopedias.

DL31 Social life and customs. Civilization — Old Norse. Earliest Scandinavian — General works

DL31.J6
Jones, Gwyn, 1907-
A history of the Vikings.   London, Oxford U.P.,
1968. xvi, 504 p.
68-124332   914.8/03/2
  Vikings. Scandinavia -- Civilization.

DL46 History — General works — 1800-

DL46.D43
Derry, T. K. 1905-
A history of Scandinavia: Norway, Sweden,
Denmark, Finland, and Iceland/ by T. K. Derry.
Minneapolis: University of Minnesota Press, 1979.
x, 447 p.
78-014284   948   0816608350
  Scandinavia -- History.

DL46.N7 2000
Nordstrom, Byron J.
Scandinavia since 1500/ Byron J. Nordstrom.
Minneapolis: University of Minnesota Press,
2000. p. cm.
 99-089029   948   0816620989
  Scandinavia -- History. Finland -- History.

DL59 History — Historiography — Political and diplomatic history

DL59.S35 1950
Scott, Franklin Daniel, 1901-
The United States and Scandinavia/ by Franklin D.
Scott. Cambridge: Harvard University Press, 1950.
xviii, 359 p.
50-007563   948
  United States -- Foreign relations --
Scandinavia. Scandinavia -- Foreign relations --
United States. Scandinavia.

DL59.U6.H36 1997
Hanhimaki, Jussi M., 1965-
Scandinavia and the United States: an insecure
friendship/ Jussi M. Hanhimaki. New York:
Twayne Publishers; c1997. xvii, 223 p.
96-044455   327.48073   0805779353
  Cold War.   United States -- Foreign relations --
1945- Sweden -- Foreign relations -- 1950-
Scandinavia -- Foreign relations -- United States.

DL61-65 History — By period — Earliest to 1387. Scandinavian Empire

DL61.S29 1993
Sawyer, Birgit.
Medieval Scandinavia: from conversion to
Reformation, circa 800-1500/ Birgit and Peter
Sawyer. Minneapolis: University of Minnesota
Press, c1993. xvi, 265 p.
93-003511   948   0816617384
  Scandinavia -- History.

DL65.H39 2000
Haywood, John, 1956-
Encyclopedia of the Viking age/ John Haywood.
New York: Thames & Hudson, 2000. 224 p.
99-066012   948/.022/03   0500019827
  Vikings -- Encyclopedias.

DL65.L63 1983
Logan, F. Donald.
The Vikings in history/ F. Donald Logan. Totowa,
N.J.: Barnes & Noble Books, 1983. 224 p.
82-025533   940/.04395   038920384X
  Vikings.

DL65.P26 1995
Page, R. I.
Chronicles of the Vikings: records, memorials, and
myths/ R.I. Page. Toronto; University of Toronto
Press, c1995. 240 p.
96-104991   948/.022   0802008038
  Vikings -- History -- Sources. Civilization,
Medieval -- Sources.

DL78 History — By period — 1524-1814

DL78.K57 1990
Kirby, D. G.
Northern Europe in the early modern period: the Baltic world, 1492-1772/ David Kirby. London; Longman, 1990. xii, 443 p.
89-028311 948 058200411X
Europe, Northern -- History. Sweden -- History -- 1523-1718. Baltic States -- History.

DL83 History — By period — 1900-1945

DL83.S35 1997
Salmon, Patrick, 1952-
Scandinavia and the great powers, 1890-1940/ Patrick Salmon. Cambridge, U.K.; Cambridge University Press, 1997. xix, 421 p.
96-053310 327.48/009/041 0521411610
Scandinavia -- History -- 20th century. Scandinavia -- Foreign relations -- Great Britain. Great Britain -- Foreign relations -- Scandinavia.

DL105 Denmark — Gazetteers. Dictionaries, etc.

DL105.T46 1998
Thomas, Alastair H.
Historical dictionary of Denmark/ Alastair H. Thomas and Stewart P. Oakley. Lanham, Md.: Scarecrow Press, 1998. xxv, 533 p.
98-038071 948.9/003 0810835444
Denmark -- History -- Dictionaries.

DL148 Denmark — History — General works

DL148.L353 1968
Lauring, Palle.
A history of the kingdom of Denmark. Translated from the Danish by David Hohnen. Drawings by Vibeke Lind. Copenhagen, Host, 1968. 274 p.
68-118267 948/.9
Denmark -- History.

DL326 Iceland — Social life and customs. Civilization — General works

DL326.L33 1998
Lacy, Terry G.
Ring of seasons: Iceland, its culture and history/ text and photos, Terry G. Lacy. Ann Arbor: University of Michigan Press, c1998. xiv, 297 p.
97-048294 949.12 047210926X
Iceland -- Civilization. Iceland -- Social life and customs.

DL338 Iceland — History — General works

DL338.G5
Gjerset, Knut, 1865-1936.
History of Iceland, by Knut Gjerset, PH.D. New York, The Macmillan company, 1924. vi p. 2 l.
24-002336
Iceland -- History. Iceland -- Civilization.

DL338.G82 1997
Gudmundur Halfdanarson, 1956-
Historical dictionary of Iceland/ Gudmundur Halfdanarson. Lanham, Md.: Scarecrow Press, 1997. xxiv, 213 p.
97-012399 949.12/003 0810833522
Iceland -- History -- Dictionaries.

DL338.H849 2000
Gunnar Karlsson.
The history of Iceland/ Gunnar Karlsson. Minneapolis, Minn.: University of Minnesota Press, c2000. xiii, 418 p.
99-054536 949.12 0816635889
Iceland -- History.

DL442 Norway — Ethnography — Individual elements in the population, A-Z

DL442.L3.O35 1992
Odner, Knut.
The Varanger Saami: habitation and economy AD 1200-1900/ Knut Odner. Oslo: Scandinavian University Press: c1992. viii, 320 p.
93-150149 8200212858
Sami (European people) -- Norway -- Nesseby (Kommune) -- History. Sami (European people) -- Norway -- Nesseby (Kommune) -- Economic conditions. Sami (European people) -- Norway -- Nesseby (Kommune) -- Antiquities. Nesseby (Norway: Kommune) -- Antiquities. Varanger Peninsula (Norway) -- Antiquities. Norway -- Antiquities.

DL448 Norway — History — General works

DL448.D4
Derry, T. K. 1905-
A short history of Norway. London, G. Allen & Unwin [1957] 281 p.
57-003947 948.1
Norway -- History.

DL449 Norway — History — Compends

DL449.G5 1969
Gjerset, Knut, 1865-1936.
History of the Norwegian people. New York, AMS Press [1969] 2 v. in 1
79-101272 914.81/03 0404028187
Norway -- History.

DL506-532 Norway — History — By period

DL506.D47
Derry, T. K. 1905-
A history of modern Norway, 1814-1972 [by] T. K. Derry. Oxford, Clarendon Press, 1973. xiii, 506 p.
73-168733 948.1/03 0198225032
Norway -- History.

DL529.Q5.H38 1972
Hayes, Paul M.
Quisling: the career and political ideas of Vidkun Quisling, 1887-1945 [by] Paul M. Hayes. Bloomington, Indiana University Press [1972, c1971] 368 p.
78-184523 948.1/04/0924 0253347602
Quisling, Vidkun, -- 1887-1945.

DL529.Q5.H6513 1989
Hoidal, Oddvar K.
Quisling: a study in treason/ Oddvar K. Hoidal. Oslo: Norwegian University Press; c1989. 913 p.
90-145884 948.104/092 8200184005
Quisling, Vidkun, -- 1887-1945. Fascists -- Norway -- Biography. Politicians -- Norway -- Biography. Norway -- Politics and government -- 1905-

DL532.S8 1995
Stokker, Kathleen, 1946-
Folklore fights the Nazis: humor in occupied Norway, 1940-1945/ Kathleen Stokker. Madison [N.J.]: Fairleigh Dickinson University Press; c1995. 273 p.
95-007915 949.104 0838635946
Norwegian wit and humor. Norway -- History -- German occupation, 1940-1945 -- Humor.

DL607 Sweden — Guidebooks

DL607.M75
Muirhead, L. Russell 1896-
Sweden. With a complete atlas of Sweden and 25 other maps and plans. Chicago, Rand McNally [1952] 350 p.
52-002784 914.85
Sweden -- Description and travel -- Guide books.

DL648 Sweden — History — General works

DL648.M62 1972
Moberg, Vilhelm, 1898-1973.
A history of the Swedish people. Translated from the Swedish by Paul Britten Austin. New York, Pantheon [1972] 210 p.
72-003411 948.5 0394481925
Sweden -- History.

DL648.S36 1977
Scott, Franklin Daniel, 1901-
Sweden, the nation's history/ Franklin D. Scott. Minneapolis: University of Minnesota Press, c1977. xviii, 654 p.
76-051154 948.5 0816608040
Sweden -- History.

DL649 Sweden — History — Compends

DL649.S8
Svanstrom, Ragnar, 1904-
A short history of Sweden, by Ragnar Svanstrom and Carl Fredrik Palmstierna. Translated by Joan Bulman and published under the auspices of the Anglo-Swedish Literary Foundation. Oxford, Clarendon Press, 1934. x, 443 p.
34-028322 948.5
Sweden -- History.

DL658.8 Sweden — History — Political and diplomatic history. Foreign and general relations

DL658.8.L4513 1988
Lewin, Leif, 1941-
Ideology and strategy: a century of Swedish politics/ Leif Lewin; translated by Victor Kayfetz. Cambridge [Cambridgeshire]; Cambridge University Press, 1988. xii, 344 p.
88-002615 320.9485 0521343305
Sweden -- Politics and government -- 1872-1907. Sweden -- Politics and government -- 20th century.

DL661-727 Sweden — History — By period

DL661.S73 1963
Stenberger, Marten, 1898-1973.
Sweden. Translated from the Swedish by Alan Binns. New York, Praeger [1963, c1962] 229 p.
62-019107 948.501
Sweden -- History -- To 1397. Sweden -- Antiquities.

DL701.R63
Roberts, Michael, 1908-
The Swedish imperial experience, 1560-1718/ Michael Roberts. Cambridge; Cambridge University Press, 1979. x, 156 p.
78-058799 948.5/02 0521225027
Sweden -- History -- 1523-1718.

DL727.U67 1998
Upton, Anthony F.
Charles XI and Swedish absolutism/ A.F. Upton. Cambridge; Cambridge University Press, 1998. xxiv, 281 p.
97-025197 948.5/03 0521573904
Charles -- XI, -- King of Sweden, -- 1655-1697. Sweden -- Politics and government -- 1660-1697.

DL976.3 Sweden — Local history and description — Cities, towns, etc.

DL976.3.G68 1997
Gould, D. E.
Historical dictionary of Stockholm/ Dennis E. Gould. Lanham, Md.: Scarecrow Press, 1997. xxvii, 257 p.
96-038621 948.7/3/003 0081083238
Stockholm (Sweden) -- History -- Dictionaries.

DL1032 Finland — History — General works

DL1032.F56 1989
Finland: people, nation, state/ edited by Max Engman & David Kirby. London: C. Hurst & Co.; c1989. xviii, 254 p.
88-033057 948.97 0253320674
Finland -- History.

DL1032.J8713 1962
Jutikkala, Eino, 1907-
A history of Finland [by] Eino Jutikkala, with Kauko Pirinen. Translated by Paul Sjoblom. New York, Praeger [1962] 291 p.
62-013488 947.1
Finland -- History.

DL1032.S55 1989
Singleton, Frederick Bernard.
A short history of Finland/ Fred Singleton. Cambridge; Cambridge University Press, 1989. xii, 211 p.
89-031419 948.97 0521322758
Finland -- History.

DL1065.5-1141.6 Finland — History — By period

DL1065.5.B62.P6413 1995
Polvinen, Tuomo.
Imperial borderland: Bobrikov and the attempted Russification of Finland, 1898-1904/ Tuomo Polvinen; translated by Steven Huxley. Durham, N.C.: Duke University Press, c1995. ix, 342 p.
94-038507 948.97/02 0822315637
Bobrikov, Nikolai Ivanovich, -- 1839-1904. Governors -- Finland -- Biography. Finland -- Politics and government -- 1809-1917.

DL1066.5.J35 1998
Jakobson, Max.
Finland in the new Europe/ Max Jakobson; foreword by George Kennan. Westport, Conn.: Praeger, 1998. xiv, 176 p.
98-021290 948.9703/4 0275963721
Finland -- History -- 20th century. Finland -- Foreign relations -- Europe. Finland -- Foreign relations -- Soviet Union.

DL1066.7.C43 1998
Charting an independent course: Finland's place in the Cold War and in U.S. foreign policy/ edited by T. Michael Ruddy. Claremont, Calif.: Regina Books, c1998. 223 p.
98-005995 327.4897 0941690830
Cold war. Finland -- Foreign relations -- 1945- Finland -- Foreign relations -- 1917-1945.

DL1097.T76 1991
Trotter, William R., 1943-
A frozen hell: the Russo-Finnish winter war of 1939-1940/ William R. Trotter. Chapel Hill, N.C.: Algonquin Books of Chapel Hill, 1991. xv, 283 p.
90-019968 948.9703/2 094557522X
Russo-Finnish War, 1939-1940.

DL1141.6.K65.A3 1997
Koivisto, Mauno.
Witness to history/ by Mauno Koivisto; translated by Klaus Tornudd; with an introduction by David Kirby. Carbondale, Ill.: SIU press, 1997. p. cm.
97-008735 948.9703/4/092 0809320452
Koivisto, Mauno. Presidents -- Finland -- Biography. Finland -- Foreign policy -- 1981-

DP12-402 History of Spain

DP12 Gazetteers. Dictionaries, etc.

DP12.S59 1996
Smith, Angel, 1958-
Historical dictionary of Spain/ Angel Smith. Lanham, Md.: Scarecrow Press, c1996. xxviii, 435 p.
95-040511 946/.003 0810830809
Spain -- History -- 19th century -- Dictionaries. Spain -- History -- 20th century -- Dictionaries.

DP14 Guidebooks

DP14.F74
Frommer's Spain. New York, NY: Macmillan, c1997- v.
97-649672 914.212
Spain -- Guidebooks.

DP14.R86
The rough guide to Spain. London; Routledge & Kegan Paul, 1983- v.
97-649639 914.604/05.221
Spain -- Guidebooks.

DP17 General works

DP17.F5 1966
Fisher, W. B.
Spain; an introductory geography, by W. B. Fisher and H. Bowen-Jones. New York, Praeger [1966] 222 p.
66-017362 914.6
Spain -- Geography.

DP17.S67 1990
Spain: a country study/ Federal Research Division, Library of Congress; edited by Eric Solsten and Sandra W. Meditz. 2nd ed. Washington, D.C.: For sale by the Supt. of Docs., U.S. G.P.O., xxxviii, 406 p.
90-006127 946.220
Spain.

DP17.V56 1994
Vincent, Mary.
Cultural atlas of Spain and Portugal/ Mary Vincent and R.A. Stradling. New York, NY: Facts on File, c1994. 240 p.
94-031211 946.220 0816030146
Spain. Portugal.

DP17.Z99 S54 1985
Shields, Graham J.
Spain/ Graham J. Shields, compiler. Oxford, England; Clio Press, c1985. xxxvi, 340 p.
86-672955 1851090037
Spain -- Bibliography.

DP43 Description and travel — 1951-1980

DP43.B66 1976
Brenan, Gerald.
The face of Spain/ by Gerald Brenan. New York: Octagon Books, 1976, c1956. ix, 310 p.
76-046224 946.082 0374909776
Spain -- Description and travel.

DP43.M45
Michener, James A. 1907-
Iberia; Spanish travels and reflections [by] James A. Michener. Photos. by Robert Vavra. New York, Random House [1968] 818 p.
67-022623 914.6/04/82
Spain -- Description and travel. Spain -- Civilization -- 20th century.

DP44 Antiquities

DP44.M27 1994
Marken, Mitchell W.
Pottery from Spanish shipwrecks, 1500-1800/ Mitchell W. Marken. Gainesville: University Press of Florida, c1994. xvi, 264 p.
93-034787　738/.0946/0903　0813012686
Pottery, Spanish. Shipwrecks. Underwater archaeology. Spain -- History, Naval. Spain -- Antiquities.

DP48 Social life and customs. Civilization — General works

DP48.A3 1959
Adams, Nicholson B. 1895-1970.
The heritage of Spain: an introduction to Spanish civilization. New York: Holt, [1959] 380 p.
58-007188　914.6
Spain -- Civilization.

DP48.C8 1975
Crow, John Armstrong.
Spain: the root and the flower: a history of the civilization of Spain and of the Spanish people/ by John A. Crow. New York: Harper & Row, 1975. xii, 475 p.
74-001802　946　006010919X
National characteristics, Spanish.　Spain -- Civilization.

DP48.E5 1937
Ellis, Havelock, 1859-1939.
The soul of Spain, by Havelock Ellis. Boston, Houghton Miffin company, 1937. xvi, 420 p.
37-034619
National characteristics, Spanish.　Spain -- Description and travel. Spain -- Social life and customs.

DP48.K45 1995
Kern, Robert W. 1934-
The regions of Spain: a reference guide to history and culture/ Robert W. Kern; photographs by Chuck Smith. Westport, Conn.: Greenwood Press 1995. xii 411 p.
95-006481　946　0313292248
Regionalism -- Spain.　Spain -- History, Local. Spain -- Civilization.

DP48.T72 1965
Trend, J. B. 1887-1958.
The origins of modern Spain, by J.B. Trend. New York, Russell & Russell, 1965. x, 220 p.
65-017925　946.08
Education -- Spain -- History.　Spain -- Intellectual life. Spain -- Biography. Spain -- History -- Revolutionary period, 1868-1875.

DP52 Ethnography — General works

DP52.D68 1997
Douglass, Carrie B., 1948-
Bulls, bullfighting, and Spanish identities/ Carrie B. Douglass. Tucson: University of Arizona Press, c1997. xii, 245 p.
96-045806　946　0816516510
National characteristics, Spanish. Fighting bull -- Spain. Bullfights -- Social aspects -- Spain. Spain -- Civilization.

DP52.G29
Ganivet, Angel, 1865-1898.
Spain: an interpretation; with introduction by R.M. Nadal. London, Eyre & Spottiswoode, 1946. 136 p.
47-020750　914.6
National characteristics, Spanish.

DP52.M4 1950a
Menendez Pidal, Ramon, 1869-1968.
The Spaniards in their history; translated with a prefatory essay on the author's work by Walter Starkie. New York, Norton [1950] viii, 251 p.
50-009474　914.6
National characteristics, Spanish.

DP53 Ethnography — Individual elements in the population, A-Z

DP53.I2.R813 1998
Ruiz, Arturo.
The archaeology of the Iberians/ Arturo Ruiz and Manuel Molinos; translated from the Spanish by Mary Turton. Cambridge, United Kingdom; Cambridge University Press, 1998. xiv, 335 p.
97-044332　936.6　0521564026
Iberians. Excavations (Archaeology) -- Spain. Spain -- Antiquities. Spain -- Civilization -- To 711.

DP56 History — Dictionaries. Chronological tables, outlines, etc.

DP56.H57 1992
Historical dictionary of the Spanish Empire, 1402-1975/ James S. Olson, editor-in-chief; Sam L. Slick, senior editor; Samuel Freeman ... [et al.], associate editors. New York: Greenwood Press, 1992. x, 702 p.
91-008250　909/.0971246/003　0313264139
Spain -- Colonies -- History -- Dictionaries. Spain -- Territories and possessions -- History -- Dictionaries. Spain -- History -- Dictionaries.

DP60 History — Biography (Collective) — Houses, noble families, etc.

DP60.M4.N3
Nader, Helen, 1936-
The Mendoza family in the Spanish Renaissance, 1350 to 1550/ Helen Nader. New Brunswick, N.J.: Rutgers University Press, c1979. xiv, 275 p.
79-009945　946/.02/0922　0813508762
Mendoza family. Renaissance -- Spain. Spain -- Civilization -- 711-1516.

DP66 History — General works — 1801-

DP66.A9
Atkinson, William C. 1902-
A history of Spain & Portugal. [Harmondsworth, Middlesex, Penguin Books [1960] 382 p.
60-003356　946
Spain -- History. Portugal -- History.

DP66.K3 1973b
Kamen, Henry Arthur Francis.
A concise history of Spain [by] Henry Kamen. New York, Scribner [c1973] 191 p.
74-000982　946　0684138506
Spain -- History.

DP66.P4 1956
Peers, E. Allison 1891-1952.
Spain; a companion to Spanish studies. London, Methuen [1956] xii, 319 p.
56-058806　914.6
Spanish literature -- History and criticism. Art, Spanish. Music, Spanish Spain -- Civilization -- History.

DP66.S63 2000
Spain: a history/ edited by Raymond Carr. New York: Oxford University Press, 2000. 318 p.
99-042639　946.221　0198206194
Spain -- History.

DP66.V513
Vicens Vives, Jaime.
Approaches to the history of Spain. Translated and edited by Joan Connelly Ullman. Berkeley, University of California Press, 1967. xxviii, 189 p.
67-027127　946
Spain -- History.

DP68 History — Compends

DP68.V5513 1967
Vilar, Pierre, 1906-
Spain; a brief history. Translated by Brian Tate. Oxford, Pergamon Press [1967] vii, 140 p.
67-026694　946
Spain -- History.

DP75 History — Special topics (not A-Z)

DP75.P34 1990
Pagden, Anthony.
Spanish imperialism and the political imagination: studies in European and Spanish-American social and political theory, 1513-1830/ Anthony Pagden. New Haven: Yale University Press, 1990. viii, 184 p.
89-022644　325/.346　0300046766
Spain -- Foreign public opinion. Spain -- Colonies -- Administration -- History. Latin America -- History -- To 1830.

DP81.5 History — General special — Naval history

DP81.5.G6 1997
Goodman, David C.
Spanish naval power, 1589-1665: reconstruction and defeat/ David Goodman. Cambridge; Cambridge University Press, 1997. xvi, 305 p.
96-002953　359/.00946/09031　0521580633
Sea-power -- Spain -- History -- 16th century. Sea-power -- Spain -- History -- 17th century. Shipbuilding -- Spain -- History -- 16th century. Spain -- History, Naval -- 16th century. Spain -- History, Naval -- 17th century.

DP86 History — General special — Political and diplomatic history. Foreign and general relations

DP86.G7.L6
Loomie, Albert J. 1922-
The Spanish Elizabethans; the English exiles at the court of Philip II. New York, Fordham University Press, 1963. xii, 280 p.
63-014407   327.42046
British in Spain. Refugees, Religious. Great Britain -- Foreign relations -- Spain. Spain -- Foreign relations -- Great Britain.

DP94-96 History — By period — Earliest to 711

DP94.R54 1996
Richardson, J. S.
The Romans in Spain/ J.S. Richardson. Cambridge, Mass.: Blackwell Publishers, 1996. vii, 341 p.
95-050447   936.6/03   063117706X
Spain -- History -- Roman period, 218 B.C.-414 A.D.

DP96.O25
O'Callaghan, Joseph F.
A history of medieval Spain/ Joseph F. O'Callaghan. Ithaca: Cornell University Press, 1975. 729 p.
74-007698   946/.02   0801408806
Spain -- History -- Gothic period, 414-711. Spain -- History -- 711-1516. Portugal -- History -- To 1385.

DP96.V57
Visigothic Spain: new approaches/ edited by Edward James. Oxford: Clarendon Press; 1980. xiii, 303 p.
79-040337   946/.01   0198225431
Spain -- History -- Gothic period, 414-711.

DP99-138.3 History — By period — Moorish domination and the Reconquest, 711-1516

DP99.C58 1989
Collins, Roger, 1949-
The Arab conquest of Spain, 710-797/ Roger Collins. Oxford, UK; B. Blackwell, 1989. xii, 239 p.
88-033356   946/.02   0631159231
Spain -- History -- 711-1516.

DP99.G46 1995
Glick, Thomas F.
From Muslim fortress to Christian castle: social and cultural change in medieval Spain/ Thomas F. Glick.   Manchester   [England];   Manchester University Press: c1995. xxi, 201 p.
95-002195   946/.02   0719033489
Social history -- Medieval, 500-1500. Irrigation -- Social aspects -- Spain. Archaeology and history -- Spain. Spain -- History -- 711-1516 -- Historiography. Spain -- History -- 711-1516.

DP99.G47
Glick, Thomas F.
Islamic and Christian Spain in the early Middle Ages/ by Thomas F. Glick. Princeton, N.J.: Princeton University Press, c1979. xi, 376 p.
78-070296   946   0691052743
Civilization, Islamic. Spain -- Civilization -- 711-1492.

DP99.M23 1977
MacKay, Angus, 1939-
Spain in the Middle Ages: from frontier to empire, 1000-1500/ Angus MacKay. New York: St. Martin's Press, 1977. xii, 245 p.
76-052257   946/.02   0312749783
Spain -- History -- 711-1516.

DP102.H34 1990
Harvey, L. P.
Islamic Spain, 1250 to 1500/ L.P. Harvey. Chicago: University of Chicago Press, 1990. xiv, 370 p.
90-030225   946/.02   0226319601
Muslims -- Spain -- History. Mudejares. Nasrides. Spain -- History -- 711-1516. Granada (Kingdom) -- History.

DP102.K46 1996
Kennedy, Hugh
Muslim Spain and Portugal: a political history of al-Andalus/ Hugh Kennedy. London; Longman, 1996. xvi, 342 p.
96-022764   946/.02   0582495156
Muslims -- Spain -- History. Muslims -- Portugal -- History. Portugal -- History -- To 1385. Spain -- History -- 711-1516.

DP102.R4 1975
Read, Jan.
The Moors in Spain and Portugal/ Jan Read. Totowa, N.J.: Rowman and Littlefield, 1975, c1974. 268 p.
75-312213   946/.02   0874716446
Muslims -- Spain -- History. Spain -- History -- Arab period, 711-1492. Portugal -- History -- To 1385.

DP103.L38 1992
The legacy of Muslim Spain/ edited by Salma Khadra Jayyusi; chief consultant to the editor, Manuela Marin. Leiden; E.J. Brill, 1992. xix, 1098 p.
92-029604   946/.02   9004095993
Muslims -- Spain. Andalusia (Spain) -- Civilization. Spain -- Civilization -- 711-1516.

DP124.8.P413 1991
Pedro IV, King of Aragon, 1319?-1387 1319?-1387.
The chronicle of San Juan de la Pena: a fourteenth-century official history of the crown of Aragon/ translated and with an introduction and notes by Lynn H. Nelson. Philadelphia: University of Pennsylvania Press, c1991. xix, 141 p.
91-008495   946/.55   081223068X
Aragon (Spain) -- History. Aragon (Spain) -- Kings and rulers. Catalonia (Spain) -- Kings and rulers.

DP127.6.S7 1995
Stalls, Clay.
Possessing the land: Aragon's expansion into Islam's Ebro frontier under Alfonso the Battler, 1104-1134/ by Clay Stalls. Leiden; New York: 1995. xiii, 337 p.
95-011140   946/.5502   9004103678
Alfonso -- I, -- King of Aragon and Navarre, -- ca. 1073-1134.   Land settlement -- Spain -- Ebro River Region -- History -- To 1500.   Aragon (Spain) -- History -- Alfonso I, 1104-1134. Ebro River Region (Spain) -- History. Aragon (Spain) -- Territorial expansion.

DP138.3.R45 1998
Reilly, Bernard F., 1925-
The Kingdom of Leon-Castilla under King Alfonso VII, 1126-1157/ Bernard F. Reilly. Philadelphia: University of Pennsylvania Press, c1998. xv, 431 p.
98-006677   946/.202   0812234529
Alfonso -- VII, -- The Emperor, King of Castile, -- 1104-1157.   Leon (Kingdom) -- History. Castile (Spain) -- History -- Alfonso VII, 1126-1157.

DP162-272 History — By period — Modern, 1479/1516-

DP162.D3
Davies, Reginald Trevor.
The golden century of Spain, 1501-1621, by R. Trevor Davies. London, Macmillan and co., limited, 1937. xi, 327 p.
38-014927   946.03
Spain -- History -- Ferdinand and Isabella, 1479-1516. Spain -- History -- House of Austria, 1516-1700.

DP162.P8 1962a
Prescott, William Hickling, 1796-1859.
History of the reign of Ferdinand and Isabella, the Catholic. Abridged and edited by C. Harvey Gardiner. Carbondale, Ill., Southern Illinois University Press [1962] 303 p.
62-016246   946.03
Ferdinand -- V, -- King of Spain, -- 1452-1516. Isabella -- I, -- Queen of Spain, -- 1451-1504. Ferdinand -- V, -- King of Spain, -- 1452-1516. Spain -- History -- Ferdinand and Isabella, 1479-1516.

DP164.E39 2000
Edwards, John, 1949-
The Spain of the Catholic Monarchs, 1474-1520/ John Edwards. Malden, Mass.: Blackwell Publishers, 2000. xi, 324 p.
00-009574   946/.03   0631161651
Spain -- Civilization -- 711-1516. Spain -- History -- Ferdinand and Isabella, 1479-1516.

DP171.E4 1964
Elliott, John Huxtable.
Imperial Spain, 1469-1716.   New York, St. Martin's Press [1964, c1963] 411 p.
64-013365   946.04
Spain -- History -- House of Austria, 1516-1700. Spain -- History -- Ferdinand and Isabella, 1479-1516.

DP171.5.H54 2000
Hillgarth, J. N.
The mirror of Spain, 1500-1700: the formation of a myth/ J.N. Hillgarth. Ann Arbor: University of Michigan Press, c2000. xxii, 584 p.
00-008541   946/.04   0472110926
Public opinion -- Europe. Spain -- Foreign public opinion, European. Spain -- Civilization -- 1516-1700 -- Public opinion.

DP178.K36 1997
Kamen, Henry Arthur Francis.
Philip of Spain/ Henry Kamen. New Haven, [Conn.]: Yale University Press, c1997. xiii, 384 p.
96-052421   946/.043/092   0300070810
Philip -- II, -- King of Spain, -- 1527-1598. Spain -- History -- Philip II, 1556-1598. Spain -- Kings and rulers -- Biography.

DP179.P39 1998
Parker, Geoffrey, 1943-
The grand strategy of Philip II/ Geoffrey Parker. New Haven [Conn.]: Yale University Press, 1998. xx, 446 p.
98-007352 946/.043/092 0300075405
Philip -- II, -- King of Spain, -- 1527-1598. Spain -- History -- Philip II, 1556-1598. Spain -- Strategic aspects.

DP182.L96 1992
Lynch, John, 1927-
The Hispanic world in crisis and change, 1598-1700/ John Lynch. Oxford, UK; Blackwell, 1992. p. cm.
91-027601 946/.05 0631176977
Spain -- History -- Philip IV, 1621-1665. Spain -- History -- Charles II, 1665-1700. Spain -- History -- Philip III, 1598-1621.

DP183.F47 2000
Feros, Antonio.
Kingship and favoritism in the Spain of Philip III, 1598-1621/ Antonio Feros. Cambridge, UK; Cambridge University Press, 2000. xvi, 299 p.
99-054217 946/.043 0521561132
Philip -- III, -- King of Spain, -- 1578-1621. Lerma, Francisco Sandoval y Rojas, -- duque de, -- 1552-1625. Spain -- Politics and government -- 1598-1621.

DP183.S26 1998
Sanchez, Magdalena S.
The empress, the queen, and the nun: women and power at the court of Philip III of Spain/ Magdalena S. Sanchez. Baltimore, Md.: Johns Hopkins University Press, 1998. xii, 267 p.
97-042171 946/.051 0801857910
Philip -- III, -- King of Spain, -- 1578-1621 -- Family. Habsburg, House of. Women in politics -- Spain -- History -- 17th century. Power (Social sciences) -- Spain -- History -- 17th century. Spain -- Politics and government -- 1598-1621.

DP186.K35
Kamen, Henry Arthur Francis.
Spain in the later seventeenth century, 1665-1700/ Henry Kamen. London; Longman, 1980. xiii, 418 p.
79-042884 946/.053 0582490367
Civilization, Modern -- 17th century. Spain -- History -- Charles II, 1665-1700.

DP192.H57 1990
Historical dictionary of modern Spain, 1700-1988/ Robert W. Kern, editor-in-chief, Meredith D. Dodge, associate editor. New York: Greenwood Press, 1990. xxv, 697 p.
89-007471 946/.003 0313259712
Spain -- History -- Bourbons, 1700- -- Dictionaries.

DP194.K3613 2001
Kamen, Henry Arthur Francis.
Philip V of Spain: the king who reigned twice/ Henry Kamen. New Haven, CT: Yale University Press, c2001. viii, 277 p.
00-067192 946/.055/092 0300087187
Philip -- V, -- King of Spain, -- 1683-1746. Spain -- History -- Philip V, 1700-1746. Spain -- Kings and rulers -- Biography.

DP203.C3
Carr, Raymond.
Spain 1808-1939. Oxford Univ. press/Clarendon, 1966. xxix, 766 p.
66-072222 946
Spain -- Politics and government -- 19th cent. Spain -- Politics and government -- 20th cent. Spain -- Social conditions.

DP203.F58 1999
Flynn, M. K.
Ideology, mobilization, and the the nation: the rise of Irish, Basque, and Carlist national movements in the nineteenth and early twentieth centuries/ M.K. Flynn. New York: St. Martin's Press, 1999. p. cm.
99-016304 320.54/0946/6 0312224338
Nationalism -- Spain -- History. Nationalism -- Spain -- Pais Vasco -- History. Carlists -- History. Spain -- History -- Autonomy and independence movements. Pais Vasco (Spain) -- History -- Autonomy and independence movements. Ireland -- History -- Autonomy and independence movements.

DP208.E82 1988
Esdaile, Charles J.
The Spanish army in the Peninsular War/ Charles J. Esdaile. Manchester, UK; Manchester University Press; c1988. xii, 232 p.
88-010274 946/.06 0719025389:
Sociology, Military -- Spain. Spain -- History -- Napoleonic Conquest, 1808-1813. Spain -- History -- Charles IV, 1788-1808. Spain -- History, Military.

DP219.2.C68 1984
Coverdale, John F., 1940-
The Basque phase of Spain's first Carlist war/ John F. Coverdale. Princeton, N.J.: Princeton University Press, c1984. ix, 332 p.
83-043068 946/.07 0691054118
Carlists. Spain -- History -- Carlist War, 1833-1840. Pais Vasco (Spain) -- History -- 19th century.

DP233.5.E63 1999
Encyclopedia of contemporary Spanish culture/ edited by Eamonn Rodgers, honorary assistant editor, Valerie Rodgers. London; Routledge, 1999. xxii, 591 p.
98-042158 946.082 0415131871
Spain -- Civilization -- 20th century -- Encyclopedias.

DP233.5.S65 2000
Smith, Paul Julian.
The moderns: time, space, and subjectivity in contemporary Spanish culture/ Paul Julian Smith. Oxford; Oxford University Press, 2000. xii, 206 p.
00-710226 0198160003
Spain -- Intellectual life -- 20th century.

DP243.B28 1997
Balfour, Sebastian.
The end of the Spanish empire, 1898-1923/ Sebastian Balfour. Oxford: Clarendon Press, 1997. vi, 269 p.
96-026833 946/.071 0198205074
Spanish-American War, 1898 -- Influence. Public opinion -- Spain. Spain -- Politics and government -- 1886-1931.

DP243.P39 1999
Payne, Stanley G.
Fascism in Spain, 1923-1977/ Stanley G. Payne. Madison: University of Wisconsin Press, 1999. xii, 601 p.
99-023078 946.08 0299165604
Fascism -- Spain -- History -- 20th century. Francoism. Spain -- Politics and government -- 20th century.

DP247.B39
Ben-Ami, Shlomo.
The origins of the Second Republic in Spain/ by Shlomo Ben-Ami. Oxford; Oxford University Press, 1978. xii, 356 p.
78-040079 320.9/46/08 0198218710
Republicanism -- Spain. Spain -- Politics and government -- 1923-1930. Spain -- Politics and government -- 1931-1939.

DP257.A54 1993
Alpert, Michael, 1936-
A New international history of the Spanish Civil War/ Michael Alpert. New York: St. Martin's Press, 1994. ix, 209 p.
93-032764 946.081 0312120168
Spain -- History -- Civil War, 1936-1939. Spain -- Foreign relations -- 1931-1939.

DP257.P34
Payne, Stanley G.
Falange: a history of Spanish fascism. Stanford, Calif.: Stanford University Press, 1961, 1967 pr ix, 316 p.
61-012391 946.081 0804700583
Fascism -- Spain. Spain -- Politics and government -- 1939-1945. Spain -- Politics and government -- 1931-1939.

DP264.F7 H63 2002
Hodges, Gabrielle Ashford.
Franco: a concise biography/ Gabrielle Ashford Hodges. 1st U.S. ed. New York: St. Martin's Press, 2002. xii, 290 p.
2002-024859 946.082/092. 221 0312282850
Franco, Francisco, 1892-1975. Heads of state--Spain--Biography. Generals--Spain--Biography.

DP269.D35 2001
De Meneses, Filipe Ribeiro,
Franco and the Spanish Civil War/ Filipe Ribeiro de Meneses. New York: Routledge, 2001. p. cm.
00-045041 946.081.221 0415239257
Franco, Francisco, 1892-1975.

DP269.F62 2000
Forrest, Andrew, 1947-
The Spanish Civil War/ Andrew Forrest. London; Routledge, 2000. 150 p.
99-056393 946.081 0415182115
Spain -- History -- Civil War, 1936-1939.

DP269.H54 1982
Historical dictionary of the Spanish Civil War, 1936-1939/ edited by James W. Cortada. Westport, Conn.: Greenwood Press, 1982. xxviii, 571 p.
81-013424 946.081/03/21 0313220549
Spain -- History -- Civil War, 1936-1939 -- Dictionaries.

DP269.T46 1977
Thomas, Hugh, 1931-
The Spanish Civil War/ Hugh Thomas. New York: Harper & Row, c1977. xx, 1115 p.
76-005531 946.081 0060142782
Spain -- History -- Civil War, 1936-1939.

DP269.27.G8.S69
Southworth, Herbert Rutledge.
Guernica! Guernica!: A study of journalism, diplomacy, propaganda, and history/ Herbert Rutledge Southworth. Berkeley: University of California Press, c1977. xxvi, 537 p.
74-082850 946.081 0520028309
Propaganda -- Spain. Spain -- History -- Civil War, 1936-1939 -- Journalism, Military. Spain -- History -- Civil War, 1936-1939 -- Diplomatic history. Spain -- History -- Civil War, 1936-1939 -- Propaganda.

DP269.47.A46.C37 1994
Carroll, Peter N.
The odyssey of the Abraham Lincoln Brigade: Americans in the Spanish Civil War/ Peter N. Carroll. Stanford, Calif.: Stanford University Press, 1994. xiv, 440 p.
93-021131   946.081   0804722765
Americans -- Spain -- History -- 20th century. Spain -- History -- Civil War, 1936-1939 -- Participation, American.

DP269.47.A46.F58 1998
Fisher, Harry, 1911-
Comrades: tales of a brigadista in the Spanish Civil War/ Harry Fisher. Lincoln: University of Nebraska, 1998. xx, 197 p.
98-004953   946.081/8   0803220065
Fisher, Harry, -- 1911- Soldiers -- Spain -- Biography. Americans -- Spain -- Biography. Spain -- History -- Civil War, 1936-1939 -- Personal narratives, American.

DP269.47.B7.H66 1998
Hopkins, James K., 1941-
Into the heart of the fire: the British in the Spanish Civil War/ James K. Hopkins. Stanford, Calif.: Stanford University Press, 1998. xxii, 474 p.
98-007835   946.081/4/09222   0804731268
British -- Spain -- History -- 20th century. Spain -- History -- Civil War, 1936-1939 -- Participation, British.

DP269.8.R3.M34 1990
MacMaster, Neil, 1945-
Spanish fighters: an oral history of civil war and exile/ Neil MacMaster. New York: St. Martin's Press, 1990. ix, 250 p.
90-033781   946.081   031204738X
Granda, David, -- 1914- Granda, Consuelo. Political refugees -- Spain -- Asturias -- Biography. Political refugees -- France -- Biography. Oral history. Spain -- Politics and government -- 1931-1939. Spain -- Politics and government -- 1939-1975. Spain -- History -- Civil War, 1936-1939 -- Refugees.

DP269.8.W7.N38 1995
Nash, Mary, 1947-
Defying male civilization: women in the Spanish Civil War/ by Mary Nash. Denver, Colo.: Arden Press, c1995. xvi, 261 p.
95-018301   946.081   0912869151
Feminism -- Spain -- History -- 20th century. Women -- Spain -- History -- 20th century. Spain -- History -- Civil War, 1936-1939 -- Women.

DP270.C258
Carr, Raymond.
Spain, dictatorship to democracy/ Raymond Carr and Juan Pablo Fusi Aizpurua. London; G. Allen & Unwin, 1979. xxi, 282 p.
78-041081   946.082   0049460129
Spain -- History -- 1939-1975. Spain -- History -- 1975-

DP270.G78 1997
Grugel, Jean.
Franco's Spain/ Jean Grugel and Tim Rees. London; Arnold: 1997. xii, 206 p.
97-008760   946.082   0340663235
Francoism. Spain -- Politics and government -- 1939-1975.

DP270.S624 1976b
Preston, Paul.
Spain in crisis: the evolution and decline of the Franco regime/ editor Paul Preston. New York: Barnes & Noble Books, c1976. 341 p.
76-375103   946.082   006495711X
Spain -- History -- 1939-1975.

DP271.F7.G56 1999
Gilmour, John, 1945-
Manuel Fraga Iribarne and the rebirth of Spanish conservatism, 1939-1990/ John Gilmour. Lewiston [NY]: E. Mellen Press, c1999. xvii, 342 p.
99-021895   946.083/092   0773480293
Fraga Iribarne, Manuel. Statesmen -- Spain -- Biography. Spain -- Politics and government -- 1975- Spain -- Politics and government -- 1939-1975.

DP272.A35 1995
Aguero, Felipe.
Soldiers, civilians, and democracy: post-Franco Spain in comparative perspective/ Felipe Aguero. Baltimore: Johns Hopkins University Press, 1995. xii, 316 p.
95-003399   322/.5/094609047   0801850851
Civil supremacy over the military -- Spain -- History -- 20th century. Comparative government. Democracy. Spain -- Politics and government -- 1975-

DP272.G545 1985
Gilmour, David, 1952-
The transformation of Spain: from Franco to the constitutional monarchy/ David Gilmour. London; Quartet Books, 1985. xi, 322 p.
85-118311   946.083   070432461X
Spain -- History -- 1975- Spain -- History -- 1939-1975.

DP272.M39 1994
Maxwell, Kenneth, 1941-
The new Spain: from isolation to influence/ Kenneth Maxwell and Steven Spiegel. New York: Council on Foreign Relations Press, c1994. xi, 126 p.
93-044751   946.083   087609163X
Spain -- Politics and government -- 1975-

DP302 Local history and description — Provinces, regions, etc., A-Z

DP302.B28.G74 1990
Gregory, Desmond, 1916-
Minorca, the illusory prize: a history of the British occupations of Minorca between 1708 and 1802/ Desmond Gregory. Rutherford [NJ?]: Fairleigh Dickinson University Press; c1990. 295 p.
89-045528   946/.752   0838633897
British -- Spain -- Minorca -- History -- 18th century. Minorca (Spain) -- History -- Invasions.

DP302.B53.C55
Clark, Robert P., 1940-
The Basques, the Franco years and beyond/ Robert P. Clark. Reno, Nev.: University of Nevada Press, c1979. xvii, 434 p.
79-024926   946/.004/9992   0874170575
Nationalism -- Spain -- Pais Vasco. Pais Vasco (Spain) -- History -- Autonomy and independence movements.

DP302.B53.D54 1995
Diez Medrano, Juan.
Divided nations: class, politics, and nationalism in the Basque Country and Catalonia/ Juan Diez Medrano. Ithaca: Cornell University Press, c1995. xvii, 236 p.
94-047526   320.5/4/09466   0801430925
Nationalism -- Spain -- Pais Vasco. Nationalism -- Spain -- Catalonia. Pais Vasco (Spain) -- Politics and government. Catalonia (Spain) -- Politics and government.

DP302.B53.S85 1988
Sullivan, John, 1932-
ETA and Basque nationalism: the fight for Euskadi, 1890-1986/ John Sullivan. London; Routledge, 1988. vii, 298 p.
88-004405   946/.6   0415003660
Nationalism -- Spain -- Pais Vasco -- History -- 20th century. Pais Vasco (Spain) -- History -- Autonomy and independence movements.

DP302.B55.C66 1997
Conversi, Daniele.
The Basques, the Catalans, and Spain: alternative routes to nationalist mobilisation/ Daniele Conversi. Reno: University of Nevada Press, c1997. xx, 312 p.
95-045484   320.5/4/094660904   0874172780
Nationalism -- Spain -- Pais Vasco. Basques -- Ethnic identity. Nationalism -- Spain -- Catalonia. Catalonia (Spain) -- History -- Autonomy and independence movements. Pais Vasco (Spain) -- History -- Autonomy and independence movements.

DP302.C42.F47 1982
Fernandez-Armesto, Felipe.
The Canary Islands after the conquest: the making of a colonial society in the early sixteenth century/ Felipe Fernandez-Armesto. Oxford: Clarendon Press; 1982. ix, 244 p.
81-014204   964/.907   0198218885
Canary Islands -- History.

DP302.C67.B3513 1995
Balcells, Albert.
Catalan nationalism: past and present/ Albert Balcells; edited and introduced by Geoffrey J. Walker; translated by Jacqueline Hall with the collaboration of Geoffrey J. Walker. New York: St. Martin's Press, 1996. xviii, 226 p.
94-047389   320.5/4/0946   0312126115
Nationalism -- Spain -- Catalonia -- History. Catalonia (Spain) -- History.

DP302.G38.J19 1987
Jackson, W. G. F. 1917-
The Rock of the Gibraltarians: a history of Gibraltar/ Sir William G.F. Jackson; illustrated by George Palao; photographs by John Fernandez. Rutherford: Farleigh Dickinson University Press, c1987. 379 p.
84-046113   946/.89   0838632378
Gibraltar -- History.

DP302.L13.C4
Cela, Camilo Jose, 1916-
Viaje a La Alcarria. Edited by Philip Polack. Boston, Heath [1962] 272 p.
62-019397
La Alcarria -- Description and travel.

DP302.N33
MacClancy, Jeremy.
The decline of Carlism/ Jeremy MacClancy. Reno: University of Nevada Press, c2000. xix, 349 p.
00-009887   946/.5207   0874173442
Carlists -- Spain -- Navarre -- History -- 20th century. Oral history. Navarre (Spain) -- Politics and government -- 20th century.

DP302.V205.B85 1984
Burns, Robert Ignatius.
Muslims, Christians, and Jews in the crusader kingdom of Valencia: societies in symbiosis/ Robert I. Burns. Cambridge [Cambridgeshire]; Cambridge University Press, 1984. xx, 363 p.
83-002007   946/.76   0521243742
Muslims -- Spain -- Valencia (Region) Christians -- Spain -- Valencia (Region) Jews -- Spain -- Valencia (Region) Valencia (Spain: Region) -- Civilization.

DP402 Local history and description — Other cities, towns, etc., A-Z

DP402.D395.W3 1996
Waldren, Jacqueline, 1937-
Insiders and outsiders: paradise and reality in Mallorca/ Jacqueline Waldren. Providence: Berghahn Books, 1996. xxii, 260 p.
95-042239 946/.754 1571818898
Aliens -- Spain -- Deia. Visitors, Foreign -- Spain -- Deia. Tourism -- Social aspects -- Spain -- Deia. Deia (Spain) -- Ethnic relations. Deia (Spain) -- Social life and customs.

DP517-702 History of Portugal

DP517 General works

DP517.M63 1998
Modern Portugal/ edited by Antonio Costa Pinto. Palo Alto, Calif.: Society for the Promotion of Science and Scholar c1998. xvii, 312 p.
97-045654 946.9 0930664175
Portugal.

DP532.3 Social life and customs. Civilization — Through 1500

DP532.3.M3413
Marques, Antonio Henrique R. de Oliveira.
Daily life in Portugal in the late Middle Ages [by] A. H. de Oliveira Marques. Translated by S. S. Wyatt. Drawings by Vitor Andre. Madison, University of Wisconsin Press, 1971. xvi, 355 p.
78-106040 914.69/03/2 0299055809
Social history -- Medieval, 500-1500. Portugal -- Social life and customs.

DP538 History — General works — 1801-

DP538.A56 2000
Anderson, James Maxwell,
The history of Portugal/ James M. Anderson. Westport, Conn: Greenwood Press, 2000. xxiii, 222 p.
99-043637 946.9.221 0313311064
Spain -- History.

DP538.B57 1993
Birmingham, David.
A concise history of Portugal/ David Birmingham. Cambridge [England]; Cambridge University Press, xiii, 209 p.
92-033824 946.9.220 0521438802
Portugal -- History.

DP538.L72
Livermore, H. V., 1914-
A new history of Portugal [by] H. V. Livermore. Cambridge, Cambridge U.P., 1966. xi, 365 p.
65-019147 946.9
Portugal -- History.

DP538.M37
Marques, Antonio Henrique R. de Oliveira.
History of Portugal [by] A. H. de Oliveira Marques. New York, Columbia University Press, 1972. 2 v.
77-184748 946.9 0231031599
Portugal -- History.

DP556 History — Political and diplomatic history. Foreign

DP556.O64 1991
Opello, Walter C.
Portugal: from monarchy to pluralist democracy/ Walter C. Opello, Jr. Boulder: Westview Press, 1991. ix, 177 p.
90-027257 946.904 0813304881
Representative government and representation -- Portugal -- History -- 20th century. Portugal -- Politics and government.

DP675-681 History — By period — 1580-

DP675.G34 1983
Gallagher, Tom, 1954-
Portugal: a twentieth-century interpretation/ Tom Gallagher. Manchester: Manchester University Press, c1983. xii, 278 p.
82-020379 946.9/04 071900876X
Portugal -- Politics and government -- 1910-1974. Portugal -- Politics and government -- 1974-

DP675.W47
Wheeler, Douglas L.
Republican Portugal: a political history, 1910-1926/ Douglas L. Wheeler. Madison: University of Wisconsin Press, 1978. xii, 340 p.
77-015059 946.9/04 0299074501
Portugal -- Politics and government -- 1910-1926.

DP680.I53 1983
In search of modern Portugal: the revolution & its consequences/ edited by Lawrence S. Graham & Douglas L. Wheeler. Madison, Wis.: University of Wisconsin Press, 1983. xv, 380 p.
81-069819 946.9/044 0299089908
Portugal -- Politics and government -- 1974- -- Congresses. Portugal -- History -- Revolution, 1974 -- Influence -- Congresses.

DP681.D68 1989
Downs, Charles, 1950-
Revolution at the grassroots: community organizations in the Portuguese revolution/ Charles Downs. Albany, N.Y.: State University of New York Press, c1989. x, 215 p.
88-031217 946.9/043 0791400662
Social movements -- Portugal -- History -- 20th century. Sociology, Urban -- Portugal -- History -- 20th century. Community organization -- Portugal -- History -- 20th century. Portugal -- History -- Revolution, 1974 -- Social aspects. Portugal -- Politics and government -- 1974- Setubal (Portugal) -- Social conditions.

DP702 Local history and description — Provinces, regions, etc., A-Z

DP702.M18.G74 1988
Gregory, Desmond, 1916-
The beneficent usurpers: a history of the British in Madeira/ Desmond Gregory. Rutherford, [N.J.]: Fairleigh Dickinson University Press; c1988. 160 p.
87-046083 946.9/8 0838633269
British -- Madeira Islands -- History. Madeira (Madeira Islands) -- History. Madeira (Madeira Islands) -- Church history. Madeira (Madeira Islands) -- Economic conditions.

DQ History of Switzerland

DQ17 General works

DQ17.H8 1975
Hughes, Christopher
Switzerland/ Christopher Hughes. New York: Praeger, 1975, c1974. 303 p.
73-015169 914.94/03/7 0275333205
Switzerland.

DQ17.S64 1982
Soloveytchik, George,
Switzerland in perspective/ by George Soloveytchik. Westport, Conn.: Greenwood Press, 1982, c1954. vii, 306 p.
82-011872 949.4.219 0313233632
Switzerland. Switzerland -- Foreign relations.

DQ17.S7 1996
Steinberg, Jonathan.
Why Switzerland?/ Jonathan Steinberg. 2nd ed. Cambridge [England]; Cambridge University Press, 1996. xix, 300 p.
95-043246 949.4.220 052128144X
National characteristics, Swiss.

DQ55 History — Compends

DQ55.G513 1978
Gilliard, Charles,
A history of Switzerland/ by Charles Gilliard; with concluding pages brought up-to-date by J. C. Biaudet; translated by D. L. B. Hartley. Westport, Conn.: Greenwood Press, 1978, c1955. 116 p.
78-017481 949.4 0313205299
Switzerland -- History.

DQ69 History — Political and diplomatic history. Foreign and general relations — General works

DQ69.M35 2000
The making of modern Switzerland, 1848-1998/ edited by Michael Butler, Malcolm Pender, and Joy Charnley. New York: St. Martin's Press , 2000. xiii, 163 p.
00-027824 949.407 0312234597
Political ethics -- Switzerland -- Congresses. Switzerland -- Politics and government -- 1848- -- Congresses.

DQ70 History — Political and diplomatic history. Foreign and general relations — General special

DQ70.L55 1980
Lloyd, William Bross,
Waging peace: the Swiss experience/ William Bross Lloyd, Jr.; foreword by Quincy Wright; pref. by William E. Rappard. Westport, Conn.: Greenwood Press, 1980, c1958. vii, 101 p.
80-015577 327.1/72/09494 0313225060
Federal government--Switzerland.

DQ70.R322513 1984
Rappard, William E. 1883-1958.
Collective security in Swiss experience, 1291-1948/ by William E. Rappard. Westport, Conn.: Greenwood Press, 1984. xvi, 150 p.
84-010758 949.4 0313243816
National security -- Switzerland. Switzerland -- Politics and government.

DR History of Balkan Peninsula

DR23 Social life and customs. Civilization. Intellectual life

DR23.N67 1993
Norris, H. T.
Islam in the Balkans: religion and society between Europe and the Arab world/ H.T. Norris. Columbia, S.C: University of South Carolina Press, c1993. xxii, 304 p.
93-001637 949.6 0872499774
Balkan Peninsula -- Civilization -- Islamic influences. Islam -- Balkan Peninsula -- History. Muslims -- Balkan Peninsula -- History.

DR23.S758 1994
Stoianovich, Traian.
Balkan worlds: the first and last Europe/ Traian Stoianovich. Armonk, NY: M.E. Sharpe, c1994. xix, 433 p.
94-016917 949.6 1563240327
Balkan Peninsula -- Civilization.

DR24 Ethnography — General works

DR24.O77 2000
Ortakovski, Vladimir, 1950-
Minorities in the Balkans/ Vladimir Ortakovski. Ardsley, NY: Transnational Publishers, c2000. xvi, 384 p.
00-023470 305.8/009496 1571051295
Minorities -- Balkan Peninsula. Nationalism -- Balkan Peninsula. Balkan Peninsula -- Ethnic relations.

DR24.5 Ethnography — National characteristics

DR24.5.N67 1999
Norris, David A.
In the wake of the Balkan myth: questions of identity and modernity/ David A. Norris. New York: St. Martin's Press, 1999. p. cm.
99-011217 949.6/0072 0312221754
National characteristics, Balkan -- Historiography. Yugoslav literature -- 20th century -- History and criticism. Yugoslav War, 1991-1995 -- Literature and the war. Balkan Peninsula -- History -- 19th century -- Historiography. Balkan Peninsula -- History -- 20th century -- Historiography.

DR27 Ethnography — Other individual elements in the population, A-Z

DR27.M87.M33 1995
McCarthy, Justin, 1945-
Death and exile: the ethnic cleansing of Ottoman Muslims, 1821-1922/ by Justin McCarthy. Princeton, N.J.: Darwin Press, c1995. xv, 368 p.
95-001282 949.61/015 0878500944
Muslims -- Relocation -- History. Turks -- Relocation -- History. Muslims -- Balkan Peninsula -- Relocation. Turkey -- Emigration and immigration -- History -- 20th century. Turkey -- Emigration and immigration -- History -- 19th century.

DR36 History — General works — 1801-

DR36.D9
Dvornik, Francis, 1893-
The making of central and eastern Europe. London, Polish Research Centre, 1949. 350 p.
49-029625
Europe, Central -- History.

DR36.G4
Gewehr, Wesley Marsh, 1888-
The rise of nationalism in the Balkans, 1800-1930, by Wesley M. Gewehr. New York, H. Holt and company [1931] xi, 137 p.
31-023664 949.6
Eastern question (Balkan) Balkan Peninsula -- History. Balkan Peninsula -- Politics.

DR36.H87 2002
Hupchick, Dennis P.
The Balkans: from Constantinople to Communism/ Dennis P. Hupchick. Houndmills, Basingstoke, Hampshire; Palgrave, 2001. xxviii, 468 p.
00-062590 949.6.221 0312217366
Balkan Peninsula -- History.

DR36 .J37 1983
Jelavich, Barbara,
History of the Balkans/ Barbara Jelavich. Cambridge; Cambridge University Press, 1983. 2 v.
82-022093 949.6 19 0521274591
Balkan Peninsula -- History.

DR36.P3 1970b
Palmer, Alan Warwick.
The lands between; a history of East-Central Europe since the Congress of Vienna [by] Alan Palmer. New York] Macmillan [1970] ix, 405 p.
74-083064 943
Europe, Eastern -- History. Europe, Central -- History.

DR36.S5
Seton-Watson, R. W. 1879-1951.
The rise of nationality in the Balkans, by R.W. Seton-Watson. With four maps. London, Constable and Company Limited, 1917. viii, 308 p.
17-028918
Eastern question (Balkan) Balkan Peninsula -- History.

DR36.S83
Stavrianos, Leften Stavros.
The Balkans since 1453. New York, Rinehart [1958] xxi, 970 p.
58-007242 949.6 0030096855
Balkan Peninsula -- History.

DR37 History — General special

DR37.S94
Sugar, Peter F.
Nationalism in Eastern Europe. Edited by Peter F. Sugar and Ivo J. Lederer. Seattle, University of Washington Press [1969] ix, 465 p.
74-093026 320.1/58/0947
Nationalism -- Europe, Eastern.

DR38.2 History — Political and diplomatic history

DR38.2.W48 2000
White, George W., 1963-
Nationalism and territory: constructing group identity in Southeastern Europe/ George W. White. Lanham, MD: Rowman & Littlefield, c2000. xv, 311 p.
99-039940 323.1/496 0847698084
Nationalism -- Balkan Peninsula. Territory, National -- Balkan Peninsula. Nationalism -- Hungary. Balkan Peninsula -- Politics and government. Hungary -- Politics and government.

DR38.3 History — Balkan relations with individual regions or countries, A-Z

DR38.3.S65.J45 1991
Jelavich, Barbara, 1923-
Russia's Balkan entanglements, 1806-1914/ Barbara Jelavich. Cambridge [England]; Cambridge University Press, 1991. xi, 291 p.
90-020036 949.6 0521401267
Eastern question (Balkan) Russia -- Foreign relations -- Balkan Peninsula. Balkan Peninsula -- Foreign relations -- Russia. Russia -- Foreign relations -- 1801-1917.

DR39 History — By period — Early and medieval to 1500

DR39.S76 2000
Stephenson, Paul.
Byzantium's Balkan frontier: a political study of the Northern Balkans, 900-1204/ Paul Stephenson. Cambridge; Cambridge University Press, 2000. xii, 352 p.
99-042114   949.6/0144   0521770173
Balkan Peninsula -- Politics and government. Byzantine Empire -- Politics and government -- 527-1081. Byzantine Empire -- Politics and government -- 1081-1453.

DR43 History — By period — 1800-1900

DR43.R513 1971
Ristelhueber, Rene, 1881-1960.
A history of the Balkan peoples. Edited and translated by Sherman David Spector. New York, Twayne Publishers [1971] 470 p.
78-147184   949.6
Ethnology -- Balkan Peninsula.   Balkan Peninsula -- History -- 19th century.

DR46.3-48.6 History — By period — 20th century (General)

DR46.3.H4 1969
Helmreich, Ernst Christian.
The diplomacy of the Balkan wars, 1912-1913. New York, Russell & Russell [1969, c1938] xiv, 523 p.
68-027063   949.6
Balkan Peninsula -- History -- War of 1912-1913.

DR48.S38 1962
Seton-Watson, Hugh.
Eastern Europe between the wars, 1918-1941. With a new pref. written for this ed. Hamden, Conn.] Archon Books, 1962. 425 p.
62-053112   914.7
Europe, Eastern -- History. Europe, Eastern -- Politics and government.

DR48.5.B698 1992
Brown, J. F. 1928-
Nationalism, democracy, and security in the Balkans/ J.F. Brown. Aldershot, Hants, England; Dartmouth Pub. Co., c1992. x, 205 p.
92-023927   949.6   1855213168
Nationalism -- Balkan Peninsula.   Balkan Peninsula -- Politics and government -- 1989- Balkan Peninsula -- Politics and government -- 1945-1989.

DR48.5.P74 1990
Problems of Balkan security: Southeastern Europe in the 1990s/ Paul S. Shoup, editor; George W. Hoffman, project director. Washington, D.C.: Wilson Center Press; c1990. xii, 286 p.
89-077744   949.6   0943875226
Balkan Peninsula -- Politics and government -- 20th century. Balkan Peninsula -- Foreign relations -- 20th century.

DR48.5.S4 1956
Seton-Watson, Hugh.
The East European revolution. London, Methuen [1956] 435 p.
57-001670   940.55
Europe, Eastern -- History. Europe, Eastern -- Politics.

DR48.5.W6 1974
Wolff, Robert Lee.
The Balkans in our time/ by Robert Lee Wolff. Cambridge, Mass.: Harvard University Press, 1974. xxi, 647 p.
73-092497   949.6   0674060512
Communism -- Balkan Peninsula.   Balkan Peninsula -- History.

DR48.6.T36 1999
Tanter, Raymond.
Balancing in the Balkans/ Raymond Tanter and John Psarouthakis. New York: St. Martin's Press, 1999. p. cm.
98-052842   327/.09496/09049   031221457X
National security -- Balkan Peninsula. Yugoslav War, 1991-1995 -- Diplomatic history.   Balkan Penisula -- Politics and government -- 1989- Balkan Peninsula -- Foreign relations -- 1989-

DR65 Bulgaria — History — Dictionaries. Chronological tables, outlines, etc.

DR65.D48 1997
Detrez, Raymond, 1948-
Historical dictionary of Bulgaria/ Raymond Detrez. Lanham, Md.: Scarecrow Press, 1997. lvii, 466 p.
96-033921   949.77/003   0810831775
Bulgaria -- History -- Dictionaries. Bulgaria -- Chronology.

DR67 Bulgaria — History — General works

DR67.C72 1997
Crampton, R. J.
A concise history of Bulgaria/ R.J. Crampton. Cambridge [Eng.]; Cambridge University Press, 1997. xv, 259 p.
96-007778   949.77.220   052156719X
Bulgaria -- History.

DR67.C73 1987
Crampton, R. J.
A short history of modern Bulgaria/ R.J. Crampton. Cambridge [Cambridgeshire];   Cambridge University Press, 1987. xiii, 221 p.
86-017528   949.7/7   0521253403
Bulgaria -- History.

DR89-90 Bulgaria — History — By period

DR89.G76 1987
Groueff, Stéphane.
Crown of thorns/ Stephane Groueff. Lanham, MD: Madison Books, c1987. xvi, 411 p.
87-010727   949.7/702/0924. 219   0819157783
Boris III, Czar of Bulgaria, 1894-1943.

DR90.B7
Brown, J. F. 1928-
Bulgaria under Communist rule [by] J. F. Brown. New York, Praeger [1970] ix, 339 p.
78-083329   320.9/497/7
Communism -- Bulgaria.   Bulgaria -- Economic policy -- 1944-1989. Bulgaria -- History -- 1944-1990.

DR205 Romania — General works

DR205.R65 1998
Siani-Davies, Peter.
Romania/ Peter Siani-Davies and Mary Siani-Davies, compilers. Oxford, England: Clio Press, c1998. xxxv, 347 p.
1851092447
Romania -- Bibliography.

DR215 Romania — History — Dictionaries. Chronological tables, outlines, etc.

DR215.T74 1996
Treptow, Kurt W.
Historical dictionary of Romania/ by Kurt W. Treptow and Marcel Popa. Lanham, Md.: Scarecrow Press, 1996. p. cm.
96-007322   949.8   0810831791
Romania -- History -- Dictionaries.

DR217 Romania — General works

DR217.G4613 1990
Georgescu, Vlad.
The Romanians: a history/ Vlad Georgescu; edited by Matei Cælinescu; translated by Alexandra Bley-Vroman. Columbus: Ohio State University Press, c1991. xiv, 357 p.
90-007720   949.8.220   0814205119
Romania -- History.

DR217.I77 1970
Iorga, Nicolae, 1871-1940.
A history of Roumania; land, people, civilisation. Translated from the 2d enl. ed. by Joseph McCabe. New York, AMS Press [1970] xii, 284 p.
79-124616   914.98   0404035043
Romania -- History.

DR241-269.6 Romania — History — By period

DR241.H575 1996
Hitchins, Keith, 1931-
The Romanians, 1774-1866/ Keith Hitchins. Oxford, Eng.: Clarendon Press, 1996. 337 p.
95-038279   949.8/01   0198205910
Romania -- History -- 1711-1821. Romania -- History -- 1821-1859. Romania -- History -- 1859-1866.

DR244.M54 1998
Michelson, Paul E., 1945-
Romanian politics, 1859-1871: from Prince Cuza to Prince Carol/ Paul E. Michelson. Iasi, Romania; Center for Romanian Studies, c1998. 344 p.
98-161666   949.8/016   9739809197
Alexandru Ioan -- I Cuza, -- Prince of Romania, -- 1820-1873. Carol -- I, -- King of Romania, -- 1839-1914. Romania -- Politics and government -- 1821-1866. Romania -- Politics and government -- 1866-1914.

DR250.H58 1994
Hitchins, Keith,
Rumania, 1866-1947/ by Keith Hitchins. Oxford: Clarendon Press; viii, 579 p.
93-031575   949.8/02.220   0198221266
Romania -- History -- Charles I, 1866-1914. Romania -- History -- 1914-1944. Romania -- History -- 1944-1989.

DR264.L58 1995
Livezeanu, Irina.
Cultural politics in Greater Romania: regionalism, nation building & ethnic struggle, 1918-1930/ Irina Livezeanu. Ithaca: Cornell University Press, 1995. xvii, 340 p.
94-032401   949.8/02   0801424453
Nationalism -- Romania. Romania -- Politics and government -- 1914-1944. Romania -- Intellectual life -- 20th century. Romania -- Ethnic relations.

DR267.I65
Ionescu, Ghita.
Communism in Rumania, 1944-1962. London, Oxford University Press, 1964. xvi, 378 p.
64-055367   949.803
Communism -- Romania. Romania -- History -- 1944-1989.

DR267.R47 2000
Retegan, Mihai.
In the shadow of the Prague spring: Romanian foreign policy and the crisis in Czechoslovakia, 1968/ Mihai Retegan. Iasi; Center for Romanian Studies, 2000. 248 p.
00-711857   327.498/009/046
Romania -- Foreign relations -- 1914-1944. Romania -- Foreign relations -- 1944-1989. Czechoslovakia -- History -- Intervention, 1968.

DR267.5.C4.F567 1989
Fischer, Mary Ellen.
Nicolae Ceausescu: a study in political leadership/ Mary Ellen Fischer. Boulder: L. Rienner Publishers, 1989. x, 324 p.
88-036391   949.8/03/0924   0931477832
Ceausescu, Nicolae. Presidents -- Romania -- Biography. Romania -- Politics and government -- 1944-1989.

DR267.5.P38
Levy, Robert, 1957-
Ana Pauker: the rise and fall of a Jewish Communist/ Robert Levy. Berkeley: University of California Press, c2001. xii, 407 p.
99-087890   949.803/1/092   0520223950
Pauker, Ana, -- 1893-1960. Cabinet officers -- Romania -- Biography. Communists -- Romania -- Biography. Jews -- Romania -- Biography. Romania -- Politics and government -- 1944-1989.

DR268.G35 1995
Gallagher, Tom, 1954-
Romania after Ceausescu: the politics of intolerance/ Tom Gallagher. Edinburgh: Edinburgh University Press, c1995. 267 p.
96-119569   0748606130
Nationalism -- Romania -- History -- 20th century. Romania -- Politics and government -- 1989- Romania -- Ethnic relations.

DR268.P67 2001
Post-Communist Romania: coming to terms with transition/ edited by Duncan Light and David Phinnemore. Houndmills, Basingstoke, Hampshire; Palgrave, 2001. xvii, 299 p.
00-042209   330.9498/032   0333791878
Post-communism -- Romania. Romania -- Politics and government -- 1989- Romania -- Economic policy -- 1989- Romania -- Foreign relations.

DR269.5.R38 1991
Ratesh, Nestor, 1933-
Romania: the entangled revolution/ Nestor Ratesh; foreword by Edward N. Luttwak. Washington, D.C.: Center for Strategic and International Studies; 1991. xxiv, 179 p.
91-119567   949.803   0275941450
Romania -- History -- Revolution, 1989. Romania -- Politics and government -- 1989-

DR269.6.C63 1991
Codrescu, Andrei, 1946-
The hole in the flag: a Romanian exile's story of return and revolution/ Andrei Codrescu. New York: W. Morrow, c1991. 249 p.
90-026046   949.803   0688088058
Codrescu, Andrei, -- 1946- Romania -- History -- Revolution, 1989 -- Personal narratives.

DR309-370 Yugoslavia

DR309.W47 1968
West, Rebecca, 1892-
Black lamb and grey falcon: the record of a journey through Jugoslavia in 1937. London, Macmillan, 1967 [i.e. 19 xv, 653 p.
68-118073   914.9/7
Eastern question (Balkan) Yugoslavia -- Description and travel. Yugoslavia -- History. Serbia -- History.

DR317.I8613
History of Yugoslavia, by Vladimir Dedijer [and others. Translator: Kordija Kveder] New York, McGraw-Hill Book Co. [1974] ix, 752 p.
74-006164   949.7   0070162352
Yugoslavia -- History.

DR359.T5.D4
Dedijer, Vladimir.
Tito. New York, Simon and Schuster, 1953 [i.e. 19 443 p.
53-006161   923.5497   0405045654
Tito, Josip Broz, -- 1892-1980. Yugoslavia -- Presidents -- Biography. Yugoslavia -- Politics and government -- 1945-

DR370.C33
Campbell, John Coert, 1911-
Tito's separate road; America and Yugoslavia in world politics, by John C. Campbell. New York, Published for the Council on Foreign Relations b [1967] viii, 180 p.
67-015967   949.7/02
Yugoslavia -- Politics and government -- 1945-1980. Yugoslavia -- Foreign relations -- 1945-1980.

DR370.D62
Doder, Dusko.
The Yugoslavs/ Dusko Doder. New York: Random House, c1978. xiv, 256 p.
77-090287   309/.1/49702   0394425383
Yugoslavia -- Politics and government -- 1945- Yugoslavia -- Social conditions.

DR370.N4
Neal, Fred Warner.
Titoism in action; the reforms in Yugoslavia after 1948. Berkeley, University of California Press, 1958. 331 p.
58-010291   949.7
Yugoslavia -- Politics and government -- 1945-1980.

DR370.U4 1971
Ulam, Adam Bruno, 1922-
Titoism and the Cominform [by] Adam B. Ulam. Westport, Conn., Greenwood Press [1971, c1952] viii, 243 p.
70-100246   321.9/2   0837134048
Communism -- Yugoslavia. Communism -- History.

DR417 Turkey — General works

DR417.D48 1971
Dewdney, John C.
Turkey: an introductory geography [by] J. C. Dewdney. New York, Praeger [1971] x, 214 p.
79-101658   915.61
Turkey.

DR417.R54 1980
Nyrop, Richard F.
Turkey, a country study/ Richard F. Nyrop. Washington, D.C.: Foreign Area Studies, American University: for 1980. xxvii, 370 p.
80-607042   956.1
Turkey.

DR417.T874 1996
Turkey, a country study/ Federal Research Division, Library of Congress; edited by Helen Chapin Metz. 5th ed. Washington, D.C.: Federal Research Division, Library of Congress: xxxix, 458 p.
95-049612   956.1 20   0844408646
Turkey.

DR432 Turkey — Social life and customs. Civilization

DR432.F2313 2000
Faroqhi, Suraiya, 1941-
Subjects of the Sultan: culture and daily life in the Ottoman Empire/ Suraiya Faroqhi. London; I.B. Tauris, 2000. x, 358 p.
1860642896
Architecture -- Turkey. Turkey -- Intellectual life. Turkey -- History -- Ottoman Empire, 1288-1918. Turkey -- Social life and customs.

DR435 Turkey — Ethnography — Individual elements in the population, A-Z

DR435.B74.G64 1998
Goffman, Daniel, 1954-
Britons in the Ottoman Empire, 1642-1660/ Daniel Goffman. Seattle: University of Washington Press, c1998. xv, 310 p.
97-025422 956.1/00421 0295976683
British -- Turkey -- History -- 17th century. Turkey -- Relations -- Great Britain. Great Britain -- Relations -- Turkey.

DR435.G8.A94 1992
Augustinos, Gerasimos,
The Greeks of Asia Minor: confession, community, and ethnicity in the nineteenth century/ Gerasimos Augustinos. Kent, Ohio: Kent State University Press, c1992. x, 270 p.
92-001308 956.1/004893 0873384598
Greeks -- Turkey -- Ethnic identity. Greeks -- Turkey -- Economic conditions. Greeks -- Turkey -- Politics and government -- History -- 19th century. Turkey -- Ethnic relations.

DR435.K87.B37 1998
Barkey, Henri J.
Turkey's Kurdish question/ Henri J. Barkey and Graham E. Fuller. Lanham, Md.: Rowman & Littlefield Publishers, c1998. xix, 239 p.
97-030696 956.1/00491597 0847685527
Kurds -- Turkey. Kurds -- Turkey -- Ethnic identity. Turkey -- Politics and government -- 1980- Turkey -- Ethnic relations.

DR435.K87.K57 1997
Kirisci, Kemal, 1954-
The Kurdish question and Turkey: an example of a trans-state ethnic conflict/ Kemal Kirisci and Gareth M. Winrow. London; Frank Cass, 1997. xvi, 237 p.
97-008572 956.1/00491597 0714647462
Kurds -- Turkey. Nationalism -- Turkey. Turkey -- Politics and government -- 1909- Turkey -- Ethnic relations.

DR435.K87.O45 1998
Olson, Robert W.
The Kurdish question and Turkish-Iranian relations: from World War I to 1998/ Robert Olson. Costa Mesa, Calif.: Mazda Publishers, 1998. xx, 105 p.
98-009898 327.561055 1568590679
Kurds -- Turkey -- Politics and government. Kurds -- Iran -- Politics and government. Turkey -- Foreign relations -- Iran. Iran -- Foreign relations -- Turkey. Turkey -- Ethnic relations.

DR436 Turkey — History — Dictionaries. Chronological tables, outlines, etc.

DR436.H47 1994
Heper, Metin.
Historical dictionary of Turkey/ by Metin Heper. Metuchen, N.J.: Scarecrow Press, 1994. xv, 593 p.
93-043208 949.61/003 0810828170
Turkey -- History -- Dictionaries.

DR440 Turkey — History — General works

DR440 .L8 1955
Luke, Harry,
The old Turkey and the new: from Byzantium to Ankara. [2d ed.] London, Bles [1955] 243 p.
55-036624 949.6
Turkey -- History.

DR440.S5
Shaw, Stanford J. 1930-
History of the Ottoman Empire and modern Turkey/ Stanford Shaw. Cambridge; Cambridge University Press, 1976-1977. 2 v.
76-009179 956.1 0521212804
Turkey -- History -- Ottoman Empire, 1288-1918. Turkey -- History -- 1918-1960. Turkey -- History -- 1960-

DR441 Turkey — History — Compends

DR441.D2
Davis, William Stearns, 1877-1930.
A short history of the near East from the founding of Constantinople (330 A.D. to 1922) New York, The Macmillan company, 1922. 408 p.
22-023804
Islam. Turkey -- History.

DR441.H69 2001
Howard, Douglas A. 1958-
The history of Turkey/ Douglas A. Howard. Westport, Conn.: Greenwood Press, 2001. xxii, 241 p.
00-061720 956.1 0313307083
Turkey -- History.

DR471-477 Turkey — History — Political and diplomatic history

DR471.V38 1976
Vaughan, Dorothy Margaret.
Europe and the Turk: a pattern of alliances, 1350-1700/ Dorothy M. Vaughan. New York: AMS Press, 1976. viii, 305 p.
78-180382 327.561/04 0404563325
Turkey -- Foreign relations. Europe -- Politics and government.

DR473.S53 2001
Sicker, Martin.
The Islamic world in decline: from the Treaty of Karlowitz to the disintegration of the Ottoman Empire/ Martin Sicker. Westport, Conn.: Praeger, 2001. x, 249 p.
00-032386 956.1/015 027596891X
Turkey -- History -- 1683-1829. Turkey -- History -- 1829-1878. Turkey -- History -- 1878-1909.

DR474.H35 2000
Hale, William M.
Turkish foreign policy, 1774-2000/ William Hale. London; Frank Cass, 2000. ix, 375 p.
00-031605 327.561/009/04 0714650714
Turkey -- Foreign relations. Turkey -- Politics and government -- 19th century. Turkey -- Politics and government -- 20th century.

DR476.T7
Toynbee, Arnold Joseph, 1889-1975.
Turkey, by Arnold J. Toynbee and Kenneth P. Kirkwood. New York, Scribner, 1927. xviii, 329 p.
27-000422
Turkey. Turkey -- Politics and government -- 1918-1960.

DR477.D44 1989
Deringil, Selim, 1951-
Turkish foreign policy during the Second World War: an "active" neutrality/ Selim Deringil. Cambridge; Cambridge University Press, 1989. 238 p.
88-011989 327.561 0521344662
Nonalignment -- Turkey. World War, 1939-1945 -- Turkey. Turkey -- Foreign relations -- 1918-1960.

DR477.T79 1996
Turkey between East and West: new challenges for a rising regional power/ edited by Vojtech Mastny and R. Craig Nation. Boulder, Colo.: Westview Press, 1996. xiii, 279 p.
95-039563 327.561 0813324203
Turkey -- Foreign relations. Turkey -- Foreign economic relations. Turkey -- Politics and government -- 1980-

DR477.T795 2001
Turkey in world politics: an emerging multiregional power/ edited by Barry Rubin, Kemal Kirisci. Boulder, Co.: Lynne Rienner Publishers, 2001. ix, 270 p.
00-045983 327.561 1555879543
Turkey -- Foreign relations. Turkey -- Politics and government -- 20th century.

DR481-603 Turkey — History — By period

DR481.C3313 2001
Cahen, Claude.
The formation of Turkey: the Seljukid Sultanate of Rum: eleventh to fourteenth century/ Claude Cahen; translated and edited by P. M. Holt. New York: Longman, 2001. p. cm.
00-069015 956.1/015 0582414911
Turkey -- History -- To 1453.

DR485 .Q37 2000
Quataert, Donald,
The Ottoman Empire, 1700-1922/ Donald Quataert. New York: Cambridge University Press, 2000. xxii, 205 p.
99-053406 956.1/015 21 0521633605
Turkey -- History -- Ottoman Empire, 1288-1918.

DR486.I5 1973b
Inalcik, Halil, 1916-
The Ottoman Empire; the classical age, 1300-1600. Translated by Norman Itzkowitz and Colin Imber. New York, Praeger Publishers [1973] xii, 257 p.
76-187274 914.96/1/031
Turkey -- History -- 1288-1453. Turkey -- History -- 1453-1683.

DR486.K34 1995
Kafadar, Cemal, 1954-
Between two worlds: the construction of the Ottoman state/ Cemal Kafadar. Berkeley: University of California Press, c1995. xx, 221 p.
94-021024 956.1/0072 0520088077
Turkey -- History -- Ottoman Empire, 1288-1918. Turkey -- History -- Ottoman Empire, 1288-1918 -- Historiography.

DR486.P35 1993
Palmer, Alan Warwick.
The decline and fall of the Ottoman Empire/ Alan Palmer. London: J. Murray, 1993. ix, 306 p.
93-147378 956.1/015 0719552818
Turkey -- History -- Ottoman Empire, 1288-1918.

DR501.B313
Babinger, Franz, 1891-1967.
Mehmed the Conqueror and his time/ Franz Babinger; translated from the German by Ralph Manheim; edited, with a pref., by William C. Hickman. Princeton, N.J.: Princeton University Press, c1978. xx, 549 p.
77-071972 956.1/01/0924 0691099006
Mehmed -- II, -- Sultan of the Turks, -- 1432-1481. Turkey -- History -- Mehmed II, 1451-1481.

DR506.M4
Merriman, Roger Bigelow, 1876-
Suleiman the Magnificent, 1520-1566, by Roger Bigelow Merriman. Cambridge, Mass., Harvard University Press, 1944. viii p.
44-005977
Sulaiman I, -- the Magnificent, sultan of the Turks, -- 1494-1566. Turkey -- History -- 1453-1683.

DR557.B4
Berkes, Niyazi.
The development of secularism in Turkey. Montreal, McGill University Press, 1964. xiii, 537 p.
64-008158 320.9561
Islam and state -- Turkey. Turkey -- History.

DR569.D3
Davison, Roderic H.
Reform in the Ottoman Empire, 1856-1876/ by Roderic H. Davison. Princeton, N.J.: Princeton University Press, 1963. xiii, 479 p.
63-012669 956.101 0877521352
Turkey -- Politics and government -- 1829-1878.

DR572 .K28 2001
Karpat, Kemal H.
The politicization of Islam: reconstructing identity, state, faith, and community in the late Ottoman state/ Kemal H. Karpat. New York: Oxford University Press, 2001. viii, 533 p.
99-053429   320.54/09561/09034   21
0195136187
Turkey -- History -- 1878-1909. Turkey -- History -- Mehmed V, 1909-1918. Islam and state--Turkey. Panislamism.

DR572.R3 1970
Ramsaur, Ernest Edmondson.
The Young Turks; prelude to the revolution of 1908. New York, Russell & Russell [1970, c1957] xii, 180 p.
79-081465 956.1/01
Turkey -- Politics and government -- 1878-1909.

DR572.5.A73 1991
Arai, Masami.
Turkish nationalism in the Young Turk era/ by Masami Arai. Leiden; E.J. Brill, 1992. x, 168 p.
90-021862 320.94961 9004093532
Nationalism -- Turkey -- History -- 19th century. Press and politics -- Turkey. Turkey -- Politics and government -- 1878-1909.

DR572.5.H37 1995
Hanioglu, M. Sukru.
The Young Turks in opposition/ M. Sukru Hanioglu. New York: Oxford University Press, 1995. ix, 390 p.
94-018606 320.9561 0195091159
Turkey -- Politics and government -- 1878-1909. Turkey -- Politics and government -- 1909-1918.

DR576.K73 2000
Kramer, Heinz.
A changing Turkey: the challenge to Europe and the United States/ Heinz Kramer. Washington, D.C.: Brookings Institution Press, c2000. xv, 304 p.
99-050446 956.103/9 0815750234
Turkey -- Politics and government -- 20th century. Turkey -- Foreign relations -- Europe. Turkey -- Foreign relations -- United States.

DR583.L48 2002
Lewis, Bernard.
The emergence of modern Turkey/ Bernard Lewis. 3rd ed. New York: Oxford University Press, 2002. xx, 524 p.
2001-031411 956.1.221 0195134605
Turkey -- History -- 20th century.

DR590.B5
Bisbee, Eleanor.
The new Turks; pioneers of the Republic, 1920-1950. Philadelphia, University of Pennsylvania Press, 1951. xiv, 298 p.
51-010780 956
Turks. Turkey -- History -- 1918-1960.

DR590.M35
Mango, Andrew.
Turkey.   London, Thames and Hudson, 1968. 192 p.
68-092250 956.1/02
Turkey -- History -- 1918-1960. Turkey -- History -- 1960- Turkey -- Politics and government -- 1918-1960.

DR592.K4.A855 1981
Ataturk, founder of a modern state/ Ali Kazancigil and Ergun Ozbudun, editors. Hamden, Conn.: Archon Books, 1981. vi, 243 p.
81-019094 956.1/024/0924 0208019685
Ataturk, Kemal, -- 1881-1938. Turkey -- Politics and government -- 1918-1960.

DR592.K4 M36 2000
Mango, Andrew.
Atatürk/ Andrew Mango. Woodstock, N.Y.: Overlook Press, 2000. xiii, 666 p.
99-086845 956.1/024/092. 221 1585670111
Atatürk, Kemal, 1881-1938. Presidents--Turkey--Biography.

DR593.T86 2001
Turkey since 1970: politics, economics and society/ edited by Debbie Lovatt. New York: Palgrave, 2001 xxiv, 224 p.
00-052455 956.103 033375378X
Turkey -- Politics and government -- 1960-1980. Turkey -- Politics and government -- 1980- Turkey -- Economic conditions -- 1960-

DR603.M36 1994
Mango, Andrew.
Turkey: the challenge of a new role/ Andrew Mango; foreword by Heath W. Lowry. Westport, Conn.: Praeger, 1994. xvi, 144 p.
94-010581 327.561 0275949850
Turkey -- Politics and government -- 1980- Turkey -- Foreign relations -- 1980- Turkey -- Social conditions -- 1960-

DR701 Turkey — Local history and description (European Turkey) — Provinces, regions, etc., A-Z

DR701.S5.M3213 1975
Marmullaku, Ramadan, 1939-
Albania and the Albanians/ by Ramadan Marmullaku; translated from the Serbo-Croatian by Margot and Bosko Milosavljevic. Hamden, Conn.: Archon Books, 1975. x, 178 p.
76-350538 949.65 0208015582
Albania.

DR701.S5.S83 1971
Swire, Joseph, 1903-
Albania; the rise of a kingdom [by] J. Swire. New York, Arno Press, 1971. xxiv, 560 p.
79-135835 949.6/501 040502777X
Albania -- History.

DR701.S86.P3
Pano, Nicholas C.
The People's Republic of Albania [by] Nicholas C. Pano. Baltimore, Johns Hopkins Press [1968] xvi, 185 p.
68-027736 949.6/5/03
Albania -- Politics and government -- 1944-1990.

DR701.S86.T3
Tang, Peter S. H., 1919-
The twenty-second Congress of the Communist Party of the Soviet Union and Moscow-Tirana-Peking relations. Washington, Research Institute on the Sino-Soviet Bloc [1962] vii, 141 p.
62-017213
Albania -- Foreign relations -- Soviet Union. Soviet Union -- Foreign relations -- Albania. Communist countries.

DR722-729 Turkey — Local history and description — Istanbul (Constantinople)

DR722.L5
Liddell, Robert, 1908-
Byzantium and Istanbul. New York, Macmillan, 1956. 256 p.
56-058952 915.61
Istanbul (Turkey) -- Description. Istanbul (Turkey) -- History. Istanbul -- Description and travel.

DR726.L4
Lewis, Bernard.
Istanbul and the civilization of the Ottoman Empire. Norman, University of Oklahoma Press [1963] xiii, 189 p.
63-017161 914.961 0806105674
Istanbul -- Civilization. Constantinople -- Civilization.

DR729.D6
Downey, Glanville.
Constantinople in the age of Justinian.   Univ. of Oklahoma Pr., 1960. 181 p.
60-013473   949.501
Justinian -- I, -- Emperor of the East, -- 483?-565. Istanbul

DR927 Albania — History — Dictionaries. Chronological tables, outlines, etc

DR927.H88 1996
Hutchings, Raymond.
Historical dictionary of Albania/ Raymond Hutchings. Lanham, Md.: Scarecrow Press, 1996. xvi, 277 p.
95-026304   949.65/003 20   0810831074
Albania -- History -- Dictionaries.

DR941 Albania — History — General works

DR941.J33 1995
Jacques, Edwin E., 1908-
The Albanians: an ethnic history from prehistoric times to the present/ by Edwin E. Jacques. Jefferson, N.C.: McFarland & Co., c1995. xvii, 730 p.
93-042598   949.65   0899509320
Albania -- History.

DR941.V53 1995
Vickers, Miranda.
The Albanians: a modern history/ Miranda Vickers. London; I.B. Tauris, c1995. 262 p.
93-060688   949.65/02
Albania -- History.

DR978.3 Albania — History — By period

DR978.3.V53 2000
Vickers, Miranda.
Albania: from anarchy to a Balkan identity/ Miranda Vickers, James Pettifer. New York: New York University Press, 2000. p. cm.
99-054483   949.65.221   081478805X
Albania -- Politics and government -- 1990-

DR1230 Yugoslavia — Ethnography — Individual elements in the population, A-Z

DR1230.S45.J83 1997
Judah, Tim, 1962-
The Serbs: history, myth, and the destruction of Yugoslavia/ Tim Judah. New Haven: Yale University Press, c1997. xvii, 350 p.
96-052212   949.6/00491822   0300071132
Serbs -- Yugoslavia -- History. Yugoslav War, 1991-1995 -- Causes. Yugoslavia -- History.

DR1232 Yugoslavia — History — Dictionaries. Chronological tables, outlines, etc.

DR1232.C66 1998
Conflict in the former Yugoslavia: an encyclopedia/ edited by John B. Allcock, Marko Milivojevic, and John J. Horton; foreword by Martin Bell. Denver, Colo.: ABC-CLIO, c1998. xxxiv, 410 p.
98-041772   949.703   0874369355
Yugoslav War, 1991-1995 -- Dictionaries. Yugoslavia -- History -- Dictionaries. Former Yugoslav republics -- History -- Dictionaries.

DR1232.S87 1998
Suster, Zeljan E., 1958-
Historical dictionary of the Federal Republic of Yugoslavia/ Zeljan E. Suster. Lanham, Md.: Scarecrow Press, 1999. c, 421 p.
98-014337   949.7   0810834669
Yugoslavia -- History -- Dictionaries.

DR1246 Yugoslavia — History — General works

DR1246.B46 1995
Bennett, Christopher.
Yugoslavia's bloody collapse: causes, course and consequences/ Christopher Bennett. New York: New York University Press, 1995. xv, 272 p.
94-030170   949.7   0814712347
Yugoslav War, 1991-1995.   Yugoslavia -- History.

DR1246.B87 1997
Burn this house: the making and unmaking of Yugoslavia/ Jasminka Udovicki & James Ridgeway, editors. Durham, N.C.: Duke University Press, 1997. x, 337 p.
97-021606   949.703   0822320010
Yugoslav War, 1991-1995 -- Causes. Yugoslav War, 1991-1995 -- Protest movements. Yugoslavia -- History.

DR1246.L36 1996
Lampe, John R.
Yugoslavia as history: twice there was a country/ John R. Lampe. Cambridge; Cambridge University Press, 1996. xx, 421 p.
96-010390   949.7   0521461227
Yugoslavia -- History.

DR1246 .S56 1985
Singleton, Frederick Bernard.
A short history of the Yugoslav peoples/ Fred Singleton.   Cambridge   [Cambridgeshire]; Cambridge University Press, xiii, 309 p.
84-017625   949.7 19   0521274850
Yugoslavia -- History.

DR1282-1313.8 Yugoslavia — History — By period

DR1282.P37 1997
Pavkovic, Aleksandar.
The fragmentation of Yugoslavia: nationalism in a multinational state/ Aleksandar Pavkovic. New York: St. Martin's Press, 1997. xii, 222 p.
96-025631   949.702   0312163428
Yugoslav War, 1991-1995 -- Diplomatic history. Nationalism -- Yugoslavia. Yugoslavia -- History -- 1980-1992. Yugoslavia -- History -- 1918-1945. Yugoslavia -- History -- 1945-1980.

DR1282.R49 1995
Rezun, Miron.
Europe and war in the Balkans: toward a new Yugoslav identity/ Miron Rezun. Westport, Conn.: Praeger, 1995. xi, 241 p.
95-004289   949.7   027595238X
Yugoslavia -- History. Yugoslavia -- Ethnic relations.

DR1282.Y84 1995
Yugoslavia, the former and future: reflections by scholars from the region/ Payam Akhavan, general editor; Robert Howse, contributing editor. Washington: Brookings Institution; c1995. xxvi, 188 p.
95-007556   949.7   081570254X
Nationalism -- Yugoslavia. Yugoslav War, 1991-1995 -- Causes. Yugoslavia -- History. Yugoslavia -- Ethnic relations.

DR1300.W47 1995
West, Richard,
Tito: and the rise and fall of Yugoslavia/ Richard West. 1st Carroll & Graf ed. New York: Carroll & Graf, 1995. xii, 436 p.
95-010404   949.702/3/092. 220   0786702028
Tito, Josip Broz, 1892-1980.   Presidents-- Yugoslavia--Biography.

DR1302.I78 1993
Irvine, Jill A.
The Croat question: partisan politics in the formation of the Yugoslav socialist state/ Jill A. Irvine; with a foreword by Ivo Banac. Boulder: Westview Press, c1993. xviii, 318 p.
92-027252   949.702   0813385423
Nationalism -- Yugoslavia. Yugoslavia -- Politics and government -- 1918-1945. Yugoslavia -- Ethnic relations. Yugoslavia -- Politics and government -- 1945-1992.

DR1302.R36 1992
Ramet, Sabrina P., 1949-
Nationalism and federalism in Yugoslavia, 1962-1991/ Sabrina P. Ramet. Bloomington: Indiana University Press, c1992. 346 p.
91-023623   320.5/09497   0253347947
Nationalism -- Yugoslavia. Yugoslavia -- Politics and government -- 1945-1980. Yugoslavia -- Politics and government -- 1980-1992.

DR1302.S7713 1997
Stojanovic, Svetozar.
The fall of Yugoslavia: why communism failed/ Svetozar Stojanovic. Amherst, N.Y.: Prometheus Books, 1997. p. cm.
97-007426   949.702/3   1573921467
Communism -- Yugoslavia.   Yugoslavia -- Politics and government -- 1945-1980. Yugoslavia -- Politics and government -- 1980-1992.

DR1308.R36 1992
Ramet, Sabrina P., 1949-
Balkan babel: politics, culture, and religion in Yugoslavia/ Sabrina Petra Ramet. Boulder: Westview Press, 1992. xvi, 230 p.
91-033354   949.702   0813381843
Yugoslavia -- Civilization -- 20th century.

DR1309.C644 2001
Cohen, Lenard J.
Serpent in the bosom: the rise and fall of Slobodan Milosevic/ Lenard J. Cohen. Boulder, Colo.: Westview Press, c2001. xviii, 438 p.
00-049965   949.71/02   0813329027
Milosevic, Slobodan, -- 1941- Authoritarianism -- Yugoslavia.   Yugoslavia -- Politics and government -- 1980-1992. Yugoslavia -- Politics and government -- 1992-

DR1313 .S55 1997
Silber, Laura.
Yugoslavia: death of a nation/ Laura Silber and
Allan Little. Rev. and updated ed. New York:
Penguin Books, 1997. 403 p.
96-036086 949.702/4 20 0140262636
Yugoslav War, 1991-1995.

DR1313.3.C64 1998
Cohen, Roger.
Hearts grown brutal: sagas of Sarajevo/ Roger
Cohen. New York: Random House, c1998. xlix,
523 p.
99-204500 949.703 0679452435
*Yugoslav War, 1991-1995 -- Bosnia and
Hercegovina. Yugoslav War, 1991-1995 --
Atrocities. Bosnia and Hercegovina -- History --
1992- Bosnia and Hercegovina -- Biography.
Yugoslavia -- History.*

DR1313.3.C67 1999
Corwin, Phillip.
Dubious Mandate: a memoir of the UN in Bosnia,
summer 1995/ Phillip Corwin. Durham, NC: Duke
University Press, 1999. p. cm.
98-039289 949.703 0822321262
*Yugoslav War, 1991-1995 -- Bosnia and
Hercegovina. Bosnia and Hercegovina -- History
-- 1992-*

DR1313.7.A85.S83 1998
Sudetic, Chuck.
Blood and vengeance: one family's story of the war
in Bosnia/ Chuck Sudetic. New York: W.W.
Norton, c1998. xxxvii, 393 p.
97-046476 949.703 0393046516
*Sudetic, Chuck. Yugoslav War, 1991-1995 --
Bosnia and Hercegovina -- Srebrenica. Yugoslav
War, 1991-1995 -- Personal narratives, American.
Genocide -- Bosnia and Hercegovina. Srebrenica
(Bosnia and Hercegovina) -- History.*

DR1313.7.D58.G69 1997
Gow, James.
Triumph of the lack of will: international
diplomacy and the Yugoslav War/ James Gow.
New York: Columbia University Press, c1997. xii,
343 p.
96-048545 949.703 0231109164
*Yugoslav War, 1991-1995 -- Diplomatic history.
Yugoslavia -- Foreign relations.*

DR1313.7.D58.H65 1998
Holbrooke, Richard C.
To end a war/ Richard Holbrooke. New York:
Random House, c1998. xx, 408 p.
97-045741 949.703 037550057X
*Holbrooke, Richard C. Yugoslav War, 1991-1995
-- Bosnia and Hercegovina. Yugoslav War, 1991-
1995 -- Personal narratives, American. Yugoslav
War, 1991-1995 -- Diplomatic history. Bosnia and
Hercegovina -- History -- 1992-*

DR1313.7.P43.B87 1999
Burg, Steven L., 1950-
The war in Bosnia-Herzegovina: ethnic conflict
and international intervention/ Steven L. Burg &
Paul S. Shoup. Armonk, N.Y.: M.E. Sharpe, c1999.
xviii, 499 p.
98-028005 949.703 1563243083
*Yugoslav War, 1991-1995 -- Peace. Yugoslav
War, 1991-1995 -- Bosnia and Hercegovina.
Yugoslav War, 1991-1995 -- Diplomatic history.
Bosnia and Hercegovina -- History -- 1992- Bosnia
and Hercegovina -- Ethnic relations.*

DR1313.7.P73.S23 1998
Sadkovich, James J., 1945-
The U.S. media and Yugoslavia, 1991-1995/ James
J. Sadkovich. Westport, Conn.: Praeger, 1998. xx,
272 p.
97-019233 949.703 0275950468
*Yugoslav War, 1991- -- Press coverage -- United
States. Yugoslav War, 1991- -- Mass media and
the war. Yugoslav War, 1991- -- Foreign public
opinion, American.*

DR1313.7.W65
Women, violence, and war: wartime victimization
of refugees in the Balkans/ edited by Vesna
Nikolic-Ristanovic; [English translation by
Borislav Radovic]. Budapest, Hungary: Central
European University Press, 2000. xiv, 245 p.
00-060345 949.703 9639116599
*Yugoslav War, 1991-1995 -- Women. Yugoslav
War, 1991-1995 -- Personal narratives. Women
refugees -- Yugoslavia -- Serbia -- Biography.*

DR1313.8.C58 2001
Clark, Wesley K.
Waging modern war: Bosnia, Kosovo, and the
future of combat/ by General Wesley K. Clark.
New York: Public Affairs, 2001. p. cm.
01-019717 949.703 158648043X
*Clark, Wesley K. Yugoslav War, 1991-1995 --
Bosnia and Hercegovina. Yugoslav War, 1991-
1995 -- Personal narratives, American. Kosovo
(Serbia) -- History -- Civil War, 1998- -- Personal
narratives, American.*

DR1360 Yugoslavia — Local history and description — Slovenia

DR1360.G68 2000
Gow, James.
Slovenia and the Slovenes: a small state and the
new Europe/ James Gow, Cathie Carmichael.
Bloomington, Ind.: Indiana University Press, 2000.
xi, 234 p
99-038472 949.73 0253336635
Slovenes. Slovenia.

DR1507.5-1628 Yugoslavia — Local history and description — Croatia

DR1507.5 .S74 1995
Stallaerts, Robert.
Historical dictionary of the Republic of Croatia/ by
Robert Stallaerts and Jeannine Laurens. Metuchen,
N.J.: Scarecrow Press, 1995. xlii, 341 p.
95-003787 949.72 20 0810829991
Historical dictionary of the Republic of Croatia

DR1510.C37 1999
Carmichael, Cathie.
Croatia/ Cathie Carmichael, compiler. Oxford,
England; Clio Press, c1999. xxv, 194 p.
　　1851092854
　　Croatia -- Bibliography.

DR1524.S47.M55 1997
Miller, Nicholas John, 1963-
Between nation and state: Serbian politics in
Croatia before the First World War/ Nicholas J.
Miller. Pittsburgh, Pa.: University of Pittsburgh
Press, c1997. xiv, 223 p.
97-004821 320.94972/009/041 0822939894
*Serbs -- Croatia -- Politics and government.
Croatia -- Politics and government -- 1800-1918.*

DR1535.T36 1997
Tanner, Marcus.
Croatia: a nation forged in war/ Marcus Tanner.
New Haven, CT: Yale University Press, c1997.
xiii, 338 p.
96-044513 949.72 0300069332
Croatia -- History.

DR1589.R33
Biondich, Mark.
Stjepan Radic, the Croat Peasant Party, and the
politics of mass mobilization, 1904-1928/ Mark
Biondich. Toronto; University of Toronto Press,
c2000. xi, 344 p.
00-702960 949.72/01/092 0802047270
*Radic, Stjepan, -- 1871-1928. Croatia --
Politics and government -- 1800-1918. Croatia --
Politics and government -- 1918-1945.*

DR1628.W65 2001
Wolff, Larry.
Venice and the Slavs: the discovery of Dalmatia in
the Age of Enlightenment/ Larry Wolff. Stanford,
Calif.: Stanford University Press, 2001. x, 408 p.
00-067121 949.72 0804739455
*Dalmatia (Croatia) -- History -- 18th century.
Venice (Italy) -- Relations -- Croatia -- Dalmatia.
Dalmatia (Croatia) -- Relations -- Italy -- Venice.*

DR1673-1752 Yugoslavia — Local history and description — Bosnia and Hercegovina

DR1673.M3413 2000
Mahmutcehajic, Rusmir, 1948-
Bosnia the good: tolerance and tradition/ Rusmir
Mahmutcehajic. Budapest; Central European
University Press, 2000. 233 p.
00-055593 305.8/00949742 9639116866
*Pluralism (Social sciences) -- Bosnia and
Hercegovina. Bosnia and Hercegovina --
Religion. Bosnia and Hercegovina -- Ethnic
relations.*

DR1675.5.C88 1997
Cuvalo, Ante.
Historical dictionary of Bosnia and Herzegovina/
by Ante Cuvalo. Lanham, Md.: Scarecrow Press,
1997. lvi, 355 p.
97-014417 949.742 0810833441
*Bosnia and Hercegovina -- History --
Dictionaries.*

DR1685 .M35 1994
Malcolm, Noel.
Bosnia: a short history/ Noel Malcolm. New York:
New York University Press, 1994. xxiv, 340 p.
94-011560 949.7/42 20 0814755208
*Bosnia and Hercegovina -- History. Bosnia and
Hercegovina -- Ethnic relations.*

DR1752.C49 1999
Chandler, David, 1962-
Bosnia: faking democracy after Dayton/ David
Chandler. London; Pluto Press, 1999. x, 239 p.
98-042752 949.74203 0745314082
*Yugoslav War, 1991-1995 -- Peace. Bosnia and
Hercegovina -- Politics and government -- 1992-*

DR1752.M3313 2000
Mahmutcehajic, Rusmir, 1948-
The denial of Bosnia/ Rusmir Mahmutcejavic; translated by Francis R. Jones and Marina Bowder; foreword by Ivo Banac. University Park, PA: Pennsylvania University Press, c2000. xv, 156 p.
99-056307 949.74203 027102030X
Bosnia and Hercegovina -- Politics and government -- 1992- Bosnia and Hercegovina -- Historiography. Yugoslav War, 1991-1995 -- Bosnia and Hercegovina -- Causes.

DR1846 Yugoslavia — Local history and description — Montenegro

DR1846.A9 T73 1983
Treadway, John D.
The falcon & the eagle: Montenegro and Austria-Hungary, 1908-1914/ John D. Treadway. West Lafayette, Ind.: Purdue University Press, c1983. xix, 349 p.
81-082728 327.497/45/0436.219 0911198652
Montenegro -- Foreign relations -- Austria. Austria -- Foreign relations -- Montenegro. Montenegro -- Foreign relations. Europe -- Politics and government -- 1871-1918. Balkan Peninsula -- History -- 20th century.

DR1965-2087 Yugoslavia — Local history and description — Serbia

DR1965.C69 2002
Cox, John K.,
The history of Serbia/ John K. Cox. Westport, CT: Greenwood Press, 2002. xix, 225 p.
2001-040599 949.71 21 0313312907
Serbia -- History.

DR2053.M55 S45 2002
Sell, Louis,
Slobodan Milosevic and the destruction of Yugoslavia/ Louis Sell. Durham, NC: Duke University Press, 2002. xviii, 412 p.
2001-055581 949.7103/092. 221 0822328550
Miloˇseviâc, Slobodan, 1941- Politicians--Yugoslavia--Biography.

DR2082 .M35 1998
Malcolm, Noel.
Kosovo: a short history/ Noel Malcolm. New York: New York University Press, 1998. xxxvi, 492 p.
97-027456 949.71 21 0814755984
Kosovo (Serbia) -- History. Kosovo (Serbia) -- Ethnic relations.

DR2082.V53 1998
Vickers, Miranda.
Between Serb and Albanian: a history of Kosovo/ Miranda Vickers. New York: Columbia University Press, c1998. xix, 328 p.
98-016581 949.71 023111382X
Albanians -- Yugoslavia -- Kosovo (Serbia) Kosovo (Serbia) -- Ethnic relations. Kosovo (Serbia) -- History.

DR2087.C75 2000
Kosovo: contending voices on Balkan interventions / edited by William Joseph Buckley. Grand Rapids, MI: William B. Eerdmans Pub., c2000. xix, 528 p.
99-059275 949.71 0802838898
Kosovo (Serbia) -- History -- Civil War, 1998- Kosovo (Serbia) -- Politics and government.

DR2087.D33 2000
Daalder, Ivo H.
Winning ugly: NATO's war to save Kosovo/ Ivo H. Daalder, Michael E. O'Hanlon. Washington, D.C.: Brookings Institution Press, c2000. xi, 343 p.
00-009198 949.71 0815716966
Kosovo (Serbia) -- History -- Civil War, 1998-

DR2087.J83 2000
Judah, Tim,
Kosovo: war and revenge/ Tim Judah. New Haven: Yale University Press, 2000. xx, 348 p.
99-089404 949.703 21 0300083130
Kosovo (Serbia) -- History -- Civil War, 1998-

DR2087.R49 2001
Rezun, Miron.
Europe's nightmare: the struggle for Kosovo/ Miron Rezun. Westport, Conn.: Praeger, 2001. xviii, 202 p.
00-032378 949.71 0275970728
Kosovo (Serbia) -- History -- Civil War, 1998- Europe -- Politics and government -- 1989-

DR2173-2185 Yugoslavia — Local history and description — Macedonia

DR2173.D36 1995
Danforth, Loring M., 1949-
The Macedonian conflict: ethnic nationalism in a transnational world/ Loring M. Danforth. Princeton, N.J.: Princeton University Press, c1995. xvi, 273 p.
95-013319 949.5/6 0691043574
Nationalism -- Macedonia. Nationalism -- Greece. Macedonians -- Australia. Macedonia -- Name. Australia -- Ethnic relations. Macedonia -- Ethnic relations.

DR2175.5.G46 1998
Georgieva, Valentina, 1964-
Historical dictionary of the Republic of Macedonia/ Valentina Georgieva and Sasha Konechni. Lanham, Md.: Scarecrow Press, 1998. xxvii, 359 p.
97-020589 949.76/003 0810833360
Macedonia (Republic) -- History -- Dictionaries.

DR2185.P68 1995
Poulton, Hugh.
Who are the Macedonians?/ Hugh Poulton. Bloomington: Indiana University Press, c1995. xvii, 218 p.
94-010136 949.5/6 20 0253345987
Macedonia -- History. Macedonia -- Ethnic relations.

DS History of Asia

DS1 Societies. Serials

DS1.F3
The Far East and Australasia. London: Europa Publications, c1969- v.
74-417170 950/.05
Encyclopedias -- periodicals. Oceania -- Periodicals. Asia -- Periodicals.

DS2 Sources and documents

DS2.S8
Studies on Asia. Lincoln, Neb.: University of Nebraska Press, 1960-1974. v.
60-015432 950.04
Asia -- Study and teaching -- Periodicals.

DS3 Collected works (nonserial)

DS3.A2.P76 1
Berger, Morroe.
Bureaucracy and society in modern Egypt; a study of the higher civil service. Princeton, Princeton University Press, 1957. xiii, 231 p.
57-005445 351.1
Civil service -- Egypt.

DS4 Gazetteers. Dictionaries, etc.

DS4.A8
Asian annual: the "Eastern World" handbook. London: Foreign Correspondents Ltd., v.
55-018104 950
Asia -- Periodicals.

DS5 General works

DS5.A79 1991
Asia and the Pacific/ edited by Robert H. Taylor. New York: Facts on File, c1991. 2 v.
89-023376 950 081601826X
Asia. Australasia. Islands of the Pacific.

DS5.W5
Wint, Guy, 1910-1969.
Asia; a handbook. New York, Praeger [1966] xiii, 856 p.
65-013263 915
Asia.

DS6 Description and travel — Through 1491

DS6.D3
Dawson, Christopher, 1889-1970.
The Mongol mission: narratives and letters of the Franciscan missionaries in Mongolia and China in the thirteenth and fourteenth centuries/ translated by a nun of Stanbrook Abbey; edited and with an introduction by Christopher Dawson. New York: Sheed and Ward, 1955. xxxix, 246 p.
55-010925   951.7
Mongols -- History.   Asia -- Description and travel.

DS6.O373
Olschki, Leonardo, 1885-
Marco Polo's Asia: an introduction to his "Description of the world: called 'Il milione'"/ translated from the Italian by John A. Scott, and revised by the author.   University of California Press, 1960. 459 p.
60-008315   950.1
Polo, Marco, -- 1254-1323?   Travelers -- Italy -- Biography. Travelers -- Asia -- Biography. Asia -- Description and travel.

DS7 Description and travel — 1492-1800

DS7.P5513 1989
Pinto, Fernao Mendes, d. 1583.
The travels of Mendes Pinto/ Fernao Mendes Pinto; edited and translated by Rebecca D. Catz. Chicago: University of Chicago Press, 1989. xlvi, 663 p.
88-039778   910.4   0226669513
Pinto, Fernao Mendes, -- d. 1583 -- Journeys -- Asia.   Asia -- Description and travel -- Early works to 1800.

DS8 Description and travel — 1801-1900

DS8.H43 1935
Hedin, Sven Anders, 1865-1952.
My life as an explorer [by] Sven Hedin; illustrated by the author; translated by Alfhild Huebsch. Garden City, N.Y., Garden City publishing co., inc. [1935] xi p.
35-002572   915
Asia -- Description and travel.

DS9 Description and travel — 1901-1950

DS9.M443
Michaux, Henry, 1899-
A barbarian in Asia; English translation by Sylvia Beach. [New York] New Directions [1949] vi, 185 p.
49-008940   915
National characteristics.   East Asia -- Description and travel. Asia -- Description and travel.

DS10 Description and travel — 1951-

DS10.D59 1967
Dobby, Ernest Henry George.
Monsoon Asia [by] E. H. G. Dobby. London, University of London P., [1967]. 381 p.
67-111124   915
Asia -- Description and travel.

DS11 Antiquities

DS11.C52 1953
Childe, V. Gordon 1892-1957.
New light on the most ancient East. New York, F. A. Praeger [1953] xiii, 255 p.
52-013107   913.3
Oriental antiquities.   Man, Prehistoric. Civilization, Ancient.

DS12 Social life and customs. Civilization. Intellectual life

DS12.K74 1990
Krejci, Jaroslav, 1916-
Before the European challenge: the great civilizations of Asia and the Middle East/ Jaroslav Krejci; assisted by Anna Krejcova. Albany: State University of New York Press, c1990. xvi, 348 p.
89-011594   950   0791401685
Civilization, Oriental.   Asia -- Civilization. Middle East -- Civilization.

DS12.N35 1964
Nakamura, Hajime, 1912-
Ways of thinking of Eastern peoples: India, China, Tibet, Japan. Rev. English translation, edited by Philip P. Wiener. Honolulu, East-West Center Press [c1964] xx, 712 p.
64-063438   915
Philosophy, Asian.   Asia -- Intellectual life. Asia -- Civilization.

DS13 Ethnography — General works

DS13.G68 1997
Government policies and ethnic relations in Asia and the Pacific/ editors, Michael E. Brown, Sumit Ganguly. Cambridge, Mass.: MIT Press, c1997. xiv, 607 p.
97-025825   305.8/0095   0262522454
Multiculturalism -- Asia. Multiculturalism -- Pacific Area.   Asia -- Ethnic relations -- Government policy. Pacific Area -- Ethnic relations -- Government policy. Asia -- Politics and government -- 1945-

DS19 Ethnography — Mongols — General works

DS19.A62 1998
Amitai-Preiss, Reuven, 1955-
The Mongol empire and its legacy/ by Reuven Amitai-Preiss. Leiden; Brill, 1998. p. cm.
98-004197   950/.2   9004110488
Mongols -- History.

DS19.B85 1998
Bulag, Uradyn Erden.
Nationalism and hybridity in Mongolia/ Uradyn E. Bulag. Oxford: Clarendon Press; 1998. xv, 302 p.
97-039268   306/.09517/3   0198233574
Mongols. Ethnology -- China -- Inner Mongolia. Inner Mongolia (China) -- Social life and customs.

DS19.H3613 1972
Haydar Mirza, 1499 or 1500-
A history of the Moghuls of Central Asia; being the Tarikh-i-Rashidi of Mirza Muhammad Haidar, Dughlat. An English version edited, with commentary, notes and map by N. Elias. The translation by E. Denison Ross. London, Curzon Press; [1972] xxv, 535 p.
73-158183   958   0389016647
Mongols -- History.   Asia, Central -- History.

DS19.H862
Howorth, Henry H. 1842-1923.
History of the Mongols, from the 9th to the 19th century. New York, B. Franklin [1965] 4 v. in 5
70-006598   909/.09/74942
Mongols -- History.   Asia -- History.

DS19.S5613 1972
Spuler, Bertold, 1911-
History of the Mongols, based on Eastern and Western accounts of the thirteenth and fourteenth centuries. Translated from the German by Helga and Stuart Drummond. Berkeley, University of California Press, 1972. x, 221 p.
68-008720   950/.2   0520019601
Mongols -- History.

DS22 Ethnography — Mongols — Jenghis Khan, 1162-1227

DS22.H3413 1989
Hartog, Leo de.
Genghis Khan, conqueror of the world/ Leo de Hartog. New York: St. Martin's Press, 1989. vii, 230 p.
89-024064   950/.2   0312037279
Genghis Khan, -- 1162-1227.   Mongols -- History.

DS22.R3713 1992
Ratchnevsky, Paul.
Genghis Khan: his life and legacy/ Paul Ratchnevsky; translated and edited by Thomas Nivison Haining. Oxford, UK; Blackwell, 1992. xvii, 313 p.
91-002295   950/.2/092   0631167854
Genghis Khan, -- 1162-1227.   Mongols -- Kings and rulers -- Biography.

DS22.3 Ethnography — Mongols — Ogotai dynasty (China, etc.)

DS22.3.A45 1987
Allsen, Thomas T.
Mongol imperialism: the policies of the Grand Qan Mongke in China, Russia, and the Islamic lands, 1251-1259/ Thomas T. Allsen. Berkeley: University of California Press, c1987. xvii, 278 p.
86-000010   950/.2   0520055276
Mongke, -- Grand Khan, -- 1208-1259.   Mongols -- History. Imperialism.

DS23 Ethnography — Mongols — Timur, 1336-1405

DS23.M28 1989
Manz, Beatrice Forbes.
The rise and rule of Tamerlane/ Beatrice Forbes Manz. Cambridge; Cambridge University Press, 1989. xi, 227 p.
88-025679   950/.2/0924   0521345952
Timur, -- 1336-1405.   Conquerors -- Asia -- Biography. Civilization, Islamic. Asia -- History.

DS26 Ethnography — Turkic people — General works

DS26.H6 1993
Hostler, Charles Warren.
The Turks of Central Asia/ Charles Warren Hostler. Westport, Conn.: Praeger, 1993. xi, 233 p.
92-037525   958/.0049435   0275939316
Turkic peoples. Turks. Pan-Turanianism.

DS27 Ethnography — Turkic people — Seljuks

DS27.K28 1988
Kafesoglu, Ibrahim.
A history of the Seljuks: Ibrahim Kafesoglu's interpretation and the resulting controversy/ translated, edited, and with an introduction by Gary Leiser. Carbondale: Southern Illinois University Press, c1988. x, 208 p.
87-026377   956.1/01   0809314142
Kafesoglu, Ibrahim. Turan, Osman. Ates, Ahmed, -- 1917-1966. Seljuks.   Islamic Empire -- History -- 750-1258.

DS27.R5
Rice, Tamara Talbot.
The Seljuks in Asia Minor. New York, Praeger [1961] 280 p.
61-013433   956.1
Seljuks.

DS31 History — Dictionaries. Chronological tables, outlines, etc.

DS31.E53 1988
Encyclopedia of Asian history/ prepared under the auspices of the Asia Society; Ainslie T. Embree, editor in chief. New York: Scribner; c1988. 4 v.
87-009891   950   0684186195
Asia -- History -- Dictionaries.

DS32 History — Biography (Collective)

DS32.A8
The Asia who's who.   Hong Kong, Pan-Asia Newspaper Alliance. v.
57-035338   920.05
Biography -- Dictionaries.   Asia -- Biography. Asia -- Biography.

DS33 History — General works

DS33.C63 2000
Columbia chronologies of Asian history and culture/ edited by John S. Bowman. New York: Columbia University Press, c2000. xvi, 751 p.
99-047017   950   0231110057
Asia -- History -- Chronology.

DS33.1 History — General special

DS33.1.L6
University of London.
Handbook of oriental history, by members of the Dept. of Oriental History, School of Oriental and African Studies, University of London. Edited by C.H. Philips. London, Offices of the Royal Historical Society, 1951. viii, 265 p.
51-004902   950.02
Asia -- History -- Outlines, syllabi, etc.

DS33.3 History — Political and diplomatic history — General works

DS33.3.L44 1995
Lee, Steven Hugh, 1962-
Outposts of empire: Korea, Vietnam and the origins of the Cold War in Asia, 1949-1954/ Steven Hugh Lee. Montreal: McGill-Queen's University Press, 1995. xiv, 295 p.
97-135057   327.7305/09645   0773513264
World politics -- 1945-1955.   Asia -- Foreign relations.

DS33.4 History — Political and diplomatic history — Asian relations of individual countries, A-Z

DS33.4.G7.P53 1998
Pickering, Jeffrey, 1967-
Britain's withdrawal from east of Suez: the politics of retrenchment/ Jeffrey Pickering. New York: St. Martin's Press in association with Institute 1998. xi, 231 p.
98-004957   327.4105   0312214367
Decolonization.   Great Britain -- Foreign relations -- Asia. Great Britain -- Foreign relations -- 1945- Great Britain -- Colonies -- History.

DS33.4.R8
Russia and Asia: the emerging security agenda / edited by Gennady Chufrin. Oxford, UK; Oxford University Press, 1999. xvi, 534 p.
99-057197   327.4705   0198296541
National security -- Asia. National security -- Russia (Federation) Asia -- Foreign relations -- Russia (Federation) Russia (Federation) -- Foreign relations -- Asia.

DS33.4.R8.R86 1998
Russia, China and Eurasia: a bibliographic profile of selected international literature/ Aleksei D. Voskressenski (editor and compiler). New York: Nova Science, 1998. 209 p.
98-020042   016.3274705   1560725702
China -- Foreign relations -- Asia -- Bibliography.   Russia -- Foreign relations -- Asia -- Bibliography. Asia -- Foreign relations -- Soviet Union -- Bibliography. Soviet Union -- Foreign relations -- Asia -- Bibliography.

DS33.4.S65.S686 1989
The Soviet Union and the Asia-Pacific Region: view from the region/ edited by Pushpa Thambipillai and Daniel C. Matuszewski. New York: Praeger, 1989. p. cm.
88-027506   327.47095   0275932125
Asia -- Foreign relations -- Soviet Union. Soviet Union -- Foreign relations -- Asia. Pacific Ocean Region -- Foreign relations -- Soviet Union.

DS33.4.U6.H35
Harrison, Selig S.
The widening gulf: Asian nationalism and American policy/ Selig S. Harrison. New York: Free Press, c1978. xi, 468 p.
76-057881   327.73/05   0029140803
Nationalism -- Asia.   Asia -- Foreign relations -- United States. United States -- Foreign relations -- Asia.

DS33.4.U6.S46 1990
Shavit, David.
The United States in Asia: a historical dictionary/ David Shavit. New York: Greenwood Press, 1990. xxvi, 620 p.
90-036740   303.48/27305   031326788X
Asia -- Relations -- United States -- Dictionaries. United States -- Relations -- Asia -- Dictionaries.

DS33.7 History — By period — Early modern

DS33.7.A4313 1982
Albertini, Rudolf von.
European colonial rule, 1880-1940: the impact of the West on India, Southeast Asia, and Africa/ Rudolf von Albertini with Albert Wirz; translated by John G. Williamson. Westport, Conn.: Greenwood Press, c1982. xxix, 581 p.
81-004264   909/.09719   0313212759
Colonies.   Asia -- History. Africa -- History -- 1884-1960.

DS35-35.2 History — By period — 20th century

DS35.A87
Asia's nuclear future/ William H. Overholt, editor; contributors, Lewis A. Dunn ... [et al.]. Boulder, Colo.: Westview Press, c1977. xvi, 285 p.
77-000778   327/.174/095   0891582177
Nuclear weapons.   Asia -- Politics and government -- 1945- Asia -- Defenses.

DS35.J38 1996
The Japanese wartime empire, 1931-1945/ edited by Peter Duus, Ramon H. Myers, and Mark R. Peattie; contributors Wan-yao Chou ... [et al.]. Princeton, N.J.: Princeton University Press, c1996. xlvii, 375 p.
95-037203 950.4/1 0691043825
World War, 1939-1945 -- Asia -- Congresses. World War, 1939-1945 -- Occupied territories -- Congresses. Sino-Japanese Conflict, 1937-1945 -- Occupied territories -- Congresses. Asia -- History -- 20th century -- Congresses. Asia -- Military relations -- Japan -- Congresses. Japan -- Military relations -- Asia -- Congresses.

DS35.S347
Scalapino, Robert A.
Asia and the road ahead: issues for the major powers/ by Robert A. Scalapino. Berkeley: University of California Press, c1975. x, 337 p.
75-015219 320.9/5/042 0520030664
Asia -- Politics and government -- 1945- Asia -- Foreign relations. United States -- Foreign relations -- Asia.

DS35.2.L37 1996
Lasater, Martin L.
The new Pacific community: U.S. strategic options in Asia/ Martin L. Lasater. Boulder, Colo.: Westview Press, 1996. xi, 177 p.
96-019487 303.48/27305 0813388694
Asia -- Politics and government -- 1945- Asia -- Relations -- United States. United States -- Relations -- Asia.

DS35.32 The Islamic world — Congresses

DS35.32.I57 1962
New nations in a divided world; the international relations of the Afro-Asian states. New York, Published for the Institute for Sino-Soviet Stud [1964, c1963] xv, 336 p.
64-013364 327
Newly independent states -- Politics and government -- Congresses.

DS35.53 The Islamic world — Gazetteers. Guidebooks. Dictionaries. Directories, etc.

DS35.53.E53 1987
E.J. Brill's first encyclopaedia of Islam, 1913-1936/ edited by M.Th. Houtsma ... [et al.]. Leiden; E.J. Brill, 1987. 9 v.
87-010319 909/.097671 9004082654
Civilization, Islamic -- Encyclopedias. Islam -- Encyclopedias. Islamic countries -- Encyclopedias.

DS35.6 The Islamic world — General works

DS35.6.R6 1982
Robinson, Francis.
Atlas of the Islamic World since 1500/ by Francis Robinson. New York, N.Y.: Facts On File, [c1982] 238 p.
82-675002 911/.17671 0871966298
Islamic countries. Islamic countries -- Historical geography -- Maps.

DS35.625 The Islamic world — Ethnography

DS35.625.A1.M87 1984
Muslim peoples: a world ethnographic survey/ edited by Richard V. Weekes; maps by John E. Coffman; Paul Ramier Stewart, consultant. Westport, Conn.: Greenwood Press, 1984. 2 v.
83-018494 305.6/971 0313233926
Muslims. Ethnology -- Islamic countries. Islamic countries -- Social life and customs.

DS35.63 The Islamic world — History — General works

DS35.63.I64 1988
Islam, politics, and social movements/ edited by Edmund Burke, III, and Ira M. Lapidus; contributors, Ervand Abrahamian ... et al. Berkeley: University of California Press, c1988. xvii, 332 p.
87-017352 909/.097671 0520057589
Islam and politics. Islamic countries -- History.

DS35.65 The Islamic world — History — Historiography

DS35.65.L37 2000
Lassner, Jacob.
The Middle East remembered: forged identities, competing narratives, contested spaces/ Jacob Lassner. Ann Arbor: University of Michigan Press, 2000. xvii, 428 p.
00-020212 909/.097671 0472110837
Jews -- Islamic Empire -- Historiography. Jewish-Arab relations -- Historiography. Islamic Empire -- History -- Study and teaching. Islamic Empire -- Historiography.

DS35.69 The Islamic world — Political history

DS35.69.E37 1996
Eickelman, Dale F., 1942-
Muslim politics/ Dale F. Eickelman and James Piscatori. Princeton, N.J.: Princeton University Press, c1996. xi, 235 p.
95-041203 320.956 0691031843
Islamic countries -- Politics and government.

DS35.7 The Islamic world — Political history — Panislamism

DS35.7.L36 1989
Landau, Jacob M.
The politics of Pan-Islam: ideology and organization/ Jacob M. Landau. Oxford, England: Clarendon Press; 1989. p. cm.
89-023007 320.5/49/0917671 0198277091
Panislamism -- History. Islamic countries -- Politics and government.

DS35.74 The Islamic world — Foreign and general relations — By region or country, A-Z

DS35.74.H53 1997
Hibbard, Scott W., 1962-
Islamic activism and U.S. foreign policy/ Scott W. Hibbard and David Little. Washington, D.C.: United States Institute of Peace Press, 1997. p. cm.
97-021908 327.73017/671 1878379712
Islam and politics. Islam -- 20th century. Islamic countries -- Foreign relations -- United States. United States -- Foreign relations -- Islamic countries.

DS35.74.I7.I73 1990
The Iranian revolution: its global impact/ edited by John L. Esposito. Miami: Florida International University Press; c1990. viii, 346 p.
90-003083 327.55017671 0813009987
Islam -- 20th century. Islamic countries -- Relations -- Iran. Iran -- Relations -- Islamic countries. Islamic countries -- Politics and government.

DS36.2 Arab countries — Societies. Serials — League of Arab States

DS36.2.P64 1987
Pogany, Istvan S.
The Arab League and peacekeeping in the Lebanon/ Istvan Pogany. New York: St. Martin's Press, 1987. xxi, 214 p.
87-012873 341.5/8 0312007825
Lebanon -- History -- Civil War, 1975-1990.

DS36.55 Arab countries — Gazetteers. Guidebooks. Itineraries. Directories, etc.

DS36.55.C57 2001
Clements, Frank, 1942-
Historical dictionary of Arab and Islamic organizations/ Frank A. Clements. Lanham, Md.: Scarecrow Press, 2001. xx, 346 p.
00-052644 909/.0974927 0810839776
Arab countries -- Dictionaries. Islamic countries -- Dictionaries.

DS36.7 Arab countries — General works

DS36.7.D45 1983
Dempsey, Michael W.
Atlas of the Arab world: a concise introduction to the economic, social, political, and military status of the Arab World/ by Michael Dempsey and Norman Barrett. New York, NY: Facts on File, 1983. p. cm.
83-001725 909/.0974927 0871961385
Arab countries.

DS36.77 Arab countries — Social life and customs. Civilization. Intellectual life — General works

DS36.77.P79 1989
Pryce-Jones, David, 1936-
The closed circle: an interpretation of the Arabs/ David Pryce-Jones. New York: Harper & Row, c1989. xii, 464 p.
88-045546   909/.0974927   0060160470
National characteristics, Arab. Civilization, Arab. Arab countries -- Politics and government. Arab countries -- Social life and customs.

DS36.85-36.88 Arab countries — Social life and customs. Civilization. Intellectual life — Civilization and culture. Intellectual life

DS36.85.I8 no. 5
Bosworth, Clifford Edmund.
The Islamic dynasties; a chronological and genealogical handbook. Edinburgh, University P., 1967. xviii, 245 p.
67-017613   909/.09/176/7
Islamic countries -- Kings and rulers. Islamic countries -- History -- Outlines, syllabi, etc.

DS36.85.I8 no. 6
Watt, W. Montgomery
Islamic political thought: the basic concepts [by] W. Montgomery Watt. Edinburgh, Edinburgh U.P., 1968. xi, 186 p.
68-022846   320/.09176/7   0852240325
Political science -- Islamic Empire -- History. Islamic Empire -- Politics and government.

DS36.85.I8 no. 8
Bell, Richard, b. 1876.
Bell's introduction to the Quran.   Edinburgh, Edinburgh U.P., 1970. xi, 258 p.
77-106474   297/.122
Koran -- Introductions.

DS36.85.I8 no. 9
Watt, W. Montgomery
The influence of Islam on Medieval Europe [by] W. Montgomery Watt. Edinburgh, University Press [1972] viii, 125 p.
70-182902   910/.031/17671 s   0852242182
Civilization, Western -- Islamic influences. Islamic Empire -- Relations -- Europe. Europe -- Relations -- Islamic Empire.

DS36.85.I8 no. 11
Ullmann, Manfred.
Islamic medicine/ Manfred Ullmann; [translated by Jean Watt]. Edinburgh: Edinburgh University Press, c1978. xiv, 138 p.
78-310925   909/.09/7671 s   0852243251
Medicine, Arab.

DS36.85.K4 1985
Khalidi, Tarif, 1938-
Classical Arab Islam: the culture and heritage of the Golden Age/ Tarif Khalidi. Princeton, NJ, USA: Darwin Press, c1985. 158 p.
84-070416   909/.097671   0878500472
Civilization, Islamic.

DS36.855.I47 1999
Insoll, Timothy.
The archaelogy of Islam/ Timothy Insoll. Malden, Mass.: Blackwell Publishers, 1999. p. cm.
98-026727   909/.097671   0631201149
Civilization, Islamic. Social archaeology -- Islamic countries. Material culture -- Islamic countries.

DS36.88.B36 1993
Barakat, Halim Isber.
The Arab world: society, culture, and state/ Halim Barakat. Berkeley: University of California Press, 1993. xiii, 348 p.
92-023342   909/.0974927   0520079078
Civilization, Arab -- 20th century.

DS36.9 Arab countries — Ethnography

DS36.9.B4.J3313 1995
Jabbur, Jibrail Sulayman.
The Bedouins and the desert: aspects of nomadic life in the Arab East/ Jibrail S. Jabbur; translated from the Arabic by Lawrence I. Conrad; edited by Suhayl J. Jabbur and Lawrence I. Conrad. Albany: State University of New York Press, c1995. xxix, 670 p.
95-031533   953/.004927   0791428516
Bedouins.   Arab countries -- Social life and customs.

DS37 Arab countries — History — Dictionaries. Chronological tables, outlines, etc.

DS37.S53 1987
Shimoni, Yaacov, 1915-
Political dictionary of the Arab world/ Yaacov Shimoni. New York: Macmillan, c1987. 520 p.
87-012392   909/.0974927   0029162300
Arab countries -- Politics and government -- Dictionaries.

DS37.4 Arab countries — History — Historiography

DS37.4.C46 1989
Choueiri, Youssef M., 1948-
Arab history and the nation-state: a study in modern Arab historiography, 1820-1980/ by Youssef M. Choueiri. London; Routledge, 1989. p. cm.
88-025852   909/.04924/0072   0415031133
Nationalism -- Arab countries. Arab countries -- Historiography.

DS37.6 Arab countries — History — Study and teaching

DS37.6.A2.T48 1990
Theory, politics, and the Arab world: critical responses/ edited by Hisham Sharabi. New York: Routledge, 1990. ix, 261 p.
90-035848   956   0415903610
Arab countries -- Study and teaching -- Philosophy.

DS37.7 Arab countries — History — General works

DS37.7.H58 1970
Hitti, Philip Khuri, 1886-
History of the Arabs from the earliest times to the present [by] Philip K. Hitti. [London] Macmillan; [1970] xxiv, 822 p.
74-102765   953
Arabs -- History. Civilization, Arab.   Islamic Empire -- History.

DS37.7.H67 1991
Hourani, Albert Habib.
A history of the Arab peoples/ Albert Hourani. Cambridge, Mass.: Belknap Press of Harvard University Press, 1991. xx, 551 p.
90-048708   909/.0974927   0674395654
Arab countries -- History.

DS37.7.M33 1976
Mansfield, Peter, 1928-
The Arab world: a comprehensive history/ Peter Mansfield. New York: Crowell, c1976. 572 p.
76-045442   909/.04/927   0690011709
Arab countries -- History.

DS37.8 Arab countries — History — Political and diplomatic history

DS37.8.J36 1997
Jandora, John Walter.
Militarism in Arab society: an historiographical and bibliographical sourcebook/ John Walter Jandora. Westport, Conn.: Greenwood Press, 1997. xxxvii, 142 p.
96-035019   355/.00917/4927   0313293708
Arab countries -- History, Military.

DS38-39 Arab countries — History — By period

DS38.B72
Brockelmann, Carl, 1868-1956.
History of the Islamic peoples/ by Carl Brockelmann; with a review of events, 1939-1947, by Moshe Perlmann; translated by Joel Carmichael and Moshe Perlmann. New York: Putnam, 1947. xx, 582 p.
47-005836
Islam -- History.   Islamic Empire -- History.

DS38.G243 1961a
Gabrieli, Francesco, 1904-
The Arab revival.   New York, Random House [1961] 178 p.
61-012141   956
Islamic countries -- History.

DS38.G485
Gibb, H. A. R. 1895-1971.
Islamic society and the west; a study of the impact of western civilization on Moslem culture in the Near East, by H. A. R. Gibb and Harold Bowen. London, Oxford University Press, 1950- v.
50-009162   949.6
Civilization, Islamic -- Western influences.

DS38.M24 1960
Mahmud, S. F.
A short history of Islam.   Karachi, Pakistan Branch, Oxford University Press, 1960. 724 p.
63-002507   956
Islamic countries -- History.

DS38.N8
Nuseibeh, Hazem Zaki.
The ideas of Arab nationalism.   Ithaca, Cornell University Press [1956] 227 p.
56-014326   956
Nationalism -- Islamic countries.   Islamic countries -- Politics and government.

DS38.O38
O'Leary, De Lacy, b. 1872.
How Greek science passed to the Arabs.   London, Routledge and K. Paul [1949] vi, 196 p.
49-006444   915
Church history -- Primitive and early church. Civilization, Arabic -- Greek influences. Hellenism.

DS38.S37
Sayegh, Fayez A. 1922-1980.
Arab unity: hope and fulfillment.   Devin, 1958. 272 p.
58-013901   953
Arabs. Nationalism -- Middle East.

DS38.S56
Smith, Wilfred Cantwell, 1916-
Islam in modern history.   Princeton, Princeton University Press, 1957. 317 p.
57-005458   297
Islam -- History. Civilization, Islamic. Islam -- 20th century.

DS38.1.D66
Donner, Fred McGraw, 1945-
The early Islamic conquests/ by Fred McGraw Donner. Princeton, N.J.: Princeton University Press, c1981. xviii, 489 p.
80-008544   909/.09767101   0691053278
Islamic Empire -- History -- 622-661.

DS38.1.M336 1997
Madelung, Wilferd.
The succession to Muhammad: a study of the early Caliphate/   Wilferd   Madelung.   Cambridge; Cambridge University Press, 1997. xviii, 413 p.
95-026105   909/.097671   0521561817
Islamic Empire -- History -- 622-661.

DS38.16.K445 1994
Khalidi, Tarif, 1938-
Arabic historical thought in the classical period/ Tarif Khalidi. Cambridge [England]; Cambridge University Press, 1994. xiii, 250 p.
93-051021   909/.097671/0072   0521465540
Historiography -- Islamic Empire.   Islamic Empire -- Historiography.

DS38.2.S53 2000
Sicker, Martin.
The Islamic world in ascendancy: from the Arab conquests to the siege of Vienna/ Martin Sicker. Westport, Conn.: Praeger, 2000. vi, 232 p.
00-037326   909/.09/7671   0275968928
Islamic Empire -- History.

DS38.3.R35 1989
Rahman, H. U. 1940-
A chronology of Islamic history, 570-1000 CE/ H.U. Rahman. Boston, Mass.: G.K. Hall, 1989. ix, 181 p.
88-012710   909/.097671   0720119820
Muhammad, -- Prophet, -- d. 632 -- Chronology. Islamic Empire -- History -- Chronology.

DS38.6.H55 2000
Hillenbrand, Carole.
The Crusades: Islamic perspectives/ Carole Hillenbrand. New York: Routledge, 2000. lvi, 648 p.
00-044642   909/.097671   0415929148
Crusades.   Islamic Empire -- History -- 750-1258.

DS39.A94 1995
Ayubi, Nazih N. M.
Over-stating the Arab state: politics and society in the Middle East/ Nazih N. Ayubi. London; I.B. Tauris, 1995. xiii, 514 p.
94-060881   320.9174927   1850438277
Arab countries -- Politics and government -- 1945-

DS39.K43 2000
Khashan, Hilal, 1951-
Arabs at the crossroads: political identity and nationalism/   Hilal   Khashan.   Gainesville: University Press of Florida, c2000. xi, 189 p.
99-047602   320.9174927   0813017378
Nationalism -- Arab countries. Islam and politics -- Arab countries.   Arab countries -- Politics and government -- 20th century.

DS39.M53 1999
Middle East dilemma: the politics and economics of Arab integration/ Michael C. Hudson, editor. New York: Columbia University Press, c1999. xii, 341 p.
98-023052   320.956/09/048   023111138X
Arab countries -- Politics and government -- 20th century.   Arab countries -- Economic integration.

DS39.N34 1987 vol. 4
The Politics of Arab integration/ edited by Giacomo Luciani and Ghassan Salame. London; Croom Helm, c1988. 334 p.
87-030368   956   070994148X
Panarabism.   Arab countries -- Politics and government -- 1945-

DS41 Middle East. Southwestern Asia. Ancient Orient. Arab East. Near East — Societies. Serials

DS41.M44
The Middle East, abstracts and index. Pittsburgh, Northumberland Press [etc.] v.
78-645468   016.956/005
Middle East -- Abstracts -- Periodicals.

DS42 Middle East. Southwestern Asia. Ancient Orient. Arab East. Near East — Sources and documents

DS42.H87 1975
Hurewitz, J. C., 1914-
The Middle East and North Africa in world politics: a   documentary   record/   compiled, translated, and edited by J. C. Hurewitz. New Haven: Yale University Press, 1975- v.
74-083525   909/.09/7671   0300012942
Middle East -- History -- 1517- -- Sources. Africa, North -- History -- 1882- -- Sources. Middle East -- Foreign relations -- Sources.

DS42.4 Middle East. Southwestern Asia. Ancient Orient. Arab East. Near East — Collected works (nonserial) — Several authors

DS42.4.M5 3
Ahmed, Jamal Mohammed, 1917-
The intellectual origins of Egyptian nationalism. London, Oxford University Press, 1960. 135 p.
60-052161   962
Muhammad Abduh, -- 1848-1905.   Nationalism -- Egypt.

DS43 Middle East. Southwestern Asia. Ancient Orient. Arab East. Near East — Gazetteers. Guidebooks. Dictionaries. Directories, etc.

DS43.E53 1996
Encyclopedia of the modern Middle East/ edited by Reeva S. Simon, Philip Mattar, Richard W. Bulliet. New York: Macmillan Reference USA, 1996. p. cm.
96-011800   956/.003   0028960114
Middle East -- Encyclopedias. Africa, North -- Encyclopedias.

DS43.H57 1996
Hiro, Dilip.
Dictionary of the Middle East/ Dilip Hiro. New York: St. Martin's Press, 1996. ix, 367 p.
96-004395   956/.003   0312125542
Middle East -- Dictionaries.

DS44 Middle East. Southwestern Asia. Ancient Orient. Arab East. Near East — General works

DS44.H418 2000
Held, Colbert C.
Middle East patterns: places, peoples, and politics/ Colbert C. Held; with the assistance of Mildred McDonald Held; cartography by John V. Cotter. Boulder, CO: Westview Press, 2000. xxi, 562 p.
00-061434   915.6   0813334888
Middle East.

DS44.M495 1987
The Middle East/ edited by Michael Adams. New York, N.Y.: Facts on File, 1987, c1988. xviii, 865 p.
86-029274   956   0816012687
Middle East.

DS44.9 Middle East. Southwestern Asia. Ancient Orient. Arab East. Near East — Historical geography

DS44.9.L6 1966
Le Strange, G. 1854-1933.
The lands of the Eastern Caliphate: Mesopotamia, Persia, and Central Asia, from the Moslem conquest to the time of Timur. New York, Barnes & Noble [1966] xvii, 536 p.
66-001733   911.56
Iraq -- Geography, Historical. Iran -- Geography, Historical. Asia, Central -- Geography, Historical.

DS44.96 Middle East. Southwestern Asia. Ancient Orient. Arab East. Near East — Geography

DS44.96.A53 2000
Anderson, Ewan W.
The Middle East: geography and geopolitics/ Ewan W. Anderson. London; Routledge, 2000. xiv, 342 p.
99-049755   956   0415076676
Geopolitics -- Middle East.   Middle East -- Geography.

DS48-48.2 Middle East. Southwestern Asia. Ancient Orient. Arab East. Near East — Description and travel — 1801-1900

DS48.C97x 1983
Curzon, Robert, 1810-1873.
Visits to monasteries in the Levant/ Robert Curzon; introduction by John Julius Norwich. London: Century Publishing: 1983. xxiv, 423 p.
84-673047   071260104X
Monasteries -- Middle East.   Middle East -- Description and travel.

DS48.2.G86 1991
Guest, John S.
The Euphrates expedition/ John S. Guest. London; K. Paul International, 1992. xiv, 182 p.
91-008581   956.7   0710304293
Steam navigation -- Euphrates River -- History -- 19th century.   Euphrates River Valley -- Discovery and exploration -- British.

DS49-49.5 Middle East. Southwestern Asia. Ancient Orient. Arab East. Near East — Description and travel — 1901-1950

DS49.R87 1958
Royal Institute of International Affairs.
The Middle East; a political and economic survey. London, Oxford University Press, 1958. xviii, 569 p.
58-003353   950
Middle East.

DS49.5.D62
Douglas, William O. 1898-
West of the Indus. Garden City, N.Y., Doubleday, 1958. 513 p.
58-013276   915.6
Middle East -- Description and travel.

DS49.7 Middle East. Southwestern Asia. Ancient Orient. Arab East. Near East — Description and travel — 1951-

DS49.7.B36
Beaumont, Peter.
The Middle East: a geographical study/ Peter Beaumont, Gerald H. Blake, J. Malcolm Wagstaff. London; Wiley, c1976. xvii, 572 p.
74-028284   330.9/56/04   0471061174.
Middle East -- Description and travel.

DS49.7.C7
Cressey, George Babcock, 1896-1963.
Crossroads; land and life in southwest Asia. Chicago, Lippincott [1960] xiv, 593 p.
60-011518   915.6
Middle East -- Description and travel. Middle East -- Geography.

DS51 Middle East. Southwestern Asia. Ancient Orient. Arab East. Near East — Local history and description — Turkish provinces, regions, cities, islands, etc., A-Z

DS51.A6
Cross, Toni M. 1945-
A brief history of Ankara/ by Toni M. Cross and Gary Leiser. Vacaville, Calif.: Indian Ford Press, 2000. 159 p.
99-095447   956.3   0965595811
Ankara (Turkey) -- History.

DS51.B3.W5
Wiet, Gaston, 1887-
Baghdad; metropolis of the Abbasid caliphate. Translated by Seymour Feiler. Norman, University of Oklahoma Press [1971] vii, 184 p.
72-123348   956.7   080610922X
Baghdad (Iraq) -- History.

DS51.K7.B613
Bois, Thomas, 1900-
The Kurds. Translated from the French by M. W. M. Welland. Beirut, Khayats, 1966. 159 p.
67-066415   915.66/7/03
Kurds.

DS51.S94.M3
Magnarella, Paul J.
Tradition and change in a Turkish town [by] Paul J. Magnarella. [Cambridge, Mass.] Schenkman Pub. Co.; [distributed by Halsted Pres 1974] xiii, 199 p.
74-014927   309.1/562   0470563389
Susurluk (Turkey)

DS54-54.95 Middle East. Southwestern Asia. Ancient Orient. Arab East. Near East — Local history and description — Cyprus

DS54.A3.K43 1980
American University (Washington, D.C.)
Cyprus, a country study/ edited by Frederica M. Bunge ... [et al.] Washington, D.C.: Foreign Area Studies, American University: for c1980. xxx, 306 p.
80-607041   956.45
Cyprus.

DS54.3.C25
Casson, Stanley, 1889-1944.
Ancient Cyprus, its art and archaeology, by Stanley Casson ... With 16 plates and a map. London, Methuen [1937] xii, 214 p.
38-014642   913.3937
Bronze age -- Cyprus. Cypriote syllabary. Cyprus -- Antiquities.

DS54.5.C97 1998
Cyprus and its people: nation, identity, and experience in an unimaginable community, 1955-1997/ edited by Vangelis Calotychos. Boulder, Colo.: Westview Press, 1998. viii, 336 p.
98-019812   956.9304   0813335159
Nationalism -- Cyprus -- Congresses. Ethnicity -- Cyprus -- Congresses. Cyprus -- Foreign relations -- Congresses. Cyprus -- History -- 20th century -- Congresses.

DS54.5.S24
Salih, Halil Ibrahim.
Cyprus, the impact of diverse nationalism on a state/ Halil Ibrahim Salih. University: University of Alabama Press, c1978. x, 203 p.
76-021743   956.4/5   0817357068
Cyprus -- History.

DS54.6.E33 1991
Edbury, P. W.
The kingdom of Cyprus and the Crusades, 1191-1374/ Peter W. Edbury. Cambridge [England]; Cambridge University Press, 1991. xiv, 241 p.
90-040488   956.45   0521268761
Crusades.   Cyprus -- History.

DS54.7.J46 1993
Jennings, Ronald C., 1941-
Christians and Muslims in Ottoman Cyprus and the Mediterranean world, 1571-1640/ Ronald C. Jennings. New York: New York University Press, c1993. xi, 428 p.
92-003108   956.45/02   0814741819
Cyprus -- History -- Turkish rule, 1571-1878.

DS54.9.J68 1997
Joseph, Joseph S., 1952-
Cyprus: ethnic conflict and international politics: from independence to the threshold of the European Union/ Joseph S. Joseph. New York: St. Martin's Press, 1997. xv, 213 p.
97-013513   956.9304   0333678362
Cyprus -- Politics and government -- 1960- Cyprus -- Ethnic relations. Cyprus -- Foreign relations -- q960-

DS54.95.K68.S67 1988
Soren, David.
Kourion: the search for a lost Roman city/ David Soren and Jamie James. New York: Anchor Press, 1988. xi, 223 p.
87-035206   939/.37   0385241410
Romans -- Cyprus -- Kourion (Extinct city) Earthquakes -- Cyprus -- Kourion (Extinct city) Excavations (Archaeology) -- Cyprus -- Kourion (Extinct city) Cyprus -- Antiquities, Roman. Kourion (Extinct city).

DS54.95.N67I55 1991
Ioannides, Christos P., 1946-
In Turkey's image: the transformation of occupied Cyprus into a Turkish province/ Christos P. Ioannides. New Rochelle, N.Y.: A.D. Caratzas, c1991. xi, 254 p.
91-004295   956.4504   0892415096
Cyprus -- History.

DS56 Middle East. Southwestern Asia. Ancient Orient. Arab East. Near East — Antiquities. Social antiquities

DS56.D4
Deuel, Leo.
The treasures of time; firsthand accounts by famous archaeologists of their work in the Near East. Cleveland, World Pub. Co. [1961] 318 p.
61-012019
Archaeology. Middle East -- Antiquities.

DS56.D5 2000
Dictionary of the ancient Near East/ edited by Piotr Bienkowski and Alan Millard. Philadelphia, PA: University of Pennsylvania Press, 2000. p. cm.
00-021715   939.4   0812235576
Middle East -- Antiquities -- Dictionaries. Middle East -- Civilization -- To 622 -- Dictionaries.

DS56.O9 1997
The Oxford encyclopedia of archaeology in the Near East/ prepared under the auspices of the American Schools of Oriental Research; Eric M. Meyers, editor in chief. New York: Oxford University Press, 1997. 5 v.
96-017152   939/.4   0195065123
Middle East -- Antiquities -- Encyclopedias. Africa, North -- Antiquities -- Encyclopedias.

DS56.P7
Pritchard, James Bennett, 1909-
The ancient Near East in pictures relating to the Old Testament.   Princeton, N. J., Princeton University Press, 1954. xvi, 351 p.
53-010151   913.3945
Oriental literature -- Translations into English. Oriental literature -- Translations into English.

DS57 Middle East. Southwestern Asia. Ancient Orient. Arab East. Near East — Social life and customs. Civilization. Intellectual life

DS57.B34 1983
Bates, Daniel G.
Peoples and cultures of the Middle East/ Daniel G. Bates, Amal Rassam. Englewood Cliffs, NJ: Prentice-Hall, c1983. xiv, 289 p.
82-021547   956   0136567932
Middle East -- Social life and customs.

DS57.D68 1988
Downey, Susan B., 1938-
Mesopotamian religious architecture: Alexander through the Parthians/ Susan B. Downey. Princeton, N.J.: Princeton University Press, c1988. xvii, 197 p.
87-003336   939/.4   069103589X
Architecture -- Middle East.   Middle East -- Civilization -- To 622. Middle East -- Religion. Middle East -- Antiquities.

DS57.G84
Gulick, John, 1924-
The Middle East: an anthropological perspective/ John Gulick. Pacific Palisades, Calif.: Goodyear Pub. Co., c1976. xvii, 244 p.
75-026052   956   0876205783.
Ethnology -- Middle East. Middle East -- Social life and customs.

DS57.M37 1990
Maisels, Charles Keith.
The emergence of civilization: from hunting and gathering to agriculture, cities, and the state in the Near East/ Charles Keith Maisels. London; Routledge, 1990. xx, 395 p.
89-006381   939/.2   0415001684
Middle East -- Civilization -- To 622.

DS57.P3 1962
Patai, Raphael, 1910-
Golden River to Golden Road; society, culture, and change in the Middle East.   Philadelphia, University of Pennsylvania Press [c1962] 422 p.
62-007199   915.6
Ethnology -- Middle East. Middle East -- Social life and customs.

DS57.P44
Peoples of Old Testament times, edited by D. J. Wiseman for the Society for Old Testament Study. Oxford, Clarendon Press, 1973. xxi, 402 p.
73-179589   221.9/1   0198263163
Middle East -- Civilization -- To 622. Middle East -- History -- To 622.

DS57.P67 1997
Potts, Daniel T.
Mesopotamian civilization: the material foundations/ D.T. Potts. Ithaca, N.Y.: Cornell Unviersity Press, 1997. xx, 366 p.
96-034832   939.4   0801433398
Ethnology -- Middle East. Physical geography -- Middle East. Middle East -- Civilization -- To 622.

DS57.R4
Redman, Charles L.
The rise of civilization: from early farmers to urban society in the ancient Near East/ Charles L. Redman. San Francisco: W. H. Freeman, c1978. viii, 367 p.
78-001493   939   0716700565.
Middle East -- Civilization.

DS57.S28 1989
Saggs, H. W. F.
Civilization before Greece and Rome/ H.W.F. Saggs. New Haven: Yale University Press, 1989. 322 p.
88-050828   939/.4   0300044402
Middle East -- Civilization -- To 622.

DS58 Middle East. Southwestern Asia. Ancient Orient. Arab East. Near East — Ethnography — General works

DS58.C48 1982
Christians and Jews in the Ottoman empire: the functioning of a plural society/ edited by Benjamin Braude and Bernard Lewis. New York: Holmes & Meier Publishers, 1982. 2 v.
80-011337   956/.01   0841905193
Christians -- Middle East -- Congresses. Jews -- Middle East -- Congresses. Christians -- Turkey -- Congresses. Turkey -- History -- Ottoman Empire, 1288-1918 -- Congresses.

DS59 Middle East. Southwestern Asia. Ancient Orient. Arab East. Near East — Ethnography — Individual elements in the population, A-Z

DS59.D78.B47 1988
Betts, Robert Brenton.
The Druze/ Robert Brenton Betts. New Haven: Yale University Press, c1988. xiv, 161 p.
87-022696   305.6/97   0300041004
Druzes.

DS59.K86.H68 2001
Houston, Christopher.
Islam, Kurds and the Turkish nation state/ Christopher Houston. Oxford; Berg, 2001. ix, 215 p.
 956.103   1859734723
Islam and politics -- Turkey. Turkey -- Politics and government -- 1980- Turkey -- Ethnic relations -- Political aspects.

DS59.K86.O23 1996
O'Ballance, Edgar.
The Kurdish struggle, 1920-94/ Edgar O'Ballance. Houndmills, Basingstoke [England]: Macmillan Press; 1996. xxi, 251 p.
95-026255   305.891/59   0333644786
Kurds -- History -- 20th century. Middle East -- Ethnic relations.

DS59.K86.W34 1999
Wahlbeck, Osten, 1965-
Kurdish diasporas: a comparative study of Kurdish refugee communities/ Osten Wahlbeck. New York: St. Martin's Press in association with Centre fo 1999. p. cm.
98-044644   305.891/597041   0312220677
Kurds -- Relocation -- Great Britain. Kurds -- Relocation -- Finland. Refugees, Kurdish.

DS61 Middle East. Southwestern Asia. Ancient Orient. Arab East. Near East — History — Dictionaries. Chronological tables, outlines, etc.

DS61.Z58 1992
Ziring, Lawrence, 1928-
The Middle East: a political dictionary/ Lawrence Ziring. Santa Barbara, Calif.: ABC-CLIO, c1992. x, 401 p.
92-015379   956/.003   0874366127
Middle East -- Politics and government -- Dictionaries. Middle East -- Dictionaries.

DS61.7 Middle East. Southwestern Asia. Ancient Orient. Arab East. Near East — History — Historiography

DS61.7.A1.M45 1992
Melman, Billie.
Women's Orients--English women and the Middle East, 1718-1918: sexuality, religion, and work/ Billie Melman. Ann Arbor: University of Michigan Press, 1992. xix, 417 p.
91-032433   956/.0072   0472103326
Women Orientalists -- Great Britain -- Biography. Women -- Great Britain -- Attitudes. Ethnology -- Middle East -- History. Middle East -- Study and teaching -- History.

DS62 Middle East. Southwestern Asia. Ancient Orient. Arab East. Near East — History — General works

DS62.G64 1983
Goldschmidt, Arthur, 1938-
A concise history of the Middle East/ Arthur Goldschmidt, Jr. Boulder, Colo.: Westview Press; 1983. xvi, 416 p.
83-050061   956   0865315981
Middle East -- History.

DS62.H8233
Hottinger, Arnold.
The Arabs: their history, culture and place in the modern world. Berkeley, University of California Press, 1963. 344 p.
64-001108   953
Nationalism -- Arab countries. Arab countries.

DS62.Y3
Yale, William.
The Near East, a modern history. Ann Arbor, University of Michigan Press [1958] x, 485 p.
58-062524   956
Middle East -- History -- 1517-

DS62.2-63.1 Middle East. Southwestern Asia. Ancient Orient. Arab East. Near East — History — By period

DS62.2.L45 1999
Leick, Gwendolyn, 1951-
Who's who in the Ancient Near East/ Gwendolyn Leick. London; Routledge, 1999. xv, 229 p.
00-268297   0415132304
Middle East -- History -- To 622 -- Biography -- Dictionaries.

DS62.2.S54 2000
Sicker, Martin.
The pre-Islamic Middle East/ Martin Sicker. Westport, Conn.: Praeger, 2000. 231 p.
99-054421   939/.4   0275968901
Middle East -- History -- To 622.

DS62.2.V35 1983
Van Seters, John.
In search of history: historiography in the ancient world and the origins of Biblical history/ John Van Seters. New Haven: Yale University Press, c1983. xiii, 399 p.
82-048912   939/.4   0300028776
Jews -- History -- To 586 B.C. -- Historiography. Greece -- History -- To 146 B.C. -- Historiography. Middle East -- History -- To 622 -- Historiography.

DS62.23.S65 1997
Snell, Daniel C.
Life in the ancient Near East, 3100-332 B.C.E./ Daniel C. Snell. New Haven: Yale University Press, c1997. xvii, 270 p.
96-032549   016.956   0300066155
Middle East -- History -- To 622. Middle East -- Social conditions. Middle East -- Economic conditions.

DS62.4.B679 1996
Imperial legacy: the Ottoman imprint on the Balkans and the Middle East/ edited by L. Carl Brown. New York: Columbia University Press, c1996. xvi, 337 p.
95-015506   909/.09712561   0231103042
Middle East -- History -- 1517- Africa, North -- History -- 1517-1882.

DS62.4.C53 1994
Cleveland, William L.
A history of the modern Middle East/ William L. Cleveland. Boulder: Westview Press, 1994. xix, 503 p.
93-015020   956   0813305624
Middle East -- History -- 1517- Middle East -- History -- 20th century.

DS62.4.H82
Hudson, Michael C.
Arab politics: the search for legitimacy/ Michael C. Hudson. New Haven: Yale University Press, 1977. xi, 434 p.
77-075379   320.9/17/4927   0300020430
Arab countries -- Politics and government.

DS62.4.M36 1991
Mansfield, Peter, 1928-
A history of the Middle East/ Peter Mansfield. New York: Viking, 1991. 373 p.
90-050580   956   0670815152
Middle East -- History -- 1517- Middle East -- History -- 20th century.

DS62.4.Y35 1987
Yapp, Malcolm.
The making of the modern Near East, 1792-1923/ M.E. Yapp. London; Longman, 1987. xii, 404 p.
87-002068   956/.01   0582493803
Middle East -- History -- 1517-

DS62.7.C46 2000
Choueiri, Youssef M., 1948-
Arab nationalism-- a history: nation and state in the Arab world/ Youssef M. Choueiri. Oxford; Blackwell Pub., 2000. xiii, 267 p.
00-009406   320.54/089927   0631217282
Nationalism -- Arab countries -- History -- 19th century. Nationalism -- Arab countries -- History -- 20th century. Arab countries -- Politics and government -- 19th century. Arab countries -- Politics and government -- 20th century.

DS62.8.B76 1984
Brown, L. Carl 1928-
International politics and the Middle East: old rules, dangerous game/ L. Carl Brown. Princeton, N.J.: Princeton University Press, c1984. xii, 363 p.
83-043063   956   069105410X
Middle East -- Politics and government.

DS62.8.L46 1980
Lenczowski, George.
The Middle East in world affairs/ George Lenczowski. Ithaca: Cornell University Press, 1980. 863 p.
79-017059   956   0801412730
Middle East -- History -- 20th century. Middle East -- Politics and government.

DS62.8.M348 1973b
Mansfield, Peter, 1928-
The Ottoman Empire and its successors.   New York, St. Martin's Press [1973] 210 p.
73-086362   949.6
Middle East -- History -- 20th century.

DS62.8.S54 2001
Sicker, Martin.
The Middle East in the twentieth century/ Martin Sicker. Westport, Conn.: Praeger, 2001. vi, 293 p.
00-064943   956.04   0275968936
Middle East -- History -- 20th century.

DS62.9.S23 1969
Sachar, Howard Morley, 1928-
The emergence of the Middle East: 1914-1924 [by] Howard M. Sachar. New York, Knopf, 1969. xiii, 518 p.
76-079349   956
Middle East -- History -- 20th century. Middle East -- History -- 1914-1923.

DS63.H282 1996
Halliday, Fred.
Islam and the myth of confrontation: religion and politics in the Middle East/ Fred Halliday. London; I.B. Tauris, 1996, c1995. 255 p.
95-061524   322/.1/0956   1860640044
Islam and politics -- Middle East. Middle East -- Relations. Middle East -- Study and teaching. Middle East -- Politics and government.

DS63.H62 1966a
Holt, P. M.
Egypt and the Fertile Crescent, 1516-1922; a political history [by] P. M. Holt. Ithaca, N.Y., Cornell University Press [1966] xii, 337 p.
66-018429   956
Turkey -- History. Egypt -- Relations -- Middle East. Middle East -- Relations -- Egypt.

DS63.K86
Kuniholm, Bruce Robellet, 1942-
The origins of the cold war in the Near East: great power conflict and diplomacy in Iran, Turkey, and Greece/ Bruce Robellet Kuniholm. Princeton, N.J.: Princeton University Press, c1980. xxiii, 485 p.
79-083999   327/.09/045   0691046654
Middle East -- Politics and government -- 1945-1979. United States -- Foreign relations -- Soviet Union. Soviet Union -- Foreign relations -- United States.

DS63.M23 1993
Maddy-Weitzman, Bruce.
The crystallization of the Arab state system, 1945-1954/ Bruce Maddy-Weitzman. Syracuse: Syracuse University Press, 1993. xvi, 253 p.
92-020835   909/.09749270825   0815625758
Arab countries -- Politics and government -- 1945-

DS63.M58
Middle East record.   Tel Aviv: Israel Oriental Society, Reuven Shiloah Research 1960- v.
63-048859
Middle East -- Politics and government -- Periodicals.

DS63.P5 1990
Pipes, Daniel, 1949-
Greater Syria: the history of an ambition/ Daniel Pipes. New York: Oxford University Press, 1990. viii, 240 p.
89-034775   956   0195060210
Arab countries -- Politics and government. Syria -- Politics and government. Syria -- Foreign relations -- Arab countries.

DS63.R6413 1961
Rondot, Pierre, 1904-
The changing patterns of the Middle East. [Translated by Mary Dilke] New York, Praeger [1961] 221 p.
61-010517   956
Middle East -- History -- 20th century.

DS63.R67 1990
Roshwald, Aviel.
Estranged bedfellows: Britain and France in the Middle East during the Second World War/ Aviel Roshwald. New York: Oxford University Press, 1990. xii, 315 p.
89-026669   940.53/2241/0944   0195062663
World War, 1939-1945 -- Middle East. World War, 1939-1945 -- Diplomatic History. France -- Foreign relations -- Great Britain. Middle East -- History -- 20th century. Great Britain -- Foreign relations -- France.

DS63.1.A246 1997
Abi-Aad, Naji, 1959-
Instability and conflict in the Middle East: people, petroleum, and security threats/ Naji Abi-Aad and Michel Grenon; foreword by Robert Mabro. New York: St. Martin's Press, 1997. xvii, 224 p.
96-046169   956.05   0333689364
Middle East -- Politics and government -- 1979- Middle East -- Strategic aspects.

DS63.1.A35
Ajami, Fouad.
The Arab predicament: Arab political thought and practice since 1967/ Fouad Ajami. Cambridge; Cambridge University Press, 1981. xvi, 220 p.
80-027457   320.917/4927   0521239141
Arab countries -- Politics and government -- 1945-

DS63.1.F34 1993
Faour, Muhammad, 1952-
The Arab world after Desert Storm/ Muhammad Faour. Washington, D.C.: United States Institute of Peace, 1993. xii, 161 p.
93-029014   909/.09749270829   1878379305
Arab countries -- Politics and government -- 1945-

DS63.1.H365 2001
Hansen, Birthe.
Unipolarity and the Middle East/ Birthe Hansen. New York: St. Martin's Press, 2001. x, 245 p.
00-059178   327/.0956   0312215215
Middle East -- Politics and government -- 1979- United States -- Foreign relations -- Middle East. Middle East -- Foreign relations -- United States.

DS63.1.K44 1997
Kemp, Geoffrey.
Strategic geography and the changing Middle East/ Geoffrey Kemp and Robert E. Harkavy. Washington, D.C.: Brookings Institution Press, c1997. xv, 493 p.
97-012997   355/.033056   0870030221
Geopolitics -- Middle East. Military geography -- Middle East.

DS63.1.M4842 1990
The Middle East from the Iran-Contra affair to the Intifada/ edited by Robert O. Freedman. Syracuse, N.Y.: Syracuse University Press, 1991. x, 441 p.
90-009977   956.05   0815625022
Middle East -- Politics and government -- 1979-

DS63.1.S3 1993
Sandstorm: Middle East conflicts & America/ edited by Daniel Pipes. Lanham [Md.]: University Press of America; c1993. ix, 411 p.
92-029688   956.05   081918893X
Middle East -- Politics and government -- 1979- Middle East -- Foreign relations -- United States. United States -- Foreign relations -- Middle East.

DS63.1.W75 1985
Wright, Robin B., 1948-
Sacred rage: the crusade of modern Islam/ Robin Wright. New York: Linden Press/Simon and Schuster, 1985. 315 p.
85-018126   956.04   067160113X
Islam and politics -- Middle East. Terrorism -- Middle East. Terrorism -- Religious aspects -- Islam. Lebanon -- History -- Civil War, 1975-1990. Middle East -- Politics and government -- 1945-

DS63.2-63.6 Middle East. Southwestern Asia. Ancient Orient. Arab East. Near East — History — Political and diplomatic history. Foreign and general relations

DS63.2.A357.O34 1987
Oded, Arye.
Africa and the Middle East conflict/ Arye Oded. Boulder, Colo.: L. Rienner, 1987. xii, 244 p.
87-009536   327.5606   1555870570
Arab countries -- Relations -- Africa, Sub-Saharan. Africa, Sub-Saharan -- Relations -- Arab countries. Israel -- Relations -- Africa, Sub-Saharan.

DS63.2.C5.C35 1990
Calabrese, John.
China's changing relations with the Middle East/ John Calabrese. London; Pinter Publishers, c1991. 183 p.
90-037187   327.51056   0861871383
Middle East -- Foreign relations -- China. China -- Foreign relations -- Middle East.

DS63.2.E7.E75 1994
Erlikh, Hagai.
Ethiopia and the Middle East/ Haggai Erlich. Boulder, Colo.: L. Rienner Publishers, 1994. xi, 227 p.
94-018824   303.48/263056   1555875203
Middle East -- Relations -- Ethiopia. Ethiopia -- Relations -- Middle East.

DS63.2.E8.L48 1982
Lewis, Bernard.
The Muslim discovery of Europe/ by Bernard Lewis. New York: W.W. Norton, c1982. 350 p.
81-019009   303.4/82   0393015297
Middle East -- Relations -- Europe. Europe -- Relations -- Middle East.

DS63.2.G7.A34 1995
Adelson, Roger.
London and the invention of the Middle East: money, power, and war, 1902-1922/ Roger Adelson. New Haven: Yale University Press, 1995. xii, 244 p.
94-036262   327.41056/09/041   0300060947
Middle East -- Foreign relations -- Great Britain. Great Britain -- Foreign relations -- Middle East.

DS63.2.G7.B34 1990
Balfour-Paul, Glen.
The end of empire in the Middle East: Britain's relinquishment of power in her last three Arab dependencies/ Glen Balfour-Paul. Cambridge [England]; Cambridge University Press, 1991. xxiii, 278 p.
89-077371   327.41017/671   0521382599
Middle East -- Foreign relations -- Great Britain. Great Britain -- Foreign relations -- Middle East.

DS63.2.G7.F496 1999
Fisher, John, 1968-
Curzon and British imperialism in the Middle East, 1916-19/ John Fisher. London; Frank Cass, 1999. xvi, 342 p.
98-017117   327.56041   0714648752
Curzon, George Nathaniel Curzon, -- Marquis of, -- 1859-1925.   Great Britain -- Foreign relations -- Middle East. Middle East -- Foreign relations -- Great Britain. Great Britain -- Foreign relations -- 1901-1936.

DS63.2.G7.I56 1992
Ingram, Edward.
Britain's Persian connection, 1798-1828: prelude to the great game in Asia/ by Edward Ingram. Oxford: Clarendon Press; c1992. xv, 351 p.
92-005535   956/.015   0198202431
Middle East -- Foreign relations -- Great Britain. Great Britain -- Foreign relations -- Middle East. Great Britain -- Foreign relations -- Iran.

DS63.2.G7.K38 1978
Kedourie, Elie.
England and the Middle East: the destruction of the
Ottoman Empire, 1914-1921/ Elie Kedourie.
Hassocks [Eng.]: Harvester Press, 1978. 236 p.
78-320786   956/.02   0855278498
*Middle East -- Foreign relations -- Great
Britain. Great Britain -- Foreign relations --
Middle East. Middle East -- Politics and
government -- 1914-1945.*

DS63.2.G7.K65 1999
Kolinsky, Martin.
Britain's war in the Middle East: strategy and
diplomacy, 1936-42/ Martin Kolinsky. New York:
St. Martin's Press, 1999. xii, 308 p.
99-012410   303.48/256041   0312222572
*World War, 1939-1945 -- Middle East. World
War, 1939-1945 -- Great Britain. Middle East --
Relations -- Great Britain. Great Britain --
Relations -- Middle East.*

DS63.2.G7.M6 1981
Monroe, Elizabeth.
Britain's moment in the Middle East, 1914-1971/
Elizabeth Monroe. Baltimore, Md.: Johns Hopkins
University Press, 1981. 254 p.
80-008869   327.41056
*Middle East -- Foreign relations -- Great
Britain. Great Britain -- Foreign relations --
Middle East. Middle East -- Politics and
government -- 1914-1945.*

DS63.2.G7.O93 1996
Ovendale, Ritchie.
Britain, the United States, and the transfer of
power in the Middle East, 1945-1962/ Ritchie
Ovendale. London; New York: 1996. viii, 264 p.
96-006321   327.41056   0718514386
*Middle East -- Foreign relations -- Great
Britain. Great Britain -- Foreign relations --
Middle East. Middle East -- Foreign relations --
United States.*

DS63.2.I68.I68 1993
Iran and the Arab world/ edited by Hooshang
Amirahmadi and Nader Entessar. New York: St.
Martin's Press, 1993. ix, 264 p.
91-042170   327.550174927   0312060114
*Arab countries -- Foreign relations -- Iran.
Iran -- Foreign relations -- Arab countries.*

DS63.2.S65.F72 1991
Freedman, Robert Owen.
Moscow and the Middle East: Soviet policy since
the invasion of Afghanistan/ Robert O. Freedman.
Cambridge [England]; Cambridge University
Press, 1991. xii, 426 p.
90-031056   327.47056   0521351847
*Middle East -- Foreign relations -- Soviet
Union. Soviet Union -- Foreign relations -- Middle
East. Soviet Union -- Foreign relations -- 1975-
1985.*

DS63.2.S65.G648 1990
Golan, Galia.
Soviet policies in the Middle East: from World
War Two to Gorbachev/ Galia Golan. Cambridge
[England]; Cambridge University Press, 1990. viii,
319 p.
89-020986   327.47056/09/04   0521353327
*Middle East -- Foreign relations -- Soviet
Union. Soviet Union -- Foreign relations -- Middle
East.*

DS63.2.S65.S657 1987
The Soviet Union and the Middle East 1917-1985/
Basil Dmytryshyn and Frederick Cox. Princeton,
NJ, USA: Kingston Press, c1987-1994 v. 1-2
87-080845   327.47056   0940670240
*Middle East -- Foreign relations -- Soviet
Union -- Sources. Soviet Union -- Foreign
relations -- Middle East -- Sources.*

DS63.2.S65.S67 1982
The Soviet Union in the Middle East: policies and
perspectives/ edited by Adeed Dawisha and Karen
Dawisha. New York, N.Y.: Published by Holmes &
Meier Publishers for the R 1982. 172 p.
82-000953   327.47056   084190796X
*Middle East -- Foreign relations -- Soviet
Union. Soviet Union -- Foreign relations -- Middle
East.*

DS63.2.S95.Y67 1988
Yorke, Valerie, 1946-
Domestic politics and regional security: Jordan,
Syria, and Israel: the end of an era?/ Valerie Yorke.
Aldershot [England]; Published for the
International Institute for St c1988. xvii, 400 p.
88-010486   956/.04   0566056526
*Middle East -- Politics and government --
1945- Syria -- Politics and government. Jordan --
Politics and government.*

DS63.2.T8.K39 1997
Kayali, Hasan.
Arabs and Young Turks: Ottomanism, Arabism,
and Islamism in the Ottoman Empire, 1908-1918/
Hasan Kayali. Berkeley: University of California
Press, c1997. xv, 291 p.
96-011474   327.56017/4927   0520204441
*Arab countries -- Foreign relations -- Turkey.
Turkey -- Foreign relations -- Arab countries.
Turkey -- Politics and government -- 1909-1918.*

DS63.2.T8.O47 2001
Olson, Robert W.
Turkey's relations with Iran, Syria, Israel, and
Russia, 1991-2000: the Kurdish and Islamist
questions/ Robert Olson. Costa Mesa, Calif.:
Mazda Publishers, 2001. p. cm.
00-054895   327.561/009/049   1568591330
*Kurds. Islam and politics -- Middle East. Turkey
-- Foreign relations -- 1980- Middle East --
Foreign relations -- Turkey. Turkey -- Foreign
relations -- Middle East.*

DS63.2.U5.A824 1993
The United States and the Middle East: a search for
new perspectives/ edited by Hooshang
Amirahmadi. Albany, N.Y.: State University of
New York Press, c1993. xvii, 491 p.
91-038541   327.73056   0791412253
*Middle East -- Foreign relations -- United
States. United States -- Foreign relations -- Middle
East. United States -- Foreign relations -- 1945-*

DS63.2.U5.A865 1996
Ashton, Nigel John.
Eisenhower, Macmillan, and the problem of
Nasser: Anglo-American relations and Arab
nationalism, 1955-59/ Nigel John Ashton. New
York: St. Martin's Press, 1996. viii, 273 p.
96-010395   327.730174927   0312161085
*Arab countries -- Foreign relations -- United
States. United States -- Foreign relations -- Arab
countries. United States -- Foreign relations --
1953-1961.*

DS63.2.U5.B79
Bryson, Thomas A., 1931-
American diplomatic relations with the Middle
East, 1784-1975: a survey/ by Thomas A. Bryson.
Metuchen, N.J.: Scarecrow Press, c1977. viii,
431 p.
76-044344   327.56/073   0810809885
*Middle East -- Foreign relations -- United
States. United States -- Foreign relations -- Middle
East.*

DS63.2.U5.H34 1992
Hadar, Leon T.
Quagmire: America in the Middle East/ Leon T.
Hadar. Washington, D.C.: Cato Institute, c1992. ix,
233 p.
92-013488   327.73056   0932790941
*Israel-Arab conflicts. United States -- Foreign
relations -- Middle East. Middle East -- Foreign
relations -- United States.*

DS63.2.U5.H46 2000
Hemmer, Christopher M. 1969-
Which lessons matter?: American foreign policy
decision making in the Middle East, 1979-1987/
Christopher Hemmer. Albany: State University of
New York Press, c2000. x, 217 p.
99-087139   327.73056/09/048   0791446492
*Middle East -- Foreign relations -- United
States. United States -- Foreign relations -- Middle
East. United States -- Foreign relations -- 1977-
1981.*

DS63.2.U5.L43 1990
Lenczowski, George.
American presidents and the Middle East/ George
Lenczowski. Durham [N.C.]: Duke University
Press, 1990. vi, 321 p.
89-017056   327.73056   0822309637
*Middle East -- Foreign relations -- United
States. United States -- Foreign relations -- Middle
East. United States -- Foreign relations -- 1945-
1989.*

DS63.2.U5.M43 1996
The Middle East and the United States: a historical
and political reassessment/ edited by David W.
Lesch. Boulder, Colo.: Westview Press, 1996. xiii,
460 p.
95-052651   327.73056   0813324041
*Middle East -- Foreign relations -- United
States. United States -- Foreign relations -- Middle
East.*

DS63.2.U5.P48 2000
Petersen, Tore T., 1954-
The Middle East between the great powers: Anglo-
American conflict and cooperation, 1952-7/ Tore
T. Petersen. Houndmills, Basingstoke, Hampshire:
Macmillan Press; 2000. xiii, 170 p.
00-026980   327.56073   0312234813
*Middle East -- Foreign relations -- United
States. United States -- Foreign relations -- Middle
East. Great Britain -- Foreign relations -- Middle
East.*

DS63.2.U5.S33 1991
Shaban, Fuad, 1935-
Islam and Arabs in early American thought: roots
of orientalism in America/ Fuad Shaban. Durham,
N.C.: Acorn Press, 1991. xxi, 244 p.
89-082248   303.48/273056   0893860298
*Islam -- Public opinion. Public opinion -- United
States -- History -- 19th century. Islam -- Relations
-- Christianity. Middle East -- Foreign public
opinion, American. Middle East -- Study and
teaching -- United States -- History -- 19th century.*

DS63.2.U5.S6 1988
The Soviet-American competition in the Middle East/ edited by Steven L. Spiegel, Mark A. Heller, Jacob Goldberg; [sponsored by] Institute on Global Conflict and Cooperation ... [et al.]. Lexington, Mass.: Lexington Books, c1988. xiii, 392 p.
86-046313   956/.05   0669153575
Middle East -- Relations -- United States. United States -- Relations -- Middle East. Middle East -- Relations -- Soviet Union.

DS63.2.U5.S62 1985
Spiegel, Steven L.
The other Arab-Israeli conflict: making America's Middle East policy, from Truman to Reagan/ Steven L. Spiegel. Chicago: University of Chicago Press, c1985. xvi, 522 p.
84-016253   327.73056   0226769615
Jewish-Arab relations -- 1949- Israel-Arab conflicts. United States -- Foreign relations -- 1945-1989. Middle East -- Foreign relations -- United States. United States -- Foreign relations -- Middle East.

DS63.2.U5.T39 1991
Taylor, Alan R.
The superpowers and the Middle East/ Alan R. Taylor. Syracuse, N.Y.: Syracuse University Press, 1991. xiii, 212 p.
91-007639   327.56073   081562543X
Middle East -- Foreign relations -- United States. United States -- Foreign relations -- Middle East. Middle East -- Foreign relations -- Soviet Union.

DS63.2.U5.U18 1995
The U.S. media and the Middle East: image and perception/ edited by Yahya R. Kamalipour; foreword by George Gerbner. Westport, Conn.: Greenwood Press, c1995. xxi, 242 p.
94-033136   956   0313292795
Mass media -- United States. Public opinion -- United States. Middle East -- Foreign public opinion, American. Middle East -- In mass media.

DS63.6.A46 1981
Antonius, George.
The Arab awakening: the story of the Arab national movement/ by George Antonius. New York: Gordon Press, 1981. p. cm.
81-006586   909/.0974927   0849014441
Nationalism -- Arab countries. Arab countries -- History -- 1798-

DS63.6.D8713 1987
Duri, Abd al-Aziz.
The historical formation of the Arab nation: a study in identity and consciousness/ A.A. Duri; translated by Lawrence I. Conrad. London; Croom Helm, c1987. 371 p.
87-017116   909/.0974927   0709934718
Nationalism -- Arab countries. Arabism. Arab countries -- History -- 1798-

DS66 Middle East. Southwestern Asia. Ancient Orient. Arab East. Near East — History — Hittites

DS66.B75 1998
Bryce, Trevor, 1940-
The kingdom of the Hittites/ Trevor Bryce. Oxford: Clarendon Press; 1998. xiv, 464 p.
97-014411   939/.2   0198140959
Hittites.

DS66.M23 1975
Macqueen, J. G.
The Hittites and their contemporaries in Asia Minor/ J. G. Macqueen. Boulder, Colo.: Westview Press, 1975. 206 p.
75-026838   939.2   0891585206
Hittites. Turkey -- Civilization.

DS68 Iraq (Assyria, Babylonia, Mesopotamia) — Sources and documents

DS68.L57
Lloyd, Seton.
The archaeology of Mesopotamia: from the Old Stone Age to the Persian conquest/ Seton Lloyd. London: Thames and Hudson, c1978. 252 p.
78-052961   935   0500780072
Iraq -- Antiquities.

DS68.L8 1968
Luckenbill, Daniel David, 1881-1927.
Ancient records of Assyria and Babylonia. New York, Greenwood Press [1968, c1926] 2 v.
68-057626   935/.03/08
Assyria -- History -- Sources.

DS69 Iraq (Assyria, Babylonia, Mesopotamia) — Antiquities — Museums, exhibitions, etc.

DS69.D5
Delaporte, Louis, 1874-1944.
Mesopotamia: the Babylonian and Assyrian civilization, by L.Delaporte. London, K.Paul, Trench, Trubner & Co., Ltd.; 1925. xvi,371 p.
25-021907
Civilization, Assyro-Babylonian.

DS69.5 Iraq (Assyria, Babylonia, Mesopotamia) — Antiquities — General works

DS69.5.B6813 1992
Bottero, Jean.
Mesopotamia: writing, reasoning, and the gods/ Jean Bottero; translated by Zainab Bahrani and Marc Van De Mieroop. Chicago: University of Chicago Press, c1992. x, 311 p.
91-025917   935   0226067262
Babylonia -- Civilization.

DS69.5.O6 1977
Oppenheim, A. Leo, 1904-1974.
Ancient Mesopotamia: portrait of a dead civilization/ by A. Leo Oppenheim. Chicago: University of Chicago Press, 1977. xvi, 445 p.
76-028340   935   0226631869
Civilization, Assyro-Babylonian.   Iraq -- Civilization -- To 634.

DS69.5.P64 1992
Postgate, J. N.
Early Mesopotamia: society and economy at the dawn of history/ J.N. Postgate. London; Routledge, 1992. xxiii, 367 p.
91-033767   935   0415008433
Iraq -- Civilization -- To 634. Iraq -- Economic conditions.

DS69.5.V36 1997
Van de Mieroop, Marc.
The ancient Mesopotamian city/ Marc Van de Mieroop. Oxford: Clarendon Press; 1997. xv, 269 p.
97-008199   935/.009732   0198150628
Cities and towns, Ancient -- Iraq.   Iraq -- Civilization -- To 634.

DS70 Iraq (Assyria, Babylonia, Mesopotamia) — Antiquities — History of excavations

DS70.L48 1980b
Lloyd, Seton.
Foundations in the dust: the story of Mesopotamian exploration/ Seton Lloyd. London: Thames and Hudson, c1980. 216 p.
81-170132   935   0500050384
Excavations   (Archaeology)   --   Iraq. Assyriologists. Archaeologists -- Iraq. Iraq -- Antiquities.

DS70.5 Iraq (Assyria, Babylonia, Mesopotamia) — Antiquities — Local antiquities, A-Z

DS70.5.B3.C413
Champdor, Albert.
Babylon. Translated from the French and adapted by Elsa Coult. London, Elek Books; [c1958] 184p.
58-011668
Babylon

DS70.5.N47.R86 1998
Russell, John Malcolm.
The final sack of Nineveh: the discovery, documentation, and destruction of King Sennacherib's throne room at Nineveh, Iraq/ John Malcolm Russell. New Haven: Yale University Press, c1998. 247 p.
98-015067   935   0300074182
Sculpture, Assyro-Babylonian -- Iraq -- Nineveh (Extinct city)

DS70.6 Iraq (Assyria, Babylonia, Mesopotamia) — General works

DS70.6.H3
Harris, George Lawrence, 1910-
Iraq: its people, its society, its culture. In collaboration with Moukhtar Ani [and others] New Haven, HRAF Press [1958] 350 p.
58-014179   915.67
Iraq.

DS70.6.L6
Longrigg, Stephen Hemsley.
Iraq, by Stephen Hemsley Longrigg and Frank Stoakes. New York, Praeger [1959] 264 p.
58-013221   956.7
Iraq.

DS70.6.S6 1979
American University (Washington, D.C.)
Iraq, a country study/ Foreign Area Studies, the American University; edited by Richard F. Nyrop. Washington, D.C.: The University: for sale by the Supt. of Docs., c1979. xxi, 320 p.
79-024184   956.7
Iraq.

DS70.7 Iraq (Assyria, Babylonia, Mesopotamia) — Social life and customs. Civilization

DS70.7.C47 1993
Charvat, Petr.
Ancient Mesopotamia: humankind's long journey into civilization/ by Petr Charvat. Prague: Oriental Institute, c1993. 368 p.
94-221984   935   8085425114
Excavations (Archaeology) -- Iraq.   Iraq -- Antiquities. Iraq -- Civilization -- To 634.

DS70.8 Iraq (Assyria, Babylonia, Mesopotamia) — Ethnography

DS70.8.K8.I37 1995
Iraq's crime of genocide: the Anfal campaign against the Kurds/ Human Rights Watch/Middle East. New Haven: Yale University Press, c1995. xxx, 373 p.
94-034779   305.89159   0300064276
Kurds -- Iraq. Massacres -- Iraq. Genocide -- Iraq. Iraq -- Ethnic relations.

DS70.8.S55.N35 1994
Nakash, Yitzhak.
The Shiis of Iraq/ Yitzhak Nakash. Princeton, N.J.: Princeton University Press, c1994. xiv, 312 p.
93-031786   297/.82/09567   0691034311
Shiites -- Iraq -- History. Shiah -- Iraq. Iraq -- History -- 1534-1921. Iraq -- History -- 1921- Iraq -- Religious life and customs.

DS70.88 Iraq (Assyria, Babylonia, Mesopotamia) — History — Historiography

DS70.88.L3.W3
Waterfield, Gordon, 1903-
Layard of Nineveh/ Gordon Waterfield. London: J. Murray, c1963. x, 535 p.
64-004433
Layard, Austen Henry, -- Sir, -- 1817-1894. Middle East -- History.

DS70.96 Iraq (Assyria, Babylonia, Mesopotamia) — History — Political and diplomatic history. Foreign and general relations

DS70.96.I72.S54 1992
Shemesh, Haim.
Soviet-Iraqi relations, 1968-1988: in the shadow of the Iraq-Iran conflict/ Haim Shemesh. Boulder: Lynne Rienner Publishers, 1992. x, 285 p.
91-030996   327.567047   155587293X
Iraq -- Foreign relations -- Soviet Union. Soviet Union -- Foreign relations -- Iraq. Soviet Union -- Foreign relations -- 1945-1991.

DS71-79.755 Iraq (Assyria, Babylonia, Mesopotamia) — History — By period

DS71.K5 1969
King, L. W. 1869-1919.
A history of Babylon, from the foundation of the monarchy to the Persian conquest. New York, AMS Press [1969] xxiii, 340 p.
74-098633   935/.02
Babylonia -- History.

DS71.S75
Smith, Sidney, 1889-
Early history of Assyria, by Sidney Smith. London, Chatto & Windus, 1928- v.
28-011237
Assyria -- History.

DS72.K7 1981
Kramer, Samuel Noah, 1897-
History begins at Sumer: thirty-nine firsts in man's recorded history/ Samuel Noah Kramer. Philadelphia: University of Pennsylvania Press, 1981. xxvii, 388 p.
81-051144   935/.01   0812278127
Sumerians.

DS72.K73
Kramer, Samuel Noah, 1897-
The Sumerians: their history, culture, and character. [Chicago] University of Chicago Press [1963] xiv, 355 p.
63-011398   913.35
Sumerians.

DS73.2.L313
Laessoe, Jorgen, 1924-
People of ancient Assyria, their inscriptions and correspondence. Translated from the Danish by F. S. Leigh-Browne. New York, Barnes & Noble [1963] 169 p.
63-003294   935
Cuneiform inscriptions. Assyria -- History.

DS75.S6.C63
Contenau, G. b. 1877.
Everyday life in Babylon and Assyria/ [Authorized translation by K. R. & A. R. Maxwell-Hyslop] New York, St. Martin's Press 1954. xv. 324 p.
54-010269   913.352
Babylonia -- Social life and customs. Assyria -- Social life and customs.

DS76.M67 1984
Morony, Michael G., 1939-
Iraq after the Muslim conquest/ Michael G. Morony. Princeton, N.J.: Princeton University Press, c1984. ix, 689 p.
83-042569   955/.02   0691053952
Ethnology -- Iraq.   Iraq -- History -- 634-1534. Iraq -- Social conditions.

DS76.4.P6613 1998
Popovic, Alexandre.
The revolt of African slaves in Iraq in the IIIrd/IXth century/ by Alexandre Popovic; translated from French by Leon King; introduction to the American edition by Henry Louis Gates, Jr. Princeton, N.J.: Markus Wiener Publishers, 1998. p. cm.
98-035899   956.7/02   1558761624
Iraq -- History -- Zanj Rebellion, 868-883.

DS79.H27 1997
Haj, Samira, 1945-
The making of Iraq, 1900-1963: capital, power, and ideology/ Samira Haj. Albany, NY: State University of New York Press, c1997. viii, 215 p.
96-007618   956.704   0791432416
Iraq -- History -- Hashemite Kingdom, 1921-1958. Iraq -- History -- 1958-

DS79.K43 1960
Khadduri, Majid, 1909-
Independent Iraq, 1932-1958; a study in Iraqi politics. London, Oxford University Press, 1960. vii, 388 p.
60-050855   956.7
Iraq -- Politics and government.

DS79.L85 1995
Lukitz, Liora.
Iraq: the search for national identity/ Liora Lukitz. London; F. Cass, 1995. xi, 212 p.
94-031533   320.5/4/09567   0714645508
Nationalism -- Iraq.   Iraq -- Politics and government.

DS79.S57 1986
Simon, Reeva S.
Iraq between the two world wars: the creation and implementation of a nationalist ideology/ Reeva S. Simon. New York: Columbia University Press, 1986. xv, 233 p.
85-029893   956.7/04   0231060742
Nationalism -- Iraq -- History. Iraq -- History -- Hashemite Kingdom, 1921-1958. Iraq -- Armed Forces -- Political activity.

DS79.65.I74 1991
The Iraqi revolution of 1958: the old social classes revisited/ edited by Robert A. Fernea and Wm. Roger Louis. London; I.B. Tauris, 1991. xxiv, 232 p.
90-063392   1850433186
Social classes -- Iraq -- Congresses.   Iraq -- History -- Revolution, 1958 -- Congresses.

DS79.65.K49
Khadduri, Majid, 1908-
Socialist Iraq: a study in Iraqi politics since 1968/ Majid Khadduri. Washington: Middle East Institute, 1978. 265 p.
78-051916   320.9/567/04   0916808165
Iraq -- Politics and government.

DS79.65.M33 1985
Marr, Phebe.
The modern history of Iraq/ Phebe Marr. Boulder, Colo.: Westview; 1985. xvii, 382 p.
83-051519   956.7/04   0865311196
Iraq -- History -- 1921-

DS79.7.B4613 1998
Bengio, Ofra.
Saddam's word: political discourse in Iraq/ Ofra Bengio. New York: Oxford University Press, 1998. xiii, 266 p.
97-002308   320.9567/01/4   0195114396
Hussein, Saddam, -- 1937- Government and the press -- Iraq. Mass media policy -- Iraq. Discourse analysis -- Political aspects -- Iraq. Iraq -- Politics and government -- 1991-

DS79.7.C67 1997
Cordesman, Anthony H.
Iraq: sanctions and beyond/ Anthony H. Cordesman and Ahmed S. Hashim. Boulder, Colo.: Westview Press, 1997. xiii, 393 p.
96-046046   956.704/3   0813332354
Iraq -- Politics and government -- 1991- Iraq -- Foreign relations -- 1991-

DS79.7.I725 1994
Iraq since the Gulf war: prospects for democracy/ edited by Fran Hazelton for CARDRI. London; Zed Books, 1994. x, 260 p.
94-111832   1856492311
  Iraq -- Politics and government -- 1991-

DS79.7.R49 1992
Rezun, Miron.
Saddam Hussein's Gulf wars: ambivalent stakes in the Middle East/ Miron Rezun. Westport, Conn.: Praeger, c1992. xxi, 140 p.
92-004197   956.704/3/092   0275943240
Hussein, Saddam, -- 1937-   Iraq -- Politics and government. United States -- Foreign relations -- Iraq. Iraq -- Foreign relations -- United States.

DS79.72.B85 1991
Bulloch, John.
Saddam's war: the origins of the Kuwait conflict and the international response/ John Bulloch and Harvey Morris. London; Faber and Faber, 1991. xviii, 194 p.
91-011737   956.704/3   0571163874
Hussein, Saddam, -- 1937-   Iraq-Kuwait Crisis, 1990- . Iraq -- Foreign relations. Iraq -- Military policy.

DS79.72.G818 1991
Gulf crisis chronology/ compiled by BBC World Service. High, Harlow, Essex, United Kingdom: Longman Current Affairs; c1991. ix, 454 p.
92-125935   0582090059
  Persian Gulf War, 1991 -- Chronology. Persian Gulf War, 1991 -- Indexes.

DS79.72.H56 1992
Hilsman, Roger.
George Bush vs. Saddam Hussein: military success! political failure?/ Roger Hilsman. Novato, CA: Presidio, c1992. xiv, 273 p.
92-011929   956.704/3   0891414703
  Persian Gulf War, 1991.   Middle East -- Politics and government -- 1979- Iraq -- Politics and government. Middle East -- Foreign relations -- United States.

DS79.72.H88 1995
Hutchison, Kevin Don.
Operation Desert Shield/Desert Storm: chronology and fact book/ Kevin Don Hutchison; foreword by John H. Admire. Westport, Conn.: Greenwood Press, 1995. vxii, 269 p.
95-021530   956.7044/2   0313296065
  Persian Gulf War, 1991.

DS79.72.K397 1997
Khadduri, Majid, 1908-
War in the Gulf, 1990-91: the Iraq-Kuwait conflict and its implications/ Majid Khadduri, Edmund Ghareeb. New York: Oxford University Press, 1997. x, 299 p.
96-033658   956.7044/2   0195083849
  Persian Gulf War, 1991.

DS79.72.M384 1993
Mazarr, Michael J., 1965-
Desert Storm: the Gulf War and what we learned/ Michael J. Mazarr, Don M. Snider, and James A. Blackwell, Jr. Boulder: Westview Press, 1993. xi, 207 p.
92-029687   956.704/42   0813315980
  Persian Gulf War, 1991.

DS79.72.N48 1998
Newell, Clayton R., 1942-
Historical dictionary of the Persian Gulf War, 1990-1991/ Clayton R. Newell. Lanham, Md.: Scarecrow Press, 1998. lix, 363 p.
98-018944   956.7044/2/03   0810835118
  Persian Gulf War, 1991 -- Dictionaries.

DS79.72.P64 1993
The Political psychology of the Gulf War: leaders, publics, and the process of conflict/ Stanley A. Renshon, editor. Pittsburgh: University of Pittsburgh Press, c1993. xxiii, 376 p.
92-034182   956.704/42   0822954958
  Persian Gulf War, 1991. Persian Gulf War, 1991 -- Psychological aspects.

DS79.72.S39 1998
Schwartz, Richard Alan, 1951-
Encyclopedia of the Persian Gulf War/ Richard A. Schwartz. Jefferson, N.C.: McFarland & Co., c1998. vii, 216 p.
97-051886   956.7044/2/03   0786404515
  Persian Gulf War, 1991 -- Encyclopedias.

DS79.72.V37 1992
Vaux, Kenneth L., 1939-
Ethics and the Gulf War: religion, rhetoric, and righteousness/ Kenneth L. Vaux. Boulder: Westview Press, 1992. xiv, 187 p.
91-044903   956.704/3   0813314593
  Persian Gulf War, 1991 -- Moral and ethical aspects. Just war doctrine.

DS79.72.Y48 1997
Yetiv, Steven A.
The Persian Gulf crisis/ Steve A. Yetiv. Westport, Conn.: Greenwood Press, 1997. xxi, 197 p.
96-006554   956.7044/2   0313299439
  Persian Gulf War, 1991.

DS79.724.A8.M55 1994
Miller, Ronnie, 1956-
Following the Americans to the Persian Gulf: Canada, Australia, and the development of the new world order/ Ronnie Miller. Rutherford, [N.J.]: Fairleigh Dickinson University Press; c1994. 188 p.
92-055107   956.7044/2   0838635369
  Persian Gulf War, 1991 -- Australia. Persian Gulf War, 1991 -- Canada. Australia -- Foreign relations -- Middle East. Middle East -- Foreign relations -- Australia. Canada -- Foreign relations -- Middle East.

DS79.724.U6.A887 1993
Atkinson, Rick.
Crusade: the untold story of the Persian Gulf War/ Rick Atkinson. Boston: Houghton Mifflin, 1993. xii, 575 p.
93-014388   956.7044/2373   0395602904
  Persian Gulf War, 1991 -- United States. United States -- History, Military -- 20th century.

DS79.724.U6.M84 1994
Mueller, John E.
Policy and opinion in the Gulf War/ John Mueller. Chicago: University of Chicago Press, 1994. xviii, 379 p.
93-021226   956.704/42   0226545644
  Persian Gulf War, 1991 -- Public opinion. Persian Gulf War, 1991 -- United States. Public opinion -- United States.

DS79.739.T35 1994
Taken by storm: the media, public opinion, and U.S. foreign policy in the Gulf War/ edited by W. Lance Bennett and David L. Paletz. Chicago: University of Chicago Press, c1994. xvi, 308 p.
93-045527   956.7044/28   0226042588
  Persian Gulf War, 1991 -- Press coverage -- United States. Press -- United States -- History -- 20th century. Persian Gulf War, 1991 -- Foreign public opinion, American.

DS79.744.C46.H37 1999
Haselkorn, Avigdor.
The continuing storm: Iraq, poisonous weapons and deterrence/ Avigdor Haselkorn. New Haven: Yale University Press, c1999. xxvi, 374 p.
98-036785   956.7044/21   0300075820
  Persian Gulf War, 1991. Weapons of mass destruction -- Iraq. United States -- Military policy.

DS79.744.N38
Marolda, Edward J.
Shield and sword: the United States Navy and the Persian Gulf War/ Edward J. Marolda and Robert J. Schneller, Jr. Annapolis, Md.: Naval Institute Press; 2001. xxi, 517 p.
00-051566   956.7044/245/0973   1557504857
  Persian Gulf War, 1991 -- Naval operations, American.

DS79.744.N38.P645 1999
Pokrant, Marvin, 1943-
Desert at sea: what the Navy really did/ Marvin Pokrant; foreword by Admiral Hank Mauz and Stan Arthur. Westport, Conn.: Greenwood Press, 1999. p. cm.
98-048907   956.7044/2450973   0313310238
  Persian Gulf War, 1991 -- Naval operations, American.

DS79.75.C63 1999
Cockburn, Andrew, 1947-
Out of the ashes: the resurrection of Saddam Hussein/ Andrew Cockburn and Patrick Cockburn. New York, NY: HarperCollins, 1999. 322 p.
98-053879   956.7044/3   0060192666
Hussein, Saddam, -- 1937-   Iraq -- Politics and government -- 1991- Despotism -- Iraq.

DS79.75.G734 1999
Graham-Brown, Sarah.
Sanctioning Saddam: the politics of intervention in Iraq/ Sarah Graham-Brown. London; I.B. Tauris in association with MERIP; 1999. xvii, 380 p.
      1860644732
Hussein, Saddam, -- 1937- Economic sanctions -- Iraq.   Iraq -- Politics and government -- 1991- Iraq -- Foreign relations -- 1991- Iraq -- History -- 1958-

DS79.755.B88 2000
Butler, Richard, 1942-
The greatest threat: Iraq, weapons of mass destruction, and the crisis of global security/ Richard Butler. New York: PublicAffairs , c2000. xxiv, 262 p.
00-029098   327.1/745/09567   1891620533
  Weapons of mass destruction -- Iraq. Arms control -- Verification -- Iraq. Security, International. Iraq -- Military policy.

DS80 Lebanon (Phenicia) — General works

DS80.G67 1983
Gordon, David C.
The Republic of Lebanon: nation in jeopardy/ David C. Gordon. Boulder, Colo.: Westview Press; 1983. xiv, 171 p.
82-020108   956.92   0865314500
Lebanon.

DS80.55 Lebanon (Phoenicia) — Ethnography — Individual elements in the population, A-Z

DS80.55.P34.P47 1991
Peteet, Julie Marie.
Gender in crisis: women and the Palestinian resistance movement/ by Julie M. Peteet. New York: Columbia University Press, c1991. x, 245 p.
90-025824   305.4/095692   0231074468
Women, Palestinian Arab -- Lebanon -- Political activity. Women revolutionaries -- Palestine. National liberation movements -- Palestine.

DS80.9 Lebanon (Phoenicia) — History — General works

DS80.9.A28 1998
AbuKhalil, Asad.
Historical dictionary of Lebanon/ Asad AbuKhalil. Lanham, Md.: Scarecrow Press, 1998. xxi, 269 p.
97-026849   956.92/003   0810833956
Lebanon -- History -- Dictionaries.

DS80.9.S26 1988
Salibi, Kamal S. 1929-
A house of many mansions: the history of Lebanon reconsidered/ Kamal Salibi. Berkeley: University of California Press, c1988. v, 247 p.
88-020679   956.92   0520065174
Lebanon -- History.

DS82-87.54 Lebanon (Phoenicia) — History — By period

DS82.G73 1992
Grainger, John D., 1939-
Hellenistic Phoenicia/ John D. Grainger. Oxford [England]: Clarendon Press; 1991. ix, 228 p.
91-013961   939/.44   0198147708
Phoenicians. Hellenism.

DS84.A35 1993
Akarli, Engin Deniz.
The long peace: Ottoman Lebanon, 1861-1920/ Engin Deniz Akarli. Berkeley: University of California Press, c1993. xviii, 288 p.
92-018987   956.92/034   0520080149
Lebanon -- History -- 1516-1918.

DS84.M35 2000
Makdisi, Ussama Samir, 1968-
The culture of sectarianism: community, history, and violence in nineteenth-century Ottoman Lebanon/ Ussama Makdisi. Berkeley, Calif.: University of California Press, c2000. xv, 259 p.
99-047861   956.92/034   0520218450
Religion and politics -- Lebanon -- History -- 19th century. Elite (Social sciences) -- Lebanon -- History -- 19th century. Lebanon -- Politics and government -- 19th century. Turkey -- Politics and government -- 19th century.

DS84.P6 1963
Polk, William Roe, 1929-
The opening of south Lebanon, 1788-1840: A study of the impact of the West on the Middle East. Cambridge, Harvard University Press, 1963. xx, 299 p.
63-013815   956.92
Lebanon -- History.

DS86.Z37 1997
Zamir, Meir.
Lebanon's quest: the road to statehood, 1926-1939/ Meir Zamir. London; I.B. Tauris, 1997. xii, 313 p.
97-169698   956.9204   1860641075
Lebanon -- History -- French occupation, 1918-1946. Lebanon -- Politics and government -- 20th century.

DS87.H3723 1997
Harris, William W.
Faces of Lebanon: sects, wars, and global extensions/ William W. Harris. Princeton, NJ: Markus Wiener Publishers, c1997. viii, 354 p.
96-008855   956.9204/4   1558761152
Lebanon -- History -- Civil War, 1975-1990.

DS87.P43 1994
Peace for Lebanon?: from war to reconstruction/ edited by Deirdre Collings. Boulder: Lynne Rienner Publishers, 1994. ix, 338 p.
93-039746   956.9204/4   1555873677
Lebanon -- History -- 1975-

DS87.P5 1995
Phares, Walid, 1957-
Lebanese Christian nationalism: the rise and fall of an ethnic resistance/ Walid Phares. Boulder, Colo.: L. Rienner, 1995. xi, 251 p.
94-028297   956.92/00882   1555875351
Christians -- Lebanon -- Politics and government. Nationalism -- Lebanon. Nationalism -- Religious aspects -- Christianity. Lebanon -- Politics and government.

DS87.2.S24.A3 1995
Salem, Elie Adib.
Violence and diplomacy in Lebanon: the troubled years, 1982-1988/ Elie A. Salem. London; I.B. Tauris; 1995. vii, 296 p.
94-060697   1850438358
Salem, Elie Adib.   Statesmen -- Lebanon -- Biography. Lebanon -- Politics and government -- 1975-1990.

DS87.5.A29 1998
Abul-Husn, Latif.
The Lebanese conflict: looking inward/ Latif Abul-Husn. Boulder, Colo.: Lynne Rienner Publishers, 1998. ix, 171 p.
97-036617   956.9204/4   155587665X
Lebanon -- History -- Civil War, 1975-1990 -- Causes. Lebanon -- Social conditions. Lebanon -- Politics and government -- 1975-1990.

DS87.5.O14 1998
O'Ballance, Edgar.
Civil war in Lebanon, 1975-92/ Edgar O'Ballance. New York, N.Y.: St. Martin's Press, 1998. xxiii, 234 p.
98-017681   956.9204/4   0312215932
Lebanon -- History -- Civil War, 1975-1990.

DS87.5.R367 1997
Ranstorp, Magnus.
Hizb'allah in Lebanon: the politics of the western hostage crisis/ Magnus Ranstorp; foreword by Terry Waite. New York: St. Martin's Press, 1997. xvi, 257 p.
96-020970   956.92   031216288X
Hostages -- Lebanon.   Lebanon -- History -- Civil War, 1975-1990.

DS87.53.E87 1987
Evron, Yair.
War and intervention in Lebanon: the Israeli-Syrian deterrence dialogue/ Yair Evron. Baltimore: Johns Hopkins University Press, 1987. x, 246 p.
87-002851   956.92/044   0801835690
Deterrence (Strategy) -- Case studies. Lebanon -- History -- Israeli intervention, 1982-1984. Israel -- Foreign relations -- Syria. Syria -- Foreign relations -- Israel.

DS87.54.D34 2000
Dagher, Carole.
Bring down the walls: Lebanon's postwar challenge/ Carole H. Dagher. New York: St. Martin's Press, 2000. xv, 248 p.
99-041936   956.9204/4   0312229208
Religion and politics -- Lebanon. Political culture -- Lebanon. Lebanon -- Politics and government -- 1990-

DS89 Lebanon (Phoenicia) — Regions, cities, etc.

DS89.A42.G55 1996
Gilsenan, Michael.
Lords of the Lebanese marches: violence and narrative in an Arab society/ Michael Gilsenan. Berkeley: University of California Press, c1996. xv, 377 p.
95-050482   956.92   0520205898
Akkar (Lebanon) -- Politics and government. Political anthropology -- Lebanon -- Akkar. Power (Social sciences) -- Lebanon -- Akkar. Lebanon -- Kings and rulers. Akkar (Lebanon) -- Social conditions.

DS90 Lebanon (Phoenicia) — Philistines

DS90.D613 1982
Dothan, Trude Krakauer.
The Philistines and their material culture/ Trude Dothan. New Haven: Yale University Press, c1982. xxii, 310 p.
80-022060   933   0300022581
Philistines -- Material culture.   Palestine -- Antiquities.

DS92.3 Syria — Congresses

DS92.3.S97 1991
Syria: society, culture, and polity/ edited by Richard T. Antoun and Donald Quataert. Albany: State University of New York Press, c1991. p. cm.
90-010251   956.91   0791407136
Syria -- Congresses.

DS93 Syria — General works

DS93.Q85 1999
Quilliam, Neil.
Syria/ Neil Quilliam, compiler Oxford, England;
Clio Press, c1999. xxvi, 284 p.
　016.95691　1851093176
　Syria -- Bibliography.　Syria -- Bibliography.

DS94 Syria — Description and travel

DS94.F4 1955
Fedden, Robin, 1908-1977.
Syria; an historical appreciation, by Robin Fedden.
Illustrated from photos. mainly by A. Costa.
London, Hale [1955] 243 p.
55-004421　956.9
　Syria -- Description and travel. Syria --
History.

DS94.5 Syria — Antiquities

DS94.5.B87 1999
Burns, Ross.
Monuments of Syria: an historical guide/ Ross
Burns. New York: New York University Press,
1992. xvii, 297 p.
92-025220　939/.43　0814712002
　Syria -- Antiquities.

DS94.8 Syria — Ethnography — Individual elements in the population, A-Z

DS94.8.D8.A24 1984
Abu Izzeddin, Nejla M.
The Druzes: a new study of their history, faith, and
society/ by Nejla M. Abu-Izzeddin. Leiden: E.J.
Brill, 1984. 259 p.
84-226664　956.92/009/7671　9004069755
　Druzes.

DS94.9 Syria — History — Dictionaries. Chronological tables, outlines, etc.

DS94.9.C66 1996
Commins, David Dean.
Historical dictionary of Syria/ David Commins.
Lanham, Md.: Scarecrow Press, 1996. p. cm.
96-012372　956.91/003　0810831767
　Syria -- History -- Dictionaries.

DS95 Syria — History — General works

DS95.S24
Salibi, Kamal S. 1929-
Syria under Islam: empire on trial, 634-1097/ by
Kamal S. Salibi. Delmar, N.Y.: Caravan Books,
1977. 193 p.
77-024197　956.91　0882060139
　Syria -- History.

DS95.6 Syria — History — Political and diplomatic history

DS95.6.I75.M36 1995
Maoz, Moshe.
Syria and Israel: from war to peacemaking/ Moshe
Maoz. Oxford; Clarendon Press, 1995. ix, 280 p.
95-005775　　　　　327.569105694/09/045
0198280181(al
　Jewish-Arab relations -- 1949-　Israel --
Relations -- Syria. Syria -- Relations -- Israel.

DS96.2-98.2 Syria — History — By period

DS96.2.G72 1990
Grainger, John D., 1939-
The cities of Seleukid, Syria/ John D. Grainger.
Oxford [England]: Clarendon Press; 1990. xi,
253 p.
89-048353　939/.43　0198146949
　Cities and towns, Ancient -- Syria. Seleucids.
Syria -- History -- 333 B.C.-634 A.D.

DS98.G45 1998
Gelvin, James L., 1951-
Divided loyalties: nationalism and mass politics in
Syria at the close of Empire/ James L. Gelvin.
Berkeley: University of California Press, 1998. ix,
335 p.
98-003204　956.9104　0520210697
　Nationalism -- Syria. Mandates -- Syria. Elites
(Social sciences) -- Syria. Syria -- History -- 20th
century.

DS98.K46 1987
Khoury, Philip S. 1949-
Syria and the French mandate: the politics of Arab
nationalism, 1920-1945/ Philip S. Khoury.
Princeton, N.J.: Princeton University Press, c1987.
xix, 698 p.
86-042859　946.08　069105486X
　Nationalism -- Syria -- History. Nationalism --
Arab countries -- History.　Syria -- History -- 20th
century.

DS98.2.M68 2000
Moubayed, Sami M.
Damascus between democracy and dictatorship/
Sami M. Moubayed. Lanham [Md.]: University
Press of America, 2000. xxv, 212 p.
00-034332　956.9104/2　0761817441
　Coups d'etat -- Syria.　Syria -- Politics and
government -- 1946-1971.

DS98.2.S4 1987
Seale, Patrick.
The struggle for Syria: a study of post-war Arab
politics, 1945-1958/ Patrick Seale; with a foreword
by Albert Hourani. New Haven: Yale University
Press, 1987, c1986. xv, 352 p.
87-008265　956.91/042　0300039441
　Syria -- Politics and government. Arab
countries -- Politics and government -- 1945-

DS99 Syria — Provinces, regions, cities, etc., A-Z

DS99.A6
Asbridge, Thomas S.
The creation of the principality of Antioch, 1098-
1130 Thomas S. Asbridge. Woodbridge, Suffolk,
UK Boydell Press, 2000. xi, 233 p.
00-026143　956.4　0851156614
　Antioch (Principality) -- History.

DS99.A6.D6
Downey, Glanville, 1908-
A history of Antioch in Syria: from Seleucus to the
Arab conquest.　　Princeton, N.J., Princeton
University Press, 1961. xvii, 752 p.
61-006288　939.42
　Antioch (Turkey) -- History.

DS99.D3.C48 1994
Chamberlain, Michael, 1953-
Knowledge and social practice in medieval
Damascus, 1190-1350/ Michael Chamberlain.
Cambridge; Cambridge University Press, 1994.
xiii, 199 p.
93-046181　956.91/4402　0521454069
　Learning and scholarship -- History -- Medieval,
500-1500. Elite (Social sciences) -- Syria --
Damascus -- History. Social history -- Medieval,
500-1500. Damascus (Syria) -- Intellectual life.
Damascus (Syria) -- Politics and government.

DS102 Israel (Palestine). The Jews — Sources and documents

DS102.C56 no. 1
Yerushalmi, Yosef Hayim, 1932-
From Spanish court to Italian ghetto; Isaac
Cardoso; a study in seventeenth-century marranism
and Jewish apologetics.　New York, Columbia
University Press, 1971. xx, 524 p.
76-109544　914.6/06/9240924　0231032862
　Cardoso, Isaac, -- 1603 or 4-1683. Jews -- Italy --
Biography. Marranos -- Biography. Judaism --
Apologetic works -- History and criticism.

DS102.J43
The Jew in the modern world: a documentary
history/ edited by Paul R. Mendes-Flohr, Jehuda
Reinharz. New York: Oxford University Press,
1980. xix, 556 p.
79-015050　909/.04/924　0195026314
　Jews -- History -- 17th century -- Sources. Jews -
- History -- 18th century -- Sources. Jews --
History -- 1789-1945 -- Sources.

DS102.L54 1988
The Literature of destruction: Jewish responses to
catastrophe/ edited by David G. Roskies.
Philadelphia: Jewish Publication Society, 1988,
c1989. xi, 652 p.
88-002774　909/.04924　0827603142
　Jews -- Persecutions -- History -- Sources.
Jewish literature. Holocaust, Jewish (1939-1945) -
- Literary collections.

DS102.4-102.5 Israel (Palestine). The Jews — Collected works (nonserial) — Several authors

DS102.4.F5 1960
Finkelstein, Louis, 1895-
The Jews: their history, culture, and religion. New
York, Harper [1960] 2 v.
60-007383　956.93
　Jews -- History. Judaism -- History. Jewish
literature -- History and criticism.

DS102.5.V5313 1996
Vidal-Naquet, Pierre, 1930-
The Jews: history, memory, and the present/ Pierre Vidal-Naquet; translated and edited by David Ames Curtis; with a foreword by Paul Berman and a new preface by the author. New York: Columbia University Press, 1996. xxiii, 337 p.
95-020960   944/.004924   0231102089
Jews -- History -- 168 B.C.-135 A.D. Jews -- France -- History. Jewish-Arab relations. France -- Ethnic relations.

DS102.8 Israel (Palestine). The Jews — Encyclopedias. Dictionaries

DS102.8.B46 1989
The Blackwell companion to Jewish culture: from the eighteenth century to the present/ edited by Glenda Abramson; advisory editors, Dovid Katz ... [et al.]. Oxford, UK; Blackwell Reference, 1989. xxii, 853 p.
89-001008   909/.04924   0631151117
Jews -- Encyclopedias. Jews -- Civilization -- Encyclopedias. Civilization, Modern -- Jewish influences -- Encyclopedias.

DS102.8.E495 1982
Encyclopaedia Judaica, 1972-1981. Jerusalem: Encyclopaedia Judaica, [1982] xii, 684 p.
83-213800   909/.049240827.219
Jews--Encyclopedias.

DS102.8.E49652 1994
Encyclopaedia Judaica. events of 1982-1992/ [editor, Geoffrey Wigoder; managing editor, Fern Seckbach; indexer, Hillel Wiseberg]. Jerusalem: Encyclopaedia Judaica, c1994. ix, 429 p.
95-100427   909/.04924/09048   9650703969
Jews -- Encyclopedias.

DS102.8.J4 1964
The Jewish encyclopedia: a descriptive record of the history, religion, literature, and customs of the Jewish people from the earliest times to the present day/ Prepared under the direction of Cyrus Adler [and others]; Isidore Singer, managing editor. New York: KTAV Publishing House, 1964. 12 v.
64-009359
Jews -- Dictionaries and encyclopedias.

DS102.8.N397 1997
Nazzal, Nafez.
Historical dictionary of Palestine/ by Nafez Y. Nazzal and Laila A. Nazzal . Lanham, Md.: Scarecrow Press, 1997. p. cm.
96-030594   956.94/003   0810832399
Jewish-Arab relations -- Dictionaries. Arab-Israeli conflict -- Dictionaries. Palestine -- History -- Dictionaries.

DS102.8.S73 1992
The New standard Jewish encyclopedia/ Geoffrey Wigoder, editor-in-chief. New York: Facts on File, 1992. 1001 p.
92-018351   909/.04924/003   0816026904
Jews -- Encyclopedias.

DS102.9 Israel (Palestine). The Jews — Directories

DS102.9.F4 1959a
Federbusch, Simon, 1892-1969.
World Jewry today. New York, T. Yoseloff [1959] 748 p.
61-001748   956.93
Jews -- Directories. Jews -- Statistics.

DS102.95 Israel (Palestine). The Jews — General works

DS102.95.W65 1987
Wolffsohn, Michael.
Israel: polity, society, economy, 1882-1986: an introductory handbook/ Michael Wolffsohn; translated by Douglas Bokovoy. Atlantic Highlands, NJ: Humanities Press International, 1987. xxxii, 302 p.
87-003702   956.94   0391035401
Zionism. Israel.

DS102.95.Y3313 1999
Yablonka, Hanna.
Survivors of the Holocaust: Israel after the war/ Hanna Yablonka; translated from Hebrew by Ora Cummings. New York: New York University Press, 1999. xiii, 337 p.
98-036899   940.53/18/09225694   0814796923
Holocaust survivors -- Israel. Kibbutzim. Social integration -- Israel.

DS107 Israel (Palestine). The Jews — Description and travel — 1800-1900

DS107.S6 1932
Smith, George Adam, 1856-1942.
The historical geography of the Holy Land, by George Adam Smith. New York, R. Long & R. R. Smith, inc., 1932. xxviii, 744 p.
32-026753   915.69
Palestine -- Historical geography. Jordan -- Historical geography.

DS107.4 Israel (Palestine). The Jews — Description and travel — 1948-1980

DS107.4.B37 1976
Bellow, Saul.
To Jerusalem and back: a personal account/ Saul Bellow. New York: Viking Press, 1976. 182 p.
76-042198   915.694/4/0450924   0670717290
Bellow, Saul -- Journeys -- Israel. Authors, American -- 20th century -- Journeys -- Israel. Jewish-Arab relations -- 1973- Israel-Arab conflicts. Israel -- Description and travel.

DS107.4.R43
Rennert, Maggie.
Shelanu: an Israel journal/ Maggie Rennert. Englewood Cliffs, N.J.: Prentice-Hall, c1979. viii, 446 p.
78-009561   956.94/05   013808808X
Rennert, Maggie -- Homes and haunts -- Israel -- Beersheba. Authors, American -- 20th century -- Biography. Israel -- Description and travel.

DS108.9 Israel (Palestine). The Jews — Historical geography. History of Palestine exploration, etc.

DS108.9.L28 1990
The Land that became Israel: studies in historical geography/ edited by Ruth Kark; [translated from the Hebrew by Michael Gordon]. New Haven: Yale University Press; 1990. x, 332 p.
89-051752   911/.5694   0300047185
Agricultural colonies -- Palestine -- History. Zionism -- Palestine -- History. Palestine -- Historical geography. Palestine -- History -- 1799-1917.

DS109-109.15 Israel (Palestine). The Jews — Jerusalem — Description. Antiquities and exploration — To 1981

DS109.K39
Kenyon, Kathleen Mary,
Digging up Jerusalem, by Kathleen M. Kenyon. New York, Praeger [1974] xxxi, 288 p.
73-010948   913.33   0275466008
Jerusalem -- Antiquities. Jerusalem -- History.

DS109.15.K65 1990
Kollek, Teddy,
My Jerusalem: twelve walks in the world's holiest city/ Teddy Kollek and Shulamith Eisner; photographs by Richard Nowitz. New York: Summit Books, c1990. 160 p.
89-021831   915.694/420454.220   0671702459
Jerusalem -- Tours.

DS109.86-109.95 Israel (Palestine). The Jews — Jerusalem — History

DS109.86.P39.A3 1992
Patai, Raphael, 1910-
Journeyman in Jerusalem: memories and letters, 1933-1947/ Raphael Patai. Salt Lake City: University of Utah Press, c1992. xiii, 478 p.
91-051095   956.94/4204/092   0874803837
Patai, Raphael, -- 1910- Patai, Raphael, -- 1910- -- Correspondence. Jewish scholars -- Jerusalem -- Biography. Folklorists -- Jerusalem -- Biography. Jews -- Jerusalem -- Biography. Jerusalem -- Biography.

DS109.9.J4576 1998
Jerusalem: its sanctity and centrality to Judaism, Christianity, and Islam/ edited by Lee I. Levine. New York: Continuum, 1998. p. cm.
98-015267   956.94/42   0826410243
Jerusalem in Judaism. Jerusalem in Christianity. Jerusalem in Islam. Jerusalem -- History.

DS109.9.J459 1989
Jerusalem in history/ edited by K.J. Asali. Brooklyn, N.Y.: Olive Branch Press, 1990. 295 p.
89-016000   956.94/42   094079344X
Jerusalem -- History.

DS109.916.G73 1996
Grabar, Oleg.
The shape of the holy: early Islamic Jerusalem/ Oleg Grabar; with contributions by Mohammad al-Asad, Abeer Audeh, Said Nuseibeh. Princeton, N.J.: Princeton University Press, c1996. xiv, 232 p.
95-050443 956.94/4203 0691036535
Jerusalem -- History. Temple Mount (Jerusalem) Jerusalem -- Antiquities.

DS109.916.P48 1993
Peters, F. E.
The distant shrine: the Islamic centuries in Jerusalem/ F.E. Peters. New York: AMS Press, c1993. 275 p.
89-045876 956.94/42 0404616291
Jerusalem -- History.

DS109.925.G54 1985
Gilbert, Martin.
Jerusalem: rebirth of a city/ Martin Gilbert 1st American ed. New York: Viking, 1985. xvii, 238 p.
85-040071 956.94/4.219 0670807893
Jews--Jerusalem--History--19th century.

DS109.93.B68 1971
Bovis, H. Eugene, 1928-
The Jerusalem question, 1917-1968 [by] H. Eugene Bovis. Stanford, Calif., Hoover Institution Press [1971] xiii, 175 p.
73-149796 320.9/5694/4 0817932917
Jerusalem -- Politics and government.

DS109.93.G55 1996
Gilbert, Martin.
Jerusalem in the twentieth century/ Martin Gilbert. New York: J. Wiley & Sons, 1996. xvi, 412 p.
96-018458 956.94/42.220 0471163082
Jerusalem -- History. Palestine -- History -- 1917-1948. Israel -- History.

DS109.93.S56 1998
Slonim, Shlomo, 1931-
Jerusalem in America's foreign policy, 1947-1997/ by Shlomo Slonim. The Hague; Kluwer Law International, c1998. xiv, 421 p.
98-034298 327.7305694 9041110399
Jerusalem -- International status. United States -- Foreign relations -- 1945-1989 -- Decision making. United States -- Foreign relations -- 1989- -- Decision making.

DS109.93.W37 2001
Wasserstein, Bernard.
Divided Jerusalem: the struggle for the Holy City/ Bernard Wasserstein. New Haven: Yale University Press, 2001. xix, 412 p.
2001-026053 956.94/42.221 0300091648
Jews--Jerusalem--History. Christians--Jerusalem--History. Muslims--Jerusalem--History.

DS109.94.B4513
Benvenisti, Meron, 1934-
Jerusalem, the torn city/ Meron Benvenisti. Minneapolis: University of Minnesota Press, c1976. xv, 407 p.
76-012226 956.94/4/05 0816607958
Jerusalem -- Politics and government.

DS109.94.C49 1999
Cheshin, Amir.
Separate and unequal: the inside story of Israeli rule in East Jerusalem/ Amir Cheshin, Bill Hutman, Avi Melamed. Cambridge, MA: Harvard University Press, 1999. 275 p.
98-053991 323.1/192740569442 0674801369
Palestinian Arabs -- Government policy -- Jerusalem. Jerusalem -- Politics and government.

DS109.94.D86 1996
Dumper, Michael.
The politics of Jerusalem since 1967/ Michael Dumper. New York: Columbia University Press, c1997. x, 365 p.
96-034820 956.94/4205 0231106408
City planning -- Jerusalem. Jewish-Arab relations -- 1949- -- Jerusalem. Jerusalem -- Politics and government. Jerusalem -- Population. Jerusalem -- Ethnic relations.

DS109.94.N45 2000
Negotiating Jerusalem/ Jerome M. Segal ... [et al.]. New York: State University of New York Press, 2000. x, 341 p.
99-041586 341.2/9/09569442 0791445372
Arab-Israeli conflict -- 1993- -- Peace. Jerusalem -- International status.

DS109.95.K55 2001
Klein, Menachem.
Jerusalem: the contested city/ Menachem Klein; translated by Haim Watzman. New York: New York University Press in association with th c2001. viii, 363 p.
01-030187 956.94/42054 081474754X
Arab-Israeli conflict -- 1993- -- Peace. Jerusalem -- Politics and government -- 20th century. Jerusalem -- International status. Jerusalem -- Ethnic relations.

DS110-110.5 Israel (Palestine). The Jews — Regions, towns, etc., A-Z

DS110.A3.T67 2000
Torstrick, Rebecca L., 1954-
The limits of coexistence: identity politics in Israel/ Rebecca L. Torstrick. Ann Arbor: University of Michigan Press, c2000. xii, 284 p.
00-037739 956.94/5 0472111248
Palestinian Arabs -- Israel -- Acre -- Politics and government. Jews -- Israel -- Acre -- Politics and government. Acre (Israel) -- Ethnic relations. Acre (Israel) -- Politics and government.

DS110.E645.S59 1998
Slyomovics, Susan.
The object of memory: Arab and Jew narrate the Palestinian village/ Susan Slyomovics. Philadelphia: University of Pennsylvania Press, c1998. xxv, 294 p.
98-005346 956.94 0812232151
Palestinian Arabs -- Israel -- Ayn Hawd -- History. Ayn Haud (Israel) -- History. En Hod (Israel) -- History.

DS110.G2.G66 1983
Goodman, Martin, 1953-
State and society in Roman Galilee, A.D. 132-212/ Martin Goodman. Totowa, NJ: Rowman & Allanheld, 1983. x, 305 p.
82-024281 956.94/5 0865980896
Jews -- History -- 70-638. Tannaim. Galilee (Israel) -- History. Rome -- History -- Empire, 30 B.C.-284 A.D.

DS110.G2.H619 1996
Horsley, Richard A.
Archaeology, history, and society in Galilee: the social context of Jesus and the rabbis/ Richard A. Horsley. Valley Forge, Pa: Trinity Press International, c1996. xii, 240 p.
96-042950 933 1563381826
Jesus Christ -- Biography. Jews -- History -- 586 B.C.-70 A.D. Judaism -- History -- Post-exilic period, 586 B.C.-210 A.D. Galilee (Israel) -- Antiquities. Galilee (Israel) -- History. Galilee (Israel) -- Social life and customs.

DS110.H28.Y39 1998
Yazbak, Mahmud.
Haifa in the late Ottoman period, 1864-1914: a Muslim town in transition/ by Mahmoud Yazbak. Leiden; Brill, 1998. xiv, 262 p.
98-014405 956.94/603 9004110518
Palestinian Arabs -- Israel -- Haifa -- History -- 19th century. Haifa (Israel) -- History -- 19th century.

DS110.J3.K3713 1990
Kark, Ruth.
Jaffa: a city in evolution, 1799-1917/ Ruth Kark; [translated by Gila Brand]. Jerusalem: Yad Izhak Ben-Zvi Press, 1990. 328 p.
90-196014 956.94/8 9652170658
Jaffa (Tel Aviv, Israel) -- History.

DS110.M33.Y33
Yadin, Yigael, 1917-1984.
Masada; Herod's fortress and the Zealot's last stand. [Translated from the Hebrew by Moshe Pearlman] New York, Random House [1966] 272 p.
66-023094 913.031028
Masada Site (Israel) Israel -- Antiquities.

DS110.N28.R33 1997
Rabinowitz, Dan, 1954-
Overlooking Nazareth: the ethnography of exclusion in Galilee/ Dan Rabinowitz. Cambridge; Cambridge University Press, 1997. xiv, 222 p.
96-011922 956.94/5 0521563615
Palestinian Arabs -- Israel -- Natsrat Ilit -- Politics and government. Natsrat Ilit (Israel) -- Politics and government.

DS110.N4.M38 1997
Meir, Avinoam.
As nomadism ends: the Israeli bedouin of the Negev/ Avinoam Meir. Boulder, Colo.: Westview Press, 1997. xi, 253 p.
96-011295 305.892/7056949 0813389593
Bedouins -- Israel -- Negev -- Sedentarisation. Negev (Israel) -- Ethnic relations.

DS110.Q8.V313 1973
Vaux, Roland de, 1903-1971.
Archaeology and the Dead Sea scrolls. London, published for the British Academy by the Oxford 1973. xv, 142 p.
73-174845 221/.44 0197259316
Qumran Site (West Bank)

DS110.W47.A29 1993
Aburish, Said K., 1935-
Cry Palestine: inside the West Bank/ Said K. Aburish. Boulder: Westview Press, 1993. xvii, 205 p.
92-041651 956.95/3044 0813317975
Palestinian Arabs -- West Bank -- Social conditions. Intifada, 1987- -- Influence. Jewish-Arab relations -- 1973- West Bank -- Social conditions. Israel -- Politics and government.

DS110.W47.I555 1991
The Intifada: its impact on Israel, the Arab World, and the superpowers/ edited by Robert O. Freedman. Miami: Florida International University Press, c1991. xxii, 417 p.
90-048019 956.9405/4 0813010403
Intifada, 1987- -- Influence. Israel -- Politics and government.

DS110.W47.I56 1990
Intifada: Palestine at the crossroads/ edited by Jamal R. Nassar and Roger Heacock. New York: Praeger, 1990. xiii, 347 p.
89-022879 956.9405/4 027593411X
Intifada, 1987-

DS110.W47.S24 1988
Sahliyeh, Emile F.
In search of leadership: West Bank politics since 1967/ Emile Sahliyeh. Washington, D.C.: Brookings Institution, c1988. xii, 201 p.
88-015083 956.95/3 0815776985
Palestinian Arabs -- West Bank -- Politics and government. Political parties -- West Bank. West Bank -- Politics and government.

DS110.5.D313 1966a
Dayan, Moshe, 1915-1981.
Diary of the Sinai Campaign. New York, Harper & Row [1966] 236 p.
66-015731 956/.044
Dayan, Moshe, -- 1915-1981 -- Diaries. Sinai Campaign, 1956 -- Personal narratives, Israeli. Israel -- Armed Forces -- Biography.

DS110.5.G634 1998
Golani, Moti.
Israel in search of a war: the Sinai Campaign, 1955-1956/ Motti Golani; foreword by Avi Shlaim. Brighton; Sussex Academic Press, 1998. x, 236 p.
97-039710 956.04/4 189872346X
Sinai Campaign. 1956.

DS111.A2 Israel (Palestine). The Jews — Antiquities — Sources and documents

DS111.A2.A73 2001
Archaeological encyclopedia of the Holy Land / edited by Avraham Negev and Shimon Gibson. New York: Continuum, 2001. 559 p.
00-069409 220.9/3 0826413161
Excavations (Archaeology) -- Palestine -- Encyclopedias. Palestine -- Antiquities -- Encyclopedias.

DS111.A2.E5813 1993
The New encyclopedia of archaeological excavations in the Holy Land/ Ephraim Stern, editor; Ayelet Lewinson-Gilboa, assistant editor; Joseph Aviram, editorial director. Jerusalem: Israel Exploration Society & Carta; c1993. 4 v.
92-017712 933/.003 0132762889
Excavations (Archaeology) -- Palestine -- Encyclopedias. Palestine -- Antiquities -- Encyclopedias.

DS111.A2.M3513 1992
The archaeology of ancient Israel/ edited by Amnon Ben-Tor; translated by R. Greenberg. New Haven: Yale University Press; c1992. xxi, 398 p.
91-009016 933 0300047681
Excavations (Archaeology) -- Palestine. Palestine -- Antiquities.

DS111.C36 Israel (Palestine). The Jews — Antiquities — Antiquities — General works

DS111.C36 1990
Canby, Courtlandt.
A guide to the archaeological sites of Israel, Egypt, and North Africa/ Courtlandt Canby with Arcadia Kocybala. New York: Facts on File, c1990. ix, 278 p.
89-011810 916.104/49 0816010544
Palestine -- Antiquities -- Guidebooks. Egypt -- Antiquities -- Guidebooks. Africa, North -- Antiquities -- Guidebooks.

DS111.1 Israel (Palestine). The Jews — Antiquities — General special

DS111.1.S74 1998
Sperber, Daniel.
The city in Roman Palestine/ Daniel Sperber. New York: Oxford University Press, 1998. viii, 200 p.
98-028559 933/.009732 019509882X
Cities and towns, Ancient -- Palestine. Jews -- History -- 70-638. Rabbinical literature -- History and criticism. Palestine -- Civilization -- History -- To 1500. Palestine -- Antiquities.

DS111.9 Israel (Palestine). The Jews — Antiquities — Other (Costumes, etc.)

DS111.9.D38 1993
Daviau, P. M. Michele.
Houses and their furnishings in Bronze Age Palestine: domestic activity areas and artefact [sic] distribution in the middle and late Bronze Ages/ P.M. Michele Daviau. Sheffield, England: JSOT Press, c1993. 489 p.
94-108929 933/.01 1850753555
Architecture, Domestic -- Palestine -- History. Dwellings -- Palestine. Bronze age -- Palestine. Palestine -- Antiquities.

DS112 Israel (Palestine). The Jews — Social life and customs. Civilization. Intellectual life — General works

DS112.B3152
Baron, Salo Wittmayer, 1895-
A social and religious history of the Jews. New York, Columbia University Press, 1952-1983 v. 1-18
52-000404 909/.04924 0231088507
Jews -- History. Judaism -- History.

DS112.K373
Katz, Jacob, 1904-
Tradition and crisis; Jewish society at the end of the Middle Ages. [New York] Free Press of Glencoe [1961] 280 p.
61-009168 915.693
Jews -- History -- 70-1789. Jews -- Social life and customs.

DS112.L65 1983
Liebman, Charles S.
Civil religion in Israel: traditional Judaism and political culture in the Jewish state/ Charles S. Liebman, Eliezer Don-Yehiya. Berkeley: University of California Press, c1983. 305 p.
82-017427 306/.2/095694 0520048172
Civil religion -- Israel. Zionism -- Israel. Political culture -- Israel. Israel -- Politics and government. Israel -- Civilization.

DS112.R755 1999
Roskies, David G., 1948-
The Jewish search for a usable past/ David G. Roskies. Bloomington, IN: Indiana University Press, c1999. xii, 217 p.
98-046951 909/.04924 0253335051
Jews -- Civilization. Jews -- Persecutions. Memory -- Religious aspects -- Judaism.

DS112.Z37
Zborowski, Mark.
Life is with people; the Jewish little-town of eastern Europe [by] Mark Zborowski and Elizabeth Herzog. Foreword by Margaret Mead. New York, International Universities Press [1952] 456 p.
52-007181 296
Jews -- Social life and customs.

DS113 Israel (Palestine). The Jews — Antiquities — Social life and customs. Civilization. Intellectual life — Intellectual life Culture

DS113.M424 1990
Mendes-Flohr, Paul R.
Divided passions: Jewish intellectuals and the experience of modernity/ Paul Mendes-Flohr. Detroit: Wayne State University Press, c1991. 449 p.
89-022557 909/.04924 0814320309
Jews -- Intellectual life -- 20th century. Philosophy, Jewish -- History -- 20th century.

DS113.M58 1999
Modern Jewish mythologies/ edited by Glenda Abramson. Cincinnati, OH: Hebrew Union College Press, 1999. p. cm.
99-026975 305.892/4 0878202161
Jews -- Intellectual life -- 20th century. Jews -- Identity.

DS113.S377 1998
Schwarcz, Vera, 1947-
Bridge across broken time: Chinese and Jewish cultural memory/ Vera Schwarcz. New Haven, CT: Yale University Press, 1998. xiii, 232 p.
97-040057 305.892/4 0300066147
Jews -- Civilization. Memory -- Religious aspects -- Judaism. Memory -- Cross-cultural studies. China -- Civilization.

DS113.S38 1956
Schwarz, Leo W. 1906-1967,
Great ages and ideas of the Jewish people, by Salo W. Baron [and others] New York, Modern Library [c1956] 515 p.
62-004323 956.93
Judaism -- History.

DS113.2 Israel (Palestine). The Jews — Ethnography. Tribes of Israel — General works

DS113.2.B464 1991
Ben Rafael, Eliezer.
Ethnicity, religion, and class in Israeli society/ Eliezer Ben-Rafael and Stephen Sharot. Cambridge [England]; Cambridge University Press, 1991. x, 287 p.
89-078199 305.8/0095694 0521392292
Ethnicity -- Israel. Social classes -- Israel. Judaism -- Israel. Israel -- Ethnic relations.

DS113.3 Israel (Palestine). The Jews — Ethnography. Tribes of Israel — Israeli national characteristics, identity, etc.

DS113.3.A5613 2000
Almog, Oz.
The Sabra: the creation of the new Jew/ Oz Almog; Haim Watzman, translator. Berkeley: University of California Press, c2000. xv, 313 p.
00-042613 305.892/405694 0520216423
National characteristics, Israeli. Sabras. Jews -- Israel -- Identity.

DS113.7-113.72 Israel (Palestine). The Jews — Ethnography. Tribes of Israel — Arabs. Palestinian Arabs

DS113.7.G38 2001
Ganim, Asad.
The Palestinian-Arab minority in Israel, 1948-2000: a political study/ Asad Ghanem. Albany: State University of New York Press, 2001. xiv, 238 p.
00-058826 956.94/0049274 0791449971
Palestinian Arabs -- Israel -- history. Israel -- Ethnic relations.

DS113.7.K53 1997
Khalidi, Rashid.
Palestinian identity: the construction of modern national consciousness/ Rashid Khalidi. New York: Columbia University Press, c1997. xvi, 309 p.
96-045757 305.892/740569442 0231105142
Palestinian Arabs -- Israel -- Ethnic identity. Arab-Israeli conflict. Palestinian Arabs -- Jerusalem.

DS113.72.F57 1999
Firro, Kais.
The Druzes in the Jewish state: a brief history/ by Kais M. Firro. Leiden; Brill, 1999. viii, 266 p.
98-037437 956.94/0088/2971 9004112510
Druzes -- Israel -- History. Israel -- Ethnic relations.

DS113.72.P37 2000
Parsons, Laila.
The Druze between Palestine and Israel, 1947-49/ Laila Parsons. Houndmills, Basingstoke, Hampshire: Macmillan Press; 2000. xvii, 180 p.
99-054117 956.94 0312231075
Druzes -- Israel -- History. Jewish-Arab relations -- History -- 1917-1948. Druzes -- Palestine -- History. Israel -- Ethnic relations.

DS113.8 Israel (Palestine). The Jews — Ethnography. Tribes of Israel — Other elements in the population, A-Z

DS113.8.F34.W34 1993
Wagaw, Teshome G., 1930-
For our soul: Ethiopian Jews in Israel/ Teshome G. Wagaw. Detroit: Wayne State University Press, c1993. xi, 293 p.
93-007494 956.94/004924063 0814324584
Jews, Ethiopian -- Israel -- History. Ethiopia -- Emigration and Immigration -- History. Israel -- Emigration and immigration -- History. Israel -- Ethnic relations.

DS113.8.Y4.L49 1989
Lewis, Herbert S.
After the eagles landed: the Yemenites of Israel/ Herbert S. Lewis. Boulder, Colo.: Westview Press, 1989. xix, 277 p.
89-024877 305.8/92405332 0813378036
Jews, Yemenite -- Israel. Jews -- Yemen. Immigrants -- Israel. Israel -- Ethnic relations. Yemen -- Ethnic relations.

DS114 Israel (Palestine). The Jews — History — Dictionaries. Chronological tables, outlines, etc.

DS114.G68 1993
Gribetz, Judah.
The timetables of Jewish history: a chronology of the most important people and events in Jewish history/ Judah Gribetz and Edward L. Greenstein and Regina Stein. New York: Simon & Schuster, c1993. vi, 808 p.
93-017295 909/.04924 0671640070
Jews -- History -- Chronology.

DS115 Israel (Palestine). The Jews — History — Biography

DS115.W49 1991
Wigoder, Geoffrey, 1922-
Dictionary of Jewish biography/ Geoffrey Wigoder. New York: Simon & Schuster, c1991. 567 p.
90-029276 920/.0092924 013210105X
Jews -- Biography -- Dictionaries.

DS115.5 Israel (Palestine). The Jews — History — Historiography

DS115.5.K37 2000
Karsh, Efraim.
Fabricating Israeli history: the "new historians"/ Efraim Karsh. London; Frank Cass, 2000. xliv, 236 p.
00-035876 956.94/04 0714650110
Jewish-Arab relations -- Historiography. Israel-Arab War, 1948-1949 -- Historiography. Great Britain -- Foreign relations -- Jordan -- Historiography. Jordan -- Foreign relations -- Great Britain -- Historiography. Palestine -- History -- 1917-1948 -- Historiography.

DS115.5.M48
Meyer, Michael A.,
Ideas of Jewish history. Edited, with introductions and notes, by Michael A. Meyer. New York, Behrman House [1974] xiv, 360 p.
73-019960 909/.04/924 0874412021
Jews -- Historiography. Jews -- History -- Philosophy.

DS115.5.S64 2000
Spero, Shubert.
Holocaust and return to Zion: a study in Jewish philosophy of history/ by Shubert Spero. Hoboken, NJ: KTAV, c2000. xviii, 398 p.
99-029442 909/.04924 0881256366
Jews -- History -- Philosophy. Jews -- Historiography.

DS115.5.Y47 1982
Yerushalmi, Yosef Hayim, 1932-
Zakhor, Jewish history and Jewish memory/ Yosef Hayim Yerushalmi. Seattle: University of Washington Press, c1982. xvii, 144 p.
82-015989 909/.04924/0072 0295959398
Jews -- Historiography.

DS115.95 Israel (Palestine). The Jews — History — Study and teaching

DS115.95.A6
Agus, Jacob B. 1911-1986.
The meaning of Jewish history. Foreword by Salo W. Baron. London, Abelard-Schuman [1963] 2 v.
63-016295 956.93
Jews -- History -- Philosophy.

DS117 Israel (Palestine). The Jews — History — General works

DS117.D7213
Dubnov, Simon, 1860-1941.
History of the Jews/ by Simon Dubnov; translated from the Russian 4th definitive rev. ed. by Moshe Spiegel. South Brunswick, N.J.: T. Yoseloff, c1967-73. 5 v.
66-014785 910/.03/924 0498075370
Jews -- History.

DS117.S3 1965
Sachar, Abram Leon, 1899-
A history of the Jews. New York, Knopf, 1965. xvi, 478 p.
64-017704 956.93
Jews -- History.

DS117.T613 1976
A History of the Jewish people/ A. Malamat ... [et al.]; edited by H. H. Ben-Sasson. Cambridge, Mass.: Harvard University Press, 1976. xii, 1170 p.
75-029879 909/.04/924 0674397304
Jews -- History.

DS118 Israel (Palestine). The Jews — History — Compends. Popular and juvenile works

DS118.E465 1986b
Encyclopedia of Jewish history: events and eras of the Jewish people/ [editor of the English edition Joseph Alpher]. New York, N.Y.: Facts on File Publications, c1986. 287 p.
85-023941 909/.04924/0321 0816012202
Jews -- History. Israel -- History.

DS119-119.2 Israel (Palestine). The Jews — History — Questions and answers on Palestine problem. Arab-Israeli conflict

DS119.G58
Goitein, S. D., 1900-
Jews and Arabs, their contacts through the ages. New York, Schocken Books [1955] 257 p.
55-007968   956.94*
Jews -- Islamic countries. Jewish-Arab relations -- History.

DS119.2.H47 1982
Herzog, Chaim, 1918-
The Arab-Israeli wars: war and peace in the Middle East/ Chaim Herzog. New York: Random House, c1982. 392 p.
80-005291   956/.04   0394503791
Israel-Arab conflicts.

DS119.2.N33 1988
Nachmias, Nitza, 1935-
Transfer of arms, leverage, and peace in the Middle East/ Nitza Nachmias. New York: Greenwood Press, 1988. xii, 196 p.
88-017777   956/.04   0313263000
Israel-Arab conflicts. Military assistance, American -- Israel. Israel -- History, Military. United States -- Military relations -- Israel. Israel -- Military relations -- United States.

DS119.6-119.8 Israel (Palestine). The Jews — History — Political and diplomatic history. Foreign and general relations

DS119.6.K54 1990
Klieman, Aaron S.
Israel & the world after 40 years/ Aaron S. Klieman. Washingon, [D.C.]: Pergamon-Brassey's International Defense Publish c1990. xvii, 275 p.
89-034182   327.5694   0080349420
Israel -- Foreign relations -- Philosophy.

DS119.6.L49 1997
Levey, Zach.
Israel and the western powers, 1952-1960/ Zach Levey. Chapel Hill: University of North Carolina Press, c1997. xi, 203 p.
97-012363   327.5694   0807823686
Military assistance, American -- Israel. Military assistance, European -- Israel. World politics -- 1945-1955. Israel -- Foreign relations.

DS119.6.S33 1999
Sachar, Howard Morley, 1928-
Israel and Europe: an appraisal in history/ Howard M. Sachar. New York: Alfred Knopf, 1999. xiii, 398 p.
98-015453   327.5694   0679454349
Israel -- Foreign relations.

DS119.65.C64 1987
Cohen, Saul Bernard.
The geopolitics of Israel's border question/ Saul B. Cohen. Boulder, Colo.: Westview Press, [1987], c1986 124 p.
86-033985   327.1/01/1095694   0813304601
Israel -- Boundaries.

DS119.7.A67234 1988
The Arab-Israeli conflict: two decades of change/ edited by Yehuda Lukacs and Abdalla M. Battah. Boulder: Westview Press, 1988. ix, 402 p.
88-015375   956.04/8   0813375169
Jewish-Arab relations -- 1967-1973 -- Congresses. Jewish-Arab relations -- 1973- Congresses. Israel-Arab War, 1967 -- Influence -- Congresses. Israel -- Politics and government -- Congresses. Middle East -- Politics and government -- 1945-1979 -- Congresses.

DS119.7.A6785.W35 1997
Wallach, Janet.
Arafat: in the eyes of the beholder/ Janet Wallach and John Wallach. Secaucus, N.J.: Carol Pub. Group, 1997. p. cm.
97-005565   322.4/2/092   155972403X
Arafat, Yasir, -- 1929- Palestinian Arabs -- Biography. Arab-Israeli conflict. Jewish-Arab relations -- 1949- Middle East -- Politics and government -- 1945-

DS119.7.B2832 1996
Bar-On, Mordechai, 1928-
In pursuit of peace: a history of the Israeli peace movement/ Mordechai Bar-On. Washington, D.C.: United States Institute of Peace Press, 1996. xix, 470 p.
96-004787   956.9405   1878379542
Peace movements -- Israel -- History. Jewish-Arab relations -- 1949- Israel -- Politics and government.

DS119.7.B698 1996
Bowker, Robert, 1949-
Beyond peace: the search for security in the Middle East/ Robert Bowker. Boulder, Colo.: Lynne Rienner Publishers, 1996. xii, 211 p.
96-015504   956.03   1555876633
Jewish-Arab relations -- 1973- Peace. National security -- Arab countries. Arab countries -- Politics and government -- 1945- Israel -- Politics and government.

DS119.7.C633 1987
Cohen, Michael Joseph, 1940-
The origins and evolution of the Arab-Zionist conflict/ Michael J. Cohen. Berkeley: University of California Press, c1987. xiv, 183 p.
86-016060   956/.03   0520058216
Jewish-Arab relations -- 1917-1949. Palestine -- History -- 1917-1948.

DS119.7.D54 1980
Dimbleby, Jonathan.
The Palestinians/ Jonathan Dimbleby; photographs by Donald McCullin. New York, N.Y.: Quartet Books: 1980. 256 p.
81-017711   956/.04   0704322560
Palestinian Arabs. Jewish-Arab relations.

DS119.7.E353 1998
Eisenberg, Laura Zittrain.
Negotiating Arab-Israeli peace: patterns, problems, possibilities/ Laura Zittrain Eisenberg and Neil Caplan. Bloomington: Indiana University Press, c1998. ix, 252 p.
97-027408   956.04   0253333687
Arab-Israeli conflict.

DS119.7.F336 1997
Farsoun, Samih K.
Palestine and the Palestinians/ Samih K. Farsoun with Christina E. Zacharia. Boulder, Colo.: Westview Press, 1997. xviii, 375 p.
97-021954   956.9405/4   0813303400
Palestinian Arabs -- Economic conditions. Palestinian Arabs -- Social conditions. Palestinian Arabs -- Politics and government.

DS119.7.F595 1996
Flamhaft, Ziva.
Israel on the road to peace: accepting the unacceptable/ Ziva Flamhaft. Boulder, Colo.: Westview Press, 1996. xviii, 252 p.
96-018527   956.9405   0813324149
Jewish-Arab relations -- 1973- Israel-Arab conflicts. Diplomatic negotiations in international disputes. Israel -- Politics and government.

DS119.7.F75 1998
Frisch, Hillel.
Countdown to statehood: Palestinian state formation in the West Bank and Gaza/ Hillel Frisch. Albany: State University of New York Press, c1998. xiii, 221 p.
97-035899   956.94/0049274   0791437116
Nationalism -- Palestine. Palestinian Arabs -- Politics and government.

DS119.7.G389 1997
Gelber, Yoav.
Jewish-Transjordanian relations, 1921-48/ Yoav Gelber. London; Frank Cass, 1997. 320 p.
96-027429   956.94/04   071464675X
Jewish-Arab relations -- History -- 1917-1948. Jordan -- Politics and government. Palestine -- Politics and government -- 1917-1948.

DS119.7.G425 1991
Gerner, Deborah J.
One land, two peoples: the conflict over Palestine/ Deborah J. Gerner. Boulder: Westview Press, 1991. xv, 220 p.
90-043497   0813309085
Jewish-Arab relations -- 1949- Israel-Arab conflicts.

DS119.7.G4313 1987
Gorni, Yosef.
Zionism and the Arabs, 1882-1948: a study of ideology/ Yosef Gorny; [English translation by Chaya Galai]. Oxford [Oxfordshire]: Clarendon Press; 1987. x, 342 p.
86-028582   956.94/001   0198227213
Jewish-Arab relations -- History -- To 1917. Jewish-Arab relations -- History -- 1917-1948. Zionism -- History.

DS119.7.H3855 1983
Heller, Mark.
A Palestinian state: the implications for Israel/ Mark A. Heller. Cambridge, Mass.: Harvard University Press, 1983. x, 190 p.
82-015698   956/.04   0674652215
Israel-Arab conflicts. Jewish-Arab relations -- 1973- Palestinian Arabs -- Politics and government.

DS119.7.J224 1997
Jaber, Hala.
Hezbollah: born with a vengeance/ Hala Jaber. New York: Columbia University Press, c1997. xvi, 240 p.
97-003053   956.92   0231108346
Hizballah (Lebanon) Israel-Arab Border Conflicts, 1949- -- Lebanon. Islam and politics -- Lebanon. Lebanon -- Politics and government -- 1975-1990.

DS119.7.K2996 1997
Kass, Ilana.
The deadly embrace: the impact of Israeli and Palestinian rejectionism on the peace process/ Ilana Kass, Bard O'Neill. Fairfax, Va.: National Institute for Public Policy; c1997. xvii, 347 p.
96-041463   956   0761805346
Israel-Arab conflicts. Insurgency -- Israel. Conflict management -- Israel.

DS119.7.K49256 1991
Kimche, David.
The last option: after Nasser, Arafat, & Saddam Hussein: the quest for peace in the Middle East/ David Kimche. New York: Charles Scribner's Sons; c1991. 328 p.
91-037775 956.04 0684194228
Jewish-Arab relations -- 1973- Israel-Arab conflicts. Jewish-Arab relations -- 1967-1973.

DS119.7.K4943 1993
Kimmerling, Baruch.
Palestinians: the making of a people/ Baruch Kimmerling, Joel S. Migdal. New York: Free Press, c1993. xix, 396 p.
92-025208 956.94/0049274 0029173213
Palestinian Arabs -- History. Jewish-Arab relations.

DS119.7.M253 1996
Makovsky, David.
Making peace with the PLO: the Rabin government's road to the Oslo Accord/ David Makovsky. Boulder, Colo.: Westview Press, c1996. xi, 239 p.
95-039631 320.95694 0813324254
Palestinian Arabs -- Politics and government. Jewish-Arab relations. Israel-Arab conflicts. Israel -- Politics and government.

DS119.7.M263
Mandel, Neville J.
The Arabs and Zionism before World War I/ by Neville J. Mandel. Berkeley: University of California Press, c1976. xxiv, 258 p.
73-078545 327.5694/017/4927 0520024664
Jewish-Arab relations -- History -- To 1917.

DS119.7.M471784 1998
The Middle East peace process: interdisciplinary perspectives/ edited by Ilan Peleg. Albany, N.Y.: State University of New York Press, c1998. xi, 300 p.
97-001208 327.569405695 0791435415
Jewish-Arab relations -- 1973- Palestinian Arabs -- Politics and government. Israel -- Politics and government. Israel -- Foreign relations -- Jordan. Jordan -- Foreign relations -- Israel.

DS119.7.M656 1993
Morris, Benny, 1948-
Israel's border wars, 1949-1956: Arab infiltration, Israeli retaliation, and the countdown to the Suez War/ Benny Morris. Oxford: Clarendon Press; 1993. xii, 451 p.
93-015065 956.9405/2 0198278500
Israel-Arab Border Conflicts, 1949- Jewish-Arab relations -- 1949-1967. Sinai Campaign, 1956 -- Causes.

DS119.7.N6 1992
Nisan, Mordechai.
Toward a new Israel: the Jewish state and the Arab question/ Mordechai Nisan. New York: AMS Press, c1992. xv, 276 p.
91-011936 956.94 0404616313
Jewish-Arab relations. Zionism and Judaism. Judaism -- Relations -- Islam.

DS119.7.O88 1980
Ott, David H.
Palestine in perspective: politics, human rights & the West Bank/ David H. Ott. London; Quartet Books, 1980. 157 p.
81-017686 956.95/044 0704322633
Jewish-Arab relations -- 1973- Israel-Arab conflicts. West Bank -- Politics and government.

DS119.7.P5534 1997
The PLO and Israel: from armed conflict to political solution, 1964-1994/ edited by Avraham Sela and Moshe Ma'oz. New York: St. Martin's Press, 1997. x, 310 p.
97-010190 956.9405/4 0312129068
Jewish-Arab relations -- 1973- -- Congresses. Intifada, 1987- -- Congresses. Israel -- Politics and government -- Congresses. Palestinian National Authority -- History -- Congresses.

DS119.7.Q69 1993
Quandt, William B.
Peace process: American diplomacy and the Arab-Israeli conflict since 1967/ William B. Quandt. Washington, D.C.: Brookings Institution; c1993. xv, 612 p.
93-018804 327.73056 0520083881
Jewish-Arab relations -- 1967-1973. Jewish-Arab relations -- 1973- United States -- Foreign relations -- Middle East. Middle East -- Foreign relations -- United States. United States -- Foreign relations -- 20th century.

DS119.7.Q722 1990
Quigley, John B.
Palestine and Israel: a challenge to justice/ John Quigley. Durham: Duke University Press, 1990. viii, 337 p.
89-039218 956.9405 0822310236
Jewish-Arab relations -- 1949- Palestinian Arabs -- Israel. Israel -- History. West Bank. Gaza Strip.

DS119.7.R374 1998
Rejwan, Nissim.
Israel's place in the Middle East: a pluralist perspective/ Nissim Rejwan. Gainesville, Fl.: University Press of Florida, c1998. 216 p.
98-006104 327.5605694 0813016010
Jewish-Arab relations -- History. Judaism -- Relations -- Islam. Islam -- Relations -- Judaism. Israel -- Politics and government. Israel -- Foreign relations -- Middle East. Middle East -- Foreign relations -- Israel.

DS119.7.R754 1994
Rubin, Barry M.
Revolution until victory?: the politics and history of the PLO/ Barry Rubin. Cambridge, Mass.: Harvard University Press, 1994. xiii, 271 p.
93-031651 322.4/2/095694 0674768035
Palestinian Arabs -- Politics and government. Jewish-Arab relations -- 1949- Israel-Arab conflicts.

DS119.7.S3738 1997
Sayigh, Yazid.
Armed struggle and the search for state: the Palestinian national movement, 1949-1993/ Yezid Sayigh. Oxford: Clarendon Press; 1997. xxxiv, 953 p.
97-023852 956.9405 0198292651
Nationalism -- Palestine. Palestinian Arabs -- Politics and government.

DS119.7.S38195 1989
Sicker, Martin.
Between Hashemites and Zionists: the struggle for Palestine, 1908-1988/ Martin Sicker. New York: Holmes & Meier, 1989. xii, 176 p.
88-032834 956 0841911762
Jewish-Arab relations. Hashimites. Jordan -- Foreign relations.

DS119.7.S4762 2000
Shlaim, Avi.
The iron wall: Israel and the Arab world/ Avi Shlaim. New York: W.W. Norton, c2000. xxv, 670 p.
99-023121 956.04 0393048160
Arab-Israeli conflict. Israel -- Foreign policy.

DS119.7.T443 1994
Tessler, Mark A.
A History of the Israeli-Palestinian conflict/ Mark Tessler. Bloomington: Indiana University Press, c1994. xvii, 906 p.
93-034049 956 0253358485
Jewish-Arab relations -- 1917- Israel-Arab conflicts.

DS119.75.F73 1993
Framing the Intifada: people and media/ edited by Akiba A. Cohen and Gadi Wolfsfeld. Norwood, N.J.: Ablex Pub. Corp., c1993. xxviii, 214 p.
92-042664 956.9405/4 0893918997
Intifada, 1987- -- Public opinion. Public opinion -- Israel. Palestinian Arabs -- Attitudes.

DS119.75.O22 1998
O'Ballance, Edgar.
The Palestinian Intifada/ Edgar O'Ballance. New York: St. Martin's Press, 1998. xvii, 252 p.
97-038060 956.95/3044 0312211724
Intifada, 1987- Arab-Israeli conflict -- 1993-

DS119.75.R54 1991
Rigby, Andrew.
Living the Intifada/ Andrew Rigby. London; Zed Books, c1991. 233 p.
92-114682 1856490394
Intifada, 1987- Palestinian Arabs -- Politics and government. Israel -- Politics and government.

DS119.75.S4813 1991
Shalev, Aryeh, 1926-
The intifada: causes and effects/ Aryeh Shalev. Jerusalem, Israel: Jerusalem Post; c1991. 256 p.
91-002786 956.94 081338303X
Intifada, 1987-

DS119.76.B49 2001
Bentsur, Eytan.
Making peace: a first-hand account of the Arab-Israeli peace process/ Eytan Bentsur. Westport, Conn.: Praeger, 2001. viii, 281 p.
00-032383 956.05/3 0275968766
Bentsur, Eytan. Arab-Israeli conflict -- 1993- -- Peace. Israel -- Politics and government -- 1993-

DS119.76.B74 2000
Bregman, Ahron.
Israel's wars, 1947-1993/ Ahron Bregman. New York: Routledge, 2000. p. cm.
99-054115 956.04 041521467X
Arab-Israeli conflict.

DS119.76.G89 1998
Guyatt, Nicholas, 1973-
The absence of peace: understanding the Israeli-Palestinian conflict/ Nicholas Guyatt. London; Zed Books, c1998. xviii, 188 p.
98-019783 956/.04 1856495795
Arab-Israeli conflict -- 1993- -- Peace Palestinian Arabs -- Government policy -- Israel.

DS119.76.K354 2001
Kaye, Dalia Dassa.
Beyond the handshake: multilateral cooperation in the Arab-Israeli peace process/ Dalia Dassa Kaye. New York: Columbia University Press, 2001. xxii, 319 p.
00-059031   956.05/3   0231120028
Arab-Israeli conflict -- 1993- -- Peace. Arab countries -- Foreign economic relations -- Israel. Israel -- Foreign economic relations -- Arab countries.

DS119.76.R67 1997
Rosenberg, Jerry Martin.
Encyclopedia of the Middle East peace process and the Middle East/North Africa economic community/ Jerry M. Rosenberg. Greenwich, Conn.: JAI Press, c1997. x, 451 p.
97-039512   956.05/3/03   0762303506
Arab-Israeli conflict -- 1993- -- Peace -- Encyclopedias. Middle East -- Economic conditions -- Encyclopedias.

DS119.76.R83 1999
Rubin, Barry M.
The transformation of Palestinian politics: from revolution to state-building/ Barry Rubin. Cambridge, Mass.: Harvard University Press, 1999. xi, 288 p.
99-034447   321.09/095695/309049   0674000714
Arab-Israeli conflict -- 1993- -- Peace. Palestinian Arabs -- Politics and government. Palestinian National Authority.

DS119.8.J67.L85 1997
Lukacs, Yehuda.
Israel, Jordan, and the peace process/ Yehuda Lukacs. Syracuse, N.Y.: Syracuse University Press, 1997. xiv, 258 p.
96-020089   327.569405695   0815627203
Jewish-Arab relations -- 1967-1973. Jewish-Arab relations -- 1973- Israel -- Foreign relations -- Jordan. Jordan -- Foreign relations -- Israel.

DS119.8.L4.S38 1998
Schulze, Kirsten E.
Israel's covert diplomacy in Lebanon/ Kirsten E. Schulze. New York: St. Martin's Press, 1998. xiv, 213 p.
97-005484   327.5694045692   0333711238
Maronites -- Politics and government. Israel -- Foreign relations -- Lebanon. Lebanon -- History -- Israeli intervention, 1982-1984. Lebanon -- Foreign relations -- Israel.

DS119.8.S65.G6813 1998
Govrin, Yosef.
Israeli-Soviet relations, 1953-67: from confrontation to disruption/ Yosef Govrin. London; Frank Cass, 1998. xxxvi, 347 p.
97-045497   327.5694047   0714648728
Israel -- Foreign relations -- Soviet Union. Soviet Union -- Foreign relations -- Israel. Soviet Union -- Foreign relations -- 1953-1975.

DS119.8.S95.R33 1998
Rabinovich, Itamar, 1942-
The brink of peace: the Israeli-Syrian negotiations/ Itamar Rabinovich. Princeton, N.J.: Princeton University Press, c1998. xv, 283 p.
98-014418   327.56940569   0691058687
Rabinovich, Itamar, -- 1942- Arab-Israeli conflict -- 1993- -- Peace. Israel -- Foreign relations -- Syria. Syria -- Foreign relations -- Israel.

DS119.8.T9.N33 1987
Nachmani, Amikam.
Israel, Turkey, and Greece: uneasy relations in the East Mediterranean/ Amikam Nachmani. London; F. Cass, 1987. x, 130 p.
87-005144   327.560495   0714633216
Sasson, Eliahu, -- 1902-   Israel -- Foreign relations -- Turkey. Turkey -- Foreign relations -- Israel. Israel -- Foreign relations -- Greece.

DS121-128.2 Israel (Palestine). The Jews — History — By period

DS121.I87 1998
Isserlin, B. S. J.
The Israelites/ B.S.J. Isserlin. New York, N.Y.: Thames and Hudson, 1998. 304 p.
97-061347   933   0500050821
Jews -- History -- To 586 B.C. Jews -- Civilization. Palestine -- History -- To 70 A.D.

DS121.O4 1931
Olmstead, A. T. 1880-1945.
History of Palestine and Syria to the Macedonian conquest. New York, London, C. Scribner's sons, 1931. xxxii, 664 p.
31-032522   933   0837160340
Palestine -- History. Syria -- History.

DS121.T48 1992
Thompson, Thomas L.
Early history of the Israelite people: from the written and archaeological sources/ by Thomas L. Thompson. Leiden; Brill, 1992. xv, 489 p.
92-025804   939.4   9004094830
Jews -- History -- To 586 B.C. Jews -- History -- To 586 B.C. -- Historiography. Palestine -- History -- To 70 A.D. Palestine -- History -- To 70 A.D. -- Historiography.

DS121.4.T83 1998
Tubb, Jonathan N.
Canaanites/ Jonathan N. Tubb. Norman: University of Oklahoma Press, c1998. 160 p.
98-008841   933/.004926   080613108X
Canaanites -- History.

DS121.65.B53 1988
Bickerman, E. J. 1897-
The Jews in the Greek Age/ Elias J. Bickerman. Cambridge, Mass.: Harvard University Press, 1988. xii, 338 p.
87-023771   909/.04924   0674474902
Jews -- History -- 586 B.C.-70 A.D. Judaism -- History -- Post-exilic period, 586 B.C.-210 A.D. Jews -- Civilization -- Greek influences.

DS121.65.V36 2001
VanderKam, James C.
An introduction to early Judaism/ James C. VanderKam. Grand Rapids, Mich.: William B. Eerdmans, c2001. xii, 234 p.
00-063605   296/.09/014   0802846416
Judaism -- History -- Post-exilic period, 586 B.C.-210 A.D. Jews -- History -- 586 B.C.-70 A.D. Apocryphal books (Old Testament) -- Criticism, interpretation, etc.

DS121.7.S53 2001
Sicker, Martin.
Between Rome and Jerusalem: 300 years of Roman-Judaean relations/ Martin Sicker. Westport, Conn.: Praeger, 2001. xii, 201 p.
00-058009   933   0275971406
Jews -- History -- 168 B.C.-135 A.D. Jews -- History -- 70-638. Palestine -- History -- 70-638.

DS121.8.J8.B3713 1989
Bar-Kochva, Bezalel.
Judas Maccabeus: the Jewish struggle against the Seleucids/ Bezalel Bar-Kochva. Cambridge [Cambridgeshire]; Cambridge University Press, 1989. xvi, 672 p.
86-023212   933/.04/0924   0521323525
Judas, -- Maccabeus, -- d. 161 B.C. -- Military leadership. Jews -- History -- 168 B.C.-135 A.D. Seleucids. Jews -- Kings and rulers -- Biography. Palestine -- History, Military. Syria -- History, Military.

DS122.B66 1998
Bond, Helen K.
Pontius Pilate in history and interpretation/ Helen K. Bond. Cambridge; Cambridge University Press, 1998. xxvi, 249 p.
97-045970   933/.05/092   0521631149
Pilate, Pontius, -- 1st cent. Philo, -- of Alexandria - - Contributions in the biography of Pontius Pilate. Josephus, Flavius -- Contributions in the biography of Pontius Pilate. Governors -- Palestine -- Biography. Jews -- History -- 168 B.C.-135 A.D.

DS122.S422 1973
Schürer, Emil,
The history of the Jewish people in the age of Jesus Christ (175 B.C.-A.D. 135)/ by Emil Schürer; [translated by T. A. Burkill ... and others]; revised and edited by Geza Vermes & Fergus Millar. Edinburgh: Clark, 1973- v. <1-3 pt. 1-2 >
75-327141   933   0567022420
Jews--History--168 B.C.-135 A.D. Greek literature--Jewish authors--History and criticism. Judaism--History--Post-exilic period, 586 B.C.-210 A.D.

DS122.8.J83.J67 1982
Josephus, the Jewish war; newly translated with extensive commentary and archaeological background illustrations/ Gaalya Cornfeld, general editor; Benjamin Mazar, Paul L. Maier, consulting editors. Grand Rapids, Mich.: Zondervan Pub. House, c1982. 526 p.
82-001946   933   0310392101
Josephus, Flavius. -- De bello Judaico. Jews -- History -- Rebellion, 66-73. Jews -- History -- 168 B.C.-135 A.D.

DS122.9.A23 2000
Aberbach, Moses.
The Roman-Jewish wars and Hebrew cultural nationalism/ Moshe Aberbach, David Aberbach. New York: St. Martin's Press, 2000. xix, 170 p.
99-054791   909/.04924   0312231911
Jews -- History -- 168 B.C.-135 A.D. Jews -- History -- Rebellion, 66-73. Jews -- History -- Bar Kokhba Rebellion, 132-135.

DS122.9.Y3
Yadin, Yigael, 1917-1984.
Bar-Kokhba: the rediscovery of the legendary hero of the second Jewish revolt against Rome. Random House, 1971. 271 p.
76-152554   933   0394471849
Bar Kokhba, -- d. 135. Jews -- History -- Bar Kokhba Rebellion, 132-135. Masada Site (Israel) -- Siege, 72-73. Palestine -- Antiquities.

DS123.P35 1949a
Parkes, James William, 1896-
A history of Palestine from 135 A.D. to modern times. New York, Oxford Univ. Press, 1949. 391 p.
49-009004
Palestine -- History.

DS123. P68
Polk, William Roe, 1929-
Backdrop to tragedy; the struggle for Palestine, by William R. Polk, David Stamler, and Edmund Asfour. Boston, Beacon Press [1957] 399 p.
57-012743 956.94*
Zionism. Palestinian Arabs. Palestine -- History.

DS124.C43 1997
Chazan, Robert.
Medieval stereotypes and modern antisemitism/ Robert Chazan. Berkeley: University of California Press, c1997. xiii, 189 p.
96-029259 909/.04924 0520203941
Jews -- History -- 70-1789. Antisemitism -- History. Judaism -- Controversial literature -- History and criticism.

DS124.F6213 2000
Foa, Anna.
The Jews of Europe after the black death/ Anna Foa; translated from the Italian by Andrea Grover. Berkeley: University of California Press, c2000. xii, 276 p.
00-022315 909/.04924 0520087658
Jews -- History -- 70-1789. Jews -- Europe -- History. Europe -- Ethnic relations.

DS124.G37 2001
Gartner, Lloyd P., 1927-
History of the Jews in modern times/ Lloyd P. Gartner. Oxford; Oxford University Press, 2001. xi, 468 p.
00-044622 909/.0492408 0192892592
Jews -- History -- 1789-1945. Jews -- History -- 1945- Judaism -- History -- Modern period, 1750-

DS124.R625 1992
Roth, Cecil,
A history of the Marranos/ by Cecil Roth.5th ed. New York: Sepher-Hermon Press, 1992. xxiv, 424 p.
93-116552 0872031381
Marranos--History. Inquisition--Spain.

DS125.I35 1998
Idinopulos, Thomas A.
Weathered by miracles: a history of Palestine from Bonaparte and Muhammad Ali to Ben-Gurion and the mufti/ Thomas A. Idinopulos. Chicago: Ivan R. Dee, 1998. xiv, 283 p.
98-014411 956.94/03 1566631890
Jewish-Arab relations. Palestine -- History -- 1917-1948. Palestine -- History -- 1799-1917. Palestine -- Ethnic relations.

DS125.S284 1988
Sanders, Ronald.
Shores of refuge: a hundred years of Jewish emigration/ Ronald Sanders. New York: Holt, c1988. xiii, 673 p.
87-010923 973/.04924 0805005633
Jews -- Persecutions -- Soviet Union. Jews, East European -- United States. Immigrants -- United States. Soviet Union -- Emigration and immigration. United States -- Emigration and immigration. Soviet Union -- Ethnic relations.

DS125.3.B37.A5 1967
Ben-Gurion, David, 1886-1973.
Days of David Ben-Gurion, seen in photographs and with text from his speeches and writings. Edited by Ohad Zmora [and others] Design: Eliezer Weishoff. Introd. by S. Y. Agnon. New York, Grossman, 1967. 157 p.
67-015209 956.94/05/0924
Ben-Gurion, David, -- 1886-1973.

DS125.3.B37.G3513 1991
Gal, Allon.
David Ben-Gurion and the American alignment for a Jewish state/ Allon Gal; [translated from the Hebrew, David S. Segal]. Bloomington: Indiana University Press; c1991. 280 p.
91-018446 956.94/05/092 025332534X
Ben-Gurion, David, -- 1886-1973 -- Relations with American Jews. Jews -- United States -- Politics and government. Zionism -- United States. Prime ministers -- Israel -- Biography. Palestine -- Politics and government -- 1917-1948.

DS125.3.H79.M37 1988
Mattar, Philip, 1944-
The Mufti of Jerusalem: Al-Hajj Amin al-Husayni and the Palestinian national movement/ Philip Mattar. New York: Columbia University Press, 1988. xiv, 158 p.
87-033314 956.94/4 0231064624
Husayni, Amin, -- Grand Mufti of Jerusalem, -- 1893-1974. Palestinian Arabs -- Biography. Politicians -- Palestine -- Biography. Jewish-Arab relations -- 1917-1949. Palestine -- History -- 1917-1948.

DS125.3.L4.A3
Levin, Meyer, 1905-
In search, an autobiography. New York, Horizon Press, 1950. 524 p.
50-004306 296
Jews -- Palestine. Jews -- Political and social conditions. Palestine -- Politics and government. -- cm

DS125.3.W45.R44 1993
Reinharz, Jehuda.
Chaim Weizmann: the making of a statesman/ Jehuda Reinharz. New York: Oxford University Press, 1993. xii, 536 p.
91-030376 320.5/4/095694092 0195072154
Weizmann, Chaim, -- 1874-1952. Zionism -- History. Presidents -- Israel -- Biography. Zionists -- Great Britain -- Biography. Great Britain -- Biography.

DS125.5.F73 1973b
Friedman, Isaiah.
The question of Palestine, 1914-1918; British-Jewish-Arab relations. New York, Schocken Books [1973] xiii, 433 p.
73-080510 956.94/001 0805235248
Zionism -- Great Britain. Great Britain -- Foreign relations -- Middle East. Middle East -- Foreign relations -- Great Britain. Middle East -- History -- 1914-1923.

DS126.B375 1977
Begin, Menachem, 1913-
The revolt/ Menachem Begin. New York: Nash Pub. Co., c1977. xxvii, 386 p.
77-010806 956.94/04/0924 0840213700
Begin, Menachem, -- 1913- Prime ministers -- Israel -- Biography. Palestine -- History -- 1929-1948.

DS126.F76 2000
Friedman, Isaiah.
Palestine, a twice-promised land?/ Isaiah Friedman. New Brunswick, N.J.: Transaction Publishers, c2000. v. 1
99-030396 327.41056/09/041 156000391X
Jewish-Arab relations -- History -- 1917-1948. Palestine -- Politics and government -- 1917-1948. Palestine -- History -- 1917-1948. Great Britain -- Foreign relations -- Middle East.

DS126.K38 1998
Kats, Yosef.
Partner to partition: the Jewish Agency's partition plan in the mandate era/ Yossi Katz. London; Frank Cass, 1998. xii, 209 p.
97-028250 956.94/04 0714648469
Zionism -- Palestine -- History. Palestine -- History -- Proposed partition, 1937.

DS126.K65 1993
Kolinsky, Martin.
Law, order, and riots in mandatory Palestine, 1928-35/ Martin Kolinsky. New York: St. Martin's Press, 1993. xx, 295 p.
92-034580 956.94/04 0312091648
Jews -- Palestine -- Politics and government. Palestinian Arabs -- Politics and government. Jewish-Arab relations -- History -- 1917-1948. Palestine -- History -- Arab riots, 1929. Palestine -- Politics and government -- 1917-1948.

DS126.L37
Lesch, Ann Mosely.
Arab politics in Palestine, 1917-1939: the frustration of a nationalist movement/ Ann Mosely Lesch. Ithaca, N.Y.: Cornell University Press, c1979. 257 p.
78-032059 956.94/04 0801412374
Palestinian Arabs -- Politics and government. Palestine -- Politics and government -- 1917-1948.

DS126.S287
Samuel, Maurice, 1895-1972.
Level sunlight. New York, Knopf, 1953. 302 p.
53-009475 956.94
Weizmann, Chaim, -- President of Israel, 1874-1952. Zionism. Palestine -- History -- 1948-

DS126.S447 1998
Sherman, A. J.
Mandate days: British lives in Palestine, 1918-1948/ A.J. Sherman. New York, N.Y.: Thames and Hudson, 1998. 264 p.
97-060324 956.94/04 0500251169
British -- Palestine. Palestine -- History -- 1917-1948. Great Britain -- Foreign relations -- 1917-1948.

DS126.4.C645 1982
Cohen, Michael Joseph, 1940-
Palestine and the Great Powers, 1945-1948/ Michael J. Cohen. Princeton: Princeton University Press, c1982. viii, 417 p.
82-003858 956.94/04 0691053715
Palestine -- History -- Partition, 1947.

DS126.4.E86 1992
Evensen, Bruce J.
Truman, Palestine, and the press: shaping conventional wisdom at the beginning of the Cold War/ Bruce J. Evensen. New York: Greenwood Press, 1992. 243 p.
91-030604 956.94 0313277737
Public opinion -- United States. United States -- Foreign relations -- Palestine. Palestine -- Foreign relations -- United States. United States -- Foreign relations -- 1945-1953.

DS126.4.F57 1987
Flapan, Simha.
The birth of Israel: myths and realities/ Simha Flapan. New York: Pantheon Books, c1987. x, 277 p.
86-042985 956.94/05
Palestine -- History -- Partition, 1947. Israel -- History -- 1948-1949.

DS126.4.P57 1986
Podet, Allen Howard.
The success and failure of the Anglo-American Committee of Inquiry, 1945-1946: last chance in Palestine/ Allen Howard Podet. Lewiston, N.Y., USA: E. Mellen Press, c1986. 381 p.
87-001635   327.73041   0889462550
Holocaust survivors. Jewish-Arab relations -- 1917-1949. Great Britain -- Foreign relations -- United States. United States -- Foreign relations -- Great Britain. United States -- Foreign relations -- 1945-1953.

DS126.4.R6
Robinson, Jacob, 1889-
Palestine and the United Nations; prelude to solution. Washington, Public Affairs Press [1947] viii, 269 p.
47-011828   956.9
Palestine -- Politics and government.

DS126.5.A914 1990
Avishai, Bernard.
A new Israel: democracy in crisis, 1973-1988: essays/ Bernard Avishai. New York: Ticknor & Fields, 1990. xxiv, 420 p.
89-020674   320.95694/09/047   0899199666
Jewish-Arab relations -- 1973- Jews -- United States -- Attitudes toward Israel. Israel -- Politics and government.

DS126.5.E48 1989
The Emergence of a binational Israel: the second republic in the making/ edited by Ilan Peleg and Ofira Seliktar. Boulder: Westview Press, 1989. x, 243 p.
88-038580   320.95694   0813375282
Palestinian Arabs -- Israel -- Politics and government. Jewish-Arab relations -- 1973- Israel -- Politics and government.

DS126.5.G357 1997
Garfinkle, Adam M., 1951-
Politics and society in modern Israel: myths and realities/ Adam Garfinkle. Armonk, N.Y.: M.E. Sharpe, c1997. xii, 322 p.
96-035070   320.95694   0765600056
National characteristics, Israeli -- Anecdotes. Israel -- Social conditions. Israel -- Foreign relations. Israel -- Politics and government.

DS126.5.H357213 1988
Harkabi, Yehoshafat, 1921-
Israel's fateful hour/ Yehoshafat Harkabi; translated by Lenn Schramm. New York: Harper & Row, c1988. xxiv, 256 p.
88-045513   956.94   006016039X
Begin, Menachem, -- 1913- Jewish-Arab relations -- 1973- Israel-Arab conflicts. Religious Zionism. Israel -- Politics and government.

DS126.5.H58 1998
Hohenberg, John.
Israel at 50: a journalist's perspective/ John Hohenberg. Syracuse, N.Y.: Syracuse University Press, 1998. xiv, 356 p.
97-051946   956.9405   0815605188
Israel -- History.

DS126.5.I7 1987
Yishai, Yael, 1933-
Land or peace: whither Israel?/ Yael Yishai. Stanford, Calif.: Hoover Institution Press, c1987. xxii, 265 p.
86-033747   320.95694   0817985212
Israel-Arab War, 1967 -- Occupied territories. Political parties -- Israel. Israel -- Politics and government.

DS126.5.P62 1993
Political dictionary of the State of Israel/ Susan Hattis Rolef, editor. New York: Macmillan; 1993. p. cm.
93-020521   320.95694/03   0028971930
Israel -- Politics and government -- Dictionaries.

DS126.5.R385 2000
Reich, Bernard.
Political dictionary of Israel/ Bernard Reich and David H. Goldberg. Lanham, Md.: Scarecrow Press, 2000. cv, 448 p.
00-021979   956.94/003   0810837781
Israel -- Politics and government -- Dictionaries. Israel -- History -- Dictionaries.

DS126.5.T495 1999
Thomas, Baylis, 1932-
How Israel was won: a concise history of the Arab-Israeli conflict/ Baylis Thomas. Lanham, Md.: Lexington Books, c1999. xviii, 326 p.
99-010673   956.94   0739100637
Arab-Israeli conflict. Israel -- History. Palestine -- History -- 1917-1948. Israel -- Politics and government.

DS126.6.A2.B74 1998
Brenner, Frederic, 1959-
Exile at home/ photographs by Frederic Brenner; poems by Yehuda Amichai = Galut bayit. New York, NY: Harry N. Abrams, 1998. 77 p.
98-190119   779/.93058924   0810932695
Brenner, Frederic, -- 1959- -- Themes, motives. Photography, Artistic. Israelis -- Portraits. Israel -- Biography.

DS126.6.D3.A35
Dayan, Moshe, 1915-1981.
Moshe Dayan: story of my life/ by Moshe Dayan. New York: Morrow, 1976. 640 p.
76-018144   956.94/05/0924   0688030769
Dayan, Moshe, -- 1915-1981. Statesmen -- Israel -- Biography. Generals -- Israel -- Biography. Israel -- Armed Forces -- Biography.

DS126.6.E2.A32
Eban, Abba Solomon, 1915-
Abba Eban: an autobiography.   New York: Random House, c1977. xii, 628 p.
77-006003   956.94/05/0924   0394493028
Eban, Abba Solomon, -- 1915- Statesmen -- Israel -- Biography. Israel -- Foreign relations.

DS126.6.M42.A37 1975
Meir, Golda, 1898-1978.
My life/ by Golda Meir. New York: Putnam, 1975. 480 p.
75-025620   956.94/05/0924   0399116699
Meir, Golda -- 1898-1978. Women prime ministers -- Israel -- Biography. Zionists -- Biography.

DS126.6.P47.A5 1998
Peres, Shimon, 1923-
For the future of Israel/ Shimon Peres and Robert Littell. Baltimore, Md.: Johns Hopkins University Press, 1998. xiv, 206 p.
97-047041   956.9405/092   080185928X
Peres, Shimon, -- 1923- -- Interviews. Statesmen -- Israel -- Interviews. Arab-Israeli conflict. Israel -- Politics and government.

DS126.6.R32
The assassination of Yitzhak Rabin/ edited by Yoram Peri. Stanford, CA: Stanford University Press, c2000. viii, 386 p.
00-024100   956.9405/4   0804738351
Rabin, Yitzhak, -- 1922- -- Assassination. Right-wing extremists -- Israel. Israel -- Politics and government -- 1993-

DS126.92.I425 1996
Ilan, Amitzur, 1932-
The origin of the Arab-Israeli arms race: arms, embargo, military power and decision in the 1948 Palestine war/ Amitzur Ilan. New York: New York University Press, c1996. xiii, 287 p.
95-002923   956.04/2   0814737587
Israel-Arab War, 1948-1949 -- Diplomatic history. Arms race -- Middle East -- History -- 20th century.

DS126.93.G7.P36 1988
Pappe, Ilan.
Britain and the Arab-Israeli conflict, 1948-51/ Ilan Pappe. New York: St. Martin's Press, 1988. xxi, 273 p.
87-022509   0312015739
Israel-Arab War, 1948-1949 -- Diplomatic history. Great Britain -- Foreign relations -- Jordan. Jordan -- Foreign relations -- Great Britain.

DS126.954.B46 2000
Benvenisti, Meron, 1934-
Sacred landscape: the buried history of the Holy Land since 1948/ Meron Benvenisti; translated by Maxine Kaufman-Lacusta. Berkeley: University of California Press, 2000. 366 p.
99-037874   956.04/2   0520211545
Israel-Arab War, 1948-1949 -- Refugees. Names, Geographical -- Israel -- History. Arab-Israeli conflict -- Social aspects. Israel -- Historical geography. Israel -- Ethnic relations.

DS126.99.J6.B37 1987
Bar-Joseph, Uri.
The best of enemies: Israel and Transjordan in the war of 1948/ Uri Bar-Joseph. London; F. Cass, 1987. x, 254 p.
86-031715   956/.042   0714632112
Israel-Arab War, 1948-1949 -- Jordan. Israel-Arab War, 1948-1949 -- Armistices. Israel -- Foreign relations -- Jordan. Jordan -- Foreign relations -- Israel.

DS128.1.H467 1975
Herzog, Chaim, 1918-
The War of Atonement, October, 1973/ Chaim Herzog. Boston: Little, Brown, [1975] viii, 300 p.
75-016118   956/.048   0316359009
Israel-Arab War, 1973.

DS128.183.Q36 1986
Quandt, William B.
Camp David: peacemaking and politics/ William B. Quandt. Washington, D.C.: Brookings Institution, c1986. xvi, 426 p.
85-048174   327.73056   0815772904
Israel-Arab War, 1973 -- Peace. United States -- Foreign relations -- Middle East. Middle East -- Foreign relations -- United States. United States -- Foreign relations -- 1977-1981.

DS128.2.F76 1997
From Rabin to Netanyahu: Israel's troubled agenda/ edited by Efraim Karsh. Portland, OR: Frank Cass, 1997. p. cm.
97-023517   956.9404/4   0714648310
Rabin, Yitzhak, -- 1922- Netanyahu, Binyamin. Jews -- Israel -- Identity. Arab-Israeli conflict -- 1993- National characteristics, Israeli. Israel -- Politics and government -- 1993-

DS132 Israel (Palestine). The Jews — Special topics — The Jewish state and Jews outside of Palestine. Israel and the diaspora

DS132.B3413 2000
Beilin, Yossi.
His brother's keeper: Israel and Diaspora Jewry in the twenty-first century/ Yossi Beilin. New York: Schocken Books, c2000. xxxvi, 232 p.
99-089429   305.892/4   0805241752
Israel and the diaspora. Jewish diaspora. Jews -- Attitudes toward Israel.

DS134-151 Israel (Palestine). The Jews — Special topics — Jews outside of Palestine

DS134.W48 1996
Wexler, Paul.
The non-Jewish origins of the Sephardic Jews/ Paul Wexler. Albany: State University of New York Press, c1996. xviii, 321 p.
95-022275   946/.004924   0791427951
Sephardim -- Origin. Jews -- Spain -- Origin. Jews -- Africa, North -- Origin. Africa, North -- Social life and customs. Spain -- Ethnic relations.

DS135.A25.L36 1994
Laskier, Michael M., 1949-
North African Jewry in the twentieth century: the Jews of Morocco, Tunisia, and Algeria/ Michael M. Laskier. New York: New York University Press, c1994. xiv, 400 p.
93-029377   961/.004924   0814750729
Jews -- Africa, North -- History -- 20th century. Africa, North -- Ethnic relations.

DS135.A68.J47 1996
Jews among Muslims: communities in the precolonial MiddleEast/ edited by Shlomo Deshen and Walter P. Zenner. New York: New York University Press, 1996. ix, 292 p.
96-030595   956/.004924   0814796753
Jews -- Arab countries. Arab countries -- Ethnic relations.

DS135.A9.G55 1998
Gilman, Sander L.
Love+marriage=death: and other essays on representing difference/ Sander L. Gilman. Stanford, Calif.: Stanford University Press, c1998. vi, 247 p.
98-023979   305.8924   0804732612
Jews -- Austria -- Intellectual life. Ethnicity. Jews in literature. Austria -- Intellectual life -- 20th century.

DS135.A9.M34 1989
McCagg, William O.
A history of Habsburg Jews, 1670-1918/ William O. McCagg, Jr. Bloomington: Indiana University Press, c1989. xi, 289 p.
88-000544   943.6/004924   0253331897
Jews -- Austria -- History. Jews -- Cultural assimilation -- Austria. Jews -- Hungary -- History. Austria -- Ethnic relations. Hungary -- Ethnic relations.

DS135.A9.R69 2001
Rozenblit, Marsha L., 1950-
Reconstructing a national identity: the Jews of Habsburg Austria during World War I/ Marsha L. Rozenblit. New York: Oxford University Press, 2001. xiv, 252 p.
99-053423   943.6/0049424   0195134656
Jews -- Austria -- History. Jews -- Austria -- Identity. Jews -- Cultural assimilation -- Austria. Austria -- Ethnic relations.

DS135.A92.V5214 1988
Berkley, George E.
Vienna and its Jews: the tragedy of success: 1880s-1980s/ George E. Berkley. Cambridge, MA: Abt Books; c1988. xxi, 422 p.
88-001521   943.6/13004924   0819168165
Jews -- Austria -- Vienna -- History. Vienna (Austria) -- Ethnic relations.

DS135.A92.V543 1987
Jews, antisemitism, and culture in Vienna/ edited by Ivar Oxaal, Michael Pollak, and Gerhard Botz. London; Routledge & Kegan Paul, 1987. xiv, 300 p.
87-004756   943.6/004924   0710208995
Jews -- Austria -- Vienna -- History -- 20th century. Antisemitism -- Austria -- Vienna. Jews -- Austria -- Vienna -- Intellectual life. Vienna (Austria) -- Ethnic relations.

DS135.A92.V583 1989
Wistrich, Robert S., 1945-
The Jews of Vienna in the age of Franz Joseph/ Robert S. Wistrich. Oxford; Published for the Littman Library by Oxford Univ 1989. xiv, 696 p.
88-006618   943.6/13004924   0197100708
Jews -- Austria -- Vienna -- History. Jews -- Austria -- Vienna -- Intellectual life. Zionism -- Austria -- Vienna -- History. Vienna (Austria) -- Intellectual life. Vienna (Austria) -- Ethnic relations.

DS135.A93.W53913 1989
Wiesenthal, Simon.
Justice, not vengeance/ Simon Wiesenthal; translated from the German by Ewald Osers. New York: Grove Weidenfeld, c1989. xi, 372 p.
89-023283   940.53/18/092   0802112781
Wiesenthal, Simon. Holocaust survivors -- Austria -- Vienna -- Biography. War criminals. War crime trials. Vienna (Austria) -- Biography.

DS135.B8.H37 1994
Haskell, Guy H., 1956-
From Sofia to Jaffa: the Jews of Bulgaria and Israel/ Guy H. Haskell; foreword by Raphael Patai. Detroit, Mich.: Wayne State University Press, c1994. 235 p.
94-012661   304.8/569404977/089924   0814325025
Jews -- Bulgaria -- History. Jews -- Bulgaria -- Folklore. Folklore -- Bulgaria. Bulgaria -- Ethnic relations. Bulgaria -- Social life and customs. Israel -- Ethnic relations.

DS135.B85.A75313 1998
Arie, Gabriel, 1863-1939.
A Sephardi life in Southeastern Europe: the autobiography and journal of Gabriel Arie, 1863-1939/ edited by Esther Benbassa and Aron Rodrigue; translated by Jane Marie Todd. Seattle: University of Washington Press, c1998. xv, 317 p.
97-033415   949.9/004924/0092   0295976748
Arie, Gabriel, -- 1863-1939. Jews -- Bulgaria -- Sofia -- Biography. Sephardim -- Bulgaria -- Sofia -- Biography. Sofia (Bulgaria) -- Biography.

DS135.C5.P6
Pollak, Michael, 1918-
Mandarins, Jews, and missionaries: the Jewish experience in the Chinese Empire/ Michael Pollak. Philadelphia: Jewish Publication Society of America, 1980. xviii, 436 p.
79-084732   951/.004/924   0827601204
Jews -- China -- History. Missions -- China. China -- History.

DS135.C5.R69 2001
Zhou, Xun.
Chinese perceptions of the 'Jews' and Judaism: a history of the Youtai/ Zhou Xun. Richmond, Surrey, [England]: Curzon, 2001. x, 202 p.
305.8924051   0700712496
Jews -- China. Public opinion -- China. Jews -- Public opinion.

DS135.C95.K54 2000
Kieval, Hillel J.
Languages of community: the Jewish experience in the Czech lands/ Hillel J. Kieval. Berkeley: University of California Press, 2000. xi, 311 p.
99-053814   943.71/004924   0520214102
Jews -- Czech Republic -- Intellectual life -- 18th century. Jews -- Czech Republic -- Intellectual life -- 19th century. Jews -- Identity. Czech Republic -- Ethnic relations.

DS135.C95.P65 1999
Pollatschek, Henriette, b. 1870.
A thousand kisses: a grandmother's Holocaust letters/ translated and edited by Renata Polt. Tuscaloosa: University of Alabama Press, c1999. xvii, 210 p.
98-009066   940.53/18/094371   0817309306
Pollatschek, Henriette, -- b. 1870 -- Correspondence. Jews -- Persecutions -- Czech Republic. Holocaust, Jewish (1939-1945) -- Czech Republic -- Personal narratives. Czech Republic -- Ethnic relations.

DS135.C96.B638 1988
Kieval, Hillel J.
The making of Czech Jewry: national conflict and Jewish society in Bohemia, 1870-1918/ Hillel J. Kieval. New York: Oxford University Press, 1988. viii, 279 p.
87-001597   305.8/924/04371   0195040570
Jews -- Cultural assimilation -- Czech Republic -- Bohemia. Zionism -- Czech Republic -- Prague. Bohemia (Czech Republic) -- Ethnic relations.

DS135.D4.R47 1987
The Rescue of the Danish Jews: moral courage under stress/ Leo Goldberger, editor. New York: New York University Press, c1987. xxvii, 222 p.
87-011253   948.9/004924   0814730108
Jews -- Denmark -- History -- 20th century. World War, 1939-1945 -- Jews -- Rescue -- Denmark. Denmark -- Ethnic relations.

DS135.E4.B45 1998
Beinin, Joel, 1948-
The dispersion of Egyptian Jewry: culture, politics, and the formation of a modern diaspora/ Joel Beinin. Berkeley: University of California Press, c1998. xii, 329 p.
97-028043   962/.004924   0520211758
Jews -- Egypt -- History -- 20th century. Jews -- Egypt -- Politics and government. Operation Susanna. Egypt -- Ethnic relations.

DS135.E5.B56 1988
Black, Eugene Charlton.
The social politics of Anglo-Jewry, 1880-1920/ Eugene C. Black. Oxford, UK; B. Blackwell, 1988. xi, 428 p.
88-019315   305.8/924/041   063116491X
Jews -- Great Britain -- Politics and government. Jews -- Great Britain -- Societies, etc. Great Britain -- Ethnic relations.

DS135.E5.E49 1990
Endelman, Todd M.
Radical assimilation in English Jewish history, 1656-1945/ Todd M. Endelman. Bloomington: Indiana University Press, c1990. viii, 246 p.
89-045475   941/.004924   0253319528
Jews -- Great Britain -- History. Jews -- Cultural assimilation -- Great Britain. Judaism -- Great Britain -- History. Great Britain -- Ethnic relations.

DS135.E5.F5 1975
Fishman, William J.
Jewish radicals: from Czarist stetl to London ghetto/ by William J. Fishman. New York: Pantheon Books, [1975] c1974. xvi, 336 p.
74-026194   914.21/06/924   0394497643
Ish Chamodot, Daniel, -- 1845-1880. Rocker, Rudolf, -- 1873-1958. Jews -- England -- London. Jewish radicals -- England -- London. East End (London, England)

DS135.E5.L46 1990
Lipman, V. D. 1921-
A history of the Jews in Britain since 1858/ V.D. Lipman. New York: Holmes & Meier, 1990. xvi, 274 p.
90-004865   941/.004924   0841912882
Jews -- Great Britain -- History. Great Britain -- Ethnic relations.

DS135.E5.L66 2000
London, Louise.
Whitehall and the Jews, 1933-1948: British immigration policy, Jewish refugees, and the Holocaust/ Louise London. New York, NY: Cambridge University Press, 2000. xiii, 313 p.
99-024282   325.41/089/924   0521631874
Refugees, Jewish -- Great Britain. Refugees, Jewish -- Government policy -- Great Britain. Holocaust, Jewish (1939-1945) -- Foreign public opinion, British. Great Britain -- Emigration and immigration.

DS135.E5.R62
Roth, Cecil, 1899-1970.
A history of the Jews in England, by Cecil Roth. Oxford, The Clarendon Press, 1941. xii, 306 p.
42-011942   296.0942
Jews in Great Britain.

DS135.E5.S56 1999
Sompolinsky, Meier.
Britain and the Holocaust: the failure of Anglo-Jewish leadership?/ Meier Sompolinsky. Portland, Or.: Sussex Academic Press, 1999. p. cm.
98-041178   940.53/18   1902210093
Jews -- Great Britain -- Politics and government. Holocaust, Jewish (1939-1945) -- Foreign public opinion, British. Great Britain -- Politics and government -- 1936-1945. Great Britain -- Ethnic relations.

DS135.E75.K35 1992
Kaplan, Steven.
The Beta Israel (Falasha) in Ethiopia: from earliest times to the twentieth century/ Steven Kaplan. New York: New York University Press, c1992. xi, 231 p.
92-001175   963/.004924   081474625X
Jews -- Ethiopia -- History. Ethiopia -- Ethnic relations.

DS135.E8.E45 2001
The Encyclopedia of Jewish life before and during the Holocaust/ edited by Shmuel Spector, Geoffrey Wigoder; forward by Ellie Wiesel. New York: New York University Press, 2001. p. cm.
01-030771   940/.04924   0814793568
Jews -- Europe -- History -- Encyclopedias. Jews -- Africa, North -- Encyclopedias. Holocaust, Jewish (1939-1945) -- Encyclopedias. Europe -- History, Local. Africa, North -- History, Local.

DS135.E81.E38 1988
Edwards, John, 1949-
The Jews in Christian Europe, 1400-1700/ John Edwards. London; Routledge, 1988. x, 190 p.
88-000731   940/.004924   0415008646
Jews -- Europe -- History. Judaism -- Relations -- Christianity. Christianity and other religions -- Judaism. Europe -- Ethnic relations.

DS135.E83.P46 2001
Penslar, Derek Jonathan.
Shylock's children: economics and Jewish identity in modern Europe/ Derek J. Penslar. Berkeley: University of California Press, 2001. p. cm.
00-048894   940/.04924   0520225902
Jews -- Europe -- Economic conditions. Jews -- Europe -- Public opinion. Public opinion -- Europe. Europe -- Economic conditions.

DS135.E83.R4 1953
Reitlinger, Gerald, 1900-
The final solution; the attempt to exterminate the Jews of Europe, 1939-1945/ Gerald Reitlinger. New York: Beechhurst Press, 1953. xii, 622 p.
53-013001   940.5315296
Holocaust, Jewish -- 1939-1945 -- Europe. Jews -- Europe. World War, 1939-1945 -- Jews. Germany -- Politics and government -- 1933-1945.

DS135.E9.A13 1967
Dawidowicz, Lucy S.
The golden tradition; Jewish life and thought in Eastern Europe [edited by] Lucy S. Dawidowicz. New York, Holt, Rinehart and Winston [1967] 502 p.
66-013203   947/.0004924
Jews -- Europe, Eastern -- Biography. Jews -- Europe, Eastern -- Intellectual life. Judaism -- Europe, Eastern. Europe, Eastern -- Ethnic relations.

DS135.F8.H96 1998
Hyman, Paula, 1946-
The Jews of modern France/ Paula E. Hyman. Berkeley: University of California Press, c1998. xii, 283 p.
97-039349   944/.004924   0520209249
Jews -- France -- History. France -- Ethnic relations.

DS135.F82.H4
Hertzberg, Arthur.
The French Enlightenment and the Jews. New York, Columbia University Press, 1968. viii, 420 p.
68-018996   301.45/296/044
Jews -- France -- History -- 18th century. Jews -- France -- Social conditions. Enlightenment -- France. France -- Ethnic relations.

DS135.F82.S38
Schwarzfuchs, Simon.
Napoleon, the Jews, and the Sanhedrin/ Simon Schwarzfuchs. London; Routledge & Kegan Paul, 1979. xii, 218 p.
78-040812   323.1/19/24044   0710089554
Napoleon -- I, -- Emperor of the French, -- 1769-1821 -- Relations with Jews. Jews -- Emancipation -- France. France -- History -- 1789-1815.

DS135.F83.C366 1999
Caron, Vicki, 1951-
Uneasy asylum: France and the Jewish refugee crisis, 1933-42/ Vicki Caron. Stanford, CA: Stanford University Press, 1999. p. cm.
98-036350   944/.004924   0804733120
Jews -- France -- History -- 20th century. Refugees, Jewish -- zFrance -- History -- 20th century. Refugees, Jewish -- Government policy -- France. France -- Ethnic relations.

DS135.F83.F75 1990
Friedlander, Judith, 1944-
Vilna on the Seine: Jewish intellectuals in France since 1968/ Judith Friedlander. New Haven: Yale University Press, c1990. xv, 249 p.
90-031502   944/.004924   0300047037
Jews -- France -- Intellectual life. Intellectuals -- France. Jewish learning and scholarship -- France. France -- Civilization -- Jewish influences. France -- Intellectual life.

DS135.F83.K43313 1996
Klarsfeld, Serge, 1935-
French children of the Holocaust: a memorial/ Serge Klarsfeld; edited by Susan Cohen, Howard M. Epstein, Serge Klarsfeld; translated by Glorianne Depondt, Howard M. Epstein. New York: New York University Press, c1996. xxi, 1881 p.
96-031206   940.53/18/083   0814726623
Jews -- Persecutions -- France. Holocaust, Jewish (1939-1945) -- France. Jewish children -- France. France -- Ethnic relations.

DS135.F83.M3813
Marrus, Michael Robert.
Vichy France and the Jews/ Michael R. Marrus and Robert O. Paxton. New York: Basic Books, c1981. xvi, 432 p.
80-070307   940.53/15039240944   0465090052
Jews -- Persecutions -- France. Holocaust, Jewish (1939-1945) -- France. World War, 1939-1945 -- Deportations from France. France -- Politics and government -- 1940-1945. France -- Ethnic relations.

DS135.F83.S84 1997
Strenski, Ivan.
Durkheim and the Jews of France/ Ivan Strenski. Chicago: University of Chicago Press, c1997. ix, 215 p.
96-047904   305.892/4044   0226777235
Durkheim, Emile, -- 1858-1917.   Jews -- France -- Intellectual life.   France -- Intellectual life -- 19th century.   France -- Intellectual life -- 20th century. France -- Ethnic relations.

DS135.F83.Z83 1993
Zuccotti, Susan, 1940-
The Holocaust, the French, and the Jews/ Susan Zuccotti. New York, NY: BasicBooks, c1993. xv, 383 p.
92-054519   940.53/18/0944   0465030343
Jews -- Persecutions -- France.   Holocaust, Jewish (1939-1945) -- France.   France -- Ethnic relations.

DS135.F85.M377 1990
Shatzmiller, Joseph.
Shylock reconsidered: Jews, moneylending, and medieval society/ Joseph Shatzmiller. Berkeley: University of California Press, c1990. viii, 255 p.
89-004970   332.7/43/089924044912   0520066359
Bondavid, -- of Draguinan -- Trials, litigation, etc. Jews -- France -- Marseille -- Economic conditions.   Debtor and creditor -- France -- Marseille -- History.   Jewish bankers -- France -- Marseille -- History.   Marseille (France) -- Ethnic relations.

DS135.F85.N675 1998
Golb, Norman.
The Jews in medieval Normandy: a social and intellectual history/ Norman Golb. New York: Cambridge University Press, 1998. xxxii, 621 p.
97-003092   944/.2004924   0521580323
Jews -- France -- Normandy -- History. Normandy (France) -- History -- To 1515. Normandy (France) -- Ethnic relations.

DS135.F9.B5713 1996
Birnbaum, Pierre.
The Jews of the Republic: a political history of state Jews in France from Gambetta to Vichy/ Pierre Birnbaum; translated by Jane Marie Todd. Stanford, Calif.: Stanford University Press, 1996. 449 p.
96-010603   944/.004924   0804726337
Jews in public life -- France -- Biography.   Jews -- France -- Biography.   Jews -- France -- History. France -- Politics and government -- 1870-1940. France -- Ethnic relations.

DS135.G3.G32 1992
Gay, Ruth.
The Jews of Germany: a historical portrait/ Ruth Gay; with an introduction by Peter Gay. New Haven: Yale University Press, c1992. xiii, 297 p.
91-030235   943/.004924   0300051557
Jews -- Germany -- History.   Germany -- Ethnic relations.

DS135.G31.C53 2000
Chazan, Robert.
God, humanity, and history: the Hebrew First Crusade narratives/ Robert Chazan. Berkeley, CA: University of California Press, c2000. xi, 270 p.
99-050352   943/.004924   0520221273
Jews -- Germany -- History -- 1096-1147 -- Sources.   Jews -- Persecutions -- Germany -- History -- Sources.   Jewish martyrs -- Germany -- Biography -- Sources.   Germany -- Ethnic relations -- Sources.

DS135.G31.K58
Kisch, Guido, 1889-
The Jews in medieval Germany; a study of their legal and social status. Chicago, Univ. of Chicago Press, [c1949] xxviii, 655 p.
49-010741   296   87068017X
Jews in Germany -- History -- 1096-1800 Jews -- Legal status, laws, etc. -- Germany.

DS135.G32.B48 1996
German-Jewish history in modern times/ edited by Michael A. Meyer, Michael Brenner, assistant editor. New York: Columbia University Press, c1996-c1998. 4 v.
96-013900   943/.004924   0231074727
Jews -- Germany -- History.   Judaism -- Germany -- History.   Haskalah -- Germany -- History. Germany -- Ethnic relations.

DS135.G33.B74 1996
Brenner, Michael.
The renaissance of Jewish culture in Weimar Germany/ Michael Brenner. New Haven, Conn.: Yale University Press, c1996. xi, 306 p.
95-030449   943/.004924   0300062621
Jews -- Germany -- Intellectual life.   Germany -- Intellectual life -- 20th century.

DS135.G33.G8
Grunfeld, Frederic V.
Prophets without honour: a background to Freud, Kafka, Einstein, and their world/ Frederic V.Grunfeld. New York: Holt, Rinehart and Winston, c1979. xiii, 349 p.
78-031645   943/.004/924   0030178711
Jews -- Germany -- Intellectual life.   Jews -- Austria -- Intellectual life.   Jews -- Biography. Germany -- Civilization -- Jewish influences. Austria -- Civilization -- Jewish influences.

DS135.G33.I42 1998
In search of Jewish community: Jewish identities in Germany and Austria, 1918-1933/ edited by Michael Brenner and Derek J. Penslar. Bloomington: Indiana University press, c1998. xv, 251 p.
98-008304   305.892/4043   0253334276
Jews -- Germany -- Social conditions -- Congresses.   Judaism -- Germany -- History -- 20th century -- Congresses.   Jews -- Austria -- Social conditions -- Congresses.   Germany -- Social conditions -- 1918-1933 -- Congresses.   Austria -- History -- 1918-1938 -- Congresses.   Germany -- Ethnic relations -- Congresses.

DS135.G33.K292 1991
Kaplan, Marion A.
The making of the Jewish middle class: women, family, and identity in Imperial Germany/ Marion A. Kaplan. New York: Oxford University Press, 1991. xvi, 351 p.
90-045234   943/.004924   0195039521
Jews -- Germany -- History -- 1800-1933.   Jewish women -- Germany.   Germany -- Ethnic relations.

DS135.G33.M63 1987
Mosse, Werner Eugen.
Jews in the German economy: the German-Jewish economic elite, 1820-1935/ W.E. Mosse. Oxford [Oxfordshire]: Clarendon Press; 1987. 420 p.
86-018080   330.943/0089924   0198219679
Jews -- Germany -- Economic conditions.   Jewish businesspeople -- Germany.   Jewish capitalists and financiers -- Germany.   Germany -- Ethnic relations -- Economic aspects.   Germany -- Economic conditions.

DS135.G33.R53 1999
Robertson, Ritchie.
The 'Jewish question' in German literature, 1749-1939: emancipation and its discontents/ Ritchie Robertson. Oxford; Oxford University Press, 1999. x, 534 p.
99-022780   830.9/35203924   0198186312 hb
Jews -- Germany -- History -- 1800-1933.   Jews -- Emancipation -- Germany.   Jews -- Cultural assimilation -- Germany.   Public opinion -- Germany.   Germany -- Intellectual life -- 19th century.

DS135.G33.S297
Scholem, Gershom Gerhard, 1897-
On Jews and Judaism in crisis: selected essays/ Gershom Scholem; edited by Werner J. Dannhauser. New York: Schocken Books, [1976] xiii, 306 p.
75-037010   943/.004/924   0805236139
Scholem, Gershom Gerhard, -- 1897- Buber, Martin, -- 1878-1965. Benjamin, Walter, -- 1892-1940.   Jews -- Germany -- History -- 1800-1933 Addresses, essays, lectures.   Germany -- History -- 20th century -- Addresses, essays, lectures.

DS135.G33.S56 1987
Sorkin, David Jan.
The transformation of German Jewry, 1780-1840/ David Sorkin. New York: Oxford University Press, 1987. 255 p.
86-028617   943/.004924   0195049926
Jews -- Germany -- History -- 1800-1933.   Jews -- Germany -- Intellectual life.   Haskalah -- Germany. Germany -- Ethnic relations.

DS135.G33.W418 1997
Weisberger, Adam M., 1960-
The Jewish ethic and the spirit of socialism/ Adam M. Weisberger. New York: Peter Lang, 1997. xiii, 270 p.
96-015393   943/.004924   082043356X
Jews -- Germany -- Politics and government. Socialism and Judaism.   Socialism -- Germany. Germany -- Ethnic relations.

DS135.G3315.B58 2001
Bitter prerequisites: a faculty for survival from Nazi terror/ Wm. Laird Kleine-Ahlbrandt. West Lafayette, Ind.: Purdue University Press, c2001. xiii, 479 p.
00-062782   943/.004924   1557532141
Jewish refugees -- Indiana -- Interviews.   Jews, German -- Indiana -- Interviews.   Holocaust survivors -- Indiana -- Interviews.   Indiana -- Interviews.

DS135.G3315.D57 1996
Dippel, John Van Houten, 1946-
Bound upon a wheel of fire: why so many German Jews made the tragic decision to remain in Nazi Germany/ John V.H. Dippel. New York: BasicBooks, c1996. xxx, 353 p.
95-045212   943/.004924/0019   0465091032
Jews -- Germany -- History -- 1933-1945.   Jewish leadership -- Germany.   Germany -- Ethnic relations.

DS135.G3315.K54513 1998
Klemperer, Victor, 1881-1960.
I will bear witness: the diaries of Victor Klemperer. New York: Random House, 1998- p. cm.
98-015429   943.086/092   0679456961
Klemperer, Victor, -- 1881-1960 -- Diaries.   Jews -- Germany -- History -- 1933-1945.   Christian converts from Judaism -- Germany -- Dresden -- Diaries.   Holocaust, Jewish (1939-1945) -- Germany -- Dresden -- Personal narratives. Dresden (Germany) -- Diaries.

DS135.G3315.L37 2001
Laqueur, Walter, 1921-
Generation exodus: the fate of young Jewish refugees from Nazi Germany/ Walter Laqueur. Hanover, NH: Brandeis University Press, Published by Universi c2001. xvii, 345 p.
00-010538   943/.004924   1584651067
Jews -- Germany -- History -- 1933-1945. Refugees, Jewish -- Biography. Jewish youth -- Germany -- Biography. Germany -- Ethnic relations.

DS135.G332.B3813 1997
Baumel, Judith Tydor, 1959-
Kibbutz Buchenwald: survivors and pioneers/ Judith Tydor Baumel. New Brunswick, N.J.: Rutgers University Press, c1997. xi, 194 p.
96-018311   940.53/18   0813523362
Holocaust survivors -- Germany -- Societies, etc. Labor Zionists -- Germany -- Societies, etc. Jews -- Germany -- History -- 1945-

DS135.G332.P7613 1998
Pross, Christian.
Paying for the past: the struggle over reparations for surviving victims of the Nazi terror/ Christian Pross; translated by Belinda Cooper. Baltimore: Johns Hopkins University Press, 1998. xxii, 265 p.
97-039245   940.53/18   0801858240
Holocaust, Jewish (1939-1945) -- Germany (West) -- Reparations. Jews -- Germany -- History -- 1945- Holocaust survivors -- Diseases -- Germany (West) Germany (West) -- Ethnic relations.

DS135.G332.R37 1997
Rapaport, Lynn.
Jews in Germany after the Holocaust: memory, identity, and Jewish-German relations/ Lynn Rapaport. Cambridge, U.K.; Cambridge University Press, 1997. xi, 325 p.
96-041211   943/.004924   0521582199
Jews -- Germany -- History -- 1945- Holocaust survivors -- Germany. Holocaust, Jewish (1939-1945) -- Germany -- Influence. Germany -- Ethnic relations.

DS135.G4.B46725 1994
Lowenstein, Steven M., 1945-
The Berlin Jewish community: enlightenment, family, and crisis, 1770-1830/ Steven M. Lowenstein. New York: Oxford University Press, 1994. xii, 300 p.
92-039884   943.1/55004924   0195083261
Jews -- Germany -- Berlin -- History -- 18th century. Jews -- Germany -- Berlin -- History -- 19th century. Jews -- Cultural assimilation -- Germany -- Berlin. Berlin (Germany) -- Ethnic relations.

DS135.G4.C684 1997
Magnus, Shulamit S., 1950-
Jewish emancipation in a German city: Cologne, 1798-1871/ Shulamit S. Magnus. Stanford, Calif.: Stanford University Press, 1997. xii, 336 p.
96-025758   943/.5514004924   0804726442
Jews -- Germany -- Cologne -- History -- 19th century. Jews -- Emancipation -- Germany -- Cologne. Cologne (Germany) -- Ethnic relations.

DS135.G4.F664 1998
Friedman, Jonathan C., 1966-
The lion and the star: gentile-Jewish relations in three Hessian communities, 1919-1945/ Jonathan C. Friedman. Lexington: University Press of Kentucky, c1998. 292 p.
97-033201   943/.4164   0813120438
Jews -- Germany -- Frankfurt am Main -- History -- 20th century. Jews -- Germany -- Giessen (Hesse) -- History -- 20th century. Jews -- Germany -- Geisenheim -- History -- 20th century. Germany -- Ethnic relations.

DS135.G5.A1263 1995
Borneman, John, 1952-
Sojourners: the return of German Jews and the question of identity/ by John Borneman and Jeffrey M. Peck. Lincoln, NE: University of Nebraska Press, 1995. xi, 309 p.
95-003125   943/.004924   0803212550
Jews -- Germany -- Berlin -- Interviews. Jews -- Germany -- Berlin -- Identity. Jews, German -- Identity. Berlin (Germany) -- Biography. Berlin (Germany) -- Ethnic relations.

DS135.G5.A155 1989
Mosse, Werner Eugen.
The German-Jewish economic elite, 1820-1935: a socio-cultural profile/ W.E. Mosse. Oxford: Clarendon Press; 1989. 369 p.
88-015934   943/.004924   0198229909
Jews -- Germany -- Biography. Jewish businesspeople -- Germany -- Biography. Jewish capitalists and financiers -- Germany -- Biography. Germany -- Ethnic relations.

DS135.G5.A753 1990
Barnouw, Dagmar.
Visible spaces: Hannah Arendt and the German-Jewish experience/ Dagmar Barnouw. Baltimore: Johns Hopkins University Press, c1990. xii, 319 p.
89-038885   320.5/092   0801839238
Arendt, Hannah. Jews -- Germany -- Biography. Jews -- Cultural assimilation -- Germany. Zionism -- History and criticism. Germany -- Ethnic relations.

DS135.G5.B57 1998
Blumenthal, W. Michael, 1926-
The invisible wall: Germans and Jews: a personal exploration/ W. Michael Blumenthal. Washington, D.C.: Counterpoint, c1998. xiv, 444 p.
97-047735   943/.004924   1887178732
Blumenthal family. Blumenthal, W. Michael, -- 1926- Jews -- Germany -- Genealogy. Germany -- Civilization -- Jewish influences. Germany -- Genealogy. Germany -- Ethnic relations.

DS135.G5.V474 1997
Arendt, Hannah.
Rahel Varnhagen: the life of a Jewess/ Hannah Arendt; edited by Liliane Weissberg; translated by Richard and Clara Winston. Baltimore: Johns Hopkins University Press, 1997. xii, 388 p.
97-006484   943/.155004924   080185587X
Varnhagen, Rahel, -- 1771-1833. Jewish women -- Germany -- Berlin -- Biography. Jews -- Germany -- Berlin -- Intellectual life. Berlin (Germany) -- Intellectual life.

DS135.G5.W338 1987
Waterford, Helen, 1909-
Commitment to the dead: one woman's journey toward understanding/ Helen Waterford. Frederick, CO: Renaissance House Publishers, c1987. 180 p.
87-020819   940.53/15/0392404341   0939650630
Waterford, Helen, -- 1909- Jews -- Germany -- Frankfurt am Main -- Biography. Holocaust, Jewish (1939-1945) -- Personal narratives. Holocaust survivors -- United States -- Biography.

DS135.G7.P56 1996
Plaut, Joshua Eli.
Greek Jewry in the twentieth century, 1913-1983: patterns of Jewish survival in the Greek Provinces before and after the Holocaust/ Joshua Eli Plaut. Madison: Fairleigh Dickinson University Press; c1996. 220 p.
92-052718   949.5/004924   083863463X
Jews -- Greece -- History -- 20th century. Holocaust, Jewish (1939-1945) -- Greece. Greece -- Ethnic relations.

DS135.H9.B74
Braham, Randolph L.
The politics of genocide: the Holocaust in Hungary/ Randolph L. Braham. New York: Columbia University Press, 1981. 2 v.
80-011096   323.1/1924/0439   0231044968
Jews -- Persecutions -- Hungary. Holocaust, Jewish (1939-1945) -- Hungary. Hungary -- Ethnic relations.

DS135.H9.K73 2000
Kramer, T. D.
From Emancipation to catastrophe: the rise and Holocaust of Hungarian Jewry/ T.D. Kramer. Lanham, Md: University Press of America, c2000. xi, 404 p.
00-041753   305.892/40439   076181759X
Jews -- Hungary -- History -- 19th century. Jews -- Hungary -- History -- 20th century. Holocaust, Jewish (1939-1945) -- Hungary. Hungary -- Ethnic relations.

DS135.H9.R36 1999
Ranki, Vera.
The politics of inclusion and exclusion: Jews and nationalism in Hungary/ Vera Ranki. New York: Holmes & Meier, 1999. p. cm.
98-045937   943.9/004924   084191401X
Jews -- Hungary -- History -- 20th century. Antisemitism -- Hungary. Nationalism -- Hungary. Hungary -- Ethnic relations.

DS135.H9.S57 1990
A Social and economic history of Central European Jewry/ edited by Yehuda Don and Victor Karady. New Brunswick, U.S.A.: Transaction Publishers, c1990. viii, 262 p.
89-005217   943/.004924   0887382118
Jews -- Hungary -- History. Jews -- Austria -- Vienna -- History. Hungary -- Ethnic relations. Vienna (Austria) -- Ethnic relations.

DS135.H9.T73 1986
The tragedy of Hungarian Jewry: essays, documents, depositions/ edited by Randolph L. Braham. Boulder: Social Science Monographs; 1986. viii, 328 p.
86-080884   943.9/004924   0880331054
Jews -- Persecutions -- Hungary. Holocaust, Jewish (1939-1945) -- Hungary. Hungary -- Ethnic relations.

DS135.H92.B83913 1999
Jewish Budapest: monuments, rites, history/ by Kinga Frojimovics ... [et al.]; edited by Geza Komoroczy. New York: Central European University Press, 1999. p. cm.
98-043496   943.9/12004924   9639116386
Jews -- Hungary -- Budapest -- History. Holocaust, Jewish (1939-1945) -- Hungary -- Budapest. Synagogues -- Hungary -- Budapest -- Pictorial works. Budapest (Hungary) -- Ethnic relations.

DS135.I6.K38 2000
Katz, Nathan.
Who are the Jews of India?/ Nathan Katz.
Berkeley: University of California Press, c2000.
xv, 205 p.
00-042617   954/.004924   0520213238
*Jews -- India -- History. Jews -- India -- Identity.
Bene-Israel. India -- Ethnic relations.*

DS135.I7.G37 1997
Gat, Moshe.
The Jewish exodus from Iraq, 1948-1951/ Moshe
Gat. London; Frank Cass, 1997. viii, 209 p.
96-030045   956.7/004924   071464689X
*Jews -- Iraq -- History. Jews -- Iraq --
Migrations. Israel -- Emigration and immigration.
Iraq -- Ethnic relations.*

DS135.I8.Z87 2000
Zuccotti, Susan, 1940-
Under his very windows: the Vatican and the
Holocaust in Italy/ Susan Zuccotti. New Haven:
Yale University Press, c2000. 408 p.
00-043307   940.53/18/0945   0300084870
*Pius -- XII, -- Pope, -- 1876-1958 -- Relations with
Jews. World War, 1939-1945 -- Religious aspects
-- Catholic Church. Jews -- Persecutions -- Italy.
Judaism -- Relations -- Catholic Church. Italy --
History -- 1914-1945.*

DS135.I85.R6356 1998
Judaism and Christianity in first-century Rome/
edited by Karl P. Donfried and Peter Richardson.
Grand Rapids, Mich.: William B. Eerdmans,
c1998. xiv, 329 p.
98-015906   937/.004924   0802842658
*Jews -- Italy -- Rome -- History. Judaism -- Italy
-- Rome -- History. Christians -- Italy -- Rome --
History. Rome (Italy) -- Church history. Rome --
History -- Empire, 30 B.C.-284 A.D.*

DS135.I85.R64
Leon, Harry J.
The Jews of ancient Rome. Philadelphia, Jewish
Publication Society of America, 1960. ix, 378 p.
60-009793   937
*Inscriptions, Jewish. Inscriptions, Greek.
Inscriptions, Latin.*

DS135.I85.T735 1999
Dubin, Lois C., 1952-
The port Jews of Habsburg Trieste: absolutist
politics and enlightenment culture/ Lois C. Dubin.
Stanford, Calif.: Stanford University Press, 1999.
ix, 335 p.
98-043111   945/.393004924   0804733201
*Jews -- Italy -- Trieste -- History -- 18th century.
Jews -- Legal status, laws, etc. -- Italy -- Trieste --
History -- 18th century. Haskalah -- Italy --
Trieste. Trieste (Italy) -- Ethnic relations.*

DS135.I85.V4 1975
Roth, Cecil, 1899-1970.
History of the Jews in Venice/ Cecil Roth. New
York: Schocken Books, 1975, c1930. x, 380 p.
74-026916   914.5/31/06924   0805204806
*Jews -- Italy -- Venice -- History. Venice (Italy)
-- History.*

DS135.I9.M595 1997
Kertzer, David I., 1948-
The kidnapping of Edgardo Mortara/ David
Kertzer. New York: Alfred Knopf, 1997. xi, 350 p.
96-039159   945/.004924   0679450319
*Mortara, Pio, -- d. 1940. Jews -- Italy -- Bologna
-- Conversion to Christianity -- History -- 19th
century. Converts from Judaism -- Italy -- Bologna
-- Biography.*

DS135.K8.B73 1993
Brauer, Erich, 1895-1942.
The Jews of Kurdistan/ by Erich Brauer; completed
and edited by Raphael Patai. Detroit: Wayne State
University Press, c1993. 429 p.
92-046105   956.6/77004924   0814323928
*Jews -- Kurdistan -- Social life and customs.
Judaism -- Kurdistan -- Customs and practices.
Jews -- Kurdistan -- Folklore. Kurdistan -- Social
life and customs.*

DS135.L3.E94 1996
Ezergailis, Andrew.
The Holocaust in Latvia, 1941-1944: the missing
center/ by Andrew Ezergailis. Riga: Historical
Institute of Latvia; c1996. xxi, 465 p.
95-042583   940.53/18/094743   9984905438
*Jews -- Persecutions -- Latvia. Holocaust, Jewish
(1939-1945) -- Latvia. Latvia -- Ethnic relations.
Latvia -- History -- German occupation, 1941-
1944.*

DS135.L44.G65 1990
Goldberg, Harvey E.
Jewish life in Muslim Libya: rivals & relatives/
Harvey E. Goldberg. Chicago: University of
Chicago Press, 1990. p. cm.
89-020593   961.2/004924   0226300919
*Jews -- Libya -- History. Jews -- Libya -- Social
life and customs. Libya -- Ethnic relations.*

DS135.L52.V5519313 1999
Abramowicz, Hirsz, 1881-1960.
Profiles of a lost world: memoirs of East European
Jewish life before World War II/ Hirsz
Abramowicz; translated by Eva Zeitlin Dobkin;
edited by Dina Abramowicz and Jeffrey Shandler;
with introductions by David E. Fishman and Dina
Abramowicz. Detroit: Wayne State University
Press, c1999. 386 p.
98-027168   947.93   0814327842
*Jews -- Lithuania -- Vilnius -- History -- 20th
century. Jews -- Lithuania -- Vilnius -- Biography.
Vilnius (Lithuania) -- Biography. Vilnius
(Lithuania) -- Ethnic relations.*

DS135.M43.B368 1996
Barclay, John M. G.
Jews in the Mediterranean diaspora: from
Alexander to Trajan (323 BCE - 117 CE)/ John
M.G. Barclay. Edinburgh: T&T Clark, 1996. xvi,
522 p.
96-197557   909/.09822   0567085007
*Jews -- Mediterranean Region -- History. Jews --
History -- 586 B.C.-70 A.D. Jews -- History -- 168
B.C.-135 A.D. Mediterranean Region -- Ethnic
relations.*

DS135.N5.A5323 1997
Bodian, Miriam, 1948-
Hebrews of the Portuguese nation: conversos and
community in early modern Amsterdam/ Miriam
Bodian. Bloomington: Indiana University Press,
c1997. xiii, 219 p.
96-048373   949.2/3520049240469   0253332923
*Sephardim -- Netherlands -- Amsterdam --
History -- 17th century. Jews -- Netherlands --
Amsterdam -- History -- 17th century. Marranos --
History. Amsterdam (Netherlands) -- Ethnic
relations.*

DS135.N5.A684 2000
Swetschinski, Daniel, 1944-
Reluctant cosmopolitans: the Portuguese Jews of
seventeenth-century Amsterdam/ Daniel M.
Swetschinski. London; Littman Library of Jewish
Civilization, 2000. xii, 380 p.
99-088379   949.2/352   1874774463
*Sephardim -- Netherlands -- Amsterdam --
History -- 17th century. Jews -- Netherlands --
Amsterdam -- History -- 17th century. Judaism --
Netherlands -- Amsterdam -- History -- 17th
century. Amsterdam (Netherlands) -- Ethnic
relations.*

DS135.N6.F73 2000
Anne Frank: reflections on her life and legacy/
edited by Hyman Aaron Enzer and Sandra
Solotaroff-Enzer; foreword by Bernd Elias.
Urbana: University of Illinois Press, c2000. xxv,
285 p.
99-006291   940.53/18/092   0252024729
*Frank, Anne, -- 1929-1945. -- Achterhuis. Frank,
Anne, -- 1929-1945. Holocaust, Jewish (1939-
1945) -- Netherlands -- Amsterdam. Jewish
children in the Holocaust -- Netherlands --
Amsterdam. Holocaust, Jewish (1939-1945) --
Influence.*

DS135.N8.A27 1990
Abrahamsen, Samuel, 1917-
Norway's response to the Holocaust/ Samuel
Abrahamsen. New York, N.Y.: Holocaust Library,
c1991. 207 p.
90-005207   948.1/004924   0896041166
*Jews -- Persecutions -- Norway. Holocaust,
Jewish (1939-1945) -- Norway. Norway -- Ethnic
relations.*

DS135.P6.C655 2000
Cooper, Leo.
In the shadow of the Polish eagle: the Poles, the
Holocaust, and beyond/ Leo Cooper. Houndmills,
Basingstoke, Hampshire; Palgrave, 2000. xiv,
255 p.
00-059125   943.8/004924   0333752651
*Jews -- Poland -- History -- 20th century.
Holocaust, Jewish (1939-1945) -- Poland.
Antisemitism -- Poland. Poland -- Ethnic relations.*

DS135.P6.D62
Dobroszycki, Lucjan.
Image before my eyes: a photographic history of
Jewish life in Poland, 1864-1939/ Lucjan
Dobroszycki and Barbara Kirshenblatt-Gimblett.
New York: Schocken Books, 1977. xviii, 269 p.
75-035448   943.8/004/924   0805236074
*Jews -- Poland -- History -- 19th century. Jews --
Poland -- History -- 20th century. Jews -- Poland -
- Pictorial works. Poland -- Ethnic relations.
Poland -- Pictorial works.*

DS135.P6.E53 1993
Engel, David.
Facing a Holocaust: the Polish government-in-exile
and the Jews, 1943-1945/ by David Engel. Chapel
Hill: University of North Carolina Press, c1993. x,
317 p.
92-028289   943.8/004924   0807820695
*Holocaust, Jewish (1939-1945) -- Poland. Jews -
- Poland -- Politics and government. Poland --
History -- Occupation, 1939-1945.*

DS135.P6.F676 1997
Fram, Edward.
Ideals face reality: Jewish law and life in Poland, 1550-1655/ Edward Fram. Cincinnati: Hebrew Union College Press, c1997. xii, 186 p.
97-002538   943.8/004924   0878204202
Jews -- Poland -- History -- 16th century. Jews -- Poland -- History -- 17th century. Jews -- Poland -- Politics and government. Poland -- Ethnic relations.

DS135.P6.H413 1988
Hertz, Aleksander.
The Jews in Polish culture/ Aleksander Hertz; translated by Richard Lourie; editor, Lucjan Dobroszycki; with a foreword by Czeslaw Milosz. Evanston, IL: Northwestern University Press, c1988. xvi, 266 p.
88-012537   943.8/004924   0810107589
Jews -- Poland -- History. Antisemitism -- Poland -- History. Poland -- Ethnic relations.

DS135.P6.J46 1986
The Jews in Poland/ edited by Chimen Abramsky, Maciej Jachimczyk, and Antony Polonsky. Oxford, UK; B. Blackwell, 1986. vi, 264 p.
86-003336   943.8/004924   0631148574
Jews -- Poland -- History -- Congresses. Holocaust, Jewish (1939-1945) -- Poland -- Congresses. Poland -- Ethnic relations -- Congresses.

DS135.P6.P49 1991
Pinchuk, Ben-Cion.
Shtetl Jews under Soviet rule: eastern Poland on the eve of the Holocaust/ Ben-Cion Pinchuk. Oxford, UK; B. Blackwell, 1991. 186 p.
90-000126   943.8/004924   0631174699
Jews -- Poland -- History -- 20th century. Jews -- Belarus -- History -- 20th century. Poland -- History -- Occupation, 1939-1945. Belarus -- Ethnic relations.

DS135.P6.R49513 1976
Ringelblum, Emanuel, 1900-1944.
Polish-Jewish relations during the Second World War/ Emmanuel Ringelblum; edited and with footnotes by Joseph Kermish, Shmuel Krakowski; trans. from the Polish by Dafna Allon, Danuta Dabrowska, and Dana Keren. New York: Fertig, 1976, c1974. xxxix, 330 p.
76-001394   943.8/004.924
Ringelblum, Emanuel, -- 1900-1944. Holocaust, Jewish (1939-1945) -- Poland. Jews -- Persecutions -- Poland. Poland -- History -- Occupation, 1939-1945. Poland -- Ethnic relations.

DS135.P6.S76 1997
Steinlauf, Michael.
Bondage to the dead: Poland and the memory of the Holocaust/ Michael Steinlauf. Syracuse, NY: Syracuse University Press, 1997. p. cm.
96-009714   940.53/18/0943   0815627297
Jews -- Persecutions -- Poland. Holocaust, Jewish (1939-1945) -- Poland. Holocaust survivors -- Poland. Poland -- Ethnic relations.

DS135.P62 J444 2001
Gross, Jan Tomasz.
Neighbors: the destruction of the Jewish community in Jedwabne, Poland/ Jan T. Gross. Princeton: Princeton University Press, c2001. x, 261 p.
00-051685   940.53/18/0943843 21   0691086672
Jews--Poland--Jedwabne--History. Holocaust, Jewish (1939-1945)--Poland--Jedwabne.

DS135.P62.L644135 1984
The chronicle of the Lodz ghetto, 1941-1944/ edited by Lucjan Dobroszycki; translated by Richard Lourie, Joachim Neugroschel, and others. New Haven: Yale University Press, c1984. lxviii, 551 p
84-003614   943.8/4   0300032080
Jews -- Persecutions -- Poland -- Lodz -- History -- Sources. Holocaust, Jewish (1939-1945) -- Poland -- Lodz -- Sources. Lodz (Poland) -- Ethnic relations -- Sources.

DS135.P62.W2613
Czerniakow, Adam, 1880-1942.
The Warsaw diary of Adam Czerniakow: prelude to doom/ edited by Raul Hilberg, Stanislaw Staron, and Josef Kermisz; translated by Staron and the staff of Yad Vashem. New York: Stein and Day, 1979. viii, 420 p.
78-009272   943.8/4   0812825233
Czerniakow, Adam, -- 1880-1942 -- Diaries. Holocaust, Jewish (1939-1945) -- Poland -- Warsaw -- Personal narratives. Jews -- Persecutions -- Poland -- Warsaw. Warsaw (Poland) -- Ethnic relations.

DS135.P62.W314 1988
Lewin, Abraham, 1893-1943.
A cup of tears: a diary of the Warsaw Ghetto/ by Abraham Lewin; edited by Antony Polonsky; translation of the diary by Christopher Hutton. Oxford, Ox., U.K.; Basil Blackwell in association with the Institut 1988. vi, 310 p.
88-016762   940.53/15/0392404384   0631162151
Lewin, Abraham, -- 1893-1943. Holocaust, Jewish (1939-1945) -- Poland -- Warsaw -- Personal narratives. Jews -- Persecutions -- Poland -- Warsaw. Warsaw (Poland) -- Ethnic relations.

DS135.P63.L3996 2000
Powell, Lawrence N.
Troubled memory: Anne Levy, the Holocaust, and David Duke's Louisiana/ Lawrence N. Powell. Chapel Hill: University of North Carolina Press, c2000. 593 p.
99-018568   940.53/18/0922   0807825042
Levy, Anne. Skorecki family. Duke, David Ernest. Holocaust, Jewish -- Poland -- Biography. Holocaust survivors -- Louisiana -- New Orleans -- Biography. Jews -- Poland -- Biography. Louisiana -- Politics and government -- 1951-

DS135.P63.N46 1999
Nelken, Halina.
And yet, I am here!/ Halina Nelken; translated by Halina Nelken with Alicia Nitecki. Amherst: University of Massachusetts Press, c1999. xii, 276 p.
98-030275   943.8/6   1558491562
Nelken, Halina -- Diaries. Jews -- Poland -- Krakow -- Diaries. Holocaust, Jewish (1939-1945) -- Poland -- Personal narratives. Krakow (Poland) -- Biography.

DS135.P63.R848 1990
Tec, Nechama.
In the lion's den: the life of Oswald Rufeisen/ Nechama Tec. New York: Oxford University Press, 1990. x, 279 p.
89-027256   940.53/18/09438   019503905X
Rufeisen, Oswald. World War, 1939-1945 -- Jewish resistance -- Poland. Converts from Judaism -- Biography. Catholic converts -- Israel -- Biography.

DS135.P63.W945 1998
Wygoda, Hermann, 1906-
In the shadow of the swastika/ Hermann Wygoda; edited by Mark Wygoda; foreword by Michael Berenbaum. Urbana: University of Illinois Press, c1998. xxiii, 167 p.
97-021147   940.53/18   025202382X
Wygoda, Hermann, -- 1906- Jews -- Poland -- Biography. Holocaust, Jewish (1939-1945) -- Personal narratives. World War, 1939-1945 -- Jewish resistance.

DS135.R7.B78 1992
Butnaru, I. C.
The silent Holocaust: Romania and its Jews/ I.C. Butnaru; foreword by Elie Wiesel. New York: Greenwood Press, 1992. xxv, 236 p.
91-021181   940.53/18/09498   0313279853
Holocaust, Jewish (1939-1945) -- Romania. Jews -- Persecutions -- Romania. Antisemitism -- Romania. Romania -- Ethnic relations.

DS135.R7.I6513 2000
Ioanid, Radu.
The Holocaust in Romania: the destruction of Jews and Gypsies under the Antonescu regime, 1940-1944/ Radu Ioanid. Chicago, Ill.: Ivan R. Dee, 2000. xxiii, 352 p.
99-043229   940.53/18/09498   1566632560
Jews -- Persecutions -- Romania. Holocaust, Jewish (1939-1945) -- Romania. World War, 1939-1945 -- Gypsies -- Romania. Romania -- Ethnic relations.

DS135.R73.S38713 2000
Sebastian, Mihail, 1907-1945.
Journal, 1935-1944/ Mihail Sebastian; translated from the Romanian by Patrick Camiller; with an introduction and notes by Radu Ioanid. Chicago: Ivan R. Dee, 2000. xxv, 641 p.
00-031535   940.53/18/092   1566633265
Sebastian, Mihail, -- 1907-1945 -- Diaries. Jews -- Romania -- Diaries. Holocaust, Jewish (1939-1945) -- Romania -- Personal narratives. Romania -- Biography. Romania -- Politics and government -- 1914-1944.

DS135.R9.B28 1976
Baron, Salo Wittmayer, 1895-
The Russian Jew under tsars and Soviets/ Salo W. Baron. New York: Macmillan, c1976. xvii, 468 p.
75-019161   323.1/19/24047   0025073001
Jews -- Soviet Union -- History. Soviet Union -- Ethnic relations.

DS135.R9.C34 1997
Cassedy, Steven.
To the other shore: the Russian Jewish intellectuals who came to America/ Steven Cassedy. Princeton, N.J.: Princeton University Press, c1997. xxiii, 197 p.
96-044604   305.892/4047
Jews -- Russia -- Intellectual life. Jews -- Cultural assimilation -- Russia. Jewish radicals -- Russia. Russia -- Ethnic relations. United States -- Ethnic relations.

DS135.R9.G444 1988
Gitelman, Zvi Y.
A century of ambivalence: the Jews of Russia and the Soviet Union, 1881 to the present/ Zvi Gitelman. New York: Schocken Books: c1988. xv, 336 p.
87-009822   947/.004924   0805240349
Jews -- Soviet Union -- History. Jews -- Soviet Union -- Pictorial works. Soviet Union -- Ethnic relations. Soviet Union -- Pictorial works.

DS135.R9.H23 1995
Haberer, Erich.
Jews and revolution in nineteenth-century Russia/ by Erich Haberer. Cambridge: Cambridge University Press, 1995. xv, 346 p.
94-001919   947/.004924   0521460093
Jews -- Russia -- History -- 19th century. Jewish radicals -- Russia -- History -- 19th century. Radicalism -- Russia -- History -- 19th century. Russia -- Ethnic relations.

DS135.R9.L33 1989
Lederhendler, Eli.
The road to modern Jewish politics: political tradition and political reconstruction in the Jewish community of tsarist Russia/ Eli Lederhendler. New York: Oxford University Press, 1989. ix, 240 p.
88-023832   947/.004924   0195058917
Jews -- Russia -- History -- 19th century. Jews -- Europe, Eastern -- Politics and government. Haskalah -- Russia. Russia -- Ethnic relations. Europe, Eastern -- Ethnic relations.

DS135.R9.P55 1991
Pogroms: anti-Jewish violence in modern Russian history/ edited by John D. Klier and Shlomo Lambroza. Cambridge; Cambridge University Press, 1992. xx, 393 p.
90-025617   947/.004924   0521405327
Jews -- Persecutions -- Russia. Pogroms -- Russia. Russia -- Ethnic relations.

DS135.R92.B78 1994
Brym, Robert J., 1951-
The Jews of Moscow, Kiev, and Minsk: identity, antisemitism, emigration/ Robert J. Brym with the assistance of Rozalina Ryvkina; editor, Howard Spier. New York: New York University Press; 1994. xvi, 142 p.
94-009893   305.892/4047/09049   0814712266
Jews -- Russia (Federation) -- Politics and government. Jews -- Ukraine -- Politics and government. Jews -- Belarus -- Politics and government. Former Soviet republics -- Ethnic relations.

DS135.R92.B89 1997
Buwalda, Piet, 1925-
They did not dwell alone: Jewish emigration from the Soviet Union, 1967-1990/ Petrus Buwalda. Washington, D.C.: Woodrow Wilson Center Press; c1997. xviii, 297 p.
96-029951   947/.004927   0801856167
Jews -- Soviet Union -- Migrations. Jews -- Persecutions -- Soviet Union. Refuseniks. Israel -- Emigration and immigration. Soviet Union -- Emigration and immigration -- Government policy.

DS135.R92.C4713 1981
The black book: the ruthless murder of Jews by German-Fascist invaders throughout the temporarily-occupied regions of the Soviet Union and in the death camps of Poland during the war of 1941-1945/ prepared under the editorship of Ilya Ehrenburg & Vasily Grossman; translated from the Russian by John Glad and James S. Levine. New York: Holocaust Publications; c1981. xliv, 595 p.
81-081517   940.53/15/03924047   0896040321
Jews -- Persecutions -- Soviet Union. Holocaust, Jewish (1939-1945) -- Soviet Union. Soviet Union -- Ethnic relations.

DS135.R92.J463 1990
Jewish culture and identity in the Soviet Union/ edited by Yaacov Roi and Avi Beker. New York: New York University Press, c1991. xxii, 482 p.
90-005483   947/.004924   0814774083
Jews -- Soviet Union -- History. Jews -- Soviet Union -- Intellectual life. Jews -- Soviet Union -- Identity. Soviet Union -- Ethnic relations.

DS135.R92.L48 1988
Levin, Nora.
The Jews in the Soviet Union since 1917: paradox of survival/ Nora Levin. New York: New York University Press, c1988. 2 v.
87-021951   947/.004924   0814750184
Jews -- Soviet Union -- History. Soviet Union -- Ethnic relations.

DS135.R92.P56 1984
Pinkus, Benjamin, 1933-
The Soviet government and the Jews, 1948-1967: a documented study/ Benjamin Pinkus; general editor, Jonathan Frankel. Cambridge [Cambridgeshire]; Cambridge University Press, 1984. xvi, 612 p.
83-018900   323.1/1924/047   0521247136
Jews -- Soviet Union -- History. Antisemitism -- Soviet Union. Soviet Union -- Ethnic relations.

DS135.R92.S28
Sawyer, Thomas E.
The Jewish minority in the Soviet Union/ Thomas E. Sawyer. Boulder, Colo.: Westview Press, 1979. xxii, 353 p.
78-020724   323.1/1924/047   0891584803
Jews -- Soviet Union -- Politics and government. Soviet Union -- Politics and government.

DS135.R92.S655 1989
Soviet Jewry in the 1980s: the politics of anti-Semitism and emigration and the dynamics of resettlement/ edited by Robert O. Freedman. Durham [N.C.]: Duke University Press, 1989. viii, 260 p.
89-001074   947/.004924   0822309068
Jews -- Soviet Union -- History. Antisemitism -- Soviet Union -- History -- 20th century. Jews -- Soviet Union -- Migrations -- History -- 20th century. Soviet Union -- Ethnic relations.

DS135.R93 G3436 1991
Jews in eastern Poland and the USSR, 1939-46/ edited by Norman Davies and Antony Polonsky. New York: St. Martin's Press, 1991. xiv, 426 p.
91-012028   947/.718004924.220   0312062001
Jews--Ukraine--Galicia, Eastern--History--20th century. Holocaust, Jewish (1939-1945)--Ukraine-- Galicia, Eastern. Jews--Belarus--History--20th century.

DS135.R93.K288 1990
Tory, Avraham.
Surviving the Holocaust: the Kovno Ghetto diary/ Avraham Tory; edited with an introduction by Martin Gilbert; textual and historical notes by Dina Porat; translated by Jerzy Michalowicz. Cambridge, Mass.: Harvard University Press, 1990. xxiv, 554 p.
89-007496   940.53/18/09475   0674858107
Tory, Avraham. Holocaust, Jewish (1939-1945) -- Lithuania -- Kaunas -- Personal narratives. Jews -- Persecutions -- Lithuania -- Kaunas. Kaunas (Lithuania) -- Ethnic relations.

DS135.R93.K7954 1989
Gelman, Charles, 1920-
Do not go gentle: a memoir of Jewish resistance in Poland, 1941-1945/ Charles Gelman. Hamden, Conn.: Archon Books, 1989. xiii, 226 p.
89-000258   0208022309
Gelman, Charles, -- 1920- Holocaust, Jewish (1939-1945) -- Belarus -- Kurenets -- Personal narratives. Jews -- Persecutions -- Belarus -- Kurenets. World War, 1939-1945 -- Jewish resistance. Kurenets (Belarus) -- Ethnic relations.

DS135.R93.V523 1989
Dawidowicz, Lucy S.
From that place and time: a memoir, 1938-1947/ Lucy S. Dawidowicz. New York: W.W. Norton, c1989. xiv, 333 p.
88-028858   947/.5
Dawidowicz, Lucy S. -- Journeys -- Lithuania -- Vilnius. Jews -- Lithuania -- Vilnius. Yiddish language -- Lithuania -- Vilnius. Holocaust, Jewish (1939-1945) Vilnius (Lithuania) -- Ethnic relations.

DS135.R95.R3713 1991
Rapoport, IA. L.
The doctors' plot of 1953/ Yakov Rapoport. Cambridge, Mass.: Harvard University Press, 1991. viii, 280 p.
90-004812   947/.00492402   0674214773:
Rapoport, IA. L. -- (IAkov Lvovich) Jews -- Soviet Union -- Biography. Political prisoners -- Soviet Union -- Biography. Pathologists -- Soviet Union -- Biography. Soviet Union -- History -- 1925-1953 -- Biography.

DS135.R95.W313 2000
Wengeroff, Pauline, 1833-1916.
Rememberings: the world of a Russian-Jewish woman in the nineteenth century/ Pauline Wengeroff; translated by Henny Wenkart; edited with an afterword by Bernard D. Cooperman. Potomac: University Press of Maryland, 2000. xvi, 306 p.
00-043945   947/.004924/0092   1883053587
Wengeroff, Pauline, -- 1833-1916. Jews -- Russia -- Biography. Jews -- Russia -- Social life and customs. Russia -- Biography.

DS135.S7.C585 1992
Convivencia: Jews, Muslims, and Christians in medieval Spain/ edited by Vivian B. Mann, Thomas F. Glick, Jerrilynn D. Dodds. New York: G. Braziller in association with the Jewish Muse 1992. xiii, 263 p.
92-010069   946/.004924   0807612839
Jews -- Spain -- Civilization. Spain -- Civilization -- 711-1516. Spain -- Civilization -- Jewish influences. Spain -- Ethnic relations.

DS135.S7.G47 1992
Gerber, Jane S.
The Jews of Spain: a history of the Sephardic experience/ Jane S. Gerber. New York: Free Press, c1992. xxv, 333 p.
92-026941   946/.004924   0029115736
Jews -- Spain -- History. Sephardim -- History. Spain -- Ethnic relations.

DS135.S7.G58 1996
Gitlitz, David M.
Secrecy and deceit: the religion of the crypto-Jews/ David M. Gitlitz. Philadelphia: Jewish Publication Society, 1996. xvi, 677 p.
95-043074   946/.004924   0827605625
Jews -- Spain -- History. Marranos -- Religious life. Spain -- Ethnic relations.

DS135.S7.R68 1994
Roth, Norman, 1938-
Jews, Visigoths, and Muslims in medieval Spain: cooperation and conflict/ by Norman Roth. Leiden; E.J. Brill, 1994. 367 p.
94-018401 946/.004924 9004099719
Jews -- Spain -- History. Spain -- History -- Gothic period, 414-711. Spain -- History -- 711-1516. Spain -- Ethnic relations.

DS135.S71.L815
Longhurst, John Edward, 1918-
The age of Torquemada. With illus. by Evelyn G. Byatt. Sandoval, N.M., Coronado Press, 1962. 170 p.
62-004424
Torquemada, Tomas de, -- 1420-1498. Jews -- Spain -- Persecutions. Inquisition -- Spain.

DS135.S75.S455 2000
Pike, Ruth, 1931-
Linajudos and conversos in Seville: greed and prejudice in sixteenth- and seventeenth-century Spain/ Ruth Pike. New York: Peter Lang, c2000. xiii, 217 p.
99-087558 946/.86004924 0820449644
Jews -- Spain -- Seville -- History. Jewish Christians -- Spain -- Seville. Antisemitism -- Spain -- Seville -- 16th century. Seville (Spain) -- Ethnic relations.

DS135.S95.F728 1997
Frankel, Jonathan.
The Damascus affair: "ritual murder," politics, and the Jews in 1840/ Jonathan Frankel. Cambridge; Cambridge University Press, 1997. xiv, 491 p.
96-005288 305.892/40594144 0521482461
Jews -- Persecutions -- Syria -- Damascus. Blood accusation -- Syria -- Damascus. Damascus (Syria) -- Ethnic relations.

DS135.T8.S46 1991
Shaw, Stanford J. 1930-
The Jews of the Ottoman Empire and the Turkish Republic/ Stanford J. Shaw. New York: New York University Press, 1991. xiii, 380 p.
91-006927 956.1/015 0814779247
Jews -- Turkey -- History. Turkey -- Ethnic relations.

DS135.Y8.G67 1999
Gordiejew, Paul Benjamin, 1954-
Voices of Yugoslav Jewry/ Paul Benjamin Gordiejew. Albany: State University of New York Press, c1999. xvi, 479 p.
98-003405 949.7/004924 0791440214
Jews -- Yugoslavia -- History. Holocaust, Jewish (1939-1945) -- Yugoslavia. Yugoslavia -- Ethnic relations.

DS140.H37 2000
Hart, Mitchell Bryan, 1959-
Social science and the politics of modern Jewish identity/ Mitchell B. Hart. Stanford, Calif.: Stanford University Press, 2000. viii, 340 p.
99-059745 305.8924 0804738246
Jews -- Social conditions -- 20th century. Jews -- Identity. Jews -- Statistics.

DS140.J475 2000
The Jewish political tradition/ editors, Michael Walzer, Menachem Lorberbaum, Noam J. Zohar; coeditor, Yair Lorberbaum. New Haven: Yale University Press, c2000- v. 1
99-059743 320/.088/296 0300078226
Jews -- Politics and government. Judaism and politics. Judaism and state.

DS140.K598 1990
Kochan, Lionel.
Jews, idols, and messiahs: the challenge from history/ Lionel Kochan. Oxford, OX, UK; B. Blackwell, 1990. vi, 231 p.
90-000202 943.1/55004924 0631154779
Jews -- Politics and government. Jews -- Germany -- Berlin -- History -- 18th century. Jews -- England -- London -- History. Berlin (Germany) -- Ethnic relations. London (England) -- Ethnic relations.

DS141.B3813 1990
Bein, Alex, 1903-
The Jewish question: biography of a world problem/ Alex Bein; translated by Harry Zohn. Rutherford, N.J.: Fairleigh Dickinson University Press, c1990. 784 p.
87-046422 909/.04924 0838632521
Antisemitism -- History. Christianity and antisemitism. Jews -- History -- 70-

DS143.B55 1996
Bernstein, Richard J.
Hannah Arendt and the Jewish question/ Richard J. Bernstein. Cambridge, Mass.: MIT Press, 1996. xiv, 233 p.
96-011506 909/.04924 0262024063
Arendt, Hannah -- Views on Jewish history. Jews -- History -- 1789-1945 -- Historiography. Antisemitism -- Historiography. Holocaust, Jewish (1939-1945) -- Historiography.

DS143.H96 1998
Hyman, Meryl, 1950-
Who is a Jew?: conversations, not conclusions/ Meryl Hyman. Woodstock, Vt.: Jewish Lights, c1998. xxx, 231 p.
98-010686 909/.04924 1879045761
Jews -- Identity. Judaism -- Essence, genius, nature. Judaism -- 20th century.

DS143.J459 1991
Jewish settlement and community in the modern western world/ edited by Ronald Dotterer, Deborah Dash Moore, and Steven M. Cohen. Selinsgrove, Pa.: Susquehanna University Press; 1991. 218 p.
93-205288 094563613X
Jews, European -- Social conditions. Jews, European -- History. Jews, American -- Social conditions.

DS143.M39 1990
Meyer, Michael A.
Jewish identity in the modern world/ Michael A. Meyer. Seattle: University of Washington Press, c1990. ix, 110 p.
89-070707 909/.04924 0295970006
Jews -- Identity -- History. Enlightenment. Antisemitism.

DS143.N27 1999
National variations in Jewish identity: implications for Jewish education/ edited by Steven M. Cohen and Gabriel Horenczyk. Albany, N.Y.: State University of New York Press, 1999. vi, 325 p.
99-019029 305.892/4 079144371X
Jews -- Identity -- Congresses. Jews -- United States -- Identity -- Congresses. Jews -- Israel -- Identity -- Congresses.

DS143.S45 2000
Seidler, Victor J., 1945-
Shadows of the Shoah: Jewish identity and belonging/ Victor Jeleniewski Seidler. Oxford; Berg, 2000. xii, 175 p.
305.8924041 1859733557
Jews -- Great Britain -- Identity. Jews -- Poland -- Identity.

DS143.W39 1996
Weinberg, David H., 1945-
Between tradition and modernity: Haim Zhitlowski, Simon Dubnow, Ahad Ha-Am, and the shaping of modern Jewish identity/ David H. Weinberg. New York: Holmes & Meier, 1996. p. cm.
96-011218 305.892/4 0841913552
Zhitlowsky, Chaim, -- 1865-1943. Dubnow, Simon, -- 1860-1941. Ahad Haam, -- 1856-1927. Jews -- Politics and government. Jews -- Identity. Jews -- Cultural assimilation -- Russia -- History -- 19th century.

DS145.C574 1997
Cohn-Sherbok, Dan.
The crucified Jew: twenty centuries of Christian anti-Semitism/ Dan Cohn-Sherbok. Grand Rapids, Mich.: W.B. Eerdmans; 1997. xx, 258 p.
96-050923 261.2/6/09 0802843115
Antisemitism -- History. Christianity and antisemitism -- History. Judaism -- Controversial literature -- History and criticism.

DS145.K354
Katz, Jacob, 1904-
From prejudice to destruction: anti-Semitism, 1700-1933/ Jacob Katz. Cambridge, MA: Harvard University Press, 1980. viii, 392 p.
80-014404 305.8/924 0674325052
Antisemitism -- History.

DS145.L32 1990
Langmuir, Gavin I.
Toward a definition of antisemitism/ Gavin I. Langmuir. Berkeley: University of California Press, c1990. x, 417 p.
90-041686 305.8/924 0520061446
Antisemitism. Christianity and antisemitism. Jews -- Legal status, laws, etc. -- France. France -- Ethnic relations.

DS145.M14 1998
MacDonald, Kevin B.
Separation and its discontents: toward an evolutionary theory of anti-Semitism/ Kevin MacDonald. Westport, Conn.: Praeger, 1998. x, 325 p.
97-026901 305.892/4 0275948706
Antisemitism. Antisemitism -- History.

DS145.T7
Trachtenberg, Joshua, 1904-
The devil and the Jews, the medieval conception of the Jew and its relation to modern antisemitism, by Joshua Trachtenberg. New Haven, Yale university press; 1943. xiv, 279 p.
43-002349 296
Jewish question.

DS145.W542 1991
Wistrich, Robert S., 1945-
Antisemitism: the longest hatred/ Robert S. Wistrich. New York: Pantheon Books, c1991. xxvi, 341 p.
91-053083 909/.04924 0679409467
Antisemitism.

DS146.F8.B5713 1992
Birnbaum, Pierre.
Anti-semitism in France: a political history from Leon Blum to the present/ Pierre Birnbaum. Oxford, UK; B. Blackwell, 1992. xi, 317 p.
91-031806 305.892/4044 1557860475
Antisemitism -- France -- History. Jewish statesmen -- France. Jews -- France -- Politics and government. France -- Politics and government -- 1789- France -- Ethnic relations.

DS146.G4.B4713 1997
Bergmann, Werner, 1950-
Anti-semitism in Germany: the post-Nazi epoch since 1945/ Werner Bergmann and Rainer Erb; translated by Belinda Cooper and Allison Brown. New Brunswick, N.J., U.S.A.: Transaction Publishers, c1997. ix, 385 p.
96-036347   943/.004924   1560002700
Antisemitism -- Germany (West)   Germany (West) -- Ethnic relations.

DS146.G4.B49 1999
Betrayal: German churches and the Holocaust/ edited by Robert P. Ericksen & Susannah Heschel. Minneapolis: Fortress Press, c1999. 224 p.
99-011275   261.2/6/094309043   0800629310
Antisemitism -- Germany -- History -- 20th century. Christianity and antisemitism. Church and state -- Germany -- History -- 1933-1945. Germany -- Religion -- 1933-1945.

DS146.G4.F57 1998
Fischer, Klaus P., 1942-
The history of an obsession: German Judeophobia and the Holocaust/ Klaus P. Fischer. New York: Continuum, 1998. viii, 532 p.
98-013846   943/.004924   0826410898
Antisemitism -- Germany -- History. Antisemitism -- Psychological aspects -- History. Holocaust, Jewish (1939-1945) -- Psychological aspects.

DS146.G4.G4813 2000
Gerlach, Wolfgang.
And the witnesses were silent: the Confessing Church and the persecution of the Jews/ by Wolfgang Gerlach; translated and edited by Victoria J. Barnett. Lincoln: University of Nebraska Press, c2000. xi, 304 p.
99-044916   261.8/348924043/099043
0803221657
Christianity and antisemitism. Jews -- Persecutions -- Germany. Antisemitism -- Germany.

DS146.G4.P75 2000
Probing the depths of German antisemitism: German society and the persecution of the Jews, 1933-1941/ edited by David Bankier. New York: Berghahn Books, c2000. 585 p.
99-056222   940.53/18   1571812385
Antisemitism -- Germany -- History -- 20th century. Jews -- Germany -- Public opinion. Public opinion -- Germany. Germany -- Ethnic relations.

DS146.G4.W43 1996
Weiss, John, 1927-
Ideology of death: why the Holocaust happened in Germany/ John Weiss. Chicago: I.R. Dee, 1996. xii, 427 p.
95-022792   305.892/4043   1566630886
Antisemitism -- Germany -- History. Antisemitism -- Austria -- History. Christianity and antisemitism.

DS146.P6.L48 1991
Levine, Hillel.
Economic origins of antisemitism: Poland and its Jews in the early modern period/ Hillel Levine. New Haven: Yale University Press, c1991. xiii, 271 p.
90-026565   943.8/004924   0300049870
Antisemitism -- Economic aspects -- Poland. Jews -- Poland -- Economic conditions. Jews -- Poland -- History. Poland -- Ethnic relations.

DS146.U6.B55 2000
Blakeslee, Spencer, 1935-
The death of American antisemitism/ Spencer Blakeslee. Westport, Conn.: Praeger, c2000. xviii, 277 p.
99-029576   305.8/00973   0275965082
Antisemitism -- United States. Jews -- United States -- Politics and government -- 20th century. United States -- Ethnic relations.

DS146.U6.D555 1994
Dinnerstein, Leonard.
Antisemitism in America/ Leonard Dinnerstein. New York: Oxford University Press, 1994. xxviii, 369 p.
93-031187   305.892/4/0973   0195037804
Antisemitism -- United States -- History. United States -- Ethnic relations.

DS148.H93 1995
Hyman, Paula, 1946-
Gender and assimilation in modern Jewish history: the roles and representation of women/ Paula E. Hyman. Seattle: University of Washington Press, c1995. xiii, 197 p.
94-037932   305.48/696   0295974257
Jews -- Cultural assimilation -- Europe. Jews -- Cultural assimilation -- United States. Jewish women -- Europe -- Social conditions. Europe -- Ethnic relations. United States -- Ethnic relations.

DS148.S34 2000
Safran, Gabriella, 1967-
Rewriting the Jew: assimilation narratives in the Russian empire/ Gabriella Safran. Stanford, Calif.: Stanford University Press, 2000. xvii, 269 p.
00-057322   305.892/4047   0804738300
Jews -- Cultural assimilation -- Russia. Jews -- Russia -- Identity. Acculturation -- Russia. Russia -- Ethnic relations.

DS149.A874
Avineri, Shlomo.
The making of modern Zionism: intellectual origins of the Jewish state/ Shlomo Avineri. New York: Basic Books, c1981. x, 244 p.
81-066102   956.94/001   0465043283
Zionism -- History -- Addresses, essays, lectures. Zionists -- Addresses, essays, lectures.

DS149.C627 1987
Cohen, Mitchell, 1952-
Zion and state: nation, class, and the shaping of modern Israel/ Mitchell Cohen. Oxford, UK; B. Blackwell, 1987. 322 p.
86-023235   956.94/001   0631152431
Zionism -- Palestine -- History. Labor Zionism -- Palestine -- History. Revisionist Zionism -- Palestine -- History. Israel -- Politics and government.

DS149.E9313 1995
Evron, Boas.
Jewish state or Israeli nation?/ Boas Evron. Bloomington: Indiana University Press, c1995. xiv, 269 p.
94-024878   320.5/4/095694   0253319633
Zionism -- Philosophy. Jews -- Israel -- Identity. Israel -- Politics and government.

DS149.H337
Halperin, Samuel, 1930-
The political world of American Zionism. Detroit, Wayne State University Press, 1961. ix, 431 p.
61-010126
Zionism -- United States.

DS149.H344 1998
Halpern, Ben.
Zionism and the creation of a new society/ Ben Halpern & Jehuda Reinharz. New York: Oxford University Press, 1998. 293 p.
97-037525   320.54/095694   0195092090
Zionism -- History. Jews -- Palestine -- History -- 20th century. Palestine -- History -- 1917-1948.

DS149.H4376
Hertzberg, Arthur.
The Zionist idea; a historical analysis and reader. Edited and with an introd. and biographical notes by Arthur Hertzberg. Foreword by Emanuel Neumann. Garden City, N.Y. Doubleday, 1959. 638 p.
59-006994   956.94
Zionism -- History -- Sources.

DS149.L315
Laqueur, Walter, 1921-
A history of Zionism [by] Walter Laqueur. London, Weidenfeld and Nicolson [1972] xvi, 640 p.
72-188323   956.94/001   0297994123
Zionism -- History.

DS149.M375 2000
Medoff, Rafael, 1959-
Historical dictionary of Zionism/ Rafael Medoff and Chaim I. Waxman. Lanham, MD: Scarecrow Press, 2000. xxix, 238 p.
99-087955   320.54/095694/03   0810837730
Zionism -- History -- Dictionaries. Israel -- History -- Dictionaries.

DS149.P424 1991
Penslar, Derek Jonathan.
Zionism and technocracy: the engineering of Jewish settlement in Palestine, 1870-1918/ Derek J. Penslar. Bloomington: Indiana University Press, c1991. xiii, 210 p.
90-025043   325/.35694   0253342902
Zionism -- History. Jews -- Colonization -- Palestine. Land settlement -- Palestine.

DS149.S497158 1992
Shapira, Anita.
Land and power: the Zionist resort to force, 1881-1948/ Anita Shapira; translated by William Templer. New York: Oxford University Press, 1992. x, 446 p.
91-028984   320.5/4/095694   0195061047
Zionism -- Philosophy. Jewish-Arab relations -- History -- To 1917 -- Public opinion. Jewish-Arab relations -- History -- 1917-1948 -- Public opinion.

DS149.S69513 1998
Sternhell, Zeev.
The founding myths of Israel: nationalism, socialism, and the making of the Jewish state/ Zeev Sternhell; translated by David Maisel. Princeton, N.J.: Princeton University Press, c1998. xiii, 419 p.
97-015871   320.54/095694   0691016941
Zionism -- History. Zionism -- Philosophy. Jewish nationalism -- Philosophy. Jews -- Palestine -- History -- 20th century.

DS149.V515 1987
Vital, David.
Zionism: the crucial phase/ David Vital. Oxford [Oxfordshire]: Clarendon Press; 1987. xvi, 392 p.
87-011320   956.94/001   0198219326
Zionism -- History.

DS149.5.G4
Miller, Rory, 1971-
Divided against Zion: anti-Zionist opposition in Britain to a Jewish state in Palestine, 1945-1948/ Rory Miller. London; Frank Cass, c2000. xii, 275 p.
00-035899   327.4105694/09/044   071465051X
Zionism -- Great Britain -- History. Jewish-Arab relations -- History -- 1917-1948. Middle East -- Foreign relations -- Great Britain. Great Britain -- Foreign relations -- Middle East.

DS149.5.U6.R35 1998
Raider, Mark A.
The emergence of American Zionism/ Mark A. Raider. New York: New York University Press, c1998. xvii, 296 p.
98-023089   320.54/095694/0973   0814774989
Zionism -- United States -- History.

DS149.5.U6M33 1997
Medoff, Rafael, 1959-
Zionism and the Arabs: an American Jewish dilemma, 1898-1948/ Rafael Medoff. Westport, Conn.: Praeger, c1997. viii, 188 p.
96-047482   320.54/095694   0275958248
Zionism -- United States -- History. Jewish-Arab relations -- History -- 1917-1948. Jews -- United States -- Identity. United States -- Ethnic relations.

DS150.R5.S52
Shavit, Jacob.
Jabotinsky and the revisionist movement, 1925-1948/ Yaacov Shavit. London, England; F. Cass, 1988. p. cm.
88-000997   956.94/001   0714633259
Jabotinsky, Vladimir, -- 1880-1940.   Revisionist Zionism -- History.

DS150.5.M47 1998
Merkley, Paul Charles.
The politics of Christian Zionism, 1891-1948/ Paul Charles Merkley. London; F. Cass, c1998. x, 223 p.
98-013351   320.54/095694/041   0714648507
Christian Zionism -- Great Britain -- History. Christian Zionism -- United States -- History. Zionism -- United States -- History.

DS151.G5.Z56 1993
Zipperstein, Steven J., 1950-
Elusive prophet: Ahad Ha'am and the origins of Zionism/ Steven J. Zipperstein. Berkeley: University of California Press, c1993. xxv, 386 p.
92-031104   320.5/4/095694092   0520081110
Ahad Haam, -- 1856-1927. Zionists -- Biography. Zionism -- Philosophy.

DS151.H4.K68 1993
Kornberg, Jacques, 1933-
Theodor Herzl: from assimilation to Zionism/ Jacques Kornberg. Bloomington: Indiana University Press, c1993. xii, 240 p.
93-018399   320.5/4/09569409436   0253332036
Herzl, Theodor, -- 1860-1904. Zionists -- Austria -- Biography.

DS151.K327.S52513 1984
Shapira, Anita.
Berl: the biography of a socialist Zionist, Berl Katznelson, 1887-1944/ Anita Shapira; [translated by Haya Galai]. Cambridge [Cambridgeshire]; Cambridge University Press, c1984. ix, 400 p.
84-007008   956.94/001/0924   0521256186
Katznelson, Berl, -- 1887-1944.

DS153.3 Jordan. Transjordan — Antiquities

DS153.3.A72 2000
The archaeology of Jordan and beyond: essays in honor of James A. Sauer/ edited by Lawrence E. Stager, Joseph A. Greene, and Michael D. Coogan. Winona Lake, Ind.: Eisenbrauns, 2000. xvi, 529 p.
00-035445   933   1575069016
Excavations (Archaeology) -- Jordan. Excavations (Archaeology) -- Middle East. Middle East -- Antiquities. Jordan -- Antiquities.

DS153.55 Jordan. Transjordan — Ethnography — Individual elements in the population, A-Z

DS153.55.B43.S57 1997
Shryock, Andrew.
Nationalism and the genealogical imagination: oral history and textual authority in tribal Jordan/ Andrew Shryock. Berkeley: University of California Press, c1997. xi, 359 p.
95-039809   956.95/004927   0520201000
Bedouins -- Jordan. Bedouins -- Jordan -- Historiography. Oral tradition -- Jordan. Jordan -- Genealogy.

DS154.55 Jordan. Transjordan — History — By period

DS154.55.D32 1999
Dallas, Roland.
King Hussein: a life on the edge/ Roland Dallas. New York: Fromm International, 1999. p. cm.
99-037260   956.9504/3/092   0880642424
Hussein, -- King of Jordan, -- 1935-   Jordan -- Politics and government -- 1952-1999.

DS175 Armenia — History — General works

DS175.A715 1997
The Armenian people from ancient to modern times/ edited by Richard G. Hovannisian. New York: St. Martin's Press, 1997- v. 2
97-005310   956.62   0312101686
Armenians -- History. Armenia -- History.

DS195.5 Armenia — History — By period

DS195.5.D337 1998
Dadrian, Vahakn N.
Warrant for genocide: key elements of Turko-Armenian conflict/ Vahakn N. Dadrian. New Brunswick, N.J.: Transaction Publishers, 1998. 214 p.
98-046214   956.6/2015   1560003898
Armenian massacres, 1915-1923.

DS204 Arabian Peninsula. Saudi Arabia — General works

DS204.L65 1997
Long, David E.
The Kingdom of Saudi Arabia/ David E. Long. Gainesville: University Press of Florida, c1997. xiii, 154 p.
96-045618   953.8   0813014719
Saudi Arabia.

DS247 Arabian Peninsula. Saudi Arabia — Local history and description — Regions, sultanates, emirates, etc., A-Z

DS247.A13.C67 1997
Cordesman, Anthony H.
Bahrain, Oman, Qatar, and the UAE: challenges of security/ Anthony H. Cordesman. Boulder, Colo.: Westview Press, 1997. p. cm.
96-046288   953.6   0813332397
National security -- Persian Gulf States. Persian Gulf States -- Strategic aspects. Persian Gulf States -- Defenses.

DS247.B23.C729 1998
Crawford, Harriet E. W.
Dilmun and its Gulf neighbours/ Harriet Crawford. Cambridge, U.K.; Cambridge University Press, 1998. xiii, 170 p.
97-009527   953.65   0521583489
Bahrain -- Antiquities. Persian Gulf Region -- Antiquities. Bahrain -- Civilization.

DS247.K88.C67 1997
Cordesman, Anthony H.
Kuwait: recovery and security after the Gulf War/ Anthony H. Cordesman. Boulder, Colo.: Westview Press, 1997. xiii, 153 p.
96-044401   953.6705/3   0813332435
Kuwait -- Politics and government. Kuwait -- Defenses.

DS247.K88.J69 1998
Joyce, Miriam.
Kuwait, 1945-1996: an Anglo-American perspective/ Miriam Joyce. London; Frank Cass, 1998. xxiii, 182 p.
97-051896   953.67   0714648639
Kuwait -- History -- Autonomy and independence movements. Kuwait -- Foreign relations -- England. England -- Foreign relations -- Kuwait.

DS247.O65.R56 1998
Riphenburg, Carol J., 1945-
Oman: political development in a changing world/ Carol J. Riphenburg. Westport, Conn.: Praeger, 1998. xii, 248 p.
97-033208   953.53   0275961443
Oman -- History. Oman -- Foreign relations. Oman -- Economic conditions.

DS247.O68.A59 2000
Allen, Calvin H.
Oman under Qaboos: from coup to constitution, 1970-1996/ Calvin H. Allen, Jr. and W. Lynn Rigsbee, II. London; Frank Cass, 2000. xix, 251 p.
99-054128   953   0714650013
Qabus bin Said, -- Sultan of Oman, -- 1940- Oman -- History.

DS266 Iran (Persia) — Social life and customs. Civilization. Intellectual life — Earliest (Zoroastrian)

DS266.G44 1998
Gheissari, Ali, 1954-
Iranian intellectuals in the 20th century/ Ali Gheissari. Austin: University of Texas Press, 1998. xvi, 247 p.
97-006742 955.05/086/31 0292728042
Intellectuals -- Iran -- Political activity. Political culture -- Iran. Iran -- Intellectual life -- 20th century.

DS269 Iran (Persia) — Ethnography — Individual elements in the population, A-Z

DS269.A75
Berberian, Houri.
Armenians and the Iranian constitutional revolution of 1905-1911: the love for freedom has no fatherland/ Houri Berberian. Boulder, Colo.: Westview Press, 2001. xii, 226 p.
00-053183 955/.00491992 0813338174
Armenians -- Iran -- Politics and government -- 20th century. Constitutional history -- Iran.

DS269.B33
Salzman, Philip Carl.
Black tents of Baluchistan/ Philip Carl Salzman. Washington, DC: Smithsonian Institution Press, c2000. ix, 390 p.
99-088316 305.891598 156098810X
Baluchi (Southwest Asian people) -- Social conditions. Baluchi (Southwest Asian people) -- Economic conditions. Baluchi (Southwest Asian people) -- Domestic animals. Sarhad Plateau (Iran) -- Social life and customs.

DS269.S53.T34 1997
Tapper, Richard.
Frontier nomads of Iran: a political and social history of the Shahsevan/ Richard Tapper. Cambridge, U.K.; Cambridge University Press, 1997. xvii, 429 p.
96-047890 955/.04 0521583365
Shahsevan (Iranian people) Iran -- History -- Qajar dynasty, 1794-1925. Iran -- History -- 20th century.

DS272 Iran (Persia) — History — General works

DS272.D36 2001
Daniel, Elton L.
The history of Iran/ Elton L. Daniel. Westport, CT: Greenwood Press, 2001. xvi, 299 p.
00-033132 955 0313307318
Iran -- History. Iran -- History -- 20th century.

DS298-318.85 Iran (Persia) — History — By period

DS298.K38 2000
Katouzian, Homa.
State and society in Iran: the eclipse of the Qajars and the emergence of the Pahlavis/ Homa Katouzian. London; I. B. Tauris; New York: 2000. xii, 351 p.
00-711855 1860643590
Iran -- Politics and government -- 20th century. Constitutional history -- Iran.

DS298.K39 1999
Keddie, Nikki R.
Qajar Iran and the rise of Reza Khan, 1796-1925/ Nikki R. Keddie. Costa Mesa, CA: Mazda Publishers, 1999. viii, 134 p.
99-012715 955/.04 1568590849
Iran -- History -- Qajar dynasty, 1794-1925. Iran -- Civilization -- 19th century.

DS307.N38.A63 1997
Amanat, Abbas.
Pivot of the universe: Nasir al-Din Shah Qajar and the Iranian Monarchy, 1831-1896/ Abbas Amanat. Berkeley: University of California Press, c1997. xix, 536 p.
95-050481 955/.04/092 0520083210
Nasir al-Din Shah, -- Shah of Iran, -- 1831-1896. Monarchy -- Iran -- History -- 19th century. Iran -- Kings and rulers -- Biography.

DS318.825.M476 2001
Menashri, David.
Post-revolutionary politics in Iran: religion, society, and power/ David Menashri. London; Frank Cass, 2001. xii, 356 p.
00-050862 955.05/4 0714650749
Iran -- Politics and government -- 1979-1997. Iran -- Politics and government -- 1997- Iran -- Foreign relations -- 1979-1997.

DS318.825.O23 1997
O'Ballance, Edgar.
Islamic fundamentalist terrorism, 1979-95: the Iranian connection/ Edgar O'Ballance. Washington Square, N.Y.: New York University Press, 1997. xx, 228 p.
96-012962 955.05/4 0814761917
State-sponsored terrorism -- Iran. Terrorism -- Islamic countries. Iran -- Foreign relations -- 1979-1997. Islamic countries -- Politics and government.

DS318.825.Z34 2000
Zahedi, Dariush.
The Iranian revolution then and now: indicators of regime instability/ Dariush Zahedi. Boulder, Co.: Westview Press, 2000. vi, 224 p.
00-020633 955.05/4 0813337488
Opposition (Political science) -- Iran. Iran -- Politics and government -- 1997- Iran -- Politics and government -- 1979-1997.

DS318.84.K48
Martin, Vanessa.
Creating an Islamic state: Khomeini and the making of a new Iran/ Vanessa Martin. London; I.B. Tauris; 2000. xv, 248 p.
00-710905 320.5/5/092 186064418X
Khomeini, Ruhollah -- Views on Islam and state. Islam and state. Islam and politics -- Iran. Iran -- Politics and government -- 1941-1979.

DS318.85.E4 1998
El-Shazly, Nadia El-Sayed, 1936-
The Gulf tanker war: Iran and Iraq's maritime swordplay/ Nadia El-Sayed El-Shazly. New York: St. Martin's Press, 1998. xxi, 403 p.
97-035534 955.05/42 0312211163
Iran-Iraq War, 1980-1988 -- Naval operations. Sea-power -- Iran. Persian Gulf Region -- Defenses. Persian Gulf Region -- Strategic aspects.

DS318.85.T866 1998
Tarock, Adam.
The superpowers' involvement in the Iran-Iraq War/ Adam Tarock. Commack, N.Y.: Nova Science Publishers, 1998. p. cm.
98-027522 955.5/422 1560725931
Iran-Iraq War, 1980-1988. United States -- Foreign relations -- Middle East. Middle East -- Foreign relations -- United States. Soviet Union -- Foreign relations -- Middle East.

DS331 Southern Asia. Indian Ocean Region — Societies. Sources and documents. Collections

DS331.A12 G66 2001
Gommans, Jos J.L.
Dutch Sources on South Asia, c. 1600-1825/ Jos Gommans, Lennart Bes, Gijs Kruijtzer. New Delhi: Manohar Publishers & Distributors, 2001- v. <1 >
2001-416655
Netherlands. Algemeen Rijksarchief -- Archives. South Asia -- Bibliography.

DS334.9 Southern Asia. Indian Ocean Region — Encyclopedias

DS334.9.C36 1989
The Cambridge encyclopedia of India, Pakistan, Bangladesh, Sri Lanka, Nepal, Bhutan, and the Maldives/ editor, Francis Robinson. Cambridge [England]; Cambridge University Press, 1989. 520 p.
88-026737 954/.003 0521334519
South Asia -- Encyclopedias.

DS338 Southern Asia. Indian Ocean Region — Antiquities

DS338.A45 1995
Allchin, F. Raymond 1923-
The archaeology of early historic South Asia: the emergence of cities and states/ F.R. Allchin; with contributions from George Erdosy ... [et al.]. Cambridge: Cambridge University Press, 1995. xvii, 371 p.
94-023181 934 0521375479
Excavations (Archaeology) -- South Asia. South Asia -- Antiquities.

DS339 Southern Asia. Indian Ocean Region — Social life and customs. Civilization. Intellectual life

DS339.A45 1997
Allchin, Bridget.
Origins of a civilization: the prehistory and early archaeology of South Asia/ Bridget and Raymond Allchin. New Delhi: Viking, 1997. xxii, 287 p.
97-904966   954.221   0670877131
Indus civilization.

DS339.4 Southern Asia. Indian Ocean Region — Ethnography — Individual elements in the population, A-Z

DS339.4.S68 1990
South Asians overseas: migration and ethnicity/ edited by Colin Clarke, Ceri Peach, and Steven Vertovec. Cambridge; Cambridge University Press, 1990. xx, 375 p.
89-034308   305.8/914   0521375436
South Asians -- Foreign countries. South Asians -- Ethnic indentity. South Asia -- Emigration and immigration.

DS339.8 Southern Asia. Indian Ocean Region — History — Study and teaching

DS339.8.O75 1993
Orientalism and the postcolonial predicament: perspectives on South Asia/ edited by Carol A. Breckenridge and Peter van der Veer. Philadelphia: University of Pennsylvania Press, c1993. viii, 355 p.
93-018290   954.220   0812214366
South Asia -- Study and teaching -- Congresses. South Asia -- Foreign public opinion, Occidental -- Congresses.

DS340 Southern Asia. Indian Ocean Region — History — General works

DS340.E85 1999
Ethnic futures: the state and identity politics in Asia/ Joanna Pfaff-Czarnecka ... [et al.]. New Delhi; Sage Publications, 1999. 209 p.
99-016908   323.1/54.221   0761993606
South Asia -- Politics and government. South Asia -- Ethnic relations. Malaysia -- Politics and government. Malaysia -- Ethnic relations.

DS340.F65 1998
Foltz, Richard,
Mughal India and Central Asia/ Richard C. Foltz. Karachi; Oxford University Press, 1998. xxx, 190 p.
99-196358   303.48/254058/0903.221
0195777824
Mogul Empire--History.

DS340.H35 1998
Hall, Richard Seymour,
Empires of the monsoon: a history of the Indian Ocean and its invaders/ Richard Hall. Pbk. ed. London: HarperCollins, 1998. xxiii, 575 p.
97-174392   909/.09824.221   0006380832
Indian Ocean Region -- History. Indian Ocean Region -- Civilization. Indian Ocean Region -- Discovery and exploration. Africa, East -- History. Africa, East -- Civilization. Africa, East -- Discovery and exploration.

DS340.H36 2001
Handcuffed to history: narratives, pathologies, and violence in South Asia/ edited by S.P. Udayakumar. Westport, Conn.: Praeger, c2001. x, 204 p.
00-042774   954.04.221   027596843X
Communalism--South Asia.

DS340.I69 1999
Invoking the past: the uses of history in South Asia/ edited by Daud Ali. New Delhi; Oxford University Press, 1999. xii, 399 p.
00-269655   954.221   0195649788
Nationalism--South   Asia--Congresses. Nationalism--South Asia--Congresses.

DS340.M36 2000
Mapping subaltern studies and the postcolonial/ edited by Vinayak Chaturvedi. London: Verso, 2000. xix, 364 p.
2001-278423   954.221   1859842143
South Asia -- History -- 20th century. South Asia -- Politics and government -- 20th century.

DS340.R57 1995
Risso, Patricia.
Merchants and faith: Muslim commerce and culture in the Indian Ocean/ Patricia Risso. Boulder, Colo.: Westview Press, 1995. xi, 152 p.
94-042937   382/.09172/4   0813316820
Muslims -- Indian Ocean Region -- History. Indian Ocean Region -- History. Indian Ocean Region -- Commerce -- History.

DS340.S83 1996
Subnational movements in South Asia/ edited by Subrata K. Mitra and R. Alison Lewis. Boulder, Colo.: Westview Press, 1996. xiii, 256 p.
94-035982   320.5/4/0954.220   0813320933
Regionalism--South Asia.

DS341-341.3 Southern Asia. Indian Ocean Region — History — Political and diplomatic history. Foreign and general relations

DS341.A38 1996
Ahmed, Ishtiaq, 1947-
State, nation, and ethnicity in contemporary South Asia/ Ishtiaq Ahmed. London and New York: Pinter Publishers: 1996. x, 326 p.
95-036993   305.8/00954   0861877470
Ethnicity -- South Asia.   South Asia -- Politics and government. South Asia -- Ethnic relations.

DS341.B35 1995
Barlas, Asma.
Democracy, nationalism, and communalism: the colonial legacy in South Asia/ Asma Barlas. Boulder, Colo.: Westview Press; 1995. xi, 241 p.
95-003113   320.954   0813387507
Democracy -- South Asia. Nationalism -- South Asia. Communalism -- South Asia. South Asia -- Politics and government.

DS341.B7313 1983
Braun, Dieter,
The Indian Ocean: region of conflict or "peace zone"?/ by Dieter Braun; translated from the German by Carol Geldart and Kathleen LLanwarne. New York: St. Martin's Press, 1983. xii, 228 p.
83-009680   327/.09182/4   0312413963
Indian   Ocean   Region -- Politics and government. Indian Ocean Region -- Strategic aspects.

DS341.J34 1995
Jalal, Ayesha.
Democracy and authoritarianism in South Asia: a comparative and historical perspective/ Ayesha Jalal. Cambridge; Cambridge University Press, 1995. xiii, 295 p.
94-017045   320.954   0521472717
South Asia -- Politics and government.

DS341.P53 2001
Phadnis, Urmila.
Ethnicity and nation-building in South Asia/ Urmila Phadnis and Rajat Ganguly. Rev. ed. New Delhi; Sage Publications, 2001. 467 p.
00-059158   320.54/0954.221   0761994394
Ethnicity--South Asia.

DS341.R35 2001
Rajagopalan, Swarna,
State and nation in South Asia / Swarna Rajagopalan. Boulder, Colo.: Lynne Rienner Publishers, 2001. x, 233 p.
2001-019069   323.1/54.221   1555879675
Nationalism--South Asia.

DS341.S75 2001
Stern, Robert W., 1933-
Democracy and dictatorship in South Asia: dominant classes and political outcomes in India, Pakistan, and Bangladesh/ Robert W. Stern. Westport, Conn.: Praeger, 2001. x, 194 p.
00-039172   320.954   0275970418
Democracy -- South Asia. Dictatorship -- South Asia. South Asia -- Politics and government.

DS341.S94 1989
Superpower rivalry in the Indian Ocean: Indian and American perspectives/ edited by Selig S. Harrison, K. Subrahmanyam. New York: Oxford University Press, 1989. viii, 309 p.
88-001480   320.9182/4   0195054970
Indian   Ocean   Region -- Politics and government. Indian Ocean Region -- Strategic aspects. Indian Ocean Region -- Economic conditions.

DS341.3.G7.M66 1987
Moore, R. J. 1934-
Making the new commonwealth/ R.J. Moore. Oxford [Oxfordshire]: Clarendon Press; 1987. xi, 218 p.
86-031215   327.41054   0198201125
Great Britain -- Foreign relations -- South Asia. South Asia -- Foreign relations -- Great Britain. Commonwealth countries.

DS341.3.U6.M35 1990
Malik, Iftikhar Haider, 1949-
US-South Asian relations, 1940-47: American attitudes towards the Pakistan movement/ Iftikhar H. Malik. New York: St. Martin's Press, 1991. xi, 322 p.
90-034611   327.73054/09/044   0312048920
South Asia -- Foreign relations -- United States. United States -- Foreign relations -- South Asia. United States -- Foreign relations -- 1933-1945.

DS351 Afghanistan — Gazetteers. Guidebooks

DS351.A62 1998
Afghanistan/ edited by Edward Girardet and Jonathan Walter. Geneva: Published for ICHR by Crosslines Communications Ltd., 524 p.
00-269253   915.810446.221   2970017601
Humanitarian assistance--Afghanistan--Handbooks, manuals. etc.

DS351.5 Afghanistan — General works

DS351.5.A34 1986
Afghanistan: a country study/ Foreign Area Studies, the American University; edited by Richard F. Nyrop and Donald M. Seekins. Washington, D.C.: The Studies: 1986. xxvii, 408 p.
86-003359   958/.1
Afghanistan.

DS354.6 Afghanistan — Ethnography — Other elements in the population, A-Z

DS354.6.H3.M68 1997
Mousavi, Sayed Askar.
The Hazaras of Afghanistan: an historical, cultural, economic and political study/ Sayed Askar Mousavi. New York: St. Martin's Press, 1997. xvii, 265 p.
97-002704   958.104/5   0312173865
Hazaras.

DS356 Afghanistan — History — General works. Dictionaries

DS356.A26 1996
Adamec, Ludwig W.
Dictionary of Afghan wars, revolutions, and insurgencies/ Ludwig W. Adamec. Lanham, Md.: Scarecrow Press, 1996. xvii, 364 p.
96-035600   958.1/003   0810832321
Afghanistan -- History -- Dictionaries. Afghanistan -- History, Military -- Dictionaries.

DS356.A27 1997
Adamec, Ludwig W.
Historical dictionary of Afghanistan/ Ludwig W. Adamec. Lanham, Md.: Scarecrow Press, 1997. xiii, 499 p.
97-002878   958.1/003   0810833123
Afghanistan -- History -- Dictionaries.

DS356.E95 2002
Evans, Martin,
Afghanistan: a short history of its people and politics/ Martin Ewans. 1st ed. New York: HarperCollins, c2002. ix, 244 p. [16] p. of plates
2002-017342   958.1.221   0060505079
Afghanistan -- History.

DS357.5-357.6 Afghanistan — History — Political and diplomatic history. Foreign and general relations

DS357.5.G42 1988
Ghaus, Abdul Samad.
The fall of Afghanistan: an insider's account/ Abdul Samad Ghaus. Washington: Pergamon-Brassey's International Defense Publish 1988. xi, 219 p.
86-030548   327.581   0080347010
Afghanistan -- Foreign relations.

DS357.6.S65.A34 1989
Afghanistan and the Soviet Union: collision and transformation/ edited by Milan Hauner and Robert L. Canfield. Boulder, Colo.: Westview Press, 1989. xi, 219 p.
88-028691   303.4/82581/047   0813375754
Afghanistan -- Relations -- Soviet Union. Soviet Union -- Relations -- Afghanistan. Afghanistan -- History -- Soviet occupation, 1979-1989.

DS358-371.3 Afghanistan — History — By period

DS358.E38 1996
Edwards, David B.
Heroes of the age: moral fault lines on the Afghan frontier/ David B. Edwards. Berkeley: University of California Press, c1996. xv, 307 p.
95-031423   958.1.220   0520200640
Afghanistan--History.

DS358.V64 2002
Vogelsang, W. J.
The Afghans/ Willem Vogelsang. Malden, MA: Blackwell Publishers, Inc., 2002. p. cm.
2001-000332   958.1.221   0631198415
Afghanistan -- History.

DS361.O43 1995
Olesen, Asta, 1952-
Islam and politics in Afghanistan/ Asta Olesen. Richmond, Surrey: Curzon, 1995. xiii, 351 p.
95-115079   0700702962
Islam and politics -- Afghanistan. Afghanistan -- Politics and government.

DS363.N64 1997
Noelle, Christine.
State and tribe in nineteenth-century Afghanistan: the reign of Amir Dost Muhammad Khan (1826-1863)/ Christine Noelle. Richmond, Surrey: Curzon, 1997. xxiv, 439 p.
2002-421181   0700706291
Dʹost Moòhammad Khʹan, Amir of Afghanistan, 1793-1863.

DS371.2.B65 1987
Bonner, Arthur.
Among the Afghans/ Arthur Bonner. Durham: Duke University Press, 1987. xvi, 366 p.
87-022260   958/.1044   0822307839
Bonner, Arthur -- Journeys -- Afghanistan. Journalists -- United States -- Biography. Afghanistan -- History -- Soviet occupation, 1979-1989. Afghanistan -- Description and travel.

DS371.2.C67 1995
Cordovez, Diego.
Out of Afghanistan: the inside story of the Soviet withdrawal/ Diego Cordovez, Selig S. Harrison. New York: Oxford University Press, 1995. ix, 450 p.
94-022301   958.104/5   0195062949
Afghanistan -- History -- Soviet occupation, 1979-1989 -- Personal narratives.

DS371.2.E38 2002
Edwards, David B.
Before Taliban: genealogies of the Afghan jihad/ David B. Edwards. Berkeley: University of California Press, 2002. xxii, 354 p.
2001-006513   958.104/5.221   0520228596
Safi, Samiullah. Amin, Qazi Muhammad.

DS371.2.G3447 1995
Galeotti, Mark.
Afghanistan, the Soviet Union's last war/ Mark Galeotti. London, England; Frank Cass, 1995. 242 p.
94-025068   958.104/5   0714645672
Afghanistan -- History -- Soviet occupation, 1979-1989.

DS371.2.G59 1999
Giustozzi, Antonio.
War, politics and society in Afghanistan, 1978-1992/ Antonio Giustozzi. Washington, DC: Georgetown University Press, 1999. xiv, 320 p.
99-017020   958.1   0878407588
Afghanistan -- History -- Soviet occupation, 1979-1989. Afghanistan -- History -- 1989- Afghanistan -- Social conditions.

DS371.2.G74 2001
Griffin, Michael.
The Taliban movement in Afghanistan/ Michael Griffin. Sterling, Virginia: Pluto Press, 2001. p. cm.
01-000249   958.104   0745312748
Taliban. Islamic fundamentalism -- Afghanistan. Islam and state -- Afghanistan. Afghanistan -- History -- 1989-

DS371.2.K35 1995
Kakar, M. Hasan.
Afghanistan: the Soviet invasion and the Afghan response, 1979-1982/ M. Hassan Kakar. Berkeley: University of California Press, c1995. x, 380 p.
93-036111   958.104/5   0520085914
Afghanistan -- History -- Soviet occupation, 1979-1989.

DS371.2.K48 1991
Khan, Riaz M.
Untying the Afghan knot: negotiating Soviet withdrawal/ Riaz M. Khan. Durham: Duke University Press, 1991. viii, 402 p.
91-011624   958.104/5   0822311550
Afghanistan -- History -- Soviet Occupation, 1979-1989. Pakistan -- Foreign relations -- Afghanistan. Afghanistan -- Foreign relations -- Pakistan.

DS371.2.M28 1998
Magnus, Ralph H.
Afghanistan: mullah, Marx, and mujahid/ Ralph H. Magnus, Eden Naby. Boulder, Colo.: Westview Press, 1998. xiii, 274 p.
97-019041   958.104/6   0865315132
Islam and politics -- Afghanistan. Communism -- Afghanistan. Afghanistan -- Politics and government.

DS371.2.M373 2002
Marsden, Peter,
The Taliban: war and religion in Afghanistan/
Peter Marsden. New expanded ed. London; Zed
Books, 2002. xiv, 162 p.
2001-058139 958.104/6.221 1842771671
*Islamic fundamentalism--Afghanistan. Islam and
politics--Afghanistan.*

DS371.2.R35 1994
Rais, Rasul Bux.
War without winners: Afghanistan's uncertain
transition after the Cold War/ Rasul Bakhsh Rais.
Karachi, Pakistan; Oxford University Press, 1994.
xi, 286 p.
95-113928 958.104/5 019577535X
*Afghanistan -- Politics and government --
1973- Afghanistan -- History -- Soviet occupation,
1979-1989.*

DS371.2.R367 2000
Rashid, Ahmed.
Taliban: militant Islam, oil, and fundamentalism in
Central Asia/ Ahmed Rashid. New Haven: Yale
University Press, c2000. xi, 274 p.
99-068718 958.104.221 0300083408
*Islamic fundamentalism--Afghanistan. Islam and
state--Afghanistan. Islam and politics--
Afghanistan.*

DS371.2.R8 1995
Rubin, Barnett R.
The fragmentation of Afghanistan: state formation
and collapse in the international system/ Barnett R.
Rubin. New Haven, CT: Yale University Press,
1995. xvii, 378 p.
94-021189 958.104/5 0300059639
*Afghanistan -- History -- Soviet occupation,
1979-1989.*

DS371.2.R82 1995
Rubin, Barnett R.
The search for peace in Afghanistan: from buffer
state to failed state/ Barnett R. Rubin. New Haven:
Yale University Press, c1995. xi, 190 p.
95-015694 958.104/5 0300063768
*Afghanistan -- Politics and government --
1973-*

DS371.3.C67 2003
Corwin, Phillip.
Doomed in Afghanistan: a UN officer's memoir of
the fall of Kabul and Najibullah's escape, 1992/
Phillip Corwin. New Brunswick, NJ: Rutgers
University Press, 2003. xx, 241 p.
2002-024831 958.104/6.221 0813531713
Najib, 1947- Corwin, Phillip.

DS371.3.F86 1998
Fundamentalism reborn?: Afghanistan and the
Taliban/ edited by William Maley. New York: New
York University Press, 1998. xiii, 253 p.
97-052616 958.104/6 0814755852
Afghanistan -- History -- 1989-

DS371.3.G66 2001
Goodson, Larry P.
Afghanistan's endless war: state failure, regional
politics, and the rise of the Taliban/ Larry P.
Goodson. Seattle: University of Washington Press,
c2001. xv, 264 p.
00-060701 958.1.221 0295980508
*Afghanistan -- History -- 1989- Afghanistan --
Social conditions.*

DS374 Afghanistan — Local history and description — Provinces, regions, etc., A-Z

DS374.B28.H66 1999
Holt, Frank Lee.
Thundering Zeus: the making of Hellenistic
Bactria/ Frank L. Holt. Berkeley: University of
California Press, c1999. xviii, 221 p.
98-006098 939/.6 0520211405
*Greeks -- Bactria -- History. Coins, Greek --
Bactria. Numismatics. Bactria -- History -- Study
and teaching. Bactria -- History.*

DS374.B28.S54 2000
Sidky, H., 1956-
The Greek kingdom of Bactria: from Alexander to
Eurcratides the Great/ H. Sidky. Lanham, Md.:
University Press of America, c2000. xvi, 284 p.
00-036365 939/.6
Bactria -- History.

DS376.9 Pakistan — General works

DS376.9.A35 1996
Ahsan, Aitzaz.
The Indus saga and the making of Pakistan/ Aitzaz
Ahsan. Karachi: Oxford University Press, 1996.
xvi, 413 p.
96-930465 954.91.221 0195776933
Pakistan -- History. India -- History.

DS376.9.P32 1997
Pakistan. [2nd ed.] Karachi: Oxford University
Press, 1997. 208 p.
97-930857 954.91.221 0195778383
Pakistan.

DS376.9.P376 1995
Pakistan: a country study/ edited by Peter R.
Blood.6th ed. Washington, D.C.: Federal Research
Division, Library of Congress: xlv, 398 p.
95-017247 954.91.220 0844408344
Pakistan.

DS380 Pakistan — Ethnography

DS380.P8 S66 1995
Spain, James W.
Pathans of the latter day/ James W. Spain. Karachi;
Oxford University Press, 1995. xi, 163 p.
97-181173 954.91/2.221 0195775767
*Spain, James W. (James William)--Journeys--
Pakistan--North-west Pushtuns--Pakistan--North-
west Frontier Province. Pushtuns--Pakistan--
North-west Frontier Province--History.*

DS382 Pakistan — History — Biography (Collective)

DS382.B87 1999
Burki, Shahid Javed.
Historical dictionary of Pakistan/ Shahid Javed
Burki. Lanham, Md.: Scarecrow Press, 1999. liii,
403 p.
99-010725 954.91/003 0810836343
Pakistan -- History -- Dictionaries.

DS382.B89 1999
Burki, Shahid Javed.
Pakistan: fifty years of nationhood/ Shahid Javed
Burki. 3rd ed. Boulder, CO: Westview Press, 1999.
xxi, 250 p.
98-055927 954.91.221 081333621X
Pakistan -- History.

DS382.H8 1997
Hussain, J.
A history of the peoples of Pakistan: towards
independence/ J. Hussain. Karachi; Oxford
University Press, 1997. viii, 487 p.
98-136158 954.9.221 0195778197
Pakistan -- History.

DS382.J66 2002
Jones, Owen Bennett.
Pakistan: in the eye of the storm/ Owen Bennett
Jones. New Haven: Yale University Press, 2002. p.
cm.
2002-006944 954.91.221 0300097603
Pakistan -- History.

DS382.T35 1998
Talbot, Ian.
Pakistan, a modern history/ Ian Talbot. New York:
St. Martin's Press, 1998. xv, 432 p.
98-017322 954.91.221 0312216068
Pakistan -- History.

DS383.5 Pakistan — History — Political and diplomatic history. Foreign and general relations

DS383.5.A3.W45 1994
Weinbaum, Marvin G., 1935-
Pakistan and Afghanistan: resistance and
reconstruction/ Marvin G. Weinbaum. Boulder:
Westview Press; 1994. xii, 190 p.
93-049473 327.54910581/09/048 0813388074
*Refugees -- Pakistan. Refugees -- Afghanistan.
Afghanistan -- History -- Soviet occupation, 1979-
1989. Pakistan -- Foreign relations -- Afghanistan.
Afghanistan -- Foreign relations -- Pakistan.*

DS384-385 Pakistan — History — By period

DS384.A69 2001
Afzal, M. Rafique.
Pakistan, history & politics, 1947-1971/ M.
Rafique Afzal. Karachi: Oxford University Press,
2001. xvi, 490 p.
2001-288994 0195796349
Pakistan -- Politics and government.

DS384.A786 2001
Arif, K. M.
Khaki shadows: Pakistan 1947-1997/ K.M. Arif.
Karachi: Oxford University Press, 2001. xvii,
452 p.
2001-300947 954.9104.221 019579396X
*Arif, K. M. (Khalid Mahmud), 1930- Generals--
Pakistan--Political activity.*

DS384.A787 1995
Arif, Khalid Mahmud, 1930-
Working with Zia: Pakistan's power politics, 1977-
1988/ Khalid Mahmud Arif. Karachi: Oxford
University Press, 1995. xx, 435 p.
95-930654 954.9105 0195775708
*Zia-ul-Haq, Mohammad. Pakistan -- Politics
and government -- 1988- Pakistan -- Politics and
government -- 1971-1988.*

DS384.B883 1991
Burki, Shahid Javed.
Pakistan under the military: eleven years of Zia ul-Haq/ Shahid Javed Burki and Craig Baxter with contributions by Robert LaPorte, Jr. and Kamal Azfar. Boulder: Westview Press; 1991. viii, 212 p.
90-049969   954.9105   0813379857
Zia-ul-Haq, Mohammad.   Pakistan -- Politics and government -- 1971-1988.

DS384.H37 2000
Hasan, Mubashir,
The mirage of power: an inquiry into the Bhutto years, 1971-1977/ Mubashir Hasan. Oxford; Oxford University Press, 2000. xi, 393 p.
2001-269442   0195793005
Bhutto, Zulfikar Ali Hasan, Mubashir, 1922- Statesmen--Pakistan--Biography.

DS384.M2718 1997
Malik, Iftikhar Haider,
State and civil society in Pakistan: politics of authority, ideology, and ethnicity/ Iftikhar H. Malik. New York: St. Martin's Press, 1997. xviii, 347 p.
96-027847   320.95491.220   0312164211
Ethnicity--Pakistan.

DS384.S2195 2000
Safdar Mahmood.
Pakistan: political roots and development, 1947-1999/ Safdar Mahmood. Karachi: Oxford University Press, 2000. x, 440 p.
00-283201   0195793730
Pakistan -- Politics and government. Pakistan -- Politics and government -- 1971-

DS384.Z572 1997
Ziring, Lawrence, 1928-
Pakistan in the twentieth century: a political history/ Lawrence Ziring. Karachi; Oxford University Press, c1997. 647 p.
98-148828
Pakistan -- History.

DS385.B45 W65 1993
Wolpert, Stanley A.,
Zulfi Bhutto of Pakistan: his life and times/ Stanley Wolpert. New York: Oxford University Press, 1993. xii, 378 p.
92-030044   954.9105/092. 220   0195076613
Bhutto, Zulfikar Ali.   Prime ministers--Pakistan--Biography.

DS385.J5.A69 1997
Ahmed, Akbar S.
Jinnah, Pakistan and Islamic identity: the search for Saladin/ Akbar S. Ahmed. London; Routledge, 1997. xxix, 274 p.
97-010613   954.03/5/092   0415149657
Jinnah, Mohamed Ali, -- 1876-1948.   Islam and state -- Pakistan. Statesmen -- Pakistan -- Biography. India -- Politics and government -- 1919-1947. Pakistan -- History -- 1947-

DS385.J5 B87 1997
Burke, S. M.
Quaid-i-Azam Mohammad Ali Jinnah: his personality and his politics/ S.M. Burke and Salim Al-Din Quraishi. Karachi; Oxford University Press, 1997. xvi, 412 p.
98-107916   954.904/2/092.221   0195777832
Jinnah, Mahomed Ali, 1876-1948.   Statesmen--Pakistan--Biography.

DS385.J5.W64 1984
Wolpert, Stanley A., 1927-
Jinnah of Pakistan/ Stanley Wolpert. New York: Oxford University Press, 1984. xii, 421 p.
83-013318   954.9/042/0924   0195034120
Jinnah, Mahomed Ali, -- 1876-1948.   Statesmen -- Pakistan -- Biography.

DS385.K498 A3 1999
Khan, Jahan Dad,
Pakistan leadership challenges/ Jahan Dad Khan. Karachi: Oxford University Press, 1999. xx, 359 p.
99-921716   954.9105/092. 221   0195779908
Khan, Jahan Dad, Lt. Gen.   Generals--Pakistan--Biography.

DS385.M39 A3 1999
Mazari, Sherbaz Khan.
A journey to disillusionment/ Sherbaz Khan Mazari. Karachi: Oxford University Press, 1999. xxxii, 646 p.
99-922213   954.9104/092. 221   0195790766
Mazari, Sherbaz Khan.   Politicians--Pakistan--Biography.

DS385.9-389.22 Pakistan — History — By period

DS385.9.G36 1994
Ganguly, Sumit.
The origins of war in South Asia: the Indo-Pakistani conflicts since 1947/ ^Sumit Ganguly. 2nd ed. Boulder: Westview Press, 1994. ix, 145 p.
93-041773   954.04.220   0813385806
India-Pakistan Conflict, 1947-1949. India-Pakistan Conflict, 1965. India-Pakistan Conflict, 1971.

DS389.P343 2001
Pakistan: founder's aspirations and today's realities/ edited by Hafeez Malik. Karachi: Oxford University Press, 2001. xi, 469 p.
2001-289561   954.9105.221
Pakistan -- Politics and government -- 1988-

DS389.P344 2001
Pakistan, nationalism without a nation/ edited by Christophe Jaffrelot. New York: Zed Books, 2001. p. cm.
2001-026999   954.9105.221   1842771175
Pakistan -- Politics and government -- 1988- Pakistan -- Ethnic relations.

DS389.22.B48 A44 2000
Akhund, Iqbal.
Trial and error: the advent and eclipse of Benazir Bhutto/ Iqbal Akhund. Karachi; Oxford University Press, 2000. xviii, 346 p.
00-710318   954.9105/092. 221   0195791606
Bhutto, Benazir. Bhutto, Benazir.   Prime ministers--Pakistan--Biography.

DS392 Pakistan — Local history and description — Minor kingdoms, states, regions, etc., A-Z

DS392.N67 A45 2001
Allen, Charles, 1940-
Soldier sahibs: the daring adventurers who tamed India's northwest frontier/ Charles Allen. New York: Carroll & Graf, 2001. xii, 368 p.
2001-025902   0786708611
Afghan Wars. British -- India -- Biography. Soldiers -- India -- Biography. North-west Frontier Province (Pakistan) -- History, Military. India -- History -- British occupation, 1765-1947. India -- History -- 19th century.

DS392.N67 B36 2000
Banerjee, Mukulika.
The Pathan unarmed: opposition & memory in the North West Frontier/ Mukulika Banerjee. Santa Fe, N.M.: School of American Research Press, c2000. 238 p.
00-066147   954.91/205.221   0933452691
Khudai Khidmatgar movement. Pushtuns--Pakistan--North-west Frontier Province--Politics and Nonviolence--Pakistan--North-west Frontier Province.

DS392.N67.M67 1998
Moreman, T. R.
The army in India and the development of frontier warfare, 1849-1947/ T.R. Moreman. New York, N.Y.: St. Martin's Press, 1998. xxiii, 258 p.
98-018858   355/.0095491/2   031221703X
North-west Frontier Province (Pakistan) -- History, Military.

DS392.N67.R57 1988
Rittenberg, Stephen Alan.
Ethnicity, nationalism, and the Pakhtuns: the independence movement in India's North-west Frontier Province/ Stephen Alan Rittenberg. Durham, N.C.: Carolina Academic Press, c1988. xii, 286 p.
84-070181   954.91/2   0890892776
Pushtuns -- Politics and government. Nationalism -- Pakistan -- North-west Frontier Province -- History. Ethnicity -- Pakistan -- North-west Frontier Province. North-west Frontier Province (Pakistan) -- Politics and government.

DS392.S58 J66 2002
Jones, Allen Keith,
Politics in Sindh, 1907-1940: Muslim identity and the demand for Pakistan/ Allen Keith Jones. Karachi: Oxford University Prss, 2002. xxii, 214 p.
2002-343069   0195795938
Pakistan movement.

DS392.W3.W37 2000
Warren, Alan.
Waziristan, the Faqir of Ipi, and the Indian Army: the North West Frontier Revolt of 1936-37/ Alan Warren. Oxford; Oxford University Press, 2000. xxxii, 324 p.
00-699913   954.91/20359   0195790162
Insurgency -- Pakistan -- Waziristan -- History. Armies -- India -- History. Waziristan (Pakistan) -- History. Pakistan -- History -- 20th century.

DS392.2 Pakistan — Local history and description — Cities, towns, etc., A-Z

DS392.2.P47 N53 2001
Nichols, Robert.
Settling the Frontier: land, law and society in the Peshawar valley, 1500-1900/ Robert Nochols. Karachi: Oxford University Press, 2001. xxxvii, 321 p.
2001-289331   954.91/23.221   0195793803
Pushtuns--Pakistan--Peshawar Region--History.

DS393.8 Bangladesh. East Pakistan — Social life and customs. Civilization. Intellectual life

DS393.8.B39 1997
Baxter, Craig.
Bangladesh: from a nation to a state/ Craig Baxter. Boulder, Colo.: Westview Press, 1997. xv, 176 p.
96-041187   954.92   0813328543
Bangladesh -- Civilization.

DS394.73 Bangladesh. East Pakistan — History — Political and diplomatic history. Foreign and general relations

DS394.73.I4 J33 1999
Jacques, Kathryn,
Bangladesh, India, and Pakistan: international relations and regional tensions in South Asia/ Kathryn Jacques. New York: St. Martin's Press, 1999. p. cm.
99-033849   327.5491054.221   0312223862
Bangladesh -- Foreign relations -- India.

DS405 India (Bharat) — Gazetteers. Dictionaries. Directories, etc.

DS405.I64
India, a reference annual. Delhi: Publications Division, Ministry of Information a [1953?- v.
54-002074   915.4
India -- Periodicals.

DS407 India (Bharat) — General works

DS407.I4465 1996
India: a country study/ Federal Research Division, Library of Congress; edited by James Heitzman and Robert L. Worden. 5th ed. Washington, D.C.: The Division: lii, 850 p.
96-019266   954.220   0844408336
India.

DS407.I51325 2000
India: a mosaic/ Ian Buruma ... [et al.]; edited by Robert B. Silvers and Barbara Epstein; preface by N. Ram, introduction by Arundhati Roy. New York: New York Review Books, c2000. xxxiv, 285 p.
99-032297   954.221   0940322080
India.

DS407.S82 1998
Stein, Burton,
A history of India/ Burton Stein. Oxford [England]; Blackwell Publishers, 1998. xvi, 432 p.
97-037370   954.221   0631205462
India -- History. Pakistan -- Ethnic relations.

DS412 India (Bharat) — Description and travel — 1762-1858

DS412.H443 1971
Heber, Reginald, 1783-1826.
Bishop Heber in northern India; selections from Heber's journal, edited by M. A. Laird. London, Cambridge U.P., 1971. x, 324 p.
70-123673   915/.4   0521078733
India -- Description and travel. India -- Social life and customs.

DS414 India (Bharat) — Description and travel — 1947-1980

DS414.P26 1992a
Palling, Bruce.
India, a literary companion/ Bruce Palling. London: John Murray, 1992. 264 p.
92-171078   0719548306
India -- Description and travel.

DS422 India (Bharat) — Social life and customs. Civilization. Intellectual life — Addresses, essays, lectures

DS422.C3 C465 1998
Challenging untouchability: Dalit initiative and experience from Karnataka/ editors, Simon R. Charsley, G.K. Karanth. New Delhi; Sage Publications, c1998. 323 p.
98-024650   305.5/68.221   0761992642
Dalits--India--Karnataka.   Caste--India--Karnataka.

DS422.C3 D22 2001
Dalit identity and politics/ editor, Ghanshyam Shah. New Delhi; Sage Publications, 2001. 363 p.
00-045815   305.5/68.221   0761995080
Dalits--India--Politics and government. Dalits--India--Economic conditions. Dalits--India--Social conditions.

DS422.C3.D245 1998
Dalits in modern India: vision and values/ editor, S.M. Michael. Thousand Oaks, CA: Sage Publications, 1998. p. cm.
98-037909   305.5/68/0954   0761992901
Untouchables -- India -- Politics and government. Untouchables -- India -- Social conditions. Untouchables -- India -- Economic conditions. India -- Politics and government -- 1947-

DS422.C3 D58 2001
Dirks, Nicholas B.,
Castes of mind: colonialism and the making of modern India/ Nicholas B. Dirks. Princeton, N.J.: Princeton University Press, c2001. xiii, 372 p.
2001-021236   305.5/122/0954.221   0691088950
Caste--India. Social classes--India.

DS422.C3 E46 2002
Encyclopaedia of Dalits in India/ editors, Sanjay Paswan, Pramanshi Jaideva. Delhi: Kalpaz Publications, 2002. 11 v.
2002-287774   8178350270
Dalits--India.

DS422.C3 I57 2000
Gupta, Dipankar,
Interrogating caste: understanding hierarchy and difference in Indian society/ Dipankar Gupta. New Delhi; Penguin Books, 2000. ix, 300 p.
99-949852   305.5/122/0954.221   0140297065
Caste--India. Social stratification--India.

DS422.C3.M39 1998
Mendelsohn, Oliver.
The untouchables: subordination, poverty, and the state in modern India/ Oliver Mendelsohn and Marika Vicziany. Cambridge, U.K.; Cambridge University Press, 1998. xviii, 289 p.
97-027947   305.5/68   0521553628
Untouchables -- India -- Politics and government. Untouchables -- India -- Economic conditions. Untouchables -- India -- Social conditions. India -- Politics and government -- 1947-

DS422.C3.P728 2000
Prashad, Vijay.
Untouchable freedom: a social history of Dalit community/ Vijay Prashad. New Delhi; Oxford University Press, 2000. xx, 176 p.
99-952353   305.5/68   0195650751
Dalits -- India -- Social conditions. Sanitation workers -- India -- Social conditions.

DS422.C3.V49613 1997
Viramma.
Viramma, life of an untouchable/ Viramma, Josiane Racine and Jean-Luc Racine; translated by Will Hobson. London; Verso; 1997. viii, 312 p.
97-039447   305.5/68   1859848176
Viramma.   Untouchables -- India, South -- Biography.   India, South -- Social conditions. India, South -- Economic conditions.

DS422.C64 C66 1996
Contesting the nation: religion, community, and the politics of democracy in India/ edited by David Ludden. Philadelphia: University of Pennsylvania Press, c1996. ix, 346 p.
95-052811   320.954.220   0812215850
Communalism--India. Hindus--India. Muslims--India.

DS422.C64.D39 1999
Datta, Pradip Kumar.
Carving blocs: communal ideology in early twentieth-century Bengal/ Pradip Kumar Datta. New Delhi; Oxford University Press, c1999. 312 p.
99-937583
Communalism -- India -- Bengal. Hindus -- India -- Bengal. Muslims -- India -- Bengal. Bengal (India) -- Ethnic relations.

DS422.C64 E55 1995
Engineer, Asgharali,
Lifting the veil: communal violence and communal harmony in contemporary India/ Asghar Ali Engineer. Hyderabad, [India]: Sangam Books: vi, 347 p.
94-906906   8173700400
Communalism--India. Muslims--India. Hindus--India.

DS422.C64 K35 1996
Kakar, Sudhir.
The colors of violence: cultural identities, religion, and conflict/ Sudhir Kakar. Chicago: University of Chicago Press, 1996. xiii, 217 p.
95-035971   303.6/0954.220   0226422852
Communalism--India. Violence--India. Violence--Religious aspects.

DS422.C64 V37 2002
Varshney, Ashutosh,
Ethnic conflict and civic life: Hindus and Muslims in India/ Ashutosh Varshney. New Haven, CT: Yale University Press, c2002. ix, 382 p.
2001-046526   954/.0088/2971.221   0300085303
Communalism--India. Ethnic conflict--India. Hindus--India.

DS423-428 India (Bharat) — Social life and customs. Civilization. Intellectual life — Civilization and culture. Intellectual life

DS423.C577 1995
Consuming modernity: public culture in a South Asian world/ Carol A. Breckenridge, editor. Minneapolis: University of Minnesota Press, 1995. ix, 261 p.
94-046772   306/.0954.220   0816623066
Popular culture--India.

DS423.E53 1998
Encyclopaedia of ancient Indian culture/ edited by N.N. Bhattacharyya. New Delhi: Manohar Publishers & Distributors, 1998. 459 p.
98-909720   954.02/03.221   817304077X
India -- Civilization -- Encyclopedias.

DS423.P54 2001
Pleasure and the nation: the history, politics, and consumption of public culture in India/ edited by Rachel Dwyer, Christopher Pinney. New Delhi; Oxford University Press, 2001. vi, 366 p.
00-440671   954.221   0195650905
popular culture--India. India--Intellectual life.

DS425.A65 1968b
Allchin, Bridget.
The birth of Indian civilization; India and Pakistan before 500 B.C. [by] Bridget and Raymond Allchin. Baltimore, Penguin Books [1968] 365 p.
79-001722   913.3/4/03
India -- Civilization -- To 1200.

DS425.B79 2001
Bryant, Edwin.
The quest for the origins of Vedic culture: the Indo-Aryan migration debate/ Edwin Bryant. Oxford [England]; Oxford University Press, 2001. xi, 387 p.
99-086274   934/.02.221   0195137779
Indo-Aryans--Origin. Indus civilization.

DS425.K576 2002
Kosambi, D. D.
Combined methods in Indology and other writings/ compiled, edited, and introduced by Brajadulal Chattopadhyaya. New Delhi; Oxford University Press, 2002. xxxvii, 832 p.
2002-285548   0195642392
India -- Civilization. India -- History.

DS425.M34 2002
McIntosh, Jane.
A peaceful realm: the rise and fall of the Indus civilization/ Jane R. McIntosh. Boulder, CO: Westview Press, 2001. 224 p.
2001-017688   934.221   0813335329
Indus civilization.

DS425.T68 1997
Trautmann, Thomas R.
Aryans and British India/ Thomas R. Trautmann. Berkeley: University of California Press, c1997. xiv, 260 p.
96-034953   954.03/1   0520205464
Indo-Aryans -- History.   India -- History -- British occupation, 1765-1947.

DS428.P76 2002
Procida, Mary A.
Married to the empire: gender, politics and imperialism in India, 1883-1947/ Mary A. Procida. Manchester; Manchester University Press: p. cm.
2001-057981   954.03/5.221   0719060737
British--India. Colonial administrators' spouses--India. Imperialism.

DS428.S93 1997
Schwarz, Henry.
Writing cultural history in colonial and postcolonial India/ Henry Schwarz. Philadelphia, Pa.: University of Pennsylvania Press, c1997. x, 199 p.
97-002875   954   0812233735
Social change -- India.   India -- Civilization -- 1947- India -- Civilization -- 1765-1947.

DS428.2 India (Bharat) — Social life and customs. Civilization. Intellectual life — Civilization and culture. Intellectual life

DS428.2.T47 1997
Tharoor, Shashi,
India: from midnight to the millennium/ by Shashi Tharoor. 1st ed. New York: Arcade Pub.: xiv, 392 p.
97-008376   954.04.221   1559703849
India -- Civilization -- 1947-

DS430 India (Bharat) — Ethnography. Sects — General works

DS430.G66 2000
Gottschalk, Peter, 1963-
Beyond Hindu and Muslim: multiple identity in narratives from village India/ Peter Gottschalk. Oxford; Oxford University Press, 2000. xviii, 215 p.
99-046737   305.8/00954   0195135148
Group identity -- India. Ethnicity -- India. Muslims -- India. India -- Ethnic relations.

DS430.I3 1997
Identity, consciousness and the past: forging of caste and community in India and Sri Lanka/ edited by H.L. Seneviratne. Delhi; Oxford University Press, 1997. viii, 207 p.
97-175770   0195640012
Ethnology--India. Ethnology--Sri Lanka. Caste--India.

DS430.S543 2000
Singh, Gurharpal.
Ethnic conflict in India: a case-study of Punjab/ Gurharpal Singh. New York: St. Martin's Press, 2000. xv, 231 p.
99-042137   305.8/00954/552.221   0312228384
Communalism--India--Punjab--Case studies. Nationalism--India--Punjab--Case studies.

DS430.S545 1992
Singh, K. Suresh
People of India/ K.S. Singh. Calcutta: Anthropological Survey of India, 1992-<1998 > v. <1-3, 7-12, 14, 18-21, 23, 25, 28, 31-34,38-39>
92-906415   8185579091
Ethnology--India.

DS430.Z35 1995
Zakaria, Rafiq,
The widening divide: an insight into Hindu-Muslim relations/ Rafiq Zakaria. New Delhi; New York, N.Y.: 1995. xxvi, 357 p.
95-905550   305.8/00954.220   0670866814
Hindus--India. Muslims--India. Communalism--India.

DS432 India (Bharat) — Ethnography. Sects — Individual elements

DS432.B25.H62 1999
Hockings, Paul.
Kindreds of the earth: Badaga household structure and demography/ Paul Hockings with a foreword by John C. Caldwell. Walnut Creek, CA: AltaMira Press, c1999. 302 p.
98-039262   306/.089/94814   0761992928
Badaga (Indic people) -- Kinship. Badaga (Indic people) -- Population. Badaga (Indic people) -- Social life and customs. Nilgiri Hills (India) -- Social life and customs.

DS432.B32.R36 1998
Rao, Aparna.
Autonomy: life cycle, gender, and status among Himalayan pastoralists/ Aparna Rao. New York: Berghahn Books, 1998. xvii, 350 p.
97-015842   306/.089/914   1571819037
Bakrawallah (Indic people) -- Psychology. Bakrawallah (Indic people) -- Ethnic identity. Bakrawallah (Indic people) -- Social conditions. Jammu and Kashmir (India) -- Social conditions.

DS432.G7.U55 1997
Unnithan-Kumar, Maya, 1961-
Identity, gender, and poverty: new perspectives on caste nd tribe in Rajasthan/ Maya Unnithan-Kumar. Providence: Berghahn Books, 1997. xii, 291 p.
97-015986   305.42/089/914   1571819185
Grasia (Indic people) Women, Grasia. Caste -- India. India -- Scheduled tribes.

DS432.K17.M56 1984
Mines, Mattison, 1941-
The warrior merchants: textiles, trade, and territory in South India/ Mattison Mines. Cambridge [Cambridgeshire]; Cambridge University Press, 1984. xiii, 178 p.
84-005899   306/.09548 0521267145
Kaikolar. India, South -- Economic conditions. India, South -- Social conditions.

DS432.M77.R36 1992
Ram, Kalpana.
Mukkuvar women: gender, hegemony, and capitalist transformation in a South Indian fishing community/ Kalpana Ram. New Delhi: Kali for Women, 1992. xix, 266 p.
92-903104   8185107467
Mukkuvars -- India -- Kanniyakumari (District) Women -- India -- Kanniyakumari (District) -- Social conditions. Women -- India -- Kanniyakumari (District) -- Economic conditions. Kanniyakumari (India: District) -- Social conditions. Kanniyakumari (India: District) -- Economic conditions.

DS432.M84.M44 1997
Mehta, Dipaka, 1939-
Work, ritual, biography: a Muslim community in North India/ Deepak Mehta. Delhi; Oxford University Press, 1997. 283 p.
96-912041   0195640217
Muslims -- India -- Bara Banki. Hand weaving -- India -- Bara Banki. Bara Banki (India) -- Social life and customs.

DS432.R13.A37 1999
Agrawal, Arun, 1962-
Greener pastures: politics, markets, and community among a migrant pastoral people/ Arun Agrawal. Durham, N.C.: Duke University Press, 1999. p. cm.
98-021274   305.9/0691 0822322331
Rabaris. Shepherds -- India -- Rajasthan. Nomads -- India -- Rajasthan.

DS432.S359.D834 1998
Dube, Saurabh.
Untouchable pasts: religion, identity, and power among a central Indian community, 1780-1950/ Saurabh Dube. Albany: State University of New York Press, c1998. xvii, 308 p.
97-049929   954/.3 079143687X
Satnamis -- India -- Chattisagarh -- History. Chattisagarh (India) -- Social conditions. Chattisagarh (India) -- Economic conditions. Chattisagarh (India) -- Religious life and customs.

DS432.T3.H33 1999
Hancock, Mary Elizabeth.
Womanhood in the making: domestic ritual and public culture in urban South India/ Mary Elizabeth Hancock. Boulder, Colo.: Westview Press, 1999. xv, 286 p.
98-047288   305.48/8948110548 0813335833
Women, Tamil -- Rites and ceremonies. Women, Tamil -- Religion. Women, Tamil -- Social conditions. Madras (India) -- Social life and customs. Madras (India) -- Religious life and customs.

DS435 India (Bharat) — History — Historiography

DS435.C46 2002
Chakrabarty, Dipesh.
Habitations of modernity: essays in the wake of subaltern studies/ Dipesh Chakrabarty; with a foreword by Homi K. Bhabha. Chicago: University of Chicago Press, 2002. xxiv, 173 p.
2002-019210   954/.007/2.221 0226100391
Social justice--India.

DS435.8 India (Bharat) — History — Study and teaching

DS435.8.I47 1990
Inden, Ronald B.
Imagining India/ Ronald Inden. Oxford, UK; Basil Blackwell, 1990. vii, 299 p.
89-036150   954/.0072 0631169237
India -- Study and teaching -- Europe. India -- Study and teaching -- United States.

DS436 India (Bharat) — History — General works

DS436.C65 1996
Cohn, Bernard S., 1928-
Colonialism and its forms of knowledge: the British in India/ Bernard S. Cohn. Princeton, N.J.: Princeton University Press, 1996. xvii, 189 p.
96-006448   954 0691032939
India -- History -- British occupation, 1765-1947. India -- Civilization -- British influences. India -- Politics and government -- 1765-1947.

DS436.C7 vol. 2.S463
India and Indonesia from the 1830s to 1914: the heyday of colonial rule: essays/ by Mushirul Hasan ... [et al.]. Leiden; E.J. Brill, 1987. xviii, 297 p.
87-017846   954 s.a954.0319 9004083626
India -- History. Indonesia -- History.

DS436.C7 vol. 3.S452
India and Indonesia during the Ancien Regime: essays/ by P.J. Marshall ... [et al.]. Leiden; New York: 1989. xviii, 218 p.
89-164910   954 s.a954/.02 220 9004083634
India -- History -- 1000-1765. Indonesia -- History -- 1478-1798.

DS436.C7 vol. 4
India and Indonesia general perspectives: essays/ by J.C. Heesterman ... [et al.]. Leiden; E. J. Brill, 1989. xiii, 158 p.
91-155311   954 s.a95420 9004083642
India -- History. Indonesia -- History.

DS436.G36 1999
Gandhi, Rajmohan.
Revenge and reconciliation/ Rajmohan Gandhi. New Delhi; Penguin Books, 1999. xxx, 463 p.
99-947947   954.221 0140290451
India -- History. India -- Ethnic relations.

DS436.N47 1987 pt. 4, vol. 2.Q1742
Forbes, Geraldine Hancock,
Women in modern India/ Geraldine Forbes. Cambridge [England]; Cambridge University Press, c1996. xix, 289 p.
95-041202   954   s.a305.4/0954/0903420 0521268125
Women--India--History--19th century. Women--India--History--20th century.

DS436.N47 1987 pt. 1, vol. 7
Michell, George.
Architecture and art of the Deccan sultanates/ George Michell and Mark Zebrowski. New York: Cambridge University Press, 1999. xxi, 297 p.
98-024737   954 s 0521563216
Art, Islamic -- India -- Deccan. Art, Indic -- India -- Deccan.

DS436.N47 1987 pt. 2, vol. 5
Prakash, Om, 1940-
European commercial enterprise in pre-colonial India/ Om Prakash. Cambridge [England]; Cambridge University Press, 1998. xviii, 377 p.
97-025536   954 s 0521257581
India -- Commerce -- Europe -- History. Europe -- Commerce -- India -- History. India -- Economic conditions.

DS436.N47 1999 pt. 3, vol. 5
Arnold, David, 1946-
Science, technology, and medicine in Colonial India/ David Arnold. New York: Cambridge University Press, 2000. xii, 234 p.
99-027791   509.54 0521563194
Science -- India -- History. Technology -- India -- History. Medicine -- India -- History.

DS436.N47 1999 pt.4, vol.4
Ludden, David E.
An agrarian history of South Asia/ David Ludden. Cambridge, UK; Cambridge Unviersity Press, 1999. xiii, 261 p.
98-043856   630/.954 0521364248 hb
Agriculture -- Economic aspects -- India. Agriculture -- India -- History.

DS436.R63 2002
Robb, Peter
A history of India/ Peter Robb. Houndmills, Basingstoke, Hampshire; Palgrave, 2002. xiii, 344 p.
2001-058772   954.221 0333691288
India -- History.

DS436.V6 2001
Vohra, Ranbir.
The making of India: a historical survey/ Ranbir Vohra. 2nd ed. Armonk, N.Y.: M.E. Sharpe, c2001. xiv, 350 p.
00-044657   954.221 0765607115
India -- History.

DS436.W66 2000
Wolpert, Stanley A.,
A new history of India/ Stanley Wolpert.6th ed. New York: Oxford University Press, 2000. xii, 511 p.
99-017705   954.221 019512877X
India -- History.

DS442.3-450 India (Bharat) — History — General special

DS442.3.G68 2002
Gommans, Jos J. L.
Mughal warfare: Indian frontiers and highroads to empire, 1500-1700/ Jos Gommans. New York: Routledge, 2002. p. cm.
2002-068305   954.02/5.221 0415239893
Artillery--Mogul Empire--History. Military art and science--India--History.

DS450.P18 G36 2001
Ganguly, Sumit.
Conflict unending: India-Pakistan tensions since 1947/ Sumit Ganguly. New York: Columbia University Press; 187 p.
2002-019477 954.04.221 0231123698
Nuclear weapons--India. Nuclear weapons--Pakistan.

DS451-481 India (Bharat) — History — By period

DS451.T452 2000
Thapar, Romila.
Cultural pasts: essays in early Indian history/ Romila Thapar. New Delhi; Oxford University Press, 2000. xi, 1156 p.
00-440398 934.221 0195640500
India -- History -- To 324 B.C. India -- History -- 324 B.C.-1000 A.D.

DS451.T465 2000
Thapar, Romila.
History and beyond/ Romila Thapar. New Delhi; Oxford University Press, 2000. 1 v. (various pagings)
99-952723 934.221 0195647084
India -- History -- To 324 B.C. India -- History -- 324 B.C.-1000 A.D. India -- Civilization -- To 1200.

DS452.S22
Sabharwal, Gopa.
The Indian millennium, AD 1000-2000/ Gopa Sabharwal. New Delhi; Penguin Books, 2000. x, 716 p.
00-289438 954/.002/02.221 0140295216
India -- History -- 1000-1765 -- Chronology. India -- History -- British occupation, 1765-1947 -- Chronology. India -- History -- 1947- -- Chronology.

DS457.S445 2001
Sharma, Ram Sharan,
Early medieval Indian society: a study in feudalisation/ R.S. Sharma. Hyderabad: Orient Longman, 2001. x, 374 p.
2001-292348 954.02.221 8125020276
India -- History -- 1000-1526.

DS459.J27 1999
Jackson, Peter A.
The Delhi Sultanate: a political and military history/ Peter Jackson. Cambridge; Cambridge University Press, 1999. xx, 367 p.
98-030080 954/.56023.221 0521404770
Delhi (Sultanate) -- History.

DS461.E72 1997
Eraly, Abraham.
The last spring: the lives and times of the great Mughals/ Abraham Eraly. New Delhi: Viking, 1997. xviii, 955 p.
97-905180 067087518X
Mogul Empire -- History. India -- History -- 1526-1765. Mogul Empire -- Kings and rulers.

DS461.5.J28813 1999
Jahangir,
The Jahangirnama: memoirs of Jahangir, Emperor of India/ translated, edited, and annotated by Wheeler M. Thackston. New York: Freer Gallery of Art, Arthur M. Sackler Gallery in xxv, 502 p.
98-018798 954.02/56/092. 221 0195127188
Jahangir, Emperor of Hindustan, 1569-1627.

DS461.8.A43 1986
Alam, Muzaffar, 1947-
The crisis of empire in Mughal north India: Awadh and the Punjab, 1707-48/ Muzaffar Alam. Delhi; Oxford University Press, 1986. xv, 365 p.
86-900020 954.02/9 0195618920
Mogul Empire -- Politics and government. Oudh (India) -- Politics and government. Punjab (India) -- Politics and government.

DS461.9.N8 F56 1993
Findly, Ellison Banks.
Nur Jahan, empress of Mughal India/ Ellison Banks Findly. New York: Oxford University Press, 1993. 407 p.
92-008697 954.02/5/092. 220 0195074882
Nur Jah̄ an, Empress, consort of Jahangir, Emperor of Hindustan, d. Empresses--Mogul Empire--Biography.

DS463.B34 1998
Bayly, C. A.
Origins of nationality in South Asia: patriotism and ethical government in the making of modern India/ C.A. Bayly. Delhi; Oxford University Press, 1998. ix, 338 p.
99-932096 320.54/0954.221 0195644573
Nationalism--India--History. Patriotism--India--History.

DS463.N37 2001
Naregal, Veena.
Language politics, elites, and the public sphere/ Veena Naregal. New Delhi: Permanent Black: 2001. xi, 300 p.
2001-358572 954.03.221 8178240149
India -- History -- British occupation, 176501947.

DS463.P67 1999
Prakash, Gyan,
Another reason: science and the imagination of modern India/ Gyan Prakash. Princeton, N.J.: Princeton University Press, c1999. xiii, 304 p.
99-017185 954.221 0691004536
Science--India--History.

DS463.S73 1993
Stern, Robert W.,
Changing India: bourgeois revolution on the subcontinent/ Robert W. Stern. Cambridge [England]; Cambridge University Press, xv, 251 p.
92-011675 954.03/5.220 0521421063
India -- History -- British occupation, 1765-1947. India -- History -- 1947- India -- Social conditions.

DS463.Z37 1994
Zastoupil, Lynn, 1953-
John Stuart Mill and India/ Lynn Zastoupil. Stanford, Calif.: Stanford University Press, 1994. viii, 280 p.
93-002225 954.03 0804722560
Mill, John Stuart, -- 1806-1873. India -- History -- British occupation, 1765-1947.

DS468.C47 1993
Chatterjee, Partha, 1947-
The nation and its fragments: colonial and postcolonial histories/ Partha Chatterjee. Princeton, N.J.: Princeton University Press, c1993. xiii, 282 p.
93-015536 954.03 0691033056
Nationalism -- India -- History. Nationalism -- India -- Bengal -- History. India -- History -- British occupation, 1765-1947. India -- History -- 20th century.

DS470.M3 L55 1992
Llewellyn-Jones, Rosie.
A very ingenious man, Claude Martin in early colonial India/ Rosie Llewellyn-Jones. Delhi; Oxford University Press, 1992. xxi, 241 p.
92-910868 0195631315
Martin, Claude, 1735-1800. Architects--Great Britain--Biography.

DS470.T6 B75 1997
Brittlebank, Kate.
Tipu Sultan's search for legitimacy: Islam and kingship in a Hindu domain/ Kate Brittlebank. Delhi; Oxford University Press, 1997. xix, 184 p.
98-902936 0195639774
Tipu Sultan, Fath Ali, Nawab of Mysore, 1753-1799.

DS471.B68 1991
Bowen, H. V.
Revenue and reform: the Indian problem in British politics, 1757-1773/ H.V. Bowen. Cambridge [England]; Cambridge University Press, 1991. xi, 204 p.
90-022178 954.02/9 0521403162
India -- History -- 18th century. Great Britain -- Politics and government -- 1760-1789.

DS473.B45 2000
Bernstein, Jeremy, 1929-
Dawning of the Raj: the life and trials of Warren Hastings/ Jeremy Bernstein. Chicago: Ivan R. Dee, 2000. p. cm.
99-088030 954.02/98/092 1566632811
Hastings, Warren, -- 1732-1818. Colonial administrators -- India -- Biography. Colonial administrators -- Great Britain -- Biography. India -- History -- British occupation, 1765-1947.

DS475.N354 1998
Nandy, Ashis.
Exiled at home: comprising, At the edge of psychology, The intimate enemy, Creating a nationality/ Ashis Nandy. Delhi; Oxford University Press, 1998. xx, 133 p.
98-902993 954.221 0195641779
Communalism--India.

DS475.2.R18 A25 1999
Rammohun Roy,
The essential writings of Raja Rammohan Ray/ edited by Bruce Carlisle Robertson. Delhi: Oxford University Press, 1999. xxxix, 299 p.
99-932755 082.221 0195647319

DS478.I44 1998
Indian people in the struggle for freedom: five essays. New Delhi: SAHMAT, c1998. 135 p.
99-934001 954.03/5.221 8186219293
Nationalism--India--History.

DS479.K75 1998
Krishnaswamy, Revathi, 1960-
Effeminism: the economy of colonial desire/ Revathi Krishnaswamy. Ann Arbor: University of Michigan Press, c1998. vi, 191 p.
98-025517 954.03 0472109758
English literature -- 19th century -- History and criticism. English literature -- 20th century -- History and criticism. India -- History -- British occupation, 1765-1947. India -- Politics and government -- 1765-1947.

DS479.L36 1997
Hasan, Mushirul.
Legacy of a Divided Nation: India's Muslims since independence/ Mushirul Hasan. Boulder, Colo.: WestviewPress, c1997. xv, 383 p.
97-003721   954.03/088/2971   0813333393
Muslims -- India -- Politics and government. Islam and politics -- India. India -- Politics and government -- 1857-1919. India -- Politics and government -- 1919-1947.

DS479.N352 1998
Nanda, B. R.
The making of a nation: India's road to independence/ B.R. Nanda. New Delhi: HarperCollins, 1998. xxxii, 362 p.
98-903066   954.03/5.221   8172233019
India -- Politics and government -- 1857-1919. India -- Politics and government -- 1919-1947.

DS479.P42 1999
Paxton, Nancy L., 1949-
Writing under the Raj: gender, race, and rape in the British colonial imagination, 1830-1947/ Nancy L. Paxton. New Brunswick, NJ: Rutgers University Press, c1999. xi, 338 p.
98-019522   954.03   0813526000
English literature -- 19th century -- History and criticism. English literature -- 20th century -- History and criticism. India -- History -- British occupation,1765-1947. India -- Politics and government -- 1765-1947.

DS479.R38 1998
Read, Anthony.
The proudest day: India's long road to independence/ Anthony Read and David Fisher. New York: Norton, c1998. xxv, 565 p.
98-010707   954.03   0393045943
India -- History -- British occupation, 1765-1947.

DS479.S265 1988
Sarkar, Sumit, 1939-
Modern India, 1885-1947/ Sumit Sarkar; foreword by D.A. Low. New York: St. Martin's Press, 1989. xxv, 489 p.
87-028930   954.03/5   0312012993
India -- History -- 1765-1947.

DS479.S52 1989
Shaikh, Farzana.
Community and consensus in Islam: Muslim representation in colonial India, 1860-1947/ Farzana Shaikh. Cambridge [England]; Cambridge University Press, 1989. xiv, 257 p.
88-023472   954.03/5   0521363284
Muslims -- India -- Politics and government. India -- Politics and government -- 1857-1919. India -- Politics and government -- 1919-1947.

DS480.3.P66 1995
Popplewell, Richard J.
Intelligence and imperial defence: British intelligence and the defence of the Indian Empire, 1904-1924/ Richard J. Popplewell. London; F. Cass, c1995. x, 354 p.
95-016884   327.1241/054/09041   071464580X
India -- Politics and government -- 1857-1919. India -- Politics and government -- 1919-1947.

DS480.4.G67 1995
Gordon, A. D. D.
India's rise to power in the twentieth century and beyond/ Sandy Gordon. New York: St. Martin's Press, 1995. xxii, 414 p.
94-030738   954.03/5   031212452X
India -- Politics and government -- 20th century.

DS480.4.S78 1991
Studdert-Kennedy, Gerald.
British Christians, Indian nationalists, and the Raj/ Gerald Studdert-Kennedy. Delhi; Oxford University Press, 1991. x, 274 p.
91-900822   0195627334
British -- India. Christians -- India. Nationalists -- India. India -- Politics and government -- 20th century.

DS480.45.A782 2000
Alter, Joseph S.
Gandhi's body: sex, diet, and the politics of nationalism/ Joseph S. Alter. Philadelphia: University of Pennsylvania Press, c2000. xviii, 207 p.
00-023421   954.03/5/092   0812235568
Gandhi, -- Mahatma, -- 1869-1948. Nationalism -- India. Sexual ethics -- India. Medicine, Ayurvedic. India -- Politics and government -- 20th century.

DS480.45.C46 1988
Chaudhuri, Nirad C., 1897-
Thy hand, great anarch!: India, 1921-1952/ Nirad C. Chaudhuri. Reading, Mass.: Addison-Wesley, [1988], c1987 xxviii, 979 p.
88-015355   954.03/5   020115577X
Chaudhuri, Nirad C., -- 1897- Scholars -- India -- Biography. India -- History -- 1919-1947. India -- History -- 1947-

DS480.45.C69 1997
Copland, Ian, 1943-
The princes of India in the endgame of empire, 1917-1947/ Ian Copland. Cambridge; Cambridge University Press, 1997. xiii, 302 p.
96-018313   954.03   0521571790
India -- Politics and government -- 1919-1947. India -- Kings and rulers. India -- History -- British occupation, 1765-1947.

DS480.45.G675 1999
Gossman, Patricia A.
Riots and victims/ Patricia A. Gossman. Boulder, Colo.: Westview Press, 1999. p. cm.
98-050487   303.6/0954/14   0813336252
Communalism -- India -- Bengal. Muslims -- India -- Bengal. Violence -- India -- Bengal. India -- History -- 20th century.

DS480.45.S72 1998
Studdert-Kennedy, Gerald.
Providence and th Raj: imperial mission and missionary imperialism/ Gerald Studdert-Kennedy. Thousand Oaks, Calif.: Sage Publications, 1998. p. cm.
98-020644   325/.3410954   0761992774
British -- India. Christians -- India. Nationalists -- India. India. India -- Politics and government -- 20th century.

DS480.45.W32 1994
Wainwright, A. Martin.
Inheritance of Empire: Britain, India, and the balance of power in Asia, 1938-55/ A. Martin Wainwright. Westport, Conn.: Praeger, 1994. xiv, 237 p.
93-024853   954   0275947335
India -- Politics and government -- 1919-1947. India -- Politics and government -- 1947- Great Britain -- Politics and government -- 1936-1945.

DS480.45.W4 1997
Weber, Thomas,
On the Salt March: the historiography of Gandhi's march to Dandi/ Thomas Weber. New Delhi: HarperCollins Publishers India, 1997. xxii, 594 p.
97-913709   8172232632
Gandhi, Mahatma, 1869-1948. Civil disobedience--India.

DS480.82.I44 1987
Inder Singh, Anita.
The origins of the partition of India, 1936-1947/ Anita Inder Singh. Delhi; Oxford University Press, 1987. xiv, 271 p.
87-900005   954.03/59   0195619552
India -- Politics and government -- 1919-1947. India -- History -- Partition, 1947.

DS480.84.C45 1997
Chadda, Maya, 1943-
Ethnicity, security, and separatism in India/ Maya Chadda. New York: Columbia University Press, c1997. xvii, 286 p.
96-048962   327.54   0231107366
Ethnicity -- India. India -- Foreign relations -- 1947-1984. India -- Foreign relations -- 1984- India -- History -- Autonomy and independence movements.

DS480.84.C545 1997
Chatterjee, Partha, 1947-
A possible India: essays in political criticism/ Partha Chatterjee. Delhi; Oxford University Press, 1997. xii, 301 p.
97-914022   954.05   019564333X
India -- Politics and government -- 1947-

DS480.84.C783 2000
Corbridge, Stuart.
Reinventing India: liberalization, Hindu nationalism and popular democracy/ Stuart Corbridge and John Harriss. Malden, Mass.: Polity Press, 2000. p. cm.
00-039986   954.04   0745620760
India -- Politics and government -- 1947-

DS480.84.D572 2000
Dissenting knowledges, open futures: the multiple selves and strange destinations of Ashis Nandy/ edited by Vinay Lal. New Delhi; Oxford University Press, 2000. xiv, 352 p.
2001-270738   306.2/0954.221   0195651154
Nandy, Ashis. Politics and culture--India. Political psychology.

DS480.84.I4854 1999
India and Pakistan: the first fifty years/ edited by Selig S. Harrison, Paul H. Kreisberg, and Dennis Kux. Washington, D.C.: Woodrow Wilson Center Press, 1999. xii, 216 p.
98-036434   954.04   0521641853
India -- Politics and government -- 1947- Pakistan -- Politics and government.

DS480.84.I535 1999
India briefing: a transformative fifty years/ Marshall Bouton and Philip Oldenburg, editors. Armonk, NY: M.E. Sharpe c1999. xi, 324 p.
00-698344   954.04   0765603381
India -- History -- 1947-

DS480.84.S3853 1982
Select documents on India's foreign policy and relations, 1947-1972/ [edited by] A. Appadorai. Delhi; Oxford University Press, 1982-1985. 2 v.
83-122485   327.54   0195613090
India -- Foreign relations -- Sources.

DS480.84.T287 2000
Talbot, Ian.
India and Pakistan/ Ian Talbot. London: Arnold;
2000. xxi, 312 p.
2001-269407   954.04.221   0340706333
Nationalism--India. Nationalism--Pakistan.

DS480.842.K355 2002
Kamra, Sukeshi.
Bearing witness: partition, independence, end of
the Raj/ Sukeshi Kamra. Calgary: University of
Calgary Press, c2002. xvi, 414 p.
2002-391839 954.04.221 1552380416
*India -- History -- Partition, 1947. India -- Politics
and government -- 1919-1947. Punjab (India) --
History -- Partition, 1947. Pakistan -- History.*

DS480.842.M46 1998
Menon, Ritu.
Borders & boundaries: women in India's Partition/
Ritu Menon & Kamla Bhasin. New Brunswick,
N.J.: Rutgers University Press, 1998. xiii, 274 p.
98-017638 954.04.221 0813525527
Oral history. Women--India--History.

DS480.852.D49 2000
Dhar, P. N.
Indira Gandhi, the "emergency", and Indian
democracy/ P.N. Dhar. New Delhi; Oxford
University Press, 2000. xii, 424 p.
99-952058   0195648994
*Gandhi, Indira, -- 1917-1984.   India -- Politics
and government -- 1975-1977.*

DS480.853.C53 1996
Class formation and political transformation in
post-colonial India/ edited by T.V. Sathyamurthy.
Delhi; Oxford University Press, 1996. xii, 490 p.
96-906242 954.04 0195634594
*India -- Politics and government -- 1977- India
-- Social conditions -- 1947-*

DS480.853.C634 2001
Cohen, Stephen P.,
India: emerging power/ Stephen Philip Cohen.
Washington, D.C.: Brookings Institution Press,
c2001. xii, 377 p.
2001-000219 954.05/2.221 0815700067
*India -- Politics and government -- 1977- India --
Economic conditions -- 1947- India -- Foreign
relations -- 1984-*

DS480.853.C67 1998
Community conflicts and the state in India/ edited
by Amrita Basu, Atul Kohli. Delhi; Oxford
University Press, 1998. viii, 287 p.
98-902939 320.954/09/049.221 0195642368
Religion and politics--India.

DS480.853.D383 2001
Sawhney, Pravin.
The defence makeover: 10 myths that shape India's
image/ Pravin Sawhney. New Delhi; Sage
Publications, 2002. 458 p.
2001-059017 327.54.221 0761996133
*India -- Politics and government -- 1977- Jammu
and Kashmir (India) -- Politics and government.
India -- Foreign relations -- Pakistan. Pakistan --
Foreign relations -- India. India -- Foreign
relations -- China. China -- Foreign relations --
India.*

DS480.853.D384 1995
De Silva, K. M.
Regional powers and small state security: India and
Sri Lanka, 1977-1990/ K.M. De Silva. Washington,
D.C.: Woodrow Wilson Center Press; c1995. xv,
388 p.
95-008097 327.5405493/09/048 0801851491
*National security -- India. National security --
Sri Lanka. India -- Politics and government --
1977- Sri Lanka -- Politics and government --
1978- India -- Foreign relations -- Sri Lanka.*

DS480.853.T475 1994
Thakur, Ramesh Chandra,
The politics and economics of India's foreign
policy/ Ramesh Thakur. London: Hurst; c1994. xi,
306 p.
93-044718 327.54.220 0312121059
*India -- Foreign relations -- 1984- India -- Politics
and government -- 1977- India -- Economic policy
-- 1980-*

DS481.G23.J38 1992
Jayakar, Pupul.
Indira Gandhi: an intimate biography/ Pupul
Jayakar. New York: Pantheon Books, c1992. xviii,
410 p.
93-010815 954.04/5/092 0679424792
*Gandhi, Indira, -- 1917-1984.   Prime ministers --
India -- Biography.*

DS481.G23.M314 1991
Malhotra, Inder.
Indira Gandhi: a personal and political biography/
Inder Malhotra. Boston: Northeastern University
Press, 1991. 363 p.
90-049859 954.04/5/092 1555530958
*Gandhi, Indira, -- 1917-1984.   Prime ministers --
India -- Biography.   India -- Politics and
government -- 1947-*

DS481.G3.B735 1989
Brown, Judith M. 1944-
Gandhi: prisoner of hope/ Judith M. Brown. New
Haven: Yale University Press, 1989. vii, 440 p.
89-051020 954.03/5/092 0300045956
*Gandhi, -- Mahatma, -- 1869-1948.   Nationalists -
- India -- Biography. Statesmen -- India --
Biography.*

DS481.G3.D215 1993
Dalton, Dennis.
Mahatma Gandhi: nonviolent power in action/
Dennis Dalton. New York: Columbia University
Press, c1993. xii, 279 p.
93-022634 954.03/5/092 0231081189
*Gandhi, -- Mahatma, -- 1869-1948.   Statesmen --
India -- Biography. Nationalists -- India --
Biography.*

DS481.G3.J7184 1998
Jordens, J. T. F.
Gandhi's religion: a homespun shawl/ G.T.F.
Jordens. New York: St. Martin's Press, 1998. ix,
283 p.
97-041964 294.5/092 0312212402
*Gandhi, -- Mahatma, -- 1869-1948 -- Religion.
Gandhi, -- Mahatma, -- 1869-1948 -- Views on
Hinduism. Hinduism.*

DS481.G3 N3395 2002
Nanda, B. R.
In search of Gandhi: essays and reflections/ B.R.
Nanda. New Delhi; Oxford University Press, 2002.
x, 270 p.
2002-285550   0195656490
*Gandhi, Mahatma, 1869-1948.   Statesmen--
India--Biography.*

DS481.G3 P3465 1997
Parekh, Bhikhu C.
Gandhi/ Bhikhu Parekh. Oxford; Oxford University
Press, 1997. viii, 111 p.
97-010822 954.03/5/092.221 0192876929
*Gandhi, Mahatma, 1869-1948--Political and
social views.*

DS481.G3.T43 1998
Terchek, Ronald, 1936-
Gandhi: struggling for autonomy/ Ronald J.
Terchek. Lanham, MD: Rowman & Littlefield
Publishers, c1998. x, 265 p.
98-022847 954.03/5/092 0847692140
*Gandhi, -- Mahatma, -- 1869-1948 -- Political and
social views.   Nationalists -- India -- Biography.
India -- Politics and government -- 1919-1947.*

DS481.G73.C43 1997
Chadha, Yogesh.
Gandhi: a life/ Yogesh Chadha. New York: John
Wiley, c1997. 546 p.
97-037406 954.03/5/092 0471243787
*Gandhi, -- Mahatma, -- 1869-1948 -- Political and
social views.   Statesmen -- India -- Biography.
India -- Politics and government -- 1919-1947-*

DS481.N35.A73 1988
Akbar, M. J.
Nehru: the making of India/ M.J. Akbar. London,
England; Viking, 1988. xii, 609 p.
88-050691 954.04/2/092 067081699X
*Nehru, Jawaharlal, -- 1889-1964.   Prime ministers
-- India -- Biography.*

DS481.N35 N285 1995
Nanda, B. R.
Jawaharlal Nehru: rebel and statesman/ B.R.
Nanda. New Delhi; Oxford University Press, 1995.
x, 312 p.
95-236342 954.04/2/092. 220 0195636848
*Nehru, Jawaharlal, 1889-1964.   Prime ministers--
India--Biography.*

DS481.N35 N453 1991
The Nehru legacy: an appraisal/ editors, Amal Ray,
N. Bhaskara Rao, Vinod Vyasulu. New Delhi:
Oxford & IBH Pub. Co., c1991. viii, 332 p.
91-904765   8120405560
*Nehru, Jawaharlal, 1889-1964--Political and
social views--Congresses.*

DS484.4-484.7 India (Bharat) — Local history and description — Larger geographical divisions

DS484.4.B39 1989
Bayly, Susan.
Saints, goddesses, and kings: Muslims and
Christians in South Indian Society, 1700-1900/
Susan Bayly. Cambridge [England]; Cambridge
University Press, 1989. xv, 504 p.
89-000543 954/.8 0521372011
*Muslims -- India, South -- History. Islam -- India,
South -- History. Christians -- India, South --
History. India, South -- Civilization.*

DS484.4.M57 1994
Mines, Mattison, 1941-
Public faces, private voices: community and
individuality in South India/ Mattison Mines.
Berkeley: University of California Press, c1994. x,
232 p.
93-035609 954/.8 0520084780
*National characteristics, East Indian.   India,
South -- Social life and customs.*

DS484.65.S86 2001
Subrahmanyam, Sanjay.
Penumbral visions: making polities in early modern South India/ Sanjay Subrahmanyam. Ann Arbor: University of Michigan Press, 2001. ix, 295 p.
2001-034777   954/.8025.221   0472112163
India, South -- Politics and government -- 17th century. India, South -- Politics and government -- 18th century.

DS484.7.I77 1994
Irschick, Eugene F.
Dialogue and history: constructing South India, 1795-1895/ Eugene F. Irschick. Berkeley: University of California Press, c1994. xiii, 263 p.
93-010238   954/.8031   0520084047
India, South -- History.

DS485 India (Bharat) — Local history and description — Minor kingdoms, states, regions, etc., A-Z

DS485.B38.S86 1997
Sundar, Nandini.
Subalterns and sovereigns: an anthropological history of Bastar, 1854-1996/ Nandini Sundar. Delhi; Oxford University Press, 1997. xxiv, 296 p.
97-906439   954/.3   0195641167
Bastar (India: District) -- History.

DS485.B46.E16 1993
Eaton, Richard Maxwell.
The rise of Islam and the Bengal frontier, 1204-1760/ Richard M. Eaton. Berkeley: University of California Press, c1993. xxvii, 359 p.
92-034002   954/.14   0520080777
Islam -- India -- Bengal -- History. Bengal (India) -- History.

DS485.B493.C49 1994
Chatterji, Joya.
Bengal divided: Hindu communalism and partition, 1932-1947/ Joya Chatterji. Cambridge, [England]; Cambridge University Press, 1994. xvii, 303 p.
93-030544   954/.140359   0521411289
Communalism -- India -- Bengal -- History. Bengal (India) -- History -- Partition, 1947.

DS485.B5.K456 2000
Khan, Sharharyar M.
The begums of Bhopal: a dynasty of women rulers in Raj India/ Shaharyar M. Khan. London; I.B. Tauris Publishers; 2000. x, 276 p.
   954.303   1860645283
Queens -- India -- Bhopal -- Biography. Bhopal (India) -- Kings and rulers -- Biography. Bhopal (India) -- History -- 18th century Bhopal (India) -- History -- 19th century.

DS485.B51.D26 1992
Damodaran, Vinita.
Broken promises: popular protest, Indian nationalism, and the Congress Party in Bihar, 1935-1946/ Vinita Damodaran. Delhi; Oxford University Press, 1992. xii, 398 p.
92-908080
Peasant uprisings -- India -- Bihar. Bihar (India) -- Politics and government.

DS485.D155 S55 1999
Skaria, Ajay.
Hybrid histories: forests, frontiers, and wildness in western India/ Ajay Skaria. Delhi; Oxford University Press, 1999. xxiv, 324 p.
99-933483   954/.75.221   0195643100
Dangs (India) -- History.

DS485.H6 S442 1988
Singh, Amar Kaur Jasbir.
Himalayan triangle: a historical survey of British India's relations with Tibet, Sikkim, and Bhutan, 1765-1950/ Amar Kaur Jasbir Singh. London: British Library, 1988. xi, 408 p.
88-176756   954.220   0712306307
Himalaya Mountains Region -- Foreign relations -- India. India -- Foreign relations -- Himalaya Mountains Region. Himalaya Mountains Region -- Politics and government.

DS485.H6.Z87 1999
Zurick, David.
Himalaya: life on the edge of the world/ by David Zurick and P.P. Karan; maps by Julsun Pacheco. Baltimore: Johns Hopkins University Press, 1999. xiv, 355 p.
99-011037   954.96   0801861683
Himalaya Mountains Region.

DS485.K23.T39 2000
Taylor, David D.
Kashmir/ David Taylor, compiler. -- Oxford, England; Clio Press, c2000. xx, 135 p.
   016.9546   1851092870
Cachemire -- Bibliographie.

DS485.K25.S38 1996
Schofield, Victoria.
Kashmir in the crossfire/ Victoria Schofield. London; I.B. Tauris, 1996. xiii, 354 p.
95-062326   954/.6   1860640362
Kashmir, Vale of (India) -- History. Jammu and Kashmir (India) -- History. India -- Foreign relations -- Pakistan.

DS485.K27.G37 1997
Ganguly, Sumit.
The crisis in Kashmir: portents of war, hopes of peace/ Sumit Ganguly. [Washington, D.C.]: Woodrow Wilson Center Press; 1997. xv, 182 p.
96-039401   954/.6   0521590663
Jammu and Kashmir (India) -- Politics and government.

DS485.K27.R33 1996
Rahman, Mushtaqur.
Divided Kashmir: old problems, new opportunities for India, Pakistan, and the Kashmiri people/ by Mushtaqur Rahman. Boulder, Colo.: Lynne Rienner Publishers, 1996. xviii, 218 p.
95-018416   954/.6   1555875890
Jammu and Kashmir (India) -- Politics and government. India -- Foreign relations -- Pakistan. Pakistan -- Foreign relations -- India.

DS485.K48.M46 1994
Menon, Dilip M.
Caste, nationalism, and communism in South India: Malabar, 1900-1948/ Dilip M. Menon. Cambridge [England]; Cambridge University Press, 1994. xv, 209 p.
93-006609   954/.83   0521418798
Caste -- India -- Kerala Nationalism -- India -- Kerala. Communism -- India -- Kerala. Kerala (India) -- Politics and government. Malabar Coast (India) -- Politics and government.

DS485.M28.M867 1989
Stein, Burton, 1926-
Thomas Munro: the origins of the colonial state and his vision of empire/ Burton Stein. Delhi; Oxford University Press, 1989. vi, 374 p.
89-900079   954/.82031/092   0195623312
Munro, Thomas, -- Sir, -- 1761-1827. Governors -- India -- Tamil Nadu -- Biography. India, South -- Politics and government.

DS485.M28.P74 1996
Price, Pamela G.
Kingship and political practice in colonial India/ Pamela G. Price. Cambridge; Cambridge University Press, 1996. xvi, 220 p.
95-017917   954.03   0521552478
Tamil Nadu (India) -- Politics and government. Ramanathapuram (Princely State) -- Politics and government. Civakankai (India) -- Politics and government.

DS485.M348.G84 1999
Guha, Sumit.
Environment and ethnicity in India, 1200-1991/ Sumit Guha. New York: Cambridge University Press, c1999. xv, 217 p.
98-040358   954/.792   0521640784
Ethnicity -- India -- Maharashtra. Human ecology -- India -- Maharashtra. Maharashtra (India) -- Civilization.

DS485.M348.P74 1989
Preston, Laurence W.
The Devs of Cincvad: a lineage and the state in Maharashtra/ Laurence W. Preston. Cambridge [England]; Cambridge University Press, 1989. xi, 273 p.
88-010857   954/.792   0521346339
Cincvad, Devs of. Land tenure -- India -- Maharashtra -- History. Maharashtra (India) -- History.

DS485.M35.P22 1989
Panikkar, K. N.
Against lord and state: religion and peasant uprisings in Malabar, 1836-1921/ K.N. Panikkar. Delhi; Oxford University Press, 1989. xiii, 232 p.
89-900070   954.03/57   0195621395
Moplah Rebellion, India, 1921. Malabar Coast (India) -- History.

DS485.P2.G54 1988
Gilmartin, David.
Empire and Islam: Punjab and the making of Pakistan/ David Gilmartin. Berkeley: University of California Press, c1988. xii, 258 p.
88-008592   954/.5   0520062493
Pakistan movement. Muslims -- India -- Punjab -- Politics and government. Islam and politics -- India -- Punjab. Punjab (India) -- Politics and government.

DS485.P3.M39 1989
McLeod, W. H.
The Sikhs: history, religion, and society/ W.H. McLeod. New York: Columbia University Press, c1989. ix, 161 p.
88-025620   954/.00882946   023106814X
Sikhs -- History. Sikhism.

DS485.P87.B87 2000
Butalia, Urvashi.
The other side of silence: voices from the partition of India/ Urvashi Butalia. Durham, NC: Duke University Press, 2000. p. cm.
99-050297   954/.504   0822324571
Punjab (India) -- History -- Partition, 1947.

DS485.P87.D44 2000
Deol, Harnik, 1966-
Religion and nationalism in India: the case of the Punjab/ Harnik Deol. London; Routledge, 2000. p. cm.
99-058052   954/.5   041520108X
Nationalism -- India -- Punjab. Religion and politics -- India -- Punjab.

DS485.P88.M25 1997
Mahmood, Cynthia Keppley.
Fighting for faith and nation: dialogues with Sikh militants/ Cynthia Keppley Mahmood. Philadelphia: University of Pennsylvania Press, 1997. xi, 314 p.
96-034959 954.91/4/00882946 0812233611
Sikhs -- Politics and government. Human rights -- India -- Punjab. Sikhism. Punjab (India) -- Politics and government.

DS485.R19 A85 2000
Amar Singh,
Reversing the gaze: Amar Singh's diary, a colonial subject's narrative of Imperial India/ editing and commentary by Susanne Hoeber Rudolph & Lloyd L. Rudolph with Mohan Singh Kanota. New Delhi; Oxford University Press, 2000. xvii, 625 p.
00-410452 0195647521
Amar Singh, 1878-1942--Diaries. Kings and rulers--India--Rajasthan--Diaries.

DS485.U64.H38 1998
Hasan, Zoya.
Quest for power: oppositional movements and post-Congress politics in Uttar Pradesh/ Zoya Hasan. Delhi; Oxford University Press, 1998. vii, 280 p.
98-902987 0195641841
Uttar Pradesh (India) -- Politics and government -- 20th century.

DS486 India (Bharat) — Local history and description — Cities, towns, etc., A-Z

DS486.A3.E34 1998
Edensor, Tim.
Tourists at the Taj: performance and meaning at a symbolic site/ Tim Edensor. London: Routledge, 1998. ix, 223 p.
98-005286 954/.2 0415167124
Taj Mahal (Agra, India) Tourist trade -- India. Popular culture -- India. India -- Civilization -- British influences. India -- Politics and government -- 1765-1947. India -- Public opinion.

DS486.A485.M36 1992
Mann, E. A., 1952-
Boundaries and identities: Muslims, work and status in Aligarh/ E.A. Mann. New Delhi; Sage Publications, 1992. 212 p.
92-003334 954/.2 0803994222(U.
Muslims -- India -- Aligarh. Aligarh (India) -- Social conditions.

DS486.C464.A45 1995
Amin, Shahid.
Event, metaphor, memory: Chauri Chaura, 1922-1992/ Shahid Amin. Berkeley: University of California Press, c1995. xiv, 256 p.
94-000737 954/.2 0520087798
Chauri Chaura (India) -- Politics and government.

DS486.D3.B55 1990
Blake, Stephen P.
Shahjahanabad: the sovereign city in Mughal India, 1639-1739/ Stephen P. Blake. Cambridge [England]; Cambridge University Press, 1991. xvi, 226 p.
89-077373 954/.56025 0521390451
Urbanization -- India -- History. Mogul Empire -- History. Delhi (India) -- History.

DS486.L9.O42 1984
Oldenburg, Veena Talwar.
The making of colonial Lucknow, 1856-1877/ Veena Talwar Oldenburg. Princeton, N.J.: Princeton University Press, c1984. xxv, 287 p.
83-016008 954/.2 069106590X
Urbanization -- India -- Lucknow. Lucknow (India) -- History.

DS489.5 Sri Lanka — History — General works

DS489.5.S26 2001
Sabaratnam, Lakshmanan.
Ethnic attachments in Sri Lanka: social change and cultural continuity/ Lakshmanan Sabaratnam. 1st ed. New York, NY: Palgrave, 2001. viii, 272 p.
2001-032754 305.8/0095493.221 0312293488
Ethnicity--Sri Lanka. Tamil (Indic people)--Politics and government.

DS489.5.S33 1997
Samarasinghe, S. W. R. de A.
Historical dictionary of Sri Lanka/ S.E.R. de A. Samarasinghe and Vidyamali Samarasinghe. Lanham, MD: Scarecrow Press, 1997. p. cm.
96-029614 954.93/003 0810832801
Sri Lanka -- History -- Dictionaries.

DS489.8-489.83 Sri Lanka — History — By period

DS489.8.W53 1988
Wilson, A. Jeyaratnam.
The break-up of Sri Lanka: the Sinhalese-Tamil conflict/ A. Jeyaratnam Wilson. Honolulu: University of Hawaii Press, c1988. xiii, 240 p.
88-009753 954.9/303 0824812115
Sri Lanka -- Politics and government. Sri Lanka -- Ethnic relations -- Political aspects.

DS489.83.B3.M36 1989
Manor, James.
The expedient utopian: Bandaranaike and Ceylon/ James Manor. Cambridge [England]; Cambridge University Press, 1989. xiii, 338 p.
89-000724 954.9/303/0924 0521371910
Bandaranaike, S. W. R. D. -- (Solomon West Ridgeway Dias), -- 1899-1959. Prime ministers -- Sri Lanka -- Biography. Sri Lanka -- Politics and government.

DS489.83.J3.D4 1988
De Silva, K. M.
J.R. Jayewardene of Sri Lanka: a political biography/ K.M. de Silva and Howard Wriggins. Honolulu: University of Hawaii Press, c1988-1994 v. 1-2
88-010828 954.9/3 0824811836
Jayewardene, Junius Richard. Presidents -- Sri Lanka -- Biography. Sri Lanka -- Politics and government.

DS489.84 Sri Lanka — History — By period

DS489.84.B67 1994
Bose, Sumantra,
States, nations, sovereignty: Sri Lanka, India, and the Tamil Eelam Movement/ Sumantra Bose. New Delhi; Sage Publications, in association 236 p.
93-049452 954.93/00494811.220 0803991703
Tamil (Indic people)--Sri Lanka--Politics and government.

DS489.84.D4 1998
De Silva, K. M.
Reaping the whirlwind: ethnic conflict, ethnic politics in Sri Lanka / K.M. de Silva. New Delhi; Penguin Books, 1998. xi, 388 p.
98-906094 0140270655
Tamil (Indic people)--Sri Lanka--Politics and government.

DS491.4 Bhutan — General works

DS491.4.N46 1993
Nepal and Bhutan: country studies/ edited by Andrea Matles Savada. 3rd ed. Wahington, D.C.: Federal Research Division, Library of Congress: xxxix, 424 p.
93-012226 954.96.220 0844407771
Nepal. Bhutan.

DS493.9 Nepal — Ethnography — Individual elements in the population, A-Z

DS493.9.M3 A54 2001
Ahearn, Laura M.,
Invitations to love: literacy, love letters, and social change in Nepal/ Laura M. Ahearn. Ann Arbor: University of Michigan Press, 2001. xiv, 295 p.
2001-053049 306.81/089/954.221 0472067842
Magar (Nepalese people)--Marriage customs and rites. Magar (Nepalese people)--Social conditions. Love letters--Nepal.

DS493.9.N4.P36 1996
Parish, Steven M.
Hierarchy and its discontents: culture and the politics of consciousness in caste society/ Steven M. Parish. Philadelphia: University of Pennsylvania Press, c1996. xxiii, 270 p.
96-003608 306/.089/95 0812233131
Newar (Nepalese people) -- Social life and customs. Caste -- Nepal -- Bhaktapur. Hinduism -- Nepal -- Bhaktapur. Bhaktapur (Nepal) -- Social conditions.

DS493.9.N92.L48 1988
Levine, Nancy E.
The dynamics of polyandry: kinship, domesticity, and population on the Tibetan border/ Nancy E. Levine. Chicago: University of Chicago Press, 1988. xvii, 309 p.
87-034478 306.8/08991495 0226475689
Nyinba (Nepalese people) -- Social life and customs. Kinship -- Nepal. Polyandry -- Nepal.

DS493.9.N94.S64 2000
Spenger, Wim van, 1949-
Tibetan border worlds: a geo-historical analysis of trade and traders/ Wim van Spengen. New York: Kegan Paul International, 1998. p. cm.
97-047356 306/.095496 0710305923
Nyishangba (Nepalese people) -- Commerce. Nyishangba (Nepalese people) -- Social conditions. Nyishangba (Nepalese people) -- Economic conditions. Manang (Nepal) -- Social conditions. Manang (Nepal) -- Economic conditions.

DS493.9.N94.W37 1996
Watkins, Joanne C.
Spirited women: gender, religion, and cultural
identity in the Nepal Himalaya/ Joanne C. Watkins.
New York: Columbia University Press, c1996. xi,
347 p.
95-037003   305.3/095496   0231102143
*Nyishangba (Nepalese people) -- Social
conditions. Women, Nyishangba. Sex role -- Nepal.
Nepal -- Social conditions.*

DS493.9.R34 H37 2000
Hardman, Charlotte.
Other worlds: notions of self and emotion among
the Lohorung Rai/ Charlotte E. Hardman. Oxford;
Berg, 2000. xix, 315 p.
2001-270099   305.895/4.221   1859731554
*Rai (Nepalese people)--Social life and customs.
Ethnology--Nepal. Self.*

DS493.9.S5.A33 1996
Adams, Vincanne, 1959-
Tigers of the snow and other virtual Sherpas: an
ethnography of Himalayan encounters/ Vincanne
Adams. Princeton, N.J.: Princeton University
Press, c1996. xiv, 304 p.
95-004618   305.8/0095496   0691034419
Sherpa (Nepalese people) Ethnology -- Nepal.

DS493.9.S5.F57 1990
Fisher, James F.
Sherpas: reflections on change in Himalayan
Nepal/ James F. Fisher; with a foreword by Sir
Edmund Hillary. Berkeley: University of
California Press, c1990. xxv, 205 p.
89-027155   915.496   0520067703
*Sherpa (Nepalese people) Education -- Nepal --
Solukhumbu. Tourist trade -- Nepal -- Solukhumbu.
Solukhumbu (Nepal) -- Description and travel.*

DS493.9.T35 F75 1994
Fricke, Thomas E.
Himalayan households: Tamang demography and
domestic processes/ by Tom Fricke. Columbia
University Press Morningside ed. New York:
Columbia University Press, 1994. xiv, 243 p.
93-037643   306.4/08991495.220   0231100078
*Tamang (Nepalese people) Demographic
anthropology--Nepal. Households--Nepal--Case
studies.*

DS493.9.T35.H65 1989
Holmberg, David H., 1948-
Order in paradox: myth, ritual, and exchange
among Nepal's Tamang/ David H. Holmberg.
Ithaca: Cornell University Press, 1989. xvi, 265 p.
88-043238   306/.09549/6   0801422477
Tamang (Nepalese people)

DS493.9.T45 F57 2001
Fisher, William F.,
Fluid boundaries: forming and transforming
identity in Nepal/ William F. Fisher. New York:
Columbia University Press, c2001. xviii, 295 p.
2001-032461   305.891/495.221   0231110871
*Thakali (Nepalese people)--Ethnic identity.
Thakali (Nepalese people)--Social life and
customs.*

DS493.9.T45 V65 1998
Vinding, Michael,
The Thakali: a Himalayan ethnography/ Michael
Vinding. London: Serindia Publications, c1998.
470 p.
99-175615   305.895.221   0906026504
Thakali (Nepalese people)

DS493.9.T47 G85 2002
Guneratne, Arjun,
Many tongues, one people: the making of Tharu
identity in Nepal/ Arjun Guneratne. Ithaca: Cornell
University Press, 2002. xvii, 236 p.
2001-006193   305.8/0095496.221   0801487285
Tharu (South Asian people)--Ethnic identity.

DS495.592 Nepal — History — By period

DS495.592.A34 F57 1997
Fisher, James F.
Living martyrs: individuals and revolution in
Nepal/ James F. Fisher with Tanka Prasad
Acharya and Rewanta Kumari Acharya. Delhi;
Oxford University Press, 1997. xix, 314 p.
97-170128   954.96. 221   0195640004
*Acharya, Tanka Prasad, 1912-1992. Acharya,
Rewanta Kumari, 1918- Prime ministers--Nepal--
Biography. Prime ministers' spouses--Nepal--
Biography.*

DS495.8 Nepal — Local history and description, A-Z

DS495.8.B456 C36 1998
Cameron, Mary M.,
On the edge of the auspicious: gender and caste in
Nepal/ Mary M. Cameron. Urbana: University of
Illinois Press, c1998. xi, 314 p.
97-045408   305.48/9694.221   0252067169
*Caste--Nepal--Bhalara. Poor women--Nepal--
Bhalara--Social conditions. Women peasants--
Nepal--Bhalara--Social conditions.*

DS498 Goa. Portuguese in India — General works

DS498.S5 1998
Sinners and saints: the successors of Vasco da
Gama/ edited by Sanjay Subrahmanyam. Delhi;
Oxford University Press, 1998. 212 p.
98-903534   954/.004691.221   0195464263
*Portuguese--India--History. Portuguese--Asia--
History.*

DS502 East Asia. The Far East — Yearbooks. Directories, etc.

DS502.A27
AccessAsia: a guide to specialists and current
research. Seattle, Wash.: National Bureau of Asian
and Soviet Research, 1991- v.
93-641476   950/.025
Orientalists -- Directories.

DS503 East Asia. The Far East — Sources and documents

DS503.C35 no. 6
Nevadomsky, Joseph-john.
The Chinese in Southeast Asia; a selected and
annotated bibliography of publications in Western
languages,   1960-1970,   by   Joseph-john
Nevadomsky and Alice Li. Berkeley, Center for
South and Southeast Asia Studies, Uni 1970. xvi,
119 p.
70-635248   915.4 s
Chinese -- Asia, Southeastern -- Bibliography.

DS503.M28 1962
Maki, John M. 1909-
Conflict and tension in the Far East: key
documents, 1894-1960.   Seattle, University of
Washington Press, 1961 [i.e. 19 245 p.
61-017709   950.4082
East Asia -- History -- Sources.

DS503.S77 vol. 22
Ortiz, Valerie Malenfer.
Dreaming the southern song landscape: the power
of illusion in Chinese painting/ by Valerie
Malenfer Ortiz. Boston: Brill, c1999. xi, 214 p.
99-042727   758/.1/0951   9004110119
Landscape painting -- Japan -- Tokyo.

DS504.5 East Asia. The Far East — Collected works — Individual authors

DS504.5.F35 1994
Fallows, James M.
Looking at the sun: the rise of the new East Asian
economic and political system/ James Fallows.
New York: Pantheon Books, c1994. vii, 517 p.
93-038367   950   067942251X
East Asia.

DS504.5.N67 1982
Northeast Asian security after Vietnam/ edited by
Martin E. Weinstein. Urbana: University of Illinois
Press, c1982. xii, 182 p.
82-001909   327/.095   0252009665
*National security -- East Asia.   East Asia --
Politics and government.*

DS504.5.R57 1997
The rise of East Asia: critical visions of the Pacific
century/ edited by Mark T. Berger and Douglas A.
Borer. London; Routledge, 1997. xi, 308 p.
96-043154   950.220   0415161681
East Asia. Asia, Southeastern.

DS504.5.T54 2001
Tigers' roar: Asia's recovery and its impact/ Julian
Weiss, editor. Armonk, N.Y.: M.E. Sharpe, c2001.
xx, 354 p.
2001-020480   950.221   0765607840
East Asia. Asia, Southeastern.

DS507 East Asia. The Far East — Description and travel — 1801-1900

DS507.C63
Cole, Allan Burnett, 1914-
Yankee surveyors in the Shogun's seas: records of the United States Surveying Expedition to the North Pacific Ocean, 1853-1856. Princeton,: Princeton Univ. Press, 1947. 161 p.
47-011678   915
Pacific Ocean. Japan -- Description and travel.

DS508 East Asia. The Far East — Description and travel — 1901-1950

DS508.P43 1957
Peterson, A. D. C. 1908-
The Far East, a social geography.   London, Duckworth, 1957. 334 p.
58-030003
East Asia -- Description and travel.

DS508.2 East Asia. The Far East — Description and travel — 1951-

DS508.2.D6 1973
Dobby, Ernest Henry George.
Southeast Asia/ [by] E. H. G. Dobby. London: University of London Press, 1973. 429 p.
75-300405   915.9   0340173858
Asia, Southeastern -- Description and travel.

DS508.2.F5 1966
Fisher, Charles Alfred.
South-East Asia: a social, economic and political geography [by] Charles A. Fisher. London, Methuen; 1966. xix, 831p.
66-072859   915.9   0416424805
Asia, Southeastern -- Description and travel.

DS508.2.S56 1991
Snow, Edgar,
Edgar Snow's journey south of the clouds/ edited with commentary by   Robert M. Farnsworth. Columbia: University of Missouri Press, c1991. xv, 297 p.
91-006790   915.404/358.220   0826207774
East Asia -- Description and travel. Asia, Southeastern -- Description and travel. South Asia -- Description and travel.

DS509 East Asia. The Far East — Antiquities

DS509.C64 1973
Early South East Asia: essays in archaeology, history, and historical geography/ edited by R. B. Smith and W. Watson. New York: Oxford University Press, 1979. xv, 561 p.
79-112301   959   0197135870
Excavations (Archaeology) -- Asia, Southeastern -- Congresses. Asia, Southeastern -- History -- Congresses. Asia, Southeastern -- Antiquities -- Congresses.

DS509.3 East Asia. The Far East — Social life and customs. Civilization. Intellectual life

DS509.3.C67 1996
Confucian traditions in east Asian modernity: moral education and economic culture in Japan and the four mini-dragons/ edited by Tu Weiming. Cambridge, Mass.: Harvard University Press, 1996. xii, 418 p.
95-030852   950.220   0674160878
East Asia -- Civilization -- Confucian influences.

DS509.3.C85 1993
Cultural nationalism in East Asia: representation and identity/ edited by Harumi Befu. Berkeley, Calif.: Institute of East Asian Studies, University of viii, 196 p.
92-047016   951.220   1557290393
Nationalism--East Asia--History--20th century.

DS509.3.D43 1988
De Bary, William Theodore, 1919-
East Asian civilizations: a dialogue in five stages/ Wm. Theodore de Bary. Cambridge, Mass.: Harvard University Press, 1988. xi, 160 p.
87-014928   950   0674224051
East Asia -- Civilization.

DS509.3.F57 1997
Formations of colonial modernity in East Asia/ Tani E. Barlow, editor. Durham: Duke University Press, c1997. vi, 453 p.
96-043148   950.220   0822319438
Anti-imperialist movements--East Asia--History--20th century.

DS509.3.K6313 1971
Kolb, Albert, 1906-
East Asia: China, Japan, Korea, Vietnam; geography of a cultural region. Translated by C. A. M. Sym. London, Methuen, 1971. xvi, 591 p.
72-175950   915/.03/42   0416184206
East Asia -- Civilization. Vietnam -- Civilization.

DS509.5 East Asia. The Far East — Ethnography

DS509.5.B8
Burling, Robbins.
Hill farms and padi fields; life in mainland Southeast Asia. Englewood Cliffs, N.J., Prentice-Hall [1965] viii, 180 p.
65-013575   572.959
Ethnology -- Asia, Southeastern.

DS509.5.L4
LeBar, Frank M.
Ethnic groups of mainland Southeast Asia [by] Frank M. LeBar, Gerald C. Hickey [and] John K. Musgrave. Contributing authors: Robbins Burling [and others] New Haven, Human Relations Area Files Press [1964] x, 288 p.
64-025414   572.959
Ethnology -- Asia, Southeastern -- Dictionaries.

DS509.5.M8
Murdock, George Peter, 1897-
Social structure in Southeast Asia.   Chicago, Quadrangle Books, 1960. ix, 182 p.
61-000981   572.959
Ethnology -- Asia, Southeastern.

DS509.5.P8 1965   *have 1951*
Purcell, Victor William Williams Saunders, 1896-1964.
The Chinese in Southeast Asia/ by Victor Purcell . Kuala Lumpur; Oxford University Press, 1965 xvi, 623 p.
65-004234   301.451   0195804635
Chinese in Southeastern Asia.

DS509.5.S63
Southeast Asian tribes, minorities, and nations, edited by Peter Kunstadter. Princeton, N.J., Princeton University Press, 1967. 2 v.
66-017703   301.3/5/0954
Minorities -- Asia, Southeastern -- Addresses, essays, lectures. Minorities -- China. Minorities -- India.

DS509.5.T45
Thompson, Virginia McLean, 1903-
Minority problems in Southeast Asia, by Virginia Thompson and Richard Adloff. Stanford, Stanford University Press, 1955. viii, 295 p.
55-006688   301.45
Minorities -- Asia, Southeastern.

DS511 East Asia. The Far East — History — General works

DS511.B8
Buchanan, Keith M.
The Southeast Asian world; an introductory essay [by] Keith Buchanan. New York, Taplinger [1967] 176 p.
67-020243   309.1/59
Asia, Southeastern.

DS511.C3 1960
Cameron, Meribeth Elliott, 1905-
China, Japan, and the powers; a history of the modern Far East [by] Meribeth E. Cameron, Thomas H. D. Mahoney [and] George E. McReynolds. With a foreword by Kenneth Scott Latourette. New York, Ronald Press Co. [1960] 714 p.
60-007761   950
East Asia -- History. Eastern question (Far East)

DS511.C67 1971
Clyde, Paul Hibbert, 1896-
The Far East; a history of the Western impact and the Eastern response (1830-1970) [by] Paul H. Clyde [and] Burton F. Beers. Englewood Cliffs, N.J., Prentice-Hall [1971] xxiii, 536 p.
72-144100   950   013302976X
East Asia -- History.

DS511.C7713 1968
Coedes, George.
The Indianized states of Southeast Asia, by G. Coedes. Edited by Walter F. Vella. Translated by Susan Brown Cowing. Honolulu, East-West Center Press [1968] xxi, 403 p.
67-029224   959
East Indians -- Asia, Southeastern.   Asia, Southeastern -- History.

DS511.C786 2000
Cohen, Warren I.
East Asia at the center: four thousand years of engagement with the   world/ Warren I. Cohen. New York: Columbia University Press, 2000. xviii, 516 p.
00-031615   303.4/8259.221   0231101090
East Asia -- Relations -- Foreign countries. Asia, Southeastern -- Relations -- Foreign countries.

DS511.C82 1994
Cotterell, Arthur.
East Asia: from Chinese predominance to the rise of the Pacific rim/ Arthur Cotterell. New York: Oxford Uinv. Press, 1994. x, 339 p.
93-026263   950.220   0195088417
East Asia -- History.

DS511.E15 1995
East Asia in transition: toward a new regional order/ Robert S. Ross, editor. Armonk, N.Y.: M.E. Sharpe, c1995. xx, 368 p.
94-023743   327.5.220   1563245612
East Asia -- Foreign relations. East Asia -- Foreign economic relations. East Asia -- Politics and government.

DS511.F28 1989
Fairbank, John King,
East Asia: tradition & transformation/ John K. Fairbank, Edwin O. Reischauer, Albert M. Craig. Rev. ed. Boston: Houghton Mifflin Co., c1989. xv, 1027 p.
87-081263   950.220   0395450233
East Asia -- History.

DS511.H15 1968
Hall, D. G. E. 1891-
A history of South-east Asia, by D. G. E. Hall. London, Macmillan; 1968. xxiv, 1019 p.
68-015302   959
Asia, Southeastern -- History.

DS511.I5 1971
In search of Southeast Asia; a modern history [by] David Joel Steinberg [and others] Edited by David Joel Steinberg. New York, Praeger Publishers [1971] xii, 522 p.
70-121850   915.9/03
Asia, Southeastern -- History.

DS511.L3 1964
Latourette, Kenneth Scott, 1884-1968.
A short history of the Far East.   New York, Macmillan [1964] viii, 776 p.
64-014965   950
East Asia -- History.

DS511.L4
Le May, Reginald, b. 1885.
The culture of South-East Asia; the heritage of India, by Reginald Le May. Foreword by R. A. Butler. London, George Allen & Unwin [1954] 218 p.
54-001347   915.9
Asia, Southeastern -- Civilization.

DS511.L68
Lower, J. Arthur, 1907-
Ocean of destiny: a concise history of the North Pacific, 1500-1978/ J. Arthur Lower. Vancouver: University of British Columbia Press, c1978. xiv, 242 p.
81-472415   909/.09644   0774801018
North Pacific region -- History. Canada -- Relations -- North Pacific Ocean Region. North Pacific Ocean Region -- Relations -- Canada.

DS511.M88 1967
Morse, Hosea Ballou, 1855-1934.
Far Eastern international relations/ by Hosea Ballou Morse and Harley Farnsworth MacNair. New York: Russell & Russell, 1967, c1931. 2 v.
67-015998   327.5
Eastern question (Far East)   China -- Foreign relations. Japan -- Foreign relations -- 1912-1945.

DS511.P45 1966a
Penkala, Maria.
A correlated history of the Far East: China, Korea, Japan, With 26 maps by Edward Penkala, five maps by N. Bellin [and] one map by Nic. Witsen. The Hague, Mouton, 1966. 76 p.
67-000797   951
East Asia -- History -- Chronology. East Asia - - Historical geography -- Maps.

DS511.W66
Williams, Lea E.
Southeast Asia: a history/ Lea E. Williams. New York: Oxford University Press, 1976. xiii, 299 p.
75-032358   959   0195019997
Asia, Southeastern -- History.

DS514-518.1 East Asia. The Far East — History — By period

DS514.H65 2001
Holcombe, Charles,
The Genesis of East Asia, 221 B.C.-A.D. 907/ Charles Holcombe. Honolulu: Association for Asian Studies and University of Hawai'i   viii, 332 p.
00-066664   950.221   0824824652
East Asia -- History.

DS515.H57 2000
Historical perspectives on contemporary East Asia/ edited by Merle   Goldman, Andrew Gordon. Cambridge, Mass.: Harvard University Press, 2000. xi, 362 p.
00-024008   950.4.221   0674000986
East Asia -- History -- 19th century. East Asia -- History -- 20th century.

DS515.M28 1977
Malozemoff, Andrew, 1910-1952.
Russian Far Eastern policy, 1881-1904: with special emphasis on the causes of the Russo-Japanese War/ Andrew Malozemoff. New York: Octagon Books, 1977, c1958. 358 p.
76-054935   327.47/05   0374952620
Eastern question (Far East) Russo-Japanese War, 1904-1905 -- Causes. Soviet Union -- Foreign relations -- East Asia. East Asia -- Foreign relations -- Soviet Union.

DS515.N38 2000
Nation work: Asian elites and national identities/ edited by Timothy Brook and Andre Schmid. Ann Arbor: University of Michigan Press, c2000. 270 p.
99-006574   320.54/095.221   0472110322
Nationalism--East Asia--History. Elite (Social sciences)--East Asia--History.

DS515.Z45 1997
Zhao, Suisheng,
Power competition in East Asia: from the old Chinese world order to post-cold war regional multipolarity/ Suisheng Zhao. 1st ed. New York: St. Martin's Press, 1997. xv, 346 p.
96-028351   327.5.220   0312162588
East Asia -- Foreign relations.

DS517.R93 1999
The Russo-Japanese war in cultural perspective, 1904-1905/ edited by David Wells and Sandra Wilson. New York: St. Martin's Press, 1999. p. cm.
99-010727   952.03/1.221   0312221614
Russo-Japanese War, 1904-1905--Social aspects--Japan.

DS517.W34 1974
Walder, David.
The short victorious war; the Russo-Japanese conflict, 1904-5. New York, Harper & Row [1974, c1973] 321 p.
74-000801   952.03/1   0060145161
Russo-Japanese War, 1904-1905.

DS517.W37
Warner, Denis Ashton, 1917-
The tide at sunrise; a history of the Russo-Japanese War, 1904-1905, by Denis and Peggy Warner. [Maps by Don Coutts. New York, Charterhouse [1974] xi, 659 p.
74-175084   952.03/1
Russo-Japanese War, 1904-1905.

DS517.13.O37
Okamoto, Shumpei.
The Japanese oligarchy and the Russo-Japanese War. New York, Columbia University Press, 1970. x, 358 p.
74-114259   952.03/1   0231034040
Russo-Japanese War, 1904-1905.   Japan -- Politics and government -- 1868-1912.

DS517.3 .H3
Hargreaves, Reginald.
Red sun rising: the siege of Port Arthur. Philadelphia, Lippincott [1962] 210 p.
62-009344   952.031
Port Arthur (China) -- Siege, 1904-1905.

DS517.7.E88 1988
Esthus, Raymond A.
Double Eagle and Rising Sun: the Russians and Japanese at Portsmouth in 1905/ Raymond A. Esthus. Durham: Duke University Press, 1988. x, 265 p.
87-020183   952.03/1   0822307782
Russo-Japanese War, 1904-1905 -- Treaties.

DS518.C66 2001
Constructing nationhood in modern East Asia/ edited by Kai-wing Chow, Kevin M. Doak, Poshek Fu. Ann Arbor: University of Michigan Press, 2001. 404 p.
00-051176   951.05.221   0472067354
Nationalism--East Asia--History--20th century.

DS518.J38
Japan's Greater East Asia Co-prosperity Sphere in World War II: selected readings and documents/ edited and introduced by Joyce C. Lebra. Kuala Lumpur; Oxford University Press, 1975. xxi, 212 p.
75-319240   327.52/05   0196382653
Greater East Asia Co-prosperity Sphere -- Addresses, essays, lectures. Greater East Asia Co-prosperity Sphere -- History -- Sources.

DS518.M2 1991
MacMurray, John Van Antwerp, 1881-1960.
How the peace was lost: the 1935 memorandum, Developments affecting American policy in the Far East/ prepared for the State Department by John Van Antwerp MacMurray; edited, and with introduction and notes by Arthur Waldron. Stanford, Calif.: Hoover Institution Press, c1992. x, 165 p.
91-025737   327.7305   0817991514
East Asia -- Foreign relations -- United States. United States -- Foreign relations -- East Asia.

DS518.P55
Pluvier, Jan M.
South-East Asia from colonialism to independence/ Jan Pluvier. Kuala Lumpur; Oxford University Press, 1974. xxii, 571 p.
74-941414   959   0196382637
Asia, Southeastern -- History.

DS518.Q46
Quigley, Harold Scott, 1889-
Far Eastern war, 1937-1941, by Harold S. Quigley ... Boston, World peace foundation, 1942. xi, 369 p.
42-014269   950
Eastern question (Far East)   East Asia -- History. Japan -- Foreign relations. China -- Politics and government -- 1912-1949.

DS518.1.B64 1998
Borthwick, Mark.
Pacific century: the emergence of modern Pacific Asia/ Mark Borthwick with contributions by selected scholars. 2nd ed. Boulder, Colo.: Westview Press, 1998. xv, 582 p.
97-042756   950.221   0813334713
East Asia -- Politics and government. Asia, Southeastern -- Politics and government -- 1945- East Asia -- Economic conditions. Asia, Southeastern -- Economic conditions.

DS518.1.C23
Cady, John Frank, 1901-
The history of post-war Southeast Asia/ John F. Cady. Athens: Ohio University Press, c1974. xxii, 720 p.
74-082497   959   0821401602
Asia, Southeastern -- History.

DS518.1.C4926 1997
China, Taiwan, Japan, the United States, and the world/ Edited by Kenneth W. Thompson. Lanham, MD: University Press of America, 1997. p. cm.
97-042721   303.48/25   0761809899
East Asia -- Relations -- Foreign countries. China.

DS518.1.C587
Colbert, Evelyn S. 1918-
Southeast Asia in international politics, 1941-1956/ Evelyn Colbert. Ithaca, N.Y.: Cornell University Press, 1977. 372 p.
76-028008   327/.0959   0801409713
World politics -- 20th century.   Asia, Southeastern -- Foreign relations.

DS518.1.E33 1987
East Asia, the West, and international security/ edited by Robert O'Neill. Hamden, CT: Archon Books, 1987. viii, 253 p.
87-019377   355/.03305   0208021981
National security -- East Asia -- Congresses. Security, International -- Congresses.

DS518.1.E44
Elsbree, Willard H
Japan's role in Southeast Asian nationalist movements, 1940 to 1945. Issued under the auspices of the International Secretariat, Institute of Pacific Relations. Cambridge, Harvard University Press, 1953. 182 p.
53-013171   959
Nationalism -- Asia, Southeastern.   Japan -- Foreign relations -- 1912-1945. Asia, Southeastern -- Politics and government.

DS518.1.F47
Fifield, Russell H. 1914-
The diplomacy of Southeast Asia: 1945-1958. New York, Harper [1958] xv, 584 p.
58-008354   959
Asia, Southeastern -- Politics.

DS518.1.G6
Gordon, Bernard K., 1932-
The dimensions of conflict in Southeast Asia [by] Bernard K. Gordon. Englewood Cliffs, N.J., Prentice-Hall [1966] xiv, 201 p.
66-014699   327.0959
Asia, Southeastern -- Politics and government -- 1945-

DS518.1.H6
Holland, W. L. 1907-
Asian nationalism and the West; a symposium based on documents and reports of the eleventh conference, Institute of Pacific Relations. New York, Macmillan, 1953. viii, 449 p.
53-001116   991
Nationalism -- Asia, Southeastern.

DS518.1.K5
King, John Kerry.
Southeast Asia in perspective.   New York, Macmillan, 1956. 309 p.
56-011449   959
Asia, Southeastern -- Politics.

DS518.1.L315 1949
Lattimore, Owen, 1900-
The situation in Asia/ Owen Lattimore. Boston: Little, Brown, 1949. 244 p.
49-002218   950
Eastern question (Far East)   Asia -- Politics and government.

DS518.1.P44 1988
Peace, politics & economics in Asia: the challenge to cooperate/ edited by Robert A. Scalapino and Masataka Kosaka. Washington: Pergamon-Brassey's International Defense Publish 1988. xiv, 209 p.
87-025840   320.95   0080359612
East Asia -- Politics and government. Asia, Southeastern -- Politics and government. East Asia -- Economic conditions.

DS518.1.P62 1999
Politics and economics in northeast Asia: nationalism and regionalism in contention/ edited by Tsuneo Akaha. New York: St. Martin's Press, 1999. p. cm.
99-025809   320.95   0312222882
Regionalism (International organization)   East Asia -- Foreign economic relations. East Asia -- Military relations. East Asia -- Relations -- Russia -- Russian Far East.

DS518.1.R43
Reischauer, Edwin O. 1910-
Wanted: an Asian policy. New York, Knopf, 1955. 276 p.
55-005615   327.73095
United States -- Foreign relations -- Asia. Asia -- Politics.

DS518.1.R74
Royal Institute of International Affairs.
Collective defence in South East Asia; the Manila treaty and its implications. A report by a Chatham House study group. London, [1956] xiv, 197 p.
57-000126   959
Asia, Southeastern -- Defenses. Asia, Southeastern -- Politics.

DS518.1.S47
Shaplen, Robert, 1917-
Time out of hand; revolution and reaction in Southeast Asia. New York, Harper & Row [1969] x, 465 p.
68-028217   320.9/59
Asia, Southeastern -- Politics and government -1945-

DS518.1.S68 1995
The strategic quadrangle: Russia, China, Japan, and the United States in East Asia/ Michael Mandelbaum, editor. New York: Council on Foreign Relations Press, c1995. vii, 221 p.
94-040867   327.5   0876091680
East Asia -- Foreign relations. East Asia -- Strategic aspects.

DS518.1.T7
Trager, Frank N.
Marxism in Southeast Asia; a study of four countries. Edited, with an introd. and conclusion. With contributions by Jeanne S. Mintz [and others] Stanford, Calif., Stanford University Press, 1959. 381 p.
59-012469   335.40959
Communism -- Asia, Southeastern.   Asia, Southeastern -- Politics.

DS518.1.V28
Vandenbosch, Amry, 1894-
Southeast Asia among the world powers, by Amry Vandenbosch and Richard A. Butwell. Lexington, University of Kentucky Press [1957] 336 p.
57-009768   959
Asia, Southeastern -- Politics and government.

DS518.1.V43
Vinacke, Harold Monk, 1893-
Far eastern politics in the postwar period.   New York, Appleton-Century-Crofts [1956] 497 p.
55-010400   950
East Asia -- Politics and government.

DS518.15-518.9 East Asia. The Far East — History — Relation of individual countries to East Asia

DS518.15.T38
Taylor, Jay, 1931-
China and Southeast Asia; Peking's relations with revolutionary movements.   New York, Praeger [1974] xx, 384 p.
74-003511   327.51/059   027508910X
Communism -- Asia.   Asia, Southeastern -- Foreign relations -- China. China -- Foreign relations -- Asia, Southeastern. Asia, Southeastern -- Politics and government -- 1945-

DS518.2.C3
Cady, John Frank, 1901-
The roots of French imperialism in Eastern Asia. Ithaca, N.Y., Published for the American Historical Associatio [1954] xii, 322 p.
54-013440 325.344095
French -- East Asia. France -- Colonies -- East Asia.

DS518.2.D74 1991
Dreifort, John E.
Myopic grandeur: the ambivalence of French foreign policy toward the Far East, 1919-1945/ John E. Dreifort. Kent, Ohio: Kent State University Press, c1991. xiv, 334 p.
91-011434 327.4405 0873384415
Great powers -- History -- 20th century. France -- Foreign relations -- East Asia. France -- Foreign relations -- 20th century. Indochina -- History.

DS518.4.L675 1981
Lowe, Peter, 1941-
Britain in the Far East: a survey from 1819 to the present/ Peter Lowe. London; Longman, 1981. 264 p.
79-042619 950/.3 0582487307
East Asia -- Foreign relations -- Great Britain. Great Britain -- Foreign relations -- East Asia.

DS518.4.L676 1997
Lowe, Peter, 1941-
Containing the Cold War in East Asia: British policies towards Japan, China, and Korea, 1948-53/ Peter Lowe. Manchester; Manchester University Press; 1997. xii, 288 p.
97-165203 0719025087
Cold War. Great Britain -- Foreign relations -- East Asia. Great Britain -- Foreign relations -- 1945- East Asia -- Foreign relations -- Great Britain.

DS518.4.R6
Rose, Saul.
Britain and South-east Asia. Baltimore, Johns Hopkins Press [1962] 208 p.
62-018415 327.42059
Great Britain -- Relations (general) with Southeastern Asia. Asia, Southeastern -- Relations (general) with Great Britain.

DS518.4.T37
Tarling, Nicholas.
Imperial Britain in South-East Asia/ Nicholas Tarling. Kuala Lumpur; Oxford University Press, 1975. viii, 273 p.
75-940341 327.41/059 0196382629
British -- Asia, Southeastern -- History. Great Britain -- Foreign relations -- Asia, Southeastern. Asia, Southeastern -- Foreign relations -- Great Britain.

DS518.45.H44
Hellmann, Donald C., 1933-
Japan and East Asia; the new international order [by] Donald C. Hellmann. New York, Praeger [1972] xii, 243 p.
78-101663 327.52/05
East Asia -- Foreign relations -- Japan. Japan -- Foreign relations -- East Asia.

DS518.45.J363 2001
Japan and East Asian regionalism/ edited by S Javed Maswood. London; Routledge, 2001. p. cm.
00-058262 327.5205/09/049.221 0415237475
East Asia -- Foreign relations -- Japan. Japan -- Foreign relations -- East Asia. Asia, Southeastern -- Foreign relations -- Japan. Japan -- Foreign relations -- Asia, Southeastern. Japan -- Foreign relations -- 1989-

DS518.45.K59 1995
Kirby, Stuart.
Japan and East Asia: documentary analyses, 1921-1945/ Stuart Kirby. London: Tauris Academic Studies; 3, 202 p.
93-060684 1850437025
East Asia -- Relations -- Japan -- Sources. Japan -- Relations -- East Asia -- Sources.

DS518.7.B42
Beloff, Max, 1913-
Soviet policy in the Far East, 1944-1951. London, Oxford University Press, 1953. vi, 278 p.
53-012887 327.47095
Eastern question (Far East) Soviet Union -- Foreign relations -- 1945-1991. Soviet Union -- Foreign relations -- Asia.

DS518.7.D3 1971
Dallin, David J., 1889-1962.
Soviet Russia and the Far East. [Hamden, Conn.] Archon Books, 1971 [c1948] vii, 398 p.
76-150769 327.47/05 0208009965
Soviet Union -- Foreign relations -- Asia. Asia -- Foreign relations -- Soviet Union.

DS518.7.M34 1988
Manning, Robert A.
Asian policy: the new Soviet challenge in the Pacific/ by Robert A. Manning. New York: Priority Press Publications, 1988. vi, 150 p.
88-031634 327.4705 0870782452
East Asia -- Foreign relations -- Soviet Union. Soviet Union -- Foreign relations -- East Asia. Soviet Union -- Foreign relations -- 1975-

DS518.7.M66
Moore, Harriet Lucy, 1912-
Soviet Far Eastern policy, 1931-1945, by Harriet L. Moore. Princeton, N.J., Princeton University Press, 1945. xv, p.
45-005523 327.47095
Eastern question (Far East) Asia -- Politics and government. -- cm Soviet Union -- Asiatic relations. -- cn

DS518.7.S68 1982
Soviet policy in East Asia/ edited by Donald S. Zagoria. New Haven: Yale University Press, c1982. xiii, 360 p.
82-050445 327.4705 0300027389
East Asia -- Foreign relations -- Soviet Union. Soviet Union -- Foreign relations -- East Asia.

DS518.7.Z53 1993
Ziegler, Charles E.
Foreign policy and East Asia: learning and adaption in the Gorbachev era/ Charles E. Ziegler. Cambridge [England]; Cambridge University Press, 1993. xii, 197 p.
92-036268 327.4705 0521415470
National security -- Soviet Union. Soviet Union -- Foreign relations -- East Asia. East Asia -- Foreign relations -- Soviet Union. Soviet Union -- Foreign relations -- 1985-1991.

DS518.8.A856 1962
American Assembly.
The United States and the Far East. [Edited by Willard L. Thorp] Englewood Cliffs, N.J., Prentice-Hall [1962] 188 p.
62-012831 327.73095
Eastern question (Far East) United States -- Foreign relations -- East Asia.

DS518.8.A858
American-East Asian relations: a survey. Contributions by Burton F. Beers [and others] Edited by Ernest R. May and James C. Thomson Jr. Cambridge, Mass., Harvard University Press, 1972. xv, 425 p.
70-188970 327.73/05 0674022858
United States -- Foreign relations -- East Asia -- Addresses, essays, lectures. East Asia -- Foreign relations -- United States -- Addresses, essays, lectures.

DS518.8.B34
Battistini, Lawrence Henry, 1907-
The rise of American influence in Asia and the Pacific. [East Lansing] Michigan State University Press, 1960. 241 p.
59-015833 327.7305
United States -- Foreign relations -- East Asia. East Asia -- Politics.

DS518.8.B58 1982
Blum, Robert M.
Drawing the line: the origin of the American containment policy in East Asia/ Robert M. Blum. New York: Norton, c1982. xii, 273 p.
82-002187 327.7305 0393015653
East Asia -- Foreign relations -- United States. United States -- Foreign relations -- East Asia.

DS518.8.C4 1989
Carter, K. Holly Maze.
The Asian dilemma in U.S. foreign policy: national interest versus strategic planning/ K. Holly Maze Carter. Armonk, N.Y.: M.E. Sharpe, c1989. xxiv, 247 p.
88-034619 327.7305 0873325125
East Asia -- Foreign relations -- United States. United States -- Foreign relations -- East Asia. Asia, Southeastern -- Foreign relations -- United States.

DS518.8.C48
Christy, Arthur, 1899-1946.
The Asian legacy and American life; essays arranged and edited by Arthur E. Christy. New York, The John Day company [1945] x p. 1 l. 2
45-004340 327.73095
East Asia -- Relations (general) with the U.S. United States -- Relations (general) with the East (Far East)

DS518.8.C57
Clubb, Oliver E. 1929-
The United States and the Sino-Soviet bloc in Southeast Asia [by] Oliver E. Clubb, Jr. Washington, Brookings Institution [1962] ix, 173 p.
62-021276 959
Asia, Southeastern -- Foreign relations -- United States. United States -- Foreign relations -- Asia, Southeastern.

DS518.8.C76 1999
Cumings, Bruce, 1943-
Parallax visions: making sense of American-East Asian relations at the end of the century/ Bruce Cumings. Durham, NC: Duke University Press, 1999. p. cm.
98-032017 303.18/27305 0822322765
East Asia -- Relations -- United States. United States -- Relations -- East Asia.

DS518.8.C8 1968
Curry, Roy Watson.
Woodrow Wilson and Far Eastern policy, 1913-1921. New York, Octagon Books, 1968 [c1957] 411 p.
68-022300   973.91/3/0924
Wilson, Woodrow, -- 1856-1924. Eastern question (Far East) United States -- Foreign relations -- East Asia. East Asia -- Foreign relations -- United States.

DS518.8.D55 1941
Dennett, Tyler, 1883-1949.
Americans in eastern Asia. New York, Barnes & Noble, Inc., 1941. xviii, 725 p.
43-047688   950
Eastern question (Far East) United States -- Commerce -- East Asia. East Asia -- Commerce -- United States. United States -- Foreign relations.

DS518.8.E22 2002
East Asia and the United States: an encyclopedia of relations since 1784/ edited by James I. Matray. Westport, Conn.: Greenwood Press, 2002. 2 v. cm.
2002-019542   303.48/25073/03.221
0313324476
East Asia -- Relations -- United States -- Encyclopedias. United States -- Relations -- East Asia -- Encyclopedias.

DS518.8.F48
Fifield, Russell H. 1914-
Southeast Asia in United States policy. New York, Published for the Council on Foreign Relations b [1963] xi, 488 p.
63-020144   327.73059
Asia, Southeastern -- Politics and government. United States -- Foreign relations -- Asia, Southeastern.

DS518.8.F57
Flynn, John Thomas, 1883-1964.
While you slept; our tragedy in Asia and who made it. New York, Devin-Adair, c1951. 192 p.
51-014369   950
Eastern question (Far East) United States -- Foreign relations -- Asia.

DS518.8.G33 1988
Gallicchio, Marc S.,
The Cold War begins in Asia: American East Asian policy and the fall of the Japanese empire/ Marc S. Gallicchio. New York: Columbia University Press, 1988. xvi, 188 p.
87-023917   327.7305.219   0231065027
East Asia -- Foreign relations -- United States. United States -- Foreign relations -- East Asia. United States -- Foreign relations -- 1945-1953.

DS518.8.G75 1962
Griswold, Alfred Whitney, 1906-1963.
The Far Eastern policy of the United States. New Haven, Yale University Press [1964, c1938] 530 p.
62-000809   327.73095
Eastern question (Far East) United States -- Foreign relations.

DS518.8.H4
Henderson, William, 1922-
Southeast Asia: problems of United States policy. Cambridge, Mass., M.I.T. Press [1964, c1963] xiv, 273 p.
63-022438   327.73059
Asia, Southeastern -- Politics. United States -- Foreign relations -- Foreign relations -- Asia, Southeastern.

DS518.8.I73
Iriye, Akira.
Across the Pacific; an inner history of American-East Asian relations. Introd. by John K. Fairbank. New York, Harcourt, Brace & World [1967] xvii, 361 p.
67-019202   301.29/5/073
United States -- Relations -- East Asia. East Asia -- Relations -- United States.

DS518.8.L28
Latourette, Kenneth Scott, 1884-1968.
The American record in the Far East, 1945-1951. New York, Macmillan, 1952. 208 p.
52-012394   950
Eastern question (Far East) United States -- Foreign relations -- Asia.

DS518.8.M7
Morin, Relman, 1907-1973.
East wind rising; a long view of the Pacific crisis. New York, Knopf, 1960 359 p.
60-007298   950.42
United States -- Relations (general) with the East (Far East) East Asia -- Relations (general) with the United States.

DS518.8.P336 1996
Pacific passage: the study of American--East Asian relations on the eve of the twenty-first century/ edited, and with an introduction by Warren I. Cohen. New York: Columbia University Press, c1996. xxi, 407 p.
95-044851   327.7305   0231104065
East Asia -- Relations -- United States. United States -- Relations -- East Asia.

DS518.9.C3.A7
Angus, Henry Forbes, 1891-
Canada and the Far East, 1940-1953. By H. F. Angus. [Toronto] University of Toronto Press, 1953. 129 p.
53-013495
East Asia -- Relations (general) with Canada. Canada -- Relations (general) with the East Asia.

DS518.9.C3.L6 1973   *have 1941*
Lower, Arthur Reginald Marsden, 1889-
Canada and the Far East--1940, by A. R. M. Lower. Westport, Conn., Greenwood Press [1973, c1940] ix, 152 p.
73-003016   301.29/71/05   0837168317
Canada -- Relations -- East Asia. East Asia -- Relations -- Canada.

DS523 Southeastern Asia — Antiquities

DS523.H55 1996
Higham, Charles.
The Bronze Age of Southeast Asia/ Charles Higham. Cambridge [England]; Cambridge University Press, 1996. xvi, 381 p.
95-039223   959/.01   0521565057
Bronze age -- Asia, Southeastern. Asia, Southeastern -- Antiquities.

DS523.2 Southeastern Asia — Social life and customs. Civilization. Intellectual life

DS523.2.D86 1991
Dumarcay, Jacques.
The palaces of South-East Asia: architecture and customs/ Jacques Dumarcay; translated and edited by Michael Smithies. Singapore; Oxford University Press, 1991. xiii, 143 p.
90-044017   959   0195889673
Palaces -- Asia, Southeastern. Architecture -- Asia, Southeastern. Asia, Southeastern -- Kings and rulers. Asia, Southeastern -- Social life and customs.

DS523.4 Southeastern Asia — Ethnography

DS523.4.M35.J66 1994
Jones, Gavin W.
Marriage and divorce in Islamic South-East Asia/ Gavin W. Jones. Kuala Lumpur; Oxford University Press, 1994. xvii, 348 p.
93-038170   306.81/0959/0917671   9676530476
Malays (Asian people) -- Asia, Southeastern -- Marriage customs and rites. Muslims -- Asia, Southeastern -- Marriage customs and rites. Marriage (Islamic law) -- Asia, Southeastern. Asia, Southeastern -- Religious life and customs.

DS524.8 Southeastern Asia — History — Study and teaching

DS524.8.E85.D55 1998
Dijk, Kees van.
European directory of South-east Asian studies/ compiled and edited by Kees van Dijk and Jolanda Leemburg-den Hollander. Leiden, The Netherlands: KITLV Press, 1998. x, 618 p.
98-234159   959/.07/04   9067181358
Scholars -- Europe -- Directories. Asia, Southeastern -- Study and teaching -- Europe -- Directories.

DS525 Southeastern Asia — History — General works

DS525.T37 1992
The Cambridge history of Southeast Asia/ edited by Nicholas Tarling. Cambridge, UK; Cambridge University Press, 1992. 2 v.
91-008808   959   0521355052
Asia, Southeastern -- History.

DS525.7 Southeastern Asia — History — Political history

DS525.7.A53 1998
Anderson, Benedict R. O'G. 1936-
The spectre of comparisons: nationalism, Southeast Asia, and the world/ Benedict Anderson. New York: Verso, 1998. p. cm.
98-035495   320.959   1859848133
Nationalism -- Asia, Southeastern. Nationalism. Asia, Southeastern -- Politics and government.

DS525.9 Southeastern Asia — History — Foreign and general relations

DS525.9.G7.T37 1996
Tarling, Nicholas.
Britain, Southeast Asia and the onset of the Pacific War/ Nicholas Tarling. Cambridge [England]; Cambridge University Press, 1996. xii, 434 p.
95-042787   327.41059   0521553466
World War, 1939-1945 -- Asia, Southeastern. Great Britain -- Foreign relations -- Asia, Southeastern. Asia, Southeastern -- Foreign relations -- Great Britain. Asia, Southeastern -- History.

DS525.9.J3.J37 1991
Japanese cultural policies in Southeast Asia during World War 2/ edited by Grant K. Goodman. New York: St. Martin's Press, 1997. xi, 223 p.
90-039913   303.48/252059   031205243X
World War, 1939-1945 -- Social aspects -- Asia, Southeastern. Japan -- Relations -- Asia, Southeastern. Japan -- Cultural policy. Asia, Southeastern -- Relations -- Japan.

DS525.9.M628.V66 1993
Von der Mehden, Fred R.
Two worlds of Islam: interaction between Southeast Asia and the Middle East/ Fred R. von der Mehden. Gainesville: University Press of Florida, c1993. xiii, 128 p.
92-044707   959/.0097671   0813012082
Muslims -- Asia, Southeastern -- Politics and government. Middle East -- Relations -- Asia, Southeastern. Asia, Southeastern -- Relations -- Middle East.

DS526.4-526.7 Southeastern Asia — History — By period

DS526.4.T37 1993
Tarling, Nicholas.
The fall of Imperial Britain in South-East Asia/ Nicholas Tarling. Singapore; Oxford University Press, 1993. ix, 229 p.
92-021081   325/.3141/0959   0195886119
British -- Asia, Southeastern -- History. Asia, Southeastern -- History. Great Britain -- Colonies -- History.

DS526.4.W43 1998
Webster, Anthony.
Gentlemen capitalists: British imperialism in South East Asia, 1770-1890/ Anthony Webster. London; Tauris Academic Studies, 1998. vi, 282 p.
98-150959   959   1860641717
British -- Asia, Southeastern -- History. Asia, Southeastern -- Relations -- Great Britain. Great Britain -- Relations -- Asia, Southeastern. Asia, Southeastern -- History.

DS526.7.S687 1998
Southeast Asian identities: culture and the politics of representation in Indonesia, Malaysia, Singapore, and Thailand/ edited by Joel S. Kahn. New York: St. Martin's Press; c1998. viii, 273 p.
97-049584   306/.0959   0312213433
Nationalism -- Asia, Southeastern -- History. Asia, Southeastern -- Ethnic relations. Asia, Southeastern -- Politics and government -- 1945-

DS526.7.T36 1998
Tarling, Nicholas.
Nations and states in Southeast Asia/ Nicholas Tarling. Cambridge, U.K.; Cambridge University Press, 1998. x, 136 p.
97-029973   959.05/3   052162245X
Nationalism -- Asia, Southeastern -- History. National state. Asia, Southeastern -- History -- 1945- Asia, Southeastern -- Historiography.

DS528.4-530.4 Southeastern Asia — Burma — History

DS528.4.A96 1998
Aung-Thwin, Michael.
Myth and history in the historiography of early Burma: paradigms, primary sources, and prejudices/ Michael A. Aung-Thwin,. Athens, OH: Ohio University Center for International Studies 1998. p. cm.
97-049191   929.1/02   0896802019
Burma -- Historical geography. Burma -- History -- To 1824.

DS530.4.B867 1997
Burma: the challenge of change in a divided society/ edited by Peter Carey; foreword by Aung San Suu Kyi. Houndmills, Basingstoke, Hampshire: Macmillan Press; 1997. xxiv, 254 p.
96-046502   320.9591   0333595726
Burma -- Politics and government -- 1948- Burma -- Foreign relations -- 1948- Burma -- Ethnic relations.

DS550-553.3 Southeastern Asia — French Indochina — History

DS550.D8 1994
Duiker, William J., 1932-
U.S. containment policy and the conflict in Indochina/ William J. Duiker. Stanford, Calif.: Stanford University Press, 1994. 453 p.
93-041544   327.730597   0804722838
Vietnamese Conflict, 1961-1975 -- United States. United States -- Foreign relations -- Indochina. Indochina -- Foreign relations -- United States. Indochina -- Politics and government -- 1945-

DS550.S54 1996
Shipway, Martin.
The road to war: France and Vietnam, 1944-1947/ Martin Shipway. Providence: Berghahn Books, 1996. xii, 306 p.
96-024310   959.7/03   1571818944
Indochina -- History -- 1945- France -- Colonies.

DS553.3.D5.N67 1995
Nordell, John R. 1947-
The undetected enemy: French and American miscalculations at Dien Bien Phu, 1953/ by John R. Nordell, Jr. College Station: Texas A&M University Press, c1995. xvi, 217 p.
94-037073   959.704/2   0890966451
Dien Bien Phu (Vietnam), Battle of, 1954.

DS554.8-554.98 Southeastern Asia — French Indochina — Cambodia

DS554.8.D397 1997
Deac, Wilfred P., 1934-
Road to the killing fields: the Cambodian war of 1970-1975/ Wilfred P. Deac; foreword by Harry G. Summers, Jr. College Station: Texas A&M University Press, c1997. xx, 307 p.
97-013661   959.604/2   0890967504
Cambodia -- History -- Civil War, 1970-1975.

DS554.8.P443 1999
Peou, Sorpong.
Intervention & change in Cambodia: towards democracy ?/ Sorpong Peou. New York: St. Martin's Press, 1999. xxiii, 572 p.
99-034595   320.9596/09/04   0312227175
Democracy -- Cambodia. Cambodia -- Foreign relations. Cambodia -- Politics and government.

DS554.98.A5.M36 1996
Mannikka, Eleanor.
Angkor Wat: time, space, and kingship/ Eleanor Mannikka. Honolulu: University of Hawaii Press, c1996. xv, 341 p.
96-004368   959.6   0824817206
Temples, Buddhist -- Cambodia -- Angkor (Extinct city) Astronomy, Khmer. Angkor (Extinct city) -- Buildings, structures, etc.

DS555.3-555.5 Southeastern Asia — French Indochina — Laos

DS555.3.L34 1995
Laos: a country study/ edited by Andrea Matles Savada. Washington, DC: Federal Research Division, Library of Congress: 1995. xliii, 366 p.
95-017235   959.404   0844408328
Laos.

DS555.45.M5.I74 1996
Ireson, Carol J.
Field, forest, and family: women's work and power in rural Laos/ Carol J. Ireson. Boulder, Colo: Westview Press, 1996. xxiii, 285 p.
96-027143   305.4/09594   0813389364
Women, Hmong -- Social conditions. Women, Lao -- Social conditions. Women, Khmu' -- Social conditions. Louangphrabang (Laos: Province) -- Social conditions. Louangphrabang (Laos: Province) -- Economic conditions.

DS555.5.S79 1997
Stuart-Fox, Martin, 1939-
A history of Laos/ Martin Stuart-Fox. Cambridge, U.K.; Cambridge University Press, 1997. xiii, 253 p.
97-012091   959.4   0521592356
Laos -- History.

DS556.45-559.93 Southeastern Asia — French Indochina — Vietnam. Annam

DS556.45.A43.B38 1996
Bass, Thomas A.
Vietnamerica: the war comes home/ Thomas A. Bass. New York: Soho, c1996. 278 p.
95-049994   959.7/00413   1569470502
Amerasians -- Vietnam. Children of military personnel -- Vietnam. Abandoned children -- Vietnam.

DS556.45.A43.D43 1995
DeBonis, Steven, 1949-
Children of the enemy: oral histories of Vietnamese Amerasians and their mothers/ by Steven DeBonis. Jefferson, N.C.: McFarland, c1995. x, 297 p.
94-028735   959.7/00413   0899509754
Amerasians -- Vietnam -- Social conditions. Children of military personnel -- Vietnam. Abandoned children -- Vietnam.

DS556.5.C47 1995
Chapuis, Oscar.
A history of Vietnam: from Hong Bang to Tu Duc/ Oscar Chapuis. Westport, Conn.: Greenwood Press, 1995. xix, 216 p.
94-048169   959.7   0313296227
Vietnam -- History.

DS556.57.V54 1999
Vietnamese foreign policy in transition/ edited by Carl Thayer and Ramses Amer. New York: St. Martin's Press, 1999. ix, 294 p.
99-041755   327.597/009/049   0312228848
Vietnam -- Foreign relations.

DS556.8.B732000
Bradley, Mark.
Imagining Vietnam and America: the making of postcolonial Vietnam, 1919-1950/ Mark Philip Bradley; foreword by John Lewis Gaddis. Chapel Hill: University of North Carolina Press, c2000. xiv, 304 p.
99-088185   959.7/03   0807825492
Vietnam -- Politics and government -- 20th century. Vietnam -- Foreign relations -- United States. United States -- Foreign relations -- Vietnam.

DS556.8.D83 1996
Duiker, William J., 1932-
The communist road to power in Vietnam/ William J. Duiker. Boulder, Colo.: Westview Press, 1996. xvi, 435 p.
95-053084   959.704   0813385865
Communism -- Vietnam -- History. Vietnam -- History -- 20th century.

DS556.8.L25 2000
Lam, Truong Buu.
Colonialism experienced: Vietnamese writings on colonialism, 1900-1931/ Truong Buu Lam. Ann Arbor, Mich.: University of Michigan, 2000. viii, 328 p.
99-058296   959.703   0472097121
Vietnam -- Politics and government -- 20th century -- Sources.

DS556.83.P46.A3 1997
Phan, Boi Chau, 1867-1940.
Overturned chariot: the autobiography of Phan-Boi-Chau/ translated with an introduction and notes by Vinh Sinh and Nicholas Wickenden. Honolulu, Ha.: University of Hawai'i Press, c1999. x, 296 p.
97-019313   959.7/03   082481875X
Phan, Boi Chau, -- 1867-1940. Revolutionaries -- Vietnam -- Biography.

DS556.9.P74 2001
Prelude to tragedy: Vietnam, 1960-1965/ edited by Harvey Neese and John O'Donnell. Annapolis, Md.: Naval Institute Press, c2001. xviii, 309 p.
00-063837   959.704/31   1557504911
Vietnamese Conflict, 1961-1975 -- United States. Vietnam -- Politics and government -- 1945-1975. Vietnam (Republic) -- Foreign relations -- United States. United States -- Foreign relations -- Vietnam (Republic)

DS557.4.J64 1997
Johnson, Lyndon B. 1908-1973.
Lyndon B. Johnson's Vietnam papers: a documentary collection/ edited by David M. Barrett. College Station, Tex.: Texas A&M University Press, c1997. xxxiv, 869 p.
96-037250   959.704/3373   0890967415
Johnson, Lyndon B. -- (Lyndon Baines), -- 1908-1973. Vietnamese Conflict, 1961-1975 -- United States. Vietnamese Conflict, 1961-1975 -- Sources. United States -- Politics and government -- 1963-1969 -- Sources.

DS557.4.V58 1996
The Vietnam War: how the U.S. became involved/ edited and introduced by Mitch Yamasaki. Carlisle, MA: Discovery Enterprises, c1996. 64 p.
96-084744   1878668617
Vietnamese Conflict, 1961-1975 -- United States -- Sources. United States -- Foreign relations -- 20th century -- Sources.

DS557.7.A5 1998
An, Tai Sung, 1931-
The Vietnam war/ Tai Sung An. Madison: Fairleigh Dickinson University Press; c1998. 471 p.
97-045141   959.704/3   0838637655
Vietnamese Conflict, 1961-1975.

DS557.7.B76 1991
Brown, T. Louise, 1963-
War and aftermath in Vietnam/ T. Louise Brown. London; Routledge, 1991. vii, 295 p.
90-047899   959.704/3   0415014034
Vietnamese Conflict, 1961-1975.

DS557.7.E53 2000 *have 1998 in Ref*
Encyclopedia of the Vietnam War: a political, social, and military history/ Spencer C. Tucker, editor, David Coffey ... [et al.], associate editors. New York, NY: Oxford University Press, 2000. xix, 578 p.
99-036873   959.7/003   0195135245
Vietnamese Conflict, 1961-1975 -- Encyclopedias.

DS557.7.I82 1983
Isaacs, Arnold R.
Without honor: defeat in Vietnam and Cambodia/ Arnold R. Isaacs. Baltimore: Johns Hopkins University Press, c1983. xv, 559 p.
83-048054   959.704/3   0801830605
Vietnamese Conflict, 1961-1975. Indochina -- History -- 1945-

DS557.73.D48 1995
Devine, Jeremy M., 1958-
Vietnam at 24 frames a second: a critical and thematic analysis of over 400 films about the Vietnam war/ by Jeremy M. Devine. Jefferson, NC: McFarland, c1995. xiii, 401 p.
92-056639   959.704/3   0899508480
Vietnamese Conflict, 1961-1975 -- Motion pictures and the conflict. Indochinese War, 1946-1954 -- Motion pictures and the war. War films -- United States -- History and criticism.

DS557.73.H55 1998
Hillstrom, Kevin, 1963- *Ref*
The Vietnam experience: a concise encyclopedia of American literature, songs, and films/ Kevin Hillstrom and Laurie Collier Hillstrom. Westport, Conn.: Greenwood Press, 1998. xiii, 322 p.
97-021965   959.704/3   0313301832
Vietnamese Conflict, 1961-1975 -- Motion pictures and the conflict -- Encyclopedias. Vietnamese Conflict, 1961-1975 -- Literature and the conflict -- Encyclopedias. Vietnamese Conflict, 1961-1975 -- Music and the conflict -- Encyclopedias.

DS557.8.C3.S5 *have 2002 rev'd ed*
Shawcross, William.
Sideshow: Kissinger, Nixon, and the destruction of Cambodia/ William Shawcross. New York: Simon and Schuster, c1979. 467 p.
78-031826   959.704/342/09596   0671230700
Kissinger, Henry, -- 1923- Nixon, Richard M. -- (Richard Milhous), -- 1913- Vietnamese Conflict, 1961-1975 -- Campaigns -- Cambodia. Cabinet officers -- United States -- Biography. Cambodia -- History -- Civil War, 1970-1975. United States -- Politics and government -- 1969-1974.

DS557.8.T6.M65 1996
Moise, Edwin E., 1946-
Tonkin Gulf and the escalation of the Vietnam War/ Edwin E. Moise. Chapel Hill: University of North Carolina Press, c1996. xviii, 304 p.
96-012159   959.704/3   0807823007
Tonkin Gulf Incidents, 1964. Vietnamese Conflict, 1961-1975.

DS557.8.T6.S54 1999
Siff, Ezra Y., 1942-
Why the senate slept?: the Gulf of Tonkin resolution and the beginning of America's Vietnam war/ Ezra Y. Siff; foreword by Lt. Col. Anthony B. Herbert. Westport, Conn.: Praeger, 1999. xix, 172 p.
98-025612   959.704/3   0275963896
Tonkin Gulf Incidents, 1964. Vietnamese Conflict, 1961-1975 -- United States.

DS558.A67 1993
Appy, Christian G.
Working-class war: American combat soldiers and Vietnam/ Christian G. Appy. Chapel Hill: University of North Carolina Press, c1993. x, 365 p.
92-018318   959.704/3373   0807820571
Vietnamese Conflict, 1961-1975 -- United States. Soldiers -- United States.

DS558.B4 1998
Beattie, Keith, 1954-
The scar that binds: American culture and the Vietnam War/ Keith Beattie. New York: New York University Press, c1998. ix, 230 p.
97-045456   959.704/3373   0814713262
Vietnamese Conflict, 1961-1975 -- United States. Vietnamese Conflict, 1961-1975 -- Influence. United States -- Civilization -- 1945-

DS558.B92 1999
Buzzanco, Robert.
Vietnam and the transformation of American life/ Robert Buzzanco. Malden, MA: Blackwell Publishers, 1999. p. cm.
98-045677   959.704/3373   1577180933
Vietnamese Conflict, 1961-1975 -- United States. Vietnamese Conflict, 1961-1975 -- Influence. United States -- Civilization -- 1970-

DS558.C5 1993
Chomsky, Noam.
Rethinking Camelot: JFK, the Vietnam War, and U.S. political culture/ Noam Chomsky. Boston, MA: South End Press, c1993. 172 p.
93-000297 959.704/3373 0896084590
Kennedy, John F. -- (John Fitzgerald), -- 1917-1963. Vietnamese Conflict, 1961-1975 -- United States. United States -- Politics and government -- 1961-1963.

DS558.C58 1988
Clarke, Jeffrey J.
Advice and support: the final years, 1965-1973/ by Jeffrey J. Clarke. Washington, D.C.: Center of Military History, U. S. Army: 1988. xxi, 561 p.
87-600379 959.704/33/73
Vietnamese Conflict, 1961-1975 -- United States. Vietnam -- Politics and government -- 1945-1975.

DS558.E29 1998
Edmonds, Anthony O.
The war in Vietnam/ Anthony O. Edmonds. Westport, Conn.: Greenwood Press, 1998. xxiii, 192 p.
98-015591 959.704/3373 0313298475
Vietnamese Conflict, 1961-1975 -- United States.

DS558.G6 2000
Glenn, Russell W.
Reading Athena's dance card: men against fire in Vietnam/ Russell W. Glenn. Annapolis, MD: Naval Institute Press, 2000. xii, 214 p.
00-024977 959.704/3373 1557503168
Vietnamese Conflict, 1961-1975 -- United States. Vietnamese Conflict, 1961-1975 -- Campaigns.

DS558.H443 2000
Helsing, Jeffrey W.
Johnson's war/Johnson's great society: the guns and butter trap/ Jeffrey W. Helsing. Westport, Conn.: Praeger, 2000. xii, 279 p.
99-055224 959.704/3373 0275964493
Johnson, Lyndon B. -- (Lyndon Baines), -- 1908-1973. Vietnamese Conflict, 1961-1975 -- United States. United States -- Politics and government -- 1963-1969.

DS558.H448 1997
Hennessy, Michael A.
Strategy in Vietnam: the Marines and revolutionary warfare in I Corps, 1965-1972/ Michael A. Hennessy. Westport, Conn.: Praeger, 1997. xiv, 210 p.
96-033989 959.704/3373 0275956679
Vietnamese Conflict, 1961-1975 -- United States.

DS558.H454 1994
Herring, George C., 1936-
LBJ and Vietnam: a different kind of war/ by George C. Herring. Austin: University of Texas Press, 1994. xiv, 228 p.
93-036793 959.704/3373 0292730853
Johnson, Lyndon B. -- (Lyndon Baines), -- 1908-1973. Vietnamese Conflict, 1961-1975 -- United States. United States -- Politics and government -- 1963-1969.

DS558.I84 1997
Isaacs, Arnold R.
Vietnam shadows: the war, its ghosts, and its legacy/ Arnold R. Isaacs. Baltimore: Johns Hopkins University Press, 1997. xii, 236 p.
97-010823 959.7/3373 0801856051
Vietnamese Conflict, 1961-1975 -- United States. Vietnamese Conflict, 1961-1975 -- Influence. United States -- History -- 1969-

DS558.J44 1999
Jeffreys-Jones, Rhodri.
Peace now!: American society and the ending of the Vietnam War/ Rhodri Jeffreys-Jones. New Haven: Yale University Press, c1999. ix, 308 p.
99-019725 959.704/3373 0300078110
Vietnamese Conflict, 1961-1975 -- United States. Vietnamese Conflict, 1961-1975 -- Protest movements -- United States. United States -- Politics and government -- 1963-1969. United States -- Politics and government -- 1969-1974. United States -- Social conditions -- 1960-1980.

DS558.L36 2000
Langguth, A. J., 1933-
Our Vietnam: the war, 1954-1975/ A.J. Langguth. New York: Simon & Schuster, c2000. 766 p.
00-057384 959.704/3373 0684812029
Vietnamese Conflict, 1961-1975 -- United States. Vietnam -- Politics and government -- 1945-1975. United States -- History -- 1945-

DS558.L64 1996
Lomperis, Timothy J., 1947-
From people's war to people's rule: insurgency, intervention, and the lessons of Vietnam/ Timothy J. Lomperis. Chapel Hill: University of North Carolina Press, 1996. xvi, 440 p.
95-036667 959.704/3373 0807822736
Vietnamese Conflict, 1961-1975 -- United States Insurgency -- Asia, Southeastern. Asia, Southeastern -- Politics and government -- 1945- Vietnam -- History -- 1945-1975. United States -- Foreign relations -- 1963-1969.

DS558.M34 2001
Mann, Robert, 1958-
A grand delusion: America's descent into Vietnam/ Robert Mann. New York: Basic Books, 2000. p. cm.
00-049824 959.704/3 0465043690
Vietnamese Conflict, 1961-1975 -- United States. Asia -- Politics and government -- 1945- Vietnam -- Politics and government -- 1945-1975. United States -- Politics and government -- 20th century.

DS558.M439 1999
McNamara, Robert S., 1916-
Argument without end: in search of answers to the Vietnam tragedy/ Robert S. McNamara, James G. Blight, and Robert K. Brigham. New York: Public Affairs, c1999. xxiii, 479 p.
99-011830 959.704/3373 1891620223
Vietnamese Conflict, 1961-1975 -- United States. Vietnam -- History -- 1945-1975. United States -- History -- 1945- United States -- Foreign relations -- Vietnam.

DS558.S39 1998
Schwab, Orrin, 1956-
Defending the free world: John F. Kennedy, Lyndon Johnson, and the Vietnam War, 1961-1965/ Orrin Schwab. Westport, Conn.: Praeger, 1998. x, 243 p.
98-017639 959.704/3 0275962792
Kennedy, John F. -- (John Fitzgerald), -- 1917-1963. Johnson, Lyndon B. -- (Lyndon Baines), -- 1908-1973. Vietnamese Conflict, 1961-1975 -- United States. United States -- Foreign relations -- 1961-1963. United States -- Foreign relations -- 1963-1969.

DS558.S737 1996
Steinberg, Blema S.
Shame and humiliation: presidential decision making on Vietnam/ Blema S. Steinberg. Pittsburgh, Pa.: University of Pittsburgh Press, c1996. ix, 397 p.
95-052140 959.704/3 082293941X
Vietnamese Conflict, 1961-1975 -- United States. Vietnamese Conflict, 1961-1975 -- Psychological aspects.

DS558.T66 1998
Tomes, Robert R.
Apocalypse then: American intellectuals and the Vietnam War, 1954-1975/ Robert R. Tomes. New York: New York University Press, c1998. xi, 293 p.
98-019769 959.704/3373 0814782345
Vietnamese Conflict, 1961-1975 -- United States. Vietnamese Conflict, 1961-1975 -- Influence. Intellectuals -- United States -- Political activity -- History -- 20th century.

DS558.V38 1997
Vandiver, Frank Everson, 1925-
Shadows of Vietnam: Lyndon Johnson's wars/ Frank E. Vandiver. College Station: Texas A&M University Press, c1997. xv, 396 p.
96-050121 959.704/3373 0890967474
Johnson, Lyndon B. -- (Lyndon Baines), -- 1908-1973. Vietnamese Conflict, 1961-1975 -- United States. United States -- Politics and government -- 1963-1969.

DS558.7.L37 1997
Larzelere, Alex, 1936-
The Coast Guard at war: Vietnam, 1965-1975/ Alex Larzelere. Annapolis, Md.: Naval Institute Press, c1997. xxv, 345 p.
96-032130 959.704/345 1557505292
Vietnamese Conflict, 1961-1975 -- Naval operations, American.

DS559.4.R63 1999
Rochester, Stuart I., 1945-
Honor bound: American prisoners of war in Southeast Asia, 1961-1973/ Stuart I. Rochester and Frederick Kiley. Annapolis, MD: Naval Institute Press, 1999. xvii, 706 p.
98-039818 959.704/37 1557506949
Vietnamese Conflict, 1961-1975 -- Prisoners and prisons, North Vietnamese. Prisoners of war -- United States. Prisoners of war -- Indochina.

DS559.46.H37 1996
Hammond, William M.
Public affairs: the military and the media, 1968-1973/ by William M. Hammond. Washington, D.C.: Center of Military History, United States Army,s 1996. xix, 659 p.
94-035531 070.4/4995970434 0160485428
Vietnamese Conflict, 1961-1975 -- Press coverage. Armed Forces and mass media -- United States -- History.

DS559.46.H38 1998
Hammond, William M.
Reporting Vietnam: media and military at war/ William H. Hammond. Lawrence, Kan.: University Press of Kansas, c1998. xi, 362 p.
98-023810 959.704/38 0700609113
Vietnamese Conflict, 1961-1975 -- Press coverage -- United States. Armed Forces and mass media -- United States -- History.

DS559.5.E28 2000
Edwards, Fred L., 1932-
The bridges of Vietnam: from the journals of U.S. Marine intelligence officer/ by Fred L. Edwards, Jr. Denton, Tex.: University of North Texas Press, c2000. xv, 273 p.
00-028678   959.704/38   1574411233
Edwards, Fred L., -- 1932- -- Diaries. Vietnamese Conflict, 1961-1975 -- Personal narratives, American.

DS559.5.S29 1999
Savage, David, 1939-
Through the wire: action with the SAS in Borneo and the Special Forces in Vietnam/ David Savage. St. Leonards NSW, Australia: Allen & Unwin, 1999. xiv, 239 p.
99-458581   1864488689
Savage, David, -- 1939- Vietnamese Conflict, 1961-1975 -- Regimental histories. Vietnamese Conflict, 1961-1975 -- Participation, Australian. Vietnamese Conflict, 1961-1975 -- Personal narratives, Australian.

DS559.5.S72 1997
Stacewicz, Richard.
Winter soldiers: an oral history of the Vietnam Veterans Against the War/ Richard Stacewicz. New York: Twayne Publishers, 1997. p. cm.
97-035825   959.704/3/0922   0805745793
Vietnamese Conflict, 1961-1975 -- Personal narratives, American. Vietnamese Conflict, 1961-1975 -- Protest movements -- United States. Vietnamese Conflict, 1961-1975 -- Veterans -- United States. United States -- Armed Forces -- Political activity.

DS559.62.A8.E38 1997
Edwards, P. G.
A nation at war: Australian politics, society and diplomacy during the Vietnam War 1965-1975/ Peter Edwards. St. Leonards, NSW: Allen & Unwin in association with the Australian 1997. xx, 460 p.
97-179298   959.704/3394   1864482826
Vietnamese Conflict, 1961-1975 -- Protest movements -- Australia. Australia -- Politics and government -- 1945- Australia -- Foreign relations -- 1945-

DS559.62.U6.B89 1996
Buzzanco, Robert.
Masters of war: military dissent and politics in the Vietnam era/ Robert Buzzanco. New York: Cambridge University Press, 1996. xiv, 386 p.
95-016226   959.704/3373   0521480469
Vietnamese Conflict, 1961-1975 -- Protest movements -- United States. United States -- Armed Forces -- Political activity. United States -- Politics and government -- 1963-1969.

DS559.62.U6.D38 1997
Davis, James Kirkpatrick.
Assault on the Left: the FBI and the sixties antiwar movement/ James Kirkpatrick Davis. Westport, Conn.: Praeger, 1997. x, 226 p.
96-044675   959.704/3373   0275954552
Vietnamese Conflict, 1961-1975 -- Protest movements -- United States.   United States -- Politics and government, -- 1963-1969.

DS559.62.U6.D53 1999
Dickerson, James.
North to Canada: men and women against the Vietnam War/ James Dickerson. Westport, Conn.: Praeger, 1999. xviii, 199 p.
98-023568   959.704/31   0275962113
Vietnamese Conflict, 1961-1975 -- Protest movements -- United States. Americans -- Canada. Vietnamese Conflict, 1961-1975 -- Conscientious objectors. Canada -- Emigration and immigration. United States -- Emigration and immigration.

DS559.62.U6.F73 2000
Franklin, H. Bruce 1934-
Vietnam and other American fantasies/ H. Bruce Franklin. Amherst, Mass.: University of Massachusetts Press, c2000. xii, 256 p.
00-030275   959.704/31   1558492798
Vietnamese Conflict, 1961-1975 -- Public opinion -- United States. Vietnamese Conflict, 1961-1975 -- Influence.   United States -- Civilization -- 1970-

DS559.62.U6.H86 1999
Hunt, Andrew E., 1968-
The turning: a history of Vietnam Veterans Against the War/ Andrew Hunt. New York: New York University Press, 1999. xi, 259 p.
99-006137   959.704/31   0814735819
Vietnamese Conflict, 1961-1975 -- Protest movements -- United States. Veterans -- United States -- Political activity -- History -- 20th century.

DS559.62.U6.M67 1996
Moser, Richard R., 1952-
The new winter soldiers: GI and veteran dissent during the Vietnam era/ Richard R. Moser. New Brunswick, NJ: Rutgers University Press, 1996. xi, 219 p.
95-004631   959.704/373   0813522412
Vietnamese Conflict, 1961-1975 -- Protest movements -- United States. Soldiers -- United States. Vietnamese Conflict, 1961-1975 -- Veterans -- United States. United States -- Armed Forces -- Political activity.

DS559.62.U6.R47 2001
Rhodes, Joel P., 1967-
The voice of violence: performative violence as protest in the Vietnam era/ Joel P. Rhodes. Westport, Conn.: Praeger, 2001. 224 p.
00-064959   959.704/3   0275970558
Vietnamese Conflict, 1961-1975 -- Protest movements -- United States. United States -- Politics and government -- 1963-1969. United States -- Politics and government -- 1969-1974.

DS559.73.L28.C37 1999
Castle, Timothy N.
One day too long: top secret site 85 and the bombing of North Vietnam/ Timothy N. Castle. New York: Columbia University Press, 1999. xiv, 371 p.
98-043117   959.704/348   0231103166
Vietnamese Conflict, 1961-1975 -- Secret service -- United States. Vietnamese Conflict, 1961-1975 -- Aerial operations, American. Vietnamese Conflict, 1961-1975 -- Laos.

DS559.73.U6.L46 1998
Lembcke, Jerry, 1943-
The spitting image: myth, memory, and the legacy of Vietnam/ Jerry Lembcke; consulting editor: Harvey J. Kaye. New York: New York University Press, c1998. xi, 217 p.
98-009048   959.704/3373   0814751466
Vietnamese Conflict, 1961-1975 -- Veterans -- United States. Vietnamese Conflict, 1961-1975 -- Public opinion. Public opinion -- United States.

DS559.8.B55.W47 1997
Westheider, James E., 1956-
Fighting on two fronts: African Americans and the Vietnam War/ James E. Westheider. New York: New York University Press, c1997. x, 238 p.
96-045832   959.704/3/08996073   0814793010
Vietnamese Conflict, 1961-1975 -- Afro-Americans.   United States -- Armed Forces -- Afro-Americans. United States -- Race relations.

DS559.8.D7.H33 2001
Hagan, John, 1946-
Northern passage: American Vietnam War resisters in Canada/ John Hagan. Cambridge, MA: Harvard University Press, 2001. xiii, 269 p.
00-054012   959.707/704/38   067400471X
Vietnamese Conflict, 1961-1975 -- Draft resisters -- United States. Vietnamese Conflict, 1961-1975 -- Desertions -- United States. Vietnamese Conflict, 1961-1975 -- Protest movements -- United States. United States -- Emigration and immigration. Canada -- Emigration and immigration.

DS559.8.P65.P34 1996
Page, Caroline, 1953-
U.S. Official propaganda during the Vietnam War, 1965-1973: the limits of persuasion/ Caroline Page. London; New York: 1996. 325 p.
95-041263   959.704/38   071851999X
Vietnamese Conflict, 1961-1975 -- Propaganda. Propaganda, American. Public opinion -- Great Britain.

DS559.8.W6.T39 1999
Taylor, Sandra C.
Vietnamese women at war: fighting for Ho Chi Minh and the revolution/ Sandra C. Taylor. Lawrence: University Press of Kansas, c1999. x, 170 p.
98-035715   959.704/3/082   070060927X
Vietnamese Conflict, 1961-1975 -- Women -- Interviews. Vietnamese Conflict, 1961-1975 -- Personal narratives, Vietnamese. Women -- Vietnam -- Interviews.

DS559.93.H36
Logan, William Stewart, 1942-
Hanoi, biography of a city/ William S. Logan. Seattle, WA: University of Washington Press, 2000. xvi, 304 p.
00-060704   959.7   0295980141
Hanoi (Vietnam) -- History. Hanoi (Vietnam) -- Description and travel.

DS560.3 Southeastern Asia — French Indochina — Democratic Republic (North Vietnam)

DS560.3.N4513
Nguyen, Khac Vien.
Tradition and revolution in Vietnam/ Nguyen Khac Vien: foreword by George McT. Kahin; edited with a pref. by David Marr and Jayne Werner; translation by Linda Yarr, Jayne Werner, and Tran Tuong Nhu. Berkeley, Calif.: Indochina Resource Center, [1974] xx, 169 p.
74-194705   959.704
Vietnam (Democratic Republic)

DS578-586 Thailand (Siam) — History — By period

DS578.32.K84.V36 1996
Van Praagh, David.
Thailand's struggle for democracy: the life and times of M.R. Seni Pramoj/ David van Praagh; foreword by Stephen J. Solarz. New York: Holmes & Meier, 1996. xviii, 358 p.
96-004393   959.304   0841913218
Seni Pramoj, -- M.R., -- 1905-   Democracy -- Thailand -- History. Prime ministers -- Thailand. Thailand -- Politics and government.

DS578.32.P55.K63 1995
Kobkua Suwannathat-Pian, 1944-
Thailand's durable Premier: Phibun through three decades, 1932-1957/ Kobkua Suwannathat-Pian. Kuala Lumpur; Oxford University Press, 1995. xii, 332 p.
94-034395   959.304/092   9676530530
Plaek Phibunsongkhram, -- 1897-1964.   Prime ministers -- Thailand -- Biography.

DS586.F56 1997
Fineman, Daniel, 1962-
A special relationship: the United States and military government in Thailand, 1947-1958/ Daniel Fineman. Honolulu: University of Hawaii Press, c1997. viii, 357 p.
96-025657   327.593073/09/045   0824818180
Thailand -- Politics and government. Thailand -- Armed Forces -- Political activity. United States -- Foreign relations -- Thailand.

DS586.M37 1995
Marks, Thomas A.
Maoist insurgency since Vietnam/ Thomas A. Marks. London; Frank Cass, 1996. 303 p.
95-005364   959.05   0714646067
Insurgency -- Thailand. Insurgency -- Philippines. Insurgency -- Sri Lanka. Thailand -- Politics and government. Sri Lanka -- Politics and government -- 1978- Philippines -- Politics and government -- 1946-

DS595.2 Malaysia. Malay Peninsula. Straits Settlements — Ethnography — Individual elements in the population

DS595.2.S3.L43 1995
Leary, John.
Violence and the dream people: the Orang Asli in the Malayan emergency, 1948-1960/ John D. Leary. Athens, OH: Ohio University Center for International Studies c1995. xiii, 238 p.
95-010758   959.5/104   0896801861
Senoi (Malaysian people) -- History. Indigenous peoples -- Malaysia -- History. Jakun (Malaysian people) -- History. Malaya -- History -- Malayan Emergency, 1948-1960.

DS595.2.S3.R67 1991
Roseman, Marina, 1952-
Healing sounds from the Malaysian rainforest: Temiar music and medicine/ Marina Roseman. Berkeley: University of California Press, c1991. xvii, 233 p.
90-011253   615.8/82/09595   0520066820
Senoi (Malaysian people) -- Rites and ceremonies. Senoi (Malaysian people) -- Medicine. Senoi (Malaysian people) -- Music.

DS596.6-597 Malaysia. Malay Peninsula. Straits Settlements — History — By period

DS596.6.K73 1997
Kratoska, Paul H.
The Japanese occupation of Malaya: a social and economic history/ Paul H. Kratoska. Honolulu: University of Hawaii Press, c1997. xxi, 404 p.
96-034310   959.5/103   082481889X
Malaya -- History -- Japanese occupation, 1942-1945. Malaya -- Economic conditions. Malaya -- Social conditions.

DS596.6.M55 1995
Milner, Anthony Crothers, 1945-
The invention of politics in colonial Malaya: contesting nationalism and the expansion of the public sphere/ Anthony Milner. Cambridge; Cambridge University Press, 1995. vi, 328 p.
94-015759   959.5/103   0521465656
Nationalism -- Malaysia -- Malaya. Political culture -- Malaysia -- Malaya. Public opinion -- Malaysia -- Malaya.

DS596.6.S65 1995
Smith, Simon C., 1967-
British relations with the Malay rulers from decentralization to Malayan independence, 1930-1957/ Simon C. Smith. Kuala Lumpur; Oxford University Press, 1995. viii, 234 p.
95-001993   959.5/105   9676530891
Malaya -- Politics and government. Malaya -- Kings and rulers.

DS596.6.W47 1996
White, Nicholas J., 1967-
Business, government, and the end of empire: Malaya, 1942-1957/ Nicholas J. White. Kuala Lumpur; Oxford University Press, 1996. xxii, 331 p.
96-008155   959.5/104   9835600082
Malaya -- Politics and government. Malaya -- Economic policy. Malaya -- Economic conditions.

DS597.D46 1996
Dennis, Peter, 1945-
Emergency and confrontation: Australian military operations in Malaya & Borneo 1950-1966/ Peter Dennis and Jeffrey Grey. St. Leonards, NSW, Australia: Allen & Unwin in association with the Australian 1996. xvi, 381 p.
96-151190   959.5/04   1863733027
Malaya -- History -- Malayan Emergency, 1948-1960 -- Participation, Australian. Borneo -- History, Military. Australia -- Armed Forces -- Foreign service -- Malaysia -- Malaya.

DS597.37 Malaysia. Malay Peninsula. Straits Settlements — Local history and description — East Malaysia (General)

DS597.37.O65 1999
Ooi, Keat Gin, 1959-
Rising sun over Borneo: the Japanese occupation of Sarawak, 1941-1945/ Ooi Keat Gin. New York, N.Y.: St. Martin's Press, 1999. xix, 158 p.
98-038442   940.53/5954   0312217145
Sarawak -- History -- Japanese occupation, 1941-1945.

DS597.37.P67 1997
Porritt, Vernon L., 1926-
British colonial rule in Sarawak, 1946-1963/ Vernon L. Porritt. Kuala Lumpur; Oxford University Press, 1997. xxv, 424 p.
96-032333   959.5/404   9835600090
Sarawak -- History.

DS601 Malay Archipelago — General works. Description and travel

DS601.S4 1997
Severin, Timothy.
The Spice Islands voyage: the quest for Alfred Wallace, the man who shared Darwin's discovery of evolution/ Tim Severin; photographs by Joe Beynon and Paul Harris; illustrationsby Leonard Sheil. New York: Carroll & Graf Publishers, c1997. 267 p.
98-006819   959.8   0786705183
Wallace, Alfred Russel, -- 1823-1913. Severin, Timothy -- Journeys -- Malay Archipelago. Natural history -- Malay Archipelago. Malay Archipelago -- Environmental conditions. Malay Archipelago -- Description and travel.

DS632 Indonesia (Dutch East Indies) — Ethnography — Individual elements in the population, A-Z

DS632.A52.K43 1997
Keane, Webb, 1955-
Signs of recognition: powers and hazards of representation in an Indonesian society/ Webb Keane. Berkeley: University of California Press, c1997. xxix, 297 p.
96-018064   306/.09598/6   0520204743
Anakalang (Indonesian people) -- Rites and ceremonies. Anakalang (Indonesian people) -- Social conditions. Anakalang (Indonesian people) -- Psychology. Sumba Island (Indonesia) -- Social life and customs.

DS632.D68
Just, Peter.
Dou Donggo justice: conflict and morality in an Indonesian society/ Peter Just. Lanham, MD: Rowman & Littlefield Publishers, 2001. xi, 263 p.
00-045827   306/.09598/6   0847683273
Dou Donggo (Indonesian people) -- Social conditions. Dou Donggo (Indonesian people) -- Legal status, laws, etc. Philosophy, Indonesian -- Indonesia -- Sumbawa. Sumbawa (Indonesia) -- Moral conditions. Sumbawa (Indonesia) -- Social life and customs.

DS632.L33.B37 1996
Barnes, R. H. 1944-
Sea hunters of Indonesia: fishers and weavers of Lamalera/ R.H. Barnes. Oxford: Clarendon Press; 1996. xvi, 467 p.
96-022391   959.8/6   019828070X
Lamaholot (Indonesian people) -- Fishing. Lamaholot (Indonesian people) -- Economic conditions. Lamaholot (Indonesian people) -- Social life and customs. Lamalerap (Indonesia) -- Economic conditions. Lamalerap (Indonesia) -- Social life and customs.

DS632.M4.B53 2000
Blackwood, Evelyn.
Webs of power: women, kin, and community in a Sumatran village/ Evelyn Blackwood. Lanham: Rowman & Littlefield, c2000. xv, 219 p.
99-045666   305.3/09598/1   0847699102
Women, Minangkabau -- Social conditions. Minangkabau (Indonesian people) -- Social conditions. Sex role -- Indonesia -- Sumatera Barat.

DS632.S89
Forshee, Jill.
Between the folds: stories of cloth, lives, and travels from Sumba/ Jill Forshee. [Honolulu]: University of Hawai'i Press, c2000. xiv, 265 p.
00-033781   305.89/922   0824822889
Sumbanese (Indonesian people) -- Costume. Sumbanese (Indonesian people) -- Industries. Sumbanese (Indonesian people) -- Commerce. Sumba Island (Indonesia) -- Social life and customs.

DS632.T62.R63 1997
Rodenburg, Janet, 1960-
In the shadow of migration: rural women and their households in North Tapanuli, Indonesia/ Janet Rodenburg. Leiden: KITLV Press, 1997. viii, 241 p.
97-223724   9067181080
Toba-Batak (Indonesian people) -- Migrations. Women, Toba-Batak -- Social conditions. Women, Toba-Batak -- Economic conditions. Tapanuli Utara (Indonesia) -- Emigration and immigration. Tapanuli Utara (Indonesia) -- Social conditions.

DS632.T7.H65 1994
Hollan, Douglas Wood.
Contentment and suffering: culture and experience in Toraja/ Douglas W. Hollan, Jane C. Wellenkamp. New York: Columbia University Press, c1994. xiii, 276 p.
93-004619   155.8/49922   0231084226
Toraja (Indonesian people) -- Psychology. Ethnopsychology.

DS632.W48.K84 1998
Kuipers, Joel Corneal.
Language, identity, and marginality in Indonesia: the changing nature of ritual speech on the Island of Sumba/ Joel C. Kuipers. Cambridge; Cambridge University Press, 1998. xvii, 183 p.
97-038770   306.44/089/992205986   0521624088
Wewewa (Indonesian people) -- Rites and ceremonies. Language and culture -- Indonesia -- Sumba Island. Ethnology -- Indonesia -- Sumba Island

DS641-644.5 Indonesia (Dutch East Indies) — History — By period

DS641.S54 1995
Slamet-Velsink, Ina E.
Emerging hierarchies: processes of stratification and early state formation in the Indonesian archipelago: prehistory and the ethnographic present/ Ina E. Slamet-Velsink. Leiden: KITLV Press, 1995. vi, 279 p.
95-233638   959.8/01   9067180866
Anthropology -- Indonesia. Ethnology -- Indonesia. Indonesia -- History -- To 1478. Indonesia -- Politics and government.

DS642.N3413 1996
Nagtegaal, Lucas Wilhelmus, 1955-
Riding the Dutch tiger: the Dutch East Indies Company and the northeast coast of Java, 1680-1743/ Luc Nagtegaal; translated by Beverley Jackson. Leiden: KITLV Press, 1996. 250 p.
96-231818   906718103X
Java (Indonesia) -- Commerce. Java (Indonesia) -- Economic conditions. Java (Indonesia) -- Social conditions.

DS643.I53
Indonesia: selected documents on colonialism and nationalism, 1830-1942/ edited and translated by Chr. L. M. Penders. St. Lucia: University of Queensland Press, 1977. xi, 367 p.
77-371030   325/.3492/09598   0702213241.
Nationalism -- Indonesia -- History -- Sources. Indonesia -- History -- 1798-1942 -- Sources.

DS643.S54 1997
Siegel, James T., 1937-
Fetish, recognition, revolution/ James T. Siegel. Princeton, N.J.: Princeton University Press, c1997. x, 275 p.
96-032041   959.8/022   069102653X
Nationalism -- Indonesia -- History. Indonesian language -- History. Language and culture -- Indonesia. Indonesia -- Social conditions. Indonesia -- Politics and government -- 1942-1949. Indonesia -- Literatures -- History and criticism.

DS644.4.D45 2001
Dijk, Kees van, 1946-
A country in despair: Indonesia between 1997 and 2000/ Kees van Dijk. Leiden: KITLV Press, 2001. viii, 620 p.
    9067181609
Soeharto, -- 1921- -- Resignation from office. Indonesia -- Politics and government -- 1966-1998. Indonesia -- Politics and government -- 1998-

DS644.4.R347 1995
Ramage, Douglas E., 1963-
Politics in Indonesia: democracy, Islam, and the ideology of tolerance/ Douglas E. Ramage. New York: Routledge, 1995. xvii, 272 p.
95-022104   320.9598/09/049   0415125480
Islam and politics -- Indonesia. Democracy -- Indonesia. Indonesia -- Politics and government -- 1966-1998.

DS644.5.V74 1999
Vredenbregt, Jacob, 1926-
Reformasi/ Jacob Vredenbregt. Baarn: De Prom, c1999. 187 p.
99-496083   9068016334
Indonesia -- Politics and government -- 1998- Indonesia -- Economic conditions -- 1945- Indonesia -- Social conditions.

DS646.15 Indonesia (Dutch East Indies) — Islands — Sumatra

DS646.15.S77.A53 1993
Andaya, Barbara Watson.
To live as brothers: southeast Sumatra in the seventeenth and eighteenth centuries/ Barbara Watson Andaya. Honolulu, Hawaii: University of Hawaii Press, c1993. xvii, 324 p.
93-001347   959.8/1   0824814894
Sumatera Selatan (Indonesia) -- History. Jambi (Indonesia: Province) -- History.

DS646.27 Indonesia (Dutch East Indies) — Islands — Java

DS646.27.R536 1998
Ricklefs, M. C.
The seen and unseen worlds in Java, 1726-1749: history, literature, and Islam in the court of Pakubuwana II/ M.C. Ricklefs. St. Leonards, NSW: Asian Studies Association of Australia in associ c1998. xxiv, 391 p.
97-042719   959.8/2021   0824820525
Paku Buwana -- II, -- Sunan of Surakarta, -- 1710?-1749. Javanese literature -- History and criticism. Islam -- Indonesia -- Java -- History. Java (Indonesia) -- History.

DS646.32 Indonesia (Dutch East Indies) — Islands — Borneo. Kalimantan, Indonesia

DS646.32.D9.T75 1993
Tsing, Anna Lowenhaupt.
In the realm of the diamond queen: marginality in an out-of-the-way place/ Anna Lowenhaupt Tsing. Princeton, N.J.: Princeton University Press, c1993. xvi, 350 p.
93-010521   323.1/19922   0691033358
Dayaks (Indonesian people) -- Government relations. Dayaks (Indonesian people) -- Social conditions. Sex role -- Indonesia -- Meratus Mountains Region.

DS646.32.P85.S4513 1994
Sellato, Bernard.
Nomads of the Borneo rainforest: the economics, politics,and ideology of settling down/ Bernard Sellato; translated by Stephanie Morgan. Honolulu: University of Hawaii Press, c1994. xxiii, 280 p.
94-004291   306.3/09598/3   0824815661
Punan (Bornean people) -- Social conditions. Punan (Bornean people) -- Economic conditions. Punan (Bornean people) -- Agriculture.

DS646.57 Indonesia (Dutch East Indies) — Islands — Timor

DS646.57.G87 2000
Guns and ballot boxes: East Timor's vote for independence/ edited by Daniel Kingsbury. Clayton: Monash Asia Institute, c2000. xii, 201 p.
00-340467   959.8/6   0732611881
Referendum -- Indonesia -- Timor Timur. Self-determination, National -- Indonesia -- Timor Timur. Atrocities -- Indonesia -- Timor Timur. Timor Timur (Indonesia) -- Politics and government. Indonesia -- Politics and government -- 1998-

DS647 Indonesia (Dutch East Indies) — Islands — Other islands, regions, and political jurisdictions larger than islands, A-Z

DS647.A78.S69 2000
Spyer, Patricia, 1957-
The memory of trade/ Patricia Spyer. Durham, NC: Duke University Press, 2000. p. cm.
99-037251   959.8/5   0822324059
Economic anthropology -- Indonesia -- Aru Islands. Aru Islands (Indonesia) -- Social life and customs. Aru Islands (Indonesia) -- Commerce -- History.

DS647.B2.B67 1990
Boon, James A.
Affinities and extremes: crisscrossing the bittersweet ethnology of East Indies history, Hindu-Balinese culture, and Indo-European allure/ James A. Boon. Chicago: University of Chicago Press, c1990. xviii, 246 p.
89-020326   959.8/6   0226064611
Ethnology -- Indonesia -- Bali Island.   Bali Island (Indonesia) -- Civilization.

DS647.B2.H58 1996
Hobart, Angela.
The peoples of Bali/ Angela Hobart, Urs Ramseyer, and Albert Leemann. Oxford; Blackwell, c1996. xiii, 274 p.
95-051998   959.8/6   063117687X
Bali Island (Indonesia)

DS647.B2.R63 1995
Robinson, Geoffrey, 1957-
The dark side of paradise: political violence in Bali/ Geoffrey Robinson. Ithaca: Cornell University Press, 1995. xxii, 341 p.
95-009754   959.8/6   080142965X
Political violence -- Indonesia -- Bali Island. Bali Island (Indonesia) -- Politics and government.

DS647.S952.B554 1996
Hitchcock, Michael.
Islam and identity in Eastern Indonesia/ Michael Hitchcock. [Hull]: University of Hull Press, 1996. ix, 208 p.
96-207917   305.6/9710598   0859586464
Muslims -- Indonesia -- Bima -- Ethnic identity. Islam -- Indonesia -- Bima.

DS650.5 Brunei — History — General works

DS650.5.S56 1997
Singh, D. S. Ranjit, 1944-
Historical dictionary of Brunei Darussalam/ D.S. Ranjit Singh and Jatswan S. Sidhu. Lanham, Md.: Scarecrow Press, 1997. xxxiv, 178 p.
96-052065   959.55/003   0810832763
Brunei -- History -- Dictionaries.

DS650.6 Brunei — History — By period

DS650.6.H87 1995
Hussainmiya, B. A.
Sultan Omar Ali Saifuddin III and Britain: the making of Brunei Darussalam/ B.A. Hussainmiya. Oxford; Oxford University Press, 1995. xxx, 447 p.
95-031531   959.5505   9676531065
Omar Ali Saifuddin -- III, -- Haji, Sultan of Brunei, -- 1914-1986.   Brunei -- Politics and government. Brunei -- Foreign relations -- Great Britain. Great Britain -- Foreign relations -- Brunei.

DS663 Philippines — Social life and customs. Civilization. Intellectual life

DS663.C35 1999
Cannell, Fenella
Power and intimacy in the Christian Philippines/ Fenella Cannell. New York: Cambridge University Press, 1999. xxvi, 312 p.
98-024883   306/.09599   0521641470
Philippines -- Social life and customs. Philippines -- Religious life and customs.

DS666 Philippines — Ethnography — Individual elements in the population, A-Z

DS666.A3.B76 1990
Brosius, J. Peter.
After Duwagan: deforestation, succession, and adaptation in Upland Luzon, Philippines/ J. Peter Brosius. [Ann Arbor]: Center for South and Southeast Asian Studies, Un c1990. xxiv, 188 p.
89-081764   631.58180959   0891480617
Shifting cultivation -- Philippines -- Zambales. Aeta (Philippine people)

DS666.A3.E37 1998
Early, John D.
Population dynamics of a Philippine rain forest people: the San Ildefonso Agta/ John D. Early, Thomas N. Headland. Gainesville: University Press of Florida, c1998. xii, 208 p.
97-041150   304.6/2/089991105991   0813015553
Aeta (Philippine people) -- Population. Aeta (Philippine people) -- Social conditions. Aeta (Philippine people) -- Economic conditions. San Ildefonso (Philippines) -- Population. San Ildefonso (Philippines) -- Social conditions. San Ildefonso (Philippines) -- Economic conditions.

DS666.I15.K85 1998
Kwiatkowski, Lynn M.
Struggling with development: the politics of hunger and gender in the Philippines/ Lynn M. Kwiatkowski. Boulder, Colo.: Westview Press, c1998. p. cm.
98-018420   306.4/61/095991   081333408X
Women, Ifugao -- Nutrition. Women, Ifugao -- Health and hygiene. Women, Ifugao -- Economic conditions. Philippines -- Social policy. Philippines -- Economic policy.

DS666.K3.K35 1994
Kalinga ethnoarchaeology: expanding archaeological method and theory/ edited by William A. Longacre and James M. Skibo. Washington: Smithsonian Institution Press, c1994. xvi, 250 p.
93-046225   392/.3/09599   1560982721
Kalinga (Philippine people) -- Material culture. Pottery, Kalinga -- Philippines -- Dangtalan -- Classification. Ethnoarchaeology -- Philippines -- Dangtalan. Dangtalan (Philippines) -- Social life and customs.

DS666.T6.S36 1998
Schlegel, Stuart A.
Wisdom from a rainforest: the spiritual journey of an anthropologist/ Stuart A. Schlegel. Athens: University of Georgia Press, c1998. xiv, 269 p.
98-007608   959.9/7   0820320579
Tiruray (Philippine people) -- Social conditions. Tiruray (Philippine people) -- Psychology. Tiruray (Philippine people) -- Ethnic identity. Mindanao Island (Philippines) -- Politics and government.

DS667.28 Philippines — History — Dictionaries. Chronological tables, outlines, etc.

DS667.28.P485
Philippine studies: history, sociology, mass media, and bibliography/ Bruce Cruikshank ... [et al.]; Donn V. Hart, editor. [De Kalb]: Northern Illinois University, Center for Southea c1978. xi, 402 p.
79-123115   959.9
Philippines -- Study and teaching. Philippines -- Bibliography.

DS673 Philippines — History — Political and diplomatic history. Foreign and general relations

DS673.U6 S65 1994
Solarz, Stephen J.
Clinton's Asia policy/ Stephen J. Solarz. Singapore: Institute of Southeast Asian Studies, c1994. viii, 22 p.
94-945469   327.7305.221   9813016884
Asia -- Foreign relations -- United States. United States -- Foreign relations -- Asia.

DS676.8-686.614 Philippines — History — By period

DS676.8.B66.M39 1996
May, Glenn Anthony.
Inventing a hero: the posthumous re-creation of Andres Bonifacio/ Glenn Anthony May. Madison, Wisconsin, USA: University of Wisconsin, Center for Southeast As 1996. x, 200 p.
96-085119   959.9/02/092   1881261182
Bonifacio, Andres, -- 1863-1897.   Revolutionaries -- Philippines -- Biography.   Philippines -- Politics and government.

DS679.M59 1982
Miller, Stuart Creighton, 1927-
"Benevolent assimilation": the American conquest of the Philippines, 1899-1903/ Stuart Creighton Miller. New Haven: Yale University Press, c1982. xii, 340 p.
82-001957   959.9/03   0300026978
Philippines -- History -- Philippine American War, 1899-1902. Philippines -- History -- 1898-1946.

DS682.A2 1989
Linn, Brian McAllister.
The U.S. Army and counterinsurgency in the Philippine war, 1899-1902/ Brian McAllister Linn. Chapel Hill: University of North Carolina Press, c1989. xiii, 258 p.
88-020741 959.9/031 0807818348
Counterinsurgency -- Philippines. Philippines -- History -- Philippine American War, 1899-1902.

DS685.G75
Grunder, Garel A.
The Philippines and the United States/ by Garel A. Grunder and William E. Livezey. Norman: University of Oklahoma Press, c1951. xi, 315 p.
51-006997 991.4
Philippines -- Foreign relations -- United States. United States -- Foreign relations -- Philippines. Philippines -- History -- 1898-1946.

DS685.R24 2000
Rafael, Vicente L.
White love and other events in Filipino history/ by Vicente L. Rafael. Durham: Duke University Press, 2000. p. cm.
99-050790 959.904 0822325055
Philippines -- History -- 20th century.

DS686.5.M84 1988
Muego, Benjamin N.
Spectator society: the Philippines under martial rule/ by Benjamin N. Muego. Athens, Ohio: Ohio University Center for International Studies 1988. x, 222 p.
88-025304 959.9/046 0896801381
Martial law -- Philippines. Philippines -- Politics and government -- 1946-1986.

DS686.5.R43 1993
Rempel, William C.
Delusions of a dictator: the mind of Marcos as revealed in his secret diaries/ William R. Rempel. Boston: Little, Brown, c1993. xv, 245 p.
92-027531 320.9599 0316740152
Marcos, Ferdinand E. -- (Ferdinand Edralin), 1917- Philippines -- Politics and government -- 1973-1986.

DS686.614.K57 1998
Kirk, Donald, 1938-
Looted: the Philippines after the bases/ Donald Kirk. New York: St. Martin's Press, 1998. vii, 248 p.
97-021844 327.599073 0312174233
Philippines -- Politics and government -- 1986- Philippines -- Foreign relations -- United States. United States -- Foreign relations -- Philippines

DS686.614.R44 1995
Reid, Robert H., 1947-
Corazon Aquino and the brushfire revolution/ Robert H. Reid and Eileen Guerrero. Baton Rouge: Louisiana State University Press, c1995. xiii, 260 p.
95-030684 959.904/7 0807119806
Aquino, Corazon Cojuangco.   Philippines -- Politics and government -- 1986-

DS688 Philippines — Local history and description — Provinces, islands, etc., A-Z

DS688.B3.M39 1991
May, Glenn Anthony.
Battle for Batangas: a Philippine province at war/ Glenn Anthony May. New Haven: Yale University Press, c1991. xxiii, 382 p.
90-045074 959.9/1 0300048505
Batangas (Philippines: Province) -- History. Philippines -- History -- Philippine American War, 1899-1902.

DS688.N5.A34 1998
Aguilar, Filomeno V.
Clash of spirits: the history of power and sugar planter hegemony on a Visayan island/ Filomeno V. Aguilar. Honolulu: University of Hawai'i Press, c1998. xiii, 313 p.
98-016629 959.9/5 0824819926
Sugar trade -- Philippines -- Negros Island. Plantations -- Philippiness -- Negros Island. Negros Island (Philippines) -- Economic conditions. Negros Island (Philippines) -- Civilization. Negros Island (Philippines) -- Social conditions.

DS689 Philippines — Local history and description — Cities, towns, etc., A-Z

DS689.C67.M35 1998
McKenna, Thomas M., 1952-
Muslim rulers and rebels: everyday politics and armed separatism in the southern Philippines/ Thomas M. McKenna. Berkeley: University of California Press, 1998. xv, 364 p.
97-049422 959.9/7 0520210158
Muslims -- Philippines -- Mindanao Island -- Politics and government. Muslims -- Philippines -- Cotabato City Region. Cotabato City Region (Philippines) -- Politics and government. Mindanao Island (Philippines) -- History -- Autonomy and independence movements.

DS703.5 China — Collected works — Individual authors

DS703.5.Y3
Yang, Lien-sheng, 1914-
Studies in Chinese institutional history. Cambridge, Harvard University Press, 1961. 229 p.
61-008844 951.0081
China -- History.

DS705 China — Gazetteers. Dictionaries, etc. Guidebooks

DS705.C35
The Cambridge encyclopedia of China/ general editor, Brian Hook. Cambridge [Cambridgeshire]; Cambridge University Press, 1982. 492 p.
81-009927 951/.003/21 0521230993
China -- Encyclopedias.

DS705.O63 1987
O'Neill, Hugh B.
Companion to Chinese history/ Hugh B. O'Neill. New York, N.Y.: Facts on File, c1987. x, 397 p.
83-011685 951 087196841X
China -- Handbooks, manuals, etc.

DS705.P47 1999
Perkins, Dorothy.
Encyclopedia of China: the essential reference to China, its history and culture/ Dorothy Perkins. New York: Facts on File, c1999. ix, 662 p.
97-052622 951/.003 0816026939
China -- Encyclopedias.

DS705.T46 1986
Through the Moon Gate: a guide to China's historic monuments. Hong Kong; Oxford University Press, 1986. xiii, 313 p.
86-021701 915.1/0458.219 019584176X
Historic sites--China--Guidebooks. Monuments--China--Guidebooks.

DS706 China — General works

DS706.C489 1981
China, a country study/ Foreign Area Studies, the American University; edited by Frederica M. Bunge and Rinn-Sup Shinn. Washington, D.C.: For sale by the Supt. of Docs., U.S. G.P.O., 1981. xxxi, 590 p.
81-012878 951
China.

DS706.E37 1996
Ebrey, Patricia Buckley,
The Cambridge illustrated history of China/ Patricia Buckley Ebrey. Cambridge; Cambridge University Press, 1996. 352 p.
95-038548 951.220 0521435196
China -- History. China -- Civilization.

DS706.H8
Hu, Chang-tu, 1920-
China: its people, its society, its culture. In collaboration with Samuel C. Chu [and others] Editor: Hsiao Hsia. New Haven, HRAF Press [1960] 610 p.
60-007382 915.1
China.

DS706.I5 1988
Information China: the comprehensive and authoritative reference source of new China/ organized by the Chinese Academy of Social Sciences; compiled and translated by the China Social Sciences Publishing House; edited for Pergamon Press by C.V. James. Oxford; Pergamon Press, 1989. 3 v.
88-019603 951 0080347649
China.

DS706.K464 1997
Kemenade, Willem van.
China, Hong Kong, Taiwan, Inc./ Willem van Kemenade; translated from the Dutch by Diane Webb. New York: Knopf, c1997. xiii, 444 p.
97-071923 0679454845
Chinese reunification question, 1949- Hong Kong (China) Taiwan. China.

DS706.L3 1964
Latourette, Kenneth Scott, 1884-
The Chinese, their history and culture. New York, Macmillan [1964] 2 v. in 1
64-017372 915.1
China. China -- History. China -- Civilization.

309

DS706.M24 2001
Mackerras, Colin.
The new Cambridge handbook of contemporary China/ Colin Mackerras. Cambridge, UK; Cambridge University Press, 2001. xi, 313 p.
2001-035783   951.221   0521786746
China -- Handbooks, manuals, etc.

DS706.M245 2000
Mackerras, Colin.
Sinophiles and sinophobes: Western views of China/ an anthology selected and edited by Colin Mackerras. Oxford; Oxford University Press, 2000. xxvi, 268 p.
00-057996   951.221   0195918924
China.

DS706.P38 1979
The People's Republic of China: a handbook/ edited by Harold C. Hinton. Boulder, Colo.: Westview Press, 1979. xvii, 443 p.
78-010306   951.05   0891584196
   China.

DS706.S62 1998
Spence, Jonathan D.
The Chan's great continent: China in western minds/ Jonathan D. Spence. New York: W. W. Norton, c1998. xviii, 279 p.
98-010823   951   0393027473
   China. China -- Civilization.

DS706.T39 1987
Taylor, Jay, 1931-
The dragon and the wild goose: China and India/ Jay Taylor. New York: Greenwood Press, 1987. xvii, 289 p.
87-007563   951   0313258996
   China. India.

DS706.U53 1999
Understanding contemporary China/ edited by Robert E. Gamer. Boulder, Colo.: Lynne Rienner Publishers, c1999. p. cm.
98-024305   951   1555876870
   China.

DS706.W46
Whitaker, Donald P.
Area handbook for the People's Republic of China [by] Donald P. Whitaker, Rinn-Sup Shinn [and others. Washington, For sale by the Supt. of Docs., U.S. Govt. Print 1972. xvi, 729 p.
72-600022   915.1/03/5
   China.

DS706.5 China — Historical geography

DS706.5.L3 1951
Lattimore, Owen.
Inner Asian frontiers of China. Irvington-on-Hudson, N.Y., Capitol Pub. Co., 1951. lxi, 585 p.
52-000655   915.1
   China -- Historical geography. China -- Boundaries.

DS706.7 China — Geography

DS706.7.L44 1993
Leeming, Frank.
The changing geography of China/ Frank Leeming. Oxford; Blackwell, 1993. xiii, 197 p.
92-014969   915.1   0631176756
   China -- Geography.

DS707 China — Description and travel — Earliest through 1500

DS707.C36 1989
Cameron, Nigel.
Barbarians and mandarins: thirteen centuries of western travellers in China/ Nigel Cameron. Hong Kong; Oxford University Press, 1989, c1970. 443 p.
89-025534   303.48/251.220   019585005X
China -- Description and travel. China -- Relations -- Foreign countries.

DS707.E512
Ennin, 794-864.
Diary; the record of a pilgrimage to China in search of the law; translated from the Chinese by Edwin O. Reischauer. New York, Ronald Press Co. [1955] xvi, 454 p.
55-005553   951.016
Ennin, -- 794-864 -- Diaries. Buddhism -- China. China -- Description and travel -- Early works to 1800. China -- History -- Tang dynasty, 618-907 -- Sources.

DS707.L5
Li, Chih-Ch'ang, 1193-1278.
The travels of an alchemist; the journey of the Taoist, Ch'ang-Ch'un, from China to the Hindukush at the summons of Chingiz Khan, recorded by his disciple, Li Chih-Ch'ang.   Translated, with an introduction, by Arthur Waley. London, G. Routledge & Sons, ltd. [1931] xi, 166 p.
31-031754   915.1
Chiu, Chang-chun, -- 1148-1227.   China -- Description and travel. Mongolia -- Description and travel. Asia, Central -- Description and travel.

DS707.R45
Reischauer, Edwin O. 1910-
Ennin's travels in Tang China. New York, Ronald Press Company [1955] xii, 341 p.
55-006273   951.016
Ennin, -- 793-864.   China -- Description and travel.

DS708 China — Description and travel — 1501-1800

DS708.M14
Macartney, George Macartney, 1737-1806.
An embassy to China; being the journal kept by Lord Macartney during his embassy to the Emperor Chien-lung, 1793-1794. Edited with an introd. and notes by J. L. Cranmer-Byng. Hamden, Conn., Archon Books, 1963. 421 p.
63-006504   915.1
   China -- Description and travel.

DS709 China — Description and travel — 1801-1900

DS709.C634 2001
Clifford, N. J.
"A truthful impression of the country": British and American travel   writing in china, 1880---1949/ Nicholas Clifford. Ann Arbor: University of Michigan Press, 2001. xxi, 231 p.
00-012313   915.104/4.221   0472111973
Travelers' writings, English--History and criticism. Travelers' writings, American--History and criticism. British--China--History--19th century.

DS709.F64 1996
Fogel, Joshua A.,
The literature of travel in the Japanese rediscovery of China, 1862-1945/ Joshua A. Fogel. Stanford, Calif.: Stanford University Press, c1996. xvii, 417 p.
95-000448   915.104/35.220   0804725675
Travelers' writings, Japanese--History and criticism. Travelers--China--History.

DS709.R49 1990
Ricalton, James.
James Ricalton's photographs of China during the Boxer Rebellion: his   illustrated travelogue of 1900/ edited, with introduction and notes by Christopher J. Lucas. Lewiston, NY: E. Mellen Press, c1990. x, 248 p.
89-013574   951/.035.220   0889465088
Ricalton, James--Journeys--China.

DS709.T475 1982
Thomson, J.
China and its people in early photographs: an unabridged reprint of the classic 1873/4 work/ by John Thomson; with a new foreword by Janet Lehr. New York: Dover Publications, 1982. 272 p.
82-004587   951/.03/0222.219   0486243931
Thomson, J. (John), 1837-1921.

DS710 China — Description and travel — 1901-1948

DS710.C294
Candlin, Enid Saunders.
The breach in the wall; a memoir of the Old China. New York, Macmillan [1973] viii, 340 p.
72-011955   915.1/04/42
   China -- Description and travel.

DS710.C73
Cressey, George Babcock, 1896-1963.
Land of the 500 million; a geography of China. New York, McGraw-Hill, 1955. xv, 387 p.
55-008895   915.1
   China -- Geography.

DS710.H58 1938
Hedin, Sven Anders, 1865-1952.
The Silk road, by Sven Hedin, translated from the Swedish by F. H. Lyon; with 31 plates and a map. New York, E. P. Dutton & company, inc. [c1938] viii, 322 p.
38-034570   915.1
   Trade routes.   China -- Description and travel. Sinkiang Province (China) -- Description and travel.

DS711 China — Description and travel — 1949-1975

DS711.G7
Greene, Felix.
Awakened China; the country Americans don't know. Garden City, N.Y., Doubleday, 1961. 425 p.
61-009512   915.1
   China -- Description and travel.

DS711.S288
Schell, Orville.
In the People's Republic: an American's first-hand view of living and working in China/ Orville Schell. New York: Random House, c1977. ix, 271 p.
76-053458   951.05   0394499050
Schell, Orville.   China -- Description and travel.

DS711.S57
Snow, Edgar, 1905-1972.
The long revolution. New York, Random House [1972] x, 269 p.
72-004838 951.05 0394468597
China -- Description and travel.

DS711.T68 1966
Tregear, T. R.
A geography of China, by T. R. Tregear. Chicago, Aldine Pub. Co. [1966, c1965] xvii, 342 p.
65-026752 915.1
China -- Geography.

DS715 China — Antiquities — General works

DS715.C38 1986
Chang, Kwang-chih.
The archaeology of ancient China/ Kwang-chih Chang. New Haven, Conn.: Yale University Press, c1986. xxv, 450 p.
86-009186 931 0300037848
Prehistoric peoples -- China. Antiquities, Prehistoric -- China. China -- Antiquities. China -- Civilization.

DS715.C42
Cheng, Te-kun, 1908-
Archaeology in China. [Toronto] University of Toronto Press [1961, c1959- v.
62-030119 913.31
China -- Antiquities.

DS715.G65 1999
The golden age of Chinese archaeology: celebrated discoveries from the People's Republic of China/ edited by Xiaoneng Yang. Washington: National Gallery of Art; 584 p.
99-016620 931/.0074/753.221 0894682458
Antiquities, Prehistoric--China--Exhibitions. Prehistoric peoples--China--Exhibitions.

DS715.M97 1996
Mysteries of ancient China: new discoveries from the early dynasties / edited by Jessica Rawson. New York: G. Braziller, 1996. p. cm.
96-015451 931.220 0807614122
China -- Antiquities. China -- Civilization.

DS715.Q513
Qian, Hao.
Out of China's earth: archeological discoveries in the People's Republic of China/ Qian Hao, Chen Heyi, Ru Suichu. New York: H.N. Abrams; 1981. 206 p.
81-002058 931 0810907666
China -- Antiquities.

DS715.R43 1984
Recent archaeological discoveries in the People's Republic of China/ the Institute of Archaeology, Academy of Social Sciences, People's Republic of China. Tokyo, Japan: Centre for East Asian Cultural Studies; xi, 103 p.
85-149229 931.219 4896564014
China -- Antiquities.

DS715.W32 1966a
Watson, William, 1917-
Early civilization in China. New York, McGraw-Hill [1966 143 p.
66-016974 915.103
China -- Antiquities.

DS721-724 China — Social life and customs. Civilization. Intellectual life — General works

DS721.A8
Ayscough, Florence Wheelock, 1878-1942.
A Chinese mirror: being reflections of the reality behind appearance/ Florence Ayscough; with drawings by Lucille Douglass. London: J. Cape; 1925. 464 p.
26-026222
China -- Social life and customs. China -- Description and travel. China -- Religion.

DS721.B213
Balazs, Etienne, 1905-1963.
Chinese civilization and bureaucracy; variations on a theme. Translated by H.M. Wright. Edited by Arthur F. Wright. New Haven, Yale University Press, 1964. xix, 309 p.
64-020909 915.1
China -- Civilization.

DS721.B38
Beckmann, George M.
The modernization of China and Japan. New York, Harper & Row [1962] 724 p.
62-016641 915.1
China -- Civilization. Japan -- Civilization -- 1868-1945.

DS721.B44 2002
Benn, Charles D.,
Daily life in traditional China: the Tang dynasty/ Charles Benn. Westport, Conn.: Greenwood Press, 2002. xxii, 317 p.
2001-023839 951/.017.221 0313309558
China -- Social life and customs. China -- History -- Tang dynasty, 618-907.

DS721.B45 2000
Berkowitz, Alan J.
Patterns of disengagement: the practice and portrayal of reclusion in early medieval China/ Alan J. Berkowitz. Stanford, Calif.: Stanford University Press, 2000. xii, 296 p.
99-057586 951.221 0804736030
Recluses--China.

DS721.B56 1998 *have 1983 Ref*
Blunden, Caroline.
Cultural atlas of China/ by Caroline Blunden and Mark Elvin. New York: Facts on File, 1998. p. cm.
98-034322 951 0816038147
China -- Civilization.

DS721.B6
Bodde, Derk, 1909-
China's cultural tradition, what and whither? New York, Rinehart [1957] 90 p.
57-059558 915.1
China -- Civilization.

DS721.C517 1993 *have 1981*
Chinese civilization: a sourcebook/ edited by Patricia Buckley Ebrey. 2nd ed., rev. and expanded. New York: Free Press, c1993. xix, 524 p.
92-047017 951.220 0029087651
China -- Civilization -- Sources. China -- History -- Sources.

DS721.C98 1997
Culture & state in Chinese history: conventions, accommodations, and critiques/ edited by Theodore Huters, R. Bin Wong, and Pauline Yu. Stanford, Calif.: Stanford University Press, 1997. x, 500 p.
97-006109 951.221 0804728682
Chinese literature--History and criticism.

DS721.D357
Dawson, Raymond Stanley.
The Chinese chameleon: an analysis of European conceptions of Chinese civilization [by] Raymond Dawson. London, Oxford U.P., 1967. xvi, 235 p.
67-081516 915.1/03
China -- Civilization.

DS721.D37 1999
De Bary, William Theodore,
Sources of Chinese tradition/ compiled by Wm. Theodore De Bary and Irene Bloom; with the collaboration of Wing-tsit Chan ... [et al.] and contributions by Joseph Adler ... [et al.]. 2nd ed. New York: Columbia University Press, c1999- v. <1-2 >
98-021762 951.221 023111270X
China -- Civilization -- Sources.

DS721.E32613 1986 *Ref*
Eberhard, Wolfram,
A dictionary of Chinese symbols: hidden symbols in Chinese life and thought/ Wolfram Eberhard; translated from the German by G.L. Campbell. London; Routledge & Kegan Paul, 1986. 332 p.
85-008187 951/.003/21.219 0710201915
Symbolism in art--China--Dictionaries.

DS721.E336 1991
Ebrey, Patricia Buckley, 1947-
Confucianism and family rituals in imperial China: a social history of writing about rites/ Patricia Buckley Ebrey. Princeton, N.J.: Princeton University Press, 1991. x, 272 p.
91-007488 951 0691031509
Confucianism -- China -- Rituals. China -- Social life and customs.

DS721.F26
Fairbank, John King, 1907-
Chinese thought and institutions. With contributions by Tung-tsu Chu [and others]. Chicago] University of Chicago Press [1957] xiii, 438 p.
57-005272 915.1
China -- Intellectual life.

DS721.F55 1954 *have 3d ed 1961*
Fitzgerald, C. P. 1902-
China: a short cultural history. New York, Praeger [1954] xviii, 621 p.
54-006804 915.1
Art, Chinese. China -- Civilization -- History. China -- History. China -- Religion.

DS721.G37
Gentzler, J. Mason.
A syllabus of Chinese civilization, by J. Mason Gentzler. New York, Columbia University Press, 1968. x, 107 p.
68-055814 915.1/03/0202
China -- Civilization.

DS721.G413 1962b
Gernet, Jacques.
Daily life in China, on the eve of the Mongol invasion, 1250-1276. Translated from the French by H. M. Wright. Stanford, Calif., Stanford University Press [1962] 254 p.
73-110281   915.1/03/2   0804707200
China -- Social life and customs -- 960-1644.
China -- History -- Sung dynasty, 960-1279.

DS721.G788
Granet, Marcel, 1884-1940.
Chinese civilization, by Marcel Granet. London, K. Paul, Trench, Trubner & co.,; 1930. xxiii, 444 p.
30-028700   951
China -- Social life and customs. China -- History -- To 1643.

DS721.H254 1996
The handbook of Chinese psychology/ edited by Michael Harris Bond. Hong Kong; Oxford University Press, 1996. xx, 588 p.
95-037341   155.8/951.220   0195865987
Chinese--Psychology. National characteristics, Chinese.

DS721.H45 1990
Heritage of China: contemporary perspectives on Chinese civilization/ edited by Paul S. Ropp; contributors, T.H. Barrett ... [et al.]. Berkeley: University of California Press, c1990. xxi, 369 p.
89-037365   951   0520064402
China -- Civilization.

DS721.H685 1970
Hsu, Francis L. K., 1909-
Americans and Chinese: purpose and fulfillment in great civilizations. Garden City, N.Y., Published for the American Museum of Natural His [1970] xxviii, 493 p.
72-116215   915.1
China -- Civilization. United States -- Civilization -- 20th century.

DS721.H687
Hsu, Francis L. K., 1909-
Religion, science and human crises; a study of China in transition and its implications for the West. London, Routledge & K. Paul [1952] x, 142 p.
52-002962   915.1
Medicine, Magic, mystic, and spagiric   China -- Social life and customs. West Town, China.

DS721.H69
Hsu, Francis L. K., 1909-
Under the ancestors' shadow; Chinese culture and personality. New York, Columbia Univ. Press, 1948. xiv, 317 p.
48-007782
Ancestor worship.   China -- Social life and customs. West Town, China.

DS721.H724
Hucker, Charles O.
China's imperial past: an introduction to Chinese history and culture/ Charles O. Hucker. Stanford, Calif.: Stanford University Press, 1975. xii, 474 p.
74-025929   951   0804708878
China -- Civilization. China -- History.

DS721.I66 2001
An introduction to Chinese culture through the family/ edited by Howard Giskin and Bettye S. Walsh. Albany: State University of New York Press, c2001. xii, 237 p.
2001-020807   951.221   0791450473
Family--China.

DS721.I8
Isaacs, Harold Robert, 1910-
Scratches on our minds; American images of China and India. New York, J. Day Co. [1958] 416 p.
58-005692   915
China -- Civilization. India -- Civilization.

DS721.K85
Kulp, Daniel Harrison.
Country life in South China; the sociology of familism. Volume I. Phenix village, Kwantung, China. By Daniel Harrison Kulp II. New York city, Bureau of publications, Teachers college, Columb 1925. xxx p.
25-021663
Country life -- China. Family.   China -- Social life and customs.

DS721.L345 1998
Landscape, culture, and power in Chinese society/ edited by Wen-hsin Yeh. Berkeley: Institute of East Asian Studies, University of California, xv, 152 p.
97-048842   951.221   155729061X
China -- Civilization. China -- Social life and customs.

DS721.L538
Levenson, Joseph Richmond, 1920-1969.
Confucian China and its modern fate: the problem of intellectual continuity. Berkeley, University of California Press, 1958. 223 p.
58-002791   915.1
Communism -- China.   China -- Civilization -- History. China -- Intellectual life.

DS721.L5483
Liang, Chi-chao, 1873-1929.
Intellectual trends in the Ching period (Ching-tai hsueh-shu kai-lun) Translated with introd. and notes by Immanuel C. Y. Hsu. Foreword by Benjamin I. Schwartz. Cambridge, Harvard University Press, 1959. xxii, 147 p.
59-006158   915.1
China -- Intellectual life.

DS721.M3
MacNair, Harley Farnsworth, 1891-1947.
The Real conflict between China and Japan: an analysis of opposing ideologies/ by Harley Farnsworth MacNair. Chicago, Ill.: University of Chicago Press, c1938. xvi, 215 p.
38-027812   915.1
Eastern question (Far East)   China -- Civilization. Japan -- Civilization. China -- Relations -- Japan.

DS721.N39
Needham, Joseph, 1900-
Science and civilisation in China, by Joseph Needham. Cambridge [Eng.] University Press, 1954-1999 v. 1-4; v. 5,
54-004723   509.51   052132727X
Science -- China -- History. Technology -- China -- History. Science and civilization. China -- Civilization.

DS721.N392
Needham, Joseph, 1900-
The shorter Science and civilisation in China: an abridgement of Joseph Needham's original text/ Colin A. Ronan. Cambridge; Cambridge University Press, 1978-1995 v. 1-5
77-082513   951   0521218217
Science -- China -- History.   China -- Intellectual life. China -- Civilization.

DS721.P684 1994
The Power of culture: studies in Chinese cultural history/ edited by Willard J. Peterson, Andrew Plaks, Ying-shih Yü. Hong Kong: Chinese University Press, c1994. xii, 366 p.
97-178511   951.221   9622015964
China -- Civilization -- History.

DS721.P78 1986
The Psychology of the Chinese people/ editor, Michael Harris Bond; contributors, Michael Harris Bond ... [et al.]. Hong Kong; Oxford University Press, 1986. xii, 354 p.
86-008715   155.8/951.219   0195840518
National characteristics, Chinese.

DS721.P794 2001
Puett, Michael J.,
The ambivalence of creation: debates concerning innovation and artifice in early China/ Michael Puett. Stanford, Calif.: Stanford University Press, 2001. viii, 299 p.
00-049290   951.221   0804736235
China -- Civilization -- History.

DS721.S37
Scott, A. C. 1909-
Literature and the arts in twentieth century China. Garden City, N.Y., Doubleday [1963] 212 p.
63-008760   915.1
China -- Intellectual life.

DS721.S39
Self and society in Ming thought, by Wm. Theodore de Bary and the Conference on Ming Thought. New York, Columbia University Press, 1970. xii, 550 p.
78-101229   915.1/03/2   0231032714
China -- Civilization -- 960-1644. China -- History -- Ming dynasty, 1368-1644.

DS721.T528 1995
Time and space in Chinese culture/ edited by Chun-chieh Huang and Erik Zürcher. Leiden; E.J. Brill, 1995. vi, 400 p.
95-020958   951.220   9004102876
Space and time.

DS721.T59 1989
Tom, K. S.,
Echoes from old China: life, legends, and lore of the Middle Kingdom / K.S. Tom. Honolulu: Hawaii Chinese History Center: xi, 160 p.
89-020224   951.220   0824812859
China -- Social life and customs.

DS721.T67 1973
Toynbee, Arnold Joseph, 1889-1975.
Half the world: the history and culture of China and Japan. Texts E. Glahn [and others] Edited by Arnold Toynbee. New York, Holt, Rinehart and Winston [1973] 368 p.
73-004198   915.1/03   0030107164
China -- Civilization. Japan -- Civilization.

DS721.W3
Waln, Nora, 1895-
The House of exile, by Nora Waln; with illustrations by C. Le Roy Baldridge. Boston, Little, Brown, and Company, 1933. 7 p.
33-027105   915.1
China -- Social life and customs. China -- History -- Republic, 1912-1949.

DS721.W334
Wang, Y. C. 1916-
Chinese intellectuals and the West, 1872-1949, by Y.C. Wang. Chapel Hill, University of North Carolina Press [1966] xiv, 557 p.
66-010207   915.1033
Multicultural education. Returned students -- China. China -- Civilization -- Western influences.

DS721.W53 1950
Winfield, Gerald Freeman, 1908-
China, the land and the people. New York, W. Sloane Associates [1950] vii, 431 p.
50-058305
Reconstruction (1939-1951) -- China. China.

DS721.Z48 1999
Zhang, Longxi.
Mighty opposites: from dichotomies to differences in the comparative study of China/ Zhang Longxi. Stanford, Calif.: Stanford University Press, c1998. 248 p.
98-026223   951   0804732590
Comparative civilization. East and West. China -- Civilization -- Western influences.

DS723.C38
Chang, Kwang-chih.
Early Chinese civilization: anthropological perspectives/ K. C. Chang. Cambridge, Mass.: Harvard University Press, 1976. xv, 229 p.
75-014094   931   0674219996
China -- Civilization -- To 221 B.C.

DS723.C7 1954
Creel, Herrlee Glessner, 1905-
The birth of China; a study of the formative period of Chinese civilization. New York, F. Ungar Pub. Co. [1954, c1937] 402 p.
54-005633   913.31
Excavations (Archaeology) -- China. Bronze age -- China. China -- Civilization. China -- Antiquities.

DS724.C7 1970
Croizier, Ralph C.,
China's cultural legacy and communism. Edited by Ralph C. Croizier. New York, Praeger Publishers [1970] xiii, 313 p.
77-083334   915.1/03/5
China -- Civilization -- 1949-

DS727 China — Social life and customs. Civilization. Intellectual life — Other special

DS727.A74 1990
Anderson, Mary M.
Hidden power: the palace eunuchs of imperial China/ Mary M. Anderson. Buffalo, N.Y.: Prometheus Books, c1990. 318 p.
89-070053   305.9/066/0951.220   0879755741
Eunuchs--China--History.

DS730 China — Ethnography — General works

DS730.E17 1982
Eberhard, Wolfram, 1909-
China's minorities: yesterday and today/ Wolfram Eberhard. Belmont, Calif.: Wadsworth, c1982. xi, 176 p.
82-002629   305.8/00951   0534010806
Ethnology -- China. China -- Race relations.

DS730.H4213 1989
Heberer, Thomas.
China and its national minorities: autonomy or assimilation?/ Thomas Heberer. Armonk, N.Y.: M.E. Sharpe, c1989. xiii, 165 p.
88-038363   305.8/00951   0873325494
Ethnology -- China. China -- Ethnic relations.

DS730.L5 1967
Li, Chi, 1896-1979.
The formation of the Chinese people; an anthropological inquiry. New York, Russell & Russell [1967] 283 p.
66-027117   572.9/51
Ethnology -- China.

DS730.L596 1994
The living tree: the changing meaning of being Chinese today/ edited by Tu Wei-ming. Stanford, Calif.: Stanford University Press, 1994. xvi, 295 p.
93-041416   305.8/00951.220   0804721378
Chinese--Ethnic identity. National characteristics, Chinese. Nationalism--China.

DS730.M336 1994
Mackerras, Colin.
China's minorities: integration and modernization in the twentieth century/ Colin Mackerras. Hong Kong; Oxford University Press, 1994. 355 p.
93-043882   951/.004   019585988X
Minorities -- China -- History -- 20th century. Ethnology -- China -- History -- 20th century. China -- History -- Autonomy and independence movements.

DS730.M338 1995
Mackerras, Colin.
China's minority cultures: identities and integration since 1912/ Colin Mackerras. Melbourne, Australia: Longman; 1995. x, 252 p.
95-020956   305.8/00951   0582806712
Ethnology -- China -- History -- 20th century. China -- Ethnic relations.

DS730.N33 1998
Nationalism and ethnoregional identities in China/ edited by William Safran. London; Frank Cass, 1998. 197 p.
98-026002   305.8/00951   071464921X
Ethnology -- China -- Case studies. Nationalism -- China -- Case studies. China -- Ethnic relations -- Political aspects -- Case studies.

DS730.O47 1998
Olson, James Stuart, 1946-
An ethnohistorical dictionary of China/ James S. Olson. Westport, Conn.: Greenwood Press, 1998. ix, 434 p.
97-027110   305.8/00951   0313288534
Ethnology -- China -- Dictionaries. China -- Ethnic relations -- Dictionaries.

DS730.W5 1954
Wiens, Herold J. 1912-
China's march toward the tropics; a discussion of the southward penetration of China's culture, peoples, and political control in relation to the non-Han-Chinese peoples of south China and in the pe Hamden, Conn., Shoe String Press [1954]. xv, 441 p.
54-013401   951.2
Migration, Internal -- China. Ethnology -- China.

DS731 China — Ethnography — Individual elements in the population, A-Z

DS731.H3.G83 1996
Guest people: Hakka identity in China and abroad/ edited by Nicole Constable. Seattle: University of Washington Press, c1996. x, 284 p.
95-017857   951   0295974699
Hakka (Chinese people)

DS731.H3.L46 1997
Leong, Sow-Theng.
Migration and ethnicity in Chinese history: Hakkas, Pengmin, and their neighbors/ Sow-Theng Leong; edited by Tim Wright, with an introduction and maps by G. William Skinner. Stanford, Calif.: Stanford University Press, 1997. xix, 234 p.
97-000413   305.895/1   0804728577
Hakka (Chinese people) -- Ethnic identity -- History. Migration, Internal -- China -- History. China -- Economic conditions -- To 1644 -- Regional disparities. China -- Economic conditions -- 1644-1912 -- Regional disparities.

DS731.J3.K87 1999
Kuramoto, Kazuko, 1927-
Manchurian legacy: memoirs of a Japanese colonist/ Kazuko Kuramoto. xii, 189 p.
99-006503   951/.8042/092   0870135104
Kuramoto, Kazuko, -- 1927- Japanese -- China -- Manchuria -- Biography. Women -- China -- Manchuria -- Biography. Agricultural colonies -- China -- Manchuria. Manchuria (China) -- History -- 1931-1945. Japan -- History -- 1945- Manchuria (China) -- Biography.

DS731.K38.B46 1998
Benson, Linda.
China's last Nomads: the history and culture of China's Kazaks/ Linda Benson and Ingvar Svanberg. Armonk, N.Y.: M.E. Sharpe, c1998. xiii, 251 p.
97-045582   952/.00494345   156324781X
Kazakhs -- China -- History -- 20th century. Xinjiang Uygur Zizhiqu (China) -- Ethnic relations.

DS731.M35
Elliott, Mark C.
The Manchu way; the eight banners and ethnic identity in late imperial China/ Mark C. Elliott. Stanford, Calif.: Stanford University Press, 2001. xxiii, 580 p.
00-064087   951.004/941   0804736065
Manchus -- Ethnic identity -- History -- 17th century. Manchus -- Ethnic identity -- History -- 18th century.

DS731.M35.C76 1990
Crossley, Pamela Kyle.
Orphan warriors: three Manchu generations and the end of the Qing world/ Pamela Kyle Crossley. Princeton, N.J.: Princeton University Press, c1990. xi, 305 p.
89-034963   951/.03   0691055831
Manchus -- Social life and customs. China -- History -- Ching dynasty, 1644-1912.

DS731.M87.G53 1991
Gladney, Dru C.
Muslim Chinese: ethnic nationalism in the People's Republic/ Dru C. Gladney. Cambridge, Mass.: Council on East Asian Studies, Harvard Universit 1991. xxiv, 473 p.
90-026582   305.6/971051   0674594967
Muslims -- China. China -- Ethnic relations.

DS731.U4.M33 1973
Mackerras, Colin.
The Uighur Empire according to the Tang dynastic histories: a study in Sino-Uighur relations, 744-840. Colin Mackerras, editor and translator. Columbia, University of South Carolina Press [1973, c1972] viii, 226 p.
73-001708   951/.01   0872492796
Uigurs.   China -- History -- Tang dynasty, 618-907.

DS731.Y3
Litzinger, Ralph A., 1959-
Other Chinas: the Yao and the politics of national belonging/ Ralph A. Litzinger. Durham, NC: Duke University Press, 2000. xxiv, 331 p.
99-087369   305.895/94   082232525X
Yao (Southeast Asian people) -- Ethnic identity. Yao (Southeast Asian people) -- History. Yao (Southeast Asian people) -- Government relations. China -- Ethnic relations. China -- Politics and government. China -- Social conditions.

DS732 China — Chinese in foreign countries (General)

DS732.C9 2001
Cultural curiosity: thirteen stories about the search for Chinese roots/ edited by Josephine M.T. Khu. Berkeley: University of California Press, c2001. xiv, 272 p.
00-067224   305.895/1.221   0520223411
Chinese--Foreign countries. Ethnicity--China. National characteristics, Chinese.

DS732.E53 1999
The encyclopedia of the Chinese overseas/ general editor, Lynn Pan. Cambridge, Mass.: Harvard University Press, 1999. 399 p.
98-035466   304.8/0951   0674252101
Chinese -- Foreign countries. China -- Emigration and immigration.

DS732.F56
Fitzgerald, Stephen.
China and the overseas Chinese; a study of Peking's changing policy, 1949-1970. Cambridge [Eng.] University Press, 1972. xii, 268 p.
77-177938   301.29/51   0521084105
Chinese -- Foreign countries. China -- Foreign relations -- 1949-1976.

DS732.M39 2001
McKeown, Adam.
Chinese migrant networks and cultural change: Peru, Chicago, Hawaii, 1900-1936/ Adam McKeown. Chicago: The University of Chicago Press, 2001. xi, 349 p.
00-011903   304.8/0951/09041.221   0226560252
Chinese--Foreign countries.

DS732.P36 1990
Pan, Lynn.
Sons of the yellow emperor: a history of the Chinese diaspora/ Lynn Pan. Boston: Little, Brown, c1990. xvii, 408 p.
90-006258   951/.004924   0316690104
Chinese -- Foreign countries -- History. Immigrants -- History. China -- Emigration and immigration -- History.

DS732.W346 2000
Wang, Gungwu.
The Chinese overseas: from earthbound China to the quest for autonomy / Wang Gungwu. Cambridge, Mass.: Harvard University Press, 2000. 148 p.
99-053438   909/.04951.221
Chinese--Foreign countries--History.

DS733 China — History — Dictionaries. Chronological tables, outlines, etc.

DS733.C58523 1998
China: a historical and cultural dictionary/ edited by Michael Dillon. Richmond, Surrey: Curzon, 1998. viii, 391 p.
98-128565   951/.003.221   0700704396
China -- History -- Dictionaries. China -- Civilization -- Dictionaries.

DS733.M6 1957a
Moule, A. C. 1873-1957.
The rulers of China, 221 B.C.- A.D. 1949; chronological tables. With an introductory section on the earlier rulers c. 2100-249 B.C. by W. Perceval Yetts. New York, F. A. Praeger [1957] xxiii, 131 p.
57-011146   951.002
China -- History -- Chronology. China -- Kings and rulers.

DS734 China — History — Biography (Collective)

DS734.P285 1998
Paludan, Ann,
Chronicle of the Chinese emperors: the reign-by-reign record of the rulers of Imperial China/ Ann Paludan. New York: Thames and Hudson, 1998. 224 p.
98-060041   951/.009/9. 221   0500050902
Emperors--China.

DS734.S75
Ssu-ma, Chien, ca. 145-ca. 8
Statesman, patriot, and general in ancient China; three biographies of the Chin dynasty (255-206 B.C.) translated and discussed by Derk Bodde. New Haven, Conn., American Oriental Society, 1940. xi, 75 p.
40-011696   923.251
Lu, Pu-wei, -- d. B.C. 235. Ching, Ko, -- d. B.C. 227. Meng, Tien, -- d. B.C. 210?

DS734.U65
Library of Congress.
Eminent Chinese of the Ching period (1644-1912) Edited by Arthur W. Hummel ... Washington, U.S. Govt. Print. Off., 1943-44. 2 v.
43-053640   920.051
China -- Biography.

DS734.W63 1994
Wills, John E. 1936-
Mountain of fame: portraits in Chinese history/ John E. Wills, Jr. Princeton, N.J.: Princeton University Press, c1994. xvi, 403 p.
93-046773   920.051   0691055424
China -- Biography.

DS734.7-734.97 China — History — Historiography

DS734.7.D57
Dirlik, Arif.
Revolution and history: the origins of Marxist historiography in China, 1919-1937/ Arif Dirlik. Berkeley: University of California Press, c1978. x, 299 p.
77-080469   951.04/07/2   0520035410
Marxian historiography--China. Revolutions--China.

DS734.7.D83 1995
Duara, Prasenjit.
Rescuing history from the nation: questioning narratives of modern China/ Prasenjit Duara. Chicago: University of Chicago Press, 1995. x, 275 p.
95-003205   951/.072   0226167216
Civilization, Oriental. China -- History -- 20th century. China -- Historiography.

DS734.7.F4
Feuerwerker, Albert.
Chinese Communist studies of modern Chinese history, by Albert Feuerwerker and S. Cheng. Cambridge, East Asian Research Center, Harvard University; 1961. xxv, 287 p.
61-019595   951.0072
China -- History -- Historiography.

DS734.7.H3
Han, Yu-shan, 1899-
Elements of Chinese historiography. Hollywood, Calif., W.M. Hawley, 1955. 246 p.
55-020273   951.007
China -- History -- Historiography.

DS734.7.H56
History in communist China, edited by Albert Feuerwerker. Cambridge, M.I.T. Press [1968] xiv, 382 p.
68-018238   951/.0072
China -- Historiography.

DS734.7.H824 1992
Hu, David Y.,
Chinese-English dictionary of Chinese historical terminology/ written by David Y. Hu; authorized by the National Institute for Compilation and Translation = [Zhongguo shi xue ci hui/ Hu Yingyuan bian zhuan; Guo li bian yi guan zhu bian]. Taipei, Taiwan: Hua Shiang Yuan Pub. Co., c1992. 2 v.
97-153203   951/.0072.221   9575240723
China -- Historiography -- Dictionaries.

DS734.7.L8 1994
Lu, Hsiao-peng.
From historicity to fictionality: the Chinese poetics of narrative/ Sheldon Hsiao-peng Lu. Stanford, Calif.: Stanford University Press, c1994. viii, 213 p.
93-031744   895.13/08109   0804723192
Chinese fiction -- History and criticism. Narration (Rhetoric) China -- Historiography.

DS734.7.W33 2001
Wang, Q. Edward, 1958-
Inventing China through history: the May Fourth approach to historiography/ Q. Edward Wang. Albany, NY: State University of New York Press, c2001. xi, 304 p.
00-020626   951/.007/2   0791447316
Historiography -- China -- History -- 20th century. China -- Historiography.

DS734.7.W5
Wilkinson, Endymion Porter.
The history of imperial China;a research guide.
Cambridge, Mass., East Asian Research Center,
Harvard University; xxi, 213 p.
72-093955 951/.007/2 0674396804
*China -- Historiography. China -- History --
Sources -- Bibliography.*

DS734.8.W58 1992
Wixted, John Timothy.
Japanese scholars of China: a bibliographical
handbook = [Nihon no Ch̄ugokugaku senmonka
handobukku]/ compiled by John Timothy Wixted.
Lewiston: Edwin Mellen Press, 1992. xlii, 474 p.
92-025299 951/.007202/252.220 0773495711
Sinologists--Japan--Handbooks, manuals, etc.

DS734.9.F3.A33 1982
Fairbank, John King, 1907-
Chinabound: a fifty-year memoir/ John King
Fairbank. New York: Harper & Row, 1982. xiv,
480 p.
81-047656 951/.04 0060390050
*Fairbank, John King, -- 1907- Sinologists --
United States -- Biography. United States --
Relations -- China. China -- Relations -- United
States.*

DS734.9.F8
Wang, Fan-shen.
Fu Ssu-nien: an intellectual biography/ Wang Fan-
shen. New York: Cambridge University Press,
2000. p. cm.
99-053801 951.04/092 0521480515
*Fu, Ssu-nien, -- 1896-1950. Historians -- China --
Biography.   China -- Intellectual life -- 1912-
1949.*

DS734.9.W55 A3 1996
Wilbur, C. Martin
China in my life: a historian's own history/ C.
Martin Wilbur; edited by Anita M. O'Brien.
Armonk, N.Y.: M.E. Sharpe, c1996. vii, 321 p.
[10] p. of plates
95-053181 951/.007202. 220 1563247631
*Wilbur, C. Martin (Clarence Martin), d1908-
Sinologists--United States--Biography.*

DS734.97.U6.C47 1993
Chow, Rey.
Writing diaspora: tactics of intervention in
contemporary cultural studies/ Rey Chow.
Bloomington: Indiana University Press, c1993. x,
223 p.
92-023064 951/.0072 025331366X
*Culture -- Study and teaching -- United States.
China -- Study and teaching -- United States.*

DS734.97.U6 K86 1986
Kuo, Tai-Chün,
Understanding Communist China: Communist
China studies in the United   States and the
Republic of China, 1949-1978/ Tai-Chün Kuo and
Ramon H. Myers. Stanford, Calif.: Hoover
Institution Press, Stanford University, xi, 172 p.
86-003126 951/.0072073.219 0817983414
*China -- Study and teaching -- United States.
China -- Study and teaching -- Taiwan.*

DS735 China —
General works

DS735.B25 1914a
Backhouse, Edmund Trelawny, 1873-
Annals & memoirs of the court of Peking (from the
16th to the 20th century) by E. Backhouse and J.
O. P. Bland. London, W. Heinemann [1914] x,
531 p.
44-037779
China -- History. China -- Kings and rulers.

DS735.F27 1998
Fairbank, John King, *have 1992*
China: a new history/ John King Fairbank and
Merle Goldman. Enl. ed. Cambridge, Mass.:
Belknap Press of Harvard University Press, 1998.
xix, 546 p.
98-009474 951.221 0674116739
China -- History.

DS735.F28 1989
Fairbank, John King,
China: tradition & transformation/ John K.
Fairbank, Edwin O. Reischauer. Rev. ed. Boston:
Houghton Mifflin Co., c1989. xii, 551 p.
88-083732 951.220 0395496926
China -- History.

DS735.F3 1983
Fairbank, John King, *have 3rd 1971*
The United States and China/ John King
Fairbank.4th ed., enl. Cambridge, Mass.: Harvard
University Press, 1983. xxvi, 632 p.
83-008492 327.51073.219 0674924371
*China -- History. United States -- Foreign
relations -- China. China -- Foreign relations --
United States.*

DS735.G5
Giles, Herbert Allen, 1845-1935.
China and the Manchus, by Herbert A. Giles.
Cambridge [Eng.] The University press; 1912. viii,
148 p.
13-006024
Manchus. China -- History.

DS735.G58 1969 *have 1943*
Goodrich, L. Carrington 1894-
A short history of the Chinese people [by] L.
Carrington Goodrich. London, Allen & Unwin,
1969. xv, 295 p.
73-454308 951 0049510150
China -- History.

DS735.G7
Grousset, Rene, 1885-1952.
The rise and splendour of the Chinese Empire.
[Translated by Anthony Watson-Gandy and
Terence Gordon. Berkeley, University of
California Press, 1953. 312 p.
53-009939
China -- History.

DS735.H25 2000
Hansen, Valerie,
The open empire: a history of China to 1600/
Valerie Hansen. 1st ed. New York: Norton, c2000.
xvii, 458 p.
99-041325 951/.01.221 0393973743
China -- History.

DS735.T75 1942
Tsui, Chi.
A short history of Chinese civilisation/ by Tsui
Chi; with a preface by Laurence Binyon. London:
V. Gollancz, 1942. 335 p.
43-002182
*China -- History. China -- Civilization --
History.*

DS735.W695 2000
Wilkinson, Endymion Porter.
Chinese history: a manual/ Endymion Wilkinson.
Rev. and enl. Cambridge, Mass.: Published by the
Harvard University Asia Center for xxiv, 1181 p.
99-056876 951.221 0674002490
China -- History -- Handbooks, manuals, etc.

DS735.W79 1997
Wong, Roy Bin.
China transformed: historical change and the limits
of European experience/ R. Bin Wong. Ithaca:
Cornell University Press, 1997. x, 327 p.
97-023232 951 0801432545
*China -- History. Europe -- History. China --
Economic conditions.*

DS736 China — History
— Addresses, essays, lectures

DS736.S625 1992
Spence, Jonathan D.
Chinese roundabout: essays in history and culture/
Jonathan D. Spence. lst ed. New York: W.W.
Norton, c1992. xiii, 400 p.
91-034393 951.220 0393033554
China -- History. China -- Civilization.

DS736.T6 1982
The Translation of things past: Chinese history and
historiography/ edited by George Kao. Hong Kong:
Chinese University Press; 200 p.
82-165579 951/.0072.219 9622012728
China -- History. China -- Historiography.

DS736.5 China — History
— Philosophy of Chinese history

DS736.5.M47 1965
Meskill, John Thomas,
The pattern of Chinese history: cycles,
development, or stagnation? Edited with an introd.
by John Meskill. Boston, Heath [1965] xx, 108 p.
65-017466 951.001
China -- History -- Philosophy.

DS737 China — History
— Several parts of the empire
treated together

DS737.C4818 1982
Chang, Luke T.
China's boundary treaties and frontier disputes: a
manuscript/ by Luke T. Chang. London; Oceana
Publications, c1982. xii, 443 p.
82-003483 341.4/2/026851.219 0379207338
*China -- Boundaries. China -- Foreign relations --
Treaties.*

DS737.T96 1990
Tzou, Byron N.
China and international law: the boundary disputes/
Byron N. Tzou. New York: Praeger, 1990. 158 p.
89-023098 911/.51 0275934624
China -- Boundaries.

DS738 China — History — Military history

DS738.L5
Liu, F. F. 1919-
A military history of modern China, 1924-1949, by F. F. Liu. Princeton, Princeton University Press, 1956. 312 p.
56-008386   951.04
China -- History, Military.

DS738.W36 2000
Warfare in Chinese history/ edited by Hans van de Ven. Leiden; Brill, 2000. 456 p.
00-039816   355/.00951   9004117741
China -- History, Military.

DS740-740.5 China — History — Political and diplomatic history

DS740.B36
Bau, Mingchien Joshua, b. 1894.
The open door doctrine in relation to China by Mingchien Joshua Bau ... New York, The Macmillan company, 1923. xxviii p.
23-010566   327.51
China -- Foreign relations.

DS740.C5
Chiang, Kai-shek, 1887-1975.
China's destiny/ by Chiang Kai-shek; authorized translation by Wang Chung-hui; with an introduction by Lin Yutang. New York: Macmillan, 1947. xi, 260 p.
47-030071   951.04
Reconstruction (1939-1951) -- China. China -- Foreign relations. China -- Politics and government -- 1912-1949.

DS740.C56
Chou, Hsiang-kuang.
Political thought of China. Foreword by S. Radhakrishnan. Delhi, S. Chand, 1954. iii, 244 p.
57-000149
China -- Politics and government.

DS740.2.H57 1992
Historical dictionary of revolutionary China, 1839-1976/ edited by Edwin Pak-wah Leung. New York: Greenwood Press, 1992. xv, 566 p.
91-015990   951   0313264570
Revolutions -- China -- History -- Dictionaries. China -- History -- 19th century -- Dictionaries. China -- History -- 20th century -- Dictionaries.

DS740.2.I8
Israel, John.
Student nationalism in China, 1927-1937. Stanford, Calif., Published for the Hoover Institution on War, Rev 1966. ix, 253 p.
66-015300   951.042
Students -- China. China -- Politics and government -- 1912-1949.

DS740.2.M4
Maverick, Lewis A. 1891-
China, a model for Europe. San Antonio, Tex., Paul Anderson, c1946. 2 v. in 1
46-006265
China -- Relations -- Europe. Europe -- Relations -- China. China -- Politics and government.

DS740.2.P47
Perry, Elizabeth J.
Rebels and revolutionaries in north China, 1845-1945/ Elizabeth J. Perry. Stanford, Calif.: Stanford University Press, 1980. xiii, 324 p.
79-065179   951/.03   0804710554
Peasant uprisings -- China. Revolutions -- China. China -- Politics and government -- 19th century. China -- Politics and government -- 20th century.

DS740.2.S33 1991
Schrecker, John E.
The Chinese revolution in historical perspective/ John E. Schrecker. New York: Greenwood Press, 1991. xx, 240 p.
90-038410   951   0313274851
Revolutions -- China -- History. China -- History -- 19th century. China -- History -- 20th century. China -- Intellectual life.

DS740.2.T4
Teng, Ssu-yu, 1906-
China's response to the West; a documentary survey, 1839-1923 [by] Ssu-yu Teng [and] John. K. Fairbank, with E-tu Zen Sun, Chaoying Fang, and others. [Prepared in Cooperation with the International Secretariat of the Institute of Pacific Relations] Cambridge, Harvard University Press, 1954. vi, 296 p.
53-005061   303.4/82/0951
China -- Relations -- Foreign countries.

DS740.4.A644 1988
Adshead, Samuel Adrian M.
China in world history/ S.A.M. Adshead. New York: St. Martin's Press, 1988. x, 422 p.
87-004516   957   0312005067
China -- Relations -- Foreign countries.

DS740.4.F26
Fairbank, John King, 1907-
Ching administration; three studies by John K. Fairbank and Ssu-yu Teng. Cambridge, Harvard University Press, 1960. x, 218 p.
60-007991   951.03
Tributary system (China) Document writing, Chinese.

DS740.4.F7185
Frodsham, J. D.,
The first Chinese embassy to the West; the journals of Kuo-Sung-Tao, Liu Hsi-Hung and Chang Te-yi; translated and annotated by J. D. Frodsham. Oxford, Clarendon Press, 1974. lxv, 222 p.
74-180206   301.29/51/04   019821555X
China -- Relations -- Europe. Europe -- Relations -- China.

DS740.4.M6
Morse, Hosea Ballou, 1855-1934.
The international relations of the Chinese empire, by Hosea Ballou Morse ... London, Longmans, Green, and Co., 1910-18. 3 v.
11-002033
Opium trade. China -- History. China -- Foreign relations. China -- Politics and government.

DS740.4.M67 2000
Mosher, Steven W.
Hegemon: China's plan to dominate Asia and the world/ Steven W. Mosher. San Francisco: Encounter Books, c2000. xi, 193 p.
00-028283   327.51/009   1893554082
China -- Relations -- Foreign countries.

DS740.4.V34 1970
Van Ness, Peter.
Revolution and Chinese foreign policy; Peking's support for wars of national liberation. Berkeley, University of California Press, 1970. xii, 266 p.
73-089893   327.51
China -- Foreign relations -- 1949-1976.

DS740.4.W23
Walker, Richard Louis, 1922-
China and the West: cultural collision; selected documents. [New Haven] Far Eastern Publications, Yale University, 1956. 254 p.
56-058515   327.51
Communism -- China. China -- Foreign relations.

DS740.5.G5 F6 1940
Fox, Grace Estelle,
British admirals and Chinese pirates, 1832-1869. London, K. Paul, Trench, Trubner & Co., ltd. [1940] xiv, 227 p.
41-000183
Pirates.

DS740.5.G5.H48 1995
Hevia, James Louis, 1947-
Cherishing men from afar: Qing guest ritual and the Macartney Embassy of 1793/ James L. Hevia. Durham: Duke University Press, 1995. xv, 292 p.
94-043610   327.51041/09/033   0822316250
Macartney, George Macartney, -- Earl, -- 1737-1806. Diplomatic etiquette -- China. China -- Foreign relations -- 1644-1912. China -- Foreign relations -- Great Britain. Great Britain -- Foreign relations -- China.

DS740.5.G5.P4 1969
Pelcovits, Nathan A. 1912-
Old China Hands and the Foreign Office [by] Nathan A. Pelcovits. New York, Octagon Books, 1969 [c1948] xi, 349 p.
78-076003   327.51/042
Merchants, British. Great Britain -- Foreign relations -- China. China -- Foreign relations -- Great Britain.

DS740.5.I5.B3 1971
Bagchi, Prabodh Chandra.
India and China; a thousand years of cultural relations. Westport, Conn., Greenwood Press [1971] vi, 234 p.
71-136053   301.29/51/054   0837152038
China -- Relations -- India. India -- Relations -- China.

DS740.5.J3 E44 2002
Elleman, Bruce A.,
Wilson and China: a revised history of the Shandong question/ Bruce A. Elleman. Armonk, N.Y.: M.E. Sharpe, c2002. xviii, 227 p.
2002-024699   327.51052.221   0765610507
China -- Foreign relations -- Japan. Japan -- Foreign relations -- China. China -- Foreign relations -- 1912-1949. Shandong Sheng (China) -- History.

DS740.5.J3.J67 1991
Jordan, Donald A., 1936-
Chinese boycotts versus Japanese bombs: the failure of China's "revolutionary diplomacy," 1931-32/ Donald A. Jordan. Ann Arbor: University of Michigan Press, c1991. xii, 363 p.
90-026383   327.51052/09/043   0472101722
China -- Foreign relations -- Japan. Japan -- Foreign relations -- China. China -- Foreign economic relations -- Japan.

DS740.5.J3.W3
Wang, Yi-tung, 1914-
Official relations between China and Japan, 1368-1549/ by Wang Yi-tung. Cambridge: Harvard University Press, 1953. xi, 128 p.
53-005062   327.510952
Japan -- Foreign relations -- China. China -- Foreign relations -- Japan.

DS740.5.J3.W48 1989
Whiting, Allen Suess, 1926-
China eyes Japan/ Allen S. Whiting. Berkeley: University of California Press, c1989. xi, 228 p.
88-038067   327.51052   0520065115
China -- Foreign relations -- Japan. Japan -- Foreign relations -- China. China -- Foreign relations -- 1976-

DS740.5.K6.L44 1996
Lee, Chae-Jin, 1936-
China and Korea: dynamic relations/ Chae-Jin Lee in collaboration with Doo-Bok Park. Stanford, Calif.: Hoover Institution Press, 1996. x, 218 p.
96-003792   327.510519   0817994211
China -- Relations -- Korea. Korea -- Relations -- China.

DS740.5.R8.B37
Barnett, A. Doak.
China and the major powers in East Asia/ A. Doak Barnett. Washington: Brookings Institution, c1977. xii, 416 p.
77-021981   327.51   0815708246
China -- Foreign relations -- Soviet Union. Soviet Union -- Foreign relations -- China. China -- Foreign relations -- Japan.

DS740.5.R8.B7
Brandt, Conrad.
Stalin's failure in China, 1924-1927.   Cambridge, Harvard University Press, 1958. xv, 226 p.
58-012963   951.042
Stalin, Joseph, -- 1879-1953.   China -- Foreign relations -- Soviet Union. Soviet Union -- Foreign relations -- China.

DS740.5.R8.C5
Cheng, Tien-fang, 1899-1967.
A history of Sino-Russian relations.   Washington, Public Affairs Press [1957] 389 p.
57-006908
China -- Foreign relations -- Russia. Soviet Union -- Foreign relations -- China.

DS740.5.R8.C6
Clemens, Walter C.
The arms race and Sino-Soviet relations [by] Walter C. Clemens, Jr. Stanford, Calif., Hoover Institution on War, Revolution and Peace, 1968. xi, 335 p.
68-021253   327.47/051
Nuclear arms control. Nuclear disarmament Arms race -- History -- 20th century. Soviet Union -- Foreign relations -- China. China -- Foreign relations -- Soviet Union.

DS740.5.R8.C63
Clubb, O. Edmund 1901-
China & Russia; the "great game" [by] O. Edmund Clubb. New York, Columbia University Press, 1971. xii, 578 p.
72-155362   327.47/051   0231027400
Soviet Union -- Foreign relations -- China. China -- Foreign relations -- Soviet Union.

DS740.5.R8.G3
Garthoff, Raymond L.,
Sino-Soviet military relations, edited by Raymond L. Garthoff. New York, F. A. Praeger [1966] xii, 285 p.
66-018900   327.47051
China -- Military relations -- Soviet Union. Soviet Union -- Military relations -- China.

DS740.5.R8.G5
Gittings, John.
Survey of the Sino-Soviet dispute: a commentary and extracts from the recent polemics 1963-1967. London, issued under the auspices of the Royal Institute 1968. xix, 410 p.
75-356659   327.51/047
China -- Foreign relations -- Soviet Union. Soviet Union -- Foreign relations -- China.

DS740.5.R8.H78
Hudson, Geoffrey Francis, 1903-
The Sino-Soviet dispute. Documented and analysed by G. F. Hudson, Richard Lowenthal and Roderick MacFarquhar. New York, Praeger [1961] 227p.
61-015894   327.47051
World politics -- 1955-1965.   China -- Foreign relations -- Soviet Union. Soviet Union -- Foreign relations -- China.

DS740.5.R8.J3 1968 *have, 962*
Jackson, W. A. Douglas 1923-
The Russo-Chinese borderlands: zone of peaceful contact or potential conflict? By W. A. Douglas Jackson. Princeton, N.J., Van Nostrand [1968] 156 p.
68-009548   327.47/051
Soviet Union -- Boundaries -- China. China -- Boundaries -- Soviet Union.

DS740.5.R8.M373
Mehnert, Klaus, 1906-
Peking and Moscow. Translated from the German by Leila Vennewitz. New York, Putnam [1963] xiv, 522 p.
63-016176   327.47051
China -- Relations -- Soviet Union. Soviet Union -- Relations -- China.

DS740.5.R8.N6 1963
North, Robert Carver.
Moscow and Chinese Communists.   Stanford, Calif., Stanford University Press [1963] 310 p.
62-018742   951.04
Communism -- China.   Soviet Union -- Foreign relations -- China. China -- Foreign relations -- Soviet Union.

DS740.5.R8.W5 1968
Whiting, Allen Suess, 1926-
Soviet policies in China, 1917-1924, by Allen S. Whiting. Stanford, Calif., Stanford University Press [1968, c1953] viii, 350 p.
68-012335   327.47/051
China -- Foreign relations -- Soviet Union. Soviet Union -- Foreign relations -- China.

DS740.5.S65.G37 1988
Garver, John W.
Chinese-Soviet relations, 1937-1945: the diplomacy of Chinese nationalism/ John W. Garver. New York: Oxford University Press, 1988. viii, 301 p.
88-001462   327.51047   0195054326
China -- Foreign relations -- Soviet Union. Soviet Union -- Foreign relations -- China. China -- Politics and government -- 1937-1945.

DS740.5.S65.G66 1993
Goncharov, S. N.
Uncertain partners: Stalin, Mao, and the Korean War/ Sergei N. Goncharov, John W. Lewis, Xue Litai. Stanford, Calif.: Stanford University Press, c1993. xi, 393 p.
93-023971   327.51047   0804721157
Korean War, 1950-1953.   Soviet Union -- Foreign relations -- China. China -- Foreign relations -- Soviet Union.

DS740.5.S65.L68 1987
Low, Alfred D.
The Sino-Soviet confrontation since Mao Zedong: dispute, detente or conflict?/ by Alfred D. Low. Boulder: Social Science Monographs; 1987. xii, 322 p.
87-060628   327.51047   0880339586
China -- Foreign relations -- Soviet Union. Soviet Union -- Foreign relations -- China.

DS740.5.S65.S56 1982
The Sino-Soviet conflict: a global perspective/ edited by Herbert J. Ellison. Seattle: University of Washington Press, c1982. xxii, 408 p.
81-051279   327.51047   0295958545
World politics -- 1975-1985 -- Congresses. Soviet Union -- Foreign relations -- China -- Congresses. China -- Foreign relations -- Soviet Union -- Congresses.

DS740.5.S65.S562 1997
Sheng, Michael M., 1950-
Battling Western imperialism: Mao, Stalin, and the United States/ Michael M. Sheng. Princeton, N.J.: Princeton University Press, c1997. x, 255 p.
97-010035   327.51047   0691016356
Mao, Tse-tung, -- 1893-1976 -- Contributions in international relations.   China -- Foreign relations -- United States. United States -- Foreign relations -- China. China -- Foreign relations -- Soviet Union.

DS740.5.S65.W55 1989
Wilbur, C. Martin 1908-
Missionaries of revolution: Soviet advisers and Nationalist China, 1920-1927/ C. Martin Wilbur and Julie Lien-ying How. Cambridge, Mass.: Harvard University Press, 1989. xii, 904 p.
88-019124   327.51047   0674576527
China -- Foreign relations -- Soviet Union. Soviet Union -- Foreign relations -- China. China -- Foreign relations -- 1912-1949.

DS740.5.T28 Z46 1993
Zhan, Jun.
Ending the Chinese civil war: power, commerce, and conciliation between Beijing and Taipei/ Jun Zhan. New York: St Martin's Press, 1993. xxi, 246 p.
92-031869   327.5105124/9.220   0312089880
China -- Relations -- Taiwan. Taiwan -- Relations -- China.

DS740.5.U5.B6 1947a
Borg, Dorothy, 1902-
American policy and the Chinese revolution, 1925-1928, by Dorothy Borg ... New York, American Institute of Pacific Relations, The Mac 1947. x p. 1 . 44
47-004150   951.042
United States -- Foreign relations -- China. China -- Foreign relations -- United States. China -- History -- Republic, 1912-1937.

DS740.5.V5 D85 1986
Duiker, William J.,
China and Vietnam: the roots of conflict/ William J. Duiker. Berkeley: Institute of East Asian Studies, University of California, x, 136 p.
86-081534   327.510597.219   0912966890
China -- Foreign relations -- Vietnam. Vietnam -- Foreign relations -- China.

DS740.5.V5.R67 1988
Ross, Robert S., 1954-
The Indochina tangle: China's Vietnam policy, 1975-1979/ Robert S. Ross. New York: Columbia University Press, 1988. xvi, 361 p.
87-015819   327.510597   0231065647
Sino-Vietnamese Conflict, 1979.   China -- Foreign relations -- Vietnam. Vietnam -- Foreign relations -- China.

DS740.63 China — History — China and the Far Eastern question

DS740.63.L48
Levi, Werner, 1912-
Modern China's foreign policy.   Minneapolis, University of Minnesota Press [1953] 399 p.
53-010470   327.51
China -- Foreign relations -- 1949- China -- Foreign relations -- 1912-1949.

DS741-779.32 China — History — By period

DS741.C5 no.6
Ling-hu, Te-fen, 583-666.
Accounts of Western nations in the history of the Northern Chou dynasty [Chou shu 50. 10b-17b] Translated and annotated by Roy Andrew Miller. Berkeley, University of California Press, 1959. 83 p.
59-009437
Sinkiang -- Historical geography. Iran -- Historical geography.

DS741.C5 no.8
Chiu Tang shu.
Biography of An Lu-shan. Translated and annotated by Howard S. Levy. Berkeley, University of California Press, 1960. 122 p.
61-063071
An, Lu-shan, -- 703-757.

DS741.3.S6813 1994
SSu-ma, Chien, ca. 145-ca. 8
The grand scribe's records/ Ssu-ma Chien; William H. Nienhauser, Jr., editor; Tsai-fa Cheng ... [et al.], translators. Bloomington: Indiana University Press, c1994- v. 1, 7
94-018408   931   0253340217
China -- History -- To 221 B.C. China -- History -- Chin dynasty, 221-207 B.C. China -- History -- Han dynasty, 202 B.C.-220 A.D.

DS741.3.S683 H37 1999
Hardy, Grant.
Worlds of bronze and bamboo: Sima Qian's conquest of history/ Grant Hardy. New York: Columbia University Press, 1999. xviii, 301 p.
98-052716   931/.04.221   0231113056
Ssu-ma, Ch ien, ca. 145-ca. 86 B.C. Shih chi.

DS741.5.C35 1999
The Cambridge history of ancient China: from the origins of civilization to 221 B.C./ edited by Michael Loewe and Edward L. Shaughnessy. Cambridge, UK; Cambridge University Press, 1999. xxix, 1148 p.
97-033203   931   0521470307
China -- History -- To 221 B.C. China -- Civilization -- To 221 B.C. China -- Antiquities.

DS741.5.W3
Watson, William, 1917-
China before the Han dynasty. New York, Praeger [c1961] 264 p.
61-014105   913.31
China -- History -- To 221 B.C.

DS741.65.C53 1983
Chang, Kwang-chih.
Art, myth, and ritual: the path to political authority in ancient China/ K.C. Chang. Cambridge, Mass.: Harvard University Press, 1983. x, 142 p.
83-000214   931   0674048075
Political science -- China -- History.   China -- Civilization -- To 221 B.C.

DS741.65.D44 1999
Defining Chu: image and reality in ancient China/ edited by Constance A. Cook and John S. Major. Honolulu: University of Hawai'i Press, c1999. ix, 254 p. [8] p. of col. plates
99-027952   931.221   0824818857
Historiography--China.

DS741.65.L514 1996
Li, Jun, 1961-
Chinese civilization in the making, 1766-221 BC/ Li Jun. New York: St. Martin's Press, 1996. ix, 206 p.
96-034821   931   0333618904
China -- Civilization -- To 221 B.C.

DS741.65.P55 2002
Pines, Yuri.
Foundations of Confucian thought: intellectual life in the Chunqiu period (722-453 B.C.E.)/ Yuri Pines. Honolulu: University of Hawai'i Press, c2002. 387 p.
2001-046286   931.221   0824823966
China -- Intellectual life -- To 221 B.C. China -- History -- Spring and Autumn period, 722-481 B.C.

DS744.K43 2000
Keightley, David N.
The ancestral landscape: time, space, and community in late Shang China, ca. 1200-1045 B.C./ David N. Keightley. Berkeley: University of California, Berkeley; xiv, 209 p.
00-029598   931/.01.221   1557290709
Oracle bones--China.

DS744.K44
Keightley, David N.
Sources of Shang history: the oracle-bone inscriptions of bronze age China/ David N. Keightley. Berkeley: University of California Press, c1978. xvii, 281 p.
74-029806   931   0520029690
Inscriptions, Chinese. Oracle bones -- China. China -- History -- Shang dynasty, 1766-1122 B.C. -- Sources.

DS745.C513
Chinese dynastic histories translations = Chung ku shih i tsung/ Institute of East Asiatic Studies, University of California. Berkeley [Calif.]: University of California Press, 1952-1968. 10 v.
52-007553   951
China -- History -- 221 B.C.-960 A.D.

DS747.H79 1988
Hsu, Cho-yun, 1930-
Western Chou civilization/ Cho-yun Hsu and Katheryn M. Linduff. New Haven: Yale University Press, c1988. xxiv, 421 p.
87-006178   931/.03   0300037724
China -- History -- Chou dynasty, 1122-221 B.C.

DS747.2.C725 1998
Crump. J. I.
Legends of the warring states: persuasions, romances, and stories from Chan-kuo ts e/ selected, translated, and edited by J.I. Crump. Ann Arbor: Center for Chinese Studies, The University of Michigan, xiv, 189 p.
98-036393   931/.03.221   0892641290
China -- History -- Warring States, 403-221 B.C. -- Anecdotes.

DS747.42.B64 1992
Bol, Peter Kees.
"This culture of ours": intellectual transitions in Tang and Sung China/ Peter K. Bol. Stanford, Calif.: Stanford University Press, 1992. x, 519 p.
91-016004   951/.01   0804719209
China -- Intellectual life -- 221 B.C.-960 A.D. China -- Intellectual life -- 960-1644.

DS747.5.B6
Bodde, Derk.
China's first unifier; a study of the Chin dynasty as seen in the life of Li Ssu ... (280?-208 B.C.) By Derk Bodde. Leiden, E. J. Brill, 1938. viii, 270 p.
38-023382   951
Li Ssu, -- B.C. 280?-208. Shih Huang Ti, -- emperor of China, -- B.C. 259-210.

DS747.5.C6
Cottrell, Leonard.
The Tiger of Chin; the dramatic emergence of China as a nation. New York, Holt, Rinehart and Winston [1962] 245 p.
62-008352   951.01
Chin Shih-huang, -- Emperor of China, -- 259-210 B.C.   China -- History -- Chin dynasty, 221-207 B.C.

DS747.5.F57
The First Emperor of China/ edited by Li Yu-ning. White Plains, N.Y.: International Arts and Sciences Press, [1975] 1xxiii, 357 p.
74-015390   931/.00994   0873320670
Chin Shih-huang, -- Emperor of China, -- 259-210 B.C.

DS747.9.C47 K47 2000
Kern, Martin.
The stele inscriptions of Ch in Shih-huang: text and ritual in early Chinese imperial representation/ by Martin Kern. New Haven, Conn.: American Oriental Society, 2000. viii, 221 p.
2001-274107   931/.04/092.221   0940490153
Qin Shihuang, Emperor of China, 259-210 B.C. Stele (Archaeology)--China. Inscriptions, Chinese.

DS748.H28 vol. 1
Chu, Tung-tsu.
Han social structure. Edited by Jack L. Dull. Seattle, University of Washington Press [1972] xix, 550 p.
69-014206   309.1/31   0295950684
China -- Social conditions -- 221 B.C.-960 A.D.

DS748.L577
Loewe, Michael.
Crisis and conflict in Han China, 104 BC to AD 9/ Michael Loewe. London: Allen & Unwin, 1974. 340 p.
75-308728　931　0049510215
China -- History -- Han dynasty, 202 B.C.-220 A.D.

DS748.P3 1974
Pan, Ku, 32-92.
Courtier and commoner in ancient China; selections from the History of the former Han. Translated by Burton Watson. New York, Columbia University Press, 1974. 282 p.
73-018003　931　0231037651
China -- History -- Han dynasty, 202 B.C.-220 A.D.

DS748.P5713 1982
Pirazzoli-t'Serstevens, Michele.
The Han Dynasty/ Michele Pirazzoli-t'Serstevens; translated by Janet Seligman. New York: Rizzoli, c1982. 240 p.
82-050109　931/.04　0847804380
China -- History -- Han dynasty, 202 B.C.-220 A.D.

DS748.S7453
Ssu-ma, Chien, ca. 145-ca. 8
Records of the grand historian of China. Translated from the Shih chi of Ssu-ma Ch'ie by Burton Watson. New York, Columbia University Press, 1961. 2 v.
60-013348　931
China -- History -- 1766 B.C.-220 A.D.

DS748.18.S73 1991
State and society in early medieval China/ edited by Albert E. Dien. Stanford, Calif.: Stanford University Press, 1991, c1990. viii, 414 p.
89-060727　951/.01　0804717451
Social history -- Medieval, 500-1500. China -- Social conditions -- 221 B.C.-960 A.D. China -- Politics and government -- 220-589.

DS748.2.L492513 2002
Liu, Yiqing,
A new account of tales of the world/ by Liu I-ch ing; with commentary by Liu Chün; translated with introduction and notes by Richard B. Mather. 2nd ed. Ann Arbor: Center for Chinese Studies, University of Michigan, p. cm.
2002-019275　931/.04.221　089264155X
China -- History -- Three kingdoms, 220-265 -- Anecdotes. China -- History -- Jin dynasty, 265-419 -- Anecdotes.

DS749.2.B5
Bingham, Woodbridge.
The founding of the T'ang dynasty; the fall of Sui and rise T'ang, a preliminary survey by Woodbridge Bingham. Baltimore, Waverly Press, inc., 1941. xiv, 183 p.
41-017978　951
Sui Yang-ti, -- Emperor of China, -- 569-618. Tang Kao-tsu, -- Emperor of China, -- 565-635. China -- History -- Early to 1643.

DS749.2.W74 1978
Wright, Arthur F., 1913-1976.
The Sui dynasty/ Arthur F. Wright. New York: Knopf, 1978. 237 p.
78-054898　951/.01　0394492765
China -- History -- Sui dynasty, 581-618.

DS749.3.F5 1971
Fitzgerald, C. P. 1902-
Son of heaven [a biography of Li Shih-Min, founder of the Tang dynasty, by C. P. Fitzgerald] New York, AMS Press [1971] ix, 232 p.
74-136382　951/.01/0924　0404024041
Tang Tai-tsung, -- Emperor of China, -- 597-649.

DS749.3.P8
Pulleyblank, Edwin G. 1922-
The background of the rebellion of An Lu-shan. London, Oxford University Press, 1955. 264p.
58-001352
China -- History -- Early to 1643

DS749.3.S3
Schafer, Edward H.
The vermilion bird; T'ang images of the South [by] Edward H. Schafer. Berkeley, University of California Press, 1967. viii, 380 p.
67-010463　915.1
Natural history -- China. China -- History -- T'ang dynasty, 618-907. China -- Description and travel.

DS749.3.W36.W42
Wechsler, Howard J.
Mirror to the Son of Heaven: Wei Cheng at the court of Tang Tai-tsung/ Howard J. Wechsler. New Haven: Yale University Press, 1974 [i.e. 19 xi, 259 p.
74-076649　951/.01/0924　0300017154
Wei, Cheng, -- 580-643. China -- History -- Tang dynasty, 618-907.

DS749.5.W3
Wang, Gungwu.
The structure of power in North China during the five dynasties. Kuala Lumpur, University of Malaya Press, 1963. viii, 257 p.
64-002651　951.01
China -- Politics and government -- Early to 1643.

DS750.64.M67 1999
Mote, Frederick W., 1922-
Imperial China, 900-1800/ F.W. Mote. Cambridge, Mass.: Harvard University Press, 1999. xix, 1107 p.
99-031840　951/.02　0674445155
China -- History -- 960-1644. China -- History -- 1644-1795.

DS751.D38 1996
Davis, Richard L., 1951-
Wind against the mountain: the crisis of politics and culture in thirteenth-century China/ Richard L. Davis. Cambridge, Mass.: Council on East Asian Studies, Harvard Universit 1996. xvii, 283 p.
96-025667　951/.024　0674953576
Martyrs -- China. Martyrdom. China -- History -- Sung dynasty, 960-1279. China -- Politics and government -- 960-1279.

DS751.J38 1991
Jay, Jennifer W.
A change in dynasties: loyalism in thirteenth-century China/ by Jennifer W. Jay. Bellingham, Wash.: Western Washington, c1991. xiv, 309 p.
91-014475　951/.024　0914584189
Loyalty. China -- History -- Yuan dynasty, 1260-1368. China -- History -- Sung dynasty, 960-1279.

DS751.O73 1993
Ordering the world: approaches to state and society in Sung Dynasty China/ edited by Robert P. Hymes and Conrad Schirokauer. Berkeley: University of California Press, c1993. xiv, 437 p.
91-043492　951/.02　0520076915
China -- History -- Sung dynasty, 960-1279 -- Congresses.

DS751.T34 1988
Tao, Jing-shen.
Two sons of heaven: studies in Sung-Liao relations/ Jing-shen Tao. Tucson: University of Arizona Press, c1988. x, 173 p.
88-001330　951/.024　0816510512
China -- History -- Sung dynasty, 960-1279. China -- History -- Liao dynasty, 947-1125.

DS751.W35 1935
Williamson, Henry Raymond.
Wang An Shih, a Chinese statesman and educationalist of the Sung dynasty. By H. R. Williamson. London, A. Probsthain, 1935-37. 2 v.
35-013711　923.251
Wang, An-shih, -- 1021-1086. China -- Politics and government.

DS751.W58 1949
Wittfogel, Karl August, 1896-
History of Chinese society: Liao, 907-1125 [by] Karl A. Wittfogel and Feng Chia-sheng, with the assistance of John DeFrancis [and others] Philadelphia, American Philosophical Society: distributed by t 1949. xv, 752 p.
49-008472　951.023
Khitan (Chinese people) -- History. China -- Social life and customs.

DS751.3.C35 1999
Chaffee, John W.
Branches of heaven: a history of the imperial clan of Sung China/ John W. Chaffee. Cambridge, Mass.: Harvard University Asia Center: xx, 441 p.
99-028564　951/.024.221　0674080491
Nobility--China.

DS751.5.S96
Sung biographies/ ed. by Herbert Franke. Wiesbaden: Steiner, 1976- v.
77-462858　3515024123
China -- History -- Sung dynasty, 960-1279 -- Biography. China -- Biography.

DS752.6.K83.R67 1988
Rossabi, Morris.
Khubilai Khan: his life and times/ Morris Rossabi. Berkeley: University of California Press, c1988. xvii, 322 p.
86-025031　950/.2/0924　0520067401
Kublai Khan, -- 1216-1294. Mongols -- History. China -- Kings and rulers -- Biography.

DS753.B76 1998
Brook, Timothy, 1951-
The confusions of pleasure: commerce and culture in Ming China/ Timothy Brook. Berkeley: University of California Press, c1998. xxv, 320 p.
97-008838　951/.026　0520210913
China -- History -- Ming dynasty, 1368-1644. China -- Commerce -- History.

DS753.F37 1994
Farmer, Edward L.
Ming History: an introduction guide to research = [Ming shih yen chiu chih nan]/ compiled by Edward L. Farmer, Romeyn Taylor, Ann Waltner; with the assistance of Jiang Yonglin. Minneapolis: Ming Studies Research Series, History Department, 152 p.
96-232253   951/.026   1886108021
China -- History -- Ming dynasty, 1368-1644 -- Research -- Methodology. China -- History -- Ming dynasty, 1368-1644 -- Bibliography.

DS753.F74
From Ming to Ching: conquest, region, and continuity in seventeenth-century China/ edited by Jonathan D. Spence and John E. Wills. Jr. New Haven: Yale University Press, 1979. xxiv, 413 p.
78-015560   951   0300022182
China -- History -- Ming dynasty, 1368-1644. China -- History -- Ching dynasty, 1644-1912.

DS753.H829
Hucker, Charles O.
The Ming dynasty, its origins and evolving institutions/ by Charles O. Hucker. Ann Arbor: Center for Chinese Studies, University of Michig 1978. viii, 105 p.
78-017354   951/.026   0892640340
China -- History -- Ming dynasty, 1368-1644.

DS753.H83
Hucker, Charles O.
The traditional Chinese state in Ming times (1368-1644) Tucson, University of Arizona Press, 1961. 85 p.
61-015391   951.026
China -- Politics and government -- Early to 1643.

DS753.J64 1995
Johnston, Alastair I.
Cultural realism: strategic culture and grand strategy in Chinese history/ Alastair Iain Johnston. Princeton, N.J.: Princeton University Press, c1995. xiii, 307 p.
95-003105   951/.02   0691029962
National security -- China. China -- History -- Ming dynasty, 1368-1644. China -- Military policy.

DS753.M5 1965
Michael, Franz H.
The origin of Manchu rule in China; frontier and bureaucracy as interacting forces in the Chinese Empire. New York, Octagon Books, 1972 [c1942] viii, 127 p.
65-025880   320.951
Manchus. China -- History -- Early to 1643. China -- History -- Tatar Conquest, 1643-1644.

DS753.2.D37 2002
Dardess, John W.,
Blood and history in China: the Donglin faction and its repression, 1620-1627/ John W. Dardess. Honolulu: University of Hawai'i Press, c2002. vii, 207 p.
2001-053063   951/.026.221   0824825160
Political parties--China.

DS753.2.S77 1998
Struve, Lynn A.,
The Ming-Qing conflict, 1619-1683: a historiography and source guide / Lynn A. Struve. Ann Arbor, Mich.: Association for Asian Studies, c1998. xiv, 423 p.
98-039736   951/.026/072.221   0924304375
China -- History -- Ming dynasty, 1368-1644 -- Historiography. China -- History -- Qing dynasty, 1644-1912 -- Historiography. China -- History -- Ming dynasty, 1368-1644 -- Bibliography. China -- History -- Qing dynasty, 1644-1912 -- Bibliography.

DS753.5.A84 1976
Association for Asian Studies.
Dictionary of Ming biography, 1368-1644/ the Ming Biographical History Project of the Association for Asian Studies; L. Carrington Goodrich, editor, Chaoying Fang, associate editor. New York: Columbia University Press, 1976. 2 v.
75-026938   951/.026/0922   0231038011
China -- History -- Ming dynasty, 1368-1644 -- Biography -- Dictionaries. China -- Biography -- Dictionaries.

DS753.6.H87 S75 2001
Statecraft and intellectual renewal in late Ming China: the cross-cultural synthesis of Xu Guangqi (1562-1633)/ edited by Catherine Jami, Peter Engelfriet, and Gregory Blue. Leiden; Brill, 2001. viii, 466 p.
2001-025667   951/.026.221   9004120580
Xu, Guangqi, 1562-1633.

DS753.6.H94 W35 1999
Wang, Chengmian.
The Life and career of Hung Ch'eng-ch'ou, 1593-1665; public service in a time of dynastic change/ Chen-main Wang. Ann Arbor, Mich. Association for Asian Studies, c1999. xiv, 322 p.
99-052253   951/.026/092. 221   0924304405
Hong, Chengchou, 1593-1665. Statesmen--China--Biography.

DS753.6.M43 T75 2001
Tsai, Shih-shan Henry
Perpetual happiness: the Ming emperor Yongle/ Shih-shan Henry Tsai. Seattle: University of Washington Press, c2001. xv, 270 p.
00-052771   951/.026/092. 221   0295981091
Ming Chengzu, Emperor of China, 1360-1424.

DS753.84.P47 1991
Perspectives on modern China: four anniversaries/ Kenneth Lieberthal ... [et al.], editors. Armonk, N.Y.: M.E. Sharpe, c1991. xiii, 433 p.
91-013410   951/.03   0873328140
China -- History -- Ching dynasty, 1644-1912 -- Congresses. China -- History -- May Fourth movement, 1919 -- Congresses. China -- History -- 1949- -- Congresses.

DS754.H74 1994
China: ancient culture, modern land/ general editor, Robert E. Murowchick. Norman, Okla.: University of Oklahoma Press, c1994. 192 p.
94-013366   951   0806126833
China -- Civilization.

DS754.M37
Marsh, Robert Mortimer.
The mandarins; the circulation of elites in China, 1600-1900. Glencoe [Ill.] Free Press of Glencoe [1961] 300 p.
60-010899
Social mobility -- China. Bureaucracy.

DS754.N4 1987
Naquin, Susan.
Chinese society in the eighteenth century/ Susan Naquin and Evelyn S. Rawski. New Haven: Yale University Press, c1987. xiii, 270 p.
86-029007   951/.03   0300038488
Social history -- 18th century. China -- Politics and government -- 1644-1912. China -- Economic conditions -- 1644-1912. China -- Social conditions -- 1644-1912.

DS754.R38 1998
Rawski, Evelyn Sakakida.
The last emperors: a social history of Qing imperial institutions/ Evelyn S. Rawski. Berkeley: University of California Press, c1998. xii, 481 p.
97-038792   951/.03   0520212894
Rites and ceremonies -- China. Political culture -- China. China -- Court and courtiers. China -- History -- Ching dynasty, 1644-1912. China -- Kings and rulers.

DS754.S65 1990 *2d ed 1999*
Spence, Jonathan D.
The search for modern China/ Jonathan D. Spence. New York: Norton, c1990. xxv, 876 p.
89-009241   951/.03   0393027082
China -- History -- Ching dynasty, 1644-1912. China -- History -- 20th century.

DS754.14.G74
Grieder, Jerome B.
Intellectuals and the state in modern China: a narrative history/ Jerome B. Grieder. New York: Free Press; c1981. xix, 395 p.
81-066436   951   0029128102
China -- Intellectual life -- 1644-1912. China -- Intellectual life -- 1912-1949.

DS754.15.W67 1999
Wortzel, Larry M.
Dictionary of contemporary Chinese military history/ Larry M. Wortzel; Robin Higham, advisory editor. Westport, Conn.: Greenwood Press, 1999. xv, 334 p.
99-010655   355/.00951/031   0313293376
China -- History, Military -- 1644-1912 -- Dictionaries. China -- History, Military -- 1912-1949 -- Dictionaries. China -- History, Military -- 1949- -- Dictionaries.

DS754.17.C76 1999
Crossley, Pamela Kyle.
A translucent mirror: history and identity in Qing imperial ideology / Pamela Kyle Crossley. Berkeley: University of California Press, 1999. xiv, 403 p.
99-011002   951/.03.221
Nationalism--China.

DS754.17.K8413 2002
Kuhn, Philip A.
Origins of the modern Chinese State/ Philip A. Kuhn. English ed. Stanford, Calif.: Standford University Press, 2002. viii, 162 p.
2002-001132   951/.033.221   0804742839
China -- Politics and government -- 19th century. China -- Politics and government -- 20th century.

DS754.18.M36 1984
Mancall, Mark.
China at the center: 300 years of foreign policy/ Mark Mancall. New York: Free Press; c1984. xviii, 540 p.
83-047981   327.51   0029198100
China -- Foreign relations -- 1644-1912. China -- Foreign relations -- 1912-1949. China -- Foreign relations -- 1949-

DS754.2.F8
Fu, Lo-shu, 1920-
A documentary chronicle of Sino-Western relations, 1644-1820, compiled, translated, and annotated by Lo-shu Fu. Tucson, Published for the Association for Asian Studies [1966] 2 v.
66-018529 951.03
China -- History -- Ching dynasty, 1644-1912 - - Sources. China -- Relations -- Foreign countries - - Sources.

DS754.2.V65 1993
Voices from the Ming-Qing cataclysm: China in tigers' jaws/ edited and translated by Lynn A. Struve. New Haven: Yale University Press, c1993. x, 303 p.
92-043916 951/.032 0300056796
China -- History -- 1644-1795.

DS754.4.C5.K3
Kahn, Harold L.
Monarchy in the emperor's eyes; image and reality in the Chien-lung reign [by] Harold L. Kahn. Cambridge, Mass., Harvard University Press, 1971. ix, 314 p.
75-135546 951/.03/0924 0674582306
Chien-lung, -- Emperor of China, -- 1711-1799. China -- History -- Chien-lung, 1736-1795.

DS754.4.C53.A33 1974
Kang-hsi, 1654-1722.
Emperor of China; self portrait of Kang Hsi, by Jonathan D. Spence. New York, Knopf; [distributed by Random House] 1974. xxv, 217 p.
73-020743 951/.03/0924 0394488350
Kang-hsi, -- Emperor of China, -- 1654-1722.

DS754.4.C53.K47
Kessler, Lawrence D.
Kang-hsi and the consolidation of Ching rule, 1661-1684/ Lawrence D. Kessler. Chicago: University of Chicago Press, 1976. xi, 251 p.
75-020897 951/.03/0924 0226432033
Kang-hsi, -- Emperor of China, -- 1654-1722. China -- History -- Kang-hsi, 1662-1722.

DS754.4.C53.W8
Wu, Silas H. L., 1929-
Passage to power: Kang-hsi and his heir apparent, 1661-1722/ Silas H. L. Wu. Cambridge: Harvard University Press, 1979. xv, 252 p.
79-004191 951/.03/0924 0674656253
Kang-hsi, -- Emperor of China, -- 1654-1722. China -- History -- Kang-hsi, 1662-1722.

DS754.74.T74 S64 2001
Spence, Jonathan D.
Treason by the book/ Jonathan D. Spence. New York, N.Y.: Viking, 2001. xvi, 300 p.
00-043805 951/.032/092. 221 0670892920
Zeng, Jing, 1679-1736. Yongzheng, Emperor of China, 1677-1735. Revolutionaries--China--Biography.

DS754.84.C45
Rowe, William T.
Saving the world: Chen Hongmou and elite consciousness in eighteenth-century China/ William T. Rowe. Stanford, Calif.: Stanford University Press, c2001. xii, 601 p.
00-061248 951/.032 0804737355
Chen, Hongmou, -- 1696-1771.   China -- Politics and government -- 18th century.

DS755.B47 1992
Bernhardt, Kathryn.
Rents, taxes, and peasant resistance: the lower Yangzi region, 1840-1950/ Kathryn Bernhardt. Stanford, Calif.: Stanford University Press, 1992. xii, 326 p.
91-015772 951/.2 0804718806
Peasant uprisings -- China -- Yangtze River Region -- History. Taxation -- China -- Yangtze River Region -- History. Rent -- China -- Yangtze RiverRegion -- History. China -- History -- Republic, 1912-1949. China -- History -- 19th century.

DS755.G72 1990
Gray, Jack, 1926-
Rebellions and revolutions: China from the 1800s to the 1980s/ Jack Gray. New York: Oxford University Press, 1990. lxiv, 456 p.
89-035997 951 0199130760
China -- History -- 19th century. China -- History -- 20th century.

DS755.K77
Kuhn, Philip A.
Rebellion and its enemies in late imperial China, militarization and social structure, 1796-1864 [by] Philip A. Kuhn. Cambridge, Mass., Harvard University Press, 1970. 254 p.
75-115476 951/.03 0674749510
China -- History -- 19th century.

DS755.L4313 1956
Li, Chien-nung.
The political history of China, 1840-1928. Translated and edited by Ssu-yu Teng and Jeremy Ingalls. Princeton, N.J., D. Van Nostrand Co. [1956] 545 p.
56-012095 951.03
China -- Politics and government -- 19th century. China -- Politics and government -- 1900-1949. China -- Foreign relations.

DS755.S294 2002
Schoppa, R. Keith,
Revolution and its past: identities and change in modern Chinese history/ R. Keith Schoppa. Upper Saddle River, N.J.: Prentice Hall, c2002. xv, 480 p.
00-140083 951/.033.221 0130224073
Revolutions--China--History.   National characteristics, Chinese.

DS755.S635 2000
Schoppa, R. Keith, 1943-
The Columbia guide to modern Chinese history/ R. Keith Schoppa. New York: Columbia University Press, c2000. xviii, 356 p.
99-053420 951.05 0231112769
China -- History -- 19th century. China -- History -- 20th century.

DS755.2.E46 2001
Elleman, Bruce A.,
Modern Chinese warfare, 1795-1989/ Bruce A. Elleman. London; Routledge, 2001. p. cm.
00-045739 951/.033.221 0415214742
China -- History -- 19th century. China -- History - - 20th century. China -- History, Military.

DS755.2.M63 1998
Modern China: an encyclopedia of history, culture, and nationalism/ editor Wang Ke-wen. New York: Garland Pub., 1998. xxxv, 442 p.
97-019299 951/.003 0815307209
Nationalism -- China -- History -- 19th century -- Encyclopedias. Nationalism -- China -- History -- 20th century -- Encyclopedias.

DS757.5.C45
Chang, Hsin-pao, 1922-
Commissioner Lin and the Opium War. Cambridge, Harvard University Press, 1964. xiv, 319 p.
64-021786 951.03
Lin, Tse-hsu, -- 1785-1850.   China -- History -- Opium War, 1840-1842.

DS757.5.C6 2002
Collis, Maurice,
Foreign mud: being an account of the opium imbroglio at Canton in the 1830's and the Anglo-Chinese war that followed/ by Maurice Collis. New York: New Directions, 2002. 318 p.
2001-055772 951/.033.221 0811215067
China -- History -- Opium War, 1840-1842.

DS757.5.F39
Fay, Peter Ward, 1924-
The Opium War, 1840-1842: barbarians in the Celestial Empire in the early part of the nineteenth century and the war by which they forced her gates ajar/ by Peter Ward Fay. Chapel Hill: University of North Carolina Press, [1975] xxi, 406 p.
74-030200 951/.03 0807812439
China -- History -- War of 1840-1842.

DS757.5.K8
Kuo, Pin-chia.
A critical study of the first Anglo-Chinese war, with documents, by P. C. Kuo. Shanghai, China, The Commercial press, limited, 1935. 315 p
35-024903 951
Opium trade. Great Britain -- Foreign relations -- Foreign relations -- China. China -- History -- Opium War, 1840-1842. China -- Foreign relations -- Foreign relations -- Great Britain.

DS757.5.T28
Tan, Chung, 1929-
China and the brave new world: a study of the origins of the Opium War (1840-42)/ Tan Chung. Durham, N.C.: Carolina Academic Press, c1978. viii, 271 p.
78-050590 951/.03 9890890862
Opium trade -- China.   China -- History -- War of 1840-1842.

DS757.5.W3 1968
Waley, Arthur.
The Opium War through Chinese eyes. Stanford, Calif., Stanford University Press [1968, c1958] 256 p.
68-012334 951/.03
China -- History -- War of 1840-1842.

DS757.55.P65 1991
Polachek, James M.
The inner Opium War/ James M. Polachek. Cambridge, Mass.: Council on East Asian Studies/Harvard University c1992. viii, 400 p.
91-030657 951/.033 0674454464
China -- History -- Opium War, 1840-1842. China -- Foreign relations.

DS758.23.H85.S64 1996
Spence, Jonathan D.
God's Chinese son: the Taiping Heavenly Kingdom of Hong Xiuquan/ Jonathan D. Spence. New York: W.W. Norton, c1996. xxvii, 400 p.
95-017245 951/.034/092 0393038440
Hung, Hsiu-chuan, -- 1814-1864.   China -- History -- Taiping Rebellion, 1850-1864.

DS758.7.C63
Clarke, Prescott.
Western reports on the Taiping: a selection of documents/ Prescott Clarke and J.S. Gregory. -- Honolulu: University Press of Hawaii, 1982. xxx, 454 p.
81-068942 951/.03 0824808096
China -- History -- Taiping Rebellion, 1850-1864 -- Sources.

DS759.B6 1972
Boardman, Eugene Powers.
Christian influence upon the ideology of the Taiping Rebellion, 1851-1864.   New York, Octagon Books, 1972 [c1952] xi, 188 p.
71-159168 951/.03 0374906971
Christians in China.   China -- History -- Taiping Rebellion, 1850-1864.

DS759.C377 1963
Cheng, James Chester, 1926-
Chinese sources for the Taiping Rebellion, 1850-1864. Pref. by William Lewisohn. [Hong Kong] Hong Kong University Press; 1963. xii, 182 p.
63-004982 951.03
China -- History -- Taiping Rebellion, 1850-1864.

DS759.H15
Hail, William James.
Tseng Kuo-fan and the Taiping Rebellion: with a short sketch of his later career/ by William James Hail. New Haven: Yale University Press; 1927. xvii, 422 p.
27-013143
Tseng, Kuo-fan, -- 1811-1872.   China -- History -- Taiping Rebellion, 1850-1864.

DS759.M48 1953
Meadows, Thomas Taylor.
The Chinese and their rebellions, viewed in connection with their national philosophy, ethics, legislation, and administration. To which is added, an essay on civilization and its present state in t Stanford, Calif., Academic Reprints [1953] lx, 656 p.
54-002175 951.037
Civilization.   China -- History -- Taiping Rebellion, 1850-1864. China -- Civilization.

DS759.M57
Michael, Franz H.
The Taiping Rebellion; history and documents, by Franz Michael, in collaboration with Chung-li Chang. [Translations by Margery Anneberg and others] Seattle, University of Washington Press, 1966-1971. 3 v.
66-013538 951.03 0295739592
China -- History -- Taiping Rebellion, 1850-1864.

DS759.S48
Shih, Yu-chung, 1902-
The Taiping ideology; its sources, interpretations, and influences, by Vincent Y. C. Shih. Seattle, University of Washington Press [1967] xix, 553 p.
66-019571 951/.03
China -- History -- Taiping Rebellion, 1850-1864.

DS759.T45
Teng, Ssu-yu, 1906-
New light on the history of the Taiping Rebellion. Cambridge, Harvard University Press, 1950. ii, 132 p.
50-002109 951.037
China -- History -- Taiping Rebellion, 1850-1864.

DS759.W455 1994
Weller, Robert P. 1953-
Resistance, chaos, and control in China: Taiping rebels, Taiwanese ghosts, and Tiananmen/ Robert P. Weller. Seattle: University of Washington Press, c1994. viii, 255 p.
93-020037 951/.035 0295972858
Ghosts -- Taiwan.   China -- History -- Tiananmen Square Incident, 1989. China -- History -- Taiping Rebellion, 1850-1864.

DS759.5.T43
Teng, Ssu-yu, 1906-
The Nien army and their guerrilla warfare, 1851-1868 [by] S. Y. Teng. Paris, Mouton, 1961. 254 p.
73-249839 951/.03
China -- History -- Nien Rebellion, 1853-1868.

DS760.B3
Banno, Masataka.
China and the West, 1858-1861: the origins of the Tsungli yamen. Cambridge, Harvard University Press, 1964. x, 367 p.
64-013419 327.51
China -- History -- Foreign intervention, 1857-1861.

DS760.W87 1998
Wong, J. Y.
Deadly dreams: opium, imperialism, and the Arrow War (1856-1860) in China/ J.Y. Wong. Cambridge [U.K.]; Cambridge University Press, 1998. xxx, 542 p.
95-017248 327.034 0521552559
China -- History -- Foreign intervention, 1857-1861 -- Causes. Great Britain -- Foreign relations -- China. China -- Foreign relations -- Great Britain.

DS760.9.T7.B3
Bales, William Leslie, 1893-
Tso Tsungt'ang, soldier and statesman of old China, by W. L. Bales. Shanghai [etc.] Kelly and Walsh, Limited, 1937. 3 p.
38-005016 923.551
Tso, Tsung-tang, -- 1812-1885.   China -- History -- Taiping Rebellion, 1850-1864. China -- History -- 1862-1899.

DS761.C3
Cameron, Meribeth Elliott, 1905-
The reform movement in China, 1898-1912, Stanford Univeristy, Calif., Stanford university press: 1931. 223 p.
31-032244
Tzu-hsi, -- Empress dowager of China, -- 1835-1908.   China -- Politics and government -- 1900-

DS761.P69 1972
Powell, Ralph L.
The rise of Chinese military power, 1895-1912, by Ralph L. Powell. Port Washington, N.Y., Kennikat Press [1972, c1955] x, 383 p.
76-159102 355/.00951 0804616450
China -- History, Military.

DS761.R47 1993
Reynolds, Douglas Robertson, 1944-
China, 1898-1912: the xinzheng revolution and Japan/ Douglas R. Reynolds. Cambridge, Mass.: Council on East Asian Studies, Harvard Universit c1993. xxi, 308 p.
92-041724 951/.035 0674116607
Education -- China -- History -- To 1912. China -- Relations -- Japan. Japan -- Relations -- China. China -- History -- 1861-1912.

DS761.2.P47 2002
Perry, Elizabeth J.
Challenging the mandate of Heaven: social protest and state power in China/ Elizabeth J. Perry. Armonk, N.Y.: M.E. Sharpe, c2002. xxxii, 343 p.
2001-034214 303.6/095.221 0765604450
Protest movements--China--History--19th century. Protest movements--China--History--20th century. Political culture--China--History--19th century.

DS761.2.R496 2000
Rhoads, Edward J. M.
Manchus & Han: ethnic relations and political power in late Qing and early republican China, 1861-1928/ Edward J.M. Rhoads. Seattle: University of Washington Press, c2000. x, 394 p.
00-008470 951/.035 0295979380
Manchus.   China -- Ethnic relations. China -- History -- 1861-1912. China -- History -- 1912-1928.

DS762.C6
Cohen, Paul A.
China and Christianity; the missionary movement and the growth of Chinese antiforeignism, 1860-1870. Cambridge, Harvard University Press, 1963. xiv, 392 p.
63-019135
Missions -- China.   China -- Foreign relations -- 1644-1912.

DS763.K3.H75
Hsiao, Kung-chuan, 1897-
A modern China and a new world: Kang Yu-wei, reformer and utopian, 1858-1927/ Kung-chuan Hsiao. Seattle: University of Washington Press, [1975] vii, 669 p.
74-028166 951/.035/092 0295953853
Kang, Yu-wei, -- 1858-1927.   China -- History -- Reform movement, 1898.

DS763.T8.H8
Hussey, Harry.
Venerable ancestor; the life and times of Tzu hsi, 1835-1908, Empress of China. Drawings by Shirley Wang. Garden City, N. Y., Doubleday, 1949. xix, 354 p.
49-011056
Tzu-hsi, -- Empress dowager of China, -- 1835-1908.

DS764.23.L52.T36 1996
Tang, Xiaobing, 1964-
Global space and the nationalist discourse of modernity: the historical thinking of Liang Qichao/ Xiaobing Tang. Stanford, Calif.: Stanford University Press, c1996. viii, 289 p.
95-018540 951/.035/092 0804725837
Liang, Chi-chao, -- 1873-1929 -- Contributions in historiography. Historiography.

DS765.L66 1994
Lone, Stewart.
Japan's first modern war: Army and society in the conflict with China, 1894-95/ Stewart Lone. Houndmills, Basingstoke, Hampshire: Macmillan Press; 1994. xi, 222 p.
94-016292 952.03/1 0312122772
Chinese-Japanese War, 1894-1895.   Japan -- Military relations -- East Asia. East Asia -- Military relations -- Japan. Japan -- Military relations -- East Asia.

DS768.R48 2002
Rethinking the 1898 reform period: political and cultural change in late Qing China/ edited by Rebecca E. Karl & Peter Zarrow. Cambridge, Mass.: Published by the Harvard University Asia Center: x, 273 p.
2001-051782   951/.035.221   0674008545
China -- History -- Reform movement, 1898.

DS771.F55 1959a
Fleming, Peter, 1907-1971.
The siege at Peking. New York, Harper [1959] 273 p.
59-010580   951.03
Beijing (China) -- History -- Siege, 1900.

DS771.P75 1989
Price, Eva Jane, 1855-1900.
China journal 1889-1900: an American missionary family during the Boxer Rebellion: with the letters and diaries of Eva Jane Price and her family/ foreword by Harrison E. Salisbury; introductory notes and annotations by Robert H. Felsing. New York: Scribner, c1989. xxiii, 289 p.
88-018483   951/.03
Price, Eva Jane, -- 1855-1900. Missions -- China. China -- History -- Boxer Rebellion, 1899-1901 -- Personal narratives, American.

DS771.T3
Tan, Chester C.
The Boxer catastrophe, by Chester C. Tan. New York, Columbia University Press, 1955. ix, 276 p.
55-007834   951.039
China -- History -- Boxer Rebellion, 1899-1901. Manchuria (China) -- History. China -- Foreign relations -- Soviet Union.

DS772.G54 1970
Giles, Lancelot, 1878-1934.
The siege of the Peking legations; a diary. Edited with introduction, Chinese anti-foreignism and the Boxer uprising, by L. R. Marchant. Foreword by Sir Robert Scott. [Nedlands, W.A.] University of Western Australia Press [1970] xxvii, 212 p.
78-123328   951/.03   0855640413
Giles, Lancelot, -- 1878-1934 -- Diaries. Beijing (China) -- History -- Siege, 1900 -- Personal narratives.

DS773.C5145
China in revolution: the first phase, 1900-1913. Edited and with an introd. by Mary Clabaugh Wright. New Haven, Yale University Press, 1968. xiii, 505 p.
68-027770   951/.03
China -- History -- Revolution, 1911-1912.

DS773.G35
Gasster, Michael, 1930-
Chinese intellectuals and the revolution of 1911; the birth of modern Chinese radicalism. Seattle, University of Washington Press [1969] xxix, 288 p.
66-019568   915.1/03
China -- History -- Revolution, 1911-1912.

DS773.M28
McAleavy, Henry.
A dream of Tartary: the origins and misfortunes of Henry Pu Yi/ by Henry McAleavy. London: G. Allen & Unwin, 1963. 292 p.
64-055659
Pu-i, -- 1906-1967. China -- History -- 20th century. Manchuria (China) -- History -- 1931-1945. China -- Kings and rulers -- Biography.

DS773.P7
Price, Don C.
Russia and the roots of the Chinese revolution, 1896-1911/ Don C. Price. Cambridge, Mass.: Harvard University Press, 1974. 303 p.
74-080443   951/.03   0674783204
China -- History -- Revolution, 1911-1912. Soviet Union -- Relations -- China. China -- Relations -- Soviet Union.

DS773.R4
Reid, John Gilbert,
The Manchu abdication and the powers, 1908-1912; an episode in pre-war diplomacy; a study of the role of foreign diplomacy during the reign of Hsuan-T'ung, by John Gilbert Reid. Berkeley, Calif., University of California Press, 1935. xiii, 497 p.
36-006448   951
Pu -- I, -- chief executive of Manchuria, -- 1906- China -- Foreign relations. China -- History -- Boxer Rebellion, 1899-1901.

DS774.H62 1989
Hoyt, Edwin Palmer.
The rise of the Chinese republic: from the last emperor to Deng Xiaoping/ Edwin P. Hoyt. New York: McGraw-Hill, c1989. x, 355 p.
88-013703   951.05   0070306192
China -- History -- 20th century.

DS774.I7 1961
Isaacs, Harold Robert, 1910-
The tragedy of the Chinese revolution. Stanford, Calif., Stanford University Press [1961] 392 p.
61-011101   951.042
Communism -- China. China -- History -- 1912-1937.

DS774.K6
Kotenev, Anatol M., 1882-
New lamps for old; an interpretation of events in modern China and whither they lead, by Anatol M. Kotenev. Shanghai, North-China Daily News and Herald, 1931. 371 p.
31-030817   951
China -- History -- Republic, 1912-1949.

DS774.L48
Linebarger, Paul Myron Anthony, 1913-1966.
The China of Chiang K'ai-shek/ a political study by Paul M. A. Linebarger. Boston: World Peace Foundation, 1941. xi, 449 p.
41-011374   951
Chiang, Kai-shek, -- 1887-1975. China -- Politics and government -- 1912-1949.

DS774.M35
MacNair, Harley Farnsworth, 1891-1947.
China in revolution: an analysis of politics and militarism under the republic/ by Harley Farnsworth MacNair. Chicago: University of Chicago Press, c1931. xi, 244 p.
31-028310   951
China -- Politics and government -- 1912-1949. China -- History -- Republic, 1912-1949.

DS774.S37
Schwartz, Benjamin Isadore, 1916-
Chinese communism and the rise of Mao. Cambridge, Harvard University Press, 1951. 258 p.
51-012067   951.04
Mao, Tse-tung, -- 1893-1976. Communism -- China. China -- History -- 20th century.

DS774.S54
Sheridan, James E.
China in disintegration: the Republican era in Chinese history, 1912-1949/ James E. Sheridan. New York: Free Press, [1975] xii, 338 p.
74-028940   951.04   0029286107
China -- History -- Republic, 1912-1949.

DS774.S59 1981
Spence, Jonathan D.
The Gate of Heavenly Peace: the Chinese and their revolution, 1895-1980/ Jonathan D. Spence. New York: Viking Press, 1981. xxii, 465 p.
81-065264   951   0670292478
China -- History -- 20th century. China -- History -- 1861-1912.

DS775.B513
Bianco, Lucien.
Origins of the Chinese revolution, 1915-1949. Translated from the French by Muriel Bell. Stanford, Calif., Stanford University Press [1971] xiii, 223 p.
75-150321   951.04   0804707464
China -- Politics and government -- 1912-1949.

DS775.C33
Chang, Chun-mai, 1886-1969.
The third force in China [by] Carsun Chang. New York, Bookman Associates [c1952] 345 p.
53-005815   951.05
Communism -- China. China -- Politics and government -- 1912-1949. China -- Politics and government -- 1949-

DS775.C5386 1960
Chou, Tse-tsung, 1916-
The May fourth movement: intellectual revolution in modern China. Cambridge, Harvard University Press, 1960. xv, 486 p.
60-010034   951.041
China -- History -- May Fourth movement, 1919. China -- History.

DS775.C53862
Chou, Tse-tsung, 1916-
Research guide to The May fourth movement; intellectual revolution in modern China, 1915-1924. Cambridge, Harvard University Press, 1963. xi, 297 p.
63-022745   951.041
China -- History -- May Fourth movement, 1919.

DS775.F5
Finney, Charles G. 1905-
The Old China Hands. Drawings by Arthur Shilstone. Garden City, N. Y., Doubleday, 1961. 258 p.
61-009506   951.04
China -- History -- 1912-1937.

DS775.L48
Linebarger, Paul Myron Anthony, 1913-1966.
Government in republican China, by Paul Myron Anthony Linebarger; foreword by Fritz Morstein Marx. New York, London, McGraw-Hill book company, inc., 1938. xv, 203 p.
38-025848   951
China -- Politics and government -- 1912-1928.

DS775.P67 1976
Powell, John Benjamin, 1888-1947.
My twenty-five years in China/ by John B. Powell. New York: Da Capo Press, 1976, c1945. 436 p.
76-027721   320.9/51/04   0306707616
Powell, John Benjamin, -- 1888-1947. Journalists -- China -- Biography. China -- Politics and government -- 1912-1949.

DS775.Q49 1962
Quigley, Harold Scott, 1889-
China's politics in perspective. Minneapolis:
University of Minnesota Press [1962] 266 p.
62-013606   951.04
China -- Politics and government -- 1900-1949.
China -- Politics and government -- 1949-

DS775.S72 1968   *have   order*
Snow, Edgar, 1905-1972.
Red star over China. New York, Grove Press
[1968] 543 p.
68-017724   951.04
Communism -- China.   China -- History --
Republic, 1912-1949.

DS775.S84
Stuart, John Leighton, 1876-1962.
My fifty years in China; the memoirs of John
Leighton Stuart, missionary and ambassador. New
York, Random House [1954] 346 p.
54-007808   951.04
China -- History -- Boxer Rebellion, 1899-
1901.

DS775.T442
Tewksbury, Donald George, 1894-
Source books on Far Eastern political ideologies.
New York: International Secretariat, Institute of
Pacific 1950- v.
53-024605   951.04
Korea -- History -- Sources.

DS775.T7 1966
Trotsky, Leon, 1879-1940.
Problems of the Chinese revolution. With
appendices by Zinoviev, Vuyovitch, Nassunov &
others. Translated with an introd. by Max
Shachtman. New York, Paragon Book Reprint
Corp., 1966. vi, 432 p.
66-017378   951.04
Communism -- China.   China -- Politics and
government -- 1912-1949.

DS775.Y3 1972
Yakhontoff, Victor A., 1881-
The Chinese soviets, by Victor A. Yakhontoff.
Westport, Conn., Greenwood Press [1972, c1934]
xiv, 296 p.
78-138195   320.9/51   0837152909
People's councils -- China. Communism -- China.
China -- Politics and government -- 1912-1949.

DS775.2.C47 1990
Chow, Rey.
Woman and Chinese modernity: the politics of
reading between West and East/ Rey Chow.
Minneapolis, MN: University of Minnesota Press,
c1991. xvii, 197 p.
90-011080   951.05   0816618704
Women -- China. Chinese literature -- 20th
century -- History and criticism.   China --
Civilization -- 20th century.

DS775.2.C4813 1983
One day in China, May 21, 1936/ translated,
edited, and introduced by Sherman Cochran and
Andrew C. K. Hsieh with Janis Cochran. New
Haven: Yale University Press, c1983. xxvi, 290 p.
82-048901   951.04/2   0300028342
China -- Social life and customs -- 1912-1949.

DS775.2.I58 2002
An intellectual history of modern China/ edited by
Merle Goldman, Leo Ou-fan Lee. New York:
Cambridge University Press, 2002. vii, 607 p.
2001-043168   951.05.221   0521797101
China -- Intellectual life -- 20th century.

DS775.4.D74 1995
Dreyer, Edward L.
China at war, 1901-1949/ Edward L. Dreyer.
London; Longman, 1995 x, 422 p.
94-032357   951.05   0582051258
China -- History, Military. China -- History --
20th century.

DS775.7.G74 2000
Gregor, A. James 1929-
A place in the sun: Marxism and Fascism in
China's long revolution/ A. James Gregor. Boulder,
CO: Westview Press, 2000. p. cm.
99-089499   320.951/09/04   0813337822
Revolutions -- China. Communism -- China.
Fascism -- China. China -- Politics and
government -- 20th century.

DS775.7.H67 1994
Hoston, Germaine A., 1954-
The State, identity, and the national question in
China and Japan/ Germaine A. Hoston. Princeton,
N.J.: Princeton University Press, c1994. xii, 628 p.
93-050669   951.04   0691078734
Communism -- China. Communism -- Japan.
Communism -- Asia. China -- Politics and
government -- 1912-1949. Japan -- Politics and
government -- 1926-1945.

DS775.7.R64 1992
Roads not taken: the struggle of opposition parties
in twentieth-century China/ edited by Roger B.
Jeans. Boulder: Westview Press, 1992. x, 385 p.
92-021651   320.951   0813386195
Political parties -- China -- History.   China --
Politics and government -- 20th century.

DS775.8.H86 1996
Hunt, Michael H.
The genesis of Chinese Communist foreign policy/
Michael H. Hunt. New York: Columbia University
Press, c1996. xiv, 343 p.
95-018885   327.51   0231103107
China -- Foreign relations -- History. China --
Foreign relations -- 1912-1949.

DS775.8.Z43 1991
Zhang, Yongjin.
China in the international system, 1918-20: the
Middle Kingdom at the periphery/ Zhang Yongjin.
New York: St. Martin's Press, 1991. xi, 262 p.
90-043360   327.51/009/041   031205341X
China -- Foreign relations -- 1912-1949.

DS776.6.F58 1996
Fitzgerald, John, 1951-
Awakening China: politics, culture, and class in the
Nationalist Revolution/ John Fitzgerald. Stanford,
Calif.: Stanford University Press, 1996. xi, 461 p.
96-000565   951.04   0804726590
Nationalism -- China -- History -- 20th century.
Intellectuals -- China -- History -- 20th century.
China -- History -- 1912-1928. China -- History --
1928-1937.

DS776.6.H37 2000
Harrison, Henrietta.
The making of the Republican citizen: political
ceremonies and symbols in China, 1911-1929/
Henrietta Harrison. Oxford; Oxford University
Press, 2000. viii, 270 p.
99-041111   951.04/1   0198295197
Political culture -- China -- History -- 20th
century.   China -- Politics and government --
1912-1928.

DS777.A25 1994
Sun, Yat-sen.
Prescriptions for saving China: selected writings of
Sun Yat-sen/ edited, with an introduction and notes
by Julie Lee Wei, Ramon H. Myers, Donald G.
Gillin; translated by Julie Lee Wei, E-su Zen,
Linda Chao. Stanford, Calif.: Hoover Institution
Press, c1994. xlv, 328 p.
93-048603   951.04/1.220   0817992820

DS777.A55 1974
Sun, Yat-sen, 1866-1925.
The triple demism of Sun Yat-sen. Translated from
the Chinese, annotated and appraised by Paschal
M. d'Elia. With introd. and index. [New York,
AMS Press, 1974] xxxvii, 747 p.
78-038069   320.5/092/4   0404569293

DS777.A55 1975   *have   1950*
Sun, Yat-sen, 1866-1925.
San min chu i = The three principles of the people/
by Sun Yat-sen; translated into English by Frank
W. Price; edited by L. T. Chen. New York: Da
Capo Press, 1975. xvii, 514 p.
75-001033   320.5/092/4   0306706989

DS777.A567.C416 1991
Chang, Hsu-Hsin.
All under heaven--: Sun Yat-sen and his
revolutionary thought/ Sidney H. Chang & Leonard
H.D. Gordon. Stanford, Calif.: Hoover Institution
Press, c1991. xvii, 253 p.
90-048071   951.04/1/092   081799081X
Sun, Yat-sen, -- 1866-1925. -- San min chu i.
China -- Politics and government -- 1912-1928.

DS777.B47 1998
Bergere, Marie-Claire.
Sun Yat-sen/ by Marie-Claire Bergere; translated
from the French by Janet Lloyd. Stanford, Calif.:
Stanford University Press, c1998. ix, 480 p.
97-035504   951.04/1/092   0804731705
Sun, Yat-sen, -- 1866-1925.   Presidents -- China --
Biography.

DS777.J3
Jansen, Marius B.
The Japanese and Sun Yat-sen. Cambridge,
Harvard University Press, 1954. viii, 274 p.
53-008021   951.041
Sun, Yat-sen, -- 1866-1925.   China -- Foreign
relations -- Japan. Japan -- Foreign relations --
China.

DS777.L4 1976   *have   1960*
Leng, Shao Chuan, 1921-
Sun Yat-sen and communism/ by Shao Chuan Leng
and Norman D. Palmer. Westport, Conn.:
Greenwood Press, 1976, c1960. viii, 234 p.
75-027683   951.04/1/0924   083718455X
Sun, Yat-sen, -- 1866-1925. Communism -- China.

DS777.L49 1936
Linebarger, Paul Myron Anthony, 1913-1966.
The political doctrines of Sun Yat-sen, an
exposition of the San min chu i ... by Paul Myron
Anthony Linebarger. Baltimore, The Johns
Hopkins press, 1937. xiv, 278 p.
37-018375   951
Sun, Yat-sen, -- 1866-1925. -- San min chu i.
Nationalism. World politics.   China -- Economic
conditions. China -- Foreign relations. China --
Politics and government.

DS777.L5 1969
Linebarger, Paul Myron Wentworth, 1871-1939.
Sun Yat Sen and the Chinese Republic. New York, AMS Press [1969] xviii, 371 p.
70-096469   951.04/1/0924
Sun, Yat-sen, -- 1866-1925.   China -- History -- 1912-1928.

DS777.S33
Schiffrin, Harold Z.
Sun Yat-sen, reluctant revolutionary/ by Harold Z. Schiffrin. Boston: Little, Brown, c1980. viii, 290 p.
80-016100   951.04/1/0924   0316773395
Sun, Yat-sen, -- 1866-1925.   Presidents -- China -- Biography.

DS777.S5 1968
Sharman, Lyon, 1872-1957.
Sun Yat-sen; his life and its meaning; a critical biography. Stanford, Calif., Stanford University Press [1968, c1934] xxi, 420 p.
68-017141   951.04/1/0924
Sun, Yat-sen, -- 1866-1925.   China -- History -- Revolution, 1911-1912. China -- History -- Republic, 1912-1949.

DS777.S8 1970
Sun, Yat-sen, 1866-1925.
Memoirs of a Chinese revolutionary, a programme of national reconstruction for China. by Sun-Yat-Sen, with a frontispiece portrait of the author. New York, AMS Press 1970. 254 p.
28-011331   951.04
China -- History -- Republic, 1912-1949.

DS777.15.C5.A4 1998
Chen, Tu-hsiu, 1879-1942.
Chen Duxiu's last articles and letters, 1937-1942/ edited and translated by Gregor Benton. Honolulu: University of Hawaii Press, 1998. x, 163 p.
98-023410   0824821122
Chen, Tu-hsiu, -- 1879-1942 -- Correspondence. Communists -- China -- Correspondence. Politicians -- China -- Correspondence.

DS777.15.C5.F44 1983
Feigon, Lee, 1945-
Chen Duxiu, founder of the Chinese Communist Party/ by Lee Feigon. Princeton, N.J.: Princeton University Press, c1983. xv, 279 p.
83-042556   324.251/075/0924   0691053936
Chen, Tu-hsiu, -- 1879-1942.   Communists -- China -- Biography. Politicians -- China -- Biography.

DS777.15.S53.S36 1995
Schoppa, R. Keith, 1943-
Blood road: the mystery of Shen Dingyi in revolutionary China/ R. Keith Schoppa. Berkeley: University of California Press, c1995. xii, 322 p.
94-022072   951.04/1/092   0520200152
Shen, Dingyi, -- dd. 1928.   Revolutionaries -- China -- Biography.   China -- History -- 1912-1928.

DS777.2.C48 1972
Chen, Jerome, 1919-
Yuan Shih-kai. Stanford, Calif., Stanford University Press, 1972. 258 p.
76-153815   951/.03/0924   0804707898
Yuan, Shih-kai, -- 1859-1916.

DS777.2.S85 1997
Sullivan, Lawrence R.
Historical dictionary of the People's Republic of China, 1949-1997/ Lawrence R. Sullivan, with the assistance of Nancy R. Hearst. Lanham, Md.: Scarecrow Press, 1997. xxxiv, 279 p.
97-015875   951.05/03   0810833492
China -- History -- 1949- -- Dictionaries.

DS777.2.Y68 1977
Young, Ernest P.
The presidency of Yuan Shih-kai: liberalism and dictatorship in early republican China/ Ernest P. Young. Ann Arbor: University of Michigan Press, c1977. viii, 347 p.
75-031057   951/.03/0924   0472089951
Yuan, Shih-kai, -- 1859-1916.   China -- History -- 1912-1937.

DS777.36.M33 1993
McCord, Edward Allen.
The power of the gun: the emergence of modern Chinese warlordism/ Edward A. McCord. Berkeley: University of California Press, c1993. ix, 436 p.
92-031375   951.04/1   0520081285
China -- History -- Warlord period, 1916-1928.

DS777.36.W34 1995
Waldron, Arthur.
From war to nationalism: China's turning point, 1924-1925/ Arthur Waldron. Cambridge; Cambridge University Press, 1995. xix, 366 p.
94-040940   951.04/1   0521472385
China -- History -- Warlord period, 1916-1928.

DS777.44.C5 1966
Chen, Kung-po, 1892-1946.
The Communist movement in China; an essay written in 1924. Edited with an introd. by C. Martin Wilbur. New York, Octagon Books, 1966 [c1960] vi, 138 p.
65-028873   951.041
Communism -- China.

DS777.45.C54
Chi, Hsi-sheng.
Warlord politics in China, 1916-1928/ Hsi-sheng Chi. Stanford, Calif.: Stanford University Press, 1976. 282 p.
75-007482   320.9/51/041   0804708940
China -- History -- Warlord period, 1916-1928.

DS777.45.S82 1953
Sun, Yat-sen, 1866-1925.
Fundamentals of national reconstruction.   Taipei] China Cutural Service [1953] vii, 266 p.
55-057070
China -- Politics and government.

DS777.47.C4273 1958
Chiang, Kai-shek, 1886-
Soviet Russia in China, a summing-up at seventy, by Chiang Chung-cheng (Chiang Kai-shek). Translated under the direction of Madam Chiang Kai-shek. New York, Farrar, Straus and Cudahy [1958] 432 p.
58-013798   951.042
Commumism -- China -- History   China -- Foreign relations -- Soviet Union. Soviet Union -- Foreign relations -- China.

DS777.47.C65 1991
Coble, Parks M., 1946-
Facing Japan: Chinese politics and Japanese imperialism, 1931-1937/ Parks M. Coble. Cambridge, Mass.: Council on East Asian Studies, Harvard Universit c1991. xi, 492 p.
91-021271   327.51052   0674775309
China -- Politics and government -- 1928-1937. China -- Foreign relations -- Japan. Japan -- Foreign relations -- China.

DS777.47.E24
Eastman, Lloyd E.
The abortive revolution: China under Nationalist rule, 1927-1937/ Lloyd E. Eastman. Cambridge, Mass.: Harvard University Press, 1974. xvii, 398 p.
74-075639   320.9/51/042   0674001753
China -- Politics and government -- 1928-1937.

DS777.47.S493 1989
Single sparks: China's rural revolutions/ Kathleen Hartford, Steven M. Goldstein, editors. Armonk, N.Y.: M.E. Sharpe, c1989. xi, 216 p.
87-004823   951   0873324277
Communism -- China -- History.   China -- History -- 1928-1937. China -- History -- 1937-1945. China -- History -- Civil War, 1945-1949.

DS777.47.W5
White, Theodore Harold, 1915-
Thunder out of China [by] Theodore H. White and Annalee Jacoby. New York, William Sloane Associates [1946] xvi, 331 p.
46-011919   951.042
World War, 1939-1945 -- China. Reconstruction (1939-1951) -- China. China -- History -- 1937-1945.

DS777.47.W56
Wilbur, C. Martin 1908-
Documents on communism, nationalism, and Soviet advisers in China, 1918-1927; papers seized in the 1927 Peking raid. Edited, with introductory essays, by C. Martin Wilbur and Julie Lien-ying How. New York, Columbia University Press, 1956. xviii, 617 p.
56-006813   951.041
Communism -- China. China -- History -- 1912-1928 -- Sources. Soviet Union -- Foreign relations -- China. China -- Foreign relations -- Soviet Union.

DS777.488.T45.K83 1997
Kwan, Daniel Y. K.
Marxist intellectuals and the Chinese labor movement: a study of Deng Zhongxia (1894-1933)/ Daniel Y.K. Kwan. Seattle: University of Washington Press, c1997. xiv, 309 p.
96-027538   322/.2/092   0295976012
Teng, Chung-hsia, -- 1894-1933.   Communists -- China -- Biography. Labor movement -- China. General Strike, Guangzhou, China, 1925.

DS777.5.C45 1948a
Chiang, Wen-han, 1908-
The ideological background of the Chinese student movement. New York, King's Crown Press, 1948. x, 176 p.
49-003831   951.04
Students -- China.   China -- History -- Republic, 1912-1949.

DS777.5134.Y36 1990
Yang, Benjamin.
From revolution to politics: Chinese communists on the long march/ Benjamin Yang. Boulder: Westview Press, 1990. xiv, 338 p.
89-049475   951.04/2   0813376726
Communism -- China -- History.   China -- History -- Long March, 1934-1935.

DS777.53.A8 1939a
Auden, W. H. 1907-1973.
Journey to a war, by W. H. Auden & Christopher Isherwood. New York, Random House [c1939] 3 p.
39-020272
China -- Description and travel. China -- History -- 1937-1945.

DS777.53.B3
Band, Claire.
Two years with the Chinese Communists, by Claire and William Band. New Haven, Yale Univ.Press, 1948. xii, 347 p.
48-005830
Communism -- China. World War, 1939-1945 -- Personal narratives, British. China -- History -- 1937-1949.

DS777.53.B32 1963
Barnett, A. Doak.
China on the eve of Communist takeover. New York, Praeger [1963] 371 p.
63-010824 354.51
China -- Politics and government -- 1937-1949. China -- Social conditions. China -- Economic conditions -- 1912-1949.

DS777.53.B38 1970
Belden, Jack, 1910-
China shakes the world. New York [Monthly Review Press, 1970] xvii, 524 p.
77-105312 951.04/2
Communism -- China. China -- Politics and government -- 1945-1949.

DS777.53.B5
Bisson, T. A. 1900-1979.
Japan in China/ by T.A. Bisson. New York: Macmillan, 1938. 417 p.
38-027434 951
China -- History -- 1937-1945. China -- Politics and government -- 1912-1949. Japan -- Politics and government.

DS777.53.B65
Boyle, John Hunter.
China and Japan at war, 1937-1945; the politics of collaboration. Stanford, Calif., Stanford University Press, 1972. ix, 430 p.
76-183886 952.03/3 0804708002
Sino-Japanese Conflict, 1937-1945 -- Collaborationists. Communism -- China.

DS777.53.C4235
Chiang, Kai-shek, 1887-1975.
The collected wartime messages of Generalissimo Chiang Kai-shek, 1937-1945, compiled by Chinese Ministry of Information. New York, The John Day company [1946] 2 v.
46-007008 951.0425
Sino-Japanese Conflict -- 1937-1945.

DS777.53.J58
Johnson, Chalmers A.
Peasant nationalism and communist power; the emergence of revolutionary China. Stanford, Calif.: Stanford University Press, 1962. xii, 256 p.
62-016949 951.042
Nationalism -- China. Communism -- China. Peasantry -- China.

DS777.53.L4634
Li, Lincoln.
The Japanese Army in North China, 1937-1941: problems of political and economic control/ Lincoln Li. Tokyo; Oxford University Press, 1975. 278 p.
76-366647 951.04/2 0195802691
Sino-Japanese Conflict, 1937-1945. China -- History -- 1937-1945.

DS777.53.L484
Liao, Kai-lung.
From Yenan to Peking; the Chinese People's War of Liberation, from reconstruction to first five-year plan. Peking, Foreign Languages Press, 1954. 187 p.
55-028352 951.042
China -- History -- 1945-

DS777.53.L573
Lindsay, Michael, 1909-
The unknown war: North China 1937-1945/ Michael Lindsay. London: Bergstrom & Boyle Books, 1975. 112 p.
76-367218 951.04/2 0903767058
Sino-Japanese Conflict, 1937-1945 -- Underground movements. Sino-Japanese Conflict, 1937-1945 -- China, Northwest.

DS777.53.P37
Peck, Graham, 1914-
Two kinds of time; illustrated by the author. Boston, Houghton Mifflin 1950. 725 p.
50-010600
World War, 1939-1945 -- China. China -- Description and travel.

DS777.53.R58 1945
Rosinger, Lawrence Kaelter, 1915-
China's wartime politics, 1937-1944, Princeton, Princeton university press, 1945. viii p.
45-010186
World War, 1939-1945 -- China. China -- History -- 1937- China -- Politics and government -- 1912-

DS777.53.S38 1959
Scott, Robert Lee, 1908-
Flying Tiger: Chennault of China.   Doubleday, 1959. 285 p.
59-007000 358.4/13/320924
Chennault, Claire Lee, -- 1890-1958. World War, 1939-1945 -- Aerial operations, Chinese. Generals -- United States -- Biography.

DS777.53.S5
Smedley, Agnes, 1892-1950.
China fights back, an American woman with the Eighth route army, by Agnes Smedley. New York, The Vanguard press [c1938] xxii, 282 p.
38-027564 951
Communism -- China. China -- History -- Republic, 1912-1949.

DS777.53.T39
Taylor, George Edward, 1905-
Struggle for north China.   International Secretariat, Institute of Pacific 1940. 250 p.
41-051528 951
China -- History -- 1937-1945. China -- Politics and government Japanese -- China.

DS777.53.T866
Tsou, Tang, 1918-
America's failure in China, 1941-50. [Chicago] University of Chicago Press [1963] 614 p.
63-013072 327.73051
China -- Politics and government -- 1937-1945. China -- Politics and government -- 1945-1949. United States -- Foreign relations -- China.

DS777.53.Y62
Young, Arthur N. 1890-
China's wartime finance and inflation, 1937-1945 [by] Arthur N. Young. Cambridge, Harvard University Press, 1965. xviii, 421 p.
65-022049 336.51
Inflation (Finance) -- China. Sino-Japanese Conflict, 1937-1945.

DS777.5316.N36 H6613 1999
Honda, Katsuichi,
The Nanjing massacre: a Japanese journalist confronts Japan's national shame/ Honda Katsuichi; edited by Frank Gibney; translated by Karen Sandness Armonk, N.Y.: M.E. Sharpe, c1999. xxvii, 367 p.
98-040563 951.04/2.221 0765603357
Sino-Japanese Conflict, 1937-1945--Atrocities. Atrocities--China--Nanjing (Jiangsu Sheng)

DS777.533.B55 H37 2002
Harris, Sheldon H.
Factories of death: Japanese biological warfare, 1932-1945, and American cover-up/ Sheldon H. Harris.Rev. ed. New York: Routledge, 2002. p. cm.
2001-045729 940.54/25.221 0415932149
Sino-Japanese Conflict, 1937-1945--Biological warfare--China

DS777.533.P825.U65 1987
MacKinnon, Stephen R.
China reporting: an oral history of American journalism in the 1930's and 1940's/ Stephen R. MacKinnon and Oris Friesen. Berkeley: University of California Press, c1987. xxx, 230 p.
86-019193 940.53 0520058437
Sino-Japanese Conflict, 1937-1945 -- Foreign public opinion, American. Foreign correspondents -- United States. Foreign correspondents -- China. China -- History -- Civil War, 1945-1949 -- Foreign public opinion, American.

DS777.533.S62.N67 2000
North China at war: the social ecology of revolution, 1937-1945/ edited by Feng Chongyi and David S. G. Goodman. Lanham, MD: Rowman & Littlefield Publishers, 2000. p. cm.
99-089422 940.53/1/09511 0847699382
Sino-Japanese Conflict, 1937-1945 -- Social aspects -- China. Social ecology -- China -- History -- 20th century. Communism -- China -- History -- 20th century.

DS777.5366.C4644.A3 1994
Chen, Li-fu, 1900-
The storm clouds clear over China: the memoir of Chen Li-fu, 1900-1993/ edited and compiled, with an introduction and notes by Sidney H. Chang and Ramon H. Myers. [Stanford, Calif.]: Hoover Press, c1994. xxvii, 359 p.
93-023214 951.05/092 0817992715
Chen, Li-fu, -- 1900- Statesmen -- China -- Biography. Statesmen -- Taiwan -- Biography.

DS777.542.Y53 1995
Yick, Joseph K. S., 1953-
Making urban revolution in China: the CCP-GMD struggle for Beiping-Tianjin, 1945-1949/ Joseph K.S. Yick. Armonk, N.Y.: M.E. Sharpe, c1995. xxv, 233 p.
95-005921   951.04/2   1563246058
China -- History -- Civil war, 1945-1949. Beijing (China) -- History. Tianjin (China) -- History.

DS777.547.C47 1986
Chinese politics: documents and analysis/ edited by James T. Myers, Jurgen Domes, Erik von Groeling. Columbia, S.C.: University of South Carolina Press, c1986-c1995 v. 1-4
85-022466   951.05   0872494756
China -- Politics and government -- 1949- -- Sources.

DS777.55.B29
Barnett, A. Doak.
China after Mao, with selected documents, by A. Doak Barnett. Princeton, N.J., Princeton University Press, 1967. 287 p.
67-014406   320.9/51
Mao, Tse-tung, -- 1893-1976.   China (People's Republic of China, 1949-   ) -- Politics and government.

DS777.55.B3
Barnett, A. Doak.
Communist China and Asia; challenge to American policy. New York] Published for the Council on Foreign Relations b 1960. 575 p.
60-005956   951.05
China. China -- Foreign relations -- 1949-1976.

DS777.55.B322
Barnett, A. Doak.
Communist China: the early years, 1949-55 [by] A. Doak Barnett. New York, F. A. Praeger [1964] xiv, 336 p.
64-022487   951.05
China -- History -- 1949-1976.

DS777.55.B346
Baum, Richard, 1940-
China in ferment; perspectives on the cultural revolution. Edited by Richard Baum, with Louise B. Bennett. Englewood Cliffs, N.J., Prentice-Hall [1971] viii, 246 p.
70-153433   951.05   0131326880
China -- History -- Cultural Revolution, 1966-1969.

DS777.55.B55
Bloodworth, Dennis.
The Chinese looking glass. New York, Farrar, Straus and Giroux [1967] xii, 432 p.
67-022047   915.1/03/5
China.

DS777.55.B6
Bodde, Derk, 1909-
Peking diary, a year of revolution. New York, Schuman [1950] xxi, 292 p.
50-010426   951.156
Communism -- China.   Peking (China) -- History. China -- Description and travel.

DS777.55.C34
Chandrasekhar, Sripati, 1917-
Red China; an Asian view. New York, Praeger [1963, c1961] 230 p.
61-009880   951.05
Communism -- China.   China -- Social conditions. Asia -- Politics and government.

DS777.55.C395
Chen, Theodore Hsi-en, 1902-
Thought reform of the Chinese intellectuals, by Theodore H. E. Chen. [Hong Kong] Hong Kong University Press, 1960. 247 p.
60-004137   951.05
Thought and thinking.   China -- Intellectual life.

DS777.55.C44684
China in crisis. Edited by Ping-ti Ho and Tang Tsou. With a foreword by Charles U. Daly. [Chicago] University of Chicago Press [1968- v.
68-020981   915.1/03
China.

DS777.55.C4573 1960
Chou, Ching-wen, 1909-
Ten years of storm; the true story of the Communist regime in China, by Chow Ching-wen. Foreword by Lin Yutang. Translated and edited by Lai MIng. New York, Holt, Rinehart and Winston [1960] xxii, 323 p.
60-012858   951.05
China.

DS777.55.C642
Communist China 1955-1959; policy documents with analysis. Prepared at Harvard University under the joint auspices of the Center for International Affairs and the East Asian Research Center. With a foreword by Robert R. Bowie and John K. Fairbank. Cambridge, Harvard University Press, 1962. xi, 611 p.
62-011394   951.05
China -- History -- 1949-1976 -- Sources.

DS777.55.C645
Communist China yearbook. Hong Kong: China Research Associates, c1963- v.
63-005429   951
China -- Periodicals.

DS777.55.C78
The cultural revolution in the provinces. Cambridge, Mass., East Asian Research Center, Harvard University; 1971. vii, 216 p.
77-162858   951.05   0674179854
China -- History -- Cultural Revolution, 1966-1969.

DS777.55.D52 1986
Dietrich, Craig.
People's China: a brief history/ Craig Dietrich. New York: Oxford University Press, 1986. xv, 327 p.
85-015217   951.05   0195036883
China -- History -- 1949-

DS777.55.E813
Esmein, Jean, 1923-
The Chinese cultural revolution. Translated from the French by W. J. F. Jenner. Garden City, N.Y., Anchor Press, 1973. xiv, 346 p.
73-079206   320.9/51/05   0385050984
China -- Politics and government -- 1949-1976.

DS777.55.F373
Faure, Edgar.
The serpent and the tortoise; problems of the new China. Translated by Lovett F. Edwards. New York, St. Martin's Press, 1958. 205 p.
58-004200   951.042
China.

DS777.55.G67
Goldman, Merle.
Literary dissent in Communist China. Cambridge, Harvard University Press, 1967. xvii, 343 p.
67-017311   895/.109005
China -- Intellectual life.

DS777.55.G686 1968
The Great cultural revolution in China, compiled and edited by the Asia Research Centre. Rutland, Vt., C. E. Tuttle Co. [1968] 507 p.
68-015016   951.05
China -- Intellectual life.

DS777.55.G823
Guillain, Robert, 1908-
600 million Chinese. Translated by Mervyn Savill. New York, Criterion Books [1957] 310 p.
57-008260   *951.05
Communism -- China.   China -- Social conditions.

DS777.55.H553
Hinton, William.
Turning point in China; an essay on the cultural revolution. New York [Monthly Review Press, 1972] 112 p.
76-178715   320.9/51/05   0853452091
China -- Politics and government -- 1949-1976.

DS777.55.H83
Hunter, Neale.
Shanghai journal; an eyewitness account of the cultural revolution. New York, Praeger [1969] v, 311 p.
71-076954   951/.05
Shanghai (China) -- Politics and government.

DS777.55.K32413 1974
Karol, K. S.
The second Chinese revolution [by] K. S. Karol. Translated from the French by Mervyn Jones. New York, Hill and Wang [1974] 472 p.
73-091174   320.9/51/05   080908516X
China -- Politics and government -- 1949-1976.

DS777.55.K75
Kuo, Pin-chia.
China: new age and new outlook, by Ping-chia Kuo. New York, Knopf, 1956. xi, 231 p.
56-005605   951.05
China -- Politics and government -- 1949- China -- Foreign relations -- 1949- China -- Economic policy.

DS777.55.L457
Lifton, Robert Jay, 1926-
Revolutionary immortality; Mao Tse-tung and the Chinese cultural revolution. New York, Random House [1968] xviii, 178 p.
68-028545   320.9/51
Mao, Tse-tung, -- 1893-1976.   China -- Politics and government -- 1949-1976.

DS777.55.L46
Lindsay, Michael, 1909-
China and the cold war; a study in international politics. [Carlton] Melbourne University Press [1955] 286 p.
55-001680   327.51
Communism -- China.   China -- Foreign relations -- 1949-

DS777.55.M455 1986
Meisner, Maurice J., 1931-
Mao's China and after: a history of the People's Republic/ Maurice Meisner. New York: Free Press; c1986. xx, 534 p.
86-004480   951.05   002920870X
China -- History -- 1949-

DS777.55.M6
Moraes, F. R.
Report on Mao's China. New York, Macmillan, 1953. 212 p.
53-009391   951.05
Communism -- China.   China -- Politics and government -- 1949-

DS777.55.M913
Myrdal, Jan.
Report from a Chinese village. Illustrated and with photos. by Gun Kessle. Translated from the Swedish by Maurice Michael. New York, Pantheon Books [1965] xxxiv, 373 p.
64-018346   309.151
China -- Social life and customs. Liu-lin (China)

DS777.55.P3
Panikkar, K. M. 1896-1963.
In two Chinas, memoirs of a diplomat. London, G. Allen & Unwin [1955] 183 p.
55-004527
China -- History -- 1945-

DS777.55.P4243
The People's Republic of China, 1949-1979: a documentary survey/ Harold C. Hinton, editor. Wilmington, Del.: Scholarly Resources, 1980. 5 v.
80-005228   951.05   0842021663
China -- History -- 1949-1976 -- Sources. China -- History -- 1976- -- Sources.

DS777.55.S35 1968
Schurmann, Franz, 1924-
Ideology and organization in Communist China [by] Franz Schurmann. Berkeley, University of California Press, 1968. lii, 642 p.
68-026124   335.43/4/0951
China -- Politics and government -- 1949-1976.

DS777.55.S455
Shabad, Theodore.
China's changing map; a political and economic geography of the Chinese People's Republic. Maps by Vaughn S. Gray. New York, F. A. Praeger [c1956] x, 295 p.
55-011530   330.9
Physical geography -- China.   China -- Economic conditions -- 1949- China -- Politics and government -- 1949-1976.

DS777.55.S455 1972
Shabad, Theodore.
China's changing map; national and regional development, 1949-71. New York, Praeger [1972] xiii, 370 p.
71-178868   330.951/05
Physical geography -- China.   China -- Economic conditions -- 1949-1976.   China -- Politics and government -- 1949-1976.

DS777.55.S6
Snow, Edgar, 1905-1972.
The other side of the river, Red China today. New York, Random House [1962] 810 p.
61-006243   951.05
China.

DS777.55.S6 1971
Snow, Edgar, 1905-1972.
Red China today.   New York, Random House [1971] 749 p.
73-102336   915.1/03/5   0394462610
China.

DS777.55.T25
Tang, Sheng-hao.
Communist China today; domestic and foreign policies. New York, F. A. Praeger [1957] xvi, 536 p.
57-005411   951.05*
*China -- Politics and government -- 1949-
China -- Foreign relations -- 1949-*

DS777.55.T4166 1992
Terrill, Ross.
China in our time: the epic saga of the People's Republic from the Communist victory to Tiananmen Square and beyond/ Ross Terrill. New York: Simon & Schuster, c1992. 366 p.
92-007699   951.05   067168096X
China -- History -- 1949-

DS777.55.T45
Thomas, S. Bernard, 1921-
Government and administration in Communist China.   New York, International Secretariat, Institute of Pacific 1953. iii, 150 p.
53-013464   *951.05
Communism -- China.   China -- Politics and government -- 1949-

DS777.55.T73 1968
Tsang, Chiu-sam, 1901-
Society, schools & progress in China.   Oxford, Pergamon Press [1968] xx, 333 p.
68-021109   370/.951   0080128440
Education -- China -- History -- 1949-1976. China.

DS777.55.V36
Van Slyke, Lyman P.
Enemies and friends; the united front in Chinese Communist history [by] Lyman P. Van Slyke. Stanford, Calif., Stanford University Press, 1967. viii, 330 p.
67-026531   951.05
Communism -- China.   China.

DS777.55.W34
Walker, Richard Louis, 1922-
China under communism, the first five years. New Haven, Yale University Press, 1955. xv, 403 p.
55-006422   951.05
Communism -- China.   China -- History -- 1945-

DS777.57.H6
Hou, Fu-wu.
To change a nation; propaganda and indoctrinatiion in Communist China, by Franklin W. Houn. New York, Free Press of Glencoe [c1961] 250 p.
61-062518
Propaganda, Chinese.

DS777.57.M3
MacFarquhar, Roderick.
The hundred flowers campaign and the Chinese intellectuals. With an epilogue by G. F. Hudson. New York, Praeger [1960] 324 p.
60-010877   951.05
Communist self-criticism.   China -- Politics and government -- 1949-

DS777.57.R5
Rickett, W. Allyn, 1921-
Prisoners of liberation [by] Allyn and Adele Rickett. New York, Cameron Associates, 1957. xiii, 288 p.
57-013896   951.05
Criminal justice, Administration of -- China. Communism -- China. China -- History -- 1945-

DS777.57.Y78
Yu, Frederick T. C., 1921-
Mass persuasion in Communist China [by] Frederick T.C. Yu. New York, Praeger [1964] viii, 186 p.
64-013389   301.15230951
Propaganda, Chinese. Public opinion -- China.

DS777.6.C46 1987
China's intellectuals and the state: in search of a new relationship/ edited by Merle Goldman with Timothy Cheek and Carol Lee Hamrin. Cambridge, Mass.: Council on East Asian Studies, Harvard Universit 1987. xv, 374 p.
87-000177   001.1/0951   067411972X
China -- Intellectual life -- 1949- China -- Politics and government -- 1949-

DS777.6.G64
Goldman, Merle.
China's intellectuals: advise and dissent/ Merle Goldman. Cambridge, Mass.: Harvard University Press, 1981. 276 p.
81-002945   951.05   0674119703
China -- Intellectual life -- 1949-

DS777.75.B78 1981
Brugger, Bill.
China, radicalism to revisionism, 1962-1979/ Bill Brugger. London: Croom Helm; 1981. 275 p.
81-102749   951.05/6   0389200875
China -- Politics and government -- 1949-

DS777.75.C66 1991
Contemporary Chinese politics in historical perspective/ edited by Brantly Womack. Cambridge [England]; Cambridge University Press, 1991. xiv, 334 p.
91-013687   951.05   0521410991
China -- Politics and government -- 1949-

DS777.75.D57 1987
Dittmer, Lowell.
China's continuous revolution: the post-liberation epoch, 1949-1981/ Lowell Dittmer. Berkeley: University of California Press, c1987. xv, 320 p.
86-001330   951.05   0520056566
China -- Politics and government -- 1949-

DS777.75.L557 1995
Lieberthal, Kenneth.
Governing China: from revolution through reform/ Kenneth Lieberthal. New York: W.W. Norton, c1995. xxii, 498 p.
94-040257   951.05   039396714X
China -- Politics and government -- 1949- China -- History -- 20th century.

DS777.75.M32 1974
MacFarquhar, Roderick.
The origins of the Cultural Revolution. New York, Published for the Royal Institute of Internation 1974-1997. 3 v.
73-015794   951.05   0231038410
China -- Politics and government -- 1949-1976. China -- History -- 1949-1976. China -- History -- Cultural Revolution, 1966-1969.

DS777.75.P64 1997
The Politics of China: the eras of Mao and Deng/
edited by Roderick MacFarquhar. New York:
Cambridge University Press, 1997. x, 608 p.
96-036090 320.951 0521581419
China -- Politics and government -- 1949-

DS777.75.T43 1999
Teiwes, Frederick C.
China's road to disaster: Mao, central politicians,
and provincial leaders in the unfolding of the great
leap forward, 1955-1959/ Frederick C. Teiwes with
Warren Sun. Armonk, N.Y.: M.E. Sharpe, c1999.
xxvii, 319 p.
98-015299 951.05/5 0765602016
China -- Politics and government -- 1949-1976.

DS777.75.T442 1990
Teiwes, Frederick C.
Politics at Mao's court: Gao Gang and party
factionalism in the early 1950s/ Frederick C.
Teiwes. Armonk, N.Y.: M.E. Sharpe, c1990. xvi,
326 p.
90-035927 951.05/5 0873325907
*Kao, Kang. China -- Politics and government --
1949-1976.*

DS777.75.W54 1995
Wild lily, prairie fire: China's road to democracy,
Yan'an to Tian'anmen, 1942-1989/ edited by
Gregor Benton and Alan Hunter. Princeton, N.J.:
Princeton University Press, c1995. x, 361 p.
95-005200 951.05 0691043590
*Dissenters -- China -- Sources. China -- Politics
and government -- 1949- -- Sources.*

DS777.8.Z388 2000
Zhai, Qiang.
China and the Vietnam wars, 1950-1975/ Qiang
Zhai. Chapel Hill: University of North Carolina
Press, 2000. 304 p.
99-016884 959.704 0807825328
*Vietnamese conflict, 1961-1975. Vietnam
(Democratic Republic) -- Foreign relations --
China. China -- Foreign relations -- 1949-1976.
China -- Foreign relations -- Vietnam (Democratic
Republic)*

DS777.8.Z39 1998
Zhang, Yongjin.
China in international society since 1949:
alienation and beyond/ Yongjin Zhang. Oxford: St.
Anthony's College; 1998. viii, 345 p.
98-017293 327.51 0312215401
China -- Foreign relations -- 1949-

DS778.A1B32 1997
Bartke, Wolfgang.
Who was who in the People's Republic of China/
by Wolfgang Bartke. München: K.G. Saur, 1997. 2
v.
98-112370 920.051.221 3598113315
*China -- History -- 1949- -- Biography --
Dictionaries. China -- Biography -- Dictionaries.*

DS778.A1.B5
Biographical dictionary of Republican China.
Howard L. Boorman, editor; Richard C. Howard,
associate editor. New York, Columbia University
Press, 1967-79. 5 v.
67-012006 920/.051 0231089570
*China -- History -- Republic, 1912-1949 --
Biography -- Dictionaries. China -- Biography --
Dictionaries.*

DS778.A1.B6
Boorman, Howard L
Men and politics in modern China: preliminary ...
biographies. New York, Columbia University,
1960- v.
60-001816 920.051
China -- Biography.

DS778.A1.E4
Elegant, Robert S.
China's Red masters; political biographies of the
Chinese Communist leaders. New York, Twayne
Publishers [1951] 264 p.
51-010445 951.042
China -- Biography.

DS778.A1.H3 1943
Hahn, Emily, 1905-
The Soong sisters, [by] Emily Hahn. New York,
Doubleday, Doran & co., inc., 1943. 8 p, . 349 p.
43-003571 920.7
*Kung, Al-ling (Sung) -- 1888- Sung, Ching-ling, --
1893-1981. Chiang, Mei-ling (Sung) -- 1892-*

DS778.A1.K55 1971
Klein, Donald W.
Biographic dictionary of Chinese communism,
1921-1965 [by] Donald W. Klein [and] Anne B.
Clark. Cambridge, Mass., Harvard University
Press, 1971. 2 v.
69-012725 951.04/922 0674074106
*Communists -- China -- Biography --
Dictionaries. China -- Biography -- Dictionaries.*

DS778.A1.S499
Wales, Nym, 1907-
The Chinese Communists: sketches and
autobiographies of the Old Guard. Book 1: Red
dust. Book 2: Autobiographical profiles and
biographical sketches. Introd. to book 1 by Robert
Carver North. Westport, Conn., Greenwood Pub.
Co. [1972] xxi, 398 p.
77-104236 335.43/4 0837163218
Communists -- China. China -- Biography.

DS778.A2.C467 1996
Shao, Kuo-kang.
Zhou Enlai and the foundations of Chinese foreign
policy/ Kuo-kang Shao. New York: St. Martin's
Press, 1996. xii, 370 p.
96-036088 0312158920
*Chou, En-lai, -- 1898-1976. China -- Foreign
relations -- 1949-1976.*

DS778.C4966.S38 1992
Schwarcz, Vera, 1947-
Time for telling truth is running out: conversations
with Zhang Shenfu/ Vera Schwarcz. New Haven:
Yale University Press, c1992. xii, 256 p.
91-000817 951.05/092 0300050097
*Chang, Shen-fu, -- 1893- Communists -- China --
Biography.*

DS778.C5.M3
McCormack, Gavan.
Chang Tso-lin in northeast China, 1911-1928:
China, Japan, and the Manchurian idea/ Gavan
McCormack. Stanford, Calif.: Stanford University
Press, 1977. vi, 334 p.
76-048028 951.04/1/0924 0804709459
*Chang, Tso-lin, -- 1875-1928. Generals -- China -
- Biography. Japanese in Manchuria. Manchoukuo
-- History.*

DS778.C5374.W57
Witke, Roxane.
Comrade Chiang Ching/ Roxane Witke. Boston:
Little, Brown, c1977. xxvi, 549 p.
77-000935 951.05/092/4 0316949000
*Chiang, Ching, -- 1910- Statesmen -- China --
Biography. Women -- China -- Biography. China -
- Biography. China -- History -- 20th century.*

DS778.C55.C7
Crozier, Brian.
The man who lost China: the first full biography of
Chiang Kai-shek/ by Brian Crozier, with the
collaboration of Eric Chou. New York: Scribner,
c1976. xv, 430 p.
76-010246 951.04/2/0924 068414686X
Chiang, Kai-shek, -- 1887-1975.

DS778.C593.L44 1994
Lee, Chae-Jin, 1936-
Zhou Enlai: the early years/ Chae-Jin Lee.
Stanford, Calif.: Stanford University Press, 1994
viii, 241 p.
93-033525 951.05/092 0804723028
*Chou, En-lai, -- 1898-1976 -- Childhood and
youth. Prime ministers -- China -- Biography.*

DS778.C593.W54 1984
Wilson, Dick, 1928-
Zhou Enlai: a biography/ Dick Wilson. New York,
N.Y.: Viking, 1984. 349 p.
83-047928 951.05/092/4 0670220116
*Chou, En-lai, -- 1898-1976. Prime ministers --
China -- Biography.*

DS778.C6.S5
Smedley, Agnes, 1890-1950.
The great road; the life and times of Chu Teh.
New York, Monthly Review Press, 1956. 461 p.
56-011272 923.551
*Chu, Te, -- 1886-1976. Communism -- China --
History. Communism -- China. China (People's
Republic of China, 1949-) -- History.*

DS778.D34.B45
Bennett, Gordon A.
Red Guard; the political biography of Dai Hsiao-ai,
by Gordon A. Bennett and Ronald N. Montaperto.
Garden City, N.Y., Doubleday, 1971. xx, 267 p.
70-116236 951.05/0924
Dai, Hsiao-ai.

DS778.H85.H7
Hsueh, Chun-tu, 1922-
Huang Hsing and the Chinese revolution.
Stanford, Calif., Stanford University Press, 1961.
260 p.
61-006531 951.03
*Huang, Hsing, -- 1874-1916. China -- History --
Revolution, 1911-1912.*

DS778.H89.A3
Hussey, Harry.
My pleasures and palaces; an informal memoir of
forty years in modern China. Introd. by V. K.
Wellington Koo. Garden City, N.Y., Doubleday,
1968. 384 p.
67-019104 951.04/0924
China -- History -- Republic, 1912-1949.

DS778.L4725.L49
The Lin Piao affair: power politics and military
coup/ edited by Michael Y. M. Kau. White Plains,
N.Y.: International Arts and Sciences Press, [1975]
lxxvii, 591 p
73-092807 951.05/092/4
*Lin, Piao, -- 1908-1971. China -- Politics and
government -- 1949-1976 -- Sources.*

DS778.L4725.T38 1996
Teiwes, Frederick C.
The tragedy of Lin Biao: riding the tiger during the Cultural Revolution, 1966-1971/ Frederick C. Teiwes, Warren Sun. Honolulu: University of Hawaii Press, c1996. xvi, 251 p.
95-044130 951.105/6 0824818113
Lin, Piao, -- 1908-1971.   China -- History -- Cultural Revolution, 1966-1971. China -- Politics and government -- 1949-1976.

DS778.L49.D57
Dittmer, Lowell.
Liu Shao-chi and the Chinese cultural revolution: the politics of mass criticism/ Lowell Dittmer. Berkeley: University of California Press, [1974] xiv, 386 p.
73-085786 951.05/092/4 0520025741
Liu, Shao-chi, -- 1898-1969.   Communist self-criticism. China -- History -- Cultural Revolution, 1966-1969.

DS778.M3.A4295
Mao, Tse-tung, 1893-1976.
Mao papers, anthology and bibliography edited by Jerome Chen. London, Oxford University Press, 1970. xxxiii, 221 p.
76-147091 016.95105/0924 0192151886
Mao, Tse-tung, -- 1893-1976 -- Bibliography.

DS778.M3.A515
Mao, Tse-tung, 1893-1976.
Selected military writings of Mao Tse-tung. Peking: Foreign Languages Press, 1963. 408 p.
65-001840
Guerrilla warfare.   China -- Politics and government -- 1912-1949.

DS778.M3.A516
Mao, Tse-tung, 1893-1976.
Mao Tse-tung: an anthology of his writings. Edited with an introd. by Anne Fremantle. [New York] New American Library [1962] 300 p.
62-014315 951.05
Communism -- China.

DS778.M3.A538 1969
Mao, Tse-tung, 1893-1976.
The political thought of Mao Tse-tung [by] Stuart R. Schram. New York, Praeger [1969] 479 p.
68-016093 320.9/51
Communism -- China.

DS778.M3 A74 2000
Andrew, Anita M.,
Autocracy and China's rebel founding emperors: comparing Chairman Mao and Ming Taizu/ written and edited by Anita M. Andrew and John A. Rapp. Lanham, MD: Rowan & Littlefield Publishers, c2000. xiii, 361 p.
99-089975 951.05/0922.221 0847695808
Mao, Zedong, 1893-1976. Ming Taizu, Emperor of China, 1328-1398. Dictatorship--China.

DS778.M3.C473
Chen, Jerome, 1919-
Mao Englewood Cliffs, N.J., Prentice-Hall [1969] x, 176 p.
69-015346 951.05/0924 013555912X
Mao, Tse-tung, -- 1893-1976

DS778.M3.C474
Chen, Jerome, 1919-
Mao and the Chinese revolution. With thirty-seven poems by Mao Tse-tung translated from the Chinese by Michael Bullock and Jerome Chen. London, Oxford University Press, 1965. ix, 419 p.
65-002375 923.151
Mao, Zedong, -- 1893-1976. Mao, Zedong, -- 1893-1976 -- Translations into English. Communism -- China.

DS778.M3 L5164 1994
Li, Zhisui.
The private life of Chairman Mao: the memoirs of Mao's personal physician/ Dr. Li Zhisui; translated by Professor Tai Hung-chao; with the editorial assistance of Anne F. Thurston; foreword by Andrew J. Nathan. 1st ed. New York: Random House, c1994. xxii, 682 p.
94-029970 951.05.220 0679400354
Mao, Zedong, 1893-1976.   Heads of state--China--Biography.

DS778.M3.P28 1963
Paloczi Horvath, Gyorgy.
Mao Tse-tung, emperor of the blue ants. Garden City, N.Y., Doubleday, 1963 [c1962] 393 p.
63-011223 923.151
Mao, Tse-tung, -- 1893-1976.

DS778.M3.P32 1961
Payne, Robert, 1911-
Portrait of a revolutionary; Mao Tse-tung. London, Abelard-Schuman [c1961] 311 p.
61-015322 923.551
Mao, Tse-tung, -- 1893-1976.

DS778.M3.P93
Pye, Lucian W., 1921-
Mao Tse-tung: the man in the leader/ Lucian W. Pye. New York: Basic Books, c1976. xviii, 346 p.
75-031832 951.05/092/4 0465043968
Mao, Tse-tung, -- 1893-1976.

DS778.M3.R8
Rue, John E.
Mao Tse-tung in opposition, 1927-1935 [by] John E. Rue, with the assistance of S. R. Rue. Stanford, Calif., Published for the Hoover Institution on War, Rev 1966. viii, 387 p.
66-015302 951.90430924
Mao, Tse-tung, -- 1893-1976.   China -- Politics and government -- 1928-1937.

DS778.M3.S3 1967
Schram, Stuart R.
Mao Tse-tung [by] Stuart Schram. New York, Simon and Schuster [1967, c1966] 351 p.
67-012918 951/.05/0924
Mao, Tse-tung, -- 1893-1976.

DS778.M3.S548 2000
Short, Philip.
Mao: a life/ Philip Short. New York: Henry Holt, 2000. xiii, 782 p.
99-041839 951.05/092 0805031154
Mao, Tse-tung, -- 1893-1976.   Heads of state -- China -- Biography.

DS778.M3 S685 1999
Spence, Jonathan D.
Mao Zedong/ Jonathan Spence. New York: Viking, 1999. xiv, 188 p.
99-027739 951.05/092. 221 0670886696
Mao, Zedong, 1893-1976. Heads of state--China--Biography.

DS778.M3.S76
Starr, John Bryan.
Continuing the revolution: the political thought of Mao/ John Bryan Starr. Princeton, N.J.: Princeton University Press, c1979. xv, 366 p.
78-063597 320.5/323/0924 0691075964
Mao, Tse-tung, -- 1893-1976 -- Political and social views. Dictatorship of the proletariat.

DS778.N53.T48 1991
Thurston, Anne F.
A Chinese odyssey: the life and times of a Chinese dissident/ Anne F. Thurston. New York: Charles Scribner's Sons; c1991. xxi, 440 p.
91-023216 951.05/092 0684192195
Ni, Yuxian.   Dissenters -- China -- Biography. China -- Politics and government -- 1949-

DS778.S8.L5 1971b
Liew, K. S.
Struggle for democracy; Sung Chiao-jen and the 1911 Chinese revolution [by] K. S. Liew. Berkeley, University of California Press, 1971. ix, 260 p.
74-123623 951/.03/0924 0520017609
Sung, Chiao-jen, -- 1882?-1913.   China -- History -- Revolution, 1911-1912.

DS778.T39.D46 1995
Deng Xiaoping: portrait of a Chinese statesman/ edited by David Shambaugh. Oxford [England]: Clarendon Press; 1995. viii, 172 p.
94-048627 951.05/8/092 0198289332
Teng, Hsiao-ping, -- 1904-   Heads of state -- China -- Biography.

DS778.T39.F7313 1988
Franz, Uli, 1949-
Deng Xiaoping/ Uli Franz; translated by Tom Artin. Boston: Harcourt Brace Jovanovich, c1988. xi, 340 p.
88-011158 951.05/8/0924 0151251770
Teng, Hsiao-ping, -- 1904-   Heads of state -- China -- Biography.

DS778.T39.R813 1994
Ruan, Ming, 1931-
Deng Xiaoping: chronicle of an empire/ Ruan Ming; translated and edited by Nancy Liu, Peter Rand, and Lawrence R. Sullivan; with a foreword by Andrew J. Nathan. Boulder: Westview Press, 1994. xxi, 288 p.
94-001944 951.05/8/092 081331920X
Teng, Hsiao-ping, -- 1904-   China -- Politics and government -- 1976-

DS778.T39.Y33 1997
Yang, Benjamin.
Deng: a political biography/ Benjamin Yang. Armonk, N.Y.: M.E. Sharpe, 1997. xix, 331 p.
97-023950 951.05/092 1563247216
Teng, Hsiao-ping, -- 1904- Heads of state -- China -- Biography.   China -- Politics and government -- 1949-

DS778.W3.B85
Bunker, Gerald E.
The peace conspiracy; Wang Ching-wei and the China war, 1937-1941 [by] Gerald E. Bunker. Cambridge, Mass., Harvard University Press, 1972. 327 p.
78-180149 940.53/12/0924 0674659155
Wang, Ching-wei, -- 1883-1944.   Sino-Japanese Conflict, 1937-1945.

DS778.Y4.G6
Gillin, Donald G.
Warlord: Yen Hsi-shan in Shansi Province, 1911-1949, by Donald G. Gillin. Princeton, N.J., Princeton University Press, 1967. xiv, 334 p.
66-014308   951.040924
Yen, Hsi-shan, -- 1883-1960.

DS778.Z47.A3 1993
Zhai, Zhenhua, 1951-
Red flower of China/ Zhai Zhenhua. New York: SOHO, c1992. 245 p.
92-044047   951.05/6   0939149834
Zhai, Zhenhua, -- 1951-   China -- History -- Cultural Revolution, 1966-1969.

DS778.7.F462513 1991
Feng, Chi-tsai.
Voices from the whirlwind: an oral history of the Chinese Cultural Revolution/ Feng Jicai; with a foreword by Robert Coles. New York, N.Y.: Pantheon Books; c1991. xvi, 252 p.
90-052565   951.05/6   039458645X
China -- History -- Cultural Revolution, 1966-1969 -- Personal narratives.

DS778.7.J56 1999
Jin, Qiu, 1956-
The culture of power: the Lin Biao incident in the Cultural Revolution/ Jin Qiu. Stanford, Calif.: Stanford University Press, 1999. xiii, 279 p.
98-054159   951.05/6   0804735298
Lin, Piao, -- 1908-1971.   China -- History -- Cultural Revolution, 1966-1976. China -- Politics and government -- 1949-1976.

DS778.7.L57 1991
Lin, Jing.
The Red Guards' path to violence: political, educational, and psychological factors/ Jing Lin. New York: Praeger, 1991. x, 187 p.
91-002272   951.05/6   0275938727
China -- History -- Cultural Revolution, 1966-1969.

DS778.7.N48 1991
New perspectives on the Cultural Revolution/ edited by William A. Joseph, Christine P.W. Wong, and David Zweig. Cambridge, Mass.: Council on East Asian Studies/Harvard University 1991. xi, 351 p.
90-020970   951.05/6   0674617584
China -- History -- Cultural Revolution, 1966-1969. China -- Politics and government -- 1949-1976. China -- Economic conditions -- 1949-1976.

DS778.7.P535 1999
Picturing power in the People's Republic of China: posters of the Cultural Revolution/ edited by Harriet Evans and Stephanie Donald. Lanham, Md.: Rowman & Littlefield, c1999. xiv, 170 p.
99-024279   951.05/6.221   0847695115
Political posters, Chinese--Exhibitions. Political posters--England--London--Exhibitions.

DS778.7.W47 1989
White, Lynn T.
Policies of chaos: the organizational causes of violence in China's Cultural Revolution/ Lynn T. White III. Princeton, N.J.: Princeton University Press, c1989. x, 367 p.
88-015235   951.05/6   0691055467
China -- History -- Cultural Revolution, 1966-1969. China -- Politics and government -- 1949-1976.

DS778.7.Y42 1997
Yang, Rae, 1950-
Spider eaters: a memoir/ Rae Yang. Berkeley: University of California Press, c1997. xi, 285 p.
96-031622   951.05/092   0520204808
Yang family. Yang, Rae, -- 1950-   Peking (China) -- Biography.   China -- History -- Cultural Revolution, 1966-1976 -- Personal narratives.

DS778.7.Y4313 1997
Yang, Xiaokai.
Captive spirits: prisoners of the Cultural Revolution/ Yang Xiguang and Susan McFadden. Hong Kong; Oxford University Press, 1997. xxx, 302 p.
97-010203   951.05/6.221   0195868455
Yang, Xiaokai.   Political prisoners--China--Anecdotes.

DS778.7.Y4613 1996
Yan, Jiaqi, 1942-
Turbulent decade: a history of the cultural revolution/ Yan Jiaqi and Gao Gao; translated and edited by D.W.Y. Kwok. Honolulu: University of Hawai'i Press, 1996. xxv, 659 p.
95-030358   951.05/8   0824816951
China -- History -- Cultural revolution, 1966-1969.

DS778.7.Z48 1998
Zhu, Xiao Di, 1958-
Thirty years in a red house: a memoir of childhood and youth in Communist China/ Zhu Xiao Di; foreword by Ross Terrill. Amherst: University of Massachusetts Press, c1998. xiv, 255 p.
97-015886   951.05/6   1558491120
Zhu, Xiao Di, -- 1958-   China -- History -- Cultural Revolution, 1966-1969 -- Personal narratives.

DS779.15.C48
China facts & figures annual. [Gulf Breeze, Fla.] Academic International Press. v.
79-640300   951/.005
China -- History -- 1976- -- Periodicals. China -- Economic conditions -- 1976- -- Periodicals. China -- Politics and government -- 1976- -- Periodicals.

DS779.23.C44145 1997
Ch en, Fang-cheng.
From Youthful manuscripts to River elegy: the Chinese popular cultural movement and political transformation 1979-1989/ Chen Fong-ching & Jin Guantao. Hong Kong: Chinese University Press, c1997. x, 343 p.
98-140321   951.05.221   9622017622
Popular culture--China. Politics and culture--China.

DS779.23.H8613 2000
Huot, Marie Claire,
China's new cultural scene: a handbook of changes/ Claire Huot. Durham: Duke University Press, 2000. viii, 258 p.
99-050299   951.05/7.221   0822324458
Popular culture--China.

DS779.23.L4 1996
Lee, Gregory B.
Troubadours, trumpeters, troubled makers: lyricism, nationalism, and hybridity in China and its others/ Gregory B. Lee. Durham: Duke University Press, 1996. xvii, 278 p.
95-005193   951.05.220   0822316714
Popular music--China--Text--History and criticism.

DS779.23.T365 2000
Tang, Wenfang, 1955-
Chinese urban life under reform: the changing social contract/ Wenfang Tang, William L. Parish. Cambridge, UK; Cambridge University Press, 2000. xi, 388 p.
99-030393   951/.009732   0521770858
City and town life -- China.   China -- Social life and customs -- 1976-

DS779.26.C47647 1999
Chinoy, Mike.
China live: people power and the television revolution/ Mike Chinoy. Lanham, Md.: Rowman & Littlefield Publishers, c1999. 437 p.
98-052035   951.05.221   084769318X
Chinoy, Mike--Journeys--China.   Television broadcasting of news--China.

DS779.26.M32 1991
Mainland China after the thirteenth party congress/ edited by King-yuh Chang. Boulder: Westview Press, c1990. xii, 492 p.
90-034395   320.951   0813378699
China -- Politics and government -- 1976-

DS779.26.M66 1983
Moody, Peter R.
Chinese politics after Mao: development and liberalization, 1976 to 1983/ Peter R. Moody, Jr. New York, N.Y., U.S.A.: Praeger, 1983. v, 210 p.
83-013925   320.951   0030635276
China -- Politics and government -- 1976-

DS779.26.N38 1990
Nathan, Andrew J.
China's crisis: dilemmas of reform and prospects for democracy/ Andrew J. Nathan. New York: Columbia University Press, c1990. x, 242 p.
89-071266   951.05   0231072848
China -- Politics and government -- 1976- Taiwan -- Politics and government -- 1988-

DS779.26.N383 1997
Nathan, Andrew J.
China's transition/ Andrew J. Nathan; with contributions by Tianjian Shi and Helena V.S. Ho. New York: Columbia University Press, 1997. 313 p.
97-024417   951.05   0231110227
China -- Politics and government -- 1976- Taiwan -- Politics and government -- 1988-

DS779.27.C44 1999
Chan, Gerald.
Chinese perspectives on international relations: a framework for analysis/ Gerald Chan. New York: St. Martin's Press; 1999. xvii, 201 p.
98-040018   327.51   0312219091
China -- Foreign relations -- 1976-

DS779.27.C4873 1989
China and the world: new directions in Chinese foreign relations/ edited by Samuel S. Kim. Boulder: Westview Press, 1989. xii, 339 p.
88-038886   327.51   0813306191
China -- Foreign relations -- 1976-

DS779.27.C5 1984
China's foreign relations in the 1980s/ edited by Harry Harding. New Haven: Yale University Press, c1984. xv, 240 p.
84-003677   327.51   0300032072
China -- Foreign relations -- 1976-

DS779.27.F38 1995
Faust, John R., 1930-
China in world politics/ John R. Faust and Judith F. Kornberg. Boulder, Colo.: Lynne Rienner Publishers, 1995. ix, 281 p.
94-038876 327.51/009/049 1555874134
China -- Foreign relations -- 1976- China -- Politics and government -- 1976-

DS779.27.I53 1999
In the eyes of the dragon: China views the world/ edited by Yong Deng and Fei-Ling Wang. Lanham: Rowman & Littlefield Publishers, c1999. xi, 279 p.
98-046956 327.51 0847693368
China -- Foreign relations -- 1976- World politics -- 1989- Nationalism -- China.

DS779.27.J53 1996
Jian, Sanqiang.
Foreign policy restructuring as adaptive behavior: China's independent foreign policy, 1982-1989/ Sanqiang Jian. Lanham, Md.: University Press of America, c1996. xii, 310 p.
96-017905 327.51 0761804196
International relations. China -- Foreign relations -- 1976-

DS779.27.R57 2000
The rise of China/ edited by Michael E. Brown ... [et al.]. Cambridge, Mass.: MIT Press, 2000. xxvii, 270 p.
00-033948 327.51 0262522764
National security -- China. Security, International. China -- Foreign relations -- 1976-

DS779.27.S89 1996
Sutter, Robert G.
Shaping China's future in world affairs: the role of the United States/ Robert G. Sutter, with the assistance of Seong-Eun Choi. Boulder, Colo.: Westview Press, 1996. vi, 194 p.
96-012425 327.51073 0813329574
International relations. United States -- Foreign relations -- China. China -- Foreign relations -- United States. China -- Foreign relations -- 1976-

DS779.29.C477.G55 1998
Gilley, Bruce, 1966-
Tiger on the brink: Jiang Zemin and China's new elite/ Bruce Gilley. Berkeley: University of California Press, c1998. xi, 395 p.
97-042753 951.05/092 0520213955
Chiang, Tse-min, -- 1926- Heads of state -- China -- Biography. China -- Politics and government -- 1976-

DS779.32.B76 1992
Brook, Timothy, 1951-
Quelling the people: the military suppression of the Beijing democracy movement/ Timothy Brook. New York: Oxford University Press, 1992. xiv, 265 p.
92-016396 951.05/8 0195074572
China -- History -- Tiananmen Square Incident, 1989.

DS779.32.C35 1994
Calhoun, Craig J., 1952-
Neither gods nor emperors: students and the struggle for democracy in China/ Craig Calhoun. Berkeley: University of California Press, c1994. xiv, 333 p.
94-009432 951.05/8 0520088263
Students -- China -- Political activity. China -- History -- Tiananmen Square Incident, 1989.

DS779.32.C46 1990
Cheng, Chu-yuan.
Behind the Tiananmen Massacre: social, political, and economic ferment in China/ Chu-yuan Cheng. Boulder, Colo.: Westview Press, 1990. xii, 256 p.
90-012384 951.05/8 0813310474
China -- History -- Tiananmen Square Incident, 1989.

DS779.32.C84 1990
Culture and politics in China: an anatomy of Tiananmen Square/ edited by Peter Li, Steven Mark, Marjorie H. Li. New Brunswick, U.S.A.: Transaction Publishers, c1991. xiv, 369 p.
90-042374 951.05/8 088738353X
Students -- China -- Political activity. China -- Politics and government -- 1976- China -- History -- Tiananmen Square Incident, 1989.

DS779.32.L54 2001
Zhang, Liang.
The Tiananmen papers/ compiled by Zhang Liang; edited by Andrew J. Nathan and Perry Link; with an afterword by Orville Schell. 1st ed. New York: Public Affairs, c2001. xlv, 513 p.
00-045823 951.05/8.221 158648012X
China -- History -- Tiananmen Square Incident, 1989. China -- Politics and government -- 1976-

DS779.32.L56 1992
Lin, Nan, 1938-
The struggle for Tiananmen: anatomy of the 1989 mass movement/ Nan Lin. Westport, Conn.: Praeger, 1992. ix, 199 p.
92-015780 951.05/8 0275936562
China -- History -- Tiananmen Square Incident, 1989.

DS779.32.M54 1996
Miles, James A. R., 1961-
The legacy of Tiananmen: China in disarray/ James A.R. Miles. Ann Arbor: University of Michigan Press, c1996. viii, 379 p.
95-052804 951.05/8 0472107313
China -- History -- Tiananmen Square Incident, 1989. China -- Politics and government -- 1976- China -- Social conditions -- 1976-

DS779.32.P4513 1989
June Four: a chronicle of the Chinese democratic uprising/ by the photographers and reporters of the Ming pao news; translated by Zi Jin and Qin Zhou. Fayetteville: University of Arkansas Press, 1989. 171 p.
89-020260 951.05/8 1557281408
China -- History -- Tiananmen Square Incident, 1989.

DS779.32.P67 1991
Popular protest and political culture in modern China: learning from 1989/ edited by Jeffrey N. Wasserstrom and Elizabeth J. Perry. Boulder: Westview Press, 1992. xi, 300 p.
91-027191 951.05/8 0813380324
Political culture -- China. China -- History -- Tiananmen Square Incident, 1989.

DS779.32.V65 1990
Voices from Tiananmen Square: Beijing Spring and the democracy movement/ edited by Mok Chiu Yu and J. Frank Harrison; introduction by George Woodcock. Montreal; Black Rose Books, c1990. xxiv, 203 p.
90-081589 951.05/8 0921689586
China -- History -- Tiananmen Square Incident, 1989 -- Sources.

DS779.32.Y5 1989
Yi, Mu.
Crisis at Tiananmen: reform and reality in modern China/ by Yi Mu and Mark V. Thompson. San Francisco: China Books & Periodicals, c1989. x, 283 p.
89-081313 951.05/8 0835122905
China -- History -- Tiananmen Square Incident, 1989.

DS783.7-784 China — Local history and description — Manchuria

DS783.7.L3 1969
Lattimore, Owen, 1900-
The Mongols of Manchuria; their tribal divisions, geographical distribution, historical relations with Manchus and Chinese, and present political problems. New York, H. Fertig, 1969 [c1934] 311 p.
68-009626 951/.7
Mongols -- History. Mongols -- China -- Manchuria. Eastern question (Far East) Mongolia -- History.

DS783.7.O4 1984
Ogata, Sadako N.
Defiance in Manchuria: the making of Japanese foreign policy, 1931-1932/ by Sadako N. Ogata. Westport, Conn.: Greenwood Press, 1984, c1964. p. cm.
84-000543 327.51/8/052 0313244286
Manchuria (China) -- History -- 1931-1945. Japan -- Foreign relations -- China -- Manchuria. Manchuria (China) -- Foreign relations -- Japan.

DS783.7.P7 1933
Price, Ernest Batson, 1890-
The Russo-Japanese treaties of 1907-1916, concerning Manchuria and Mongolia/ Ernest Batson Price. Baltimore: Johns Hopkins Press, 1933. xiv, 164 p.
33-020423 327.47/051
Eastern question (Far East) Soviet Union -- Foreign relations -- Japan. Japan -- Foreign relations -- Soviet Union. Soviet Union -- Foreign relations -- Treaties.

DS783.7.R575
Romanov, B. A. 1889-1957.
Russia in Manchuria, 1892-1906. Translated from the Russian by Susan Wilbur Jones. Ann Arbor, Mich., Published for American Council of Learned Societ [1952] x, 549 p.
53-000394 951.8
Russians in Manchuria. Manchuria (China) -- History.

DS783.7.Y6
Young, C. Walter 1902-1939.
This international relations of Manchuria; a digest and analysis of treaties, agreements, and negotiations concerning the three eastern provinces of China, prepared for the 1929 conference of the In by C. Walter Young. Chicago, Ill., Pub. for the American council. Institute of Pac [c1929] xxx, 307 p.
30-003997
Eastern question (Far East) Manchuria (China) China -- Foreign relations. China -- Foreign relations -- Treaties.

DS783.7.Y65 vol. 1
Young, C. Walter 1902-1939.
Japan's special position in Manchuria; its assertion, legal interpretation and present meaning, by C. Walter Young. Baltimore, The Johns Hopkins press; 1931. xxxiv, 412 p.
31-030527   341
Railroads -- Manchuria. Finance -- China. Japanese -- China -- Manchuria. Manchuria (China)

DS783.7.Y67 1998
Young, Louise, 1960-
Japan's total empire: Manchuria and the culture of wartime imperialism/ Louise Young. Berkeley: University of California Press, c1998. xiii, 487 p.
97-001715   325/.352/09518   0520210719
Mukden Incident, 1931. World politics -- 1933-1945. Japan -- History -- 1926-1945. Manchuria (China) -- History -- 1931-1945.

DS784.B65 1964
Borg, Dorothy, 1902-
The United States and the Far Eastern crisis of 1933-1938; from the Manchurian incident through the initial stage of the undeclared Sino-Japanese war/ Dorothy Borg. Cambridge, Mass.: Harvard University Press, 1964. x, 674 p.
64-013421
Manchuria (China) -- History -- 1931-1945. China -- Foreign relations -- Japan. Japan -- Foreign relations -- China.

DS784.K3
Kawakami, Kiyoshi Karl, 1875-1949.
Manchoukuo, child of conflict, by K. K. Kawakami ... New York, The Macmillan company, 1933. viii p.
33-008957   915.8
Japanese in Manchuria. Chinese in Manchuria. Manchuria (China) Japan -- Foreign relations -- China. China -- Foreign relations -- Japan.

DS784.W55 2001
Wilson, Sandra,
The Manchurian crisis and Japanese society, 1931-33/ Sandra Wilson. New York: Routledge, 2001. p. cm.
2001-034966   951/.804/.221   0415250560
Mukden Incident, 1931. Japanese--China--Manchuria.

DS785-786 China — Local history and description — Tibet

DS785.B53 1995
Berry, Scott, 1945-
Monks, spies, and a soldier of fortune: the Japanese in Tibet/ Scott Berry. New York: St. Martin's Press; 1995. xi, 352 p.
94-028744   951/.5   0312123981
Japanese -- China -- Tibet. Tibet (China) -- History.

DS785.C15
Cammann, Schuyler V. R.
Trade through the Himalayas, the early British attempts to open Tibet. Princeton, N.J., Princeton U. Pr. 1951 186 p.
51-010847   951.5
Tibet (China) -- History -- 18th century.

DS785.F34 1996
Feigon, Lee, 1945-
Demystifying Tibet: unlocking the secrets of the Land of the Snows/ Lee Feigon. Chicago: I.R. Dee, 1996. xi, 242 p.
95-030697   951/.5   1566630894
Tibet (China) -- History.

DS785.F56 1961a
Fleming, Peter, 1907-1971.
Bayonets to Lhasa; the first full account of the British invasion of Tibet in 1904.   New York, Harper [1961] 319 p.
61-006431   951.5
Younghusband, Francis Edward, -- Sir, -- 1863-1942. British -- China -- Tibet -- History -- 20th century.   Tibet (China) -- Foreign relations -- Great Britain. Great Britain -- Foreign relations -- China -- Tibet. Tibet (China) -- History.

DS785.H273 1954
Harrer, Heinrich, 1912-
Seven years in Tibet; translated by Richard Graves. New York, Dutton, 1954 [c1953] 314 p.
53-010851   915.15
Tibet (China) -- Description and travel. Tibet (China) -- Description and travel.

DS785.H4 1934
Hedin, Sven Anders, 1865-1952.
A conquest of Tibet. [New York, E.P. Dutton, 1934] viii,11-400 p.
34-020537
Tibet (China) -- Description and travel.

DS785.L5 1960
Li, Tieh-cheng, 1906-
Tibet, today and yesterday, by Tieh-Tseng Li. New York, Bookman Associates [1960] xv, 324 p.
60-008548   951.5
Tibet (China) -- History.

DS785.M28
McGovern, William Montgomery, 1897-
The Early empires of Central Asia: a study of the Scythians and the Huns and the part they played in world history, with special reference to the Chinese sources/ by William Montgomery McGovern. Chapel Hill: University of North Carolina Press, 1939. xiii, 529 p.
39-006490   950
Scythians. Huns. Asia, Central -- History.

DS785.P93.R38 1976b
Rayfield, Donald, 1942-
The dream of Lhasa: the life of Nikolay Przhevalsky (1839-88) explorer of Central Asia/ Donald Rayfield. [Athens]: Ohio University Press, 1976. xii, 221 p.
76-020326   915.8/04   0821403699
Przhevalskii, Nikolai Mikhailovich, -- 1839-1888. Explorers -- Asia, Central -- Biography.   Asia, Central -- Description and travel.

DS785.S43
Shen, Tsung-lien.
Tibet and the Tibetans, by Tsung-lien Shen and Shen-chi Liu. Foreword by George E. Taylor. Stanford, Calif., Stanford University Press [1953] 199 p.
52-005973   915.15
Tibet (China) -- History. Tibet (China) -- Social life and customs.

DS785.S83
Stein, Aurel, 1862-1943.
On ancient Central-Asian tracks: brief narrative of three expeditions in innermost Asia and northwestern China/ by Sir Aurel Stein. London: Macmillan, 1933. xxiv, 342 p.
33-011526
Excavations (Archaeology) -- Asia, Central. Excavations (Archaeology) -- China -- Sinkiang Province.   Asia, Central -- Antiquities. Asia, Central -- Description and travel. Sinkiang Province (China) -- Antiquities.

DS785.45
Petech, Luciano.
China and Tibet in the early 18th century; history of the establishment of Chinese protectorate in Tibet. Leiden, E. J. Brill, 1950. x, 286 p.
52-015516   951.5
China -- Foreign relations -- Tibet. Tibet (China) -- History. Tibet (China) -- Foreign relations -- China.

DS786.B38 1987
Beckwith, Christopher I., 1945-
The Tibetan Empire in central Asia: a history of the struggle for great power among Tibetans, Turks, Arabs, and Chinese during the early Middle Ages/ Christopher I. Beckwith. Princeton, N.J.: Princeton University Press, c1987. xxii, 269 p.
87-002852   958   0691054940
Tibet (China) -- History. Asia, Central -- History.

DS786.B53 1989
Bishop, Peter,
The myth of Shangri-La: Tibet, travel writing, and the western creation of sacred landscape/ Peter Bishop. Berkeley: University of California Press, c1989. x, 308 p.
89-040450   915.1/5.220   0520066863
Travel writing--History.

DS786.D6613 1994
Donnet, Pierre-Antoine.
Tibet: survival in question/ Pierre-Antoine Donnet; translated by Tica Broch. Delhi: Oxford University Press; c1994. xv, 267 p.
94-223989   951/.505   0195635736
Tibet (China) -- Politics and government -- 1951-

DS786.G635 1989
Goldstein, Melvyn C.
A history of modern Tibet, 1913-1951: the demise of the Lamaist state/ Melvyn C. Goldstein; with the help of Gelek Rimpoche. Berkeley: University of California Press, c1989. xxv, 898 p.
87-034933   951/.5   0520061403
Tibet (China) -- History.

DS786.G636 1997
Goldstein, Melvyn C.
The snow lion and the dragon: China, Tibet, and the Dalai Lama/ Melvyn C. Goldstein. Berkeley: University of California Press, c1997. xiii, 152 p.
97-002562   0520212541
Bstan-dzin-rgya-mtsho, -- Dalai Lama XIV, -- 1935- China -- Relations -- China -- Tibet. Tibet (China) -- Relations -- China.

DS786.K93
Kwanten, Luc.
Imperial nomads: a history of central Asia, 500-1500/ Luc Kwanten. [Philadelphia]: University of Pennsylvania Press, 1979. xv, 352 p.
78-053339   958   0812277503
Mongols -- History. Asia, Central -- History.

DS786.L3 1962
Lattimore, Owen, 1900-
Studies in frontier history; collected papers, 1928-1958. London, Oxford University Press, 1962. 565 p.
63-004349   950.081
Asia, Central -- History. China -- Boundaries.

DS786.M6
Moraes, F. R.
The revolt in Tibet. New York, Macmillan, 1960. 223 p.
60-006644   951.5
Tibet (China) -- Politics and government.

DS786.S5423 1991
Sinha, Nirmal Chandra.
An introduction to the history and religion of Tibet/ by Nirmal C. Sinha; foreword by K.P.S. Menon. Gangtok, India: Himalindia Publications, 1991. xiv, 100 p.
91-906862   951/.5.220
Tibet (China) -- History. Tibet (China) -- Religion.

DS786.S56 1996
Smith, Warren W.
Tibetan nation: a history of Tibetan nationalism and Sino-Tibetan relations/ Warren W. Smith, Jr. Boulder, Colo.: Westview Press, 1996. xxxi, 732 p.
96-034206   951/.5   0813331552
Nationalism -- China -- Tibet. Tibet (China) -- Politics and government. Tibet (China) -- Relations -- China. China -- Relations -- China -- Tibet.

DS786.S6 1968b
Snellgrove, David L.
A cultural history of Tibet [by] David Snellgrove [and] Hugh Richardson. New York, F. A. Praeger [1968] 291 p.
68-026668   915.15/03
Tibet (China) -- Civilization.

DS786.T48 1959
Thomas, Lowell, 1923-
The silent war in Tibet.   Garden City, N.Y., Doubleday, 1959. 284 p.
59-012648   951/.5
Tibet (China) -- History.

DS786.T679 1999
Tsering Shakya.
The dragon in the land of snows: a history of modern Tibet since 1947 / Tsering Shakya. New York: Columbia University press, c1999. xxix, 574 p.
99-014020   951/.505.221   0231118147
Tibet (China) -- History -- 20th century.

DS786.T7713
Tucci, Giuseppe, 1894-
Transhimalaya. Translated from the French by James Hogarth. Geneva, Nagel Publishers [1973] 239 p.
74-186286   951/.5   2826305751
Archaeology. Tibet (China) -- Antiquities.

DS786.T8
Tucci, Giuseppe, 1894-
Tibet, land of snows. Photos. by Wim Swaan, Edwin Smith, and others. Translated by J. E. Stapleton Driver. New York, Stein and Day [1967] 216 p.
67-024403   951/.5
Tibet (China)

DS793 China — Local history and description — Provinces, dependencies, regions, etc., A-Z

DS793.C268 F67 1990
Forster, Keith,
Rebellion and factionalism in a Chinese province: Zhejiang, 1966-1976 / Keith Forster. Armonk, N.Y.: M.E. Sharpe, c1990. xiii, 338 p.
89-049160   951/.242056.220   0873325354
Zhejiang Sheng (China) -- Politics and government. China -- History -- Cultural Revolution, 1966-1976.

DS793.C3.Y44 1996
Yeh, Wen-hsin.
Provincial passages: culture, space, and the origins of Chinese communism/ Wen-hsin Yeh. Berkeley: University of California Press, c1996. x, 403 p.
95-050179   306/.0951/242   0520200683
Intellectuals -- China -- Zhejiang Sheng. Communism -- China -- Zhejiang Sheng. Zhejiang Sheng (China) -- History. China -- History -- May Fourth Movement, 1919.

DS793.F8 D48 1990
Development and decline of Fukien Province in the 17th and 18th centuries/ edited by E.B. Vermeer. Leiden; Brill, 1990. 488 p.
90-043720   951/.245032.220   9004091718
Fujian Sheng (China) -- History -- Congresses.

DS793.G6.C3
Cable, Mildred.
The Gobi desert [by] Mildred Cable with Francesca French ... London, Hodder and Stoughton limited [1942] 303 p.
43-012196   915.1739
Gobi. Mongolia -- Description and travel.

DS793.G6.H413
Hedin, Sven Anders, 1865-1952.
Across the Gobi Desert, by Sven Hedin; with 114 illustrations and three maps. London, G. Routledge and sons, ltd. [1931?] xxi, 402 p.
32-007528   915.17
Gobi. Mongolia -- Description and travel.

DS793.G67 W25 1990
Waldron, Arthur.
The Great Wall of China: from history to myth/ Arthur Waldron. Cambridge [England]; Cambridge University Press, 1990. xiii, 296 p.
88-032689   951.219   052136518X
Great Wall of China (China)

DS793.H3.S3 1970
Schafer, Edward H.
Shore of pearls, by Edward H. Schafer. Berkeley, University of California Press, 1970 [c1969] ix, 173 p.
78-094990   915.1/27   0520015924
Chinese literature -- Hainan. Hainan -- History.

DS793.H5.D6513 1995
Domenach, Jean-Luc.
The origins of the great leap forward: the case of one Chinese province/ Jean-Luc Domenach; translated by A.M. Berrett. Boulder: Westview Press, 1995. xvii, 212 p.
94-038713   951.18055   081331710X
Henan Sheng (China) -- Politics and government.

DS793.H5 W6 1994
Wou, Odoric Y. K.,
Mobilizing the masses: building revolution in Henan/ Odoric Y.K. Wou. Stanford, Calif.: Stanford University Press, 1994. viii, 477 p.
93-020624   951/.18042.220   0804721424
Communism--China--Henan Sheng--History.

DS793.H6443525.S36 1989
Schoppa, R. Keith, 1943-
Xiang Lake--nine centuries of Chinese life/ R. Keith Schoppa. New Haven: Yale University Press, c1989. xx, 284 p.
88-010132   951/.215   0300042531
Hsiang Lake Region (China) -- History.

DS793.K2.F3
Farrer, Reginald John, 1880-1920.
On the eaves of the world, by Reginald Farrer ... London, E. Arnold, 1917. 2 v.
18-001582
Botany -- China -- Kansu. Kansu Province (China) -- Description and travel.

DS793.K6 C4413 1996
Zheng, Yi,
Scarlet memorial: tales of cannibalism in modern China/ Zheng Yi; translated and edited by T.P. Sym; with a foreword by Ross Terrill. Boulder, Colo.: Westview Press, 1996. xxii, 199 p.
96-033948   951.05/6.220   0813326168
Guangxi Zhuangzu Zizhiqu (China) -- Politics and government. China -- History -- Cultural Revolution, 1966-1976.

DS793.K6.L48 1993
Levich, Eugene William, 1937-
The Kwangsi way in Kuomintang China, 1931-1939/ Eugene William Levich. Armonk, N.Y.: bM.E. Sharpe, c1993. xx, 363 p.
92-037094   951/.28042   1563242001
Guangxi Zhuangzu Zizhiqu (China) -- History. China -- History -- 1928-1937.

DS793.K7.V64 1989
Vogel, Ezra F.
One step ahead in China: Guangdong under reform/ Ezra F. Vogel; with a contribution by John Kamm. Cambridge, Mass.: Harvard University Press, 1989. viii, 510 p.
89-031695   951/.27058   0674639103
Guangdong Sheng (China) -- Politics and government. Guangdong Sheng (China) -- Economic conditions.

DS793.K7.W3
Wakeman, Frederic E.
Strangers at the gate; social disorder in South China, 1839-1861 [by] Frederic Wakeman, Jr. Berkeley, University of California Press [c1966] 276 p.
66-025349   951.512703
Guangdong Sheng (China) -- History. China -- History -- Opium War, 1840-1842.

DS793.M7.J32
Jagchid, Sechin, 1914-
Mongolia's culture and society/ Sechin Jagchid and Paul Hyer; with a foreword by Joseph Fletcher. Boulder, Colo.: Westview Press, c1979. xvi, 461 p.
79-001438   951/.77   0891583904
Inner Mongolia (China) -- Social life and customs.

DS793.M7.L3
Lattimore, Owen, 1900-
The desert road to Turkestan/ by Owen Lattimore; with 48 illustrations and 2 maps. London, Methuen & co., ltd. [1928] xiv, p.
29-001315
Mongolia -- Description and travel.

DS793.M7.L33 1955a
Lattimore, Owen, 1900-
Nationalism and revolution in Mongolia. With a translation from the Mongol of Sh. Nachukdorji's Life of Sukebatur, by Owen Lattimore and Urgungge Onon. Leiden, E.J. Brill, 1955. x, 186 p.
56-046167   951.7
Sukebatur, -- 1893-1923.   Nationalism -- Mongolia.   Mongolia -- History.

DS793.M7.P3625 1993
Pasternak, Burton.
Cowboys and cultivators: the Chinese of Inner Mongolia/ Burton Pasternak and Janet W. Salaff. Boulder: Westview Press, 1993. xiv, 280 p.
93-222673   0813318777
Chinese -- China -- Inner Mongolia.

DS793.N6 J85 2001
Juliano, Annette L.
Monks and merchants: Silk Road treasures from Northwest China Gansu   and Ningxia 4th-7th century/ Annette L. Juliano and Judith A. Lerner; with essays by Michael Alram ... [et al.]. New York, N.Y.: Harry N. Abrams with the Asia Society, 2001. 352 p.
2001-022132   951/.4.221   0878480897
China, Northwest -- Antiquities.   Silk Road -- Antiquities.

DS793.S4.F5
Fifield, Russell H. 1914-
Woodrow Wilson and the Far East; the diplomacy of the Shantung question.   New York, Crowell [1952] xv, 383 p.
52-012518   951.14
Wilson, Woodrow, -- 1856-1924.   World War, 1914-1918 -- Territorial questions -- China. Shantung Province (China)

DS793.S62.B37 1990
Benson, Linda.
The Ili Rebellion: the Moslem challenge to Chinese authority in Xinjiang, 1944-1949/ by Linda Benson. Armonk, N.Y.: M.E. Sharpe, c1990. xxvii, 265 p.
89-037237   951/.6   0873325095
Xinjiang Uygur Zizhiqu (China) -- History. Xinjiang Uygur Zizhiqu (China) -- Ethnic relations. I-li Ha-sa-ko tzu chih chou (China) -- History.

DS793.S62.L3 1950
Lattimore, Owen, 1900-
Pivot of Asia; Sinkiang and the inner Asian frontiers of China and Russia, by Owen Lattimore with the assistance of Chang Chih-yi [and others. Boston, Little, Brown, 1950. xii, 288 p.
50-006506   951.6
Sinkiang Province (China) Asia, Central -- Politics and government.

DS793.S62.M24 1979
McMillen, Donald Hugh, 1944-
Chinese Communist power and policy in Xinjiang, 1949-1977/ Donald H. McMillen. Boulder, Colo.: Westview Press, 1979. xix, 373 p.
78-024645   320.9/51/605   0891584528
Xinjiang Uygur Zizhiqu (China) -- Politics and government.

DS793.S62.M535 1998
Millward, James A., 1961-
Beyond the pass: economy, ethnicity, and empire in Qing Central Asia, 1759-1864/ James A. Millward. Stanford, Calif.: Stanford University Press, 1998. xxii, 353 p.
97-035503   951/.6   0804729336
Ethnicity -- China -- Xinjiang Uygur Zizhiqu. Xinjiang Uygur Zizhiqu (China) -- Commerce -- History. Xinjiang Uygur Zizhiqu (China) -- History. China -- History -- Chien lung, 1736-1795.

DS793.S62.W22 1991
Waley-Cohen, Joanna.
Exile in Mid-Qing China: banishment to Xinjiang, 1758-1820/ Joanna Waley-Cohen. New Haven: Yale University Press, c1991. xv, 267 p.
90-013005   951.6   0300048270
Exiles -- China -- Xinjiang Uygur Zizhiqu. Penal colonies -- China -- Xinjiang Uygur Zizhiqu -- History.

DS793.S62 W24 1999
Wang, David D.
Under the Soviet shadow: the Yining Incident: ethnic conflicts and   international rivalry in Xinjiang, 1944-1949/ David D. Wang. Hong Kong: The Chinese University Press , 1999. viii, 577 p.
00-510338   9622018319
Xingjiang Uygur Zizhiqu (China) -- History. Asia, Central -- Politics and government.

DS793.S62 W359 1999
Wang, David D.
Clouds over Tianshan: essays on social disturbance in Xinjiang in the   1940s/ David D. Wang. Copenhagen: NIAS, 1999. 122 p.
00-694861   8787062623
Xinjiang Uygur Zizhiqu (China) -- History. Xinjiang Uygur Zizhiqu (China) -- Politics and government.

DS793.S8 A528 2001
Ancient Sichuan: treasures from a lost civilization/ edited by Robert Bagley, with contributions by Jay Xu ... [et al.]. Seattle, Wash.: Seattle Art Museum; c2001. 359 p.
00-068782   931   0691088519
Excavations (Archaeology) -- China -- Sichuan Sheng.   Sanxingdui Site (China) -- Antiquities. Sichuan Sheng (China) -- Antiquities.

DS793.S8 G66 1986
Goodman, David S. G.
Centre and province in the People's Republic of China: Sichuan and   Guizhou, 1955-1965/ David S.G. Goodman. Cambridge: Cambridge University Press, 1986. xi, 257 p.
86-008245   951/.34.219   0521325307
Sichuan Sheng (China) -- Politics and government. Guizhou Sheng (China) -- Politics and government.

DS793.Y45 D63 2001
Dodgen, Randall A.,
Controlling the dragon: Confucian engineers and the Yellow River in   the late imperial China/ Randall A. Dodgen. Honolulu: University of Hawai'i Press, c2001. ix, 243 p.
00-059940   951/.1.221   0824823664
Yellow River (China)

DS793.Y8 M83 2001
Mueggler, Erik, 1962-
The age of wild ghosts: memory, violence, and place in Southwest China/ Erik Mueggler. Berkeley: University of California Press, c2001. xv, 360 p.
00-055164   305.8/00951/35   0520226232
Ethnology -- China -- Yunnan Sheng.   Yunnan Sheng (China) -- Social conditions.

DS795-797.42 China — Local history and description — Cities, towns, etc.

DS795.L52
Lin, Yutang, 1895-1976.
Imperial Peking; seven centuries of China. With an essay on The Art of Peking, by Peter C. Swann. New York, Crown Publishers [1961] 227 p.
61-015790   951.15
Art -- Peking.   Peking (China) -- History.

DS795.O44 1997
Old Peking: city of the ruler of the world: an anthology/ selected   and edited by Chris Elder. Hong Kong; Oxford University Press, 1997. ix, 302 p.
97-018602   951/.156.221   0195903048
Beijing (China) -- Description and travel. Beijing (China) -- Social life and customs.

DS795.3.H63 2000
Hoare, James
Beijing/ J.E. Hoare and Susan Pares, compilers. -- Oxford; Clio Press, c2000. xxxiv, 218 p.
016.951156   1851092994
Pekin (Chine) -- Bibliographie.

DS795.3.N36 2000
Naquin, Susan.
Peking: temples and city life, 1400-1900/ Susan Naquin. Berkeley: University of California Press, c2000. xxxiv, 816 p.
99-032294   951/.156   0520219910
Temples -- China -- Beijing.   Beijing (China) -- History. China -- History -- Ming dynasty, 1368-1644. China -- History -- Ching dynasty, 1644-1912.

DS795.3.S82 1989
Strand, David.
Rickshaw Beijing: city people and politics in the 1920s/ David Strand. Berkeley: University of California Press, c1989. xix, 364 p.
88-015571   951/.156041   0520063112
Beijing (China) -- Politics and government. Beijing (China) -- Social life and customs.

DS796.A55.L5
Li, Chi, 1896-1979.
Anyang/ by Li Chi. Seattle: University of Washington Press, c1977. xviii, 304 p.
75-040873   951/.18   0295954905
Excavations (Archaeology) -- China -- Anyang (Henan Sheng)   Anyang (Henan Sheng, China) -- Antiquities.

DS796.C49 F67 2000
Forêt, Philippe,
Mapping Chengde: the Qing landscape enterprise/ Philippe Forêt. Honolulu: University of Hawai'i Press, c2000. xviii, 209 p.
99-088190   951/.52.221   0824822935
Chengde (China) -- History.   Chengde (China) -- Civilization.   China -- History -- Ch ing dynasty, 1644-1912.

DS796.F855 H47 2001
Hessler, Peter,
River town: two years on the Yangtze/ Peter Hessler. 1st ed. New York: HarperCollins Publishers, c2001. 402 p.
00-049872 915.1/38.221 0060195444
Hessler, Peter, 1969---Journeys--China--Fuling (Sichuan Sheng)

DS796.F86 V47 1991
Vermeer, E. B.
Chinese local history: stone inscriptions from Fukien in the Sung to Ch'ing periods/ Eduard B. Vermeer. Boulder: Westview Press, 1991. 192 p.
91-026088 951/.245.220 0813384125
Inscriptions, Chinese--China--Fujian Sheng.

DS796.H25 S38 2000
Schultheis, Eugenia Barnett,
Hangchow, my home: growing up in heaven below/ Eugenia Barnett Schultheis. Fort Bragg, Calif.: Lost Coast, c2000. vii, 262 p.
99-054123 951/.242.221 1882897463
Schultheis, Eugenia Barnett, 1913---Journeys--China--Hangzhou.

DS796.H4 W64 1999
Wolff, David,
To the Harbin Station: the liberal alternative in Russian Manchuria, 1898-1914/ David Wolff. Stanford, Calif.: Stanford University Press, 1999. xiv, 255 p.
98-029100 951/.84.221 0804732663
Russians--China--Harbin.

DS796.H7.E48
Endacott, G. B.
Fragrant harbour, a short history of Hong Kong, by G.B. Endacott and A. Hinton. Hong Kong, Oxford University Press 1962 216 p.
62-006748 951.25
Hong Kong -- History.

DS796.H7.L593
Lo, Hsiang-lin, 1905-1978.
Hong Kong and Western cultures. Tokyo, Centre for East Asian Cultural Studies; [1964, c1963] vi, 289, 56 p
65-007535
Hong Kong (China) -- Relations -- China. China -- Relations -- China -- Hong Kong. Hong Kong (China) -- Relations -- Europe.

DS796.H75.A34 1997
Abbas, M. A.
Hong Kong: culture and the politics of disappearance/ Ackbar Abbas. Minneapolis: University of Minnesota Press, 1997. vii, 155 p.
96-041269 951.25 0816629242
Hong Kong (China) -- Civilization. Hong Kong (China) -- History -- Transfer of Sovereignty from Great Britain, 1997.

DS796.H757.B83 1997
Buckley, Roger, 1944-
Hong Kong: the road to 1997/ Roger Buckley. Cambridge, U.K.; Cambridge University Press, 1997. xxi, 232 p.
96-037247 951.25 0521470080
Hong Kong (China) -- History. Hong Kong (China) -- Politics and government. Hong Kong (China) -- Relations -- China.

DS796.H757.C36 1991
Cameron, Nigel.
An illustrated history of Hong Kong/ Nigel Cameron. Hong Kong: Oxford University Press, 1991. 362 p.
90-048787 951.25 0195849973
Hong Kong (China) -- History.

DS796.H757.C44 1998
Chang, David W., 1929-
The politics of Hong Kong's reversion to China/ David Wen-Wei Chang and Richard Y. Chuang; foreword by Hungdah Chiu. New York: St. Martin's Press, 1998. xxiv, 274 p.
96-052814 951.2505 0333684621
Hong Kong (China) -- Politics and government. Hong Kong (China) -- Relations -- China. China -- Relations -- China -- Hong Kong.

DS796.H757.H645 1988
Hong Kong, a Chinese and international concern/ edited by Jurgen Domes and Yu-ming Shaw. Boulder: Westview Press, 1988. vii, 279 p.
87-029475 320.951/25 0813374499
Hong Kong (China) -- Politics and government.

DS796.H757.H6595 1999
Hong Kong the super paradox: life after return to China/ edited by James C. Hsiung. New York, N.Y.: St. Martin's Press, 1999. p. cm.
99-040500 951.2506 0312222939
Hong Kong (China) -- Politics and government -- 1997- Hong Kong (China) -- Economic conditions. Hong Kong (China) -- Social conditions.

DS796.H757.K45 1986
Kelly, Ian.
Hong Kong: a political-geographic analysis/ Ian Kelly. Honolulu, Hawaii: University of Hawaii Press, c1986. xiv, 191 p.
86-007000 951/.25 0824810244
Geopolitics -- Hong Kong. Hong Kong (China) -- Politics and government. Hong Kong (China) -- Foreign relations -- China. China -- Foreign relations -- Hong Kong.

DS796.H757.M48 2000
Meyer, David R.
Hong Kong as a global metropolis/ David R. Meyer. Cambridge, UK; Cambridge University Press, 2000. xiii, 272 p.
99-032285 951.25 0521643449
Hong Kong (China) -- History. Hong Kong (China) -- Economic conditions.

DS796.H757.M56 1987
Miners, Norman.
Hong kong under imperial rule, 1912-1941/ Norman Miners. Hong Kong; Oxford University Press, 1987. vi, 330 p.
87-021992 951/.2504 0195841719
Hong Kong (China) -- Politics and government.

DS796.H757.P39 1998
Patten, Chris, 1944-
East and west: China, power, and the future of Asia/ Christopher Patten. New York: Times Books, c1998. xiv, 304 p.
98-024150 951.25/04 0812930002
Pacific Area -- Politics and government. Hong Kong (China) -- Politics and government.

DS796.H757.R46 1999
Reporting Hong Kong: foreign media and the handover/ edited by Alan Knight and Yoshiko Nakano. New York: St. Martin's Press, 1999. xxii, 223 p.
99-011038 070.4/499512505 031222429X
Foreign correspondents -- China -- Hong Kong. Journalism -- China -- Hong Kong. Mass media -- Hong Kong. Hong Kong (China) -- History -- Transfer of Sovereignty from Great Britain, 1997 -- Public opinion. Hong Kong (China) -- History -- Transfer of Sovereignty from Great Britain, 1997 -- Press coverage.

DS796.H757.R64 1992
Roberts, Elfed Vaughan, 1946-
Historical dictionary of Hong Kong & Macau/ Elfed Vaughan Roberts, Sum Ngai Ling, Peter Bradshaw. Metuchen, N.J.: Scarecrow Press, 1992. xlvii, 357 p.
92-020816 951.25/003 0810825740
Hong Kong (China) -- History -- Dictionaries. Macau (China: Special Administrative Region) -- History -- Dictionaries.

DS796.H757.S43 1989
Scott, Ian, 1943-
Political change and the crisis of legitimacy in Hong Kong/ Ian Scott. Honolulu: University of Hawaii Press, c1989. xv, 480 p.
89-004957 951.25 0824812697
Hong Kong (China) -- Politics and government.

DS796.H757.T735 1997
Tsang, Steve Yui-Sang, 1959-
Hong Kong: appointment with China/ Steve Tsang. London; I.B. Tauris, 1997. xiii, 274 p.
1860643116
Hong Kong (China) -- Relations -- China. China -- Relations -- China -- Hong Kong. Hong Kong (China) -- History.

DS796.H757.T77 1993
Tsai, Jung-fang, 1936-
Hong Kong in Chinese history: community and social unrest in the British Colony, 1842-1913/ Jung-fang Tsai. New York: Columbia University Press, c1993. xiii, 375 p.
92-036866 951.25 023107932X
Hong Kong (China) -- History. Hong Kong (China) -- Social conditions.

DS796.H757.W36 1995
Wang, Enbao, 1953-
Hong Kong, 1997: the politics of transition/ Enbao Wang. Boulder: L. Rienner, 1995. xiv, 231 p.
95-012694 951.2505 1555875971
Hong Kong (China) -- Politics and government. Hong Kong (China) -- Relations -- China. China -- Relations -- China -- Hong Kong.

DS796.H79.E189 1994
White, Barbara-Sue, 1942-
Turbans and traders: Hong Kong's Indian communities/ Barbara-Sue White. Hong Kong; Oxford University Press, 1994. ix, 257 p.
94-007561 951.25/004914 0195852877
East Indians -- Hong Kong.

DS796.H84.J36 1993
Jankowiak, William R.
Sex, death, and hierarchy in a Chinese city: an anthropological account/ William R. Jankowiak. New York: Columbia University Press, c1993. xvi, 345 p.
92-023945 951/.77 0231079605
Mongols -- China -- Hohhot. Hohhot (China) -- Ethnic relations.

DS796.M2.B59
Boxer, C. R. 1904-
Fidalgos in the Far East, 1550-1770; fact and fancy in the history of Macao. The Hague, M. Nijhoff, 1948. xii, 297 p.
49-021659 951.26
Portuguese -- China -- Macau (Special Administrative Region) Macau (China: Special Administrative Region) -- History.

DS796.M2 P55 2002
Pina-Cabral, João de
Between China and Europe: person, culture, and emotion in Macao/ João de Pina-Cabral. New York: Continuum, 2002. p. cm.
2001-047480 951.26.221 0826457495
Macau (China: Special Administrative Region) -- History.

DS796.M2.P67 1996
Porter, Jonathan.
Macau, the imaginary city: culture and society, 1557 to the present/ Jonathan Porter. Boulder, Colo.: Westview Press, 1996. x, 240 p.
96-007544 951.26 0813328365
Macau (China: Special Administrative Region). Macau (China: Special Administrative Region) -- Civilization.

DS796.N2.C44 1997
Chang, Iris.
The rape of Nanking: the forgotten holocaust of World War II/ Iris Chang. New York, NY: BasicBooks, c1997. xi, 290 p.
97-024137 951.04/2 0465068359
Nanking Massacre, Nanjing, Jiangsu Sheng, China, 1937. Nanjing (Jiangsu Sheng, China) -- History.

DS796.N2 D63 1999
Documents on the rape of Nanking/ edited by Timothy Brook. Ann Arbor: University of Michigan Press, c1999. viii, 301 p.
99-054728 940.53.221 0472111345
Nanking Massacre, Nanjing, Jiangsu Sheng, China, 1937--Sources. Sino-Japanese Conflict, 1937-1945--Atrocities--Sources.

DS796.N2.E93 2001
Eyewitnesses to massacre: American missionaries bear witness to Japanese atrocities in Nanjing/ edited by Zhang Kaiyuan; foreword by Donald MacInnis. Armonk, N.Y.: M.E. Sharpe, 2001. xxviii, 463 p.
00-059528 940.53 0765606844
Nanking Massacre, Nanjing, Jiangsu Sheng, China, 1937 -- Personal narratives, American. Missionaries -- China -- Jiangsu Sheng. Sino-Japanese Conflict, 1937-1945 -- Atrocities. Nanjing (Jiangsu, China)

DS796.N2 R3313 1998
Rabe, John,
The good man of Nanking: the diaries of John Rabe/ edited by Erwin Wickert; translated from the German by John E. Woods. 1st American ed. New York: A.A. Knopf: 1998. xx, 294 p.
98-015885 951.04/2.221 037540211X
Rabe, John, 1882-1949--Diaries. Nanking Massacre, Nanjing, Jiangsu Sheng, China, 1937--Personal

DS796.S2.J64
Jones, Francis Clifford.
Shanghai and Tientsin, with special reference to foreign interests, by F. C. Jones; with the co-operation of certain members of the Royal Institute of International Affairs. Prepared as a report in the International Research Series of the Institute of Pacific Relations. London, Oxford University Press, H. Milford, 1940. x, 182 p.
41-009811 325.51
Aliens -- China -- Shanghai. Aliens -- China -- Tientsin. Japanese -- China. Shanghai (China) -- Politics and government. Tientsin (China) -- Politics and government.

DS796.S2 W4 1995
Wakeman, Frederic E.
Policing Shanghai, 1927-1937/ Frederic Wakeman, Jr. Berkeley: University of California Press, c1995. xvii, 507 p.
93-042415 951/.132.220 0520084888
Police--China--Shanghai.

DS796.S24 S538 1998
Shanghai and the Yangtze Delta: a city reborn/ edited by Brian Hook. Hong Kong; Oxford University Press, 1998. xx, 188 p.
97-035895 951/.2.221 0195861825
Shanghai (China) Shanghai (China) -- Economic conditions. Yangtze River Valley (China) Yangtze River Valley (China) -- Economic conditions.

DS796.S25.G66 1995
Goodman, Bryna, 1955-
Native place, city, and nation: regional networks and identities in Shanghai, 1853-1937/ Bryna Goodman. Berkeley: University of California Press, c1995. xii, 367 p.
94-024416 951/.132035 0520089170
Social networks -- China -- Shanghai -- History -- 19th century. Social networks -- China -- Shanghai -- History -- 20th century. Rural-urban migration -- China -- Shanghai -- History -- 19th century. Shanghai (China) -- Social life and customs.

DS796.S25.L43 1999
Lee, Leo Ou-fan.
Shanghai modern: the flowering of a new urban culture in China, 1930-1945/ Leo Ou-fan Lee. Cambridge, Mass.: Harvard University Press, 1999. xvii, 408 p.
98-032318 306/.0951/132 067480550X
Popular culture -- China -- Shanghai. Shanghai (China) -- Social life and customs. China -- Civilization -- 1912-1949.

DS796.S25.L8 1999
Lu, Hanchao.
Beyond the neon lights: everyday Shanghai in the early twentieth century/ Hanchao Lu. Berkeley: University of California Press, c1999. xvii, 456 p.
98-031298 951/.132 0520215648
Shanghai (China) -- Social life and customs -- 20th century. Shanghai (China) -- Social conditions -- 20th century. Shanghai (China) -- Economic conditions -- 20th century.

DS796.S257.F8 1993
Fu, Poshek, 1955-
Passivity, resistance, and collaboration: intellectual choices in occupied Shanghai, 1937-1945/ Poshek Fu. Stanford, Calif.: Stanford University Press, 1993. xvii, 261 p.
93-010239 951/.132 0804721726
Chinese literature -- China -- Shanghai -- History and criticism. Sino-Japanese Conflict, 1937-1945 -- China -- Shanghai -- Literature and the War. Shanghai (China) -- History.

DS796.S257.H4613 1993
Henriot, Christian.
Shanghai, 1927-1937: municipal power, locality, and modernization/ Christian Henriot; translated by Noel Castelino. Berkeley: University of California Press, c1993. xiii, 288 p.
92-025054 951/.132042 0520070968
Shanghai (China) -- Politics and government.

DS796.S257 J614 1995
Johnson, Linda Cooke.
Shanghai: from market town to treaty port, 1074-1858/ Linda Cooke Johnson. Stanford, Calif.: Stanford University Press, 1995. ix, 440 p.
94-025034 951/.132.220 0804722943
Shanghai (China) -- History.

DS796.S257.M36 1996
Martin, Brian G.
The Shanghai Green Gang: politics and organized crime, 1919-1937/ Brian G. Martin. Berkeley: University of California Press, c1996. x, 314 p.
95-005017 951/.132 0520201140
Tu, Yueh-sheng, -- 1888-1951. Shanghai (China) -- Politics and government.

DS796.S29.C57 1991
Clifford, Nicholas Rowland.
Spoilt children of empire: Westerners in Shanghai and the Chinese revolution of the 1920s/ Nicholas R. Clifford. [Middlebury, Vt.]: Middlebury College Press; c1991. xvi, 361 p.
90-050904 951/.132041 0874515483
Immigrants -- China -- Shanghai. Exterritoriality. China -- History -- 1912-1928.

DS796.S29.H66 1992
Honig, Emily.
Creating Chinese ethnicity: Subei people in Shanghai, 1850-1980/ Emily Honig. New Haven: Yale University Press, c1992. xv, 174 p.
92-006055 305.8/00951132 0300051050
Ethnology -- China -- Shanghai -- History. Outcasts -- China -- Shanghai -- History. Shanghai (China) -- Ethnic relations.

DS796.S484.R57 2001
Ristaino, Marcia R.,
Port of last resort: the diaspora communities of Shanghai/ Marcia Reynders Ristaino. Stanford, Calif.: Stanford University Press, c2001. xviii, 369 p.
2001-020087 305.8/00951/132.221 0804738408
Immigrants--China--Shanghai--History--20th century. Refugees--China--Shanghai--History--20th century. Jews--China--Shanghai--History.

DS796.S55 X56 2000
Xiong, Victor Cunrui.
Sui-Tang Chang an =[Sui Tang Chang'an]: a study in the urban history of medieval China/ Victor Cunrui Xiong. 1st ed. Ann Arbor: Center for Chinese Studies, University of Michigan, xiv, 370 p.
99-058182 951/.43.221 0892641371
Xi'an (Shaanxi Sheng, China) -- History. China -- Capital and capitol -- History.

DS796.T5 L53
Lieberthal, Kenneth.
Revolution and tradition in Tientsin, 1949-1952/ Kenneth G. Lieberthal. Stanford, Calif.: Stanford University Press, 1980. viii, 231 p.
79-064215 951/.15.219 0804710449
Tianjin (China) -- Politics and government.

DS796.T68.B8
Buck, David D., 1936-
Urban change in China: politics and development in Tsinan, Shantung, 1890-1949/ David D. Buck. Madison: University of Wisconsin Press, 1978. xvi, 296 p.
76-011309   309.1/51/14   0299071103
Jinan (Shandong Sheng, China) -- History.

DS796.W8.W36 1995
Wang, Shaoguang, 1954-
Failure of charisma: the Cultural Revolution in Wuhan/ Shaoguang Wang. Hong Kong; Oxford University Press, 1995. viii, 345 p.
94-034568   951.05/6   0195859502
Wu-han shih (China) -- Politics and government. China -- History -- Cultural Revolution, 1966-1976.

DS797.42.H373 C37 2002
Carter, James Hugh.
Creating a Chinese Harbin: nationalism in an international city, 1916-1932 / James H. Carter. Ithaca: Cornell University Press, 2002. xiv, 217 p.
2001-006918   951/.84.221   0801439663
Nationalism--China--Harbin--History--20th century.

DS798-798.75 China — Local history and description — Outer Mongolia. Mongolian People's Republic

DS798.B513 1963a
Bitsch, Jorgen.
Mongolia, unknown land. Translated from the Danish by Reginald Spink. New York, Dutton, 1963. 159 p.
63-011287   915.17
Mongolia -- Description and travel.

DS798.H57 1970
Historical Evaluation and Research Organization.
Area handbook for Mongolia. Co-authors: Trevor N. Dupuy [and others] Prepared for the American University by Historical Evaluation and Research Organization. Washington, For sale by the Supt. of Docs., U.S. Govt. Print 1970. xiv, 500 p.
74-607921   309.1/51/73
Mongolia.

DS798.I54 1990
Information Mongolia: the comprehensive reference source of the People's Republic of Mongolia (MPR)/ compiled and edited by the Academy of Sciences, MPR. Oxford; Pergamon Press, 1990. xxviii, 505 p.
90-007173   951.7/3   0080361935
Mongolia.

DS798.L3
Lattimore, Owen, 1900-
Nomads and commissars; Mongolia revisited. New York, Oxford University Press, 1962. 238 p.
62-016575   951.73
Mongolia -- History. Mongolia -- Social life and customs.

DS798.5.B813 1976
History of the Mongolian People's Republic/ translated from the Mongolian and annotated by William A. Brown and Urgunge Onon. Cambridge: East Asian Research Center, Harvard University: 1976. xv, 897 p.
75-037731   951/.73   0674398629
Mongolia -- History.

DS798.75.B3313 1999
Baabar, 1954-
Twentieth century Mongolia/ by Baabar; translated by D. Suhljargalmaa ... [et al.]; edited by C. Kaplonski. Cambridge: White Horse Press, 1999- v. 1
00-361297   951.7/3   1874267405
Mongolia -- History -- 20th century.

DS798.96 China — Taiwan — Gazetteers. Dictionaries, etc.

DS798.96.C67 2000
Copper, John Franklin.
Historical dictionary of Taiwan (Republic of China)/ John F. Copper. Lanham, Md.: Scarecrow Press, 2000. xliv, 269 p.
99-027946   951.24/9/003   0810836653
Taiwan -- History -- Dictionaries.

DS799 China — Taiwan — General works

DS799.C67 1990
Copper, John Franklin.
Taiwan: nation-state or province?/ John F. Copper. Boulder: Westview Press, 1990. x, 148 p.
87-015931   951/.249   081330444X
Taiwan. Taiwan -- International status.

DS799.4 China — Taiwan — Social life and customs. Civilization. Intellectual life

DS799.4.D38 1998
Davison, Gary Marvin,
Culture and customs of Taiwan/ Gary Marvin Davison and Barbara E. Reed. Westport, Conn.: Greenwood Press, 1998. xxv, 248 p.
97-043935   951.24/9.221   0313302987
Taiwan -- Civilization. Taiwan -- Social life and customs. Taiwan -- History.

DS799.5-799.848 China — Taiwan — History

DS799.5.T3114 1999
Taiwan: a New history/ Murray A. Rubinstein, ed. Armonk, N.Y.: M.E. Sharpe, c1999. xiv, 520 p.
98-006043   951.24/905.221   1563248166
Taiwan -- History. Taiwan -- Politics and government -- 1945- Taiwan -- Civilization.

DS799.7.C484 2001
Ching, Leo T. S.,
Becoming "Japanese": colonial Taiwan and the politics of identity formation/ Leo T.S. Ching. Berkeley: University of California Press, 2001. xii, 251 p.
00-051169   951.24/904.221   0520225538
Taiwan -- History -- 1895-1945. Taiwan -- Politics and government -- 1895-1945.

DS799.716.M45 2002
Memories of the future: national identity issues and the search for a new Taiwan/ Stéphane Corcuff, editor. Armonk, N.Y.: M.E. Sharpe, c2002. xxv, 285 p.
2001-049918   951.24/904.221   0765607913
Taiwan -- Politics and government -- 1895-1945. Taiwan -- Politics and government -- 1945-

DS799.812.G38 1987
Gates, Hill.
Chinese working-class lives: getting by in Taiwan/ Hill Gates. Ithaca: Cornell University Press, 1987. xii, 256 p.
87-047597   951/.24905   0801494613
Working class -- Taiwan. Taiwan -- Social conditions -- 1975-1988. Taiwan -- Social life and customs -- 1975-

DS799.816.B86 1996
Bullard, Monte R.
The soldier and the citizen: the role of the military in Taiwan's development/ Monte R. Bullard. Armonk, NY: M.E. Sharpe, c1997. xiv, 223 p.
96-038663   322/.5/0951249   1563249782
Civil-military relations -- Taiwan. Taiwan -- Politics and government -- 1945- Taiwan -- Armed Forces -- Political activity.

DS799.816.L66 1990
Long, Simon, 1955-
Taiwan: China's last frontier/ Simon Long. New York: St. Martin's Press, 1991. xix, 264 p.
90-043872   951.24/905   0312052731
Chinese reunification question, 1949- China -- Politics and government -- 1949- Taiwan -- Politics and government -- 1945-

DS799.816.M33 1998
Maguire, Keith.
The rise of modern Taiwan/ Keith Maguire. Aldershot, Hampshire, England; Ashgate, c1998. vii, 223 p.
98-028554   951.24/905   185521847X
Taiwan -- Politics and government -- 1945- Taiwan -- Economic conditions -- 1945- Taiwan -- Social conditions -- 1945-

DS799.816.O74 1994
The Other Taiwan: 1945 to the present/ Murray A. Rubinstein, editor. Armonk, N.Y.: M.E. Sharpe, 1994. ix, 485 p.
94-016058   951.24/905.220   1563241935
Taiwan -- Politics and government -- 1945- Taiwan -- Economic conditions -- 1945- Taiwan -- Civilization.

DS799.82.C437
Taylor, Jay, 1931-
The Generalissimo's son: Chiang Ching-kuo and the revolutions in China and Taiwan/ Jay Taylor. Cambridge, Mass.: Harvard University Press, 2000. xiv, 520 p.
00-035053   951.24/905/092   0674002873
Chiang, Ching-kuo, -- 1910-1988. Presidents -- Taiwan -- Biography. China -- History -- 1912-1949. Taiwan -- History -- 1945-

DS799.82.W346.M37 1996
Marks, Thomas A.
Counterrevolution in China: Wang Sheng and the Koumintang/ Thomas A. Marks. London; Frank Cass, 1996. 357 p.
96-013891   951.24/905/092   0714647004
Wang, Sheng, -- d1917- Generals -- Taiwan -- Biography. Taiwan -- Politics and government -- 1949-

DS799.823.L35 1991
Lai, Tse-han.
A tragic beginning: the Taiwan uprising of February 28, 1947/ Lai Tse-han, Ramon H. Myers, Wei Wou. Stanford, Calif.: Stanford University Press, 1991. x, 273 p.
90-039218   951.24/905   0804718296
Taiwan -- History -- February Twenty Eighth Incident, 1947.

DS799.847.C63 1994
Contemporary China and the changing international community/ edited by Bih-jaw Lin and James T. Myers. Columbia, S.C.: University of South Carolina Press, c1994. xvii, 396 p.
94-011684   951.05   1570030243
Chinese reunification question, 1949- Taiwan -- Economic conditions -- 1975- Taiwan -- Foreign relations -- 1945- China -- Economic conditions -- 1976-

DS799.847.W33 1994
Wachman, Alan.
Taiwan: national identity and democratization/ Alan M. Wachman. Armonk, N.Y.: M.E. Sharpe, c1994. xvi, 294 p.
94-012659   305.8/00951.220   1563243997
Democracy--Taiwan. Democratization--Taiwan.

DS799.847.W84 1994
Wu, Hsin-hsing, 1953-
Bridging the Strait: Taiwan, China, and the prospects for reunification/ Hsin-hsing Wu. Hong Kong; Oxford University Press, 1994. viii, 346 p.
93-042311   951.05/8   0195857658
Chinese reunification question, 1949- China -- Politics and government -- 1976- Taiwan -- Politics and government -- 1988-

DS799.848.T35 1994
Taiwan in world affairs/ edited by Robert G. Sutter and William R. Johnson. Boulder: Westview Press, 1994. viii, 328 p.
94-010740   327.5124/9   0813318955
Taiwan -- Foreign relations -- 1945- Taiwan -- Politics and government -- 1988- Taiwan -- Economic conditions -- 1975-

DS799.9 China — Taiwan — Local history and description, A-Z

DS799.9.T24.S36 1987
Sangren, Paul Steven.
History and magical power in a Chinese community/ P. Steven Sangren. Sanford, Calif.: Stanford University Press, c1987. x, 268 p.
86-023199   951/.249   0804713448
Ta-hsi chen (Tao-yuan hsien, Taiwan) -- History. Ta-hsi chen (Tao-yuan hsien, Taiwan) -- Social life and customs.

DS805 Japan — Gazetteers. Dictionaries, etc. Place names

DS805.M63 1998
Modern Japan: an encyclopedia of history, culture, and nationalism/ editor, James L. Huffman. New York: Garland Pub., 1998. xxxiii, 316 p.
97-021910   952   0815325258
Nationalism -- Japan. Japan -- History -- 1868- Japan -- Encyclopedias.

DS806 Japan — General works

DS806.H25
Hall, John Whitney, 1916-
Twelve doors to Japan, by John Whitney Hall and Richard K. Beardsley. With chapters by Joseph K. Yamagiwa [and] B. James George, Jr. New York, McGraw-Hill [1965] xxi, 649 p.
64-066015   915.203
Japan.

DS806.R35
Reischauer, Edwin O. 1910-
The Japanese/ Edwin O. Reischauer. Cambridge, Mass.: Belknap Press, 1977. 443 p.
76-030708   952   0674471768
Japan.

DS806.S43
Seidensticker, Edward, 1921-
This country, Japan/ Edward Seidensticker. Tokyo; Kodansha International, 1979. x, 332 p.
74-077958   952
Seidensticker, Edward, -- 1921- Japanese literature -- History and criticism. National characteristics, Japanese. Translators -- United States -- Biography. Japan.

DS809 Japan — Description and travel — 1801-1900

DS809.A35 1969
Alcock, Rutherford, 1809-1897.
The capital of the tycoon: a narrative of a three years' residence in Japan. London, Longman, Green, Longman, Roberts, & Green, 1863. St. Clair Shores, Mich., Scholarly Press [1969] 2 v.
73-008881   915.2
Japan -- Description and travel. Japan -- Foreign relations -- To 1868.

DS809.H18 1992
Hall, Francis.
Japan through American eyes: the journal of Francis Hall, Kanagawa and Yokohama, 1859-1866/ edited and annotated by F.G. Notehelfer. Princeton, N.J.: Princeton University Press, c1992. xiv, 652 p.
91-036385   952/.025   0691031819
Japan -- Description and travel.

DS809.H523 1964
Heusken, Henry C. J., 1832-1861.
Japan journal, 1855-1861. Translated and edited by Jeannette C. van der Corput and Robert A. Wilson. New Brunswick, Rutgers University Press [1964] xviii, 247 p.
63-023314   915.2
Japan -- Description and travel.

DS809.P456 1967
Perry, Matthew Calbraith, 1794-1858.
Narrative of the expedition of an American squadron to the China Seas and Japan, performed in the years 1852, 1853, and 1854, under the command of Commodore M.C. Perry, United States Navy, by order Compiled from the original notes and journals of Commodore Perry and his officers, at his request, and under his supervision, by Francis L. Hawks. Washington, B. Tucker, 1856. New York, AMS Press, 1967. 3 v.
67-031019   952.02/5
Japan -- Description and travel.

DS821 Japan — Social life and customs. Civilization. Intellectual life — General works

DS821.B46
Benedict, Ruth, 1887-1948.
The chrysanthemum and the sword; patterns of Japanese culture, by Ruth Benedict. Boston, Houghton Mifflin company, 1946. 324 p.
46-011843   915.2
Japan -- Social life and customs. Japan -- Civilization.

DS821.C43 1971
Chamberlain, Basil Hall, 1850-1935.
Japanese things; being notes on various subjects connected with Japan, for the use of travelers and others. Rutland, Vt., Tuttle [c1971] x, 568 p.
76-087791   915.2/03/3103   0804807132
Japan.

DS821.C62 1988
Collcutt, Martin, 1939-
Cultural atlas of Japan/ by Martin Collcutt, Marius Jansen, and Isao Kumakura. New York: Facts on File, 1988. 240 p.
88-002967   952   0816019274
Japan -- Civilization. Japan -- Civilization -- Maps.

DS821.H375 1997
Hayashi, Chikio, 1918-
Japanese culture in comparative perspective/ Chikio Hayashi and Yasumasa Kuroda; foreword by Hayward R. Alker. Westport, Conn.: Praeger, 1997. xvi, 215 p.
96-037728   306/.0952   0275958612
Comparative civilization. Japan -- Civilization.

DS821.K33
Keene, Donald.
Living Japan/ Donald Keene. Garden City, N.Y.: Doubleday, [1959] 224 p.
59-010088   915.2
Japan -- Civilization.

DS821.L346
Lebra, Takie Sugiyama, 1930-
Japanese patterns of behavior/ Takie Sugiyama Lebra. Honolulu: University Press of Hawaii, c1976. xviii, 295 p.
76-010392   301.29/52   0824803965.
National characteristics, Japanese.   Japan -- Social life and customs.

DS821.S3 1943
Sansom, George Bailey, 1883-1965.
Japan, a short cultural history/ by G.B. Sansom. New York: Appleton-Century-Crofts, c1943. xviii, 554 p.
43-018417   952
Japan -- Civilization. Japan -- History.

DS821.T76
Tsunoda, Ryusaku, 1877-1964,
Sources of the Japanese tradition, compiled by Ryusaku Tsunoda, Wm. Theodore de Bary [and] Donald Keene. New York, Columbia University Press, 1958. xxvi, 928 p.
58-007167   952.0082
Japan -- Civilization. Japan -- History -- Sources.

DS821.5 Japan — Social life and customs. Civilization. Intellectual life — Foreign influences

DS821.5.C5.H68 1996
Howland, Douglas, 1955-
Borders of Chinese civilization: geography and history at Empire's end/ by D.R. Howland. Durham, N.C.: Duke University Press, 1996. p. cm.
95-049999   303.48/251052   0822317753
Chinese -- Japan -- Ethnic identity.   Japan -- Relations -- China. China -- Relations -- Japan. Japan -- Civilization -- Chinese influences.

DS822.2-822.5 Japan — Social life and customs. Civilization. Intellectual life — By period

DS822.2.M355 2000
Masuda, Wataru, 1903-1977.
Japan and China: mutual representations in the modern era/ Masuda Wataru; translated by Joshua A. Fogel. New York, N.Y.: St. Martin's Press, 2000. ix, 298 p.
99-059682   303.48/251052   0312228406
Japan -- Intellectual life -- 1600-1868. Japan -- Foreign relations -- To 1868. Europe -- Relations -- East Asia.

DS822.4.H36 2000
Harootunian, Harry D., 1929-
Overcome by modernity: history, culture, and community in interwar Japan/ Harry Harootunian. Princeton, N.J.: Princeton University Press, c2000. xxxii, 440 p.
00-022857   952.03/3   0691006504
Civilization, Modern -- 20th century. Japan -- Civilization -- Western influences. Japan -- Relations -- Foreign countries. Japan -- Civilization -- 1912-1945.

DS822.5.F54 1997
Field, Norma, 1947-
From my grandmother's bedside: sketches of postwar Tokyo/ Norma Field. Berkeley, Calif.: University of California Press, c1997. xv, 204 p.
97-018526   952.04   0520208447
Japan -- Social life and customs -- 1945-

DS822.5.I33 2000
Igarashi, Yoshikuni, 1960-
Bodies of memory: narratives of war in postwar Japanese culture, 1945-1970/ Yoshikuni Igarashi. Princeton, N.J.: Princeton University Press, c2000. x, 284 p.
99-088263   952.04   0691049114
Japan -- Civilization -- 1945-

DS822.5 .L65 2001
Lonsdale, Sarah.
Japanese style/ Sarah Lonsdale. London: Carlton, 2001. 256 p.
2001-536231   779/.995204 21   1842220810
Japan -- Social life and customs -- 1945- -- Pictorial works.

DS827 Japan — Social life and customs. Civilization. Intellectual life — Other special, A-Z

DS827.S3.T36 1993
Tanaka, Stefan.
Japan's Orient: rendering pasts into history/ Stefan Tanaka. Berkeley: University of California Press, c1993. xi, 305 p.
92-020639   951./0072   0520077318
China -- Historiography. China -- Study and teaching -- Japan.

DS830 Japan — Ethnography — General works

DS830.M345 1996
Matsumoto, David Ricky.
Unmasking Japan: myths and realities about the emotions of the Japanese/ David Matsumoto. Stanford, Calif.: Stanford University Press, 1996. xvi, 179 p.
96-016555   152.4/0952   0804727198
Japanese -- Psychology. National characteristics, Japanese. Emotions -- Cross-cultural studies.

DS830.O33 1993
Ohnuki-Tierney, Emiko.
Rice as self: Japanese identities through time/ Emiko Ohnuki-Tierney. Princeton, N.J.: Princeton University Press, c1993. xi, 184 p.
92-043711   952   0691094772
National characteristics, Japanese. Rice -- Social aspects -- Japan. Japan -- Civilization.

DS832 Japan — Ethnography — Ainu

DS832.S66 1993
Sjoberg, Katarina, 1949-
The return of the Ainu: cultural mobilization and the practice of ethnicity in Japan/ Katarina Sjoberg. Chur, Switzerland; Harwood Academic Publishers, c1993. xii, 221 p.
93-016634   305.89/46   3718654016
Ainu. Japan -- Ethnic relations.

DS832.7 Japan — Natives of foreign countries (General) — General works

DS832.7.K6.F817 2000
Fukuoka, Yasunori, 1947-
Lives of young Koreans in Japan/ Yasunori Fukuoka; translated by Tom Gill. Melbourne: Trans Pacific Press, 2000. xxxviii, 330 p.
2001-339494   1876843004
Koreans -- Japan. Koreans -- Ethnic identity.

DS832.7.K6.K669 2000
Koreans in Japan: critical voices from the margin/ edited by Sonia Ryang. London; Routledge, 2000. viii, 229 p.
99-039943   952/.004957   041521999X
Koreans -- Japan -- History. Japan -- Ethnic relations.

DS832.7.K6.R93 1997
Ryang, Sonia.
North Koreans in Japan: language, ideology, and identity/ Sonia Ryang. Boulder, Colo.: Westview Press, 1997. xix, 248 p.
96-045336   305.895/7052   0813389526
Koreans -- Japan. Japan -- Ethnic relations.

DS834 Japan — History — Biography (Collective)

DS834.M64
Morris, Ivan I.
The nobility of failure: tragic heroes in the history of Japan/ Ivan Morris. New York: Holt, Rinehart and Winston, [1975] xxiii, 500 p.
73-003750   952/.00992   003010811X
Heroes -- Japan. Japan -- Biography.

DS834.7-834.9 Japan — History — Historiography

DS834.7.M43 1998
Mehl, Margaret.
History and the state in nineteenth-century Japan/ Margaret Mehl. New York: St. Martin's Press, 1998. x, 210 p.
97-036784   952/.007/2052   0312211600
Historiography -- Japan -- History -- 19th century. Japan -- Historiography.

DS834.9.I35
Ienaga, Saburo, 1913-
Japan's past, Japan's future: one historian's odyssey/ Ienaga Saburo; translated and introduced by Richard H. Minear. Lanham, Md.: Rowman & Littlefield Publishers, 2001. x, 203 p.
00-062695   952.03/3/092   0742509885
Ienaga, Saburo, -- 1913- Historians -- Japan -- Biography.

DS835 Japan — History — General works

DS835.B6 1970 *have 1955*
Borton, Hugh.
Japan's modern century; from Perry to 1970. New York, Ronald Press [1970] x, 610 p.
70-110544   952.03
Japan -- History.

DS835.C36 1988
The Cambridge history of Japan/ [general editors, John W. Hall ... et al.]. Cambridge [England]; Cambridge University Press, 1988-1999 v. 1-6
88-002877   952   0521223520
Japan -- History.

DS835.K2 1971
Kaempfer, Engelbert, 1651-1716.
The history of Japan, together with a description of the Kingdom of Siam, 1690-92. Translated by J. G. Scheuchzer. [New York, AMS Press, 1971] 3 v.
78-137313   915.2/03/25   0404036309
Japan -- History -- To 1868. Japan -- Description and travel -- Early works to 1800. Thailand -- Description and travel -- Early works to 1800.

DS835.R38 1970
Reischauer, Edwin O. 1910-
Japan; the story of a nation [by] Edwin O. Reischauer. New York, Knopf [1970] xv, 345 p.
77-108925   952
Japan -- History. *have 1967 3rd ed.*

DS835.R4 1953
Reischauer, Edwin O. 1910-
Japan, past and present/ by Edwin O. Reischauer; foreword by Sir George Sansom. New York: Knopf, 1961, c1952. xi, 292 p.
52-012412   952
Japan -- History.

DS835.S27
Sansom, George Bailey, 1883-1965.
A history of Japan. Stanford, Calif., Stanford University Press, 1958-63. 3 v.
58-011694   952   0804705240
Japan -- History.

DS835.T58
Totman, Conrad D.
Japan before Perry: a short history/ Conrad Totman. Berkeley: University of California Press, c1981. xv, 246 p.
80-014708   952   0520041321
Japan -- History -- To 1868.

DS838.5 Japan — History — Military history

DS838.5.F37 1992
Farris, William Wayne.
Heavenly warriors: the evolution of Japan's military, 500-1300/ William Wayne Farris. Cambridge, Mass.: Council on East Asian Studies, Harvard Universit 1992. xv, 486 p.
92-011200   952   0674387031
Japan -- History, Military -- To 1868. Japan -- History -- To 1333.

DS838.5.F75 1992
Friday, Karl F.
Hired swords: the rise of private warrior power in early Japan/ Karl F. Friday. Stanford, Calif.: Stanford University Press, c1992. ix, 265 p.
91-024615   952   0804719780
Samurai -- History. Japan -- History, Military -- To 1868.

DS849 Japan — History — Diplomatic history. — Foreign and general relations

DS849.C6.B67 2000
Brooks, Barbara J., 1953-
Japan's imperial diplomacy: consuls, treaty ports, and war in China, 1895-1938/ Barbara J. Brooks. Honolulu: University of Hawai'i Press, c2000. xi, 296 p.
00-021819   327.52051   0824820622
Japan -- Foreign relations -- China. China -- Foreign relations -- Japan. Japan -- Foreign relations -- 1868-

DS849.C6.M32 2001
Matsusaka, Yoshihisa Tak.
The making of Japanese Manchuria, 1904-1932/ Yoshihisa Tak Matsusaka. Cambridge, MA: Harvard University Asia Center, 2001. xviii, 522 p.
00-049856   951/.805   0674003691
Imperialism -- History -- 20th century. Manchuria (China) -- Relations -- Japan. Manchuria (China) -- History -- 20th century. Japan -- Relations -- China -- Manchuria.

DS849.C6.W358 2000
Wang, Qingxin Ken, 1964-
Hegemonic cooperation and conflict: postwar Japan's China policy and the United States/ Qingxin Ken Wang. Westport, Conn.: Praeger, c2000. xii, 294 p.
98-044534   327.52051   0275963144
Japan -- Foreign relations -- China. China -- Foreign relations -- Japan. Japan -- Foreign relations -- 1945-1989.

DS849.K8.K34 1997
Kang, Etsuko Hae-jin.
Diplomacy and ideology in Japanese-Korean relations: from the fifteenth to the eighteenth century/ Etsuko Hae-jin Kang. Houndmills, Basingstoke, Hampshire: Macmillan Press; 1997. xi, 312 p.
96-052880   327.520519/09/03   0333699394
Japan -- Foreign relations -- Korea. Korea -- Foreign relations -- Japan. Japan -- Foreign relations -- To 1868.

DS850-891 Japan — History — By period

DS850.A36 2000
Adolphson, Mikael S., 1961-
The gates of power: monks, courtiers, and warriors in premodern Japan/ Mikael S. Adolphson. Honolulu: University of Hawaii Press, c2000. xvii, 456 p.
00-023448   952   0824822633
Japan -- Politics and government -- 794-1600.

DS850.H36 1991
Hane, Mikiso.
Premodern Japan: a historical survey/ Mikiso Hane. Boulder: Westview Press, 1991. xii, 258 p.
90-041699   952   0813380669
Japan -- History -- To 1868.

DS850.T68 1993
Totman, Conrad D.
Early modern Japan/ Conrad Totman. Berkeley: University of California Press, c1993. xxix, 593 p.
92-022617   952/.025   0520080262
Japan -- History -- To 1868.

DS855.F37 1998
Farris, William Wayne.
Sacred texts and buried treasures: issues in the historical archaeology of ancient Japan/ William Wayne Farris. Honolulu: University of Hawai'i Press, c1998. ix, 333 p.
97-046014   952/.01   0824819667
Inscription, Japanese. Wooden tablets -- Japan -- History. Korea -- Relations -- Japan. Japan -- Capital and capitol -- History. Japan -- Antiquities.

DS855.I45 1996
Imamura, Keiji, 1946-
Prehistoric Japan: new perspectives on insular East Asia/ Keiji Imamura. Honolulu, Hawaii: University of Hawaii Press, c1996. x, 246 p.
96-012382   952/.01   0824818539
Japan -- History -- To 645. Japan -- Relations -- East Asia. East Asia -- Relations -- Japan.

DS855.P54 1997
Piggott, Joan R.
The emergence of Japanese kingship/ Joan R. Piggott. Stanford, Calif.: Stanford University Press, c1997. 434 p.
97-011323   952/.01   0804728321
Mythology, Japanese. State, The. Emperors -- Japan. Japan -- Kings and rulers. Japan -- History -- To 794.

DS859.M25
Mass, Jeffrey P.
Warrior government in early medieval Japan: a study of the Kamakura Bakufu, shugo and jito/ Jeffrey P. Mass. New Haven: Yale University Press, 1974. x, 257 p.
74-075875   320.9/52/02   0300017561
Local officials and employees -- Japan -- History. Constitutional history, Medieval. Japan -- Politics and government -- 1185-1333.

DS859.M3313 1998
The clear mirror: a chronicle of the Japanese court during the Kamakura period (1185-1333)/ translated, with notes and an introduction, by George W. Perkins. Stanford, Calif.: Stanford University Press, 1998. xiv, 342 p.
97-049585   952/.021   0804729530
Japan -- History -- Kamakura period,1185-1333. Japan -- Court and courtiers.

DS861.T313
The Taiheiki: a chronicle of medieval Japan. Translated, with an introd. and notes, by Helen Craig McCullough. New York, Columbia University Press, 1959. xlix, 401 p.
59-006662   952.02
Godaigo, -- Emperor of Japan, -- 1288-1339. Japan -- History -- To 1868.

DS863.G63 1996
Goble, Andrew Edmund.
Kenmu: Go-Daigo's revolution/ Andrew Edmund Goble. Cambridge, MA; Council on East Asian Studies, Harvard Universit 1996. xxi, 390 p.
96-017198   952/.022   0674502558
Godaigo, -- Emperor of Japan, -- 1288-1339. Japan -- History -- Kenmu Restoration, 1333-1336.

DS865.5.O75 1997
The origins of Japan's medieval world: courtiers, clerics, warriors, and peasants in the fourteenth century/ edited by Jeffrey P. Mass. Stanford, Calif.: Stanford University Press, 1997. xvi, 504 p.
97-002475   952/.02   0804728941
Japan -- History -- Period of northern and southern courts, 1336-1392. Japan -- History -- Kamakura period, 1185-1333. Japan -- Court and courtiers.

DS869.T6.B47 1982
Berry, Mary Elizabeth, 1947-
Hideyoshi/ Mary Elizabeth Berry. Cambridge, Mass.: Harvard University Press, 1982. xiv, 293 p.
82-001056   952/.023/0924   0674390253
Toyotomi, Hideyoshi, -- 1536?-1598. Generals -- Japan -- Biography. Japan -- History -- Period of civil wars, 1480-1603. Japan -- History -- Azuchi-Momoyama period, 1568-1603.

DS871.J35 2000
Jansen, Marius B.
The making of modern Japan/ Marius B. Jansen. Cambridge, Mass. Belknap Press of Harvard University Press, 2000. 871 p.
00-041352   952/.025   0674003349
Japan -- History -- Tokugawa period, 1600-1868. Japan -- History -- Meiji period, 1868-1912.

DS871.T527 1990
Tokugawa Japan: the social and economic antecedents of modern Japan/ edited by Chie Nakane and Shinzabur Oishi; translation edited by Conrad Totman. Tokyo, Japan: University of Tokyo Press, c1990. viii, 240 p.
91-105754   952/.025   4130270249

DS871.T6
Totman, Conrad D.
Politics in the Tokugawa bakufu, 1600-1843 [by] Conrad D. Totman. Cambridge, Harvard University Press, 1967. 346 p.
67-022873   952.02/5
Tokugawa family.   Japan -- Politics and government -- 1600-1868.

DS871.5.B66
Bolitho, Harold.
Treasures among men; the fudai daimyo in Tokugawa Japan. New Haven, Yale University Press, 1974. xiii, 278 p.
73-086885   320.9/52/025   0300016557
Daimyo.   Japan -- Politics and government -- 1600-1868.

DS881.B4 1963
Beasley, W. G. 1919-
The modern history of Japan. New York, Praeger [1963] xi, 352 p.
63-020665   952
Japan -- History.

DS881.3.J28 1971
Jansen, Marius B.
Sakamoto Ryoma and the Meiji Restoration, by Marius B. Jansen. Stanford, Calif., Stanford University Press, 1971. xii, 423 p.
77-153818   952.03/1   0804707847
Sakamoto, Ryoma, -- 1836-1867.   Japan -- History -- Restoration, 1853-1870.

DS881.3.T63
Totman, Conrad D.
The collapse of the Tokugawa bakufu, 1862-1868/ Conrad D. Totman. Honolulu: University Press of Hawaii, c1980. xxiv, 588 p.
79-022094   952/.025
Japan -- History -- Restoration, 1853-1870. Japan -- Politics and government -- 1600-1868.

DS881.3.W55 1992
Wilson, George M. 1937-
Patriots and redeemers in Japan: motives in the Meiji Restoration/ George M. Wilson. Chicago: University of Chicago Press, c1992. xvi, 201 p.
91-020448   952.03/1   0226900916
Japan -- History -- Restoration, 1853-1870.

DS881.5.M323.W35 1998
Walthall, Anne.
The weak body of a useless woman: Matsuo Taseko and the Meiji Restoration/ Anne Walthall. Chicago, Ill: University of Chicago Press, 1998. xvi, 412 p.
98-016365   952/.025   0226872351
Matsuo, Taseko, -- 1811-1894.   Women intellectuals -- Japan -- Biography. Nationalists -- Japan -- Biography. Women political activists -- Japan -- Biography. Japan -- History -- Restoration, 1853-1870.

DS881.8.P4
Perry, Matthew Calbraith, 1794-1858.
The Japan Expedition, 1852-1854; the personal journal of Commodore Matthew C. Perry. Edited by Roger Pineau. With an introd. by Samuel Eliot Morison. Washington, Smithsonian Institution Press, 1968. xix, 241 p.
68-009578   915.2/04/250924
Perry, Matthew Calbraith, -- 1794-1858.   United States Naval Expedition to Japan, 1852-1854.

DS881.9.F847 1996
Fujitani, Takashi.
Splendid monarchy: power and pageantry in modern Japan/ T. Fujitani. Berkeley: University of California Press, c1996. xiv, 305 p.
95-038543   952.03   0520202376
Emperor worship -- Japan. Monarchy -- Japan. Emperors -- Japan. Japan -- History -- 1868- Japan -- Kings and rulers.

DS881.9.G54 1994
Giffard, Sydney.
Japan among the powers, 1890-1990/ Sydney Giffard. New Haven: Yale University Press, 1994. xxi, 218 p.
93-036806   952   0300058470
Japan -- History -- 1868- Japan -- Relations -- Foreign countries.

DS881.9.T77 2000
Tsuzuki, Chushichi.
The pursuit of power in modern Japan, 1825-1995/ Chushichi Tsuzuki. New York: Oxford University Press, 2000. x, 550 p.
00-709361   952.03   0198205899
Japan -- History -- 1868- Japan -- History -- Tokugawa period, 1600-1868.

DS882.D88 1995
Duus, Peter, 1933-
The abacus and the sword: the Japanese penetration of Korea, 1895-1910/ Peter Duus. Berkeley: University of California Press, c1995. xiv, 480 p.
94-006118   951.9/02   0520086147
Japan -- History -- Meiji period, 1868-1912. Korea -- History -- 1864-1910. Japan -- Relations -- Korea.

DS882.S78
Storry, Richard, 1913-
A history of modern Japan. [Harmondsworth, Middlesex; Penguin Books [1960] 287 p.
60-004354   952
Japan -- History.

DS882.7.S29 1999
Seagrave. Sterling.
The Yamato dynasty: the secret history of Japan's imperial family/ by Sterling Seagrave and Peggy Seagrave. New York: Broadway Books, c1999. xvii, 394 p.
99-049888   952.03/0922   0767904966
Meiji, -- Emperor of Japan, -- 1852-1912. Meiji, -- Emperor of Japan, -- 1852-1912 -- Family. Taisho, -- Emperor of Japan, -- 1879-1926. Emperors -- Japan -- Biography.

DS889.A59 1997
Allinson, Gary D.
Japan's postwar history/ Gary D. Allinson. Ithaca, N.Y.: Cornell University Press, 1997. xiv, 208 p.
96-038163   952.04   0801483727
Japan -- History -- 1945-

DS889.K546 2001
Kingston, Jeff, 1957-
Japan in transformation, 1952-2000/ Jeff Kingston. New York: Longman, 2001. xii, 230 p.
00-067849   952.04   0582418755
Japan -- History -- 1945-

DS889.M345767 2001
Matray, James Irving, 1948-
Japan's emergence as a global power/ James I. Matray. Westport, Conn.: Greenwood Press, 2001. xxxix, 228 p.
00-039356   952   0313299722
Japan -- History -- 1945- Japan -- Economic policy -- 1945-

DS889.16.S26 2000
Sarantakes, Nicholas Evan, 1966-
Keystone: the American occupation of Okinawa and U.S.-Japanese relations/ Nicholas Evan Sarantakes. College Station, TX: Texas A&M University, c2000. xxiii, 264 p.
00-044340   952/.29404   0890969698
Japan -- History -- Allied occupation, 1945-1952. Japan -- Military relations -- United States. United States -- Military relations -- Japan.

DS890 .T29
Babb, James.
Tanaka, the making of postwar Japan/ James Babb. Harlow, England; Longman 2001. xii, 126 p.
00-061358   952.04/7/092   0582382165
Tanaka, Kakuei, -- 1918-   Prime ministers -- Japan -- Biography.   Japan -- Politics and government -- 1945-1989.

DS891.V58 1997
The vitality of Japan: sources of national strength and weakness/ edited by Armand Clesse ... [et al.]. Houndmills, Basingstoke, Hampshire: Macmillan Press; 1997. xiv, 414 p.
96-037768   957.03/3   033364820X
Japan -- Politics and government -- 1989- -- Congresses. Japan -- Foreign economic relations - - Congresses. Japan -- Relations -- Foreign countries -- Congresses.

DS894.59 Japan — Local history and description — Tohoku region

DS894.59.I53.W56 1995
Wigen, Karen, 1958-
The making of a Japanese periphery, 1750-1920/ Karen Wigen. Berkeley, Calif.: University of California Press, c1995. xv, 336 p.
93-036270   952/.1   0520384209
Ina Valley (Japan) -- History.

DS894.59.I539.K343 1993
Brown, Philip C., 1947-
Central authority and local autonomy in the formation of early modern Japan: the case of Kaga domain/ Philip C. Brown. Stanford, Calif.: Stanford University Press, 1993. xvi, 312 p.
93-010240   952/.154   0804720363
Kaga-han (Japan) -- Politics and government.

DS894.59.I838.B39 1994
Baxter, James C.
The Meiji unification through the lens of Ishikawa prefecture/ James C. Baxter. Cambridge, Mass.: Harvard University Press, 1994. xvi, 358 p.
94-038297   952.1/54   0674564669
Ishikawa-ken (Japan) -- History.

DS894.59.T698
Lewis, Michael, 1949-
Becoming apart: national power and local politics in Toyama, 1868-1945/ Michael Lewis. Cambridge, Mass.: Harvard University Asia Center, 2000. xviii, 340 p.
00-037017   952/.153   0674002423
Toyama-ken (Japan) -- Politics and government.

DS894.59.Y3485.V36 1994
Van Staaveren, Jacob.
An American in Japan, 1945-1948: a civilian view of the occupation/ Jacob Van Staaveren; introduction by Akira Iriye. Seattle: University of Washington Press, c1994. xvii, 286 p.
94-005717   952/.164044   0295973633
Yamanashi-ken (Japan) -- History. Japan -- History -- Allied occupation, 1945-1952.

DS894.79 Japan — Local history and description — Chugoku region

DS894.79.Y349.C4637
Huber, Thomas M.
The revolutionary origins of modern Japan/ Thomas M. Huber. Stanford, Calif.: Stanford University Press, 1981. 260 p.
79-064214   952.03/1/0922   0804710481
Choshu-han (Japan) -- Politics and government. Choshu-han (Japan) -- Biography. Japan -- History -- Restoration, 1853-1870.

DS895 Japan — Local history and description — Other regions, etc., A-Z

DS895.C5.C7 *have 1967*
Craig, Albert M.
Choshu in the Meiji restoration.   Cambridge, Harvard University Press, 1961. 385 p.
61-008839   952.025   0674128508
Choshu-han (Japan) -- History. Japan -- History -- Restoration, 1853-1870.

DS895.R95.S65 1999
Smits, Gregory, 1960-
Visions of Ryukyu: identity and ideology in early-modern thought and politics/ Gregory Smits. Honolulu: University of Hawai'i Press, c1999. 213 p.
98-038468   952/.29   0824820371
Ryukyu Islands -- History.

DS896.35 Japan — Tokyo — General works

DS896.35.C93 1998
Cybriwsky, Roman A.
Tokyo: the shogun's city at the twenty-first century/ by Roman Cybriwsky. Chichester; J. Wiley & Sons, c1998. xi, 260 p.
97-050189   952/.135   0471978698
Tokyo (Japan)

DS897 Japan — Other cities, towns, etc., A-Z

DS897.K85.N3313 1995
Nakano, Makiko, 1890-1978.
Makiko's diary: a merchant wife in 1910 Kyoto/ Nakano Makiko; translated with introduction and notes by Kazuko Smith. Stanford, California: Stanford University Press, 1995. xii, 256 p.
94-039864   952/.1864031/092   0804724407
Nakano, Makiko, -- 1890-1978.   Kyoto (Japan) -- Social life and customs -- 1868-1912. Kyoto (Japan) -- Biography.

DS897.K857.B47 1994
Berry, Mary Elizabeth, 1947-
The culture of civil war in Kyoto/ Mary Elizabeth Berry. Berkeley: University of California Press, c1994. xxxii, 373 p.
93-007452   952/.186   0520081706
Kyoto (Japan) -- History. Japan -- History -- Period of civil wars, 1480-1603.

DS897.S2.M63 1999
Mock, John Allan.
Culture, community and change in a Sapporo neighborhood, 1925-1988: Hanayama/ John Mock. Lewiston, N.Y.: Edwin Mellen Press, 1999. xi, 232 p.
99-023114   952/.4   0773479740
Sapporo-shi (Japan) -- History.

DS897.S3923
Smith, Kerry Douglas.
A time of crisis: Japan, the great depression, and rural revitalization/ Kerry Smith. Cambridge, Mass.: Harvard University Asia Center; c2001. xvi, 481 p.
00-046093   952/.117   0674003705
Depressions -- 1929 -- Japan -- Kitakata-shi (Japan)   Kitakata-shi (Japan) -- History. Sekishiba-machi (Kitakata-shi, Japan) -- Economic conditions.   Kitakata-shi (Japan) -- Economic conditions.

DS897.T635.B35 1991
Bailey, Jackson H.
Ordinary people, extraordinary lives: political and economic change in a Tohoku village/ Jackson H. Bailey. Honolulu: University of Hawaii Press, c1991. xii, 259 p.
91-015781   952/.11   0824812999
Tanohata-mura (Japan) -- History.

DS903 Korea — Description and travel — Antiquities

DS903.P35 2000
Pai, Hyung Il.
Constructing "Korean" origins: a critical review of archaeology, historiography, and racial myth in Korean state-formation theories/ Hyung Il Pai. Cambridge, Mass.: Harvard University Asia Center, 2000. xxv, 543 p.
99-056872   951.9/01   067400244X
Archaeology and history -- Korea.   Korea -- Historiography. Korea -- Antiquities.

DS907.18 Korea — History — General works

DS907.18.L44 1997
Lee, Kenneth B.
Korea and East Asia: the story of a Phoenix/ Kenneth B. Lee; forewords by Edward Olsen and Kyung-Cho Chung. Westport, Conn.: Praeger, 1997. xix, 285 p.
96-044693   951.9   027595823X
Korea -- History. Korea (South) -- History.

DS909 Korea — History — Military history

DS909.N34 1993 *ref.*
Nahm, Andrew C.
Historical dictionary of the Republic of Korea/ by Andrew C. Nahm. Metuchen, N.J.: Scarecrow Press, 1993. lxi, 272 p.
93-003033   951.9/003   0810826038
Korea -- History -- Dictionaries. Korea (South) -- History -- Dictionaries.

DS910.2 Korea — History — Foreign and general relations

DS910.2.J3.C483 1991
Cheong, Sung-hwa.
The politics of anti-Japanese sentiment in Korea: Japanese-South Korean relations under American occupation, 1945-1952/ Sung-hwa Cheong. New York: Greenwood Press, 1991. xv, 190 p.
90-047325   303.48/25195052   031327410X
Korea (South) -- Relations -- Japan. Japan -- Relations -- Korea (South) Korea (South) -- History -- 1948-1960.

DS915.2-922.2 Korea — History — By period

DS915.2.O45 1993
Oliver, Robert Tarbell, 1909-
A history of the Korean people in modern times: 1800 to the present/ Robert T. Oliver. Newark: Univ. of Delaware Press; 1993. 374 p.
92-050486   951.9/02   0874134773
Korea -- History -- 1864-1910.   Korea -- History -- 20th century. Korea (South) -- History.

DS916.H62 1999 *ref*
Hoare, James.
Conflict in Korea: an encyclopedia/ James Hoare and Susan Pares. Santa Barbara, Calif.: ABC-CLIO, c1999. xxvii, 260 p.
99-015211   951.904   0874369789
Korean War, 1950-1953 -- Causes.   Korea -- History -- Partition, 1945- Korea -- History -- 20th century.

DS916.M94 2001
Myers, Robert John, 1924-
Korea in the cross currents: a century of struggle and the crisis of reunification/ Robert J. Myers. New York: Palgrave, 2001. vii, 200 p.
00-069225   951.904   0312238150
Korean reunification question (1945-)   Korea -- History -- 20th century.

DS916.55.S55 1996
Shin, Gi-Wook.
Peasant protest & social change in colonial Korea/ Gi-Wook Shin. Seattle: University of Washington Press, c1996. xiii, 234 p.
96-031636   951.9/03/08624   0295975482
Peasant uprisings -- Korea -- History. Land tenure -- Korea -- History. Social movements -- Korea -- History. Korea -- History -- 1864-1910. Korea -- History -- Japanese occupation, 1910-1945.

✓**DS917.C86 1997**
Cumings, Bruce, 1943-
Korea's place in the sun: a modern history/ Bruce
Cumings. New York: W.W. Norton, c1997. 527 p.
96-015398   951.9/03   0393040119
   *Korea -- History -- 20th century. Korea (South)
-- History. Korea -- History -- 1864-1910.*

DS917.444.G75 1998
Grinker, Roy Richard, 1961-
Korea and its futures: Unification and the
unfinished war/ Roy Richard Grinker. New York:
St. Martin's Press, 1998. xix, 316 p.
97-049577   951.904/3   0312210914
   Korean reunification question (1945-)

DS918.A79 1989
Appleman, Roy Edgar.
Disaster in Korea: the Chinese confront
MacArthur/ by Roy E. Appleman. College Station:
Texas A & M University Press, c1989. xvi, 456 p.
88-028133   951.9/042   0890963444
   Korean War, 1950-1953 -- Campaigns.

DS918.A8 1990
Appleman, Roy Edgar.
Ridgway duels for Korea/ by Roy E. Appleman.
College Station: Texas A&M University Press,
c1990. xvi, 665 p.
89-048499   951.904/2   0890964327
*Ridgway, Matthew B. -- (Matthew Bunker), --
1895- Korean War, 1950-1953 -- Campaigns.*

DS918.E39 2000
Edwards, Paul M.
To acknowledge a war: the Korean War in
American memory/ Paul M. Edwards. Westport,
Conn.: Greenwood Press, 2000. x, 176 p.
99-049887   951.904/2   0313310211
   Korean War, 1950-1953.

✓**DS918.S819 1995**
Stueck, William Whitney, 1945-
The Korean War: an international history/ William
Stueck. Princeton, N.J.: Princeton University Press,
c1995. xii, 484 p.
94-046286   951.904/2   0691037671
   *Korean War, 1950-1953. Korean War, 1950-
1953 -- Diplomatic history.*

DS919.D658 2001
Donnelly, William M., 1962-
Under Army orders: the Army National Guard
during the Korean War/ William M. Donnelly.
College Station: Texas A&M University Press,
2001. xiii, 271 p.
00-011803   1585441171
   *Korean War, 1950-1953 -- United States.
United States -- National Guard -- History --
Korean War, 1950-1953.*

DS919.P54 1999
Pierpaoli, Paul G., 1962-
Truman and Korea: the political culture of the
early cold war/ Paul G. Pierpaoli, Jr. Columbia,
MO.: University of Missouri Press, 1999. p. cm.
98-033326   951.904/2373   0826212069
*Truman, Harry S., -- 1884-1972.   Korean War,
1950-1953 -- United States.   United States --
Politics and government -- 1945-1953.*

✓**DS919.5.C4513 1994**
Chen, Jian.
China's road to the Korean War: the making of the
Sino-American confrontation/ Chen Jian. New
York: Columbia University Press, c1994. xii,
339 p.
94-011240   951.904/2   0231100248
   Korean War, 1950-1953 -- China.

✓**DS919.5.Z45 1995**
Zhang, Shu Guang.
Mao's military romanticism: China and the Korean
War, 1950-1953/ Shu Guang Zhang. Lawrence:
University Press of Kansas, 1995. xiii, 338 p.
95-018532   951.904/2   0700607234
*Mao, Tse-tung, -- 1893-1976 -- Military
leadership.   Korean War, 1950-1953 -- China.
China -- Politics and government -- 1946-1974.*

✓**DS920.2.U5.S53 1996**
Sherwood, John Darrell, 1966-
Officers in flight suits: the story of American Air
Force fighter pilots in the Korean War/ John
Darrell Sherwood. New York: New York
University Press, c1996. xiii, 239 p.
96-010021   951.904/2   0814780385
   *Fighter pilots -- United States. Korean War,
1950-1953 -- Aerial operations, American. Fighter
planes -- United States -- History.*

DS921.L43 2000
Lech, Raymond B., 1940-
Broken soldiers/ Raymond B. Lech. Urbana:
University of Illinois Press, c2000. xiii, 330 p.
00-008208   951.904/27   0252025415
   *Korean War, 1950-1953 -- Prisoners and
prisons, North Korean. Prisoners of war -- United
States.*

DS921.6.D36 1999
Dannenmaier, William D. 1930-
We were innocents: an infantryman in Korea/
William D. Dannenmaier. Urbana: University of
Illinois Press, c1999. 230 p.
98-025403   951.904/2   0252024494
*Dannenmaier, William D. -- (William Deal), --
1930-   Korean War, 1950-1953 -- Personal
narratives, American. Soldiers -- United States --
Biography.*

DS921.6.M55 2000
Mills, Randy Keith, 1951-
Unexpected journey: a Marine Corps Reserve
Company in the Korean War/ Randy K. Mills and
Roxanne Mills. Annapolis, MD: Naval Institute
Press, 2000. xvi, 271 p.
00-030487   951.904/245   1557505462
*Mills, Randy Keith, -- 1951-   Korean War, 1950-
1953 -- Personal narratives, American.*

DS921.6.R57 1993
Rishell, Lyle, 1927-
With a Black Platoon in combat: a year in Korea/
Lyle Rishell. College Station: Texas A&M
University Press, c1993. xvi, 176 p.
92-027918   951.904/2/092   0890965269
*Rishell, Lyle, -- 1927- Korean War, 1950-1953 --
Personal narratives, American. Afro-American
soldiers -- Korea.*

DS922.2.O25 1997
Oberdorfer, Don.
The two Koreas: a contemporary history/ Don
Oberdorfer. Reading, Mass.: Addison-Wesley,
c1997. xvii, 472 p.
97-019302   951.904   0201409275
   *Korea (South) -- History -- 1960-1988. Korea
(South) -- History -- 1988- Korea (North) --
History.*

DS932 Korea — Democratic People's Republic, 1948- — General works

DS932.N665 1998
North Korea after Kim Il Sung/ edited by Dae-
Sook Suh, Chae-Jin Lee. Boulder: Lynne Rienner
Publishers, 1998. xi, 275 p.
97-032958   951.93   155587763X
   Korea (North)

DS935.65 Korea — Democratic People's Republic, 1948- — History

DS935.65.S69 1999
Snyder, Scott, 1964-
Negotiating on the edge: North Korean negotiating
behavior/ Scott Snyder. Washington, D.C.: United
States Institute of Peace Press, 1999. xviii, 213 p.
99-048064   327.5193   187837995X
   *Negotiation. Diplomatic negotiations in
international disputes. Korea (North) -- Foreign
relations.*

DT History of Africa

DT2 Gazetteers. Dictionaries, etc. Guidebooks

DT2.E53 1997
Encyclopedia of precolonial Africa: archaeology,
history, languages, cultures, and environments/
Joseph O. Vogel, editor; Jean Vogel, editorial
manager. Walnut Creek, Calif.: AltaMira Press,
c1997. 605 p.
96-051227   960/.2   0761989021
   Africa -- Encyclopedias.

DT6.7 Geography

DT6.7.A34 1995
Africa on file/ Mapping Specialists, Ltd. New
York: Facts On File, c1995. 2 v.
95-023088   960.3/2   0816032882
   *Africa -- Geography. Africa -- Politics and
government -- 1960- Africa -- Economic conditions
-- 1960-*

DT14 Social life and customs. Civilization. Intellectual life

DT14.G47 1997
Gershoni, Yekutiel, 1943-
Africans on African-Americans: the creation and
uses of an African-American myth/ Yekutiel
Gershoni. Washington Square, N.Y.: New York
University Press, 1997. ix, 246 p.
96-009222   305.896/07306   0814730825
   *Africa -- Civilization -- Afro-American
influences.*

DT15 Ethnography — General works

DT15.E53 2000
Encyclopedia of African peoples/ by the Diagram Group. New York: Facts on File, 2000. 400 p.
99-055125   305.896/003   0816040990
Africans -- Encyclopedias. Ethnology -- Africa -- Encyclopedias.

DT15.Y35 1999
Yakan, Muhammad Zuhdi.
Almanac of African peoples & nations/ Mohamad Z. Yakan. New Brunswick, N.J.: Transaction, c1999. vii, 847 p.
98-054917   305.8/096   1560004339
Ethnology -- Africa.   Africa -- Languages.

DT16 Ethnography — Individual elements in the population not limited to specific territorial divisions, A-Z

DT16.B2.S35 1998
Schoenbrun, David Lee.
A green place, a good place: agrarian change, gender, and social identity in the Great Lakes region to the 15th century/ David Lee Schoenbrun. Portsmouth, NH: Heinemann, c1998. xiv, 301 p.
98-018871   967.6/0049639   0325000417
Bantu-speaking peoples -- Africa, East -- History. Bantu-speaking peoples -- Agriculture -- Africa, East. Bantu-speaking peoples -- Africa, East -- Ethnic identity. Great Rift Valley -- History. Victoria, Lake -- History. Kivu, Lake (Congo and Rwanda) -- History.

DT17 History — Dictionaries. Chronological tables, outlines, etc.

DT17.C65 2001
Collins, Robert O., 1933-
Historical dictionary of pre-colonial Africa/ Robert O. Collins. Lanham, Md.: Scarecrow Press, 2001. p. cm.
00-052254   960/.02/03   0810839784
Africa -- History -- To 1884 -- Dictionaries.

DT18 History — Biography (Collective)

DT18.D55
Dictionary of African biography.   New York: Reference Publications, c1977-c1995 v. 1-3
76-017954   920/.06   091725600X
Africa -- Biography -- Dictionaries.

DT19.7 History — Historiography — Biography of historians, are studies specialists, archaeologists, etc.

DT19.7.O45.A3 1997
Oliver, Roland Anthony.
In the realms of gold: pioneering in African history/ Roland Oliver. Madison, Wis.: University of Wisconsin Press, 1997. xvi, 425 p.
97-007217   960/.07202   0299156508
Oliver, Roland Anthony.   Africanists -- United States -- Biography. Historians -- United States -- Biography.

DT19.7.V36.A3 1994
Vansina, Jan.
Living with Africa/ Jan Vansina. Madison: The University of Wisconsin Press, c1994. xv, 312 p.
94-000588   960/.07202   0299143201
Vansina, Jan.   Africanists -- United States -- Biography.   Africa -- Historiography.

DT19.8 History — Study and teaching — General works

DT19.8.Z44 1997
Zeleza, Tiyambe, 1955-
Manufacturing African studies and crises/ Paul Tiyambe Zeleza. [Dakar]: Codesria, 1997. viii, 617 p.
99-891351   2869780664
Africa -- Study and teaching. Africa -- Historiography.

DT19.8.Z45 1997
Zell, Hans M.
The African studies companion: a resource guide & directory/ Hans M. Zell & Cecile Lomer. London; H. Zell Publishers, 1997. xvi, 276 p.
97-005671   960/.07   1873836414
Africa -- Study and teaching -- Handbooks, manuals, etc.

DT19.9 History — Study and teaching — By region or country, A-Z

DT19.9.U5.G74 1999
Great ideas for teaching about Africa/ edited by Misty L. Bastian and Jane L. Parpart. Boulder: Lynne Rienner, 1999. p. cm.
98-049639   960/.07/073   1555878156
Africa -- Study and teaching -- United States.

DT20 History — General works

DT20.C28
The Cambridge history of Africa/ general editors, J. D. Fage and Roland Oliver. Cambridge; Cambridge University Press, 1975-1986. 8 v.
76-002261   960   0521209811
Africa -- History.

DT21.5 History — Military history

DT21.5.A76 1999
Arnold, Guy.
Historical dictionary of civil wars in Africa/ Guy Arnold. Lanham, Md.: Scarecrow Press, 1999. xxi, 377 p.
98-053946   960   0810836335
Revolutions -- Africa -- Dictionaries. Civil war -- Dictionaries.   Africa -- History, Military -- Dictionaries.

DT28 History — By period — 1801-1884

DT28.C66 1993
Conquest and resistance to colonialism in Africa/ edited with an introduction by Gregory Maddox. New York: Garland, 1993. xv, 367 p.
93-019790   960.3   0815313888
Africa -- Colonization. Africa -- History -- 19th century. Africa -- History -- 1884-1960.

DT28.W4713 1996
Wesseling, H. L.
Divide and rule: the partition of Africa, 1880-1914/ H.L. Wesseling; translated by Arnold J. Pomerans. Westport, Conn.: Praeger, 1996. xvi, 446 p.
95-038253   960.3/12   0275951375
Africa -- History -- To 1884. Africa -- History -- 1884-1918. Africa -- Colonization -- History -- 19th century.

DT29 History — By period — 1884-1945

DT29.A33 1993
African nationalism and independence/ edited with an introduction by Timothy K. Welliver. New York: Garland Pub., 1993. xv, 359 p.
93-027885   960   081531390X
Nationalism -- Africa -- History -- 20th century. Africa -- History -- Autonomy and independence movements. Africa -- Politics and government.

DT29.C575 1993
The colonial epoch in Africa/ edited with introduction by Gregory Maddox. New York: Garland, 1993. xvi, 387 p.
93-017822   960.3   0815313896
Colonies -- Africa.   Africa -- History -- 1884-1960.

DT30.5 History — By period — 1960-

DT30.5.A14 1992
30 years of independence in Africa: the lost decades?/ edited by Peter Anyang Nyongo. Nairobi, Kenya: Academy Science Publishers, 1992. viii, 254 p.
92-981169   996683110X
Africa -- History -- 1960- -- Congresses.

DT30.5.A35325 2000
Africa at the millennium: an agenda for mature development/ edited by Bakut tswah Bakut and Sagarika Dutt; foreword by Stephen Chan. Houndmills, Basingstoke, Hampshire; Palgrave, 2000. xi, 294 p.
00-033325   320.96/09/049   0312235194
Twenty-first century -- Forecasts.   Africa -- Economic conditions -- 1960- Africa -- Social conditions -- 1960- Africa -- Politics and government -- 1960-

DT30.5.F35 2001
Falola, Toyin.
Nationalism and African intellectuals/ Toyin Falola. Rochester, NY: University of Rochester Press, 2001. xx, 372 p.
00-059943   305.5/52/096   1580460852
Nationalism -- Africa -- History -- 20th century. Intellectuals -- Africa -- Political activity. Africa -- Politics and government -- 1960-

DT30.5.G74 1995
Griffiths, Ieuan Ll.
The African inheritance/ Ieuan Ll. Griffiths. London; Routledge, 1995. 216 p.
94-039051   960.3   0415010918
Decolonization -- Africa. Political stability -- Africa. Africa -- Economic conditions -- 1960- Africa -- Politics and government -- 1960-

DT30.5.H34 1997
Hameso, Seyoum Y.
Ethnicity and nationalism in Africa/ Seyoum Y. Hameso. Commack, NY: Nova Science Publishers, c1997. xiii, 180 p.
97-196960   320.54/096   1560724447
Nationalism -- Africa. National state. Tribal government -- Africa. Africa -- Politics and government -- 1960- Africa -- Ethnic relations -- Political aspects.

DT30.5.S44 2000
Schraeder, Peter J.
African politics and society: a mosaic in transformation/ Peter J. Schraeder. Boston: Bedford/St. Martin's, c2000. xxi, 378 p.
99-062329   960   0312076037
Africa -- Politics and government -- 1960-

DT30.5.S455 1999
Searching for peace in Africa: an overview of conflict prevention and management activities/ editors, Monique Mekenkamp, Paul van Tongeren, and Hans van de Veen. Utrecht: European Platform for Conflict Prevention and Tr 1999. 528 p.
00-268273   303.6/9/096   9057270331
Conflict management -- Africa. Civil society -- Africa. Political violence -- Africa -- Prevention. Africa -- Politics and government -- 1960-

DT30.5.S667 1996
Sovereignty as responsibility: conflict management in Africa/ Francis M. Deng [et. al.]. Washington, DC: Brookings Institution, c1996. xxiii, 265 p.
96-014159   327.1   0815718284
Conflict management -- Africa. Sovereignty. Africa -- Politics and government -- 1960-

DT30.5.S697 1999
Soyinka, Wole.
The burden of memory, the muse of forgiveness/ Wole Soyinka. New York: Oxford University Press, 1999. xii, 208 p.
97-050052   960.3/2   0195122054
Senghor, Leopold Sedar, -- 1906-   Amnesty -- Africa. African literature -- 20th century -- History and criticism. Black literature -- 20th century -- History and criticism. Nigeria -- Politics and government -- 1984-1993. Africa -- Politics and government -- 1960-

DT31 History — Political and diplomatic history. Partition. Colonies and possessions — General works

DT31.B395 1996
Bever, Edward.
Africa/ by Edward Bever. Phoenix, Ariz.: Oryx Press, 1996. x, 302 p.
96-043086   320.96   0897749545
Africa -- Politics and government.

DT31.T516 1992
Thornton, John Kelly, 1949-
Africa and Africans in the making of the Atlantic world, 1400-1680/ John Thornton. Cambridge; Cambridge University Press, 1992. xxxviii, 309 p.
91-027968   303.48/26/04   0521392330
Slavery.   Europe -- Relations -- Africa. Africa -- Relations -- America. America -- Relations -- Africa.

DT36.5-38.9 History — Political and diplomatic history. Partition. Colonies and possessions — Relations with individual countries

DT36.5.M33 1997
Macqueen, Norrie, 1950-
The decolonization of Portuguese Africa: metropolitan revolution and the dissolution of empire/ Norrie Macqueen. London; Longman, 1997. p. cm.
96-034685   960/.097569   0582259932
Decolonization -- Africa, Portuguese-speaking. Africa, Portuguese-speaking -- Politics and government.

DT36.7.C355 1997
Cann, John P., 1941-
Counterinsurgency in Africa: the Portuguese way of war, 1961-1974/ John P. Cann; foreword by Bernard E. Trainor. Westport, Conn.: Greenwood Press, 1997. xvi, 216 p.
96-038260   960.3/26   0313301891
Counterinsurgency -- Africa, Portuguese-speaking -- History -- 20th century. Counterinsurgency -- Portugal -- History -- 20th century. Africa, Portuguese-speaking -- History, Military. Portugal -- Colonies -- Africa. Portugal -- Colonies -- History.

DT38.7.H5 1993
Hickey, Dennis.
An enchanting darkness: the American vision of Africa in the twentieth century/ Dennis Hickey and Kenneth Wylie. East Lansing: Michigan State University Press, 1993. 352 p.
92-056916   960   0870133217
Public opinion -- United States.   Africa -- Foreign public opinion, American. Africa -- Relations -- United States.

DT38.7.S73 1991
Staniland, Martin.
American intellectuals and African nationalists, 1955-1970/ Martin Staniland. New Haven: Yale University Press, 1991. ix, 310 p.
90-044756   303.48/27306   0300048386
Public opinion -- United States -- History -- 20th century. Intellectuals -- United States -- Attitudes -- History -- 20th century. Nationalism -- Africa -- History -- 20th century. Africa -- Foreign public opinion, American -- History -- 20th century. Africa -- Relations -- United States. Africa -- Politics and government -- 1945-1960.

DT38.9.L75.G74 1988
The Green and the black: Qadhafi's policies in Africa/ edited by Rene Lemarchand. Bloomington: Indiana University Press, c1988. viii, 188 p.
87-046088   327.61/206   0253326788
Africa -- Foreign relations -- Libya. Libya -- Foreign relations -- Africa.

DT53 Egypt — Description and travel — 1798-1848

DT53.L36 2000
Lane, Edward William, 1801-1876.
Description of Egypt: notes and views in Egypt and Nubia, made during the years 1825, -26, -27, and -28 ... / Edward William Lane; edited and with an introduction by Jason Thompson. Cairo: American University in Cairo Press, c2000. xxxii, 588 p.
99-503178   916.204/3   9774245253
Lane, Edward William, -- 1801-1876 -- Journeys -- Egypt.   Egypt -- Description and travel.

DT58-68.8 Egypt — Antiquities — By period

DT58.B96 1990
Bunson, Margaret.
The encyclopedia of ancient Egypt/ Margaret Bunson. New York: Facts on File Publications, c1991. xv, 291 p.
89-027473   932/.003   0816020930
Egypt -- Civilization -- To 332 B.C. -- Dictionaries. Egypt -- Antiquities -- Dictionaries.

DT58.E53 1998
Encyclopedia of the archaeology of ancient Egypt/ edited by Kathryn A. Bard; with the editing assistance of Steven Blake Shubert. New York: Routledge, 1998. p. cm.
98-016350   932/.003   0415185890
Egypt -- Antiquities -- Encyclopedias.

DT58.O94 2001
The Oxford encyclopedia of ancient Egypt/ Donald B. Redford, editor in chief. Oxford; Oxford University Press, 2001. 3 v.
99-054801   932   0195102347
Egypt -- Civilization -- To 332 B.C. -- Encyclopedias. Egypt -- Civilization -- 332 B.C.-638 A.D. -- Encyclopedias. Egypt -- Antiquities -- Encyclopedias.

DT60.L33 1997
Lacovara, Peter.
The New Kingdom royal city/ Peter Lacovara. London; Kegan Paul International; 1997. xiv, 202 p.
96-011773   932   0710305443
Cities and towns, Ancient -- Egypt. City planning -- Egypt -- History. Architecture -- Egypt. Egypt -- Antiquities.

DT60.M36 1998
Mark, Samuel
From Egypt to Mesopotamia: a study of predynastic trade routes/ Samuel Mark. College Station, Tex.: Texas A&M University Press; 1998. xi, 181 p.
97-021879 382/.0939/4 0890967776
Underwater archaeology -- Middle East. Middle East -- Antiquities. Egypt -- Antiquities. Egypt -- Commerce -- Iraq.

DT60.R397 2000
Reeves, C. N. 1956-
Ancient Egypt: the great discoveries: a year-by-year chronicle/ Nicholas Reeves. New York: Thames & Hudson, 2000. 255 p.
99-069519 932 0500051054
Excavations (Archaeology) -- Egypt. Archaeologists -- Egypt. Egypt -- Antiquities.

DT61.A6313 1997
Andreu, Guillemette
Egypt in the age of the pyramids/ Guillemette Andreu; translated from the French by David Lorton Ithaca, N.Y.: Cornell University Press, 1997. 171 p.
96-048461 932 0801432227
Egypt -- Civilization -- To 332 B.C.

DT61.J35 1984
James, T. G. H.
Pharaoh's people: scenes from life in Imperial Egypt/ T.G.H. James. Chicago: University of Chicago Press, 1984. 282 p.
84-002482 932/.014 0226391930
Egypt -- Social life and customs -- To 332 B.C. Egypt -- History -- Eighteenth dynasty, ca. 1570-1320 B.C.

DT61.S644 1999
Shuter, Jane.
Egypt/ Jane Shuter. Austin, Tex.: Raintree Steck-Vaughn, 1999. 63 p.
97-040036 932 0817250581
Egypt -- Civilization -- To 332 B.C. -- Juvenile literature. Egypt -- Civilization -- To 332 B.C.

DT61.S92513 1992
Strouhal, Evzen, 1931-
Life of the ancient Egyptians/ by Eugen Strouhal; with photographs by Werner Forman; foreword by Geoffrey T. Martin; [translated by Deryck Viney]. Norman: University of Oklahoma Press, c1992. 279 p.
92-054140 080612475X
Egypt -- Social life and customs -- To 332 B.C.

DT61.T95 2000
Tyldesley, Joyce A.
Judgement of the Pharaoh: crime and punishment in ancient Egypt/ Joyce Tyldesley. London: Weidenfeld & Nicolson, 2000. 199 p.
364.932 0297646699
Crime -- Egypt -- History. Criminal justice, Administration of -- Egypt -- History. Punishment -- Egypt. Egypt -- Social life and customs -- To 332 B.C. Egypt -- History -- To 332 B.C.

DT61.U55 1997
University of Pennsylvania.
Searching for ancient Egypt: art, architecture, and artifacts from the University of Pennsylvania Museum of Archaeology and Anthropology/ David P. Silverman, editor; with essays by Edward Brovarski ... [et al.]; photography by Tom Jenkins. [Dallas, Tex.]: Dallas Museum of Art; c1997. 342 p.
97-018386 932 0801434823
Art, Egyptian -- Exhibitions. Architecture -- Egypt -- Exhibitions. Egypt -- Antiquities -- Exhibitions.

DT68.8.W55 2000
Wilkinson, Richard H.
The complete temples of ancient Egypt/ Richard H. Wilkinson. New York: Thames & Hudson, 2000. 256 p.
99-066106 299/.31 0500051003
Temples -- Egypt. Egypt -- Religion. Egypt -- Antiquities.

DT70 Egypt — Social life and customs. Civilization. Intellectual life

DT70.C47 1998
Cherry, David,
Frontier and society in Roman North Africa/ David Cherry. Oxford: Clarendon Press; 1998. xii, 291 p.
98-007230 939/.7 0198152353
Romans -- Africa, North -- History. Africa, North -- History -- To 647. Rome -- Army -- History.

DT72 Egypt — Ethnography — Individual elements in the population, A-Z

DT72.B4.H6 1989
Hobbs, Joseph J. 1956-
Bedouin life in the Egyptian wilderness/ Joseph J. Hobbs; with a foreword by Leo Tregenza. Austin: University of Texas Press, 1989. xix, 165 p.
89-032001 305.8/9270623 0292715560
Hobbs, Joseph J. -- (Joseph John), -- 1956- -- Journeys -- Egypt -- Eastern Desert. Maaza (Arab tribe) Eastern Desert (Egypt) -- Social conditions. Eastern Desert (Egypt) -- Description and travel.

DT73 Egypt — Local antiquities, A-Z

DT73.A4 F7
Fraser, P. M.
Ptolemaic Alexandria [by] P. M. Fraser. Oxford, Clarendon Press, 1972. 3 v. (xvi, 812 p.)
73-157923 932 0198142781
Alexandria (Egypt) -- Civilization.

DT73.B33
Hawass, Zahi A.
Valley of the golden mummies/ Zahi Hawass. New York, N.Y.: Harry N. Abrams, 2000. 224 p.
00-026628 932 0810939428
Mummies -- Egypt -- Bahariya Oasis. Tombs -- Egypt -- Bahariya Oasis. Bahariya Oasis (Egypt) -- Antiquities.

DT73.M5.T46 1988
Thompson, Dorothy J., 1939-
Memphis under the Ptolemies/ Dorothy J. Thompson. Princeton, N.J.: Princeton University Press, c1988. xvii, 342 p.
88-012654 932 0691035938
Ptolemaic dynasty, -- 305-30 B.C. Memphis (Extinct city) -- Civilization.

DT73.T3.H5813 2000
Hodel-Hoenes, Sigrid, 1949-
Life and death in ancient Egypt: scenes from private tombs in new kingdom Thebes/ Sigrid Hodel-Hoenes; translated from the German by David Warburton. Ithaca, N.Y.: Cornell University Press, 2000. xii, 329 p.
99-059747 932/.01 0801435064
Tombs -- Egypt -- Thebes (Extinct city) Egypt -- Social life and customs -- To 332 B.C. Thebes (Egypt: Extinct city)

DT76 Egypt — History — Biography (Collective)

DT76.D38 1992
David, A. Rosalie
A biographical dictionary of ancient Egypt/ by Rosalie and Antony E. David. London: Seaby, 1992. xxvi, 179 p.
92-226306 920.032 1852640324
Egypt -- Biography. Egypt -- History -- To 640 A.D.

DT77 Egypt — History — General works

DT77.W35 1997
Watterson, Barbara.
The Egyptians/ Barbara Watterson. Oxford, UK; Blackwell Publishers, 1997. xx, 347 p.
96-019205 962 0631182721
Egypt -- History.

DT82.5 Egypt — History — Political and diplomatic history. Foreign and general relations

DT82.5.G7.H36 1995
Hanes, William Travis, 1954-
Imperial diplomacy in the era of decolonization: the Sudan and Anglo-Egyptian relations, 1945-1956/ W. Travis Hanes III. Westport, Conn.: Greenwood Press, 1995. x, 190 p.
94-007421 327.62041 0313293414
Egypt -- Foreign Relations -- Great Britain. Great Britain -- Foreign relations -- Egypt. Sudan -- Foreign relations -- Great Britain.

DT82.5.I7.M45 1997
Meital, Yoram.
Egypt's struggle for peace: continuity and change, 1967-1977/ Yoram Meital. Gainesville, Fla.: University Press of Florida, c1997. x, 215 p.
97-029622 327.6205694 0813015332
Egypt -- Foreign relations -- Israel. Israel -- Foreign relations -- Egypt. Egypt -- Foreign relations -- 1952-

DT82.5.P19.R43 1992
Redford, Donald B.
Egypt, Canaan, and Israel in ancient times/ Donald
B. Redford. Princeton, N.J.: Princeton University
Press, c1992. xxiii, 488 p.
91-019245   303.48/26205694   0691036063
*Egypt -- Relations -- Palestine. Palestine --
Relations -- Egypt. Egypt -- History -- To 332 B.C.*

DT83-107.87 Egypt — History
— By period

DT83.O875 2000
The Oxford history of ancient Egypt/ edited by Ian
Shaw. Oxford; Oxford University Press, 2000. xv,
512 p.
01-274677   932   0198150342
Egypt -- History -- To 640 A.D.

DT83.R47 1999
Rice, Michael.
Who's who in ancient Egypt/ Michael Rice.
London; Routledge, 1999. lix, 257 p.
2001-265056   932.0099   0415154480
*Egypt -- History -- To 332 B.C. Egypt --
History -- To 332 B.C. -- Biography. Egypt --
Biography.*

DT87.38.A45 1998
Amenhotep III: perspectives on his reign/ edited by
David O'Connor and Eric H. Cline. Ann Arbor:
University of Michigan Press, c1998. xvi, 393 p.
97-033738   932/.014/092   0472107429
*Amenhotep -- III, -- King of Egypt.   Egypt --
History -- Eighteenth dynasty, ca. 1570-1320 B.C.*

DT87.4.M64 2000
Montserrat, Dominic, 1964-
Akhenaten: history, fantasy, and ancient Egypt/
Dominic Montserrat. London; Routledge, 2000.
xiii, 219 p.
99-059754   932/.014/092   0415185491
*Akhenaton, -- King of Egypt. Akhenaton, -- King of
Egypt -- Legends. Pharaohs -- Biography. Egypt
-- History -- Eighteenth dynasty, ca. 1570-1320
B.C.*

DT87.4.R44 2001
Reeves, C. N. 1956-
Akhenaten, Egypt's false prophet/ Nicholas
Reeves. New York: Thames & Hudson, 2001.
208 p.
00-108868   932/.014/092   0500051062
*Akhenaton, -- King of Egypt.   Pharaohs --
Biography.   Egypt -- History -- Eighteenth
dynasty, ca. 1570-1320 B.C.*

DT87.45.T95 1998
Tyldesley, Joyce A.
Nefertiti: Egypt's sun queen/ Joyce Tyldesley.
London; Viking, 1998. xiv, 232 p.
98-035469   932/.014/092   0670869988
*Nefertiti, -- Queen of Egypt, -- 14th cent. B.C.
Queens -- Egypt -- Biography. Egypt -- History --
Eighteenth dynasty, ca. 1570-1320 B.C.*

DT92.H6513 2001
Holbl, Gunther.
History of the Ptolemaic empire/ Gunther Holbl.
New York: Routledge, 2000. p. cm.
00-020437   932/.021   0415201454
*Ptolemaic dynasty, -- 305-30 B.C.   Egypt --
History -- 332-30 B.C.*

DT93.B33 1993
Bagnall, Roger S.
Egypt in late antiquity/ Roger S. Bagnall.
Princeton, N.J.: Princeton University Press, c1993.
xii, 370 p.
92-040332   932/.022   0691069867
Egypt -- Civilization -- 332 B.C.-638 A.D.

DT94.C36 1998
The Cambridge history of Egypt/ general editor,
M.W. Daly. Cambridge; Cambridge University
Press, 1998- v.
98-016515   962   0521471370
Egypt -- History.

DT96.7.P48 1993
Petry, Carl F., 1943-
Twilight of majesty: the reigns of the Mamluk
Sultans al-Ashraf Qaytbay and Qansuh al-Ghawri
in Egypt/ Carl F. Petry. Seattle: Distributed by
University of Washington Press, c1993. p. cm.
93-004632   962/.02   0295973072
*Qayitbay al-Mahmudi, -- Sultan of Egypt and
Syria, -- 1412-1496. Qansuh al-Ghuri, -- Sultan pf
Egypt and Syria, -- d. 1516.   Egypt -- History --
1250-1517.*

DT97.G65 1999
Goldschmidt, Arthur, 1938-
Biographical dictionary of modern Egypt/ Arthur
Goldschmidt, Jr. Boulder, CO: L. Rienner, 1999. x,
299 p.
99-033550   920.062   1555872298
*Egypt -- History -- 1517-1882 -- Biography --
Dictionaries. Egypt -- History -- 1798--
Biography -- Dictionaries.*

DT100.S66 2000
Sonbol, Amira El Azhary.
The new Mamluks: Egyptian society and modern
feudalism/ Amira El-Azhary Sonbol; with a
foreword by Robert A. Fernea. Syracuse, New
York: Syracuse University Press, 2000. xli, 292 p.
00-035820   962/.03   0815628447
*Egypt -- History -- 1798- Egypt -- Social
conditions -- 19th century. Egypt -- Social
conditions -- 20th century.*

DT107.B58 1991
Botman, Selma.
Egypt from independence to revolution, 1919-
1952/ Selma Botman. Syracuse, N.Y.: Syracuse
University Press, c1991. xiii, 170 p.
91-007246   962.05   0815625308
Egypt -- History -- 1919-

DT107.V38 1986
Vatikiotis, P. J. 1928-
The history of Egypt/ P.J. Vatikiotis. Baltimore:
Johns Hopkins University Press, 1986, c1985. xiii,
546 p.
85-024200   962   0801833256
Egypt -- History -- 1798-

DT107.82.D67 1999
Doran, Michael Scott, 1962-
Pan-Arabism before Nasser: Egyptian power
politics and the Palestine Question/ Michael Doran.
New York: Oxford University Press, 1999. 230 p.
98-023001   962.05   0195123611
*Panarabism. Arab-Israeli conflict.   Egypt --
Foreign relations -- Arab countries. Egypt --
Politics and government -- 1919-1952.*

DT107.82.G43 1995
Gershoni, I.
Redefining the Egyptian nation, 1930-1945/ Israel
Gershoni and James P. Jankowski. Cambridge;
Cambridge University Press, 1995. xvii, 280 p.
94-031795   320.5/4/0962   052147535X
*Nationalism -- Egypt -- History -- 20th century.
Egypt -- Politics and government -- 1919-1952.*

DT107.826.A76 1996
Armbrust, Walter.
Mass culture and modernism in Egypt/ Walter
Armbrust. Cambridge [England]; Cambridge
University Press, 1996. xi, 275 p.
95-039632   962/.03   0521481473
*Popular culture -- Egypt. Mass media -- Egypt --
History -- 20th century.   Egypt -- Civilization --
1798-*

DT107.83.C25 1991
Calhoun, Daniel F. 1929-
Hungary and Suez, 1956: an exploration of who
makes history/ Daniel F. Calhoun. Lanham:
University Press of America, c1991. 591 p.
90-032029   909.82/5   0819181862
*Egypt -- History -- Intervention, 1956. Hungary
-- History -- Revolution, 1956.*

DT107.83.F374 1994
Farid, Abdel Majid.
Nasser: the final years/ Abdel Magid Farid.
Reading: Ithaca Press, 1994. x, 221 p.
94-208329   0863721745
*Nasser, Gamal Abdel, -- 1918-1970.   Presidents --
Egypt. Egypt -- Politics and government -- 1952-
Egypt -- Foreign relations.*

DT107.83.G67 1991
Gordon, Joel.
Nasser's Blessed Movement: Egypt's Free Officers
and the July revolution/ Joel Gordon. New York:
Oxford University Press, 1992. vii, 254 p.
91-016836   962   0195069358
Egypt -- Politics and government -- 1952-

DT107.83.T36 1994
Templeton, Malcolm, 1924-
Ties of blood and empire: New Zealand's
involvement in Middle East defence and the Suez
Crisis, 1947-1957/ Malcolm Templeton. Auckland:
Auckland University Press in association with th
1994. xi, 278 p.
94-235566   962.05/3   1869400976
*Egypt -- History -- Intervention, 1956. New
Zealand -- Foreign relations -- 1945- Suez Canal
(Egypt) -- History.*

DT107.87.B35 1990
Baker, Raymond William, 1942-
Sadat and after: struggles for Egypt's political soul/
Raymond William Baker. Cambridge, Mass.:
Harvard University Press, 1990. xxiii, 365 p.
89-026692   962.05/4   0674784979
Egypt -- Politics and government -- 1970-

DT146-154 Egypt —
Local history and description —
Cities, towns, etc.

DT146.S26 1994
Sanders, Paula.
Ritual, politics, and the city in Fatimid Cairo/ Paula Sanders. [Albany, N.Y.]: State University of New York Press, c1994. xii, 231 p.
93-022317   962/.16   0791417816
Social history -- Medieval, 500-1500. Festivals -- Egypt -- Cairo -- History. Rites and ceremonies -- Egypt -- Cairo. Cairo (Egypt) -- Court and courtiers. Cairo (Egypt) -- Social life and customs. Egypt -- Court and courtiers.

DT148.R3913 2000
Raymond, Andre.
Cairo/ Andre Raymond; translated by Willard Wood. Cambridge, MA: Harvard University Press, 2000. 436 p.
00-056747   962/.16   0674003160
Cairo (Egypt) -- History.

DT154.A4.H36 1997
Haas, Christopher.
Alexandria in late antiquity: topography and social conflict/ Christopher Haas. Baltimore: Johns Hopkins University Press, 1997. xviii, 494 p.
96-021424   932   080185377X
Alexandria (Egypt) -- Civilization. Alexandria (Egypt) -- Social conditions. Alexandria (Egypt) -- Ethnic relations.

DT154.A4.R45 1997
Reimer, Michael J.
Colonial bridgehead: government and society in Alexandria, 1807-1882/ Michael J. Reimer. Boulder, Colo.: Westview Press, 1997. xv, 251 p.
97-025933   962/.1   0813327776
Alexandria (Egypt) -- History -- 19th century.

DT154.8 Sudan.
Anglo-Egyptian Sudan —
Antiquities

DT154.8.S94 1997
Sudan: ancient kingdoms of the Nile/ edited by Dietrich Wildung; photography by Jurgen Liepe. New York, N.Y.: Flammarion, 1997. p. cm.
96-037294   962.4/01   2080136372
Art -- Sudan -- Exhibitions. Sudan -- Civilization -- Exhibitions. Sudan -- Antiquities -- Exhibitions.

DT155.2 Sudan. Anglo-Egyptian
Sudan — Ethnography
— Individual elements in the
population, A-Z

DT155.2.B47.H65 1991
Holy, Ladislav.
Religion and custom in a Muslim society: the Berti of Sudan/ Ladislav Holy. Cambridge [England]; Cambridge University Press, 1991. x, 243 p.
90-020417   305.896/50624   0521394856
Berti (African people) Muslims -- Sudan. Sudan -- Social life and customs.

DT155.2.N82.M36 1994
Manger, Leif O.
From the mountains to the plains: the integration of the Lafofa Nuba into Sudanese society/ Leif O. Manger. Uppsala: Scandinavian Institute of African Studies, 1994. 173 p.
95-116986   9171063366
Nuba (African people)   Nuba Mountains (Sudan) Sudan -- Ethnic relations.

DT156.3-156.7 Sudan.
Anglo-Egyptian Sudan — History
— By period

DT156.3.E93 1990
Ewald, Janet, 1951-
Soldiers, traders, and slaves: state formation and economic transformation in the Greater Nile Valley, 1700-1885/ Janet J. Ewald. Madison, Wis.: University of Wisconsin Press, c1990. xiii, 270 p.
90-050084   926.5/023   0299126005
Sudan -- History -- to 1821. Sudan -- History -- 1821-1881.

DT156.4.W37 1992
Warburg, Gabriel.
Historical discord in the Nile Valley/ Gabriel R. Warburg. Evanston, Ill.: Northwestern University Press, c1992. xviii, 210 p.
92-014197   962.4/03/072   0810110571
Sudan -- History -- 1821-1881 -- Historiography. Sudan -- History -- 1821-1881.

DT156.6.D35 1997
Daly, M. W.
The Sirdar: Sir Reginald Wingate and the British Empire in the Middle East/ by M.W. Daly. Philadelphia: American Philosophical Society, 1997. vii, 345 p.
96-079457   962.4/03/092   0871692228
Wingate, F. R. -- (Francis Reginald), -- Sir, -- 1861-1953.   Generals -- Great Britain -- Biography. Governors general -- Sudan -- Biography. Sudan -- History -- 1899-1956. Egypt -- History -- British occupation, 1882-1936.

DT156.7.D35 1990
Daly, M. W.
Imperial Sudan: the Anglo-Egyptian condominium, 1934-1956/ M.W. Daly. Cambridge [England]; Cambridge University Press, 1991. xvi, 471 p.
89-077382   962.4/03   0521391636
Sudan -- History -- 1899-1956.

DT159.6 Sudan.
Anglo-Egyptian Sudan —
Local history and description —
Provinces, regions, etc., A-Z

DT159.6.B34.S55 1991
Sikainga, Ahmad Alawad.
The western Bahr al-Ghazal under British rule, 1898-1956/ by Ahmad Alawad Sikainga. Athens, Ohio: Ohio University Center for International Studies 1991. xx, 183 p.
90-041421   962.4   0896801616
Bahr al Ghazal (Sudan: Province) -- History. Sudan -- History -- 1899-1956.

DT159.6.N83.A53 1998
Ancient African civilizations: Kush and Axum/ Stanley Burstein, editor. Princeton: M. Wiener Publishers, c1998. vii, 166 p.
97-041207   939/.78   1558761470
Nubia -- History. Aksum (Ethiopia) -- History.

DT159.9.N83.W45 1998
Welsby, Derek A.
The kingdom of Kush: the Napatan and Meroitic empires/ by Derek A. Welsby. Princeton, N.J.: Markus Wiener, 1998. p. cm.
97-050451   939.78   1558761810
Nubia -- Civilization. Sudan -- Civilization.

DT193.95 Maghrib. Barbary States
— History — Historiography

DT193.95.M34 1997
The Maghrib in question: essays in history & historiography/ edited by Michel Le Gall and Kenneth Perkins. Austin: University of Texas Press, 1997. xxv, 258 p.
96-044825   961/.072   0292765762
Africa, North -- Historiography.

DT194 Maghrib. Barbary States
— History — General works

DT194.A23 1987
Abun-Nasr, Jamil M.
A history of the Maghrib in the Islamic period/ Jamil M. Abun-Nasr. Cambridge; Cambridge University Press, 1987. xvi, 455 p.
86-024407   961   0521331846
Africa, North -- History.

DT197.5 Maghrib. Barbary States
— History — Relations with
individual countries, A-Z

DT197.5.L75.D44 1989
Deeb, Mary Jane.
Libya's foreign policy in North Africa/ Mary-Jane Deeb. Boulder: Westview Press, 1991. x, 214 p.
87-014179   327.61/2/061   0813372445
Qaddafi, Muammar.   Libya -- Foreign relations -- Africa, North. Africa, North -- Foreign relations -- Libya.

DT197.5.U6.A45 1995
Allison, Robert J.
The crescent obscured: the United States and the Muslim world, 1776-1815/ Robert J. Allison. New York: Oxford University Press, 1995. xviii, 266 p.
94-005447   303.48/273061   0195086120
Islam -- Public opinion. Public opinion -- United States. Africa, North -- Relations -- United States. Africa, North -- Foreign public opinion, American. United States -- Relations -- Africa, North.

DT223.3-236 Maghrib. Barbary
States — Libya — History

DT223.3.S7 1998
St. John, Ronald Bruce.
Historical dictionary of Libya/ Ronald Bruce St John. Lanham, Md.: Scarecrow Press, 1998. p. cm.
98-006044   961.2/003   0810834952
Libya -- History -- Dictionaries.

DT236.E45 1997
El-Kikhia, Mansour O.
Libya's Qaddafi: the politics of contradiction/ Mansour O. El-Kikhia. Gainesville: University Press of Florida, c1997. xv, 213 p.
96-044107   961.204/2   0813014883
Libya -- Politics and government -- 1969-

DT236.Q27 1995
Qadhafi's Libya, 1969-1994/ edited by Dirk Vandewalle. New York: St. Martin's Press, 1995. xxxi, 252 p.
95-009835   961.204/2   0312125879
Libya -- Politics and government -- 1969-

DT238 Maghrib. Barbary States — Libya — Local history and description

DT238.C8.P47 1990
Peters, Emrys L., d. 1987.
The Bedouin of Cyrenaica: studies in personal and corporate power/ Emrys L. Peters; edited by Jack Goody and Emanuel Marx. Cambridge [England]; Cambridge University Press, 1990. xi, 310 p.
89-048036   961.2   052138561X
Bedouins -- Libya -- Barqah.   Barqah (Libya) -- Social life and customs.

DT269 Maghrib. Barbary States — Tunisia (Tunis) — Local history and description

DT269.C32.C37 1987
Carthage: a mosaic of ancient Tunisia/ edited by Aicha Ben Abed Ben Khader and David Soren; photographs by Martha Cooper. New York: American Museum of Natural History in associatio [c1987] 238 p.
87-071760   939/.73   0913424110
Carthage (Extinct city) Tunisia -- Civilization. Tunisia -- Antiquities.

DT269.C35 S67 1990
Soren, David.
Carthage: uncovering the mysteries and splendors of ancient Tunisia/ David Soren, Aicha Ben Abed Ben Khader, Hedi Slim. New York: Simon and Schuster, c1990. 304 p.
89-029984   939/.73.220   0671669028
Carthage (Extinct city) -- History.

DT283.7-295.6 Maghrib. Barbary States — Algeria — History

DT283.7.N39 1994
Naylor, Phillip Chiviges.
The historical dictionary of Algeria/ by Phillip Chiviges Naylor and Alf Andrew Heggoy. Metuchen, N.J.: Scarecrow Press, c1994. xxxix, 443 p.
93-026302   965/.003   0810827484
Algeria -- History -- Dictionaries.

DT287.5.F8
Naylor, Phillip Chiviges.
France and Algeria: a history of decolonization and transformation/ Philip C. Naylor. Gainesville, Fla.: University Press of Florida, 2000. xviii, 457 p.
00-048884   965/.04   0813018013
Algeria -- Relations -- France. France -- Relations -- Algeria. Algeria -- History -- 20th century.

DT294.5.R84 1992
Ruedy, John 1927-
Modern Algeria: the origins and development of a nation/ John Ruedy. Bloomington: Indiana University Press, c1992. x, 290 p.
92-004637   965   0253349982
Algeria -- History.

DT295.S354 1991
Schalk, David L.
War and the ivory tower: Algeria and Vietnam/ David L. Schalk. New York: Oxford University Press, 1991. p. cm.
90-021086   959.704/3373   0195068076
Vietnamese Conflict, 1961-1975 -- Protest movements -- United States. Peace movements -- France. Peace movements -- United States. Algeria -- History -- Revolution, 1954-1962 -- Protest movements -- France.

DT295.5.M34 1996
Malley, Robert, 1963-
The call from Algeria: third worldism, revolution, and the turn to Islam/ Robert Malley. Berkeley: University of California Press, c1996. x, 323 p.
95-036054   965.05   0520203003
Developing countries -- Miscellanea.   Algeria -- Politics and government.

DT295.6.G73 1998
Graffenried, Michael von, 1957-
Inside Algeria/ Michael von Graffenried. New York, N.Y.: Aperture, c1998. 158 p.
98-085810   965.05/4   0893818402
Algeria -- Politics and government -- 1990- -- Pictorial works.

DT295.6.M3713 2000
Martinez, Luis, 1965-
The Algerian Civil War, 1990-1998/ by Luis Martinez. New York: Columbia University Press, 2000. p. cm.
99-043326   965.05/4   0231119968
Islam and politics -- Algeria.   Algeria -- Politics and government -- 1990-

DT298-299 Maghrib. Barbary States — Algeria — Local history and description

DT298.K2.L57 1995
Lorcin, Patricia M. E.
Imperial identities: stereotyping, prejudice and race in colonial Algeria/ Patricia M.E. Lorcin. London: I.B. Tauris; c1995. x, 323 p.
94-061505   1850439095
Kabyles -- Study and teaching -- France. Racism -- France -- History. Algeria -- Ethnic relations. Algeria -- History -- 1830-1962.

DT299.B6.P76 1990
Prochaska, David.
Making Algeria French: colonialism in Bone, 1870-1920/ David Prochaska. Cambridge [England]; Cambridge University Press; 1990. xix, 328 p.
89-033176   965/.5   0521343038
French -- Algeria -- Bone -- History.   Bone (Algeria) -- History.

DT313.3 Maghrib. Barbary States — Morocco — Ethnography

DT313.3.R53.J67 1987
Joseph, Roger, 1938-
The rose and the thorn: semiotic structures in Morocco/ Roger Joseph and Terri Brint Joseph. Tucson: University of Arizona Press, c1987. x, 157 p.
87-010889   306.8/089933   0816509964
Rifs (Berber people) -- Marriage customs and rites. Rifs (Berber people) -- Social life and customs.

DT316-324.5 Maghrib. Barbary States — Morocco — History

DT316.G47 1999
Gershovich, Moshe, 1959-
French military rule in Morocco: colonialism and its consequences/ Moshe Gershovich. London; F. Cass, 2000. xvii, 238 p.
99-014650   964.05   071464949X
Morocco -- History, Military -- 20th century. France -- Military relations -- Morocco. Morocco -- Military relations -- France.

DT324.H54 1984
Hoisington, William A., 1941-
The Casablanca connection: French colonial policy, 1936-1943/ William A. Hoisington, Jr. Chapel Hill: University of North Carolina Press, c1984. xiv, 320 p.
83-005902   964/.04   0807815748
Morocco -- History -- 20th century.

DT324.5.A48 2001
Alvarez, Jose E., 1955-
The betrothed of death: the Spanish Foreign Legion during the Rif Rebellion, 1920-1927/ Jose E. Alvarez. Westport, Conn.: Greenwood Press, 2001. 282 p.
99-055222   946/.074   0313306974
Rif Revolt, 1921-1926.   Spain -- History, Military -- 20th century. Spain -- Foreign relations -- Morocco. Morocco -- Foreign relations -- Spain.

DT351 Central Sub-Saharan Africa — General works

DT351.E53 1997
Encyclopedia of Africa south of the Sahara/ John Middleton, editor in chief. New York: C. Scribner's Sons, c1997. 4 v.
97-031364   967/.003   0684804662
Africa, Sub-Saharan -- Encyclopedias.

DT352.4 Central Sub-Saharan Africa — Social life and customs. Civilization. Intellectual life

DT352.4.A66 1992
Appiah, Anthony.
In my father's house: Africa in the philosophy of culture/ Kwame Anthony Appiah. New York: Oxford University Press, 1992. xi, 225 p.
91-023386   960   0195068513
Africa -- Civilization -- Philosophy. Africa -- Intellectual life -- 20th century.

DT352.4.G94 1997
Gyekye, Kwame.
Tradition and modernity: philosophical reflections on the African experience/ Kwame Gyekye. New York: Oxford University Press, 1997. xix, 338 p.
96-023814   960.3/01   0195112253
Africa, Sub-Saharan -- Civilization -- Philosophy.

DT352.4.N86 1995
Nunez, Benjamin, 1912-
Dictionary of Portuguese-African civilization/ Benjamin Nunez. London, UK; Hans Zell Publishers, 1995- v. 1
94-017124   967/.003   1873836104
Africa, Sub-Saharan -- History -- Dictionaries. Africa -- Civilization -- Portuguese influences -- Dictionaries.

DT352.6 Central Sub-Saharan Africa — History — Biography and memoirs

DT352.6.L56 1987
Lipschutz, Mark R.
Dictionary of African historical biography/ Mark R. Lipschutz & R. Kent Rasmussen. Berkeley: University of California Press, c1986. xiii, 328 p.
86-019157   967/.009/92   0520051793
Africa, Sub-Saharan -- Biography -- Dictionaries. Africa, Sub-Saharan -- History.

DT352.7-352.8 Central Sub-Saharan Africa — History — By period

DT352.7.M49 1992
Meyer, Lysle E.
The farther frontier: six case studies of Americans and Africa, 1848-1936/ Lysle E. Meyer. Selinsgrove [Pa.]: Susquehanna University Press; c1992. 267 p.
90-050770   967.03/1   0945636199
Americans -- Africa, Sub-Saharan -- Biography. Africa, Sub-Saharan -- Discovery and exploration -- American. Africa, Sub-Saharan -- History -- 1884-1960. Africa, Sub-Saharan -- History -- To 1884.

DT352.8.B47 2000
Berman, Eric.
Peacekeeping in Africa: capabilities and culpabilities/ Eric G. Berman and Katie E. Sams. Geneva: United Nations Institute for Disarmament Researc c2000. xxx, 540 p.
00-361875   341.5/84   9290451335
Peacekeeping forces -- Africa, Sub-Saharan. Africa, Sub-Saharan -- Politics and government -- 1960-

DT352.8.E84 1995
Ethnic conflict and democratization in Africa/ edited by Harvey Glickman. Atlanta, Ga.: African Studies Assoc. Press, 1995. iii, 484 p.
95-034881   305.8/00967   0918456746
Democracy -- Africa, Sub-Saharan. Democratization -- Africa, Sub-Saharan. Africa, Sub-Saharan -- Ethnic relations.

DT352.8.M35 1998
Maier, Karl, 1957-
Into the house of the ancestors: inside the new Africa/ Karl Maier. New York: Wiley, c1998. x, 278 p.
97-026809   967.03/2   047113547X
Africa, Sub-Saharan -- Politics and government -- 1960- Africa, Sub-Saharan -- Social conditions -- 1960-

DT353-353.5 Central Sub-Saharan Africa — History — Political and diplomatic history. Foreign and general relations

DT353.C65 1999
Comprehending and mastering African conflicts: the search for sustainable peace and good governance/ edited by Adebayo Adedeji. London; Zed Books, in association with African Centre fo c1999. xxi, 377 p.
99-052438   967.03/2   1856497623
Civil war -- Africa, Sub-Saharan -- History -- 20th century. Peace. Africa, Sub-Saharan -- Politics and government -- 1960-

DT353.P74 1999
Press, Robert M.
The new Africa: dispatches from a changing continent/ Robert M. Press; photographs by Betty Press. Gainesville: University Press of Florida, c1999. xvii, 380 p.
99-017517   967.03/2   0813017041
Operation Restore Hope, 1992-1993. Democracy -- Africa, Sub-Saharan -- History -- 20th century. Human rights -- Africa, Sub-Saharan -- History -- 20th century. Africa, Sub-Saharan -- Politics and government -- 1960- Rwanda -- Politics and government. Africa, Sub-Saharan -- Social conditions -- 1960-

DT353.5.C9.C83 1989
Cuban internationalism in Sub-Saharan Africa/ edited by Sergio Diaz-Briquets. Pittsburgh, Pa.: Duquesne University Press, c1989. xi, 211 p.
89-016974   327.7291067   0820702013
Africa, Sub-Saharan -- Military relations -- Cuba. Cuba -- Military relations -- Africa, Sub-Saharan.

DT353.5.E9.A34 2001
Africa and the West: a documentary history from the slave trade to independence/ William H. Worger, Nancy L. Clark, and Edward A. Alpers. Phoenix, Ariz.: Oryx Press, 2001. ix, 428 p.
00-010718   967/.02   1573562475
Slave-trade -- History -- Sources. Europe -- Relations -- Africa, Sub-Saharan -- History -- Sources. Africa, Sub-Saharan -- Relations -- America -- History -- Sources. America -- Relations -- Africa, Sub-Saharan -- History -- Sources.

DT353.5.E9.R68 1994
Rouvez, Alain.
Disconsolate empires: French, British, and Belgian military involvement in post-colonial Sub-Saharan Africa/ Alain Rouvez with the assistance of: Michael Coco, Jean-Paul Paddack. Lanham, Md.: University Press of America, c1994. xiv, 451 p.
94-022104   327.44067/09/045   0819196436
Africa, Sub-Saharan -- Foreign relations -- 1960- Africa, Sub-Saharan -- History -- 1960- Africa, Sub-Saharan -- Relations -- Europe.

DT353.5.U6
Cohen, Herman J.
Intervening in Africa: superpower peacemaking in a troubled continent/ Herman J. Cohen. New York: St. Martin's Press, 2000. p. cm.
99-087453   327.67073   0312232217
Mediation, International -- History -- 20th century. Civil war -- Africa, Sub-Saharan -- History -- 20th century. Africa, Sub-Saharan -- Foreign relations -- United States. United States -- Foreign relations -- Africa, Sub-Saharan.

DT365.45 Eastern Africa — Ethnography — Individual elements in the population, A-Z

DT365.45.S93.A45 1993
Allen, J. de V.
Swahili origins: Swahili culture & the Shungwaya phenomenon/ James de Vere Allen. London: J. Currey; 1993. xii, 272 p.
92-014316   960/.0496392   082141030X
Swahili-speaking peoples -- History. Swahili-speaking peoples -- Ethnic identity.

DT365.65-365.8 Eastern Africa — History — By period

DT365.65.E37 1998
Ehret, Christopher.
An African classical age: eastern and southern Africa in world history, 1000 B.C. to A.D. 400/ Christopher Ehret. Charlottesville: University Press of Virginia; 1998. xvii, 354 p.
97-044239   967.6   0813918146
Africa, Eastern -- History. Africa, Southern -- History -- To 1899.

DT365.65.G57 1995
Glassman, Jonathon.
Feasts and riot: revelry, rebellion, and popular consciousness on the Swahili Coast, 1856-1888/ Jonathon Glassman. Portsmouth, NH: Heinemann; c1995. xvii, 293 p.
94-034509   967.6   0435089560
Africa, East -- History -- To 1886. Indian Coast (Africa) -- History.

DT365.8.A37 1998
African guerrillas/ edited by Christopher Clapham. Oxford: James Currey; 1998. xiii, 208 p.
98-015631   322.4/2/096   0852558163
Insurgency -- Africa, Eastern -- History -- 20th century. Guerrillas -- Africa, Eastern -- History -- 20th century. Insurgency -- Liberia -- History -- 20th century. Sierra Leone -- Politics and government -- 1961- Africa, Eastern -- Politics and government -- 1960- Liberia -- Politics and government -- 1980-

DT367.63-367.8 Eastern Africa — Northeast Africa — History

DT367.63.S65.P38 1990
Patman, Robert G.
The Soviet Union in the Horn of Africa: the diplomacy of intervention and disengagement/ Robert G. Patman. Cambridge [England]; Cambridge University Press, 1990. xvii, 411 p.
89-015826   327.47063   0521360226
Africa, Northeast -- Foreign relations -- Soviet Union. Soviet Union -- Foreign relations -- Africa, Northeast. Ethiopia -- Foreign relations -- Soviet Union.

DT367.75.M37 1987
Markakis, John.
National and class conflict in the Horn of Africa/ John Markakis. Cambridge; Cambridge University Press, 1987. xvii, 314 p.
87-028361   960/.3   0521333628
Nationalism -- Africa, Northeast -- History -- 20th century. National liberation movements -- Africa, Northeast -- History -- 20th century. Revolutions -- Africa, Northeast -- History -- 20th century. Africa, Northeast -- Politics and government.

DT367.8.B49 1992
Beyond conflict in the Horn: prospects for peace, recovery, and development in Ethiopia, Somalia, and the Sudan/ edited by Martin Doornbos ... [et al.]. Trenton, NJ: Red Sea Press, c1992. viii, 242 p.
92-053881   320.96   0932415814
Africa, Northeast -- Politics and government -- 1974- Africa, Northeast -- Foreign relations -- 1974- Africa, Northeast -- Economic conditions.

DT380.4 Eastern Africa — Ethiopia (Abyssinia) — Ethnography

DT380.4.G19.O55 1997
Olmstead, Judith V.
Woman between two worlds: portrait of an Ethiopian rural leader/ Judith Olmstead. Urbana: University of Illinois Press, c1997. xv, 248 p.
96-010068   963/.06/092   0252022831
Women, Gamo -- Biography. Gamo (African people) -- Politics and government.

DT381-388.35 Eastern Africa — Ethiopia (Abyssinia) — History

DT381.H465 2000
Henze, Paul B., 1924-
Layers of time: a history of Ethiopia/ Paul B. Henze. New York: St. Martin's Press, 2000. xxiv, 372 p.
99-033311   963   0312227191
Ethiopia -- History.

DT381.M33 1994
Marcus, Harold G.
A history of Ethiopia/ Harold G. Marcus. Berkeley: University of California Press, c1994. xv, 261 p.
93-017987   963   0520081218
Ethiopia -- History.

DT381.P39 1998
Pankhurst, Richard.
The Ethiopians/ Richard Pankhurst. Malden, MA: Blackwell Publishers, 1998. p. cm.
98-009224   963   0631184686
Ethnology -- Ethiopia. Ethiopia -- History.

DT387.7.H2513 1976
Haile Selassie 1892-1975.
My life and Ethiopia's progress, 1892-1937: the autobiography of Emperor Haile Sellassie I/ translated and annotated by Edward Ullendorff. Oxford [Eng.]: Oxford University Press, 1976. xxxii, 335 p.
76-366652   963/.05/0924   0197135897
Haile Selassie -- I, -- Emperor of Ethiopia, -- 1892-1975. Ethiopia -- History -- 1889-1974.

DT387.8.H36 1994
Harris, Joseph E., 1929-
African-American reactions to war in Ethiopia, 1936-1941/ Joseph E. Harris. Baton Rouge: Louisiana State University Press, c1994. xii, 185 p.
93-010343   963/.056   080711832X
Italo-Ethiopian War, 1935-1936 -- Afro-Americans. Afro-Americans -- Politics and government. Ethiopia -- Relations -- United States. United States -- Relations -- Ethiopia.

DT387.8.S37 1992
Scott, William R. 1940-
The sons of Sheba's race: African-Americans and the Italo-Ethiopian War, 1935-1941/ William R. Scott. Bloomington: Indiana University Press, c1993. xvii, 288 p.
92-007900   963/.056   025335126X
Italo-Ethiopian War, 1935-1936 -- Afro-Americans. Afro-Americans -- Politics and government. United States -- Relations -- Ethiopia. Ethiopia -- Relations -- United States.

DT387.9.T34 1991
Tareke, Gebru, 1940-
Ethiopia: power and protest: peasant revolts in the twentieth century/ Gebru Tareke. Cambridge; Cambridge University Press, 1991. xxi, 272 p.
90-022025   963/.06   0521400112
Peasant uprisings -- Ethiopia -- History. Ethiopia -- Politics and government -- 1889-1974.

DT387.95.K45 1988
Keller, Edmond J. 1942-
Revolutionary Ethiopia: from empire to people's republic/ Edmond J. Keller. Bloomington: Indiana University Press, c1988. xi, 307 p.
87-046090   963/.07   025335014X
Ethiopia -- History -- Revolution, 1974. Ethiopia -- History -- 1974-

DT387.95.T57 1993
Tiruneh, Andargachew.
The Ethiopian revolution, 1974-1987: a transformation from an aristocratic to a totalitarian autocracy/ Andargachew Tiruneh. Cambridge; Cambridge University Press, 1993. xiii, 435 p.
92-006554   963.07   0521430828
Totalitarianism. Ethiopia -- History -- Revolution, 1974. Ethiopia -- Politics and government -- 1974-1991.

DT388.35.N44 2000
Negash, Tekeste.
Brothers at war: making sense of the Eritrean-Ethiopian war/ Tekeste Negash & Kjetil Tronvoll. Oxford: J. Currey; 2000. xi, 179 p.
00-049159   963.07/2   085255849X
Eritrean-Ethiopian War, 1998-

DT390 Eastern Africa — Ethiopia (Abyssinia) — Kingdoms, regions, cities, etc., A-Z

DT390.G2.H38 1990
Hassen, Mohammed.
The Oromo of Ethiopia: a history, 1570-1860/ Mohammed Hassen. Cambridge; Cambridge University Press, 1990. xviii, 253 p.
89-009692   963/.3   0521380111
Oromo (African people) -- History. Gibbe River Valley (Ethiopia) -- History.

DT395.3-397 Eastern Africa — Eritrea — History

DT395.3.O38 1991
Okbazghi Yohannes.
Eritrea: a pawn in world politics/ Okbazghi Yohannes. Gainesville: University of Florida Press: c1991. x, 331 p.
90-044256   963/.506   0813010446
Eritrea -- Politics and government -- 1941-1952. Eritrea -- Politics and government -- 1952-1962. Eritrea -- Politics and government -- 1962-1993.

DT397.I96 1995
Iyob, Ruth, 1957-
The Eritrean struggle for independence: domination, resistance, nationalism, 1941-1993/ Ruth Iyob. Cambridge; Cambridge University Press, 1995. xiv, 198 p.
94-012845   963.505   0521473276
Eritrea -- History -- Autonomy and independence movements. Eritrea -- Politics and government -- 1941-1952. Eritrea -- Politics and government -- 1952-1962.

DT402.3 Eastern Africa — Somalia. Somaliland and adjacent territory — Ethnography

DT402.3.C37 1982
Cassanelli, Lee V., 1946-
The shaping of Somali society: reconstructing the history of a pastoral people, 1600-1900/ Lee V. Cassanelli. Philadelphia: University of Pennsylvania Press, 1982. xvi, 311 p.
81-043520   967/.7301   0812278321
Somalis -- History.

DT407-407.4 Eastern Africa — Somalia. Somaliland and adjacent territory — History

DT407.S24 1994
Sahnoun, Mohamed.
Somalia: the missed opportunities/ Mohamed Sahnoun. Washington, D.C.: United States Institute of Peace Press, 1994. xiii, 89 p.
94-003624   967.7305   1878379356
Maxamed Siyaad Barre, -- 1920- Clans -- Somalia. Insurgency -- Somalia -- History -- 20th century. Somalia -- Politics and government -- 1991- Somalia -- Politics and government -- 1960-1991.

DT407.S55 1995
Simons, Anna.
Networks of dissolution: Somalia undone/ Anna Simons. Boulder, CO: Westview Press, 1995. x, 246 p.
95-031508   967.7305   0813325803
Clans -- Somalia. Somalia -- History -- 1991- Somalia -- History -- 1960-1991.

DT407.S59 1994
The Somali challenge: from catastrophe to renewal?/ edited by Ahmed I. Samatar. Boulder: L. Rienner Publishers, 1994. xiii, 297 p.
93-038661   967.73   1555873634
Somalia -- Politics and government -- 1960- Somalia -- Social conditions -- 1960-

DT407.4.P48 2000
Peterson, Scott.
Me against my brother: at war in Somalia, Sudan, and Rwanda: a journalist reports from the battlefields of Africa/ Scott Peterson. New York: Routledge, 2000. p. cm.
99-056411   960.3/29   0415921988
Insurgency -- Somalia -- History -- 20th century. Genocide -- Rwanda -- History -- 20th century. Civil war -- Africa, Eastern -- History -- 20th century. Rwanda -- History -- Civil War, 1994. Rwanda -- History -- Civil War, 1994 -- Atrocities. Somalia -- Politics and government -- 1991-

DT411.5 Eastern Africa — Djibouti. French Territory of the Afars and Issas. French Somaliland — History

DT411.5.A34 2000
Aboubaker Alwan, Daoud.
Historical dictionary of Djibouti/ Daoud A. Alwan, Yohanis Mibrathu. Lanham, Md.: Scarecrow Press, 2000. xxviii, 165 p.
00-040001   967.71/003   0810838737
Djibouti -- History -- Dictionaries.

DT429-429.5 Eastern Africa — East Africa. British East Africa — Ethnography

DT429.F67 1999
Forster, Peter G. 1944-
Race and ethnicity in East Africa/ Peter G. Forster, Michael Hitchcock, Francis F. Lyimo. New York: St. Martin's Press, 1999. p. cm.
99-032869   305.8/009676   0312226071
Africa, East -- Ethnic relations -- History. Africa, East -- Race relations -- History. Rwanda -- Ethnic relations -- History.

DT429.5.A47.D88 1998
Du Toit, Brian M., 1935-
The Boers in East Africa: ethnicity and identity/ Brian M. Du Toit. Westport, Conn.: Bergin & Garvey, 1998. viii, 209 p.
98-018514   967.6/0043936   0897896114
Afrikaners -- Africa, East -- History. Afrikaners -- Africa, East -- Ethnic identity -- History.

DT429.5.S68.G74 1993
Gregory, Robert G.
South Asians in East Africa: an economic and social history, 1890-1980/ Robert G. Gregory. Boulder: Westview Press, 1993. xiii, 410 p.
92-003854   304.8/540676   0813314038
South Asians -- Africa, East -- Economic conditions. South Asians -- Africa, East -- Social conditions. Occupations -- Africa, East.

DT429.5.S94
Horton, Mark
The Swahili: the social landscape of a mercantile society/ Mark Horton and John Middleton. Oxford, UK; Blackwell Publishers, 2000. 282 p.
00-009633   967.6004/96392   063118919X
Swahili-speaking peoples -- History. Swahili-speaking peoples -- Commerce. Swahili-speaking peoples -- Social life and customs. Africa, East -- Social life and customs.

DT429.5.S94.M54 1992
Middleton, John, 1921-
The world of the Swahili: an African mercantile civilization/ John Middleton. New Haven: Yale University Press, c1992. xii, 254 p.
91-031617   306/.089/96392   0300052197
Swahili-speaking peoples -- Commerce. Swahili-speaking peoples -- Kinship. Swahili-speaking peoples -- Social life and customs. Lamu (Kenya) -- Commerce. Lamu (Kenya) -- Social life and customs. Zanzibar -- Commerce.

DT432 Eastern Africa — East Africa. British East Africa — History

DT432.P43 1998
Pearson, M. N. 1941-
Port cities and intruders: the Swahili Coast, India, and Portugal in the early modern era/ Michael N. Pearson. Baltimore, Md.: Johns Hopkins University Press, c1998. x, 202 p.
97-020627   967.6/01   0801856922
East Indians -- Africa, East -- History. Portuguese -- Africa, East -- History. Swahili-speaking peoples -- History. Africa, East -- History -- To 1886. Portugal -- Relations -- Africa, East. Africa, East -- Relations -- Portugal.

DT433.215-433.265 Eastern Africa — East Africa. British East Africa — Uganda

DT433.215.M39 2000
Maxon, Robert M.
Historical dictionary of Kenya/ Robert M. Maxon, Thomas P. Ofcansky. Lanham, Md.: Scarecrow Press, 2000. xxvi, 449 p.
98-050070   967.62/003   0810836165
Kenya -- History -- Dictionaries.

DT433.245.G35.R39 1991
Ray, Benjamin C., 1940-
Myth, ritual, and kingship in Buganda/ by Benjamin C. Ray. New York: Oxford University Press, 1991. ix, 239 p.
90-007127   306.6/996896395706761   0195064364
Ganda (African people) -- Kings and rulers. Ganda (African people) -- Rites and ceremonies.

DT433.265.W75 1996
Wrigley, Christopher.
Kingship and state: the Buganda dynasty/ Christopher Wrigley. Cambridge; Cambridge University Press, 1996. xv, 293 p.
95-004678   967.6/01   0521473705
Mythology, Ganda. Oral tradition -- Uganda. Ganda (African people) -- Kings and rulers. Uganda -- History -- To 1890.

DT433.542-434 Eastern Africa — East Africa. British East Africa — Kenya

DT433.542.M85
Muriuki, Godfrey.
A history of the Kikuyu, 1500-1900.   Nairobi, Oxford University Press, 1974. viii, 190 p.
74-186971   916.76/2/06963   0195723147
Kikuyu (African people) -- History.

DT433.545.G86.C55 1994
Child care and culture: lessons from Africa/ Robert A. LeVine ... [et al.]; with the collaboration of James Caron ... [et al.]. Cambridge [England]; Cambridge University Press, 1994. xx, 346 p.
93-033584   305.23/1/096762   0521331714
Children, Gusii -- Kenya -- Kisii District. Women, Gusii -- Kenya -- Kisii District -- Family relationships. Child rearing -- Kenya -- Kisii District -- Cross-cultural studies.

DT433.545.K55.R63 1997
Robertson, Claire C., 1944-
Trouble showed the way: women, men, and trade in the Nairobi area, 1890-1990/ Claire C. Robertson. Bloomington: Indiana University Press, c1997. xii, 341 p.
97-040099   338.9/0089/963954067625   0253333601
Women, Kikuyu -- Commerce. Women, Kikuyu -- Economic conditions. Women, Kikuyu -- Social conditions. Nairobi (Kenya) -- Commerce. Nairobi (Kenya) -- Economic conditions. Nairobi (Kenya) -- Social conditions.

DT433.545.K87
Fleisher, Michael L., 1942-
Kuria cattle raiders: violence and vigilantism on the Tanzania/Kenya frontier/ Michael L. Fleisher. Ann Arbor: University of Michigan Press, c2000. xiv, 198 p.
00-031521   967.62/004/96395   0472111523
Kuria (African people) -- Domestic animals. Kuria (African people) -- Social conditions. Kuria (African people) -- Economic conditions. Kenya -- Social conditions. Tanzania -- Social conditions.

DT433.545.L63.A38 1997
Abwunza, Judith M. 1937-
Women's voices, women's power: dialogues of resistance from East Africa/ Judith M. Abwunza. Peterborough, Ont.: Broadview Press, c1997. ix, 224 p.
98-118625   305.48/896395   1551111322
Women, Logooli -- Social conditions. Women, Logooli -- Economic conditions. Patriarchy -- Kenya -- Western Province.

DT433.545.M33.S64 1988
Spencer, Paul, 1932-
The Maasai of Matapato: a study of rituals of rebellion/ Paul Spencer. Bloomington: Indiana University Press in association with the c1988. xii, 296 p.
87-026035   306/.08996   0253336252
Masai (African people) -- Social life and customs. Masai (African people) -- Rites and ceremonies. Age groups -- Kenya. Matapatu (Kenya) -- Social life and customs.

DT433.545.M47.F34 1993
Fadiman, Jeffrey.
When we began there were witchmen: an oral history from Mount Kenya/ Jeffrey A. Fadiman. Berkeley: University of California Press, c1993. xi, 395 p.
92-012639   967.62/0049639   0520065077
Meru (African people) -- History. Oral tradition -- Kenya. Witchcraft -- Kenya.

DT433.545.S93.S93 1991
Swartz, Marc J.
The way the world is: cultural processes and social relations among the Mombasa Swahili/ Marc J. Swartz. Berkeley: University of California Press, c1991. xiii, 350 p.
91-013198   306.4/08996392   0520071379
Swahili-speaking peoples -- Kenya -- Mombasa. Swahili-speaking peoples -- Social life and customs. Mombasa (Kenya) -- Social life and customs.

DT433.545.T3.B73 1998
Bravman, Bill.
Making ethnic ways: communities and their transformations in Taita, Kenya, 1800-1950/ Bill Bravman. Portsmouth, NH: Heinemann, c1998. xiv, 283 p.
98-012377 305.8/0096762 0325001057
Taita (African people) -- Ethnic identity. Taita (African people) -- History. Taita (African people) -- Religion. Taita Hills (Kenya) -- Social conditions. Taita Hills (Kenya) -- Ethnic relations.

DT433.57.A43 1988
Ambler, Charles H.
Kenyan communities in the age of imperialism: the central region in the late nineteenth century/ Charles H. Ambler. New Haven: Yale University Press, c1988. x, 181 p.
87-014801 967.6/2 0300039573
Kenya -- History -- To 1895. Kenya -- Economic conditions -- To 1963.

DT433.577.C58 1998
Clough, Marshall S.
Mau Mau memoirs: history, memory, and politics/ Marshall S. Clough. Boulder, Colo.: L. Rienner, 1998. x, 283 p.
97-036869 967.62/03 1555875378
Autobiography. Kenya -- History -- Mau Mau Emergency, 1952-1960 -- Historiography.

DT433.577.K47 1996
Kershaw, Greet.
Mau Mau from below/ Greet Kershaw. Oxford: j. Currey; c1997. xxx, 354 p.
96-041339 967.62/03 0821411543
Kenya -- History -- Mau Mau Emergency, 1952-1960.

DT433.577.M35 1993
Maloba, Wunyabari O., 1950-
Mau Mau and Kenya: an analysis of a peasant revolt/ Wunyabari O. Maloba. Bloomington: Indiana University Press, 1993. x, 228 p.
92-031421 967.6204 0253336643
Nationalism -- Kenya -- History -- 20th century. Peasant uprisings -- Kenya -- History -- 20th century. Kenya -- History -- Mau Mau Emergency, 1952-1960.

DT433.582.O75.A3 1998
Otieno, Wambui Waiyaki, 1936-
Mau Mau's daughter: a life history/ Wambui Waiyaki Otieno; edited and with an introduction by Cora Ann Presley. Boulder: Lynne Rienner Publishers, 1998. xiii, 255 p.
98-010980 967.62/03/092 1555877222
Otieno, Wambui Waiyaki, -- 1936- Otieno, Silvanus Melea, -- d. 1985 -- Death and burial. Politicians -- Kenya -- Biography. Women, Kikuyu -- Biography. Women politicians -- Kenya -- Biography. Kenya -- Politics and government.

DT433.584.W53 1992
Widner, Jennifer A.
The rise of a party-state in Kenya: from "Harambee" to "Nyayo!"/ Jennifer A. Widner. Berkeley: University of California, c1992. xix, 283 p.
91-044328 967.6204 0520076249
Kenya -- Politics and government -- 1978-

DT434.L35.R66 1997
Romero, Patricia W.
Lamu: history, society, and family in an East African port city/ by Patricia W. Romero. Princeton: M. Wiener, 1997. p. cm.
96-045647 967.62/3 1558761063
Lamu (Kenya) -- History.

DT434.R75.I47 1998
Imperato, Pascal James.
Quest for the Jade Sea: colonial competition around an East African lake/ Pascal James Imperato. Boulder, Co.: Westview Press, 1998. xvi, 332 p.
98-004983 967.62/7 0813327911
Rudolf, Lake, Region (Kenya and Ethiopia) -- Discovery and exploration -- European. Rudolf, Lake, Region (Kenya and Ethiopia) -- Politics and government. Great Britain -- Foreign relations -- Ethiopia.

DT443.3-443.3 Eastern Africa — Tanzania. Tanganyika. German East Africa — Ethnography

DT443.3.B38.R54 1992
Rigby, Peter, 1938-
Cattle, capitalism, and class: Ilparakuyo Maasai transformations/ Peter Rigby. Philadelphia: Temple University Press, 1992. xviii, 247 p.
91-038186 306/.089965 0877229546
Baraguyu (African people) -- Social conditions. Baraguyu (African people) -- Economic conditions. Baraguyu (African people) -- Domestic animals.

DT443.3.H39.S24 1997
Schmidt, Peter R. 1942-
Iron technology in East Africa: symbolism, science, and archaeology/ Peter R. Schmidt. Bloomington: Indiana University Press; c1997. xii, 328 p.
96-046107 669/.141/096 0253332559
Haya (African people) -- Industries. Metal-work, Haya. Haya (African people) -- Social life and customs. Tanzania -- Antiquities.

DT443.3.H39.W45 1996
Weiss, Brad.
The making and unmaking of the Haya lived world: consumption, commoditization, and everyday practice/ Brad Weiss. Durham: Duke University Press, c1996. viii, 250 p.
95-037842 390/.089/967827 0822317257
Haya (African people) -- Economic conditions. Haya (African people) -- Commerce. Haya (African people) -- Food. Kagera Region (Tanzania) -- Economic conditions. Kagera Region (Tanzania) -- Social conditions.

DT443.3.H88.M35 1995
Malkki, Liisa H.
Purity and exile: violence, memory, and national cosmology among Hutu refugees in Tanzania/ Liisa H. Malkki. Chicago: University of Chicago Press, 1995. xiv, 352 p.
94-037099 305.896/39461 0226502716
Hutu (African people) -- Tanzania -- Ethnic identity. Political refugees -- Burundi. Political refugees -- Tanzania.

DT443.3.K33.B43 1997
Beidelman, T. O. 1931-
The cool knife: imagery of gender, sexuality, and moral education in Kaguru initiation ritual/ T.O. Beidelman. Washington: Smithsonian Institution Press, c1997. xv, 312 p.
96-043928 306/.089/96391 1560987138
Kaguru (African people) -- Rites and ceremonies. Initiation rites -- Tanzania. Kaguru (African people) -- Ethnic identity. Tanzania -- Social conditions.

DT443.3.M47.S63 1997
Spear, Thomas T.
Mountain farmers: moral economies of land & agricultural development in Arusha & Meru/ Thomas Spear. Dar es Salaam: Mkuki na Nyota; 1997. x, 262 p.
96-037622 967.8/26 0520206185
Meru (African people) -- Land tenure. Meru (African people) -- Agriculture. Meru (African people) -- Government relations. Meru, Mount, Region (Tanzania) -- Economic conditions. Meru, Mount, Region (Tanzania) -- Social conditions. Meru, Mount, Region (Tanzania) -- Race relations.

DT443.3.Z37.S93 1995
Swantz, Marja-Liisa.
Blood, milk, and death: body symbols and the power of regeneration among the Zaramo of Tanzania/ Marja-Liisa Swantz with the assistance of Salome Mjema and Zenya Wild. Westport, Conn.: Bergin & Garvey, c1995. 158 p.
94-027541 305.48/896391 0897893980
Women, Zaramo -- Rites and ceremonies. Women, Zaramo -- Social life and customs. Body, Human -- Symbolic aspects -- Tanzania. Tanzania -- Social life and customs.

DT444-447.2 Eastern Africa — Tanzania. Tanganyika. German East Africa — History

DT444.O33 1997
Ofcansky, Thomas P., 1947-
Historical dictionary of Tanzania/ Thomas P. Ofcansky, Rodger Yeager. Lanham, Md.: Scarecrow Press, 1997. xxxi, 291 p.
96-035043 967.8/003 0810832445
Tanzania -- History -- Dictionaries.

DT447.2.S34.A3 1999
Sadleir, Randal, 1924-
Tanzania, journey to republic/ Randal Sadleir; foreword by Julius Nyerere. London; Radcliffe Press; 1999. ix, 342 p.
1860644376
Sadleir, Randal, -- 1924- Colonial administrators -- Great Britain -- Biography. Tanzania -- History. Tanzania -- Politics and government -- 1964-

DT450.435 Eastern Africa — Tanzania. Tanganyika. German East Africa — History

DT450.435.G68 1998
Gourevitch, Philip, 1961-
We wish to inform you that tomorrow we will be killed with our families: stories from Rwanda/ Philip Gourevitch. New York: Farrar, Straus, and Giroux, 1998. 355 p.
98-022132 364.15/1/0967591 0374286973
Genocide -- Rwanda. Rwanda -- Politics and government. Rwanda -- Ethnic relations.

DT450.435.J36 2000
Janzen, John M.
Do I still have a life?: voices from the aftermath of war in Rwanda and Burundi/ John M. Janzen & Reinhild Kauenhoven Janzen. Lawrence: University of Kansas, c2000. x, 234 p.
2001-330217
Refugees -- Rwanda. Genocide -- Rwanda. Refugees -- Burundi. Burundi -- Ethnic relations -- History -- 20th century. Rwanda -- History -- Civil War, 1994 -- Refugees.

DT450.435.K55 1998
Klinghoffer, Arthur Jay, 1941-
The international dimension of genocide in Rwanda/ Arthur Jay Klinghoffer. New York, N.Y.: New York University Press, 1998. ix, 219 p.
98-013162   967.57104   0814747213
Genocide -- Rwanda -- History -- 20th century. Rwanda -- History -- Civil War, 1994 -- Atrocities. Rwanda -- Foreign relations. Rwanda -- History -- Civil War, 1994 -- Diplomatic history.

DT450.435.M35 2001
Mamdani, Mahmood, 1946-
When victims become killers: colonialism, nativism, and the genocide in Rwanda/ Mahmood Mamdani. Princeton, N.J.: Princeton University Press, c2001. xvi, 364 p.
00-065213   967.57104   0691058210
Genocide -- Rwanda -- History -- 20th century. Tutsi (African people) -- Crimes against -- Rwanda -- History -- 20th century. Hutu (African people) -- Rwanda -- Politics and government. Rwanda -- Politics and government. Rwanda -- Ethnic relations -- History -- 20th century.

DT450.435.U95 1998
Uvin, Peter, 1962-
Aiding violence: the development enterprise in Rwanda/ Peter Uvin. West Hartford, CT: Kumarian Press, 1998. ix, 275 p.
98-022652   967.57104   1565490843
Genocide -- Rwanda -- History -- 20th century. Economic assistance -- Rwanda -- History -- 20th century. Tutsi (African people) -- Crimes against -- Rwanda -- History -- 20th century. Rwanda -- Economic conditions. Rwanda -- Ethnic relations.

DT450.64 Eastern Africa — Burundi — Ethnography

DT450.64.L46 1994
Lemarchand, Rene.
Burundi: ethnocide as discourse and practice/ Rene Lemarchand. Washington: Woodrow Wilson Center Press; c1994. xxiii, 206 p.
93-037592   323.1/67572   0521451760
Violence -- Burundi. Genocide -- Burundi. Burundi -- Ethnic relations -- Political aspects. Burundi -- Politics and government.

DT469 Eastern Africa — Islands (East African coast) — Individual islands, A-Z

DT469.M264.K67 1980
Kottak, Conrad Phillip.
The past in the present: history, ecology, and cultural variation in highland Madagascar/ Conrad Phillip Kottak; foreword by Roy A. Rappaport. Ann Arbor: University of Michigan Press, c1980. xiv, 339 p.
80-014575   969.1/00499   0472093231
Betsileos (Malagasy people)   Madagascar -- Social conditions. Madagascar -- History.

DT469.M277.M475 2000
Larson, Pier Martin.
History and memory in the age of enslavement: becoming Merina in highland Madagascar, 1770-1822/ Pier M. Larson. Portsmouth, NH: Heinemann, c2000. xxxii, 414 p.
99-049241   969.1004/993   0325002177
Merina (Malagasy people) -- Ethnic identity. Merina (Malagasy people) -- History. Slavery -- Madagascar.

DT469.M277.S355 1991
Feeley-Harnik, Gillian, 1940-
A green estate: restoring independence in Madagascar/ Gillian Feeley-Harnik. Washington, D.C.: Smithsonian Institution Press, c1991. xxvii, 627 p.
90-026394   969.1   0874744407
Sakalava (Malagasy people) -- Kings and rulers. Sakalava (Malagasy people) -- Kinship. Ancestor worship -- Madagascar -- History. Madagascar -- History -- Colonial influences.

DT469.M277.S358 1993
Sharp, Lesley Alexandra.
The possessed and the dispossessed: spirits, identity, and power in a Madagascar migrant town/ Lesley A. Sharp. Berkeley: University of California Press, c1993. xix, 345 p.
92-037296   306/.089/993   0520080017
Sakalava (Malagasy people) -- Rites and ceremonies. Sakalava (Malagasy people) -- Religion. Sakalava (Malagasy people) -- Social conditions. Ambanja (Madagascar) -- Religious life and customs.

DT469.M277.T788 1992
Wilson, Peter J., 1933-
Freedom by a hair's breadth: Tsimihety in Madagascar/ Peter J. Wilson. Ann Arbor: University of Michigan Press, c1992. xii, 179 p.
92-028344   305.89/93   047210389X
Tsimihety (Malagasy people) Tsimihety (Malagasy people) -- Ethnic identity. Tsimihety (Malagasy people) -- Politics and government.

DT469.M445.E273 1994
Carter, Marina.
Lakshmi's legacy: the testimonies of Indian women in 19th century Mauritius/ Marina Carter. Stanley, Rose-Hill, Mauritius: Editions de l'ocean Indien, c1994. x, 282 p.
94-980912   969.8/2004914   9990301689
East Indians -- Mauritius -- History. Women -- Mauritius. Mauritius -- Emigration and immigration.

DT469.M445.E2734 1996
Carter, Marina.
Voices from indenture: experiences of Indian migrants in the British empire/ Marina Carter. London; Leicester University Press, 1996. xv, 251 p.
95-043296   306.3/63/0899141106982   0718500318
East Indians -- Mauritius -- History -- 19th century. Indentured servants -- Mauritius -- History -- 19th century. Mauritius -- Emigration and immigration -- History -- 19th century. India -- Emigration and immigration -- History -- 19th century.

DT474.6 West Africa. West Coast — Ethnography

DT474.6.I35.O33 1994
Ohadike, Don C.
Anioma: a social history of the Western Igbo people/ by Don C. Ohadike. Athens: Ohio University Press, c1994. xx, 249 p.
93-031029   960/.0496332   0821410725
Igbo (African people) -- Origin. Igbo (African people) -- History. Igbo (African people) -- Social life and customs.

DT474.6.M36.F73 1998
Frank, Barbara E.
Mande potters & leatherworkers: art and heritage in West Africa/ Barbara E. Frank. Washington, D.C.: Smithsonian Institution Press, 1998. xvi, 192 p.
97-027477   738/.089/96345   1560987944
Pottery, Mandingo. Leatherwork, Mandingo. Mandingo (African people) -- Industries.

DT474.6.M36.S73 1995
Status and identity in West Africa: Nyamakalaw of Mande/ edited by David C. Conrad and Barbara E. Frank. Bloomington: Indiana University Press, c1995. x, 204 p.
94-020215   305.5/0966   0253314097
Mandingo (African people) -- Industries. Mandingo (African people) -- Kinship. Mandingo (African people) -- Social life and customs. Africa, West -- Social life and customs.

DT476.2-476.5 West Africa. West Coast — History — By period

DT476.2.K46 1992
Kent, John, 1949-
The internationalization of colonialism: Britain, France, and Black Africa, 1939-1956/ John Kent. Oxford: Clarendon Press; 1992. xi, 365 p.
92-013210   325/.314   0198203020
Africa, West -- Politics and government -- 1884-1960. Great Britain -- Colonies -- Africa. France -- Colonies -- Africa.

DT476.2.N88 2001
Nwaubani, Ebere, 1956-
The United States and decolonization in West Africa, 1950-1960/ Ebere Nwaubani. Rochester, NY: University of Rochester Press, 2001. xxi, 338 p.
00-049445   966.03   1580460763
Decolonization -- Africa, West -- History -- 20th century. Africa, West -- Politics and government -- 1884-1960. Africa, West -- Relations -- United States. United States -- Relations -- Africa, West.

DT476.5.C66 1990
Contemporary West African states/ edited by Donal B. Cruise O'Brien, John Dunn, and Richard Rathbone. Cambridge; Cambridge University Press, 1989. viii, 227 p.
89-009695   966.03/27   0521363667
Africa, West -- Politics and government -- 1960-

DT507-516.826 West Africa. West Coast — British West Africa — Local

DT507.A45 2000
Allman, Jean Marie.
I will not eat stone: a women's history of colonial Asante/ Jean Allman and Victoria Tashjian. Portsmouth, NH: Heinemann; c2000. xlvi, 255 p.
00-024253   966.7004/963385   0325070016
Women, Ashanti -- History. Marriage -- Economic aspects -- Ghana. Ashanti (African people) -- Social conditions.

DT507.M34 1995
McCaskie, T. C.
State and society in pre-colonial Asante/ T.C. McCaskie. Cambridge; Cambridge University Press, 1995. xvii, 492 p.
94-006732   966.7/018   0521410096
Ashanti (African people) -- History. Ashanti (Kingdom) Ghana -- History.

DT510.43.A53.O93 1998
Owoahene-Acheampong, Stephen, 1956-
Inculturation and African religion: indigenous and Western approaches to medical practice/ Stephen Owoahene-Acheampong. New York: Peter Lang, c1998. xv, 225 p.
96-000478   306.4/61/09667   082043129X
Akan (African people) -- Medicine. Akan (African people) -- Religion. Traditional medicine -- Ghana. Ghana -- Social life and customs.

DT510.43.A53.Y35 1995
Yankah, Kwesi.
Speaking for the chief: okyeame and the politics of Akan royal oratory/ Kwesi Yankah. Bloomington: Indiana University Press, c1995. x, 194 p.
94-027094   808.5/1/089963385   0253368014
Akan (African people) -- Politics and government. Speeches, addresses, etc., Akan. Akan (African people) -- Rites and ceremonies. Ghana -- Social life and customs.

DT510.43.K76.W55 1991
Wilson, Louis Edward.
The Krobo people of Ghana, to 1892: a political and social history/ by Louis E. Wilson. Athens, Ohio: Ohio University Center for International Studies 1991. xiv, 253 p.
91-013764   966.7/0049633   0896801640
Krobo (African people) -- History.

DT511.R28 2000
Rathbone, Richard.
Nkrumah & the chiefs: the politics of chieftaincy in Ghana, 1951-60/ Richard Rathbone. Accra, Ghana: F. Reimmer; 2000. xi, 176 p.
99-046031   320.9667/09/045   0821413058
Nkrumah, Kwame, -- 1909-1972. Chiefdoms -- Ghana -- History -- 20th century. Tribal government -- Ghana -- History -- 20th century. Local government -- Ghana -- History -- 20th century. Ghana -- Politics and government -- 1957-1979. Ghana -- Politics and government.

DT512.A66 1992
Agyeman, Opoku, 1942-
Nkrumah's Ghana and East Africa: Pan-Africanism and African interstate relations/ Opoku Agyeman. Rutherford: Fairleigh Dickinson University Press; c1992. 234 p.
91-055093   327.6670676   0838634567
Nkrumah, Kwame, -- 1909-1972. Pan-Africanism. Ghana -- Politics and government -- 1957-1979. Ghana -- Politics and government -- 1979- Ghana -- Foreign relations -- Africa, East.

DT512.9.A3
Parker, John, 1960-
Making the town: Ga state and society in early Colonial Accra/ John Parker. Portsmouth, NH: Heinemann, c2000. xxxiii, 264 p.
00-025969   966.7   0325001901
Ga (African people) -- Ghana -- Accra -- Politics and government -- 19th century. Accra (Ghana) -- Politics and government -- 19th century.

DT512.9.E46
DeCorse, Christopher R.
An archaeology of Elmina: Africans and Europeans on the Gold Coast, 1400-1900/ Christopher R. DeCorse. Washington, DC: Smithsonian Institution Press, c2001. x, 286 p.
00-047005   966.7   1560989718
Europeans -- Ghana -- Elmina -- History. Slave trade -- Ghana -- Elmina -- History. Excavations (Archaeology) -- Ghana -- Elmina. Elmina (Ghana) -- History. Elmina (Ghana) -- Antiquities.

DT515.15.O94
Oyewole, A.
Historical dictionary of Nigeria/ Anthony Oyewole. Lanham [Md.]: Scarecrow Press, 1997. p. cm.
97-009168   966.9/003   0810832623
Nigeria -- History -- Dictionaries.

DT515.22.B45 1999
Bell-Gam, Ruby.
Nigeria/ Ruby A. Bell-Gam and David Uru Iyam, compilers. Oxford, England; Clio Press, c1999. xxvii, 342 p.
1851093273
Nigeria -- Bibliography.

DT515.45.B5.I93 1995
Iyam, David Uru.
The broken hoe: cultural reconfiguration in Biase southeast Nigeria/ David Uru Iyam. Chicago: University of Chicago Press, 1995. x, 238 p.
94-039003   307.72/09669/44   0226388484
Biase (African people) -- Social conditions. Biase (African people) -- Economic conditions. Biase (African people) -- Agriculture. Cross River State (Nigeria -- Economic conditions. Cross River State (Nigeria) -- Politics and government. Cross River State (Nigeria) -- Environmental conditions.

DT515.45.H38.C35 1987
Callaway, Barbara.
Muslim Hausa women in Nigeria: tradition and change/ Barbara J. Callaway; foreword and photographs by Enid Schildkrout. Syracuse, NY: Syracuse University Press, c1987. xx, 242 p.
87-006464   305.4/88937/06695   0815624069
Women, Hausa -- Nigeria -- Kano. Muslim women -- Nigeria -- Kano. Kano (Nigeria) -- Social conditions.

DT515.45.H38.H38 1991
Hausa women in the twentieth century/ edited by Catherine Coles and Beverly Mack. Madison, Wis.: University of Wisconsin Press, c1991. xi, 297 p.
91-014182   305.48/8937   0299130207
Women, Hausa. Muslim women.

DT515.45.H38.M55 1994
Miles, William F. S.
Hausaland divided: colonialism and independence in Nigeria and Niger/ William F.S. Miles. Ithaca: Cornell University Press, 1994. xvii, 368 p.
93-031669   966.26/004937   0801428556
Hausa (African people) -- Ethnic identity. Hausa (African people) -- Government relations. Assimilation (Sociology) -- Niger. Niger -- Colonial influence. Nigeria -- Colonial influence.

DT515.45.I33 A35 2000
Agbasiere, Joseph Therese, 1929-1998.
Women in Igbo life and thought/ Joseph Therese Agbasiere; with a biographical note by Shirley Ardener. London; Routledge, 2000. xxviii, 188 p.
99-040300   305.48/896332   0415227038
Women, Igbo. Philosophy, Igbo.

DT515.45.I33.M39 2000
McCall, John C.
Dancing histories: heuristic ethnography with the Ohafia Igbo/ John C. McCall. Ann Arbor: University of Michigan Press, c2000. xiv, 192 p.
99-059065   966.9/00496332   0472110705
Igbo (African people) -- History. Igbo (African people) -- Rites and ceremonies. Philosophy, Igbo. Ohafia (Nigeria) -- History. Ohafia (Nigeria) -- Social life and customs.

DT515.45.I33.O88 1989
Ottenberg, Simon.
Boyhood rituals in an African society: an interpretation/ Simon Ottenberg. Seattle: University of Washington Press, c1989. xxiv, 344 p.
87-021701   392./14/089963   0295965754
Igbo children. Igbo (African people) -- Rites and ceremonies. Socialization -- Case studies.

DT515.45.I35.H65 1989
Hollos, Marida, 1940-
Becoming Nigerian in Ijo society/ Marida Hollos and Philip E. Leis. New Brunswick [N.J.]: Rutgers University Press, c1989. xxii, 167 p.
88-010111   305.2/3/089963   081351360X
Children, Ijo. Ijo (African people) -- Social conditions. Nigeria -- Social conditions -- 1960-

DT515.45.K64.S76 1996
Stone, Glenn Davis.
Settlement ecology: the social and spatial organization of Kofyar agriculture/ Glenn Davis Stone. Tucson: University of Arizona Press, c1996. xv, 256 p.
96-009997   338.1/09669/5   0816515670
Kofyar (African people) -- Agriculture. Kofyar (African people) -- Land tenure. Kofyar (African people) -- Social conditions. Jos Plateau (Nigeria) -- Social conditions.

DT515.45.O88.O33 1997
Ogbomo, Onaiwu W., 1958-
When men and women mattered: a history of gender relations among the Owan of Nigeria/ Onaiwu W. Ogbomo. Rochester, N.Y., USA: University of Rochester Press, 1997. x, 220 p.
97-001501   305.3/09669/32   1878822780
Owan (African people) -- Kinship. Owan (African people) -- History. Owan (African people) -- Social life and customs. Edo State (Nigeria) -- Social life and customs.

DT515.45.Y67.R45 1995
Renne, Elisha P.
Cloth that does not die: the meaning of cloth in Bunu social life/ Elisha P. Renne. Seattle: University of Washington Press, c1995. xxi, 269 p.
94-012014   746.1/4/08996333   0295973927
Textile fabrics, Yoruba -- Nigeria -- Bunu District -- Social aspects. Yoruba (African people) -- Social life and customs. Hand weaving -- Nigeria -- Bunu District.

DT515.45.Y67.T73 2001
Trager, Lillian, 1947-
Yoruba hometowns: community, identity, and development in Nigeria/ Lillian Trager. Boulder, Co.: Lynne Rienner Publishers, 2001. p. cm.
00-066503   305.896/3330669   1555879497
Yoruba (African people) -- Kinship. Yoruba (African people) -- Ethnic identity. Philosophy, Yoruba -- Nigeria -- Ijesa Region. Ijesa Region (Nigeria) -- Social life and customs.

DT515.45.Y67.V38 2000
Vaughan, Olufemi.
Nigerian chiefs: traditional power in modern politics, 1890s-1990s/ Olufemi Vaughan. Rochester, NY: University of Rochester Press, 2000. xiv, 293 p.
99-088099 320.9669 1580460402
Yoruba (African people) -- Politics and government. Yoruba (African people) -- Kings and rulers. Yoruba (African people) -- Government relations. Nigeria -- Politics and government.

DT515.7.O36 1991
Ohadike, Don C.
The Ekumeku movement: Western Igbo resistance to the British conquest of Nigeria, 1883-1914/ Don C. Ohadike. Athens: Ohio University Press, c1991. xi, 203 p.
90-023998 966.9/03 0821409859
Igbo (African people) -- Politics and government. Nigeria -- History -- 1900-1960. Nigeria -- Relations -- Great Britain. Great Britain -- Relations -- Nigeria.

DT515.77.Y35.A3 1995
Yaji, Hamman.
The diary of Hamman Yaji: chronicle of a West African Muslim ruler/ edited and introduced by James H. Vaughan and Anthony H.M. Kirk-Greene. Bloomington: Indiana University Press, c1995. xv, 162 p.
94-027840 966.96/2 0253362067
Yaji, Hamman -- Diaries. Nigeria -- Kings and rulers -- Diaries. Sokoto State (Nigeria) -- History.

DT515.9.K32.S65 1997
Smith, M. G.
Government in Kano, 1350-1950/ M.G. Smith. Boulder, Colo.: Westview Press, 1997. xxiii, 595 p.
97-028103 966.9/78 0813332702
Hausa (African people) -- Nigeria -- Kano State -- Politics and government. Fula (African people) -- Nigeria -- Kano State -- Politics and government. Islam -- Nigeria -- Kano State -- History. Kano State (Nigeria) -- Politics and government.

DT516.45.W47
Blyden, Nemata Amelia, 1964-
West Indians in West Africa, 1808-1880: the African diaspora in reverse/ Nemata Amelia Blyden. Rochester, NY: University of Rochester Press, 2000. xi, 258 p.
00-056388 966.4/004960729 1580460461
West Indians -- Sierra Leone -- History -- 19th century. Sierra Leone -- History -- To 1896. Sierra Leone -- Ethnic relations.

DT516.7.W97 1990
Wyse, Akintola J. G.
H.C. Bankole-Bright and politics in colonial Sierra Leone, 1919-1958/ Akintola J.G. Wyse. Cambridge [England]; Cambridge University Press, 1990. xii, 278 p.
89-025427 966.4/03 0521365155
Bankole-Bright, H. C., -- d. 1958. Sierra Leone -- Politics and government -- 1896-1961.

DT516.826.H57 2001
Hirsch, John L., 1936-
Sierra Leone: diamonds and the struggle for democracy/ John L. Hirsch. Boulder, Colo.: L. Rienner, 2001. 175 p.
00-062563 966.4 1555876986

DT530.5 West Africa. West Coast — French West Africa. French Sahara. West Sahara. Sahel — Ethnography

DT530.5.M88.H37 1988
Harrison, Christopher, 1958-
France and Islam in West Africa, 1860-1960/ Christopher Harrison. Cambridge [England]; Cambridge University Press, 1988. xi, 242 p.
87-033392 966/.0097451 0521352304
Muslims -- Africa, French-speaking West -- Politics and government. Islam and politics -- Africa, French-speaking West. France -- Colonies -- Africa -- Administration. Africa, French-speaking West -- Politics and government -- 1884-1960.

DT532.23-532.5 West Africa. West Coast — French West Africa. French Sahara. West Sahara. Sahel — History

DT532.23.W75 1997
Wright, Donald R.
The world and a very small place in Africa/ Donald R. Wright. Armonk, N.Y.: M.E. Sharpe, c1997. xv, 278 p.
96-044139 966.3 1563249596
Niumi (Kingdom) -- Relations.

DT532.25.B3713 1998
Barry, Boubacar.
Senegambia and the Atlantic slave trade/ Boubacar Barry; translated from the French by Ayi Kwei Armah. Cambridge, U.K.; Cambridge University Press, 1998. xxi, 358 p.
97-006026 966.305 0521592267
Senegambia -- History.

DT532.25.C55 1999
Clark, Andrew Francis.
From frontier to backwater: economy and society in the upper Senegal Valley (West Africa), 1850-1920/ Andrew F. Clark. Lanham: University Press of America, c1999. xiii, 278 p.
0761814388
Senegambia -- Economic conditions. Senegal -- History -- To 1960. Senegal -- Civilization.

DT532.27.M63.H35 1990
Hale, Thomas A.
Scribe, griot, and novelist: narrative interpreters of the Songhay Empire/ Thomas A. Hale. Followed by The epic of Askia Mohammed/ recounted by Nouhou Malio. Gainesville: University of Florida Press: c1990. xiv, 313 p.
89-020664 966.2/018/092 0813009812
Mohammed -- I, -- Askia of Songhai, -- 1443?-1538. Songhai (African people) -- Kings and rulers -- Biography. Songhai Empire.

DT532.3.H36 1991
Hanson, John H., 1956-
After the Jihad: the reign of Ahmad Al-Kabir in the Western Sudan/ by John Hanson, David Robinson; with the assistance of Malik Balla, John Hunwick, and Malek Towghi. East Lansing: Michigan State University Press, 1991. xvi, 410 p.
91-036337 966.023 0870133055
Madani, Ahmad al-Kabir, -- 1836?-1897 -- Archives. Toucouleur Empire -- History -- Sources.

DT532.3.T35.H36 1996
Hanson, John H., 1956-
Migration, Jihad, and Muslim authority in West Africa: the Futanke colonies in Karta/ John H. Hanson. Bloomington: Indiana University Press, c1996. xi, 218 p.
95-043340 966.23/01 0253330882
Tal, Umar, -- 1794?-1864. Muslims -- Senegal -- History. Muslims -- Mali -- History. Senegal -- History -- To 1960. Mali -- History.

DT532.5.M36 1988
Manning, Patrick, 1941-
Francophone sub-Saharan Africa, 1880-1985/ Patrick Manning. Cambridge [England]; Cambridge University Press, 1988. viii, 215 p.
87-026550 966/.0097541 0521330246
Africa, French-speaking Equatorial -- History -- 1884-1960. Africa, French-speaking Equatorial -- History -- 1960- Africa, French-speaking West -- History -- 1884-1960.

DT541.45-555.45 West Africa. West Coast — French West Africa. French Sahara. West Sahara. Sahel — Local history and description

DT541.45.S65.B57 1987
Blier, Suzanne Preston.
The anatomy of architecture: ontology and metaphor in Batammaliba architectural expression/ Suzanne Preston Blier. Cambridge [Cambridgeshire]; Cambridge University Press, 1987. xx, 314 p.
86-014702 728.3/72/089963 0521321735
Architecture, Somba (African people) Somba (African people) -- Social life and customs.

DT541.65.R63 2000
Robinson, David, 1938-
Paths of accommodation: Muslim societies and French colonial authorities in Senegal and Mauritania, 1880-1920/ David Robinson. Athens, Ohio: Ohio University Press; 2000. xvi, 361 p.
00-044614 966.1/01 0821413538
Muslims -- Africa, French-speaking West -- History. Africa, French-speaking West -- History -- 1884-1960. Africa, French-speaking West -- History -- To 1884. France -- Colonies -- Africa -- History.

DT545.45.B45.O26 1992
Gottlieb, Alma.
Under the kapok tree: identity and difference in Beng thought/ Alma Gottlieb. Bloomington: Indiana University Press, c1992. xvii, 184 p.
91-025926 306/.0899634 0253326079
Beng (African people) -- Ethnic identity. Beng (African people) -- Psychology. Philosophy, Beng.

DT545.45.D85.L37 1992
Launay, Robert, 1949-
Beyond the stream: Islam and society in a West African town/ Robert Launay. Berkeley: University of California Press, c1992. xvii, 258 p.
92-002893 306.6/97/0899634 0520077180
Dyula (African people) -- Religion. Islam -- Customs and practices. Cote d'Ivoire -- Religious life and customs.

DT546.345.A35.H48 1991
Hewlett, Barry S., 1950-
Intimate fathers: the nature and context of Aka pygmy paternal infant care/ Barry S. Hewlett. Ann Arbor: University of Michigan Press, c1991. viii, 201 p.
90-048843 306.85/089965096741 0472101846
Aka (African people) -- Social life and customs. Father and child -- Central African Republic. Central African Republic -- Social life and customs.

DT546.345.A35.K57 1998
Kisliuk, Michelle Robin.
Seize the dance!: BaAka musical life and the ethnography of performance/ Michelle Kisliuk. New York; Oxford University Press, 1998. xiv, 241 p.
97-045896 390/.089/965 0195117867
Aka (African people) -- Folklore. Aka (African people) -- Music. Aka (African people) -- Rites and ceremonies.

DT546.445.B34.R53 1990
Reyna, Stephen P.
Wars without end: the political economy of a precolonial African state/ S.P. Reyna. Hanover, NH: Published for University of New Hampshire by Uni c1990. ix, 210 p.
89-040233 967.43 087451505X
Bagirmi (African people) -- Wars. Bagirmi (African people) -- Politics and government. Bagirmi (African people) -- Economic conditions. Chari-Baguirmi (Chad) -- History.

DT546.457.D4 1997
Decalo, Samuel.
Historical dictionary of Chad/ by Samuel Decalo. Lanham, Md.: Scarecrow Press, c1997. xlviii, 601 p
96-038910 967.43/003 0810832534
Chad -- History -- Dictionaries.

DT546.48.A97 1998
Azevedo, Mario Joaquim.
Chad: a nation in search of its future/ Mario J. Azevedo and Emmanuel U. Nnadozie. Boulder, Colo: Westview Press, 1998. xvii, 170 p.
97-015097 967.43 0813386772
Chad -- Politics and government -- 1960- Chad -- Economic conditions. Chad -- Social conditions.

DT546.48.N65 1996
Nolutshungu, Sam C.
Limits of anarchy: intervention and state formation in Chad/ Sam C. Nolutshungu. Charlottesville: University Press of Virginia, 1996. xiii, 348 p.
95-016954 967.4304 0813916283
Chad -- History -- Civil War, 1965- Chad -- Foreign relations -- Libya. Libya -- Foreign relations -- Chad.

DT547.45.H38.C66 1997
Cooper, Barbara MacGowan.
Marriage in Maradi: gender and culture in a Hausa society in Niger, 1900-1989/ Barbara M. Cooper. Portsmouth, NH: Heinemann; c1997. l, 228 p.
97-001610 306.81/0899376 0435074148
Hausa (African people) -- Marriage customs and rites. Hausa (African people) -- Kinship. Women, Hausa -- Social conditions. Maradi (Niger) -- Social conditions. Maradi (Niger) -- Economic conditions.

DT547.45.S65.S75 1989
Stoller, Paul.
Fusion of the worlds: an ethnography of possession among the Songhay of Niger/ Paul Stoller. Chicago: University of Chicago Press, 1989. xxi, 243 p.
88-029250 966/.2600496 0226775445
Songhai (African people) Spirit possession -- Niger.

DT547.45.S65.S765 1989
Stoller, Paul.
The taste of ethnographic things: the senses in anthropology/ Paul Stoller. Philadelphia: University of Pennsylvania Press, c1989. xv, 182 p.
89-033670 306/.096626 0812281861
Songhai (African people) Senses and sensation -- Cross-cultural studies. Ethnology -- Niger -- Field work.

DT547.5.D4 1997
Decalo, Samuel.
Historical dictionary of Niger/ by Samuel Decalo. Lanham, Md.: Scarecrow Press, 1997. xxxi, 486 p.
95-052222 966.26/003 0810831368
Niger -- History -- Dictionaries.

DT549.45.B39.S35 1988
Schloss, Marc R.
The hatchet's blood: separation, power, and gender in Ehing social life/ Marc R. Schloss. Tucson: University of Arizona Press, c1988. xv, 178 p.
88-001352 966/.3 0816510423
Bayot (African people)

DT549.45.S66.M35 1997
Manchuelle, Francois, 1953-
Willing migrants: Soninke labor diasporas, 1848-1960/ Francois Manchuelle. Athens: Ohio University Press, c1997. xvii, 371 p.
97-027492 331.6/2367044 0821412019
Soninke (African people) -- Employment -- Foreign countries. Soninke (African people) -- Migrations.

DT549.9.B68.G66 1992
Gomez, Michael Angelo, 1955-
Pragmatism in the age of Jihad: the precolonial state of Bundu/ Michael A. Gomez. Cambridge [England]; Cambridge University Press, 1992. xiii, 252 p.
91-043273 966.3 0521419409
Boundou (Senegal) -- History.

DT551.45.B35.A76 1995
Arnoldi, Mary Jo.
Playing with time: art and performance in central Mali/ Mary Jo Arnoldi. Bloomington: Indiana University Press, c1995. xx, 227 p.
94-038744 791.5/3/0899634 025330900X
Bambara (African people) -- Rites and ceremonies. Bambara (African people) -- Folklore. Bambara (African people) -- Social life and customs. Segou (Mali: Region) -- Social life and customs. Kirango (Mali) -- Social life and customs.

DT551.45.M36.P47 1997
Perinbam, B. Marie
Family identity and the state in the Bamako Kafu, c.1800-c.1900 \ B. Marie Perinbam. Bouldor, Colo.: Westview Press, 1997. x, 341 p.
96-035478 305.896/345 0813330807
Mandingo (African people) -- Ethnic identity. Mandingo (African people) -- Kinship. Legends -- Mali -- Bamako. Bamako (Mali) -- Politics and government.

DT551.9.S44.D53 1997
Djata, Sundiata A.
The Bamana empire by the Niger: kingdom, jihad, and colonization, 1712-1920/ by Sundiata A. Djata. Princeton: Markus Wiener, c1997. xv, 251 p.
96-011512 966.23/01 1558761314
Bambara (African people) -- Politics and government -- Mali -- Segou (Region) Segou (Mali: Region) -- Politics and government.

DT555.45.L94.B38 1998
Bayili, Blaise, 1954-
Religion, droit et pouvoir au Burkina Faso: les Lyelae du Burkina Faso/ Blaise Bayili; preface par Raymond Verdier. Paris: Editions L'Harmattan, c1998. 479 p.
98-204978 303.3/3/096625 2738463894
Lyelae (African people) -- Social conditions. Lyelae (African people) -- Religion. Lyelae (African people) -- Politics and government. Burkina Faso -- Social life and customs. Burkina Faso -- Politics and government.

DT564 West Africa. West Coast — Cameroon (Cameroun, Kamerun) — General works

DT564.D45 1989
DeLancey, Mark.
Cameroon: dependence and independence/ Mark W. DeLancey. Boulder, Colo.: Westview Press; 1989. x, 193 p.
86-032618 967/.11 0891588825
Cameroon.

DT570-571 West Africa. West Coast — Cameroon (Cameroun, Kamerun) — Ethnography

DT570.A35 1996
African crossroads: intersections between history and anthropology in Cameroon/ edited by Ian Fowler and David Zeitlyn. Providence: Berghahn Books, 1996. xxvii, 213 p.
96-002120 967.11 1571819266
Ethnology -- Cameroon. Cameroon -- History.

DT571.D83.A87 1999
Austen, Ralph A.
Middlemen of the Cameroons Rivers: the Duala and their hinterland, c.1600-c.1960/ Ralph A. Austen and Jonathan Derrick. Cambridge; Cambridge University Press, 1999. xii, 252 p.
99-206496 967.11/004963962 0521562287
Duala (African people) -- History. Cameroon -- History. Cameroon -- Economic conditions -- To 1960.

DT571.F84.B34 1998
Bah, M. Alpha, 1947-
Fulbe presence in Sierra Leone: a case history of twentieth-century migration and settlement among the Kissi of Koindu/ M. Alpha Bah. New York: P. Lang, c1998. x, 191 p.
93-022958 966.4 0820421804
Fula (African people) -- Sierra Leone -- Koindu -- History. Kissi (African people) -- Sierra Leone -- Koindu -- History. Koindu (Sierra Leone) -- History.

DT571.N74.G64 1996
Goheen, Miriam.
Men own the fields, women own the crops: gender and power in the Cameroon grassfields/ Miriam Goheen. Madison: University of Wisconsin Press, c1996. xx, 252 p.
95-025275 305.3/096711 0299146707
Nso (African people) -- Social conditions. Sex role -- Cameroon. Cameroon -- Social conditions - - 1960- Cameroon -- Politics and government -- 1982-

DT611.8 West Africa. West Coast — Angola

DT611.8.R44 1988
Regional conflict and U.S. policy: Angola and Mozambique/ edited by Richard J. Bloomfield. Algonac, Mich.: Reference Publications, 1988. 261 p.
88-023461 967/.304 091725645X
Angola -- Politics and government -- 1975- Angola -- Foreign relations -- United States. United States -- Foreign relations -- Angola.

DT613.76-613.78 West Africa. West Coast — Portuguese- speaking West Africa — Local history and description

DT613.76.C3.C54 1991
Chilcote, Ronald H.
Amilcar Cabral's revolutionary theory and practice: a critical guide/ Ronald H. Chilcote. Boulder, Colo.: L. Rienner Publishers, 1991. xii, 292 p.
91-011829 322.4/2/092 1555870589
Cabral, Amilcar, -- 1921-1973 -- Contributions in revolutionary theory. Revolutions -- Philosophy.

DT613.78.D47 1993
Dhada, Mustafah.
Warriors at work: how Guinea was really set free/ by Mustafah Dhada. Niwot, Colo.: University Press of Colorado, c1993. xxxiii, 324 p.
94-139187 966.57/02 0870812874
Cabral, Amilcar, -- 1921-1973. Guinea-Bissau - - History -- Revolution, 1963-1974.

DT620.9 West Africa. West Coast — Spanish West Africa — Equatorial Guinea (Spanish Guinea)

DT620.9.F47.S86 1996
Sundiata, I. K.
From slaving to neoslavery: the bight of Biafra and Fernando Po in the era of abolition, 1827-1930/ Ibrahim K. Sundiata. Madison, [Wis.]: University of Wisconsin Press, c1996. xii, 250 p.
94-039082 967.18/6 0299145107
Slavery -- Equatorial Guinea -- Fernando Po. Slavery -- Africa, West. Africa, West -- History. Fernando Po (Equatorial Guinea) -- History.

DT630.5 West Africa. West Coast — Liberia — Ethnography

DT630.5.G6.M67 1990
Moran, Mary H., 1957-
Civilized women: gender and prestige in southeastern Liberia/ Mary H. Moran. Ithaca, N.Y.: Cornell University Press, 1990. xv, 189 p.
89-022398 306/.089963306662 0801422930
Women, Grebo -- Social conditions. Women, Grebo -- Economic conditions. Harper (Liberia) -- Social conditions. Harper (Liberia) -- Economic conditions.

DT630.5.M34.K65 1996
Konneh, Augustine.
Religion, commerce, and the integration of the Mandingo in Liberia/ Augustine Konneh. Lanham, Md.: University Press of America, 1996. p. cm.
96-014958 966.62/0049634 0761803556
Mandingo (African people) -- Liberia. Islam -- Liberia -- History -- 19th century. Islam -- Liberia -- History -- 20th century. Liberia -- Commerce -- History -- 19th century. Liberia -- Commerce -- History -- 20th century.

DT631-636.5 West Africa. West Coast — Liberia — History

DT631.D95 2001
Dunn, D. Elwood.
Historical dictionary of Liberia/ D. Elwood Dunn, Amos J. Beyan, Carl Patrick Burrowes. Lanham, Md.: Scarecrow Press, 2001. xxxv, 436 p.
00-044654 966.62/003 0810838761
Liberia -- History -- Dictionaries.

DT636.5.E45 1999
Ellis, Stephen, 1953-
The mask of anarchy: the destruction of Liberia and the religious dimension of an African civil war/ Stephen Ellis. New York: New York University Press, 1999. xix, 350 p.
99-037702 966.6203 0814722113
Liberia -- Religion. Liberia -- History -- Civil War, 1989- -- Causes. Liberia -- History -- Civil War, 1989- -- Religious aspects.

DT644 West Africa. West Coast — Zaire. Congo (Democratic Republic). Belgian Congo — General works

DT644.Z3425 1994
Zaire: a country study/ Federal Research Division, Library of Congress; edited by Sandra W. Meditz and Tim Merrill. Washington, D.C.: The Division: 1994. lvii, 394 p.
94-025092 967.51 084440795X
Congo (Democratic Republic)

DT650 West Africa. West Coast — Zaire. Congo (Democratic Republic). Belgian Congo — Ethnography

DT650.E34.G75 1994
Grinker, Roy Richard, 1961-
Houses in the rain forest: ethnicity and inequality among farmers and foragers in Central Africa/ Roy Richard Grinker. Berkeley: University of California Press, c1994. xviii, 225 p.
93-036600 305.8/00967515 0520083571
Efe (African people) -- Hunting. Efe (African people) -- Ethnic identity. Hunting and gathering societies -- Congo (Democratic Republic) -- Ituri Forest. Ituri Forest (Congo) -- Ethnic relations.

DT650.K33.Y63 1992
Yoder, John Charles.
The Kanyok of Zaire: an institutional and ideological history to 1895/ John C. Yoder. Cambridge; Cambridge University Press, 1992. xv, 213 p.
91-019674 967.51/0049639 0521412986
Kanyok (African people) -- History -- Sources. Kanyok (African people) -- Folklore. Kanyok (African people) -- Social life and customs.

DT650.K66.A78 1991
Art and healing of the Bakongo, commented by themselves: minkisi from the Laman collection/ Kikongo texts translated and edited by Wyatt MacGaffey. Stockholm: Folkens museum-- etnografiska; c1991. viii, 184 p.
91-071122 9185344249
Laman, K. E. -- (Karl Edvard), -- 1867-1944 -- Ethnological collections. Kongo (African people) -- Antiquities. Sculpture, Kongo. Talismans -- Congo (Democratic Republic)

DT650.L8.F32 1990
Fabian, Johannes.
Power and performance: ethnographic explorations through proverbial wisdom and theater in Shaba, Zaire/ Johannes Fabian. Madison, Wis.: University of Wisconsin Press, c1990. xix, 314 p.
90-050085 305.8/96393067518 0299125106
Theater -- Congo (Democratic Republic) -- Katanga. Philosophy, Luba. Power (Social sciences)

DT650.P46.S77 1997
Strother, Z. S.
Inventing masks: agency and history in the art of the Central Pende/ Z.S. Strother. Chicago, Ill.: University of Chicago Press, c1998. xxvii, 348 p.
97-016344 391.4/34/08996393 0226777324
Masks, Pende. Pende (African people) -- Social life and customs. Physiognomy in art -- Congo (Democratic Republic)

DT655-658 West Africa. West Coast — Zaire. Congo (Democratic Republic). Belgian Congo — History

DT655.H63 1998
Hochschild, Adam.
King Leopold's ghost: a story of greed, terror, and heroism in Colonial Africa/ Adam Hochschild. Boston: Houghton Mifflin, 1998. 366 p.
98-016813 967.5 0395759242
Forced labor -- Congo (Democratic Republic) -- History -- 19th century. Forced labor -- Congo (Democratic Republic) -- History -- 20th century. Indigenous peoples -- Congo (Democratic Republic) -- History -- 19th century. Congo (Democratic Republic) -- Race relations -- History -- 19th century. Congo (Democratic Republic) -- Race relations -- History -- 20th century. Congo (Democratic Republic) -- Politics and government -- 1885-1908.

DT658.G53 1991
Gibbs, David N.
The political economy of Third World intervention: mines, money, and U.S. policy in the Congo crisis/ David N. Gibbs. Chicago: University of Chicago Press, 1991. x, 322 p.
91-009798 967.5103 0226290719
Investments, American -- Congo (Democratic Republic) Congo (Democratic Republic) -- History -- Civil War, 1960-1965. United States -- Foreign relations -- Congo (Democratic Republic) Congo (Democratic Republic) -- Foreign relations -- United States.

DT658.L46 1993
Leslie, Winsome J.
Zaire: continuity and political change in an oppressive state/ Winsome J. Leslie. Boulder: Westview Press, 1993. xi, 204 p.
92-046921 967.51 0865312982
Despotism -- Congo (Democratic Republic) -- History. Congo (Democratic Republic) -- Economic conditions. Congo (Democratic Republic) -- Politics and government -- 1960-1997.

DT763.5-963.42 Southern Africa

DT763.5.D4 1988
De Villiers, Marq.
White tribe dreaming: apartheid's bitter roots as witnessed by eight generations of an Afrikaner family/ Marq de Villiers. New York, N.Y., U.S.A.: Viking, 1988, c1987. xxvii, 420 p.
87-040309 968 0670817945
Villiers family. Apartheid -- South Africa -- History. Afrikaners -- South Africa -- History. South Africa -- History.

DT776.R4.R66 1988
Rotberg, Robert I.
The founder: Cecil Rhodes and the pursuit of power/ Robert I. Rotberg, with the collaboration of Miles F. Shore. New York: Oxford University Press, 1988. xxii, 800 p.
88-005960 968.04/092/4 0195049683
Rhodes, Cecil, -- 1853-1902. Statesmen -- Africa, Southern -- Biography. Capitalists and financiers -- Africa, Southern -- Biography.

DT779.9.B37 1990
Barber, James P.
South Africa's foreign policy: the search for status and security, 1945-1988/ James Barber and John Barratt. Cambridge; Cambridge University Press, 1990. ix, 398 p.
89-035773 327.68 0521373131
South Africa -- Foreign relations -- 1948-1961. South Africa -- Foreign relations -- 1961-1978. South Africa -- Foreign relations -- 1978-1989.

DT779.952.D38 1987
Davis, Stephen M., 1955-
Apartheid's rebels: inside South Africa's hidden war/ Stephen M. Davis. New Haven: Yale University Press, c1987. xvii, 238 p.
87-010680 968.06/3 0300039913
Government, Resistance to -- South Africa. South Africa -- Politics and government -- 1978-

DT779.952.S655 1989
South Africa: no turning back/ edited by Shaun Johnson; foreword by Lord Bullock. Bloomington: Indiana University Press, c1989. xxiii, 390 p.
88-022988 968.06/3 0253353955
Apartheid -- South Africa. South Africa -- Politics and government -- 1978-

DT791.C76 1988
Crowder, Michael, 1934-
The flogging of Phinehas McIntosh: a tale of colonial folly and injustice: Bechuanaland, 1933/ Michael Crowder. New Haven: Yale University Press, c1988. xii, 248 p.
87-017632 968/.1103 0300040989
McIntosh, Phinehas. Khama, Tshekedi, -- 1905-1959. Botswana -- History -- To 1966. Botswana -- Race relations.

DT963.42.P68 1988
Pottier, Johan.
Migrants no more: settlement and survival in Mambwe villages, Zambia/ Johan Pottier. Bloomington: Indiana University Press; c1988. xiii, 210 p.
88-009373 306/.089963 0253338948
Mambwe (African people) -- Social conditions. Mambwe (African people) -- Economic conditions. Migration, Internal -- Zambia. Zambia -- Economic conditions -- 1964-

DT1058 Southern Africa — Ethnography — Individual elements in the population, A-Z

DT1058.B53.B86 1992
Bunche, Ralph J. 1904-1971.
An African American in South Africa: the travel notes of Ralph J. Bunche, 28 September 1937-1 January 1938/ edited by Robert R. Edgar. Athens: Ohio University Press; c1992. xv, 398 p.
92-006621 916.804/54 0821410210
Bunche, Ralph J. -- (Ralph Johnson), -- 1904-1971 -- Journeys -- South Africa. Blacks -- South Africa -- Social conditions. Blacks -- South Africa -- Social life and customs.

DT1058.K86
Shostak, Marjorie, 1945-
Return to Nisa/ Marjorie Shostak. Cambridge, MA: Harvard University Press, 2000. 251 p.
00-033462 305.48/896106883 0674003233
Nisa. Women, !Kung -- Biography. Women, !Kung -- Social life and customs.

DT1058.S36.M57 1996
Miscast: negotiating the presence of the Bushmen/ edited by Pippa Skotnes. Cape Town, South Africa: University of Cape Town Press, 1996. 381 p.
96-193287 968/.004961 0799216526
San (African people) -- Exhibitions. Khoikhoi (African people) -- Exhibitions. San (African people) -- Public opinion -- Exhibitions.

DT1058.T78.C66 1991
Comaroff, Jean.
Of revelation and revolution/ Jean Comaroff and John Comaroff. Chicago: University of Chicago Press, 1991-c1997 v. 1-2
90-046753 303.48/241/00899639775 0226114414
Tswana (African people) -- Social conditions. Tswana (African people) -- History. Tswana (African people) -- Missions. Great Britain -- Colonies -- Africa. South Africa -- History.

DT1105 Southern Africa — History — Foreign and general relations

DT1105.G3.S45 1998
Seligmann, Matthew S., 1967-
Rivalry in Southern Africa, 1893-99: the transformation of German colonial policy/ Matthew S. Seligmann. Houndmills, Basingstoke, Hampshire: Macmilland Press; 1998. vii, 200 p.
97-046091 303.48/268043 0312211538
Africa, Southern -- Relations -- Germany. Germany -- Relations -- Africa, Southern. Germany -- Colonies -- Africa, Southern -- Administration.

DT1105.S6.S68 1998
South Africa in Southern Africa: reconfiguring the region/ edited by David Simon. Oxford: J. Currey; 1998. 259 p.
98-032009 968/.0009/045 0852554125
Africa, Southern -- Relations -- South Africa. South Africa -- Relations -- Africa, Southern.

DT1147-1166 Southern Africa — History — By period

DT1147.K35 1999
Kalley, Jacqueline A.
Southern African political history: a chronology of key political events from independence to mid-1997/ compiled by Jacqueline A. Kalley, Elna Schoeman, and L.E. Andor; assisted by Abdul Samed Bemath, Claire Kruger, and Beth Strachan; foreword by Peter Vale. Westport, Conn.: Greenwood Press, 1999. xvii, 90 p.
98-044996 968/.0009/045 0313302472
Africa, Southern -- Politics and government -- Chronology.

DT1166.U53 2000
The uncertain promise of Southern Africa/ York Bradshaw and Stephen N. Ndegwa, editors. Bloomington: Indiana University Press, c2000. xi, 424 p.
00-040714 968/.0009/0511 0253338271
Africa, Southern -- Politics and government -- 1975-1994. Africa, Southern -- Politics and government -- 1994- Africa, Southern -- Economic conditions -- 1975-

DT1308 Angola — Ethnography — Individual elements in the population, A-Z

DT1308.C67.J67 1998
Jordan, Manuel.
Chokwe/ Manuel Jordan. New York: Rosen Pub. Group, 1998. 64 p.
96-050268   306/.089/96399   0823919900
Chokwe (African people) -- History -- Juvenile literature. Chokwe (African people) -- Social life and customs -- Juvenile literature. Chokwe (African people)

DT1373-1436 Angola — History — By period

DT1373.H49 2000
Heywood, Linda Marinda, 1945-
Contested power in Angola, 1840s to the present/ Linda Heywood. Rochester, NY: University of Rochester Press, 2000. xviii, 305 p.
00-027765   323.1/19639320673/09   1580460631
Mbundu (African people) -- Politics and government. Angola -- Politics and government -- 1961-1975. Angola -- Politics and government -- 1975- Angola -- Politics and government -- 1855-1961.

DT1428.G85 1998
Guimaraes, Fernando Andresen, 1965-
The origins of the Angolan civil war: foreign intervention and domestic political conflict/ Fernando Andresen Guimaraes. New York, N.Y.: St. Martin's Press, 1998. xv, 250 p.
97-009652   967.304   0312175124
Angola -- History -- Civil War, 1975- -- Causes.

DT1436.M56 1994
Minter, William, 1942-
Apartheid's contras: an inquiry into the roots of war in Angola and Mozambique/ William Minter. Johannesburg: Witwatersrand University Press; 1994. 308 p.
94-041587   967.304   1856492656
Angola -- History -- Civil War, 1975- -- Causes. Angola -- History -- South African Incursions, 1978-1990. Mozambique -- History -- Civil War, 1976-1994 -- Causes.

DT1558 Namibia. South-West Africa — Ethnography — Individual elements in the population, A-Z

DT1558.H45.G67 1997
Gordon, Robert J., 1947-
Picturing bushmen: the Denver African Expedition of 1925/ Robert J. Gordon. Athens: Ohio University Press, c1997. xiii, 208 p.
97-002395   306.4/7   082141187X
Heikum (African people) -- Pictorial works. Photography in ethnology. Khoikhoi (African people) -- Public opinion.

DT1558.H56
Crandall, David P., 1960-
The place of stunted ironwood trees: a year in the lives of the cattle-herding Himba of Namibia/ David P. Crandall. New York: Continuum, 2000. viii, 269 p.
00-034065   305.8963906881   082641270X
Himba (African people) -- Domestic animals. Himba (African people) -- Social life and customs. Cattle herders -- Namibia -- Otutati. Otutati (Namibia) -- Social life and customs.

DT1558.S38.W53 1999
Widlok, Thomas.
Living on mangetti: 'Bushman' autonomy and Namibian independence/ Thomas Widlok. Oxford; Oxford University Press, 1999. xviii, 291 p.
0198233892
San (African people) -- Namibia -- Social life and customs. Social structure -- Namibia. Social institutions -- Namibia.

DT1625 Namibia. South-West Africa — History — By period

DT1625.C66 1990
Cooper, Allan D.
The occupation of Namibia: Afrikanerdom's attack on the British Empire/ Allan D. Cooper. Lanham, Md.: University Press of America, c1991. 215 p.
90-044921   968.8103   081917954X
Afrikaners -- Politics and government. Namibia -- Politics and government -- 1946-1990. Namibia -- Politics and government -- 1915-1946. South Africa -- Politics and government -- 20th century.

DT1680 Namibia. South-West Africa — Local history and description — Cities, towns, etc.

DT1680.P46 1996
Pendleton, Wade C.
Katutura: a place where we stay: life in a post-apartheid township in Namibia/ Wade C. Pendleton. Athens: Ohio University Center for International Studies c1996. xix, 217 p.
95-051498   968.81   0896801888
Katutura (Windhoek, Namibia)

DT1728 South Africa — Historical geography

DT1728.G46 2000
The geography of South Africa in a changing world/ edited by Roddy Fox and Kate Rowntree. Oxford; Oxford University Press, 2000. x, 509 p.
00-291591   916.8   0195716825
South Africa -- Geography.

DT1756 South Africa — Ethnography — Race relations

DT1756.D4213 1989
Debroey, Steven.
South Africa to the sources of apartheid/ Steven Debroey; translated by Lidwina Debroey. Lanham, MD: University Press of America, c1989. xii, 612 p.
88-037221   305.8/00968   0819173185
Apartheid -- South Africa -- History. South Africa -- Race relations -- History.

DT1756.K44 1996
Keegan, Timothy J.
Colonial South Africa and the origins of the racial order/ Timothy Keegan. Charlottesville: University Press of Virginia, 1996. x, 368 p.
96-035827   305.8/00968   0813917352
South Africa -- Race relations. South Africa -- History -- To 1836. South Africa -- History -- 1836-1909.

DT1756.S53 1997
Simons, H. J.
Struggles in Southern Africa for survival and equality/ H.J. Simons. New York: St. Martin's Press, 1997. xiv, 240 p.
96-002812   305.8/00968   0333656644
Ethnology -- South Africa. Women -- South Africa -- Social conditions. South Africa -- Race relations. South Africa -- Social conditions. Zambia -- Race relations.

DT1757 South Africa — Ethnography — Apartheid

DT1757.A66 1991
Apartheid unravels/ edited by R. Hunt Davis, Jr. Gainesville: University of Florida Press: c1991. x, 251 p.
91-000469   305.8/00968   0813010691
Apartheid -- South Africa. South Africa -- Politics and government -- 1978-

DT1757.D44 2001
Deegan, Heather.
The politics of the new South Africa: apartheid and after/ Heather Deegan. New York: Longman, 2001. p. cm.
00-063205   968.06   0582382270
Anti-apartheid movements -- South Africa. Apartheid -- South Africa. South Africa -- Politics and government -- 1978-1989. South Africa -- Politics and government -- 1989-1994. South Africa -- Politics and government -- 1994-

DT1757.E33 1999
Eades, Lindsay Michie, 1962-
The end of apartheid in South Africa/ Lindsay Michie Eades. Westport, Conn.: Greenwood Press, 1999. xix, 209 p.
98-045032   305.8/00968   0313299382
Apartheid -- South Africa. South Africa -- Politics and government. South Africa -- Race relations.

DT1757.L685 1998
Lowenberg, Anton David.
The origins and demise of South African apartheid: a public choice analysis/ by Anton D. Lowenberg and William H. Kaempfer. Ann Arbor: University of Michigan Press, c1998. 284 p.
97-045417   323.1/196068   0472109057
Apartheid -- South Africa. Pressure groups -- South Africa -- History -- 20th century. Social choice -- South Africa -- History -- 20th century. South Africa -- Race relations -- Economic aspects -- History -- 20th century.

DT1757.M38 1991
Marx, Anthony W.
Lessons of struggle: South African internal opposition, 1960-1990/ Anthony W. Marx. New York: Oxford University Press, 1992. xxii, 347 p.
90-026546   968.06/27   0195068157
Anti-apartheid movements -- South Africa -- History. Blacks -- South Africa -- Politics and government. Labor unions, Black -- South Africa -- Political activity. South Africa -- History -- Soweto Uprising, 1976.

DT1768 South Africa — Ethnography — Individual elements in the population, A-Z

DT1768.A57.L4 1995
Le May, G. H. L.
The Afrikaners: an historical interpretation/ G.H.L. Le May. Oxford, UK; Blackwell, 1995. 280 p.
95-011584   968   0631182047
Afrikaners -- History. Afrikaners -- Politics and government. South Africa -- History. South Africa -- Politics and government. South Africa -- Race relations -- History.

DT1768.Z95.H36 1998
Hamilton, Carolyn.
Terrific majesty: the powers of Shaka Zulu and the limits of historical invention/ Carolyn Hamilton. Cambridge, Mass.: Harvard University Press, 1998. xii, 278 p.
98-010551   968.4/039/092   0674874455
Chaka, -- Zulu Chief, -- 1787?-1828   Zulu (African people) -- Kings and rulers -- Biography. Zulu (African people) -- History. Nationalism -- South Africa.

DT1774 South Africa — History — Biography (Collective)

DT1774.G37 1990
Gastrow, Shelagh.
Who's who in South African politics/ edited by Shelagh Gastrow. London; Hans Zell Publishers, 1990. xvi, 368 p.
90-020755   968.06/3/0922   090545037X
Politicians -- South Africa -- Biography. Statesmen -- South Africa -- Biography. South Africa -- Biography. South Africa -- Politics and government -- 1978- South Africa -- Biography.

DT1776 South Africa — History — Historiography

DT1776.S63 1989
Smith, Ken.
The changing past: trends in South African historical writing/ Ken Smith. Athens: Ohio University Press, 1989, c1988. 240 p.
88-039277   968/.0072   0821409263
Social classes -- South Africa -- Historiography. Marxian historiography -- South Africa. South Africa -- Historiography. South Africa -- Race relations -- Historiography.

DT1787 South Africa — History — General works

DT1787.B43 2000
Beck, Roger B.
The history of South Africa/ Roger B. Beck. Westport, Conn.: Greenwood Press, 2000. xxx, 248 p.
99-058880   968   031330730X
South Africa -- History.

DT1787.C73 1992
Crais, Clifton C.
White supremacy and Black resistance in pre-industrial South Africa: the making of the colonial order in the Eastern Cape, 1770-1865/ Clifton C. Crais. Cambridge [England]; Cambridge University Press, 1992. xvi, 284 p.
90-025694   968   0521404797
Blacks -- South Africa -- Politics and government. Government, Resistance to -- South Africa. South Africa -- Race relations. South Africa -- History -- To 1836. South Africa -- History -- 1836-1909.

DT1787.D38 2000
Davenport, T. R. H.
South Africa: a modern history/ T.R.H. Davenport and Christopher Saunders; foreword by Desmond Tutu. Hampshire [England]: Macmillan Press; 2000. xxx, 807 p.
00-024339   968   0312233760
South Africa -- History.

DT1787.T48 1990
Thompson, Leonard Monteath.
A history of South Africa/ Leonard Thompson. New Haven: Yale University Press, c1990. xxi, 288 p.
89-022594   968   0300048157
South Africa -- History.

DT1798 South Africa — History — Political history

DT1798.E83 1997
Evans, Ivan Thomas, 1957-
Bureaucracy and race: native administration in South Africa/ Ivan Evans. Berkeley: University of California Press, c1997. xiii, 403 p.
96-023378   354.6809/1   0520206517
Indigenous peoples -- South Africa -- Politics and government. South Africa -- Politics and government -- 20th century. South Africa -- Race relations.

DT1813-1974 South Africa — History — By period

DT1813.V3613 1995
Van der Merwe, P. J. 1912-1979.
The migrant farmer in the history of the Cape colony, 1657-1842/ P.J. van der Merwe; translated by Roger B. Beck. Athens: Ohio University Press, c1995. xvi, 315 p.
94-021649   968.7   0821410903
Nigrant agricultural laborers -- South Africa -- Cape of Good Hope -- History. Cape of Good Hope (South Africa) -- History -- 1795-1872. Cape of Good Hope (South Africa) -- History -- To 1795.

DT1875.L33 1992
Laband, John, 1947-
Kingdom in crisis: the Zulu response to the British invasion of 1879/ John Laband. Manchester; Manchester University Press; c1992. x, 272 p.
91-038814   968.4/045   0719035821
Zulu War, 1879. Zulu (African people)

DT1896.N37 1990
Nasson, Bill.
Abraham Esau's war: a Black South African war in the Cape, 1899-1902/ Bill Nasson. Cambridge, England; Cambridge University Press, 1991. xxvi, 245 p.
90-001538   968.04/8   0521385121
Esau, Abraham, -- 1884-1910.   South African War, 1899-1902 -- Campaigns -- South Africa -- Calvinia Region. South African War, 1899-1902 -- Participation, Black.   Calvinia Region (South Africa) -- History.

DT1924.F87 1991
Furlong, Patrick J. 1959-
Between crown and swastika: the impact of the radical right on the Afrikaner nationalist movement in the fascist era/ Patrick J. Furlong. [Middletown, Conn.]: Wesleyan University Press; c1991. xxi, 344 p.
90-011944   320.5/3/0968   0819552291
Fascism -- South Africa -- History. South Africa -- Race relations. South Africa -- Politics and government -- 20th century.

DT1927.J34.H54 1997
Higgs, Catherine.
The ghost of equality: the public lives of D.D.T. Jabavu of South Africa, 1885-1959/ Catherine Higgs. Athens: Ohio University Press; c1997. xiii, 276 p.
96-013506   305.8/00968   0821411691
Jabavu, Davidson D. T. -- (Davidson Don Tengo), -- b. 1885.   South Africa -- Race relations.

DT1927.L46.A2 1996
Lembede, Anton Muziwakhe, 1914-1947.
Freedom in our lifetime: the collected writings of Anton Muziwakhe Lembede/ edited by Robert R. Edgar and Luyanda ka Msumza. Athens, Ohio: Ohio University Press, 1996. xx, 203 p.
96-007330   968/.00496   0821411497
Blacks -- South Africa -- Politics and government.

DT1928.H35 1999
Halisi, C. R. D., 1947-
Black political thought in the making of South African democracy/ C.R.D. Halisi. Bloomington: Indiana University Press, c1999. xxi, 198 p.
99-038817   320.54/089/96   0253335892
Blacks -- Race identity. Blacks -- Intellectual life. Nationalism -- South Africa -- History -- 20th century. South Africa -- Politics and government -- 20th century. South Africa -- History -- Autonomy and independence movements. South Africa -- Race relations.

DT1945.G35 1990
Gann, Lewis H., 1924-
Hope for South Africa?/ L.H. Gann and Peter Duignan. Stanford, Calif.: Hoover Institution Press, Stanford University, c1991. xii, 223 p.
90-005185   320.968   0817989528
Apartheid -- South Africa. Economic sanctions -- South Africa. South Africa -- Politics and government -- 1978-

DT1945.S56 1999
South Africa.
Truth and Reconciliation Commission of South Africa report/ Truth and Reconciliation Commission; foreword by Desmond Tutu. London: Macmillan Reference; 1999. p. cm.
99-014724   323.4/9/0968   1561592455
Apartheid -- South Africa. Human rights -- South Africa. South Africa -- Politics and government -- 20th century. South Africa -- Race relations.

DT1949.N75.A3 1993
Ntantala, Phyllis.
A life's mosaic: the autobiography of Phyllis Ntantala. Berkeley: University of California Press, 1993. x, 237 p.
92-020587   323/.092   0520081714
Ntantala, Phyllis.   Civil rights workers -- South Africa -- Biography. Civil rights workers -- United States -- Biography. Anti-apartheid movements -- South Africa. South Africa -- Race relations. United States -- Race relations.

DT1949.R36.A3 1996
Ramphele, Mamphela.
Across boundaries: the journey of a South African woman leader/ Mamphela Ramphele. New York: Feminist Press at the City University of New Yor c1997. xii, 244 p.
96-035474   305.4/0968/092   1558611657
Ramphele, Mamphela.   Women civil rights workers -- South Africa -- Biography. Civil rights workers -- South Africa -- Biography. Blacks -- South Africa -- Politics and government. South Africa -- Politics and government -- 1948-1994.

DT1957.B68 1997
Boynton, Graham.
Last days in cloud cuckooland: dispatches from white Africa/ Graham Boynton. New York: Random House, c1997. xiv, 299 p.
97-000894   968.05   0679432043
Boynton, Graham.   Apartheid -- South Africa. Anti-apartheid movements -- South Africa. Journalists -- South Africa -- Biography. Zimbabwe -- Social life and customs. Zimbabwe -- Race relations. South Africa -- Race relations.

DT1963.P75 1991
Price, Robert M.
The apartheid state in crisis: political transformation in South Africa, 1975-1990/ Robert M. Price. New York: Oxford University Press, 1991. x, 309 p.
90-007871   320.968   0195067495
Apartheid -- South Africa.   South Africa -- Politics and government -- 1961-1978. South Africa -- Politics and government -- 1978-

DT1963.S44 2000
Seekings, Jeremy.
The UDF: a history of the United Democratic Front in South Africa, 1983-1991/ Jeremy Seekings. Cape Town: David Philip; 2000. xiii, 371 p.
00-036706   986.06/3   0864864035
National liberation movements -- South Africa. Self-determination, National -- South Africa. South Africa -- Politics and government -- 1978-1989.

DT1967.W35 1997
Waldmeir, Patti.
Anatomy of a miracle: the end of apartheid and the birth of the new South Africa/ Patti Waldmeir. New York: W.W. Norton & Co., c1997. xvi, 303 p.
96-021150   968.06/4   0393039978
South Africa -- Politics and government -- 1978-1989. South Africa -- Politics and government -- 1989-1994. South Africa -- Race relations.

DT1974.G66 1999
Goodman, David.
Fault lines: journeys into the new South Africa/ David Goodman; photographs by Paul Weinberg. Berkeley, Calif.: University of California Press, c1999. x, 400 p.
98-043038   968.06/5   0520217365
Goodman, David, -- 1959- -- Journeys -- South Africa.   South Africa -- Politics and government -- 1994-

DT1974.S73 1998
South Africa in transition: new theoretical perspectives/ edited by David R. Howarth and Aletta J. Norval. New York, N.Y.: St. Martin's Press, 1998. xiv, 222 p.
98-011004   968.06/4   0312214308
South Africa -- Politics and government -- 1994-

DT2223-2250 South Africa — Local history and description — KwaZulu-Natal. Natal

DT2223.E38.B47 1997
Bhana, Surendra, 1939-
Gandhi's legacy: the Natal Indian Congress, 1894-1994/ Surendra Bhana. Pietermaritzburg: University of Natal Press, c1997. x, 187 p.
98-106200   369/.3914110684/09   0869809318
East Indians -- South Africa -- KwaZulu-Natal -- Politics and government -- 20th century. East Indians -- South Africa -- KwaZulu-Natal -- Politics and government -- 19th century.

DT2250.L35 1995
Lambert, John.
Betrayed trust: Africans and the state in colonial Natal/ John Lambert. Scottsville: University of Natal Press, c1995. xiv, 216 p.
95-193026   968.4/045   0869809091
Natal (South Africa) -- History -- 1843-1893. Natal (South Africa) -- History -- 1893-1910. Natal (South Africa) -- Ethnic relations.

DT2400 South Africa — Local history and description — Other regions, districts, etc., A-Z

DT2400.C58.S95 1993
Switzer, Les.
Power and resistance in an African society: the Ciskei Xhosa and the making of South Africa/ Les Switzer. Madison, Wis.: University of Wisconsin Press, c1993. xvi, 452 p.
93-010085   968.7/92   029913380X
Xhosa (African people) Nationalism -- Ciskei (South Africa) Ciskei (South Africa) -- Politics and government.

DT2405 South Africa — Local history and description — Cities, towns, etc.

DT2405.C3657.B53 1995
Bickford-Smith, Vivian.
Ethnic pride and racial prejudice in Victorian Cape Town: group identity and social practice, 1875-1902/ Vivian Bickford-Smith. Cambridge; Cambridge University Press, 1995. xxiii, 281 p.
94-012143   968.7/355   0521472032
Racism -- South Africa -- Cape Town -- History. Cape Town (South Africa) -- History. Cape Town (South Africa) -- Social life and customs.

DT2405.C369.A28 1996
Western, John.
Outcast Cape Town/ John Western; foreword by Robert Coles. Berkeley: University of California Press, c1996. xxxiv, 396 p.
96-008462   968.7/355   0520207378
Apartheid -- South Africa -- Cape Town -- History. Colored people (South Africa) -- Relocation -- South Africa -- Cape Town -- History -- 20th century. Cape Town (South Africa) -- Race relations.

DT2405.J6557.M87 1999
Musiker, Naomi.
Historical dictionary of Greater Johannesburg/ Naomi Musiker and Reuben Musiker. Lanham, Md.: Scarecrow Press, 1999. liii, 480 p.
98-021819   968.2/21/03   0810835207
Johannesburg Region (South Africa) -- History -- Dictionaries.

DT2458 Botswana. Bechuanaland — Ethnography — Individual elements in the population, A-Z

DT2458.K84.G75 1997
Griffiths, Anne M. O.
In the shadow of marriage: gender and justice in an African community/ Anne M.O. Griffiths. Chicago, Ill.: University of Chicago Press, 1997. x, 310 p.
97-019579   305.3/096883   0226308731
Women, Kwena. Kwena (African people) -- Legal status, laws, etc. Kwena (African people) -- Marriage customs and rites.

DT2458.N45.W95 1990
Wylie, Diana, 1948-
A little god: the twilight of patriarchy in a southern African chiefdom/ Diana Wylie. [Middletown, Conn.]: Wesleyan University Press; c1990. xiv, 278 p.
89-049462   968.83   0819552283
Ngwato (African people) -- Government relations. Ngwato (African people) -- Politics and government. Central District (Botswana) -- Politics and government. Central District (Botswana) -- History.

DT2714 Swaziland — Gazetteers. Dictionaries, etc.

DT2714.B66 2000
Booth, Alan R.
Historical dictionary of Swaziland/ Alan R. Booth. Lanham, Md.: Scarecrow Press, 2000. xxxi, 403 p.
99-053345   968.87/003   0810837498
Swaziland -- Encyclopedias.

DT2913 Zimbabwe. Southern Rhodesia — Ethnography — Individual elements in the population, A-Z

DT2913.S55.S36 1992
Schmidt, Elizabeth.
Peasants, traders, and wives: Shona women in the history of Zimbabwe, 1870-1939/ Elizabeth Schmidt. Portsmouth, NH: Heinemann; 1992. xiii, 289 p.
91-041251   305.48/8963975   0435080644
Women, Shona -- History -- 19th century. Women, Shona -- History -- 20th century. Women, Shona -- Social conditions. Zimbabwe -- Foreign relations. Zimbabwe -- Politics and government.

DT2913.Z49.R49 1996
Reynolds, Pamela, 1944-
Traditional healers and childhood in Zimbabwe/ Pamela Reynolds. Athens: Ohio University Press, c1996. xxxix, 183 p.
94-047391   305.23/096891   0821411217
Zezuru (African people) -- Medicine. Shona (African people) -- Medicine. Children, Shona.

DT2942-2996 Zimbabwe. Southern Rhodesia — History — By period

DT2942.P55 2001
Pikirayi, Innocent.
The Zimbabwe culture: origins and decline of southern Zambezian states/ Innocent Pikirayi. Walnut Creek, Calif.: AltaMira Press, c2001. xxx, 303 p.
00-049340   967/.9   0759100918
Bantu-speaking peoples -- History.   Zambezi River Valley -- History. Monomotapa Empire -- History. Great Zimbabwe (Extinct city)

DT2959.S86 1994
Summers, Carol, 1964-
From civilization to segregation: social ideals and social control in southern Rhodesia, 1890-1934/ Carol Summers. Athens, Ohio: Ohio University Press, c1994. xv, 311 p.
94-000196   968.91   0821410741
Zimbabwe -- History -- 1890-1965. Zimbabwe - - Social conditions -- 1890-1965. Zimbabwe -- Race relations.

DT2979.T63.M86 1999
Mungazi, Dickson A.
The last British liberals in Africa: Michael Blundell and Garfield Todd/ Dickson A. Mungazi. Westport, Conn.: Praeger, 1999. xvi, 285 p.
98-039876   325/.341/09226762   0275962830
Todd, Garfield, -- 1908- Blundell, Michael, -- Sir, - - 1907- Liberalism -- Great Britain -- History -- 20th century. Liberalism -- Africa, Sub-Saharan -- History -- 20th century. Kenya -- Politics and government -- To 1963. Kenya -- Politics and government -- 1963-1978. Great Britain -- Colonies -- Africa -- Administration.

DT2984.S65.M86 1998
Mungazi, Dickson A.
The last defenders of the laager: Ian D. Smith and F.W. de Klerk/ Dickson A. Mungazi; foreword by Donald G. Baker. Westport, Conn.: Praeger, 1998. xxii, 266 p.
97-039772   968.91/04/092   0275960307
Smith, Ian Douglas, -- 1919- De Klerk, F. W. -- (Frederik Willem) Prime ministers -- Zimbabwe -- Biography. Apartheid -- Zimbabwe. Apartheid -- South Africa. Zimbabwe -- Politics and government -- 1965-1979. South Africa -- Politics and government -- 1989-

DT2988.G64 1993
Godwin, Peter.
'Rhodesians never die': the impact of war and political change on White Rhodesia, c. 1970-1980/ Peter Godwin and Ian Hancock. Oxford; Oxford University Press, 1993. xiv, 400 p.
92-023256   968.91/04   0198203659
Whites -- Zimbabwe -- Politics and government. Zimbabwe -- History -- Chimurenga War, 1966-1980. Zimbabwe -- Ethnic relations.

DT2988.K75 1992
Kriger, Norma J.
Zimbabwe's guerrilla war: peasant voices/ Norma J. Kriger. Cambridge; Cambridge University Press, 1992. x, 303 p.
90-045311   968.91/04   0521392543
Peasants -- Zimbabwe -- Politics and government. Guerrillas -- Zimbabwe -- History -- 20th century. Peasants -- Zimbabwe -- Attitudes -- History -- 20th century. Zimbabwe -- History -- Chimurenga War, 1966-1980 -- Public opinion.

DT2996.D95 1998
Dzimba, John.
South Africa's destabilization of Zimbabwe, 1980-89/ John Dzimba. New York: St. Martin's Press, 1998. xv, 225 p.
97-019534   968.06   0312176694
Political stability -- Zimbabwe. Political stability -- Economic aspects -- Zimbabwe. Social stability -- Zimbabwe.

DT3037 Zambia. Northern Rhodesia — Gazetteers. Dictionaries, etc.

DT3037.G76 1998
Grotpeter, John J.
Historical dictionary of Zambia/ John J. Grotpeter, Brian V. Siegel, James R. Pletcher. Lanham, Md.: Scarecrow Press, 1998. xxxv, 571 p.
97-018917   968.94   081083345X
Zambia -- History -- Dictionaries.

DT3058 Zambia. Northern Rhodesia — Ethnography — Individual elements in the population, A-Z

DT3058.N44.T87 1992
Turner, Edith L. B., 1921-
Experiencing ritual: a new interpretation of African healing/ Edith Turner with William Blodgett, Singleton Kahona, and Fideli Benwa. Philadelphia: University of Pennsylvania Press, c1992. xiii, 239 p.
91-038993   299/.6839   0812231198
Ndembu (African people) -- Rites and ceremonies. Ndembu (African people) -- Religion. Ndembu (African people) -- Medicine.

DT3077 Zambia. Northern Rhodesia — History — Foreign and general relations

DT3077.S6.C46 1992
Chan, Stephen, 1949-
Kaunda and Southern Africa: image and reality in foreign policy/ Stephen Chan. London; British Academic Press, 1992. xv, 231 p.
91-068014   1850434905
Kaunda, Kenneth D. -- (Kenneth David), -- 1924- South Africa -- Foreign relations -- Zambia. Zambia -- Foreign relations -- 1964- Zambia -- Foreign relations -- South Africa.

DT3219-3227 Malawi. Nyasaland — History — By period

DT3219.C65.B35 1994
Baker, C. A.
Development governor: a biography of Sir Geoffrey Colby/ Colin Baker. London; New York: British Academic Press; 1994. xiv, 407 p.
93-061871   968.97   1850436169
Colby, Geoffrey, -- Sir, -- 1901-1958.   Malawi -- Politics and government. Malawi -- History.

DT3227.B35 1997
Baker, C. A.
State of emergency: crisis in Central Africa, Nyasaland 1959-1960/ Colin Baker. London; Tauris Academic Studies, 1997. ix, 299 p.
95-062304   968.97/03   1860640680
Banda, H. Kamuzu -- (Hastings Kamuzu), -- 1905- Malawi -- Politics and government. Malawi -- History -- 1953-1964.

DT3341 Mozambique — History — Foreign and general relations

DT3341.N48 1995
Newitt, M. D. D.
A history of Mozambique/ Malyn Newitt. Bloomington: Indiana University Press, c1995. xxii, 679 p.
93-007477   967.9   0253340063
Mozambique -- History.

DT3394 Mozambique — History — By period

DT3394.V56 1991
Vines, Alex.
Renamo: terrorism in Mozambique/ Alex Vines. London: Centre for Southern African Studies, University 1991. xi, 176 p.
91-013285   967.905   0852553544
Terrorism -- Mozambique. Guerrillas -- Mozambique. Mozambique -- History -- Civil War, 1976-1994.

DU History of Oceania (South Seas)

DU17 General works

DU17.H46 1995
Henningham, Stephen, 1950-
The Pacific island states: security and sovereignty in the post-Cold War world/ Stephen Henningham. New York: St. Martin's Press, 1995. xxiii, 174 p.
95-014906   995   0312125135
Oceania.

DU17.P3 2000
The Pacific Islands: an encyclopedia/ edited by Brij V. Lal and Kate Fortune. Honolulu: University of Hawai'i Press, c2000. xxxvi, 664 p.
99-034571   995   082482265X
Oceania.

DU18 General special

DU18.W55 2000
Wilson, Rob, 1947-
Reimagining the American Pacific: from South Pacific to Bamboo Ridge and beyond/ Rob Wilson. Durham, NC: Duke University Press, 2000. xix, 295 p.
99-056924   909/.09823   0822325004
Public opinion -- Pacific Area.   Pacific Area -- Civilization.

DU19 South Sea description and travel. Voyages — General history of voyages and discoveries

DU19.D78 1991
Dunmore, John, 1923-
Who's who in Pacific navigation/ John Dunmore. Honolulu: University of Hawaii Press, c1991. xvi, 312 p.
91-019280   910/.91823   0824813502
Explorers -- Pacific Area -- Biography.   Pacific Area -- Discovery and exploration.

DU20 South Sea description and travel. Voyages — Through 1800

DU20.W55 1987
Withey, Lynne.
Voyages of discovery: Captain Cook and the exploration of the Pacific/ Lynne Withey. New York: Morrow, c1987. 512 p.
87-007788   919/.04   0688051154
Cook, James, -- 1728-1779 -- Journeys -- Oceania.   Oceania -- Discovery and exploration.

DU22 South Sea description and travel. Voyages — 1898-1950

DU22.K776 1988
Krauss, Bob.
Keneti: South Seas adventures of Kenneth Emory/ Bob Krauss. Honolulu: University of Hawaii Press, c1988. ix, 419 p.
88-010693   919/.04/0924   0824811534
Emory, Kenneth Pike, -- 1897- -- Homes and haunts -- Oceania.   Anthropologists -- United States -- Biography.   Oceania -- Description and travel.

DU28 Social life and customs. Civilization. Intellectual life

DU28.A78 1999
Art and performance in Oceania/ edited by Barry Craig, Bernie Kernot, Christopher Anderson. Honolulu: University of Hawaii Press, c1999. viii, 318 p.
99-039638   700/.995   0824822838
Art -- Oceania -- Congresses. Performing arts -- Oceania -- Congresses. Oceania -- Social life and customs -- Congresses.

DU28.3 History — General works

DU28.3.C33 1997
The Cambridge history of the Pacific Islanders/ edited by Donald Denoon with Stewart Firth ... [et al.]. Cambridge, U.K.; Cambridge University Press, 1997. xvi, 518 p.
96-052784   995   0521441951
Pacific Islanders.   Ethnology -- Oceania.   Oceania -- History.

DU28.3.D46 2000
Denoon, Donald.
A history of Australia, New Zealand, and the Pacific/ Donald Denoon and Philippa Mein-Smith, with Marivic Wyndham. Oxford, UK; Blackwell Pub., 2000. xiv, 523 p.
00-031021   990   0631179623
Oceania -- History. Australia -- History. New Zealand -- History.

DU29 History — Political and diplomatic history. Control of the Pacific. Colonies and possessions

DU29.S43 1990
Segal, Gerald, 1953-
Rethinking the Pacific/ Gerald Segal. Oxford [England]: Clarendon Press; c1990. x, 400 p.
89-016258   327.99   0198273452
Pacific Area -- Foreign relations.

DU29.T48 1994
Thompson, Roger C., 1941-
The Pacific Basin since 1945: a history of the foreign relations of the Asian, Australasian, and American rim states and the Pacific islands/ Roger C. Thompson. London; Longman, 1994. xiv, 353 p.
93-044480   909/.09823/09045   0582021278
Pacific Area -- Politics and government. United States -- Foreign relations -- Pacific Area. Pacific Area -- Foreign relations -- United States.

DU30-50 History — Political and diplomatic history. Control of the Pacific. Colonies and possessions — By country

DU30.D83 1992
Dudden, Arthur Power, 1921-
The American Pacific: from the old China trade to the present/ Arthur Power Dudden. New York: Oxford University Press, 1992. xx, 314 p.
91-017372   973   0195058216
Pacific Area -- Relations -- United States. United States -- Relations -- Pacific Area. Pacific Area -- History.

DU30.G53 1993
Gibson, Arrell Morgan.
Yankees in paradise: the Pacific Basin frontier/ Arrell Morgan Gibson; completed with the assistance of John S. Whitehead. Albuquerque: University of New Mexico Press, c1993. xii, 495 p.
93-012957   303.48/27309   0826314422
Pacific Area -- Relations -- United States. United States -- Relations -- Pacific Area. Oceania -- Relations -- United States.

DU40.S26 1998
Samson, Jane, 1962-
Imperial benevolence: making British authority in the Pacific Islands/ Jane Samson. Honolulu: University of Hawai'i Press, c1998. xv, 240 p.
97-048936   990   0824819276
Islands of the Pacific -- History -- 19th century. Islands of the Pacific -- Relations -- Great Britain. Great Britain -- Relations -- Islands of the Pacific.

DU50.A39 1993
Aldrich, Robert, 1954-
France and the South Pacific since 1940/ Robert Aldrich. Honolulu: University of Hawaii Press, 1993 xxii, 413 p.
93-006783   996.2   0824815580
Decolonization -- Oceania.   New Caledonia -- History. Wallis and Futuna Islands -- History. Vanuatu -- History.

DU90 Australia — Gazetteers. Dictionaries, etc.

DU90.C364 1994
The Cambridge encyclopedia of Australia/ editor, Susan Bambrick. Cambridge [England]; Cambridge University Press, 1994. ix, 384 p.
94-024669   994/.003   0521365112
Australia -- Encyclopedias.

DU90.D63 1999
Docherty, J. C.
Historical dictionary of Australia/ James C. Docherty. Lanham, Md.: Scarecrow Press, 1999. xlii, 425 p.
98-041796   994/.003   0810835924
Australia -- History -- Dictionaries.

DU96.5 Australia — Historical geography

DU96.5.P69 1988
Powell, J. M.
An historical geography of modern Australia: the restive fringe/ J.M. Powell. Cambridge; Cambridge University Press, 1988. xx, 400 p.
87-019724   911/.94   0521256194
Australia -- Historical geography. Australia -- History -- 20th century.

DU99 Australia — Description and travel — 1788-1836

DU99.A78 1988
The Art of the First Fleet & other early Australian drawings/ edited by Bernard Smith & Alwyne Wheeler. New Haven: Published for the Paul Mellon Centre for Studies 1988. 256 p.
87-051377   994   0300041187
Australia in art.   Australia -- Pictorial works. Australia -- Discovery and exploration -- Pictorial works.

DU106 Australia — Antiquities

DU106.C66 1988
Connah, Graham.
Of the hut I builded: the archaeology of Australia's history/ Graham Connah; drawings by Douglas Hobbs.   Cambridge   [England];   Cambridge University Press, 1988. xvi, 176 p.
88-014920   994   0521345677
Archaeology -- Australia.   Australia -- Antiquities. Australia -- History -- 1788-1900.

DU106.M38 2000
McCarthy, Mike, 1947-
Iron and steamship archaeology: success and failure of the SS Xantho/ Michael McCarthy. New York: Kluwer   Academic/Plenum   Publishers, c2000. xiv, 234 p.
00-035704   623.8/204   0306463652
Shipwrecks -- Australia -- History. Underwater archaeology -- Australia. Australia -- Antiquities -- Collection and preservation.

DU107 Australia — Social life and customs. Civilization. Intellectual life

DU107.M4 1995
Melleuish, Gregory, 1954-
Cultural liberalism in Australia: a study in intellectual and cultural history/ Gregory Melleuish. Cambridge; Cambridge University Press, 1995. viii, 226 p.
95-011413   994   0521474442
Liberalism -- Australia -- History. Australia -- Civilization.

DU108 Australia — History — Historiography

DU108.O75 1989
The Origins of Australia's capital cities/ edited by Pamela Statham. Cambridge [England]; Cambridge University Press, 1989. xvii, 364 p.
88-020226   994   0521362423
Cities and towns -- Australia -- History. Capitals (Cities) -- Australia.   Australia -- History. Australia -- Capital and capitol -- History.

DU110 Australia — History — General works

DU110.A58 1992
Albinski, Nan Bowman.
Directory of resources for Australian studies in North America/ Nan Bowman Albinski. Clayton, Vic., Australia: National Centre for Australian Studies, Monash U 1992. xi, 211 p.
93-190600   994/.0025/73   0732604354
Library resources -- United States -- Directories. Library resources -- Canada -- Directories. Archival resources -- United States -- Directories. Australia -- History -- Library resources -- Directories. Australia -- History -- Archival resources -- Directories. Australia -- Study and teaching -- United States -- Directories.

DU110.O94 1986
The Oxford history of Australia/ [general editor, Geoffrey Bolton]. Melbourne; Oxford University Press, 1986-1992 v. 2-5
87-107443   994.04   0195546121
Australia -- History.

DU113-113.5 Australia — History — Diplomatic history. Foreign and general relations

DU113.C34 1987
Camilleri, Joseph A., 1944-
The Australia, New Zealand, US alliance: regional security in the nuclear age/ Joseph A. Camilleri. Boulder, Colo.: Westview Press, 1987. xii, 284 p.
87-050711   327.94093   0813306159
Australia -- Foreign relations -- New Zealand. Australia -- Foreign relations -- United States. New Zealand -- Foreign relations -- Australia.

DU113.5.G7
Hassam, Andrew.
Through Australian eyes: colonial perceptions of imperial Britain/ Andrew Hassam. Brighton [England]; Sussex Academic Press, 2000. ix, 220 p.
00-041301   303.48/241094   190221062X
Imperialism -- Public opinion. National characteristics, Australian. Public opinion -- Australia. Great Britain -- Relations -- Australia. Australia -- Relations -- Great Britain. Great Britain -- Foreign public opinion, Australian.

DU115-117.18 Australia — History — By period

DU115.T73 1994
Trainor, Luke.
British imperialism and Australian nationalism: manipulation, conflict, and compromise in the late nineteenth century/ Luke Trainor. Cambridge; Cambridge University Press, 1994. xi, 213 p.
93-033150   994   0521434769
Australia -- History -- 1788-1900. Nationalism -- Australia -- History. Great Britain -- History -- Victoria, 1837-1901.

DU115.2.F67
Crowley, F. K.
Big John Forrest, 1847-1918: a founding father of the Commonwealth of Australia/ Frank Crowley. Nedlands, W.A.: University of Western Australia Press, 2000. ix, 540 p.
00-421542   994.04/1/092   1876268441
Forrest, John Forrest, -- Baron, -- 1847-1918. Statesmen -- Australia -- Biography. Politicians -- Australia -- Biography. Explorers -- Australia -- Biography. Western Australia -- Politics and government. Australia -- Politics and government -- To 1900. Australia -- Politics and government -- 1901-1945.

DU117.18.A975 1997
Australian foreign policy: into the new millennium/ edited by F.A. Mediansky. South Melbourne: Macmillan Education Australia, 1997. x, 308 p.
98-175075   327.94   0732941598
Australia -- Foreign relations -- 1945-

DU122 Australia — Ethnography — Individual elements in the population, A-Z

DU122.A5.M68 1998
Mosler, David, 1941-
America and Americans in Australia/ David Mosler and Bob Catley. Westport, Conn.: Praeger, 1998. xvi, 204 p.
98-006858   994/.00413   0275962520
Americans -- Australia -- History. National characteristics, American. Australia -- Emigration and immigration. Australia -- History -- 20th century. United States -- History -- 20th century.

DU122.I7.O25 1994
Oceans of consolation: personal accounts of Irish migration to Australia/ [edited by] David Fitzpatrick. Ithaca, N.Y.: Cornell University Press, 1994. xiv, 649 p.
94-021662   994/.0049162   0801426065
Irish -- Australia -- Biography. Immigrants -- Australia -- Biography. Ireland -- Emigration and immigration -- History. Australia -- Emigration and immigration -- History.

DU125 Australia — Ethnography — Australian aborigines. By group, A-Z

DU125.M8.M65 1991
Morphy, Howard.
Ancestral connections: art and an aboriginal system of knowledge/ Howard Morphy. Chicago: University of Chicago Press, 1991. xvii, 329 p.
91-015544   306.4/7/0899915   0226538656
Murngin (Australian people) -- Rites and ceremonies. Bark painting, Yolngu. Philosophy, Australian aboriginal.

DU125.T5.V45 1995
Venbrux, Eric.
A death in the Tiwi islands: conflict, ritual, and social life in an Australian aboriginal community/ Eric Venbrux. Cambridge; Cambridge University Press, 1995. xvii, 269 p.
95-007772   994.2/95   0521473519
Tiwi (Australian people) -- Funeral customs and rites. Tiwi (Australian people) -- Social conditions. Homicide -- Australia -- Pularumpi (N.T.) Pularumpi (N.T.) -- Social life and customs.

DU125.W3.J33 1995
Jackson, Michael, 1940-
At home in the world/ Michael Jackson. Durham: Duke University Press, 1995. x, 188 p.
94-036881   306/.089/9915   0822315610
Walbiri (Australian people) -- Social conditions. Philosophy, Walbiri. Home -- Philosophy.

DU172 Australia — New South Wales — History

DU172.P58.F76 1987
Frost, Alan, 1943-
Arthur Phillip, 1738-1814: his voyaging/ Alan Frost. Melbourne; Oxford University Press, 1987. x, 320 p.
87-214146   910.4/5/0924   0195547012
Phillip, Arthur, -- 1738-1814.   Governors -- Australia -- New South Wales -- Biography.   New South Wales -- History. Great Britain -- History, Naval -- 18th century.

DU178 Australia — New South Wales — Local history and description

DU178.E37 1999
Egan, Jack, 1941-
Buried alive: Sydney 1788-1792: eyewitness accounts of the making of a nation/ Jack Egan. St. Leonards, NSW: Allen & Unwin, 1999. xvi, 351 p.
00-300418   1865081388
Frontier and pioneer life -- Australia -- New South Wales -- Social life and customs. Frontier and pioneer life -- Australia -- New South Wales -- Diaries. Prisoners -- New South Wales -- Sydney -- History. Sydney (N.S.W.) -- History. Australia -- History -- 1788-1851.

DU270 Australia — Queensland — History

DU270.W38 1987
Waterson, D. B.
From the frontier: a pictorial history of Queensland to 1920/ Duncan Waterson and Maurice French. St. Lucia; University of Queensland Press, 1987. xi, 360 p.
87-005007   994.3   0702220752
Queensland -- History -- Pictorial works.

DU370 Australia — Western Australia — History

DU370.G33 1988
Gabbedy, J. P. 1906-
Group settlement/ by J.P. Gabbedy. Nedlands, W.A.: University of Western Australia Press, 1988. 2 v.
89-151153   994.1   0855642904
Agricultural colonies -- Australia -- Western Australia. Western Australia -- History. Western Australia -- Emigration and immigration -- History.

DU420 New Zealand — History — General works

DU420.B45 1996
Belich, James, 1956-
Making peoples: a history of the New Zealanders, from Polynesian settlement to the end of the nineteenth century/ James Belich. Honolulu: University of Hawai'i Press, c1996. 497 p.
96-189332   993   0824818903
New Zealand -- History.

DU420.F555 1999
Fleras, Augie, 1947-
Recalling Aotearoa: indigenous politics and ethnic relations in New Zealand/ Augie Fleras and Paul Spoonley. Auckland; Oxford University Press, 1999. xiv, 288 p.
00-273479   305.8/00993   019558371X
Nationalism -- New Zealand. Maori (New Zealand people) New Zealand -- Ethnic relations. New Zealand -- Politics and government -- 1972-

DU420.J24 1996
Jackson, William Keith, 1928-
Historical dictionary of New Zealand/ Keith Jackson and Alan McRobie. Lanham, Md.: Scarecrow Press, c1996. xix, 313 p.
95-036075   993/.003   0810830868
New Zealand -- History -- Dictionaries.

DU420.16 New Zealand — History — 1840-1876

DU420.16.V3413 2000
Vaggioli, Felice, 1845-1921.
History of New Zealand and its inhabitants/ Dom Felice Vaggioli; translated by John Crockett. Dunedin, New Zealand: University of Otago Press, 2000. xxiii, 340 p.
00-340458   993.01   1877133523
Maori (New Zealand people) -- Politics and government -- 19th century. Missionaries -- New Zealand -- History -- 19th century. New Zealand -- Politics and government -- 19th century. New Zealand -- Social life and customs -- 19th century. New Zealand -- History -- 19th century.

DU420.32 New Zealand — History — 1945-

DU420.32.L43 1994
Leap into the dark: the changing role of the state in New Zealand since 1984/ edited by Andrew Sharp. Auckland, New Zealand: Auckland University Press, 1994. 255 p.
94-240238   993.03/7   1869400968
New Zealand -- History -- 1945- New Zealand -- Politics and government -- 1972-

DU421 New Zealand — History — Political and diplomatic history. Foreign and general relations

DU421.M35 1993
McKinnon, Malcolm.
Independence and foreign policy: New Zealand in the world since 1935/ Malcolm McKinnon. Auckland: Auckland University Press, 1993. xxiv, 329 p.
93-180960   327.93   1869400704
New Zealand -- Foreign relations.

DU421.N44
New Zealand in world affairs. Wellington: Price Milburn for the New Zealand Institute of I 1977-1999 v. 1-3
78-310317   327.931   0705506363
New Zealand -- Foreign relations -- 1945- New Zealand -- Defenses.

DU423 New Zealand — Ethnography — Maori

DU423.C57.S53 1990
Sharp, Andrew, 1906-
Justice and the Maori: Maori claims in New Zealand political argument in the 1980s/ Andrew Sharp. Auckland; Oxford University Press, 1990. vii, 310 p.
90-214550   323.1/1994/093   0195582020
Maori (New Zealand people) -- Claims. Maori (New Zealand people) -- Legal status, laws, etc. Maori (New Zealand people) -- Government relations.

DU423.F48.S25 1992
Salmond, Anne.
Two worlds: first meetings between Maori and Europeans, 1642-1772/ Anne Salmond. Honolulu: University of Hawaii Press, c1991. 477 p.
91-045422   993.01   0824814673
Maori (New Zealand people) -- First contact with Europeans. Maori (New Zealand people) -- History -- Sources. Maori (New Zealand people) -- Social life and customs. New Zealand -- Discovery and exploration. New Zealand -- History -- To 1840.

DU423.F48.S25 1997
Salmond, Anne.
Between worlds: early exchanges between Maori and Europeans, 1773-1815/ Anne Salmond. Honolulu: University of Hawaii Press, c1997. 590 p.
97-024190   993.01   0824820207
Maori (New Zealand people) -- First contact with Europeans. Maori (New Zealand people) -- History -- Sources. Maori (New Zealand people) -- Social life and customs. New Zealand -- History -- To 1840. New Zealand -- Discover and exploration. New Zealand -- Race relations.

DU423.P63.C69 1993
Cox, Lindsay, 1960-
Kotahitanga: the search for Maori political unity/ Lindsay Cox. Auckland; Oxford University Press, 1993. xi, 238 p.
94-237717   323.1/1994093   0195582802
Maori (New Zealand people) -- Politics and government. Maori (New Zealand people) -- Government relations. Maori (New Zealand people) -- Civil rights.

DU470 Tasmania (Van Diemen's Land)

DU470.R6 1983
Robson, L. L. 1931-
A history of Tasmania/ Lloyd Robson. Melbourne; Oxford Univeristy Press, 1983-1991. 2 v.
83-204405   994.6   0195543645
Tasmania -- History.

DU490 Melanesia (General)

DU490.B37 1990
Barratt, Glynn.
Melanesia and the western Polynesian fringe/ Glynn Barratt. Vancouver: University of British Columbia Press, 1990. xvii, 257 p.
90-201633   995   077480338X
Melanesia -- Relations -- Soviet Union. Soviet Union -- Relations -- Melanesis. Melanesia -- Discovery and exploration -- Russian.

DU500 Micronesia (General)

DU500.H35 1998
Hanlon, David L.
Remaking Micronesia: discourses over development in a Pacific territory, 1944-1982/ David Hanlon. Honolulu: University of Hawai'i Press, c1998. xv, 305 p.
97-036316   996.5   0824818946
Micronesia -- Politics and government. Micronesia -- Economic conditions. Micronesia -- Social conditions.

DU500.P43 1988
Peattie, Mark R., 1930-
Nanyo: the rise and fall of the Japanese in Micronesia, 1885-1945/ Mark R. Peattie. Honolulu: Center for Pacific Islands Studies, School of Ha c1988. xxii, 382 p.
87-019437   996/.5   0824810872
Micronesia -- History. Micronesia -- Relations -- Japan. Japan -- Relations -- Micronesia.

DU510 Polynesia (General)

DU510.G58 1970
Goldman, Irving, 1911-
Ancient Polynesian society. Chicago, University of Chicago Press [1970] xxviii, 625 p.
74-116028   301.29/96   0226301141
Polynesians. Prehistoric peoples -- Polynesia.

DU520 Smaller island groups — Admiralty Islands

DU520.R66 1985
Romanucci-Ross, Lola.
Mead's other Manus: phenomenology of the encounter/ Lola Romanucci-Ross. South Hadley, Mass.: Bergin and Garvey, 1985. xxi, 230 p.
84-021592   306/.0899912   0897890647
Manus (Papua New Guinea people)

DU565 Smaller island groups — Caroline Islands — History

DU565.H49 1983
Hezel, Francis X.
The first taint of civilization: a history of the Caroline and Marshall Islands in pre-colonial days, 1521-1885/ Francis X. Hezel. Honolulu: Pacific Islands Studies Program, Center for Paci c1983. xvi, 365 p.
83-010411   996/.6   0824808401
Caroline Islands -- History. Marshall Islands -- History.

DU568 Smaller island groups — Caroline Islands — Individual islands, groups of islands, cities, etc., A-Z

DU568.N44.P69 1993
Poyer, Lin, 1953-
The Ngatik massacre: history and identity on a Micronesian atoll/ Lin Poyer. Washington: Smithsonian Institution Press, c1993. xiii, 298 p.
92-037911   996.5   1560982616
Ngatik (Micronesian people) -- History. Ngatik (Micronesian people) -- Ethnic identity. Ngatik (Micronesian people) -- Social life and customs. Ngatik (Micronesia) -- History. Ngatik (Micronesia) -- Social life and customs.

DU568.P55.D35 1994
Damas, David.
Bountiful island: a study of land tenure on a Micronesian atoll/ David Damas. Waterloo, Ont.: Wilfrid Laurier University Press, c1994. xvi, 272 p.
95-137218   306.3/2/09966   0889202397
Pingelap (Micronesian people) -- Land tenure. Land tenure -- Micronesia. Pingelap (Micronesian people) -- Social life and customs.

DU568.P7.H36 1988
Hanlon, David L.
Upon a stone altar: a history of the island of Pohnpei to 1890/ David Hanlon. Honolulu: University of Hawaii Press, c1988. xxviii, 320 p.
87-034288   996/.6   0824811240
Pohnpei Island (Micronesia) -- History.

DU600 Smaller island groups — Fiji Islands

DU600.I75 1988
Islands, islanders, and the world: the colonial and post-colonial experience of Eastern Fiji/ Tim Bayliss-Smith ... [et al.]; with contributions from Muriel Brookfield. Cambridge [England]; Cambridge University Press, 1988. xvii, 323 p.
88-001372   996/.11   052126877X
Fiji -- History. Fiji -- Economic conditions.

DU600.K38 1991
Kelly, John Dunham, 1958-
A politics of virtue: Hinduism, sexuality, and countercolonial discourse in Fiji/ John D. Kelly. Chicago: University of Chicago Press, 1991. xvi, 266 p.
91-017326   996.11/00491411   0226430308
East Indians -- Fiji -- History. Fiji -- Politics and government. Fiji -- Social life and customs.

DU600.M34
Mayer, Adrian C.
Peasants in the Pacific; a study of Fiji Indian rural society. Berkeley, University of California Press, 1961. xiii, 202 p.
61-016216
East Indians in the Fiji Islands.

DU622 Smaller island groups — Hawaiian Islands. Hawaii — Gazetteers. Handbooks. Guidebooks

DU622.P8
Pukui, Mary Kawena, 1895-
Place names of Hawaii and Supplement to the third edition of the Hawaiian-English dictionary, by Mary Kawena Pukui and Samuel H. Elbert. [Honolulu] University of Hawaii Press, 1966. x, 53 p.
66-019326   919.69
Names, Geographical -- Hawaii. Hawaiian language -- Dictionaries -- English.

DU624.6-624.7 Smaller island groups — Hawaiian Islands. Hawaii — Ethnography

DU624.6.H33 1992
Haas, Michael, 1938-
Institutional racism: the case of Hawaii/ Michael Haas. Westport, Conn.: Praeger, 1992. xx, 367 p.
92-016168   305.8/009969   0275935590
Racism -- Hawaii. Hawaii -- Race relations. Hawaii -- Ethnic relations.

DU624.65.B83 1993
Buck, Elizabeth Bentzel.
Paradise remade: the politics of culture and history in Hawai'i/ Elizabeth Buck. Philadelphia: Temple University Press, 1993. viii, 242 p.
92-000310   996.9   0877229783
Hawaiians -- Social life and customs. Hawaiians -- History. Acculturation -- Case studies. Hawaii -- Historiography.

DU624.65.K46 1998
Kepler, Angela Kay, 1943-
Hawaiian heritage plants/ Angela Kay Kepler. Honolulu: University of Hawai'i Press, c1998. xii, 240 p.
97-046933   581.6/3/09969   0824819942
Hawaiians -- Ethnobotany. Ethnobotany -- Hawaii. Plants, Useful -- Hawaii.

DU624.65.K56 1992
Kirch, Patrick Vinton.
Anahulu: the anthropology of history in the Kingdom of Hawaii/ Patrick V. Kirch and Marshall Sahlins. Chicago: University of Chicago Press, 1992. 2 v.
91-033830   996.9/3   0226733637
Hawaiians -- History. Hawaiians -- Antiquities. Prehistoric peoples -- Hawaii -- Anahulu River Valley. Anahulu River Valley (Hawaii) -- History. Anahulu River Valley (Hawaii) -- Social life and customs. Anahulu River Valley (Hawaii) -- Antiquities.

DU624.65.K72 1993
Krauss, Beatrice H.
Plants in Hawaiian culture/ Beatrice H. Krauss; illustrations by Thelma F. Greig. Honolulu: University of Hawaii Press, c1993. ix, 345 p.
93-014789   581.6/1/09969   0824812255
Hawaiians -- Ethnobotany. Ethnobotany -- Hawaii. Hawaiians -- Material culture.

DU624.7.J3.A75 2000
Ariyoshi, Koji, 1914-1976.
From Kona to Yenan: the political memoirs of Koji Ariyoshi/ Koji Ariyoshi; edited by Alice M. Beechert and Edward D. Beechert. Honolulu: Published for the Biographical Research Center b 2000. xviii, 225 p.
00-060763   996.9/004956/0092   0824823761
Ariyoshi, Koji, -- 1914-1976. Japanese Americans -- Hawaii -- Biography. Industrial relations -- Hawaii -- History. Hawaii -- Politics and government -- 1959- Hawaii -- Social conditions. Hawaii -- Politics and government -- 1900-1959.

DU624.7.J3.O38 1991
Okihiro, Gary Y., 1945-
Cane fires: the anti-Japanese movement in Hawaii, 1865-1945/ Gary Y. Okihiro. Philadelphia: Temple University Press, 1991. xvii, 330 p.
90-041610   996.9/004956   0877227993
Japanese Americans -- Hawaii -- Social conditions. Japanese Americans -- Hawaii -- Economic conditions. Hawaii -- Ethnic relations.

DU624.7.J3.T36 1994
Tamura, Eileen.
Americanization, acculturation, and ethnic identity: the Nisei generation in Hawaii/ Eileen H. Tamura; foreword by Roger Daniels. Urbana: University of Illinois Press, c1994. xx, 326 p.
93-018118   996.9/004956   0252020316
Japanese Americans -- Hawaii. Acculturation -- Hawaii. Discrimination -- Hawaii. Hawaii -- Race relations.

DU624.7.K67.H983 1995
Hyun, Peter, 1906-
In the new world: the making of a Korean American/ Peter Hyun. Honolulu: University of Hawaii Press, 1995. x, 290 p.
94-030661   996.9/004957/0092   082481648X
Hyun, Peter, -- 1906- Korean Americans -- Hawaii -- Biography.

DU624.7.K67.P37 1988
Patterson, Wayne, 1946-
The Korean frontier in America: immigration to Hawaii, 1896-1910/ Wayne Patterson. Honolulu: University of Hawaii Press, c1988. xii, 274 p.
88-001163   996.9/004957   0824810902
Koreans -- Hawaii -- History. Immigrants -- Hawaii -- History. Immigrants -- Government policy -- United States. Hawaii -- Emigration and immigration. United States -- Emigration and immigration -- Government policy. United States -- Foreign relations -- Korea.

DU626-627.83 Smaller island groups — Hawaiian Islands. Hawaii — History

DU626.O28 1992
Obeyesekere, Gananath.
The apotheosis of Captain Cook: European mythmaking in the Pacific/ Gananath Obeyesekere. Princeton, N.J.: Princeton University Press; c1992. xvii, 251 p.
91-042364   996.9/02   0691056803
Cook, James, -- 1728-1779. Ethnology -- Polynesia. Hawaii -- History -- To 1893. Polynesia -- Discovery and exploration. Hawaii -- History -- To 1893 -- Historiography.

DU626.O283.S35 1995
Sahlins, Marshall David, 1930-
How "natives" think: about Captain Cook, for example/ Marshall Sahlins. Chicago: University of Chicago Press, 1995. x, 318 p.
94-034816   996.9/0072   0226733688
Obeyesekere, Gananath. -- The apotheosis of Captain Cook. Cook, James, -- 1728-1779. Ethnology -- Polynesia. Mythology, Hawaiian. Ethnology -- Hawaii -- Philosophy. Hawaii -- History -- To 1893 -- Historiography.

DU627.17.A46.D84 1997
Dye, Bob, 1928-
Merchant prince of the Sandalwood Mountains: Afong and the Chinese in Hawaii/ Bob Dye. Honolulu, Hawaii: University of Hawaii Press, c1997. x, 276 p.
96-025678   996.9/3004951   0824817729
Afong, Chun, -- 1825-1906. Chinese -- Hawaii -- Biography. Merchants -- Hawaii -- Biography. Chinese -- Hawaii -- History. Hawaii -- History -- To 1893.

DU627.17.G5.A3
Gibson, Walter Murray.
The diaries of Walter Murray Gibson: 1886, 1887. Edited with introd. and notes by Jacob Adler and Gwynn Barrett. [Honolulu] University Press of Hawaii, 1973. xvii, 199 p.
75-188977   996.9/02/0924   082480211X
Gibson, Walter Murray -- Diaries. Politicians -- Hawaii -- Diaries. Hawaii -- History -- Sources.

DU627.17.K28.A44
Kaeo, Peter Young, 1836-1880.
News from Molokai, letters between Peter Kaeo & Queen Emma, 1873-1876/ edited with introd. and notes by Alfons L. Korn. Honolulu: The University Press of Hawaii, c1976. xlv, 345 p.
76-016823   996.9/02/0922   082480399X
Kaeo, Peter, -- 1836-1880. Emma, -- consort of Kamehameha IV, King of the Hawaiian Islands, -- 1836-1885.

DU627.17.W55.A7 1996
Andrade, Ernest, 1926-
Unconquerable rebel: Robert W. Wilcox and Hawaiian politics, 1880-1903/ Ernest Andrade, Jr. Niwot, Colo.: University Press of Colorado, c1996. 299 p.
95-045470   996.9/027   0870814176
Wilcox, R. W. -- (Robert William), -- 1855-1903. Politicians -- Hawaii -- Biography. Hawaii -- Politics and government.

DU627.2.R79 1992
Russ, William Adam, 1903-
The Hawaiian Republic (1894-98): and its struggle to win annexation/ William Adam Russ, Jr.; with an introduction by Pauline N. King. Selinsgrove [Pa.]: Susquehanna University Press; c1992. xiii, 398 p.
91-043886   996.9/028   094563644X
Hawaii -- Politics and government -- 1893-1900.

DU627.83.T35.A3 1998
Takabuki, Matsuo, 1923-
An unlikely revolutionary: Matsuo Takabuki and the making of modern Hawai'i: a memoir/ by Matsuo Takabuki; assisted bu Dennis M. Ogawa with Glen Grant and Wilma Sur. Honolulu: University of Hawai'i Press, c1998. viii, 237 p.
97-048949   996.9/03/092   0824820835
Takabuki, Matsuo, -- 1923- Politicians -- Hawaii -- Biography. Hawaii -- Politics and government -- 1950-

DU629 Smaller island groups — Hawaiian Islands. Hawaii — Islands, counties, etc., A-Z

DU629.H7.B44 1990
Beechert, Edward D.
Honolulu: crossroads of the Pacific/ Edward D. Beechert. Columbia, S.C.: University of South Carolina Press, c1991. vii, 210 p.
90-044328   996.9/31   0872497194
Honolulu (Hawaii) -- History.

DU645 Smaller island groups — Northern Mariana Islands. Ladrone Islands — History

DU645.C86 1992
Cunningham, Lawrence J., 1943-
Ancient Chamorro society/ by Lawrence J. Cunningham. Honolulu, HI: Bess Press, c1992. viii, 229 p.
91-078031   996.7   1880188058
Chamorro (Micronesian people)

DU647 Smaller island groups — Northern Mariana Islands. Ladrone Islands — Individual islands, cities, etc.

DU647.R63 1995
Rogers, Robert F.
Destiny's landfall: a history of Guam/ Robert F. Rogers. Honolulu: University of Hawaii Press, 1995. xi, 380 p.
94-025845   996.7   0824816781
Guam -- History.

DU700 Smaller island groups — Marquesas Islands — General works

DU700.T46 1990
Thomas, Nicholas.
Marquesan societies: inequality and political transformation in eastern Polynesia/ Nicholas Thomas. Oxford [England]: Clarendon Press; 1990. xv, 256 p.
89-023904   306/.09963/1   0198277482
Marquesans -- History. Marquesans -- Social life and customs. Culture conflict -- French Polynesia -- Marquesas Islands. Marquesas Islands (French Polynesia) -- Politics and government. Marquesas Islands (French Polynesia) -- Social conditions.

DU710 Smaller island groups — Marshall Islands

DU710.D53 1989
Dibblin, Jane.
Day of two suns: US nuclear testing and the Pacific Islanders/ Jane Dibblin. New York: New Amsterdam, 1990, c1988. xvi, 299 p.
89-039780   996.8/3   0941533735
Nuclear weapons testing victims -- Marshall Islands. Nuclear weapons -- Testing -- Marshall Islands. Marshall Islands -- Politics and government. Marshall Islands -- Social conditions.

DU740-744.35 Smaller island groups — New Guinea

DU740.S34 1991
Schieffelin, Edward L.
Like people you see in a dream: first contact in six Papuan societies/ Edward L. Schieffelin and Robert Crittenden; with contributions by Bryant Allen ... [et al.]. Stanford, Calif.: Stanford University Press, c1991. xviii, 325 p.
90-041760   995.3   0804716625
Papuans -- History. Papuans -- Social life and customs. Purari River (Gulf Province, Papua New Guinea) -- Discovery and exploration. Purari River (Gulf Province, Papua New Guinea) -- History.

DU740.42.B39 1990
Battaglia, Debbora.
On the bones of the serpent: person, memory, and mortality in Sabarl Island society/ Debbora Battaglia. Chicago: University of Chicago Press, c1990. x, 253 p.
89-035896   393/.1/09953   0226038882
Sabarl (Papua New Guinea people) Sabarl (Papua New Guinea people) -- Funeral customs and rites.

DU740.42.B65 2000
Bolyanatz, Alexander H., 1956-
Mortuary feasting on New Ireland: the activation of matriliny among the Sursurunga/ Alexander H. Bolyanatz. Westport, Conn.: Bergin & Garvey, 2000. xvi, 182 p.
99-059735   393   0897897218
Sursurunga (Papua New Guinea people) -- Funeral customs and rites. Sursurunga (Papua New Guinea people) -- Kinship. Matrilineal kinship -- Papua New Guinea -- New Ireland Province.

DU740.42.B75 1992
Brison, Karen J.
Just talk: gossip, meetings, and power in a Papua New Guinea village/ Karen J. Brison. Berkeley: University of California Press, c1992. xviii, 287 p.
91-034511   995.3   0520077008
Kwanga (Papua New Guinea people) -- Politics and government. Kwanga (Papua New Guinea people) -- Social life and customs. Big man (Melanesia) -- Papua New Guinea -- Inakor. Inakor (Papua New Guinea) -- Politics and government. Inakor (Papua New Guinea) -- Social life and customs.

DU740.42.C595 1992
Clowning as critical practice: performance humor in the South Pacific/ William E. Mitchell, editor. Pittsburgh: University of Pittsburgh Press, c1992. x, 227 p.
92-050195   306.4/81   0822937344
Papuans -- Humor. Clowning -- Papua New Guinea. Philosophy, Papuan. Papua New Guinea -- Social life and customs.

DU740.42.D36 1990
Damon, Frederick H.
From Muyuw to the Trobriands: transformations along the northern side of the Kula Ring/ Frederick H. Damon. Tucson: University of Arizona Press, c1990. xvi, 285 p.
90-035337   306/.08991209541   0816511918
Massim (Papua New Guinea people) -- Social life and customs. Kula exchange. Social structure -- Papua New Guinea -- Woodlark Island.

DU740.42.D43 1989
Death rituals and life in the societies of the kula ring/ edited by Frederick H. Damon and Roy Wagner. DeKalb: Northern Illinois University Press, 1989. vi, 280 p.
89-008611   393/.08999509541   087580151X
Massim (Melanesian people) -- Funeral customs and rites. Kula exchange. Funeral rites and ceremonies -- Papua New Guinea -- Milne Bay Province Milne Bay Province (Papua New Guinea) -- Social life and customs.

DU740.42.D89 1990
Dwyer, Peter D., 1937-
The pigs that ate the garden: a human ecology from Papua New Guinea/ Peter D. Dwyer. Ann Arbor: University of Michigan Press, c1990. xvi, 241 p.
90-032835   338.1/9/0899912   0472101579
Etoro (Papua New Guinea people) -- Food. Etoro (Papua New Guinea people) -- Economic conditions.

DU740.42.F35 1997
Fajans, Jane.
They make themselves: work and play among the Baining of Papua New Guinea/ Jane Fajans. Chicago: University of Chicago Press, 1997. xiv, 313 p.
96-037641   306/.089/9912   0226234436
Baining (Papua New Guinea people) -- Rites and ceremonies. Baining (Papua New Guinea people) -- Social life and customs. Baining (Papua New Guinea people) -- Socialization. Gazelle Peninsula (Papua New Guinea) -- Social life and customs.

DU740.42.F44 1990
Feld, Steven.
Sound and sentiment: birds, weeping, poetics, and song in Kaluli expression/ Steven Feld. Philadelphia: University of Pennsylvania Press, c1990. xii, 297 p.
89-036978   306/.0995/3   0812212991
Kaluli (Papua New Guinea people) -- Social life and customs. Kaluli (Papua New Guinea people) -- Rites and ceremonies. Kaluli (Papua New Guinea people) -- Music -- History and criticism.

DU740.42.F67 1995
Foster, Robert John, 1957-
Social reproduction and history in Melanesia: mortuary ritual, gift exchange, and custom in the Tanga Islands/ Robert J. Foster. Cambridge; Cambridge University Press, 1995. xxii, 288 p.
94-030846   995.3   0521480302
Tanga (Papua New Guinea people) Tanga (Papua New Guinea people) -- Funeral customs and rites. Ceremonial exchange -- Papua New Guinea.

DU740.42.G47 1991
Gewertz, Deborah B., 1948-
Twisted histories, altered contexts: representing the Chambri in a world system/ Deborah Gewertz, Frederick Errington. Cambridge [England]; Cambridge University Press, 1991. xiv, 264 p.
90-043063   305.89/912   0521400120
Chambri (Papua New Guinea people) -- Social conditions. Chambri (Papua New Guinea people) -- Economic conditions. Chambri (Papua New Guinea people) -- Ethnic identity.

DU740.42.G66 1995
Goodale, Jane C. 1926-
To sing with pigs is human: the concept of person in Papua New Guinea/ Jane C. Goodale. Seattle: University of Washington Press, c1995. xvi, 269 p.
94-040671   306/.089/9912   0295974540
Kaulong (Papua New Guinea people) -- Psychology. Kaulong (Papua New Guinea people) -- Social life and customs. Identity (Psychology) -- Papua New Guinea -- New Britain Island. New Britain Island (Papua New Guinea) -- Social life and customs.

DU740.42.H42 1990
Healey, Christopher J.
Maring hunters and traders: production and exchange in the Papua New Guinea highlands/ Christopher Healey. Berkeley: University of California Press, c1990. xxii, 401 p.
89-020649   306.3/0899912   0520068408
Maring (Papua New Guinea people) -- Commerce. Maring (Papua New Guinea people) -- Hunting. Exchange -- Papua New Guinea.

DU740.42.L47 1993
Lepowsky, Maria Alexandra.
Fruit of the motherland: gender in an egalitarian society/ Maria Lepowsky. New York: Columbia University Press, c1993. xviii, 383 p.
93-008314   305.3/09953   0231081200
Tagula (Papua New Guinea people) -- Kinship. Tagula (Papua New Guinea people) -- Rites and ceremonies. Tagula (Papua New Guinea people) -- Social life and customs. Tagula Island (Papua New Guinea) -- Social life and customs.

DU740.42.L565 1997
Lipset, David, 1951-
Mangrove man: dialogics of culture in the Sepik estuary/ David Lipset. Cambridge; Cambridge University Press, 1997. xviii, 335 p.
96-050213   306/.089/9912   0521564344
Murik (Papua New Guinea people)

DU740.42.L57 1988
LiPuma, Edward, 1951-
The gift of kinship: structure and practice in Maring social organization/ Edward LiPuma. Cambridge; Cambridge University Press, 1988. x, 241 p.
87-020883   306/.0995/3   0521344832
Maring (Papua New Guinea people) Social structure -- Papua New Guinea.

DU740.42.L88 1995
Lutkehaus, Nancy.
Zaria's fire: engendered moments in Manam ethnography/ Nancy C. Lutkehaus. Durham, N.C.: Carolina Academic Press, c1995. xv, 490 p.
95-068695   306/.09953   0890898006
Wedgwood, Camilla H. -- (Camilla Hildegarde), -- 1901-1955. Ethnology -- Papua New Guinea -- Manam Island. Manam Island (Papua New Guinea) -- Social life and customs.

DU740.42.M373 1994
Maschio, Thomas.
To remember the faces of the dead: the plenitude of memory in southwestern New Britain/ Thomas Maschio. Madison, Wis.: University of Wisconsin Press, c1994. x, 245 p.
93-032388   306/.089/995   0299140903
Rauto (Papua New Guinea people) -- Rites and ceremonies. Rauto (Papua New Guinea people) -- Ethnic identity. Philosophy, Rauto. West New Britain Province (Papua New Guinea) -- Social life and customs.

DU740.42.P37 1995
Papuan borderlands: Huli, Duna, and Ipili perspectives on the Papua New Guinea highlands/ edited by Aletta Biersack. Ann Arbor: University of Michigan Press, c1995. xiv, 440 p.
95-030130   995.3   0472106015
Huli (Papua New Guinea people) Duna (Papua New Guinea people) Ipili (Papua New Guinea people)

DU740.42.S65 1994
Smith, Michael French.
Hard times on Kairiru Island: poverty, development, and morality in a Papua New Guinea village/ Michael French Smith. Honolulu: University of Hawaii Press, c1994. viii, 278 p.
93-041300   305.899/9120953   082481536X
Kairiru (Papua New Guinea people) -- Economic conditions. Kairiru (Papua New Guinea people) -- Social conditions. Subsistence economy -- Papua New Guinea -- Kragur. Kragur (Papua New Guinea) -- Economic conditions. Kragur (Papua New Guinea) -- Social conditions.

DU740.42.S79 1998
Sturzenhofecker, G.
Times enmeshed: gender, space, and history among the Duna of Papua New Guinea/ Gabriele Sturzenhofecker. Stanford, Calif.: Stanford University Press, 1998. xii, 242 p.
97-026896   305.89/912   0804728992
Duna (Papua New Guinea people) -- Social conditions. Duna (Papua New Guinea people) -- Religion. Philosophy, Duna -- Papua New Guinea -- Aluni. Aluni (Papua New Guinea) -- Social conditions.

DU740.42.T45 1998
Telban, Borut.
Dancing through time: a Sepik cosmology/ Borut Telban. Oxford: Clarendon Press; 1998. xii, 270 p.
98-004470   306/.09953   0198233760
Ambonwari (Papua New Guinea people) -- Ethnic identity. Philosophy, Ambonwari. Ambonwari (Papua New Guinea people) -- Social life and customs. East Sepik Province (Papua New Guinea) -- Social life and customs.

DU740.42.T84 1997
Tuzin, Donald F.
The Cassowary's revenge: the life and death of masculinity in a New Guinea society/ Donald Tuzin. Chicago, Ill.: University of Chicago Press, 1997. xiii, 256 p.
96-040395   306/.089/9912   0226819507
Arapesh (Papua New Guinea people) -- Rites and ceremonies. Arapesh (Papua New Guinea people) - - Religion. Arapesh (Papua New Guinea people) -- Psychology. Ilahita (Papua New Guinea) -- Social life and customs.

DU740.42.W4 1991
Weiner, James F.
The empty place: poetry, space, and being among the Foi of Papua New Guinea/ James F. Weiner. Bloomington: Indiana University Press, c1991. xiv, 218 p.
90-049766   306.4/0899912   0253363829
Foi (Papua New Guinea people) -- Philosophy. Foi (Papua New Guinea people) -- Social life and customs. Folk songs, Papuan.

DU740.42.W465 2000
Whitehead, Harriet.
Food rules: hunting, sharing, and tabooing game in Papua New Guinea/ Harriet Whitehead. Ann Arbor: University of Michigan Press, c2000. xiii, 330 p.
00-037412   394.1/6/0899912   0472097059
Seltaman (Papua New Guinea people) -- Food. Seltaman (Papua New Guinea people) -- Hunting. Seltaman (Papua New Guinea people) -- Rites and ceremonies. Western Province (Papua New Guinea) -- Social life and customs.

DU744.35.D32.H35 1999
Hampton, O. W., 1928-
Culture of stone: sacred and profane uses of stone among the Dani/ O.W. "Bud" Hampton. College Station, Tex: Texas A&M University Press, c1999. xxv, 331 p.
98-049894   306/.089/9912   0890968705
Dani (New Guinea people) -- Implements. Dani (New Guinea people) -- Industries. Dani (New Guinea people) -- Religion. Irian Jaya (Indonesia) -- Social life and customs.

DU760 Smaller island groups — New Hebrides. Vanuatu

DU760.B84 1989
Brunton, R.
The abandoned narcotic: kava and cultural instability in Melanesia/ Ron Brunton. Cambridge; Cambridge University Press, 1989. viii, 219 p.
89-031240   394.1/4   0521373751
Rivers, W. H. R. -- (William Halse Rivers), -- 1864-1922. Kava (Beverage) -- Vanuatu. Kava ceremony -- Vanuatu. Tanna (Vanuatu people) -- Drug use.

DU760.M55 1998
Miles, William F. S.
Bridging mental boundaries in a postcolonial microcosm: identity and development in Vanuatu/ William F.S. Miles. Honolulu: University of Hawaii Press, c1998. xxiv, 271 p.
98-009698   995.95   0824819799
Postcolonialism -- Vanuatu. National characteristics, Vanuatuan. Nationalism -- Vanuatu. Vanuatu -- History.

DU780 Smaller island groups — Pelew (Palau) Islands

DU780.R64 1991
Roff, Sue Rabbitt.
Overreaching in paradise: United States policy in Palau since 1945/ Sue Rabbitt Roff. Juneau, Alaska, USA: Denali Press, c1991. ix, 245 p.
90-003608   327.730966   0938737228
Palau -- Politics and government. Palau -- Foreign relations -- United States. United States -- Foreign relations -- Palau.

DU819 Smaller island groups — Samoan Islands

DU819.A2.D3
Davidson, James Wightman, 1915-
Samoa mo Samoa; the emergence of the independent state of Western Samoa [by] J. W. Davidson. Melbourne, Oxford University Press, 1967. xii, 467 p.
68-079458   996/.14
Western Samoa -- Politics and government. Western Samoa -- History.

DU850 Smaller island groups — Solomon Islands

DU850.H95 1996
Hviding, Edvard.
Guardians of Marovo Lagoon: practice, place, and politics in maritime Melanesia/ Edvard Hviding. Honolulu: University of Hawai'i Press; c1996. xxix, 473 p.
95-038976   306/.099593/1   0824816641
Marovo (Solomon Islands people) -- Land tenure. Marovo (Solomon Islands people) -- Fishing. Marovo (Solomon Islands people) -- Social conditions. New Georgia (Solomon Islands) -- Social conditions. New Georgia (Solomon Islands) -- Politics and government.

DU850.M66 1991
Monberg, Torben.
Bellona Island beliefs and rituals/ Torben Monberg; [drawings by Pernille Monberg]. Honolulu: Center for Pacific Island Studies, School of Haw c1991. xix, 449 p.
90-020224   299/.92   082481147X
Rennellese (Solomon Islands people) -- Rites and ceremonies. Rennellese (Solomon Islands people) - - Religion.

DU870 Smaller island groups — Tahiti and Society Islands

DU870.B56 1988
Bligh, William, 1754-1817.
Return to Tahiti: Bligh's second breadfruit voyage/ [edited by] Douglas Oliver. Honolulu, Hawaii: University of Hawaii Press, c1988. xx, 281 p.
88-014298   919.62/11   0824811844
Tahiti -- Social life and customs. Tahiti -- Discovery and exploration.

DU870.N48
Newbury, C. W. 1929-
Tahiti Nui: change and survival in French Polynesia, 1767-1945/ Colin Newbury. Honolulu: University Press of Hawaii, c1980. xvi, 380 p.
79-023609   996/.211   0824806301
Tahiti -- History. Tahiti -- Colonization.

DU870.N53 2001
Nicole, Robert.
The word, the pen, and the pistol: literature and power in Tahiti/ Robert Nicole. Albany: State University of New York Press, c2001. ix, 230 p.
00-028519   996.2/11   0791447391
Tahitians -- Ethnic identity. Politics and culture. East and West. Tahiti -- Civilization -- Foreign influences.

DU870.O43
Oliver, Douglas L.
Ancient Tahitian society/ Douglas L. Oliver. Honolulu: University Press of Hawaii, [1974] 3 v.
73-077010   996/.211   0824802675
Ethnology -- French Polynesia -- Tahiti. Tahiti -- History. Tahiti -- Antiquities.

DU880 Smaller island groups — Tonga Islands

DU880.D35 1999
Daly, Martin, 1939-
Tonga/ Martin Daly, compiler. Oxford, England; Clio Press, c1999. xxxvi, 185 p.
016.99612   1851092935
Tonga -- Bibliography. Tonga -- Bibliography.

DX History of Gypsies

DX115 General works

DX115.F66 1995
Fonseca, Isabel.
Bury me standing: the Gypsies and their journey/ Isabel Fonseca. New York: Knopf, 1995. 322 p.
95-014272   909/.0491497   0679406786
Gypsies -- History.

DX115.K46 1998
Kenrick, Donald.
Historical dictionary of the Gypsies (Romanies)/ Donald Kenrick with the assistance of Gillian Taylor. Lanham, Md.: Scarecrow Press, 1998. xxxvi, 231 p.
97-031419   909/.0491497/003   0810834448
Gypsies -- History -- Dictionaries.

DX118 Popular works

DX118.T66 1988
Tomasevic, Nebojsa.
Gypsies of the world/ text, Nebojsa Bato Tomasevic and Rajko Djuric; photographs, Dragoljub Zamurovic. New York, N.Y.: H. Holt, c1988. 288 p.
88-081909   909/.0491497   0805009248
Gypsies. Gypsies -- Pictorial works.

DX145 History — Modern

DX145.A47 1995
Alt, Betty Sowers.
Weeping violins: the Gypsy tragedy in Europe/ Betty Alt and Silvia Folts. Kirksville, Mo.: Thomas Jefferson University Press, 1995. p. cm.
95-025989   940.53/18   0943549310
Gypsies -- Europe. World War, 1939-1945 -- Gypsies -- Europe. World War, 1939-1945 -- Atrocities. Europe -- Ethnic relations.

DX145.L83 1998
Lucassen, Leo, 1959-
Gypsies and other itinerant groups: a socio-historical approach/ Leo Lucassen, Wim Willems, Annemarie Cottaar. New York: St. Martin's Press, 1998. viii, 226 p.
97-038692   305.891/49704   0312212585
Gypsies -- Europe -- History. Travelers -- Europe -- History. Europe -- Ethnic relations.

DX145.W5513 1997
Willems, Wim.
In search of the true gypsy: from Enlightenment to Final Solution/ Wim Willems; translated by Don Bloch. London; F. Cass, 1997. viii, 368 p.
97-022020   305.891/49704   0714646881
Gypsies -- Europe. Europe -- Ethnic relations.

DX201 By region or country — United States

DX201.S98 1988
Sway, Marlene, 1950-
Familiar strangers: gypsy life in America/ Marlene Sway. Urbana: University of Illinois Press, c1988. xi, 155 p.
87-020449   973/.0491497   0252015126
Gypsies -- United States -- Social life and customs.

DX211 By region or country — Europe — Great Britain

DX211.M39 1988
Mayall, David.
Gypsy-travellers in nineteenth-century society/ David Mayall. Cambridge [Cambridgeshire]; Cambridge University Press, 1988. x, 261 p.
87-006634   941/.00491497   0521323975
Gypsies -- Great Britain -- History -- 19th century.

DX223 By region or country — Europe — Hungary

DX223.S75 1997
Stewart, Michael, 1959-
The time of the gypsies/ Michael Stewart. Boulder, Colo.: Westview Press, 1997. xviii, 302 p.
97-009001   305.891/4970439   0813331986
Gypsies -- Hungary. Gypsies -- Hungary -- Social life and customs. Gypsies -- Hungary -- Ethnic identity. Hungary -- Ethnic relations.

DX241 By region or country — Europe — Soviet Union

DX241.C76 1995
Crowe, David.
A history of the gypsies of Eastern Europe and Russia/ David M. Crowe. New York: St. Martin's Press, c1994. xvi, 317 p.
94-031091   947/.00491497   0312086911
Gypsies -- Soviet Union -- History. Gypsies -- Russia -- History. Gypsies -- Europe, Eastern -- History. Russia -- Ethnic relations. Soviet Union -- Ethnic relations. Europe, Eastern -- Ethnic relations.

DX241.K46 2000
Lemon, Alaina, 1965-
Between two fires: Gypsy performance and Romani memory from Pushkin to post-socialism/ Alaina Lemon. Durham, NC: Duke University Press, 2000. p. cm.
99-056926   947/.00491497   0822324563
Gypsies -- Russia (Federation) -- History. Performing arts -- Russia (Federation) Russia (Federation) -- Ethnic relations.

INDEXES

Author Index

Berkhofer, Robert F. D16.B464 1995
Berkley, George E. DS135.A92.V5214 1988
Berkowitz, Alan J. DS721.B45 2000
Berlin, Isaiah. D16.9.B4
Berman, Eric. DT352.8.B47 2000
Berman, Marshall. CB425.B458 1988
Bernal, Martin. DF78.B398 1987
Bernard, Paul P. DB74.B43, DB74.7.P47.B47 1991
Bernhardt, Kathryn. DS755.B47 1992
Bernier, Olivier. DC129.B375 1987
Bernstein, Jeremy. DS473.B45 2000
Bernstein, Richard J. DS143.B55 1996
Berridge, Geoff. D1065.S6.B47 1992
Berry, Mary Elizabeth. DS869.T6.B47 1982, DS897.K857.B47 1994
Berry, Scott. DS785.B53 1995
Berstein, Serge. DC421.B4713 2000
Bertaud, Jean Paul. DC151.B4313 1988
Bertocci, Philip A. DC255.S5.B47
Best, Anthony. D750.B47 1995
Best, Geoffrey Francis Andrew. D299.B484 1982
Bethmann Hollweg, Theobald von. D515.B4665
Bettey, J. H. DA576.B45
Betts, Robert Brenton. DS59.D78.B47 1988
Bevan, Bryan. DA255.B48 1994
Bever, Edward. DT31.B395 1996
Bew, Paul. DA690.B49 1994, DA960.B48 1987, DA990.U46.B3593 1999
Bezucha, Robert J. DC733.B45 1974
Bhana, Surendra. DT2223.E38.B47 1997
Biagini, Eugenio F. DA560.B53 1992
Bialer, Seweryn. D764.B47
Bianco, Lucien. DS775.B513
Bibby, Geoffrey. CB311.B5 1973
Bickerman, E. J. DS121.65.B53 1988
Bickford-Smith, Vivian. DT2405.C3657.B53 1995
Biddle, Nicholas. DF721.B53 1993
Biek, Leo. CC75.B47
Biggs, Chester M. D805.A78.B54 1995
Billinger, Robert D. DB81.B55 1991
Billington, James H. DK32.7.B5
Billows, Richard A. DF235.48.A57.B55 1990
Bills, Scott L. D888.U6.B55 1990
Binford, Lewis Roberts. CC165.B48 2002, CC173.B56 1989
Bingham, Woodbridge. DS749.2.B5
Binski, Paul. DA687.W5.B56 1995
Biondich, Mark. DR1589.R33
Bird, Tom. D805.A2.B57 1992
Bird, William L. D743.25.B57 1998
Birket-Smith, Kaj. CB113.D3.B513
Birley, Anthony Richard. DG295.B57 1997, DG297 .B5 2000
Birmingham, David. DP538.B57 1993
Birnbaum, Pierre. DC36.9.B5713 2001, DS135.F9.B5713 1996, DS146.F8.B5713 1992
Bisbee, Eleanor. DR590.B5
Bishop, Peter. DS786.B53 1989
Bismarck, Otto. DD218.A2 1966
Bisson, T. A. DS777.53.B5
Bitsch, Jorgen. DS798.B513 1963a
Bitterli, Urs. D32.B5713 1989
Black, Eugene Charlton. DS135.E5.B56 1988
Black, Jeremy. D13.B54 1997, D214.B56 1994, D214.B58 1998, D214.B585 1998, DA67.B57 1999, DA435.B53 1991, DA498.B53 1985
Blackbourn, David. DD203.B59 1998, DD204.B5213 1984
Blackwell, Michael. DA589.8.B57 1993
Blackwood, Evelyn. DS632.M4.B53 2000
Blair, Clay. D781.B53 1996
Blake, Robert. DA564.B3.B6 1967, DA576.B53 1985
Blake, Stephen P. DS486.D3.B55 1990
Blakeslee, Spencer. DS146.U6.B55 2000
Blank, Stephen. DK266.5.B57 1994
Blaut, James M. D16.9.B493 2000

Blet, Pierre. D749.B4813 1999
Blickle, Peter. DD182.B613
Blier, Suzanne Preston. DT541.45.S65.B57 1987
Bligh, William. DU870.B56 1988
Blobaum, Robert. DK4385.B57 1995
Bloch, Ernst. DD239.B713 1990
Bloch, Marc Leopold Benjamin. D131.B513 1961, D640.B581713, D761.B562 1968
Bloch, Michael. DA580.B538 1988
Blockson, Charles L. CS21.B55
Bloodworth, Dennis. DS777.55.B55
Bloomfield, David. DA990.U46.B56 1997
Blum, Jerome. D385.B58 1993
Blum, Robert M. DS518.8.B58 1982
Blumenson, Martin. D763.I82.A55
Blumenthal, W. Michael. DS135.G5.B57 1998
Blunden, Caroline. DS721.B56 1998
Blunden, Edmund. D640.B5833 1956
Blyden, Nemata Amelia. DT516.45.W47
Boardman, Eugene Powers. DS759.B6 1972
Boardman, John. DF251.B6 1980
Boas, George. CB353.B6 1997
Boatwright, Mary Taliaferro. DG295.B62 2000, DG295.B63 1987
Bodde, Derk. DS721.B6, DS747.5.B6, DS777.55.B6
Bodian, Miriam. DS135.N5.A5323 1997
Boer, Pim den. DC36.9.B6413 1998
Boffa, Giuseppe. DK267.B585513 1992
Boggs, Marion Alexander. CT274.A43.B63 1980
Bohme, Helmut. DD210.B613
Bois, Thomas. DS51.K7.B613
Bol, Peter Kees. DS747.42.B64 1992
Bold, John. DA690.G83
Bolitho, Harold. DS871.5.B66
Bolyanatz, Alexander H. DU740.42.B65 2000
Bond, Brian. D396.B63 1983
Bond, Helen K. DS122.B66 1998
Bondanella, Peter E. CB245.B64 1987
Bonfield, Lynn A. CT274.W375.B66 1995
Bonham Carter, Violet. DA566.9.B56.A3 1996
Bonnell, Victoria E. DK266.3.B58 1997
Bonner, Arthur. DS371.2.B65 1987
Bonney, Richard. DC123.B66 1988
Bookbinder, Paul. DD240.B63 1996
Boon, James A. DS647.B2.B67 1990
Boorman, Howard L DS778.A1.B6
Boorstin, Daniel J. CB69.B66 1983
Booth, Alan R. DT2714.B66 2000
Borg, Dorothy. DS740.5.U5.B6 1947a, DS784.B65 1964
Borneman, John. DS135.G5.A1263 1995
Borsody, Stephen. D443.B58
Borthwick, Mark. DS518.1.B64 1998
Borton, Hugh. DS835.B6 1970
Borza, Eugene N. DF261.M2.B67 1990
Bose, Sumantra. DS489.84.B67 1994
Bosher, J. F. DC148.B69 1988
Bossuet, Jacques Benigne. D21.B745513 1976
Boswell, James. DC611.C811.B75
Bosworth, A. B. DF234.A773.B67, DF234.B66 1988, DF234.2.B67 1988, DF234.6.B67 1996
Bosworth, Clifford Edmund. DS36.85.I8 no. 5
Bosworth, R. J. B. DG568.5.B66 1983, DG571.16.B67 1998
Boterbloem, Kees. DK511.K157.B68 1999
Botman, Selma. DT107.B58 1991
Bottero, Jean. DS69.5.B6813 1992
Bottigheimer, Karl S. DA910.B67 1982
Bouchard, Constance Brittain. CS587.B68 2001, DC33.2.B59 1998
Boulding, Kenneth Ewart. CB425.B668
Bouloiseau, Marc. DC148.F7 1983 vol. 2
Bourne, Kenneth. DA536.P2.B68 1982, DA550.B68 1970
Bouwsma, William James. CB401.E94 2000
Bovis, H. Eugene. DS109.93.B68 1971
Bowden, Mark. DA3.P53.B69 1991
Bowen, Catherine Drinker. CS71.D77. 1970, CT21.B564

Bowen, H. V. DS471.B68 1991
Bowen, Wayne H. DD120.S7
Bowker, Mike. DK510.764.B69 1997
Bowker, Robert. DS119.7.B698 1996
Bowle, John. CB59.B6 1963
Bowsky, William M. DG535.B6, DG975.S5.B68 1981
Boxer, C. R. DS796.M2.B59
Boyce, David George. DA950.B69 1990, DA959.B69 1988
Boyer, John W. DB854.B67 1995
Boylan, Henry. CT862.B69 1998
Boyle, John Hunter. DS777.53.B65
Boynton, Graham. DT1957.B68 1997
Brackman, Roman. DK268.S8.B69 2001
Bradley, J. F. N. DB205.B68 1971
Bradley, James E. DA480.B72 1990
Bradley, Mark. DS556.8.B732000
Bradley, Omar Nelson. D756.B7
Brady, Ciaran. DA935.B69 1994
Braham, Randolph L. DS135.H9.B74
Bramsted, Ernest Kohn. DD256.5.B674
Brands, H. W. D888.U6.B73 1989
Brandt, Conrad. DS740.5.R8.B7
Brandt, Willy. DD260.8.B7413 1992, DD857.B7.A3
Bratchel, M. E. DG975.L82.B73 1995
Braudel, Fernand. D7.B7513, D973.A2.B7, DC20.5.B7313 1988
Brauer, Erich. DS135.K8.B73 1993
Braun, Dieter. DS341.B7313 1983
Bravman, Bill. DT433.545.T3.B73 1998
Brecher, Michael. D443.B713 1988, D443.B7135 2000
Bregman, Ahron. DS119.76.B74 2000
Breisach, Ernst. D13.B686 1983
Brenan, Gerald. DP43.B66 1976
Brendon, Piers. D727.B654 2000
Brenner, Frederic. DS126.6.A2.B74 1998
Brenner, Michael. DS135.G33.B74 1996
Bretton, Henry L. DD231.S83.B7
Brewer, John. DA510.B67
Brezhneva, Luba. DK275.B73.A3 1995
Brezianu, Andrei. DK509.37.B74 2000
Brian, Denis. CT21.B65 1994
Bridge, F. R. DB86.B74 1990
Briggs, Asa. DA530.B68, DA550.B75 1989, DA560.B84 1970
Briggs, Robin. DC110.B723 1998
Brinton, Crane. DC255.T3.B7
Brison, Karen J. DU740.42.B75 1992
British Bombing Survey Unit. D786.B718 1998
Britnell, R. H. DA425.B8 1997
Brittain, Vera. D640.A2.B75 1999
Britten, Thomas A. D570.8.I6.B75 1997
Brittlebank, Kate. DS470.T6 B75 1997
Brivati, Brian. DA566.9.G3.B75 1996
Brockelmann, Carl. DS38.B72
Brody, J. Kenneth. D727.B655 1999
Broers, Michael. DG618.6.B76 1997
Brogan, D. W. DC335.B75 1966
Bronowski, Jacob. CB478.B73 1978
Bronstone, Adam. D1065.U5.B67 1997
Brook, Timothy. DS753.B76 1998, DS779.32.B76 1992
Brooke, Christopher Nugent Lawrence. DA28.1.B7 1963
Brooke, Z. N. D117.B7 1969
Brooker, Paul. D445.B765 1997b
Brooks, Barbara J. DS849.C6.B67 2000
Brookshire, Jerry H. DA585.A8.B77 1995
Brosius, J. Peter. DS666.A3.B76 1990
Brothwell, Don R. CC75.B73 1970
Broughton, T. Robert S. DG83.5.A1.B73
Brown, Archie. DK288.B76 1996
Brown, Howard G. DC155.B76 1995
Brown, Ian Malcolm. D530.B76 1998
Brown, J. F. DJK50.B77 1988, DJK50.B78 1991, DJK51.B74 2001, DJK51.B75 1994, DR48.5.B698 1992, DR90.B7
Brown, Judith M. DS481.G3.B735 1989
Brown, Keith M. DA800.B76 1992

Author Index

Hickey, Dennis. DT38.7.H5 1993
Hickey, William. CT788.H5.A53 1962
Hicks, George L. D810.C698.H53 1995
Hicks, M. A. DA177.H53 1991
Hicks, Philip Stephen. DA1.H53 1996
Higgins, Trumbull. D568.3.H5
Higgs, Catherine. DT1927.J34.H54 1997
Higgs, Laquita M. DA690.C7.H54 1998
Higham, Charles. DS523.H55 1996
Higham, N. J. DA150.G483.H54 1994, DA152.H53 1995, DA152.H533 1997
Higonnet, Patrice L. R. DC178.H54 1998
Hilberg, Raul. D810.J4.H5 1985b
Hildebrand, Klaus. DD221.H5713 1989
Hilger, Gustav. DD241.R8.H5 1953
Hill, Brian W. DA480.H45 1996
Hill, C. P. DA337.H55 1988b
Hill, Christopher. DA375.H5, DA375.H54 1985, DA380.H47, DA380.H48, DA380.H5, DA380.H52 1964, DA405.H49 1984, DA426.H49 1970b, DA586.H48 1991
Hill, George Francis. DF209.5.H65 1951
Hill, Jacqueline R. DA995.D75.H55 1997
Hill, James Michael. DA784.3.M33.H55 1993
Hill, Roland. D15.A25.H487 2000
Hillenbrand, Carole. DS38.6.H55 2000
Hillgarth, J. N. DP171.5.H54 2000
Hillstrom, Kevin. DS557.73.H55 1998
Hillyar, Anna. DK219.3.H55 2000
Hilsman, Roger. DS79.72.H56 1992
Himmelfarb, Gertrude. D15.A25.H5 1952a, DA533.H55
Hinde, Wendy. DA950.3.H54 1992
Hindle, Steve. DA315.H46 2000
Hinds, Lynn Boyd. D1053.H525 1991
Hinton, William. DS777.55.H553
Hirabayashi, Lane Ryo. D769.8.A6.H58 1999
Hiro, Dilip. DS43.H57 1996
Hirsch, John L. DT516.826.H57 2001
Hirst, Derek. DA390.H57 1986
Hirst, Francis Wrigley. D651.G5.H5 1968
Hiscocks, Richard. DD259.7.A3.H5
Historical Evaluation and Research Organization. DS798.H57 1970
Hitchcock, Michael. DS647.S952.B554 1996
Hitchcock, William I. DC404.H53 1998
Hitchins, Keith. DB739.H57, DR241.H575 1996, DR250.H58 1994
Hitler, Adolf. DD247.H5.A33 1940, DD247.H5.A57513 1990, DD247.H5.A664553, DD247.H5.A685 1953a
Hitti, Philip Khuri. DS37.7.H58 1970
Hlihor, Constantin. D766.4.H55 2000
Hoare, James. DS795.3.H63 2000, DS916.H62 1999
Hobart, Angela. DS647.B2.H58 1996
Hobbs, Joseph J. DT72.B4.H6 1989
Hobsbawm, E. J. D16.8.H626 1997b, D299.H6 1969, D358.H56 1975b, D359.7.H63 1987, D421.H582 1994
Hochman, Jiri. DK267.H596 1984
Hochschild, Adam. DK267.H597 1994, DT655.H63 1998
Hockings, Paul. DS432.B25.H62 1999
Hodel-Hoenes, Sigrid. DT73.T3.H5813 2000
Hodge, A. Trevor. DC801.M37.H63 1999
Hodges, Gabrielle Ashford. DP264.F7 H63 2002
Hodges, Richard. DA152.H59 1989
Hodgkin, Thomas. DA30.P762 vol. 1
Hoensch, Jorg K. DB945.H5613 1988
Hoffman, Alice M. D811.H648 1990
Hoffman, Daniel. D790.H64 2000
Hoffman, Robert Louis. DC354.H63
Hoffmann, Peter. DD247.S342.H6413 1995, DD256.3.H59513 1988
Hogg, Ian V. D25.A2.H64 1995
Hohenberg, John. DS126.5.H58 1998
Hohne, Heinz. DD253.6.H613 1970
Hoidal, Oddvar K. DL529.Q5.H6513 1989
Hoisington, William A. DT324.H54 1984
Holbl, Gunther. DT92.H6513 2001

Holbrooke, Richard C. DR1313.7.D58.H65 1998
Holcombe, Charles. DS514.H65 2001
Holian, Timothy J. D769.8.F7.G47 1996
Hollan, Douglas Wood. DS632.T7.H65 1994
Holland, W. L. DS518.1.H6
Hollos, Marida. DT515.45.I35.H65 1989
Holloway, R. Ross. DG63.H57 1994
Holmberg, David H. DS493.9.T35.H65 1989
Holmes, Douglas R. D2009.H65 2000
Holmes, Linda Goetz. D805.J3 H58 2001
Holmes, Marjorie. CT275.H645515.A38
Holt, Frank Lee. DS374.B28.H66 1999
Holt, Mack P. DC111.3.H65 1995
Holt, P. M. DS63.H62 1966a
Holum, Kenneth G. DG322.H64 1982
Holy, Ladislav. DB2238.7.H65 1996, DT155.2.B47.H65 1991
Homans, Margaret. DA533.H74 1998
Honda, Katsuichi. DS777.5316.N36 H6613 1999
Hondros, John Louis. D802.G8.H66 1983
Honig, Emily. DS796.S29.H66 1992
Hook, J. N. CS2487.H66 1982
Hooker, J. T. DF220.H65
Hoover, Herbert. D637.H6 1959, D643.A7.H7, D743.9.H68
Hope, W. H. St. John (William Henry St. John). CR1612.H7 1953
Hopkins, James K. DP269.47.B7.H66 1998
Hopkinson, Michael. DA963.H63 1988
Hoppen, K. Theodore. DA560.H58 1998, DA950.H68 1984
Horgan, John. DA965.R63.H67 1997
Horn, David Bayne. DA47.H6
Hornblower, Simon. DF227.H67 1983, DF229.T6.H65 1991, DF229.T6.H67 1987
Horne, Alistair. D545.V3.H6, DA566.9.M33.H6 1989
Horner, Helmut. D805.A2.H67 1991
Horrox, Rosemary. DA260.H65 1989
Horsley, Richard A. DS110.G2.H619 1996
Horton, Mark. DT429.5.S94
Hosking, Geoffrey A. DK40.H66 2001, DK49.H68 1997, DK266 .H58 1993, DK286.5.H67 1992, DK288.H67 1990
Hoskins, W. G. DA600.H6 1970
Hostler, Charles Warren. DS26.H6 1993
Hoston, Germaine A. DS775.7.H67 1994
Hottinger, Arnold. DS62.H8233
Hou, Fu-wu. DS777.57.H6
Hough, Jerry F. DK266.H59 1988, DK274.H68
Hough, Richard Alexander. D581.H56 1983, D756.5.B7.H67 1989, DA89.1.M59.H68
Houghton, Walter Edwards. DA533.H85
Hourani, Albert Habib. DS37.7.H67 1991
Housley, Norman. D202.H68 1992
Houston, Christopher. DS59.K86.H68 2001
Hovell, Mark. DA559.7.H7 1967
Howard, Douglas A. DR441.H69 2001
Howard, Michael Eliot. D431.H68 1991
Howe, Stephen. DA18.H714 1993, DA963.H69 2000
Howell, Margaret. DA228.E44.H69 1998
Howland, Douglas. DS735.C5.H68 1996
Howorth, Henry H. DS19.H862
Hoyt, Edwin Palmer. D756.3.H68 1988, DS774.H62 1989
Hoyt, Robert S. CB351.H6 1966
Hrushevskyi, Mykhailo. DK508.5.H683 1970
Hsiao, Kung-chuan. DS763.K3.H75
Hsu, Cho-yun. DS747.H79 1988
Hsu, Francis L. K. DS721.H685 1970, DS721.H687, DS721.H69
Hsueh, Chun-tu. DS778.H85.H7
Hu, Chang-tu. DS706.H8
Hu, David Y. DS734.7.H824 1992
Huber, Thomas M. DS894.79.Y349.C4637
Hucker, Charles O. DS721.H724, DS753.H829, DS753.H83
Huddleston, Sisley. DC397.H83
Hudson, Benjamin T. DA777.H83 1994

Hudson, Geoffrey Francis. DS740.5.R8.H78
Hudson, John. DA195.H83 1994
Hudson, Michael C. DS62.4.H82
Huffman, Joseph P. DA47.2.H84 2000
Hughes, Christopher. DQ17.H8 1975
Hughes, H. Stuart. D15.H88.A3 1990, D424.H83 1987, DC365.H8, DG577.5.H83 1979
Hughes, Howard. CT275.H6678.A3
Hughes, Lindsey. DK131.H84 1998
Hughes, Lora Wood. CT275.M668.A3
Hughes, Michael. DD175.H84 1992
Hughes-Warrington, Marnie. D13.H75 2000
Huizinga, Johan. D7.H823, DC33.2.H83 1985
Hume, David. DA30.H92 1975
Hume, John. DA990.U46.H854 1996
Huneidi, Sahar. DA47.9.I77.H86 2001
Hunt, Andrew E. DS559.62.U6.H86 1999
Hunt, Lynn Avery. DC148.H86 1992, DC158.8.H86 1984, DC195.T8.H86
Hunt, Michael H. DS775.8.H86 1996
Hunter Blair, Peter. DA135.B59, DA152.2.H86 1977
Hunter, Neale. DS777.55.H83
Hunter, Shireen. DK509.H88 1994, DK859.5.H86 1996
Huot, Marie Claire. DS779.23.H8613 2000
Hupchick, Dennis P. DR36.H87 2002
Hurewitz, J. C. DS42.H87 1975
Hurley, Mark J. DA990.U46.H87 1990
Hurwit, Jeffrey M. DF287.A2.H87 1999
Hussain, J. DS382.H8 1997
Hussainmiya, B. A. DS650.6.H87 1995
Hussey, Harry. DS763.T8.H8, DS778.H89.A3
Hutchings, Raymond. DR927.H88 1996
Hutchings, Robert L. D1065.U5.H88 1997
Hutchinson, John. DA925.H88 1987
Hutchison, Kevin Don. DS79.72.H88 1995
Hutton, Patrick H. D13.H87 1993
Hutton, Ronald. DA320.H87 1994, DA446.H93 1989
Huxley, Aldous. DC123.9.L5.H8 1959
Huxley, Julian. CB425.H86 1962
Hviding, Edvard. DU850.H95 1996
Hyman, Meryl. DS143.H96 1998
Hyman, Paula. DS135.F8.H96 1998, DS148.H93 1995
Hynes, Samuel Lynn. D523.H96 1991
Hyppolite, Jean. D16.8.H913 1996
Hyun, Peter. DU624.7.K67.H983 1995
Iatrides, John O. DF849.I2
Ibn Khaldun. D16.7.I24, D16.7.I2413 1969
Idinopulos, Thomas A. DS125.I35 1998
Ienaga, Saburo. DS834.9.I35
Igarashi, Yoshikuni. DS822.5.I33 2000
Iggers, Georg G. D13.2.I3413 1997, DD86.I34 1983
Ikenberry, G. John. D363.I46 2001
Ilan, Amitzur. DS126.92.I425 1996
Imamura, Keiji. DS855.I45 1996
Imperato, Pascal James. DT434.R75.I47 1998
Inalcik, Halil. DR486.I5 1973b
Inden, Ronald B. DS435.8.I47 1990
Inder Singh, Anita. DS480.82.I44 1987
Ingraham, Holly. CS2305.I54 1996
Ingram, Edward. DS62.2.G7.I56 1992
Ingrao, Charles W. DB36.3.H3.I54 1994, DD801.H57.I54 1987
Inkeles, Alex. DK276.I5
Innes, Matthew. DD801.R76.I56 2000
Inoguchi, Rikihei. D792.J3.I513 1958
Inoguchi, Takashi. D860.I55 2001
Insoll, Timothy. DS36.855.I47 1999
International Military Tribunal. D804 G42.I55
Ioanid, Radu. DS135.R7.I6513 2000
Ioannides, Christos P. DS54.95.N67I55 1991
Ionescu, Ghita. DR267.I65
Iorga, Nicolae. DR217.I77 1970
Ireson, Carol J. DS555.45.M5.I74 1996
Iriye, Akira. DS518.8.I73
Irschick, Eugene F. DS484.7.I77 1994
Irvine, Jill A. DR1302.I78 1993

Author Index

Yankah, Kwesi. DT510.43.A53.Y35 1995
Yapp, Malcolm. DS62.4.Y35 1987
Yates, Keith. D582.J8.Y38 2000
Yazbak, Mahmud. DS110.H28.Y39 1998
Yegul, Fikret K. DG97.Y45 1992
Yeh, Wen-hsin. DS793.C3.Y44 1996
Yeltsin, Boris Nikolayevich. DK290.3.Y45
Yerushalmi, Yosef Hayim. DS102.C56 no. 1,
  DS115.5.Y47 1982
Yetiv, Steven A. DS79.72.Y48 1997
Yi, Mu. DS779.32.Y5 1989
Yick, Joseph K. S. DS777.542.Y53 1995
Yishai, Yael. DS126.5.I7 1987
Yoder, John Charles. DT650.K33.Y63 1992
Yoneyama, Lisa. D767.25.H6.Y66 1999
Yorke, Barbara. DA152.Y673 1995
Yorke, James. DA687.L22
Yorke, Valerie. DS63.2.S95.Y67 1988
Yoshimi, Yoshiaki. D810.C698.Y6713 2000
Yost, Charles Woodruff. D443.Y63
Young, Arthur N. DS777.53.Y62
Young, C. Walter. DS783.7.Y6, DS783.7.Y65
  vol. 1
Young, Desmond. DD247.R57.Y68 1951
Young, Donald J. D767.4.Y69 1992
Young, Ernest P. DS777.2.Y68 1977
Young, Hugo. DA591.T47 Y68 1989
Young, James Edward. D810.J4.Y58 1988
Young, John W. D843.Y68 1996, D1053.Y68
  1991, DC404.Y68 1990
Young, Louise. DS783.7.Y67 1998

Young, Michael B. DA391.Y68 2000
Young, Robert J. D742.F7.Y68 1996,
  DC373.B35.Y68 1991
Yu, Frederick T. C. DS777.57.Y78
Yu, Maochun. D810.S7.Y82 1996
Zagorin, Perez. D210.Z33 1982, DA395.Z3
  1970
Zahedi, Dariush. DS318.825.Z34 2000
Zaionchkovskii, Petr Andreevich. DK221.Z313
Zakaria, Rafiq. DS430.Z35 1995
Zamir, Meir. DS86.Z37 1997
Zamoyski, Adam. DK4140.Z36 1988
Zanger, Abby E. DC128.5.Z36 1997
Zanker, Paul. DG70.P7.Z3613 1998
Zaprudnik, Jan. DK507.37.Z37 1998,
  DK507.54.Z37 1993
Zaretsky, Robert. DC611.G217.Z37 1995
Zaslavskaia, T. I. DK288.Z37 1990
Zastoupil, Lynn. DS463.Z37 1994
Zavattini, Cesare. DG975.L95.Z3813 1997
Zborowski, Mark. DS112.Z37
Zeldin, Theodore. DC330.Z44
Zeleza, Tiyambe. DT19.8.Z44 1997
Zelikow, Philip. DD290.29.Z45 1995
Zelizer, Barbie. D804.32.Z45 1998
Zell, Hans M. DT19.8.Z45 1997
Zemtsov, Ilya. DK275.C45.Z46 1989
Zenkovsky, Serge A. DK34.T8.Z4
Zhai, Qiang. DS777.8.Z388 2000
Zhai, Zhenhua. DS778.Z47.A3 1993
Zhan, Jun. DS740.5.T28 Z46 1993

Zhang, Liang. DS779.32.L54 2001
Zhang, Longxi. DS721.Z48 1999
Zhang, Shu Guang. DS919.5.Z45 1995
Zhang, Yongjin. DS775.8.Z43 1991,
  DS777.8.Z39 1998
Zhao, Suisheng. DS515.Z45 1997
Zheng, Yi. DS793.K6 C4413 1996
Zhou, Xun. DS135.C5.R69 2001
Zhu, Xiao Di. DS778.7.Z48 1998
Zieger, Robert H. D570.A1.Z54 2000
Ziegler, Charles E. DS518.7.Z53 1993
Ziegler, Philip. D760.8.L7.Z54 1995,
  DA89.1.M59 Z54
Zielonka, Jan. D2009.Z54 1998
Zimmerman, David. D810.S2.Z56 1996
Zimmermann, T. C. Price. DG465.7.G56.Z56
  1995
Zinner, Paul E. DB215.Z55 1975, DB956.Z5
Zipperstein, Steven J. DS151.G5.Z56 1993
Ziring, Lawrence. DS61.Z58 1992,
  DS384.Z572 1997
Zmora, Hillay. DD801.F566.Z57 1997
Zola, Emile. DC354.8.Z6513 1996
Zook, Melinda S. DA435.Z66 1999
Zubok, V. M. DK267.Z78 1996
Zuccotti, Susan. DS135.F83.Z83 1993,
  DS135.I8.Z87 2000
Zuker-Bujanowska, Liliana. D810.J4.Z8413
Zurick, David. DS485.H6.Z87 1999
Zuroff, Efraim. D804.6.Z87 2000

Americans in eastern Asia / DS518.8.D55 1941

America's failure in China, 1941-50 / DS777.53.T866

America's first crusade / D643.A7.H7

America's Great War: World War I and the American experience / D570.A1.Z54 2000

America's invisible gulag: a biography of German American internment & exclusion in World War II: memory and history / D805.U5.F69 2000

America's new allies: Poland, Hungary, and the Czech Republic in NATO / DAW1051.A47 1999

America's secret war against Bolshevism: U.S. intervention in the Russian Civil War, 1917-1920 / DK265.42.U5.F64 1995

Amilcar Cabral's revolutionary theory and practice: a critical guide / DT613.76.C3.C54 1991

Ammianus Marcellinus and the representation of historical reality / DG316.B37 1998

Among the Afghans / DS371.2.B65 1987

Ana Pauker: the rise and fall of a Jewish Communist / DR267.5.P38

Anahulu: the anthropology of history in the Kingdom of Hawaii / DU624.65.K56 1992

Analytical archaeology / CC75.C535 1978

Anatomy of a dictatorship: inside the GDR, 1949-1989 / DD283.F85 1995

Anatomy of a little war: a diplomatic and military history of the Gundovald affair (568-586), The / DC65.B33 1994

Anatomy of a miracle: the end of apartheid and the birth of the new South Africa / DT1967.W35 1997

Anatomy of a naval disaster: the 1746 French naval expedition to North America / DC52.P75 1995

Anatomy of architecture: ontology and metaphor in Batammaliba architectural expression, The / DT541.45.S65.B57 1987

Anatomy of historical knowledge, The / D16.9.M26

Anatomy of the new Poland: post-Communist politics in its first phase, The / DK4449.M55 1994

Ancestor masks and aristocratic power in Roman culture / DG103.F56 1996

Ancestral connections: art and an aboriginal system of knowledge / DU125.M8.M65 1991

Ancestral landscape: time, space, and community in late Shang China, ca. 1200-1045 B.C., The / DS744.K43 2000

Ancestral trails: the complete guide to British genealogy and family history / CS414.H47 1997

Ancestry's red book: American state, county, and town sources / CS49.A55 1989

Ancien Regime: a history of France, 1610-1774, The / DC121.L4713 1996

Ancien regime, The / DC131.B4 1967

Ancient African civilizations: Kush and Axum / DT159.6.N83.A53 1998

Ancient Chamorro society / DU645.C86 1992

Ancient Crete; a social history from early times until the Roman occupation / DF261.C8.W49

Ancient Cyprus, its art and archaeology / DS54.3.C25

Ancient Egypt: the great discoveries: a year-by-year chronicle / DT60.R397 2000

Ancient Greece: a political, social, and cultural history / DF77.A595 1999

Ancient Greek France / DC801.M37.H63 1999

Ancient history / D59.G6878

Ancient history: evidence and models / DE8.F55 1986

Ancient marbles to American shores: classical archaeology in the United States / DE60.D97 1998

Ancient Mesopotamia: humankind's long journey into civilization / DS70.7.C47 1993

Ancient Mesopotamia: portrait of a dead civilization / DS69.5.O6 1977

Ancient Mesopotamian city, The / DS69.5.V36 1997

Ancient Near East in pictures relating to the Old Testament, The / DS56.P7

Ancient Polynesian society / DU510.G58 1970

Ancient records of Assyria and Babylonia / DS68.L8 1968

Ancient Rome chronology, 264-27 B.C., An / DG241.2.M38 1997

Ancient Sichuan: treasures from a lost civilization / DS793.S8 A528 2001

Ancient Tahitian society / DU870.O43

Ancient world: a beginning, The / D59.G6 1979

Ancient youth: the ambiguity of youth and the absence of adolescence in Greco-Roman society / DE61.Y68.K55 1991

And justice for all: an oral history of the Japanese American detention camps / D769.8.A6.A67 1984

And the witnesses were silent: the Confessing Church and the persecution of the Jews / DS146.G4.G4813 2000

And yet, I am here! / DS135.P63.N46 1999

Aneurin Bevan, a biography / DA585.B38.F62

Angevin legacy and the Hundred Years War, 1250-1340, The / DC96.V34 1990

Angkor Wat: time, space, and kingship / DS554.98.A5.M36 1996

Anglo-American policy towards the free French / D752.M34 1995

Anglo-Dutch moment: essays on the Glorious Revolution and its world impact, The / DA452.A54 1991

Anglo-French naval rivalry, 1840-1870 / DA88.H36 1993

Anglo-French relations and strategy on the Western Front 1914-18 / D544.P49 1996

Anglo-Irish politics in the age of Grattan and Pitt / DA948.4.O25 1987

Anglo-Irish tradition, The / DA947.B4 1976

Anglo-Norman Durham: 1093-1193 / DA690.D96.A54 1994

Anglo-Saxon achievement: archaeology & the beginnings of English society, The / DA152.H59 1989

Anglo-Saxon chronicle: a collaborative edition, The / DA150.A6 1983b

Anglo-Saxon history: basic readings / DA152.A7267 2000

Anglo-Saxon writs / CD105.H3

Anioma: a social history of the Western Igbo people / DT474.6.I35.O33 1994

Annals & memoirs of the court of Peking (from the 16th to the 20th century) / DS735.B25 1914a

Annals of St-Bertin, The / DC70.A2.A713 1991

Anne Frank: reflections on her life and legacy / DS135.N6.F73 2000

Annexation of Bosnia, 1908-1909, The / D465.S33 1970

Annotated index of medieval women, An / CT3220.A56 1992

Another country: German intellectuals, unification, and national identity / DD256.6.M85 2000

Another reason: science and the imagination of modern India / DS463.P67 1999

Anthony Eden / DA566.9.E28.R48 1987

Anthony Eden: a life and reputation / DA566.9.E28.D88 1997

Anthropological archaeology / CC72.4.G53 1984

Anthropologist looks at history, An / CB19.K686 1963

Anthropology of ancient Greece, The / DF78.G5313

Anticolonialism in British politics: the left and the end of Empire, 1918-1964 / DA18.H714 1993

Anti-fascism in Britain / DA566.7.C64 1999

Antigonos the One-eyed and the creation of the Hellenistic state / DF235.48.A57.B55 1990

Antisemitism: the longest hatred / DS145.W542 1991

Antisemitism in America / DS146.U6.D555 1994

Anti-semitism in France: a political history from Leon Blum to the present / DS146.F8.B5713 1992

Anti-semitism in Germany: the post-Nazi epoch since 1945 / DS146.G4.B4713 1997

Antler on the sea: the Yup'ik and Chukchi of the Russian Far East / DK759.C45

Antonines: the Roman empire in transition, The / DG292.G73 1994

Anvil of civilization, The / CB311.C85

Anyang / DS796.A55.L5

Anzac illusion: Anglo-Australian relations during World War I, The / D547.A8.A53 1993

Anzio: the gamble that failed / D763.I82.A55

Apartheid state in crisis: political transformation in South Africa, 1975-1990, The / DT1963.P75 1991

Apartheid unravels / DT1757.A66 1991

Apartheid's contras: an inquiry into the roots of war in Angola and Mozambique / DT1436.M56 1994

Apartheid's rebels: inside South Africa's hidden war / DT779.952.D38 1987

Aphrodite at mid-century; growing up Catholic and female in post-war America / CT275.R62.A32

Apocalypse then: American intellectuals and the Vietnam War, 1954-1975 / DS558.T66 1998

Apollodoros, the son of Pasion / DF233.8.A66.T74 1992

Apotheosis of Captain Cook: European mythmaking in the Pacific, The / DU626.O28 1992

Appeasement; a study in political decline, 1933-1939 / DA578.R68

Appeasers, The / DA47.2.G5 1963a

Application of quantitative methods in archaeology, The / CC75.H44

Approach to archaeology / CC75.P5

Approaches to social archaeology / CC72.4.R46 1984

Approaches to the history of Spain / DP66.V513

Arab awakening: the story of the Arab national movement, The / DS63.6.A46 1981

Arab conquest of Spain, 710-797, The / DP99.C58 1989

Cambridge in the age of the Enlightenment: science, religion, and politics from the Restoration to the French Revolution / DA690.C2.G37 1989

Cambridge medieval history, The / D117.C32

Cameroon: dependence and independence / DT564.D45 1989

Camp David: peacemaking and politics / DS128.183.Q36 1986

Canaanites / DS121.4.T83 1998

Canada and the Far East, 1940-1953 / DS518.9.C3.A7

Canada and the Far East--1940 / DS518.9.C3.L6 1973

Canary Islands after the conquest: the making of a colonial society in the early sixteenth century, The / DP302.C42.F47 1982

Cane fires: the anti-Japanese movement in Hawaii, 1865-1945 / DU624.7.J3.O38 1991

Capetian kings of France; monarchy & nation, 987-1328, The / DC82.F313

Capital cities at war: Paris, London, Berlin, 1914-1919 / D523.W578 1996

Capital of the tycoon: a narrative of a three years' residence in Japan, The / DS809.A35 1969

Captain Bligh: the man and his mutinies / DA87.1.B6.K46 1989

Captive mind, The / DK411.M5

Captive of the Rising Sun: the POW memoirs of rear admiral Donald T. Giles, USN / D805.J3.G54 1994

Captive spirits: prisoners of the Cultural Revolution / DS778.7.Y4313 1997

Captivity, flight, and survival in World War II / D805.L49 2000

Carausius and Allectus: the British usurpers / DA145.C37 1995

Cardinal Richelieu and the making of France / DC123.9.R5.L48 2000

Cardinal Wolsey: church, state, and art / DA334.W8.C29 1991

Carl Becker: a biographical study in American intellectual history / D15.B33.W5

Carlo Cattaneo and the politics of the Risorgimento, 1820-1860 / DG552.8.C25.L68

Carnival in Romans / DC801.R75.L4713

Carolingian renewal: sources and heritage / DC70.B84 1991

Carolingians: a family who forged Europe, The / DC70.R5313 1993

Carthage: a mosaic of ancient Tunisia / DT269.C32.C37 1987

Carthage: uncovering the mysteries and splendors of ancient Tunisia / DT269.C35 S67 1990

Carving blocs: communal ideology in early twentieth-century Bengal / DS422.C64.D39 1999

Casablanca connection: French colonial policy, 1936-1943, The / DT324.H54 1984

Casanova, a new perspective / D285.8.C4.C448 1988

Case of General Yamashita, The / D804.J33.Y36

Cassowary's revenge: the life and death of masculinity in a New Guinea society, The / DU740.42.T84 1997

Caste, nationalism, and communism in South India: Malabar, 1900-1948 / DS485.K48.M46 1994

Castes of mind: colonialism and the making of modern India / DS422.C3 D58 2001

Castlereagh / DA522.L8.D47 1976

Catalan nationalism: past and present / DP302.C67.B3513 1995

Catherine De' Medici / DC119.8.K64 1998

Catherine de Medicis / DC119.8.H44 1959

Catherine of Aragon / DA333.A6.M3 1942

Catherine the Great: a short history / DK171.D44 1990

Catherine the Great: life and legend / DK170.A58 1989

Catholic emancipation: a shake to men's minds / DA950.3.H54 1992

Catholicism in a Protestant kingdom: a study of the Irish Ancien Regime / DA948.A2.L38 1993

Catholicism, political culture, and the countryside: a social history of the Nazi Party in south Germany / DD801.B64.H3813 1998

Cattle, capitalism, and class: Ilparakuyo Maasai transformations / DT443.3.B38.R54 1992

Causes and consequences of World War II / D753.D56

Causes of the English Civil War, The / DA415.R78 1990

Cautious patriotism: the American churches & the Second World War, A / D744.5.U6.S58 1997

Cavalier Parliament and the reconstruction of the Old Regime, 1661-1667, The / DA445.S42 1989

Cavaliers & roundheads: the English Civil War, 1642-1649 / DA415.H53 1993

Cavour / DG552.8.C3.M17 1985

Cavour and Garibaldi, 1860:a study in political conflict / DG554.M3 1985

CB: a life of Sir Henry Campbell-Bannerman / DA565.C15.W54 1974

Celt and Roman: the Celts of Italy / DG225.C44.E44 1998

Celtic baby names: traditional names from Ireland, Scotland, Wales, Brittany, Cornwall & the Isle of Man / CS2377.S48 1997

Celtic Britain / DA140.L33 1979b

Celtic consciousness, The / CB206.C44 1982

Celtic Leinster: towards an historical geography of early Irish civilization, A.D. 500-1600 / DA990.L5.S63 1982

Celtic world, The / D70.C38 1995

Celts and the classical world / D70.R36 1987

Celts, The / D70.C47

Cemeteries of the U.S.: a guide to contact information for U.S. cemeteries and their records / CS44.C46

Censorship in Ireland, 1939-1945: neutrality, politics, and society / D799.I73.O37 1996

Center: a guide to genealogical research in the national capital area, The / CS44.S33 1996

Central Asia and the Caucasus after the Soviet Union: domestic and international dynamics / DK859.5.C454 1994

Central Asia since independence / DK859.5.H86 1996

Central Asia's new states: independence, foreign policy, and regional security / DK859.5.O43 1996

Central authority and local autonomy in the formation of early modern Japan: the case of Kaga domain / DS894.59.I539.K343 1993

Central Europe profiled: essential facts on society, business, and politics in central Europe / DAW1009.C46 2000

Centre and province in the People's Republic of China: Sichuan and Guizhou, 1955-1965 / DS793.S8 G66 1986

Centuries of darkness: a challenge to the conventional chronology of Old World archaeology / CC165.J35 1993

Century of ambivalence: the Jews of Russia and the Soviet Union, 1881 to the present, A / DS135.R9.G444 1988

Century of revolution, 1603-1714, The / DA375.H5

Century of total war, The / D431.A7

Century's journey: how the great powers shape the world, A / D443.C34 1999

Ceramic ethnoarchaeology / CC79.5.P6.C48 1991

Cercle social, the Girondins, and the French Revolution, The / DC158.8.K38 1985

Certain idea of France: French security policy and the Gaullist legacy, A / DC420.G67 1993

Chad: a nation in search of its future / DT546.48.A97 1998

Chaim Weizmann: the making of a statesman / DS125.3.W45.R44 1993

Challenge of coexistence, The / D843.G26

Challenging the mandate of Heaven: social protest and state power in China / DS761.2.P47 2002

Challenging untouchability: Dalit initiative and experience from Karnataka / DS422.C3 C465 1998

Chamberlain and the lost peace / DA585.C5.C48 1990

Chamberlain, Germany and Japan, 1933-4 / DA565.C4.B45 1996

Chambers dictionary of political biography / D108.C44 1991

Chancellor as courtier: Bernhard von Bulow and the governance of Germany, 1900-1909, The / DD231.B8.L47 1990

Chang Tso-lin in northeast China, 1911-1928: China, Japan, and the Manchurian idea / DS778.C5.M3

Change and continuity in seventeenth-century England / DA380.H47

Change in dynasties: loyalism in thirteenth-century China, A / DS751.J38 1991

Change in the European balance of power, 1938-1939: the path to ruin, The / D727.M87 1984

Changing anatomy of Britain, The / DA589.7.S25 1982

Changing face of empire: Charles V, Philip II, and Habsburg authority, 1551-1559, The / DD179.R62 1988

Changing geography of China, The / DS706.7.L44 1993

Changing identities in early modern France / DC33.3.C45 1997

Changing India: bourgeois revolution on the subcontinent / DS463.S73 1993

Changing past: trends in South African historical writing, The / DT1776.S63 1989

Changing patterns of the Middle East, The / DS63.R6413 1961

Changing Scottish landscape, 1500-1800, The / DA850.W48 1991

Changing Turkey: the challenge to Europe and the United States, A / DR576.K73 2000

Columbia companion to British history, The / DA34.H64 1997

Columbia dictionary of European political history since 1914, The / D424.C65 1992

Columbia dictionary of political biography, The / D108.C65 1991

Columbia guide to modern Chinese history, The / DS755.S635 2000

Columbia guide to the Holocaust, The / D804.3.N54 2000

Columbia history of Eastern Europe in the twentieth century, The / DJK42.C65 1991

Combined fleet decoded: the secret history of American intelligence and the Japanese Navy in World War II / D810.C88.P73 1995

Combined methods in Indology and other writings / DS425.K576 2002

Comfort women: Japan's brutal regime of enforced prostitution in the Second World War, The / D810.C698.H53 1995

Comfort women: sexual slavery in the Japanese military during World War II / D810.C698.Y6713 2000

Coming of the First World War, The / D511.C623 1988

Coming of the First World War; a study in the European balance, 1878-1914, The / D397.M28

Coming of the Greeks: Indo-European conquests in the Aegean and the Near East, The / DF220.D73 1988

Coming to terms with the Soviet regime: the "Changing signposts" movement among Russian emigres in the early 1920s / DK35.5.H37 1994

Command decisions / D743.C555 2000

Command on the western front: the military career of Sir Henry Rawlinson, 1914-18 / D530.P75 1991

Commentary on Thucydides, A / DF229.T6.H65 1991

Commissioner Lin and the Opium War / DS757.5.C45

Commitment to the dead: one woman's journey toward understanding / DS135.G5.W338 1987

Committee: political assassination in Northern Ireland, The / DA990.U46.M458 1998

Commodore Vanderbilt; an epic of the steam age / CT275.V23.L3

Common destiny: dictatorship, foreign policy, and war in Fascist Italy and Nazi Germany / DG571.K63 2000

Common roots of Europe, The / D21.5.G4713 1996

Commonwealth and independence in post-Soviet Eurasia / DK293.C656 1998

Commonwealth to protectorate / DA425.W59 1982

Communism in Rumania, 1944-1962 / DR267.I65

Communist China 1955-1959; policy documents with analysis / DS777.55.C642

Communist China and Asia; challenge to American policy / DS777.55.B3

Communist China today; domestic and foreign policies / DS777.55.T25

Communist China yearbook / DS777.55.C645

Communist China: the early years, 1949-55 / DS777.55.B322

Communist movement in China; an essay written in 1924, The / DS777.44.C5 1966

Communist road to power in Vietnam, The / DS556.8.D83 1996

Communist strategy and tactics in Czechoslovakia, 1918-48 / DB215.Z55 1975

Communist subversion of Czechoslovakia, 1938-1948; the failure of coexistence, The / DB215.5.K68

Communities and conflict in early modern Colmar, 1575-1730 / DC801.C657.W35 1995

Communities of violence: persecution of minorities in the Middle Ages / D164.N57 1996

Community and consensus in Islam: Muslim representation in colonial India, 1860-1947 / DS479.S52 1989

Community and society in Roman Italy / DG231.D95 1991

Community conflicts and the state in India / DS480.853.C67 1998

Community transformed: the manor and liberty of Havering, 1500-1620, A / DA685.H28.M39 1991

Companion encyclopedia of archaeology / CC70.C59 1999

Companion to Chinese history / DS705.O63 1987

Companion to historiography / D13.C626 1997

Companion to Hungarian studies, A / DB906.M3413 1999

Companion to Irish history, 1603-1921: from the submission of Tyrone to partition / DA912.N485 1991

Complete manual of field archaeology: tools and techniques of field work for archaeologists, A / CC76.J68

Complete temples of ancient Egypt, The / DT68.8.W55 2000

Complete wartime correspondence of Tsar Nicholas II and the Empress Alexandra: April 1914-March 1917, The / DK258.N458 1999

Complete works of Tacitus: The annals. The history. The life of Cnaeus Julius Agricola. Germany and its tribes. A dialogue on oratory, The / DG207.T2.C45

Complete writings: The Peloponnesian war / DF229.T5.C7 1951

Complexion of race: categories of difference in eighteenth-century British culture, The / DA125.A1.W448 2000

Comprehending and mastering African conflicts: the search for sustainable peace and good governance / DT353.C65 1999

Comrade Chiang Ching / DS778.C5374.W57

Comrades: tales of a brigadista in the Spanish Civil War / DP269.47.A46.F58 1998

Concert of Europe, The / D388.A55

Concise history of Bulgaria, A / DR67.C72 1997

Concise history of Greece, A / DF802.C57 2002

Concise history of Hungary, A / DB925.1.M6413 2001

Concise history of Portugal, A / DP538.B57 1993

Concise history of Spain, A / DP66.K3 1973b

Concise history of the Middle East, A / DS62.G64 1983

Concise history of the Russian Revolution, A / DK265 .P4742 1995

Condition of man, The / CB53.M8 1973

Condition of postmodernity: an enquiry into the origins of cultural change, The / CB428.H38 1989

Conduct unbecoming: the story of the murder of Canadian prisoners of war in Normandy / D804.G4.M3225 1998

Conferences at Malta and Yalta, 1945, The / D734.A1.U57 1976

Conflict and conciliation in Ireland, 1890-1910: Parnellites and radical agrarians / DA960.B48 1987

Conflict and tension in the Far East: key documents, 1894-1960 / DS503.M28 1962

Conflict in Korea: an encyclopedia / DS916.H62 1999

Conflict in Northern Ireland: an encyclopedia / DA990.U46.E44 1999

Conflict in the former Yugoslavia: an encyclopedia / DR1232.C66 1998

Conflict unending: India-Pakistan tensions since 1947 / DS450.P18 G36 2001

Conflict, cleavage, and change in Central Asia and the Caucasus / DK859.5.C66 1997

Conflicts of empires: Spain, the low countries and the struggle for world supremacy, 1585-1713 / D231.I55 1997

Confronting conflict: domestic factors and U.S. policymaking in the Third World / D888.U6.O43 1993

Confucian China and its modern fate: the problem of intellectual continuity / DS721.L538

Confucian traditions in east Asian modernity: moral education and economic culture in Japan and the four mini-dragons / DS509.3.C67 1996

Confucianism and family rituals in imperial China: a social history of writing about rites / DS721.E336 1991

Confusions of pleasure: commerce and culture in Ming China, The / DS753.B76 1998

Congress of Vienna, a study in allied unity: 1812-1822, The / DC249.N5 1946

Conquering the past: Austrian Nazism yesterday & today / DB97.C65 1989

Conquerors and conquered in medieval Wales / DA715.G75 1994

Conquest and colonisation: the Normans in Britain, 1066-1100 / DA197.G65 1994

Conquest and empire: the reign of Alexander the Great / DF234.B66 1988

Conquest and resistance to colonialism in Africa / DT28.C66 1993

Conquest of a continent: Siberia and the Russians, The / DK761.L56 1994

Conquest of Constantinople, The / D164.A3.C55 1996

Conquest of Tibet, A / DS785.H4 1934

Conquest, anarchy, and lordship: Yorkshire, 1066-1154 / DA670.Y4.D35 1994

Conquest, coexistence, and change Wales, 1063-1415 / DA715.D37 1987

Conquests and cultures: an international history / CB481.S58 1998

Conquete romaine, La / D20.P37 t.3, 1967

Conscience and power: an examination of dirty hands and political leadership / D744.4.G35 1996

Conscientious objectors and the Second World War: moral and religious arguments in support of pacifism / D810.C82.E45 1991

Conscripts and deserters: the army and French society during the Revolution and Empire / DC151.F6713 1989

Consequences of the war to Great Britain, The / D651.G5.H5 1968

Conservation skills: judgement, method, and decision / CC135.C29 2000

Imperial Germany 1867-1918: politics, culture, and society in an authoritarian state / DD220.M5613 1995

Imperial identities: stereotyping, prejudice and race in colonial Algeria / DT298.K2.L57 1995

Imperial ideology and provincial loyalty in the Roman Empire / DG59.A2.A64 2000

Imperial leather: race, gender, and sexuality in the colonial contest / DA16.M37 1995

Imperial legacy: the Ottoman imprint on the Balkans and the Middle East / DS62.4.B679 1996

Imperial nomads: a history of central Asia, 500-1500 / DS786.K93

Imperial Peking; seven centuries of China. With an essay on The Art of Peking / DS795.L52

Imperial policies and perspectives towards Georgia, 1760-1819 / DK68.7.G28.G88 2000

Imperial Russia: a reference handbook / DK14.P39 2001

Imperial Russia; a source book, 1700-1917 / DK3.D55 1974

Imperial Spain, 1469-1716 / DP171.E4 1964

Imperial Sudan: the Anglo-Egyptian condominium, 1934-1956 / DT156.7.D35 1990

Imperial sunset / DA566.7.B442

Imperial visions: nationalist imagination and geographical expansion in the Russian Far East, 1840-1865 / DK771.A3.B37 1999

Imperialism's new clothes: the repartition of tropical Africa, 1914-1919 / D651.A4.D54 1990

Impossible peace: Britain, the division of Germany and the origins of the cold war, The / DA47.2.D47 1990

Imprisoned apart: the World War II correspondence of an Issei couple / D769.8.A6.F49 1997

In a cold crater: cultural and intellectual life in Berlin, 1945-1948 / DD866.S3513 1998

In confidence: Moscow's ambassador to America's six Cold War presidents (1962-1986) / DK275.D63.A3 1995

In danger undaunted: the anti-interventionist movement of 1940-1941 as revealed in the papers of the America First Committee / D753.I47 1990

In defense of history / D16.8.E847 1999

In Europe's name: Germany and the divided continent / DD290.25.G37 1993

In from the cold: Germany, Russia, and the future of Europe / D1065.E852.I5 1992

In Hitler's shadow: West German historians and the attempt to escape from the Nazi past / DD256.5.E92 1989

In my father's house: Africa in the philosophy of culture / DT352.4.A66 1992

In my time / D15.S85.A3 1996

In our time: the Chamberlain-Hitler collusion / D727.L385 1998

In our time: the world as seen by Magnum photographers / D840.M23 1989

In pursuit of peace: a history of the Israeli peace movement / DS119.7.B2832 1996

In pursuit of the past:decoding the archaeological record: with a new afterword / CC165.B48 2002

In search of Gandhi: essays and reflections / DS481.G3 N3395 2002

In search of history: historiography in the ancient world and the origins of Biblical history / DS62.2.V35 1983

In search of Jewish community: Jewish identities in Germany and Austria, 1918-1933 / DS135.G33.I42 1998

In search of leadership: West Bank politics since 1967 / DS110.W47.S24 1988

In search of modern Portugal: the revolution & its consequences / DP680.I53 1983

In search of peace / D727.C5 1971

In search of Poland: the superpowers' response to Solidarity, 1980-1989 / DK4442.R33 1990

In search of Southeast Asia; a modern history / DS511.I5 1971

In search of Sugihara: the elusive Japanese diplomat who risked his life to rescue 10,000 Jews from the Holocaust / D804.66.S84.L48 1996

In search of the maquis: rural resistance in southern France, 1942-1944 / D802.F8.S675 1993

In search of the true gypsy: from Enlightenment to Final Solution / DX145.W5513 1997

In search, an autobiography / DS125.3.L4.A3

In the balance; speeches 1949 and 1950 / DA588.C57 1951

In the beginning: the advent of the modern age, Europe in the 1840's / D385.B58 1993

In the eyes of the dragon: China views the world / DS779.27.I53 1999

In the lion's den: the life of Oswald Rufeisen / DS135.P63.R848 1990

In the name of sanity / CB425.M79

In the name of the people: prophets and conspirators in prerevolutionary Russia / DK221.U38 1977

In the new world: the making of a Korean American / DU624.7.K67.H983 1995

In the People's Republic: an American's first-hand view of living and working in China / DS711.S288

In the realm of the diamond queen: marginality in an out-of-the-way place / DS646.32.D9.T75 1993

In the realms of gold: pioneering in African history / DT19.7.O45.A3 1997

In the shadow of marriage: gender and justice in an African community / DT2458.K84.G75 1997

In the shadow of migration: rural women and their households in North Tapanuli, Indonesia / DS632.T62.R63 1997

In the shadow of Olympus: the emergence of Macedon / DF261.M2.B67 1990

In the shadow of revolution: life stories of Russian women from 1917 to the second World War / DK37.2.I5 2000

In the shadow of the Holocaust: the second generation / D804.3.H374 1990

In the shadow of the Polish eagle: the Poles, the Holocaust, and beyond / DS135.P6.C655 2000

In the shadow of the Prague spring: Romanian foreign policy and the crisis in Czechoslovakia, 1968 / DR267.R47 2000

In the shadow of the swastika / DS135.P63.W945 1998

In the thick of the fight, 1930-1945 / DC389.R433

In the wake of the Balkan myth: questions of identity and modernity / DR24.5.N67 1999

In touch / CT275.S6763.A3

In Turkey's image: the transformation of occupied Cyprus into a Turkish province / DS54.95.N67I55 1991

In two Chinas, memoirs of a diplomat / DS777.55.P3

In war's dark shadow: the Russians before the Great War / DK240.L56 1983

Incompatible allies; a memoir-history of German-Soviet relations, 1918-1941, The / DD241.R8.H5 1953

Inculturation and African religion: indigenous and Western approaches to medical practice / DT510.43.A53.O93 1998

Indentured to liberty: peasant life and the Hessian military state, 1688-1815 / DD801.H57.T39 1994

Independence and foreign policy: New Zealand in the world since 1935 / DU421.M35 1993

Independence and nationhood: Scotland, 1306-1469 / DA783.G72 1984

Independent Iraq, 1932-1958; a study in Iraqi politics / DS79.K43 1960

India: a country study / DS407.I4465 1996

India: a mosaic / DS407.I51325 2000

India: emerging power / DS480.853.C634 2001

India: from midnight to the millennium / DS428.2.T47 1997

India and China; a thousand years of cultural relations / DS740.5.I5.B3 1971

India and Indonesia during the Ancien Regime: essays / DS436.C7 vol. 3.S452

India and Indonesia from the 1830s to 1914: the heyday of colonial rule: essays / DS436.C7 vol. 2.S463

India and Indonesia general perspectives: essays / DS436.C7 vol. 4

India and Pakistan / DS480.84.T287 2000

India and Pakistan: the first fifty years / DS480.84.I4854 1999

India briefing: a transformative fifty years / DS480.84.I535 1999

India, a literary companion / DS414.P26 1992a

India, a reference annual / DS405.I64

Indian millennium, AD 1000-2000, The / DS452.S22

Indian Ocean: region of conflict or "peace zone"?, The / DS341.B7313 1983

Indian people in the struggle for freedom: five essays / DS478.I44 1998

Indian summer of English chivalry: studies in the decline and transformation of chivalric idealism, The / CR4529.G7.F4

Indian voices of the Great War: solders' letters, 1914-18 / D549.I53.I53 1999

Indianized states of Southeast Asia, The / DS511.C7713 1968

India's rise to power in the twentieth century and beyond / DS480.4.G67 1995

Indira Gandhi: a personal and political biography / DS481.G23.M314 1991

Indira Gandhi: an intimate biography / DS481.G23.J38 1992

Indira Gandhi, the "emergency", and Indian democracy / DS480.852.D49 2000

Individual choice and the structures of history: Alexis de Tocqueville as historian reappraised / DC36.98.T63.M57 1996

Indochina tangle: China's Vietnam policy, 1975-1979, The / DS740.5.V5.R67 1988

Indonesia: selected documents on colonialism and nationalism, 1830-1942 / DS643.I53

Indus saga and the making of Pakistan, The / DS376.9.A35 1996

Jacobin clubs in the French Revolution, 1793-1795, The / DC178.K45 2000

Jacobin Republic, 1792-1794, The / DC148.F7 1983 vol. 2

Jacobinism and the revolt of Lyon, 1789-1793 / DC195.L9.E36 1990

Jacobitism and the English people, 1688-1788 / DA813.M86 1989

Jaffa: a city in evolution, 1799-1917 / DS110.J3.K3713 1990

Jahangirnama: memoirs of Jahangir, Emperor of India, The / DS461.5.J28813 1999

James Connolly: a political biography / DA965.C7.M67 1988

James Connolly and the Irish left / DA965.C7.A68 1994

James II / DA450.A83 1977, DA783.7.M38 1990

James IV / DA784.5.M23 1989

James Ricalton's photographs of China during the Boxer Rebellion: his illustrated travelogue of 1900 / DS709.R49 1990

James Welwood: physician to the Glorious Revolution / DA437.W4.F87 1998

Japan among the powers, 1890-1990 / DS881.9.G54 1994

Japan and China: mutual representations in the modern era / DS822.2.M355 2000

Japan and East Asia: documentary analyses, 1921-1945 / DS518.45.K59 1995

Japan and East Asia; the new international order / DS518.45.H44

Japan and East Asian regionalism / DS518.45.J363 2001

Japan at war: an oral history / D811.A2.C62 1992

Japan before Perry: a short history / DS835.T58

Japan Expedition, 1852-1854; the personal journal of Commodore Matthew C. Perry, The / DS881.8.P4

Japan in China / DS777.53.B5

Japan in transformation, 1952-2000 / DS889.K546 2001

Japan journal, 1855-1861 / DS809.H523 1964

Japan through American eyes: the journal of Francis Hall, Kanagawa and Yokohama, 1859-1866 / DS809.H18 1992

Japan, a short cultural history / DS821.S3 1943

Japan, past and present / DS835.R4 1953

Japan; the story of a nation / DS835.R38 1970

Japanese American evacuation and resettlement / D769.8.A6.J36

Japanese and Sun Yat-sen, The / DS777.J3

Japanese Army in North China, 1937-1941: problems of political and economic control, The / DS777.53.L4634

Japanese cultural policies in Southeast Asia during World War 2 / DS525.9.J3.J37 1991

Japanese culture in comparative perspective / DS821.H375 1997

Japanese occupation of Malaya: a social and economic history, The / DS596.6.K73 1997

Japanese oligarchy and the Russo-Japanese War, The / DS517.13.O37

Japanese patterns of behavior / DS821.L346

Japanese scholars of China: a bibliographical handbook = [Nihon no Chūgokugaku senmonka handobukku] / DS734.8.W58 1992

Japanese style / DS822.5 .L65 2001

Japanese things; being notes on various subjects connected with Japan, for the use of travelers and others / DS821.C43 1971

Japanese thrust into Siberia, 1918, The / D558.M6 1957

Japanese wartime empire, 1931-1945, The / DS35.J38 1996

Japanese, The / DS806.R35

Japanese-Russian relations under Brezhnev and Andropov / DK68.7.J3 K56 2000

Japan's decision to surrender / D821.J3.B8 1954

Japan's emergence as a global power / DS889.M345767 2001

Japan's first modern war: Army and society in the conflict with China, 1894-95 / DS765.L66 1994

Japan's Greater East Asia Co-prosperity Sphere in World War II: selected readings and documents / DS518.J38

Japan's imperial diplomacy: consuls, treaty ports, and war in China, 1895-1938 / DS849.C6.B67 2000

Japan's modern century; from Perry to 1970 / DS835.B6 1970

Japan's Orient: rendering pasts into history / DS827.S3.T36 1993

Japan's past, Japan's future: one historian's odyssey / DS834.9.I35

Japan's postwar history / DS889.A59 1997

Japan's role in Southeast Asian nationalist movements, 1940 to 1945 / DS518.1.E44

Japan's special position in Manchuria; its assertion, legal interpretation and present meaning / DS783.7.Y65 vol. 1

Japan's total empire: Manchuria and the culture of wartime imperialism / DS783.7.Y67 1998

Jawaharlal Nehru: rebel and statesman / DS481.N35 N285 1995

Jean Monnet: the first statesman of interdependence / D413.M56.D73 1994

Jean Paul Marat: scientist and revolutionary / DC146.M3.C57 1997

Jennie: the life of Lady Randolph Churchill / DA565.C6.M3

Jerusalem: its sanctity and centrality to Judaism, Christianity, and Islam / DS109.9.J4576 1998

Jerusalem: rebirth of a city / DS109.925.G54 1985

Jerusalem: the contested city / DS109.95.K55 2001

Jerusalem in America's foreign policy, 1947-1997 / DS109.93.S56 1998

Jerusalem in history / DS109.9.J459 1989

Jerusalem in the twentieth century / DS109.93.G55 1996

Jerusalem question, 1917-1968, The / DS109.93.B68 1971

Jerusalem, the torn city / DS109.94.B4513

Jew in the modern world: a documentary history, The / DS102.J43

Jewish Budapest: monuments, rites, history / DS135.H92.B83913 1999

Jewish claims against East Germany: moral obligations and pragmatic policy / D819.G3.T56 1997

Jewish culture and identity in the Soviet Union / DS135.R92.J463 1990

Jewish emancipation in a German city: Cologne, 1798-1871 / DS135.G4.C684 1997

Jewish emigration: the S.S. St. Louis affair and other cases / D810.J4.H655 vol. 7

Jewish encyclopedia: a descriptive record of the history, religion, literature, and customs of the Jewish people from the earliest times to the present day, The / DS102.8.J4 1964

Jewish ethic and the spirit of socialism, The / DS135.G33.W418 1997

Jewish exodus from Iraq, 1948-1951, The / DS135.I7.G37 1997

Jewish family names and their origins: an etymological dictionary / CS3010.G84 1992

Jewish identity in the modern world / DS143.M39 1990

Jewish life in Muslim Libya: rivals & relatives / DS135.L44.G65 1990

Jewish minority in the Soviet Union, The / DS135.R92.S28

Jewish political tradition, The / DS140.J475 2000

Jewish question: biography of a world problem, The / DS141.B3813 1990

'Jewish question' in German literature, 1749-1939: emancipation and its discontents, The / DS135.G33.R53 1999

Jewish radicals: from Czarist stetl to London ghetto / DS135.E5.F5 1975

Jewish responses to Nazi persecution: collective and individual behavior in extremis / D810.J4.T7

Jewish search for a usable past, The / DS112.R755 1999

Jewish settlement and community in the modern western world / DS143.J459 1991

Jewish state or Israeli nation? / DS149.E9313 1995

Jewish-Transjordanian relations, 1921-48 / DS119.7.G389 1997

Jews: history, memory, and the present, The / DS102.5.V5313 1996

Jews among Muslims: communities in the precolonial MiddleEast / DS135.A68.J47 1996

Jews and Arabs, their contacts through the ages / DS119.G58

Jews and revolution in nineteenth-century Russia / DS135.R9.H23 1995

Jews in Christian Europe, 1400-1700, The / DS135.E81.E38 1988

Jews in eastern Poland and the USSR, 1939-46 / DS135.R93 G3436 1991

Jews in Germany after the Holocaust: memory, identity, and Jewish-German relations / DS135.G332.R37 1997

Jews in medieval Germany; a study of their legal and social status, The / DS135.G31.K58

Jews in medieval Normandy: a social and intellectual history, The / DS135.F85.N675 1998

Jews in Poland, The / DS135.P6.J46 1986

Jews in Polish culture, The / DS135.P6.H413 1988

Jews in the German economy: the German-Jewish economic elite, 1820-1935 / DS135.G33.M63 1987

Jews in the Greek Age, The / DS121.65.B53 1988

Jews in the Mediterranean diaspora: from Alexander to Trajan (323 BCE - 117 CE) / DS135.M43.B368 1996

Jews in the Soviet Union since 1917: paradox of survival, The / DS135.R92.L48 1988

Jews of ancient Rome, The / DS135.I85.R64

Jews of Europe after the black death, The / DS124.F6213 2000

Jews of Germany: a historical portrait, The / DS135.G3.G32 1992

Jews of Kurdistan, The / DS135.K8.B73 1993

Life of John Bright, The / DA565.B8.T8 1971

Life of King Alfred / DA153.A88 1966

Life of King Edward, who rests at Westminster, The / DA154.8.V5

Life of Lady Mary Wortley Montagu, The / DA501.M7.H3

Life of Lenin, The / DK254.L4.F53

Life of Neville Chamberlain, The / DA585.C5.F4 1970

Life of Niccolo Machiavelli, The / DG738.14.M2.R513

Life of the ancient Egyptians / DT61.S92513 1992

Life of Thomas More, The / DA334.M8.A64 1998

Life of William Pitt, earl of Chatham, The / DA483.P6.W5 1966a

Life on a medieval barony; a picture of a typical feudal community in the thriteenth century / CB355.D3

Life unworthy of life: racial phobia and mass murder in Hitler's Germany / D804.3.G587 1997

Life with the enemy: collaboration and resistance in Hitler's Europe, 1939-1945 / D802.E9.R5613

Life's mosaic: the autobiography of Phyllis Ntantala, A / DT1949.N75.A3 1993

Lifting the veil: communal violence and communal harmony in contemporary India / DS422.C64 E55 1995

Like people you see in a dream: first contact in six Papuan societies / DU740.S34 1991

Liliana's journal: Warsaw 1939-1945 / D810.J4.Z8413

Limits of anarchy: intervention and state formation in Chad / DT546.48.N65 1996

Limits of coexistence: identity politics in Israel, The / DS110.A3.T67 2000

Limits of settlement growth: a theoretical outline, The / CC72.4.F54 1995

Limits of Soviet power in the developing world, The / D888.S65.L55 1989

Lin Piao affair: power politics and military coup, The / DS778.L4725.L49

Linajudos and conversos in Seville: greed and prejudice in sixteenth- and seventeenth-century Spain / DS135.S75.S455 2000

Lines of fire: women writers of World War I / D639.W7.L48 1999

Lines of life: theories of biography, 1880-1970, The / CT21.N68 1986

Lines of succession: heraldry of the royal families of Europe / CR1605.L68 1991

Lines that divide: historical archaeologies of race, class, and gender / CC72.4.L56 2000

Lion and the star: gentile-Jewish relations in three Hessian communities, 1919-1945, The / DS135.G4.F664 1998

Lion's share: a short history of British imperialism, 1850-1970, The / DA16.P67

Lipstick traces: a secret history of the twentieth century / CB428.M356 1989

Lisle letters: an abridgement, The / DA335.L5.L572 1983

Listening to the enemy: key documents on the role of communications intelligence in the war with Japan / D810.S7.L49 1988

Literary dissent in Communist China / DS777.55.G67

Literary lives: biography and the search for understanding / CT21.E414 2000

Literary underground of the Old Regime, The / DC133.3.D37 1982

Literature and the arts in twentieth century China / DS721.S37

Literature and the historian / D13.W42

Literature of destruction: Jewish responses to catastrophe, The / DS102.L54 1988

Literature of travel in the Japanese rediscovery of China, 1862-1945, The / DS709.F64 1996

Literature, art and the pursuit of decay in twentieth-century France / DC33.6.M33 2000

Lithuania: the rebel nation / DK505.54.V37 1997

Lithuania: the rebirth of a nation, 1991-1994 / DK505.8.A84 1999

Lithuania awakening / DK505.74.S46 1990

Lithuania in European politics: the years of first republic, 1918-1940 / DK505.74.E38 1998

Lithuania, independent again: the autobiography of Vytautas Landsbergis / DK505.85.L36

Little Czech and the Great Czech Nation: national identity and the post-communist transformation of society, The / DB2238.7.H65 1996

Little god: the twilight of patriarchy in a southern African chiefdom, A / DT2458.N45.W95 1990

Liu Shao-chi and the Chinese cultural revolution: the politics of mass criticism / DS778.L49.D57

Lives of Talleyrand, The / DC255.T3.B7

Lives of the later Caesars: the first part of the Augustan history: with newly compiled Lives of Nerva and Trajan / DG274.S32 1976

Lives of their own: rhetorical dimensions in autobiographies of women activists / CT25.W28 1999

Lives of young Koreans in Japan / DS832.7.K6.F817 2000

Living archaeology / CC79.E85.G68

Living Japan / DS821.K33

Living martyrs: individuals and revolution in Nepal / DS495.592.A34 F57 1997

Living on mangetti: 'Bushman' autonomy and Namibian independence / DT1558.S38.W53 1999

Living the Intifada / DS119.75.R54 1991

Living tree: the changing meaning of being Chinese today, The / DS730.L596 1994

Living with Africa / DT19.7.V36.A3 1994

Livy: reconstructing early Rome / DG207.L583.M5 1995

Livy's written Rome / DG241.J34 1997

Lloyd George and the challenge of Labour: the post-war coalition, 1918-1922 / DA566.9.L5.W76 1991

Lloyd George, the people's champion, 1902-1911 / DA566.9.L5.G78 1978b

Local origins of modern society: Gloucestershire 1500-1800, The / DA670.G5.R65 1992

Local scripts of archaic Greece: a study of the origin of the Greek alphabet and its development from the eighth to the fifth centuries B.C., The / CN362.J44 1990

Logic of evil: the social origins of the Nazi Party, 1925-1933, The / DD253.25.B76 1996

Logistics of the Roman army at war (264 B.C.-A.D. 235), The / DG89.R675 1998

London: a history / DA677.S54 1998

London and the invention of the Middle East: money, power, and war, 1902-1922 / DS63.2.G7.A34 1995

London at war, 1939-1945 / D760.8.L7.Z54 1995

London crowds in the reign of Charles II: propaganda and politics from the Restoration until the exclusion crisis / DA445.H24 1987

London in the age of Chaucer / DA680.M9

London perceived / DA677.P7 1962a

London, a social history / DA677.P67 1995

London--world city, 1800-1840 / DA683.L88 1992

Long eighteenth century: British political and social history, 1688-1832, The / DA480.O38 1997

Long nineteenth century: a history of Germany, 1780-1918, The / DD203.B59 1998

Long peace: Ottoman Lebanon, 1861-1920, The / DS84.A35 1993

Long presidency: France in the Mitterrand years, 1981-1995, The / DC423.F748 1998

Long revolution, The / DA566.4.W48, DS711.S57

Longest day: June 6, 1944, The / D756.5.N6.R9

Long-haired kings, The / DC65.W3 1982

Longman companion to the formation of the European empires, 1488-1920, The / D217.C46 2000

Looking at the sun: the rise of the new East Asian economic and political system / DS504.5.F35 1994

Looking back; a chronicle of growing up old in the sixties / CT275.M46518.A34

Looking forward: a guide to futures research / CB158.H415 1983

Looted: the Philippines after the bases / DS686.614.K57 1998

Lord Acton / D15.A25.H487 2000

Lord Acton; a study in conscience and politics / D15.A25.H5 1952a

Lord Beaverbrook: a life / DA566.9.B37.C49 1993

Lord Chesterfield and his world / DA501.C5.S52 1971

Lord Grey, 1764-1845 / DA536.G84.S65 1990

Lord Hailey, the Colonial Office and the politics of race and empire in the Second World War: the loss of white prestige / D750.W35 2000

Lord Haldane; scapegoat for liberalism / DA566.9.H27.K6

Lord Hervey; eighteenth-century courtier / DA501.H47.H34 1974

Lord Liverpool: the life and political career of Robert Banks Jenkinson, Second Earl of Liverpool, 1770-1828 / DA522.L7.G37 1984

Lord Lloyd and the decline of the British Empire / DA17.L56.C48 1987

Lord Macaulay, 1800-1859 / DA536.M15.K5

Lord Melbourne, 1779-1848 / DA536.M5.M58 1997

Lord Randolph Churchill / DA565.C6.C6 1952

Lords of battle: image and reality of the comitatus in Dark-Age Britain, The / DA59.E94 1997

Lords of the ascendancy: the Irish House of Lords and its members, 1600-1800 / DA940.J36 1995

Lords of the Lebanese marches: violence and narrative in an Arab society / DS89.A42.G55 1996

Lordship and military obligation in Anglo-Saxon England / DA59.A24 1988

Lordship to patronage: Scotland, 1603-1745 / DA800.M56 1983

Lordship, knighthood, and locality: a study in English society, c. 1180-c. 1280 / DA690.C75.C56 1991

Norwegian invasion of England in 1066, The / DA161.D48 1999

Norwegian resistance, 1940-1945 / D802.N7.G5413 1979

Not like us: how Europeans have loved, hated, and transformed American culture since World War II / D1065.U5.P388 1997

Notable American women: the modern period: a biographical dictionary / CT3260.N573

Notable American women, 1607-1950; a biographical dictionary / CT3260.N57

Notable North Dakotans / CT253.R65 1987

Notable twentieth-century Latin American women: a biographical dictionary / CT3290.N68 2001

Nothing sacred: Nazi espionage against the Vatican, 1939-1945 / D810.S7.A559 1997

Nur Jahan, empress of Mughal India / DS461.9.N8 F56 1993

Nuremberg diary / D804.G42.G5

Object of memory: Arab and Jew narrate the Palestinian village, The / DS110.E645.S59 1998

Obstructed path; French social thought in the years of desperation, 1930-1960, The / DC365.H8

Occupation: the policies and practices of military conquerors / D25.5.C34 1992

Occupation and resistance: the Greek agony, 1941-44 / D802.G8.H66 1983

Occupation of Namibia: Afrikanerdom's attack on the British Empire, The / DT1625.C66 1990

Ocean of destiny: a concise history of the North Pacific, 1500-1978 / DS511.L68

Oceans of consolation: personal accounts of Irish migration to Australia / DU122.I7.O25 1994

October Revolution, The / DK265.M375

October revolution; a collection of articles and speeches by Joseph Stalin, The / DK265.S668

Odyssey of the Abraham Lincoln Brigade: Americans in the Spanish Civil War, The / DP269.47.A46.C37 1994

Of battles long ago: memoirs of an American ambulance driver in World War I / D630.C8.A36

Of diamonds and diplomats / CT275.B316.A3

Of revelation and revolution / DT1058.T78.C66 1991

Of the hut I builded: the archaeology of Australia's history / DU106.C66 1988

Officers in flight suits: the story of American Air Force fighter pilots in the Korean War / DS920.2.U5.S53 1996

Official chronology of the U.S. Navy in World War II, The / D773.C74 2000

Official military historical offices and sources / D25.5.O34 2000

Official relations between China and Japan, 1368-1549 / DS740.5.J3.W3

Old China Hands and the Foreign Office / DS740.5.G5.P4 1969

Old China Hands, The / DS775.F5

Old English in Ireland, 1625-42, The / DA941.5.C5 1966a

Old Europe: a study of continuity, 1000-1800 / CB203.G47

Old men forget: the autobiography of Duff Cooper (Viscount Norwich) / DA566.9.C64.A3

Old Peking: city of the ruler of the world: an anthology / DS795.O44 1997

Old Regime and the Revolution, The / DC138.T6313 1998

Old Turkey and the new: from Byzantium to Ankara, The / DR440 .L8 1955

Old world and the new 1492-1650, The / CB401.E43

Oldest ally: Britain and the Portuguese connection, 1936-1941, The / DA47.9.P8.S76 1994

Oliver Cromwell / DA426.G38 1996, DA426.W4

Oliver Cromwell and the Puritan Revolution / DA426.A78 1958

Olivier de Clisson and political society in France under Charles V and Charles VI / DC97.C54.H46 1996

Olympia: gods, artists and athletes / DF261.O5.D713 1968

Omaha Beach: a flawed victory / D756.5.N6 L435 2001

Oman: political development in a changing world / DS247.O65.R56 1998

Oman under Qaboos: from coup to constitution, 1970-1996 / DS247.O68.A59 2000

On ancient Central-Asian tracks: brief narrative of three expeditions in innermost Asia and north-western China / DS785.S83

On cultural freedom: an exploration of public life in Poland and America / DK4440.G64 1982

On historical materialism / D16.9.E57 1979

On history / D16.8.H626 1997b, D7.B7513

On internal war: American and Soviet approaches to Third World clients and insurgents / D883.O36 1992

On Jean-Jacques Rousseau: considered as one of the first authors of the Revolution / DC138.S94 2000

On Jews and Judaism in crisis: selected essays / DS135.G33.S297

On listening to Holocaust survivors: recounting and life history / D804.195.G74 1998

On or about December 1910: early Bloomsbury and its intimate world / DA685.B65.S73 1996

On Soviet dissent / DK274.M3513

On the bones of the serpent: person, memory, and mortality in Sabarl Island society / DU740.42.B39 1990

On the eaves of the world / DS793.K2.F3

On the edge of the auspicious: gender and caste in Nepal / DS495.8.B456 C36 1998

On the philosophy of history / D16.8.M286 1973

On the Salt March: the historiography of Gandhi's march to Dandi / DS480.45.W4 1997

On war / D843.A683 1968

One day in China, May 21, 1936 / DS775.2.C4813 1983

One day too long: top secret site 85 and the bombing of North Vietnam / DS559.73.L28.C37 1999

One Europe, many nations: a historical dictionary of European national groups / D21.3.M55 2000

One hundred days: Napoleon's road to Waterloo / DC239.S36 1992

One hundred pages for the future: reflections of the president of the Club of Rome / CB161.P35 1981

One king, one faith: the Parlement of Paris and the religious reformations of the sixteenth century / DC33.3.R64 1996

One land, two peoples: the conflict over Palestine / DS119.7.G425 1991

One special summer / CT275.O552.A36

One step ahead in China: Guangdong under reform / DS793.K7.V64 1989

One thousand days in Siberia: the Odyssey of a Japanese-American POW / D811.S3228 1997

Open door doctrine in relation to China, The / DS740.B36

Open empire: a history of China to 1600, The / DS735.H25 2000

Open letters: selected writings, 1965-1990 / DB2241.H38.A5 1991b

Opening of south Lebanon, 1788-1840: A study of the impact of the West on the Middle East, The / DS84.P6 1963

Operation Desert Shield/Desert Storm: chronology and fact book / DS79.72.H88 1995

Operation Drumbeat: the dramatic true story of Germany's first U-boat attacks along the American coast in World War II / D781.G36 1990

Operation Overlord, design and reality; the Allied invasion of Western Europe / D770.N6

Operation Sea Lion; German plans for the invasion of England, 1939-1942 / D771.W38 1958

Opium War through Chinese eyes, The / DS757.5.W3 1968

Opium War, 1840-1842: barbarians in the Celestial Empire in the early part of the nineteenth century and the war by which they forced her gates ajar, The / DS757.5.F39

Opposition years: Winston S. Churchill and the Conservative Party, 1945-1951, The / DA589.7.M39 1991

Optimism at Armageddon: voices of American participants in the First World War / D570.1.M45 1997

Oral history index: an international directory of oral history interviews / D16.14.O74 1990

Ordeal of total war, 1939-1945, The / D743.W68 1968

Order and history / CB19.V58 1956

Order in paradox: myth, ritual, and exchange among Nepal's Tamang / DS493.9.T35.H65 1989

Order of terror: the concentration camp, The / DD256.5.S5813 1997

Order of the Death's Head; the story of Hitler's S.S., The / DD253.6.H613 1970

Ordering anarchy: armies and leaders in Tacitus' Histories / DG286.A84 1999

Ordering the world: approaches to state and society in Sung Dynasty China / DS751.O73 1993

Ordinary people, extraordinary lives: political and economic change in a Tohoku village / DS897.T635.B35 1991

Organise! organise! organise!: a study of reform agitations in Wales, 1840-1886 / DA722.W355 1991

Organization of ground combat troops, The / D769.A533 vol. 1, pt. 1

Oriental renaissance: Europe's rediscovery of India and the East, 1680-1880 / CB253.S3813 1984

Orientalism and the postcolonial predicament: perspectives on South Asia / DS339.8.O75 1993

Orientalizing revolution: Near Eastern influence on Greek culture in the early archaic age, The / DF78.B8513 1992

Origin and goal of history, The / D13.J314 1953a

Origin of Manchu rule in China; frontier and bureaucracy as interacting forces in the Chinese Empire, The / DS753.M5 1965

Social misconstruction of reality: validity and verification in the scholarly community, The / D13.H282 1996

Social politics of Anglo-Jewry, 1880-1920, The / DS135.E5.B56 1988

Social politics of medieval diplomacy: Anglo-German relations (1066-1307), The / DA47.2.H84 2000

Social reproduction and history in Melanesia: mortuary ritual, gift exchange, and custom in the Tanga Islands / DU740.42.F67 1995

Social science and the politics of modern Jewish identity / DS140.H37 2000

Social structure in Southeast Asia / DS509.5.M8

Social world of the Florentine humanists, 1390-1460, The / DG737.55.M3

Socialism and democracy in Czechoslovakia, 1945-1948 / DB2218.7.M9 1981

Socialist Iraq: a study in Iraqi politics since 1968 / DS79.65.K49

Society and culture in early modern France: eight essays / DC33.D33

Society and government in France under Richelieu and Mazarin, 1624-61 / DC123.B66 1988

Society and politics in revolutionary Bordeaux / DC195.B6.F67

Society and Puritanism in pre-Revolutionary England / DA380.H52 1964

Society as I have found it / CT275.M23.A3 1975

Society in crisis: France in the sixteenth century / DC116.5.S25 1975b

Society of the Enlightenment: the rise of the middle class and Enlightenment culture in Germany, The / DD65.D8513 1992

Society, schools & progress in China / DS777.55.T73 1968

Soderini and the Medici: power and patronage in fifteenth-century Florence, The / DG737.8.C57 1991

SOE in the Far East / D767.C75 1983

Sojourners: the return of German Jews and the question of identity / DS135.G5.A1263 1995

Soldier and civilian in the later Roman Empire / DG89.M13

Soldier and the citizen: the role of the military in Taiwan's development, The / DS799.816.B86 1996

Soldier sahibs: the daring adventurers who tamed India's northwest frontier / DS392.N67 A45 2001

Soldiers and politics in Eastern Europe, 1945-90: the case of Hungary / DB956.B37 1993

Soldiers and statesmen: the General Council of the Army and its debates, 1647-1648 / DA415.W63 1987

Soldiers and the Soviet state: civil-military relations from Brezhnev to Gorbachev / DK274.3.S63 1990

Soldiers of destruction: the SS Death's Head Division, 1933-1945 / D757.85.S95

Soldiers of the French Revolution, The / DC151.F68 1990

Soldier's story, A / D756.B7

Soldiers, civilians, and democracy: post-Franco Spain in comparative perspective / DP272.A35 1995

Soldiers, traders, and slaves: state formation and economic transformation in the Greater Nile Valley, 1700-1885 / DT156.3.E93 1990

Solidarity and the Soviet worker: the impact of the Polish events of 1980 on Soviet internal politics / DK288.T43 1988

Solomon Islands campaign, Guadalcanal to Rabaul: historiography and annotated bibliography, The / D767.98.R37 1997

Somali challenge: from catastrophe to renewal?, The / DT407.S59 1994

Somalia: the missed opportunities / DT407.S24 1994

Some 20th-century historians; essays on eminent Europeans / D14.H3

Son of heaven [a biography of Li Shih-Min, founder of the Tang dynasty / DS749.3.F5 1971

Sons against fathers; studies in Russian radicalism and revolution / DK219.3.L3

Sons of Sheba's race: African-Americans and the Italo-Ethiopian War, 1935-1941, The / DT387.8.S37 1992

Sons of the Revolution: radical democrats in France, 1862-1914 / DC342.8.P35.S76 1996

Sons of the yellow emperor: a history of the Chinese diaspora / DS732.P36 1990

Soong sisters, The / DS778.A1.H3 1943

Sorcerer as apprentice: Stalin as commissar of nationalities, 1917-1924, The / DK266.5.B57 1994

Sorcerer's apprentice: the life of Franz von Papen, The / DD247.P3.R65 1996

Sorrows of the ancient Romans: the gladiator and the monster, The / DG78.B37 1993

Soul of Spain, The / DP48.E5 1937

Sound and sentiment: birds, weeping, poetics, and song in Kaluli expression / DU740.42.F44 1990

Source books on Far Eastern political ideologies / DS775.T442

Sources for Greek history: between the Persian and Peloponnesian wars / DF209.5.H65 1951

Sources for Roman history, 133-70 B.C. / DG254.G8 1960

Sources of Chinese tradition / DS721.D37 1999

Sources of Shang history: the oracle-bone inscriptions of bronze age China / DS744.K44

Sources of the Japanese tradition / DS821.T76

South Africa: a modern history / DT1787.D38 2000

South Africa: no turning back / DT779.952.S655 1989

South Africa in Southern Africa: reconfiguring the region / DT1105.S6.S68 1998

South Africa in transition: new theoretical perspectives / DT1974.S73 1998

South Africa to the sources of apartheid / DT1756.D4213 1989

South Africa, the colonial powers and "African defence": the rise and fall of the white entente, 1948-60 / D1065.S6.B47 1992

South Africa's destabilization of Zimbabwe, 1980-89 / DT2996.D95 1998

South Africa's foreign policy: the search for status and security, 1945-1988 / DT779.9.B37 1990

South America and the First World War: the impact of the war on Brazil, Argentina, Peru, and Chile / D618.A42 1988

South Asians in East Africa: an economic and social history, 1890-1980 / DT429.5.S68.G74 1993

South Asians overseas: migration and ethnicity / DS339.4.S68 1990

Southeast Asia / DS508.2.D6 1973

Southeast Asia: a history / DS511.W66

Southeast Asia among the world powers / DS518.1.V28

South-East Asia from colonialism to independence / DS518.P55

Southeast Asia in international politics, 1941-1956 / DS518.1.C587

Southeast Asia in perspective / DS518.1.K5

Southeast Asia in United States policy / DS518.8.F48

South-East Asia: a social, economic and political geography / DS508.2.F5 1966

Southeast Asia: problems of United States policy / DS518.8.H4

Southeast Asian identities: culture and the politics of representation in Indonesia, Malaysia, Singapore, and Thailand / DS526.7.S687 1998

Southeast Asian tribes, minorities, and nations / DS509.5.S63

Southeast Asian world; an introductory essay, The / DS511.B8

Southeastern Europe under Ottoman rule, 1354-1804 / DJK4.S93 vol. 5

Southern African political history: a chronology of key political events from independence to mid-1997 / DT1147.K35 1999

Southern Slav question and the Habsburg Monarchy, The / DB48.S5

Sovereignty and the sword: Harrington, Hobbes, and mixed government in the English civil wars / DA413.F85 1997

Sovereignty as responsibility: conflict management in Africa / DT30.5.S667 1996

Soviet bloc, unity and conflict, The / D847.B7 1967

Soviet briefing: Gorbachev and the reform period / DK288.E35 1989

Soviet citizen; daily life in a totalitarian society, The / DK276.I5

Soviet colossus: a history of the USSR, The / DK246.K64 1985

Soviet conduct in world affairs; a selection of readings / DK63.3.D32

Soviet disunion: a history of the nationalities problem in the USSR / DK33.N26 1990

Soviet Far Eastern policy, 1931-1945 / DS518.7.M66

Soviet foreign policy after Stalin / DK63.3.D33

Soviet government and the Jews, 1948-1967: a documented study, The / DS135.R92.P56 1984

Soviet historians and perestroika: the first phase / DK38.S68 1989

Soviet history in the Yeltsin era / DK266.D28 1997

Soviet history of World War II: myths, memories, and realities, The / DK273.G3

Soviet image of the United States; a study in distortion, The / DK69.B3

Soviet impact on the Western World, The / DK265.9.I5.C3 1973

Soviet intellectuals and political power: the post-Stalin era / DK276.S48 1990

Soviet Jewry in the 1980s: the politics of anti-Semitism and emigration and the dynamics of resettlement / DS135.R92.S655 1989

Soviet leadership in transition / DK274.H68

Soviet legacy in Central Asia, The / DK859.56.G57 1999

Soviet military intelligence in war / D810.S7.G552 1990

Thera, Pompeii of the ancient Aegean: excavations at Akrotiri, 1967-79 / DF221.T38.D68 1983

There are no slaves in France: the political culture of race and slavery in the Ancien Regime / DC133.4.P43 1996

Thermidorean regime and the directory, 1794-1799, The / DC148.F7 1984 vol. 3

They called them angels: American military nurses of World War II / D807.U5.J33 2000

They came in ships / CS49.C63 1989

They did not dwell alone: Jewish emigration from the Soviet Union, 1967-1990 / DS135.R92.B89 1997

They drew fire: combat artists of World War II / D810.L36 2000

They make themselves: work and play among the Baining of Papua New Guinea / DU740.42.F35 1997

They shall grow not old: Irish soldiers and the Great War / D547.I6.D86 1997

They were expendable / D811.W45

Third force in China, The / DS775.C33

Third French Republic, 1870-1914, The / DC335.S4

Third Reich: a new history, The / DD256.5.B94 2000

Third Reich: politics and propaganda, The / DD256.5.W4324 1993

Third Reich almanac, The / DD256.5.T283 1987

Third Reich, The / DD256.5.W49 1982

Third World and South Africa: post-apartheid challenges, The / D888.S6.P39 1992

Third World security in the post-cold war era / D887.T45 1991

Thirty years in a red house: a memoir of childhood and youth in Communist China / DS778.7.Z48 1998

Thirty Years War: the Holy Roman Empire and Europe, 1618-48, The / D258.A83 1997

Thirty years war, The / D258.W4

This country, Japan / DS806.S43

This I cannot forget: the memoirs of Nikolai Bukharin's widow / DK268.B76.N4913 1993

This international relations of Manchuria; a digest and analysis of treaties, agreements, and negotiations concerning the three eastern provinces of China ... / DS783.7.Y6

This is England: British film and the People's War, 1939-1945 / D743.23.R38 2001

Thomas Attwood: the biography of a radical / DA536.A88.M67 1990

Thomas Cranmer: a life / DA317.8.C8.M34 1996

Thomas More / DA334.M8.G88 2000

Thomas More: a biography / DA334.M8.M275 1984

Thomas Munro: the origins of the colonial state and his vision of empire / DS485.M28.M867 1989

Those of my blood: constructing noble families in medieval Francia / CS587.B68 2001

Thought reform of the Chinese intellectuals / DS777.55.C395

Thousand kisses: a grandmother's Holocaust letters, A / DS135.C95.P65 1999

Three centuries; family chronicles of Turkey and Egypt / CT1474.T8

Three Christian capitals: topography and politics / DG63.K7 1983

Three eighteenth century figures: Sarah Churchill, John Wesley [and] Giacomo Casanova / D285.1.D6

Three eras of political change in Eastern Europe / DJK36.S85 1997

Three saints and a sinner: Julia Ward Howe, Louisa, Annie, Sam Ward / CS71.W26. 1956

Three who made a revolution; a biographical history / DK254.L4.W6 1964

Threshold of war: Franklin D. Roosevelt and American entry into World War II / D753.H38 1988

Through Australian eyes: colonial perceptions of imperial Britain / DU113.5.G7

Through French windows: an introduction to France in the nineties / DC33.7.C597 1994

Through the eyes of innocents: children witness World War II / D810.C4.W45 2000

Through the Moon Gate: a guide to China's historic monuments / DS705.T46 1986

Through the wire: action with the SAS in Borneo and the Special Forces in Vietnam / DS559.5.S29 1999

Thucydides / DF229.T6.H67 1987

Thucydides: narrative and explanation / DF229.T6.R64 1998

Thunder on the Dnepr: Zhukov-Stalin and the defeat of Hitler's Blitzkrieg / D764.F845 1997

Thunder out of China / DS777.47.W5

Thundering Zeus: the making of Hellenistic Bactria / DS374.B28.H66 1999

Thy hand, great anarch!: India, 1921-1952 / DS480.45.C46 1988

Tiananmen papers, The / DS779.32.L54 2001

Tibet: survival in question / DS786.D6613 1994

Tibet and the Tibetans / DS785.S43

Tibet, land of snows / DS786.T8

Tibet, today and yesterday / DS785.L5 1960

Tibetan border worlds: a geo-historical analysis of trade and traders / DS493.9.N94.S64 2000

Tibetan Empire in central Asia: a history of the struggle for great power among Tibetans, Turks, Arabs, and Chinese during the early Middle Ages, The / DS786.B38 1987

Tibetan nation: a history of Tibetan nationalism and Sino-Tibetan relations / DS786.S56 1996

Tide at sunrise; a history of the Russo-Japanese War, 1904-1905, The / DS517.W37

Tides of fortune, 1945-1955 / DA566.9.M33.A28 1969

Tides of history, The / D20.P513

Ties of blood and empire: New Zealand's involvement in Middle East defence and the Suez Crisis, 1947-1957 / DT107.83.T36 1994

Tiger of Chin; the dramatic emergence of China as a nation, The / DS747.5.C6

Tiger on the brink: Jiang Zemin and China's new elite / DS779.29.C477.G55 1998

Tigers of the snow and other virtual Sherpas: an ethnography of Himalayan encounters / DS493.9.S5.A33 1996

Tigers' roar: Asia's recovery and its impact / DS504.5.T54 2001

Time and space in Chinese culture / DS721.T528 1995

Time and the hour: Nigeria, East Africa, and the Second World War / D766.84.K47 1997

Time and tide wait for no man: the changing European geopolitical landscape / D2009.G83 1991

Time and traditions: essays in archaeological interpretation / CC75.T68 1978

Time for courage: the Royal Air Force in the European War, 1939-1945, A / D786.T44 1985

Time for telling truth is running out: conversations with Zhang Shenfu / DS778.C4966.S38 1992

Time of crisis: Japan, the great depression, and rural revitalization, A / DS897.S3923

Time of my life, The / DA591.H38.A3 1990

Time of the gypsies, The / DX223.S75 1997

Time out of hand; revolution and reaction in Southeast Asia / DS518.1.S47

Times enmeshed: gender, space, and history among the Duna of Papua New Guinea / DU740.42.S79 1998

Time's reasons: philosophies of history old and new / D13.K7 1989

Timetables of Jewish history: a chronology of the most important people and events in Jewish history, The / DS114.G68 1993

Tipu Sultan's search for legitimacy: Islam and kingship in a Hindu domain / DS470.T6 B75 1997

Titan: the life of John D. Rockefeller, Sr. / CT275.R75.C47 1998

Tito / DR359.T5.D4

Tito: and the rise and fall of Yugoslavia / DR1300.W47 1995

Titoism and the Cominform / DR370.U4 1971

Titoism in action; the reforms in Yugoslavia after 1948 / DR370.N4

Tito's separate road; America and Yugoslavia in world politics / DR370.C33

To acknowledge a war: the Korean War in American memory / DS918.E39 2000

To be young was very heaven / CT275.P488.A3

To change a nation; propaganda and indoctrinatiion in Communist China / DS777.57.H6

To command the sky: the battle for air superiority over Germany, 1942-1944 / D785.M39 1991

To die for Germany: heroes in the Nazi pantheon / DD243.B35 1990

To end a war / DR1313.7.D58.H65 1998

To foreign shores: U.S. amphibious operations in World War II / D769.45.L67 1995

To Jerusalem and back: a personal account / DS107.4.B37 1976

To live as brothers: southeast Sumatra in the seventeenth and eighteenth centuries / DS646.15.S77.A53 1993

To Marietta from Paris, 1945-1960 / DC707.A45

To remember the faces of the dead: the plenitude of memory in southwestern New Britain / DU740.42.M373 1994

To sing with pigs is human: the concept of person in Papua New Guinea / DU740.42.G66 1995

To the bitter end / DD256.5.G52

To the Harbin Station: the liberal alternative in Russian Manchuria, 1898-1914 / DS796.H4 W64 1999

To the other shore: the Russian Jewish intellectuals who came to America / DS135.R9.C34 1997

Zaire: continuity and political change in an oppressive state / DT658.L46 1993

Zakhor, Jewish history and Jewish memory / DS115.5.Y47 1982

Zaria's fire: engendered moments in Manam ethnography / DU740.42.L88 1995

Zero! / D792.J3.O38

Zhou Enlai: a biography / DS778.C593.W54 1984

Zhou Enlai: the early years / DS778.C593.L44 1994

Zhou Enlai and the foundations of Chinese foreign policy / DS778.A2.C467 1996

Zhukov's greatest defeat: the Red Army's epic disaster in Operation Mars, 1942 / D764.G5575 1999

Zimbabwe culture: origins and decline of southern Zambezian states, The / DT2942.P55 2001

Zimbabwe's guerrilla war: peasant voices / DT2988.K75 1992

Zion and state: nation, class, and the shaping of modern Israel / DS149.C627 1987

Zionism: the crucial phase / DS149.V515 1987

Zionism and technocracy: the engineering of Jewish settlement in Palestine, 1870-1918 / DS149.P424 1991

Zionism and the Arabs: an American Jewish dilemma, 1898-1948 / DS149.5.U6M33 1997

Zionism and the Arabs, 1882-1948: a study of ideology / DS119.7.G4313 1987

Zionism and the creation of a new society / DS149.H344 1998

Zionist idea; a historical analysis and reader, The / DS149.H4376

Zone of the interior: a memoir, 1942-1947 / D790.H64 2000

Zulfi Bhutto of Pakistan: his life and times / DS385.B45 W65 1993